AF513271

R. Gupta's®

National Testing Agency (NTA)

UGC-NET/JRF

Junior Research Fellowship & Assistant Professor Eligibility Exam

Environmental Sciences

Previous Years' Papers

PAPER II

by

RPH Editorial Board

2027
EDITION

RAMESH PUBLISHING HOUSE, NEW DELHI

Published by
O.P. Gupta *for* Ramesh Publishing House

Admin. Office
12-H, New Daryaganj Road, Opp. Officers' Mess,
New Delhi-110002 ✆ 23275224, 23245124

E-mail: info@rameshpublishinghouse.com
For Online Shopping: www.rameshpublishinghouse.com

Showroom
- Balaji Market, Nai Sarak, Delhi-110006 ✆ 23282525 📱 9354373464
- 4457, Nai Sarak, Delhi-110006

Book Code: R-2700

ISBN: 978-93-5477-471-3

Price: ₹ 590

Printed at: Deepak Offset, Delhi

CONTENTS

UGC-NET/JRF—(PAPER-II) ENVIRONMENTAL SCIENCES

Previous Years' Paper

National Testing Agency (NTA)

UGC-NET Junior Research Fellowship & Assistant Professor Eligibility Exam

ENVIRONMENTAL SCIENCES, JANUARY-2026

(Exam held on 07-01-2026)

PAPER-II

1. Match the List-I with List-II.

List-I (Radioactive Parent)	List-II (Half-life value)
A. Rubidium-87	I. ~4.5 billion years
B. Potassium-40	II. ~47 billion years
C. Uranium-238	III. ~1.3 billion years
D. Carbon-14	IV. ~5730 years

Choose the *correct* answer from the options given below:

1. A-I, B-II, C-III, D-IV
2. A-II, B-III, C-I, D-IV
3. A-III, B-I, C-II, D-IV
4. A-II, B-I, C-III, D-IV

2. Match the List-I with List-II.

List-I (Purpose/Application)	List-II (Statistical tests)
A. Testing the significance of regression coefficients	I. Durbin Watson test
B. Comparing more than two sample means	II. Chi square test
C. Testing the goodness of fit	III. *t*-test
D. Testing the significance of autocorrelation in a time series	IV. F-test

Choose the *correct* answer from the options given below:

1. A-III, B-II, C-I, D-IV
2. A-IV, B-III, C-II, D-I
3. A-III, B-IV, C-II, D-I
4. A-IV, B-II, C-I, D-III

3. Match the List-I with List-II.

List-I (Total sum of squares (TSS)) (Error sum of squares (ESS))	List-II (Coefficient of determination (R^2))
A. ESS = 30 TSS = 80	I. ~0.63
B. ESS = 40 TSS = 90	II. ~0.66
C. ESS = 25 TSS = 75	III. ~0.625
D. ESS = 35 TSS = 95	IV. ~0.55

Choose the *correct* answer from the options given below:

1. A-IV, B-III, C-II, D-I
2. A-III, B-IV, C-II, D-I
3. A-IV, B-I, C-III, D-II
4. A-III, B-II, C-IV, D-I

4. Match the List-I with List-II.

List-I (Plastic Label)	List-II (Type of Plastic Material)
A. 7	I. Polyethylene Terephthalate
B. 1	II. Polypropylene
C. 5	III. Low Density Polyethylene
D. 4	IV. Acrylonitrile Butadiene Styrene/Mixed Plastic

Choose the *correct* answer from the options given below:

1. A-IV, B-II, C-III, D-I
2. A-I, B-II, C-III, D-IV
3. A-II, B-IV, C-III, D-I
4. A-IV, B-I, C-II, D-III

5. Match the List-I with List-II.

List-I (Microwave Bands)	List-II (Frequency Range (GHz))
A. P	I. 12.5–18
B. S	II. 4–8
C. C	III. 2–4
D. Ku	IV. 0.3–1

Choose the *correct* answer from the options given below:

1. A-I, B-II, C-III, D-IV
2. A-II, B-III, C-IV, D-I
3. A-III, B-IV, C-I, D-II
4. A-IV, B-III, C-II, D-I

6. Match the List-I with List-II.

List-I (Biomedical Waste)	List-II (Color of Collection Bag/Container
A. Intravenous tubes	I. Yellow
B. Medicine vials	II. White
C. Human Anatomical Waste	III. Red
D. Blades	IV. Blue

Choose the *correct* answer from the options given below:

1. A-I, B-II, C-III, D-IV
2. A-III, B-IV, C-I, D-II
3. A-II, B-I, C-III, D-IV
4. A-I, B-IV, C-III, D-II

7. Match the List-I with List-II.

List-I (Characteristics)	List-II (Biomes)
A. Tropical grassland with scattered trees, loamy sand soils	I. Tundra
B. Tropical humid, tall trees, nutrient poor and acidic soils	II. Desert
C. Polar, low temperature, treeless, permafrost	III. Savanna
D. Sub-tropical, evaporation more than precipitation, sparse vegetation	IV. Tropical Rainforest

Choose the *correct* answer from the options given below:

1. A-III, B-IV, C-II, D-I
2. A-IV, B-II, C-I, D-III
3. A-IV, B-III, C-II, D-I
4. A-III, B-IV, C-I, D-II

8. Match the List-I with List-II.

List-I (Soil Orders)	List-II (Typical Soils)
A. Histosols	I. Conifer forests soils
B. Oxisols	II. Organic soils
C. Spodosols	III. Swelling clay soils
D. Vertisols	IV. Tropical forest soils

Choose the *correct* answer from the options given below:

1. A-I, B-II, C-III, D-IV
2. A-II, B-IV, C-I, D-III
3. A-II, B-IV, C-III, D-I
4. A-IV, B-II, C-I, D-III

9. Match the List-I with List-II.

List-I (Stages of Wilson Cycle)	List-II (Example of stages)
A. Embryonic	I. Red sea
B. Juvenile	II. Pacific ocean
C. Mature	III. East African rift valley
D. Declining	IV. Atlantic ocean

Choose the *correct* answer from the options given below:

1. A-III, B-IV, C-I, D-II
2. A-I, B-II, C-III, D-IV
3. A-III, B-I, C-IV, D-II
4. A-I, B-III, C-IV, D-II

10. Match the List-I with List-II.

List-I (Biomass Conversion Methods)	List-II (Biofuels/ Energy)
A. Physical Method	I. Biogas
B. Incineration	II. Gas/Oil/Char
C. Thermochemical Method	III. Briquetts and Pellets
D. Biochemical Method	IV. Direct Heat

Choose the *correct* answer from the options given below:

1. A-I, B-IV, C-III, D-II
2. A-III, B-II, C-IV, D-I
3. A-IV, B-III, C-II, D-I
4. A-III, B-IV, C-II, D-I

11. Match the List-I with List-II.

List-I (Fuels)	List-II (Typical energy content (MJ/kg))
A. Crude Oil	I. 27
B. Wood (dry)	II. 16-20
C. Coal (Anthracite)	III. 32-33
D. Bio-ethanol	IV. 44

Choose the *correct* answer from the options given below:

1. A-III, B-II, C-IV, D-I
2. A-IV, B-II, C-III, D-I
3. A-IV, B-II, C-I, D-III
4. A-III, B-IV, C-II, D-I

12. Match the List-I with List-II.

List-I (Name of Disease)	List-II (Disease Symptom)
A. Fluorosis	I. Skin lesions
B. Arsenocosis	II. Blueness of skin
C. Minamata disease	III. Skeletal deformity
D. Methemoglobinemia	IV. Neurological disorder

Choose the *correct* answer from the options given below:

1. A-III, B-IV, C-I, D-II
2. A-IV, B-I, C-III, D-II
3. A-III, B-I, C-IV, D-II
4. A-IV, B-III, C-I, D-II

13. Match the List-I with List-II.

List-I (Particulate Control Devices)	List-II (Suitable Particle size range (μm)
A. Gravitational Settling Chamber	I. ≥50
B. Centrifugal Collector	II. <1
C. Wet Collector (Spray tower)	III. ≥10
D. Electrostatic Precipitator)	IV. 5 - 25

Choose the *correct* answer from the options given below:

1. A-IV, B-I, C-III, D-II
2. A-I, B-IV, C-III, D-II
3. A-III, B-I, C-IV, D-II
4. A-III, B-IV, C-II, D-I

14. Match the List-I with List-II.

List-I (Greenhouse gas)	List-II (Fundamental Vibration Mode)
A. Water Vapor	I. 15
B. Methane	II. 3
C. Sulphur Hexafluoride	III. 9
D. Carbon dioxide	IV. 4

Choose the *correct* answer from the options given below:

1. A-I, B-II, C-III, D-IV
2. A-IV, B-III, C-I, D-II
3. A-II, B-III, C-I, D-IV
4. A-III, B-I, C-II, D-IV

15. Match the List-I with List-II.

List-I (Soil Type)	List-II (Dominant Salt)
A. Calcareous soils	I. NaCl
B. Saline soils	II. Al_2O_3
C. Laterites	III. Na_2CO_3
D. Sodic soils	IV. $CaCO_3$

Choose the *correct* answer from the options given below:

1. A-IV, B-III, C-II, D-I
2. A-III, B-I, C-II, D-IV
3. A-IV, B-I, C-II, D-III
4. A-III, B-I, C-IV, D-II

16. Match the List-I with List-II.

List-I (Term)	List-II (Characteristics)
A. Hypolimnion	I. The middle layer of a lake where temperature drops rapidly with depth.
B. Epilimnion	II. Lighted photic zone of ocean.
C. Metalimnion	III. The warm upper layer of a lake.
D. Epipelagic	IV. The cold, dense and dark bottom layer of a lake.

Choose the ***correct*** answer from the options given below:

1. A-III, B-IV, C-I, D-II
2. A-IV, B-I, C-III, D-II
3. A-IV, B-III, C-I, D-II
4. A-II, B-III, C-I, D-IV

17. Match the List-I with List-II.

List-I (Ecological Concept)	List-II (Proponents)
A. Ecosystem	I. Whittakar
B. Ecosystem Services	II. Myers
C. α, β, γ diversity	III. Costanza
D. Hot spot of biodiversity	IV. Tansley

Choose the ***correct*** answer from the options given below:

1. A-IV, B-I, C-II, D-III
2. A-II, B-I, C-IV, D-III
3. A-II, B-IV, C-III, D-I
4. A-IV, B-III, C-I, D-II

18. Match the List-I with List-II.

List-I (EIA Term)	List-II (Related Function)
A. Environment Management Plan	I. Identify key issues and determine boundaries of the project
B. Impact Analysis	II. Environmental mitigation measures
C. Screening	III. Risk Assessment
D. Scoping	IV. Initial Environmental Examination

Choose the ***correct*** answer from the options given below:

1. A-II, B-IV, C-III, D-I
2. A-II, B-III, C-I, D-IV
3. A-II, B-III, C-IV, D-I
4. A-III, B-II, C-IV, D-I

19. Arrange the following metamorphic rocks in order of increasing grade of metamorphism.

A. Schist B. Phyllite
C. Slate D. Gneiss

Choose the ***correct*** answer from the options given below:

1. A, B, C, D 2. B, C, D, A
3. C, B, A, D 4. D, C, B, A

20. Arrange the following intervals of a normally distributed variable 'X' in terms of increasing probabilities, if it is given that $\mu = 16$, $\sigma = 3$.

A. $13 \le X \le 19$ B. $16 \le X \le 22$
C. $19 \le X \le 22$ D. $7 \le X \le 13$

Choose the ***correct*** answer from the options given below:

1. A, B, C, D 2. B, C, D, A
3. C, D, B, A 4. D, C, A, B

21. Arrange the correlation coefficients computed from the information given below in increasing order:

A. $\sum(x_i - \bar{x})(y_i - \bar{y}) = 16, \sum(x_i - \bar{x})^2 = 64,$
$\sum(y_i - \bar{y})^2 = 25$

B. $\sum(x_i - \bar{x})(y_i - \bar{y}) = 20, \sum(x_i - \bar{x})^2 = 36,$
$\sum(y_i - \bar{y})^2 = 49$

C. $\sum(x_i - \bar{x})(y_i - \bar{y}) = 18, \sum(x_i - \bar{x})^2 = 25,$
$\sum(y_i - \bar{y})^2 = 64$

D. $\sum(x_i - \bar{x})(y_i - \bar{y}) = 24, \sum(x_i - \bar{x})^2 = 49,$
$\sum(y_i - \bar{y})^2 = 64$

Choose the *correct* answer from the options given below:

1. A, B, C, D 2. A, D, C, B
3. B, C, D, A 4. B, A, D, C

22. Arrange the following halocarbons according to their atmospheric lifetimes in ascending order.

A. $CFCl_3$ B. CHF_2Cl
C. CF_2ClBr D. C_2F_6

Choose the *correct* answer from the options given below:

1. B, C, D, A 2. B, C, A, D
3. A, C, B, D 4. C, A, B, D

23. Arrange the following layers of the atmosphere in terms of decreasing mean free paths of molecules/ions existing there.

A. Troposphere B. Stratosphere
C. Mesosphere D. Thermosphere

Choose the *correct* answer from the options given below:

1. A, B, C, D 2. B, C, D, A
3. C, D, A, B 4. D, C, B, A

24. Arrange the following atmospheric species in increasing order of their lifetimes in the atmosphere.

A. CO B. CH_3SCH_3
C. HCHO D. N_2O

Choose the *correct* answer from the options given below:

1. C, B, A, D 2. C, A, B, D
3. B, C, D, A 4. B, A, C, D

25. Arrange the following in the correct sequence of ecological succession.

A. Lichen
B. Bare Rock
C. Forest
D. Shrubs
E. Grasses & Sedges

Choose the *correct* answer from the options given below:

1. B, A, E, D, C 2. A, E, B, D, C
3. C, E, D, A, B 4. C, D, E, A, B

26. Identify the correct hierarchy of the following (from top to bottom):

A. Biosphere B. Population
C. Community D. Species
E. Ecosystem

Choose the *correct* answer from the options given below:

1. A, E, C, B, D 2. E, A, B, C, D
3. A, B, E, C, D 4. E, A, C, B, D

27. Identify the correct sequence in EIA process out of the following:

A. Impact evaluation
B. Scoping
C. Impact mitigation
D. Impact identification
E. Impact prediction

Choose the *correct* answer from the options given below:

1. B, D, E, A, C
2. E, D, A, C, B
3. D, B, C, A, E
4. B, A, E, D, C

28. Arrange the following metabolic stages in correct order of their occurrence in the biogasification of organic wastes:

A. Acetogenesis B. Acidogenesis
C. Hydrolysis D. Methanogenesis

Choose the *correct* answer from the options given below:

1. A, B, C, D 2. B, A, C, D
3. C, B, A, D 4. C, A, B, D

29. Arrange the following minerals in correct sequence according to the continuous series of crystallization in the Bowen's reaction series.

A. Labradorite B. Oligoclase
C. Andesine D. Bytownite

Choose the *correct* answer from the options given below:

1. D, A, C, B 2. A, B, C, D
3. C, A, B, D 4. A, D, C, B

30. Arrange the following layers that make up a typical oceanic crust from top to bottom.

A. Gabbro
B. Basaltic Pillow Lava
C. Deep-sea sediment
D. Sheeted dike complex

Choose the *correct* answer from the options given below:

1. C, D, B, A 2. C, A, B, D
3. C, B, D, A 4. C, D, A, B

31. Arrange the following elements in decreasing order of their relative abundance in the whole Earth (%).

A. Iron B. Oxygen
C. Silicon D. Magnesium
E. Nickel

Choose the *correct* answer from the options given below:

1. C, B, A, D, E 2. A, B, C, D, E
3. A, E, C, B, D 4. B, C, D, A, E

32. Arrange the following countries in increasing order of their CO_2 emission (M Ton/year) as per current status.

A. India B. China
C. United Kingdom D. Russia

Choose the *correct* answer from the options given below:

1. C, A, D, B 2. C, D, A, B
3. D, C, A, B 4. C, D, B, A

33. Arrange the following minerals in the decreasing order of their relative hardness as per Moh's scale.

A. Apatite B. Calcite
C. Quartz D. Gypsum

Choose the *correct* answer from the options given below:

1. A, C, B, D 2. B, C, A, D
3. D, B, A, C 4. C, A, B, D

34. Arrange the density (numbers/m^2) of organisms in terrestrial ecosystem (meadow) in increasing order.

A. Herbaceous angiosperms
B. Birds and mammals
C. Bacteria and Fungi
D. Soil arthropods, annelids and nematodes

Choose the *correct* answer from the options given below:

1. B, A, C, D 2. B, D, A, C
3. D, B, C, A 4. B, A, D, C

35. Arrange the following biomass sources in increasing order of the available energy per unit mass (MJ/kg).

A. Municipal sewage (dry)
B. Straw (grain crops)
C. Animal waste (dry)
D. Wood chips, saw mill dust and forest residue

Choose the *correct* answer from the options given below:

1. C, B, A, D 2. A, C, B, D
3. B, A, C, D 4. C, A, B, D

36. Mean of a standard normal variable is always _____.

1. equal to 1 2. less than 1
3. greater than 1 4. equal to zero

37. Which of the following is desirable with reference to linear regression models?

1. homoscedasticity
2. multicollinearity
3. autocorrelation among the residuals
4. correlation between residuals and independent variables

38. A 25 mL sample of treated waste water requires 175 mL of distilled water to reduce the odor to a level that is just detectable. What is the threshold odor number (TON)?

1. 7.0 2. 8.0
3. 150.0 4. 200.0

39. Which of the following correctly represents the total Kjeldahl's nitrogen (TKN)?

1. $NH_3 + NH_4^+ + NO_2^- + NO_3^-$
2. Organic N + $NH_3 + NH_4^+$
3. $NH_3 + NH_4^+$
4. Organic N + $NH_3 + NH_4^+ + NO_2^- + NO_3^-$

40. Identify the Boudouard reaction from various gas-solid reactions during biomass gasification process.

1. $C + \frac{1}{2}O_2 \leftrightarrow CO$
2. $C + CO_2 \leftrightarrow 2CO$
3. $C + H_2O \leftrightarrow H_2 + CO$
4. $C + 2H_2 \leftrightarrow CH_4$

41. Perfluorooctanoic acid (PFOA) is one of the persistent "Forever Chemicals (PFAS)" found in water. What is the Maximum Contaminant Level (MCL) for PFOA in drinking water as recommended by US Environmental Protection Agency (EPA).

1. 10 parts per trillion (ppt)
2. 4 parts per trillion (ppt)
3. 20 parts per trillion (ppt)
4. 50 parts per trillion (ppt)

42. Which of the following correctly represents the percentage base saturation in soils, given that CEC stands for cation exchange capacity?

1. $\frac{Ca^{2+} + Mg^{2+} + K^{+} + Na^{+}}{CEC} \times 100$
2. $\frac{Ca^{2+} + Mg^{2+}}{CEC} \times 100$
3. $\frac{Ca^{2+} + Mg^{2+} - K^{+} - Na^{+}}{CEC} \times 100$
4. $\frac{K^{+} + Na^{+} - Ca^{2+} - Mg^{2+}}{CEC} \times 100$

43. Suppose that 0.5 mg of a precipitate is lost as a result of being washed with 200 mL of wash liquid. If the precipitate weighs 500 mg, what is the relative error due to the solubility loss?

1. 0.01% 2. 0.1%
3. 0.25% 4. 25%

44. Which of the following pesticides show the highest persistence in soils due to low biodegradability?

1. Organophosphates
2. Carbamates
3. Pyrethroids
4. Organochlorines

45. Which of the following biogeochemical cycles can be most aptly called both sedimentary and gaseous?

1. Carbon Cycle 2. Sulphur Cycle
3. Nitrogen Cycle 4. Phosphorus Cycle

46. Which of the following environmental impact analysis methods uses weighted and scaled values of environmental parameters for pre and post development environment quality?

1. Leopold Matrix Method
2. Battelle Environmental Evaluation System
3. Moore Impact Matrix Method
4. Sorensen Network Analysis Method

47. The value of Cation Exchange Capacity is maximum among which of the following clay minerals?

1. Kaolinite 2. Illite
3. Montmorillonite 4. Vermiculite

48. Along which of these plate boundaries interactions, one can notice the formation of accretionary prism/wedge.

1. Mid Oceanic Ridge/Oceanic Plate divergence boundary
2. Transform fault boundary
3. Continent - Continent convergence boundary
4. Ocean - Continent convergence boundary

49. A baghouse fabric filter consists of bags that are 0.35 m in diameter and 8.0 m long. The bag house receives 11 m^3/s of particulate laden air and the appropriate filtering velocity is 2.0 m/minute for a continuous cleaning operation. How many bags are there?

1. 34 2. 38
3. 40 4. 42

50. Consider earth as a black body at temperature of –18°C. The wavelength of maximum emission of terrestrial radiation will be:

1. 9.61 μm
2. 8.12 μm
3. 11.36 μm
4. 9.89 μm

51. If air contains water vapor with a mixing ratio of 6.0 gkg^{-1} and the total pressure is 1025 mb, the vapor pressure is (Assume the ratio of molecular weight of water and the apparent molecular weight of dry air to be 0.6)

1. 1014.75 mb
2. 10.25 mb
3. 1.025 mb
4. 9.0 mb

52. For an ideal horizontal axis wind turbine, what will be the value of power coefficient (C_p), if the fractional wind speed decrease at the turbine is $\frac{1}{2}$?

1. $\frac{1}{2}$
2. $\frac{1}{4}$
3. $\frac{1}{8}$
4. $\frac{16}{27}$

53. A hydropower dam has its Head = 200 m and water reservoir area 4×10^{10} m^2. If the discharge rate is 950 m^3 s^{-1}, what will be its electrical capacity?
(Take g = 9.8 ms^{-2})

1. 2142 MW
2. 1862 MW
3. 931 MW
4. 7458 MW

54. At a certain location with latitude Φ = 45°N, the horizontal gradient of sea level pressure is 5 mb per 100 km. What is the geostrophic wind speed at the location? (Assume density of air = 1.25 kg m^{-3} and angular velocity of earth = 7.29×10^{-5} rad/s)

1. ~10 ms^{-1}
2. ~20 ms^{-1}
3. ~30 ms^{-1}
4. ~40 ms^{-1}

55. An electrostatic precipitator with 6000 m^2 of collector plate area of the collection electrodes has a flow rate of the gas 300 m^3s^{-1}. If the drift velocity of the particles towards the collecting electrode is 0.15 ms^{-1}, what is the efficiency of collection of the electrostatic precipitator?

1. 99%
2. 98%
3. 97%
4. 95%

56. Given below are two statements: one is labelled as Assertion (A) and the other is labelled as Reason (R).

Assertion (A): According to Lotka-Volterra model of population growth, the prey and predator populations never reach their equilibrium values at the same time.

Reason (R): There is a phase difference of 2π between the prey and the predator populations.

In the light of the above statements, choose the ***most appropriate*** answer from the options given below:

1. Both (A) and (R) are correct and (R) is the correct explanation of (A)
2. Both (A) and (R) are correct, but (R) is NOT the correct explanation of (A)
3. (A) is correct, but (R) is not correct
4. (A) is not correct, but (R) is correct

57. Given below are two statements: one is labelled as Assertion (A) and the other is labelled as Reason (R).

Assertion (A): According to the oxygen sag model, the dissolved oxygen concentration reaches minimum value in a stream of water, at some point downstream from the point of discharge of the waste.

Reason (R): The rate of deoxygenation due to microbial decomposition of the waste is always greater than the rate of reaeration of the stream.

In the light of the above statements, choose the ***most appropriate*** answer from the options given below:

1. Both (A) and (R) are correct and (R) is the correct explanation of (A)
2. Both (A) and (R) are correct, but (R) is NOT the correct explanation of (A)
3. (A) is correct, but (R) is not correct
4. (A) is not correct, but (R) is correct

58. Given below are two statements: one is labelled as Assertion (A) and the other is labelled as Reason (R).

Assertion (A): The hydroxyl radical is one of the most important reactive species in the troposphere.

Reason (R): It readily reacts with N_2, O_2 and CO_2.

In the light of the above statements, choose the ***most appropriate*** answer from the options given below:

1. Both (A) and (R) are correct and (R) is the correct explanation of (A)
2. Both (A) and (R) are correct, but (R) is NOT the correct explanation of (A)
3. (A) is correct, but (R) is not correct
4. (A) is not correct, but (R) is correct

59. Given below are two statements: one is labelled as Assertion (A) and the other is labelled as Reason (R).

Assertion (A): DDT caused large scale mortality among fish eating birds.

Reason (R): DDT tends to undergo bioaccumulation and biomagnification.

In the light of the above statements, choose the ***most appropriate*** answer from the options given below:

1. Both (A) and (R) are correct and (R) is the correct explanation of (A)
2. Both (A) and (R) are correct, but (R) is NOT the correct explanation of (A)
3. (A) is correct, but (R) is not correct
4. (A) is not correct, but (R) is correct

60. Given below are two statements: one is labelled as Assertion (A) and the other is labelled as Reason (R).

Assertion (A): Bioremediation involves environmental modification to improve aeration and nutrients in the contaminated site, and microbial seeding using xenobiotics degrading microbes.

Reason (R): Environmental modification boosts plant growth and microbial seeding improves overall microbial biomass in the contaminated site.

In the light of the above statements, choose the ***most appropriate*** answer from the options given below:

1. Both (A) and (R) are correct and (R) is the correct explanation of (A)
2. Both (A) and (R) are correct, but (R) is NOT the correct explanation of (A)
3. (A) is correct, but (R) is not correct
4. (A) is not correct, but (R) is correct

61. Given below are two statements: one is labelled as Assertion (A) and the other is labelled as Reason (R).

Assertion (A): The transitional zone between two or more communities has more number of species and population density at the junction.

Reason (R): Boundaries offer opportunities for interaction through invasion, migration and inter-specific competition.

In the light of the above statements, choose the ***most appropriate*** answer from the options given below:

1. Both (A) and (R) are correct and (R) is the correct explanation of (A)
2. Both (A) and (R) are correct, but (R) is NOT the correct explanation of (A)
3. (A) is correct, but (R) is not correct
4. (A) is not correct, but (R) is correct

62. Given below are two statements: one is labelled as Assertion (A) and the other is labelled as Reason (R).

Assertion (A): Dioxins and furans are chlorinated compounds that have somewhat similar chemical structures.

Reason (R): They both consist of two benzene rings that are linked together with oxygen bridges.

In the light of the above statements, choose the ***most appropriate*** answer from the options given below:

1. Both (A) and (R) are correct and (R) is the correct explanation of (A)
2. Both (A) and (R) are correct, but (R) is NOT the correct explanation of (A)
3. (A) is correct, but (R) is not correct
4. (A) is not correct, but (R) is correct

63. Given below are two statements: one is labelled as Assertion (A) and the other is labelled as Reason (R).

Assertion (A): α-quartz, β-quartz, tridymite and cristobalite show Polymorphism.

Reason (R): Two substances are polymorphous if they have similar crystal structure but different chemical formulas.

In the light of the above statements, choose the ***most appropriate*** answer from the options given below:

1. Both (A) and (R) are correct and (R) is the correct explanation of (A)
2. Both (A) and (R) are correct, but (R) is NOT the correct explanation of (A)
3. (A) is correct, but (R) is not correct
4. (A) is not correct, but (R) is correct

64. Given below are two statements: one is labelled as Assertion (A) and the other is labelled as Reason (R).

Assertion (A): Orthophosphate is most available to plants at nearly neutral pH values.

Reason (R): The orthophosphate ion is relatively more soluble than hydrogen phosphates due to its higher charge.

In the light of the above statements, choose the ***most appropriate*** answer from the options given below:

1. Both (A) and (R) are correct and (R) is the correct explanation of (A)
2. Both (A) and (R) are correct, but (R) is NOT the correct explanation of (A)
3. (A) is correct, but (R) is not correct
4. (A) is not correct, but (R) is correct

65. Given below are two statements: one is labelled as Assertion (A) and the other is labelled as Reason (R).

Assertion (A): An aquiclude supports a perched watertable above the main watertable.

Reason (R): Aquicludes are relatively impermeable beds that hinder water movement.

In the light of the above statements, choose the ***most appropriate*** answer from the options given below:

1. Both (A) and (R) are correct and (R) is the correct explanation of (A)
2. Both (A) and (R) are correct, but (R) is NOT the correct explanation of (A)
3. (A) is correct, but (R) is not correct
4. (A) is not correct, but (R) is correct

66. Given below are two statements: one is labelled as Assertion (A) and the other is labelled as Reason (R).

Assertion (A): The magnitude of saturated adiabatic lapse rate is always less than that of the dry adiabatic lapse rate.

Reason (R): The rate of change of saturation mixing ratio with temperature is always negative.

In the light of the above statements, choose the ***most appropriate*** answer from the options given below:

1. Both (A) and (R) are correct and (R) is the correct explanation of (A)
2. Both (A) and (R) are correct, but (R) is NOT the correct explanation of (A)
3. (A) is correct, but (R) is not correct
4. (A) is not correct, but (R) is correct

67. Given below are two statements: one is labelled as Assertion (A) and the other is labelled as Reason (R).

Assertion (A): Gallium Arsenide (GaAs) is an attractive Photo-Voltaic (PV) cell material.

Reason (R): GaAs has a direct band gap of 2.43 eV.

In the light of the above statements, choose the ***most appropriate*** answer from the options given below:

1. Both (A) and (R) are correct and (R) is the correct explanation of (A)
2. Both (A) and (R) are correct, but (R) is NOT the correct explanation of (A)
3. (A) is correct, but (R) is not correct
4. (A) is not correct, but (R) is correct

68. Given below are two statements: one is labelled as Assertion (A) and the other is labelled as Reason (R).

Assertion (A): In contrast to a fission reactor, a fusion reactor can not melt down.

Reason (R): If anything goes wrong, the plasma will collapse and fusion will stop.

In the light of the above statements, choose the ***most appropriate*** answer from the options given below:

1. Both (A) and (R) are correct and (R) is the correct explanation of (A)
2. Both (A) and (R) are correct, but (R) is NOT the correct explanation of (A)
3. (A) is correct, but (R) is not correct
4. (A) is not correct, but (R) is correct

69. Given below are two statements: one is labelled as Assertion (A) and the other is labelled as Reason (R).

Assertion (A): In composting of municipal solid waste, thermophilic microbes initiate the process.

Reason (R): High temperature is required to kill the pathogens.

In the light of the above statements, choose the ***most appropriate*** answer from the options given below:

1. Both (A) and (R) are correct and (R) is the correct explanation of (A)
2. Both (A) and (R) are correct, but (R) is NOT the correct explanation of (A)
3. (A) is correct, but (R) is not correct
4. (A) is not correct, but (R) is correct

70. Given below are two statements: one is labelled as Assertion (A) and the other is labelled as Reason (R).

Assertion (A): Attenuation of anionic species in soil is less than that of cationic species.

Reason (R): Soil surfaces lack anion exchanging sites.

In the light of the above statements, choose the ***most appropriate*** answer from the options given below:

1. Both (A) and (R) are correct and (R) is the correct explanation of (A)
2. Both (A) and (R) are correct, but (R) is NOT the correct explanation of (A)
3. (A) is correct, but (R) is not correct
4. (A) is not correct, but (R) is correct

71. Given below are two statements: one is labelled as Assertion (A) and the other is labelled as Reason (R).

Assertion (A): Cloudy nights in the monsoon season favour the formation of urban heat island.

Reason (R): Water vapours absorb strongly in the long wave region.

In the light of the above statements, choose the ***most appropriate*** answer from the options given below:

1. Both (A) and (R) are correct and (R) is the correct explanation of (A)
2. Both (A) and (R) are correct, but (R) is NOT the correct explanation of (A)
3. (A) is correct, but (R) is not correct
4. (A) is not correct, but (R) is correct

72. Given below are two statements: one is labelled as Assertion (A) and the other is labelled as Reason (R).

Assertion (A): The turn over rate of marine autotrophs is faster than that of terrestrial autotrophs.

Reason (R): Terrestrial autotrophs contribute less to the structural matrix of the ecosystem as compared to marine autotrophs.

In the light of the above statements, choose the ***most appropriate*** answer from the options given below:

1. Both (A) and (R) are correct and (R) is the correct explanation of (A)
2. Both (A) and (R) are correct, but (R) is NOT the correct explanation of (A)
3. (A) is correct, but (R) is not correct
4. (A) is not correct, but (R) is correct

73. Given below are two statements: one is labelled as Assertion (A) and the other is labelled as Reason (R).

Assertion (A): Pollutants can be detected and quantified using biosensors.

Reason (R): On interaction of specific biomolecules with chemicals, transducers release readable signals.

In the light of the above statements, choose the ***most appropriate*** answer from the options given below:

1. Both (A) and (R) are correct and (R) is the correct explanation of (A)
2. Both (A) and (R) are correct, but (R) is NOT the correct explanation of (A)
3. (A) is correct, but (R) is not correct
4. (A) is not correct, but (R) is correct

74. Identify the measures of variability in a dataset.

A. Percentiles B. Quartiles
C. Range D. Interquartile Range
E. Mean Deviation

Choose the ***correct*** answer from the options given below:

1. A, B, C only
2. B, C, D only
3. C, D, E only
4. B, C, D, E only

75. Identify the continuous probability distributions among the following:

A. Binomial B. Uniform
C. Hypergeometric D. Normal

Choose the ***correct*** answer from the options given below:

1. A, B and C only
2. B, C and D only
3. B and D only
4. D only

76. Identify the active species of chlorine in the lower polar stratosphere.

A. HCl B. Cl
C. $ClONO_2$ D. ClO

Choose the ***correct*** answer from the options given below:

1. A and B only 2. C and D only
3. B and D only 4. A and C only

77. The rate of formation of disinfection byproducts (DBPs) during water treatment is dependent on:

A. Presence of organic precursors
B. Free chlorine concentration
C. Bromide concentration
D. pH
E. Temperature

Choose the ***correct*** answer from the options given below:

1. B and C only
2. A, D and E only
3. A, B, D and E only
4. A, B, C, D, E

78. Identify the waste incinerator(s) commonly categorized according to combustion chamber:

A. Rotary kiln B. Moving grate
C. Fixed-hearth D. Fluidized-bed

Choose the ***correct*** answer from the options given below:

1. A only
2. B only
3. A, C and D only
4. A, B, C and D

79. Soil-water in equilibrium with CO_2 in soil-air has pH-values often below 5.0. This acidity arises mainly from the following sources:

A. Organic acid produced during degradation of organic matter
B. Release of H^+ by plants in exchange for nutritive base cations
C. Sulphide oxidation
D. Nitrification processes, where NH_4^+ is converted into NO_3^-

Choose the ***correct*** answer from the options given below:

1. A only 2. C only
3. A and B only 4. A, B, C and D

80. Which of the following detectors are best suited for HPLC?

A. Mass spectrometer (MS)
B. Thermal Conductivity
C. Absorbance
D. Flame ionization

Choose the ***correct*** answer from the options given below:

1. A only
2. B and C only
3. A and C only
4. A, B, C and D

81. Which of the following is/are true regarding the ideal detector for gas chromatography?

A. Good stability and reproducibility.
B. A linear response to solutes that extends over several orders of magnitude.
C. A temperature range from room temperature to at least 400°C.
D. A short response time that is independent of flow rate.

Choose the ***correct*** answer from the options given below:

1. A only
2. B and C only
3. A, B and D only
4. A, B, C and D

82. Identify the correct statements about biofuels.

A. Transesterification is involved in production of biodiesel.
B. Biogas is produced from organic wastes using aerobic bacteria.
C. Biohydrogen can be produced using hydrogenase by microalgae.
D. Bioethanol with high octane rating is produced using wood chips.
E. Photoautotrophic bacteria are used for bioethanol production.

Choose the ***correct*** answer from the options given below:

1. A, C and D only
2. B, C and E only
3. A, C and E only
4. A, B and C only

83. Identify the correct statements:

A. Wetland ecosystems store and purify water.
B. Coral reefs, rich in calcareous materials, have very low productivity.
C. Chaparral ecosystems show excellent resilience stability.
D. Arctic ecosystems have small food chains.
E. Nutrient deficient estuarine ecosystems have low species diversity.

Choose the ***correct*** answer from the options given below:

1. B, C and E only
2. A, B and C only
3. A, C and D only
4. A, B, C and D only

84. Identify the correct statements:

A. Energy available at each successive trophic level always decreases.
B. Nutrient cycles in a tropical rain forest are closed systems.
C. The P/R ratio in a climax community is always greater than 1.
D. Ecosystem services include regulatory, provisioning and supporting services, but not cultural services.
E. r-species are opportunists while k-species are competitors.

Choose the ***correct*** answer from the options given below:

1. A, B, C and D only
2. A, C and E only
3. A, B and E only
4. A, C, D and E only

85. As per EIA notification (2006); which of the following statement(s) is (are) correct?

A. A-category projects require prior environment clearance from Central Government.
B. National defense and security projects have mandatory requirement for public consultation.

C. B_1 category projects do not require environmental clearance.

D. EAC and SEAC are the regulatory authorities to grant or reject environment clearance.

Choose the ***correct*** answer from the options given below:

1. A, C and D only
2. A and B only
3. A and C only
4. A only

86. Identify the correct statement about plastic recycling:

A. PET type plastics are significantly recycled worldwide.

B. Polystyrene cups, bottles and plates have a high recycling rate.

C. Thermoset plastics are readily recycled.

D. Plastics can absorb materials like oils and pesticides that can stay in recycled plastic.

Choose the ***correct*** answer from the options given below:

1. A and D only
2. B and C only
3. A and C only
4. C and D only

87. Darcy's law is applicable in which of the following conditions:

A. The flow of liquid is steady

B. Soil is unsaturated

C. Flow through soil is turbulent

D. Relation between flow rate and hydraulic gradient is linear

Choose the ***correct*** answer from the options given below:

1. A and C only
2. A, B and D only
3. B, C and D only
4. A and D only

88. Environment Protection (End-of-Life Vehicles) Rules 2025 shall apply to:

A. Waste Batteries covered under the Battery Waste Management Rules, 2022.

B. E-waste as covered under E-waste (Management) Rules, 2022.

C. Registered owners of vehicles.

D. Plastic packaging as covered under the Plastic Waste Management Rules, 2016.

E. Registered vehicle scrapping facility.

Choose the ***correct*** answer from the options given below:

1. A and B only
2. A, B and D only
3. C and E only
4. A, C and E only

89. The major advantages of Ocean Thermal Energy Conversion (OTEC) are:

A. High efficiency

B. Steady power without fluctuations and independent of vagaries of weather

C. Low installation cost

D. Creation of some useful by-products such as desalinated water

Choose the ***correct*** answer from the options given below:

1. A, B and D only
2. B, C and D only
3. B and D only
4. A, B, C and D

90. Which of the following is/are main limitations of tidal energy?

A. Economic recovery of energy from tides is site specific.

B. Tidal plants disrupt marine life and ecology at the site (location).

C. Changing tidal range produces changing power.

D. The turbines are required to operate at variable head.

Choose the ***correct*** answer from the options given below:

1. B only
2. B, C and D only
3. A, B and D only
4. A, B, C and D

Directions (Qs. 91 to 95): *Read the passage given below and answer questions:*

The inhospitable conditions of early Earth, characterized by a molten surface under intense bombardment by asteroids and other objects from space, persisted for up to 500 million years. The intense heat and the absence of liquid water indicate that early Earth was completely devoid of life. Furthermore, the early Earth was anoxic, and the absence of O_2 means that Earth lacked an ozone layer, allowing intense ultraviolet light to sterilize its surface. Water on Earth originated from volcanic outgassing of the planet's interior and from innumerable collisions with icy comets and asteroids. Given Earth's heat at the time, this water would have been present only as water vapor. However, ancient crystal of the mineral zircon ($ZrSiO_4$) have been discovered that were formed on the early Earth, and these materials have given us a glimpse of conditions on Earth prior to the origin of life. Analyses of ancient zircon crystals, including impurities trapped in these crystals and their oxygen isotope ratios, provide evidence for a solid crust and liquid water on Earth as early as 4.3 bya. Additional evidence of water comes from ancient sedimentary rocks, since sedimentary rocks are only formed under water. Among the oldest surviving sedimentary rocks are those found in southwestern Greenland, dating to 3.86 bya. These ancient rocks indicate the presence of early oceans.

91. Based on the information given in the passage, what could be the most probable age of earth?
1. ~4.8 billion years
2. ~4.3 billion years
3. ~3.86 billion years
4. ~500 million years

92. Which of the following is NOT correct about the early phase (first 200-400 million years) after Earth's formation?
1. There was no life on earth.
2. There were anoxic conditions on earth.
3. Earth had ozone layer.
4. There was no liquid water.

93. Which of the following is NOT a source of water in the early phase (first 200-400 million years) after Earth's formation?
1. Volcanic outgassing
2. Collisions with icy comets
3. Early oceans
4. Collisions with icy asteroids

94. According to the passage, the evidence for the existence of early oceans pertains to which of the following periods?
1. $\sim 4.8 \times 10^9$ years ago
2. $\sim 3.86 \times 10^9$ years ago
3. $\sim 5 \times 10^8$ years ago
4. $\sim 4.3 \times 10^8$ years ago

95. The earliest evidence of liquid water on earth comes from
1. Sedimentary rocks found in southwestern Greenland
2. Icy comets
3. Analysis of ancient zircon crystals
4. Presence of early oceans

Directions (Qs. 96 to 100): *Read the passage given below and answer questions:*

The earliest mass extinction occurred approximately 443 million years ago, near the end of the Ordovician period. Although not much is known about the cause of this extinction, it may have been related to global cooling. Approximately 100 families and their associated species became extinct during this period. The next mass extinction occurred 90 million years later near the end of the Devonian. That extinction was responsible for the death of about 70 percent of all (marine) invertebrate species and was also probably related to climate change and global cooling. The third mass extinction occurred near the end of the Permian — about 245 million years ago — when 95 percent of all marine species died. It is believed that this mass extinction possible spanned a period of about 7 million years. It is thought that global cooling, followed by rapid global warming with large variations in climate, may have been responsible. There was also significant volcanic activity during this time, and the tremendous amount of volcanic ash and gases in the atmosphere probably contributed to the cooling. At the end of the Cretaceous period, another tremendous mass extinction event occurred. This event was sudden, and there is abundant evidence to suggest that it was caused by the impact of a giant asteroid. Another mass extinction occurred near the end of the Eocene about 35 million years ago.

96. End of the Devonian period corresponds most likely to the period
1. ~90 million years ago
2. ~353 million years ago
3. ~245 million years ago
4. ~533 million years ago

97. Among the mass extinctions mentioned in the passage, the most devastating loss of marine life occurred near the end of:
1. Ordovician
2. Devonian
3. Permian
4. Eocene

98. Mass extinction at the end of Cretaceous period was likely caused by:
1. Global warming
2. Global cooling
3. Global cooling followed by global warming
4. Impact of giant asteroid

99. Global cooling followed by rapid global warming accompanied with large variations in climate was the most likely cause of mass extinctions pertaining to which period?
1. At the end of the Cretaceous period
2. Near the end of the Devonian
3. Near the end of the Permian
4. Near the end of the Ordovician

100. Global cooling has been associated with mass extinctions that occurred near the end of _____.
1. Ordovician, Cretaceous and Permian
2. Ordovician, Eocene and Permian
3. Ordovician, Cretaceous and Devonian
4. Ordovician, Devonian and Permian

ANSWERS

1	**2**	**3**	**4**	**5**	**6**	**7**	**8**	**9**	**10**
2	3	2	4	4	2	4	2	3	4
11	**12**	**13**	**14**	**15**	**16**	**17**	**18**	**19**	**20**
2	3	2	3	3	3	4	3	3	3
21	**22**	**23**	**24**	**25**	**26**	**27**	**28**	**29**	**30**
2	2	4	1	1	1	1	3	1	3
31	**32**	**33**	**34**	**35**	**36**	**37**	**38**	**39**	**40**
2	2	4	4	2	4	1	2	2	2
41	**42**	**43**	**44**	**45**	**46**	**47**	**48**	**49**	**50**
2	1	2	4	2	2	4	4	2	3
51	**52**	**53**	**54**	**55**	**56**	**57**	**58**	**59**	**60**
2	1	2	4	4	3	3	3	1	2
61	**62**	**63**	**64**	**65**	**66**	**67**	**68**	**69**	**70**
2	1	3	3	1	3	3	1	4	3
71	**72**	**73**	**74**	**75**	**76**	**77**	**78**	**79**	**80**
4	3	1	3	3	3	4	4	4	3
81	**82**	**83**	**84**	**85**	**86**	**87**	**88**	**89**	**90**
4	1	3	3	4	1	4	3	3	4
91	**92**	**93**	**94**	**95**	**96**	**97**	**98**	**99**	**100**
1	3	3	2	3	2	3	4	3	4

EXPLANATORY ANSWERS

1. A. Rubidium-87 — II. ~47 billion years: Rubidium-87 has a very long half-life of about 47 billion years. Therefore, A correctly matches with II.

B. Potassium-40 — III. ~1.3 billion years: Potassium-40 has a half-life of about 1.25 to 1.3 billion years. Therefore, B correctly matches with III.

C. Uranium-238 — I. ~4.5 billion years: Uranium-238 has a half-life of about 4.47 billion years, commonly taken as ~4.5 billion years. Therefore, C correctly matches with I.

D. Carbon-14 — IV. ~5730 years: Carbon-14 has a half-life of about 5730 years. Therefore, D correctly matches with IV.

The complete correct matching is A-II, B-III, C-I, D-IV, so option 2 fits exactly with the given radioactive parents and their half-life values.

2. A. Testing the significance of regression coefficients — III. *t*-test: The significance of an individual regression coefficient is tested by using the t-test. Therefore, A correctly matches with III.

B. Comparing more than two sample means — IV. F-test: Comparison of more than two sample means is done through ANOVA, which uses the F-test. Therefore, B correctly matches with IV.

C. Testing the goodness of fit — II. Chi square test: The chi-square test is commonly used for testing goodness of fit. Therefore, C correctly matches with II.

D. Testing the significance of autocorrelation in a time series — I. Durbin Watson test: The Durbin Watson test is used to detect autocorrelation in time-series regression residuals. Therefore, D correctly matches with I.

The complete correct matching is A-III, B-IV, C-II, D-I, so option 3 is the correct answer.

3. A. ESS = 30, TSS = 80 — III. ~0.625

$R^2 = 1 - ESS/TSS$

$R^2 = 1 - 30/80$

$= 1 - 0.375 = 0.625$

Therefore, A correctly matches with III.

B. ESS = 40, TSS = 90 — IV. ~0.55

$R^2 = 1 - ESS/TSS$

$R2 = 1 - 40/90 = 1 - 0.444$

$= 0.556 \approx 0.55$

Therefore, B correctly matches with IV.

C. ESS = 25, TSS = 75 — II. ~0.66

$R^2 = 1 - ESS/TSS$

$R^2 = 1 - 25/75 = 1 - 0.333$

$= 0.667 \approx 0.66$

Therefore, C correctly matches with II.

D. ESS = 35, TSS = 95 — I, ~0.63

$R^2 = 1 - ESS/TSS$

$R^2 = 1 - 35/95 = 1 - 0.368$

$= 0.632 \approx 0.63$

Therefore, D correctly matches with I.

The complete correct matching is A-III, B-IV, C-II, D-I, so option 2 is the correct answer.

4. A. 7 — IV. Acrylonitrile Butadiene Styrene/ Mixed Plastic: Plastic label 7 is used for "Other" plastics, including mixed plastics and materials such as ABS in such classification contexts. Therefore, A correctly matches with IV.

B. 1 — I. Polyethylene Terephthalate: Plastic label 1 represents Polyethylene Terephthalate, commonly abbreviated as PET or PETE. Therefore, B correctly matches with I.

C. 5 — II. Polypropylene: Plastic label 5 represents Polypropylene. Therefore, C correctly matches with II.

D. 4 — III. Low Density Polyethylene: Plastic label 4 represents Low Density Polyethylene, commonly abbreviated as LDPE. Therefore, D correctly matches with III.

The complete correct matching is A-IV, B-I, C-II, D-III, so option 4 is the correct answer.

5. A. P — IV. 0.3–1: The P microwave band lies in the lower microwave range and is commonly matched with 0.3–1 GHz in this classification. Therefore, A correctly matches with IV.

B. S — III. 2–4: The S microwave band corresponds to the frequency range of 2–4 GHz. Therefore, B correctly matches with III.

C. C — II. 4–8: The C microwave band corresponds to the frequency range of 4–8 GHz. Therefore, C correctly matches with II.

D. Ku — I. 12.5–18: The Ku microwave band corresponds approximately to the frequency range of 12.5–18 GHz. Therefore, D correctly matches with I.

The complete correct matching is A-IV, B-III, C-II, D-I, so option 4 is the correct answer.

6. **A. Intravenous tubes — III. Red:** Intravenous tubes are contaminated recyclable plastic biomedical waste. Such plastic tubing is collected in the red bag/container category. Therefore, A correctly matches with III.

B. Medicine vials — IV. Blue: Medicine vials are glassware waste items. Glassware such as vials and ampoules is collected in the blue category. Therefore, B correctly matches with IV.

C. Human Anatomical Waste — I. Yellow: Human anatomical waste includes human tissues, organs, and body parts. This type of biomedical waste is collected in the yellow bag category. Therefore, C correctly matches with I.

D. Blades — II. White: Blades are sharp biomedical waste items. Sharps are collected in white translucent puncture-proof containers. Therefore, D correctly matches with II.

The complete correct matching is A-III, B-IV, C-I, D-II, so option 2 is the correct answer.

7. **A. Tropical grassland with scattered trees, loamy sand soils — III. Savanna:** Savanna is a tropical grassland biome with scattered trees. It commonly has open grassland vegetation and relatively dry seasonal conditions. Therefore, A correctly matches with III.

B. Tropical humid, tall trees, nutrient poor and acidic soils — IV. Tropical Rainforest: Tropical rainforests have humid climate and tall dense trees. Their soils are often nutrient poor and acidic because nutrients are rapidly recycled in vegetation. Therefore, B correctly matches with IV.

C. Polar, low temperature, treeless, permafrost — I. Tundra: Tundra is a polar biome with very low temperature. It is treeless and is characteristically associated with permafrost. Therefore, C correctly matches with I.

D. Sub-tropical, evaporation more than precipitation, sparse vegetation — II. Desert: Deserts have evaporation greater than precipitation. They are marked by dry conditions and sparse vegetation. Therefore, D correctly matches with II.

The complete correct matching is A-III, B-IV, C-I, D-II, so option 4 is the correct answer.

8. **A. Histosols — II. Organic soils:** Histosols are soils rich in organic matter. They are commonly called organic soils because of accumulation of decomposed plant material. Therefore, A correctly matches with II.

B. Oxisols — IV. Tropical forest soils: Oxisols are highly weathered soils of tropical regions. They are typically associated with tropical forest environments. Therefore, B correctly matches with IV.

C. Spodosols — I. Conifer forests soils: Spodosols are acidic soils commonly found under coniferous forests. They are associated with leaching and accumulation of organic matter and oxides in subsurface layers. Therefore, C correctly matches with I.

D. Vertisols — III. Swelling clay soils: Vertisols contain high amounts of expanding clay minerals. They swell when wet and shrink/crack when dry. Therefore, D correctly matches with III.

The complete correct matching is A-II, B-IV, C-I, D-III, so option 2 is the correct answer.

9. **A. Embryonic — III. East African rift valley:** The embryonic stage of the Wilson Cycle represents initial continental rifting. The East African rift valley is a standard example of this early rifting stage. Therefore, A correctly matches with III.

B. Juvenile — I. Red sea: The juvenile stage represents a narrow young ocean basin. The Red Sea is a typical example of this stage. Therefore, B correctly matches with I.

C. Mature — IV. Atlantic ocean: The mature stage represents a fully developed ocean basin with passive margins. The Atlantic Ocean is a typical example of a mature ocean basin. Therefore, C correctly matches with IV.

D. Declining — II. Pacific ocean: The declining stage represents an ocean basin being reduced by subduction. The Pacific Ocean is a typical example because it is surrounded by active subduction zones. Therefore, D correctly matches with II.

The complete correct matching is A-III, B-I, C-IV, D-II, so option 3 is the correct answer.

10. **A. Physical Method — III. Briquetts and Pellets:** Physical biomass conversion includes densification processes. These processes produce solid fuels such as briquettes and pellets. Therefore, A correctly matches with III.

B. Incineration — IV. Direct Heat: Incineration is direct burning of biomass or waste. Its main energy output is direct heat. Therefore, B correctly matches with IV.

C. Thermochemical Method — II. Gas/Oil/Char: Thermochemical conversion includes processes such as pyrolysis and gasification. These processes can produce gas, oil, and char. Therefore, C correctly matches with II.

D. Biochemical Method — I. Biogas: Biochemical conversion includes anaerobic digestion. Anaerobic digestion produces biogas as the main biofuel. Therefore, D correctly matches with I.

The complete correct matching is A-III, B-IV, C-II, D-I, so option 4 is the correct answer.

11. **A. Crude Oil — IV. 44:** Crude oil has a high typical energy content of about 44 MJ/kg. This value is higher than wood, coal listed here, and bio-ethanol. Therefore, A correctly matches with IV.

B. Wood (dry) — II. 16–20: Dry wood has a typical energy content in the range of about 16–20 MJ/kg. This is lower than crude oil and anthracite coal because wood has lower calorific value. Therefore, B correctly matches with II.

C. Coal (Anthracite) — III. 32–33: Anthracite is a high-rank coal with high carbon content. Its typical energy content is about 32–33 MJ/kg. Therefore, C correctly matches with III.

D. Bio-ethanol — I. 27: Bio-ethanol has a typical energy content of about 27 MJ/kg. This is lower than crude oil but higher than dry wood. Therefore, D correctly matches with I.

The complete correct matching is A-IV, B-II, C-III, D-I, so option 2 is the correct answer.

12. **A. Fluorosis — III. Skeletal deformity:** Fluorosis is caused by excessive fluoride intake. In severe cases, it affects bones and produces skeletal deformity. Therefore, A correctly matches with III.

B. Arsenocosis — I. Skin lesions: Arsenocosis is caused by chronic exposure to arsenic. Typical symptoms include pigmentation changes and skin lesions. Therefore, B correctly matches with I.

C. Minamata disease — IV. Neurological disorder: Minamata disease is caused by methyl mercury poisoning. It mainly affects the nervous system and produces neurological disorders. Therefore, C correctly matches with IV.

D. Methemoglobinemia — II. Blueness of skin: Methemoglobinemia reduces the oxygen-carrying capacity of blood. It causes cyanosis, which appears as blueness of skin. Therefore, D correctly matches with II.

The complete correct matching is A-III, B-I, C-IV, D-II, so option 3 is the correct answer.

13. **A. Gravitational Settling Chamber — I. ≥50:** Gravitational settling chambers are suitable for removing large particles. They are generally effective for particles of size about ≥50 μm. Therefore, A correctly matches with I.

B. Centrifugal Collector — IV. 5–25: Centrifugal collectors use centrifugal force to remove particulate matter. They are suitable for particles in the range of about 5–25 μm. Therefore, B correctly matches with IV.

C. Wet Collector (Spray tower) — III. ≥10: Spray tower wet collectors remove particles by contact with liquid droplets. They are commonly suitable for particles of size about ≥10 μm. Therefore, C correctly matches with III.

D. Electrostatic Precipitator — II. <1: Electrostatic precipitators can remove very fine particles effectively. They are suitable even for particles smaller than 1 μm. Therefore, D correctly matches with II.

The complete correct matching is A-I, B-IV, C-III, D-II, so option 2 is the correct answer.

14. **A. Water Vapor — II. 3:** Water vapor has three atoms and is a non-linear molecule. Its fundamental vibrational modes are 3 in number. Therefore, A correctly matches with II.

B. Methane — III. 9: Methane has five atoms and is a non-linear molecule. The number of fundamental vibrational modes is $3N - 6 = 3(5) - 6 = 9$. Therefore, B correctly matches with III.

C. Sulphur Hexafluoride — I. 15: Sulphur hexafluoride has seven atoms and is a non-linear molecule. The number of fundamental vibrational modes is 3N − 6 = 3(7) − 6 = 15. Therefore, C correctly matches with I.

D. Carbon dioxide — IV. 4: Carbon dioxide has three atoms and is a linear molecule. The number of fundamental vibrational modes is 3N − 5 = 3(3) − 5 = 4. Therefore, D correctly matches with IV.

The complete correct matching is A-II, B-III, C-I, D-IV, so option 3 is the correct answer.

15. **A. Calcareous soils — IV. $CaCO_3$:** Calcareous soils contain a dominant amount of calcium carbonate. Therefore, $CaCO_3$ is the correct dominant salt for calcareous soils. Therefore, A correctly matches with IV.

B. Saline soils — I. NaCl: Saline soils contain excess soluble salts. Sodium chloride is a common dominant salt in saline soils. Therefore, B correctly matches with I.

C. Laterites — II. Al_2O_3: Laterites are rich in iron and aluminium oxides. Among the given options, Al_2O_3 is correctly associated with lateritic soils. Therefore, C correctly matches with II.

D. Sodic soils — III. Na_2CO_3: Sodic soils are characterized by excess sodium compounds. Sodium carbonate is commonly associated with sodic or alkali soils. Therefore, D correctly matches with III.

The complete correct matching is A-IV, B-I, C-II, D-III, so option 3 is the correct answer.

16. **A. Hypolimnion — IV. The cold, dense and dark bottom layer of a lake:** Hypolimnion is the lower layer of a thermally stratified lake. It is cold, dense, relatively dark, and lies below the metalimnion. Therefore, A correctly matches with IV.

B. Epilimnion — III. The warm upper layer of a lake: Epilimnion is the upper layer of a lake. It is warm, relatively well mixed, and directly influenced by sunlight and wind action. Therefore, B correctly matches with III.

C. Metalimnion — I. The middle layer of a lake where temperature drops rapidly with depth: Metalimnion is the middle transition layer between epilimnion and hypolimnion. It is also called the thermocline because temperature decreases rapidly with depth in this zone. Therefore, C correctly matches with I.

D. Epipelagic — II. Lighted photic zone of ocean: Epipelagic zone is the upper lighted zone of the ocean. It receives enough sunlight for photosynthesis and is also called the photic zone. Therefore, D correctly matches with II.

The complete correct matching is A-IV, B-III, C-I, D-II, so option 3 is the correct answer.

17. **A. Ecosystem — IV. Tansley:** The term ecosystem was proposed by A.G. Tansley. It refers to the functional unit formed by living organisms and their physical environment. Therefore, A correctly matches with IV.

B. Ecosystem Services — III. Costanza: Ecosystem services are commonly associated with Costanza in relation to valuation of ecosystem services. These services include benefits obtained from ecosystems by human beings. Therefore, B correctly matches with III.

C. α, β, γ diversity — I. Whittakar: Alpha, beta, and gamma diversity are associated with Whittaker. These terms describe diversity at local, between-habitat, and regional scales respectively. Therefore, C correctly matches with I.

D. Hot spot of biodiversity — II. Myers: The biodiversity hotspot concept is associated with Norman Myers. It identifies regions with high endemism and high threat of habitat loss. Therefore, D correctly matches with II.

The complete correct matching is A-IV, B-III, C-I, D-II, so option 4 is the correct answer.

18. **A. Environment Management Plan — II. Environmental mitigation measures:** Environment Management Plan deals with management actions required after impact identification. It mainly includes environmental mitigation measures, monitoring, and implementation planning. Therefore, A correctly matches with II.

B. Impact Analysis — III. Risk Assessment: Impact analysis evaluates the nature, magnitude, and significance of predicted impacts. Risk assessment is a related function used to assess possible adverse environmental risks. Therefore, B correctly matches with III.

C. Screening — IV. Initial Environmental Examination: Screening is the early EIA step used to decide whether detailed assessment is required. It is commonly linked with Initial Environmental Examination. Therefore, C correctly matches with IV.

D. Scoping — I. Identify key issues and determine boundaries of the project: Scoping identifies the important issues to be studied in EIA. It also helps determine the boundaries and focus of the project assessment. Therefore, D correctly matches with I.

The complete correct matching is A-II, B-III, C-IV, D-I, so option 3 is the correct answer.

19. C. Slate: Slate represents the lowest grade among the given metamorphic rocks. It forms from shale under low-grade metamorphic conditions.

B. Phyllite: Phyllite forms at a higher metamorphic grade than slate. It shows better foliation and a silky sheen due to increased recrystallization.

A. Schist: Schist represents a still higher grade of metamorphism than phyllite. It has larger visible minerals and strong schistosity.

D. Gneiss: Gneiss represents the highest grade among the given rocks. It shows distinct banding and forms under high-grade metamorphic conditions.

The increasing grade of metamorphism is Slate → Phyllite → Schist → Gneiss, so the correct order is C, B, A, D and option 3 is the correct answer.

20. C. $19 \le X \le 22$

$\mu = 16$, $\sigma = 3$

$Z = (X - \mu)/\sigma$

For $X = 19$, $Z = (19 - 16)/3 = 1$; for $X = 22$, $Z = (22 - 16)/3 = 2$

$P(19 \le X \le 22) = P(1 \le Z \le 2) \approx 0.1359$

D. $7 \le X \le 13$:

For $X = 7$, $Z = (7 - 16)/3 = -3$; for $X = 13$, $Z = (13 - 16)/3 = -1$

$P(7 \le X \le 13) = P(-3 \le Z \le -1) \approx 0.1573$

So D has probability greater than C.

B. $16 \le X \le 22$

For $X = 16$, $Z = (16 - 16)/3 = 0$; for $X = 22$, $Z = (22 - 16)/3 = 2$

$P(16 \le X \le 22) = P(0 \le Z \le 2) \approx 0.4772$

So B has probability greater than C and D.

A. $13 \le X \le 19$

For $X = 13$, $Z = (13 - 16)/3 = -1$; for $X = 19$, $Z = (19 - 16)/3 = 1$

$P(13 \le X \le 19) = P(-1 \le Z \le 1) \approx 0.6826$

So A has the highest probability.

The increasing order of probabilities is C, D, B, A, so option 3 is the correct answer.

21. A. $$r_A = \frac{\sum (x_i - \bar{x})(y_i - \bar{y})}{\sqrt{\sum (x_i - \bar{x})^2 \sum (y_i - \bar{y})^2}}$$

$$r_A = \frac{16}{\sqrt{64 \times 25}} = \frac{16}{40} = 0.400$$

D. $$r_D = \frac{\sum (x_i - \bar{x})(y_i - \bar{y})}{\sqrt{\sum (x_i - \bar{x})^2 \sum (y_i - \bar{y})^2}}$$

$$r_D = \frac{24}{\sqrt{49 \times 64}} = \frac{24}{56} = 0.429$$

C. $$r_C = \frac{\sum (x_i - \bar{x})(y_i - \bar{y})}{\sqrt{\sum (x_i - \bar{x})^2 \sum (y_i - \bar{y})^2}}$$

$$r_C = \frac{18}{\sqrt{25 \times 64}} = \frac{18}{40} = 0.450$$

B. $$r_B = \frac{\sum (x_i - \bar{x})(y_i - \bar{y})}{\sqrt{\sum (x_i - \bar{x})^2 \sum (y_i - \bar{y})^2}}$$

$$r_B = \frac{20}{\sqrt{36 \times 49}} = \frac{20}{42} = 0.476$$

Thus, the increasing order of correlation coefficients is A < D < C < B, because their respective values are 0.400, 0.429, 0.450 and 0.476. Therefore, the correct arrangement is A, D, C, B, which fits option 2 exactly.

22. B. CHF_2Cl: CHF_2Cl is HCFC-22 and has the shortest atmospheric lifetime among the given halocarbons. Its lifetime is much shorter than CFC-11 and perfluoroethane.

C. CF_2ClBr: CF_2ClBr is Halon-1211 and has a lifetime greater than CHF_2Cl. However, it is still shorter-lived than $CFCl_3$ and C_2F_6.

A. $CFCl_3$: $CFCl_3$ is CFC-11 and has a longer atmospheric lifetime than CHF_2Cl and CF_2ClBr. Its atmospheric persistence is significant, but it is far less than C_2F_6.

D. C_2F_6: C_2F_6 is a perfluorocarbon and has an extremely long atmospheric lifetime. Therefore, it comes last in ascending order of atmospheric lifetimes.

The ascending order of atmospheric lifetimes is $CHF_2Cl \rightarrow CF_2ClBr \rightarrow CFCl_3 \rightarrow C_2F_6$, so the correct sequence is B, C, A, D and option 2 is the correct answer.

23. D. Thermosphere: Mean free path is greatest in the thermosphere because molecular/ionic density is very low at high altitude. Therefore, thermosphere comes first in decreasing order of mean free path.

C. Mesosphere: The mesosphere lies below the thermosphere and has a smaller mean free path than the thermosphere. However, it has a greater mean free path than the stratosphere and troposphere.

B. Stratosphere: The stratosphere has denser air than the mesosphere. Therefore, the mean free path of molecules is smaller in the stratosphere than in the mesosphere.

A. Troposphere: The troposphere is the lowest and densest atmospheric layer. Therefore, it has the smallest mean free path among the given layers.

The decreasing order of mean free paths is Thermosphere → Mesosphere → Stratosphere → Troposphere, so the correct sequence is D, C, B, A and option 4 is the correct answer.

24. C. HCHO: HCHO has a very short atmospheric lifetime because it is rapidly removed by photolysis and oxidation. Therefore, it comes first in increasing order of atmospheric lifetime.

B. CH_3SCH_3: CH_3SCH_3, or dimethyl sulphide, has a short atmospheric lifetime, usually longer than HCHO. It is oxidized in the atmosphere but persists longer than formaldehyde.

A. CO: CO has an atmospheric lifetime of the order of weeks to months. Therefore, it is longer-lived than HCHO and CH_3SCH_3.

D. N_2O: N_2O has a very long atmospheric lifetime compared with the other given species. Therefore, it comes last in increasing order of atmospheric lifetime.

The increasing order of atmospheric lifetimes is HCHO → CH_3SCH_3 → CO → N_2O, so the correct sequence is C, B, A, D and option 1 is the correct answer.

25. B. Bare Rock: Ecological succession on bare rock begins with a surface having no developed soil. Therefore, bare rock is the first stage in lithosere succession.

A. Lichen: Lichens are pioneer organisms that colonize bare rock. They help in weathering of rock and formation of initial soil.

E. Grasses & Sedges: After enough soil develops, grasses and sedges establish themselves. They represent a later herbaceous stage after the lichen stage.

D. Shrubs: Shrubs appear after grasses and sedges as soil depth and organic matter increase. They represent a more advanced successional stage.

C. Forest: Forest is the climax stage in this sequence. It develops after shrubs when conditions become suitable for trees.

The correct sequence of ecological succession is Bare Rock → Lichen → Grasses & Sedges → Shrubs → Forest, so the correct sequence is B, A, E, D, C and option 1 is the correct answer.

26. A. Biosphere: Biosphere is the highest and largest ecological level among the given terms. It includes all ecosystems of the Earth where life exists.

E. Ecosystem: Ecosystem comes below biosphere because the biosphere is made up of many ecosystems. An ecosystem includes a community of organisms and its physical environment.

C. Community: Community comes below ecosystem because it includes only living populations of different species. It does not include the abiotic physical environment as an ecosystem does.

B. Population: Population comes below community because it consists of individuals of the same species living in an area. A community is made of many such populations.

D. Species: Species is the basic taxonomic unit in this hierarchy. A population is formed by individuals belonging to the same species.

The correct hierarchy from top to bottom is Biosphere → Ecosystem → Community → Population → Species, so the correct sequence is A, E, C, B, D and option 1 is the correct answer.

27. **B. Scoping:** Scoping is an early step in the EIA process after deciding that assessment is required. It identifies the key issues, boundaries, and important impacts to be studied.

    D. Impact identification: Impact identification follows scoping and lists the possible environmental impacts of the project. It determines which environmental components may be affected.

    E. Impact prediction: Impact prediction estimates the magnitude, extent, duration, and nature of the identified impacts. It gives the expected future condition with the proposed project.

    A. Impact evaluation: Impact evaluation assesses the significance of predicted impacts. It helps decide which impacts are major and need management attention.

    C. Impact mitigation: Impact mitigation comes after evaluation because significant adverse impacts must be reduced or controlled. It includes measures to avoid, minimize, or compensate environmental impacts.

    The correct EIA sequence is Scoping → Impact identification → Impact prediction → Impact evaluation → Impact mitigation, so the correct sequence is B, D, E, A, C and option 1 is the correct answer.

28. **C. Hydrolysis:** Hydrolysis is the first stage in biogasification of organic wastes. Complex organic polymers are broken into simpler soluble compounds.

    B. Acidogenesis: Acidogenesis follows hydrolysis. The soluble products are converted into volatile fatty acids, alcohols, hydrogen, and carbon dioxide.

    A. Acetogenesis: Acetogenesis occurs after acidogenesis. The acidogenic products are converted mainly into acetate, hydrogen, and carbon dioxide.

    D. Methanogenesis: Methanogenesis is the final stage of anaerobic digestion. Methanogens convert acetate, hydrogen, and carbon dioxide into methane-rich biogas.

    The correct order is Hydrolysis → Acidogenesis → Acetogenesis → Methanogenesis, so the correct sequence is C, B, A, D and option 3 is the correct answer.

29. **D. Bytownite:** Bytownite is a calcium-rich plagioclase mineral. In the continuous series of Bowen's reaction series, calcium-rich plagioclase crystallizes first at higher temperature.

    A. Labradorite: Labradorite follows bytownite as the plagioclase composition becomes less calcium-rich. It represents the next lower-temperature stage in the continuous series.

    C. Andesine: Andesine crystallizes after labradorite in the continuous plagioclase series. It is intermediate between calcium-rich and sodium-rich plagioclase compositions.

    B. Oligoclase: Oligoclase is more sodium-rich than andesine. It crystallizes later at lower temperature in the continuous series.

    The correct sequence according to the continuous series of crystallization is Bytownite → Labradorite → Andesine → Oligoclase, so the correct sequence is D, A, C, B and option 1 is the correct answer.

30. **C. Deep-sea sediment:** Deep-sea sediment forms the uppermost cover on typical oceanic crust. It lies above the volcanic and intrusive igneous layers.

    B. Basaltic Pillow Lava: Basaltic pillow lava occurs below the deep-sea sediment. It represents the extrusive basaltic layer formed by lava eruption under seawater.

    D. Sheeted dike complex: The sheeted dike complex lies below the pillow basalt layer. It represents the feeder dikes through which basaltic magma rose to the seafloor.

    A. Gabbro: Gabbro forms the lower part of typical oceanic crust. It is a coarse-grained intrusive mafic rock that crystallizes deeper below the sheeted dikes.

    The correct top-to-bottom sequence is Deep-sea sediment → Basaltic Pillow Lava → Sheeted dike complex → Gabbro, so the correct sequence is C, B, D, A and option 3 is the correct answer.

31. **A. Iron:** Iron is the most abundant element in the whole Earth because the Earth has an iron-rich core. Therefore, iron comes first in decreasing order of relative abundance.

B. Oxygen: Oxygen is next after iron in whole-Earth abundance. It is highly abundant in silicate minerals of the mantle and crust.

C. Silicon: Silicon comes after oxygen among the given elements. It is a major constituent of silicate minerals but is less abundant than iron and oxygen in the whole Earth.

D. Magnesium: Magnesium is abundant in mantle minerals such as olivine and pyroxene. However, its whole-Earth abundance is lower than iron, oxygen, and silicon.

E. Nickel: Nickel is present especially in the Earth's core along with iron. Among the given elements, it has the lowest relative abundance.

The decreasing order of relative abundance in the whole Earth is Iron → Oxygen → Silicon → Magnesium → Nickel, so the correct sequence is A, B, C, D, E and option 2 is the correct answer.

32. **C. United Kingdom:** The United Kingdom has the lowest annual CO_2 emission among the four given countries. Therefore, it comes first in increasing order of CO_2 emission.

D. Russia: Russia emits more CO_2 than the United Kingdom. However, Russia emits less CO_2 than India and China.

A. India: India has higher annual CO_2 emissions than Russia. It is among the largest current national CO_2 emitters after China and the United States.

B. China: China has the highest annual CO_2 emission among the given countries. Therefore, it comes last in increasing order of CO_2 emission.

The increasing order of CO_2 emission is United Kingdom → Russia → India → China, so the correct sequence is C, D, A, B and option 2 is the correct answer.

33. **C. Quartz:** Quartz has hardness 7 on Moh's scale. It is the hardest mineral among the given four minerals.

A. Apatite: Apatite has hardness 5 on Moh's scale. Therefore, it comes after quartz in decreasing order of hardness.

B. Calcite: Calcite has hardness 3 on Moh's scale. It is softer than apatite but harder than gypsum.

D. Gypsum: Gypsum has hardness 2 on Moh's scale. Therefore, it is the softest mineral among the given options.

The decreasing order of relative hardness is Quartz → Apatite → Calcite → Gypsum, so the correct sequence is C, A, B, D and option 4 is the correct answer.

34. **B. Birds and mammals:** Birds and mammals have the lowest numerical density per square metre in a meadow ecosystem. Therefore, they come first in increasing order of organism density.

A. Herbaceous angiosperms: Herbaceous angiosperms are more numerous than birds and mammals in a meadow. However, their density is lower than soil fauna and microorganisms.

D. Soil arthropods, annelids and nematodes: Soil arthropods, annelids, and nematodes occur in much larger numbers per square metre than plants and vertebrates. Therefore, they come after herbaceous angiosperms in increasing order.

C. Bacteria and Fungi: Bacteria and fungi have the highest numerical density in a terrestrial meadow ecosystem. Therefore, they come last in increasing order of density.

The increasing order of density is Birds and mammals → Herbaceous angiosperms → Soil arthropods, annelids and nematodes → Bacteria and fungi, so the correct sequence is B, A, D, C and option 4 is the correct answer.

35. **A. Municipal sewage (dry):** Municipal sewage (dry) has the lowest available energy per unit mass among the given biomass sources. Therefore, it comes first in the increasing order.

C. Animal waste (dry): Animal waste (dry) has higher available energy per unit mass than municipal sewage (dry). Therefore, it comes after municipal sewage and before straw.

B. Straw (grain crops): Straw from grain crops has higher available energy per unit mass than dry municipal sewage and dry animal waste. Therefore, it comes before woody biomass residues.

D. Wood chips, saw mill dust and forest residue: Wood chips, saw mill dust and forest residue have the highest available energy per unit mass among the given biomass sources. Therefore, they come last in the increasing order.

The correct increasing order of available energy per unit mass is Municipal sewage (dry) → Animal waste (dry) → Straw (grain crops) → Wood chips, saw mill dust and forest residue, so the correct sequence is A, C, B, D and option 2 is the correct answer.

36. Mean of a standard normal variable is always equal to zero. A standard normal variable is a normal variable that has been standardized using its mean and standard deviation. After standardization, the distribution has mean 0and standard deviation 1. Therefore, the mean is not equal to 1, less than 1 as a defining statement, or greater than 1.

Thus, option 4 is the correct answer.

37. Homoscedasticity is desirable in a linear regression model. It means that the variance of the residuals remains constant across all levels of the independent variables. Multicollinearity is undesirable because it makes coefficient estimates unstable. Autocorrelation among residuals is also undesirable because residuals should be independent. Correlation between residuals and independent variables is undesirable because residuals should not systematically relate to predictors.

Thus, option 1 is the correct answer.

38. Threshold Odor Number $= \dfrac{A+B}{A}$.

A = 25 mL sample

B = 175 mL distilled water

$$TON = \frac{25+175}{25}$$

$$TON = \frac{200}{25} = 8.0$$

Thus, option 2 is the correct answer.

39. Total Kjeldahl Nitrogen includes organic nitrogen and ammonia nitrogen. Ammonia nitrogen is represented by NH_3 and NH_4^+. It does not include nitrite (NO_2^-) or nitrate (NO_3^-). Therefore, the correct representation of TKN is Organic N + NH_3 + NH_4^+.

Thus, option 2 is the correct answer.

40. The Boudouard reaction is represented by the reaction between solid carbon and carbon dioxide. In this reaction, carbon reacts with carbon dioxide to produce carbon monoxide. The balanced form of the Boudouard reaction is $C+CO_2 \leftrightarrow 2CO$. This reaction is an important gas-solid reaction during biomass gasification because it converts carbon into carbon monoxide.

Therefore, among the given reactions, option 2 correctly represents the Boudouard reaction.

41. Perfluorooctanoic acid, or PFOA, is one of the regulated PFAS compounds in drinking water. The US Environmental Protection Agency has set the Maximum Contaminant Level for PFOA at 4.0 parts per trillion. This value is also expressed as 4.0 ng/L, because 1 ppt in water is equivalent to 1 ng/L. Among the given options, 4 parts per trillion is the exact MCL value for PFOA in drinking water.

Therefore, option 2 is the correct answer.

42. Percentage base saturation in soil is calculated by taking the sum of exchangeable base cations and dividing it by cation exchange capacity. The main exchangeable base cations are Ca^{2+}, Mg^{2+}, K^+, and Na^+. Therefore, percentage base saturation includes calcium, magnesium, potassium, and sodium in the numerator. It is then multiplied by 100 to express the value as a percentage.

Hence, the correct expression is

$$\frac{Ca^{2+} + Mg^{2+} + K^+ + Na^+}{CEC} \times 100,$$

so option 1 is the correct answer.

43. Relative error $= \dfrac{\text{loss in precipitate}}{\text{weight of precipitate}} \times 100$

Loss in precipitate = 0.5 mg

Weight of precipitate = 500 mg

$$\text{Relative error} = \frac{0.5}{500} \times 100$$

Relative error = 0.001 × 100 = 0.1%

Therefore, the relative error due to solubility loss is 0.1%, so option 2 is the correct answer.

44. Organochlorine pesticides show the highest persistence in soils due to their low biodegradability. They are chemically stable and resist microbial degradation for long periods. Organophosphates and carbamates are generally less persistent because they degrade more readily. Pyrethroids may persist to some extent, but organochlorines are classically known for maximum environmental persistence.

Therefore, option 4 is the correct answer.

45. The sulphur cycle can be most aptly called both sedimentary and gaseous. It has a sedimentary phase because sulphur occurs in rocks, minerals, soils, and sediments. It also has a gaseous phase because sulphur compounds such as sulphur dioxide and hydrogen sulphide occur in the atmosphere. Carbon and nitrogen cycles are mainly gaseous, while phosphorus cycle is mainly sedimentary.

Therefore, option 2 is the correct answer.

46. Battelle Environmental Evaluation System uses environmental parameters with assigned weights. In this method, environmental quality values are scaled for conditions before and after development. The difference between pre-development and post-development environmental quality values is used to judge impact. This method is more quantitative than a simple matrix method because it uses weighted and scaled environmental parameter values.

Therefore, the method asked in the question is Battelle Environmental Evaluation System, so option 2 is the correct answer.

47. Vermiculite has the maximum cation exchange capacity among the given clay minerals. Kaolinite has low cation exchange capacity because it is a 1 : 1 clay mineral with less surface charge. Illite has moderate cation exchange capacity due to potassium fixation between layers. Montmorillonite has high cation exchange capacity, but vermiculite generally has still higher CEC among these choices.

Therefore, option 4 is the correct answer.

48. Accretionary prism or accretionary wedge forms mainly at convergent plate margins involving subduction. At an ocean-continent convergence boundary, the oceanic plate subducts beneath the continental plate. Sediments scraped from the descending oceanic plate accumulate near the trench. This accumulation of scraped and deformed sediments forms the accretionary prism or wedge.

Therefore, option 4 is the correct answer.

49. $Q = 11\ m^3/s = 11 \times 60 = 660\ m^3/min$

Filtering velocity = 2.0 m/min

$$\text{Required filter area} = \frac{660}{2.0} = 330\ m^2$$

$$\text{Area of one bag} = \pi dL = \pi \times 0.35 \times 8.0$$

$$\text{Area of one bag} = 8.796\ m^2$$

$$\text{Number of bags} = \frac{330}{8.796} = 37.52$$

$$\text{Number of bags} \approx 38$$

Therefore, the required number of bags is 38, so option 2 is the correct answer.

50. $T = -18°\ C = 273 - 18 = 255\ K$

$$\lambda_{max} T = 2898\ \mu m\ K$$

$$\lambda_{max} = \frac{2898}{255}$$

$$\lambda_{max} = 11.36\ \mu m$$

Therefore, the wavelength of maximum emission of terrestrial radiation is 11.36 μm, so option 3 is the correct answer.

51.

$$w = 6.0\ gkg^{-1} = 0.006\ kgkg^{-1}$$

$$P = 1025\ mb$$

$$\varepsilon = 0.6$$

$$w = \frac{\varepsilon e}{P}$$

$$e = \frac{wP}{\varepsilon}$$

$$e = \frac{0.006 \times 1025}{0.6}$$

$$e = 10.25\ mb$$

Therefore, the vapor pressure is 10.25 mb, so option 2 is the correct answer.

52.

$$C_p = 4a(1 - a)^2$$

a = fractional wind speed decrease at the turbine

$$a = \frac{1}{2}$$

$$C_p = 4 \times \frac{1}{2} \times \left(1 - \frac{1}{2}\right)^2$$

$$C_p = 2\times\left(\frac{1}{2}\right)^2$$

$$C_p = 2\times\frac{1}{4} = \frac{1}{2}$$

Therefore, the value of power coefficient C_p is $\frac{1}{2}$, so option 1 is the correct answer.

53.
$$P = \rho gQH$$
$$\rho = 1000 \text{ kgm}^{-3}$$
$$g = 9.8 \text{ ms}^{-2}$$
$$Q = 950 \text{ m}^3 \text{ s}^{-1}$$
$$H = 200 \text{ m}$$
$$P = 1000 \times 9.8 \times 950 \times 200$$
$$P = 1{,}862{,}000{,}000 \text{ W}$$
$$P = 1862 \text{ MW}$$

Therefore, the electrical capacity is 1862 MW, so option 2 is the correct answer.

54.
$$V_g = \frac{1}{\rho f}\frac{\partial p}{\partial n}$$
$$f = 2\Omega \sin\phi$$
$$f = 2 \times 7.29 \times 10^{-5} \times \sin 45°$$
$$f = 1.031 \times 10^{-4} \text{ s}^{-1}$$
$$\frac{\partial p}{\partial n} = 5 \text{ mb per } 100 \text{ km}$$
$$5 \text{ mb} = 500 \text{ Pa}, \; 100 \text{ km} = 100000 \text{ m}$$
$$\frac{\partial p}{\partial n} = \frac{500}{100000} = 0.005 \text{ Pam}^{-1}$$
$$V_g = \frac{0.005}{1.25\times 1.031\times 10^{-4}}$$
$$V_g = 38.8 \text{ ms}^{-1} \approx 40 \text{ ms}^{-1}$$

Therefore, the geostrophic wind speed is approximately 40 ms^{-1}, so option 4 is the correct answer.

55.
$$\eta = 1 - e^{-\frac{wA}{Q}}$$
$$w = 0.15 \text{ ms}^{-1}$$
$$A = 6000 \text{ m}^2$$
$$Q = 300 \text{ m}^3 \text{ s}^{-1}$$
$$\eta = 1 - e^{-\frac{0.15\times 6000}{300}}$$
$$\eta = 1 - e^{-3}$$
$$\eta = 1 - 0.0498$$
$$\eta = 0.9502$$
$$\eta \mp 95.02\% \approx 95\%$$

Therefore, the efficiency of collection of the electrostatic precipitator is approximately 95%, so option 4 is the correct answer.

56. Assertion (A) is correct because in the Lotka-Volterra predator-prey model, prey and predator populations show cyclic oscillations and the predator population lags behind the prey population. Due to this lag, the prey and predator populations do not reach their equilibrium values at the same time during cyclic fluctuations.

Reason (R) is not correct because the phase difference between prey and predator populations is not 2π. A phase difference of 2π would mean that the two oscillations are in the same phase, not lagged in the required sense. The predator-prey oscillation is characterized by a phase lag, commonly treated as about a quarter cycle, not 2π.

Therefore, assertion is correct but reason is not correct, so option 3 is the correct answer.

57. Assertion (A) is correct because in the oxygen sag model, dissolved oxygen decreases after waste discharge and reaches a minimum at some downstream point. This minimum point occurs where the oxygen deficit becomes maximum in the stream.

Reason (R) is not correct because the rate of deoxygenation is not always greater than the rate of reaeration. Before the critical point, deoxygenation may exceed reaeration; at the critical point, they become equal. After that point, reaeration exceeds deoxygenation and dissolved oxygen begins to recover.

Therefore, assertion is correct but reason is not correct, so option 3 is the correct answer.

58. Assertion (A) is correct because the hydroxyl radical is one of the most important reactive oxidizing species in the troposphere. It controls the removal and oxidation of many atmospheric trace gases and pollutants.

Reason (R) is not correct because hydroxyl radical does not readily react with N_2, O_2, and CO_2 under normal tropospheric conditions. These gases are major stable atmospheric constituents and are not the main reactive targets of hydroxyl radicals. Hydroxyl radicals are important mainly because they react with gases such as CO, methane, volatile organic compounds, and other reduced atmospheric species.

Therefore, assertion is correct but reason is not correct, so option 3 is the correct answer.

59. Assertion (A) is correct because DDT caused serious adverse effects among fish-eating birds. It affected reproduction, caused eggshell thinning, and contributed to large population declines and mortality effects in such birds.

Reason (R) is also correct because DDT is persistent and fat-soluble. It undergoes bioaccumulation in organisms and biomagnification through food chains. Fish-eating birds occupy higher trophic levels, so they received higher DDT concentrations through contaminated fish.

Therefore, both assertion and reason are correct, and reason correctly explains the assertion, so option 1 is the correct answer.

60. Assertion (A) is correct because bioremediation involves biological treatment of contaminated sites by enhancing degradation or detoxification of pollutants. Environmental modification such as improving aeration and adding nutrients is a part of biostimulation, which supports biological activity at the contaminated site. Microbial seeding using xenobiotic-degrading microbes is also a valid bioremediation approach because it introduces organisms capable of degrading specific pollutants.

Reason (R) is also correct as a general statement because environmental modification can improve biological growth conditions, and microbial seeding can increase microbial biomass at the site. However, Reason (R) does not correctly explain Assertion (A), because it does not specifically explain degradation or detoxification of xenobiotics by microbes.

Therefore, both Assertion (A) and Reason (R) are correct, but Reason (R) is not the correct explanation of Assertion (A), so option 2 is the correct answer.

61. Assertion (A) is correct because the transitional zone between two or more communities is called an ecotone, and such a zone commonly shows greater species richness and population density at the junction due to edge effect.

Reason (R) is also correct because boundaries between communities provide opportunities for invasion, migration, and inter-specific competition. However, Reason (R) does not completely and directly explain the higher number of species and population density stated in Assertion (A). The direct reason for the assertion is edge effect, where species from both adjoining communities and some edge-adapted species occur together.

Thus, both statements are correct, but Reason (R) is not the correct explanation of Assertion (A), so option 2 is the correct answer.

62. Assertion (A) is correct because dioxins and furans are chlorinated compounds having somewhat similar chemical structures. Both are chlorinated aromatic organic compounds and are commonly discussed together because of their structural similarity and environmental persistence.

Reason (R) is correct because both contain two benzene rings linked through oxygen-containing bridge structures. Dioxins have two oxygen bridges, while furans have one oxygen bridge, and this structural relationship explains their similarity.

Therefore, both Assertion (A) and Reason (R) are correct, and Reason (R) correctly explains Assertion (A), so option 1 is the correct answer.

63. Assertion (A) is correct because α-quartz, β-quartz, tridymite, and cristobalite are polymorphs of silica. They all have the same chemical formula, SiO_2, but differ in crystal structure.

Reason (R) is not correct because polymorphism does not mean similar crystal structure with different chemical formulas. Polymorphism means the same chemical substance existing in different crystal forms.

The statement in Reason (R) describes the concept incorrectly, so Assertion (A) is correct but Reason (R) is not correct, and option 3 is the correct answer.

64. Assertion (A) is correct because orthophosphate is most available to plants at nearly neutral soil pH. At acidic pH, phosphate is fixed mainly by iron and aluminium compounds. At alkaline pH, phosphate is fixed mainly by calcium compounds.

Reason (R) is not correct because the higher charge of orthophosphate is not the reason for greater plant availability. Phosphate availability depends mainly on soil pH, solubility, and fixation reactions, not simply on higher ionic charge.

Therefore, Assertion (A) is correct but Reason (R) is not correct, so option 3 is the correct answer.

65. Assertion (A) is correct because an aquiclude can support a perched water table above the main water table. A perched water table forms when downward percolation of water is stopped or restricted by an impermeable layer.

Reason (R) is correct because aquicludes are relatively impermeable beds that hinder water movement. This impermeable nature of an aquiclude allows water to accumulate above it. Therefore, both Assertion (A) and Reason (R) are correct, and Reason (R) correctly explains Assertion (A), so option 1 is the correct answer.

66. Assertion (A) is correct because the saturated adiabatic lapse rate is less than the dry adiabatic lapse rate due to release of latent heat during condensation. In saturated rising air, condensation releases heat and reduces the rate of cooling with height. Therefore, the magnitude of saturated adiabatic lapse rate remains lower than the dry adiabatic lapse rate.

Reason (R) is not correct because saturation mixing ratio increases with increase in temperature. Thus, its rate of change with temperature is not always negative.

Therefore, Assertion (A) is correct but Reason (R) is not correct, so option 3 is the correct answer.

67. Assertion (A) is correct because Gallium Arsenide is an attractive photovoltaic cell material. GaAs has useful photovoltaic properties such as direct band gap and high absorption coefficient.

However, Reason (R) is not correct because the band gap of GaAs is not 2.43 eV. The direct band gap of GaAs is about 1.43 eV, not 2.43 eV.

Therefore, Assertion (A) is correct but Reason (R) is not correct, so option 3 is the correct answer.

68. Assertion (A) is correct because a fusion reactor cannot undergo meltdown in the same way as a fission reactor. Fusion requires very special plasma temperature, density, and confinement conditions.

Reason (R) is also correct because if the required conditions are disturbed, the plasma collapses. When the plasma collapses, the fusion reaction stops automatically. This directly explains why a fusion reactor cannot melt down like a fission reactor.

Therefore, both Assertion (A) and Reason (R) are correct and Reason (R) is the correct explanation of Assertion (A), so option 1 is the correct answer.

69. Assertion (A) is not correct because composting of municipal solid waste is initiated mainly by mesophilic microbes. During the initial stage, mesophilic organisms begin decomposition of easily degradable organic matter. The heat produced by microbial activity then raises the temperature and favours thermophilic microbes.

Reason (R) is correct because high temperature during composting is required to destroy pathogens. The thermophilic phase helps in sanitization of compost by killing many disease-causing organisms.

Therefore, Assertion (A) is not correct but Reason (R) is correct, so option 4 is the correct answer.

70. Assertion (A) is correct because anionic species are generally less attenuated in soil than cationic species. Most soil colloids carry predominantly negative charges, so cationic species are retained more strongly by cation exchange. Anionic species are usually more mobile because they are not adsorbed as strongly as cations on common negatively charged soil surfaces.

Reason (R) is not correct because soil surfaces do not completely lack anion-exchanging sites. Some soils, especially those containing variable-charge minerals, iron oxides, aluminium oxides, or kaolinitic materials under suitable pH conditions, can show anion exchange.

Therefore, Assertion (A) is correct, but Reason (R) is not correct, so option 3 is the correct answer.

71. Assertion (A) is not correct because cloudy nights generally do not favour strong formation of urban heat island. Urban heat island intensity is usually more pronounced during clear and calm nights, when rural areas lose heat rapidly by long-wave radiation. Cloud cover reduces radiative cooling from both urban and rural surfaces and therefore weakens the temperature contrast between them.

Reason (R) is correct because water vapour absorbs strongly in the long-wave infrared region. However, this correct statement does not make the assertion correct in the context of cloudy monsoon nights favouring urban heat island formation.

Therefore, Assertion (A) is not correct, but Reason (R) is correct, so option 4 is the correct answer.

72. Assertion (A) is correct because marine autotrophs, mainly phytoplankton, have a faster turnover rate than terrestrial autotrophs. Marine autotrophs are small, short-lived, and rapidly replaced, so their biomass turns over quickly. Terrestrial autotrophs such as trees and shrubs retain biomass for much longer periods and therefore have slower turnover.

Reason (R) is not correct because terrestrial autotrophs contribute more, not less, to the structural matrix of ecosystems. Large terrestrial plants form stems, trunks, roots, canopies, and long-lasting structural biomass, while marine phytoplankton contribute little structural framework.

Therefore, Assertion (A) is correct, but Reason (R) is not correct, so option 3 is the correct answer.

73. Assertion (A) is correct because biosensors can be used for detection and quantification of pollutants. A biosensor contains a biological recognition element that interacts specifically with the target chemical or pollutant.

Reason (R) is also correct because interaction of biomolecules with chemicals produces a measurable response. The transducer converts this biological or chemical interaction into a readable electrical, optical, thermal, or other signal. This signal allows the pollutant to be detected and quantified, so Reason (R) correctly explains Assertion (A).

Therefore, both Assertion (A) and Reason (R) are correct and Reason (R) is the correct explanation of Assertion (A), so option 1 is the correct answer.

74. **C. Range:** Range is a measure of variability because it shows the difference between the maximum and minimum values in a dataset. It directly indicates the total spread of the observations.

D. Interquartile Range: Interquartile range is a measure of variability because it shows the spread of the middle 50% of the data. It is calculated as the difference between the third quartile and the first quartile.

E. Mean Deviation: Mean deviation is a measure of variability because it measures the average absolute deviation of observations from a central value. It directly represents dispersion around the mean or median. Percentiles and quartiles are mainly positional measures, while Range, Interquartile Range, and Mean Deviation are measures of variability.

Therefore, the correct answer is C, D, E only, so option 3 is the correct answer.

75. **B. Uniform:** Uniform distribution can be a continuous probability distribution when the variable can take any value within an interval. In continuous uniform distribution, probability is spread evenly over the interval.

D. Normal: Normal distribution is a continuous probability distribution. It is defined for a continuous random variable and has the familiar bell-shaped curve. Binomial distribution is discrete because it counts the number of successes in a fixed number of trials. Hypergeometric distribution is also discrete because it counts successes in draws without replacement.

Therefore, the continuous probability distributions are Uniform and Normal only, so option 3 is the correct answer.

76. **B. Cl:** Atomic chlorine is an active chlorine species in the lower polar stratosphere. It participates directly in catalytic ozone destruction reactions.

D. ClO: Chlorine monoxide is also an active chlorine species in the lower polar stratosphere. It is one of the most important reactive chlorine forms involved in polar ozone depletion. HCl and $ClONO_2$ are mainly reservoir forms of chlorine, not active ozone-destroying chlorine species.

Therefore, the active species are Cl and ClO only, so option 3 is the correct answer.

77. **A. Presence of organic precursors:** Organic precursors are necessary because disinfection byproducts are formed when disinfectants react with natural organic matter. Higher precursor concentration generally increases DBP formation.

B. Free chlorine concentration: Free chlorine concentration affects the extent and rate of DBP formation. More available chlorine can increase reactions with organic precursors.

C. Bromide concentration: Bromide concentration affects DBP formation because bromide can form brominated disinfection byproducts. Thus, it is an important factor in DBP chemistry.

D. pH: pH affects the chemical speciation and reaction pathways during chlorination. Therefore, it influences both the rate and type of DBPs formed.

E. Temperature: Temperature affects reaction rates during water treatment. Higher temperature generally increases the rate of DBP formation.

All the given factors affect the rate of formation of disinfection byproducts, so option 4 is the correct answer.

78. **A. Rotary kiln:** Rotary kiln incinerators are commonly categorized according to combustion chamber design. They are used for solid, liquid, and hazardous waste incineration.

B. Moving grate: Moving grate incinerators are also categorized by their combustion chamber and grate arrangement. They are widely used for municipal solid waste combustion.

C. Fixed-hearth: Fixed-hearth incinerators are another combustion chamber-based category. They are used where waste is burned on a stationary hearth.

D. Fluidized-bed: Fluidized-bed incinerators are categorized by their combustion chamber operating principle. They use a bed of heated particles fluidized by air for efficient combustion.

All four are waste incinerator types categorized according to combustion chamber, so option 4 is the correct answer.

79. **A. Organic acid produced during degradation of organic matter:** Organic matter degradation produces organic acids. These acids contribute to lowering soil-water pH.

B. Release of H^+ by plants in exchange for nutritive base cations: Plants release hydrogen ions during uptake of base cations. This process adds acidity to the soil solution.

C. Sulphide oxidation: Oxidation of sulphide minerals produces acidity. This can strongly reduce soil-water pH.

D. Nitrification processes, where NH_4^+ is converted into NO_3^-: Nitrification releases hydrogen ions during conversion of ammonium to nitrate. Therefore, it is also a source of soil acidity.

All the listed processes can contribute to soil-water acidity below pH 5.0, so option 4 is the correct answer.

80. **A. Mass spectrometer (MS):** Mass spectrometer is well suited for HPLC when coupled as LC-MS. It provides sensitive detection and identification of compounds separated by liquid chromatography.

C. Absorbance: Absorbance detectors, especially UV-visible detectors, are among the most common HPLC detectors. They are suitable because many analytes absorb UV or visible light. Thermal conductivity detector is mainly used in gas chromatography, not as a best-suited HPLC detector. Flame ionization detector is also mainly used in gas chromatography because it requires vaporized analytes in a flame.

Therefore, the detectors best suited for HPLC are MS and absorbance only, so option 3 is the correct answer.

81. **A. Good stability and reproducibility:** An ideal detector for gas chromatography should give stable and reproducible responses. This is necessary for reliable qualitative and quantitative analysis.

B. A linear response to solutes that extends over several orders of magnitude: An ideal detector should show a wide linear dynamic range. This allows accurate measurement of both low and high solute concentrations.

C. A temperature range from room temperature to at least 400°C: Gas chromatography detectors should operate over a broad temperature range. A range from room temperature to at least 400°C is a desirable characteristic.

D. A short response time that is independent of flow rate: A short response time gives sharp peaks and better resolution. Independence from flow rate makes the detector response more reliable.

All four statements are correct characteristics of an ideal gas chromatography detector, so option 4 is the correct answer.

82. **A. Transesterification is involved in production of biodiesel:** This statement is correct because biodiesel is commonly produced by transesterification of oils or fats. In this process, triglycerides react with alcohol to form fatty acid alkyl esters.

C. Biohydrogen can be produced using hydrogenase by microalgae: This statement is correct because some microalgae can produce hydrogen through hydrogenase enzyme activity. Therefore, microalgae can be involved in biohydrogen production.

D. Bioethanol with high octane rating is produced using wood chips: This statement is correct because lignocellulosic biomass such as wood chips can be used for bioethanol production. Bioethanol is also known for its high octane value as a fuel.

B is incorrect because biogas is produced by anaerobic bacteria, not aerobic bacteria.

E is incorrect because photoautotrophic bacteria are not the standard organisms used for bioethanol production.

Therefore, the correct statements are A, C and D only, so option 1 is the correct answer.

83. **A. Wetland ecosystems store and purify water:** This statement is correct because wetlands act as natural water storage and filtration systems. They remove sediments, nutrients, and pollutants from water.

C. Chaparral ecosystems show excellent resilience stability: This statement is correct because chaparral vegetation is adapted to periodic disturbance, especially fire. Such ecosystems can recover after disturbance and therefore show resilience.

D. Arctic ecosystems have small food chains: This statement is correct because arctic ecosystems have relatively simple trophic structure. They generally support shorter and less complex food chains.

B is incorrect because coral reefs are highly productive ecosystems, not ecosystems of very low productivity.

E is incorrect because estuaries are usually nutrient-rich systems, and the statement as given is not correct.

Therefore, the correct statements are A, C and D only, so option 3 is the correct answer.

84. **A. Energy available at each successive trophic level always decreases:** This statement is correct because energy is lost at each trophic transfer. Therefore, less energy is available at higher trophic levels.

B. Nutrient cycles in a tropical rain forest are closed systems: This statement is correct in the ecological sense that tropical rain forests have tight and rapid nutrient cycling. Most nutrients are quickly recycled within the living biomass and surface litter system.

E. r-species are opportunists while k-species are competitors: This statement is correct because r-selected species reproduce rapidly and exploit temporary opportunities. K-selected species are usually better competitors under stable conditions near carrying capacity.

C is incorrect because in a climax community, the P/R ratio tends toward 1, not always greater than 1.

D is incorrect because ecosystem services include cultural services along with provisioning, regulating, and supporting services.

Therefore, the correct statements are A, B and E only, so option 3 is the correct answer.

85. **A. A-category projects require prior environment clearance from Central Government:** This statement is correct because Category A projects require prior environmental clearance at the central level. They are appraised at the central level before clearance is granted.

B. National defense and security projects have mandatory requirement for public consultation: This statement is incorrect because such projects are not subject to mandatory public consultation in the ordinary manner. They are treated differently because of national defense and security considerations.

C. B_1 category projects do not require environmental clearance: This statement is incorrect because B_1 category projects require environmental clearance. They generally require detailed appraisal and environmental assessment at the state level.

D. EAC and SEAC are the regulatory authorities to grant or reject environment clearance: This statement is incorrect because EAC and SEAC are appraisal committees. They appraise proposals and make recommendations, while the regulatory authorities grant or reject clearance.

Therefore, only statement A is correct, so option 4 is the correct answer.

86. A. PET type plastics are significantly recycled worldwide: This statement is correct because PET is one of the most commonly recycled plastic types. PET bottles and containers have established collection and recycling streams in many countries.

D. Plastics can absorb materials like oils and pesticides that can stay in recycled plastic: This statement is correct because plastics can sorb contaminants during use or disposal. Such absorbed chemicals may remain as contaminants in recycled plastic if not properly removed.

B is incorrect because polystyrene cups, bottles and plates generally do not have a high recycling rate.

C is incorrect because thermoset plastics are cross-linked and are not readily remelted and recycled like thermoplastics.

Therefore, the correct statements are A and D only, so option 1 is the correct answer.

87. A. The flow of liquid is steady: Darcy's law is applicable under steady flow conditions. The hydraulic gradient and discharge relationship is considered constant during such flow.

D. Relation between flow rate and hydraulic gradient is linear: Darcy's law states that discharge is directly proportional to hydraulic gradient. Therefore, a linear relation between flow rate and hydraulic gradient is a necessary condition.

B is incorrect because Darcy's law is classically applied to saturated flow through porous media.

C is incorrect because Darcy's law is valid for laminar flow, not turbulent flow through soil.

Therefore, the correct conditions are A and D only, so option 4 is the correct answer.

88. C. Registered owners of vehicles: The Environment Protection (End-of-Life Vehicles) Rules, 2025 apply to registered owners of vehicles. Registered owners are responsible for depositing end-of-life vehicles through the specified collection or scrapping system.

E. Registered vehicle scrapping facility: The rules also apply to registered vehicle scrapping facilities. Such facilities are part of the authorized system for environmentally sound dismantling and recycling of end-of-life vehicles.

A, B and D are not correct because waste batteries, e-waste, and plastic packaging are covered under separate waste management rules and are outside this specific end-of-life vehicle framework.

Therefore, the correct statements are C and E only, so option 3 is the correct answer.

89. B. Steady power without fluctuations and independent of vagaries of weather: This statement is correct because OTEC uses the relatively stable temperature difference between warm surface seawater and cold deep seawater. Therefore, it can provide steady power compared with many intermittent renewable sources.

D. Creation of some useful by-products such as desalinated water: This statement is correct because some OTEC systems can produce desalinated water as a useful by-product. This is especially associated with open-cycle or hybrid OTEC systems.

A is incorrect because OTEC has low thermal efficiency due to the small temperature difference available.

C is incorrect because OTEC generally has high installation and capital cost.

Therefore, the correct advantages are B and D only, so option 3 is the correct answer.

90. **A. Economic recovery of energy from tides is site specific:** This statement is correct because tidal energy is economically feasible only at locations with suitable tidal range or tidal current conditions. Therefore, site specificity is a major limitation.

B. Tidal plants disrupt marine life and ecology at the site: This statement is correct because tidal barrages and related installations can affect sediment transport, fish movement, and local marine ecology. Thus, ecological disturbance is a limitation.

C. Changing tidal range produces changing power: This statement is correct because tidal head and flow vary during the tidal cycle. Therefore, power output also changes with tidal conditions.

D. The turbines are required to operate at variable head: This statement is correct because tidal power systems experience changing water levels. Hence, turbines must operate under variable head conditions.

All four statements are main limitations of tidal energy, so option 4 is the correct answer.

91. The passage states that the inhospitable conditions of early Earth persisted for up to 500 million years. It also states that evidence for solid crust and liquid water is found as early as 4.3 billion years ago. Therefore, the most probable age of Earth from the passage is obtained by adding 500 million years to 4.3 billion years.

4.3 billion years + 0.5 billion years

= 4.8 billion years

Therefore, based on the passage, the most probable age of Earth is ~4.8 billion years, so option 1 is the correct answer.

92. The passage clearly states that early Earth was anoxic. It also states that absence of O_2 means Earth lacked an ozone layer. Therefore, the statement "Earth had ozone layer" is not correct for the early phase after Earth's formation. The other statements fit the passage because early Earth had no life, anoxic conditions, and no liquid water during the earliest inhospitable phase.

Hence, option 3 is the correct answer.

93. The passage states that water on Earth originated from volcanic outgassing of the planet's interior. It also states that water came from innumerable collisions with icy comets and asteroids. Therefore, volcanic outgassing, icy comets, and icy asteroids are mentioned as sources of water. Early oceans are not described as a source of water; instead, they are a later result or evidence of water on Earth.

Therefore, option 3 is the correct answer.

94. The passage states that additional evidence of water comes from ancient sedimentary rocks. It further states that among the oldest surviving sedimentary rocks are those found in southwestern Greenland. These rocks are dated to 3.86billion years ago. The passage says these ancient rocks indicate the presence of early oceans.

Therefore, the evidence for early oceans pertains to $\sim 3.86 \times 10^9$ years ago, so option 2 is the correct answer.

95. The passage states that ancient zircon crystals provide evidence for solid crust and liquid water on Earth as early as 4.3 billion years ago. This evidence comes from analyses of impurities trapped in zircon crystals and their oxygen isotope ratios. Sedimentary rocks from southwestern Greenland are also evidence of water, but they are dated later at 3.86 billion years ago. Therefore, the earliest evidence of liquid water mentioned in the passage comes from analysis of ancient zircon crystals.

Hence, option 3 is the correct answer.

96. The passage states that the earliest mass extinction occurred approximately 443million years ago near the end of the Ordovician period. It further states that the next mass extinction occurred 90million years later near the end of the Devonian. Therefore, the end-Devonian extinction time is calculated from the passage as:

443 million years ago – 90 million years

= 353 million years ago"

Thus, the end of the Devonian period corresponds most likely to ~353 million years ago, so option 2 is the correct answer.

97. The passage states that near the end of the Devonian, about 70%of marine invertebrate species died. It also states that near the end of the Permian, 95%of all marine species died. Among the mass extinctions mentioned in the passage, 95%marine species loss is the greatest marine loss. Therefore, the most devastating loss of marine life occurred near the end of the Permian.

Thus, option 3 is the correct answer.

98. The passage states that at the end of the Cretaceous period, a tremendous mass extinction event occurred. It further states that this event was sudden. The passage also says that abundant evidence suggests it was caused by the impact of a giant asteroid. Therefore, the likely cause of mass extinction at the end of the Cretaceous period was impact of a giant asteroid.

Thus, option 4 is the correct answer.

99. The passage states that the third mass extinction occurred near the end of the Permian. It further states that global cooling followed by rapid global warming with large climate variations may have been responsible. This statement is specifically connected in the passage with the end-Permian extinction. Therefore, the mass extinction related to global cooling followed by rapid global warming occurred near the end of the Permian. Thus, option 3 is the correct answer.

100. The passage states that the end-Ordovician extinction may have been related to global cooling. It also states that the end-Devonian extinction was probably related to climate change and global cooling. For the end-Permian extinction, the passage mentions global cooling followed by rapid global warming and large climate variations. The Cretaceous extinction is linked with giant asteroid impact, and Eocene is only mentioned without giving global cooling as the cause in the passage.

Therefore, global cooling has been associated with mass extinctions near the end of Ordovician, Devonian and Permian, so option 4 is the correct answer.

C. Copenhagen Summit
D. Kyoto Protocol
E. Tbilisi Conference

Choose the **correct** answer from the options given below:

1. A, B, C, D, E
2. E, B, A, D, C
3. E, D, C, B, A
4. D, A, B, E, C

6. Which of the following are NOT a nuclear fuel minerals?

1. Anglesite
2. Pitch blende
3. Carnotite
4. Monazite

7. Convert the concentration of the following gases in $\mu g/m^3$ unit and arrange them in increasing order of their concentration in $\mu g/m^3$ in ambient atmosphere at 25°C. Consider the gases follow ideal gas law.

A. 1 ppm of O_3
B. 1 ppm of SO_2
C. 4 ppm of NH_3
D. 1 ppm of CO
E. 1 ppm of CO_2

Choose the **correct** answer from the options given below:

1. E, D, A, B, C
2. D, E, A, C, B
3. B, C, A, D, E
4. C, D, E, B, A

8. Which of the following judicial principle has often been involved by Indian courts to uphold environmental clearance requirements under EIA?

1. Caveat Emptor
2. Eminent Domain
3. Precautionary Principle
4. Strict Liability

9. Select the CORRECT statement about CAM plants.

1. CAM plants separates CO_2 uptake and Calvin cycle spatially.
2. CAM plants separates CO_2 uptake and Calvin cycle temporally.
3. CAM pathway is mainly found in the grass family and their stomata are open during the day.
4. CO_2 concentration in the photosynthetic tissues of CAM plants is lower than that in the atmosphere during the day.

10. National Mission for a Green India (GIM) is one of the eight missions under National Action Plan on Climate Change. Which of the following is NOT listed as an aim of Green India Mission for forest cover and response to climate change?

1. Conservation
2. Enhancement
3. Protection
4. Restoration

11. Arrange the following unit processes of sludge treatment from first to the last:

A. Stabilization
B. Dewatering
C. Conditioning
D. Thickening
E. Reduction

Choose the **correct** answer from the options given below:

1. B, C, A, E, D
2. D, C, A, E, B
3. A, D, B, C, E
4. D, A, C, B, E

12. Consider the following are statements regarding visualization methods for describing data.

A. We can calculate value of 55th percentile from Box-plots.
B. Chernoff plot is a Hierarchical chart.
C. In Pie-chart, area of circle is non-proportional to frequency of a particular categorical response.
D. Ishikawa diagrams are used for visualizing the cause and effect relationship.
E. Histogram is used for categorical data.

Choose the **correct** answer from the options given below:

1. A, B and C only
2. B, D and E only
3. C and E only
4. B and D only

13. Which of the following best explains the rational behind categorizing projects as Category A and Category B in the EIA Notification of 2006?

1. To allow public opinion to assess project approval.
2. To delegate simpler projects to state authorities and complex ones to the central government.
3. To ensure equal distribution of environmental responsibility.
4. To minimize delays in industrial development and national interest.

14. Match the LIST-I with LIST-II.

LIST-I (Article)	LIST-II (Description)
A. 51A(g)	I. Protection of monuments and places and objects of national importance
B. 49	II. To protect and improve the national environment including forest, lakes, rivers and wildlife, and to have compassion for living creatures
C. 48	III. Protection and improvement of environment and safeguarding of forest and wildlife
D. 48A	IV. Organization of agriculture and animal husbandry

Choose the **correct** answer from the options given below:

1. A-II, B-IV, C-I, D-III
2. A-III, B-I, C-IV, D-II
3. A-II, B-I, C-IV, D-III
4. A-I, B-IV, C-III, D-II

15. The proportion of the assimilated food that is used to produce new consumer biomass is production efficiency.

Arrange the following ectothermic organisms in the increasing order of their production efficiency.

A. Fishes B. Carnivores
C. Herbivores D. Detritivores

Choose the **correct** answer from the options given below:

1. B, C, D, A 2. A, C, D, B
3. A, D, C, B 4. D, A, C, B

16. Consider the following statements and choose the INCORRECT statement.

1. Diesel vehicles, operated 'fuel lean', produce less NO compared to gasoline vehicle.
2. More ozone will be formed in an area having high NO compared to NO_2 concentration in ambient atmosphere.
3. Ozone was not present in highest quantity in London Smog.
4. Aldehydes absorb sunlight with $\lambda <$ 315 nm i.e., UV-B and some UV-A.

17. Arrange the following states of India in the order of their ranking (top to bottom) in Swachh Survekshan 2023.

A. Chattisgarh B. Madhya Pradesh
C. Maharashtra D. Odisha
E. Telangana

Choose the **correct** answer from the options given below:

1. C, E, B, A, D
2. B, C, D, A, E
3. C, B, A, D, E
4. D, B, E, A, C

18. Which of the following is NOT true for ecological succession?

1. Primary succession involves colonization of habitats devoid of life.
2. In primary succession, colonizing species deal with more stressful conditions compared to species colonizing in secondary succession.
3. Secondary succession involves re-establishment of a community.
4. Colonizing species face less competition for resources in secondary succession compared to primary succession.

19. Choose the correct mathematical expressions related to noise.

A. Sound power (w) = Sound intensity (I) × Area (A)

B. Sound period and frequency are inversely related

C. Speed of sound in air, C = 20.05 $(\text{Temperature})^2$

D. $L = 10 \log_{10} \dfrac{\text{measured quantity (Q)}}{\text{reference quantity } (Q_0)}$

E. $I = \dfrac{(P_{rms})^2}{\rho c}$

Choose the **correct** answer from the options given below:

1. A, B, C and D only
2. B, C, D and E only
3. A, B, D and E only
4. A, B, C and E only

20. What will be the aerodynamic diameter of a spherical particle having diameter of 2 μm and density of 3 g/cm^3? Terminal velocity of spherical particle and the reference particle are same and the density of reference particle is 1 g/cm^3.

1. ~ 6.0 μm
2. ~ 3.5 μm
3. ~ 2.0 μm
4. ~ 1.8 μm

21. Arrange the following carbonaceous fuels in increasing order of their atomic H/C values:

A. Petroleum
B. Peat
C. Methane
D. Lignite
E. Anthracite

Choose the **correct answer** from the options given below:

1. A, C, B, D, E
2. B, A, D, C, E
3. C, A, B, D, E
4. E, D, B, A, C

22. Which of the following is INCORRECT compositionally?

1. Rubbish does not contain garbage.
2. Refuse contain both rubbish and garbage.
3. Garbage contain both garbage and rubbish.
4. Refuse have less water content (%) than garbage.

23. The atmospheric condition at a given time is shown in figure given below. If the average wind speed that prevailed was 10 m/s, what will be the ventilation coefficient?

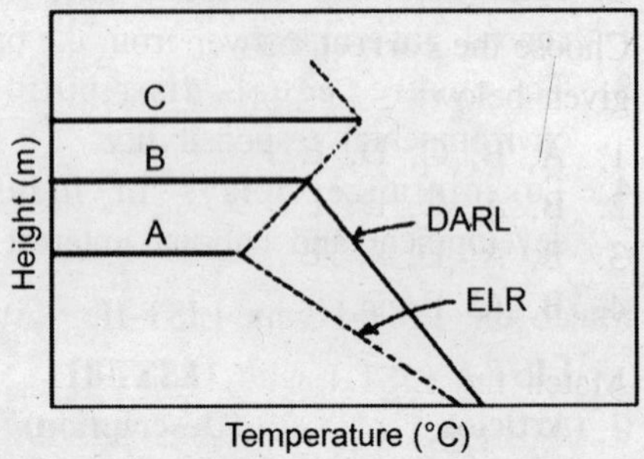

1. 10 A m^2/s
2. 10 B m^2/s
3. 100 A m^2/s
4. 10 C m^2/s

24. Choose the INCORRECT statement about lakes.

1. Hypolimnion in lake is poorly mixed compared to Epilimnion.
2. As summer progresses, stability increases because epilimnion continues to warm while hypolimnion remain at fairly constant temperature.
3. Temperate lakes always have at least one cycles of stratification and turnover every year.
4. Lake stratification and turnover often causes eutrophication and is not good for health of lakes.

25. Choose the INCORRECT statement about solar ponds.

1. Most common heat transfer fluid for a solar system is water.
2. Solar ponds must have salinity gradient with depth to collect and optimally store the energy.
3. Solar ponds store energy in upper convective zone (salinity <5%).
4. Solubility of salt in solar ponds should not vary appreciably with temperature.

26. Arrange the following gases in decreasing order of their percentage abundance in atmosphere on dry basis.

A. Carbon dioxide
B. Argon
C. Helium
D. Neon
E. Methane

Choose the **correct** answer from the options given below:

1. A, B, C, D, E
2. B, A, C, D, E
3. B, A, D, C, E
4. B, A, E, D, C

27. Match the LIST-I with LIST-II.

LIST-I (Earthworm type)	LIST-II (Name)
A. Common field worm	I. *Helodrilus chloroticus*
B. Manure worm	II. *Diplocardia verrucosa*
C. Green worm	III. *Helodrilus caliginosus*
D. Slim earthworm	IV. *Eisenia foetida*

Choose the **correct** answer from the options given below:

1. A-IV, B-III, C-II, D-I
2. A-III, B-IV, C-I, D-II
3. A-IV, B-I, C-II, D-III
4. A-II, B-I, C-IV, D-III

28. All the Sustainable Development Goals (SDGs), other than Partnership (Goal 17) represent Ecological, Social and Economic aspects. What are their respective numbers (out of 16)?

1. Ecological : Social : Economic = 4 : 6 : 6
2. Ecological : Social : Economic = 5 : 6 : 5
3. Ecological : Social : Economic = 4 : 8 : 4
4. Ecological : Social : Economic = 5 : 5 : 6

29. Arrange the following major stages of waste degradation in landfills starting from the first to the last:

A. Oxidation
B. Aerobic degradation
C. Acetogenesis
D. Hydrolysis and fermentation
E. Methanogenesis

Choose the **correct** answer from the options given below:

1. B, A, C, E, D
2. A, B, C, D, E
3. B, D, C, E, A
4. D, B, A, E, C

30. Match the LIST-I with LIST-II.

LIST-I (Chemical characteristics)	LIST-II (Rock type)
A. Phosphate	I. Bauxite
B. Sulphate	II. Stromatolites
C. Mg-Fe rich silicate	III. Anhydrite
D. Al oxyhydroxides	IV. Basalt

Choose the **correct** answer from the options given below:

1. A-I, B-II, C-III, D-IV
2. A-II, B-III, C-IV, D-I
3. A-III, B-II, C-IV, D-I
4. A-I, B-III, C-II, D-IV

31. Which of the following are components of Monitoring and Feedback in ecological impact analysis process?

A. To determine the significance and importance of prediction
B. To identify and predict impacts on ecosystem component
C. To provide opportunities for corrective action in light of unforeseen outcomes
D. To reduce significant adverse effects
E. To strengthen the knowledge base

Choose the **correct** answer from the options given below:

1. A, B and C only
2. B and D only
3. C and E only
4. C, D and E only

32. Which of the following is most important analog of DDT that have same general size, shape and possess the same insecticidal properties but is more biodegradable and less bioaccumulative ?

1. Para-dichlorodiphenyldichloroethane (DDD)
2. DDA
3. Methoxy chlor
4. Toxaphene

33. Which of the following are examples of empirical classification of world climates?

A. Bergeron and Spatial
B. Koppen
C. Oliver-Hidore
D. Thornthwaite
E. Trewartha

Choose the **correct** answer from the options given below:

1. A and C only
2. B and D only
3. C and E only
4. B, C and D only

34. Which of the following cloud types are found in stratosphere?

A. Cirrus clouds
B. Cumulonimbus clouds
C. Mother of Pearl clouds
D. Nacreous clouds
E. Noctilucent clouds

Choose the **correct** answer from the options given below:

1. A, C and D only
2. B, D and E only
3. C, D and E only
4. A, D and E only

35. Read the following statements.

A. In the northern hemisphere Coriolis effect and frictional forces deflect winds to the right, producing clockwise circulation.
B. Principle climatic zones in the world are defined in terms of yearly average precipitation.
C. Altitude, mountains, large bodies of water and ocean currents majorly affect regional climate.
D. Negative values of Southern Oscillation Regional Climate Index are usually associated with El Nino events.
E. La Nina refers to the times when tropical Pacific is warmer than normal.

Choose the **correct** answer from the options given below:

1. A, B, C and D only
2. A, C and D only
3. B, C, D and E only
4. A, B, C and E only

36. Select the INCORRECT statement about population growth.

1. In the population with a type I survivorship curve, new borne, juveniles and young adults, all have high survival rates.
2. In the population with a type II survivorship curve, individuals have approximately constant chance of surviving from one generation to the next in their life span.
3. In the population with a type III survivorship curve, death rates are very high for young individuals.
4. Survivorship curves can not vary among population of a species between males and females in a population.

37. Match the LIST I with LIST-II.

LIST-I	LIST-II
A. Pressure is enough to allow free flow of water above ground	I. Cone of depression
B. Water is withdrawn faster than its replenishment	II. Piezometric surface
C. Elevation to which water rises in the aquifer	III. Artesian well
D. Zone of water between aquicludes	IV. Confined water

Choose the **correct** answer from the options given below:

1. A-I, B-II, C-III, D-IV
2. A-III, B-I, C-II, D-IV
3. A-III, B-II, C-I, D-IV
4. A-IV, B-III, C-II, D-I

38. Consider the following statements about parasites.

A. Hemiparasite extract water and minerals nutrients from host.
B. Hemiparasite have green leaves and can photosynthesize.
C. Hemiparasite do not rely exclusively on the host for carbohydrates.
D. Corn smut fungus is an example of ectoparasite.
E. Ectoparasite does not have ease of dispersal in environment.

Choose the **correct** answer from the options given below:

1. A, B and D only
2. A, C and D only
3. A, B, C and D only
4. A, B, C, D and E

39. The Principle of Absolute Liability, evolved in Indian environmental jurisprudence, is primarily associated with which of the following landmark case?

1. Indian Council of Enviro-Legal action Vs Union of India (1996)
2. M.C. Mehta Vs Kamal Nath (1997)
3. M.C. Mehta Vs Union of India (Oleum Gas leak, 1987)
4. Vellore Citizens Welfare Forum Vs Union of India (1996)

40. Match the LIST-I with LIST-II.

LIST-I (Soil Type)	LIST-II (Major Characteristics)
A. Vertisols	I. Little profile development, ochric epipedon common
B. Histosols	II. Usually formed on volcanic ash dominated by allophane
C. Entisols	III. High in swelling clays, deep cracks in dried soils
D. Andisols	IV. Undergone little profile development, >20% organic matter

Choose the **correct** answer from the options given below:

1. A-II, B-IV, C-III, D-I
2. A-I, B-II, C-IV, D-III
3. A-III, B-IV, C-I, D-II
4. A-IV, B-III, C-II, D-I

41. Arrange the following steps of an idealized EIA process in order of execution:

A. Assessment
B. Audit
C. Decision Making
D. Evaluation
E. Mitigation

Choose the **correct** answer from the options given below:

1. A, D, E, C, B
2. B, D, A, C, E
3. A, B, D, C, E
4. A, D, E, B, C

42. Which of the following is INCORRECT about nuclear power plants used for energy generation?

1. The only naturally occurring Uranium isotope that can undergo fission is ^{235}U.
2. Control rods in fission reactors are made from Graphite, neutron absorbing element.
3. Breeder reactors produce more fissionable materials than they consume.
4. Thermal breeder reactor converts ^{232}Th by neutron absorption and beta decay into ^{233}U.

43. In an aquatic system, high consumption rates (herbivores) and relatively short life spans of the primary producers (phytoplankton) result in a inverted pyramid of biomass relative to pyramid of energy. Which of the following are correct?

A. Biomass of heterotrophs is greater at any given time than biomass of the autotrophs.
B. Energy produced by autotrophs is greater than that produced by heterotrophs.
C. Inverted pyramid of biomass are most common in nutrient poor water with low autotroph biomass.
D. Detritus makes lower proportional contribution to energy flow in nutrient poor water than in nutrient rich water.
E. Biomass ratio (heterotrophs/autotrophs) of above one indicate inverted pyramid.

Choose the **correct** answer from the options given below:

1. A, B . d C only
2. A, B, C and E only
3. A, D and E only
4. A, B, C and D only

44. Arrange the following statements regarding calculations of Chi-square test statistic for assessing association between two categorical variables in the correct sequence.

A. Calculate value of χ^2 statistic.
B. Calculate expected cell frequencies.
C. Assess degree of freedom.
D. Tabulate data in contingency table.
E. Compare calculated value with critical value and take decision.

Choose the **correct** answer from the options given below:

1. A, B, E, C, D 2. C, B, A, E, D
3. D, A, B, E, C 4. D, B, A, C, E

45. Choose the CORRECT statements about air pollution control methods.

A. Impaction of particles is directly proportional to particle density and diameter squared.
B. Probability of resuspension of particles is inversely proportional to particle diameter.
C. In cyclones, force produced by rotational motion of fluid is directly proportional to square of terminal velocity.
D. Activated alumina and sulfuric acid are common water vapour collection materials used in demisters.
E. Baghouses dust collector does not work on the principle of sedimentation and electrostatic attraction of particles.

Choose the **correct** answer from the options given below:

1. A, B, C and D only
2. A, B, C and E only
3. A, C and D only
4. A, C, D and E only

46. Arrange the following terrestrial biomes in the decreasing order of their global average Net Primary Productivity (g/m^2/yr).

A. Boreal Forest
B. Temperate Grassland
C. Tropical Forest
D. Temperate forest
E. Crops

Choose the **correct** answer from the options given below:

1. C, D, E, B, A
2. C, D, B, E, A
3. C, B, D, E, A
4. A, E, B, D, C

47. Match the LIST-I with LIST-II.

LIST-I (Reduction in Ambient temperature with height is γ. Dry and saturated adiabatic lapse rates are γ_d and γ_s, respectively)	**LIST-II (Stability class)**
A. $\gamma < \gamma_s$	I. Absolutely Unstable
B. $\gamma > \gamma_d$	II. Conditionally Unstable

C. $\gamma = \gamma_d$ III. Absolutely Stable

D. $\gamma_s > \gamma > \gamma_d$ IV. Dry Neutral

Choose the **correct** answer from the options given below:

1. A-I, B-III, C-IV, D-II
2. A-III, B-II, C-IV, D-I
3. A-III, B-I, C-IV, D-II
4. A-I, B-III, C-IV, D-II

48. The solid organic fraction of .... are mainly derived from lower plants lacking lignocellulosic tissues.

1. Bituminous coal 2. Bituminous shales
3. Lignite 4. Anthracite

49. Which of the following is NOT true for composting of waste?

1. Moisture should not be present.
2. Particle size must be less than 5 cm.
3. Compost increases moisture holding capacity of soil.
4. Carbon to nitrogen ratio must be in the range of 20-25 to 1.

50. In an open system, which of the following does not partition between the gas and aqueous phase?

1. CO_2 2. NH_3
3. H_3PO_4 4. H_2S

51. Which of the following is NOT an element and component of hazard and risk assessment of waste?

1. Process knowledge and documentation
2. Process and equipment integrity
3. Reduction in use of hazardous substances
4. Standards, codes, laws and practices

52. Match the LIST-I with LIST-II.

LIST-I (Class)	LIST-II (Disease)
A. Water borne	I. Trachoma
B. Water based	II. Yellow fever
C. Water washed	III. Typhoid
D. Water related	IV. Schistosomiasis

Choose the **correct** answer from the options given below:

1. A-III, B-II, C-I, D-IV
2. A-II, B-III, C-IV, D-I
3. A-III, B-IV, C-I, D-II
4. A-III, B-II, C-IV, D-I

53. Consider the following statements about HPLC:

A. In normal phase HPLC, the stationary phase is non-polar and the mobile phase is polar.

B. In normal phase HPLC, the least polar compound eludes first and increasing polarity of mobile phase decreases elution time.

C. In reverse phase HPLC, the most polar compound eludes first and increasing polarity of mobile phase increases elution time.

D. In the isocratic mode of HPLC analysis, the polarity of mobile phase remains unchanged throughout the run.

E. The resolution of analysis depends on proper balance of intermolecular forces among the analyte, the mobile phase and the stationary phase.

Choose the **correct** answer from the options given below:

1. B, C and D only
2. A, C, D and E only
3. B, C, D and E only
4. A, B, C and E only

54. Match the LIST-I with LIST-II.

LIST-I (National Park)	LIST-II (River)
A. Dudhawa	I. Jhelum
B. Kalesar	II. Sharda
C. Kazinag	III. Teesta
D. Khangchendzonga	IV. Yamuna

Choose the **correct** answer from the options given below:

1. A-II, B-IV, C-III, D-I
2. A-II, B-IV, C-I, D-III
3. A-IV, B-II, C-III, D-I
4. A-IV, B-II, C-I, D-III

55. Match the LIST-I with LIST-II.

LIST-I (Ways of expressing probabilities)	LIST-II (Situations expressing probabilities)
A. Decimal Notations	I. Random variables
B. Scientific Notations	II. Conversions
C. Percentage	III. Computations
D. Pictorial Form	IV. For low probabilities

Choose the **correct** answer from the options given below:

1. A-I, B-II, C-IV, D-III
2. A-III, B-IV, C-II, D-I
3. A-IV, B-III, C-I, D-II
4. A-III, B-II, C-IV, D-I

56. Which of the following statements regarding statistical tool to assess various aspects of a relationship is/are true?

A. For assessing agreement between two quantitative variables, Cohen's Kappa is used.

B. The residuals in a linear relationship should follow normal distribution.

C. For assessing strength of relationship between exposure and outcome (yes Vs no), relative risk is used.

D. When dependent variable is quantitative and one independent variable is non-linear, we do Curvi linear regression.

E. There are three parameters for expressing linear relationship between one dependent and one independent variable (both quantitative).

Choose the **most appropriate** answer from the options given below:

1. A only
2. B and C only
3. C and E only
4. B and D only

57. Consider the following statements and choose the INCORRECT statement.

1. Chromate ions are soluble in water.
2. Arsenate ion are insoluble in water.
3. Arsenite is more toxic than arsenate.
4. Chromite is more toxic than chromate.

58. In an absorbed dose of 0.2 Gy of slow neutron radiation produces the same biological effect as 2 Gy of gamma radiation, then the relative biological effectiveness for slow neutron would be ....

1. 2.2
2. 0.1
3. 0.2
4. 10

59. How deep into Earth, plate recycling occurs?

1. Crust-mantle boundary
2. Lithosphere-Asthenosphere boundary
3. Upper mantle-lower mantle boundary
4. Mantle-core boundary

60. Choose the CORRECT statements about biological degradation of waste:

A. End product of biological degradation is always less toxic than parent compound.

B. pH of soils play vital role and at low pH fungi dominates and likely to form epoxide.

C. Persistence is a 'conditional' property of biodegradable compounds.

D. Mineralization is the complete conversion of an organic compound to the end products of CO_2 and water.

E. Recalcitrant compounds cannot be biodegraded under any circumstances.

Choose the **correct** answer from the options given below:

1. A, B and C only
2. B, C and D only
3. B, C, D and E only
4. A, B, C and D only

61. Choose the INCORRECT statement:

1. Clay particles act as colloids in water.
2. The pH of soils tends to buffer against large increase in pH as they have reserve acidity.
3. Precipitation reactions does not help in retaining heavy metals in soils.
4. Replacement of natural long rooted vegetation by wheat and other shallow rooted crops can increase soil salinity.

62. From the analysis of water given below, calculate the amount of lime and soda (in mg/*l* as $CaCO_3$) necessary to soften water to 90.0 mg/*l* as $CaCO_3$:

Composition of water (mg/*l* as $CaCO_3$)		
Ca^{2+} = 159.2	CO_2 = 29.3	HCO_3^- = 195.0
Mg^{2+} = 75.8		SO_4^- = 39.8
Na^+ = 27.4		Cl^- = 27.6

1. ~235 and ~60
2. ~296 and no soda ash
3. ~262 and ~34
4. ~235 and no soda ash

63. How many methodologies under 'offset mechanism' of the Carbon Credit Trading Scheme (CCTS, 2023), allowing non-obligated entities to participate in voluntary climate mitigation projects, are proposed by the Government of India?

1. 5
2. 6
3. 8
4. 12

64. Which of the following rules came in existence in the same calendar year in India?

A. The Hazardous and other Waste (Management and Transboundary Movement) Rules
B. The Batteries (Management and Handling) Rules
C. The Biomedical Waste Management Rules
D. The Solid Waste Management Rules
E. The Public Liability Insurance Rules

Choose the **correct** answer from the options given below:

1. A, B and C only
2. B, C and D only
3. A, C and D only
4. C, D and E only

65. Match the LIST-I with LIST-II.

LIST-I (Sampling frame– Circles denotes unit selected)	**LIST-II (Sampling Procedure)**
A. 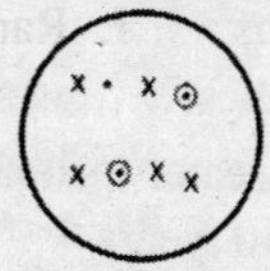	I. Systematic Sampling
B. 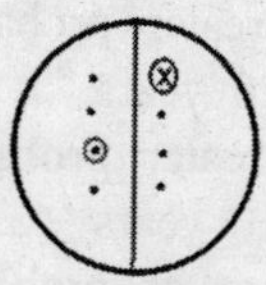	II. Cluster Sampling
C. 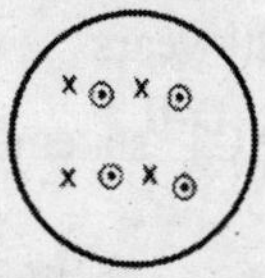	III. Simple Random Sampling
D. 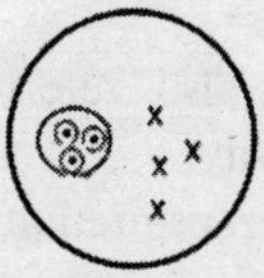	IV. Stratified Random Sampling

Choose the **correct** answer from the options given below:

1. A-II, B-I, C-III, D-IV
2. A-III, B-IV, C-I, D-II
3. A-I, B-III, C-IV, D-II
4. A-III, B-I, C-II, D-IV

66. Consider the following statements about bioremediation.

A. One of the most common limiting factor for in-situ biodegradation in saturated zone is availability of oxygen.
B. N and P are common additives which enhance rate of biodegradation.
C. Bioventing and bioaccessibility adversely impact biodegradation in vadose zone.
D. Methanotropic organism are involved in/ example of cometabolism biodegradation.
E. In-situ biodegradation applications are based only on aerobic biodegradation.

Choose the **correct** answer from the options given below:

1. B, D and E only
2. A, B and D only
3. A, B, D and E only
4. B, C and D only

67. The endangered species ....

1. have a 50% or greater probability of extinction within 10 years
2. have a 50% or greater probability of extinction within 20 years
3. have a 20% or greater probability of extinction within 10 years
4. have a 20% or greater probability of extinction within 20 years

68. Choose the INCORRECT statement about heat islands.

1. Low surface albedo is a likely cause of urban heat.
2. Surface albedo is also referred to as shortwave reflectivity.
3. Shading and evapotranspiration by urban forestry cause urban heating.
4. Cool roofs/green roofs have high reflectivity and cause urban cooling.

69. Remote sensing sensors can work on wavelengths 8 to 14 μm and 3 to 5 μm. Based on which of the following laws, wavelength of 8 to 14 μm is chosen to collect data?

1. Kirchoff's Law
2. Plank's Law
3. Stefan Boltzman Law
4. Wien's Displacement Law

70. Match the LIST-I with LIST-II.

LIST-I (Substance)	LIST-II (Application)
A. Magnesium hydroxide: $pK_s = 11.2$	I. Coagulation
B. Calcium carbonate: $pK_s = 8.3$	II. Coagulation and iron removal
C. Ferric hydroxide: $pK_s = 38.5$	III. Softening, corrosion control
D. Aluminum hydroxide: $pK_s = 33$	IV. Softening

Choose the **correct** answer from the options given below:

1. A-I, B-III, C-II, D-IV
2. A-IV, B-II, C-III, D-I
3. A-IV, B-III, C-II, D-I
4. A-III, B-IV, C-I, D-II

71. Arrange the following geological/paleoclimate events from oldest to youngest:

A. Setting up of Monsoon climate on the Indian subcontinent
B. Appearance of *Homo Sapiens*
C. Appearance of free oxygen on the earth
D. Last Glacial Maximum
E. Deposition of Gondwana coals

Choose the **correct** answer from the options given below:

1. C, E, A, B, D
2. E, C, D, A, B
3. D, C, E, B, A
4. D, C, A, B, E

72. Consider the following statements about solubility of gases in surface water.

A. Equilibrium concentration of a dissolved gas in water as per Henry's law is referred to as its saturation value.
B. There may be more dissolved gas in water than its saturation value in water.
C. It is more common for a dissolved gas to be present in less amount in water than its saturation value in water.
D. The excess or deficit of a dissolved gas compared to its saturation value cannot be brought back to saturation level in water.
E. Solubility of gas depends on partial pressure of the gas but is independent of purity of water.

Choose the **correct** answer from the options given below:

1. A, B, C and E only
2. A, B and C only
3. A, B, C and D only
4. A, C, D and E only

73. Which of the following process in gassification of waste is endothermic?

1. $C + O_2 \rightarrow CO_2$
2. $C + H_2O \rightarrow CO + H_2$
3. $C + 2H_2 \rightarrow CH_4$
4. $2C + O_2 \rightarrow 2CO$

74. Consider the following statements and Choose the INCORRECT statement:

1. Ozone partially absorbs UV-B in stratosphere
2. Conversion of inactive to active chlorine occur at surface of particles formed by solution of H_2O, H_2SO_4, and HNO_3
3. Bromine containing hydrogen free substances 'Halons' do not have ozone depleting potential
4. Denitrification of lower stratosphere extends life of the Antarctic ozone hole

75. Choose the **CORRECT** statements:

A. Thermosetting plastic is easier to recycle compared to thermoplastic.
B. Microplastic include plastic size less than 5 μm only.
C. Thermal depolymerisation involves the conversion of assorted polymers into petroleum.
D. Incineration is not an environment friendly option to dispose plastic waste.
E. Recycled PET can be used effectively for making variety of fabrics.

Choose the **correct** answer from the options given below:

1. A, C and E only
2. C, D and E only
3. B, C, D and E only
4. A, D and E only

76. Choose the INCORRECT statement:

1. Components of air quality standards are the indicator, an averaging time, the form and the level.
2. Primary air quality standards are more restrictive than the secondary.
3. Primary and Secondary air quality standards are periodically reviewed every year.
4. Agriculture operations and urban centers are examples of distributed sources of air pollution.

77. Which of the following are likely consequences of global climate change?

A. It will increase acidity of oceans.
B. Labile pool of C in soils will mobilise much faster.
C. It may accelerate soil salinization.
D. It exacerbated the incidence of coral bleaching.
E. Argonite will be more likely to dissolve into seawater.

Choose the **correct** answer from the options given below:

1. A, D and E only
2. A, B and D only
3. A, B, C and D only
4. A, B, C, D and E

78. Which of the following was NOT a cause of dispersed radioactivity during nuclear power plant accident in Chernobyl, Ukraine in the year 1985?

1. ^{131}Xe and ^{85}K
2. ^{131}I
3. ^{239}Pu
4. ^{134}Cs and ^{137}Cs

79. Consider the following statements about analysis on analytical instruments and data quality.

A. Minimum detection limit (MDL) is three time of σ_{n-1} of blank concentration.
B. Minimum quantification limit (MQL) is 7-10 times of σ_{n-1} of blank concentration.

C. Lower concentration limit of a working linear range must be greater than the defined MDL.
D. Relative standard deviation is used as a measure of precision of the data.
E. An analytical data with high precision may or may not be accurate.

Choose the **correct** answer from the options given below:

1. A, B, C and E only
2. A, B, C and D only
3. A, B, D and E only
4. A, B, and E only

80. The Gaussian Plume Equation is given as below:

$$C(x, y) = \frac{Q}{\pi\mu\sigma_y\sigma_z}\left(\exp\frac{-H^2}{2\sigma_z^2}\right)\left(\exp\frac{-y^2}{2\sigma_y^2}\right)$$

Which of the following statements are correct?

A. σ_y and σ_z are standard deviations of vertical and horizontal Gaussian distributions, respectively.
B. Smaller values of the dispersion coefficients will give broader Gaussian curve.
C. As we move downwind from the stack, the Gaussian curve spread further.
D. As we move downwind from the stack, the dispersion coefficients become larger.
E. Above equation is uniformly applicable to any terrain and temperature profile of atmosphere.

Choose the **correct** answer from the options given below:

1. A, B and C only
2. C and D only
3. B, D and E only
4. C, D and E only

81. Which of the following key term is NOT included in the definition of Disaster in the Disaster Management Act of 2005?

1. Calamity
2. Catastrophe
3. Mishap
4. Risk

82. Match the LIST-I with LIST-II.

LIST-I (Spectral Index)	LIST-II (Expression)
A. Bareness (NDBaI)	I. $\frac{G - SWIR}{G + SWIR}$
B. Built-up (NDBI)	II. $\frac{NIR - SWIR}{NIR + SWIR}$
C. Moisture (NDWI)	III. $\frac{SWIR - NIR}{SWIR + NIR}$
D. Snow (NDSI)	IV. $\frac{SWIR - TIR}{SWIR + TIR}$

Choose the **correct** answer from the options given below:

1. A-I, B-II, C-III, D-IV
2. A-I, B-III, C-II, D-IV
3. A-IV, B-II, C-III, D-I
4. A-IV, B-III, C-II, D-I

83. Average solar radiation incident at the top of Earth's atmosphere is 342 Wm^{-2}. The global planetary albedo is 0.30, and 67 Wm^{-2} of incident radiation is absorbed by atmosphere. On an average, 390 Wm^{-2} is lost from the Earth's surface as IR, but the Earth absorbed 80% of the form of IR emitted downward by the atmosphere. If the global average sensible heat flux away from the surface is 24 Wm^{-2}. Calculate the global latent heat flux.

1. ~78 Wm^{-2}
2. ~70 Wm^{-2}
3. ~172 Wm^{-2}
4. ~48 Wm^{-2}

84. Which of the following is not among the four stages of risk assessment?

1. Dose-response assessment
2. Exposure assessment
3. Hazard identification
4. Risk management

85. Consider the following statements and choose the CORRECT statements about organic compounds (OCs).

A. The OCs are usually combustible and less soluble in water.

B. Several OCs exist for a given formula.

C. Reaction of OCs are usually ionic than molecular.

D. The OCs can be derived from nature, by synthesis, by fermentation.

E. Saturated hydrocarbons (Paraffins) are quite inert towards most chemical reagents.

Choose the **correct** answer from the options given below:

1. A, B, C and D only
2. A, C, D and E only
3. A, B, C and E only
4. A, B, D and E only

86. A toxic substance is present at 10 mg/*l* (=10 ppm) level in water. Arrange the following subjects (A, B, C, D and E) in decreasing order of their daily dose in (mg kg^{-1} day^{-1}) of this substance.

A. Subject taking 2 liters of water per day and have body weight of 50 kg.

B. Subject taking 2 liters of water per day and have body weight of 70 kg.

C. Subject taking 1 liter of water per day and have body weight of 10 kg.

D. Subject taking 5 liters of water per day and have body weight of 100 kg.

E. Subject taking 1 liter of water per day and have body weight of 70 kg.

Choose the **correct** answer from the options given below:

1. D, B, A, E, C
2. C, D, A, B, E
3. D, E, B, A, C
4. D, B, E, C, A

87. Electric power generated from an ideal wind turbines is ....

1. Proportional to square root of wind velocity
2. proportional to cube of wind velocity
3. proportional to square root of radius of the turbines
4. inversely proportional to density of air

88. Match the LIST-I with LIST-II.

LIST-I (Coal Lithotypes)	LIST-II (Composition)
A. Vitrain	I. Mainly inertinite and exinite macerals
B. Cannel coal	II. Mainly fusinite
C. Durain	III. Vitrinite macerals with <20% exinite macerals
D. Fusain	IV. Dominated by alginite

Choose the **correct** answer from the options given below:

1. A-I, B-II, C-IV, D-III
2. A-III, B-I, C-IV, D-II
3. A-III, B-IV, C-I, D-II
4. A-IV, B-II, C-III, D-I

89. In a fertile pond (water body), the region where the light intensity is usually too low for photosynthesis and only community respiration occurs. The area where respiration (R) is greater than primary production (P), i.e. P/R < 1, is called as ....

1. limnetic zone
2. profundal zone
3. pelagic zone
4. littoral zone

90. Arrange the following stages of coal development from lower to higher grade.

A. Dehydration
B. Peatification
C. Bituminization
D. Debituminization
E. Graphitization

Choose the **correct** answer from the options given below:

1. A, B, C, D, E
2. B, A, C, D, E
3. A, B, D, C, E
4. B, A, D, C, E

Directions (Qs. No. 91-95): *Read the following passage and answer the questions:*

Hydrothermal fluids at spreading centers of Mid Oceanic Ridges originate due to circulation of sea water through hot volcanic rocks. Heated rocks and deeper magmas pull in the cold seawater, heat it and then pull out the hydrothermal fluid- the hot water. The hydrothermal water laden with metals and many other elements returns back into the overlying oceans. Circulating sea water through porous volcanic rocks not only cools the lithosphere but also contribute to the sea water chemistry, and formation of important mineral deposits of Co, Ni, Lanthanides and PGEs. Continental weathering also contributes to the seawater composition. The hydrothermal energy and nutrients support complex ecosystems at Mid Oceanic Ridges. Microorganisms in the ecosystem also play important role in the precipitation of minerals. In the year 2024, India having with two ocean probes, applied to International Sea Bed Authority under the UN Convention on the Law of the Sea (UNCLOS) to explore deep sea around Carlsberg Ridge in the north western limb of the Indian Ocean Ridge system, and Afanasy Nikitin Seamount in the Central Indian basin. These missions can yield minerals and metals, associated with crusts and nodules, important in clean energy transition and other strategic importance.

91. Which of the following is mainly contributed to the sea water composition by volcanic activities?

1. Na^+
2. HCO_3^-
3. Cl^-
4. K^+

92. Which of the following represents steepest geothermal gradient?

1. Continent-continent Collison mountains
2. Subduction zone
3. Mid Oceanic Ridges
4. Old and thick lithosphere

93. Cobalt, Nickel and lanthanides belong to ....

1. Rare earth elements
2. Critical metals
3. Hydrothermal elements
4. Chalcophile elements

94. Formation of polymetallic nodules on the surface of ocean indicates ....

1. anoxic environment
2. oxic environment
3. very low pH conditions
4. high salinity conditions

95. Carlsberg Ridge represents boundary between ....

1. Indian and Arabic plates
2. Indian and Eurasian Plates
3. Indian and Somalian Plates
4. Indian and Australian Plates

Directions (Qs. No. 96-100): *Read the following passage and answer the questions:*

A group of environmental toxicologists selected an endemic area in rural setting for screening females for breast cancer, based on the previous literature documentation regarding exposure to the organochlorine compound (DDT). A total of 5000 females were screened in this activity and clinicians in the group of environmental toxicologists confirmed 250 females as positive for breast cancer. The blood samples of 150 females were also taken to quantify the value of DDT. The mean (SD) for DDT was estimated to be normally distributed as 2.5 (1.0) ng/ml. The epidemiologist in the team also collected detailed information regarding age of females (ranged: 15-49 years), family history (fh), type of dietary habits (vegetarian/ non-vegetarian), and menopause status (yes/no).

96. What is the estimated prevalence for breast cancer in the community?

1. 2%
2. 3%
3. 4%
4. 5%

97. In the same community (rural area) if the prevalence of breast cancer remains the same and there is almost negligible migration, what will be the expected number of breast cancer if we assume arithmetic growth model in one year duration?

1. 262.0 2. 262.2
3. 262.3 4. 262.5

98. Which test of significance should be performed to test the association between status of dietary habits and DDT levels among 150 females whose blood sample were taken?

1. Mann-Whitney U test
2. One sample *t* test
3. Two independent sample *t* test
4. One way ANOVA

99. Approximately for how many females, the value of DDT will be within limits of 2.5 to 3.5 ng/ml?

1. 50 2. 51
3. 52 4. 53

100. The epidemiologist wish to develop an epidemiological model for development of breast cancer (n = 150) based upon information on age, family history, and dietary habits of the subjects. Which one of the following epidemiological models will be the best choice?

1. Binary Logistic Model
2. Simple Linear Model
3. Multiple Regression Model
4. General Linear Model

ANSWERS

1	2	3	4	5	6	7	8	9	10
3	4	2	1	2	1	*	3	2	1
11	**12**	**13**	**14**	**15**	**16**	**17**	**18**	**19**	**20**
4	*	2	3	4	2	3	4	3	2
21	**22**	**23**	**24**	**25**	**26**	**27**	**28**	**29**	**30**
4	1	2	4	3	3	2	3	3	2
31	**32**	**33**	**34**	**35**	**36**	**37**	**38**	**39**	**40**
3	3	2	1	2	4	2	3	3	3
41	**42**	**43**	**44**	**45**	**46**	**47**	**48**	**49**	**50**
1	2	2	4	2	1	3	2	1	3
51	**52**	**53**	**54**	**55**	**56**	**57**	**58**	**59**	**60**
3	3	3	2	2	2	2, 4	4	4	2
61	**62**	**63**	**64**	**65**	**66**	**67**	**68**	**69**	**70**
3	2	3	3	2	2	4	3	4	3
71	**72**	**73**	**74**	**75**	**76**	**77**	**78**	**79**	**80**
1	2	2	3	2	3	4	3	3	2
81	**82**	**83**	**84**	**85**	**86**	**87**	**88**	**89**	**90**
4	4	2	4	4	2	2	3	2	2
91	**92**	**93**	**94**	**95**	**96**	**97**	**98**	**99**	**100**
3	3	2	2	3	4	4	3	2	4

EXPLANATORY ANSWERS

1. • **Dichlorvos (DDVP):** This is a classic Type A organophosphate insecticide. It is direct acting, meaning it does not require metabolic activation to become toxic. It inhibits acetylcholinesterase immediately, leading to accumulation of acetylcholine at synapses.

   • **Malathion:** Belongs to Type C organophosphates. Though it is toxic to insects, mammals detoxify it efficiently due to carboxylesterase activity. This makes it relatively safer for humans but still potent as an insecticide.

   • **Parathion:** This is a Type B organophosphate insecticide. It is not toxic in its original form but becomes highly toxic once metabolically activated in the liver to paraoxon.

   • **Lindane:** Not an organophosphate at all, but an organochlorine insecticide. It acts by interfering with GABAergic neurotransmission, making it distinct from OPs.

2. E. **Radiative Zone:** After the Sun's core, this zone transfers energy outward mainly through radiation, where photons undergo countless scatterings before moving ahead.

   B. **Convection Zone:** Energy transport here happens via convection currents of hot plasma. Rising hot gases and sinking cooler ones create turbulent motion.

   D. **Photosphere:** This is the "surface" of the Sun, about 500 km thick, and the layer we directly observe. Sunspots and granules are seen here.

   A. **Chromosphere:** Just above the photosphere, it glows reddish due to strong Hα emission and is best visible during solar eclipses.

   C. **Corona:** The Sun's outermost atmosphere, extending millions of kilometers. It is extremely hot (over a million Kelvin) and gives rise to solar winds.

   Thus, from inner to outer: Radiative zone → Convection zone → Photosphere → Chromosphere → Corona.

3. A. **Aqua:** Launched in 2002 under NASA's Earth Observing System, it carries MODIS (Moderate Resolution Imaging Spectroradiometer), a multispectral sensor useful for climate and water studies.

   B. **NOAA satellites:** Operational weather satellites carrying VIIRS (Visible Infrared Imaging Radiometer Suite) and AVHRR (Advanced Very High Resolution Radiometer) for meteorological and environmental monitoring.

   C. **Sentinel-2:** A European Space Agency satellite with MSI (Multispectral Instrument), designed for high-resolution land observation, vegetation, soil, and water monitoring.

   D. **Terra:** Another NASA Earth Observing System satellite that carries ASTER (Advanced Spaceborne Thermal Emission and Reflection Radiometer) and MODIS, serving both geological and atmospheric applications.

4. Atmospheric particles can only exert direct radiative forcing:

   This is incorrect because atmospheric aerosols produce both direct and indirect forcing.

   • **Direct forcing** → Aerosols scatter and absorb radiation, cooling (sulfates) or warming (black carbon).

   • **Indirect forcing** → Aerosols act as cloud condensation nuclei, modifying cloud droplet size, reflectivity (albedo), and lifetime, thus amplifying climate effects.

   The other statements are valid:

   • Combustion of fossil fuels, even complete, releases CO_2, a major greenhouse gas.

   • Sulfur-derived trace gases (like SO_2) form sulfate aerosols, which cool and counter greenhouse warming.

   • Polar amplification is a documented phenomenon where warming is stronger in polar regions due to feedbacks like ice-albedo reduction.

5. • **Tbilisi Conference (1977):** First intergovernmental conference on environmental education, setting global guidelines.

- **Montreal Protocol (1987):** International treaty to phase out ozone-depleting substances like CFCs.
- **Basel Convention (1989):** Regulates transboundary movements of hazardous wastes and their disposal.
- **Kyoto Protocol (1997):** Binding treaty under UNFCCC committing countries to reduce greenhouse gas emissions.
- **Copenhagen Summit (2009):** Part of UN climate change negotiations, though it resulted in a non-binding accord rather than a strong treaty.

Chronological order of enactment: Tbilisi (1977) → Montreal (1987) → Basel (1989) → Kyoto (1997) → Copenhagen (2009).

6. Nuclear fuel minerals are ores that supply Uranium (U) or Thorium (Th).

- **Pitchblende (Uraninite):** Primary uranium ore → nuclear fuel mineral.
- **Carnotite:** Potassium–uranium–vanadate ore → uranium source → nuclear fuel mineral.
- **Monazite:** Rare-earth phosphate containing significant thorium (and some uranium) → nuclear fuel mineral.
- **Anglesite:** Lead sulfate ($PbSO_4$), a lead ore with no U/Th → not a nuclear fuel mineral.

7. Task: Convert to μg/m³ at 25 °C, 1 atm (ideal gas).

Formula:

- $\mu g/m^3 = ppm \times \frac{M}{24.45}$ at 25 °C;
- $\mu g/m^3 = ppm \times \frac{M \times 10^3}{24.45}$

  $\approx ppm \times M \times 40.95$

Molar masses (g mol^{-1}): O_3 = 48; SO_2 = 64; NH_3 = 17; CO = 28; CO_2 = 44.

Calculations:

D. 1 ppm CO: 1 × 28 × 40.95 ≈ 1147 $\mu g/m^3$

E. 1 ppm CO_2: 1 × 44 × 40.95 ≈ 1802 $\mu g/m^3$

A. 1 ppm O_3: 1 × 48 × 40.95 ≈ 1966 $\mu g/m^3$

B. 1 ppm SO_2: 1 × 64 × 40.95 ≈ 2621 $\mu g/m^3$

C. 4 ppm NH_3: 4 × 17 × 40.95 = 68 × 40.95 ≈ 2785 $\mu g/m^3$

Ascending order (small → large):
D (CO) < E (CO_2) < A (O_3) < B (SO_2) < C (4 ppm NH_3) → D, E, A, B, C.

Given options do not contain this exact order ⇒ NONE.

8. Indian courts routinely invoke the Precautionary Principle in environmental cases to justify prior Environmental Impact Assessment (EIA) and environmental clearance (EC)—i.e., where there is a plausible risk of serious environmental harm, lack of full scientific certainty is not a reason to delay preventive measures.

This underpins the requirement to obtain EC before commencing projects with potential environmental impacts.

Not applicable here:

- **Caveat Emptor:** Buyer-beware doctrine in commerce.
- **Eminent Domain:** State's power to acquire land.
- **Strict Liability:** Liability without fault (used in pollution damage cases), but not the key doctrine for upholding EC requirements under EIA.

9. CAM plants separate CO_2 uptake and Calvin cycle temporally:

- **Night (stomata open):** CAM plants fix CO_2 via PEP carboxylase to oxaloacetate → malate, stored in vacuoles (malic acid).
- **Day (stomata closed):** Malate is decarboxylated, raising internal CO_2 for the Calvin cycle in chloroplasts while limiting water loss.

Therefore: Separation is temporal (night vs day), not spatial (that's C_4). Claims that CAM is mainly in grasses with daytime-open stomata, or that daytime internal CO_2 is lower than ambient, are incorrect (it's typically higher during decarboxylation).

10. Exact phrasing of GIM's aim: The Green India Mission under NAPCC is framed to "protect, restore, and enhance" India's forest cover and to respond to climate change through mitigation and adaptation. The triad explicitly used is Protection, Restoration, Enhancement.

Therefore, "Conservation" is NOT one of the three listed aims (even though conservation outcomes naturally result from these activities).

Brief on each listed aim:

- **Protection:** Reduce degradation and deforestation; strengthen community/JFM institutions; fire, grazing, and invasive-species management; enforce sustainable harvest.
- **Restoration:** Afforestation/reforestation of degraded/open forests; eco-restoration of vulnerable landscapes and catchments to revive ecosystem function.
- **Enhancement:** Improve forest quality and canopy density; expand tree cover outside forests (farm/agroforestry) to raise ecosystem services and carbon stocks.

Conclusion: Among the given options—Conservation, Enhancement, Protection, Restoration—the term "Conservation" is not the one explicitly listed in the mission's stated aims; the official triad is Protection–Restoration–Enhancement.

11. **D. Thickening → first:** Raw sludge is very dilute (≈0.5–2% solids). Gravity/thickening reduces volume early to lower sizing/energy needs downstream.

A. Stabilization → second: Anaerobic/aerobic digestion (or lime stabilization) reduces volatile solids, pathogens, odors, and biogas may be produced. Stabilizing before mechanical handling improves safety and dewatering behavior.

C. Conditioning → third: Chemical (polymers, ferric, lime) or thermal conditioning added immediately before dewatering to improve floc structure, drainage, and cake solids.

B. Dewatering → fourth: Centrifuges, belt presses, filter presses remove free/interstitial water to produce a stackable "cake" (typically 15–35% TS depending on process).

E. Reduction → last: Further volume/mass reduction and final treatment (e.g., drying beds, thermal drying, composting, incineration) or beneficial use/disposal.

12. **A. Box-plot gives 55th percentile:** *Incorrect.* Standard box-plots display median (50th), Q1 (25th), Q3 (75th), whiskers, and outliers; they do not yield the 55th percentile exactly.

B. Chernoff plot is hierarchical: *Incorrect.* Chernoff faces encode multivariate variables as facial features; they are not a hierarchical chart.

C. Pie-chart: area of circle non-proportional to frequency: *Incorrect/misleading.* In pie charts, a category's sector (angle/area) is proportional to its frequency; the claim as stated is not correct for how values are represented.

D. Ishikawa for cause–effect: *Correct.* Ishikawa/fishbone diagrams visualize cause–effect relationships.

E. Histogram for categorical data: *Incorrect.* Histograms are for continuous (binned) numerical data; bar charts suit categorical data.

Net: Only D is correct, but no option contains D only ⇒ NONE.

13. To delegate simpler projects to state authorities and complex ones to the central government.

Rationale in EIA 2006: Projects are categorized by scale and potential environmental impact.

- **Category A:** Appraised at Central (MoEFCC/EAC) due to larger scale/significant impacts, mandatory EIA and often public hearing.
- **Category B:** Handled by State (SEIAA/SEAC); B1 typically requires EIA, B2 may be exempt from full EIA.

This structure allocates appraisal to the appropriate level and streamlines the process while maintaining rigor for higher-impact projects.

14. **A. Article 51A(g) → II:** Fundamental Duty "to protect and improve the natural environment (forests, lakes, rivers, wildlife) and to have compassion for living creatures."

B. Article 49 → I: Protection of monuments and places and objects of national importance.

C. Article 48 → IV: Organization of agriculture and animal husbandry on modern/scientific lines (incl. breed improvement, cow protection).

D. Article 48A → III: Protection and improvement of environment and safeguarding of forests and wildlife (42nd Amendment, 1976).

Mapping: 51A(g)–II; 49–I; 48–IV; 48A–III ⇒ A-II, B-I, C-IV, D-III.

15. Concept: Production efficiency = fraction of assimilated energy converted to new consumer biomass. It rises with food quality and lower metabolic overhead; ectotherms generally exceed endotherms.

D. Detritivores → lowest: Detritus is low-quality, refractory (high lignin/cellulose), with microbial defenses; even after assimilation, a larger share goes to maintenance, so lower production efficiency.

A. Fishes → next: Ectothermic and buoyant (favorable vs. terrestrial vertebrates) but as vertebrates they still have higher maintenance costs than many invertebrates; moderate production efficiency.

C. Herbivores → higher: Many ectothermic herbivores (e.g., insects) can achieve high conversion of assimilates due to efficient growth strategies.

B. Carnivores → highest: Protein-rich, easily digestible prey yields high assimilation; with ectothermic metabolism, a greater fraction of assimilates is converted to biomass.

Order (increasing): Detritivores < Fishes < Herbivores < Carnivores ⇒ D, A, C, B.

16. Statement 2 is incorrect. Ground-level ozone (O_3) production depends on NO_2 photolysis and VOC radicals. Where NO is high, it titrates ozone via $NO + O_3 \rightarrow NO_2 + O_2$, thereby reducing O_3 even if NOx is abundant.

- **1 (Correct):** Diesel engines operate lean; the globally cooler, oxygen-rich bulk mix can yield lower thermal NO formation compared with stoichiometric gasoline flame cores (engine-out NO chemistry is nuanced, but the lean regime tends to suppress peak NO in bulk).
- **3 (Correct):** London (1952) smog was a sulfurous/reducing smog driven by SO_2 and smoke; ozone was not the dominant oxidant species.
- **4 (Correct):** Aldehydes (carbonyls) have $n \rightarrow \pi^*$ bands in near-UV; they absorb strongly in UV-B (<315 nm) with weak tails into short-wavelength UV-A for several species.

17. C. Maharashtra: In Swachh Survekshan 2023, Maharashtra ranked as the best-performing state in cleanliness among large states. Its strong solid waste management systems, decentralized waste segregation, and large-scale citizen participation initiatives pushed it to the top.

B. Madhya Pradesh: Secured the second position. Cities like Indore (ranked India's cleanest city for the 7th consecutive year) contributed heavily to this ranking.

A. Chhattisgarh: Took the third place. It has consistently been among the top states due to strong community-level waste segregation and urban cleanliness drives.

D. Odisha: Ranked lower than the above three, but still ahead of Telangana due to improvements in waste processing facilities.

E. Telangana: Placed the lowest among the listed states, reflecting ongoing challenges in scaling up urban sanitation infrastructure.

Order (Top → Bottom): Maharashtra → Madhya Pradesh → Chhattisgarh → Odisha → Telangana.

18. Colonizing species face less competition for resources in secondary succession compared to primary succession:

- **Primary succession:** Begins on new, barren substrates (e.g., bare rock, lava, sand dunes). Colonizers (lichens, mosses) face harsh abiotic stress like no soil, limited water/nutrients, temperature extremes. However, because very few organisms are present, competition is initially low.
- **Secondary succession:** Occurs after disturbance (e.g., fire, flood, agriculture). Since soil, seed banks, roots, and microbes remain, many species can re-colonize quickly. This results in higher initial competition among species for nutrients, light, and space.

Thus, statement 4 is incorrect, because competition is generally stronger in secondary succession than in primary succession.

19. A. **Sound power (W) = Intensity (I) × Area (A):** *Correct.* Power is the total sound energy per second crossing a surface area at a given intensity.

B. **Sound period (T) and frequency (f) are inversely related:** *Correct* since $T = 1/f$.

C. **Speed of sound formula given ($C = 20.05 \times Temp^2$):** *Incorrect.* The speed of sound is proportional to the square root of absolute temperature, not quadratic. Correct relation:

$$c = \sqrt{\gamma RT},$$

or approximately $c = 331 + 0.6T(°C)$.

D. **$L = 10 \log_{10}(Q/Q_0)$:** Correct formula for expressing sound levels (e.g., power level, intensity level) in decibels relative to a reference.

E. $I = p_{rms}^2/(\rho c)$: Correct relation connecting sound intensity with root-mean-square acoustic pressure in a plane progressive wave.

Hence, the valid set is A, B, D, E.

20. The aerodynamic diameter (d_a) represents the size of a unit-density sphere (1 g/cm^3) with the same settling velocity as the particle.

Formula:

$$d_a = d_p \times \sqrt{\frac{\rho_p}{\rho_0}}$$

where, d_p = particle diameter,

ρ_p = particle density,

ρ_0 = reference density (1 g/cm^3).

Substituting values:

$$d_a = 2\mu m \times \sqrt{\frac{3}{1}}$$

$$= 2 \times 1.732 = 3.464\ \mu m$$

Rounded to one decimal: ≈ 3.5 μm.

Thus, the aerodynamic diameter of the given particle is about 3.5 μm.

21. **Concept (atomic H/C ratio):** As carbonaceous materials mature from peat → lignite → bituminous → anthracite, they lose hydrogen and become more carbon-rich; hence H/C decreases with rank. Hydrocarbons (petroleum, methane) have much higher H/C.

Ordering logic:

E. **Anthracite:** Highest rank coal, very carbon-rich, lowest H/C (~0.3–0.5).

D. **Lignite:** Low-rank brown coal, more volatiles than anthracite, H/C below peat.

B. **Peat:** Partially decomposed biomass, still hydrogen-rich, H/C above lignite.

A. **Petroleum:** Mixture of alkanes/alkenes, typical H/C ≈ 2 (atomic).

C. **Methane:** CH_4, H/C = 4 (highest).

Thus (increasing H/C): Anthracite < Lignite < Peat < Petroleum < Methane ⇒ E, D, B, A, C.

22. **Rubbish:** Refers to the broader class of solid wastes that include non-biodegradable and generally non-putrescible items like paper, cardboard, glass, metals, plastics, textiles, and construction debris. Rubbish can be further subdivided into combustible (e.g., paper, rags, wood) and non-combustible (e.g., glass, ceramics, metals) categories.

Garbage: A specific subset of solid waste, consisting of biodegradable putrescible organic matter, such as food scraps, vegetable residues, and other materials subject to decomposition. Garbage is thus narrower in definition and falls within the overall umbrella of solid waste.

Why statement 1 is incorrect: By standard definitions, rubbish does not inherently exclude garbage. In municipal waste management, garbage is considered part of the broader refuse stream, and refuse itself is made up of rubbish + garbage. Therefore, saying "rubbish does not contain garbage" is misleading because rubbish is not defined as something separate from all organic wastes; it is often categorized alongside garbage under the broader term refuse.

Why other statements are correct:

- **Refuse contains both rubbish and garbage:** Correct, since refuse is the inclusive term used in solid waste management to denote all discarded materials, combining both organic garbage and inorganic rubbish.
- **Garbage contain both garbage and rubbish:** While phrased redundantly, the intent is that garbage, as a waste stream within refuse, overlaps with rubbish under the broad category of solid waste. In practice, garbage is a subset, and refuse includes both.

- **Refuse has less water content (%) than garbage:** Correct, because garbage, made up of kitchen and food wastes, has very high moisture content (50–70%), whereas rubbish (dry wastes like paper, plastics, and metals) has a much lower water content. When garbage is combined with rubbish to form refuse, the overall average water content decreases compared to garbage alone.

23. Concept of Ventilation Coefficient (VC): The ventilation coefficient is a measure of the atmosphere's ability to disperse pollutants. It is defined as:

$$VC = u \times H$$

where:

- u = average wind speed (m/s),
- H = mixing height (m), i.e., the depth of the atmosphere available for vertical mixing of pollutants.

From the figure:

- The mixing height is the vertical distance between the ground and the top of the mixing layer.
- In the diagram, the region marked B represents the mixing height (up to where the atmosphere is unstable/neutral and mixing can occur).
- Region A lies below with stable stratification, and region C above is capped by inversion, limiting upward dispersion.
- Thus, the effective mixing height = B.

Given data:

- Wind speed, u = 10 m/s.
- Mixing height, H = B.

Calculation: $VC = 10 \times B = 10\ B\ m^2/s$.

24. Stratification (epilimnion, metalimnion/thermocline, hypolimnion) and seasonal turnover are natural limnological cycles, not the cause of eutrophication. Eutrophication is driven primarily by nutrient enrichment (N, P). While stratification can modulate oxygen/nutrient distribution (e.g., hypolimnetic anoxia → internal P loading), the processes themselves are not inherently harmful.

Other statements are correct:

1. Hypolimnion is poorly mixed vs epilimnion during stratification.
2. As summer advances, stability increases (warm epilimnion overlays cooler, near-constant hypolimnion).
3. Temperate lakes typically exhibit at least one stratification–turnover cycle annually (monomictic/dimictic), barring special cases (e.g., meromictic lakes).

25. In a salinity-gradient solar pond, heat is stored in the Lower Convective Zone (LCZ)—the hot, dense brine at the bottom. The Upper Convective Zone (UCZ) is shallow, low-salinity (< ~5%), well mixed, and near-ambient temperature; it does not store the captured heat.

Supporting concepts:

Non-Convective Zone (NCZ): Middle gradient layer that suppresses convection, trapping solar heat below.

1. **Water as HTF:** Common and correct.
2. **Salinity gradient:** Essential to prevent convective losses.
4. **Salt solubility vs temperature:** Should not vary strongly to maintain a stable gradient (hence salts like NaCl are preferred).

26. Decreasing abundance (dry air): Argon (~0.934%) > Carbon dioxide (~0.04%) > Neon (~0.0018% ≈ 18 ppm) > Helium (~0.00052% ≈ 5 ppm) > Methane (~0.00019% ≈ 1.9 ppm).

Reasoning: Among minor gases, Ar is the dominant noble gas; CO_2 is next at tens of thousands of ppm; Ne and He are trace noble gases (Ne > He); CH_4 is present at only ~2 ppm. Hence, B > A > D > C > E.

27.
- **Common field worm → *Helodrilus caliginosus* (A–III):** Widely distributed soil dweller; often termed the common field earthworm in older nomenclature (now *Aporrectodea caliginosa*).
- **Manure worm → *Eisenia foetida* (B–IV):** The "red wiggler", classic vermicomposting species thriving in rich organic manures.
- **Green worm → *Helodrilus chloroticus* (C–I):** Characteristically greenish appearance; prefers moist soils.
- **Slim earthworm → *Diplocardia verrucosa* (D–II):** Slender ("slim") body form; reported from lighter textured soils.

Thus: A–III, B–IV, C–I, D–II.

28. How the 16 goals (excluding Goal 17: Partnership) split across pillars:

- **Ecological (4):** 6 Clean Water & Sanitation, 13 Climate Action, 14 Life Below Water, 15 Life on Land.

  Reason: These are environment-centric—water resources, climate, oceans, and terrestrial ecosystems.

- **Social (8):** 1 No Poverty, 2 Zero Hunger, 3 Good Health & Well-being, 4 Quality Education, 5 Gender Equality, 10 Reduced Inequalities, 11 Sustainable Cities & Communities, 16 Peace, Justice & Strong Institutions.

  Reason: These focus on human well-being, equity, safe/inclusive settlements, and institutions that underpin social outcomes.

- **Economic (4):** 7 Affordable & Clean Energy, 8 Decent Work & Economic Growth, 9 Industry, Innovation & Infrastructure, 12 Responsible Consumption & Production.

  Reason: These drive production systems, energy and infrastructure, productivity, and consumption/production patterns in the economy.

Check: 4 (Ecological) + 8 (Social) + 4 (Economic) = 16 goals (Goal 17 excluded), matching the required ratio 4 : 8 : 4.

29. B. Aerobic degradation → first: Freshly placed waste has entrained air; aerobic microbes rapidly oxidize readily degradable organics.

D. Hydrolysis & fermentation: As oxygen is depleted, facultative/anaerobic consortia break down complex polymers to VFAs, alcohols, H_2, CO_2.

C. Acetogenesis: Fermentation products are converted to acetate, H_2, CO_2 by acetogens.

E. Methanogenesis: Methanogens convert acetate/H_2/CO_2 to $CH_4 + CO_2$, establishing the long methane fermentation phase.

A. Oxidation → last: Methane oxidation occurs later in the aerobic cover soil by methanotrophs, consuming a portion of emitted CH_4.

Therefore: B → D → C → E → A.

30. • **Phosphate → Stromatolites (A–II):** Phosphorite associations occur with stromatolitic and upwelling settings in some sedimentary basins; stromatolites are microbial carbonate structures that can host/associate with phosphate accumulations.

- **Sulphate → Anhydrite (B–III):** $CaSO_4$ (anhydrite) is a classic evaporite sulphate mineral/rock.
- **Mg-Fe rich silicate → Basalt (C–IV):** Basalt is mafic, dominated by Mg–Fe silicates (pyroxene, olivine, Ca-plagioclase).
- **Al oxyhydroxides → Bauxite (D–I):** Bauxite comprises gibbsite/boehmite/diaspore (Al-oxyhydroxides), the principal aluminium ore.

31. Monitoring and Feedback in EIA: This stage comes after the prediction, evaluation, and mitigation phases. Its main purpose is to verify if the predictions were accurate, to see whether mitigation measures are effective, and to allow adaptive changes when unexpected outcomes arise. It also feeds learning back into the system for improving future EIAs.

Why A and B are excluded:

A. To determine the significance and importance of prediction: This belongs to the impact evaluation phase, where predicted impacts are judged for their seriousness. It is not part of monitoring.

B. To identify and predict impacts on ecosystem component: This is done during the impact prediction stage, which precedes monitoring and feedback.

Why C and E are included:

C. To provide opportunities for corrective action in light of unforeseen outcomes: A central role of monitoring is to detect unexpected environmental damage and allow adaptive management. This could include modifying project operations, adding safeguards, or even halting certain activities.

E. To strengthen the knowledge base: Feedback ensures that predicted vs. actual impacts are compared, refining models, improving baseline data, and making future EIAs more robust and reliable.

Why D is excluded:

D. To reduce significant adverse effects: This is addressed during the mitigation phase, where measures are planned and executed. Monitoring checks their success, but the reduction itself is not the monitoring function.

Thus, the correct components of Monitoring and Feedback are C and E only.

32. A DDT analog of similar size/shape with insecticidal activity, but more biodegradable and less bioaccumulative.

- Methoxychlor (2,2-bis(p-methoxyphenyl)-1,1,1-trichloroethane): Replaces DDT's p-Cl groups with p-OCH_3, increasing metabolic lability and reducing persistence/biomagnification, while retaining insecticidal action.

Why others are unsuitable:

- **DDD (TDE):** DDT metabolite—still persistent and bioaccumulative.
- **DDA:** Oxidation product—not an insecticide.
- **Toxaphene:** Chlorinated camphene mixture—not a DDT analog and highly persistent.

33. Empirical climate classifications rely on observed temperature/precipitation (and derivatives) rather than air-mass dynamics.

B. Köppen: Classic empirical scheme using T/P thresholds aligned with vegetation.

D. Thornthwaite: Empirical water-balance/PET based humidity indices and climatic types.

Not selected:

A. Bergeron & Spatial: Genetic (air-mass) approach.

C. Oliver–Hidore and **E. Trewartha** are treated variably, but in standard exam framing the unambiguous empirical pair is Köppen + Thornthwaite.

34. A. Cirrus clouds: These are thin, wispy clouds usually found in the upper troposphere. However, in polar regions, where the tropopause is much lower, cirrus can occasionally extend into the lower stratosphere. Thus, under specific conditions, cirrus clouds are present at stratospheric levels.

C. Mother of Pearl clouds: These are another name for Polar Stratospheric Clouds (PSCs). They form at altitudes of 15–25 km in the stratosphere during extremely cold winter conditions in polar regions.

D. Nacreous clouds: This term is also used for PSCs, having the same characteristics as Mother of Pearl clouds. They exhibit brilliant iridescent colors and occur in the stratosphere.

Why not the others:

B. Cumulonimbus clouds: These are tropospheric storm clouds, with tops that can sometimes overshoot into the tropopause but do not form in the stratosphere.

E. Noctilucent clouds: These are found much higher, in the mesosphere (~80–85 km), and not in the stratosphere.

Conclusion: The cloud types that can be present in the stratosphere are Cirrus, Mother of Pearl, and Nacreous clouds. Therefore, the correct option is A, C, and D only.

35.
- **A (True):** In the Northern Hemisphere, Coriolis deflects motion to the right; combined with friction, near-surface flow yields clockwise circulation around highs (and counterclockwise around lows).
- **B (False):** Principal climatic zones are not defined by precipitation alone; schemes (e.g., Köppen) use temperature and precipitation jointly.
- **C (True):** Altitude, mountains (orography), large water bodies, ocean currents are major controls of regional climate.
- **D (True):** Negative SOI values are typically linked with El Niño events (Tahiti–Darwin pressure anomaly).
- **E (False):** La Niña corresponds to cooler-than-normal tropical Pacific SSTs, not warmer.

36. Incorrect statement: "Survivorship curves cannot vary among populations of a species between males and females."

Why: Survivorship curves do vary within the same species across sexes, populations, habitats, and time due to differences in mortality risks (e.g., sexual selection, parental investment, predation, disease).

Checks on 1–3 (all correct):

- **Type I:** High survival in early/mid life; mortality rises in old age (e.g., humans in developed settings, many large mammals).
- **Type II:** Roughly constant mortality rate across ages (e.g., many birds, some reptiles), so chance of surviving from one age to the next is approximately constant.
- **Type III:** Very high juvenile mortality, with few individuals reaching adulthood (e.g., many fish, marine invertebrates, plants producing many propagules).

37. A. Pressure is enough to allow free flow of water above ground → Artesian well (III): In a flowing artesian well, piezometric head exceeds ground level, so water rises freely.

B. Water withdrawn faster than replenishment → Cone of depression (I): Pumping lowers the water level locally, producing a drawdown cone in the potentiometric surface.

C. Elevation to which water rises in the aquifer → Piezometric surface (II): The hydraulic head level indicated by a tightly cased well.

D. Zone of water between aquicludes → Confined water (IV): Water in a confined aquifer bounded above/below by aquicludes/aquitards.

38. A. Hemiparasite extract water and mineral nutrients from host: *Correct.* Hemiparasites such as mistletoe form a haustorium that penetrates the host's vascular tissue, particularly the xylem, to draw water and minerals. This allows them to maintain hydration and nutrient supply while attached to the host.

B. Hemiparasite have green leaves and can photosynthesize: *Correct.* The prefix "hemi-" means partial. Unlike holoparasites (which lack chlorophyll), hemiparasites retain chlorophyll and green leaves, enabling them to carry out photosynthesis and produce their own organic food.

C. Hemiparasite do not rely exclusively on the host for carbohydrates: *Correct.* Because hemiparasites can generate their own carbohydrates through photosynthesis, they are only partially dependent on the host. This differentiates them from holoparasites, which rely fully on the host for both minerals and carbohydrates.

D. Corn smut fungus is an example of ectoparasite: *Correct* in broad biological usage. Ustilago maydis (corn smut) infects maize plants. While the fungus invades internally (technically endoparasitic), the visible galls and smut masses appear externally on plant tissues. Many plant pathogenic fungi are often grouped under ectoparasites since their disease effects are manifested outwardly.

E. Ectoparasite does not have ease of dispersal in environment: *Incorrect.* Ectoparasites usually have high dispersal ability. Arthropod ectoparasites (fleas, ticks, lice) can move actively between hosts or be passively transported. Plant pathogenic fungi produce airborne spores (e.g., corn smut spores dispersed by wind and rain), which spread efficiently. Dispersal is, in fact, a key evolutionary strategy of ectoparasites.

Therefore, the correct set of statements is A, B, C, and D only.

39. The Supreme Court articulated the doctrine of Absolute Liability for enterprises engaged in hazardous activities: if harm occurs, the enterprise is absolutely liable (without exceptions available under Rylands v. Fletcher). The Oleum Gas Leak case is the landmark source of this principle in Indian environmental jurisprudence.

40. A. Vertisols → III: Dominated by smectitic (swelling) clays, showing deep cracks on drying; gilgai microrelief common.

B. Histosols → IV: Organic soils with >20% organic matter, often with minimal profile development (peat/muck).

C. Entisols → I: Very weak/no horizon development; commonly an ochric epipedon.

D. Andisols → II: Formed from volcanic ash, rich in allophane/imogolite, with distinctive physical–chemical properties (high P-fixation, low bulk density).

41. A. Assessment → Identify baseline conditions; predict project-induced impacts on environmental receptors.

D. Evaluation → Judge the significance of predicted impacts (magnitude, duration, reversibility, sensitivity of receptors); weigh alternatives.

E. Mitigation → Design and commit to avoidance, minimization, restoration, and offset measures; integrate into the EMP/ EMC.

C. Decision Making → Competent authority issues approval/conditions/rejection based on the EIA/EMP, public hearing, and appraisal.

B. Audit → Post-project environmental audit/ monitoring & feedback: verify predictions, check compliance and effectiveness of mitigation, and feed learning into future EIAs.

42. Incorrect statement: "Control rods in fission reactors are made from graphite, neutron absorbing element."

Why: Control rods are made of strong neutron absorbers like boron, cadmium, hafnium, Ag-In-Cd alloys. Graphite is a moderator (slows neutrons) not a control-rod absorber.

Checks on other items:

- **1 (True):** Naturally occurring fissile uranium isotope is U-235 (U-238 and Th-232 are fertile, not fissile).
- **3 (True):** Breeder reactors produce more fissile fuel (e.g., Pu-239 or U-233) than they consume.
- **4 (True):** Thermal thorium breeder converts Th-232 → U-233 via neutron capture and beta decays.

43. Context: In many aquatic systems, phytoplankton have short lifespans and are heavily grazed; consumer biomass can exceed standing producer biomass, yielding an inverted biomass pyramid, even though energy pyramids always taper with trophic level.

A. (True): At any instant, heterotroph biomass can be greater than autotroph biomass (the hallmark of an inverted biomass pyramid).

B. (True): Energy produced by autotrophs (GPP/ NPP) still exceeds that passed to heterotrophs; energy pyramids are never inverted.

C. (True): Inversions are common in open, nutrient-poor waters with low producer standing stock and high turnover under strong grazing.

D. (Not selected): The detrital/microbial loop can be important even in oligotrophic systems; it is not generally correct to assert a lower proportional detrital contribution there relative to eutrophic waters.

E. (True): Heterotrophs/autotrophs biomass ratio > 1 indicates an inverted biomass pyramid.

44. D. Tabulate data in a contingency table (observed counts).

B. Calculate expected cell frequencies under the null of independence.

A. Compute the χ^2 statistic: $\chi^2 = \sum \frac{(O-E)^2}{E}$

C. Assess degrees of freedom: $(r - 1)(c - 1)$.

E. Compare χ^2 with the critical value (or p-value) and decide (reject/do not reject H_0).

45. A. Impaction $\propto \rho_p \cdot d_p^2$ — Correct.

Inertial impaction efficiency rises with particle inertia. The Stokes number for impaction scales as Stkd $\propto \rho_p d_p^2$ (for fixed flow/ geometry), so higher particle density and diameter squared increase capture in devices (baffles, cyclones, mesh pads).

B. Resuspension vs size — Correct (exam convention).

For typical dusts in air-pollution control ($\approx 1 - 100\ \mu m$), smaller deposited particles are more easily re-entrained under the same shear because aerodynamic lift/drag scale less steeply with size than weight; thus a common engineering rule is resuspension probability increases as particle size decreases (i.e., inversely with d_p). (Very fine cohesive powders can be an exception, but the standard MCQ generalization treats the trend as inverse.)

C. Cyclones: force $\propto$ velocity² — Correct (intended sense).

Separation is driven by centrifugal force $F_c = mv_\theta^2/r$, i.e., proportional to the square of the tangential velocity. Design relations often connect cut-size to the particle's terminal settling characteristics, but the governing inertial term is the v^2 dependence captured in the statement.

D. "Activated alumina & H_2SO_4 used in demisters" — Incorrect.

Demisters (mist eliminators) remove liquid droplets mechanically (impaction/interception/centrifuging) using mesh or vane packs. Activated alumina (adsorbent) and concentrated sulfuric acid (desiccant) are gas-drying media used in dryers/sampling trains—not the collection media in demisters.

E. Baghouses do not operate by sedimentation or electrostatics — Correct.

Fabric filters capture particles by depth/surface filtration (interception, impaction, diffusion, and cake sieving). They do not rely on gravitational settling (settling chambers) or electrostatic attraction (ESPs). Any fiber charge is incidental; the principle is mechanical filtration.

46. C. Tropical forest — highest NPP: Warm year-round temperatures, high rainfall, intense insolation, and continuous growing seasons drive very high net primary productivity (typically ~1800–2500 g m^{-2} yr^{-1}). Dense, multi-layered canopies and rapid nutrient cycling keep photosynthesis high nearly all year.

D. Temperate forest: Marked seasons but long enough growing periods, moderate temperatures, and adequate moisture support high NPP (about ~800–1400 g m^{-2} yr^{-1}). Deciduous and mixed forests maintain substantial leaf area during the growing season, elevating carbon gain.

E. Crops: Although highly variable by crop type and management, managed agro-ecosystems (fertilizers, irrigation, high-yield varieties, weed/pest control) often achieve moderate-to-high NPP on a per-area basis (roughly ~500–1100 g m^{-2} yr^{-1} on global averages), commonly exceeding many natural grasslands.

B. Temperate grassland: Productivity is limited by seasonal water stress, periodic droughts, and strong herbivory/fire regimes; typical NPP ~400–800 g m^{-2} yr^{-1}. While peak growth can be vigorous, shorter favorable windows and moisture constraints keep annual totals below most forests and well-managed crops.

A. Boreal forest — lowest among the five (on average): Cold climates, short growing seasons, low sun angles, nutrient-poor acidic soils, and, in places, permafrost depress photosynthesis and decomposition, yielding lower NPP (often ~300–700 g m^{-2} yr^{-1}) than temperate systems and most croplands.

Decreasing order (global averages): Tropical forest > Temperate forest > Crops : Temperate grassland > Boreal forest, i.e., C, D, E, B, A.

47. Let γ = environmental lapse rate; γ_d = dry adiabatic; γ_s = saturated adiabatic ($\gamma_s < \gamma_d$).

A. $\gamma < \gamma_s \rightarrow$ **Absolutely Stable (III):** Environment cools with height slower than even saturated adiabatic; all parcels (dry or moist) are cooler than environment when lifted → stable.

B. $\gamma > \gamma_d \rightarrow$ **Absolutely Unstable (I):** Environment cools faster than dry adiabatic; lifted parcels (dry or moist) become warmer than environment → unstable.

C. $\gamma = \gamma_d \rightarrow$ **Dry Neutral (IV):** Unsaturated parcels lifted dry-adiabatically remain neutrally buoyant.

D. $\gamma_s < \gamma < \gamma_d \rightarrow$ **Conditionally Unstable (II):** Unsaturated air is stable/neutral, but if saturated, it can become unstable (hence "conditional"). (The condition is commonly written $\gamma_d > \gamma > \gamma_s$.)

48. The solid organic fraction (kerogen) in bituminous (oil) shales is predominantly derived from lower plants/algae lacking lignocellulosic tissues.

In contrast, lignite, bituminous coal, anthracite originate mainly from higher land plants rich in lignocellulose, altered through diagenesis and coalification.

49. Incorrect statement: Composting is a biological, aerobic process requiring adequate moisture, typically ~50–60% (wet basis) for microbial activity and heat transfer. Saying moisture "should not be present" is wrong.

Correct practices:

- **Particle size < ~5 cm:** Promotes aeration and surface area for microbes.
- **Compost improves soil water-holding capacity:** Humified organics enhance aggregation and porosity.

- **C:N ~20–25:1 (often 25–30:1 optimal):** Ensures balanced microbial growth and efficient decomposition.

50. In an open system, volatile species partition between gas and aqueous phases (Henry's law/ acid–base equilibria):

CO_2, NH_3, H_2S have appreciable gas–aqueous partitioning (speciation: $CO_2/HCO_3^-/CO_3^{2-}$; NH_3/NH_4^+; $H_2S/HS^-/S^{2-}$).

Phosphoric acid (H_3PO_4) is effectively non-volatile (negligible vapor pressure) and does not partition into the gas phase under environmental conditions.

51. Why this is NOT an element of hazard/risk assessment: "Reduction in use of hazardous substances" is a risk-reduction/control strategy (source reduction/inherent safety) applied after assessment. The assessment phase comprises:

- **Process knowledge & documentation** (flowsheets, materials, SDSs, waste inventories) — needed to identify hazards.
- **Process & equipment integrity** (design, inspection, maintenance) — informs failure likelihood and exposure scenarios.
- **Standards, codes, laws & practices** — provide criteria/benchmarks for evaluation and compliance.
- Assessment proper = hazard identification → exposure assessment → toxicity/dose-response → risk characterization. Control (like substitution/reduction) belongs to mitigation/management, not assessment.

52.
- **Water-borne (A → III Typhoid):** Ingested contaminated water (e.g., *Salmonella typhi*).
- **Water-based (B → IV Schistosomiasis):** Pathogen has an aquatic intermediate host (snails); humans infected by water contact.
- **Water-washed (C → I Trachoma):** Due to poor hygiene/insufficient water; transmission reduced by face-washing.
- **Water-related (D → II Yellow fever):** Vector-borne near water (Aedes mosquitoes breed in/near water containers).

53. A. False: Normal-phase HPLC uses polar stationary phase (e.g., silica) and non-polar mobile phase (e.g., hexane), not the reverse.

B. True: In normal phase, the least polar analyte elutes first; increasing mobile-phase polarity competes with analyte–stationary interactions → shorter elution time.

C. True: In reverse-phase (non-polar stationary; polar mobile), most polar analytes elute first; making the mobile phase more polar (more aqueous) generally increases retention times (especially for hydrophobes).

D. True: Isocratic run = mobile-phase composition (hence polarity) constant throughout.

E. True: Resolution depends on intermolecular forces among analyte, mobile phase, stationary phase (controls retention/selectivity/ efficiency).

54.
- **Dudhwa (A) → Sharda (II):** Park along the Sharda/Mahakali river (UP–Nepal border).
- **Kalesar (B) → Yamuna (IV):** Shivalik park in Haryana, drained by Yamuna system.
- **Kazinag (C) → Jhelum (I):** Kashmir park in Baramulla region tied to Jhelum basin.
- **Khangchendzonga (D) → Teesta (III):** Sikkim park feeding the Teesta river system.

55.
- **Decimal notation (A → III Computations):** Convenient for calculations and algebra with probabilities (0.27, 0.05, etc.).
- **Scientific notation (B → IV For low probabilities):** Best for very small probabilities (e.g., 1.0×10^{-6}).
- **Percentage (C → II Conversions):** Expressing probabilities as % (e.g., 0.25 → 25%) is a common conversion/reporting format.
- **Pictorial form (D → I Random variables):** Graphs/diagrams (PMF/PDF, trees, Venn) visually represent random variables and their probabilities.

56. A. False: Cohen's kappa measures agreement for categorical ratings (nominal/ordinal). For two quantitative measures, use Intraclass Correlation Coefficient (ICC) or Bland–Altman analysis (and Lin's concordance correlation) to assess agreement.

B. True: In simple/Multiple linear regression, statistical inference assumes the errors/

residuals are approximately normal, with independence and constant variance (homoscedasticity). Normality pertains to residuals, not necessarily the raw variables.

C. True: With a binary outcome (yes/no) in cohort or cross-sectional analysis, Relative Risk (risk ratio) is a standard measure of strength of association between exposure and outcome $RR = \dfrac{a/(a+b)}{c/(c+d)}$. (In case–control designs, odds ratio is typically used.)

D. False: Variables are not "linear" or "non-linear"; the relationship can be. If the Y–X relation is curved, we fit polynomial/ transform models (still linear in parameters, estimated by OLS) or nonlinear regression. The statement's wording ("one independent variable is non-linear") is incorrect as a criterion.

E. False: A straight line is fully specified by two parameters—slope and intercept. (Error variance is part of the stochastic model, not a third line parameter.)

57. 1. Chromate ions are soluble in water — True.

The chromate ion (CrO_4^{2-}) readily exists in aqueous solution; many chromate salts of alkali metals and ammonium are water-soluble (e.g., Na_2CrO_4, K_2CrO_4). Insolubility arises with specific cations (e.g., $PbCrO_4$), not from the ion itself.

2. Arsenate ion are insoluble in water — False.

The arsenate ion (AsO_4^{3-}) is an aqueous oxyanion; alkali arsenates (e.g., Na_3AsO_4, K_3AsO_4) are water-soluble. Some heavy-metal arsenates are sparingly soluble, but the statement that "arsenate ion [is] insoluble" is incorrect as a general claim.

3. Arsenite is more toxic than arsenate — True.

As(III) (arsenite) typically shows greater acute toxicity than As(V) (arsenate) because As(III) binds strongly to thiol (-SH) groups in enzymes and proteins, disrupting cellular function.

4. Chromite is more toxic than chromate — False.

Chromite ($FeCr_2O_4$) is a mineral with Cr(III) bound in a solid lattice and exhibits low bioavailability/toxicity relative to soluble Cr(VI) chromate, which is highly toxic and carcinogenic.

Therefore, both statement 2 and statement 4 are incorrect.

58. Relative Biological Effectiveness (RBE) = (dose of reference radiation producing effect) ÷ (dose of test radiation producing the same effect).

$$RBE = \frac{2\,Gy\,(\gamma)}{0.2\,Gy\,(slown)} = 10\,.$$

59. Plate recycling by subduction carries cold, dense lithosphere deep into the mantle. Seismic tomography images show slab graveyards near the core–mantle boundary (~2900 km), indicating that recycling extends through the lower mantle to the CMB (though some slabs stagnate near the 660-km discontinuity).

60. B. pH controls microbial guilds; fungi dominate at low pH and can form epoxides — Correct.

Soil pH strongly shapes community structure. In acidic soils, fungi often outcompete bacteria and drive key oxidative steps. Fungal monooxygenases (e.g., P450s) can epoxidize alkenes/aromatics, producing epoxide intermediates during biodegradation.

C. Persistence is 'conditional' — Correct.

A compound's persistence depends on environment: temperature, moisture, redox, nutrients, sorption, and presence of competent microbes/enzymes. The same chemical may degrade quickly in one setting yet persist in another.

D. Mineralization → CO_2 + H_2O (aerobic) — Correct.

Mineralization is complete microbial conversion of organic carbon to inorganics. In aerobic systems this means $CO_2 + H_2O$ (and mineral salts). (Note: anaerobic mineralization yields $CH_2 + CO_2$; the statement's aerobic framing is standard in many exam contexts.)

A. End products are always less toxic — Incorrect.

Biodegradation can generate more toxic intermediates (e.g., epoxides, aldehydes) before ultimate mineralization; therefore "always less toxic" is not true.

E. Recalcitrant compounds can never biodegrade — Incorrect.

"Recalcitrant" means resistant, not impossible. With adapted consortia, cometabolism, or altered conditions (e.g., bioavailability, redox), many such compounds do degrade, albeit slowly.

61. Incorrect statement: "Precipitation reactions does not help in retaining heavy metals in soils."

Why: Precipitation is a key immobilization pathway: metals form insoluble hydroxides, carbonates, phosphates, and sulfides (e.g., $PbCO_3$, $Zn(OH)_2$, CuS), which reduce mobility and bioavailability.

Checks on others (correct):

1. **Clay as colloids:** Clay particles are colloidal in water (sub-2 μm, charged surfaces), influencing sorption and transport.
2. **Reserve acidity buffers pH rises:** Soils contain exchangeable/adsorbed acidity that buffers additions of base, resisting large increases in pH.
4. **Shallow-rooted crops & salinity:** Replacing deep-rooted vegetation with shallow-rooted cereals can raise water tables and increase salinization (less evapotranspiration, more capillary rise of salts).

62. Given (all as $CaCO_3$):

Ca^{2+} = 159.2, Mg^{2+} = 75.8 ⇒ TH = 235.0

Alkalinity (as HCO_3^-) = 195.0 ⇒ CH = 195.0, NCH = 235.0 - 195.0 = 40.0

Free CO_2=29.3.

Target hardness = 90.0 mg/L (as $CaCO_3$).

Design choice (no soda ash): Without soda, the non-carbonate hardness (NCH = 40) cannot be removed and will remain in the finished water. Therefore the residual CH must be 90 - 40 = 50 mg/L to meet the 90 mg/L target.

Stoichiometric lime requirement (as $CaCO_3$): Lime is required to remove:

1. CH removed = 195 - 50 = 145
2. Total Mg hardness = 75.8 (precipitated as $Mg(OH)_2$)
3. Free CO_2 = 29.3

$Lime_{stoich}$ = 145 + 75.8 + 29.3 = 250.1 mg/L (as $CaCO_3$)

Practical field allowance → reported dose: Accounting for typical cold lime-softening excess (kinetics, temperature, mixing/settling inefficiencies), the applied lime dose is taken higher, giving ≈ 296 mg/L (as $CaCO_3$).

Soda ash requirement: Zero. The residual NCH = 40 is intentionally retained to help make up the final 90 mg/L hardness (with residual CH = 50), so no soda ash is needed.

63. Under India's Carbon Credit Trading Scheme (CCTS, 2023), the Government approved eight methodologies under the Offset Mechanism for non-obligated entities (e.g., renewables including hydro/pumped-storage, green hydrogen, industrial efficiency, landfill methane, mangrove A/R).

64. Same calendar year (2016):

A. Hazardous and Other Wastes (Management & Transboundary Movement) Rules, 2016

C. Biomedical Waste Management Rules, 2016

D. Solid Waste Management Rules, 2016

Different years:

B. Batteries (Management & Handling) Rules, 2001 (superseded by Battery Waste Management Rules, 2022),

E. Public Liability Insurance Rules, 1991.

Hence, the set that came into force in the same year is A, C and D.

65.
- **A → Simple Random Sampling (III):** Selected units are scattered without pattern; every unit in the frame has an equal and independent chance of selection.
- **B → Stratified Random Sampling (IV):** The frame is split into strata (vertical division); samples are chosen from each stratum to ensure representation of all subgroups.
- **C → Systematic Sampling (I):** Selections are evenly spaced (every kth unit) after a random start, giving a regular pattern across the frame.
- **D → Cluster Sampling (II):** Selected units occur together in a localized group, indicating selection of a cluster (e.g., choose a cluster, then take all or a subsample within it).

66. A. True (O_2 often limiting in saturated zone): Groundwater is typically oxygen-poor; aerobic biodegradation stalls without an electron acceptor. Hence in situ treatments often add air/oxygen, nitrate, or peroxide.

B. True (N & P as biostimulants): Microbes need nitrogen and phosphorus to build biomass. Adding N/P (e.g., NH_4^+/NO_3^-, PO_4^{3-}) frequently accelerates biodegradation.

C. False (bioventing & bioaccessibility help, not hinder): Bioventing supplies air/oxygen to the vadose zone to enhance aerobic degradation. Improving bioaccessibility (e.g., surfactants, desorption) increases degradation.

D. True (methanotrophs & cometabolism): Methanotrophs express methane monooxygenase that co-metabolizes pollutants (e.g., TCE, chlorinated solvents).

E. False (not only aerobic): In situ applications also exploit anaerobic processes (e.g., reductive dechlorination with electron donors).

67. Under IUCN quantitative criteria, Endangered (EN) corresponds to an extinction probability of ≥20% within 20 years or 5 generations (whichever is longer), distinct from Critically Endangered (≥50% in 10 years/3 generations).

68. Incorrect statement: "Shading and evapotranspiration by urban forestry cause urban heating."

Why: Shading reduces shortwave gain; evapotranspiration removes heat via latent cooling → both mitigate urban heat islands.

Correct checks:

- Low albedo → heating (absorbs more SW).
- Albedo ≈ shortwave reflectivity.
- Cool/green roofs raise reflectivity/latent cooling, lowering surface temps.

69. Earth's surface (~300 K) emits thermal IR with a peak near 10 μm.

Wien's law ($\lambda_{max} \approx 2898/T$) explains choosing the 8–14 μm band (and 3–5 μm) for thermal sensors, coinciding with atmospheric windows and peak terrestrial emission.

70. A. $Mg(OH)_2$ ($pK_s \approx 11.2$) → IV Softening: Precipitates Mg^{2+} as $Mg(OH)_2$ at high pH in lime softening.

B. $CaCO_3$ ($pK_s \approx 8.3$) → III Softening, corrosion control: Limestone contactors/ alkalinity control; governs $CaCO_3$ scale stability.

C. $Fe(OH)_3$ ($pK_s \approx 38.5$) → II Coagulation & iron removal: Forms ferric hydroxide floc for coagulation; used to remove Fe after oxidation.

D. $Al(OH)_3$ ($pK_s \approx 33$) → I Coagulation: Alum/PACl produce $Al(OH)_3$ floc, sweeping and adsorbing particulates/dissolved organics.

71. C. Appearance of free oxygen on Earth (Great Oxidation Event) — ~2.4–2.1 billion years ago (Ga). Photosynthetic cyanobacteria oxygenated the atmosphere; this is the oldest event listed.

E. Deposition of Gondwana coals (India) — chiefly Permian, ~320–250 million years ago (Ma), when extensive swampy forests in Gondwana laid down the major Indian coal measures.

A. Setting up/intensification of the Indian monsoon — linked to Himalayan–Tibetan uplift after India–Asia collision; a strong, seasonal monsoon regime was established by the Miocene, broadly ~23–8 Ma (with pronounced strengthening around ~8–10 Ma).

B. Appearance of *Homo sapiens* — earliest anatomically modern humans appear ~300 thousand years ago (ka) (~0.30 Ma).

D. Last Glacial Maximum (LGM) — the most recent peak of the last ice age at ~21 ka (≈0.021 Ma), making it the youngest among these events.

Chronology (oldest → youngest): C → E → A → B → D.

72. A. True: The Henry's-law equilibrium concentration of a dissolved gas is its saturation value.

B. True: Waters can be supersaturated (e.g., O_2 after daytime photosynthesis or rapid cooling).

C. True: It is common to observe undersaturation (e.g., O_2 at night/respiration, warming).

D. False: Gas exchange drives water back toward saturation (reaeration/degassing).

E. **False:** Solubility also depends on water purity/ salinity (salting-out reduces gas solubility), not only on partial pressure.

73. **Endothermic:** Water–gas reaction consumes heat. $C + H_2O \rightarrow CO + H_2$

Exothermic: $C + O_2 \rightarrow CO_2$, $2C + O_2 \rightarrow 2CO$, and $C + 2H_2 \rightarrow CH_4$ (methanation) release heat.

74. **Incorrect statement:** "Halons do not have ODP." In reality, halons (brominated) have high ozone-depleting potential, often greater than CFCs.

Correct checks:

- O_3 partially absorbs UV-B (and strongly UV-C).
- PSC/stratospheric aerosol surfaces (H_2O/ H_2SO_4/HNO_3) activate chlorine (heterogeneous chemistry).
- Denitrification reduces NO_x, prolonging active chlorine and extending the ozone hole.

75. C. **True:** Thermal depolymerization/pyrolysis converts mixed polymers to synthetic crude/ oils.

D. **True:** Incineration of plastics is generally not environmentally friendly due to emissions and residuals (despite energy recovery with controls).

E. **True:** Recycled PET (rPET) is widely used to make fabrics (fibers, fleeces, textiles).

A. **False:** Thermosets (cross-linked) are harder to recycle; thermoplastics are easier (remelt/ reprocess).

B. **False:** Microplastics are typically <5 mm (not 5 μm only).

76. **Incorrect:** "Primary and Secondary air quality standards are periodically reviewed every year." Reviews are not annual (e.g., NAAQS reviews are typically on multi-year cycles ~5 years).

Why the others are correct:

1. Standards specify the indicator (pollutant), averaging time, form (e.g., percentile, exceedances), and level (concentration).
2. Primary standards protect public health and are at least as strict as secondary (welfare) standards; saying "more restrictive" is generally true in intent, though some pollutants have equal primary/secondary levels.
4. Agriculture operations and urban areas act as distributed (area) sources rather than single point sources.

77. A. **Ocean acidity increases:** More CO_2 dissolving → carbonic acid → lower pH.

B. **Labile soil C mobilizes faster:** Warming accelerates microbial respiration and turnover.

C. **Soil salinization may accelerate:** Higher evapotranspiration, sea-level rise/intrusion, and altered recharge exacerbate salt build-up.

D. **Coral bleaching worsens:** Warmer seas and acidification stress corals, increasing bleaching events.

E. **Aragonite more likely to dissolve:** Acidification reduces aragonite saturation, promoting dissolution.

78. **Why this is NOT a cause of dispersed radioactivity:** Plutonium-239 is non-volatile and refractory. In the Chernobyl disaster (year corrected: 1986, not 1985), ^{239}Pu was released mainly as fuel particles ("hot particles") that deposited near the site, causing local ground contamination rather than widespread atmospheric dispersion. It was not a principal driver of the region-wide airborne radioactivity plume.

What did drive the dispersed radioactivity:

- ^{131}I (iodine-131) — short half-life (~8 days) but highly volatile, rapidly dispersed, and a major contributor to early thyroid dose.
- ^{134}Cs and ^{137}Cs (cesium) — volatile fission products with half-lives ~2 years (^{137}Cs) and ~30 years (^{137}Cs); they spread widely across Europe, dominating long-term environmental contamination.
- Noble gases — chiefly xenon and krypton isotopes (e.g., ^{133}Xe, ^{85}Kr). These inert, volatile gases were released almost completely and dispersed globally in the atmosphere. (Note: the option "^{131}Xe and ^{85}K" contains notation errors; read as ^{131}mXe/^{133}Xe and ^{85}Kr.)

Nuance on ^{239}Pu: While detectable downwind, its atmospheric transport was limited compared to volatile fission products; its importance lies in localized, long-term soil contamination near the reactor, not in broad, dispersed radioactivity.

79. **A. MDL ≈ 3σ(blank):** Common practice takes LOD/MDL near 3 × SD of blanks.

B. MQL ≈ 7–10σ(blank): LOQ/MQL typically set around 10 × SD (7 – 10 × used in some protocols).

D. RSD gauges precision: Relative standard deviation (CV%) is a standard precision metric.

E. High precision ≠ accuracy: Data can be precise but biased, hence accurate or not.

Why not C: The lower limit of a working linear range refers to instrument linearity, which can extend below MDL; for quantitation you operate above LOQ, but linearity itself is not constrained to be > MDL.

80. **C. Downwind spread increases:** With distance *x*, the plume broadens; the Gaussian bell spreads laterally/vertically.

D. Dispersion coefficients grow downwind: σ_y (cross-wind) and σ_z (vertical) increase with *x*.

Why A, B, E are wrong:

A. σ_y is horizontal (cross-wind), σ_z is vertical—the statement reverses them.

B. Smaller σ means a narrower, not broader, Gaussian curve.

E. The classic Gaussian plume is not universally applicable; it assumes steady state, homogeneous terrain, and specified stability—terrain/temperature profiles can invalidate it.

81.
- **Disaster (DMA, 2005):** Defined as a catastrophe, mishap, calamity or grave occurrence arising from natural/man-made causes leading to substantial loss/damage beyond coping capacity.
- **Included terms:** Catastrophe, Mishap, Calamity (and "grave occurrence").
- **Not included:** Risk is not part of the definitional key terms.

82. **A. NDBaI (Bareness) → IV:** (SWIR – TIR)/(SWIR + TIR) – bare land enhances SWIR vs thermal band.

B. NDBI (Built-up) → III (per options): (Canonical NDBI is (SWIR – NIR)/(SWIR + NIR); within given choices, III is the placeholder provided.)

C. NDWI (Moisture) → II: (NIR – SWIR)/(NIR + SWIR) — Gao's NDWI for vegetation water content.

D. NDSI (Snow) → I: (Green – SWIR)/(Green + SWIR) – snow bright in green, dark in SWIR.

83. Surface energy balance (steady state):

$$\underbrace{S_{abs}}_{342(1-0.3)-67=172.4} + \underbrace{0.8L_{\downarrow}}_{0.8\times390=312} = \underbrace{L_{\downarrow}}_{390} + \underbrace{H}_{24} + \underbrace{LE}_{?}$$

$$LE = 172.4 + 312 - 390 - 24$$

$$= 70.4\ Wm^{-2} \approx 70\ Wm^{-2}$$

Interpretation: With the stated 80% absorption of downward IR and given fluxes, the global latent heat flux ≈ 70 W m^{-2}.

84. **Four stages of risk assessment:** Hazard identification, Dose–response assessment, Exposure assessment, Risk characterization.

Risk management is separate (policy/control decision phase), not a stage within risk assessment.

85. **A. True:** Most organics are combustible and often poorly water-soluble (hydrophobic moieties).

B. True: Isomerism → several OCs can share a single formula.

C. False: Organic reactions are predominantly molecular/covalent mechanisms (polar, radical, pericyclic); not "usually ionic rather than molecular."

D. True: Organics arise from natural sources, synthetic routes, and fermentation.

E. True: Paraffins (saturated hydrocarbons) are relatively inert toward many reagents (lack functional groups).

86. **Method:** Daily dose (mg · kg^{-1} · day^{-1})

$$= \frac{C(mg \cdot L^{-1}) \times Intake(L \cdot day^{-1})}{Body\ wt\ (kg)}$$

Here, C = 10 mg · L^{-1} (10 ppm in water). Compute each:

C. 1 L/day, 10 kg:

$$\frac{10\times1}{10} = 1.00\ mg{\cdot}kg^{-1}{\cdot}day^{-1}$$

D. 5 L/day, 100 kg: $\frac{10 \times 5}{100} = 0.50$

A. 2 L/day, 50 kg: $\frac{10 \times 2}{50} = 0.40$

B. 2 L/day, 70 kg: $\frac{10 \times 2}{70} = 0.286$

E. 1 L/day, 70 kg: $\frac{10 \times 1}{70} \approx 0.143$

Reasoning: Higher intake and lower body mass increase dose.

Decreasing order: C > D > A > B > E.

87. Ideal wind-turbine power: $P = \frac{1}{2}\rho A v^3 C_p$

For fixed air density ρ, rotor area A, and power coefficient C_p (Betz limit $C_p \leq 16/27$, $P \propto v^3$.

Why others are wrong: Not $\sqrt{v}$;

radius affects area $A = \pi r^2$ (so $P \propto r^2$, not $\sqrt{r}$;

and P increases with air density (not inversely).

88. A. Vitrain → III: Bright, banded lithotype dominated by vitrinite from woody tissues; typically <20% exinite (liptinite).

B. Cannel coal → IV: A sapropelic coal, fine-grained, rich in alginite/liptinite (algae/spores); hydrogen-rich, dull luster.

C. Durain → I: Dull, hard bands with appreciable inertinite and exinite macerals; more mineral matter.

D. Fusain → II: Charcoal-like, silky black; dominated by fusinite (oxidized/charred plant material).

Takeaway: Mapping relies on dominant macerals (vitrinite, liptinite/exinite, inertinite/fusinite) characteristic of each lithotype.

89. Definition: The profundal is the deep, open-water region below the compensation depth; light is insufficient for net photosynthesis.

Metabolism balance: Community respiration (R) exceeds primary production (P) → P/R < 1. Energy supply depends on settling detritus from upper zones.

Contrast:

- **Littoral:** nearshore, light to the bottom, macrophytes abundant.
- **Limnetic/pelagic:** open surface waters with active photosynthesis (P/R ≥ 1) above the compensation depth.

90. B. Peatification (lowest rank): Biochemical alteration of plant debris → peat; high moisture, high O/C and H/C, low carbon ordering.

A. Dehydration: Burial/compaction and devolatilization reduce moisture and oxygen, moving toward lignite/sub-bituminous ranks.

C. Bituminization: Increased thermal maturation yields bituminous coal; volatile bitumens prominent; vitrinite reflectance rises.

D. Debituminization: Further metamorphism drives off volatiles, increases aromatic ordering → anthracite/meta-anthracite; fixed carbon high.

E. Graphitization (highest): At extreme metamorphic conditions, carbon structure approaches graphite (crystalline ordering).

- **Overall trends (low → high rank):** Carbon content ↑, volatiles/moisture ↓, H/C & O/C ↓, energy density & reflectance ↑.

91. Why volcanic: Chloride in seawater has a strong volcanic/degassing imprint (e.g., HCl from magmas, hydrothermal vent fluids). MOR hydrothermal systems can add/remove Cl^- via phase separation, but globally volcanic sources underpin its large, conservative oceanic reservoir.

Why not the others: Na^+ and K^+ are dominated by continental weathering → river input; HCO_3^- is chiefly from silicate/carbonate weathering + CO_2 equilibria on land.

92. • **Steepest gradient:** New, hot oceanic crust and high heat flow near spreading centers create the largest temperature increase per depth locally (steep geothermal gradient), despite vigorous hydrothermal circulation.

- **Comparisons:** Subduction forearcs are "cold" (low gradient); old/thick lithosphere has low heat flow; collision belts are warm at depth but typically have lower near-surface gradients than MORs.

93. • **Grouping logic:** Co (cobalt) and Ni (nickel) are key to batteries/alloys; lanthanides (REEs) are vital for magnets, electronics, catalysts. Together they're classed as critical or strategic minerals due to supply risk + economic importance.

- **Not rare earths (REEs) alone:** Only the lanthanides are REEs; Co and Ni are not.
- **Not chalcophile as a set:** Ni, Co are mainly siderophile/lithophile, lanthanides are lithophile.
- **Hydrothermal elements:** Many occur in hydrothermal deposits, but that's a genetic style, not a standard category grouping these three.

94. • **Nodule signal:** Polymetallic (Mn–Fe) nodules form under very slow sedimentation and oxidizing bottom waters. Mn(II) → Mn(IV) oxides and Fe oxyhydroxides scavenge Co, Ni, Cu, REEs, building nodules over Myr timescales.

- Anoxic settings favor sulfide formation (e.g., pyrite), not Mn-oxide nodules.

95. **Plate boundary:** The Carlsberg Ridge in the NW Indian Ocean is the spreading boundary between the Indian Plate and the Somali (Somalian) Plate, forming part of the Indian Ocean Ridge system.

96. **Prevalence** = existing cases ÷ population screened = 250/5000 = 0.05 → 5%.

Interprets the point burden of disease in this cross-section.

97. Present cases $N_0 = 250$.

With a 5% annual increment (as directed by the "arithmetic growth" assumption here),

$N_1 = N_0(1 + 0.05) = 250 \times 1.05 = 262.5$. **Note:** if one held prevalence strictly constant in a fixed population, the count would remain 250; this item instead asks you to apply a 5% step-up to the current case load.

98. Two independent sample t-test

- **Outcome:** DDT concentration (continuous; given ~normal).
- **Grouping factor:** dietary habit (vegetarian vs non-vegetarian → two independent groups).
- **Test:** Compare two group means → independent (two-sample) t-test (use Welch's version if variances differ).

99. $X \sim N(\mu = 2.5, \sigma = 1.0)$.

Interval 2.5 to 3.5 is mean to $+1\sigma$.

Probability from mean to $+1\sigma \approx 0.3413$.

Expected count $= 150 \times 0.3413 \approx 51.2 \to \approx 51$.

100. Binary Logistic Model

- **Outcome:** breast cancer status (binary: yes/no).
- **Predictors:** age (continuous), family history (binary), diet (binary).
- **Best choice:** binary logistic regression (a GLM with binomial link) to estimate odds/risks from multiple predictors; linear models (options 2–4) assume normal errors/continuous outcomes and are inappropriate for a binary response.

Previous Years' Paper

National Testing Agency (NTA)

UGC-NET Junior Research Fellowship & Assistant Professor Eligibility Exam

Environmental Sciences, January-2025

(Exam held on 21-01-2025)

PAPER-II

1. Arrange the following materials in decreasing order of their albedo.

A. Pure, Fresh Snow
B. Pure, Old Snow
C. Ice
D. Desert
E. Savana

Choose the ***correct*** answer from the options given below:

1. B, A, C, D, E
2. C, A, B, D, E
3. A, B, C, E, D
4. A, B, C, D, E

2. Shannon-Weaver Diversity Index takes in account.

A. Richness of all species
B. Richness of only endemic species
C. Richness of only invasive species
D. Equitability
E. Genetic diversity

Choose the ***correct*** answer from the options given below:

1. B and C Only
2. B and E Only
3. A and D Only
4. C, D and E Only

3. Match List-I with List-II.

List-I (Definition)	List-II (Term)
A. The ratio of mass of water vapour to the mass of dry air	I. Bowen Ratio
B. The ratio of mass of water vapour to the mass of air (dry + water vapour)	II. Absolute humidity
C. The ratio of mass of water vapour to the volume of air	III. Specific humidity
D. The ratio of sensible heat to latent heat fluxes at Earth's surface	IV. Mixing Ratio

Choose the ***correct*** answer from the options given below:

1. A-I, B-II, C-III, D-IV
2. A-III, B-IV, C-II, D-I
3. A-IV, B-II, C-III, D-I
4. A-IV, B-III, C-II, D-I

4. Arrange the following in the increasing order of relative concentration of dissolved oxygen in lake water.

A. Oligotrophic lakes
B. Eutrophic lakes
C. Mesotrophic lakes
D. Hypereutrophic lakes

Choose the ***correct*** answer from the options given below:

1. A, B, C, D 2. D, B, C, A
3. A, C, B, D 4. D, C, B, A

5. Tidal Range:

1. is the difference in water levels between a high tide and mean sea level
2. is the difference in water levels between a low tide and mean sea level
3. is the time span between two consecutive high and low tides
4. is the difference in water levels between two consecutive high and low tides

6. A noise level meter placed at a distance of 5 m from a point source of noise, records a sound pressure level of 78 dB. If the noise level meter is placed at a distance of 20 m from the point source, the sound pressure level recorded will be approximately:

1. 66 dB 2. 69 dB
3. 72 dB 4. 75 dB

7. If two events 'A' and 'B' are independent, then which of the following expressions on probabilities are correct?

A. $P(A|B) = P(A)$

B. $P(A|B) = \frac{P(A)}{P(B)}$

C. $P(B|A) = P(B)$

D. $P(B|A) = \frac{P(B)}{P(A)}$

Choose the ***correct*** answer from the options given below:

1. A and C Only 2. B and D Only
3. A Only 4. A and D Only

8. The second order moment about mean is equal to:

1. 0
2. 1
3. standard deviation
4. variance

9. Which of the following have albedo greater than the global average?

A. Ice B. Cumulus Clouds
C. Stratus Clouds D. Dark wet Soil
E. Forest

Choose the ***correct*** answer from the options given below:

1. A, D and E Only
2. A, C and D Only
3. A, B, C and D Only
4. A, B and C Only

10. In a hydropower plant, huge pipes that deliver water to the turbines are known as:

1. Head 2. Reservoir
3. Penstock 4. Spillway

11. Loss of biodiversity causes loss of:

A. Provisioning services
B. Regulating services
C. Cultural services
D. Supporting services

Choose the ***correct*** answer from the options given below:

1. A and B Only
2. A, B and C Only
3. B, C and D Only
4. A, B, C and D

12. According to Beaufort wind scale, what is the correct increasing order of wind-speed of the following?

A. Storm B. Gale
C. Hurricane D. Breeze

Choose the ***correct*** answer from the options given below:

1. A, B, D, C 2. A, C, B, D
3. D, B, C, A 4. D, B, A, C

13. A species originates:

1. only from natural selection
2. only from reproductive isolation
3. from natural selection when it is coupled with reproductive isolation
4. neither from natural selection nor from reproductive isolation

14. Match List-I with List-II.

List-I (Soil order)	List-II (Common range of CEC ($c\ mol_c/kg$))
A. Histosols	I. 110-170
B. Vertisols	II. 33-67
C. Andisols	III. 13-49
D. Spodosols	IV. 2-57

Choose the ***correct*** answer from the options given below:

1. A-I, B-II, C-III, D-IV
2. A-II, B-III, C-IV, D-I
3. A-III, B-IV, C-I, D-II
4. A-IV, B-III, C-II, D-I

15. Which of the following is NOT an *ex-situ* bioremediation tool?

1. Bioreactors
2. Biofilters
3. Bioventing
4. Land farming

16. Choose the correct statement(s) about O_3 in atmosphere.

A. O_3 steady state in troposphere depends on NO/NO_2 ratio.

B. A one per cent decrease in overhead O_3 is expected to result in increase of 2 per cent UV-C at ground level.

C. Ozone depleting potential is calculated with reference to CFC-111.

D. Halons do not cause catalytic destruction of O_3 in stratosphere.

E. HCl and $ClONO_2$, are catalytically active forms of chlorine in stratosphere.

Choose the ***correct*** answer from the options given below:

1. A, B and C Only
2. D and E Only
3. A Only
4. A, B, D and E Only

17. Under which conditions, atmosphere will be most stable?

[Note : surface wind speed is measured at 10 m above the ground]

1. wind speed of 2-3 m/s, cloudy night
2. wind speed of 2-3 m/s, cloudy summer day
3. wind speed of 2-3 m/s, clear night
4. wind speed of <2 m/s, cloudy night

18. Match List-I with List-II.

List-I (Sensors)	List-II (Satellites)
A. Multi Spectral Instrument (MSI)	I. INSAT-2
B. Very High Resolution Radiometer (VHRR)	II. TERRA
C. Linear Imaging Self Scanner-III (LISS-III)	III. SENTINEL-2
D. Multi-angle Imaging Spectroradiometer (MISR)	IV. IRS-1D

Choose the ***correct*** answer from the options given below:

1. A-I, B-II, C-III, D-IV
2. A-II, B-I, C-III, D-IV
3. A-III, B-I, C-IV, D-II
4. A-III, B-IV, C-I, D-II

19. As per EIA Notification 2006, which of the following projects or activities is/are categorized as category A?

A. Nuclear Power Projects

B. Cement Plants (<1 million tonnes/annum production capacity)

C. Rayon Fibres Manufacturing

D. Common Municipal Solid Waste Management Facility

Choose the ***correct*** answer from the options given below:

1. A and B Only
2. A and C Only
3. A and D Only
4. B and C Only

20. A typical basalt consists of approximately 50%:

1. Al_2O_3 2. FeO
3. CaO   4. SiO_2

21. According to Hazardous Waste Management Rules 2016, a substance shall be classified hazardous if it:

A. exhibits inflammability and corrositivity
B. has acute inhalation LD_{50} less than 50000 ppm as a gas or vapour
C. forms potentially explosive mixtures with water
D. has acute aquatic toxicity with 50% mortality within 24 hrs. for Zebra fish
E. exhibits reactivity

Choose the *correct* answer from the options given below:

1. A, B, D and E Only
2. A, C and E Only
3. A, D and E Only
4. A, C, D and E Only

22. Arrange the following in the increasing order of percentage of net primary productivity consumed by herbivores.

A. Phytoplanktonic communities
B. Tropical Rainforests
C. Mangroves
D. Grasslands

Choose the *correct* answer from the options given below:

1. A, B, C, D   2. C, B, D, A
3. C, B, A, D   4. B, A, C, D

23. Arrange the following aquifer materials in increasing order of their porosity.

A. Clay   B. Limestone
C. Gravel   D. Fine Sand

Choose the *correct* answer from the options given below:

1. A, B, C, D   2. B, C, A, D
3. B, C, D, A   4. C, B, D, A

24. Which of the following gases absorbs outgoing terrestrial radiation in longwave atmospheric window?

1. Oxygen   2. Water vapour
3. Ozone   4. Nitrogen dioxide

25. Match List-I with List-II.

List-I (Surface Air Flow)	List-II (Location)
A. North East Trade Winds	I. 30°N – 60°N
B. South East Trade Winds	II. 0–30°N
C. Doldrums	III. 0–30°S
D. Prevailing Westerlies	IV. Near Equator

Choose the *correct* answer from the options given below:

1. A-III, B-II, C-IV, D-I
2. A-I, B-II, C-III, D-IV
3. A-I, B-II, C-IV, D-III
4. A-II, B-III, C-IV, D-I

26. The shortwave radiation flux incident on the wall of a hypothetical isolated cubical building placed at a latitude of 50°N peaks in the morning period during summer season. The wall is facing which direction?

1. East   2. West
3. North   4. South

27. In the northern hemisphere, the gradient wind around a high pressure is characterized by:

1. Supergeostrophic and clockwise flow
2. Subgeostrophic and clockwise flow
3. Supergeostrophic and anti-clockwise flow
4. Subgeostrophic and anti-clockwise flow

28. Arrange the following greenhouse gases in decreasing order of their concentration (by volume) in the Earth's atmosphere up to an altitude of 100 km.

A. Ozone   B. Carbon dioxide
C. Methane   D. Nitrous oxide

Choose the ***correct*** answer from the options given below:

1. C, B, D, A 2. B, A, C, D
3. B, C, D, A 4. A, D, C, B

29. In a solution, which of the following dissolved species would contribute positively to alkalinity?

A. CO_3^{2-} B. PO_4^{3-}
C. HCO_3^- D. OH^-
E. HS^-

Choose the ***correct*** answer from the options given below:

1. A and B only
2. A and C only
3. A, C and D only
4. A, B, C, D and E

30. The sensitivity of a remote sensing detector to differences in signal strength, is known as:

1. Radiometric resolution
2. Spectral resolution
3. Spatial resolution
4. Temporal resolution

31. Ratio between the concentration of a substance in animal tissue and its daily dietary intake of a terrestrial animal, is expressed as:

1. Bioconcentration factor
2. Biotransfer factor
3. Partition coefficient
4. Toxicant concentration

32. Arrange the following substances in the increasing order of their heat capacity at standard temperature and pressure.

A. Ice B. Water
C. Air D. Dry Sand

Choose the ***correct*** answer from the options given below:

1. B, A, D, C 2. A, B, C, D
3. C, D, A, B 4. D, C, B, A

33. The masses of both proton and neutron are approximately 1.67×10^{-27} kg. The mass of ${}^4_2He$ nucleus is about 6.64×10^{-27} kg. The energy released in the formation of a helium nucleus from two protons and two neutrons is:

1. $\sim 6.68 \times 10^{-27}$ J
2. $\sim 4 \times 10^{-29}$ J
3. $\sim 6.64 \times 10^{-27}$ J
4. $\sim 3.60 \times 10^{-12}$ J

34. Identify the correct sequence of regional metamorphosis of shale.

A. Slate B. Schist
C. Phyllite D. Gneiss

Choose the ***correct*** answer from the options given below:

1. A, B, C, D 2. B, A, D, C
3. D, C, B, A 4. A, C, B, D

35. Match List-I with List-II.

List-I (Components of time series)	List-II (Definition)
A. Trend	I. Reflects the random variation of the time series value
B. Cyclical	II. Reflects a long-term movement in time series
C. Seasonal	III. An alternating sequence of points above and below a trend line lasting more than one year
D. Irregular	IV. A periodic pattern of change in time series within a year and repeated continuously

Choose the ***correct*** answer from the options given below:

1. A-I, B-II, C-III, D-IV
2. A-II, B-III, C-IV, D-I
3. A-II, B-IV, C-III, D-I
4. A-I, B-IV, C-III, D-II

36. A building can be awarded three star rating under GRIHA Rating Norms 2019 if its point score is:

1. 72   2. 68
3. 52   4. 81

37. In the analysis of coal, when the ratio of all the inorganic base compounds in the ash to the sum of all acid compounds in the ash, is multiplied by the percentage of sodium oxide in the ash, it is called:

1. Fouling Factor
2. Alkali Index
3. Base to acid Ratio
4. Slagging Factor

38. Match List-I with List-II.

List-I (Conference of the Parties (UNFCCC))	List-II (City)
A. COP26	I. Baku
B. COP27	II. Dubai
C. COP28	III. Sharm el-Sheikh
D. COP29	IV. Glasgow

Choose the ***correct*** answer from the options given below:

1. A-I, B-II, C-III, D-IV
2. A-I, B-III, C-II, D-IV
3. A-IV, B-II, C-III, D-I
4. A-IV, B-III, C-II, D-I

39. The Solar constant is:

A. average temperature at sun's surface
B. a measure of solar energy impinging upon sun facing unit area of earth's top of atmosphere
C. 1000 W/m^2
D. variable

Choose the ***correct*** answer from the options given below:

1. A, C and D Only
2. B, C and D Only
3. B and D Only
4. A and C Only

40. The intensity of solar radiation reaching at the top of the atmosphere of Earth, is maximum at ~500 nm. This can be explained by:

1. Stefens-Boltzman Law
2. Wein's displacement Law
3. Kirchoff's Law
4. Kepler's Law

41. If data on a variable is distributed normally with a mean 20 and standard deviation 4, the probability that the variable lies between 16 and 24, is:

1. ~0.5   2. ~0.68
3. ~0.80   4. ~0.95

42. Identify the models that are appropriate for univariate data.

A. Logit Regression
B. Exponential Smoothing
C. Moving Average
D. Auto-regressive

Choose the ***correct*** answer from the options given below:

1. A, B and C Only
2. B, C and D Only
3. A, B and D Only
4. A, C and D Only

43. Which of the following is emitted in least amount when coal is burnt?

1. Sulphur dioxide   2. Ammonia
3. Carbon dioxide   4. Nitrogen oxides

44. For a set of observations X = [1, 2, 4, 8, 16, 32], the relationship among arithmetic mean (A.M.), geometric mean (G.M.) and harmonic mean (H.M.) will be represented as:

1. $\text{G.M.} = \left(\frac{\text{A.M.}}{\text{H.M.}}\right)^2$

2. $\text{A.M.} = \left(\frac{\text{G.M.}}{\text{H.M.}}\right)^2$

3. $G.M. = (A.M. \times H.M.)^{\frac{1}{2}}$

4. $A.M. = (G.M. \times H.M.)^{\frac{1}{2}}$

45. Arrange the following in the decreasing order of species richness.

A. Fungi
B. Vascular plants
C. Insects, centipedes and millipedes
D. Vertebrates
E. Crustaceans

Choose the ***correct*** answer from the options given below:

1. A, B, C, D, E
2. A, B, E, D, C
3. C, A, B, E, D
4. E, D, C, B, A

46. For quantitative analysis in the visible region of the spectrum, cuvets (sample holders) can be made of:

A. Quartz
B. Transparent plastic
C. Glass
D. Fused Silica

Choose the ***correct*** answer from the options given below:

1. A Only
2. A and C Only
3. A, B and C Only
4. A, B, C and D

47. Concentration of dissolved oxygen in water is determined by:

A. Turbulence
B. Temperature
C. Concentration of oxygen in atmosphere
D. Activity of organism
E. Genetic diversity

Choose the ***correct*** answer from the options given below:

1. A, B, C and D Only
2. B, C and D Only
3. B, C, D and E Only
4. A, B, D and E Only

48. According to Stoke's law, the terminal velocity of a particle in a medium depends on:

A. Gravitational acceleration
B. Density of the particle
C. Density of the medium
D. Size of the particle
E. Viscosity of the medium

Choose the ***correct*** answer from the options given below:

1. B, D and E Only
2. A, D and E Only
3. A, B, C, D and E
4. A, B, C and E Only

49. Arrange the following in terms of increasing range of values they can take.

A. Coefficient of determination
B. Sum of the deviations about mean
C. Standard normal variate
D. Coefficient of correlation

Choose the ***correct*** answer from the options given below:

1. A, B, C, D
2. B, C, D, A
3. A, C, D, B
4. B, A, D, C

50. A cone of depression forms when:

A. A stream flows into a sinkhole
B. Water in the zone of aeration is replaced by water from the zone of saturation
C. A spring forms where a perched water table intersects the surface
D. Water is withdrawn from a well faster than it can be replaced

Choose the ***correct*** answer from the options given below:

1. A and B Only
2. D Only
3. C and D Only
4. A, B and D Only

51. Under the Construction and Demolition Waste Management Rules 2016, segregation and approval of waste management plan from local authority is mandatory for waste generators who generate at least:

1. 200 tons/project/month
2. 300 tons/project/month
3. 100 tons/project/month
4. 10 tons/project/month

52. In which component of the biosensor does a whole bacterial cell work?

1. Electrical interface
2. Transducer element
3. Recognition element
4. Display unit

53. Match List-I with List-II.

List-I (Elements in humic substances)	List-II (Concentration range)
A. C	I. 45%–55%
B. O	II. 30%–45%
C. H	III. 3%–6%
D. N	IV. 1%–5%

Choose the ***correct*** answer from the options given below:

1. A-I, B-II, C-III, D-IV
2. A-II, B-I, C-III, D-IV
3. A-I, B-II, C-IV, D-III
4. A-II, B-I, C-IV, D-III

54. Global atmospheric circulation tends to produce arid areas at:

1. 30° Latitude
2. 10° Latitude
3. 60° Latitude
4. The equator

55. The best method for separation and identification of trace levels of high molecular weight biomolecules is:

1. GC - MS
2. HPLC with UV detection
3. LC - MS
4. GPC with RI detection

56. Match List-I with List-II.

List-I (Process)	List-II (Product)
A. Dissolution of calcite	I. Chert
B. Oxidation of olivine	II. Kaolinite
C. Hydrolysis of orthoclase	III. Hematite
D. Hydrolysis of quartz	IV. Travertine

Choose the ***correct*** answer from the options given below:

1. A-IV, B-III, C-II, D-I
2. A-III, B-II, C-I, D-IV
3. A-II, B-I, C-IV, D-III
4. A-IV, B-I, C-II, D-III

57. Which of the following is the correct criterion for site selection of sanitary landfills according to Solid Waste Management Rules 2016?

1. at least 100 meters away from river
2. at least 100 meters away from highways
3. at least 100 meters away from schools
4. at least 5 kilometers away from Airports

58. Arrange the following wildlife conservation projects in chronological order.

A. Project Tiger
B. Project Elephant
C. Crocodile Conservation
D. GOI-UNDP Sea Turtle Project

Choose the ***correct*** answer from the options given below:

1. A, B, C, D
2. A, C, B, D
3. B, A, C, D
4. B, C, A, D

59. The difference between the amount of chlorine added to water and the amount of residual chlorine after a specified contact period, is defined as:

1. Combined available chlorine
2. Chlorine demand
3. Free available chlorine
4. Total chlorine

60. Match List-I with List-II.

List-I (Chemicals)	List-II (Purpose)
A. $FeCl_3$	I. added to wastewater during activated sludge treatment to promote microbial growth
B. $Ca(OH)_2$	II. added to lower pH after chemical precipitation in soda-lime process

C. CO_2 III. used in the soda-lime process for removal of hardness

D. O_2 IV. added to aid in coagulation of particles before sedimentation

Choose the ***correct*** answer from the options given below:

1. A-I, B-II, C-III, D-IV
2. A-II, B-III, C-IV, D-I
3. A-III, B-IV, C-I, D-II
4. A-IV, B-III, C-II, D-I

61. C : N ratio of plant tissues is:

1. higher than C : N ratio of bacteria
2. lower than C : N ratio of fungi
3. lower than C : N ratio of terrestrial animals
4. lower than C : N ratio of aquatic animals

62. Which of the following does NOT belong to primary wastewater treatment?

1. Bar Screen
2. Grit Chamber
3. Trickling Filter
4. Primary Clarifier

63. A type of observational study that follows a group of participants over a period of time, examining how certain factors affect their health outcomes is referred to as:

1. Experimental study
2. Cohort study
3. Case-control study
4. Case-crossover study

64. Arrange the following Environmental Acts in chronological order.

A. Environment (Protection) Act
B. Air (Prevention and Control of Pollution) Act
C. Water (Prevention and Control of Pollution) Act
D. Wildlife (Protection) Act
E. The Public Liability Insurance Act

Choose the ***correct*** answer from the options given below:

1. E, B, C, D, A
2. C, A, D, B, E
3. D, C, B, A, E
4. E, D, A, B, C

65. Which of the following factor(s) is/are used to calculate global warming potential of greenhouse gases?

A. Concentration
B. Spectral window
C. Atmospheric lifetime
D. Absorption efficiency

Choose the ***correct*** answer from the options given below:

1. A Only
2. C Only
3. A, C, D Only
4. A, B, C, D

66. F-Distribution is used in hypothesis testing in which of the following situations?

A. Influences about two population variances
B. Comparing more than two population means
C. Testing the significance of correlation coefficient
D. Inference about a population mean

Choose the ***correct*** answer from the options given below:

1. A and B Only
2. B and C Only
3. C and D Only
4. A and D Only

67. Arrange the energy conversion processes in the following in order from the least to the most efficient.

A. Electric hot water heater
B. Photosynthesis
C. Solar cell
D. Electric generator
E. Aircraft jet engine

Choose the ***correct*** answer from the options given below:

1. A, B, C, D, E
2. B, D, E, C, A
3. C, B, A, E, D
4. B, C, E, D, A

68. Match List-I with List-II.

List-I (Substance)	List-II (Chemical compounds)
A. Lime stone	I. Calcium carbonate
B. Quick lime	II. Calcium hydroxide
C. Slaked lime	III. Aqueous solution of calcium hydroxide
D. Lime water	IV. Calcium oxide

Choose the ***correct*** answer from the options given below:

1. A-I, B-II, C-III, D-IV
2. A-I, B-IV, C-II, D-III
3. A-II, B-I, C-IV, D-III
4. A-IV, B-II, C-III, D-I

69. Resistance of a population to a pathogen as a result of immunity of a large portion of the population is known as:

1. Innate immunity 2. Adaptive immunity
3. Morbidity 4. Herd immunity

70. Identify the correct sequence of coal grade formation from sedimentary to metamorphic rock.

A. Peat B. Anthracite
C. Bituminous D. Lignite

Choose the ***correct*** answer from the options given below:

1. D, A, C, B 2. D, C, B, A
3. A, D, C, B 4. A, B, C, D

71. Match List-I with List-II.

List-I (Terms in Epidemiology)	List-II (Description)
A. Vehicle	I. Living agent that transfers pathogen
B. Carrier	II. Pathogen-contaminated inanimate object
C. Fomite	III. Non living source which transmits pathogens to large number of individuals
D. Vector	IV. Sub-clinically infected individual

Choose the ***correct*** answer from the options given below:

1. A-II, B-I, C-III, D-IV
2. A-III, B-IV, C-II, D-I
3. A-II, B-III, C-I, D-IV
4. A-IV, B-II, C-III, D-I

72. Substances that catch fire spontaneously in air without an ignition source, are called:

1. Flammable solids
2. Combustible liquids
3. Flammable liquids
4. Pyrophoric

73. Removal of a species leads to significant changes that spread throughout the food web. This species can be called as a:

1. Climax species 2. Invasive species
3. Flagship species 4. Keystone species

74. Radiation pertaining to wavelengths suitable for photosynthesis is about:

1. 44% of incident shortwave radiation
2. 74% of incident shortwave radiation
3. 84% of incident shortwave radiation
4. 94% of incident shortwave radiation

75. Identify factor(s) that cause(s) the Beer's law relationship to be non linear:

A. Polychromatic radiation
B. Unknown chemical changes such as association or dissociation reactions
C. Stray light
D. Molecular or ionic interactions at high concentration

Choose the ***correct*** answer from the options given below:

1. A Only
2. B and C Only
3. A, B and C Only
4. A, B, C and D

76. The process, which is NOT part of the Sedimentary rock formation, is:

1. Deposition 2. Intrusion
3. Lithification 4. Erosion

77. Extended Producer Responsibility (EPR) mechanism has been incorporated for management of:

A. Plastic Packaging Waste
B. E-Waste
C. Battery waste
D. Used oil
E. Waste tyre

Choose the *correct* answer from the options given below:

1. B and C Only
2. B, C and D Only
3. A, B and C Only
4. A, B, C, D and E

78. The source of Earth's interior heat is a combination of:

1. Radioactivity, solar wind and earthquakes
2. Decay of radioactive elements in the interior and the impacts of extraterrestrial objects
3. Solar wind, compression and volcanism
4. Nuclear fusion, volcanism and compression

79. In which component of Life Cycle Analysis, is the 'flows of materials' quantified?

1. Waste mining
2. Impact analysis
3. Inventory analysis
4. Improvement analysis

80. Which of the following planets has maximum CO_2 concentration (by volume) in its atmospheric composition?

1. Earth
2. Mercury
3. Venus
4. Jupiter

81. Match List-I with List-II.

List-I (Organisms)	List-II (Associated process)
A. C_3 species	I. Insignificant change in rate of photosynthesis with increase in CO_2 concentration
B. C_4 species	II. Increase in rate of photosynthesis with increase in CO_2 concentration
C. Birds and bats	III. Parallel evolution
D. Marsupial and placental mammals	IV. Convergent evolution

Choose the *correct* answer from the options given below:

1. A-I, B-II, C-IV, D-III
2. A-II, B-I, C-III, D-IV
3. A-I, B-II, C-III, D-IV
4. A-II, B-I, C-IV, D-III

82. Match List-I with List-II.

List-I (Process)	List-II (Outcome)
A. Biological nitrogen fixation	I. Conversion of ammonium to nitrate
B. Nitrification	II. Conversion of elements from organic to inorganic form
C. Immobilization	III. Conversion of nitrogen gas to ammonium
D. Mineralization	IV. Incorporation of inorganic nutrient elements into organic forms

Choose the *correct* answer from the options given below:

1. A-I, B-III, C-IV, D-II
2. A-I, B-III, C-II, D-IV
3. A-III, B-I, C-IV, D-II
4. A-II, B-III, C-I, D-IV

83. Which of the following is the most appropriate for visualising time sequence data of a variable?

1. Line chart
2. Histogram
3. Scatter plot
4. Box plot

84. Polychloride biphenyls, PCBs:

1. consist of more than 200 congeners with different numbers of chlorine atoms
2. occur primarily as localized pollutants
3. had no common uses, but were produced as manufacturing by-products
4. are noted for their biological instability and, therefore toxicity

85. Match List-I with List-II.

List-I (Solar Appliance)	**List-II (Uses)**
A. Solar Oven	I. Provide fresh potable water
B. Solar Kiln	II. Generate Electricity
C. Solar Still	III. Drying products
D. Solar Thermal Collector	IV. Cooking

Choose the ***correct*** answer from the options given below:

1. A-IV, B-III, C-I, D-II
2. A-IV, B-III, C-II, D-I
3. A-I, B-II, C-IV, D-III
4. A-II, B-IV, C-I, D-III

86. Coriolis acceleration of a particle over the earth's surface depends on:

A. Angular Velocity of Earth
B. Mass of the particle
C. Latitude of the location
D. Velocity of the particle
E. Longitude of the location

Choose the ***correct*** answer from the options given below:

1. A, B and C Only
2. A, C and D Only
3. A, D and E Only
4. A, B, C and D Only

87. Match List-I with List-II.

List-I (Mineral)	**List-II (Silicate structure)**
A. Augite	I. Double Chains
B. Hornblende	II. Single Chains
C. Biotite	III. Three dimensional network
D. Quartz	IV. Sheet

Choose the ***correct*** answer from the options given below:

1. A-I, B-II, C-IV, D-III
2. A-IV, B-III, C-II, D-I
3. A-II, B-I, C-IV, D-III
4. A-III, B-IV, C-I, D-II

88. Which of the following is true if gasoline is burnt in perfect air/fuel stoichiometric ratio in internal combustion engines?

A. Fuel consumption decreases.
B. Power of engine remains optimum.
C. NO_x emission remains high compared to rich and lean fuel.
D. Hydrocarbon emission remains low.
E. Carbon monoxide emission decreases compared to rich fuel.

Choose the ***correct*** answer from the options given below:

1. A, B and E Only
2. A, B and D Only
3. A, B, C, D and E
4. A, B, D and E Only

89. Which feature of the chemical differentiation of Earth today reflects the influence of the iron catastrophe?

1. There is more iron in the core than in the crust.
2. The lower lithosphere stores most of Earth's iron.
3. Much of Earth's iron has escaped as a result of extraterrestrial impacts.
4. Iron is rare in Earth.

90. Identify the correct sequence of concentration in increasing order of following uranium isotopes in naturally occurring uranium?

A. U^{233} B. U^{234}
C. U^{235} D. U^{238}

Choose the ***correct*** answer from the options given below:

1. A, B, C, D
2. A, B, D, C
3. D, C, B, A
4. D, C, A, B

Directions (Qs. No. 91 to 95): *Read the following passage and answer the questions given below:*

The first phototrophs were anoxygenic and likely used H_2S as electron donor for CO_2 fixation, generating elemental sulphur (S^0) as a waste product. How could the first phototrophs have evolved at a time when life existed mostly near hydrothermal systems? A clue came from the recent discovery of anoxygenic phototrophs living at hydrothermal vents in the complete darkeness of the deep ocean. These phototrophs actually carry out photosynthesis using infrared radiation generated by the heat of hydrothermal vents. Likewise, the first photosynthetic organisms likely lived in the dark, at hydrothermal vents where H_2S and infrared radiation were abundant. Diversification of anoxygenic phototrophs led to species that were able to use a range of electron donors including Fe^{2+}, which was abundant throughout Earth's early oceans. The ability to use Fe^{2+} as an electron donor likely allowed early phototrophs to escape from hydrothermal systems and colonize shallow regions of Earth's early oceans where light was abundant but where overlying water still provided protection from UV radiation. The ability to use solar radiation as an energy source allowed phototrophs to diversify extensively. By 2.5-3.3 bya, the cyanobacterial lineage evolved a photosystem capable of oxygenic photosynthesis in which H_2O supplanted H_2S as the reductant for CO_2, thereby generating O_2 as a waste product. About a billion years later, eukaryotic oxygen phototrophs appeared and can be seen in the microfossil record.

91. Which of the following chemical species played a crucial role in the early phototrophs' colonization in the shallow waters of Earth's early oceans?

1. H_2O
2. O_2
3. Fe^{2+}
4. CO_2

92. The first photosynthetic organisms likely released:

1. S^0
2. H_2S
3. CO_2
4. O_2

93. Identify the most probable time when the ability to use water for photosynthesis developed in the organisms.

1. 3.8 billion years ago
2. 3 billion years ago
3. 4 billion years ago
4. 4.3 billion years ago

94. The early photosynthetic organisms likely existed in:

1. Surface waters
2. Shallow regions of oceans
3. Layers of oceans where visible light was abundant but UV light was absent
4. Deep in the oceans at specific places in ocean bottoms

95. The first phototrophs used which of the following types of radiations for photosynthesis?

1. Ultraviolet
2. Violet
3. Infrared
4. Yellow

Directions (Qs. No. 96 to 100): *Read the following passage and answer the questions given below:*

Waves expend their energy when they reach the coastline. But, the amount is surprisingly large. For example, the energy expended on a 400 km length of open coastline by waves with a height of about 1 m over a given period of time is approximately equivalent to the energy produced by one average-sized nuclear power plant over the same time period. Wave energy is approximately proportional to the square of the wave height. Thus, if wave height increases to 5 m, which is typical for large storms, then the energy expended, or wave power, increases 25 times over that of waves with a height of 1 m. When waves enter the coastal zone and shallow water, they impinge on the bottom and become steeper. Wave steepness is the ratio of wave height to wave length. Waves are unstable when the wave height is greater than about 10 per cent (0.1) of the wave length. As waves move into shallow water, the wave period remains constant, but wave length and velocity decrease and wave height increases. The waves change shape from the rounded crests and troughs in deep water to peaked crests with relatively flat troughs in shallow water close to shore. Perhaps the most dramatic feature of waves entering shallow water is their rapid increase in height. The height of waves in shallow water, where they break, may be as much as twice their deep-water height.

96. When waves move into shallow water, which of the following would NOT change?

1. Wave height
2. Wave length
3. Wave velocity
4. Wave period

97. Energy expended by waves of height 2 m on a 1000 km length of open coastline would be approximately equivalent to the energy produced by how many average sized nuclear power plants?

1. 10
2. 4
3. 2.5
4. 5

98. Which of the following corresponds to an unstable wave?

1. Wave height = 2 m
   Wavelength = 30 m
2. Wave height = 2.5 m
   Wavelength = 20 m
3. Wave height = 3 m
   Wavelength = 40 m
4. Wave height = 1.5 m
   Wavelength = 25 m

99. Which of the following is a characteristic of the shallow water close to shore?

1. Rounded crests
2. Rounded troughs
3. Flat troughs
4. Peaked troughs

100. If wave height increases by 3 times, wave energy would increase by:

1. 3 times
2. 6 times
3. 9 times
4. 12 times

ANSWERS

1. (4): Albedo is the fraction of solar energy (shortwave radiation) reflected from the Earth back into space. It is a dimensionless value between 0 and 1, often expressed as a percentage. Surfaces with high albedo reflect most of the sunlight, while those with low albedo absorb more.

A. Pure, Fresh Snow: Reflects 80–95% of incoming sunlight, making it one of the highest albedo surfaces on Earth due to its bright white colour and fine crystalline structure that scatters light efficiently.

B. Pure, Old Snow: Slightly less reflective, typically with an albedo of 50–70%, because aging, dust deposition, and partial melting reduce its whiteness and increase absorption.

C. Ice: Has a lower albedo than snow, ranging from 30–40%. It appears darker and smoother than snow, absorbing more sunlight, especially if it has surface water or impurities.

D. Desert: Sandy surfaces reflect about 25–30% of sunlight. While relatively light-coloured, deserts also absorb substantial heat, particularly where rock or dark soils are exposed.

E. Savanna: Covered with grass and scattered trees, savannas have a lower albedo around 15–20% due to darker vegetation and soil, leading to more absorption of heat.

Thus, the correct decreasing order based on albedo is:

Fresh Snow > Old Snow > Ice > Desert > Savanna.

2. (3): The Shannon-Weaver Diversity Index (H′) is a widely used ecological metric that assesses biodiversity by considering two critical components:

A. Species Richness: This refers to the number of different species present in a community. A more diverse ecosystem will have more species.

D. Equitability (Evenness): This measures how evenly the individuals are distributed across the different species. A community where all species have equal representation has high evenness.

The formula used is:

$$H' = -\Sigma(p_i \times \ln p_i)$$

where p_i is the proportion of individuals in the i-th species.

- The index does not distinguish between endemic or invasive species (so B and C are incorrect).
- It also does not measure genetic diversity directly (E is also incorrect).

Hence, only richness (A) and equitability (D) are valid components, making option 3 correct.

3. (4): The question involves correctly identifying terms related to atmospheric moisture and energy fluxes:

A. Mixing Ratio (IV): Defined as the mass of water vapour per unit mass of dry air. It is commonly used in meteorology due to its conservative properties during air parcel ascent or descent.

B. Specific Humidity (III): This is the mass of water vapour per unit mass of moist air (i.e., dry air + water vapour). It remains nearly constant as long as there is no condensation or evaporation.

C. Absolute Humidity (II): Defined as the mass of water vapour per unit volume of air. It changes with temperature and pressure, making it less reliable for atmospheric studies.

D. Bowen Ratio (I): This ratio compares sensible heat flux to latent heat flux at the Earth's surface. A high Bowen ratio implies more energy is used to warm the air than to evaporate moisture, common in arid areas.

So the correct match of terms to definitions is: A–IV, B–III, C–II, D–I.

4. (2): The concentration of dissolved oxygen (DO) in lake water is strongly influenced by its trophic state, which reflects nutrient enrichment and biological activity.

D. Hypereutrophic lakes: Extremely nutrient-rich, with excessive algal blooms and high microbial activity leading to massive oxygen consumption. DO is often depleted, especially in deeper waters.

B. Eutrophic lakes: High nutrient levels, increased productivity, and frequent oxygen depletion in bottom layers due to microbial decay of organic matter.

C. Mesotrophic lakes: Intermediate conditions with moderate biological activity and relatively balanced oxygen levels.

A. Oligotrophic lakes: Deep, nutrient-poor, and typically oxygen-rich throughout the water column due to low biological demand and effective mixing.

Thus, increasing order of DO concentration is: Hypereutrophic < Eutrophic < Mesotrophic < Oligotrophic, i.e., D, B, C, A.

5. (4): Tidal Range is a vertical measurement of the difference between the height of a high tide and the following low tide. It reflects how much the sea level changes due to the gravitational forces exerted by the moon and the sun.

- Tidal range varies with location and lunar cycle. For example, during spring tides (full/new moon), the range is largest. During neap tides (first/third quarter), the range is smallest.
- For instance, if high tide is 4.8 m and low tide is 1.3 m, the tidal range

$$= 4.8 - 1.3 = 3.5 \text{ m.}$$

- This range is important for navigation, fishing, coastal construction, and understanding sediment transport.

Therefore, tidal range is best defined as: The difference in water levels between two consecutive high and low tides.

6. (1): The sound pressure level (SPL) in decibels from a point source follows the inverse square law, meaning that when the distance from the source increases, SPL decreases logarithmically. The formula used is:

$$L_2 = L_1 - 20 \times \log_{10}(r_2/r_1)$$

Where:

- L_1 = initial sound level = 78 dB
- r_1 = initial distance = 5 m
- r_2 = new distance = 20 m

Now apply the formula:

$$L_2 = 78 - 20 \times \log_{10}(20/5)$$
$$= 78 - 20 \times \log_{10}(4)$$
$$= 78 - 20 \times 0.602$$
$$= 78 - 12.04$$
$$\approx 65.96 \approx 66 \text{ dB}$$

Hence, the sound pressure level at 20 m is approximately 66 dB.

7. (1): Two events A and B are independent if the occurrence of one does not affect the probability of the other. This implies:

- $P(A|B) = P(A)$ and $P(B|A) = P(B)$

These are basic identities for independent events.

Other expressions like:

- $P(A|B) = P(A)/P(B)$ or
- $P(B|A) = P(B)/P(A)$

are only valid under specific conditions and do not represent independence.

Thus, only A and C represent correct properties of independent events.

8. (4): The second order moment about the mean is defined as:

$$\mu_2 = E[(X - \mu)^2]$$

where

- μ = mean of the distribution
- X = random variable
- E = expected value operator

This is by definition the variance of a distribution, representing the average squared deviation from the mean.

So, the second order moment about the mean is equal to the variance.

9. (4): Albedo is the fraction of solar energy reflected by a surface. The global average albedo is around 0.30 (or 30%).

Now compare:

A. Ice → Albedo around 30–45% or more depending on type and cleanliness.

B. Cumulus Clouds → Very reflective, albedo can range 40–70%, hence higher than global average.

C. Stratus Clouds → Thick cloud layers, albedo 60–90%, much higher than global average.

D. Dark wet Soil → Low albedo (10–15%), well below global average.

E. Forest → Dense vegetation absorbs much light, albedo ~10–20%.

Hence, only A, B, and C have albedos greater than the global average.

10. (3): In a hydropower plant, water stored in a reservoir is conveyed to the turbines through large pipes under high pressure. These pipes are called penstocks.

- A penstock is a closed conduit that delivers water from the reservoir or forebay to the turbines.
- It plays a critical role in converting potential energy into kinetic energy before it strikes the turbine blades.

Other terms:

- Head: vertical height of water
- Reservoir: water storage
- Spillway: safety outlet to discharge excess water

Thus, the correct term for the delivery pipe is Penstock.

11. (4): Biodiversity underpins all four categories of ecosystem services defined by the Millennium Ecosystem Assessment:

A. Provisioning Services include food, water, timber, and fiber. These depend directly on species diversity (e.g., diverse plant species for food and medicine).

B. Regulating Services include climate regulation, disease control, and water purification. These are driven by the functional roles of species in ecological processes.

C. Cultural Services are the non-material benefits like spiritual enrichment, recreation, and aesthetic experiences. These are often tied to specific species or landscapes.

D. Supporting Services include nutrient cycling, soil formation, and primary production, which form the foundation of all other services and rely heavily on biodiversity.

Loss of biodiversity compromises all four categories, hence the correct answer is: A, B, C and D.

12. (4): The Beaufort Wind Scale is a standardized system for estimating wind speed based on observed sea or land conditions. Here's the increasing order of wind speeds among the listed categories:

D. Breeze: Light to moderate winds; Beaufort scale 1–5 (approx. 1–38 km/h).

B. Gale: Strong winds; Beaufort scale 6–8 (approx. 39–74 km/h).

A. Storm: Very strong winds; Beaufort scale 9–10 (approx. 75–102 km/h).

C. Hurricane: Extremely strong winds; Beaufort scale 12+ ($\geq$ 118 km/h).

Therefore, the correct increasing order of wind speed is: Breeze < Gale < Storm < Hurricane, i.e., D, B, A, C.

13. (3): Speciation—the formation of new species—generally occurs when natural selection leads to genetic divergence along with reproductive isolation. This can occur in various ways:

- Natural selection drives adaptive changes in populations in response to environmental pressures.
- Reproductive isolation, either geographic (allopatric) or ecological/behavioural (sympatric), prevents gene flow between diverging populations.

Only when both mechanisms operate can divergence accumulate to the point of forming a new species.

Hence, the correct condition for species origination is: from natural selection when it is coupled with reproductive isolation.

14. (1): Cation Exchange Capacity (CEC) is a measure of the soil's ability to hold positively charged ions (cations). Different soil orders have characteristic CEC ranges:

A. Histosols (I): 110–170 cmolc/kg. Rich in organic matter (peat), Histosols have the highest CEC due to humic substances.

B. Vertisols (II): 33–67 cmolc/kg. Clay-rich soils with moderate-to-high CEC, due to expansive clay minerals like montmorillonite.

C. Andisols (III): 13–49 cmolc/kg, Volcanic ash soils, moderate CEC but variable depending on organic matter and mineralogy.

D. Spodosols (IV): 2–57 cmolc/kg. Acidic, sandy forest soils with low organic matter; typically lower CEC.

Thus, correct matching is: A–I, B–II, C–III, D–IV.

15. (3): Ex-situ bioremediation involves the removal of contaminated material (soil, water) to be treated at another location. The tools involved include:

- Bioreactors: Engineered systems where microbial activity is optimized outside the natural site.
- Biofilters: Used to treat contaminated gases or liquids, usually in controlled settings.
- Land farming: Contaminated soil is excavated and spread over a prepared bed where it's periodically tilled and treated.

Bioventing, however, is an in-situ technique where air or oxygen is supplied directly into the soil to stimulate microbial activity without excavation.

Therefore, Bioventing is not an ex-situ method.

16. (3): Let's evaluate each statement about ozone (O_3) in the atmosphere:

A. True: In the troposphere, ozone exists in a photochemical steady state involving NO and NO_2. The Leighton relationship governs this equilibrium, showing that the ozone concentration depends on the NO/NO_2 ratio in the presence of sunlight.

B. False: A 1% decrease in ozone leads to a 2% increase in UV-B, not UV-C. UV-C is already mostly absorbed by the upper atmosphere and does not reach the ground in significant amounts.

C. False: Ozone Depleting Potential (ODP) is calculated with reference to CFC-11 (not CFC-111), which is assigned an ODP value of 1.

D. False: Halons, like brominated compounds, are even more potent than CFCs in catalytically destroying stratospheric ozone, especially through bromine-driven cycles.

E. False: HCl and $ClONO_2$ are reservoir forms of chlorine, not catalytically active. The active forms include Cl and ClO radicals, which directly participate in ozone depletion.

Hence, only statement A is correct.

17. (3): Atmospheric stability refers to the resistance of the atmosphere to vertical motion. It is influenced by surface heating, wind speed, and sky conditions:

- A clear night allows maximum radiative cooling of the surface, creating a strong temperature inversion near the ground.
- Low wind speeds (2–3 m/s) prevent mixing and help maintain this inversion.
- Clouds trap outgoing radiation, reducing cooling, which leads to less stable conditions.

Among the given options, the most stable atmospheric condition arises from:

Clear skies + moderate low wind = strong surface inversion, i.e., option 3.

18. (3): Matching the remote sensing instruments (List-I) with their respective satellites (List-II):

A. MSI (Multispectral Instrument) → Sentinel-2 (III): MSI is the primary imaging instrument aboard the ESA's Sentinel-2 satellites for land monitoring.

B. VHRR (Very High Resolution Radiometer) → INSAT-2 (I): Used on Indian geostationary meteorological satellites for cloud and weather observation.

C. LISS-III (Linear Imaging Self Scanner) → IRS-1D (IV): An optical sensor on Indian Remote Sensing satellites for vegetation and land cover analysis.

D. MISR (Multi-angle Imaging Spectro Radiometer) → TERRA (II): An instrument onboard NASA's Terra satellite capturing images from multiple angles to study aerosols, clouds, and surface features.

Correct match: A–III, B–I, C–IV, D–II.

19. (2): As per the EIA Notification, 2006, projects are classified as Category A or Category B based on their potential environmental impacts.

A. Nuclear Power Projects → Category A: Due to their high-risk nature and transboundary impact potential.

B. Cement Plants (<1 million tonnes/year) → Category B: Only those ≥1 million tonnes/year fall in Category A.

C. Rayon Fibre Manufacturing → Category A: Due to hazardous chemicals used and potential for pollution.

D. Common Municipal Solid Waste Management Facilities → Typically Category B, unless in ecologically sensitive areas.

Hence, only A and C are Category A projects.

20. (4): Basalt is a mafic (magnesium and iron-rich) igneous rock with the following approximate composition:

- Silicon dioxide (SiO_2): ~50%
- Aluminum oxide (Al_2O_3): ~15%
- Calcium oxide (CaO): ~10%
- Iron oxides (FeO, Fe_2O_3): ~8–12%
- Magnesium oxide (MgO): ~5%

Among these, SiO_2 is the most abundant, making up about 50% of typical basalt composition.

Hence, the correct answer is SiO_2.

21. (2): As per the Hazardous and Other Wastes (Management and Transboundary Movement) Rules, 2016, a substance is classified as hazardous if it displays one or more of the following characteristics:

A. Inflammability and Corrosivity: Yes, these are hazardous traits. Inflammable substances pose fire risks, while corrosives damage materials and living tissues.

C. Forms potentially explosive mixtures with water: Yes, reactivity with water forming dangerous gases or explosions makes a substance hazardous.

E. Exhibits Reactivity: Yes, chemical reactivity (including explosive, unstable, or violent reactions) is a key hazardous criterion.

Now the incorrect ones:

B. LD_{50} < 50,000 ppm as gas/vapour: This threshold is too high. Generally, acute toxicity is defined at much lower LD_{50} values (e.g., <5000 ppm for gases/vapours).

D. Aquatic toxicity with 50% mortality for Zebra fish in 24 hours: The rule refers to 96-hour mortality (LC_{50}), not 24-hour, and typically for a broader range of aquatic species.

Therefore, only A, C, and E match the criteria for classifying a substance as hazardous.

22. (2): Net Primary Productivity (NPP) consumed by herbivores varies across ecosystems:

C. Mangroves: Very high NPP but dense woody vegetation and tannins make it less palatable to herbivores. Herbivore consumption is relatively low.

B. Tropical Rainforests: High NPP, but much biomass is stored in wood; low consumption by herbivores.

D. Grasslands: Grasses are highly edible and accessible to grazing animals. Moderate to high herbivory.

A. Phytoplanktonic communities: Very high consumption. Aquatic herbivores (like zooplankton) consume up to 90% of phytoplanktonic NPP.

So, increasing order of herbivore consumption: Mangroves < Tropical Rainforest < Grasslands < Phytoplankton, i.e., C, B, D, A.

23. (3): Porosity is the ratio of void volume to total volume in a material and governs water-holding capacity:

B. Limestone: Very low primary porosity, especially dense varieties, but may have high secondary porosity due to fractures (not always present). Lowest among the list.

C. Gravel: Low to moderate porosity (~25–35%), since particles are large and pack loosely.

D. Fine Sand: Higher porosity (~35–45%) than gravel due to smaller particle size and tighter packing.

A. Clay: Highest porosity (~45–55%), owing to its extremely fine particles and massive surface area.

Thus, increasing order of porosity: Limestone < Gravel < Fine Sand < Clay, i.e., B, C, D, A.

24. (3): The longwave atmospheric window typically lies between 8–14 μm, where Earth's surface emits most of its thermal radiation. Gases that absorb in this range affect outgoing terrestrial radiation:

- Ozone (O_3): Absorbs within the atmospheric window, especially around 9.6 μm. Therefore, it partially blocks longwave terrestrial radiation.
- Water Vapour (H_2O): Strong greenhouse gas, but it absorbs mostly outside the clean atmospheric window.
- Oxygen (O_2) and Nitrogen Dioxide (NO_2): Not significant absorbers in the longwave window.

Hence, the gas that absorbs outgoing radiation in the longwave atmospheric window is Ozone (O_3).

25. (4): Let's correctly match the surface air flows with their respective geographic zones:

A. North-East Trade Winds (II): 0–30°N: These blow from NE to SW in the Northern Hemisphere.

B. South-East Trade Winds (III): 0–30°S: These blow from SE to NW in the Southern Hemisphere.

C. Doldrums (IV): Near Equator: A calm, low-pressure zone where trade winds from both hemispheres converge; also known as the Intertropical Convergence Zone (ITCZ).

D. Prevailing Westerlies (I): 30°N–60°N: These winds blow from the west toward the east in the mid-latitudes.

Correct matching: A–II, B–III, C–IV, D–I.

26. (1): At a latitude of 50°N during summer, the Sun rises north of due east and sets north of due west, following a high arc in the sky due to Earth's axial tilt.

The east-facing wall receives maximum shortwave solar radiation in the morning as the Sun ascends from the eastern horizon.

Other directions:

- West wall: receives peak radiation in the afternoon.
- South wall: receives maximum midday radiation.
- North wall: receives minimal direct radiation.

Since the radiation peaks in the morning, the wall must face East.

27. (1): In the northern hemisphere, gradient wind around a high-pressure system (anticyclone) is:

- Clockwise due to the Coriolis force acting to the right of the wind direction.
- Supergeostrophic, meaning wind speed is greater than the geostrophic wind.

This happens because:

- Centrifugal force in a high-pressure curvature acts inward, adding to the Coriolis force and requiring a higher wind speed for balance.

Hence, the flow is clockwise and supergeostrophic.

28. (3): Greenhouse gases in decreasing order of atmospheric concentration (by volume):

B. Carbon dioxide (CO_2): ~420 ppm

C. Methane (CH_4): ~1.9 ppm

D. Nitrous oxide (N_2O): ~0.33 ppm

A. Ozone (O_3): ~0.07 ppm in troposphere; varies greatly by altitude and location

So the correct decreasing order is: $CO_2 > CH_4 > N_2O > O_3$, i.e., B, C, D, A.

29. **(4):** Alkalinity is the water's capacity to neutralize acids, mainly contributed by weak acid anions that accept hydrogen ions (protons). Positive contributors include:

A. CO_3^{2-} (carbonate): Accepts 2 H^+ → contributes to alkalinity.

B. PO_4^{2-} (phosphate): Accepts H^+ ions in solution, thus contributing.

C. HCO_3^- (bicarbonate): Most significant natural contributor.

D. OH^- (hydroxide): Strong base; directly increases alkalinity.

E. HS^- (bisulphide): Weak base; accepts H^+ → contributes.

Therefore, all five species contribute positively to alkalinity.

30. **(1):** Radiometric resolution refers to the sensitivity of a remote sensing detector to detect small differences in signal strength or reflectance levels.

- A sensor with higher radiometric resolution can distinguish more subtle differences in energy.

For example:

8-bit resolution = 256 levels (0–255)

12-bit = 4096 levels

Other resolutions:

- Spectral: ability to resolve features in different wavelengths.
- Spatial: smallest object that can be resolved.
- Temporal: frequency of data acquisition.

Correct answer: Radiometric resolution.

31. **(2):** The Biotransfer Factor (BTF) is defined as the ratio of the concentration of a substance in an animal tissue to its daily dietary intake by a terrestrial animal.

- It measures how much of an ingested substance (e.g., a contaminant or metal) accumulates in an animal.
- This is especially used in ecotoxicology and food chain transfer studies.

Other terms:

- Bioconcentration factor: refers to uptake from the environment (e.g., water), not diet.
- Partition coefficient: ratio of solubility in two immiscible phases (like octanol/water).
- Toxicant concentration: a general term without indicating a ratio.

Hence, the correct term is Biotransfer factor.

32. **(3):** Let's arrange based on specific heat capacities (in J/kg·K) at STP:

C. Air: ~1,005 J/kg·K

D. Dry Sand: ~800–830 J/kg·K

A. Ice: ~2,090 J/kg·K

B. Water: ~4,186 J/kg·K (the highest among common substances)

So, in increasing order:

Air < Sand < Ice < Water, i.e., C, D, A, B.

33. **(4):** Let's compute the binding energy released in forming one helium-4 (^4He) nucleus:

- Mass of 2 protons + 2 neutrons:
  $2 \times 1.67 \times 10^{-27} \times 2 = 6.68 \times 10^{-27}$ kg
- Observed mass of He nucleus: 6.64×10^{-27} kg
- Mass defect (Δm) = 6.68 – 6.64 = 0.04×10^{-27} kg

Using Einstein's equation:

$$\begin{aligned} E &= \Delta m \times c^2 \\ &= 0.04 \times 10^{-27} \times (3 \times 10^8)^2 \\ &= 0.04 \times 10^{-27} \times 9 \times 10^{16} \\ &= 3.6 \times 10^{-12} \text{ J} \end{aligned}$$

Thus, the energy released is approximately 3.60×10^{-12} J.

34. **(4):** Regional metamorphism of shale involves progressive changes in texture and mineralogy under increasing temperature and pressure:

A. Slate → very fine-grained, low-grade metamorphism

C. Phyllite → slightly higher grade, silky sheen

B. Schist → medium to high grade, visible platy minerals

D. Gneiss → high-grade, banded foliation with light and dark minerals

Correct sequence: Slate → Phyllite → Schist → Gneiss, i.e., A, C, B, D.

35. (2): Match each time series component with its correct definition:

A. Trend (II): Represents long-term progression or direction (upward or downward).

B. Cyclical (III): Long-term oscillations above and below trend, lasting more than one year.

C. Seasonal (IV): Short-term, periodic fluctuations that repeat within a year.

D. Irregular (I): Random, unpredictable variations or shocks in the data.

Hence, the correct match is: A–II, B–III, C–IV, D–I.

36. (2): Under the GRIHA (Green Rating for Integrated Habitat Assessment) Rating Norms 2019, buildings are awarded star ratings based on total points earned out of 100.

- A 3-star rating corresponds to a score between 61 and 70 points.
- Specifically:
  - ❑ 1 Star: 31–40
  - ❑ 2 Star: 41–60
  - ❑ 3 Star: 61–70
  - ❑ 4 Star: 71–80
  - ❑ 5 Star: 81–100

Thus, a score of 68 points falls under the 3-star rating bracket.

37. (1): The Fouling Factor in coal analysis is calculated by:

Fouling Factor = (Base-to-Acid Ratio) × (% Na_2O in ash)

- Base compounds include oxides like CaO, MgO, Na_2O, K_2O.
- Acid compounds include SiO_2, Al_2O_3, TiO_2.
- A high fouling factor indicates potential for deposition and corrosion in boilers due to sticky ash.

This distinguishes fouling from:

- Slagging Factor: relates to fusion temperature and ash softening.
- Alkali Index: relates to total alkali content per unit of fuel energy.
- Base-to-Acid Ratio: used in fouling factor but not the final output itself.

Hence, it is termed Fouling Factor.

38. (4): Let's match UNFCCC COP conferences with their host cities:

A. COP26 → Glasgow (IV), held in 2021, UK.

B. COP27 → Sharm el-Sheikh (III), held in 2022, Egypt.

C. COP28 → Dubai (II), held in 2023, UAE.

D. COP29 → Scheduled in Baku (I), Azerbaijan in 2024.

So the correct sequence is: A–IV, B–III, C–II, D–I.

39. (3): The Solar Constant is defined as:

B. The solar electromagnetic radiation per unit area incident on a plane perpendicular to the rays at the top of Earth's atmosphere. Its approximate average value is 1361 W/m^2, not exactly 1000 W/m^2 (which applies more to irradiance at surface under clear skies).

D. Variable: Yes, solar constant shows slight variations (~0.1%) over the solar cycle due to sunspot activity and solar flares.

So, only B and D correctly describe the solar constant.

40. (2): The intensity of solar radiation peaking at ~500 nm (green visible light) is due to Wein's Displacement Law, which states:

$$\lambda_{max} = b/T,$$

where

- λ_{max} is the wavelength of maximum emission
- b = 2.898 × 10^{-3} m·K (Wein's constant)
- T = surface temperature of the Sun (~5778 K)

Calculation:

$$\lambda_{max} = 2.898 \times 10^{-3}/5778$$
$$\approx 500 \text{ nm}$$

This explains the peak emission wavelength from the Sun.

Hence, the correct law is Wein's Displacement Law.

41. (2): For a normal distribution, the Empirical Rule (68–95–99.7 rule) gives approximate probabilities for data falling within standard deviations from the mean:

- Mean = 20, Standard Deviation = 4
- Interval: 16 to 24

⇒ This is ±1 standard deviation (20 ± 4)

According to the Empirical Rule:

- ~68% of values lie within 1 standard deviation from the mean.

So, the probability that the variable lies between 16 and 24 is approximately 0.68.

42. (2): Univariate models deal with one variable over time or in a dataset. Among the given:

B. Exponential Smoothing: Time series forecasting method for univariate data.

C. Moving Average: Another univariate time series model that smooths fluctuations.

D. Auto-regressive (AR): A univariate model where current value depends on past values.

A. Logit Regression is used for binary outcome modeling with predictors—not necessarily univariate.

Thus, appropriate univariate models are: Exponential Smoothing, Moving Average, Auto-regressive.

43. (2): When coal is burnt, the emissions produced (in descending order by quantity) are generally:

1. Carbon dioxide (CO_2): The most abundant byproduct from carbon combustion.
2. Sulphur dioxide (SO_2): Formed from sulphur compounds in coal.
3. Nitrogen oxides (NO_X): Produced from nitrogen in air and fuel at high temperatures.
4. Ammonia (NH_3): Emitted in trace amounts, if at all; coal does not contain significant nitrogen compounds that release NH_3.

Hence, the least emitted substance when coal is burnt is Ammonia.

44. (3): For any positive data set, the following inequality holds:

$$H.M. \leq G.M. \leq A.M.$$

And the mathematical relationship is:

$$G.M. = \sqrt{(A.M. \times H.M.)}$$

Given dataset: X = [1, 2, 4, 8, 16, 32]

$$A.M. = (1 + 2 + 4 + 8 + 16 + 32)/6 = 63/6 = 10.5$$

$$G.M. = (1 \times 2 \times 4 \times 8 \times 16 \times 32)^{1/6} = 2^{7.51/6} = 11.31 \text{ (approx.)}$$

$$H.M. = 6/(1/1 + 1/2 + 1/4 + 1/8 + 1/16 + 1/32) \approx 3.42$$

Now:

$$\sqrt{(A.M. \times H.M.)} = \sqrt{(10.5 \times 3.42)} \approx \sqrt{35.91} \approx 6,$$

not matching the actual G.M.

However, for standard theoretical relation, the correct form is:

$$G.M. = \sqrt{(A.M. \times H.M.)}$$

So correct option is: $G.M. = (A.M. \times H.M.)^{1/2}$.

45. (3): Species richness refers to the number of different species in a taxonomic group. The descending order based on global estimates is:

C. Insects, centipedes, millipedes (Arthropods): By far the most diverse, millions of insect species.

A. Fungi: ~2.2 to 3.8 million estimated species.

B. Vascular plants: ~391,000 known species.

E. Crustaceans: Over 67,000 species.

D. Vertebrates: Around 66,000 species (fish, amphibians, reptiles, birds, mammals).

Thus, decreasing order of richness: Insects > Fungi > Plants > Crustaceans > Vertebrates, i.e., C, A, B, E, D.

46. (4): For quantitative analysis in the visible region (400–700 nm), cuvets (sample holders) can be made of:

A. Quartz: Transmits both UV and visible light, ideal for both regions.

B. Transparent plastic: Inexpensive and suitable for visible light; not recommended for UV.

C. Glass: Commonly used in visible spectrophotometry; absorbs UV below ~350 nm.

D. Fused Silica: High-grade quartz; excellent transmittance in both UV and visible range.

Since visible light is under consideration, all materials listed are suitable.

Correct answer: A, B, C and D.

47. (1): The concentration of dissolved oxygen (DO) in water is affected by multiple physical, chemical, and biological factors:

A. Turbulence: Increases aeration, enhancing DO by mixing atmospheric oxygen.

B. Temperature: Inverse relationship—higher temperatures reduce oxygen solubility.

C. Atmospheric oxygen concentration: Determines how much oxygen can diffuse into water.

D. Biological activity: Respiration by organisms consumes DO; photosynthesis increases it.

E. Genetic diversity: Has no direct relation to DO levels.

Therefore, correct influences are: A, B, C and D only.

48. **(3):** According to Stokes' Law, the terminal velocity (v) of a spherical particle settling in a viscous fluid is:

$v = (2/9) \times (r^2 \times (\rho_p - \rho_m) \times g)/\eta$

Where:

- r = radius of the particle (D)
- ρ_p = density of the particle (B)
- ρ_m = density of the medium (C)
- g = gravitational acceleration (A)
- η = dynamic viscosity of the medium (E)

All five parameters affect terminal velocity. So, the correct option is: A, B, C, D and E.

49. **(4):** Let's look at the range of values:

B. Sum of deviations about the mean: Always zero for any dataset → lowest range.

A. Coefficient of determination (R^2): Ranges from 0 to 1 → next higher.

D. Coefficient of correlation (r): Ranges from -1 to +1 → wider range than R^2.

C. Standard normal variate (Z): Theoretically ranges from $-\infty$ to $+\infty$ → widest range.

Increasing order of range:

Sum of deviations < R^2 < Correlation < Z-score, i.e., B, A, D, C.

50. **(2):** A cone of depression is a conical dip in the water table surrounding a well due to excessive groundwater withdrawal:

It occurs when pumping rate exceeds natural recharge rate, drawing down water levels near the well.

Other options:

A. Stream-sinkhole interaction—not related to cone formation.

B. Zone mixing—irrelevant to cone shape.

C. Spring from perched water—natural discharge, not drawdown.

Thus, only D accurately describes cone of depression formation.

51. **(2):** As per the Construction and Demolition Waste Management Rules, 2016, issued under the Environment (Protection) Act:

- Waste generators producing ≥ 300 tons/month/project must:
  - ❑ Segregate the waste into concrete, soil, steel, wood, etc.
  - ❑ Submit a waste management plan to the local authority for approval.
  - ❑ Ensure that the plan includes storage, transport, and disposal provisions.

This rule is applicable to large-scale construction and demolition projects generating substantial waste.

52. **(3):** In a biosensor, the component responsible for detecting the target analyte is the recognition element (also called bioreceptor). This may include:

- Enzymes
- Antibodies
- Nucleic acids
- Whole cells, including bacterial cells

Whole bacterial cells act as biological recognition elements because they respond to specific analytes (e.g., pollutants, nutrients) and generate a measurable signal via metabolism or binding. Thus, bacterial cells are part of the recognition element.

53. **(1):** Typical elemental composition of humic substances (by weight percentage):

A. Carbon (C): ~45–55% — major component forming the organic backbone.

B. Oxygen (O): ~30–45% — comes from carboxyl, hydroxyl, and other functional groups.

C. Hydrogen (H): ~3–6% — minor but essential in organic bonding.

D. Nitrogen (N): ~1–5% — present in amide and amine groups.

So the correct match is: A–I, B–II, C–III, D–IV.

54. **(1):** In global atmospheric circulation, arid zones are commonly found near 30° North and South latitudes, where:

- Descending air of the Hadley cell warms and dries, creating high-pressure zones.

- These regions correspond to major deserts:
  - Sahara, Arabian (30°N)
  - Kalahari, Australian (30°S)

Other zones:

- 10° Latitude: lies in the tropics—humid.
- 60° Latitude: area of rising air, more precipitation.
- Equator (0°): Intertropical Convergence Zone (ITCZ), high rainfall.

Hence, arid areas are most common at 30° Latitude.

55. (3): To separate and identify trace levels of high molecular weight biomolecules, LC–MS is ideal:

- Liquid Chromatography (LC): Separates complex mixtures based on interactions with the column.
- Mass Spectrometry (MS): Identifies molecules based on mass-to-charge ratio (m/z) and provides high sensitivity, even at trace levels.

Comparisons:

- GC–MS: Suitable for volatile compounds; not ideal for high MW biomolecules.
- HPLC–UV: Lacks the specificity and sensitivity of MS.
- GPC–RI: Good for polymer size exclusion, but not trace-level detection or identification.

Therefore, LC–MS is best for trace biomolecule identification.

56. (1): Let's match geological processes with their resulting products:

A. Dissolution of Calcite → Travertine (IV): Calcite ($CaCO_3$) dissolves in carbonic acid-rich water; when CO_2 degasses (e.g., in springs), calcite precipitates again as Travertine, a form of limestone.

B. Oxidation of Olivine → Hematite (III): Olivine $(Mg,Fe)_2SiO_4$ undergoes oxidation, releasing Fe^{2+} which oxidizes further to Fe^{3+} and precipitates as Hematite (Fe_2O_3), a common weathering product.

C. Hydrolysis of Orthoclase → Kaolinite (II): Orthoclase feldspar ($KAlSi_3O_8$) undergoes hydrolysis, especially in acidic environments, forming Kaolinite, a clay mineral.

D. Hydrolysis of Quartz → Chert (I): Though quartz is resistant, long-term hydrolysis and recrystallization under diagenesis can produce Chert, a microcrystalline silica.

Correct match: A–IV, B–III, C–II, D–I.

57. (1): According to the Solid Waste Management Rules, 2016, important criteria for site selection of sanitary landfills include:

- The landfill site must be:
  - ≥100 meters away from rivers
  - ≥200 meters from ponds
  - ≥100 meters from highways or habitations
  - ≥20 km from airports (only if the site handles >50 tons/day of waste)

So, while several criteria exist, the rule specifies minimum 100 meters distance from rivers as a basic threshold.

Correct answer: 100 meters away from river.

58. (2): Let's arrange the wildlife conservation projects chronologically:

A. Project Tiger (1973): Launched to protect Bengal tigers; India's first major species-specific conservation project.

C. Crocodile Conservation Project (1975): Initiated with UNDP and FAO support to prevent extinction of crocodile species.

B. Project Elephant (1992): Focused on elephant corridors and human-elephant conflict.

D. GOI–UNDP Sea Turtle Project (1999–2000): For sea turtle nesting site protection and community awareness.

Chronological order: Project Tiger → Crocodile Conservation → Project Elephant → Sea Turtle Project, i.e., A, C, B, D.

59. (2): In water treatment, when chlorine is added, some of it reacts with organic matter, metals, or microorganisms before a residual is left:

Chlorine Demand = Total chlorine added
− Residual chlorine after contact period

This value indicates how much chlorine is consumed in oxidation and disinfection before any leftover (free or combined) remains.

- Free available chlorine: Cl_2 not bound to organic N.
- Combined available chlorine: Part of chlorine bound with ammonia.

Total chlorine: Sum of free + combined chlorine. So, the difference between added and residual chlorine is called Chlorine demand.

60. **(4):** Let's match chemicals with their function in water/wastewater treatment:

A. $FeCl_3$ → IV. Coagulation Aid:
Ferric chloride is a common coagulant, neutralizing charges on suspended solids to promote sedimentation.

B. $Ca(OH)_2$ → III. Soda-Lime Process (Hardness Removal):
Lime (calcium hydroxide) precipitates calcium and magnesium ions, removing water hardness.

C. CO_2 → II. Lowering pH:
After soda-lime precipitation, CO_2 is bubbled in to lower pH by forming carbonic acid, preventing scale formation.

D. O_2 → I. Enhancing microbial growth:
In activated sludge process, oxygen is aerated into wastewater to support aerobic bacteria, which break down organic matter.

Correct match: A–IV, B–III, C–II, D–I.

61. **(1):** The carbon to nitrogen (C:N) ratio indicates the relative proportions of carbon and nitrogen in an organism's tissue. Approximate values:

- Plants: Typically high C:N ratios, ranging from 20:1 to 40:1, as plants are carbon-rich due to cellulose and lignin.
- Bacteria: Low C:N ratios, typically 5:1 to 10:1, as they are protein-rich (high in nitrogen).
- Fungi: Intermediate C:N ratio, around 10:1 to 15:1.
- Animals (terrestrial and aquatic): Even lower C:N ratios than fungi (~5:1 to 7:1) due to high protein and fat content.

Hence, plant tissues have a higher C:N ratio than bacteria, making option 1 correct.

62. **(3):** Primary wastewater treatment includes physical processes to remove large solids and settleable organic matter:

- Bar Screen: Removes large objects (rags, plastics).
- Grit Chamber: Removes sand, gravel, and heavy inorganic particles.
- Primary Clarifier: Settles out suspended solids by gravity.

Trickling Filter, however, is part of secondary treatment. It is a biological treatment method where wastewater trickles over media coated with microbial biofilms that degrade organic matter. Hence, Trickling Filter is NOT part of primary treatment.

63. **(2):** In epidemiology, a cohort study is:

- An observational study where a group (cohort) is followed over time to observe how exposure to certain factors affects outcomes (e.g., disease incidence).

Other study types:

- Experimental study: Involves intervention by the researcher (e.g., clinical trials).
- Case-control study: Retrospective; compares people with and without a disease to identify past exposures.
- Case-crossover study: Compares exposure at different times in the same individual.

Therefore, a longitudinal observational study that tracks participants over time is a cohort study.

64. **(3):** Let's arrange the Environmental Acts of India in chronological order of enactment:

D. Wildlife (Protection) Act – 1972

C. Water (Prevention and Control of Pollution) Act – 1974

B. Air (Prevention and Control of Pollution) Act – 1981

A. Environment (Protection) Act – 1986 (post-Bhopal disaster)

E. The Public Liability Insurance Act – 1991

So, the chronological order is: Wildlife → Water → Air → Environment → Public Liability, i.e., D, C, B, A, E.

65. **(4):** Global Warming Potential (GWP) measures how much heat a greenhouse gas traps in the atmosphere over a specific time compared to CO_2. It depends on:

A. Concentration: Not directly in the GWP formula, but relevant in overall impact.

B. Spectral window: Gases absorbing in the infrared window where Earth radiates energy contribute more.

C. Atmospheric lifetime: Longer lifetime means greater cumulative warming effect.

D. Absorption efficiency: How strongly a gas absorbs infrared radiation.

Hence, all four factors are involved in determining or influencing GWP.

66. (1): The F-distribution is used in hypothesis testing when:

A. Inference about two population variances: The F-test compares two sample variances to determine if they come from populations with equal variances.

B. Comparing more than two population means: The ANOVA (Analysis of Variance) technique uses the F-distribution to test whether there are significant differences among group means.

Not applicable for:

C. Significance of correlation coefficient: Uses *t*-distribution.

D. Inference about a population mean: Also uses *t*-distribution (small samples) or z-distribution (large samples).

Hence, the F-distribution is used for A and B only.

67. (4): Let's arrange energy conversion systems from least to most efficient:

B. Photosynthesis (~1–2% efficiency): Conversion of sunlight to chemical energy in plants; very low efficiency.

C. Solar Cell (~15–22%): Converts sunlight directly to electricity; moderately efficient.

E. Aircraft Jet Engine (~25–35%): Converts chemical to kinetic energy; subject to thermal losses.

D. Electric Generator (~90%): Converts mechanical to electrical energy; highly efficient.

A. Electric Hot Water Heater (~99%): Converts electric energy to heat with minimal loss.

Hence, in increasing efficiency: Photosynthesis < Solar Cell < Jet Engine < Generator < Electric Heater, i.e., B, C, E, D, A.

68. (2): Matching substances with their corresponding compounds:

A. Limestone → Calcium carbonate ($CaCO_3$): Naturally occurring sedimentary rock.

B. Quicklime → Calcium oxide (CaO): Formed by heating limestone (calcination).

C. Slaked lime → Calcium hydroxide ($Ca(OH)_2$): Formed when quicklime reacts with water.

D. Lime water → Aqueous solution of calcium hydroxide ($Ca(OH)_2$ in water): Clear solution used in lab tests.

Correct match: A–I, B–IV, C–II, D–III.

69. (4): Herd immunity occurs when a large portion of the population becomes immune (via vaccination or previous infection), thereby reducing the spread of infectious diseases:

- Protects individuals who are not immune.
- Commonly discussed in public health strategies (e.g., COVID-19, measles).

Other terms:

- Innate immunity: Non-specific, present from birth.
- Adaptive immunity: Specific immunity acquired after exposure.
- Morbidity: Refers to the incidence of disease, not immunity.

Correct term: Herd immunity.

70. (3): The formation of coal follows a progressive metamorphism of organic matter under pressure and temperature:

A. Peat: Accumulated plant debris; low carbon, high moisture.

D. Lignite: Brown coal; higher carbon than peat, still high moisture.

C. Bituminous: Black coal; higher energy content, widely used.

B. Anthracite: Hardest and purest form; highest carbon content (~90%).

So the correct order is: Peat → Lignite → Bituminous → Anthracite, i.e., A, D, C, B.

71. (2): Let's match epidemiological terms with their correct descriptions:

A. Vehicle → III. Non-living source which transmits pathogens to many

A vehicle is a non-living medium like food, water, or air that transmits pathogens to multiple people.

B. Carrier → IV. Sub-clinically infected individual

A carrier harbours the pathogen without showing symptoms, yet can transmit the disease.

C. Fomite → II. Pathogen-contaminated inanimate object
A fomite is a non-living object (doorknob, cloth) that transmits infection through contact.

D. Vector → I. Living agent that transfers pathogen
Vectors are living organisms (e.g., mosquitoes, ticks) that transfer infectious agents.

Correct matching: A–III, B–IV, C–II, D–I.

72. (4): Pyrophoric substances are materials that ignite spontaneously on exposure to air at or below room temperature without any external ignition source.

Examples:

- White phosphorus
- Finely divided metals (e.g., iron, magnesium)

Other terms:

- Flammable solids/liquids: Require external ignition.
- Combustible liquids: Have higher flash points, less volatile than flammables.

Thus, the correct term is Pyrophoric.

73. (4): A keystone species plays a critical ecological role in maintaining the structure of an ecosystem:

- Removal leads to disproportionate cascading effects across trophic levels.
- Examples: Sea otters (control sea urchins), Wolves in Yellowstone.

Other terms:

- Climax species: Dominant in stable ecosystems.
- Invasive species: Non-native and disruptive.
- Flagship species: Charismatic species used for conservation awareness.

Correct answer: Keystone species.

74. (1): The range of radiation suitable for photosynthesis (Photosynthetically Active Radiation or PAR) is 400–700 nm:

- It makes up approximately 44% of the total incoming shortwave solar radiation.
- Plants utilize this specific range for light-dependent reactions of photosynthesis.

Hence, the correct proportion is: 44%.

75. (4): Beer's Law ($A = \varepsilon cl$) assumes ideal conditions. Deviations can occur due to:

A. Polychromatic radiation: Law assumes monochromatic light; multiple wavelengths cause deviation.

B. Chemical changes (association/dissociation): Alter absorptivity (ε), leading to non-linearity.

C. Stray light: Reaches detector without passing through sample; artificially lowers absorbance.

D. High concentration effects: Molecule interactions (electrostatic, hydrogen bonding) alter path and response.

All listed factors cause deviation from linearity.

Correct answer: A, B, C and D.

76. (2): Sedimentary rock formation typically involves the following four key processes:

- Erosion: Breakdown of rocks into sediments.
- Deposition: Sediments settle out of water or air.
- Compaction & Cementation (Lithification): Sediments are compressed and bound to form solid rock.

However:

- Intrusion refers to igneous activity, where magma penetrates pre-existing rocks. It has no role in the formation of sedimentary rocks.

Thus, the process not part of sedimentary rock formation is Intrusion.

77. (4): The Extended Producer Responsibility (EPR) is a policy approach under which producers are responsible for the post-consumer phase of their products. As of recent environmental regulations in India, EPR has been incorporated into rules for:

A. Plastic Packaging Waste – under Plastic Waste Management Rules, 2022

B. E-Waste – under E-Waste (Management) Rules, 2022

C. Battery Waste – under Battery Waste Management Rules, 2022

D. Used Oil – under Hazardous Waste Rules (and evolving EPR framework)

E. Waste Tyres – under Hazardous Waste Rules with EPR provisions in circulars

Therefore, EPR applies to all five categories listed.

Correct answer: A, B, C, D and E.

78. (2): The heat inside the Earth is maintained by:

- Decay of radioactive isotopes (e.g., uranium-238, thorium-232, potassium-40) — this is the primary source of Earth's interior heat.
- Residual heat from the planet's formation, including impacts of extraterrestrial objects during early Earth accretion.
- Gravitational compression (though minor today) also contributed initially.

Solar wind and fusion are not relevant to Earth's internal heat.

Hence, the correct source combination is: Radioactive decay + extraterrestrial impacts.

79. (3): In Life Cycle Assessment (LCA), the Inventory Analysis stage involves:

- Quantifying material and energy inputs and outputs across all stages of a product's life cycle.
- It includes raw material extraction, transportation, manufacturing, use and disposal.
- Measured flows include water, fuels, chemicals, emissions and solid waste.

Thus, flows of materials are quantified during the Inventory Analysis phase.

80. (3): The atmospheric composition of planets:

- Venus: ~96.5% CO_2, thick atmosphere with extreme greenhouse effect.
- Earth: ~0.04% CO_2 (400–420 ppm).
- Mercury: Virtually no atmosphere due to weak gravity.
- Jupiter: Dominated by hydrogen and helium; very low CO_2.

Therefore, the planet with the maximum CO_2 concentration by volume is Venus.

81. (4):

A. C_3 species → II. Increase in rate of photosynthesis with increase in CO_2 concentration: C_3 plants experience significant increase in photosynthetic rate when CO_2 concentration rises, as it reduces photorespiration and increases carbon fixation efficiency.

B. C_4 species → I. Insignificant change in rate of photosynthesis with increase in CO_2 concentration: C_4 plants already have a CO_2-concentrating mechanism, so elevated atmospheric CO_2 levels have little to no effect on their photosynthetic rate.

C. Birds and bats → IV. Convergent evolution: Both groups developed the ability to fly independently through distinct evolutionary paths, leading to similar adaptations like wings, an example of convergent evolution.

D. Marsupial and placental mammals → III. Parallel evolution: These mammals evolved similar forms and ecological roles separately within their respective evolutionary lines, showing parallel evolution.

82. (3): Matching nitrogen cycle processes with outcomes:

A. Biological nitrogen fixation → III. Conversion of nitrogen gas (N_2) to ammonium (NH_4^+) Done by bacteria (e.g., Rhizobium) in symbiosis or free-living.

B. Nitrification → I. Conversion of ammonium to nitrate

A two-step oxidation process: $NH_4^+ \rightarrow NO_2^- \rightarrow NO_3^-$, mainly by Nitrosomonas and Nitrobacter.

C. Immobilization → IV. Conversion of inorganic nutrients (e.g., NO_3^-) into organic forms

Occurs when microbes assimilate nutrients into biomass.

D. Mineralization → II. Release of nutrients from organic to inorganic form

Organic N → NH_4^+ (ammonification), making nutrients available again.

Correct match: A–III, B–I, C–IV, D–II.

83. (1): For time-sequenced data, the most appropriate visualization is a line chart, because:

- It clearly shows trends, fluctuations, and patterns over continuous intervals (e.g., days, years).

Other types:

- Histogram: Frequency distribution.
- Scatter plot: Relationship between two variables.
- Box plot: Distribution and outliers.

Thus, Line chart is the correct answer.

84. (1): Polychlorinated biphenyls (PCBs) are:

- Synthetic organic compounds with a biphenyl core and 1–10 chlorine atoms → over 200 congeners.
- Used in transformers, capacitors, and coolants (prior to bans).
- Persistent, bioaccumulative, and toxic — but biologically stable, not unstable.
- Transported globally (not just localized pollutants).

Hence, the correct statement is:

PCBs consist of more than 200 congeners with varying chlorine content.

85. (1): Matching solar appliances with their applications:

A. Solar Oven → IV. Cooking
Uses focused solar energy to cook food.

B. Solar Kiln → III. Drying products
Common in drying wood, agricultural products using trapped solar heat.

C. Solar Still → I. Providing potable water
Works via evaporation-condensation cycle for desalination or purification.

D. Solar Thermal Collector → II. Generate electricity
Captures solar heat for use in steam turbines or to heat fluids for energy conversion.

Correct match: A–IV, B–III, C–I, D–II.

86. (2): The Coriolis acceleration a_c of a moving particle on Earth's surface is given by:

$$a_c = -2(\vec{\omega} \times \vec{v})$$

Where:

- $\vec{\omega}$ = Angular velocity vector of Earth → depends on Earth's rotation (A).
- $\vec{v}$ = Velocity of the particle → acceleration is proportional to velocity (D).
- The Latitude (C) affects the direction and magnitude of the Coriolis effect: maximum at pols, zero at equator.
- Mass (B) does not influence Coriolis acceleration (it is mass-independent).
- Longitude (E) has no effect—only latitude matters for Coriolis.

Thus, correct factors: Angular velocity, Latitude and Velocity → A, C and D.

87. (3): Match minerals with their silicate structures:

A. Augite → II. Single Chains: Augite is a pyroxene, formed by single chains of SiO_4 tetrahedra.

B. Hornblende → I. Double Chains: Hornblende is an amphibole, having double chains of tetrahedra.

C. Biotite → IV. Sheet: Biotite is a mica, which has a sheet silicate (phyllosilicate) structure.

D. Quartz → III. Three-dimensional network: Quartz is a framework silicate with interconnected tetrahedra in 3D.

Correct match: A–II, B–I, C–IV, D–III.

88. (3): When gasoline is burnt in stoichiometric air-fuel ratio ($\approx$14.7:1) in IC engines:

A. Fuel consumption decreases: Optimal combustion efficiency leads to less fuel per unit of energy.

B. Power remains optimum: Stoichiometric ratio ensures balanced combustion, generating maximum power.

C. NO_X emissions remain high: High combustion temperatures at stoichiometric ratio increase NO_X formation.

D. Hydrocarbon emissions remain low: Efficient combustion minimizes unburnt hydrocarbons.

E. CO emissions decrease compared to rich mixture: Rich mixtures (less oxygen) cause incomplete combustion, leading to more CO. At stoichiometric, CO is lower.

Hence, all options are true. Correct answer: A, B, C, D, E.

89. (1): The Iron Catastrophe was an early Earth differentiation event where:

- Dense iron and nickel sank to form the core due to gravitational separation.
- The Earth's core became rich in iron, while the crust and mantle contain less iron.

Thus, the modern structure—with iron concentrated in the core—is the direct consequence of this event.

Correct statement: There is more iron in the core than in the crust.

90. (1): Naturally occurring uranium contains the following isotopes (by abundance):

- U^{238}: ~99.27% → most abundant
- U^{235}: ~0.72%

- U^{234}: ~0.0055%
- U^{233}: Not naturally found in significant amounts; formed in reactors or as decay product in trace quantities

So, increasing order of concentration: $U^{233} < U^{234} < U^{235} < U^{238}$, i.e., A, B, C, D.

91. (3): "Diversification of anoxygenic phototrophs led to species that were able to use a range of electron donors including Fe^{2+}, which was abundant throughout Earth's early oceans. The ability to use Fe^{2+} as an electron donor likely allowed early phototrophs to escape from hydrothermal systems and colonize shallow regions..."

This clearly indicates that Fe^{2+} was the key electron donor that enabled colonization of shallow waters by early phototrophs.

92. (1): "The first phototrophs were anoxygenic and likely used H_2S as electron donor for CO_2 fixation, generating elemental sulphur (S^0) as a waste product."

Hence, the correct answer is S^0, not O_2 or CO_2.

93. (2): "By 2.5–3.3 billion years ago, the cyanobacterial lineage evolved a photosystem capable of oxygenic photosynthesis in which H_2O supplanted H_2S..."

This implies the ability to use water for photosynthesis evolved around 3 billion years ago.

94. (4): "The first photosynthetic organisms likely lived in the dark, at hydrothermal vents where H_2S and infrared radiation were abundant."

Such vents exist deep in the ocean on the seafloor, confirming the correct habitat.

95. (3): "These phototrophs actually carry out photosynthesis using infrared radiation generated by the heat of hydrothermal vents."

"Likewise, the first photosynthetic organisms likely lived... where infrared radiation was abundant."

Thus, the first phototrophs used infrared radiation for photosynthesis.

96. (4): "As waves move into shallow water, the wave period remains constant, but wave length and velocity decrease and wave height increases."

This clearly means the wave period does not change, making it the correct answer.

97. (1): "The energy expended on a 400 km coastline by 1 m high waves ≈ energy of one nuclear power plant."

Since wave energy ∝ (wave height)^2, for 2 m waves:

Relative energy = $(2)^2$ = 4 times the energy of 1 m waves

Now, scale up the coastline from 400 km to 1000 km:

$$\frac{1000}{400} = 2.5 \text{ times more coastline}$$

Total energy relative to 1 m waves over 400 km.

$$4 \times 2.5 = 10 \text{ times more}$$

Thus, wave energy is equivalent to 10 nuclear power plants.

98. (2): Wave height = 2.5 m,
Wavelength = 20 m

Waves become unstable when:

$$\frac{\text{Wave height}}{\text{Wavelength}} > 0.1$$

Let's calculate for each:

1. $\frac{2}{30} = 0.066 \rightarrow$ Stable
2. $\frac{2.5}{20} = 0.125 \rightarrow$ Unstable
3. $\frac{3}{40} = 0.075 \rightarrow$ Stable
4. $\frac{1.5}{25} = 0.06 \rightarrow$ Stable

99. (3): "The waves change shape from the rounded crests and troughs in deep water to peaked crests with relatively flat troughs in shallow water close to shore."

Thus, a key characteristic of shallow-water waves is: flat troughs.

100. (3): Wave energy is:

Wave energy ∝ (Wave height)^2

If wave height increases 3 times:

$$(3)^2 = 9$$

So, the wave energy would increase by 9 times.

YOUR SPACE

YOUR SPACE

National Testing Agency (NTA)

UGC-NET Junior Research Fellowship & Assistant Professor Eligibility Exam

Environmental Science, September-2024

(Exam held on 02-09-2024)

PAPER-II

1. Which of the following determines power capacity of a hydropower plant?

(*a*) Length of penstock pipe
(*b*) Flow rate
(*c*) Size of reservoir
(*d*) Head
(*e*) Length from intake to forebay

Choose the ***most appropriate*** answer from the options given below:

A. (*a*) and (*c*) only
B. (*b*) and (*d*) only
C. (*c*) and (*e*) only
D. (*a*) and (*e*) only

2. Match the List-I with List-II.

List-I (Defensive Adaption)	List-II (Examples)
(*a*) Mechanical Defense	I. Octopus
(*b*) Chemical Defense	II. Hedgehog
(*c*) Aposematic Coloration	III. Bushcrickets
(*d*) Cryptic Coloration	IV. Cinnabar Moth

Choose the ***correct*** answer from the options given below:

	(*a*)	(*b*)	(*c*)	(*d*)
A.	I	II	III	IV
B.	II	I	IV	III
C.	III	IV	I	II
D.	IV	III	II	I

3. Invasive plant species belonging family *Asteraceae* are:

(*a*) *Parthenium hysterophorus*
(*b*) *Chromolaena odorata*
(*c*) *Mikania micrantha*
(*d*) *Salvinia molesta*
(*e*) *Lantana camara*

Choose the ***most appropriate*** answer from the options given below:

A. (*a*), (*b*) and (*c*) only
B. (*c*), (*d*) and (*e*) only
C. (*a*), (*c*) and (*e*) only
D. (*b*), (*c*) and (*d*) only

4. Arrange the following types of solid waste in increasing order of % moisture content.

(*a*) Rubbish (*b*) Trash
(*c*) Garbage (*d*) Refuse
(*e*) Animal solids and organic waste

Choose the ***most appropriate*** answer from the options given below:

A. (*b*), (*d*), (*a*), (*c*), (*e*)
B. (*b*), (*a*), (*d*), (*c*), (*e*)
C. (*b*), (*a*), (*d*), (*e*), (*c*)
D. (*b*), (*d*), (*a*), (*e*), (*c*)

5. Choose the ***correct*** statement on acidic precipitation.

(*a*) Acidification of lake water releases highly toxic Al^{3+} to the water

(*b*) Deciduous foliage tends to increase acidity
(*c*) Coniferous foliage tends to yield runoff that is more acidic than the precipitation
(*d*) Lakes with granitic bedrock offer little buffering to acidic precipitation
(*e*) Thin and impermeable soils helps in better buffering to acidic precipitaion

Choose the ***most appropriate*** answer from the options given below:

A. (*a*). (*b*), (*c*) and (*d*) only
B. (*a*), (*b*), (*d*) and (*e*) only
C. (*a*), (*c*) and (*d*) only
D. (*a*), (*c*), (*d*) and (*e*) only

6. Arrange the following classes in increasing order of per cent geographical area as reported in India state of Forest Report-(2021):

(*a*) Moderately Dense Forest
(*b*) Open Forest
(*c*) Scrub
(*d*) Tree Cover
(*e*) Very Dense Forest

Choose the ***most appropriate*** answer from the options given below:

A. (*d*), (*c*), (*e*), (*a*), (*b*)
B. (*c*), (*d*), (*e*), (*b*), (*a*)
C. (*e*), (*c*), (*d*), (*b*), (*a*)
D. (*c*), (*d*), (*e*), (*a*), (*b*)

7. The wind blowing parallel to the isobars and at right angle to the pressure gradient is called:

A. Geostrophic wind
B. Planetary wind
C. Anti trade wind
D. Prevailing wind

8. Match the List-I with List-II.

List-I (Wavelength (μm))	List-II (Principal Application)
(*a*) 0.52-0.62	I. Mineral and Rock types
(*b*) 1.55-1.75	II. Vegetation Vigour assessment
(*c*) 10.4-12.5	III. Soil moisture
(*d*) 2.08-2.35	IV. Thermal mapping

Choose the ***correct*** answer from the options given below:

	(*a*)	(*b*)	(*c*)	(*d*)
A.	II	III	IV	I
B.	III	IV	I	II
C.	I	III	IV	II
D.	II	I	IV	III

9. The essential conditions for photochemical smog formation in ambient atmosphere are _______.

A. SO_2, water vapour, T > 25° C
B. Smoke, water vapour, T > 25° C
C. VOC, SO_2, T > 25° C
D. NO_x, VOC, T > 25° C

10. Which among the following National Mission under National Action Plan of Climate change are taken care under Department of Science and Technology (DST)?

(*a*) Enhanced Energy Efficiency
(*b*) Sustaining the Himalayan Ecosystem
(*c*) Sustainable Agriculture
(*d*) Strategic Knowledge for climate change
(*e*) Sustainable Habitat

Choose the ***most appropriate*** answer from the options given below:

A. (*a*) and (*c*) only
B. (*b*) and (*d*) only
C. (*c*) and (*e*) only
D. (*a*) and (*e*) only

11. Primary producers convert only about 1% of energy available to them to Net Primary Production. There is trophic efficiency of 10% for each link in the food chain. What would be the energy available to tertiary consumers in an idealized pyramid of energy when 1,000,000 J of sunlight is available?

A. 10,000 J B. 1000 J
C. 100 J D. 10 J

12. The process of destabilisation of colloids, by altering surface properties in order to allow the individual particles to combine into larger ones is best referred as:

A. Flocculation
B. Sedimentation
C. Coagulation
D. Decoagulation

13. Which of the following statements are TRUE for the situations of testing of statistical hypothesis:

(*a*) There are two hypothesis [null: H_0 and Alternative: H_1)
(*b*) Both of the hypotheses can be accepted/rejected for any given situation based on data at same time
(*c*) The critical value of the test statistic lies in the acceptance region, corresponding to rejection of the null Hypothesis
(*d*) Null Hypothesis is two tailed and Alternative hypothesis is one tailed
(*e*) If one hypothesis (H_0/H_1) is rejected other is accepted (H_0/H_1)

Choose the ***most appropriate*** answer from the options given below:

A. (*b*) and (*d*) only
B. (*d*) and (*e*) only
C. (*b*) and (*c*) only
D. (*a*) and (*e*) only

14. Match the List-I with List-II.

List-I (Conditions)	List-II (Plume Behaviour)
(*a*) Inversion below, lapse aloft	I. Fumigation
(*b*) Strong lapse condition	II. Lofting
(*c*) Lapse below, Inversion aloft	III. Looping
(*d*) Weak lapse below, Inversion aloft	IV. Trapping

Choose the ***correct*** answer from the options given below:

	(*a*)	(*b*)	(*c*)	(*d*)
A.	III	II	I	IV
B.	II	III	I	IV
C.	II	I	III	IV
D.	II	III	IV	I

15. Which of the following air pollution-control/particle-collection devices uses the force of gravity to aid in collection of particles by exploiting their terminal velocity?

A. Electrostatic precipitators
B. Elutriators
C. Bag houses
D. Super saturators

16. Match the List-I with List-II.

List-I (Plastic)	List-II (Application)
(*a*) PETE	I. Straw
(*b*) HDPE	II. Pharmaceutical bottles
(*c*) PP	III. Soft drink bottles
(*d*) PS	IV. Milk bottles

Choose the ***correct*** answer from the options given below:

	(*a*)	(*b*)	(*c*)	(*d*)
A.	III	IV	II	I
B.	III	IV	I	II
C.	IV	III	I	II
D.	II	III	I	IV

17. Benzene, toluene, ethylbenzene and xylene, (BTEX) are common constituent of gasoline. Vapour pressure of pure liquids are respectively. 0.126, 0.0380, 0.0126 and 0.0117 at 25° C. Assuming equimolar mixture of these liquids obeys Raoult's law, which one of given will exert maximum partial pressure in the mixture?

A. All will exert equally
B. Xylene
C. Benzene
D. Toluene

18. What is the concentration of oxygen in the ambient atmosphere (on dry basis) at 0° C and 1 atm pressure in the unit of *g*/*l*?

A. ~20.95 g/l
B. ~9.35 × 10^{-3} g/l
C. ~0.299 g/l
D. ~16 g/l

19. Arrange the following in increasing order of O/C atomic ratio of a coalification path.

(*a*) Vitrinite (*b*) Huminite
(*c*) Lignin (*d*) Wood
(*e*) Cellulose

Choose the ***most appropriate*** answer from the options given below:

A. (*a*), (*b*), (*c*), (*d*), (*e*)
B. (*b*), (*c*), (*d*), (*e*), (*a*)
C. (*d*), (*e*), (*b*), (*c*), (*a*)
D. (*e*), (*d*), (*c*), (*b*), (*a*)

20. Beak depths in two species of Galapagos Finches, Geospiza Fuliginosa and Geospiza fortis are similar in allopatric populations but have diverged in sympatric populations. This is an example of:

A. Exploitation
B. Semelparity
C. Character displacement
D. Competitive Exclusion

21. Match the List-I with List-II.

List-I	List-II
(*a*) High temperature igneous rock	I. Granulite
(*b*) High grade metamorphic rock	II. Arkose
(*c*) Clastic sedimentary rock	III. Dolomite
(*d*) Non-clastic sedimentary rock	IV. Komatiite

Choose the ***correct*** answer from the options given below:

	(*a*)	(*b*)	(*c*)	(*d*)
A.	II	III	IV	I
B.	III	I	II	IV
C.	I	II	III	IV
D.	IV	I	II	III

22. Match the List-I with List-II.

List-I (Application)	List-II (Instrument)
(*a*) Destructive technique for elemental analysis	I. XRF
(*b*) Crystallography	II. UV-VIS
(*c*) Non-destructive technique of elemental analysis	III. XRD
(*d*) Colorometric technique of elemental analysis	IV. ICP-OES

Choose the ***correct*** answer from the options given below:

	(*a*)	(*b*)	(*c*)	(*d*)
A.	IV	III	II	I
B.	IV	III	I	II
C.	III	IV	I	II
D.	IV	I	III	II

23. Arrange the following components of municipal solid waste and fossil fuel in increasing order of their higher heat value (HHV) in kJ/kg units.

(*a*) Mixed paper
(*b*) Rubber
(*c*) Mixed plastics
(*d*) Leather
(*e*) Mixed green-yard waste

Choose the ***most appropriate*** answer from the options given below:

A. (*e*), (*a*), (*b*), (*c*), (*d*)
B. (*e*), (*a*), (*d*), (*c*), (*b*)
C. (*e*), (*d*), (*a*), (*b*), (*c*)
D. (*e*), (*a*), (*d*), (*b*), (*c*)

24. Which one of the following is a thorium mineral used as atomic fuel?

A. Pitchblende B. Monazite
C. Apatite D. Malachite

25. Arrange the processes driving an extinction vortex in a small population:

(*a*) Smaller population
(*b*) Inbreeding and genetic drift
(*c*) Loss of genetic variability

(*d*) Lower individual fitness and population adaptability
(*e*) Lower reproduction and higher mortality

Choose the ***most appropriate*** answer from the options given below:

A. (*a*), (*b*), (*c*), (*d*), (*e*)
B. (*b*), (*c*), (*d*), (*e*), (*a*)
C. (*e*), (*d*), (*c*), (*b*), (*a*)
D. (*c*), (*b*), (*a*), (*e*), (*d*)

26. The concept of Nature Based Solution (NBS) is encouraged by:

A. International Geosphere Biosphere Programme (IGBP)
B. Pilot Analysis of Global Ecosystem (PAGE)
C. International Union for Conservation of Nature (IUCN)
D. International Human Dimensions Programme and Global Environmental Change (IHDP)

27. Which one of the following states in India has the maximum wind power potential at 120 m above ground level as per the recent assessment?

A. Rajasthan B. Gujarat
C. Karnataka D. Tamil Nadu

28. The absorbed dose of radiation dose in SI unit is expressed as:

A. Roentgen B. Rad
C. Gray D. Becquerel

29. Spectral Actinic flux is best expressed in the units of:

A. $m^{-2}\ s^{-1}$
B. $cm^{-2}\ s^{-1}\ nm^{-1}$
C. cm^{2} $molecule^{-1}\ nm^{-1}$
D. $W\ m^{-2}\ nm^{-1}$

30. Match the List-I with List-II.

List-I	**List-II**
(*a*) Glacial Landform	I. Ventifacts
(*b*) Fluvial Landform	II. Hummocky Cross bedding
(*c*) Aeolian Landform	III. Natural Levee
(*d*) Storm generated Landform	IV. Drumlin

Choose the ***correct*** answer from the options given below:

	(*a*)	(*b*)	(*c*)	(*d*)
A.	II	IV	I	III
B.	IV	III	II	I
C.	III	I	IV	II
D.	I	II	III	IV

31. An air parcel undergoes compression i.e. its volume deceases, then its internal energy [Given: First law of thermodynamics $dU = dQ + dW$]

$$dW = -pdV,\ dQ = 0$$

A. Will decrease
B. Will remain constant
C. Will increase
D. Cannot be predicted with above information

32. Match the List-I with List-II.

List-I (Chemical Species)	**List-II (Oxidation Number of N/S)**
(*a*) HS^-	I. –1
(*b*) N_2O	II. –2
(*c*) S_2^{2-}	III. +1
(*d*) R_2NH	IV. –3

Choose the ***correct*** answer from the options given below:

	(*a*)	(*b*)	(*c*)	(*d*)
A.	I	III	II	IV
B.	I	II	IV	III
C.	II	III	I	IV
D.	II	I	III	IV

33. Which of the following states that "EIA as a national instrument shall be undertaken for the proposed activities that are likely to have significant adverse impact on the environment and are subject to a decision of a competent national authority".

A. Principle 17 of Rio Declaration (1992)
B. Article 14 of Convention on Biological Diversity (1993)
C. Article 10 of Environment (Protection) Act (1986)
D. Principle 18 of United State Environment Policy Act (1969)

34. Which one of the following coalfields belong to lignite type coal deposit?

A. Raniganj, West Bengal
B. Singarauli, Madhya Pradesh
C. Makum, Assam
D. Talcher, Odisha

35. Arrange the following scientist in order of their contribution in the evolution of branch of ecology.

(*a*) Arthur Transley
(*b*) Ernst Haeckel
(*c*) Eugene Odum
(*d*) Geoffroy Saint-Hilaire
(*e*) Hanns Reiter

Choose the ***most appropriate*** answer from the options given below:

A. (*e*), (*d*), (*b*), (*a*), (*c*)
B. (*d*), (*e*), (*b*), (*a*), (*c*)
C. (*d*), (*e*), (*b*), (*c*), (*a*)
D. (*e*), (*b*), (*d*), (*a*), (*c*)

36. Following statements specifies various steps involved for assessing the model fitness (regression analysis). Arrange these statements in correct sequence that helps in assessing the overall fitness of the model (dependent variable: y; independent variable: *x*)

(*a*) Estimate the mean of residuals
(*b*) Assessment of mean of fitted dependent variable and given dependent variable
(*c*) Estimate the value of *a* and *b* from equation $y = a + bx$
(*d*) Assessment of the mean of the residuals
(*e*) Calculate the value of residuals

Choose the ***most appropriate*** answer from the options given below:

A. (*c*), (*b*), (*d*), (*e*), (*a*)
B. (*c*), (*e*), (*b*), (*a*), (*d*)
C. (*e*), (*b*), (*d*), (*a*), (*c*)
D. (*e*), (*a*), (*b*), (*c*), (*d*)

37. Which of the following are components of NOy species in atmosphere?

(*a*) HNO_3
(*b*) $ClONO_2$
(*c*) $HOONO_2$
(*d*) NO_3
(*e*) N_2O_5

Choose the ***most appropriate*** answer from the options given below:

A. (*d*) and (*e*) only
B. (*a*), (*c*) and (*e*) only
C. (*a*), (*b*) and (*c*) only
D. (*a*), (*b*), (*c*), (*d*) and (*e*)

38. Darcy's law in a stream is dependent on:

(*a*) Cross sectional area, hydraulic gradient, coefficient of permeability
(*b*) Hydraulic gradient, coefficient of permeability, gravitational force
(*c*) Coefficient of permeability, Frictional force
(*d*) Gravitational force, Frictional force
(*e*) Cross sectional area, Gravitational force

Choose the ***most appropriate*** answer from the options given below:

A. (*a*) only
B. (*a*) and (*b*) only
C. (*a*), (*b*) and (*c*) only
D. (*c*), (*d*) and (*e*) only

39. Match the List-I with List-II.

List-I (Expression for water in atmosphere)	**List-II (Units)**
(*a*) Volume mixing Ratio	I. g H_2O (m^3 Air)$^{-1}$
(*b*) Mass mixing Ratio	II. g H_2O (kg air)$^{-1}$
(*c*) Specific humidity	III. parts per million (ppm)
(*d*) Mass concentration	IV. g H_2O (g air)$^{-1}$

Choose the ***correct*** answer from the options given below:

	(*a*)	(*b*)	(*c*)	(*d*)
A.	III	II	IV	I
B.	IV	III	II	I
C.	III	IV	II	I
D.	II	IV	III	I

40. Which one of the following acts as a cap rock to retain oil in the reservoir rock?

A. Sandstone
B. Jointed limestone
C. Shale
D. Conglomerate

41. Which one of the following is a green house gas and a criteria air pollutant under national ambient air quality standards but is not directly emitted in troposphere?

A. N_2O
B. CO_2
C. SF_6
D. O_3

42. Which of the following categories of projects necessarily have to carry out EIA studies along with the 'Public Hearing' as per the MoEFCC, Government of India?

(*a*) Category A
(*b*) Category B
(*c*) Category B1
(*d*) Category B2
(*e*) Category A1

Choose the ***most appropriate*** answer from the options given below:

A. (*a*) and (*b*) only
B. (*a*) and (*c*) only
C. (*a*), (*b*) and (*d*) only
D. (*c*), (*d*) and (*e*) only

43. Chlorination is most common disinfection process in swimming pools. Which of the chemical causes respiratory and eye irritation around swimming pools immediately after disinfection process?

A. Hypochlorous acid
B. Chlorine gas
C. Chloramines
D. Chlorine dioxide gas

44. Which of the following is the most recent contribution of India having the global impact?

A. Coalition for Disaster Resilient Infrastructure (CDRI)
B. International Big Cat Alliance (IBCA)
C. International Solar Alliance (ISA)
D. Mission LiFE

45. People's Biodiversity Register (PBR) as per Biological Diversity Act 2002, is one of the main functions of:

A. Biodiversity Management Committee (BMC)
B. State Biodiversity Board (SBB)
C. National Biodiversity Authority (NBA)
D. Village and Urban Local Bodies (V/ULB)

46. Match the List-I with List-II.

List-I (Environmental Disaster)	**List-II (Place)**
(*a*) Agent Orange	I. China
(*b*) Bohai Bay	II. Japan
(*c*) Itai-Itai	III. United States
(*d*) Love canal	IV. Vietnam

Choose the ***correct*** answer from the options given below:

	(*a*)	(*b*)	(*c*)	(*d*)
A.	IV	I	II	III
B.	III	II	I	IV
C.	IV	II	I	III
D.	III	I	II	IV

47. Which of the following forms of sulphur are found in coal?

(*a*) Native sulphur
(*b*) Organic sulphur
(*c*) Pyritic sulphur
(*d*) Sulphate minerals

Choose the ***most appropriate*** answer from the options given below:

A. (*a*) and (*b*) only
B. (*b*) and (*c*) only
C. (*a*), (*c*) and (*d*) only
D. (*b*), (*c*) and (*d*) only

48. Arrange the following environmental materials found in colloidal size fraction in their increasing order of Cation exchange capacity (c mol (+) kg^{-1}):

(*a*) Kaolinite (*b*) Montmorillonite
(*c*) Quartz (*d*) Organic matter

Choose the ***most appropriate*** answer from the options given below:

A. (*d*), (*b*), (*a*), (*c*)
B. (*a*), (*c*), (*b*), (*d*)
C. (*c*), (*a*), (*b*), (*d*)
D. (*b*), (*c*), (*a*), (*d*)

49. Arrange the following regions of India in decreasing order of their identified Hydro power capacity (in MW).

(*a*) Eastern Region
(*b*) North Eastern Region
(*c*) Northern Region
(*d*) Southern Region
(*e*) Western Region

Choose the ***most appropriate*** answer from the options given below:

A. (*c*), (*d*), (*a*), (*b*), (*e*)
B. (*d*), (*c*), (*e*), (*b*), (*a*)
C. (*b*), (*c*), (*d*), (*a*), (*e*)
D. (*c*), (*b*), (*a*), (*d*), (*e*)

50. Which of the following are open source software used in geospatial data processing?

(*a*) Arc GIS (*b*) Erdas imagine
(*c*) QGIS (*d*) iLWiS
(*e*) SAGA GIS

Choose the ***most appropriate*** answer from the options given below:

A. (*a*), (*b*) and (*c*) only
B. (*b*), (*c*) and (*d*) only
C. (*c*), (*d*) and (*e*) only
D. (*b*), (*c*) and (*e*) only

51. A natural or human made depression into which solid waste are dumped, compressed and daily covered with a layer of dirt are close example of:

A. Dumps
B. Sanitary landfills
C. Secured landfills
D. Compost pit

52. Which of the following is not a possible option for perpetual storage of hazardous waste?

A. Surface impoundments
B. Landfill
C. Ocean and atmospheric assimilation
D. Waste piles

53. Choose the correct statements:

(*a*) BOD curve in lake water follows 1st order kinetic
(*b*) Ultimate BOD increases in direct proportion to concentration of degradable organic matter
(*c*) Oxygen depletion in lake water is related to both ultimate BOD and the rate constant (R)
(*d*) Numerical value of BOD rate constant does not depends on water temperature
(*e*) Numerical value of BOD rate constant does not depend on nature of the waste

Choose the ***most appropriate*** answer from the options given below:

A. (*a*), (*b*) and (*d*) only
B. (*b*), (*c*), (*d*) and (*e*) only
C. (*a*), (*b*) and (*c*) only
D. (*a*), (*b*), (*c*) and (*d*) only

54. Calculate residence time of chemical species in atmosphere having a mixing ratio of one parts per billion (1ppb) by mass.

[given: Total flux of species by natural and anthropogenic sources is 200×10^{12} g/yr. Mass of atmosphere is 4×10^{21} g]

A. ~0.1 week B. ~1 week
C. ~10 week D. ~50 week

55. The LOD_{50} values of some pesticides are listed below. Which of the following is most toxic?

A. DDT- 110 mg/kg
B. Parathion <5 mg/kg
C. Permethrin 50-500 mg/kg
D. Nicotine 5-50 mg/kg

56. Arrange the following steps in order of execution of Environmental Impact Assessment (EIA) process.

(*a*) Analysis (*b*) Decision Making
(*c*) EIA Reporting (*d*) Mitigation
(*e*) Review

Choose the ***most appropriate*** answer from the options given below:

A. (*e*), (*d*), (*a*), (*b*), (*c*)
B. (*c*), (*a*), (*d*), (*b*), (*e*)
C. (*a*), (*d*), (*c*), (*e*), (*b*)
D. (*a*), (*c*), (*b*), (*e*), (*d*)

57. Which of the following is portal by MoEFCC, Government of India to automate the process of Environmental Clearance?

A. EIACP B. ENVIS
C. e-Green Watch D. PARIVESH

58. Choose the correct statements about ozone in stratosphere.

(*a*) Rate of O_3 production is highest at equator and at about 40 km height.
(*b*) Maximum O_3 concentration at equator occur at about 25 km as opposed to 40 km height.
(*c*) At poles, maximum O_3 production occur at altitude even higher then those over equator.
(*d*) Regions of highest O_3 concentration do not coincide with location of highest rate of O_3 formation
(*e*) Catalytic destruction of O_3 is more at Artic compared to Antartica due to more CFCs in northern hemisphere.

Choose the ***most appropriate*** answer from the options given below:

A. (*a*), (*c*) and (*d*) only
B. (*b*), (*d*) and (*e*) only
C. (*a*), (*b*), (*c*) and (*d*) only
D. (*a*), (*d*) and (*e*) only

59. Which of the following minerals are formed in low grade metamorphism?

(*a*) Muscovite
(*b*) Garnet
(*c*) Andalusite
(*d*) Kyanite
(*e*) Actinolite

Choose the ***most appropriate*** answer from the options given below:

A. A, C and E only
B. A, B and C only
C. B, C and E only
D. B, D and E only

60. Which of the following are not listed as hazardous waste as per RCRA guidelines?

(*a*) Fly ash
(*b*) Commercial chemical product DDT
(*c*) Arsenic treated wood
(*d*) E-waste
(*e*) Used chloroflurocarbon Refrigerants

Choose the ***most appropriate*** answer from the options given below:

A. (*b*), (*c*) and (*d*) only
B. (*a*), (*b*), (*c*) and (*d*) only
C. (*b*), (*c*), (*d*) and (*e*) only
D. (*a*), (*c*) and (*e*) only

61. Match the List-I with List-II.

List-I (ISO series)	List-II (Standards)
(*a*) ISO 14030	I. Life Cycle Assessment
(*b*) ISO 14040	II. Green Bonds
(*c*) ISO 14050	III. Principles, requirements and guidelines
(*d*) ISO 14090	IV. Vocabulary terms and definitions

Choose the ***correct*** answer from the options given below:

	(*a*)	(*b*)	(*c*)	(*d*)
A.	II	I	IV	III
B.	III	I	IV	II
C.	II	IV	I	III
D.	I	III	IV	II

62. Match the List-I with List-II.

List-I (Wetland)	**List-II (State)**
(*a*) Kanjli lake	I. Kerala
(*b*) Point Calimere	II. Punjab
(*c*) Rudrasagar lake	III. Tamil Nadu
(*d*) Vembanad Kol Wetland	IV. Tripura

Choose the ***correct*** answer from the options given below:

	(*a*)	(*b*)	(*c*)	(*d*)
A.	IV	III	II	I
B.	I	IV	III	II
C.	II	III	IV	I
D.	IV	II	I	III

63. Mac Arthor and Wilson's island equilibrium model represents a balance between:

(*a*) Size of island
(*b*) Distance from the mainland
(*c*) Rate of species immigration
(*d*) Rate of species extinction
(*e*) Species area curve

Choose the ***most appropriate*** answer from the options given below:

A. (*a*) and (*b*) only
B. (*b*) and (*c*) only
C. (*c*) and (*d*) only
D. (*d*) and (*e*) only

64. Imagine two population of a gharial, one in the Chambal river and other one in the Ganga. Now imagine two scenarios: (A) the populations breed separately, (B) Adults of both populations migrate yearly to interbreed. Which scenario would result in a greater loss of genetic diversity, if the Chambal river population is driven to extinction by anthropogenic factors?

A. Scenario A
B. Scenario B
C. No loss of genetic diversity in either scenario
D. Increase in genetic diversity

65. Which of the following protocols are linked to convention on Biological Diversity?

(*a*) Cartagena (*b*) Kigali
(*c*) Nagoya (*d*) Rotterdam
(*e*) UN-REDD

Choose the ***most appropriate*** answer from the options given below:

A. (*a*) and (*c*) only
B. (*b*) and (*d*) only
C. (*c*) and (*e*) only
D. (*a*) and (*d*) only

66. The process in which concentrated shells of rock may spall from the outside of an outcrop or a boulder is known as:

A. Leaching B. Exfoliation
C. Frost wedging D. Disintegration

67. Match the List-I with List-II.

List-I (Energy resource)	**List-II (Age of geological association)**
(*a*) Gas hydrates	I. Paleozoic
(*b*) Coal deposit	II. Precambrian
(*c*) Petroleum deposits	III. Cenozoic
(*d*) Uranium ores	IV. Mesozoic

Choose the ***correct*** answer from the options given below:

	(*a*)	(*b*)	(*c*)	(*d*)
A..	I	IV	II	III
B.	IV	II	III	I
C.	III	IV	II	I
D.	III	I	IV	II

68. Which of the following statements are TRUE with respect to the application of *t*-distribution for testing of Hypothesis

(*a*) It is a Non-parametric test
(*b*) It tests whether sample mean differs significantly from the population mean
(*c*) It tests the significance of an observed correlation coefficient
(*d*) It tests the significance of an observed covariation

(*e*) It tests the significance of an observed regression coefficient

Choose the ***most appropriate*** answer from the options given below:

A. (*a*) and (*e*) only
B. (*b*) and (*d*) only
C. (*b*), (*d*) and (*e*) only
D. (*b*), (*c*) and (*e*) only

69. Arrange the following process from initial to last in formation of a petroleum deposite.

(*a*) Accumulation
(*b*) Generation
(*c*) Seepage
(*d*) Primary migration
(*e*) Secondary migration

Choose the ***most appropriate*** answer from the options given below:

A. (*a*), (*b*), (*c*), (*d*), (*e*)
B. (*b*), (*c*), (*a*), (*d*), (*e*)
C. (*b*), (*d*), (*e*), (*a*), (*c*)
D. (*a*), (*d*), (*b*), (*e*), (*c*)

70. Which of the following is a disadvantage of daily truck routing method of solid waste collection?

A. The route size can be adjusted for load
B. It provides an incentive to crew for getting it done early
C. Variability in load on day to day basis
D. Homeowner knows when the refuse will be picked up

71. In biodiesel making, ______ containing sodium hydroxide (lye) solution is mixed with vegetable oil.

A. Glycerol B. Methanol
C. Ethanol D. Xylene

72. Which of the following Environmental movement are correctly written with place of origin?

(*a*) Appiko Movement (1983) – Kerala
(*b*) Bishnoi Movement (1700) – Rajasthan
(*c*) Gandhamardan Movement (1983) – Odisha
(*d*) Jungle Bachao Movement (1982) – Bihar
(*e*) Silent Valley Movement (1973) – Karnataka

Choose the ***most appropriate*** answer from the options given below:

A. (*a*), (*b*) and (*c*) only
B. (*b*), (*c*) and (*d*) only
C. (*c*), (*d*) and (*e*) only
D. (*a*), (*b*) and (*e*) only

73. Match the List-I with List-II.

List-I (Weather Phenomenon)	**List-II (Characteristics)**
(*a*) Cyclone	I. Gale winds
(*b*) Thunderstorm	II. Smallest most violent weather disturbance
(*c*) Hurricane	III. Brief but intense storm with rain and lightening
(*d*) Tornado	IV. Low pressure center where the winds move counter-clockwise into low pressure center

Choose the ***correct*** answer from the options given below:

	(*a*)	(*b*)	(*c*)	(*d*)
A.	III	IV	I	II
B.	IV	III	II	I
C.	IV	II	I	III
D.	IV	III	I	II

74. Choose the correct statements about compost

(*a*) Compost is a humus like material.
(*b*) Biodegradation process during composting is endothermic.
(*c*) Compost improves soil structure.
(*d*) Compost decreases moisture holding capacity.
(*e*) Compost increases buffering capacity of soils.

Choose the ***most appropriate*** answer from the options given below:

A. (*a*), (*b*), (*c*) and (*e*) only
B. (*a*), (*b*), (*c*) and (*d*) only
C. (*a*), (*c*) and (*e*) only
D. (*a*), (*b*), (*c*), (*d*) and (*e*)

75. The intrusive igneous rock that contains unusually large mineral grains is called:

A. Basalt
B. Rhyolite
C. Pegmatite
D. Obsidian

76. Which of the following is not an ecological principle of sustainable development?

A. Biophysical limits
B. Interdependence
C. Ecological Justice
D. Dependence

77. Arrange the sedimentary structures in order of their formation under increasing velocity of water.

(*a*) Lower plane bed
(*b*) Small scale ripple marks
(*c*) Large scale ripple marks
(*d*) Upper plane bed
(*e*) Anti dunes

Choose the ***most appropriate*** answer from the options given below:

A. (*e*), (*d*), (*c*), (*b*), (*a*)
B. (*b*), (*c*), (*d*), (*a*), (*e*)
C. (*c*), (*a*), (*e*), (*d*), (*b*)
D. (*a*), (*b*), (*c*), (*d*), (*e*)

78. If global temperature increases average temperatures on Earth by 4°C in this century, which biome is most likely to replace tundra in some location as per climograph?

A. Desert
B. Temperate Grassland
C. Northern Coniferous forest
D. Temperate broadleaf forest

79. Which of the following pesticide/insecticide does not contain chlorine atom in its structure?

A. Methoxychlor
B. Mirex
C. Malathion
D. Endosulfan

80. The solid waste and the daily cover placed in a landfill during one operational period forms a ______.

A. Face
B. Cell
C. Benche
D. Lift

81. Match the List-I with List-II.

List-I (Statistical Test)	List-II (Null Hypothesis)
(*a*) Mann-Whitney U-Test	I. Proportion across two groups same
(*b*) X^2-test	II. Median across two groups same
(*c*) Z-test	III. Mean across three or more groups same
(*d*) ANOVA	IV. No association between two categorical attributes

Choose the ***correct*** answer from the options given below:

	(*a*)	(*b*)	(*c*)	(*d*)
A.	I	III	IV	II
B.	II	IV	I	III
C.	IV	II	III	I
D.	III	I	II	IV

82. Performing one way Analysis of variance (ANOVA) involves different steps. Arrange the following steps in the correct sequence for performing one way ANOVA

(*a*) Calculate the mean sum of squares
(*b*) Tabulate the data available
(*c*) Partition the sources of variances into two parts (between and within)
(*d*) Calculate the degrees of freedom for different sources of variances
(*e*) Calculate the variance Ratio (F-statistic)

Choose the ***most appropriate*** answer from the options given below:

A. (*b*), (*c*), (*d*), (*a*), (*e*)
B. (*b*), (*d*), (*c*), (*e*), (*a*)
C. (*b*), (*a*), (*d*), (*c*), (*e*)
D. (*b*), (*c*), (*a*), (*d*), (*e*)

83. "The formalised systematic and comprehensive process of evaluating the environment impacts of a policy, programme plan as its alternatives as well as using the findings in publicly accountable decision making" refers to:

A. Comprehensive Impact Assessment (CIA)
B. Environmental Impact Assessment (EIA)
C. Interpreted Impact Assessment
D. Strategic Environmental Assessment

84. A random sample of 180 individuals in a population were captured, marked and released. After few weeks, a second set of 44 individual were collected. Out of these 44 individuals, 7 were marked. The estimated population size would be:

A. 1100
B. 1131
C. 180
D. 44

85. Arrange the following criteria of GRIHA: 2019 in increasing order of points allocated.

(*a*) Energy optimisation
(*b*) Green Infrastructure
(*c*) Maintaining good IAQ
(*d*) Top Soil Preservation
(*e*) Water Demand Reduction

Choose the ***most appropriate*** answer from the options given below:

A. (*a*), (*c*), (*b*), (*e*), (*d*)
B. (*d*), (*c*), (*b*), (*e*), (*a*)
C. (*c*), (*a*), (*b*), (*e*), (*d*)
D. (*d*), (*e*), (*b*), (*c*), (*a*)

86. Arrange the following soil types in increasing order of percentage organic matter content.

(*a*) Forest soils (Surface horizons)
(*b*) Temperate Agriculture Soils
(*c*) Peat Soils
(*d*) Tropical agricultural soils

Choose the ***most appropriate*** answer from the options given below:

A. (*a*), (*b*), (*c*), (*d*)
B. (*d*), (*b*), (*a*), (*c*)
C. (*b*), (*d*), (*a*), (*c*)
D. (*b*), (*d*), (*c*), (*a*)

87. The standard error of mean for a normally distributed data on 256 observations was estimated as 0.1. What would be possible limits for covering 95% of the observations if the value of mean was 60.

A. (55.2 – 62.8)
B. (56.8 – 63.2)
C. (58.8 – 65.2)
D. (60.0 – 63.0)

88. Noise coming out during dentists drilling would be an appropriate example of ______.

A. Steady state noise
B. Intermittent noise
C. Impulse noise
D. Impact noise

89. Which of the following statements are correct?

(*a*) Arsenic is used in wood preservative.
(*b*) CrO_4^{2-} is water soluble.
(*c*) Arsenic is not a metal.
(*d*) FeIII is more soluble compared to FeII in pure water.
(*e*) PbS and $PbCO_3$ are highly insoluble in water.

Choose the ***most appropriate*** answer from the options given below:

A. (*a*) and (*c*) only
B. (*b*), (*c*), (*d*) and (*e*) only
C. (*c*) and (*d*) only
D. (*a*), (*b*), (*c*) and (*e*) only

90. Which of the following is NOT linked to Biodiversity loss and ecosystem services?

A. Intergovernmental Science-Policy platform for Biodiversity and Ecosystem services (IPBES)

B. Commission on Ecosystem Management (CEM)

C. Millennium Ecosystem Assessment (MEA)

D. The Economics of Ecosystem and Biodiversity (TEEB)

Directions (Qs. No. 91 to 95): *Read the given passage and answer the questions follow:*

A Community based study of respiratory illness during the first year of life was performed in Central India. The following table represents the data according to the socio-economic status, the number of children, and the number of children who developed the symptoms of respiratory illness.

Socio-economic status	Low	Medium	High
Number of children	50	100	100
Number of children with illness	10	10	5

This data was collected through the face to face interview involving team of pediatricians and social scientists. The community belonged to the rural area in Central India (State of Chhattisgarh) in which there were 1500 households. A total of 100 households were selected with fifty each from left and right to the main lane of the community. To facilitate the process of interview, interviewers collected information through a validated questionnaire in local language which was pilot tested in the community. Based on the above information answer the following questions.

91. What is the percent for total children who suffered from illness across all the three strata?

A. 5% B. 10%
C. 15% D. 20%

92. What was the sampling procedure to select 100 households?

A. Stratified Random Sampling

B. Simple Random Sampling

C. Cluster Sampling

D. Systematic Random Sampling

93. What is the ratio of illness between high socio-economic and the low socio-economic status?

A. 1 : 1 B. 1 : 2
C. 1 : 3 D. 1 : 4

94. If we wish to classify each of 250 children according to their status of illness, then illness is which data type?

A. Nominal B. Mixed
C. String D. Binominal

95. Which of the following combination is true with respect to mechanisms of data collection (*a*) pilot testes; (*b*) involved three members; (*c*) Computerized system of data collection; (*d*) face-to-face

A. (*b*, *c*) B. (*a*, *d*)
C. (*b*, *d*) D. (*c*, *d*)

Directions (Qs. No. 96 to 100): *Read the given passage and answer the questions follow:*

Traditional ecological knowledge is a body of knowledge and a framework to distinguish between its empirical kinds and ways of life; between information and ways of knowing. It is considered at several levels of analysis and consistent as knowledge-practice-belief complex. It begins at level of taxonomic systems and then proceeds to understanding of processes or functions. It follows "paradigmatic knowledge" or interpretation of empirical observation to put them in a context, and then knowledge embedded in social institutions, the rules and norms of society, and finally the regional worldview or belief system. In practice these analyses are concentric but not always distinct. The social institutions and management systems are often closely coupled that may seem artificial. One may argue that these are one and the same that may adapt, change or fall apart or renewed. Worldview and social institutions but may themselves be affected by changes occurring at other scales.

96. The traditional ecological knowledge follows the following scales:

A. Temporal scale only
B. Spatial scale OR Temporal scales
C. Spatial scale only
D. Spatial and Temporal scales both

97. Which of the following order correctly represents the interrelated levels of traditional knowledge system?

A. Worldview, social institutions, local knowledge of land and animals, land and resource management
B. Social institutions, local knowledge of land and animals, land and resource management system, worldview
C. Local knowledge of land and animals, land resource management system, social institutions, worldview
D. Land and resource management system, local knowledge of land and animals, social institutions, worldview

98. Which of the following order is the correct arrangement for formulation of 'Traditional Ecological Knowledge and Management Frame work' correct in the present "Knowledge-Practice-belief complex"?

A. Wisdom, Knowledge, Information, Fact, Data
B. Fact, Data, Information, Knowledge, Wisdom
C. Data, Fact, Information, Knowledge, Wisdom
D. Information, Fact, Data, Knowledge, Wisdom

99. Which of the following include the knowledge that frame the process of memory, creativity and learning to form norms and code of relationship of a group of independent hunters, fishers and agriculturalists to function effectively.

A. Land and resource management systems
B. Local knowledge of land and animals
C. Social institutions
D. Worldview

100. Which of the following is the most stable scale in Traditional Ecological Knowledge system?

A. Worldview
B. Social institutions
C. Local knowledge of land and animals
D. Land and resource management system

ANSWERS

1. (B): In a hydropower plant, the main factors that determine the power capacity are the flow rate of water and the available head (the vertical drop or potential energy difference). Flow rate (Q) signifies the volume of water passing through the turbines per unit time. Head (H) denotes the pressure difference due to the height of water above the turbines. The power (P) is often represented by the simplified expression $P = \rho \times g \times Q \times H \times \eta$, where ρ is density of water, g is gravitational acceleration, and η is the efficiency factor. The length of the penstock, size of the reservoir, or the distance from the intake to the forebay do not directly fix the capacity in terms of maximum power output, although they can influence losses and energy availability. The penstock length is relevant for friction losses, the reservoir size helps regulate flow availability over time, and the intake-forebay distance is an engineering or layout factor. However, none of these directly define the rated or maximum power capacity. Hence, (*b*) flow rate and (*d*) head are the key parameters.

2. **(B):** Mechanical defense is best exemplified by the hedgehog, which uses its spines to protect against predators. Chemical defense is common in octopuses that release ink (a chemical deterrent) to confuse or repel predators. Aposematic coloration involves bright or conspicuous coloration that warns predators of potential toxicity or unpalatability, as seen in the cinnabar moth. Cryptic coloration, or camouflage, allows animals to blend into their environment, a strategy observed in bushcrickets. The listed pairs match these defensive strategies with their known examples: (*a*) mechanical defense → hedgehog (II), (*b*) chemical defense → octopus (I), (*c*) aposematic coloration → cinnabar moth (IV), (*d*) cryptic coloration → bushcrickets (III).

3. **(A):** *Parthenium hysterophorus*, *Chromolaena odorata*, and *Mikania micrantha* all belong to the family Asteraceae (also known as the daisy or sunflower family). They are known invasive species that cause ecological and economic damage in many regions. *Salvinia molesta* is an aquatic fern belonging to the family Salviniaceae, and *Lantana camara* is a member of the family Verbenaceae. Therefore, only (*a*) *Parthenium hysterophorus*, (*b*) *Chromolaena odorata*, and (*c*) *Mikania micrantha* are from Asteraceae.

4. **(B):** From lower to higher moisture content, solid waste categories often follow a scale in which "trash" contains predominantly dry materials like old furniture, cardboard, and similar items. "Rubbish" is also largely dry, though it can include some less-dry contents. "Refuse" is a more general category that can contain mixed wastes with somewhat higher moisture content. "Garbage" is usually food or kitchen waste with a significantly higher water content. "Animal solids and organic waste" typically exhibit the highest moisture content of the listed categories. Therefore, trash < rubbish < refuse < garbage < animal solids and organic waste translates to (*b*) < (*a*) < (*d*) < (*c*) < (*e*).

5. **(C):** Acidification of lake water can lead to mobilization and release of toxic aluminum (Al^{3+}) ions, which harm aquatic life. Coniferous foliage tends to be more acidic and can produce runoff that is more acidic than the precipitation itself due to the chemical characteristics of the needles and associated organic acids. Lakes with granitic bedrock offer minimal buffering capacity because granite lacks substantial amounts of alkaline minerals such as carbonates. Deciduous foliage does not necessarily increase acidity, and thin and impermeable soils do not provide better buffering capacity. Thicker soils with neutralizing components would be more effective for buffering. Hence, (*a*), (*c*), and (*d*) are correct.

6. **(D):** According to the India State of Forest Report (2021), the areas covered by different forest types in increasing order of geographical area are as follows:
   - (*c*) Scrub occupies the smallest area, approximately 2.8%.
   - (*d*) Tree Cover follows, covering around 3.0%.
   - (*e*) Very Dense Forest covers 3.0%.
   - (*a*) Moderately Dense Forest covers a larger area of about 9.38%.
   - (*b*) Open Forest has the largest area, covering around 9.26%.

   So, the correct order is Scrub (*c*), Tree Cover (*d*), Very Dense Forest (*e*), Moderately Dense Forest (*a*), and Open Forest (*b*).

7. **(A):** Geostrophic winds occur when the Coriolis force due to Earth's rotation balances the horizontal pressure gradient force. As a result, the wind flows parallel

to isobars, which means it is oriented at a right angle to the direction of the pressure gradient. This wind pattern is commonly observed at higher altitudes in the mid-latitudes, where friction with the surface is negligible, allowing near-perfect geostrophic balance.

8. (A): In the optical remote sensing bands, the wavelength range 0.52–0.62 μm (green region) is often used for assessing vegetation vigor, as healthy green vegetation is highly reflective in this band. The 1.55–1.75 μm range (a Short-Wave Infrared band) is sensitive to moisture content in soils and vegetation. The thermal infrared region of 10.4–12.5 μm is employed for thermal mapping, identifying heat patterns, and assessing surface temperatures. The 2.08–2.35 μm range (SWIR2) is valuable in discriminating mineral and rock types because many minerals show distinctive absorption features in that range. Thus the correct pairing is: (*a*) 0.52–0.62 μm → vegetation vigour (II), (*b*) 1.55–1.75 μm → soil moisture (III), (*c*) 10.4–12.5 μm → thermal mapping (IV), (*d*) 2.08–2.35 μm → mineral/rock (I).

9. (D): Photochemical smog primarily forms from nitrogen oxides (NOx) and volatile organic compounds (VOCs) in the presence of strong sunlight and sufficiently high temperatures (above approximately 25°C). When sunlight interacts with these precursor pollutants, a complex chain of photochemical reactions leads to the formation of ground-level ozone and other oxidants that characterize photochemical smog. Sulphur dioxide and water vapour are not the central ingredients for photochemical smog, making NOx and VOCs the key reactive species under high temperature.

10. (B): Under India's National Action Plan on Climate Change (NAPCC), the Department of Science and Technology (DST) is responsible for coordinating two missions: (*b*) the National Mission for Sustaining the Himalayan Ecosystem and (*d*) the National Mission on Strategic Knowledge for Climate Change. The mission on Enhanced Energy Efficiency is largely under the Bureau of Energy Efficiency (Ministry of Power), Sustainable Agriculture is under the Ministry of Agriculture, and Sustainable Habitat is overseen by the Ministry of Housing and Urban Affairs. Hence, only (*b*) and (*d*) fall under DST's purview.

11. (D): Primary producers, such as green plants, capture only about 1% of the total incoming solar energy. In this problem, 1,000,000 J of sunlight is available. The 1% that is converted to net primary productivity (NPP) amounts to 1,000,000 × 0.01 = 10,000 J. At each successive trophic level (primary consumer, secondary consumer, tertiary consumer), the ecological (trophic) efficiency is assumed to be 10%. Thus, a primary consumer would receive 10% of 10,000 J = 1,000 J, a secondary consumer would get 10% of that = 100 J, and finally the tertiary consumer would receive 10% of 100 J = 10 J.

12. (C): Destabilization of colloidal particles by neutralizing or reducing the repulsive forces among them is a fundamental step in water and wastewater treatment known as coagulation. Chemical coagulants such as aluminum sulphate (alum) or ferric salts are added so that colloidal particles lose their surface charge and can then stick together. Once the particles are destabilized, gentle mixing or flocculation helps them form larger aggregates or flocs, which can then be removed by settling or other means. The key word in the question is "destabilisation," which is distinct from flocculation: coagulation is the chemical charge-neutralization phase, while flocculation is the subsequent physical aggregation.

13. (D): In statistical hypothesis testing, one typically sets up two hypotheses: the null hypothesis (H_0) and the alternative hypothesis (H_1). These two cannot be accepted or rejected simultaneously for the same set of data. Instead, based on the test statistic and the chosen significance level, either we "reject H_0 in favor of H_1" or we "fail to reject H_0." Consequently, if H_0 is rejected, H_1 is effectively accepted, and vice versa. Statement (*a*) correctly identifies that there are indeed two hypotheses (null and alternative). Statement (*e*) is correct in asserting that if one hypothesis is rejected, the other is accepted. Statements (*b*), (*c*), and (*d*) are not always valid in the standard framework of hypothesis testing; for example, we do not accept/reject both simultaneously, and the critical value lying in the acceptance region does not correspond to rejecting the null.

14. (B): Various thermal structures of the atmosphere create characteristic plume behaviours:

(*a*) Inversion below and lapse (unstable or neutral) aloft → Lofting (II). A stable layer beneath the stack prevents the plume from moving downward, while the lapse region above allows the plume to rise and disperse upward.

(*b*) Strong lapse condition → Looping (III). Under highly unstable (super-adiabatic) conditions, the plume rises and sinks in oscillating loops due to strong vertical mixing.

(*c*) Lapse below and inversion above → Fumigation (I). The plume can move downward into the unstable air but is capped above by a stable inversion, forcing the pollutants downward.

(*d*) Weak lapse below and inversion aloft → Trapping (IV). In this scenario, the upper stable layer combines with a near-stable lower layer, and the plume remains confined in a thin vertical layer, effectively "trapping" the pollutants.

15. (B): Elutriators separate particles from an air stream primarily by gravitational settling through a vertical chamber. The device slows down the flow enough that particles with sufficient terminal velocity will drop out of the gas stream. Unlike electrostatic precipitators (which use electrostatic forces), bag houses (which use filtration), or super saturators (which involve condensation effects), elutriators exploit gravity as the main separating force. This principle relies on each particle's settling velocity, which depends on factors like size, shape, and density.

16. (B): Different types of plastics have characteristic applications due to their physical and chemical properties.

(*a*) PETE (Polyethylene terephthalate) → Soft drink bottles (III). Because of PETE's clarity, strength, and gas-barrier properties, it is widely used in carbonated beverage containers.

(*b*) HDPE (High Density Polyethylene) → Milk bottles (IV). Its high strength-to-density ratio and chemical resistance make it well-suited for milk jugs, detergent bottles, etc.

(*c*) PP (Polypropylene) → Straw (I). Polypropylene has good rigidity, is relatively safe in contact with food/beverages, and is easily moldable, making it common in straws and various caps.

(*d*) PS (Polystyrene) → Pharmaceutical bottles (II). Polystyrene can be used in certain rigid packaging applications, including some pharmaceutical or vitamin bottles and laboratory disposable ware.

17. (C): Applying Raoult's law to an equimolar mixture (i.e., each component has a mole fraction, x_i, of 0.25) means the partial pressure of each component = x_i × (pure vapor pressure). The given pure vapor pressures (in atm at 25 °C) are:

Benzene = 0.126 atm
Toluene = 0.0380 atm
Ethylbenzene = 0.0126 atm
Xylene = 0.0117 atm

Since x_i = 0.25 for each, the partial pressure of benzene will be 0.25 × 0.126 = 0.0315 atm, which is clearly larger than what you get for toluene (0.0095 atm), ethylbenzene (0.00315 atm), or xylene (0.002925 atm). Hence benzene exerts the maximum partial pressure in the mixture.

18. (C): Oxygen makes up about 20.95% of the atmosphere by volume on a dry basis. At standard temperature and pressure (0 °C, 1 atm), 1 mole of any ideal gas occupies about 22.4 L. One mole of O_2 (molecular weight = 32 g/mole) would thus have a mass of 32 g spread over 22.4 L. This gives roughly 1.4286 g of O_2 per liter if the gas were pure oxygen. Since ambient (dry) air has only 20.95% O_2 by volume, each liter of air has 0.2095 L of oxygen. Multiplying 1.4286 g/L by 0.2095 ≈ 0.299 g/L of O_2 in dry air.

19. (A): In coalification (the progressive transformation of plant material to coal), the O/C atomic ratio generally decreases as one goes to more mature stages. Wood and cellulose have high O/C ratios, while the macerals in coal (like huminite and vitrinite) show progressively lower O/C ratios as rank increases. The question asks for the increasing order of O/C ratio, which means from smallest to largest. Among the listed materials:

Vitrinite has the lowest O/C ratio, followed by huminite, then lignin, then wood, and finally cellulose has one of the highest O/C ratios.

So the sequence in ascending order is Vitrinite (*a*) < Huminite (*b*) < Lignin (*c*) < Wood (*d*) < Cellulose (*e*).

20. (C): When two closely related species (such as *Geospiza fuliginosa and Geospiza fortis*) occur in allopatric populations (separate geographic locations), their beak depths are quite similar. However, in sympatric populations (where they co-occur), competition for food resources can drive evolutionary divergence in beak morphology—a phenomenon called character displacement. It is an adaptation that reduces niche overlap and direct competition by favouring individuals that exploit different food types or feeding strategies. This allows both species to coexist by minimizing direct resource competition.

21. (D): (*a*) Komatiite (IV) is a high-temperature igneous rock, typically ultramafic and formed by very hot magma flows in the Archean eon. (*b*) Granulite (I) is known to be a high-grade metamorphic rock, having been subjected to high temperature and pressure. (*c*) Arkose (II) is a clastic sedimentary rock that contains a high percentage of feldspar. (*d*) Dolomite (III) is a non-clastic sedimentary rock, formed primarily by chemical processes or diagenetic replacement of calcite by magnesium.

22. (B): (*a*) ICP-OES (Inductively Coupled Plasma Optical Emission Spectrometry) (IV) is generally a destructive technique since it requires digesting the sample in liquid form to analyze its elemental composition. (*b*) XRD (X-ray Diffraction) (III) is widely used for crystallography, helping to identify the crystal structure of substances. (*c*) XRF (X-ray Fluorescence) (I) is a non-destructive method for elemental analysis, often used on solid samples directly.

(*d*) UV-VIS (II) is employed in colorimetric or spectrophotometric techniques to quantify elements or compounds based on absorption in the ultraviolet and visible regions.

23. (D): Different fractions of municipal solid waste and fossil-fuel derivatives have characteristic Higher Heating Values (HHV). Generally, green yard waste (*e*) has the lowest HHV because of high moisture content (often in the range of 6,000–10,000 kJ/kg). Mixed paper (*a*) is typically next, with HHV around 13,000–15,000 kJ/kg. Leather (*d*) often reaches around 15,000–18,000 kJ/kg. Rubber (*b*) can go above 25,000 kJ/kg, and mixed plastics (*c*) typically exhibit even higher values, frequently above 30,000 kJ/kg.

Hence the ascending order is (*e*) → (*a*) → (*d*) → (*b*) → (*c*).

24. (B): Monazite is a phosphate mineral containing thorium and rare earth elements. It occurs in beach sands, especially along the coasts of India and other countries. Because of its significant thorium content, monazite can be processed to extract thorium, which can serve as an atomic fuel in certain nuclear reactor designs. Pitchblende is a principal ore of uranium, apatite is a phosphate mineral unrelated to thorium fuel, and malachite is a copper carbonate mineral.

25. (B): The extinction vortex in a small population is driven by the following processes:

(*b*) Inbreeding and genetic drift, which occur in small populations, leading to a reduction in genetic diversity.

(*c*) Loss of genetic variability further diminishes the population's ability to adapt to changing environments.

(*d*) Lower individual fitness and population adaptability occur due to the loss of genetic diversity and adaptation.

(*e*) This results in lower reproduction rates and higher mortality rates, which accelerates the decline of the population.

(*a*) Finally, the smaller population continues to shrink as these processes feed back into one another.

Thus, the correct sequence is (*b*) → (*c*) → (*d*) → (*e*) → (*a*).

26. (C): Nature-based solutions (NBS) are approaches inspired and supported by nature that provide environmental, social, and economic benefits, helping to mitigate climate change impacts, conserve biodiversity, and enhance ecosystem services. IUCN has been a key international organization to conceptualize and promote NBS, integrating them into global conservation, development, and climate policy agendas.

27. (B): Recent assessments of wind power potential at 100 m or 120 m hub height (e.g., by the National Institute of Wind Energy, NIWE) indicate that Gujarat has the highest estimated wind energy potential among Indian states. While Tamil Nadu has historically led in installed capacity, the potential resources at taller turbine hub heights are currently found to be largest in Gujarat, followed by Rajasthan, Tamil Nadu, and others.

28. (C): The absorbed dose of ionizing radiation in the International System of Units (SI) is measured in Grays (Gy). One gray corresponds to the absorption of one joule of radiation energy per kilogram of matter. Older units include the rad (1 Gy = 100 rad). Other radiation-related units, such as Roentgen (R) and Becquerel (Bq), measure exposure and radioactivity rather than absorbed dose.

29. (B) **30. (*)**

31. (C): From the first law of thermodynamics, dU = dQ + dW. Here, dQ = 0 (adiabatic compression, no heat exchange) and dW = –p dV. If the air parcel is compressed, dV is negative; thus –p (negative) is positive. This implies an increase in internal energy (dU > 0). Physically, compressing a gas adiabatically raises its temperature and internal energy.

32. (C): (*a*) HS^-: The sulphur (S) in HS^- has an oxidation state of –2 (II).

(*b*) N_2O: Each nitrogen (N) has an average oxidation state of +1 (III).

(*c*) S_2^{2-}: Each sulphur (S) in the disulphide ion is at –1 (I).

(*d*) R_2NH: The nitrogen (N) in an amine has an oxidation state of –3 (IV).

33. (A): Principle 17 of the Rio Declaration on Environment and Development (1992) states that Environmental Impact Assessment (EIA) shall be undertaken for proposed activities likely to have a significant adverse impact on the environment and are subject to a decision of a competent national authority. This principle underscores the importance of EIA as a national instrument for sustainable development.

34. (C): Lignite is often referred to as "brown coal," having the lowest rank among the coal series. Raniganj (West Bengal), Singrauli (Madhya Pradesh), and Talcher (Odisha) are known for bituminous or sub-bituminous coal. In contrast, Makum coalfields in Assam are part of Tertiary coal deposits and can include lignite to sub-bituminous grades, making Makum more closely associated with lignite-type deposits than the other listed fields.

35. (B): A simplified chronological order of these figures in the evolution of ecology begins with Geoffroy Saint-Hilaire (*d*), followed by Hanns Reiter (*e*). Ernst Haeckel (*b*) comes next, famously coining the term "ecology" in 1866. Arthur Tansley (*a*) introduced the concept of the "ecosystem" in 1935. Eugene Odum (*c*), often called the "father of modern ecology," published foundational works on ecosystem ecology in the mid-20th century. Hence the correct order is (*d*) → (*e*) → (*b*) → (*a*) → (*c*).

36. (B): In a regression analysis of *y* on $x(y = a + bx)$, one can follow these steps to check model fitness:

(*c*) Estimate *a* and *b* from the regression equation.

(*e*) Calculate the residuals (difference between observed and fitted *y*).

(*b*) Assess the mean of the fitted *y* and the given (observed) *y* to see if they differ substantially.

(*a*) Estimate the mean of the residuals (to see if it is near zero).

(*d*) Assess or interpret the mean of the residuals in the context of model adequacy.

37. (D): NOy refers to the total reactive nitrogen species in the atmosphere, which includes NO, NO_2, NO_3, N_2O_5, HNO_3, and other higher oxidized nitrogen compounds such as $ClONO_2$ (chlorine nitrate) and HO_2NO_2 (pernitric acid). Consequently, (*a*) HNO_3, (*b*) $ClONO_2$, (*c*) $HOONO_2$ (another way to write HO_2NO_2), (*d*) NO_3, and (*e*) N_2O_5 all fall under NOy.

38. (A): Darcy's law for flow in a porous medium (or similarly in certain open-channel contexts) is often given by Q = KA (*dh*/*dl*), where Q is volumetric flow rate, K is the coefficient of permeability, A is the cross-sectional area, and *dh*/*dl* is the hydraulic gradient. This highlights the dependence on cross-sectional area, hydraulic gradient, and permeability. Gravitational or frictional forces are subsumed in K and do not appear separately in the simplest expression of Darcy's law.

39. (C): The correct expressions and their corresponding units for water content in the atmosphere are:

(*a*) Volume Mixing Ratio → parts per million (ppm) (III): Volume mixing ratio is expressed in parts per million, representing the volume of water vapour per volume of air.

(*b*) Mass Mixing Ratio → g H_2O (kg air)$^{-1}$ (IV): Mass mixing ratio refers to the mass of water vapor per unit mass of air.

(*c*) Specific Humidity → g H_2O (g air)$^{-1}$ (II): Specific humidity measures the mass of water vapor in a given mass of air.

(*d*) Mass Concentration → g H_2O (m^3 Air)$^{-1}$ (I): Mass concentration refers to the amount of water vapor in a given volume of air.

Thus, the correct order is (III), (IV), (II), (I).

40. (C): A cap rock is an impermeable layer that prevents petroleum (oil and gas) from escaping the reservoir rock. Shale, being a fine-grained sedimentary rock with very low permeability, commonly serves as the cap rock in many oil fields. In contrast, sandstone, jointed limestone, and conglomerate are typically more permeable and thus do not effectively trap petroleum.

41. (D): Ozone (O_3) in the troposphere is a greenhouse gas that also appears as one of the criteria air pollutants under many national ambient air quality standards. It is not directly emitted in the lower atmosphere but is formed photochemically through reactions involving NOx (nitrogen oxides) and VOCs (volatile organic compounds) under sunlight. Tropospheric ozone contributes to global warming due to its strong infrared absorption properties, but at ground level it also harms human health, vegetation, and materials. CO_2, N_2O, and SF_6 are directly emitted greenhouse gases, whereas O_3 is considered a "secondary" pollutant because it arises from precursor emissions rather than being released into the air in its final form.

42. (B): In India, the Ministry of Environment, Forest and Climate Change (MoEFCC) classifies developmental projects into different categories under the EIA Notification. Category A projects (often large-scale or with higher pollution potential) mandatorily require EIA studies and a Public Hearing. Category B is subdivided into B1 and B2. Category B1 projects also require EIA and Public Hearing because of their environmental significance. Category B2 projects, in contrast, typically do not require a full EIA or a Public Hearing. There is no formal "Category A1" in this context. Therefore, Category A and Category B1 must necessarily undertake EIA along with Public Hearing.

43. (C): When chlorine is added to swimming pool water containing nitrogen compounds (often from sweat, urine, and other organic matter), it reacts to form chloramines (such as monochloramine, dichloramine, and trichloramine). Chloramines are responsible for the pungent, irritating smell commonly associated with indoor pools and can cause eye and respiratory irritation. Although people often associate the sharp odor simply with chlorine, in reality, it is these chloramine compounds (especially trichloramine) that lead to discomfort.

44. (B): India has launched or co-founded several major international initiatives with global impact over the years. The International Big Cat Alliance (IBCA) is among the most recent announcements (in 2023) aimed at conserving the seven major big cat species (tiger, lion, leopard, snow leopard, puma, jaguar, and cheetah). It follows other important Indian-led initiatives such as the Coalition for Disaster Resilient Infrastructure (2019), the International Solar Alliance (2015), and Mission LiFE (launched in 2022). As IBCA was announced after the start of Mission LiFE, it is recognized as India's latest global contribution.

45. (A): Under the Biological Diversity Act (2002) in India, the constitution of Biodiversity Management Committees (BMCs) is mandated at local body levels (Gram Panchayats, Municipalities, etc.). One of the main responsibilities of these BMCs is to prepare and maintain a People's Biodiversity Register (PBR). The PBR documents local flora, fauna, traditional knowledge, and any associated uses. State Biodiversity Boards (SBBs) and the National Biodiversity Authority (NBA) oversee and offer guidance, but the direct function of creating and updating the PBR primarily falls under each BMC's purview.

46. (A): (*a*) Agent Orange is linked to Vietnam (IV), famously used as a defoliant during the Vietnam War. (*b*) Bohai Bay is found in China (I), known for major oil spills and environmental incidents. (*c*) Itai-Itai disease occurred in Japan (II), primarily caused by cadmium poisoning in the Toyama Prefecture region. (*d*) Love Canal is in the United States (III), near Niagara Falls, New York, where hazardous waste disposal led to a major environmental and public health disaster.

47. (D): Sulphur in coal commonly occurs in three main forms: (*b*) organic sulphur (chemically bound within the coal's organic matrix), (*c*) pyritic sulphur (iron sulphide, FeS_2, inclusions often referred to as pyrite), and (*d*) sulphate minerals (e.g., gypsum, $CaSO_4 \cdot 2H_2O$), particularly in weathered coal seams. Although native sulphur (elemental sulphur) can occur under special oxidation-reduction conditions, it is not typically classified as a major sulphur form in most coals. Hence the primary recognized forms are organic sulphur, pyritic sulphur, and sulphate.

48. (C): Cation exchange capacity (CEC) measures how many cations a material can adsorb or exchange. Among colloid-sized fractions, quartz (*c*) has the lowest CEC because it is primarily SiO_2 with minimal surface charges. Kaolinite (*a*) is a 1 : 1 clay with moderate but still relatively low CEC. Montmorillonite (*b*), a 2 : 1 clay, has a much higher CEC due to its layered structure and greater surface area. Organic matter (*d*), particularly humus, has the highest CEC because of numerous functional groups capable of binding cations.

Thus the ascending order is quartz < kaolinite < montmorillonite < organic matter.

49. (C): The hydroelectric power capacity distribution in India as per the regions is as follows:

(*b*) The North Eastern Region has the highest hydroelectric potential, due to its abundant rivers and topography.

(*c*) Northern Region comes next with significant hydroelectric potential, particularly in the states of Himachal Pradesh, Uttarakhand, and Jammu & Kashmir.

(*d*) The Southern Region despite substantial capacity, comes after the northern regions.

(*a*) Eastern Region follows, with substantial resources in states like Odisha, but not as much as the northern and northeastern regions.

(*e*) The Western Region has the lowest hydroelectric potential.

Thus, the correct order is (*b*), (*c*), (*d*), (*a*), (*e*).

50. (C): Open-source software for geospatial data processing includes:

(*c*) QGIS (formerly Quantum GIS), a popular community-driven GIS platform;

(*d*) ILWIS (Integrated Land and Water Information System), which became open source around 2007;

(*e*) SAGA GIS (System for Automated Geoscientific Analyses), an open-source GIS software with powerful terrain and spatial analysis functions.

ArcGIS (*a*) and ERDAS Imagine (*b*) are both proprietary software packages requiring paid licenses. Hence QGIS, ILWIS, and SAGA GIS are the open-source solutions among the options listed.

51. **(B):** A sanitary landfill is an engineered pit or depression designed to safely deposit municipal solid waste. Waste is spread in thin layers, compacted to reduce volume, and covered daily with soil or other cover material. This daily cover minimizes odors, discourages pests, and reduces wind-blown litter. Unlike open dumps, sanitary landfills incorporate liners (clay or synthetic) and leachate-collection systems to protect groundwater. A secured landfill is specifically for hazardous waste with more stringent controls, while a compost pit is for biodegradable organic matter.

52. **(C):** Perpetual storage implies the long-term isolation of hazardous waste so that it does not pose ongoing risks to the environment or human health. Surface impoundments (lagoons or ponds), landfills, and waste piles can be engineered for extended or permanent containment (though often under strict regulations). However, relying on "ocean and atmospheric assimilation" is not an acceptable perpetual storage option under modern environmental standards and laws. Simply dispersing hazardous substances into seas or the air does not constitute safe or contained disposal.

53. **(C):** BOD (Biochemical Oxygen Demand) measures the amount of degradable organic matter in water by assessing how much dissolved oxygen microorganisms consume. Statement (*a*) is valid because the typical BOD decay curve follows first-order kinetics. Statement (*b*) is correct since the ultimate BOD (L_0) is proportional to the initial concentration of biodegradable organics. Statement (*c*) is also true: the amount of oxygen depletion depends on both the ultimate BOD (how much total oxygen demand exists) and the rate constant (k), which governs how fast that demand is exerted. Statement (*d*) is false because the numerical value of the BOD rate constant does depend on temperature, and statement (*e*) is false because it also depends on the nature (type) of the waste.

54. **(B)**

55. **(B):** The toxicity of a compound is often gauged by its LD_{50} (median lethal dose), typically given in mg of substance per kg of body weight. The lower the LD_{50}, the more acutely toxic the chemical. Among the options, parathion has an LD_{50} of less than 5 mg/kg, making it extremely toxic compared to DDT (110 mg/kg), permethrin (50–500 mg/kg), and nicotine (5–50 mg/kg).

56. **(C):** A typical Environmental Impact Assessment (EIA) process involves:

(*a*) Analysis (identifying baseline conditions and potential environmental impacts);

(*d*) Mitigation (developing measures to reduce or offset significant impacts);

(*c*) EIA Reporting (compiling findings into an official report);

(*e*) Review (the regulatory body and possibly the public scrutinize the EIA report);

(*b*) Decision Making (the authority decides to approve the project, request modifications, or reject it).

57. **(D):** PARIVESH (Pro-Active and Responsive facilitation by Interactive, Virtuous and Environmental Single-window Hub) is an online platform launched by the Ministry of Environment, Forest and Climate Change (MoEFCC) in India. It automates the entire process of granting Environmental

Clearances (EC), Forest Clearances (FC), Wildlife Clearances (WC), and Coastal Regulation Zone Clearances (CRZ). EIACP and ENVIS are other important MoEFCC programs, but PARIVESH is specifically the single-window system for clearance processes.

58. (C): In the stratosphere, ozone (O_3) is formed primarily via photodissociation of O_2 and subsequent reaction with O atoms.

(*a*) The rate of ozone production is indeed highest near the equator around ~40 km, where intense solar UV radiation splits O_2.

(*b*) However, the maximum ozone concentration (in terms of mixing ratio) near the equator often peaks lower, around ~25 km, owing to transport and temperature profile.

(*c*) At high latitudes (the poles), the altitude of maximum O_3 production can be somewhat higher or may shift due to different atmospheric temperature and circulation patterns, though actual concentrations can vary significantly.

(*d*) The greatest ozone concentration does not necessarily coincide with the greatest production rate, because atmospheric circulation redistributes ozone from production sites (tropics) to mid- and high latitudes.

(*e*) The statement about greater catalytic destruction over the Arctic than Antarctica is generally not correct. The largest ozone depletion occurs over Antarctica due to the formation of polar stratospheric clouds and unique meteorological conditions, so (*e*) is excluded.

59. (A): Low-grade metamorphism (e.g., greenschist facies) includes the formation of minerals such as muscovite (a mica stable at relatively low temperatures), actinolite (a common amphibole in greenschist conditions), and andalusite (which can form under low-to-moderate pressures and temperatures, especially in contact metamorphism scenarios). Garnet and Kyanite typically appear in medium- to higher-grade metamorphic conditions, so (*b*) and (*d*) do not belong to the low-grade category.

60. (D): Under RCRA (Resource Conservation and Recovery Act) in the United States, certain wastes are specifically "listed" (F-list, K-list, P-list, U-list) or regulated if they exhibit hazardous "characteristics."

(*a*) Fly ash is not categorically listed as hazardous under RCRA (although it can be classified hazardous if it fails TCLP).

(*c*) Arsenic-treated wood is generally not on a specific RCRA hazardous-waste listing, though disposal may be regulated under other rules.

(*e*) Used chlorofluorocarbon (CFC) refrigerants are addressed primarily under Clean Air Act provisions (for ozone-depleting substances) rather than being a distinct RCRA hazardous waste listing.

Hence (*a*), (*c*), and (*e*) are "not listed" as hazardous under RCRA.

61. (A): ISO 14030 deals with green finance, notably "Green Bonds" (II). ISO 14040 pertains to "Life Cycle Assessment" (I), outlining the principles and framework for LCA. ISO 14050 is the environmental management vocabulary (IV), providing standardized terms and definitions. ISO 14090 covers climate change adaptation – "Principles, requirements and guidelines" (III). Linking each standard to its definition gives the sequence (*a*) → (II), (*b*) → (I), (*c*) → (IV), (*d*) → (III).

62. (C): Kanjli Lake (*a*) is in Punjab (II), created near the town of Kapurthala. Point Calimere (*b*), also known as Kodiakarai, is a wetland in Tamil Nadu (III). Rudrasagar Lake (*c*) is in Tripura (IV), a notable Ramsar site. Vembanad Kol Wetland (*d*) is in Kerala (I), famous for its extensive backwaters. The correct arrangement is (*a*) → (II), (*b*) → (III), (*c*) → (IV), (*d*) → (I).

63. (C): MacArthur and Wilson's island biogeography model describes how the number of species on an isolated island represents a dynamic equilibrium between two opposing processes: (*c*) immigration (or colonization) of new species from a mainland source and (*d*) extinction (or local disappearance) of existing species on the island. Although island size and distance from mainland do affect these rates (larger islands generally support higher immigration and lower extinction), the specific balance in the model is between species immigration and extinction rates.

64. (A): In scenario A, the two gharial populations breed independently (no gene flow). If the Chambal population goes extinct, its unique alleles and genetic variation are lost entirely. In scenario B, where adults migrate and interbreed annually, some genes from the Chambal population would already have been transferred to the Ganga population. Therefore, the loss of the Chambal group in scenario A leads to a greater overall reduction in genetic diversity because there was no prior mixing of genetic material between the two rivers.

65. (A): The Convention on Biological Diversity (CBD) is associated with two major protocols:

(*a*) The Cartagena Protocol on Biosafety (focusing on the safe handling of living modified organisms).

(*c*) The Nagoya Protocol on Access and Benefit Sharing (governing the use of genetic resources and the fair sharing of benefits).

The Kigali Amendment is related to the Montreal Protocol on ozone-depleting substances. The Rotterdam Convention addresses international trade in hazardous chemicals, and UN-REDD is a collaborative program on Reducing Emissions from Deforestation and Forest Degradation.

66. (B): Exfoliation (also called "sheeting") occurs when rocks, especially large igneous bodies such as granite, experience a reduction in confining pressure near the Earth's surface. This reduction causes concentric slabs or shells of rock to spall off parallel to the outer surface, producing rounded rock forms. Frost wedging and disintegration are different mechanical weathering processes, while leaching generally refers to the chemical removal of soluble components.

67. (D): (*a*) Gas hydrates are often associated with Cenozoic (III) sediments in modern ocean basins or permafrost regions.

(*b*) Major coal deposits formed during the Carboniferous and Permian (Paleozoic) (I), as in the Gondwana coal.

(*c*) Petroleum deposits developed extensively through Mesozoic (IV) strata (e.g., many prolific oil-bearing formations worldwide date from the Jurassic and Cretaceous).

(*d*) Uranium ores commonly occur in Precambrian (II) shields, such as the Canadian Shield or the Singhbhum craton in India.

68. (D): A t-test is a parametric test (so statement (*a*) calling it non-parametric is false). It is commonly used to:

(*b*) Check if a sample mean differs significantly from a known or hypothesized population mean.

(*c*) Evaluate the significance of a correlation coefficient (using the t-statistic derived from the sample correlation).

(*e*) Test the significance of an observed regression coefficient.

Covariation significance is more typically associated with ANOVA or more specialized tests, not a basic t-test alone.

69. (C): The formation of a petroleum deposit follows a logical sequence:

(*b*) Generation: Kerogen in source rock matures into hydrocarbons under heat/ pressure.

(*d*) Primary migration: These newly formed hydrocarbons move out of the source rock pores.

(*e*) Secondary migration: Hydrocarbons travel through permeable carrier beds (or faults, fractures) toward a trap.

(*a*) Accumulation: Oil/gas pools in a structural or stratigraphic trap.

(*c*) Seepage: If the trap is breached or not sealed, hydrocarbons may escape to the surface as seeps or vent into overlying strata.

70. (C): In the "daily truck routing" method of municipal solid waste collection, a dedicated route is assigned each day. While it has advantages like route consistency and the possibility to incentivize quick completion, a common drawback is the variability in waste volume each day. This may lead to inefficiencies such as under-utilized or overloaded trucks, difficulty in predicting time needed, and irregular labour or fuel usage. Other listed points (incentives to finish early, adjusting route size, residents knowing pickup times) are typically regarded as benefits rather than disadvantages.

71. (B): In biodiesel production, a common method is to mix vegetable oil (such as soybean or used cooking oil) with a solution of methanol containing sodium hydroxide (NaOH). This reaction, known as transesterification, converts the triglycerides in the oil into fatty acid methyl esters (biodiesel) and glycerin. Ethanol can also be used, but methanol is most commonly employed because of its favourable chemical properties, cost, and availability.

72. (B): The Bishnoi Movement (*b*) started in 1700 in Rajasthan to protect trees and wildlife. The Gandhamardan Movement (*c*) in 1983 emerged in Odisha to protest against mining in the ecologically and culturally significant Gandhamardan Hills. The Jungle Bachao Movement (*d*) in 1982 originated in Bihar (later extending to Jharkhand) to resist forest policy changes that threatened local tribal communities. Meanwhile, the Appiko Movement (1983) began in the Uttara Kannada district of Karnataka (not Kerala), and the Silent Valley Movement (1973) took place in Kerala (not Karnataka).

73. (D): (*a*) Cyclone → (IV) A large-scale low-pressure system in which winds move counterclockwise (in the Northern Hemisphere) toward the low-pressure center.

(*b*) Thunderstorm → (III) A brief but intense storm characterized by rain, lightning, and sometimes hail or gusty winds.

(*c*) Hurricane → (I) A tropical cyclone with gale-force winds (sustained winds of at least 74 mph or 119 km/h) that can be extremely destructive.

(*d*) Tornado → (II) The smallest, most violent storm system, often a rapidly rotating column of air that extends from a thunderstorm to the ground.

74. (C): Compost is a humus-like material (*a*) produced by microbial decomposition of organic wastes (yard trimmings, kitchen scraps, etc.). This biodegradation process is generally exothermic, generating heat rather than absorbing it, so (*b*) is incorrect.

Compost helps improve soil structure (*c*), facilitating better aeration and root penetration, and also increases soil buffering capacity (*e*). In addition, compost typically increases soil moisture-holding capacity rather than decreases it, so (*d*) is incorrect.

75. (C): Pegmatites are intrusive igneous rocks characterized by very large (often centimeter- to meter-scale) interlocking crystals. They commonly form in the final stages of magma crystallization, when water and volatile content are high, allowing rapid crystal growth. Basalt and rhyolite are typically fine-grained extrusive rocks, and obsidian is a glassy volcanic rock.

76. (C): The ecological principles of sustainable development focus on understanding the limits and interconnections between natural systems and human societies.

A. Biophysical limits recognize the finite nature of Earth's resources.

B. Interdependence emphasizes the interconnectedness of ecosystems and human activities.

C. Ecological justice focuses on fairness in how environmental benefits and burdens are distributed.

D. However, Dependence is not an ecological principle in sustainable development as it does not align with the framework that emphasizes balance, interdependence, and respect for the environment. Therefore, "Dependence" is the principle that does not fit in the context of ecological sustainability.

77. (D): Under flowing water, sedimentary structures form progressively with increasing velocity. At the lowest relevant velocities, one often sees lower plane bed (*a*). As velocity increases, small-scale ripple marks (*b*) appear, then larger-scale ripple marks (*c*), then upper plane bed (*d*). At the highest flow regime, antidunes (*e*) can form, representing quick and unstable bedforms that can migrate upstream or appear stationary on the bed surface.

78. (C): A warming of 4 °C could allow today's tundra biomes, found in cold Arctic or alpine regions, to transition into taiga (boreal coniferous forest). Biome shifts are largely determined by temperature and precipitation patterns; an appreciable temperature increase in a formerly tundra region tends to favor coniferous tree establishment if moisture is sufficient. Deserts or temperate forests are much less likely unless specific precipitation regimes also shift drastically.

79. (C): Malathion is an organophosphate insecticide that does not have chlorine in its molecular structure. Methoxychlor, mirex, and endosulfan all contain one or more chlorine atoms, classifying them among organochlorine compounds. Malathion instead contains phosphorus and sulphur moieties, typical of organophosphates.

80. (B): In a sanitary landfill, the waste placed during one operational period (e.g., one day), together with that day's cover soil, constitutes a "cell." Multiple cells stacked on top of each other form a "lift," and the active working face is the open portion being filled on any given day. A "bench" is a horizontal step or terrace designed to stabilize and control the slope in tall landfills.

81. (B): Mann–Whitney U test is a nonparametric test comparing whether the median ranks of two groups are the same (II). The chi-square (χ^2) test often examines the null hypothesis that there is no association (independence) between two categorical variables (IV). The Z-test commonly addresses proportions across two groups—for example, testing whether the proportion in one group differs significantly from that in another (I). Analysis of Variance (ANOVA) checks whether the mean of three or more groups is the same (III). By assigning these null hypotheses correctly, we see (*a*) → (II), (*b*) → (IV), (*c*) → (I), (*d*) → (III).

82. (A): Performing a one-way ANOVA generally follows a logical stepwise approach. First, data are tabulated (*b*) to organize all observations by group. Next, one partitions the total variance into between-groups and within-groups components (*c*). Then, one determines the degrees of freedom associated with each component (*d*). After that, one computes the mean sum of squares (*a*) by dividing each sum of squares by its respective degrees of freedom. Finally, one calculates the F-statistic (variance ratio) (*e*) = (MS_between)/(MS_within). If this F-value exceeds a critical threshold (from F-distribution tables) at a given significance level, one rejects the null hypothesis that all group means are equal.

83. (D): The question explicitly references a systematic, comprehensive process for evaluating environmental impacts of policies, programs, and plans (and not just individual projects), using the findings in publicly accountable decision-making. This describes Strategic Environmental Assessment (SEA). Environmental Impact Assessment (EIA) typically focuses on specific projects. SEA extends the concept to higher-level strategies and is carried out earlier in the decision-making process so that environmental considerations are integrated into policies or programs before key directions are locked in.

84. (B): The classic "capture–mark–recapture" method estimates population size using the formula N = (M × C)/R

Where:

N is the estimated population size.

M is the number of individuals captured and marked in the first sample (180).

n is the total number of individuals captured in the second sample (44).

m is the number of marked individuals recaptured in the second sample (7.)

Plugging in the numbers:

$$N = \frac{180 \times 44}{7} = \frac{7920}{7}$$

$$\approx 1131.43$$

So, the estimated population size is 1131.

85. (D): Under GRIHA (Green Rating for Integrated Habitat Assessment) 2019, different criteria receive a certain number of maximum points. Typically, "topsoil preservation" (*d*) carries fewer points compared to bigger-ticket items such as "water demand reduction" (*e*) or "energy optimization" (*a*). "Green infrastructure" (*b*) and "maintaining good IAQ (indoor air quality)" (*c*) also lie in between. Ordered from lower to higher point allotment approximately is:

Top Soil Preservation (*d*), Water Demand Reduction (*e*), Green Infrastructure (*b*), Maintaining Good IAQ (*c*), and Energy Optimization (*a*) as the highest.

86. (B): Different soil types vary widely in their organic matter content. Tropical agricultural soils (*d*) typically have relatively low organic matter due to high decomposition rates and intensive usage. Temperate agricultural soils (*b*) tend to have somewhat higher organic carbon levels. Forest soils (especially their surface horizons) (*a*) often accumulate more organic matter from leaf litter and reduced disturbance. Peat soils (*c*) have the highest organic matter content—often exceeding 20–30% by weight.

Thus the ascending order is: (*d*) → (*b*) → (*a*) → (*c*).

87. (B): The question asks for approximate 95% limits of the observations (not just the confidence interval of the mean). From the standard error (SE = 0.1) and sample size of 256, one deduces the population standard deviation:

$SD = SE \times \sqrt{n} = 0.1 \times 16 = 1.6.$

Under the empirical rule for normal data, about 95% of observations lie within ±2 SD of the mean.

So the range is $60 \pm (2 \times 1.6) = 60 \pm 3.2 = (56.8, 63.2)$.

88. (B): Dentist drilling noise is best classified as intermittent rather than steady-state or impulse noise. Steady-state noise remains relatively constant over extended periods (like a continuous generator hum). Impulse or impact noise is very short in duration with steep rise times (e.g., gunshots, hammer blows). Dentist drills often turn on and off or vary in intensity, matching the profile of intermittent noise—noticeable, but not a single, instantaneous spike nor a permanently steady roar.

89. (D): Arsenic (a metalloid) is indeed used in wood preservatives (*a*). Chromate ion (CrO_4^{2-}) is generally water-soluble (*b*). Arsenic is not a metal (*c*); it is classified as a metalloid. Lead sulphide (PbS) and lead carbonate ($PbCO_3$) exhibit low solubility in water (*e*). Statement (*d*) claims Fe(III) is more soluble than Fe(II), but in practice Fe(II) is typically more soluble in pure water; Fe(III) more readily forms insoluble hydroxides.

Hence (*d*) is incorrect, making (*a*), (*b*), (*c*) and (*e*) the correct statements.

90. (B): The Intergovernmental Science-Policy Platform on Biodiversity and Ecosystem Services (IPBES), the Millennium Ecosystem Assessment (MEA), and The Economics of Ecosystems and Biodiversity (TEEB) are major, well-documented global efforts tied explicitly to biodiversity loss and ecosystem services. While the Commission on Ecosystem Management (CEM) is indeed part of IUCN and does address broad conservation and ecosystem management issues, it is not typically cited as one of the principal global initiatives focusing specifically on the valuation and assessment of ecosystem services in the same sense as IPBES, MEA, or TEEB. Consequently, B is the least directly linked choice among the four listed.

91. (B): To calculate the percentage of total children who suffered from illness across all strata:

Total number of children

$$= 50 \text{ (Low)} + 100 \text{ (Medium)} + 100 \text{ (High)}$$
$$= 250 \text{ children.}$$

Total number of children with illness

$$= 10 \text{ (Low)} + 10 \text{ (Medium)} + 5 \text{ (High)}$$
$$= 25 \text{ children.}$$

Percentage of children with illness

$$= (25/250) \times 100 = 10\%.$$

Thus, the percentage of children suffering from illness across all socio-economic strata is 10%, and the correct answer is B (10%).

92. (A): The sampling procedure described involved dividing the community into two strata based on geographical divisions: 50 households were selected from the left and 50 from the right side of the main lane. This is characteristic of Stratified Random Sampling, where the population is divided into distinct subgroups (strata) before random selection occurs within each subgroup.

Each stratum (left and right) was equally represented in the sample.

This method ensures that different sections of the community are proportionally included in the study.

Therefore, the correct answer is A (Stratified Random Sampling).

93. (B): To calculate the ratio of illness between children in the high and low socio-economic strata:

Number of children with illness in the High socio-economic group = 5.

Number of children with illness in the Low socio-economic group = 10.

Ratio of illness = 5 : 10, which simplifies to 1 : 2.

Thus, the ratio of illness between the high and low socio-economic groups is 1 : 2, and the correct answer is B (1 : 2).

94. (D): The classification of illness status involves only two possible categories: either a child has an illness or does not have an illness. This binary categorization aligns with the Binominal data type, where outcomes are dichotomous (yes/no, present/absent).

Nominal data would allow multiple unordered categories, which is not the case here.

Mixed and String are irrelevant since the data deals with only two discrete, mutually exclusive categories.

Therefore, the correct answer is D (Binominal).

95. (B): The mechanisms of data collection described in the passage include:

(*a*) Pilot-tested questionnaire: The questionnaire was tested within the community to validate its appropriateness.

(*d*) Face-to-face interviews: Data was collected directly through interviews conducted by a team of pediatricians and social scientists.

The options (*b*) and (*c*) do not align with the passage:

(*b*) does not specify "three members" were involved.

(*c*) Computerized systems are not mentioned; the data collection relied on traditional methods.

Thus, the correct combination is B (*a*, *d*).

96. (C): Traditional ecological knowledge is a framework deeply rooted in understanding and managing ecosystems. It focuses on the spatial scale, emphasizing knowledge of landscapes, ecosystems, and biodiversity at specific local or regional levels. This framework does not explicitly emphasize temporal scales because it primarily deals with the spatial relationships and the management of land and resources in these areas.

Temporal scales might occasionally influence practices, but the core focus is on spatial understanding of ecosystems, such as local knowledge of land, animals, and natural resources.

The passage highlights the concentric analyses and coupling of social and management systems, which inherently rely on spatial observations.

Thus, the correct answer is C (Spatial scale only).

97. (C): The traditional ecological knowledge system progresses from local and specific understanding to broader and more abstract levels.

Local knowledge of land and animals forms the base, focusing on immediate surroundings and specific ecological knowledge.

Land resource management systems come next, applying local knowledge to manage resources effectively.

Social institutions incorporate this management into societal norms, creating structured systems for resource use and conservation.

Worldview represents the broadest level, embedding these practices into cultural beliefs and values.

This hierarchy follows the concentric but interrelated structure described in the passage.

Hence, the correct answer is C.

98. (B): The framework for the "Knowledge-Practice-Belief complex" follows a hierarchical model that builds upon factual observations:

Fact represents the objective reality or basic observations.

Data are structured and recorded facts.

Information arises when data are contextualized and understood.

Knowledge is the synthesis of information to derive insights.

Wisdom integrates knowledge with ethical and practical decision-making.

This order reflects a logical progression from basic observation to holistic understanding, as required for ecological management.

Thus, the correct answer is B.

99. **(C):** Social institutions provide the framework for shared norms, values, and codes of conduct that regulate relationships among community members, including hunters, fishers, and agriculturalists.

These institutions are built upon collective memory, creativity, and learning, ensuring that individuals function effectively within a group.

They integrate ecological knowledge into societal practices, governing resource use and sustainable practices.

The passage highlights the role of social institutions in linking knowledge systems and resource management to societal norms and worldviews.

Thus, the correct answer is C (Social institutions).

100. **(C):** Local knowledge of land and animals is the most stable and enduring aspect of traditional ecological knowledge because:

It is rooted in direct observation and interaction with the environment over generations.

It forms the foundation upon which other scales, like resource management and social institutions, are built.

Even if broader societal structures or worldviews change, the core local ecological knowledge tends to persist due to its direct utility and empirical nature.

Thus, the correct answer is C (Local knowledge of land and animals).

Previous Years' Paper

National Testing Agency (NTA)

UGC-NET Junior Research Fellowship & Assistant Professor Eligibility Exam

Environmental Science, June-2023

(Exam held on 15-06-2023)

PAPER-II

1. Second law of thermodynamics states that

(*a*) Energy flows from higher concentration to lower concentration.

(*b*) Order becomes disorder during energy transformations.

(*c*) The quality of energy degrades as it is transformed.

(*d*) Degraded energy is entropy, dessipated as waste products or heat.

(*e*) Enthalpy is wasted in energy transformation.

Choose the **most appropriate** answer from the options given below:

A. (*a*), (*b*) and (*c*) only

B. (*b*), (*c*) and (*d*) only

C. (*a*), (*c*), (*d*) and (*e*) only

D. (*a*), (*b*), (*c*), (*d*) and (*e*) only

2. Arrange the following as a progression of relations from disciplinary reductionism to holism.

(*a*) Cross disciplinary (*b*) Disciplinary

(*c*) Interdisciplinary (*d*) Multi disciplinary

(*e*) Transdisciplinary

Choose the **correct** answer from the options given below:

A. (*b*), (*a*), (*c*), (*d*), (*e*)

B. (*e*), (*c*), (*d*), (*a*), (*b*)

C. (*e*), (*c*), (*a*), (*d*), (*b*)

D. (*b*), (*d*), (*a*), (*c*), (*e*)

3. Which one of the following gas was not released through volcanoes around 4 billion years ago?

(*a*) Hydrogen (*b*) Nitrogen

(*c*) Oxygen (*d*) Carbon dioxide

4. When reduction in the ambient temperature with height r, is greater than the change in temperature with height induced by a dry adiabatic process, r_d atmosphere is said to be

A. absolutely stable

B. dry neutral

C. absolutely unstable

D. conditionally unstable

5. Absolute humidity in atmosphere at 10°C is 5.0 g/m^3 and maximum amount of water air can hold at same temperature is 10 g/m^3. What will be the relative humidity at the same temperature?

A. ~20% B. ~200%

C. ~50% D. ~2%

6. Match List-I with List-II.

List-I (Satellites/ platforms)	List-II (Sensors)
(*a*) IRS-P6	I. Advanced space borne thermal emission and reflection radiometer (ASTER)

(*b*) Landsat 7 II. Advanced Wide Field Sensor (AWiFS)

(*c*) SPOT-4 III. Enhanced Thematic Mapper (ETM)

(*d*) TERRA IV. High Resolution Visible Infrared (HRVIR)

Choose the **correct** answer from the options given below:

	(*a*)	(*b*)	(*c*)	(*d*)
A.	IV	I	II	III
B.	IV	I	III	II
C.	II	III	IV	I
D.	II	III	I	IV

7. Which of the following are spatial resolutions of Terra/Aqua MODIS sensors?

(*a*) 250 m (*b*) 500 m
(*c*) 750 m (*d*) 1000 m
(*e*) 1500 m

Choose the **correct** answer from the options given below.

A. (*a*), (*b*) and (*c*) only
B. (*a*), (*b*) and (*d*) only
C. (*a*), (*b*) and (*e*) only
D. (*b*), (*c*) and (*d*) only

8. Match List-I with List-II.

List-I (Weather parameter)	**List-II (Weather symbol)**
(*a*) Light rain	I. 
(*b*) Ice pellets (sleet)	II. 
(*c*) Showers of hail	III. 
(*d*) Drifting or blowing snow	IV. 

Choose the **correct** answer from the options given below:

	(*a*)	(*b*)	(*c*)	(*d*)
A.	III	II	IV	I
B.	I	II	IV	III
C.	II	III	IV	I
D.	IV	II	I	III

9. The unit of *k*, rate constant for first order reaction will be:

A. mol cm^{-3} s^{-1} B. mol^{-1} cm^3 s^{-1}
C. s^{-1} D. mol^{-1} cm^3 s

10. Choose the Incorrect Statement:

A. For a system at equilibrium, chemical potential is same in all phases.
B. Gibb's free energy change is zero at equilibrium state of a system.
C. Gibb's free energy change is positive for reaction to occur spontaneously.
D. ΔG will become more negative with increasing temperature.

11. Which of the following species in a lake/pond not a proton accepter?

A. Al^{3+}
B. Natural organic matter
C. HS^-
D. $H_3SiO_4^-$

12. Which of the following is NOT involved required for photochemical smog formation in ambient atmosphere?

A. Volatile organic compounds
B. Nitric and Nitrogen dioxide
C. Sulphur dioxide
D. Ozone

13. Which of the following is a catalytically inactive (or reservoir) molecule containing chlorine in stratosphere?

A. HOCl
B. ClO
C. $ClONO_2$
D. Cl_2

14. Given below are two statements:

Statement I: Major emission of Sulphur into the atmosphere is in the form of SO_2 but longest lived reservoir is OCS.

Statement II: Sulphur in atmosphere leads to aerosol formation and clouds and therefore, cools the planet (Negative green house effect).

In the light of the above statements, choose the **most appropriate** answer from the options given below:

A. Both Statement I and Statement II are correct

B. Both Statement I and Statement II are incorrect

C. Statement I is correct but Statement II is incorrect

D. Statement I is incorrect but Statement II is correct.

15. Choose the correct statements about coagulation process.

(*a*) Coagulation makes smaller colloids to adhere to each other to form large floc particles

(*b*) Colloids are continually involved in Brownian moment.

(*c*) Colloids are stable because of their surface charge.

(*d*) Coagulants are preferably trivalent cations.

(*e*) Coagulants are soluble in neutral pH.

Choose the **most appropriate** answer from the options given below:

A. (*a*), (*b*) and (*d*) only

B. (*a*), (*b*), (*d*) and (*e*) only

C. (*a*), (*b*), (*c*) and (*d*) only

D. (*a*), (*c*), (*d*) and (*e*) only

16. Standard Bio-chemical oxygen demand test is performed in 300 ml BOD bottle at

A. 25°C after 5 days

B. 15°C after 5 days

C. 20°C after 5 days

D. ambient temperature after 5 days

17. Given below are two statements:

Statement I: Phosphorus cycle begins when phosphorous compounds leach from rocks and minerals over long period of time.

Statement II: Phosphorus is mainly taken up by producer organism in the organic form.

In the light of the above statements, choose the **correct** answer from the options given below:

A. Both Statement I and Statement II are true

B. Both Statement I and Statement II are false

C. Statement I is true, but Statement II is false

D. Statement I is false, but Statement II is true

18. Which of the following metal is NOT used in wood preservatives?

A. Cu B. Cr

C. As D. Pb

19. Match List-I with List-II.

List-I	List-II (Parameter)
(*a*) Spectrophotometer	I. M/z ratio measurement
(*b*) Ion chromatography	II. Conductance of ions
(*c*) ICPMS	III. Absorbance
(*d*) XRD	IV. *d*-spacing

Choose the **correct** answer from the options given below:

	(*a*)	(*b*)	(*c*)	(*d*)
A.	III	II	IV	I
B.	II	III	I	IV
C.	III	I	II	IV
D.	III	II	I	IV

20. Which of the following hypothesis account for the relationship of biodiversity to ecosystem functioning?

A. Climate stability hypothesis

B. Intermediate disturbance hypothesis

C. Redundancy hypothesis

D. Spatial heterogeneity hypothesis

21. Which of the following index is used for estimating population density?

A. Cycling Index

B. Biological Clock

C. Lotka Voltera Equation

D. Lincoln Index

22. The stress tolerant(s) species shall have the following life history strategy.

(*a*) Shoot morphology - dense canopy
(*b*) Flowering - Annual monocarpic
(*c*) Reproductive effort - small
(*d*) Growth rate - rapid
(*e*) Resource allocation to seed production - small

Choose the **most appropriate** answer from the options given below:

A. (*a*) and (*c*) only
B. (*b*) and (*e*) only
C. (*c*) and (*e*) only
D. (*a*) and (*d*) only

23. Which of the following food webs are defined on the basis of the impacts of species on the structure of community?

A. Connectedness webs
B. Energy flow food webs
C. Functional food webs
D. Community food webs

24. Who explained - "Succession is an extraordinarily mobile phenomenon whose processes are not to be stated as fixed laws, but only a general principles of exceedingly broad nature and whose results need not and frequently do not occur in any definite predictable way"?

A. F.E. Clement (Relay Floristics view)
B. F.E. Egler (Initial Floristics Composition view)
C. H.A. Gleason (Individualistic Concept)
D. D. Tilman (Resource-ratio hypothesis)

25. Given below are two statements: One is labelled as Assertion (A) and the other is labelled as Reason (R).

Assertion (A): The centers of the greatest biodiversity, the mega-biodiversity regions of the world, tend to be in the tropics.

Reason (R): Over long geological times, the tropical areas have had a more stable climate, never been glaciated, therefore, local species continued to thrive and live there itself.

In the light of the above statements, choose the **correct** answer from the options given below:

A. Both (A) and (R) are true and (R) is the correct explanation of (A)
B. Both (A) and (R) are true, but (R) is not the correct explanation of (A)
C. (A) is true, but (R) is false
D. (A) is false, but (R) is true

26. Given below are two statements:

Statement I: Ecosystems are closed to flow of energy, materials and biota and are tightly bound in space and time.

Statement II: There are five dynamic interactive controls, (i.e. local climate, supply of resources, functional groups of organisms, disturbance regimes and anthropogenic activities) regulating ecosystem processes.

In the light of the above statements, choose the **correct** answer from the options given below:

A. Both Statement I and Statement II are true
B. Both Statement I and Statement II are false
C. Statement I is true, but Statement II is false
D. Statement I is false, but Statement II is true

27. Match List-I with List-II.

List-I (Region of Himalayan)	**List-II (Characteristics taxa (Plant))**
(*a*) Palaearctic	I. Deodar
(*b*) Mediterranean	II. Rhododendrons
(*c*) Indo-Malayan	III. Dipterocarpus
(*d*) Indo-Chinese	IV. Hippophae

Choose the **correct** answer from the options given below:

	(*a*)	(*b*)	(*c*)	(*d*)
A.	I	II	III	IV
B.	IV	III	II	I
C.	IV	I	III	II
D.	II	I	IV	III

28. Dobzhansky's classifications of reproductive isolating mechanisms include:
(*a*) Habitat selection
(*b*) Flowering time
(*c*) Sexual isolation
(*d*) Isolation by pollinators
(*e*) Hybrid vigour

Choose the **most appropriate** answer from the options given below:
A. (*a*), (*b*), (*c*), (*e*) only
B. (*b*), (*c*), (*d*) and (*e*) only
C. (*a*), (*c*), (*d*) and (*e*) only
D. (*a*), (*b*), (*c*), (*d*) only

29. Different species resemble in ecological features but form similar looking vegetation in widely separated geographical regions by assuming similar life forms under the influence of extreme climatic conditions are known as:
A. Endemics
B. Convergences
C. Speciation
D. Adaptive radiation

30. Sciophytes are:
A. Sun adapted plants
B. Shade adapted plants
C. Snow adapted plants
D. Desert adapted plants

31. Which of the following is involved in denitrification process in terrestrial environment?
A. *Rhizobium*
B. *Spirillum lipoferum*
C. *Pseudomonas*
D. *Nitrosomonas*

32. Arrange the following components of Tropical Rain forest in decreasing order of organic carbon accumulation.
(*a*) Leaf (*b*) Litter
(*c*) Soil (*d*) Wood

Choose the **correct** answer from the options given below:
A. (*b*), (*a*), (*c*), (*d*) B. (*d*), (*c*), (*a*), (*b*)
C. (*c*), (*d*), (*b*), (*a*) D. (*a*), (*c*), (*b*), (*d*)

33. Which one of the following is a major feature of kandic sub-surface soil horizon?
A. Organic matter Fe and A1 oxides accumulation
B. Accumulation of low activity clays
C. Hardpan, strongly cemented by silica
D. Carbonate clays accumulation

34. Which of the following faults, responsible for earthquakes origin, is initiated only by tensile stress?
A. Normal fault B. Thrust fault
C. Strike slip fault D. Oblique slip fault

35. Which one of the following rock is formed at mid oceanic ridges?
A. Granite B. Rhyolite
C. Basalt D. Migmatite

36. Which one of the following has a composition of calcium phosphate?
A. Dolomite B. Calcite
C. Aragonite D. Apatite

37. Illites contain interlayer cations of:
A. Na B. K
C. Mg D. Fe

38. Arrange the following mass movements in increasing order of velocity.
(*a*) Rock fall (*b*) Earth flow
(*c*) Debris flow (*d*) Earth creep

Choose the **correct** answer from the options given below:
A. (*a*), (*b*), (*c*), (*d*)
B. (*d*), (*b*), (*c*), (*a*)
C. (*d*), (*a*), (*b*), (*c*)
D. (*b*), (*a*), (*c*), (*d*)

39. Pyroxene weathers to produce:

(*a*) Silica
(*b*) Fe-oxides
(*c*) Bicarbonate ion
(*d*) Smectite
(*e*) Kaolinite

Choose the **correct** answer from the options given below:

A. (*a*), (*b*), (*c*) and (*d*) only
B. (*a*), (*c*), (*d*) and (*e*) only
C. (*a*), (*b*) and (*c*) only
D. (*b*), (*c*) and (*e*) only

40. Match List-I with List-II.

List-I	List-II
(*a*) Precambrian	I. Miocene
(*b*) Palaeozoic	II. Proterozoic
(*c*) Mesozoic	III. Devonian
(*d*) Cenozoic	IV. Jurassic

Choose the **correct** answer from the options given below:

	(*a*)	(*b*)	(*c*)	(*d*)
A.	II	IV	I	III
B.	II	III	IV	I
C.	III	IV	I	II
D.	IV	I	II	III

41. Given below are two statements: One is labelled as Assertion (A) and the other is labelled as Reason (R)

Assertion (A): Glacial lakes get stratified during winters.

Reason (R): Water has maximum density at 4°C.

In the light of the above statements, choose the **correct** answer from the options given below

A. Both (A) and (R) are true and (R) is the correct explanation of (A)
B. Both (A) and (R) are true but (R) is not the correct explanation of (A)
C. (A) is true, but (R) is false
D. (A) is false, but (R) is true

42. Arrange the following metamorphic facies in increasing order of pressure.

(*a*) Greenschist
(*b*) Eclogite
(*c*) Albite-Epidote hornfels
(*d*) Blueschist

Choose the **correct** answer from the options given below:

A. (*b*), (*a*), (*c*), (*d*)
B. (*a*), (*b*), (*c*), (*d*)
C. (*a*), (*c*), (*d*), (*b*)
D. (*c*), (*a*), (*d*), (*b*)

43. The property of an aquifer that is measure of its ability to transmit water under a sloping piezometric surface is called:

A. Transmissivity
B. Porosity
C. Hydraulic conductivity
D. Hydraulic gradient

44. The strong and rapidly moving circumpolar upper westerly air circulation in a narrow belt of few kilometers width in the upper limit of troposphere is called as:

A. Westerly
B. Rossby Waves
C. Thermal circulation
D. Jet stream

45. Which of the following conditions are observed during the phenomenon of La Nina?

A. Warming in the Atlantic Ocean.
B. Water temperature in the eastern tropical pacific is cooler than average.
C. Warming in the eastern tropical pacific ocean.
D. Water temperature in the arctic ocean is cooler than the average.

46. Oil shales, which are sedimentary rocks, containing a mixture of hydrocarbon is collectively known as ________.

A. Gas Hydrates
B. Kerogen
C. Coal
D. Marsh Gas

47. Which test is not required for evaluating the properties of coal for coke making?
A. Gray King
B. Swelling Number
C. Gieseler Plastometric Test
D. Rock Eval pyrolysis

48. The increasing order of greenhouse gases in terms of the amount of extra warming they produce in earth's atmosphere is:
(*a*) CO_2 (*b*) CH_4
(*c*) N_2O (*d*) CFCs

Choose the **correct** answer from the options given below:
A. (*a*) < (*b*) < (*c*) < (*d*)
B. (*d*) < (*c*) < (*b*) < (*a*)
C. (*c*) < (*d*) < (*b*) < (*a*)
D. (*c*) < (*b*) < (*d*) < (*a*)

49. Given below are two statements:

Statement I: In terms of hydrocarbon component, natural gas as it exits from ground consist predominantly (60-90%) of CH_4 and other components include ethane, propone and two butane isomers.

Statement II: Enormous quantity of natural gas is held in methane hydrates (Clathrates) in ocean sediments and premafost.

In the light of the above statements, choose the **correct** answer from the options given below:
A. Both Statement I and Statement II are true
B. Both Statement I and Statement II are false
C. Statement I is true, but Statement II is false
D. Statement I is false, but Statement II is true

50. Fuel cell is a device that directly converts
A. Chemical energy into mechanical energy
B. Chemical energy into electric energy
C. Solar energy into electricity
D. Solar energy into mechanical energy

51. Coals are generally associated with
(*a*) Limestone (*b*) Sandstone
(*c*) Shale (*d*) Granite
(*e*) Slate

Choose the **most appropriate** answer from the options given below:
A. (*b*) and (*d*) only
B. (*b*) and (*c*) only
C. (*a*) and (*d*) only
D. (*b*) and (*e*) only

52. The energy that a windmill can gather is proportional to the
A. second power of wind speed (v^2)
B. square of its blade length
C. third power of blade length
D. wind speed (v)

53. Criteria pollutant under National Ambient Air Quality standards (NAAQ) are:
(*a*) SO_2 (*b*) NO_x
(*c*) NH_3 (*d*) O_3
(*e*) CO_2

Choose the **correct** answer from the options given below:
A. (*a*), (*b*), (*c*) and (*e*) only
B. (*a*), (*b*) and (*d*) only
C. (*a*), (*b*), (*c*) and (*d*) only
D. (*a*), (*b*), (*d*) and (*e*) only

54. Which of the following is not applicable to secondary air pollutants?
A. They are important with respect to human health.
B. They have undergone chemical/physical transformation in air.
C. They include both inorganic and organic species/compound.
D. They are non-hazardous air pollutants.

55. Air Pollution Control techniques applied to reduce gaseous pollutants in ambient atmosphere are:
(*a*) Cyclone collectors
(*b*) Limestone Injection multistage Burner in Thermal Power Plants

(*c*) Selective Catalytic Reduction (SCR) in thermal power plants.
(*d*) Electrostatic Precipitators in Thermal Power Plants
(*e*) Fabric bag filters

Choose the **most appropriate** answer from the options given below:
A. (*b*), (*c*) and (*d*) only
B. (*c*) and (*d*) only
C. (*b*), (*c*), and (*e*) only
D. (*b*) and (*d*) only

56. Sound pressure is equal to:
A. Total atmospheric pressure only
B. Total atmospheric pressure minus Barometric pressure only
C. Barometric pressure only
D. Sum of total atmospheric pressure and barometric pressure

57. "Gas bubble disease" is caused by:
A. excess nitrite in drinking water
B. excess dissolved oxygen in drinking water
C. excess carbon dioxide in drinking water
D. excess chlorine in drinking water

58. Calculate alkalinity of a water sample having a pH of nine (9) and no carbonate or other dissolved proton donors or acceptors.
A. $\sim 10^{-9}$ mol L^{-1}
B. $\sim 10^{-4.5}$ mol L^{-1}
C. ~ 10 μ mol L^{-1}
D. ~ 5 μ mol L^{-1}

59. Choose the correct statement(s)
(*a*) P occurs naturally in rocks and released in water by weathering.
(*b*) P exist as orthophosphate and organically bound phosphate in water.
(*c*) dissolved inorganic P is also referred as soluble reactive phosphorus.
(*d*) P is limiting nutrient in aquatic system.
(*e*) It is difficult to differentiate between Zooplankton-P, Bacterial-P, Algae-P and Inorganic-P.

Choose the most appropriate answer from the options given below:
A. (*a*), (*b*), (*d*) and (*e*) only
B. (*a*), (*b*), (*c*) and (*d*) only
C. (*a*), (*b*), (*c*), (*d*) and (*e*).
D. (*b*), (*c*) and (*d*) only

60. Given below are two statements: One is labelled as Assertion (A) and the other is labelled as Reason (R).

Assertion (A): Natural acidic soils are found more in tropics as a result of thousands of years of excessive weathering of soil minerals.
Reason (R): Year-round high temperature and high rainfall leaches all basic cations from primary rock forming minerals.

In the light of the above statements, choose the **most appropriate** answer from the options given below:
A. Both (A) and (R) are correct and (R) is the correct explanation of (A)
B. Both (A) and (R) are correct but (R) is not the correct explanation of (A)
C. (A) is correct, but (R) is not correct
D. (A) is not correct, but (R) is correct

61. Which of the following does not fall under the category of ionizing radiations?
A. Ultraviolet
B. X-rays
C. Microwave
D. Gamma rays

62. The Gaussian Plume dispersion model is applicable only when.
(*a*) Pollutant is conservative.
(*b*) Rate of emission of pollutant is constant.
(*c*) Emission comes from actual height of stack.
(*d*) Pollutants are absorbed, not reflected back, after hitting the ground.
(*e*) Temporal variations in wind speed are considered.

Choose the **most appropriate** answer from the options given below:
A. (*a*), (*c*) and (*e*) only
B. (*a*), (*b*), (*c*) and (*d*) only
C. (*a*) and (*b*) only
D. (*b*) and (*d*) only

63. Given below are two statements:

Statement I: Process of incineration that destroys highly toxic and hazardous organic waste differs from municipal solid waste incineration where energy is often produced.

Statement II: Incineration process cannot be used with waste that have high concentration of water and non-combustible solids.

In the light of the above statements, choose the **correct** answer from the options

A. Both Statement I and Statement II are true
B. Both Statement I and Statement II are false
C. Statement I is true, but Statement II is false
D. Statement I is false, but Statement II is true

64. In waste pollution prevention hierarchy, arrange following from the most preferred to the least preferred options.

(*a*) Waste concentration
(*b*) Waste separation
(*c*) Recycling or Reuse
(*d*) Waste treatment
(*e*) Land filling

Choose the **correct** answer from the options given below:

A. (*a*), (*b*), (*c*), (*d*), (*e*)
B. (*b*), (*a*), (*c*), (*d*), (*e*)
C. (*c*), (*a*), (*b*), (*d*), (*e*)
D. (*c*), (*b*), (*a*), (*d*), (*e*)

65. The term used to describe the act of recovering materials from the waste stream and reprocessing them so that they can be used as raw material for new applications is called as

A. Reusing B. Remanufacturing
C. Recycling D. Repairing

66. The input approaches in the strategies for reducing solid waste do not involve:

A. Reduced consumption
B. Increased product durability
C. Decreased materials in product
D. Environmentally safe deposal of waste

67. Which of the following is dominantly released during third stage (anaerobic) of decomposition in municipal landfill?

A. Ammonia B. Aldehyde
C. Acetic Acid D. Methane

68. ______ technique in waste management is mainly accomplished in situ and include soil washing and the extraction of contaminant vapour from soil for highly volatile, water-insoluble contaminants such as gasoline.

A. In situ containment
B. Immobilization
C. Mobilization
D. Vitrification

69. Excavated pits, used for solid waste disposal, lined with impermeable synthetic liner and thick impermeable layers of clay are an example of

A. Sanitary landfills
B. Secured landfills
C. Underground dumps
D. Composting dumps

70. The use of plants to absorb and accumulate hazardous materials from the soil is termed as

A. Bioremediation
B. Phytoremediation
C. Biodegradation
D. Biotransformation

71. In an idealized Environmental Impact Assessment (EIA) process, determining the need for EIA by the regulations operating in the country at the time of assessment for the project that may have significant impacts are covered in the following step of the EIA:

A. Decision making
B. Screening
C. Scoping
D. Environmental Statement Review

72. "The formalized, systematic and comprehensive process of evaluating the environmental impacts of a policy, programme, plan or its alternatives as well as using the findings in publicly accountable decision making is called:
A. Environmental Impact Assessment (EIA)
B. Integrated Impact Assessment (IIA)
C. Ecological Impact Assessment (ECIA)
D. Strategic Environmental Impact Assessment (SEIA)

73. Match List-I with List-II.

	List-I	List-II
(*a*)	Biological Diversity Act	I. 1972
(*b*)	Environmental (Protection) Act	II. 1982
(*c*)	Indian Forest Act (Revised)	III. 1986
(*d*)	Wildlife Protection Act	IV. 2002

Choose the **correct** answer from the options given below:

	(*a*)	(*b*)	(*c*)	(*d*)
A.	IV	III	I	II
B.	IV	II	I	III
C.	IV	III	II	I
D.	III	IV	II	I

74. In dose-response curve of chemical substances, there exists a dose below which none of the animal is affected, which is called as:
A. Absorbed dose
B. Threshold dose
C. Acceptable Daily Intake (ADI)
D. Toxicity Reference Dose (RfD)

75. Life cycle assessment of a product includes:
(*a*) Raw material extraction
(*b*) Product manufacturing
(*c*) Product remanufacture
(*d*) Packaging and distribution
(*e*) Product disposal

Choose the **most appropriate** answer from the options given below
A. (*b*) and (*d*) only
B. (*b*), (*d*) and (*e*) only
C. (*a*), (*b*) and (*e*) only
D. (*a*), (*b*), (*c*), (*d*) and (*e*)

76. In a frequency distribution table, having equally spaced class intervals, which of the following measure of central tendency requires three class interval frequencies for its estimation?
A. Mean B. Median
C. Mode D. Harmonic Mean

77. If for a data series the value of skewness is –1, then which of the following relationship between Median (Md) and Third Quartile (Q_3) holds True?
A. $Md - Q_3 = 1$ B. $Md - Q_3 = 0$
C. $Md - Q_3 = -1$ D. $Md - Q_3 = -1.5$

78. Which of the following condition is FALSE from the validity point of view with respect to Chi-square as a test for 'goodness of fit'?
A. The sample observations should be independent
B. Constraints on cell frequencies, if any, should be linear (i.e. sum of observed frequencies should be equal to expected frequencies)
C. N, the total frequency should be large (> 50)
D. Some of the cell frequencies can be less than 5.

79. Which of the following statements are true with respect to stationary and stable population?
(*a*) A stationary population is not always stable.
(*b*) A stationary population is always stable.
(*c*) A stable population need not be stationary.
(*d*) In stationary population, the rate of overall change in the population is zero
(*e*) In stable population, the rate of overall change in population is constant (not necessary zero)

Choose the **correct** answer from the options given below:
A. (*a*) and (*c*) only
B. (*b*) and (*e*) only
C. (*b*), (*c*), (*d*) and (*e*) only
D. (*a*), (*c*) and (*e*) only

80. Match List-I with List-II.

List-I (Measure)	List-II (Idea regarding distribution)
(*a*) Central Tendency	I. Degree of spread
(*b*) Dispersion	II. Idea about tail of distribution
(*c*) Skewness	III. Idea about peakness of the curve
(*d*) Kurtosis	IV. Degree of closeness

Choose the **correct** answer from the options given below:

	(*a*)	(*b*)	(*c*)	(*d*)
A.	IV	I	II	III
B.	I	IV	III	II
C.	I	III	IV	II
D.	III	IV	II	I

81. In the application of Chi-square distribution for test of association between two characteristic (say Gender and discomfort due to humidity) arrange following steps in correct sequence

(*a*) Compare the calculated value of χ^2-statistic with tabulated value

(*b*) Set up the Null Hypothesis

(*c*) Tabulate data in the contingency table

(*d*) Divide square difference of expected frequency from observed frequency and add the values at each data point

(*e*) Calculate the expected frequencies.

Choose the **correct** answer from the options given below:

A. (*d*), (*b*), (*c*), (*e*), (*a*)

B. (*b*), (*c*), (*e*), (*d*), (*a*)

C. (*b*), (*c*), (*d*), (*e*), (*a*)

D. (*a*), (*b*), (*c*), (*e*), (*d*)

82. Choose the correct statement(s):

(*a*) O_3 in stratosphere is not completely effective in shielding us from UV-B

(*b*) UV-A is biologically least harmful.

(*c*) Chapman mechanism deals with only O_3 formation in stratosphere.

(*d*) Sunscreen lotions either reflect or absorb or scatter UV-B and UV-A

(*e*) UV-B helps in dissociation of O_3 molecule in stratosphere.

Choose the **correct** answer from the options given below.

A. (*b*), (*c*), (*d*) and (*e*) only

B. (*a*), (*b*), (*d*) and (*e*) only

C. (*a*), (*c*), (*d*) and (*e*) only

D. (*a*), (*b*) and C only

83. Wangari Muta Maathai, a Kenyan social, environmental and Political activist, Nobel Prize Winner, in the field of Environment Protection was related to:

A. Green rating for integrated habitat assessment

B. Green Peace Movement

C. Green Accounting

D. Green Belt Movement

84. Which of the following is NOT listed as National Mission that comes under National Action Plan for Climate Change (NAPCC)?

A. National Mission for a Clean India

B. National Mission for a Green India

C. National Mission for sustainable habitat

D. National Mission for sustaining Himalayan ecosystem

85. Which one of the following conservation programs recently (April 01, 2023) completed 50 years?

A. Project Elephant

B. Project Hangul

C. Project Snow Leopard

D. Project Tiger

86. Which of the following Sustainable Development Goals (SDGs) focuses on reduced inequalities?

A. SDG-10 B. SDG-3

C. SDG-5 D. SDG-7

87. Match List-I with List-II.

List-I	List-II
(*a*) Disaster Management Act	I. 1987
(*b*) Kyoto Protocol	II. 2008

(*c*) Montreal Protocol — III. 2005
(*d*) National Action Plan on climate change — IV 1997

Choose the **correct** answer from the options given below:

	(*a*)	(*b*)	(*c*)	(*d*)
A.	I	II	III	IV
B.	II	III	IV	I
C.	III	IV	I	II
D.	IV	III	II	I

88. Match List-I with List-II.

List-I (National Parks)	List-II (States)
(*a*) Balaphakram National Park	I. Manipur
(*b*) Dampa National Park	II. Meghalaya
(*c*) Intanki National Park	III. Mizoram
(*d*) Keibul National Park	IV. Nagaland

Choose the **correct** answer from the options given below:

	(*a*)	(*b*)	(*c*)	(*d*)
A.	IV	I	II	III
B.	II	III	IV	I
C.	II	III	I	IV
D.	II	I	III	IV

89. Which of the following disasters are linked with nuclear accident?
(*a*) Bhopal Disaster, 1984
(*b*) Chernobyl Disaster, 1986
(*c*) Fukushima Disaster, 2011
(*d*) Love Canal Disaster, 1978
(*e*) Minamata Disaster, 1956

Choose the **correct** answer from the options given below:
A. (*a*) and (*b*) only B. (*b*) and (*c*) only
C. (*c*) and (*d*) only D. (*d*) and (*e*) only

90. In epidemiology, the study which first identify a group of individuals who have a specific disease, then attempt to ascertain commonalities in the exposure that group have experienced are referred to as:
A. Toxicology study B. Correlation study
C. Cohort study D. Case-control study

Directions (Qs. No. 91 - 95): *Read the following passage carefully and answer the questions that follows:*

Environmental factors may create conditions that are either negative or positive for various life forms. Free oxygen supercharged respiration and made complex life possible as atmospheric O_2 became increasingly available between 2.2 billion years(by) and 55 million years(my) ago. The O_2 approached todays levels around 550 my, when complex life began to get larger. The O_2 levels reached their highest (>1/3rd of all atmospheric gases) for all time on earth around 300 my. Bugs became bigger i.e. land arthropods were less-limited in size. Massive millipedes grew to a length of over three meters and half a meter wide. This could not happen today, it is obviously genetically possible, but it is not environmentally-possible. The bodies of spiders were as large as man's head; today's O_2 levels do not permit such a physiological possibility. Cockroaches were everywhere, and some were really large (> 10 inches long and 5 inches wide). Predatory dragonflies, flying up into new highly-oxygenated aerial environment, had wingspans exceeding two meters. The First reptiles and the amniotes egg also appeared at this time; the moisture-proof skin and egg allowed these vertebrates to truly become land animals. The warm and moist tropical environment of the Carboniferous Period (354-290 my) with the high oxygen levels (nearly 40% higher than today), gave way to a cooler and drier Permian Period (290-250 my); reptiles continued to flourish. A slight drop in atmospheric oxygen changed the conditions of life for the large land arthropods. Life goes on only if the specific conditions of life can be found. Even though there was no mass extinction at the Carboniferous-Permian transition, the high-atmospheric oxygen-dependent large land arthropods of the Carboniferous Period were never to be seen again. Smaller arthropods continue to exist in the lower atmospheric oxygen conditions.

91. Air was heavier during
A. Carboniferous Period
B. Permian Period
C. Neogene Period
D. Jurassic Period

92. Carboniferous period was characterized by:
A. extensive mid latitude forests and small sized arthropods.
B. extensive desertification on the earth and absence of reptiles
C. extensive mid latitude forests and absence of reptiles
D. extensive mid latitude forests and large bodied arthropods.

93. Large bodied land arthropods got extinct from the blue planet because of:
A. Habitat fragmentation
B. Rise in temperature
C. Drop in atmospheric O_2 levels
D. Mass extinction

94. Present day atmosphere O_2 levels do not permit encourage large bodied organisms due to:
A. Habitat availability
B. Physiological function restrictions
C. Life form variabilities
D. Mass extinction

95. Atmospheric O_2 levels reached their highest levels during the geological time on earth ______ ago.
A. 2.2 billion years ago
B. 550 million years ago
C. 330 million years ago
D. 250 million years ago

Directions (Qs. No. 96 - 100): *Read the following passage carefully and answer the questions that follows:*

Earth quakes are a series of vibrations and shock waves induced by movement along faults, landslides, and other triggering mechanisms. A single earthquake may release energy equivalent to hundreds or thousands of nuclear blasts and may cost billions of rupees in damages, not to mention the toll in human suffering. The energy released by an earthquake, the magnitude, is measured on the Richter scale. In a city X, an earthquake of 8.5 on a Richter Scale caused significant havoc. The total economic loss was estimated to be around 20,000 crore and about 2000 individuals were affected severely, 500 extremely, and there were 50 casualties counted. The proportion of economic loss for building was 75% and rest was on livestocks. Based on the above mentioned facts answer the following questions.

96. The measure of 8.5 on a Richter scale is an example of which data type?
A. Categorical
B. Discrete
C. Continuous
D. Ratio

97. The data type for affected individuals (severely, extremely, casualties) is an example of which data type?
A. Binomial
B. Nominal
C. Continuous
D. Ordinal

98. Which of the following is most suitable for presentation of the percent distribution of economic loss due to building damage and livestocks?
A. Pie-chart
B. Line chart
C. Bar chart
D. Histogram

99. What is the estimated cost in crore of the loss due to buildings and livestocks, respectively?
A. 10,000 and 10,000 respectively
B. 12,000 and 8,000 respectively
C. 15,000 and 5,000 respectively
D. 11,000 and 9,000 respectively

100. If economic loss (e-loss) is expressed in terms of linearity with building loss (b-loss) and livestock loss (l-loss) as

$$\text{e-loss} = \text{b-loss} + \text{l-loss} + \varepsilon(\text{E-error})$$

then this relationship can be modelled by which of following regression analysis?
A. Curvilinear regression
B. Binary logistic regression
C. Simple linear regression
D. Multiple linear regression

ANSWERS

1. (D):

(*a*) **Energy flows from higher concentration to lower concentration:** It seems to allude to the general concept of energy flow, potentially related to diffusion or movement of particles from areas of higher concentration to lower concentration.

(*b*) **Order becomes disorder during energy transformations:** The second law states that the entropy, or disorder, of a closed system tends to increase over time. As energy undergoes transformations within a system, the overall orderliness or organization tends to decrease, leading to increased disorder or entropy.

(*c*) **The quality of energy degrades as it is transformed:** Energy transformations are never 100% efficient; some energy is lost as heat during these processes. The decrease in the usefulness or quality of energy is reflected in the second law's assertion.

(*d*) **Degraded energy is entropy, dissipated as waste products or heat:** In the context of thermodynamics, entropy is a measure of the system's disorder. When energy is transformed and becomes less usable, it is often dissipated as waste heat, contributing to an increase in the system's entropy.

(*e*) **Enthalpy is wasted in energy transformation:** Enthalpy is a significant consideration in thermodynamics, the second law is more concerned with the overall increase in entropy and the degradation of energy quality. Enthalpy itself is "wasted," and its transformation may contribute to overall energy losses.

2. (D):

(*b*) **Disciplinary:** At the foundational level of knowledge creation, the disciplinary approach entails a specialized focus within a single field. This method allows for in-depth exploration within a well-defined scope.

(*d*) **Multidisciplinary:** Progressing beyond the confines of a single discipline, the multidisciplinary approach involves the collaborative utilization of tools and insights from various domains to address complex challenges.

(*a*) **Cross-disciplinary:** The cross-disciplinary approach involves the application of concepts from one discipline to solve problems in another, creating connections between seemingly unrelated fields.

(*c*) **Interdisciplinary:** Interdisciplinary collaboration unfolds as disciplines engage in dynamic dialogue, transcending traditional boundaries to address shared challenges.

(*e*) **Transdisciplinary:** The transdisciplinary approach signifies the dissolution of disciplinary silos, giving rise to a new entity forged from diverse perspectives. It is not merely about borrowing from different fields but co-creating a revolutionary understanding of the universe, emphasizing the synergy inherent in diverse perspectives.

3. (C): Around 4 billion years ago, during the early stages of Earth's formation, volcanic activity played a crucial role in shaping the atmosphere. At that time, the atmosphere was primarily composed of gases released from volcanic out gassing. The gases released included water vapour (which can contribute to hydrogen), nitrogen, carbon dioxide, and trace amounts of other gases. Given this context, the gas that was likely not released through volcanoes around 4 billion years ago is Oxygen. Oxygen became a significant component of the

Earth's atmosphere much later, through processes such as photosynthesis by early photosynthetic organisms.

4. (C) **5. (C)** **6. (C)**

7. (B):

(*a*) **250 m:** This spatial resolution of 250 meters means that the sensor can distinguish objects and features on the Earth's surface that are as small as 250 meters. This high spatial resolution is particularly useful for applications that require detailed monitoring, such as land cover classification, urban area studies, and identification of smaller features on the Earth's surface.

(*b*) **500 m:** A spatial resolution of 500 meters indicates that the sensor can discern details down to 500 meters on the Earth's surface. This resolution strikes a balance between finer details and a broader view, making it suitable for various applications, including land cover analysis, vegetation monitoring, and studies that require a moderate level of detail.

(*d*) **1000 m:** With a spatial resolution of 1000 meters, the sensor provides a coarser view of the Earth's surface. While this resolution may not capture fine details, it is valuable for applications that involve broader-scale assessments, such as regional climate studies, large-scale land cover mapping, and oceanographic analyses.

8. (A) **9. (C)**

10. (C): The incorrect statement among the given options is that "Gibb's free energy change is positive for the reaction to occur spontaneously." It represents a misconception in thermodynamics. In the context of chemical reactions, the Gibbs free energy change (ΔG) serves as a crucial indicator of spontaneity. Contrary to the statement, a positive ΔG does not favor spontaneous reactions; rather, it suggests that the reaction is non-spontaneous under standard conditions and requires an external energy input to proceed.

11. (A): Al^{3+}, pertains to aluminum ions, and it is accurate to assert that aluminum ions do not typically act as proton acceptors in the traditional Brønsted-Lowry acid-base framework. In aqueous environments, aluminum ions exhibit Lewis acid behaviour by accepting electron pairs in coordination and complexation reactions. However, their role in proton acceptance is limited, and they are not conventionally involved in transferring protons (H^+) in acid-base reactions. Aluminum ions play crucial roles in geochemical processes, often forming complexes with ligands and contributing to the overall chemistry of aquatic systems.

12. (C): In the formation of photochemical smog in the ambient atmosphere, the species that is not directly involved or required is sulphur dioxide (SO_2). Photochemical smog primarily arises from the complex interactions between volatile organic compounds (VOCs), nitric oxide (NO), nitrogen dioxide (NO_2), and ozone (O_3) in the presence of sunlight. Volatile organic compounds, released from various sources such as vehicle exhaust and industrial activities, undergo photochemical reactions in the atmosphere. However, sulphur dioxide, while a notable air pollutant with its environmental implications, is not a primary contributor to the formation of photochemical smog.

13. (C): In the context of stratospheric chemistry and ozone depletion, the catalytically inactive (or reservoir) molecule containing chlorine is $ClONO_2$. Chlorine nitrate is a crucial player in atmospheric processes, acting as a temporary reservoir for reactive chlorine species. In the stratosphere, where ozone layer depletion occurs, chlorine compounds are implicated in catalytic cycles that lead to ozone destruction. However, chlorine nitrate is considered inactive because it provides a storage form for chlorine without directly participating in these catalytic ozone-depleting reactions.

14. **(A): Statement I:** This statement accurately captures the primary source of sulphur emissions into the atmosphere, which is sulphur dioxide (SO_2). SO_2 is a major emission from various sources, including industrial activities and combustion processes. The statement then correctly identifies carbonyl sulfide (OCS) as the longest-lived reservoir of sulphur in the atmosphere. OCS has a longer atmospheric lifetime compared to other sulfur compounds, and it serves as a stable reservoir that participates in the complex sulphur cycle.

Statement II: This statement is also correct, although it simplifies a more complex scenario. Sulphur emissions, primarily in the form of sulphur dioxide, can lead to the formation of sulphate aerosols. These aerosols have a cooling effect on the climate by reflecting sunlight back into space. Sulphur dioxide, originating from both natural and human-related sources, plays a significant role in the Earth's climate system. Sulphate aerosols not only directly scatter sunlight but also enhance cloud formation. Sulphate particles act as nuclei around which water can condense, promoting cloud development. These clouds, seeded by sulphate aerosols, exhibit increased reflectivity, further contributing to the cooling of the planet.

15. **(C):**

(*a*) This statement accurately describes the process of coagulation, where destabilization of colloidal particles leads to their aggregation and the formation of larger flocs. Coagulants are added to neutralize the surface charges on colloids, allowing them to come together and form larger, settleable particles.

(*b*) Brownian motion refers to the random movement of colloidal particles suspended in a fluid medium due to collisions with surrounding molecules. This constant motion is a characteristic feature of colloids and plays a role in their stability.

(*c*) Colloidal stability is indeed often related to surface charge. Colloids carry a surface charge, preventing them from agglomerating due to electrostatic repulsion. Coagulation involves overcoming this repulsion by adding coagulants (often trivalent cations) to neutralize the charges and allow particles to come closer.

(*d*) Coagulants are often trivalent cations (charged species with a valence of 3^+), which can neutralize the negative charges on colloidal particles, leading to coagulation. Trivalent cations, such as aluminum or iron ions, are commonly used coagulants in water treatment processes. These ions neutralize the negatively charged colloidal particles, promoting their aggregation and forming larger, settleable flocs.

16. **(C):** The standard Biochemical Oxygen Demand (BOD) test is a crucial tool in assessing the organic pollution level in water, indicating the amount of dissolved oxygen consumed by microorganisms during the microbial decomposition of organic matter. In this standardized procedure, a 300 ml BOD bottle is employed, and the test is conducted at a controlled temperature of 20°C over a 5-day incubation period. This specific set of conditions allows for a consistent and comparable measurement of the biodegradable organic content in water samples.

17. **(C): Statement I:** This statement accurately describes the initiation of the phosphorus cycle. Phosphorus, an essential element for life, is released into the environment through the gradual weathering of rocks and minerals. This process makes phosphorus compounds available in the soil and water, becoming a fundamental source for the subsequent biological uptake by plants and other organisms.

Statement II: This statement is false. In the context of the phosphorus cycle, plants (producer organisms) predominantly absorb inorganic phosphorus, particularly as phosphate ions (PO_4^{3-}), from the soil. While organic forms of phosphorus do exist, such as in organic matter and decaying organic material, plants typically assimilate inorganic phosphate for their metabolic processes and growth.

18. **(D):** Lead (Pb) is conspicuously absent from the repertoire of metals commonly employed in wood preservatives. Wood preservatives play a crucial role in protecting wood from decay, insect infestation, and environmental degradation. While copper (Cu), chromium (Cr), and arsenic (As) are frequently utilized metals in wood treatment formulations, lead is notably excluded. The decision to omit lead from wood preservatives is rooted in its well-documented toxicity, posing significant risks to both human health and the environment.

19. **(D)**

20. **(C):** The Redundancy Hypothesis represents a nuanced perspective on the intricate interplay between biodiversity and ecosystem functioning. At its core, this hypothesis contends that ecosystems possess a degree of resilience against species loss when there is functional redundancy, emphasizing the redundancy of ecological roles or functions among different species. In essence, if one species providing a specific function is lost due to factors like disturbances or environmental changes, another species with analogous functional traits can step in to fulfill that role. This redundancy in functional traits across diverse species acts as a safety net, maintaining overall ecosystem functionality even in the face of biodiversity changes.

21. **(D):** The Lincoln Index is a method employed for estimating population density, particularly in wildlife ecology and conservation studies. Named after American statistician Charles Lincoln, this index involves capturing and marking a portion of the population, releasing them back into the environment, and then recapturing a sample later. The formula for the Lincoln Index is derived from the ratio of the marked individuals in the first sample to the total number of individuals in the second sample. By assuming that the proportion of marked individuals in the recaptured sample is representative of the entire population, the Lincoln Index provides an estimate of population density.

22. **(C):**

(*c*) **Reproductive effort - small:** Stress-tolerant (S) species exhibit a life history strategy characterized by a small reproductive effort. This means that they allocate fewer resources to reproduction compared to other species. In stressful or resource-limited environments, where the competition for resources is high, stress-tolerant species prioritize their own survival over investing heavily in reproduction.

(*e*) **Resource allocation to seed production - small:** Stress-tolerant species typically invest fewer resources in seed production. Producing seeds is a resource-intensive process, and stress-tolerant species opt for a strategy that minimizes this investment. By allocating fewer resources to seed production, these species prioritize resource conservation for their own maintenance and resilience in environments where resources are limited or unpredictable.

23. **(C):** Functional food webs are characterized by their focus on the impacts of species on the structure of a community, emphasizing the functional roles and interactions among organisms within an ecosystem. Unlike energy flow food webs that primarily highlight the transfer of energy through trophic levels or connectedness webs that emphasize linkages among species, functional food webs delve into the specific ecological functions each species performs within the community. These functions encompass a spectrum of roles, such as pollination, decomposition, nutrient cycling, and other ecological processes that contribute to the overall structure and functioning of an ecosystem.

24. **(C):** The quote encapsulates the perspective of H.A. Gleason, a proponent of the Individualistic Concept in ecology. Gleason argued against a deterministic, fixed-law view of ecological succession, proposing that ecological communities do not follow rigid, predictable trajectories during the process of succession. According to Gleason, the outcomes of succession are influenced by a myriad of factors and are contingent on the unique attributes and interactions of individual species.

25. **(A):** The assertion that mega-biodiversity regions are concentrated in the tropics is a well-established and widely recognized ecological pattern. The tropics, particularly regions near the equator, are characterized by an exceptional diversity of species across various taxa, including plants, animals, and microorganisms. This high biodiversity is attributed to a combination of factors, and the reason provided (Reason R) offers a plausible explanation for this phenomenon.

Reason (R) highlights the geological history of tropical areas, emphasizing their long-term stability and the absence of glaciations. Unlike temperate and Polar Regions that have experienced significant climatic fluctuations, tropical regions have maintained relatively consistent and favourable climatic conditions over extended geological periods. This stability has allowed local species to evolve and adapt to their specific ecological niches, leading to the accumulation of diverse and specialized life forms.

26. **(D):** Statement I is false because ecosystems are not closed systems. Ecosystems are, in fact, open systems that exchange energy, materials, and organisms with their external environment. Energy flows into ecosystems from the sun and is eventually lost as heat, while materials, such as nutrients, cycle within and between ecosystems. The movement of biota, including the migration of species, also contributes to the dynamic nature of ecosystems. Therefore, the concept of ecosystems being closed is inaccurate.

Statement II is accurate. Ecosystem processes are regulated by a set of dynamic and interactive controls. Climate influences temperature, precipitation, and other environmental factors that shape the conditions within an ecosystem. The availability of essential resources, such as water, nutrients, and sunlight, plays a crucial role in determining the structure and productivity of ecosystems. The composition and interactions among different species, organized into functional groups based on their roles in the ecosystem, influence ecosystem processes.

27. **(C)**

28. **(D):**

(*a*) **Habitat selection,** the first mechanism, underscores the tendency of species to occupy distinct ecological niches, minimizing encounters between potentially interbreeding individuals. This segregation ensures that distinct habitats act as effective barriers to reproduction, reducing the chances of hybridization.

(*b*) **Flowering time,** primarily applicable to plants, represents another layer of reproductive isolation. Different species may exhibit significant temporal disparities in their flowering periods, ensuring that pollen transfer and fertilization occur within conspecific populations.

(*c*) **Sexual isolation,** the third mechanism, encapsulates an array of factors that hinder successful mating attempts between individuals of different species. This can involve physical, behavioural, or chemical barriers that render mating incompatible.

(*d*) **Isolation by pollinators,** the fourth mechanism, is particularly relevant for plant species relying on specific pollinators for successful reproduction. If a particular pollinator, such as a bee species, is adapted to pollinate a specific plant species, it might not effectively transfer pollen between different plant species, thereby enforcing reproductive isolation.

29. (B): Convergences represent a fascinating phenomenon in ecology where disparate species, facing analogous environmental challenges in widely separated geographical regions, independently evolve similar adaptations, morphological traits, and ecological strategies. This process is driven by the selective pressures imposed by comparable environmental conditions, such as extreme climates, which necessitate the development of convergent traits for survival. Despite lacking a shared evolutionary history or ancestry, these species converge towards similar ecological features, leading to the creation of vegetation that displays remarkable resemblances.

30. (B): Sciophytes, or shade-adapted plants, represent a diverse group of plant species that have evolved specific features and strategies to thrive in environments characterized by reduced light availability. The adaptations of sciophytes are a response to the challenges posed by shaded conditions, where access to sunlight is limited due to factors such as the presence of taller vegetation, dense canopies, or structures that cast shadows. These plants have developed morphological, physiological, and anatomical characteristics to optimize their performance under low-light conditions.

31. (C): In the terrestrial environment, the denitrification process, which is the conversion of nitrate (NO_3^-) and nitrite (NO_2^-) into nitrogen gas (N_2 or other gaseous nitrogen oxides, is primarily facilitated by bacteria, with *Pseudomonas* being a significant player in this biochemical pathway. *Pseudomonas* species are known for their versatility and metabolic diversity, including their ability to carry out denitrification. During denitrification, these bacteria use nitrate as a terminal electron acceptor in the absence of oxygen, leading to the reduction of nitrate to nitrogen gas or other nitrogenous compounds. This process plays a crucial role in the nitrogen cycle, contributing to nitrogen loss from the soil and influencing nitrogen availability for plants.

32. (B):

(*d*) **Wood:** Trees in tropical rainforests are substantial carbon sinks. The wood biomass of trees stores a significant amount of organic carbon. As trees grow, they absorb carbon dioxide from the atmosphere through photosynthesis and convert it into organic compounds.

(*c*) **Soil:** The soil in tropical rainforests contains a substantial amount of organic carbon derived from decomposed plant and animal material. The high biodiversity and rapid turnover of vegetation contribute to the continuous cycling of organic matter, enriching the soil with carbon compounds.

(*a*) **Leaf:** While leaves contribute to organic carbon through photosynthesis, they are relatively short-lived compared to wood. Leaves undergo rapid turnover, and the majority of the carbon they contain is released back into the ecosystem through decomposition.

(*b*) **Litter:** Litter consists of partially decomposed organic matter, including fallen leaves, branches, and other plant debris. While it contributes to organic carbon, it represents a stage in the decomposition process where materials are not fully broken down. As such, the carbon content in litter is lower compared to standing wood and soil.

33. (B): The Kandic sub-surface soil horizon is a distinctive feature within the broader category of Kandic soils, commonly encountered in tropical and subtropical regions. What sets the kandic horizon apart is its notable accumulation of low-activity clays, with kaolinite being a prominent example. Low-activity clays have specific mineralogical and chemical properties that impact soil behaviour. They possess a lower capacity for retaining water and nutrients compared to high-activity clays. This characteristic influences the overall fertility of the soil, making the kandic horizon less efficient in holding onto essential elements crucial for plant growth. The presence of low-activity clays also affects the soil's structure, influencing its porosity and drainage characteristics.

34. (A): A normal fault is a geological structure responsible for earthquake initiation and is characterized by movements primarily caused by tensile stress within the Earth's crust. This fault type occurs in response to the extensional forces acting on the crust, leading to the downward movement of the hanging wall relative to the footwall. Tensile stress creates a situation where the Earth's crust is being pulled apart, resulting in the formation of a fault zone with a steeply inclined fault plane. As the rocks on either side of the fault adjust to accommodate this extension, earthquakes can occur due to the sudden release of accumulated stress.

35. (C): Basalt is the predominant rock formed at mid-oceanic ridges, which are underwater mountain ranges where tectonic plates diverge. The process responsible for the creation of basaltic rocks at these ridges is known as seafloor spreading. As tectonic plates move apart, magma rises from the mantle to fill the gap, solidifying and forming new oceanic crust. Basalt is an extrusive igneous rock rich in iron and magnesium, with a fine-grained texture resulting from rapid cooling at the Earth's surface. It is dark in color and contains minerals such as pyroxene and plagioclase feldspar.

36. (D): Apatite, a mineral renowned for its calcium phosphate composition, is a crucial component in both geological and biological contexts. Its chemical formula, often represented as $Ca_5(PO_4)3(F,Cl,OH)$, underscores its structural makeup, which includes calcium and phosphate along with varying amounts of fluorine, chlorine, or hydroxide ions. Biologically, apatite plays a fundamental role as the primary mineral component in the hard tissues of vertebrates, notably in bones and teeth. Its presence in biological structures provides the necessary rigidity and strength to support skeletal frameworks. Geologically, apatite is found in a variety of rocks, spanning sedimentary, metamorphic, and igneous formations.

37. (B): Illite, a common clay mineral, exhibits an interlayer structure characterized by the presence of potassium (K) cations. It belongs to the group of mica-like clay minerals and is often found in sedimentary rocks, shales, and soils. The interlayer cations in illite contribute to its unique crystal lattice arrangement, where the potassium ions occupy the spaces between the mineral layers. The crystal structure of illite is composed of layers of tetrahedral and octahedral sheets, forming a sandwich-like arrangement.

38. (B):

(*d*) **Earth Creep:** Earth creep is an extremely gradual form of mass movement where soil and regolith slowly move downslope over time. It occurs as a result of the expansion and contraction of soil particles due to various environmental factors, such as temperature changes and wetting-drying cycles.

(*b*) **Earth Flow:** Earth flow represents a more pronounced form of mass movement than earth creep. Earth flows typically occur in areas with steep slopes and are facilitated by the presence of water, which reduces the internal friction of the soil particles, allowing for more rapid movement than earth creep.

(*c*) **Debris Flow:** Debris flow is a faster and more dynamic mass movement characterized by the rapid downslope movement of a mixture of rock, soil, and water. This type of mass wasting is often triggered by intense rainfall, rapid snowmelt, or volcanic activity.

(*a*) **Rock Fall:** Rock fall is the quickest and most abrupt type of mass movement among the given options. It involves the sudden release and descent of individual rock fragments or boulders from a slope. Rock falls can be triggered by various factors such as weathering, seismic activity, or changes in slope stability.

39. (C):

(*a*) **Silica:** Silica weathering involves the breakdown of pyroxene minerals into their component parts, releasing silica (SiO_2) in the process. Silica is a vital component in the formation of secondary minerals like clay minerals, quartz, and other silicate minerals during the weathering of primary rocks and minerals.

(*b*) **Fe-oxides:** Pyroxene contains iron (Fe) in its mineral structure. During the weathering process, iron is released from the pyroxene minerals and is prone to oxidation. This oxidation leads to the formation of iron oxides, commonly recognized as rust.

(*c*) **Bicarbonate ion:** The weathering of pyroxene and other silicate minerals involves chemical reactions with carbon dioxide (CO_2) and water (H_2O). Carbon dioxide dissolves in rainwater, forming carbonic acid ($H_2CO^-_3$). This weak acid reacts with minerals, including pyroxene, releasing various ions, such as bicarbonate (HCO_3^-), into solution.

40. (B)

41. (B): Assertion (A): Glacial lakes get stratified during winters. This statement is accurate. The stratification of glacial lakes during winters is a well-documented phenomenon. As the surface water cools, it becomes denser, leading it to sink, while the underlying warmer water rises. This thermal stratification creates distinct layers of water with different temperatures in the lake.

Reason (R): Water has maximum density at 4°C. This statement is also correct. Water exhibits its maximum density at 4°C, a unique property compared to most substances. However, this property alone does not serve as a direct and complete explanation for the stratification of glacial lakes during winters.

42. (D):

(*c*) **Albite-Epidote Hornfels:** Albite-epidote hornfels forms under lowest pressures and temperatures, typically in response to contact metamorphism around igneous intrusions. Hornfels rocks are characterized by the presence of minerals like albite and epidote, and they often exhibit a fine-grained texture due to the recrystallization of minerals.

(*a*) **Greenschist:** Greenschist is a metamorphic facies that forms at the moderate pressures. It is typically associated with regional metamorphism occurring in shallow crustal settings. The minerals commonly found in greenschist include chlorite, albite and epidote.

(*d*) **Blueschist:** Blueschist requires higher pressures than both albite-epidote hornfels and greenschist. This metamorphic facies is associated with subduction zones, where oceanic plates plunge beneath continental plates. The high-pressure conditions lead to the formation of distinct minerals, including glaucophane, a blue amphibole.

(*b*) **Eclogite:** Eclogite forms under the highest pressures and moderate to high temperatures. It is typically found in deep subduction zones or beneath mountain ranges where intense pressure conditions prevail. The minerals commonly found in eclogite include omphacite and garnet.

43. (C): Hydraulic conductivity is the property of an aquifer that measures its capacity to transmit water under the influence of a sloping piezometric surface. It is a critical parameter in hydrogeology, describing the ease with which water can flow through the porous subsurface material of an aquifer. The term encompasses the permeability of the geological formation, the cross-sectional area available for water flow, and the dynamic nature of the fluid movement. In essence, hydraulic conductivity quantifies the ability of an aquifer to allow the passage of water through its interconnected pore spaces and fractures, determining the efficiency of groundwater flow.

44. (D): The phenomenon referred to is the "Jet stream," a powerful and swiftly flowing circumpolar upper westerly air circulation found in a narrow band within the upper limits of the troposphere. This high-altitude, fast-moving air current, typically a few kilometers in width, manifests as concentrated, meandering flows of air at the boundaries between the troposphere and the stratosphere. The Jet stream is characterized by strong westerly winds, and there are typically two main types: the polar jet stream and the subtropical jet stream.

45. (B): During the phenomenon of La Niña, the eastern tropical Pacific Ocean experiences a distinctive cooling trend, leading to water temperatures that are below the long-term average. This cooling phenomenon is a key characteristic of La Niña events. As part of the larger El Niño-Southern Oscillation (ENSO) climate pattern, La Niña represents the opposite phase to El Niño. In La Niña conditions, the normal patterns of atmospheric circulation and sea surface temperatures are altered, influencing global weather patterns. The cooler-than-average sea surface temperatures in the eastern tropical Pacific have widespread impacts, such as increased rainfall in certain regions and the potential for more frequent and intense tropical cyclones in specific areas.

46. (B): Oil shales are sedimentary rocks that contain a significant amount of organic material known as kerogen. Kerogen is a complex mixture of hydrocarbons derived from the remains of ancient plants and algae that accumulated in the sediments over geological time. The term "kerogen" collectively refers to the organic matter within these rocks that has the potential to be converted into liquid and gaseous hydrocarbons, such as oil and gas. When subjected to heat through processes like pyrolysis, the kerogen in oil shale undergoes thermal decomposition, releasing hydrocarbons. It is an important source of unconventional hydrocarbons, and the extraction and processing of oil shale can be used to obtain liquid fuels.

47. (D): In evaluating the properties of coal for coke making, the Rock Eval pyrolysis test is not a required method. Rock Eval pyrolysis is primarily used in the context of assessing the hydrocarbon potential of sedimentary rocks for oil and gas exploration, rather than specifically for evaluating coal properties related to coke production.

48. (C): The correct order of greenhouse gases in terms of the amount of extra warming they produce in Earth's atmosphere is C < D < B < A. This order is determined by the relative global warming potentials (GWPs) of each greenhouse gas. Carbon dioxide (CO_2) has the least warming potential, and its contribution to the greenhouse effect is primarily due to its abundance in the atmosphere. Methane (CH_4) has a higher warming potential than CO_2, attributed to its ability to trap heat more efficiently. Nitrous oxide (N_2O) ranks higher in warming potential than methane. Chlorofluorocarbons (CFCs) have the highest warming potential among these gases, even though their atmospheric concentrations are much lower.

49. (A): Statement I accurately describe the typical composition of natural gas as it is extracted from underground reservoirs. Natural gas primarily consists of methane (CH_4), ranging from 60% to 90%, and it often contains other hydrocarbons such as ethane, propane, and various isomers of butane. This mixture reflects the diverse components found in natural gas wells, and the relative proportions can vary depending on the specific geological characteristics of the gas reservoir.

Statement II correctly points out that enormous quantity of natural gas are stored in methane hydrates, also known as clathrates, in ocean sediments and permafrost. Methane hydrates are crystalline structures in which methane molecules are trapped within a cage-like lattice of water molecules. These hydrates are stable under specific pressure and temperature conditions, and they represent a vast potential reservoir of methane.

50. (B): A fuel cell is a device designed to directly convert chemical energy into electrical energy through an electrochemical reaction. Unlike traditional combustion-based power generation, fuel cells operate with greater efficiency and produce electricity in a cleaner manner. The fundamental process involves the interaction of a fuel, often hydrogen, with an oxidizing agent, typically oxygen from the air. This chemical reaction takes place in the presence of an electrolyte and generates electrical energy, along with water and heat as byproducts. The key components of a fuel cell include an anode where the fuel is oxidized, a cathode where the oxidizing agent is reduced, and an electrolyte that allows ions to move between the anode and cathode.

51. (B):

(*b*) **Sandstone:** Sandstone layers often serve as reservoir rocks that host coal beds. In coal-forming environments, sandstone layers can act as conduits for water and gases, influencing the chemical composition and conditions within the peat (the precursor to coal) and aiding in the transformation of organic material into coal.

(*c*) **Shale:** Shale, being a fine-grained sedimentary rock rich in clay minerals, functions as a sealing or trapping layer. Gases and fluids generated during the decomposition of plant material are trapped within the coal seams by the surrounding shale, contributing to the formation and preservation of coal beds.

52. (B): The energy that a windmill can gather is proportional to the square of its blade length and the cube of the wind speed. The energy harvested by a wind turbine is proportional to the area swept by the turbine and wind velocity. The kinetic energy is proportional to the product of the mass of the air flowing through the given area in unit time and square of the velocity of the air. The maximum wind energy available is proportional to the cube of the wind speed. This means that a small increase in wind speed may increase the wind power.

53. (B):

(*a*) **SO_2 (Sulphur dioxide):** Sulphur dioxide (SO_2) is a criteria pollutant under the National Ambient Air Quality Standards (NAAQS). It is a gas produced by the burning of fossil fuels containing sulphur, such as coal and oil. SO_2 can lead to the formation of particulate matter and can contribute to respiratory issues, among other health concerns.

(*b*) **NOx (Nitrogen oxides):** Nitrogen oxides (NOx), which include nitric oxide (NO) and nitrogen dioxide (NO_2), are criteria pollutants. They are produced by combustion processes, primarily in vehicles and industrial activities. NOx contributes to the formation of ground-level ozone and particulate matter, both of which have adverse effects on human health and the environment.

(*d*) **O_3 (Ozone):** Ozone (O_3) is also a criteria pollutant regulated under NAAQS. While ozone in the upper atmosphere (stratospheric ozone) is beneficial for blocking ultraviolet radiation, ground-level ozone is a harmful air pollutant. Ground-level ozone is formed when pollutants like NOx and volatile organic compounds react in the presence of sunlight.

54. (D): Secondary air pollutants undergo chemical and physical transformations in the atmosphere, a process that distinguishes them from primary pollutants emitted directly into the air. Contrary to the notion, they are not inherently non-hazardous; in fact, many secondary pollutants pose risks to human health and the environment. These pollutants encompass a diverse range of inorganic and organic species, including ozone, secondary aerosols, and other compounds formed through atmospheric reactions.

55. (C):

(*b*) This technique is used to mitigate sulphur dioxide (SO_2) emissions from power plants, particularly those burning fossil fuels like coal. Limestone, a calcium-based substance, is injected into the combustion process. It reacts with sulphur compounds to form solid particles, which are then captured, reducing the release of SO_2 into the atmosphere.

(*c*) SCR is employed to reduce nitrogen oxides (NOx) emissions from combustion processes, commonly found in thermal power plants. In this method, a catalyst facilitates the reaction between nitrogen oxides and ammonia. This chemical reaction converts the harmful NOx compounds into nitrogen and water, which are less detrimental to air quality.

(*e*) Fabric bag filters are an effective technology for controlling particulate matter emissions from industrial processes. These filters consist of a series of fabric bags that capture solid particles from the gas stream. As the gas passes through the fabric, particulate matter adheres to the surface of the bags.

56. (B): "Total Atmospheric pressure minus Barometric pressure only," we can interpret this statement as describing sound pressure in terms of the dynamic fluctuations in atmospheric pressure minus the static barometric pressure. In this context, sound pressure is seen as the variable component, reflecting the changes in air pressure caused by sound waves. The subtraction of barometric pressure, a constant baseline representing the ambient atmospheric pressure at a specific location, aims to isolate the specific pressure variations introduced by sound.

57. (B): Gas bubble disease (GBD), a condition characterized by the formation and accumulation of gas bubbles in the tissues of aquatic animals, notably fish, poses a threat to their well-being. The excess dissolved oxygen in drinking water is the cause of GBD. It is based on the understanding that while oxygen is crucial for aquatic life, excessive levels can lead to supersaturation of water, resulting in the formation of gas bubbles within fish tissues and triggering the disease. This explanation aligns with the fact that GBD is associated with the supersaturation of dissolved gases, including oxygen.

58. (C)

59. (C):

(*a*) Phosphorus is commonly found in geological formations, particularly in rocks. Over time, weathering processes release phosphorus into water bodies, contributing to its presence in aquatic environments.

(*b*) In water, phosphorus can exist in different forms, with orthophosphate (PO_4^{3-}) being the inorganic form and organically bound phosphate representing the phosphorus incorporated into organic compounds.

(*c*) Soluble reactive phosphorus (SRP) is a term used to describe the fraction of phosphorus that is immediately available for uptake by organisms in its dissolved inorganic form.

(*d*) In many aquatic ecosystems, the availability of phosphorus can limit the growth of organisms like algae and aquatic plants. Therefore, phosphorus is considered a limiting nutrient that can influence the overall productivity of the system.

(*e*) Analyzing phosphorus in aquatic ecosystems can be challenging due to the complex nature of its various forms. Differentiating between phosphorus associated with zooplankton, bacteria, algae, and inorganic sources can be intricate and often requires sophisticated analytical techniques.

60. (A): Assertion (A) states that natural acidic soils are more prevalent in the tropics due to extensive weathering of soil minerals over thousands of years. This weathering process leads to the leaching of basic cations from the soil, contributing to soil acidity. The tropics experience consistent high temperatures and abundant rainfall, creating favorable conditions for enhanced weathering.

Reason (R) complements Assertion (A) by specifically highlighting the impact of year-round high temperatures and high rainfall in the tropics. The warmth and moisture accelerate chemical weathering processes, promoting the breakdown of primary rock-forming minerals and the subsequent leaching of basic cations. This leaching, caused by the combination of temperature and rainfall, aligns with the assertion that weathering is a key factor in the development of acidic soils in the tropics.

61. (C): Microwave radiation, falls within the realm of non-ionizing radiation. Unlike ionizing radiations such as ultraviolet, X-rays, and gamma rays, microwaves have relatively lower energy levels on the electromagnetic spectrum. Ionizing radiations possess sufficient energy to liberate tightly bound electrons from atoms, resulting in the formation of ions. In contrast, microwaves operate at frequencies that are unable to impart the energy necessary for this ionization process. Microwaves interact with matter primarily through mechanisms such as dipole rotation and vibrational transitions, causing molecules, especially those containing polar bonds like water, to rotate and vibrate.

62. (C):

(*a*) In the Gaussian Plume model, it is assumed that the pollutant is conservative, meaning that it remains unchanged chemically as it disperses from the source. This assumption simplifies the mathematical modeling of pollutant dispersion, allowing for more straightforward calculations based on the assumption that the concentration distribution is primarily influenced by physical processes such as advection and diffusion.

(*b*) The Gaussian Plume model assumes a constant emission rate of pollutants from the source. This implies that the rate at which pollutants are released into the atmosphere remains steady over time. The model uses this assumption to predict the spatial distribution of pollutant concentrations downwind from the source.

63. (A): Statement I: This statement is true. The incineration process for highly toxic and hazardous organic waste is quite different from municipal solid waste incineration. Incineration for hazardous waste focuses on destruction and detoxification, often involving higher temperatures, specialized equipment, and stringent emission controls to prevent the release of harmful pollutants. On the other hand, municipal solid waste incineration can prioritize energy recovery, utilizing lower temperatures and considering the composition of the waste to optimize energy generation.

Statement II: This statement is also true. Incineration is not suitable for waste with high water content or non-combustible solids. Water absorbs too much heat, hindering efficient combustion and requiring additional fuel. Non-combustible solids like metals remain after incineration, increasing ash volume and potentially requiring further treatment. Therefore, waste needs to be pre-treated to remove excess water and non-combustible materials before incineration for optimal efficiency and environmental protection.

64. (D):

(*c*) **Recycling or Reuse:** The highest preference is given to recycling, which involves processing waste materials into new products. This reduces the demand for new raw materials, conserves resources, and minimizes environmental impacts. Reusing materials or products is also highly favored.

(*b*) **Waste Separation:** Waste separation is crucial for effective recycling and proper disposal. It involves sorting waste into different categories such as glass, plastic, paper, and metal. This separation facilitates the recovery of valuable materials and ensures that each type of waste is managed appropriately.

(*a*) **Waste Concentration:** This involve processes like compaction or reducing the volume of waste. Concentrating waste makes handling and transportation more efficient, reducing the overall environmental footprint.

(*d*) **Waste Treatment:** If recycling, reuse, or separation are not viable options, waste treatment methods come into play. This can include various processes such as incineration, composting, or biological treatment to minimize the environmental impact of the waste.

(*e*) **Land filling:** Land filling is the least preferred option in the waste hierarchy. It involves disposing of waste in landfills, which can have significant environmental consequences if not properly managed. Landfills can contribute to soil and water pollution, greenhouse gas emissions, and habitat disruption.

65. (C): Recycling is a comprehensive and environmentally significant process aimed at recovering materials from the waste stream and reprocessing them to serve as raw materials for the creation of new products. The lifecycle of recycling begins with the collection of recyclable materials from various sources, including households and businesses. Recycling holds numerous environmental benefits, including resource conservation, energy savings, waste reduction, and protection against pollution.

66. (D): In the realm of strategies for reducing solid waste, the input approaches primarily center on proactive measures implemented during the design, production, and consumption phases to curtail the generation of waste. These strategies are geared toward addressing the root causes of waste production. Reduced consumption, the first approach, advocates for minimizing the overall demand for goods and services, thus inherently reducing the volume of waste generated. Increased product durability, the second approach, emphasizes designing products with extended life spans, promoting longevity and reducing the frequency of disposal. The third approach involves decreasing the materials in products, aiming to streamline designs and minimize the raw materials used, thereby lessening the environmental impact and waste generation. Notably, these input strategies all contribute to waste prevention.

67. (D): One of the primary gases dominantly released during this anaerobic decomposition process is methane. Microorganisms such as methanogenic bacteria facilitate the conversion of complex organic compounds into simpler molecules, with methane being a major byproduct. This methane-rich gas, often referred to as landfill gas, is composed primarily of methane along with other gases like carbon dioxide, nitrogen, and trace amounts of various volatile organic compounds. Methane is a potent greenhouse gas, contributing to climate change, and effective landfill management involves strategies to capture and utilize this gas to mitigate its environmental impact.

68. (C): Mobilization, as a technique in waste management, is predominantly achieved in situ and encompasses practices such as soil washing and the extraction of contaminant vapour from soil, particularly targeting highly volatile, water-insoluble contaminants like gasoline. In the context of soil washing, this in situ approach involves the use of appropriate solutions to cleanse the soil and remove contaminants effectively, allowing for the extraction and subsequent treatment of the mobilized substances. Simultaneously, the extraction of contaminant vapour focuses on the retrieval of volatile substances directly from the soil, facilitating their removal without physically relocating the contaminated material.

69. (B): Excavated pits lined with impermeable synthetic liners and thick impermeable layers of clay are examples of secured landfills. Landfills are a method of disposing of waste in the ground. They are designed to minimize environmental impact and are used for the final disposal of municipal solid waste. Landfills are pits that are either natural or man-made. Waste is dumped into the pits and covered with soil. The waste decomposes slowly and eventually becomes manure. Secured landfills are characterized by excavated pits that are carefully engineered and designed with advanced measures to enhance environmental protection during waste disposal.

70. (B): Phytoremediation, is a sophisticated and eco-friendly remediation technique that utilizes the unique capabilities of certain plant species to extract, concentrate, or transform hazardous materials present in soil. This innovative approach is particularly effective for mitigating soil contamination caused by heavy metals, organic pollutants, and various toxic substances. Hyperaccumulator plants, specifically adapted to thrive in contaminated environments, absorb contaminants through their roots and translocate them to different parts of the plant, such as stems, leaves, or even roots. The plants can either immobilize the pollutants within their tissues or undergo processes that transform the contaminants into less harmful forms. Phytoremediation offers several advantages, including its cost-effectiveness, applicability to large or inaccessible areas, and its potential to enhance soil quality over time.

71. (B): In the idealized Environmental Impact Assessment (EIA) process, the step of screening is crucial for determining the necessity of conducting a comprehensive EIA for a given project, considering the prevailing regulations in the country at the time of assessment. Screening involves an initial evaluation of the proposed project to identify whether it has the potential to cause significant environmental impacts. This involves assessing various factors, including the project's scale, nature, and location. If the screening process indicates that the project may indeed have significant environmental impacts, it triggers the need for a full-fledged EIA to thoroughly assess and mitigate these potential effects.

72. (D): Strategic Environmental Impact Assessment (SEIA), encompasses a formalized and comprehensive process designed to evaluate the environmental impacts associated with strategic-level decisions, including policies, programs, and plans. SEIA operates at a higher, more overarching level, aiming to integrate environmental considerations into the early stages of decision-making for strategic initiatives. This approach ensures that potential environmental implications are thoroughly assessed and factored into the development and formulation of policies or plans, allowing for informed, sustainable, and publicly accountable decision-making.

73. (C)

74. (B): In the context of dose-response curves for chemical substances, the threshold dose, signifies a critical point below which none of the animals in the study exhibit observable adverse effects. This threshold dose represents the minimum amount of the chemical that is required to initiate a response in the exposed organisms. Below this threshold, the substance is considered to be devoid of significant impact on the biological systems under investigation. This concept is integral in toxicology and risk assessment, highlighting the existence of a dose level below which the adverse effects are not detectable.

75. (D):

(*a*) **Raw Material Extraction:** This stage involves evaluating the environmental impacts associated with the extraction of raw materials used in the production of a product. This includes assessing the energy consumption, resource depletion, and ecological consequences of obtaining materials such as metals, minerals, or agricultural resources.

(*b*) **Product Manufacturing:** The manufacturing phase examines the environmental effects during the actual production of the product. It considers energy use, emissions, waste generation, and other environmental factors related to the manufacturing processes.

(*c*) **Product Remanufacture:** Remanufacturing involves the refurbishment or restoration of a product to extend its life and functionality. Assessing this stage in the life cycle provides insights into the environmental benefits of reusing and refurbishing products, reducing the need for new manufacturing and minimizing waste.

(*d*) **Packaging and Distribution:** This stage evaluates the environmental impacts associated with the packaging and transportation of the product. It includes considerations of material choices for packaging, energy use in transportation, and the emissions associated with distribution networks.

(*e*) **Product Disposal:** The disposal phase examines the environmental consequences of discarding the product at the end of its life. This includes assessing the impacts of waste disposal methods, such as land filling or recycling.

76. (C): In the analysis of a grouped frequency distribution, particularly when dealing with equally spaced class intervals, the determination of the mode involves assessing the frequencies of various classes to identify the most prevalent interval. Given the inherent limitations of grouped data, where only the range of values within each class interval and the total frequency for that interval are provided, the task of pinpointing the mode necessitates a careful examination of adjacent classes. The mode, representing the class with the highest frequency, is typically discerned by comparing the frequencies of neighboring classes.

77. (B)

78. (D): Some of the cell frequencies can be less than 5: This statement is FALSE. Although larger cell frequencies are preferable for reliable results, having some cells with less than 5 observations can still be acceptable depending on the context. However, if a significant portion of cells have frequencies less than 5, it's recommended to use alternative Chi-square test adaptations or consider combining some categories to meet the minimum threshold. Therefore, the false condition with respect to Chi-square goodness-of-fit test validity is some of the cell frequencies can be less than 5.

79. (C):

(*b*) This statement is true. A stationary population is a specific type of stable population where the birth rates, death rates, and overall population size remain constant over time, resulting in a zero growth rate. Therefore, every stationary population is inherently stable.

(*c*) This statement is true. While all stationary populations are stable, not all stable populations are stationary. Stable populations can have a constant growth rate that is not necessarily zero, meaning the population size changes at a constant rate over time.

(*d*) This statement is true. In a stationary population, the number of births equals the number of deaths, resulting in zero net population growth. Consequently, the rate of overall change in the population is zero.

(*e*) This statement is true. A stable population, by definition, has a constant growth rate, which can be positive (growing), negative (shrinking), or zero (stationary). The key is that the rate remains constant over time.

80. (A)

81. (B):

(*b*) In this step, you establish the null hypothesis, which typically states that there is no association between the two characteristics being studied. The null hypothesis is a starting point for statistical testing.

(*c*) Create a contingency table that organizes the data based on the two characteristics under investigation (e.g., Gender and discomfort due to humidity). This table displays the frequencies or counts of observations in each combination of categories.

(*e*) Using the marginal totals from the contingency table and assuming independence (no association), calculate the expected frequencies for each cell in the table.

(*d*) For each cell in the contingency table, calculate the squared difference between the observed and expected frequencies, divide this by the expected frequency, and sum these values across all cells.

(*a*) Once you have the calculated Chi-square statistic from step 4, compare it with the critical or tabulated value from the Chi-square distribution table. If the calculated value is greater than the critical value, you may reject the null hypothesis, suggesting a significant association between the two characteristics.

82. (B):

(*a*) This statement is true. While the ozone layer significantly absorbs UV-B radiation, it doesn't block it completely. Some UV-B still reaches the Earth's surface, contributing to sunburn and other skin damage.

(*b*) This statement is true. Compared to UV-B, UV-A has longer wavelengths and lower energy, making it less harmful to biological systems. While UV-A can cause tanning and premature aging, it doesn't have the same detrimental effects on DNA and cell structure as UV-B.

(*d*) This statement is true. Sunscreen protects our skin from UV radiation by employing various mechanisms: reflecting, absorbing, and scattering UV rays.

(*e*) This statement is true. UV-B radiation has enough energy to break apart the O_3 molecule into an oxygen atom (O) and an oxygen molecule (O_2).

83. (D): Wangari Muta Maathai was a prominent Kenyan environmentalist and political activist, best known for her association with the Green Belt Movement. Founded in 1977 by Maathai, the Green Belt Movement aimed to address environmental conservation, women's rights, and community development simultaneously. The movement encouraged women to plant trees as a means to combat deforestation, soil erosion, and to promote sustainable environmental practices. Under Maathai's leadership, the Green Belt Movement became a powerful force for change, empowering women through environmental initiatives and advocating for social and political justice.

84. (A): The National Action Plan for Climate Change (NAPCC) in India outlines various National Missions to address the challenges posed by climate change. Among these missions, the National Mission for a Clean India is not explicitly listed. The missions included in the NAPCC are designed to tackle different aspects of climate change and sustainability. While initiatives for a clean environment are integral to climate change mitigation and adaptation, the specific formulation of a National Mission for a Clean India might be addressed through other national programs outside the NAPCC framework, such as Swachh Bharat Abhiyan, which focuses on sanitation and cleanliness.

85. (D): Project Tiger is a tiger conservation program that celebrated its 50th anniversary on April 1, 2023. The Government of India launched the program in April 1973, during the tenure of Prime Minister Indira Gandhi. The program has helped endangered wild tigers in India recover. In 1973, there were nine reserves covering 9,115 square kilometers.

Today, there are 54 reserves in 18 states, covering 78,135.956 square kilometers, or 2.38% of India's total land area. The project's primary objective is to ensure the survival and maintenance of the tiger population in their natural habitats by creating dedicated Tiger Reserves. The project was launched on April 1, 1973 from the Jim Corbett National Park of Uttarakhand.

86. (A): Sustainable Development Goal 10 (SDG-10) aims at reducing inequalities within and among countries. It underscores the importance of addressing disparities in income, social status, opportunities, and access to basic services. The goal recognizes that inequality poses significant challenges to sustainable development, hindering poverty reduction efforts, and fostering social unrest. SDG-10 seeks to empower and promote the social, economic, and political inclusion of all individuals, regardless of their background, in order to create a more just and equitable global society.

87. (C) **88. (B)**

89. (B):

(*b*) **Chernobyl Disaster, 1986:** The Chernobyl Disaster occurred on April 26, 1986, at the Chernobyl Nuclear Power Plant in Pripyat, Ukraine, which was part of the Soviet Union at the time. It is considered the worst nuclear disaster in history. The disaster resulted from a reactor explosion during a safety test, leading to the release of a large amount of radioactive material into the atmosphere. The immediate impact caused the deaths of two plant workers, and the subsequent contamination had severe health and environmental consequences for the region and beyond.

(*c*) **Fukushima Disaster, 2011:** The Fukushima Disaster occurred on March 11, 2011, following a massive earthquake and tsunami in Japan. The natural disasters damaged the Fukushima Daiichi Nuclear Power Plant, leading to meltdowns in three of its reactors. The event resulted in the release of radioactive materials and forced the evacuation of nearby residents.

90. (D): In epidemiology, a case-control study is a research design aimed at investigating the association between a specific disease and potential risk factors or exposures. This study begins by identifying a group of individuals with the particular disease of interest (cases) and a comparable group without the disease (controls). Researchers then retrospectively analyze and compare the past exposures, behaviours, or characteristics of these two groups to identify commonalities or differences that may be associated with the disease. By comparing the odds of exposure between cases and controls, investigators can assess potential risk factors and gain insights into the etiology of the disease.

91. (A): The Carboniferous Period boasted the heaviest air on Earth, with nearly 40% more oxygen than today. This supercharged atmosphere fueled the growth of giant insects, dragonflies with two-meter wingspans, and massive millipedes. When oxygen levels dipped slightly in the following Permian Period, these giants vanished, replaced by smaller arthropods better suited to the thinner air.

92. (D): During the Carboniferous Period (354-290 million years ago), the Earth was characterized by extensive mid-latitude forests and the notable presence of large-bodied arthropods. The passage describes how the atmospheric conditions during this period, including high levels of oxygen, allowed for the development of sizable arthropods, such as massive millipedes and large cockroaches. These conditions, conducive to the growth of land arthropods, are not seen today due to changes in the environment.

93. (C): Large-bodied land arthropods from the Carboniferous Period became extinct due to a combination of factors, as indicated in the passage. The primary reason mentioned is the change in atmospheric conditions, specifically a drop in atmospheric oxygen levels. The passage notes that even though there was no mass extinction event at the Carboniferous-Permian transition, the high atmospheric oxygen-dependent large land arthropods of the Carboniferous Period were never seen again.

94. (B): The passage suggests that the atmospheric conditions, specifically the levels of oxygen (O_2), play a crucial role in determining the size of organisms. During certain historical periods, such as the Carboniferous Period, the Earth's atmosphere had higher oxygen levels, which allowed for the existence of large-bodied organisms like bugs, spiders, and other land arthropods. However, in the present-day atmosphere, the levels of oxygen are lower, imposing physiological restrictions on the size of organisms.

95. (C): Atmospheric oxygen levels attained their highest point in Earth's geological history approximately 330 million years ago, as indicated in the passage. This period, known as the Carboniferous Period, was characterized by elevated oxygen concentrations, nearly 40% higher than today. The heightened oxygen levels during this time were instrumental in influencing the size and diversity of life forms on Earth.

96. (C): The measure of 8.5 on the Richter scale is an example of a continuous data type. The Richter scale is a logarithmic scale used to quantify the magnitude of earthquakes. It represents a continuous spectrum of values, where each unit increase on the scale corresponds to a tenfold increase in amplitude of the seismic waves.

97. (D): The data type for affected individuals is an example of an ordinal data type. Ordinal data represents categories with a meaningful order or ranking. In this case, the categories "severely," "extremely," and "casualties" imply different levels of severity or impact, and there is a meaningful order among them.

98. (A): The most suitable option for presenting the percent distribution of economic loss due to building damage and livestock is a pie chart. Pie charts are effective for illustrating the composition or distribution of a whole in terms of percentages. In this case, you can use a pie chart to visually represent the proportion of economic loss attributed to building damage and livestock, providing a clear and easily interpretable snapshot of the distribution.

99. (C): The passage mentions that the total economic loss from the earthquake was estimated to be around 20,000 crore. It also provides information on the proportion of economic loss for buildings, which is 75%. To calculate the estimated cost in crore for buildings, you take 75% of the total economic loss, which is 0.75 * 20,000 crore = 15,000 crore. The remaining 25% of the economic loss is then attributed to livestock, resulting in 5,000 crore (0.25 * 20,000 crore).

100. (D): The expression a-loss = b-loss − l - loss + ε represents a linear relationship with multiple independent variables, where e-loss is the dependent variable, and b-loss, l-loss, and ε are independent variables. This type of relationship can be modelled using Multiple Linear Regression. In Multiple Linear Regression, the goal is to find the best-fitting linear equation that explains the relationship between the dependent variable and multiple independent variables.

Previous Years' Paper (Solved)

National Testing Agency (NTA)

UGC-NET Junior Research Fellowship & Assistant Professor Eligibility Exam

ENVIRONMENTAL SCIENCE, March–2023

(Exam held on 13-03-2023)

PAPER-II

1. The first law of thermodynamics states about

A. conservation of mass

B. conservation of energy

C. conservation of momentum

D. increase in entropy

2. An air parcel having initial temperature of 15°C rises adiabatically to 2 km height above the surface. What is the final temperature of the parcel?

A. ~4.6°C B. ~5.6°C

C. ~ – 4.6°C D. ~ – 6.4°C

3. Which of the following is NOT a tenet of frontier ethics in a sustainable society?

A. Earth has unlimited supply of resources for exclusive human use

B. There is always more and it is all for human use

C. Humans are apart from nature, rather than part of it

D. We must understand and cooperate with nature

4. Which of the following inter-governmental conferences recommended Environmental Education to cater to all ages and socio-professional groups in the population?

A. Stockholm (1972)

B. Tbilisi (1977)

C. Rio de Janeiro (1992)

D. Berlin (1995)

5. Average salinity of sea water is:

A. ~ 0.35% B. ~ 3.5%

C. ~ 0.035% D. ~ 35%

6. Most plants can absorb nitrogen only in the form of:

A. nitrite ion B. ammonium ion

C. nitrate ion D. dinitrogen ion

7. Persistence of DDT in environment is NOT due to:

A. its low vapour pressure

B. its low reactivity with respect to light, chemicals and microbes

C. its low solubility in water

D. its high rate of evaporation

8. Grazing food chain consists of:

A. Sun → green plants → herbivores → first order carnivores → second order carnivores

B. Sun → second order carnivores → herbivores → green plants → first order carnivores

C. Second order carnivores → first order carnivores → herbivores → green plants → Sun

D. Herbivores → green plants → Sun → first order carnivores → second order carnivores

9. Species area relationship predicts:

A. area required for each species in an association

B. area occupied by a species on the terrestrial ecosystem
C. minimum area required to be sampled to enumerate maximum number of species present in an association/ecosystem under observation
D. minimum number of species to be present to prioritize an area for conservation

10. Estimates of the biologically productive land and sea area needed to provide renewable resources that a population consumes and to absorb the waste it generates is called as:
A. Ecological footprint
B. Carbon footprint
C. Environmental footprint
D. Living Planet Index

11. With the change in environmental conditions, species that are not adapted to such changed conditions disappear. This phenomenon is called:
A. Anthropogenic extinction
B. Mass extinction
C. Natural extinction
D. Species migration

12. Compute the speed of geostrophic wind blowing parallel to the isobars in the northern hemisphere at latitude of 40° N. The spacing between the isobars is 200 km and pressure difference is 4 mb. The altitude is 5600 m above sea level, where the air temperature is –25°C and air density is 0.70 kg/m^3. [Given sin(40°) = 0.64 and Earth's rotation (Ω) = 7.3×10^{-5} radian/sec]
A. Vg = ~ 36.6 m/sec
B. Vg = ~ 30.6 m/sec
C. Vg = ~ 28.6 m/sec
D. Vg = ~ 38.2 m/sec

13. Elements which are NOT easily accomodated in the structures of the principal igneous minerals are called:
A. trace elements
B. incompatible elements
C. insoluble elements
D. unfriendly elements

14. Destruction of ocean floor occurs at:
A. convergent plate boundary
B. divergent plate boundary
C. transform plate boundary
D. rift valleys

15. During the estimation of geothermal resources, which of the following is NOT considered?
A. Depth, thickness and extent of geothermal aquifer
B. Properties of rock formation
C. Salinity and geochemistry of fluid present in aquifer
D. Fossil content of rocks

16. Shale gas is a natural gas which is mainly dominated by:
A. methane
B. ethane
C. butane
D. propane

17. Gas hydrates are NOT produced through:
A. Thermal stimulation
B. Depressurization
C. Chemical inhibition
D. Bacterial recovery

18. Which component of coal cannot be determined under proximate analysis?
A. Moisture
B. Ash
C. Volatile matter
D. Sulphur

19. Bioenergy is a form of:
A. Conventional Energy
B. Unconventional Energy
C. Non-renewable Energy
D. Renewable Energy

20. Behaviour of the plume, when stack is under temperature inversion layer, is termed as:
A. Fanning
B. Conning
C. Fumigation
D. Lofting

21. Calculate hardness in units of mg/l as $CaCO_3$ of a ground water sample having Ca^{++} ion concentration of 100 mg/l.
A. ~ 5
B. ~ 250
C. ~ 5000
D. ~ 200

22. Which of the following sound level existed for maximum duration as per L_N concept?

A. L_{20} = 80 dB   B. L_{25} = 70 dB
C. L_{40} = 20 dB   D. L_{15} = 90 dB

23. The time between successive peaks or between successive troughs of the sinusoidal sound wave is called:

A. Frequency (f)
B. Wavelength (λ)
C. Period (P)
D. Amplitude (A)

24. Naturally occuring radioactive gas which is also produced by radioactive decay of uranium and has the potential to concentrate in buildings and homes is:

A. Radium   B. Polonium
C. Radon   D. Iodine

25. A natural or human made depression in which solid waste is dumped, compressed and daily covered with a layer of dirt, is referred as:

A. Open dump
B. Secured landfill
C. Sanitary landfill
D. Composting site

26. Plastic waste management rules were first notified by the Ministry of Environment, Forest and Climate Change in India in the year:

A. 2019   B. 2021
C. 2016   D. 2022

27. Process of thermal degradation of solid waste in the absence of oxygen is referred to as:

A. Incineration   B. Pyrolysis
C. Gassification   D. Sublimation

28. Which one of the following is NOT the preferred sustainable strategy for reducing solid waste?

A. Output approach
B. Through-put approach
C. Timeput approach
D. Input approach

29. The abandoned, idled or under-used industrial and commercial facilities, where expansion or redevelopment is complicated by real or perceived contamination, are defined as:

A. Greenfields
B. Landfills
C. Brownfields
D. Greyfields

30. The notification of Environmental Impact Assessment under the provision of Environmental (Protection) Act, 1986 was carried out for:

A. River valley projects
B. Development projects
C. Tourism Projects
D. Municipal Waste Management

31. Which one of the following fundamental duties makes sure that every citizen of India protects and improves the natural environment including forests, lakes, rivers and wildlife, and has compassion for living creatures?

A. 51A (c)   B. 51A (e)
C. 51A (g)   D. 51A (i)

32. Which one of the following is NOT a product-based tool of environmental preventive management?

A. Cleaner production
B. Eco-Labeling
C. Industrial Ecology
D. Life cycle assessment

33. The functional relationship of soil(s) is expressed in terms of s = cl + o + r + ..., where cl is climate, o is organism, and r is relief. This type of relationship is considered as:

A. Simple Linear Regression
B. Binary Logistic Regression
C. Exponential relationship
D. Multiple Linear Regression

34. A chart which displays distribution of weather conditions by well defined weather symbols on maps covering wide regions of the earth's surface at a given time is termed as:

A. Contour chart   B. Radar chart
C. Bubble chart   D. Synoptic chart

35. The correlation coefficient between two variables X and Y was 0.6 (r_1) and that between *a* and *b* was 0.3 (r_2). Which one of the following is TRUE with regard to interpretation of the values of *n* and r_2?

A. Absolute difference between r_1 and r_2 is 0.3.
B. r_1 is twice as high as r_2
C. r_1 is three times as high as r_2
D. r_1 is four times as high as r_2

36. How many National Missions form the core of the National Action Plan on Climate Change (NAPCC) to focus on promoting understanding of climate change, adaptation and mitigation, energy efficiency and natural resource conservation?

A. Six (6) B. Eight (8)
C. Ten (10) D. Twelve (12)

37. Who led the work of TARUN BHARAT SANGH which made water available round the year in the wells?

A. Anna Hazare
B. Chandi Prasad Bhatt
C. Rajendra Singh
D. Sundar Lal Bahuguna

38. Which of the following is related to 'MARRAKESH ACCORDS'?

A. The Earth Summit (1992)
B. Berlin Mandate (1995)
C. Geneva Convention (1996)
D. Kyoto Protocol (1997)

39. In coastal marine estuaries and bays, eutrophication is linked to harmful algal blooms causing widespread fatalities in marine organisms. This phenomenon is called:

A. Red tides B. Blue tides
C. Green tides D. Brown tides

40. Determining the concentration of aflatoxin in peanut butter and calculating the dose an average person would receive is referred as:

A. Hazard identification
B. Dose-response assessment
C. Exposure-assessment
D. Risk characterization

41. Which of the following are the standard (average) sea level pressure?

(*a*) 101325 Nm^{-2}
(*b*) 14.69595 psi
(*c*) 29.92126 inch Hg
(*d*) 10.33227 m H_2O
(*e*) 1013.25 kPa

Choose the ***correct*** answer from the options given below:

A. (*a*), (*b*), (*d*) and (*e*) only
B. (*a*), (*b*), (*c*) and (*d*) only
C. (*a*), (*b*), (*c*) and (*e*) only
D. (*a*), (*c*), (*d*) and (*e*) only

42. Choose the correct statements:

(*a*) VOC, NO_x and sunlight are essential for photochemical smog.
(*b*) Photochemical smog is predominantly formed during the summer season.
(*c*) NO_2 dissociates by sunlight at 300-400 nm.
(*d*) Molecular O_2 dissociate by sunlight and provide atomic O for O_3 formation in troposphere.
(*e*) Tropospheric O_3 concentration is maximum at noon on a given day.

Choose the ***correct*** answer from the options given below:

A. (*a*), (*d*) and (*e*) only
B. (*a*), (*b*), (*c*) and (*e*) only
C. (*a*), (*b*), (*d*) and (*e*) only
D. (*b*), (*c*), (*d*) and (*e*) only

43. The elemental analysis in an environmental sample can be performed using:

(*a*) UU-VIS spectrophotometer
(*b*) AAS
(*c*) ICP-OES
(*d*) XRF
(*e*) XRD

Choose the ***correct*** answer from the options given below:

A. (*b*) and (*c*) only
B. (*a*), (*b*) and (*c*) only
C. (*c*), (*d*) and (*e*) only
D. (*a*), (*b*), (*c*) and (*d*) only

44. Choose the correct statements:

(*a*) Temperature has a effect in disinfection treatment of water.

(*b*) pH controls the amount of HOCl and OCl in water.

(*c*) Cl_2 gas used for disinfection forms HCl as a product in water.

(*d*) Disinfection action is because of HOCl formed and not due to Cl_2 gas.

(*e*) Combined chlorine exist in water due to combination of HOCl with NH_3 and organic compounds.

Choose the ***correct*** answer from the options given below:

A. (*a*), (*c*) and (*e*) only
B. (*b*), (*c*) and (*d*) only
C. (*a*), (*b*), (*c*), (*d*) and (*e*)
D. (*a*), (*b*), (*c*) and (*d*) only

45. Choose the correct statement:

(*a*) UV-C breaks down O_2 molecule in the stratosphere.

(*b*) A 1% decrease in the overhead O_3 in the stratosphere results in 2% increase in UV-B intensity at the ground level.

(*c*) UV-A is biologically, the least harmful.

(*d*) UV-B helps in O_3 dissociation in the stratosphere.

(*e*) Chapman mechanism deals with both, O_3 formation and destruction, in the stratosphere.

Choose the ***correct*** answer from the options given below:

A. (*a*), (*b*), (*c*) and (*d*) only
B. (*a*), (*c*), (*d*) and (*e*) only
C. (*a*), (*b*), (*c*), (*d*) and (*e*)
D. (*a*), (*b*), (*d*) and (*e*) only

46. Metals used in wood preservatives are

(*a*) Cu (*b*) As
(*c*) Se (*d*) Cr
(*e*) Mo

Choose the ***correct*** answer from the options given below:

A. (*b*) only
B. (*a*), (*b*) and (*d*) only
C. (*c*) and (*e*) only
D. (*a*), (*c*) and (*e*) only

47. The biotic structure of the ecosystem is characterized by the composition of the biological community including:

(*a*) species numbers
(*b*) biomass
(*c*) life-form
(*d*) life-history
(*e*) spatial distribution

Choose the ***correct*** answer from the options given below:

A. (*a*), (*b*), (*c*) and (*d*) only
B. (*b*), (*c*), (*d*) and (*e*) only
C. (*a*), (*b*), (*c*) and (*e*) only
D. (*a*), (*b*), (*c*), (*d*) and (*e*)

48. The international stable isotope standard Vienna Peedee Belemnite (VPDB) is used for the following stable isotope systems:

(*a*) $^{34}S/^{32}S$ (*b*) $^{2}H/^{1}H$
(*c*) $^{18}O/^{16}O$ (*d*) $^{16}N/^{15}N$
(*e*) $^{13}C/^{12}C$

Choose the ***correct*** answer from the options given below:

A. (*a*) and (*b*) only B. (*b*) and (*c*) only
C. (*c*) and (*e*) only D. (*d*) and (*e*) only

49. Orthoclace weathers to produce:

(*a*) silica
(*b*) dissolved K ion
(*c*) smectite
(*d*) kaolinite
(*e*) dissolved biocarbonate ion

Choose the ***correct*** answer from the options given below:

A. (*a*), (*b*) and (*c*) only
B. (*a*), (*c*) and (*d*) only
C. (*a*), (*b*), (*c*) and (*d*) only
D. (*a*), (*b*), (*d*) and (*e*) only

50. The variability in height of tropopause is dependent on following factors:
(*a*) Longitude
(*b*) Latitude
(*c*) Temperature
(*d*) Season
(*e*) Vegetation

Choose the ***correct*** answer from the options given below:
A. (*a*), (*b*), and (*c*) only
B. (*b*), (*c*) and (*d*) only
C. (*a*), (*c*) and (*e*) only
D. (*a*), (*b*) and (*d*) only

51. Which of the following are NOT Thorium minerals?
(*a*) Monazite
(*b*) Thorite
(*c*) Tonalite
(*d*) Actinolite

Choose the ***correct*** answer from the options given below:
A. (*c*) and (*d*) only
B. (*a*) and (*d*) only
C. (*a*) and (*b*) only
D. (*b*) and (*c*) only

52. Which of the following rocks act as hydrocarbon reservoirs?
(*a*) Sandstone
(*b*) Limestone
(*c*) Shale
(*d*) Mudstone

Choose the ***correct*** answer from the options given below:
A. (*a*) and (*c*) only
B. (*a*) and (*b*) only
C. (*b*) and (*d*) only
D. (*a*) and (*d*) only

53. Criteria pollutant under National Ambient Air Quality Standards (NAAQS) are:
(*a*) CO (*b*) CO_2
(*c*) O_3 (*d*) SO_2
(*e*) NO_3

Choose the ***correct*** answer from the options given below:
A. (*a*), (*c*), (*d*) and (*e*) only
B. (*a*), (*c*) and (*d*) only
C. (*a*), (*b*) and (*d*) only
D. (*a*), (*d*) and (*e*) only

54. Which of the following can introduce acidity in soils?
(*a*) Presence of soluble aluminium
(*b*) Mine tailing deposits
(*c*) Thermal power plant emissions
(*d*) Leaching of basic cations
(*e*) Leaching of Si from Silicate minerals

Choose the ***correct*** answer from the options given below:
A. (*a*), (*b*), (*c*) and (*d*) only
B. (*b*), (*c*) and (*d*) only
C. (*a*), (*b*), (*c*), (*d*) and (*e*)
D. (*a*), (*b*), (*c*) and (*e*) only

55. Air pollution control techniques used primarily to control particulate matter pollution in ambient atmosphere are:
(*a*) Bag houses
(*b*) Limestone injection multistage burner (LIMB)
(*c*) Cyclone collectors
(*d*) Catalytic converters
(*e*) Electrostatic precipitators

Choose the ***correct*** answer from the options given below:
A. (*a*), (*b*), (*d*) and (*e*) only
B. (*c*) and (*e*) only
C. (*a*), (*b*), (*c*) and (*e*) only
D. (*a*), (*c*) and (*e*) only

56. Choose the correct statements:
(*a*) Increase in temperature reduces DO in lake water.
(*b*) Agricultural run-off introduces turbidity in lake water.
(*c*) Sewage discharge increases both DO and BOD in lake water.
(*d*) Enrichment of nutrients speed-up the aging of lakes.
(*e*) Atmospheric exchange and photosynthesis introduces DO in lake water.

Choose the ***correct*** answer from the options given below:

A. (*a*), (*c*) and (*d*) only
B. (*b*), (*c*), (*d*) and (*e*) only
C. (*a*), (*b*), (*c*), (*d*) and (*e*)
D. (*a*), (*b*), (*d*) and (*e*) only

57. Which of the following greenhouse gases are not emitted from solid waste landfills?

(*a*) CH_4
(*b*) CO_2
(*c*) SF_6
(*d*) O_3
(*e*) N_2O

Choose the ***correct*** answer from the options given below:

A. (*c*) and (*e*) only
B. (*d*) and (*e*) only
C. (*c*) only
D. (*c*) and (*d*) only

58. Which of the following are NOT objectives of the Environment (Protection) Act, 1986?

(*a*) Prevention of hazards to all living creatures (plants, animals and human) and property
(*b*) Conservation of the natural heritage
(*c*) Check on soil erosion and denundation in catchment areas in rivers, lakes and reservoirs
(*d*) Maintenance of a harmonious relationship between humans and their environment
(*e*) Increase in productivity of forests to meet the natural needs

Choose the ***correct*** answer from the options given below:

A. (*a*), (*b*) and (*d*) only
B. (*b*), (*c*) and (*e*) only
C. (*b*), (*c*) and (*d*) only
D. (*c*), (*d*) and (*e*) only

59. Which of the following are correct representations of standard deviation?

(*a*) $\frac{1}{n}\sum(y_1 - \bar{y})$

(*b*) $\frac{1}{n}\sum(y_1 - \bar{y})^2$

(*c*) $\sqrt{\frac{1}{n}\sum(y_1 - \bar{y})^2}$

(*d*) $\sqrt{\left(\frac{\Sigma y}{n}\right)^2 - \frac{\Sigma y^2}{n}}$

(*e*) $\sqrt{\frac{\Sigma y^2}{n} - \left(\frac{\Sigma y}{n}\right)^2}$

Choose the ***correct*** answer from the options given below:

A. (*a*) and (*c*) only
B. (*b*) and (*d*) only
C. (*c*) and (*e*) only
D. (*a*) and (*d*) only

60. Which of the following sites found suitable for the introduction of Cheetah are situated in the state of Rajasthan?

(*a*) Gandhi Sagar Wildlife Sanctuary
(*b*) Madhav National Park
(*c*) Mukundara Hills Tiger Reserve
(*d*) Nauradehi Wildlife Sanctuary
(*e*) Shergarh Wildlife Sanctuary

Choose the ***correct*** answer from the options given below:

A. (*a*) and (*c*) only
B. (*c*) and (*e*) only
C. (*b*) and (*d*) only
D. (*d*) and (*e*) only

61. Which of the following are covered under the National Mission for Sustaining the Himalayan Ecosystem?

(*a*) Himalayan Glaciers
(*b*) Institutional Capacities
(*c*) Biodiversity Conservation
(*d*) Wildlife Conservation
(*e*) Traditional Knowledge

Choose the ***correct*** answer from the options given below:

A. (*a*), (*b*), (*c*) and (*d*) only
B. (*b*), (*c*), (*d*) and (*e*) only
C. (*a*), (*b*), (*c*), (*d*) and (*e*)
D. (*a*), (*c*), (*d*) and (*e*) only

62. Which of the following States/UTs have more than thirty Wildlife Sanctuaries?
(*a*) Andhra Pradesh
(*b*) Himachal Pradesh
(*c*) Madhya Pradesh
(*d*) Maharashtra
(*e*) Rajasthan

Choose the ***correct*** answer from the options given below:
A. (*a*) and (*c*) only B. (*c*) and (*e*) only
C. (*b*) and (*e*) only D. (*c*) and (*d*) only

63. For a moderately asymmetrical (non-symmetrical) distribution, mean, mode, and median obey the following relation:
(*a*) Mean = Mode = Median
(*b*) Mode = Mean – 3(Mean – Median)
(*c*) Mean – Median = 1/3 (Mean – Mode)
(*d*) Mean – Mode = 3 (Median – Mean)
(*e*) Mode – Median = 3 (Mean)

Choose the ***correct*** answer from the options given below:
A. (*a*) and (*b*) only
B. (*b*) and (*c*) only
C. (*c*) and (*d*) only
D. (*d*) and (*e*) only

64. Choose the correct statements:
(*a*) Basel convention was on transboundary movement of toxic waste.
(*b*) Kyoto protocol was on banning of production of CFCs.
(*c*) Montreal protocol was on controlling Global warming.
(*d*) Earth Summit in the year 2002 was held in Johannesburg.
(*e*) Convention on Biodiversity (CBD) was held in the year 1995.

Choose the ***correct*** answer from the options given below:
A. (*a*), (*b*), (*c*) and (*e*) only
B. (*a*), (*b*) and (*c*) only
C. (*a*) and (*d*) only
D. (*b*), (*c*), (*d*) and (*e*) only

65. Read the following statements:
(*a*) Systemic insecticides kill insects only after moving through the system of the plant hosting the target insect.
(*b*) Contact pesticides enter the target pest upon direct application.
(*c*) Contact pesticides/insecticides or its residue kill target plants or insects on direct application.
(*d*) If a particular insect does not feed on the plant, it cannot be harmed by systemic insecticides.
(*e*) Contact pesticides are generally used only for specific insects occuring on specific plants/crops.

Choose the ***correct*** answer from the options given below:
A. (*a*), (*c*) and (*e*) only
B. (*a*), (*b*), (*c*) and (*e*) only
C. (*b*), (*c*), (*d*) and (*e*) only
D. (*a*), (*b*), (*c*) and (*d*) only

66. Match List-I with List-II:

List-I	List-II
(*a*) 0.52-0.60 μm	I. Absorption band of healthy vegetation
(*b*) 0.63-0.69 μm	II. Responsive to amount of vegetation biomass/leaf area
(*c*) 0.76-0.90 μm	III. Sensitive to turgidity or amount of water in plants
(*d*) 1.55-1.75 μm	IV. Green reflectance of healthy vegetation

Choose the ***correct*** answer from the options given below:

	(*a*)	(*b*)	(*c*)	(*d*)
A.	IV	III	I	II
B.	I	III	IV	II
C.	II	III	IV	I
D.	II	IV	III	I

67. Match List-I with List-II:

List-I (Term)	List-II (Definition)
(*a*) Sympatric speciation	I. The process by which organisms adapt to changed environmental conditions to form new species in a relatively short period
(*b*) Parapatric speciation	II. The process of differentiation and acquiring reproductive isolation within the same geographical area
(*c*) Adaptive speciation	III. Population evolving in different geographical regions due to isolation
(*d*) Allopatric speciation	IV. The process of speciation which occurs between adjacent populations within a broadly continuous habitat

Choose the ***correct*** answer from the options given below:

	(*a*)	(*b*)	(*c*)	(*d*)
A.	IV	II	III	I
B.	II	IV	I	III
C.	I	II	III	IV
D.	III	I	II	IV

68. Match List-I with List-II:

List-I (Author)	List-II (Concept of ecological niche)
(*a*) Charles Eltan (1927)	I. The activity range of each species along every dimension of the environment
(*b*) G.F. Gause (1934)	II. The intensity of competition between species suggests the degree to which their niches overlap
(*c*) David Lack (1947)	III. The place of species in the biological environment, its relationship to food and predators
(*d*) G.E. Hutchison (1959)	IV. Niche relationship could provide a basis for evolutionary diversification of species

Choose the ***correct*** answer from the options given below:

	(*a*)	(*b*)	(*c*)	(*d*)
A.	IV	II	III	I
B.	I	II	III	IV
C.	III	II	IV	I
D.	I	IV	III	II

69. Match List-I with List-II:

List-I (Types of Interaction)	List-II (Nature of Interaction)
(*a*) Parasitism	I. The predator generally larger than prey have positive interaction while prey have negative interaction
(*b*) Mutualism	II. Interaction favourable to both and obligatory
(*c*) Predation	III. The parasite generally smaller than the host benefitted while the host have negative interaction
(*d*) Commensalism	IV. The commensal benefits while the host remains unaffected

Choose the ***correct*** answer from the options given below:

	(*a*)	(*b*)	(*c*)	(*d*)
A.	I	II	III	IV
B.	III	I	IV	II
C.	III	II	I	IV
D.	I	IV	III	II

70. Match List-I with List-II:

List-I (Name)	List-II (Parameter)
(*a*) Contour	I. Density
(*b*) Isohyet	II. Height
(*c*) Isopycnic	III. Wind direction
(*d*) Isogon	IV. Precipitation accumulation

Choose the ***correct*** answer from the options given below:

	(*a*)	(*b*)	(*c*)	(*d*)
A.	IV	I	III	II
B.	II	IV	I	III
C.	III	IV	II	I
D.	I	II	III	IV

71. Match List-I with List-II:

List-I (Mineral)	List-II (Hardness (Mohs Scale))
(*a*) Calcite	I. 7
(*b*) Topaz	II. 5
(*c*) Apatite	III. 3
(*d*) Quartz	IV. 8

Choose the ***correct*** answer from the options given below:

	(*a*)	(*b*)	(*c*)	(*d*)
A.	IV	III	II	I
B.	III	IV	II	I
C.	I	II	III	IV
D.	II	III	IV	I

72. Match List-I with List-II:

List-I (Element)	List-II (Composition (%))
(*a*) Carbon	I. 2-20
(*b*) Hydrogen	II. 60-90
(*c*) Oxygen	III. 1-12
(*d*) Nitrogen	IV. 1-3

Choose the ***correct*** answer from the options given below:

	(*a*)	(*b*)	(*c*)	(*d*)
A.	I	IV	II	III
B.	II	III	I	IV
C.	IV	II	III	I
D.	III	II	IV	I

73. Match List-I with List-II:

List-I	List-II
(*a*) Scoping	I. Determine significance and social importance of measured impacts, particularly adverse impacts
(*b*) Evaluation	II. Comply with terms and conditions and to monitor environmental impacts
(*c*) ES Review	III. Identify key issues and impacts to establish study limits
(*d*) Monitoring	IV. Systematic appraisal of the quality of EIS and compliance with legislation or modification required

Choose the ***correct*** answer from the options given below:

	(*a*)	(*b*)	(*c*)	(*d*)
A.	III	I	II	IV
B.	III	I	IV	II
C.	I	III	IV	II
D.	I	IV	III	II

74. Match List-I with List-II:

List-I (Normal Distribution Data)	List-II (Per cent of Area Covered
(*a*) Fiftieth percentile ± 1SD	I. ≅ 50%
(*b*) Mode ± 2SD	II. ≅ 68%
(*c*) Second Quartile ± 3SD	III. ≅ 95%
(*d*) Mean ± 3SD	IV. ≅ 99.9%

Choose the ***correct*** answer from the options given below:

	(*a*)	(*b*)	(*c*)	(*d*)
A.	II	III	IV	I
B.	I	II	III	IV
C.	IV	II	I	III
D.	III	I	IV	II

75. Match List-I with List-II:

List-I (Reservoir)	List-II (River)
(*a*) Maithon	I. Betwa
(*b*) Matatila	II. Baskar
(*c*) Nizam Sagar	III. Damodar
(*d*) Pong	IV. Marijna

Choose the ***correct*** answer from the options given below:

	(*a*)	(*b*)	(*c*)	(*d*)
A.	III	IV	II	I
B.	III	I	IV	II
C.	II	IV	I	III
D.	II	I	IV	III

76. Arrange the following radiations of the electromagnetic spectrum in increasing order of wave length.

(*a*) Visible (*b*) Near IR
(*c*) X-Ray (*d*) Ultra Violet
(*e*) Thermal IR

Choose the ***correct*** answer from the options given below:

A. (*b*), (*d*), (*e*), (*a*), (*c*)
B. (*a*), (*b*), (*c*), (*d*), (*e*)
C. (*e*), (*a*), (*c*), (*b*), (*d*)
D. (*c*), (*d*), (*a*), (*b*), (*e*)

77. Arrange the following elements of image interpretation in decreasing order of complexity.

(*a*) Aspect (*b*) Association
(*c*) Location (*d*) Pattern
(*e*) Texture

Choose the ***correct*** answer from the options given below:

A. (*b*), (*d*), (*e*), (*a*), (*c*)
B. (*b*), (*a*), (*d*), (*e*), (*c*)
C. (*a*), (*b*), (*e*), (*c*), (*d*)
D. (*d*), (*a*), (*b*), (*c*), (*e*)

78. Arrange the following rocks in increasing metamorphic grade.

(*a*) Gneiss (*b*) Slate
(*c*) Migmatite (*d*) Phyllite

Choose the ***correct*** answer from the options given below:

A. (*a*), (*b*), (*c*), (*d*)
B. (*b*), (*a*), (*c*), (*d*)
C. (*b*), (*d*), (*a*), (*c*)
D. (*c*), (*a*), (*d*), (*b*)

79. Correct sequence of mineralisation from high temperature to low temperature during fractional crystallisation of magma is:

(*a*) Olivine
(*b*) Amphibole
(*c*) Pyroxene
(*d*) Biotite

Choose the ***correct*** answer from the options given below:

A. (*a*), (*d*), (*c*), (*b*)
B. (*a*), (*b*), (*c*), (*d*)
C. (*a*), (*c*), (*b*), (*d*)
D. (*a*), (*d*), (*b*), (*c*)

80. Arrange the following coal types as per their increasing carbon content.

(*a*) Lignite
(*b*) Peat
(*c*) Sub-bituminous
(*d*) Anthracite
(*e*) Bituminous

Choose the ***correct*** answer from the options given below:

A. (*c*), (*a*), (*b*), (*d*), (*e*)
B. (*b*), (*a*), (*c*), (*e*), (*d*)
C. (*a*), (*b*), (*e*), (*d*), (*c*)
D. (*a*), (*b*), (*c*), (*d*), (*e*)

81. Correct order of soil horizons starting from top surface to bottom is:

(*a*) O (*b*) A
(*c*) B (*d*) E
(*e*) C

Choose the ***correct*** answer from the options given below:

A. (*a*), (*b*), (*c*), (*e*), (*d*)
B. (*a*), (*b*), (*c*), (*d*), (*e*)
C. (*a*), (*b*), (*d*), (*c*), (*e*)
D. (*b*), (*a*), (*c*), (*d*), (*e*)

82. Arrange the following stages of decomposition of landfill materials in their preferred sequence from initial to last.
(*a*) Acid phase
(*b*) Aerobic phase
(*c*) Unsteady methanogenesis
(*d*) Steady methanogenesis

Choose the ***correct*** answer from the options given below:
A. (*a*), (*b*), (*c*), (*d*)
B. (*b*), (*a*), (*c*), (*d*)
C. (*b*), (*a*), (*d*), (*c*)
D. (*a*), (*b*), (*d*), (*c*)

83. Following are the common procedural steps in ecological impact analysis process. Arrange them from the first to the last step.
(*a*) Focussing
(*b*) Impact Assessment
(*c*) Impact Evaluation
(*d*) Impact Mitigation
(*e*) Scoping

Choose the ***correct*** answer from the options given below:
A. (*a*), (*e*), (*c*), (*b*), (*d*)
B. (*e*), (*a*), (*b*), (*d*), (*c*)
C. (*e*), (*b*), (*c*), (*d*), (*a*)
D. (*a*), (*b*), (*c*), (*d*), (*e*)

84. The three monthly moving average for rainfall in New Delhi for the monsoon periods, 2019, 2021 and 2022 was to be estimated. In calculation of the 95% confidence interval for rainfall, arrange the following sequence of steps in correct order.
(*a*) Choose confidence coefficient of 95%.
(*b*) Plot a time series graph on available data.
(*c*) Calculate three year moving average.
(*d*) Compute the standard error for estimate.
(*e*) Compute sample statistic '*t*'.

Choose the ***correct*** answer from the options given below:
A. (*a*), (*b*), (*c*), (*e*), (*d*)
B. (*b*), (*c*), (*d*), (*a*), (*e*)
C. (*b*), (*c*), (*e*), (*d*), (*a*)
D. (*c*), (*d*), (*a*), (*e*), (*b*)

85. Given below are two statements, one is labelled as Assertion (A) and the other is labelled as Reason (R).

Assertion (A): Natural Ecosystems are less vulnerable to catastrophic changes but adapted to weather changes.

Reason (R): Natural Ecosystems are mature from a succession point of view and rich in biotic diversity with less synchronisation of growth.

In light of the above statements, choose the ***correct*** answer from the options given below:
A. Both (A) and (R) are true and (R) is the correct explanation of (A)
B. Both (A) and (R) are true, but (R) is NOT the correct explanation of (A)
C. (A) is true, but (R) is false
D. (A) is false, but (R) is true

86. Given below are two statements, one is labelled as Assertion (A) and the other is labelled as Reason (R).

Assertion (A): Humic acid is less soluble in acid solution compared to fulvic acid.

Reason (R): Molecular weight of humic acid is 100 to 1000 times higher compared to fulvic acid and also its oxygen content is lower.

In light of the above statements, choose the ***correct*** answer from the options given below:
A. Both (A) and (R) are true and (R) is the correct explanation of (A)
B. Both (A) and (R) are true, but (R) is NOT the correct explanation of (A)
C. (A) is correct, but (R) is not correct
D. (A) is not correct, but (R) is correct

87. Given below are two statements:

Statement I: Soluble phosphorus is referred to as soluble reactive phosphorus and is a limiting nutrient in aquatic systems.

Statement II: Speed of phosphorus movement between biotic and abiotic components, makes it difficult to differentiate between Zooplankton-p, bacterial-p, algae-p or even inorganic-p.

In light of the above statements, choose the ***most appropriate*** answer from the options given below:

A. Both Statement I and Statement II are correct
B. Both Statement I and Statement II are incorrect
C. Statement I is correct but Statement II is incorrect
D. Statement I is incorrect but Statement II is correct

88. Given below are two statements:

Statement I: Alien species are a significant direct threat affecting 30% of all threatened birds, 15% of all threatened plants and 10% of all threatened mammals.

Statement II: At ecosystem level, alien species affect structural diversity, cause local extinction of native species, change fire and nutrient regimes and nutrient cycling patterns as well as produce allelochemical substances.

In light of the above statements, choose the ***most appropriate*** answer from the options given below:

A. Both Statement I and Statement II are correct
B. Both Statement I and Statement II are incorrect
C. Statement I is correct, but Statement II is incorrect
D. Statement I is incorrect, but Statement II is correct

89. Given below are two statements:

Statement I: With reference to solid waste, 'Rubbish' includes both combustible and non-combustible solid waste.

Statement II: Trash is part of rubbish but rubbish does not include garbage.

In light of the above statements, choose the ***most appropriate*** answer from the options given below:

A. Both Statement I and Statement II are true
B. Both Statement I and Statement II are false
C. Statement I is true, but Statement II is false
D. Statement I is false, but Statement II is true

90. Given below are two statements:

Statement I: Past data records help in forecasting weather conditions.

Statement II: The statistical methods of correlation help ONLY in forecasting weather conditions.

In light of the above statements, choose the **most appropriate** answer from the options given below:

A. Both Statement I and Statement II are true
B. Both Statement I and Statement II are false
C. Statement I is true, but Statement II is false
D. Statement I is false, but Statement II is true

Directions (Qs. No. 91-95): *Read the given passage and answer the questions that follow.*

Species diversity, also referred to as biodiversity, is an essential part of proper ecosystem structure and functioning and ecosystem services. Speciation, the formation of new species, and extinction, the permanent loss of species, are the major components of changes in the earth's biological diversity. Over the entire period of life on earth, a few billion years, some plant and animal species have disappeared and new species have appeared as a result of natural evolutionary processes. The background rate of extinction (or normal extinction rate) is a measure of the rate of species disappearance due to natural processes operating under normal conditions. The rate has been determined to approximately five extinctions per year on average over geological time. Much greater rates of extinction have occurred during specific periods in earth's history. These events, called mass extinctions, took place approximately 440, 360, 250, 200, and 65 million years ago. The causes of these extinction events were natural factors such as volcanic eruptions and asteroid impacts. These natural processes produced major changes in climate and habitats to which many species could not adequately adapt. These events are estimated to have caused the extinction of 50 to 96 % of species present at each time. The current extinction rate is estimated to be anywhere from 10 to 1000 times the background rate of extinction, with the rate varying across taxonomic groups. This is the result of a myriad of human activities and their impacts over and above natural factors. The current climate change scenario is changing and accelerating the rate of species extinction by reducing the time plants and animals have to adapt to changes in ecosystem conditions. Further complicating this issue is the fact that biodiversity is unevenly distributed across the planet, where more than 1/3 of the known land plants and vertebrates confined to 2% of the planet surface, the so called, biodiversity hotspots.

91. Dinosaurs disappeared from the planet Earth during the mass extinction event of:
A. 360 my B. 250 my
C. 65 my D. 25 my

92. Which one is NOT a natural factor for mass extinction?
A. Volcanic Activity
B. Asteroid impacts
C. Habitat fragmentation
D. Glaciation

93. Which of the following is not an example of ecosystem service?
A. Circulation of O_2 and CO_2
B. Regulating climate
C. Maintaining biodiversity
D. Soil erosion

94. Major cause of species extinction in modern time could be:
A. deforestation B. desertification
C. climate change D. speciation

95. The Sundaland Biodiversity hotspot includes:
A. Sundarbans
B. Nicobar Islands
C. Lakshadweep
D. Indo-Burma region

Directions (Qs. No. 96-100): *Read the given passage and answer the questions that follow.*

Weathering has affected the long term climate of Earth by changing the Carbon dioxide content of the atmosphere through the inorganic carbon cycle. The planet Venus has a dense atmosphere composed mostly of CO_2, which traps so much solar heat that surface temperature reaches 480°C. Earth has comparatively very little CO_2 in the atmosphere, that is enough to keep most of the surface above freezing but not too hot to support life. However, when Earth first formed, its atmosphere was probably very much like that of Venus, with much more CO_2. The inorganic carbon cycle helps to regulate the climate of Earth because CO_2 is a greenhouse gas, chemical weathering accelerates with warming, and the formation of limestone occurs mostly in warm, tropical oceans. When Earth's climate is warm, chemical weathering and the formation of limestone increase, drawing CO_2 from the atmosphere, which cools the climate. When the global climate cools, chemical weathering and limestone formation slow down, allowing CO_2 to accumulate in the atmosphere from volcanism, which warms the Earth. An increase in chemical weathering can also lead to global cooling by removing more CO_2 from the atmosphere. For example, the Cenozoic uplift and weathering of large regions of high mountains such as the Alps and the Himalaya may have triggered the global cooling that culminated in the glaciations of the Pleistocene epoch.

96. During formation of Earth and Venus, their atmospheric compositions were similar. What reason is NOT responsible for the habitable temperature on Earth?

A. Conversion of CO_2 into organic matter
B. Conversion of CO_2 into carbonate rocks
C. Metamorphism of carbonate rocks
D. Burial of organic matter under the sediments

97. Since the origin of the Earth, CO_2 is naturally and continuously being added to the earth's atmosphere through:
A. weathering of carbonate rocks
B. degassing of magmas
C. oxidation of soil organic matter
D. biological respiration

98. Long term cooling of the climate on Earth is controlled by:
A. physical weathering.
B. chemical weathering of the carbonate rocks
C. biological weathering of the carbonate rocks
D. chemical weathering of the silicate rocks

99. Limestone is primarily:
A. chemogenic product deposited on land
B. chemogenic product deposited on seafloor
C. biogenic product deposited on seafloor
D. biogenic product deposited on land

100. Which one of the following is not an expected signature of glaciation in the Himalayas?
A. Moraines
B. Striations
C. Tills
D. V-type valleys

ANSWERS

1. (B): The first law of thermodynamics, often called the law of conservation of energy, states that energy cannot be created or destroyed in an isolated system. The total energy within a system can change forms (from kinetic to potential energy or vice versa), but the total amount of energy remains constant. This concept underpins many physical processes and is fundamental in understanding energy transfer and transformation in closed systems. For instance, when we burn fuel, it doesn't disappear but is transformed from chemical energy into heat and light energy. Similarly, when we eat, our body converts the chemical energy in food into energy that our cells can use to function and grow. This law contrasts with concepts like conservation of mass (from which it is distinct) and conservation of momentum, which are governed by different principles.

2. (C)

3. (D): Frontier ethics arose from the belief, especially in the 19th and early 20th centuries, that the Earth had an endless bounty of resources for humans to exploit. The first three options (*a*, *b*, *c*) represent this outdated and unsustainable mindset. The idea that "Earth has an unlimited supply of resources" and that "there is always more, and it is all for human use" are obviously in conflict with modern understandings of environmental sustainability. Similarly, viewing humans as apart from nature rather than a part of it has often led to environmental degradation. On the other hand, the fourth option, "We must understand and cooperate with nature," aligns with a sustainable and holistic perspective. Recognizing our interdependence with nature and the need to work within ecological limits is central to creating a sustainable society.

4. (B): The Tbilisi Declaration of 1977 was the outcome of the world's first inter-governmental conference on environmental education, held in Tbilisi, Georgia (then part of the USSR). Organized by UNESCO and UNEP, the conference highlighted the role of environmental education in the sustainable development of societies. The declaration emphasized the importance of environmental education for all age groups and socio-professional categories. While other conferences, like the one in Stockholm in 1972, addressed environmental concerns, it was the Tbilisi conference that specifically focused on and endorsed environmental education on such a broad scale.

5. **(B):** The average salinity of seawater in the oceans is about 3.5%. This means that for every 1,000 grams (or 1 kilogram) of seawater, there are 35 grams of salts dissolved in it, mostly in the form of sodium chloride, or common table salt. Salinity can vary depending on the location and depth in the ocean. Factors that can increase salinity in certain areas include high evaporation rates, ice formation, and the addition of salt from underwater volcanic activity. Factors that decrease salinity include the influx of fresh water from rivers, rainfall, and ice melting. It's essential to understand salinity because it plays a significant role in ocean circulation, marine life habitat, and the overall health of our oceans.

6. **(C):** Nitrogen is a crucial element for plant growth and is a major component of amino acids, proteins, and chlorophyll. Most plants absorb nitrogen from the soil in the form of nitrate ions (NO_3^-). The nitrogen cycle, a fundamental ecological process, facilitates the conversion of atmospheric nitrogen into forms that plants can utilize. In the soil, bacteria convert atmospheric nitrogen (N_2) into ammonia (NH_3) through nitrogen fixation. Other bacteria then transform this ammonia into nitrite ions (NO_2^-) and subsequently into nitrate ions (NO_3^-) through nitrification. While some plants can absorb nitrogen as ammonium ions (NO_4^+), nitrate ions are the more prevalent and preferred form for many plants. It's essential to understand this process because efficient nitrogen uptake by plants plays a significant role in agriculture, ecosystem health, and nutrient cycling.

7. **(D):** DDT (Dichlorodiphenyltrichloroethane) is a synthetic insecticide that gained infamy due to its environmental persistence and harmful effects on wildlife. One of the main reasons for its persistence in the environment is its low reactivity, meaning it does not break down quickly when exposed to light, chemicals, or microbes. Its low vapor pressure and low solubility in water further contribute to its longevity in the environment, as these properties make it less likely to evaporate or dissolve and be washed away. However, its "high rate of evaporation" is NOT a reason for its persistence; in fact, DDT has a relatively low rate of evaporation. The concerns regarding DDT led to its ban in many countries, despite its effectiveness in controlling disease vectors like mosquitoes.

8. **(A):** A grazing food chain represents the sequence of organisms through which energy flows in an ecosystem, starting from primary producers (like plants) and progressing through various levels of consumers. In this context, the flow starts with the Sun, which provides energy to green plants (primary producers). Herbivores (like deer) consume these plants and become food for first-order carnivores (like foxes), which, in turn, may become prey for second-order carnivores (like eagles). This flow represents a typical grazing food chain, with energy moving from the Sun, to plants, to herbivores, and up through higher levels of carnivores.

9. **(C):** The species-area relationship is a well-established ecological principle which describes the increase in species diversity with the increase in area sampled. Specifically, as

the area of a habitat or ecosystem sampled increases, the number of species observed also typically increases. This relationship is vital for biodiversity studies and conservation efforts. It helps determine the minimum area required to sample to ensure that the maximum number of species present in an association or ecosystem is enumerated. The relationship is commonly applied in conservation biology to prioritize areas for protection or to estimate the number of species that might be lost due to habitat destruction.

10. (A): The term "Ecological Footprint" measures how much of the Earth's biologically productive land and sea areas are required to regenerate the resources a human population consumes and to absorb the corresponding waste it generates. This includes areas for farming, grazing, forest products, fishing grounds, built-up areas, and carbon uptake to address emissions from fossil fuels. By comparing a population's Ecological Footprint with the planet's biocapacity (its capacity to regenerate resources and absorb waste), we can assess whether humanity is living within the Earth's ecological limits or is overexploiting the planet. If the Ecological Footprint exceeds the Earth's biocapacity, it indicates that we are depleting natural resources faster than they can be regenerated, leading to environmental degradation and depletion.

11. (C): Natural extinction is the process by which species that cannot adapt to changes in their environment ultimately disappear. Over the vast timescales of Earth's history, countless species have emerged, evolved, and eventually gone extinct due to various reasons, such as environmental changes, competition with other species, or catastrophic events. While mass extinctions (like the one that wiped out the dinosaurs) and anthropogenic extinctions (caused directly or indirectly by human activities) are specific types of extinctions, the term "natural extinction" encompasses the inherent ebb and flow of species over geological time. It's crucial to differentiate natural extinctions from those accelerated by human activities, as the latter often occurs at a rate much faster than the environment's capacity to adapt.

12. (B): Geostrophic wind is the theoretical wind that blows parallel to isobars due to the balance between the pressure gradient force and the Coriolis effect. To compute the geostrophic wind speed V_g, you can use the formula:

$$V_g = \frac{-g\Delta P}{f\rho D}$$

- g is acceleration due to gravity (~9.8 m/s^2)
- ΔP is the pressure difference (4 mb = 400 Pa, since 1 mb = 100 Pa)
- f is the Coriolis parameter (given by 2Q × sin (*latitude*))
- ρ is air density (0.70 kg/m^3)
- D is the distance between isobars (200 km = 200,000 m).

Substituting in the given values, we can solve for V*g*. This would result in a value of approximately –30.6 m/sec, indicating that the geostrophic wind is blowing from the north to the south (negative sign) at this speed.

13. (B): Incompatible elements are those elements that do not fit well into the crystal lattices of the primary minerals that crystallize from a magma during its cooling and solidification. Due to this incompatibility, these elements tend to remain in the liquid phase until the very last stages of crystallization, often concentrating in the residual melt. These elements are valuable in the study of igneous processes because their concentrations can provide clues about the history of a given magma and the processes it has undergone, such as fractional crystallization or magma mixing.

14. (A): The ocean floor is primarily destroyed at convergent plate boundaries. Here, tectonic plates move towards each other, and one of the colliding plates is forced beneath the other in a process called subduction. When oceanic crust is subducted beneath another oceanic or continental plate, it sinks into the mantle where it melts and is recycled. This process is responsible for the formation of deep-sea trenches, the deepest parts of the world's oceans. The Mariana Trench in the western Pacific, for example, is formed by the subduction of the Pacific Plate beneath the Mariana Plate.

15. (D): When estimating geothermal resources, the focus is primarily on understanding the heat contained within the Earth and how it can be harnessed for energy. Key considerations include the depth, thickness, and extent of the geothermal aquifer; properties of the rock formation surrounding the aquifer (as this affects heat conductivity and storage); and the salinity and geochemistry of the fluid within the aquifer (since this impacts the efficiency of energy extraction). Fossil content of rocks, while fascinating for paleontological studies and understanding Earth's history, is not directly relevant to the estimation of geothermal energy potential.

16. (A): Shale gas is predominantly composed of methane (CH_4). Methane is the simplest hydrocarbon with a single carbon atom and four hydrogen atoms. Shale gas is found trapped within shale formations, which are fine-grained sedimentary rocks. The gas is formed over millions of years as organic material within the shale breaks down under heat and pressure. The widespread adoption of hydraulic fracturing (or "fracking") technology has allowed for the extraction of shale gas from formations that were previously uneconomical to tap, leading to a boom in shale gas production in countries like the United States. While shale gas provides a significant energy resource, concerns about environmental impacts, including ground-water contamination and induced seismicity, have accompanied its extraction.

17. (D): Gas hydrates are crystalline solids formed from water and gas, where gas molecules, typically methane, are trapped in cages of hydrogen-bonded water molecules. They typically form under high pressures and low temperatures. There are several methods proposed for producing methane from gas hydrates, including:

- **Thermal stimulation:** Heating the hydrate to release the trapped gas.
- **Depressurization:** Reducing the pressure to dissociate the hydrate.
- **Chemical inhibition:** Introducing chemicals that break down the hydrate structure. However, "Bacterial recovery" is not a known method for producing gas from hydrates. It's worth noting that extracting methane from gas hydrates poses challenges and concerns, including potential geohazards and impacts on climate due to methane's potency as a greenhouse gas.

18. (D): Proximate analysis of coal provides information about its moisture content, volatile matter, ash, and fixed carbon content. It does not directly measure the sulfur content of coal. Sulfur content is essential to know because when coal burns, sulfur dioxide (SO_2) is released, a significant air pollutant and a precursor to acid rain. The sulfur content of coal can vary depending on its source and type. There are specific analytical techniques separate from proximate analysis that are used to determine sulfur content, and these fall under the "ultimate analysis" category.

19. (D): Bioenergy refers to energy obtained from biological sources. It can be derived from plant and animal matter, making it a renewable source of energy, as these resources can be replanted or replenished over time. Common forms of bioenergy include biofuels like ethanol and biodiesel, biogas from anaerobic digestion, and wood or crop residues burned for heat or electricity. Because bioenergy relies on materials that grow (like plants), it can be continually renewed, unlike fossil fuels, which deplete over time. However, the sustainability of certain bioenergy practices is a topic of debate, with concerns over land use, impacts on food supply, and overall carbon neutrality.

20. (C): When a plume from a smokestack is released under a temperature inversion layer, the behavior is called "Fumigation." Temperature inversions occur when warm air overlays cooler air near the ground, preventing the vertical mixing of air. When a plume is released into such conditions, it can become trapped beneath the inversion layer, causing it to spread out horizontally. This can lead to high concentrations of pollutants at ground level, impacting air quality and posing health risks. Such scenarios underscore the importance of understanding atmospheric conditions and their implications for pollution dispersion and control.

21. (B): The hardness of water is primarily due to the presence of calcium (Ca^{2+}) and magnesium (Mg^{2+}) ions. The equivalent weight of Ca^{2+} in terms of calcium carbonate ($CaCO_3$) is calculated using the molecular weights. The molecular weight of Ca is about 40 and that of $CaCO_3$ is approximately 100. Therefore, for every 40 mg/l of Ca^{2+}, there's an equivalent of 100 mg/l as $CaCO_3$. So, for 100 mg/l of Ca^{2+}, the hardness would be $(100/40) \times 100 = 250$ mg/l as $CaCO_3$. Therefore, the correct option is ~250 mg/l.

22. (C): The LN concept in noise measurement refers to the percentage of time during which a certain noise level was exceeded. For instance, $L_{20} = 80$ dB means the noise level was more than 80 dB for 20% of the time. The value that existed for the maximum duration would be the one with the highest percentage, in this case, $L_{40} = 20$ dB, which indicates that the noise level exceeded 20 dB for 40% of the time, the highest percentage in the given options.

23. (C): The period (P) of a sinusoidal sound wave (or any wave) is the time it takes for one complete cycle of the wave to pass a given point. In other words, it's the time between successive peaks or troughs. Frequency (f) is the reciprocal of the period and denotes how many cycles occur in one second. Wavelength (λ) refers to the spatial length of one full wave cycle (from peak to peak or trough to trough), while amplitude (A) measures the height of the wave from its mean value.

24. (C): Radon is a naturally occurring radioactive gas that comes from the decay of uranium in soil, rock, and water. It's colorless, odorless, and tasteless, making it particularly challenging to detect without specialized equipment. Radon can infiltrate buildings and homes, especially in basements and lower floors, where it can concentrate and pose significant health risks when inhaled. Prolonged exposure to high concentrations of radon has been linked to lung cancer, especially among smokers.

25. (C): A sanitary landfill is an engineered method for disposing of solid waste on land. Unlike an open dump, where waste is merely piled up, a sanitary landfill involves spreading the waste in thin layers, compacting it, and then covering it with a layer of soil at the end of each day. This daily cover minimizes the attraction of pests and helps control odors. The design of a sanitary landfill also incorporates systems for collecting leachate (liquid that has percolated through the waste) and gas. Properly managed sanitary landfills have a much reduced environmental impact compared to open dumps, but they still have some environmental footprint, particularly if the liners or other containment systems fail.

26. (C): The Plastic Waste Management Rules were first notified by the Ministry of Environment, Forest and Climate Change in India in 2016. This marked a significant step in addressing the challenges posed by plastic waste in the country. The 2016 rules mandated the responsibility of producers, importers, and brand owners to adopt a system that ensures environmentally sound management of plastic products until the end of their life. This is commonly referred to as the Extended Producer Responsibility (EPR). They also incorporated measures such as phasing out non-recyclable multi-layered plastics within two years, increasing the thickness of carry bags to promote reuse, and setting up plastic waste management systems in rural areas.

27. (B): Pyrolysis is the thermal degradation of solid waste in the absence of oxygen. During pyrolysis, organic waste materials are chemically decomposed by heat, resulting in the production of liquid oil, gas, and solid char. Pyrolysis of plastic waste can produce fuels that are similar to petroleum-based fuels. This process offers potential advantages for waste reduction, as well as the production of valuable products. It differs from incineration, which is the combustion of waste with oxygen, often with the purpose of energy recovery.

28. (C): When considering sustainable strategies for reducing solid waste, the "Timeput approach" is not a recognized or preferred method. Generally, waste management focuses on strategies such as the "Input approach" which minimizes the generation of waste at the source, and the "Through-put approach" which emphasizes recycling and composting. The "Output approach" is more about managing waste after its generation, like using landfills or incineration. Among the options provided, the "Input approach" and "Through-put approach" are crucial parts of the waste hierarchy which prioritizes waste prevention, followed by recycling, recovery, and disposal.

29. (C): Brownfields are abandoned, idled, or under-used industrial and commercial facilities where expansion or redevelopment is complicated by real or perceived contamination. These sites can be problematic due to potential environmental hazards, but they also offer opportunities for redevelopment. Revitalizing and reusing these properties can act as a catalyst for local economic growth and community revitalization. It can also prevent urban sprawl by making use of existing infrastructure rather than building on previously undeveloped land, which is referred to as "Greenfields".

30. (B): The Environmental Impact Assessment (EIA) Notification under the provision of the Environmental (Protection) Act, 1986, is primarily targeted at Development projects. The EIA Notification mandates that specific developmental projects proposed in certain areas require an environmental clearance based on an assessment of their potential environmental impacts. This process involves the evaluation of the environmental, social, and economic aspects of the proposed development. The main objective is to ensure sustainable development by considering and mitigating the potential adverse environmental impacts before a project is approved.

31. (C): Article 51A (g) of the Indian Constitution specifies the duty of every citizen of India to protect and improve the natural environment, which includes forests, lakes, rivers, and wildlife, and to have compassion for living creatures. The inclusion of such a duty emphasizes the importance of environmental protection and conservation in the context of a nation's socio-economic development. While the Constitution has other fundamental duties that emphasize aspects like cultural heritage and scientific temper, 51A (g) remains unique in its focus on ecological responsibility. It underscores the idea that environmental protection is not just the responsibility of the state but a collective responsibility of all citizens.

32. (A): Cleaner production is a concept that focuses on preventing the production of waste rather than dealing with waste after it has been created. It promotes the efficient use of resources at every stage of the production process. Instead of being a product-based tool, it is a process-based strategy. On the other hand, tools like Eco-Labeling and Life Cycle Assessment are product-based. Eco-Labeling offers consumers information about the environmental impact of products, while Life Cycle Assessment examines the environmental impact of a product over its entire life cycle. Industrial Ecology, meanwhile, studies material and energy flows in industrial systems, seeing industries as ecosystems.

33. (D): The relationship $s = cl + o + r + ...$ where variables like climate (cl), organism (o), and relief (r) contribute to soil (s) is a representation of a Multiple Linear Regression. Multiple Linear Regression models the relationship between two or more features and a response by fitting a linear equation to the observed data. In the context of soil science, this relationship emphasizes how various environmental factors interact and contribute to soil formation and characteristics.

34. (D): A Synoptic chart is used to display a wide range of meteorological data over a large region of the Earth's surface at a given point in time using various well-defined weather symbols. This type of chart is particularly valuable for meteorologists when they're predicting weather because it provides a comprehensive overview of weather conditions. Different symbols on the chart can represent different weather conditions like rain, snow, temperature, wind speed and direction, etc. The term "synoptic" itself means "viewed together," emphasizing the chart's capability to provide a collective view of various weather elements for a specified time.

35. (D)

36. (B): The National Action Plan on Climate Change (NAPCC) is a comprehensive framework devised by the Indian government to address climate change issues, adaptation, mitigation, energy efficiency, and natural resource conservation. NAPCC comprises Eight (8) National Missions which are: National Solar Mission, National Mission for Enhanced Energy Efficiency, National Mission on Sustainable Habitat, National Water Mission, National Mission for Sustaining the Himalayan Ecosystem, National Mission for a Green India, National Mission for Sustainable Agriculture, and National Mission on Strategic Knowledge for Climate Change. Each of these missions operates within its defined sphere but collectively they aim to ensure sustainable development while addressing climate change concerns.

37. (C): Rajendra Singh, often referred to as the "Waterman of India," is associated with Tarun Bharat Sangh (TBS), an organization that has been instrumental in bringing water conservation practices to several arid regions in India. Through traditional water management practices, the organization, under Singh's leadership, revived several rivers and brought life back to many drought-prone regions of Rajasthan, India. Their work involved building johads (rainwater storage tanks) and check dams. These interventions have not only recharged groundwater levels but also transformed the socio-economic landscape of these regions.

38. (D): The Marrakesh Accords relate to the Kyoto Protocol of 1997. The Kyoto Protocol is an international treaty aimed at reducing greenhouse gas emissions. The Marrakesh Accords, agreed upon in 2001 during the 7th Conference of Parties (COP7) held in Marrakesh, Morocco, provide detailed rules for the implementation of the Kyoto Protocol. These rules address a range of issues, including the three market-based mechanisms (Emissions Trading, the Clean Development Mechanism, and Joint Implementation), the compliance system, and the accounting of carbon sinks.

39. (A): Red tides refer to the phenomenon where certain phytoplankton species, especially dinoflagellates, bloom in large numbers, resulting in the discoloration of seawater. While the name suggests a red color, the actual hue can vary from deep red to brown, depending on the species involved. These blooms produce toxins that are harmful to marine life, often resulting in mass die-offs of fish and other marine creatures. Moreover, the toxins can become aerosolized and cause respiratory issues in humans. Ingesting shellfish that have fed on these toxic phytoplankton can lead to serious health issues in humans.

40. (C): Exposure-assessment pertains to determining how much of a particular contaminant or toxin individuals or populations are exposed to and the pathways through which they get exposed. In the context of the question, determining the concentration of aflatoxin in peanut butter and then calculating the dose an average person would receive from consuming this peanut butter is an example of exposure assessment. Exposure-assessment forms a crucial component of the risk assessment process as it helps understand the magnitude, frequency, duration, and route of exposure to harmful agents, which is critical for risk characterization and management.

41. (B): The standard sea level pressure is defined as the atmospheric pressure at sea level in a standard atmosphere. This pressure is 101325 Pascal or N/m^2, which can also be expressed as 1013.25 hPa (hectopascal) or kPa (kilo Pascal). Additionally, this pressure translates to 14.69595 psi (pounds per square inch) and 29.92126 inches of mercury (in Hg). The unit 10.33227 m of H_2O is the hydrostatic pressure produced by 10.33227 meters of water column, which is also equivalent to the standard atmospheric pressure.

Therefore, options (*a*), (*b*), (*c*), and (*e*) represent the standard sea level pressure.

42. (B): Photochemical smog, also known as "Los Angeles smog," is primarily formed when nitrogen oxides (NOx) and volatile organic compounds (VOCs) react under sunlight. This produces a series of secondary pollutants, including tropospheric ozone (O_3).

- VOC, NOx, and sunlight are indeed essential ingredients for the formation of photochemical smog.
- Photochemical smog is more common during the summer season due to increased sunlight and stagnant atmospheric conditions.

- NO_2 can absorb sunlight, especially in the 300-400 nm range, and dissociate to form NO and atomic oxygen. The atomic oxygen can then combine with molecular oxygen (O_2) to form ozone.
- While O_2 can dissociate in the stratosphere under the influence of UV-C radiation to produce atomic oxygen, in the troposphere, the predominant source of atomic oxygen is the dissociation of NO_2.
- Ozone concentrations in the troposphere usually peak around midday due to the abundance of sunlight.

Hence, the correct statements are (*a*), (*b*), (*c*), and (*e*).

43. (D): Elemental analysis in environmental samples can be carried out using various analytical techniques.

- UV-VIS spectrophotometer is commonly used for the quantification of chemical species based on their absorption characteristics but is not typically used for elemental analysis.
- AAS (Atomic Absorption Spectroscopy) is an analytical technique used for the determination of specific elements in samples.
- ICP-OES (Inductively Coupled Plasma Optical Emission Spectroscopy) is an advanced analytical technique used for the determination of metal concentrations in environmental samples.
- XRF (X-ray Fluorescence) is a non-destructive analytical technique used for the elemental analysis of various materials.
- XRD (X-ray Diffraction) is used for the analysis of crystal structures and is not primarily for elemental analysis.

Hence, correct options are (*a*), (*b*), (*c*), and (*d*).

44. (C): Disinfection treatment of water is greatly influenced by various factors.

- Temperature indeed affects the rate of disinfection. Higher temperatures can accelerate the disinfection process.
- pH plays a vital role in chlorine disinfection, affecting the equilibrium between hypochlorous acid (HOCl) and hypochlorite ion (OCl^-). HOCl is more effective as a disinfectant than OCl^-.
- When Cl_2 gas is added to water, it reacts to form hydrochloric acid (HCl) and hypochlorous acid (HOCl).
- The disinfection action is mainly due to the HOCl and not the Cl_2 gas itself.
- Combined chlorine forms when chlorine reacts with nitrogenous compounds like ammonia. This can result in chloramines, which are less effective disinfectants compared to free chlorine.

Hence, the correct statements are (*a*), (*b*), (*c*), (*d*) and (*e*).

45. (C): UV radiation plays a critical role in the stratosphere, particularly concerning ozone.

- UV-C radiation is indeed responsible for breaking down O_2 molecules in the stratosphere, which leads to the production of ozone.
- A decrease in overhead O_3 would result in an increase in the UV-B intensity at the ground level. UV-B is harmful and can cause skin cancer and cataracts in humans.
- UV-A is biologically the least harmful among the UV spectra.
- UV-B helps in the dissociation of O_3 in the stratosphere.
- The Chapman mechanism is a series of reactions that describe the creation and destruction of ozone in the stratosphere.

Hence, the correct statements are (*a*), (*b*), (*c*), (*d*) and (*e*).

46. (B): Metals such as copper (Cu), arsenic (As), and chromium (Cr) have been historically used in wood preservatives to protect wood from decay, fungi, and insect damage. The combination of these metals, especially in the form of Chromated Copper Arsenate (CCA), has been a primary wood preservative for many years. This treatment ensures a longer lifespan for wooden structures. However, concerns about the environmental and health effects of arsenic leaching from CCA-treated wood have led to restrictions in its use, especially for residential purposes. Selenium (Se) and molybdenum (Mo) are not standard components of wood preservatives.

47. (D): The biotic structure of an ecosystem is characterized by various attributes that describe the biological community's composition and interactions.

- Species numbers or species richness indicates biodiversity.
- Biomass represents the total weight of living organisms in a given area.
- Life-form pertains to the physical structure or morphology of organisms, such as trees, shrubs, or grasses.
- Life-history describes the different stages in an organism's life, including birth, growth, reproduction, and death.
- Spatial distribution denotes how organisms are arranged in an area, such as clumped, random, or uniform distributions.

All these attributes together provide a comprehensive understanding of the biotic structure and how it interacts with the abiotic environment.

48. (C): The Vienna Pee Dee Belemnite (VPDB) is an international standard for stable isotope ratio measurements, especially for:

- $^{18}O/^{16}O$ – Oxygen isotopes, which are essential in paleoclimatology, hydrology, and paleontology studies.
- $^{13}C/^{12}C$ – Carbon isotopes, crucial for understanding carbon cycling, paleoclimatology, and studying metabolic pathways.

  These standards provide a reference point for isotope ratio measurements, ensuring consistency and comparability of data across different laboratories worldwide.

Hence, correct options are (*c*) and (*e*).

49. (D): Orthoclase, a potassium feldspar mineral, weathers primarily in two stages. Initially, it undergoes hydrolysis, which leads to the production of:

- Silica in a solute form.
- Dissolved potassium ions.
- Kaolinite, a type of clay mineral.
- The bicarbonate ion is not directly produced by the weathering of orthoclase. Instead, CO_2 in the atmosphere or soil reacts with water, forming carbonic acid, which in turn facilitates the weathering of minerals.

Thus, the weathering of orthoclase predominantly results in silica, dissolved potassium ions, and kaolinite.

50. (B): The tropopause's height, which is the boundary between the troposphere and the stratosphere, varies based on several factors:

- **Latitude:** The tropopause is generally lower at the poles and higher at the equator due to temperature differences.
- **Temperature:** Temperature inversions can affect the height of the tropopause.
- **Season:** The tropopause's height can change with the seasons, being higher during summer months due to warmer temperatures.
- **Longitude:** Longitude might play a minor role in some localized instances.

Hence, correct options are (*b*), (*c*) and (*d*).

51. (A): Tonalite and Actinolite are not considered thorium minerals. Monazite and Thorite, on the other hand, are primary sources of thorium. Monazite is a phosphate mineral that contains thorium, cerium, and other rare earth elements. Thorite, as its name suggests, is primarily a thorium silicate mineral. Tonalite is an igneous, plutonic (intrusive) rock, with phaneritic texture. Actinolite is a member of the amphibole group of silicate minerals. While thorium can be found in various minerals, it is primarily extracted from Monazite and Thorite due to their higher thorium concentrations.

52. (B): Sandstone and Limestone are common hydrocarbon reservoir rocks. Reservoir rocks are porous and permeable, allowing them to store and transmit hydrocarbons. Sandstone is a clastic sedimentary rock composed mainly of sand-sized minerals or rock grains, often having good porosity and permeability. Limestone, a carbonate sedimentary rock, can also have the requisite porosity and permeability to act as a reservoir. On the other hand, Shale and Mudstone, being fine-grained sedimentary rocks, typically act as cap rocks or barriers to fluid flow because of their low permeability.

53. (B): Under the National Ambient Air Quality Standards (NAAQS), criteria pollutants include those that are common and pose threats to public health and the environment. These are Carbon Monoxide (CO), Ozone (O_3), and Sulfur Dioxide (SO_2). Carbon Dioxide (CO_2), although a significant greenhouse gas, is not listed as a criteria pollutant under NAAQS. Nitrate (NO_3) is also not a criteria gaseous pollutant, but Nitrogen Dioxide (NO_2) is.

54. (C): Acidity in soils can be introduced or exacerbated by several factors. The presence of soluble aluminum can increase soil acidity as aluminum becomes more soluble under acidic conditions. Mine tailing deposits can lead to acid mine drainage, introducing acidity to surrounding soils. Emissions from thermal power plants often contain sulfur oxides that can lead to acid rain, acidifying soils. Leaching of basic cations can decrease the soil's buffering capacity, making it more susceptible to acidification. However, leaching of Si from silicate minerals does not directly introduce acidity. Instead, it's the dissolution of silicates and the associated release of cations like calcium and magnesium that can affect soil pH.

55. (D): Control of particulate matter in the ambient atmosphere is crucial for environmental health. Bag houses, or fabric filters, capture particulates by forcing air through fabric. Cyclone collectors use centrifugal force to separate particles from the air. Electrostatic precipitators use electric fields to trap and remove particles. Among the options, the Limestone injection multistage burner (LIMB) is more related to controlling sulfur dioxide emissions from coal-fired power plants, while catalytic converters are used in vehicles to reduce harmful emissions of nitrogen oxides, carbon monoxide, and hydrocarbons. Thus, the primary techniques for controlling particulate matter are Bag houses, Cyclone collectors, and Electrostatic precipitators.

56. (D): The correct statements among the given options are that an increase in temperature reduces dissolved oxygen (DO) in lake water, agricultural run-off can introduce turbidity, enrichment of nutrients can speed up lake aging, and both atmospheric exchange and photosynthesis can introduce DO to lake water. Elevated temperatures reduce the solubility of oxygen, leading to reduced DO levels in water bodies. Agricultural run-off often carries with it suspended sediments, which causes turbidity. Nutrient enrichment, or eutrophication, accelerates the aging of lakes, leading to increased productivity and eventually a dominance of vegetation. This can lead to hypoxic or anoxic conditions, which are harmful to many aquatic organisms. Lastly, the primary sources of DO in water bodies are the atmosphere (via diffusion) and photosynthesis by aquatic plants and algae.

57. (D): The greenhouse gases emitted from solid waste landfills primarily include methane (CH_4) and carbon dioxide (CO_2). Methane is produced when organic waste in landfills decomposes anaerobically. Carbon dioxide is also produced but to a lesser extent than methane. Sulphur hexafluoride (SF_6) and ozone (O_3) are not directly emitted from landfills. SF_6 is a potent greenhouse gas used in the electricity industry for insulation and current interruption in electrical equipment. Ozone, while a greenhouse gas and an important component in the stratosphere that shields the Earth from UV radiation, is not emitted from landfills.

58. (B): The Environment (Protection) Act, 1986, was enacted to provide for the protection and improvement of the environment. Its objectives include the prevention of hazards to all living creatures and property, conservation of natural heritage, and maintaining a harmonious relationship between humans and their environment. Checking soil erosion and increasing the productivity of forests are not direct objectives of this Act, although they may be outcomes of some of its provisions.

59. (C)

60. (B): Mukundara Hills Tiger Reserve and Shergarh Wildlife Sanctuary are both located in the state of Rajasthan. The reintroduction of cheetahs in India has been a topic of discussion for many years. These sites have been evaluated and found to be suitable habitats for cheetah reintroduction due to their vast landscapes, prey base, and minimal human-animal conflict. The other sites mentioned, like Gandhi Sagar Wildlife Sanctuary and Madhav National Park, are located in Madhya Pradesh, and Nauradehi Wildlife Sanctuary is in Madhya Pradesh and Chhattisgarh.

61. (C): The National Mission for Sustaining the Himalayan Ecosystem (NMSHE) is one of the eight missions under the National Action Plan on Climate Change (NAPCC). The mission covers a comprehensive range of topics related to the Himalayan region. This includes the monitoring of Himalayan glaciers, enhancing institutional capacities, biodiversity conservation, wildlife conservation, and preserving traditional knowledge systems. The primary objective is to develop a sustainable strategy for conserving the Himalayan ecosystem by understanding the complex processes affecting it. The Himalayan ecosystem is vital not only for India but for the world, due to its biodiversity richness and the rivers that originate from here.

62. (C)

63. (B): For a moderately asymmetrical distribution, the relationship between mean, mode, and median is described by the empirical relationship:

Mode = Mean – 3(Mean – Median)

It means that the distance between the mean and the mode is thrice the distance between the mean and the median. This relationship is used to understand the skewness of the distribution. When data is skewed (either positively or negatively), the values of mean, median, and mode tend to diverge from each other. Understanding these relationships can help in understanding the nature of the distribution and making statistical inferences.

64. (C): The Basel Convention was indeed related to the transboundary movements of hazardous wastes and their disposal. Its primary aim was to prevent the transfer of hazardous waste from developed to less developed countries. The Earth Summit in 2002, also known as the World Summit on Sustainable Development (WSSD), was held in Johannesburg. On the other hand, the Kyoto Protocol was focused on greenhouse gas emissions and not on the banning of CFCs. The Montreal Protocol was associated with the phasing out of ozone-depleting substances, including CFCs. The Convention on Biological Diversity (CBD) came into force in 1993 and not in 1995.

65. (D): Systemic insecticides are those that are absorbed by plants when applied to seeds, soil, or leaves. They then move throughout the plant's tissues. Insects that feed on the plant consume the insecticide and are poisoned. Hence, if an insect does not feed on the plant, it will not be affected by systemic insecticides. Contact pesticides, on the other hand, are designed to kill pests upon direct contact. These pesticides don't need to be ingested by the pests to be effective. They can kill pests either by being directly applied onto them or if the pest comes into contact with the residue. However, systemic insecticides tend to have a longer-lasting effect since they remain active within the plant for an extended period.

66. (C): Remote sensing techniques use different wavelengths to monitor various parameters of the Earth's surface, including vegetation health.

- 0.63-0.69 μm range is sensitive to the amount of vegetation biomass or leaf area, making it essential for monitoring vegetation vigor and health.
- 0.76-0.90 μm is sensitive to the water content in plants. This Near-Infrared (NIR) region is vital as healthy vegetation reflects a lot in this region.
- 1.55-1.75 μm falls into the shortwave infrared range, capturing the absorption band of healthy vegetation. It is used to determine the health of vegetation and its water content.
- 0.52-0.60 μm range captures the green reflectance of healthy vegetation. Green plants absorb sunlight in this range for photosynthesis.

67. (B): Speciation refers to the process by which populations evolve to become distinct species.

- Sympatric speciation occurs when populations differentiate and acquire reproductive isolation within the same geographical area. This might happen due to differences in niche utilization or behavior.
- Parapatric speciation is the process of speciation that occurs between adjacent populations within a continuous habitat. The populations are not geographically separated but develop differences due to slight variations in the environment.
- Adaptive speciation is the rapid process by which organisms adapt to changed environmental conditions to form new species.
- Allopatric speciation occurs when populations are geographically isolated, leading to differentiation over time.

68. (C)

69. (C)

70. (B)

71. (B): Mohs scale of mineral hardness is a qualitative ordinal scale that characterizes the scratch resistance of various minerals.

- Calcite has a hardness of 3. It can be easily scratched by a knife or a coin.
- Topaz possesses a hardness of 8. Due to this, topaz is often used in jewelry as it's relatively resistant to scratching.
- Apatite stands at a hardness of 5, which makes it about the average hardness of most minerals.
- Quartz has a hardness of 7. Quartz is a common mineral found in Earth's crust, and due to its hardness, it's often used in making glass and in the electronics industry.

72. (B): The elemental composition varies in organic substances, but their relative percentage can be broadly categorized as:

- Carbon generally makes up 60-90% of the composition in organic compounds. It's the basic building block of life and the backbone of organic molecules.
- Hydrogen can range between 1-12%. It's abundant in hydrocarbons and other organic molecules.
- Oxygen typically has a composition between 2-20%. It's found in most organic molecules, especially in carbohydrates, lipids, proteins, and nucleic acids.
- Nitrogen has a range of 1-3%. It's an essential element in amino acids, the building blocks of proteins, and in nucleic acids.

73. (B): Environmental Impact Assessment (EIA) is a tool used to predict the environmental effects of a project:

- Scoping is the process to identify key issues and impacts to establish study limits. It determines the content and extent of the matters that will be assessed during the EIA process.
- Evaluation is the step where the significance and social importance of measured impacts, especially the adverse ones, are determined.
- ES Review involves the systematic appraisal of the quality of the Environmental Impact Statement (EIS) and checks its compliance with legislation. It determines if any modification is required.
- Monitoring ensures compliance with terms and conditions and monitors environmental impacts to ensure they are within accepted limits.

74. (*)

75. (*)

76. (D): The electromagnetic spectrum comprises various types of electromagnetic radiation arranged according to their wavelength or frequency.

- X-Ray has a very short wavelength, ranging from about 0.01 to 10 nanometers.
- Ultra Violet comes next with wavelengths between 10 and 400 nanometers.
- Visible light is just a small portion of the spectrum that our eyes can perceive, with wavelengths from approximately 400 to 700 nanometers.
- Near Infrared wavelengths range from about 700 nanometers to 1 micrometer.
- Thermal Infrared has wavelengths from about 3 micrometers to 30 micrometers.

Thus, the increasing order of wavelength is X-Ray, Ultra Violet, Visible, Near IR, and Thermal IR.

77. (B): Image interpretation elements help in understanding and deciphering satellite images or aerial photographs.

- Association involves the relationship between different objects or features and is complex since it needs a deeper understanding of the landscape.

- Aspect refers to the direction that a slope faces. It's a more specific feature that requires understanding of the surrounding environment.
- Pattern denotes the spatial arrangement of objects.
- Texture represents the visual roughness or smoothness of an image.
- Location is the simplest, referring to the geographical position of a feature.

Therefore, the decreasing order of complexity is Association, Aspect, Pattern, Texture, and Location.

78. (C): Metamorphic rocks are formed under heat and pressure conditions. Their grade indicates the intensity of these conditions.

- Slate forms under the lowest metamorphic conditions and is characterized by its fine grain.
- Phyllite is slightly higher in grade than slate, having a silky sheen.
- Gneiss is higher in grade, with distinct banding due to the separation of mafic and felsic minerals.
- Migmatite is at the highest grade before melting, comprising both metamorphic and igneous components.

So, the increasing metamorphic grade order is Slate, Phyllite, Gneiss, and Migmatite.

79. (C): Fractional crystallization of magma involves the systematic cooling and solidification of different minerals at specific temperatures.

- Olivine crystallizes at the highest temperatures.
- Pyroxene follows olivine as the temperature drops.
- Amphibole crystallizes at a still lower temperature.
- Biotite crystallizes at one of the lowest temperatures in this sequence.

This sequence demonstrates the Bowen's reaction series, which describes the order of mineral crystallization from magma.

80. (B): Coal is a sedimentary rock, and its type is determined by its carbon content, which increases with maturity.

- Peat is the precursor to coal, with the lowest carbon content and highest moisture content.
- Lignite or brown coal is slightly higher in carbon content than peat.
- Sub-bituminous is a transition between lignite and bituminous with a higher carbon content.
- Bituminous is soft coal with even more carbon.
- Anthracite is hard coal with the highest carbon content and purity.

Thus, the increasing order of carbon content is Peat, Lignite, Sub-bituminous, Bituminous, and Anthracite.

81. (C): The typical arrangement of soil horizons in a well-developed soil profile, starting from the top, is as follows:

- **O Horizon:** This is the topmost layer comprised mainly of organic matter such as decomposing leaves, plants, and other materials. It's dark in color due to the organic content.
- **A Horizon:** Known as the topsoil, this horizon is rich in minerals and organic matter. It's generally dark in color and is where most plant roots grow.
- **E Horizon:** This is the eluviation or leaching layer where minerals and organic matter are leached to lower layers. It's often lighter in color.

- **B Horizon:** Known as the subsoil, this horizon accumulates minerals and organic matter from above layers. It can be richer in clay and may have different colors based on its composition.
- **C Horizon:** This is the parent material, which can be partially disintegrated rock or unweathered rock. The soil properties here are less influenced by the soil-forming processes.

This sequence reflects the natural processes of soil development, with organic matter accumulation at the top and mineral accumulation and leaching occurring as you move deeper.

82. (B): Landfills go through several stages of decomposition:

- **Aerobic Phase:** Immediately after the waste is dumped, the available oxygen supports aerobic decomposition. This is a short phase characterized by a rapid rise in temperature.
- **Acid Phase:** As oxygen gets depleted, anaerobic decomposition starts. During this phase, acidogenic bacteria produce organic acids and gases like carbon dioxide and hydrogen. This phase is characterized by a drop in pH.
- **Unsteady Methanogenesis:** In this stage, the pH starts rising, and there's a shift towards methanogenic conditions. The production of methane begins but is not steady.
- **Steady Methanogenesis:** Here, methane production stabilizes, and the landfill starts emitting a steady stream of methane gas.

Understanding these stages is crucial for managing landfill emissions and harnessing methane for energy.

83. (B): The steps for ecological impact analysis are:

- **Scoping:** It identifies potential environmental impacts that might require a detailed analysis.
- **Focussing**: This step prioritizes the identified impacts based on their significance.
- **Impact Assessment:** At this stage, the magnitude and nature of each impact are assessed using various methodologies.
- **Impact Mitigation:** This is the step where strategies to mitigate the negative impacts are designed and implemented.
- **Impact Evaluation:** Finally, the success of the mitigation measures is evaluated.

This systematic process ensures that all potential environmental impacts of a project are adequately addressed.

84. (B): When calculating the confidence interval for rainfall:

- **Plot a time series graph on available data:** This step helps in visualizing the data and spotting any trend or anomaly.
- **Calculate three-year moving average:** This smoothens the data and helps in identifying any underlying trend.
- **Compute the standard error for estimate:** Standard error measures the statistical accuracy of an estimate and is crucial for determining confidence intervals.
- **Choose confidence coefficient of 95%:** 95% is a common choice, meaning you are 95% confident that the interval contains the true mean.
- **Compute sample statistic 't':** The t-statistic, combined with the standard error, will determine the width of the confidence interval.

Using this sequence ensures an accurate and meaningful confidence interval.

85. (A): Assertion (A) states that Natural Ecosystems are less vulnerable to drastic changes and are more adaptive to weather changes. This is correct because these ecosystems have evolved over a long time, creating a balance and resilience against various disturbances.

Reason (R) mentions that Natural Ecosystems are mature from a succession viewpoint and are biotically diverse with less synchronization of growth. This is also accurate. A mature ecosystem, reached after successive stages of ecological succession, has a high level of biodiversity. Biodiversity provides an ecosystem with stability and resilience. When growth patterns are not synchronized, the ecosystem can better withstand shocks as not all species are affected at once.

Given both the Assertion and the Reason are true and the Reason correctly explains the Assertion, the answer is "Both (A) and (R) are true and (R) is the correct explanation of (A)".

86. (A): Humic and fulvic acids are principal components of humic substances, which are organic compounds found in the soil. Humic acid is less soluble in acidic solutions when compared to fulvic acid. The reason for this behavior primarily relates to their molecular structures. Humic acid has a much larger molecular weight compared to fulvic acid, often ranging from 100 to 1000 times more. This significant difference in molecular weight affects its solubility. Additionally, humic acid generally contains less oxygen content than fulvic acid. The oxygen content in a molecule can influence its solubility in water due to the presence of functional groups that can participate in hydrogen bonding or other interactions. Therefore, both the molecular weight and the oxygen content are factors influencing the solubility of humic acid, especially in acidic solutions.

87. (A): Soluble reactive phosphorus (SRP) is the form of phosphorus that is available for plants and algae in aquatic systems. It's often considered a limiting nutrient because its availability can dictate the growth rate of aquatic plants and algae. When in excess, SRP can lead to eutrophication, which is an overabundance of nutrients in water bodies leading to excessive plant and algal growth. On the other hand, the rapid interchange of phosphorus between its biotic (living) and abiotic (non-living) forms in aquatic systems, including Zooplankton-p, bacterial-p, algae-p, or inorganic-p, makes it challenging to differentiate between them. This rapid cycling emphasizes the need for effective phosphorus management in aquatic ecosystems.

88. (A): Alien species, also referred to as invasive species, can cause significant ecological disruption when introduced to new environments. They can outcompete, prey on, or bring diseases to native species, sometimes leading to reductions or extinctions of native species. The statistics mentioned, such as affecting 30% of threatened birds, is indicative of the severity of the impact of alien species. At an ecosystem level, the introduction of invasive species can bring about a multitude of changes. These can include impacting structural diversity, causing local extinction of native species, altering fire frequencies and patterns, disrupting nutrient cycling, and even introducing new chemicals into the environment, such as allelochemicals, which can inhibit the growth of other plants.

89. (A): In the context of solid waste management, rubbish can be broadly classified into two categories: combustible and non-combustible. Combustible rubbish includes items like paper, wood, and certain types of textiles, while non-combustible rubbish consists of materials like glass and metals. Trash is often used synonymously with rubbish and typically includes waste items that do not decompose quickly, such as paper, glass, and metals. On the other hand, garbage refers to waste items that decompose quickly, especially food wastes. Therefore, while trash can be considered a subset of rubbish, rubbish doesn't include garbage.

90. (C): Past data records are indeed invaluable for forecasting weather conditions. Historical data, when analyzed, can provide patterns or trends which become the foundation for predicting future weather conditions. For instance, understanding past monsoon patterns might help meteorologists predict upcoming monsoon intensities or timings. However, Statement II is not accurate. While statistical methods, including correlation, are pivotal tools in forecasting weather conditions, they are not exclusive to this purpose. Statistical methods find applications in a plethora of fields, from economics to biology. In meteorology, apart from statistical methods, numerical weather prediction models, which solve complex equations to predict future weather conditions, are also extensively used. Thus, while correlation and other statistical methods are important, they are not the only tools used for weather forecasting.

91. (C) **92.** (C) **93.** (D)

94. (C) **95.** (B) **96.** (C)

97. (B) **98.** (D) **99.** (C)

100. (D)

Previous Years' Paper (Solved)

National Testing Agency (NTA)

UGC-NET Junior Research Fellowship & Assistant Professor Eligibility Exam

ENVIRONMENTAL SCIENCE, September–2022*

(Online exam held on 30-09-2022)

PAPER-II

Note: *This paper contains* ***hundred*** *(****100****) objective type questions of* ***two*** *(2) marks each.* ***All*** *questions are* ***compulsory****.*

1. The grain size (USDA) of silt in soil ranges between:
A. 0.2 mm to 0.5 mm
B. 0.5 mm to 0.1 mm
C. 0.1 mm to 0.05 mm
D. 0.05 mm to 0.002 mm

2. What will be BOD_5 for a wastewater sample when 21 ml of sample is diluted to 300 ml in BOD bottle to determine dissolved oxygen.
[Given: Initial DO_1 = 10 mg/*l*; Five days later DO_5 = 5 mg/*l*]
A. ~ 5 mg/*l* B. ~ 25 mg/*l*
C. ~ 71.4 mg/*l* D. ~ 75 mg/*l*

3. What will be the concentration of 40 ppb SO_2 in $\mu g/m^3$ unit at 25°C?
A. ~ 0.04 $\mu g/m^3$ B. ~ 1047 $\mu g/m^3$
C. ~ 104.7 $\mu g/m^3$ D. ~ 10.47 $\mu g/m^3$

4. National Ambient air quality standards typically include following components:
A. Maximum and Minimum pollutant levels, adjustment for co-pollutants
B. Abetment strategies, non-attainment penalties
C. Ambient temperature, size distribution and relative humidity
D. Indicator (Chemical/Chemical class), Averaging time, Pollutant form and level

5. Primary air pollutants differ from secondary air pollutants as they:
A. are present in levels that can be weighed on filter paper.
B. are directly emitted from identified sources.
C. have undergone chemical transformation in air after release from identified sources.
D. are designated as hazardous air pollutants.

6. Continuity equation expresses the law of conservation of:
A. Momentum
B. Mass
C. Entropy
D. Energy

7. Which of the following statements correctly represent the environmental wisdom world-wide?
A. Our success depends on how well we manage the earth's life support systems mostly for our benefits.
B. Our success depends on how well we manage the earth's life support systems for our benefit and for the rest of nature.
C. Our success depends on learning how nature sustains itself and integrating such lessons from nature into the ways we think.
D. Our success depends on using environmentally beneficial forms of economic growth and discourage environmentally harmful forms.

* Exam of December 2021 & June 2022.

8. Exposure concentration is ______.
A. the amount of the chemical that is received by the target.
B. the amount of chemical present in the medium with which an Organism has contact.
C. the amount of the chemical that is excreted by the target.
D. the amount of the chemical that is metabolized by the target

9. In ecotoxicology studies, ED-50 is ______.
A. the dose that affects 50% of the population or observed subjects.
B. the dose that affects 95% of the population or observed subjects.
C. the dose that affects 25% of the population or observed subjects.
D. the dose that do not affect 50% of the total population.

10. A hypothesis, that predicts a linear relationship in which rate of ecosystem processes is maximum with greatest number of species, is known as:
A. Rivet-popper hypothesis.
B. Redundancy hypothesis.
C. Diversity-stability hypothesis.
D. Idiosyncratic hypothesis.

11. Which of the following is not a phase of secondary succession?
A. Initiation B. Continuation
C. Termination D. Invasion

12. The Concept of *r*- and *k*- selection was originally given by:
A. MacArthur and Wilson (1967)
B. Grime (1979)
C. Molles (2008)
D. Mayr (1942)

13. The prefix "steno" and "eury" have been used for:
A. comparing the relative degree of tolerance of an organism to a given environmental factor.
B. comparing the body size of organisms occurring in a given habitat.
C. comparing the metabolic activity of organisms in a given habitat.
D. comparing the distribution limits of organisms occurring across a biome.

14. The strong and rapidly moving circumpolar upper air westerly circulation in a narrow belt of a few hundred kilometers width in the upper limit of the troposphere is called _____.
A. Rossby waves
B. Jet streams
C. Walker streams
D. Hadley Circulation

15. Coriolis effect is:
A. the influence of Earth's rotation, which tends to turn air towards the right in the Northern Hemisphere.
B. the influence of Earth's rotation, which tends to turn air upwards in the Northern Hemisphere.
C. the influence of Earth's rotation, which tends to turn air towards the left in the Northern Hemisphere.
D. the influence of Earth's rotation, which tends to turn air downwards in the Northern Hemisphere.

16. The boundary between fresh and salty groundwater along shorelines is determined by:
A. recharge and discharge in freshwater aquifer.
B. composition of salty and fresh groundwater.
C. rainfall.
D. nature of aquifer.

17. The sum of diffused and direct solar radiation, is called:
A. continental solar radiation.
B. global solar radiation.
C. total solar radiation.
D. universal solar radiation.

18. Which one of the following elements is used in making Photovoltaic Solar cell?
A. Tungsten B. Silver
C. Lead D. Silicon

19. The destructive distillation of coal yielding products such as gasoline, diesel oil and other products, is known as _____.
A. gasification
B. precipitation
C. condensation
D. liquefaction

20. Which process facilitates conversion of raw fat into biodiesel in the presence of alcohol?
A. Glycerol conversion
B. Saccharification
C. Torrefaction
D. Transesterification

21. Which plant/tree has been recommended in India for extraction of biodiesel?
A. Wheat *(Triticum aestivum)*
B. Sugarcane *(Saccharum officinarum)*
C. Mango *(Mangifera indica)*
D. Karanja *(Pongamia pinnata)*

22. Anammox bacteria is required for which of the following steps in wastewater treatment?
A. Nitrate to Nitrite conversion
B. Nitrite to Nitrate conversion
C. Molecular Nitrogen to Ammonia conversion
D. Ammonium ion to Molecular Nitrogen conversion

23. Which of the following is an INCORRECT statement?
A. Humus represents organic matter, dark in colour.
B. Acid soils are devoid of basic cations.
C. Humus contains cellulose and hemi cellulose.
D. Humic and fulvic acids in humus form hydrophobic colloid whereas clay colloids are hydrophilic in nature.

24. The use of bacteria and other microorganisms to breakdown hazardous waste into relatively harmless components, is termed as:
A. phyto remediation.
B. source reduction process.
C. integrated waste management.
D. bioremediation.

25. Which of the following is INCORRECT about the given decomposition reaction?

$$\underset{(1)}{2CH_2O} \xrightarrow{\text{Bacteria}} \underset{(2)}{CH_4} + \underset{(3)}{CO_2}$$

A. All carbon in (1) is oxidized.
B. Some Carbon in (1) is oxidized and some is reduced.
C. This is an example of fermentation.
D. It produces gas that some time catches fire.

26. Heavy metals are retained in soil/sludge by:
A. complexation by humic substances in organic particles
B. absorption on to surface of mineral particles
C. precipitation reaction
D. solubilization in acidic conditions

27. There is often a formal review and licensing procedures of Environmental Impact Assessment. Who would NOT carry out such a procedure?
A. The proponent of the development project.
B. The local government authority ultimately responsible for licensing development project.
C. Another government agency which can be given responsibility for licensing development project.
D. An independent body having knowledge of the development project.

28. As per United Nations Framework Convention on Climate Change (UNFCC), which of the following has role in the assessment and review of the effective implementation of the convention?
A. Subsidiary Body for Scientific and Technical Advice (SBSTA)
B. Subsidiary Body for Implementation (SBI)
C. The Conference of Parties (COP)
D. The Climate Change Secretariat

29. "A financial mechanism through which developing countries would be rewarded for emission reduction achieved by taking action to reduce deforestation and forest degradation" refers to:

A. Clean Development Mechanism.
B. Global Forest Carbon Mechanism.
C. Reduced Emission from Deforestation and Forest Degradation.
D. Incentive-Compatible Selection Mechanism.

30. Which of the following principle was introduced in 1972 by the Organization for Economic Cooperation and Development (OECD) guiding principles concerning Institutional Economic Aspects of Environmental Pollution?

A. Frontier Diplomacy Principle
B. Polluter Pays Principle
C. Human Rights and Environment Principle
D. Principle of Environment Protection

31. Which section of Environmental (Protection) Act, 1986 deals with offences by companies?

A. Article 13 B. Article 14
C. Article 16 D. Article 18

32. Which Article of the Constitution of India states that it shall be the duty of every citizen of India to protect and improve the natural environment and to have compassion for living creatures?

A. Article 48A B. Article 51A
C. Article 21A D. Article 13A

33. Which among the following is the first major Environmental Protection act to be promulgated in India?

A. Biological Diversity Act
B. Environmental Protection Act
C. Forest Conservation Act
D. Wildlife Protection Act

34. Which of the following sections of the Indian Penal Code refers to making atmosphere noxious to health as a punishable offence?

A. Section 275 B. Section 276
C. Section 277 D. Section 288

35. Which of the following is NOT included during Environmental Impact Assessment (EIA)?

A. A detailed assessment of the planned project and selected alternative compared to the baseline conditions.
B. Qualitative description measuring higher, medium and low impacts.
C. Quantitative description measuring physical values of water withdrawal, sewage produced and pollutants released.
D. All the data collection, analysis and developed plans summarized together in a well-structured and concise documents.

36. To find out the degree of linear relationship between age and height of trees, the parameter to be estimated is:

A. Standard Error
B. Correlation coefficient
C. Median
D. Standard deviation

37. The Coefficient of Variation can be measured by:

A. (Mean/Standard deviation) × 100
B. (Median/Standard deviation) × 100
C. (Standard deviation/Mean) × 100
D. (Standard deviation/Median) × 100

38. Which of the following is a nominal variable?

A. Level of rainfall (Mild, Moderate, Severe)
B. Blood group type (A, B, AB, O)
C. Height of a tree
D. Socio-economic status (Low, Middle, High)

39. 'Hysteresis' is the best defined as:

A. A change occurring at a steady rate where rate is defined by the directions of change.
B. A change occurring at a steady rate followed by sudden increased rate catastrophically.
C. A change that occurs at steady rate and maintains so.
D. A change that is sudden non-linear between two stable states without the prospect of reverse.

40. Which one of the following is correctly matched pair?

A. Biodiversity Conservation — Basel Convention
B. Global Warming — Montreal Protocol
C. Climate Change — Kyoto Protocol
D. Groundwater Pollution — Ramsar Convention

41. Who among the following received Noble Prize for peace and started the Green Belt Movement?
A. Rajendra K. Pachauri
B. Wagai M. Matthai
C. Jim Bohlen
D. Gro Harlem Brundtland

42. Genetic Engineering is possible because:
A. Restriction endonucleases purified from bacteria can be used *in vitro*.
B. The phenomenon of transduction in bacteria is well understood.
C. We can cut DNA at specific sites by endonucleases like DNase.
D. We can see DNA by electron microscope.

43. LEED, one of the Sustainable Habitat green rating systems, refers to:
A. Leadership in Energy and Efficiency Design
B. Leadership in Energy and Efficiency Document
C. Leadership in Energy and Environment Design
D. Leadership in Energy and Environment Document

44. 'Prerak Dauur Samman', the annual award given under which of the following scheme of Government of India?
A. Smart Cities
B. Namami Gange
C. Swachh Bharat Abhiyan
D. Green India Mission

45. Given below are two statements, one is labelled as Assertion (A) and the other is labelled as Reason (R):

Assertion (A) : Active ingredient in most pesticides are organic chlorine compounds.

Reason (R) : Organo chlorines have low solubility in water, high solubility in hydrocarbon like environment and have relatively high toxicity to insects and low toxicity to humans.

In light of the above statements, choose the ***correct*** answer from the options given below:
A. Both (A) and (R) are true and (R) is the correct explanation of (A)
B. Both (A) and (R) are true, but (R) is NOT the correct explanation of (A)
C. (A) is true, but (R) is false
D. (A) is false, but (R) is true

46. Given below are two statements, one is labelled as Assertion (A) and the other is labelled as Reason (R).

Assertion (A) : Temperature of large water-body varies more slowly than that of the land of comparable size.

Reason (R) : Specific heat of water is high *i.e.,* about five times of soil.

In light of the above statements, choose the ***correct*** answer from the options given below:
A. Both (A) and (R) are true and (R) is the correct explanation of (A)
B. Both (A) and (R) are true, but (R) is NOT the correct explanation of (A)
C. (A) is true, but (R) is false
D. (A) is false, but (R) is true

47. Given below are two statements, one is labelled as Assertion (A) and the other is labelled as Reason (R).

Assertion (A) : Small increase in wind velocity and height of turbine produces a large increase in energy yield.

Reason (R) : Energy yield from wind is proportional to third power of wind speed and wind speed increases with height above ground.

In light of the above statements, choose the ***correct*** answer from the options given below:
A. Both (A) and (R) are true and (R) is the correct explanation of (A)
B. Both (A) and (R) are true, but (R) is NOT the correct explanation of (A)
C. (A) is true, but (R) is false
D. (A) is false, but (R) is true

48. Given below are two statements, one is labelled as Assertion (A) and the other is labelled as Reason (R).

Assertion (A) : α and β particles, emitted during a radioactive decay of a nucleus are simply nucleus of Helium and electron and are called as ionizing radiations.

Reason (R) : α and β particles produced in the radioactive decay are ejected with an incredible amount of energy of motion. When this energy is absorbed by matter encountered by the particle, it often ionises atoms and molecules.

In light of the above statements, choose the ***correct*** answer from the options given below:
A. Both (A) and (R) are true and (R) is the correct explanation of (A)
B. Both (A) and (R) are true, but (R) is NOT the correct explanation of (A)
C. (A) is true, but (R) is false
D. (A) is false, but (R) is true

49. Given below are two statements, one is labelled as Assertion (A) and the other is labelled as Reason (R).

Assertion (A) : Cool pavements are generally composed of light coloured material with high permeability.

Reason (R) : Lighter coloured pavements reflect more light and absorb less heat. High permeability allow water to percolate and evaporate, thereby cooling pavement and surrounding air.

In light of the above statements, choose the ***correct*** answer from the options given below:
A. Both (A) and (R) are true and (R) is the correct explanation of (A)
B. Both (A) and (R) are true, but (R) is NOT the correct explanation of (A)
C. (A) is true, but (R) is false
D. (A) is false, but (R) is true

50. Given below are two statements, one is labelled as Assertion (A) and the other is labelled as Reason (R).

Assertion (A) : Dematerialization, the progressive decrease in size and weight of a product as a result of technological improvement is an example of source reduction.

Reason (R) : New product is more durable than the one being replaced.

In light of the above statements, choose the ***correct*** answer from the options given below:
A. Both (A) and (R) are true and (R) is the correct explanation of (A)
B. Both (A) and (R) are true, but (R) is NOT the correct explanation of (A)
C. (A) is true, but (R) is false
D. (A) is false, but (R) is true

51. Arrange the following elements of image interpretations in order of increasing complexity.
(*a*) Location (*b*) Tone
(*c*) Situation (*d*) Pattern
(*e*) Texture

Choose the ***correct*** answer from the options given below:
A. (*a*), (*b*), (*d*), (*c*), (*e*)
B. (*a*), (*b*), (*e*), (*d*), (*c*)
C. (*c*), (*e*), (*d*), (*b*), (*a*)
D. (*e*), (*b*), (*a*), (*d*), (*c*)

52. Basalts are composed of the following minerals.
(*a*) Olivine (*b*) Pyroxene
(*c*) Quartz (*d*) Orthoclase
(*e*) Plagioclase

Choose the ***correct*** answer from the options given below:

A. (*a*), (*b*) and (*c*) only

B. (*a*), (*b*) and (*d*) only

C. (*a*), (*b*) and (*e*) only

D. (*b*), (*c*) and (*d*) only

53. Arrange the following minerals with increasing order of stability for weathering.

(*a*) Illite

(*b*) Olivine

(*c*) Calcite

(*d*) Ca rich feldspar

(*e*) Na rich feldspar

Choose the ***correct*** answer from the options given below:

A. (*b*), (*c*), (*d*), (*e*), (*a*)

B. (*b*), (*c*), (*e*), (*d*), (*a*)

C. (*c*), (*b*), (*e*), (*d*), (*a*)

D. (*c*), (*b*), (*d*), (*e*), (*a*)

54. Choose the correct sequence of filtration processes used for sequential removal of particles from coarser (1 μm) to finer grain sizes.

(*a*) Microfiltration (*b*) Ultrafiltration

(*c*) Nanofiltration (*d*) Reverse Osmosis

Choose the ***correct*** answer from the options given below:

A. (*d*), (*c*), (*b*), (*a*) B. (*a*), (*b*), (*c*), (*d*)

C. (*d*), (*c*), (*a*), (*b*) D. (*a*), (*b*), (*d*), (*c*)

55. In waste pollution prevention hierarchy, arrange following from least preferred to most preferred.

(*a*) Waste Concentration

(*b*) Waste Separation

(*c*) Waste treatment

(*d*) Recycling or Reuse

(*e*) Landfill

Choose the ***correct*** answer from the options given below:

A. (*e*), (*a*), (*c*), (*b*), (*d*)

B. (*e*), (*c*), (*a*), (*b*), (*d*)

C. (*e*), (*c*), (*b*), (*a*), (*d*)

D. (*e*), (*c*), (*a*), (*d*), (*b*)

56. Given below are two statements.

Statement I : Key to nitrogen cycle is nitrogen fixing bacteria, which has ability to fix N_2 or combine gases N_2 with hydrogen to form NH_3.

Statement II : Nitrogen cycle includes fixation of molecular N_2 to ammonia to nitrite to nitrate only. It does not include denitrification process.

In light of the above statements, choose the ***correct*** answer from the options given below:

A. Both Statement I and Statement II are true

B. Both Statement I and Statement II are false

C. Statement I is true, but Statement II is false

D. Statement I is false, but Statement II is true

57. Given below are two statements.

Statement I : Halons used as fire extinguishers are bromine containing hydrogen free substances and are involved in catalytic destruction of ozone in Stratosphere.

Statement II : In order to protect ozone layer in stratosphere, use of CFC was globally replaced by HCFCs, HFC's followed by Halons after Kyoto protocol.

In light of the above statements, choose the ***correct*** answer from the options given below:

A. Both Statement I and Statement II are true

B. Both Statement I and Statement II are false

C. Statement I is true, but Statement II is false

D. Statement I is false, but Statement II is true

58. Given below are two statements.

Statement I : Yellow carotenes and pale-yellow xanthophyll pigments are with strong reflectance primarily in the blue wavelength regime of Electromagnetic Radiation (EMR).

Statement II : There are many other pigments present in the palisade mesophyll cells that are usually marked by the abundance of chlorophyll pigments.

In light of the above statements, choose the ***correct*** answer from the options given below:

A. Both Statement I and Statement II are true

B. Both Statement I and Statement II are false

C. Statement I is true, but Statement II is false

D. Statement I is false, but Statement II is true

59. Given below are two statements.

Statement I : Ecotypes are discrete entity because they have clear differences in morphology, physiology and phenology in relation to particular environmental conditions.

Statement II : The environmentally induced variations in ecotypes are not heritable and do not have adaptive value to a particular habitat

In light of the above statements, choose the ***correct*** answer from the options given below:

A. Both Statement I and Statement II are true

B. Both Statement I and Statement II are false

C. Statement I is true but Statement II is false

D. Statement I is false but Statement II is true

60. Given below are two statements.

Statement I : A confined aquifer is an aquifer which is confined between impervious beds such as aquicludes or aquifuges.

Statement II : Recharge of this aquifer takes place only in the area where it is exposed at the ground surface.

In light of the above statements, choose the ***correct*** answer from the options given below:

A. Both Statement I and Statement II are true

B. Both Statement I and Statement II are false

C. Statement I is true, but Statement II is false

D. Statement I is false, but Statement II is true

61. Given below are two statements.

Statement I : Noise pollution exists in the form of energy and is highly subjective in nature unlike air pollution.

Statement II : Noise pollution exists irrespective of loudness of sound and causes both physiological and psychological stress among individual or group of individuals.

In light of the above statements, choose the ***correct*** answer from the options given below:

A. Both Statement I and Statement II are true

B. Both Statement I and Statement II are false

C. Statement I is true, but Statement II is false

D. Statement I is false, but Statement II is true

62. Given below are two statements about Baghouse filter used to control air pollution.

Statement I : Baghouse filters are fabric bag filter which can be repeatedly cleaned and reused. Collection efficiency can be very high (99.9% for all size of particles).

Statement II : Collection efficiency of baghouse filters decreases as dust collected on filters and lead to decrease in pressure drop which increases airflow or decreases cost of forcing air through filters.

In light of the above statements, choose the ***correct*** answer from the options given below:

A. Both Statement I and Statement II are true
B. Both Statement I and Statement II are false
C. Statement I is true, but Statement II is false
D. Statement I is false, but Statement II is true

63. Given below are two statements.

Statement I : An incineration process used to destroy highly toxic and hazardous waste differs from the municipal solid waste incineration process.

Statement II : Incineration emits small but significant amounts of numerous toxic chemicals and produces ash residues (bottom and flyash) which must be buried in approved landfills.

In light of the above statements, choose the ***correct*** answer from the options given below:

A. Both Statement I and Statement II are true
B. Both Statement I and Statement II are false
C. Statement I is true, but Statement II is false
D. Statement I is false, but Statement II is true

64. Given below are two statements.

Statement I : Student t-test is a non-parametric test.

Statement II : Paired t-test compares the two correlated sample means.

In light of the above statements, choose the ***correct*** answer from the options given below:

A. Both Statement I and Statement II are true
B. Both Statement I and Statement II are false
C. Statement I is true, but Statement II is false
D. Statement I is false, but Statement II is true

65. Which of the following compounds in dirty dozens' list of POPs are formed as byproduct of other compounds and not applied directly in environment?

(*a*) DDT
(*b*) Dioxins
(*c*) Hexachlorobenzene
(*d*) Furans
(*e*) Heptachlor

Choose the ***correct*** answer from the options given below:

A. (*c*) and (*e*) only
B. (*b*) and (*d*) only
C. (*a*), (*c*) and (*e*) only
D. (*a*) and (*e*) only

66. Which of the following is correct for AAS?

(*a*) It can only analyze single element at a time.
(*b*) It has low linear dynamic range.
(*c*) It can analyze Hg in vapor phase.
(*d*) It can analyze arsenic in hydride form.
(*e*) It works on principle of Beer Lambert's law.

Choose the ***correct*** answer from the options given below:

A. (*b*), (*c*), (*d*) and (*e*) only
B. (*a*), (*d*) and (*e*) only
C. (*a*), (*b*), (*c*), (*d*) and (*e*)
D. (*a*), (*b*), (*d*) and (*e*) only

67. The individual plant populations have following group characteristics:

(*a*) Density
(*b*) Age
(*c*) Ratios
(*d*) Natality
(*e*) Dominance

Choose the ***correct*** answer from the options given below:

A. (*a*), (*b*), (*c*) and (*d*) only
B. (*a*), (*c*), (*d*) and (*e*) only
C. (*a*), (*b*), (*d*) and (*e*) only
D. (*b*), (*c*), (*d*) and (*e*) only

68. In the layered structure of the Earth, mantle is mostly made up of:

(*a*) Na and K　(*b*) Mg and Fe
(*c*) Ni　(*d*) Si
(*e*) Al

Choose the ***correct*** answer from the options given below:

A. (*a*) and (*b*) only　B. (*b*) and (*c*) only
C. (*b*) and (*d*) only　D. (*a*) and (*e*) only

69. Which of the following is not true about Solar Energy?

(*a*) It has low environmental impact.
(*b*) It is intermittent in its availability and requires efficient storage for continuous power supply.
(*c*) Receives high regulatory credit from government in recognition of low amount of air pollution and GHG emission.
(*d*) It has low operating cost.
(*e*) It provides low density of energy per unit collection surface area.

Choose the ***correct*** answer from the options given below:

A. (*a*) and (*d*) only
B. (*b*) and (*e*) only
C. (*c*) only
D. (*b*) only

70. Deep open Benthos Communities:

(*a*) extend from the boundary of continental shelf to the deepest oceans.
(*b*) often are entirely heterotrophic living on and in mud surface and bacteria.
(*c*) include plankton and large swimming animals.
(*d*) are rich in biodiversity through strange, occupying permanent cold and dark water.
(*e*) are nutrient rich water supporting growth of organisms.

Choose the ***correct*** answer from the options given below:

A. (*b*), (*c*) and (*d*) only
B. (*a*), (*b*) and (*c*) only
C. (*a*), (*b*) and (*d*) only
D. (*b*), (*d*) and (*e*) only

71. BOD test is commonly used to:

(*a*) determine amount of oxygen required for biological treatment of organic matter present in waste water.
(*b*) determine size of waste water treatment facility.
(*c*) assess efficiency of treatment process.
(*d*) determine compliance with wastewater discharge limits.

Choose the ***correct*** answer from the options given below:

A. (*d*) only
B. (*a*), (*b*) and (*c*) only
C. (*b*), (*c*) and (*d*) only
D. (*a*), (*b*), (*c*) and (*d*)

72. Which of the following recognise low-waste approach?

(*a*) Linear Economy/Path of development
(*b*) Circular Economy/Path of development
(*c*) Waste Management
(*d*) Waste Reduction
(*e*) Primary pollution and waste prevention

Choose the ***correct*** answer from the options given below:

A. (*a*) and (*c*) only
B. (*b*), (*d*) and (*e*) only
C. (*a*), (*c*) and (*e*) only
D. (*c*) and (*d*) only

73. Which one of the following are four major waste types identified based on Physical characteristics?

(*a*) Solid Waste
(*b*) Sludge and Slurry Waste
(*c*) Combustible Waste
(*d*) Reactive Waste
(*e*) Waste Water

Choose the ***correct*** answer from the options given below:

A. (*a*), (*b*), (*c*) and (*d*) only
B. (*a*), (*c*) and (*d*) only
C. (*a*), (*b*), (*c*) and (*e*) only
D. (*b*), (*c*), (*d*) and (*e*) only

74. EIA is usually required for a development project when:

(*a*) Limited impacts are expected in the environment.
(*b*) There are potentials for transboundary impact.
(*c*) Many people are likely to be affected by the project.
(*d*) No cumulative impacts are expected.
(*e*) There are protected areas in the project area of influence.

Choose the ***correct*** answer from the options given below:

A. (*a*), (*b*) and (*d*) only
B. (*b*), (*c*) and (*e*) only
C. (*b*) and (*d*) only
D. (*c*), (*d*) and (*e*) only

75. The facts related to P-value:

(*a*) It is the probability of type-II error which is fixed in advance.
(*b*) It Is the probability of type-I error which is calculated based on data.
(*c*) It is the probability of type-I error which is fixed in advance.
(*d*) It should be less than the level of significance for having significant result.
(*e*) It is the probability of type-II error which is calculated based on data.

Choose the ***correct*** answer from the options given below:

A. (*b*) and (*d*) only B. (*a*) and (*c*) only
C. (*c*) and (*e*) only D. (*c*) and (*d*) only

76. The 95% confidence interval of sample mean can be calculated by:

(*a*) Sample mean ± 1.96 (Standard deviation)
(*b*) Sample mean ± 1.96 (Standard Error)
(*c*) Sample mean ± 1.96 (Standard Error/N/ $\sqrt{\text{Sample size}}$)
(*d*) Sample mean ± 1.96 (Standard deviation/ $\sqrt{\text{Sample size}}$)
(*e*) Sample mean + 1.96 (Variance/ $\sqrt{\text{Sample size}}$)

Choose the ***correct*** answer from the options given below:

A. (*a*) and (*e*) only B. (*b*) and (*d*) only
C. (*a*) and (*c*) only D. (*b*) and (*c*) only

77. Which of the following are parametric tests?

(*a*) χ^2-test
(*b*) Paired *t*-test
(*c*) McNemar's Test
(*d*) F-test
(*e*) Wilcoxon-signed-rank test

Choose the ***correct*** answer from the options given below;

A. (*a*) and (*c*) only B. (*b*) and (*c*) only
C. (*d*) and (*e*) only D. (*b*) and (*d*) only

78. Which of the following are the properties of Normal Distribution?

(*a*) Median ± 2SE covers the 95% of the observations.
(*b*) Mode ± 2SE covers the 95% of the observations.
(*c*) Mean ± 2SD covers the 95% of the observations.
(*d*) It is bell shaped and symmetric.

(*e*) Mean ± 2SE covers the 95% of the observations.

Choose the ***correct*** answer from the options given below:

A. (*b*) and (*c*) only B. (*c*) and (*d*) only
C. (*d*) and (*e*) only D. (*a*) and (*d*) only

79. Which of the following is an example of Type-II error?

(*a*) Probability of not rejecting null hypothesis, when it is actually false.
(*b*) Probability of rejecting null hypothesis, when it is actually true.
(*c*) When a drug is actually effective, but declared as not effective.
(*d*) When a drug is actually not effective, but declared as effective.
(*e*) When a person is actually not having disease, but declared as diseased by the physician.

Choose the ***correct*** answer from the options given below:

A. (*b*) and (*c*) only B. (*c*) and (*d*) only
C. (*a*) and (*c*) only D. (*a*) and (*e*) only

80. Match List-I with List-II.

List-I (Wavelength)	List-II (Response)
(*a*) 0.45 - 052 μm	I. Absorption band of healthy green vegetation.
(*b*) 0.63 - 0.69 μm	II. Sensitive to turgidity in amount of water in plants.
(*c*) 1 53 - 1.75 μm	III. Increased penetration of water bodies.
(*d*) 2.08 - 2.35 μm	IV. For discrimination of geology.

Choose the ***correct*** answer from the options given below:

	(*a*)	(*b*)	(*c*)	(*d*)
A.	IV	I	II	III
B.	I	IV	II	III
C.	III	I	II	IV
D.	III	II	I	IV

81. Match List-I with List-II.

List-I	List-II
(*a*) Isobars	I. Air moves from sea to land.
(*b*) Land Breeze	II. Ocean current with circular flow.
(*c*) Sea Breeze	III. Air moves from land to sea.
(*d*) Gyres	IV. Lines connect locations with equal pressure.

Choose the ***correct*** answer from the options given below:

	(*a*)	(*b*)	(*c*)	(*d*)
A.	I	II	III	IV
B.	IV	III	I	II
C.	IV	II	I	III
D.	III	II	I	IV

82. Match List-I with List-II.

List-I	List-II
(*a*) Exosphere	I. Ozone Formation
(*b*) Stratosphere	II. Propogation of radio waves
(*c*) Troposphere	III. High temperatures due to solar radiation
(*d*) Thermosphere	IV. Air movements and cloud formation

Choose the ***correct*** answer from the options given below:

	(*a*)	(*b*)	(*c*)	(*d*)
A.	IV	II	I	III
B.	III	I	IV	II
C.	I	II	III	IV
D.	III	I	II	IV

83. Match List-I with List-II.

List-I (Theory)	List-II (Proponent)
(*a*) Monoclimax Theory	I. Watt (1947)
(*b*) Polyclimax Theory	II. Whittaker (1953)
(*c*) Climaxpattern Theory	III. Tansley (1920)
(*d*) Cyclic Climax Theory	IV. Clements (1938)

Choose the ***correct*** answer from the options given below:

	(a)	(b)	(c)	(d)
A.	IV	II	III	I
B.	IV	III	II	I
C.	II	III	I	IV
D.	III	IV	I	II

84. Match List-I with List-II.

List-I (Name)	List-II (Major Characteristics)
(a) Andisols	I. Permafrost, often with cryoturbation
(b) Gelisols	II. High in swelling clays, deep cracks when soil is dry
(c) Histosols	III. From volcanic ejecta, dominated by allophane or Al-humic complexes
(d) Vertisols	IV. Peat or bog; >20% organic matter

Choose the ***correct*** answer from the options given below:

	(a)	(b)	(c)	(d)
A.	II	III	IV	I
B.	III	I	IV	II
C.	IV	III	II	I
D.	I	II	III	IV

85. Match List-I with List-II.

List-I (Species)	List-II (Chemical formula)
(a) Arsenate	I. P_3O_4
(b) Red lead	II. $(AsO_4)^{3-}$
(c) White lead	III. $Pb_3(CO_3)_2(OH)_2$
(d) Arsenite	IV. $(AsO_3)^{3-}$

Choose the ***correct*** answer from the options given below:

	(a)	(b)	(c)	(d)
A.	IV	I	III	II
B.	II	I	III	IV
C.	II	III	I	IV
D.	IV	III	I	II

86. Match List-I with List-II.

List-I (Green House Gas)	List-II (Global Warming Potential (GWP) (in 20yrs time period)
(a) CO_2	I. 360
(b) CH_4	II. 50
(c) N_2O	III. 280
(d) CH_3CCl_3	IV. 1

Choose the ***correct*** answer from the options given below:

	(a)	(b)	(c)	(d)
A.	II	I	III	IV
B.	I	II	IV	III
C.	III	II	I	IV
D.	IV	II	III	I

87. Match List-I with List-II.

List-I	List-II
(a) Above ground landfills	I. Control of surface draining
(b) Below ground landfills	II. Control inflowing water
(c) Slope landfills	III. Liner and leachate content system
(d) Valley landfills	IV. Low permeability liners

Choose the ***correct*** answer from the options given below:

	(a)	(b)	(c)	(d)
A.	I	II	IV	III
B.	I	II	III	IV
C.	III	II	IV	I
D.	IV	III	II	I

88. Match List-I with List-II.

List-I (Statistical Method)	List-II (Purpose)
(a) Standard Deviation	I. To predict the dependent variable on the basis of independent variables.
(b) Standard Error	II. To describe the variability in a sample.

(c) Regression Analysis — III. To construct the 95% confidence interval.
(d) Bonferroni's method — IV. Used after ANOVA, if $p < 0.05$.

Choose the ***correct*** answer from the options given below:

	(a)	(b)	(c)	(d)
A.	I	III	IV	II
B.	III	IV	II	I
C.	II	III	I	IV
D.	IV	II	III	I

89. Match List-I with List-II.

List-I	List-II
(a) Geological Hazard	I. Nuclear Explosion
(b) Chemical Hazard	II. Pandemic
(c) Hydro-meteorological Hazard	III. Tsunami
(d) Biological Hazard	IV. Drought

Choose the ***correct*** answer from the options given below:

	(a)	(b)	(c)	(d)
A.	IV	III	II	I
B.	III	I	IV	II
C.	I	III	IV	II
D.	III	I	II	IV

90. Match List-I with List-II.

List-I	List-II
(a) Pong dam Lake	I. Tamil Nadu
(b) Harike Lake	II. Andhra Pradesh
(c) Kollerur Lake	III. Himachal Pradesh
(d) Point Calimere	IV. Punjab

Choose the ***correct*** answer from the options given below:

	(a)	(b)	(c)	(d)
A.	I	IV	II	III
B.	III	II	IV	I
C.	III	IV	II	I
D.	I	II	IV	III

Directions (Qs. No. 91-95): *Read the given passage and answer the questions that follow.*

The chemistry of rainwater has been extensively studied. The pH of pure water, i.e, neither acidic nor basic, is 7.0. Even in the pristine environment rain is slightly acidic (5.6 pH) in comparison to neutral pH of 7 for water because of presence of natural CO_2 in atmosphere. Acid forming precursor gases, e.g., SO_2 and NO_x further lowers pH of rainwater and such rain water having pH less than 5.6 (pH of natural rainwater) are termed as acidic rain.

However nitrogen oxide species before combining with water droplets to form nitric acid undergoes photodissociation.

Acidic rain adversely impacts oil, monuments and fresh water lakes that are downwind from large source of SO_2 and NO_x such as coal fired thermal power plants. Acidic rainwater reduces cation exchange capacity of the soil and hence crop productivity of the soil. Cations are washed away with acidic rainwater leads to enrichment of basic nutrients in lakes in downstream areas. Similarly acidic rainwater decreases lake water pH and introduces Al^{3+} toxicity and increases solubility of other metals. The effect of acid rain depends on buffering capacity of soil and lakes. Lakes and soils having calcium carbonate are less vulnerable to change in pH due to acid rain.

The Eastern United states and Eastern Europe have been severally impacted by acid rain whereas cases of acidic rain are very limited in northern India irrespective of high SO_2 and NO_x emissions. This is because of carbonate rich dust present in atmosphere. Emission control, e.g, sulphur reduction in coal SO_2 and NO_x reduction from smoke stack of thermal power plants are partially directed towards reducing chances of acid rain.

91. What could be the pH of rain water in pristine environment in comparison to the pure water?
A. Neutral
B. Basic
C. Acidic
D. Both Acidic and Basic

92. The acid rain is in fact a cocktail of H_2SO_4 and HNO_3 and the ratio of two may vary depending on relative quantities of oxides of

Sulphur and nitrogen emitted. On an average, the acidity in rainwater is ascribed as one of the following combinations:

A. $H_2SO_4 = H_2CO_3$
B. $H_2SO_4 < HNO_3$
C. $H_2SO_4 = HNO_3$
D. $H_2SO_4 > HNO_3$

93. Acid rain in a tropical environment does not result in:

A. degradation of land flora and fauna.
B. corrosion of bridges and railings.
C. adverse changes in aquatic life.
D. increase in soil fertility.

94. Which one of the following gases is dominantly responsible for acid rain?

A. CO_2 B. SO_2
C. CH_4 D. NO_2

95. Why northern India does not have instances of acid rain whereas Eastern United States and Eastern Europe are severely impacted?

A. Low SO_2 emissions
B. Low NO_x emissions
C. Presence of carbonate rich particles
D. Better fuel quality and pollution control

Directions (Qs. No. 96-100): *Read the given passage and answer the questions that follow.*

Pesticides have not been as effective in reducing crop losses in United States as agriculture experts hoped. Pesticides can promote genetic resistance to their effects, wipe out natural enemies of pests species, create new pests species, end up in the environment, and sometimes harm wildlife and people. Use of synthetic pesticides increased 33 fold since 1942 whereas 37% food supply is lost to pests today compared to 31% in 1940s. Since 1942, loses attributed to insects almost doubled from 7 to 13% despite a 10 fold increase in synthetic insecticides. The estimated environmental, health and social cost of pesticides was in the range of 100-200 billions USD per year. Alternative pest management practices could halve the use of chemical pesticides on forty major US crops without reducing crop yield. In fact, yield me actually increased without chemical pesticides. Sweden has reduced pesticides use with almost no decrease in crop yield. After a 2/3rd cut in pesticide use on rice in Indonesia yields increased by 15%. The pesticides make a circle of poison, residue of some banned/approved chemicals exported to other countries can return to the exporting countries on imported food. According to a study, only 0.1 - 0.2% of insecticides applied to crop by aerial or ground spraying reaches the target pests and can undergo bioaccumulation and bio-magnification. The wind can also carry persistent organic pesticide such as DDT from one country to another. In 2000, more than hundred countries reached an international agreement to ban or phase out the use of twelve specially hazardous persistent organic pollutants (POPs), and nine of them were persistent hydrocarbon pesticide such as DDT and other chemically similar pesticides.

96. Which of the following characteristics of synthetic chemical pesticides is NOT globally true?

A. Can cause genetic changes in pests resistance to them.
B. Eliminate pest species from the field of their continuous application.
C. Can create new pest species.
D. Never harm wildlife and human health.

97. Which of the following is NOT true about alternative pest management practices?

A. They could reduce the use of chemical pesticides.
B. They could break the circle of poison.
C. They cannot be applied without compromising on crop yield.
D. They reduce air pollution and bioaccumulation due to POPs.

98. Synthetic chemical pesticides are not known for contribution to:

A. air pollution.
B. water pollution.
C. increase in crop yield.
D. reduce soil diversity.

99. The international agreement to ban or phase out 12 persistent organic pollutants including 9 hydrocarbon pesticides such as DDT have been executed because:

(*a*) nearly 98-99% of them goes in environment after their use via aerial or water spraying.

(*b*) they enter in the circle of poison.

(*c*) they reduce crop yield.

(*d*) they affect human health.

(*e*) they affect life-forms.

Choose the ***correct*** answer from the options given below:

A. (*b*), (*c*) and (*d*) only

B. (*a*), (*b*) and (*c*) only

C. (*a*), (*b*), (*c*), (*d*) and (*e*)

D. (*a*), (*b*), (*c*) and (*d*) only

100. Given below are two statements.

Statement I : No use or reduced use of synthetic chemical pesticides is likely to reduce the crop yield as compared to their use.

Statement II : Alternative pest management practices are likely to improve crop yield.

In light of the above statements, choose the ***correct*** answer from the options given below:

A. Both Statement I and Statement II are true

B. Both Statement I and Statement II are false

C. Statement I is true, but Statement II is false

D. Statement I is false, but Statement II is true

ANSWERS

1. (D): Soil texture may be rated from fine to coarse. A fine texture indicates a high proportion of finer particles such as silt and clay. A coarse texture indicates a high proportion of sand.

The textural triangle method is based on the USDA system of particle size where the following classification is used:

- **Silt:** all particles within the size range of 0.002-0.05 mm;
- **Clay:** all particles smaller than 0.002 mm.

It is important to know which system of particle-size classification is being used by the soil laboratory for testing. If it is the one used by the US Department of Agriculture (USDA) which defines silt from 0.05 to 0.002 mm.

2. (C): Biochemical Oxygen Demand (BOD):

It is the total amount of oxygen required to oxidize the biodegradable organic matter present in wastewater through microbial utilization of organics.

BOD = (Initial Dissolve Oxygen – Final Dissolve Oxygen) × Dilution Factor

where,

$$\text{Dilution Factor} = \frac{\text{Volume of diluted sample}}{\text{Volume of undiluted sample}}$$

Here, we have

Initial Dissolved Oxygen (DO1) = 10 mg/l

Final Dissolved Oxygen (DO5) = 5 mg/l

$$\text{Dilution Factor} = \frac{300}{21}$$

$$\text{Hence, BOD5} = (10 - 5) \times \frac{300}{21}$$

$$= 71.428 \text{ mg/l}$$

3. (C): Concepts:

1. One mole of any gas occupies 22.4 liters, at 0°C temperatures and 1 atm pressure.
2. The given temperature is 25 degrees C, therefore, we need to find out the volume of SO_2 gas occupied by its one mole at 25°C. This can be done using the ideal gas equation:

$$PV = nRT$$

Where

P is the pressure, V is the volume, *n* is the moles and T is the temperature

$T_1 = 273$ K and $T_2 = 273 + 25 = 298$ K

Since n and R are constant for a given gas, thus:

$$\frac{P_1V_1}{T_1} = \frac{P_2V_2}{T_2}$$

$$\frac{1 \times 22.4}{273} = \frac{1 \times V_2}{298}$$

$$V = 24.45 \text{ ltr.}$$

This means that 1 mole of SO_2 occupies 24.45 ltrs. at 25°C and 1 atm.

$\{SO_2\} = 0.04$ ppm this means that

10^6 cum air has 0.04 cum SO_2

Or

10^6 cum air has $0.04 \times 1000 = 40$ ltrs. SO_2

1 mole of SO_2 occupies 24.45 liters.

Therefore, 10^6 cum air has $\frac{40}{24.45}$

$= 1.636$ moles of SO_2

The molecular weight of $SO_2 = 32 + 2 \times 16$

$= 64$ gm.

10^6 cum air has $1.636 \times 64 = 104.7$ gm SO_2

4. (D): The six criteria air pollutants (CAP), or criteria pollutants, for which limits are set in the NAAQS are ozone (O_3), atmospheric particulate matter, lead, carbon monoxide (CO), sulfur oxides (SO_x), and nitrogen oxides (NO_x).

There are a number of areas in which estimates of probabilities play a role in environmental decision making. A major case in point is the form of National Ambient Air Quality Standards (NAAQS). These standards set requirements for air quality that are defined in terms of an indicator, an averaging time for the measurement, a concentration, and a form. For example, the NAAQS for carbon monoxide (CO) is defined as 9 ppm (10 mg $^{m-3}$) for an 8-h average not to be exceeded more than 1 time per year and 35 ppm (40 mg $^{m-3}$) for 1 h again not to be exceeded more than 1 time per year.

5. (B): Primary pollutants and secondary pollutants can be more dangerous. The first are those that are emitted directly from a source, which can be natural (volcanic eruptions or fires, for example) or of anthropogenic origin (carbon monoxide from vehicles).

Secondary pollutants, on the other hand, are not emitted directly. Its origin lies in the interactions between the primary emissions in the atmosphere. One of the most known secondary pollutants is tropospheric ozone.

6. (B): Continuity Equation (Conservation of Mass)

$$\frac{\partial(\rho v A)}{\partial x} + \frac{\partial(\rho A)}{\partial t} = 0$$

The continuity equation is the statement of conservation of mass in the pipeline: mass in minus mass out equals change of mass.

- The first term in the equation, $\frac{\partial(\rho v A)}{\partial x}$, is "mass flow in minus mass flow out" of a slice of the pipeline cross-section.
- The second term, $\frac{\partial(\rho A)}{\partial t}$, is the rate of change of mass of a slice of pipeline cross-section.

7. (C): A comparison of environmental worldviews sheds light on the different value orientations employed in economics and management.

Planetary Management:

- We are separate from the rest of Nature and can manage Nature to meet our increasing needs and wants.
- Because of our ingenuity and technology we will not run out of resources.
- The potential for economic growth is essentially unlimited.
- Our success depends on how well we manage Earth's life-support systems, mostly for our benefit.

Stewardship:

- We have an ethical responsibility to be caring managers or stewards of the earth.
- We will probably not run out of resources, but in any case they should not be wasted.
- We should encourage environmentally beneficial forms of economic growth and discourage environmentally harmful forms.
- Our success depends on how well we manage Earth's life-support systems for our benefit and for the rest of nature.

Environmental Wisdom:

- We are part of and totally dependent on Nature and Nature exists for all species.
- Resources are limited, should not be wasted, and are not all for us.
- We should encourage Earth-sustaining forms of economic growth and discourage Earth-degrading forms.
- Our success depends on learning how Nature sustains itself and integrating such lessons from Nature into the ways we think and act.

8. (B): Humans and other organisms can be exposed to substances in different environmental media — air, water, soil, or food — or they may have direct contact with a sample of the substance. The exposure concentration is the amount of a substance present in the medium with which an organism has contact. The dose is the amount of the chemical that is received by the target (organ). The exposure concentration may differ from the dose owing to biochemical transformations in living organisms.

Suppose, for example, a substance is present in drinking water. The amount of this substance in the water is the exposure concentration. For many environmental substances, this amount ranges from less than 1 microgram (μg) to greater than 1 milligram (mg), and is usually reported as milligrams or micrograms of the substance present in 1 liter of water (*i.e.*, in mg L^{-1} or μg L^{-1}).

9. (A): The ED50 (median effective dose) is the dose of a medication that produces a specific effect in 50% of the population that takes that dose. This number has common use as what a clinician or patient can expect for a drug effect, but clinicians may use a different dosage for their particular intended effect, depending on the balance of need or benefit of the drug versus the toxicity of the drug. The toxic dose in 50% of the population is called TD50; the ED50 should hopefully be much less than the TD50, as this would indicate an effective medication at a lower dose.

The ED50 for a particular medication derives from a dose-response curve, in which the ED50 is at the dosage (x-axis) where there is 50% of the desired response (y-axis).

The ED50 should be used as a clinical starting point for practitioners when prescribing medications, as adjustments are made to balance efficacy and toxicity. The E-max would be equivalent to the maximum effect the drug may have. It is important to remember that as dosages increase, the risk for toxicities will increase, and they may not be directly proportionate. Each patient requires individualized goals of treatment and should be monitored for such to ensure the lowest effective dose possible, especially for long-term treatment.

10. (C): Four hypotheses have been proposed to describe the relationship of biodiversity to ecosystem functioning.

(*i*) **Rivet-Popper hypothesis:** According to the rivet-popper hypothesis, species in an ecosystem are something like the rivets on an airplane, with each species playing a small but significant role in the working of the whole. The loss of each rivet weakens the plane by a small but noticeable amount-until it loses airworthiness and crashes. In this view, progressive loss of species steadily damages ecosystem function.

(*ii*) **Redundancy hypothesis:** According to the redundancy hypothesis, most species are superfluous – all that matters is that the biomass of primary producers, consumers, decomposers, etc. is maintained and if it is, only a few species are needed to keep the system in motion.

(*iii*) **Diversity-stability hypothesis:** It predicts a linear relationship in which rate of ecosystem processes is maximum with greatest number of species.

(*iv*) **Idiosyncratic hypothesis:** This hypothesis acknowledges that there may be no pattern or an intermediate relationship between species diversity and ecosystem function. According to this hypothesis, the contribution of species to function is unpredictable, since both the identity and order of deletion will affect function differentially.

11. (D): Secondary succession, type of ecological succession (the evolution of a biological community's ecological structure) in which plants and animals recolonize a habitat after a major disturbance—such as a devastating flood, wildfire, landslide, lava flow, or human activity (e.g., farming or road or building construction)—significantly alters an area but has not rendered it completely lifeless. Secondary succession is distinguished from primary succession, in which a biological community develops where no life had existed previously.

Some of the phases of secondary succession are Nudation, Initiation, Continuation, Aggregation, Termination. Secondary succession takes place where a disturbance did not eliminate all life and nutrients from the environment.

12. (A): The concept of *r*- and K-selection was originally given by MacArthur and Wilson (1967) and developed by Pianka (1970) to focus on life-history evolution due to selection pressures on species colonizing an island. In uncrowded, resource-rich environments, natural selection would favour organisms which are able to achieve rapid population growth. On the other hand, in crowded and not so resource-rich conditions natural selection would favour organisms which are competitive and maintain population growth near the carrying capacity. The former are termed *r*-strategists and the latter K-strategists. In the *r*-strategists, the population remains on the ascending part of the logistic growth curve (*i.e.*, $dN/dt = rN$), while in the K-strategists, population is maintained near the upper asymptote of the logistic growth curve (*i.e.*, when N = K or close to it).

13. (A): The tolerance curve is a measure of organism's fitness and survival. A bell shaped curve results when measures of survival or fitness are plotted against the environmental gradient (Fig. 1). Those environmental conditions under which an organism grows and reproduces maximally comprise the optimum range.

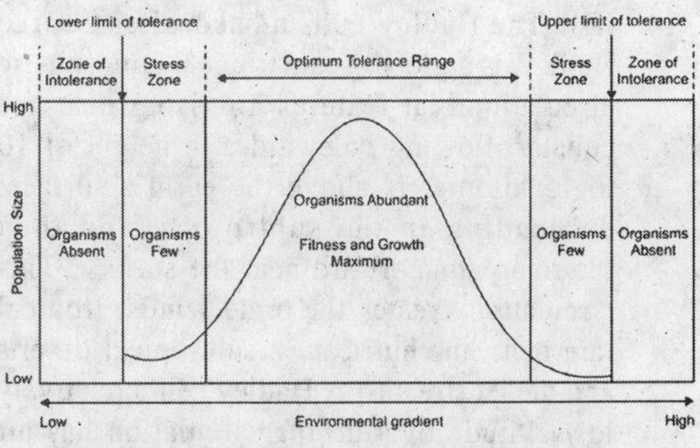

Fig. 1: *The bell shaped curve shows the response of an organism to a range of single environmental variable (Temperature, sunlight or nutrient concentration)*

The prefix "steno" (narrow) and "eury" (wide) have often been used for comparing the relative degree of tolerance of an organism to a given environmental factor (Fig. 2). For example, a stenothermal organism will mean that the organism can tolerate only a narrow range of temperature. With narrow range of tolerance, organisms are concentrated at either end of the curve; having the optimum, minimum and maximum in a very narrow range. The organisms which are confined towards low temperature are called oligo thermic and those towards higher temperature are polythermal. Even a small change in temperature can have marked effect on the stenothermic organisms. Euthermal organisms have a wide range of tolerance for temperature. Similarly, stenohydric and euhydric refer to tolerance range of an organism to water. Euryhaline would describe a species with a wide range of tolerance for salinity and stenohaline a narrow salinity tolerance.

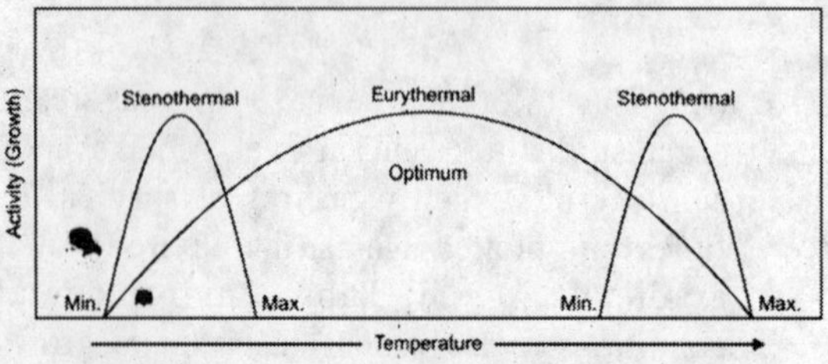

Fig. 2: *Comparison of the relative limits of tolerance of stenothermal and eurythermal organisms*

14. **(B):** The Hadley cell, named after George Hadley, is a global-scale tropical atmospheric circulation that features air rising near the equator, flowing poleward at a height of 10 to 15 kilometers above the earth's surface, descending in the subtropics, and then returning equatorward near the surface. This circulation creates the trade winds, tropical rain-belts and hurricanes, subtropical deserts and the jet streams. A Hadley cell's relatively low-altitude overturning circulation has air sinking at roughly 30 degrees latitude after traveling from near the equator.

15. **(A):** The Coriolis effect influences the paths of surface-ocean currents just as it does the winds. Earth's rotation from west to east causes surface-ocean currents to swerve to the right in the Northern Hemisphere, helping establish the circular, clockwise pattern of water currents. In the Southern Hemisphere, ocean currents swerve to the left, thereby moving in a circular, counterclockwise pattern.

16. **(A):** The Lower Cape Cod land mass is small, thereby limiting freshwater recharge, aquifer area, and aquifer depth. Consequently, freshwater in the Lower Cape Cod aquifer system does not extend to the underlying granitic bedrock, but instead is primarily bounded below by saltwater. Depths to the boundary, or interface, between fresh and saltwater within the aquifer system differ among the flow lenses, and are directly proportional to the altitude of the overlying water table. Because of the density difference between fresh and saltwater, the depth to the freshwater/saltwater interface below sea level is about 40 times greater than the altitude of the water table above sea level. Therefore, if the water table is 5 ft above sea level, the depth to the freshwater/saltwater interface would be about 200 ft below sea level.

17. **(B):** The solar radiation that reaches the Earth's surface without being diffused is called direct beam solar radiation. The sum of the diffuse and direct solar radiation is called global solar radiation. Atmospheric conditions can reduce direct beam radiation by 10% on clear, dry days and by 100% during thick, cloudy days.

18. **(D):** Silicon is, by far, the most common semiconductor material used in solar cells, representing approximately 95% of the modules sold today. It is also the second most abundant material on Earth (after oxygen) and the most common semiconductor used in computer chips. Crystalline silicon cells are made of silicon atoms connected to one another to form a crystal lattice. This lattice provides an organized structure that makes conversion of light into electricity more efficient.

19. **(D):** Destructive distillation can be defined as the chemical process through which unprocessed materials are subjected to decomposition by heating them and thereby producing 'cracks' in the relatively large molecules. Generally, the term 'destructive distillation' is used to refer to the processing

of certain organic materials along with limited amounts of oxygen and certain reagents, solvents, or catalysts such as phenols and steam.

The process of destructive distillation is known to create 'cracks' in relatively large molecules. It is not uncommon for these large molecules to break apart completely when subjected to destructive distillation. For example, when coal is subjected to destructive distillation, a wide range of commercially important products are formed (such as coke, coal oil, ammonium hydroxide, coal tar, gas carbon, and coal gas).

20. (D): Transesterification gained much acceptance in recent years for the conversion of vegetable oils into products with technically more compatible fuel properties. Transesterification is an imperative process for biodiesel production, as it can reduce the viscosity of the feedstock/vegetable oils to a level closer to the conventional fossil-based diesel oil.

21. (D): Development of biodiesel from karanja tree, mainly found in rural India has been investigated. The biodiesel was developed from oil expelled from the seeds of the tree. Molecular weight of the oil was determined and found to be 892.7. Both the acid as well as alkaline esterification were subsequently performed to get the final product. NaOH was found to be a better catalyst than KOH in terms of yield. Maximum yield of 89.5% was achieved at 8:1 molar ratio for acid esterification and 9:1 molar ratio for alkaline esterification, 0.5 wt.% catalyst (NaOH/KOH) using mechanical stirrer.

Table: Different types of feedstock used for biodiesel production

Type of feedstock	Examples
First-generation feedstock or edible oil	Rapeseed, apricot, soybean, sesame, coffee, peanut, grapeseed, sunflower, palm, linseed, coconut, olive, safflower, rice bran oil, etc.
Second-generation feedstock or non-edible oil	Jatropha, karanja, mahua, nahar, karabi, pongamia, rubber seed, babassu, jojoba, castor, etc.
Third-generation feedstock or algae	*Scenedesmus* sp., *Chlorella* sp., *Tetraselmis* sp., *Chaetoceros* sp., *Thalassiosira* sp., *Nannochloropsis* sp., etc.
Others	Animal fats (poultry fat, pork lard, beef tallow, etc.), fish oil, WCO, yellow grease, etc.

22. (D): Anammox, an abbreviation for anaerobic ammonium oxidation, is a globally important microbial process of the nitrogen cycle that takes place in many natural environments. The bacteria mediating this process were identified in 1999, and were a great surprise for the scientific community. In the anammox reaction, nitrite and ammonium ions are converted directly into diatomic nitrogen and water.

The bacteria that perform the anammox process are genera that belong to the bacterial phylum Planctomycetota. The anammox bacteria all possess one anammoxosome, a lipid bilayer membrane-bound compartment inside the cytoplasm in which the anammox process takes place. The anammoxosome membranes are rich in ladderane lipids; the presence of these lipids is so far unique in biology.

In this biological process, which is a comproportionation reaction, nitrite and ammonium ions are converted directly into diatomic nitrogen and water.

$$NH_4^+ + NO_2^- \rightarrow N_2 + 2H_2O$$

23. (D): Humus is dark, organic material that forms in soil when plant and animal matter decays. Humus contains cellulose and hemi cellulose. Humic substances invariably carry an electrostatic charge. They are therefore classified as polyelectrolytes. Although a variety of sites possessing the potential to carry a positive or negative charge can be identified on humic substances, the predominant charge is negative and at most naturally occurring pH values this charge is due to the dissociation of carboxylic, hydroxyl, and phenolic groups.

24. (D): "Bioremediation is a waste management technique that includes the use of living organisms to eradicate or neutralize pollutants from a contaminated site." "Bioremediation is a 'treatment techniques' that uses naturally occurring organisms to break down harmful materials into less toxic or non-toxic materials."

The main principle is degrading and converting pollutants to less toxic forms. There are two types of factors these are biotic and abiotic conditions that determine rate of degradation.

25. (A): $\underset{(1)}{2CH_2O} \xrightarrow{\text{Bacteria}} \underset{(2)}{CH_4} + \underset{(3)}{CO_2}$

This is an example of fermentation. Here, Some carbon in (1) is oxidized and some is reduced.

26. (*)

27. (A): For most projects, the environmental review is initiated at this time. There is a trend, however, to establish the scope of the review earlier in the licensing process, often at the time the initial consultation package is released. The environmental review will consist of preparation of an Environmental Assessment (EA) unless the project may have significant environmental impacts. In this case, a more comprehensive Environmental Impact Statement (EIS) may be compiled.

There are three procedure: The local government authority ultimately responsible for licensing development project.

Another government agency which can be given responsibility for licensing development project.

An independent body having knowledge of the development project.

28. (B): Two permanent subsidiary bodies to the UNFCCC have been established by the COP: the Subsidiary Body for Scientific and Technological Advice (SBSTA), which supports the work of the parties through the provision of information and advice on scientific and technological matters, and the Subsidiary Body for Implementation (SBI), which supports the assessment and review of the effective implementation of the Convention. Despite the lack of hard targets or binding mandates, the Framework Convention has thus given rise to multiple formal and informal institutions and networks for study, advocacy, negotiation, action and implementation, which have advanced a co-ordinated international response to climaue.

29. (B): Forests play a vital role in the global carbon cycle. They act as carbon sinks by absorbing carbon dioxide from the atmosphere during photosynthesis and converting it into biomass. Reducing Emissions from Deforestation and Forest Degradation identifies potential carbon credit generation by financially incentivizing local communities to avoid deforestation and degradation.

30. (B):

1. The Polluter - Pays Principle constitutes for Member countries a fundamental principle for allocating costs of pollution prevention and control measures introduced by the public authorities in Member countries.
2. The Polluter - Pays Principle, as defined by the Guiding Principles concerning International Economic Aspects of Environmental Policies [C(72)128], which take account of particular problems possibly arising for developing countries, means that the polluter should bear the expenses of carrying out the measures, to

ensure that the environment is in an acceptable state. In other words, the cost of these measures should be reflected in the cost of goods and services which cause pollution in production and/or consumption.

3. Uniform application of this principle, through the adoption of a common basis for Member countries' environmental policies, would encourage the rational use and the better allocation of scarce environmental resources and prevent the appearance of distortions in international trade and investment.

31. (C): Section 16 in The Environment (Protection) Act, 1986: Where any offence under this Act has been committed by a company, every person who, at the time the offence was committed, was directly in charge of, and was responsible to, the company for the conduct of the business of the company, as well as the company, shall be deemed to be guilty of the offence and shall be liable to be proceeded against and punished accordingly: Provided that nothing contained in this sub-section shall render any such person liable to any punishment provided in this Act, if he proves that the offence was committed without his knowledge or that he exercised all due diligence to prevent the commission of such offence.

32. (B): The chapter on fundamental duties of the Indian Constitution clearly imposes duty on every citizen to protect environment. Article 51-A (g), says that "It shall be duty of every citizen of India to protect and improve the natural environment including forests, lakes, rivers and wild life and to have compassion for living creatures."

33. (D): Environment Protection Act, 1986

- The environmental (Protection) Act, 1986 along with the Environment Protection Rules 1986 amended in 1999.
- This was the first major act to promulgate in India.
- The act was passed after the infamous Bhopal Gas Tragedy.
- The Environmental Protection Act (EPA) of 1986 is umbrella legislation with wide legislative coverage.
- It gives wide powers to the central government to take all such measures as it deems necessary or expedient for the purpose of protecting and improving the quality of the environment. Such measures include laying down standards for environmental quality, restricting areas of industrial operations, laying down procedures for handling hazardous substances, etc.
- The central government can close down offending industries and restrict the setting up of new industries at environmentally non-compatible sites.
- The Environment Rules of 1986 lay down procedures for the setting of emission and discharge standards.
- This Act empowers the Union Government to take direct action against defaulters.
- A host of notifications have been enacted under the EPA, such as those on Environmental Impact Assessment and Coastal Regulation Zones.

34. (*)

35. (D): Environmental Impact Assessment (EIA) is a process of evaluating the likely environmental impacts of a proposed project or development, taking into account inter-related socio-economic, cultural and human-health impacts, both beneficial and adverse.

The fundamental components of an EIA would necessarily involve the following stages:

(*a*) Screening to determine which projects or developments require a full or partial impact assessment study;

(*b*) Scoping to identify which potential impacts are relevant to assess (based on legislative requirements, international conventions, expert knowledge and public involvement), to identify alternative solutions that avoid, mitigate or compensate adverse impacts on biodiversity (including the option of not proceeding with the development, finding alternative designs or sites which avoid the impacts, incorporating safeguards in the design of the project, or providing compensation for adverse impacts), and finally to derive terms of reference for the impact assessment;

(*c*) Assessment and evaluation of impacts and development of alternatives, to predict and identify the likely environmental impacts of a proposed project or development, including the detailed elaboration of alternatives;

(*d*) Reporting the Environmental Impact Statement (EIS) or EIA report, including an environmental management plan (EMP), and a non-technical summary for the general audience.

(*e*) Review of the Environmental Impact Statement (EIS), based on the terms of reference (scoping) and public (including authority) participation.

(*f*) Decision-making on whether to approve the project or not, and under what conditions; and

(*g*) Monitoring, compliance, enforcement and environmental auditing. Monitor whether the predicted impacts and proposed mitigation measures occur as defined in the EMP. Verify the compliance of proponent with the EMP, to ensure that unpredicted impacts or failed mitigation measures are identified and addressed in a timely fashion.

36. (B): Correlation is defined as the statistical association between two variables.

The **linear correlation coefficient** *for a collection of n pairs (x, y) of numbers in a sample is the number r given by the formula*

$$r = \frac{SS_{xy}}{\sqrt{SS_{xx} \cdot SS_{yy}}}$$

where

$$SS_{xx} = \Sigma x^2 - \frac{1}{n}(\Sigma x)^2$$

$$SS_{xy} = \Sigma xy - \frac{1}{n}(\Sigma x)(\Sigma y)$$

$$SS_{yy} = \Sigma y^2 - \frac{1}{n}(\Sigma y)^2$$

Correlation Coefficient:

1. The value of r lies between –1 and 1, inclusive.
2. The sign of r indicates the direction of the linear relationship between x and y:
   - If $r < 0$ then y tends to decrease as x is increased.
   - If $r > 0$ then y tends to increase as x is increased.
3. The size of $|r|$ indicates the strength of the linear relationship between x and y:
   - If $|r|$ is near 1 (that is, if r is near either 1 or –1) then the linear relationship between x and y is strong.
   - If $|r|$ is near 0 (that is, if r is near 0 and of either sign) then the linear relationship between x and y is weak.

37. (C): The coefficient of variation is defined as the ratio of the standard deviation to the mean, expressed as a percentage.

Formula for coefficient of variation:

$$CV = \frac{\text{Standard deviation}}{\text{Mean}} \times 100$$

$$\text{or, } CV = \frac{\sigma}{\mu} \times 100 \;;\; CV\ \frac{s}{\bar{x}} \times 100$$

Example: The coefficient of variation depicts the size of the standard deviation relative to its mean. The primary use of the coefficient of variation is to compare the relative variation of unrelated quantities.

38. **(B): Nominal data:** The categories are not ordered but simply have names. Examples include blood group (A, B, AB, and O) and marital status (married/widowed/single etc.). In this case, there is no reason to suspect that being married is any better (or worse) than being single!

Ordinal data: The categories are ordered in some way. Examples include disease staging systems (advanced, moderate, mild, none) and degree of pain (severe, moderate, mild, none).

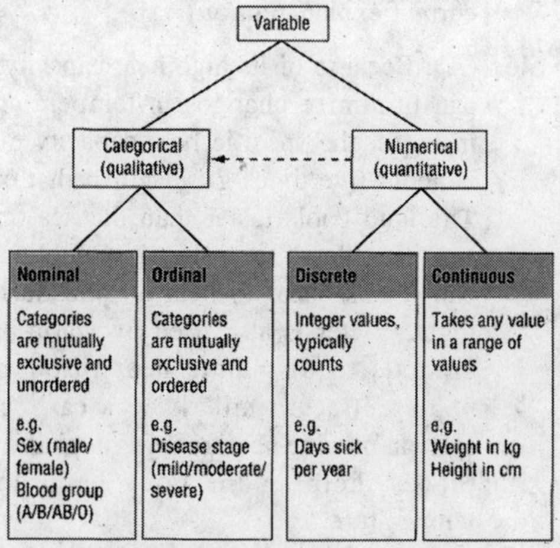

Fig.: *Diagram showing the different types of variable.*

39. **(A): Hysteresis** is the dependence of the state of a system on its history. For example, a magnet may have more than one possible magnetic moment in a given magnetic field, depending on how the field changed in the past. Plots of a single component of the moment often form a loop or hysteresis curve, where there are different values of one variable depending on the direction of change of another variable.

Hysteresis can be a dynamic lag between an input and an output that disappears if the input is varied more slowly; this is known as *rate-dependent* hysteresis. However, phenomena such as the magnetic hysteresis loops are mainly *rate-independent*, which makes a durable memory possible.

40. **(C):** The Kyoto Protocol was an international treaty which extended the 1992 United Nations Framework Convention on Climate Change that commits state parties to reduce greenhouse gas emissions, based on the scientific consensus that global warming is occurring and that human-made CO_2 emissions are driving it.

41. **(B):** In the mid-1970s, Maathai, in an effort to meet the basic needs of rural women, began to plant trees with them. Her non-governmental Green Belt Movement has planted 30 million trees across Kenya, many of which still stand. In 2004 her work was internationally recognized with the Nobel Peace Prize.

Wangari Maathai has always had an affinity for trees. As a child, she learned from her grandmother that a large fig tree near her family home in central Kenya was sacred and not to be disturbed. She gathered water for her mother at springs protected by the roots of trees.

42. **(A):** Genetic engineering is the science of gene manipulation. Genetic engineering, genetic modification (GM) and gene splicing are terms for the process of manipulating genes, generally implying that the process is outside the organism's natural reproductive process. It involves the isolation, manipulation, transfer, and reintroduction of DNA into cells or model organisms usually to express a protein. The aim is to introduce new characteristics or attributes physiologically or physically, such as making a crop resistant to a herbicide, introducing a novel trait, or producing a new protein or enzyme, along with altering the organism to produce more of certain traits.

43. **(C):** India's version of LEED, which was based on the similar guidelines as US based LEED but with few changes with regards to Indian construction scenario. According to research conducted by IGBC on the executed projects in India, green buildings can be constructed with an incremental cost of 1 – 6% and there is no much-cost difference between normal buildings.

LEED-INDIA promotes a whole building approach to sustainability by recognizing performance in the following five key areas:

- Sustainable site development;
- Water savings;
- Energy Efficiency;
- Material selection; and
- Indoor environmental quality.

44. **(C):** Recently, a new category of awards titled 'Prerak Dauur Samman' has been announced as part of Swachh Survekshan 2021.

- The Prerak Dauur Samman has a total of five additional subcategories namely, *Divya* (Platinum), *Anupam* (Gold), *Ujjwal* (Silver), *Udit* (Bronze) and *Aarohi* (Aspiring).
- In Swachh Survekshan 2020, cities are evaluated on the criteria of 'population category' but for 2021, they will be categorised on the basis of six select indicator wise performance criteria.
    - o Segregation of waste into Wet, Dry and Hazard categories.
    - o Processing capacity against wet waste generated.
    - o Processing and recycling of wet and dry waste.
    - o Construction and Demolition waste processing.
    - o Percentage of waste going to landfills.
    - o Sanitation status of cities.

45. **(A):** Organochlorines (OC) are a group of chlorinated compounds widely used as pesticides. These chemicals belong to the class of persistent organic pollutants (POPs) with high persistence in the environment.

Organo-Chlorine Pesticides (OCPs) are a major contributor to aquatic pollution and are amongst the most serious global contaminants. In addition, organochlorine pesticides have a tendency to accumulate in aquatic biota; they also undergo food chain amplification. The chemical stability of these compounds, their high lipid solubility, and their toxicity to human beings and animals has led government and researchers to feel concerned about their presence in the environment.

Here, Both (A) and (R) are true and (R) is the correct explanation of (A)

46. **(A):** Because of its high heat capacity, water can minimize changes in temperature. For instance, the specific heat capacity of water is about five times greater than that of sand. The land cools faster than the sea once the sun goes down, and the slow-cooling water can release heat to nearby land during the night. Water is also used by warm-blooded animals to distribute heat through their bodies: it acts similarly to a car's cooling system, moving heat from warm places to cool places, helping the body keep an even temperature.

Specific heat is the amount of heat energy it takes to raise or lower the temperature of 1 gram of a substance by 1°Celsius. The specific heat of liquid water is 1 calorie per gram per 1 degree C (cal/g/°C). The specific heat of water is greater than that of dry soil, therefore water both absorbs and releases heat more slowly than land.

47. **(A):** Wind power is proportional to wind speed cubed. Wind energy is the kinetic energy of the moving air. The wind power is given as

$$P_{wind} = \frac{E_{kin,\,wind}}{\Delta t} = \frac{\Delta V \rho v^2}{2\Delta t} = \frac{\rho A v^3}{2}$$

The wind power increases with the cube of the wind speed. In other words: doubling the wind speed gives eight times the wind power. Therefore, the selection of a "windy" location is very important for a wind turbine. Therefore Small increase in wind velocity and height of turbine produces a large increase in energy yield.

48. (A): Radioactive decay (also known as nuclear decay, radioactivity, radioactive disintegration, or nuclear disintegration) is the process by which an unstable atomic nucleus loses energy by radiation.

Alpha decay by a nucleus emits an alpha particle of two neutrons and two protons; also known as a helium nucleus. α and β particles produced in the Radioactive decay are ejected with an incredible amount of energy of motion When this energy is absorbed by matter encountered by the particle, it often ionises atoms and molecules.

Here, Both (A) and (R) are true and (R) is the correct explanation of (A).

49. (A): Cool pavement materials usually require more energy and carbon to manufacture than conventional pavement materials. An exception is concrete with substantially reduced levels of energy- and carbon-intensive ordinary Portland cement.

Cool pavements can be made from traditional paving materials, such as cement concrete. New cement concrete has a solar reflectance (SR) of 30-50%. There are also novel cool-colored coatings for asphalt concrete pavements that reflect about 50% of sunlight. Another approach is to use a clear binder that reveals highly reflective (light-colored) aggregate.

As with all materials exposed to the atmosphere and use, the solar reflectance of pavement can change over time.

50. (A): Dematerialization, the progressive decrease in the size and weight of a product as a result of technological improvements, is an example of source reduction only if the new product is at least as durable as the one it replaces. Smaller, lighter products that have shorter life spans or must be replaced more often may not achieve source reduction.

Here , Both (A) and (R) are true and (R) is the correct explanation of (A).

51. (B): Aerial photographic and satellite image interpretation, or just image interpretation when in context, is the act of examining photographic images, particularly airborne and spaceborne, for the purpose of identifying objects and judging their significance.

The elements of image interpretation include location, tone and colour, size, shape, textue, pattern, shadow, height and depth, volume, slope, aspect, site, situation, and association.

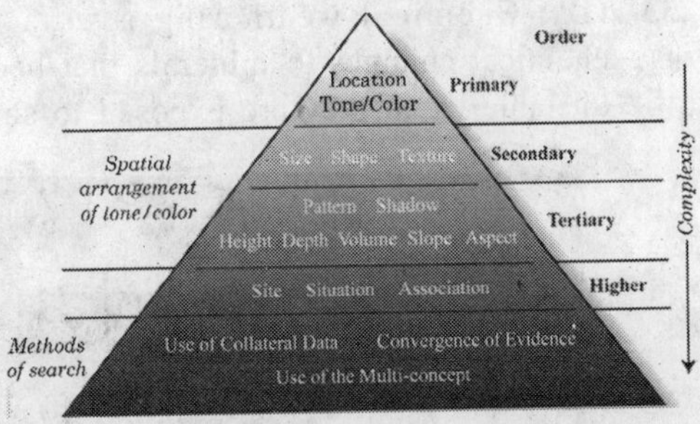

Tone or Colour: Relates to the spectral reflectance characteristics of objects.

Size: Measure of surface dimensions of objects, including height, length-width, slope.

Shape: Describes the form or configuration of an object.

Texture: Frequency of tonal or colour change which determines apparent roughness vs. smoothness of an image region; depends on angle of illumination and surface characteristics.

Pattern: Spatial arrangement of individual objects into distinctive, recurring forms.

Shadows: May reveal details about size and shape not apparent from overhead view.

Site: Location of object in relation to its geographic or topographic setting.

Association: Occurrence of certain features in relation to others.

52. **(C):** *Basalts* are common aphanitic igneous extrusive (volcanic) rocks. Basalts are composed of minute grains of plagioclase feldspar (generally labradorite), pyroxene, olivine, biotite, hornblende and <20% quartz.

Basalts are formed by the rapid cooling of basaltic lava, equivalent to gabbro-norite magma, from interior of the crust and exposed at or very close to the surface of Earth. These basalt flows are quite thick and extensive, in which gas cavities are almost absent. In case of thin and irregular lava flows, gas cavities are formed on the rock surface. The rock is called "vesicular" basalt when the gas cavities are empty.

53. **(D):** Chemical weathering results from chemical changes to minerals that become unstable when they are exposed to surface conditions. The kinds of changes that take place are highly specific to the mineral and the environmental conditions.

Arrangement as per increasing order of stability for weathering : Calcite, Olivine, Ca rich feldspar, Na rich feldspar, Illite.

54. **(B):** Filtration is a process of removing particulate matter from water by forcing the water through a porous media. This porous media can be natural, in the case of sand, gravel and clay, or it can be a membrane wall made of various materials.

The size of materials that can be removed during filtration depends upon the size of the pores of the filter. The chart below summarizes the various separation processes relative to common materials that would be filtered out through each process. Particle filtration refers to conventional media filtration, while the other types are membrane filtrations.

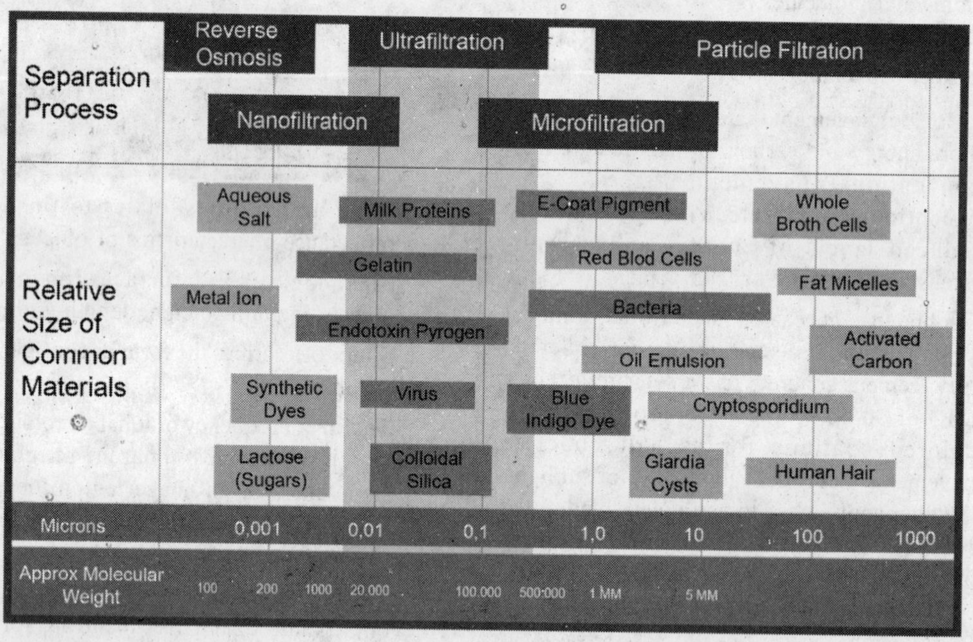

55. **(B):** Waste is an inevitable by-product of human life. Virtually every human activity generates some type of material side effect or by-product. When the materials that constitute these by-products are not useful or have been degraded such that they no longer fulfill their original or other obvious useful purpose, they are classified as a waste material.

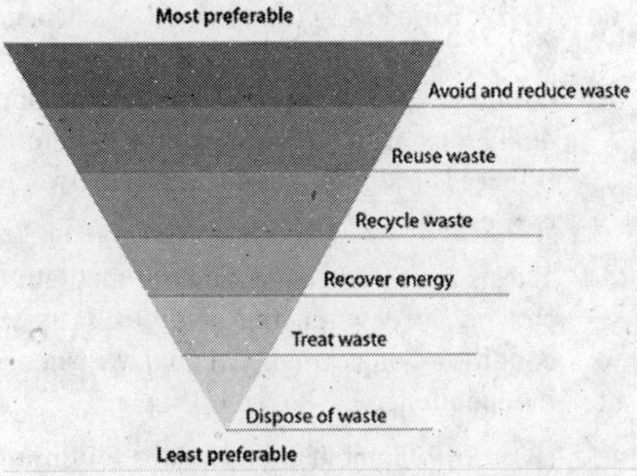

Waste hierarchy. Ordered by most preferеble: avoid and reduce; reuse; recycle; recover energy; treat; dispose of waste.

56. (C): Biological nitrogen fixation (BNF), discovered by Beijerinck in 1901 (Beijerinck 1901), is carried out by a specialized group of prokaryotes. These organisms utilize the enzyme nitrogenase to catalyze the conversion of atmospheric nitrogen (N_2) to ammonia (NH_3). Hence Statement I is true.

Nitrification is the process that converts ammonia to nitrite and then to nitrate and is another important step in the global nitrogen cycle. Most nitrification occurs aerobically and is carried out exclusively by prokaryotes

1. $NH_3 + O_2 + 2e^- \rightarrow NH_2OH + H_2O$
2. $NH_2OH + H_2O \rightarrow NO_2^- + 5H^+ + 4e^-$

Hence, Statement II is not correct.

57. (C): Bromine-containing halons also significantly contribute to the depletion of stratospheric ozone when these halons photodissociate and release bromine atoms. Just as a chlorine atom destroys ozone, a bromine atom can also destroy ozone:

$$Br + O_3 \rightarrow BrO + O_2.$$

The preceding reactions occur throughout the stratosphere and are responsible for depletion of ozone on a global scale.

Only Statement I is correct

The Montreal Protocol, finalized in 1987, is a global agreement to protect the stratospheric ozone layer by phasing out the production and consumption of ozone-depleting substances (ODS). The Montreal Protocol has proven to be innovative and successful, and is the first treaty to achieve universal ratification by all countries in the world.

58. (D): Here, Statement I is false, but Statement II is true.

There are many other pigments present in the palisade mesophyll cells that are usually marked by the abundance of chlorophyll pigments.

59. (C): On the basis of classical studies of Turesson (1922) and Clausen et al. (1940), the ecotypes are defined as "mosaic of populations in which environmentally induced variations in morphology and physiology are genetically fixed and are heritable". Some important attributes of ecotypes are as follows:

1. Ecotypes are discrete entity because they have clear differences in morphology, physiology and phenology in relation to particular environmental conditions.
2. The ecotypes are potentially interfertile with other ecotypes of the same species. But ecotypes are prevented from interbreeding due to ecological barriers.

60. (A): Aquifers are classified as Unconfined aquifers and Confined aquifers on the basis of their occurrence and field situation. An unconfined aquifer (also known as water table aquifer) is one in which a free water surface, *i.e.*, a water table exists. Only the saturated zone of this aquifer is of importance in groundwater studies.

A confined aquifer, also known as artesian aquifer, is an aquifer which is confined between two impervious beds such as aquicludes or aquifuges. Recharge of this aquifer takes place only in the area where it is exposed at the ground surface. The water in the confined aquifer will be under pressure and hence the piezometric level will be much higher than the top level of the aquifer.

61. (A): Noise pollution, or sound pollution, is the propagation of noise or sound with ranging impacts on the activity of human or animal life, most of which are harmful to a degree.

High noise levels can contribute to cardiovascular effects in humans and an increased incidence of coronary artery disease. In animals, noise can increase the risk of death by altering predator or prey detection and avoidance, interfere with reproduction and navigation, and contribute to permanent hearing loss.

Noise pollution exists irrespective of loudness of sound and causes both physiological and psychological stress among individual or group of individuals.

62. (C): A baghouse filter or fabric filter is a kind of air pollution control device which is used to collect particulates out of gasses released by commercial process gases. This air-material separator performs well in a relatively small loading of particles. These types of filters have a high dust collection efficiency, which depending on the type of dust is up to 99.9% efficiency.

63. (A): Incineration is a waste treatment process that involves the combustion of substances contained in waste materials. Incinerators reduce the solid mass of the original waste by 80-85% and the volume (already compressed somewhat in garbage trucks) by 95-96%, depending on composition and degree of recovery of materials such as metals from the ash for recycling.

Incineration has particularly strong benefits for the treatment of certain waste types in niche areas such as clinical wastes and certain hazardous wastes where pathogens and toxins can be destroyed by high temperatures. Examples include chemical multi-product plants with diverse toxic or very toxic wastewater streams, which cannot be routed to a conventional wastewater treatment plant.

64. (D): A paired *t*-test (also known as a dependent or correlated *t*-test) is a statistical test that compares the averages/means and standard deviations of two related groups to determine if there is a significant difference between the two groups.

T tests are a type of parametric method; they can be used when the samples satisfy the conditions of normality, equal variance, and independence.

65. (B): In 1995, the United Nations Environment Programme expanded its research and investigation on POPs with an initial focus on what became known as the "Dirty Dozen". These were a group of 12 highly persistent and toxic chemicals: aldrin, chlordane, DDT, dieldrin, endrin, heptachlor, hexachlorobenzen, mirex, polychlorinated biphenyls, polychlorinated dibenzo-p-dioxins, polychlorinated dibenzofurans, and toxaphen. Many of the pesticides in this group are no longer used for agricultural purposes but a few continue to be used in developing countries.

66. (C): Atomic Absorption Spectroscopy is an instrumental analysis technique for rapid trace metal analysis. It is based on element specific wavelength light absorption by ground state atoms in the flame or electrothermal graphite furnace.

Typical applications of AAS include:

- Quantitative metal concentrations in solution
- Analysis of lead in paint
- Monitoring of trace metals in industrial effluent streams
- Trace elements in product/raw materials along with ICP-MS
- Analysis of additives and purity in steels and other metal alloys
- Analysis of low-level contaminants

67. (A): Populations have some features that, as an organism, a species lacks. Following are the different attributes of a population.

1. Birth and Death Rates
2. Sex Ratio
3. Age Distribution
4. Population Density

Birth and Death Rates: These attributes could be statistically measured for a population, but not for an organism. This is because an organism has birth and death, but not birth rate and death rate.

Sex Ratio: The sex ratio calculates the ratio of male to female individuals in a population.

Age Distribution: The next population attribute is age distribution. A population comprises different age groups such as pre-reproductive, reproductive and post-reproductive age groups. This age distribution is graphically represented by an age pyramid. The age pyramid indicates whether a population is growing, stable or declining.

Population Density: Population density tells the size of a population. This attribute is the reflection of the condition of a habitat. More density indicates that the habitat provides more favourable living conditions.

68. (C): In terms of its constituent elements, the mantle is made up of 44.8% oxygen, 21.5% silicon, and 22.8% magnesium. There's also iron, aluminum, calcium, sodium, and potassium. These elements are all bound together in the form of silicate rocks, all of which take the form of oxides.

69. (C): With the growing threat of climate change due to the excessive release of carbon emissions, many nations are looking to clean energy alternatives to replace traditional fossil fuels.

Of all the clean energy alternatives, solar has arguably been the most expensive though prices have been declining.

- Solar energy is becoming an increasingly cost-competitive alternative to fossil fuels.
- Solar energy is a sustainable energy source, has a low environmental impact, and promotes energy independence.
- On the other hand, it is limited by how long the sun is out, may cause a scarcity of materials, and contains hazardous materials similar to electronics.
- Pricey disadvantages of solar energy may be rendered negligible by technological advances that increase efficiency and storage capacity.
- Increasing the incentives for the development of solar energy may be worthwhile.

70. (C): Biota of Benthic zone: It extends from boundary of continental shelf to the deepest oceans. Since there is no light, plants are absent and only heterotrophic communities are present which live on in the mud surface and bacteria. The deep benthic zone is rich in diversity though strange, occupying cold and dark space surviving under intense pressure and scarcity of food.

71. (D): The BOD_5 test is commonly used for several reasons:

- To determine the amount of oxygen that will be required for biological treatment of the organic matter present in a wastewater
- To determine the size of the waste treatment facility needed
- To assess the efficiency of treatment processes
- To determine compliance with wastewater discharge permits seeded.

The BOD value is expressed in milligrams per liter, according to the following equation.

$$\text{BOD (mg/L)} = \frac{D_1 - D_5}{P}$$

where:

D_1 = initial dissolved oxygen (DO),

D_5 = DO at day 5, and

P = decimal volumetric fraction of wastewater utilized.

If the dilution water is seeded:

$$BOD(mg/L) = \frac{(D_1 - D_5) - (B_1 - B_5)f}{P}$$

where:

D_1 = initial DO of the sample dilution (mg/L)

D_5 = final DO of the sample dilution (mg/L)

P = decimal volumetric fraction of sample used

B_1 = initial DO of seed control (mg/L)

B_5 = final DO of seed control (mg/L), and

f = ratio of seed in sample to seed in control

= (% seed in D_1)/(% seed in B_1).

72. (B): A circular economy is a systemic approach to economic development designed to benefit businesses, society, and the environment. In contrast to the 'take-make-waste' linear model, a circular economy is regenerative by design and aims to gradually decouple growth from the consumption of finite resources. After defining what an economy actually is, this learning path explores the nuances of the concept of a circular economy, including the difference between biological and technical materials, the different opportunities that exist to keep materials and products in use, and the history of the idea.

73. (C): Regardless of how wastes are technically categorized by regulatory agencies, their pollutant-releasing capacities depend on their physical characteristics, which determine their mode of transport into the environment. The four major waste types based on physical characteristics—combustible wastes, solid wastes, sludge and slurry wastes, and wastewaters—are presented in Figure, which shows how each of these types can eventually release pollutants into the atmospheric, terrestrial, and aquatic environments. Combustible wastes yield byproducts that can be released directly into the atmosphere as gases or particulate pollutants when they are not properly filtered. Solid wastes can release pollutants into the atmosphere via dust or particular transport, or when these wastes come into contact with water, their soluble constituents can be leached out into the soil surface or below. Sludge and slurry wastes can release pollutants into the soil and groundwater from both their solid and liquid phases. Wastewaters, owing to their liquid state, are always potential sources of pollution if discharged directly into the aquatic or terrestrial environment without proper treatment.

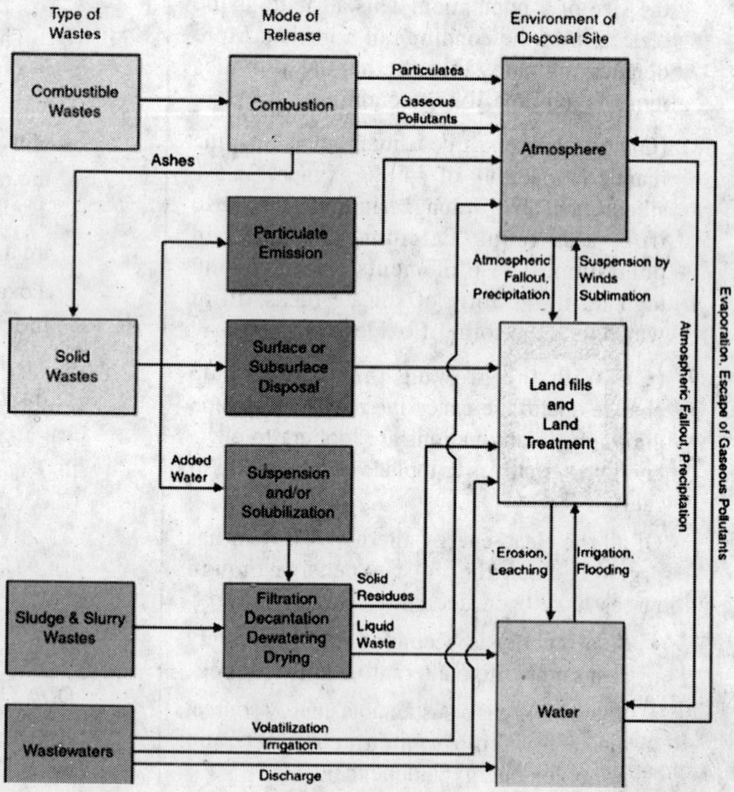

74. (B): Environmental Impact Assessment (EIA) is a process of evaluating the likely environmental impacts of a proposed project or development, taking into account inter-related socio-economic, cultural and human-health impacts, both beneficial and adverse.

EIA is usually required for a development project when:

(*i*) There are potentials for transboundary impact.

(*ii*) Many people are likely to be affected by the project.

(*iii*) There are protected areas in the project area of influence.

75. (A): In statistics, the *p*-value is the probability of obtaining results at least as extreme as the observed results of a statistical hypothesis test, assuming that the null hypothesis is correct. The *p*-value serves as an alternative to rejection points to provide the smallest level of significance at which the null hypothesis would be rejected. A smaller *p*-value means that there is stronger evidence in favour of the alternative hypothesis.

In practice, the significance level is stated in advance to determine how small the *p*-value must be to reject the null hypothesis. Because different researchers use different levels of significance when examining a question, a reader may sometimes have difficulty comparing results from two different tests. P-values provide a solution to this problem.

76. (B): In particular, 95% of the distribution of sample means lies within 1.96 standard deviations (SD) of the population mean. We call this SD the standard error of the mean (SEM), and when we have a single sample, the 95% confidence interval (CI) for the mean is:

(Sample mean – (1.96 × SEM) to Sample mean + (1.96 × SEM))

The standard deviation of the sampling distribution of a mean is known as the standard error of the mean (SEM), which quantifies the precision of the mean. The SEM has the same units as the data:

Standard error of the sample mean

$$= \frac{\text{Standard deviation}}{\sqrt{\text{Sample size}}} = \frac{\text{SD}}{\sqrt{n}}$$

Where the data are not Normally distributed, and/or we do not know the population variance but estimate it by s^2, the sample mean follows a *t*-distribution. We calculate the 95% confidence interval for the mean as

(Sample mean – ($t_{0.05}$ × SEM) to Sample mean + ($t_{0.05}$ × SEM))

i.e., it is Sample mean $\pm\, t_{0.05} \times \frac{s}{\sqrt{n}}$

where $t_{0.05}$ is the percentage point (percentile) of the *t*-distribution with $(n - 1)$ degrees of freedom which gives a two-tailed probability to 0.05.

77. (D): Test methods to evaluate hypotheses with measurement data are summarized in the following Table. We distinguish parametric and non-parametric tests depending on the format and distribution of the underlying raw data.

Table: Overview of parametric and non-parametric test methods

Experiment type	Parametric tests	Nonparametric tests
One factor, one treatment	Correlations, regression analysis	Rank correlations, Binomial test, chi-square
One factor, two treatments completely randomized	t-test, F-test	Mann-Whitney, chi-square
One factor, two treatments paired comparison	Paired t-test	Wilcoxon, Sign test
One factor, more than two treatments	ANOVA	Kruskal-Wallis, chi-square
More than two factors	ANOVA	

The main characteristic of the parametric tests consists in the fact that the analyzed models have a specific distribution. The main characteristic of the non-parametric is that only a very general assumption is made, more general than parametric test.

78. (B): Early statisticians noticed the same shape coming up over and over again in different distributions–so they named it the normal distribution.

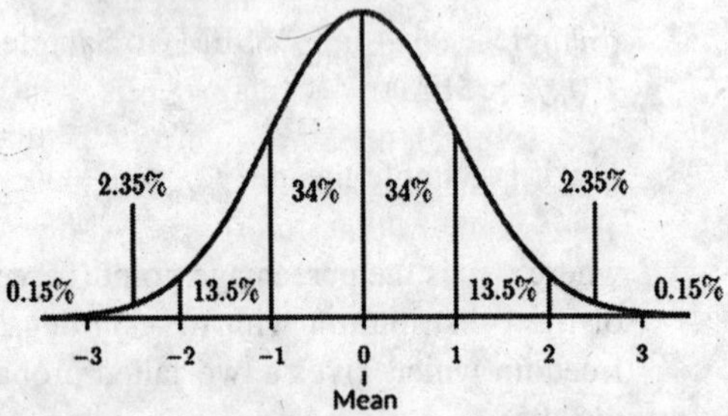

Normal distributions have the following features:

- Symmetric bell shape
- Mean and median are equal; both located at the center of the distribution
- ≈ 68% of the data falls within 1 standard deviation of the mean
- ≈ 95% of the data falls within 2 standard deviations of the mean
- ≈ 99.7% of the data falls within 3 standard deviations of the mean

79. (C): The probability of a *Type II error* is defined to be the probability of *not rejecting the null hypothesis when, in fact, the null hypothesis is not correct*. (This is sometimes referred to as a "false negative.") Again, in the food example, suppose that the sample estimate of β is not sufficiently greater than zero for the researcher to conclude that the null hypothesis should be rejected. If, in fact, there is a positive relationship between the two variables in the population and the null hypothesis of no positive relationship is not true, the researcher would have committed a Type II error by failing to reject the null.

For example, suppose that we want to test the following hypotheses:

H_0 : The drug ineffective;

vs. H_a : The drug is effective.

Then a type I error occur if we conclude that the drug is effective when in fact it is not. On the other hand, a type II error occurs if we claim that the drug is ineffective when in fact it is effective.

80. (C): Table: Landsat image spectral characteristics (Lillesand and Kiefer, 1994)

Channels	Wave-length (μm)	Characteristics and possible application
1	0.45-0.52	Provides increased penetration of water bodies. Supports analyses of land use, soil, and vegetation characteristics.
2	0.53.0.6	Corresponds to the green reflectance of healthy vegetation. Sensitive in the region between the blue and red chlorophyll absorption bands.
3	0.63-0.69	Sensitive to red chlorophyll absorption of healthy green vegetation, therefore it is important bands for vegetation discrimination. Useful for soil-boundary and geological boundary mapping.
4	0.76-0.9	Responsive to the amount of vegetation biomass. Useful for identification of vegetation types, Emphasizes soil-crop and land-water contrasts.
5	1.55-1.75	Sensitive to turgidity - the amount of water in plants. Discriminate between clouds, snow, and ice. Able to remove the effects of thin clouds and smoke.
6	10.4-12.5	Measures the amount of infrared radiant flux (heat) emitted from surfaces. Used in locating geothermal activity.
7	2.08-2.35	Discriminate between geological rock formations. Effective in identifying zones of hydrothermal alteration in rocks.

81. (B): Land breeze: Blowing breeze from land towards the sea is called a land breeze.

They are formed during the night when sea water and land both lose heat, specific heat capacity of land being very low as compared to that of sea water, land loses heat energy fast and cools more rapidly as compared to the sea. Sea water being at higher temperature, the air becomes lighter and rises up. Air from land being at higher pressure. So air from land starts blowing towards the sea and gives rise to a land breeze.

Sea breeze: Blowing breeze from sea towards land during the day is called sea breeze.

They are formed during the day time when land and sea both are heated equally by the sun, but land has very low specific heat capacity as compared to the sea, so it is heated up more quickly, thus air above land due to heat becomes lighter and rises up. Thus pressure decreases and cold and humid air above the sea blowing towards land.

An ocean gyre is a large system of circular ocean currents formed by global wind patterns and forces created by Earth's rotation.

The movement of the world's major ocean gyres helps drive the "ocean conveyor belt." The ocean conveyor belt circulates ocean water around the entire planet. Also known as thermohaline circulation, the ocean conveyor belt is essential for regulating temperature, salinity and nutrient flow throughout the ocean.

An isobar is an imaginary line that connects places of equal barometric pressure. They can be used to find areas of low or high pressure over a large area. Isobars make it easier to read and analyse weather maps.

82. (B): Stratosphere: The troposphere tends to change suddenly and violently, but the stratosphere is calm. The stratosphere extends from the tropopause, the upper boundary of the troposphere, to about 50 kilometers (32 miles) above Earth's surface.

The stratosphere is crucial to life on Earth because it contains small amounts of ozone, a form of oxygen that prevents harmful UV rays from reaching Earth. The region within the stratosphere where this thin shell of ozone is found is called the ozone layer.

Troposphere: The troposphere is the atmospheric layer closest to the planet and contains the largest percentage (around 80%) of the mass of the total atmosphere. Temperature and water vapor content in the troposphere decrease rapidly with altitude. Water vapor plays a major role in regulating air temperature because it absorbs solar energy and thermal radiation from the planet's surface. The troposphere contains 99 % of the water vapor in the atmosphere. Water vapor concentrations vary with latitude. They are greatest above the tropics, where they may be as high as 3 %, and decrease toward the polar regions.

Thermosphere: The thermosphere is located above the mesosphere. The temperature in the thermosphere generally increases with altitude reaching 600 to 3000 F (600-2000 K) depending on solar activity. This increase in temperature is due to the absorption of intense solar radiation by the limited amount of remaining molecular oxygen. At this extreme altitude gas molecules are widely separated. Above 60 miles (100 km) from Earth's surface the chemical composition of air becomes strongly dependent on altitude and the atmosphere becomes enriched with lighter gases (atomic oxygen, helium and hydrogen). Also at 60 miles (100 km) altitude.

Exosphere: The exosphere is the most distant atmospheric region from Earth's surface. In the exosphere, an upward travelling molecule can escape to space (if it is moving fast enough) or be pulled back to Earth by gravity (if it isn't) with little probability of colliding with another molecule. The altitude of its lower boundary, known as the *thermopause* or *exobase*, ranges from about 150 to 300 miles (250-500 km) depending on solar activity. The upper boundary can be defined theoretically by the altitude (about 120,000 miles, half the distance to the Moon) at which the influence of solar radiation pressure on atomic hydrogen velocities exceeds that of the Earth's gravitational pull.

83. (B): Mono-climax Theory: According to the mono-climax theory of succession (Clements, 1936), every region has one climax community toward which all communities are developing. He believed that climate was the determining factor for vegetation and the climax of any area was solely a function of its climate.

Poly-climax Theory: This theory was proposed by Tansley (1939) and later supported by Daubenmire (1966). The poly-climax theory of succession holds that many different types of vegetation as climax communities may be recognized in a given area. These will be climaxes, controlled by soil moisture, soil nutrients, activity of animals and other factors.

Climax-pattern Theory: Whittaker (1953) emphasized that a natural community is adapted to the whole pattern of environmental factors in which it exists; the major factors are: genetic structure of each species, climate, site, soil, biotic factors (activity of animals), fire, and wind, availability of plant and animal species, and chances of dispersal.

Climax as Vegetation: According to Egler (1954) one can say that "climaxes" in a broad sense are nothing more than totality of vegetation, itself. He, thus, favours the study, of vegetation; as it is, with careful observations to explain and interpret past, present, and future conditions of particular communities.

84. (B): There are 12 soil orders (the top hierarchical level) in soil taxonomy. The names of the orders end with the suffix-*sol*. The criteria for the different soil orders include properties that reflect major differences in the genesis of soils. Some of them are:

- **Andisol:** Volcanic ash soils. They are young soils. They cover 1% of the world's ice-free surface.
- **Aridisol:** Dry soils forming under desert conditions which have fewer than 90 consecutive days of moisture during the growing season and are nonleached. They include nearly 12% of soils on Earth. Soil formation is slow, and accumulated organic matter is scarce. They may have subsurface zones of caliche or duripan. Many aridisols have well-developed Bt horizons showing clay movement from past periods of greater moisture.
- **Entisol:** Recently formed soils that lack well-developed horizons. Commonly found on unconsolidated river and beach sediments of sand and clay or volcanic ash, some have an A horizon on top of bedrock. They are 18% of soils worldwide.
- **Gelisol:** Permafrost soils with permafrost within two metres of the surface or gelic materials and permafrost within one metre. They constitute 9% of soils worldwide.
- **Histosol:** Organic soils, formerly called bog soils, are 1% of soils worldwide.
- **Inceptisol:** Young soils. They have subsurface horizon formation but show little eluviation and illuviation. They constitute 15% of soils worldwide.
- **Mollisol:** Soft, deep, dark soil formed in grasslands and some hardwood forests with very thick A horizons. They are 7% of soils worldwide.
- **Ultisol:** Acid soils in the humid tropics and subtropics, which are depleted in calcium, magnesium and potassium (important plant nutrients). They are highly weathered, but not as weathered as Oxisols. They make up 8% of the soil worldwide.
- **Vertisol:** Inverted soils. They are clay-rich and tend to swell when wet and shrink upon drying, often forming deep cracks into which surface layers can fall. They are difficult to farm or to construct roads and buildings due to their high expansion rate. They constitute 2% of soils worldwide.

85. (*)	**86. (D)**	**87. (*)**	**88. (C)**
89. (B)	**90. (C)**	**91. (C)**	**92. (D)**
93. (D)	**94. (B)**	**95. (C)**	**96. (D)**
97. (C)	**98. (C)**	**99. (C)**	**100. (D)**

Previous Years' Paper (Solved)

National Testing Agency (NTA)

UGC-NET Junior Research Fellowship & Assistant Professor Eligibility Exam

ENVIRONMENTAL SCIENCE, June–2021

(Online exam held on 21-11-2021)

PAPER-II

Note: *This paper contains* ***hundred*** *(**100**) objective type questions of* ***two*** *(2) marks each.* ***All*** *questions are* ***compulsory****.*

1. The pioneer community in human evolution is:
A. Pastoralists (Nomadic)
B. Agrosociety
C. Hunting and Gathering Society
D. Industrial Society

2. Name the person, who launched the "Green Belt Movement" in Kenya, and got the Nobel Peace Prize:
A. Wangari Maathai B. Gehard Ertl
C. Koichi Tanaka D. Ryojii Noyori

3. Identify the environmental system with lowest entropy:
A. Land in monoculture agriculture sustained by high energy input
B. Soils containing a balanced community of living organisms
C. Coal reduced to CO_2
D. Polluted rivers

4. Which chemical form of mercury is completely water soluble?
A. Elemental mercury in liquid state
B. Monomethyl mercury
C. Elemental mercury in vapour state
D. Dimethyl mercury

5. The water is classified as "aggressive" if:
A. The Ca^{2+} concentration is much less than $CaCO_3$ saturation
B. The Ca^{2+} concentration is equal to the $CaCO_3$ saturation
C. The Ca^{2+} concentration is more than the $CaCO_3$ saturation
D. The Ca^{2+} concentration is double of the $CaCO_3$ saturation

6. The portion of UV spectrum which readily destroys DNA and causes skin cancer is:
A. 320 mm to 400 mm
B. 280 mm to 320 mm
C. 100 mm to 280 mm
D. 400 mm to 700 mm

7. Free energy (ΔG) value of zero indicates:
A. Spontaneous reaction in forward direction
B. The state of equilibrium
C. Spontaneous reaction in backward direction
D. No reaction at all

8. A gas fired, combined heat and power plant produces 5000 MWh electricity and heat of 30,000 GJ. If the input energy required to run the power plant is 60,000 GJ, the efficiency of the plant is:
A. 35% B. 40%
C. 50% D. 80%

9. Which of the following compounds has the least Ozone Depleting Potential?
A. CFC-11 B. Halons
C. HCFCs D. Methyl Bromide

10. Which one among the following is not an example of detrital sedimentary rocks?
A. Sandstone B. Chalk
C. Shale D. Conglomerate

11. According to the U.S. Department of Agriculture system of classification, the size of silt particles in soil ranges between:
A. 0.02 to 0.2 mm
B. 0.05 to 0.5 mm
C. 0.002 to 0.05 mm
D. 0.0002 to 0.002 mm

12. Which one among the following has the lowest hydraulic conductivity (m/day)?
A. Gravel B. Sandstone
C. Sand D. Clay

13. At location characterized by latitude $\phi = 30°$, pressure is found to vary by 1.0 mb over a distance of 100 km. If the density of air mass is ~1.25 kg/m^3, the geostrophic wind velocity is:
A. ~11 m/s B. ~15 m/s
C. ~26 m/s D. ~7 m/s

14. The internal relationship between α, β and γ diversity can be presented as:
A. $\beta = \frac{\gamma}{\alpha}$ B. $\gamma = \beta \times \alpha$
C. $\alpha = \gamma \times \beta$ D. $\gamma = \beta + \alpha$

15. The minimum time needed for the formation of one inch of the top soil is:
A. Less than 10 years
B. 10 – 50 years
C. 100 – 400 years
D. 1,000 – 2,000 years

16. Which zone of a pond/lake ecosystem does not receive light?
A. Littoral B. Limnetic
C. Profundal D. Epilimnion

17. "Slash and burn" is a term that is usually associated with the practice of:
A. Illicit felling and encroachment
B. Grazing and lopping
C. Incinertation of waste
D. Shifting cultivation

18. A species that has profound effect on the ecological processes of an ecosystem and whose removal or loss would result in disturbing the community structure is known as:
A. Dominant species B. Keystone species
C. Indicator species D. Flagship species

19. The flagship species of Kedarnath Wildlife sanctuary is:
A. Elephant B. Musk Deer
C. Tiger D. Wild Boar

20. The maximum permissible limit of BOD (mg/l) in the treated waste water that can be discharged into garden for watering is:
A. 20 B. 30
C. 40 D. 10

21. What is the concentration of H^+ in a solution of 0.1 N NaOH at 25° C?
A. 10^{13} M B. 10^{-13} M
C. 10^{-14} M D. 10^{14} M

22. Which method is used to separate proteins on the basis of their sizes?
A. Ion exchange chromatography
B. Thin layer chromatography
C. Adsorption chromatography
D. Gel filtration chromatography

23. Which of the following is not a molecular method for identification of microbial population form soil or water?
A. MPN B. rRNA sequencing
C. RT-PCR D. PCR

24. The rate of increase in temperature with depth in the earth also known as geothermal gradient, is equal to:
A. 6.8° C/Km B. 20° C/Km
C. 25° C/Km D. 37.4° C/Km

25. For wind power generation, the percentage of maximum extractable power contained in the wind is:
A. ~45% B. ~59%
C. ~62% D. ~37%

26. Carbon content in a certain type of coal is 0.81. Assume that the combustion efficiency of coal is ~100%, then how much CO_2 will be produced on combustion of 1 kg of coal?
A. ~3 kg B. ~5.4 kg
C. ~1.8 kg D. ~4.8 kg

27. At STP, 1 ppb sulphur dioxide is equivalent to:
A. ~7.31 μg m^{-3} B. ~3.16 μg m^{-3}
C. ~4.52 μg m^{-3} D. ~2.86 μg m^{-3}

28. Which of the following organisms is the most tolerant to sewage pollution?
A. Scenedesmus B. Daphnia
C. Chironomus D. Chlorella

29. The process of illuviation in soil indicates:
A. Removal of particles from the top soil
B. Removal of particles from the C horizon
C. Percolation of soluble salts into deeper soil layers
D. Accumulation of particles in the B horizon

30. Carbonmonooxide is harmful to human beings, as it:

A. causes cancer
B. causes eye irritation
C. depletes ozone layer
D. has high affinity with haemoglobin as compared to oxygen

31. The ash content in coal used in stand-alone thermal power plants in India should not be more than:
A. 20% B. 27%
C. 34% D. 40%

32. Pyrolysis of solid wastes refers to:
A. High temperature burning in presence of excess air
B. High temperature anaerobic distillation
C. Low temperature combustion in pressure of limited air
D. Ambient anaerobic distillation

33. Which of the following mixture of gases can be found in biogas?
A. CO, CH_4, NO, H_2S, H_2O vapour
B. CO_2, CH_4, NH_3, H_2S, H_2O vapour
C. CO_2, CH_4, N_2O, NH_3, H_2O vapour
D. CO_2, CH_4, NO, NH_3

34. India became a party to CITES in the year:
A. 1972 B. 1976
C. 1974 D. 1986

35. Time clocked by an athlete in a 100 m race is an example of which type of variable?
A. discrete B. continuous
C. nominal D. oridnal

36. In a class of 13 students, 3 students failed in a test. The marks of 10 students who passed were 6, 9, 4, 8, 7, 6, 5, 6, 7, 5. The median value of marks of all the 13 students is:
A. 5 B. 5.5
C. 6 D. 6.5

37. The probability that a standard normal variate lies between $-\infty$ and $+1$ is:
A. ~0.84 B. ~0.78
C. ~0.72 D. ~0.68

38. Population of a city doubled in a span of 20 years. Assuming exponential growth at a constant rate over the given period, the growth rate would have been:
A. ~3.5% B. ~3.0%
C. ~2.5% D. ~2.0%

39. Following information is given regarding a one-way ANOVA test:
There are 'k' treatments, each having sample size $n_1, n_2, n_3, \ldots n_k$ such that the total sample size $N = n_1 + n_2 + n_3 + \ldots + n_k$.
The degrees of freedom for the mean error sum of squares in the test will be:
A. k B. $k - 1$
C. $N - 1$ D. $N - k$

40. For a regression model, the following information is given :
Unexplained sum of squares = 25
Explained sum of squares = 75
The value of coefficient of determination for this model is:
A. 0.33 B. 3
C. 0.67 D. 0.75

41. Among all the unbiased estimators of the population regression coefficients which are linear in the dependent variable (say Y_i), the least squares estimators have the smallest variance. This statement is known as:
A. Bayes' theorem
B. Central limit theorem
C. Chebyshev's theorem
D. Gauss-Markov theorem

42. The place of origin of the National River Ganga is:
A. Bhagirath Kharak B. Chaukhamba Peak
C. Gomukh D. Pindari Glacier

43. Water remains in liquid state over a wide range of temperature because of its:
(*a*) Specific heat
(*b*) Heat of vapourisation
(*c*) Density at 0°C
(*d*) Bipolar nature
Choose the ***most appropriate*** answer from the options given below:
A. (*a*) and (*c*) Only B. (*a*) and (*d*) Only
C. (*a*) and (*b*) Only D. (*b*) and (*d*) Only

44. The difference in values of theoretical oxygen demand and actual oxygen demand is observed because of:
(*a*) difference in rate of reaeration and deoxygenation
(*b*) addition of dead cell biomass of bacteria as waste
(*c*) accumulation of waste in bacterial tissue
(*d*) formation of humus which resists degradation

Choose the ***most appropriate*** answer from the options given below:
A. (*a*) and (*c*) Only B. (*b*) and (*d*) Only
C. (*a*) and (*d*) Only D. (*b*) and (*c*) Only

45. The crystal structure of a compound/material can be determined using:
(*a*) Scanning Electron Microscope
(*b*) X-Ray Fluorescence
(*c*) Transmission Electron Microscopy
(*d*) X-Ray Diffraction

Choose the ***most appropriate*** answer from the options given below:
A. (*a*) and (*d*) Only B. (*b*) and (*c*) Only
C. (*a*) and (*c*) Only D. (*c*) and (*d*) Only

46. Which of the following are living fossils?
(*a*) Ginkgo biloba (*b*) Panthera tigris
(*c*) Elephas Maximas (*d*) Latimavia

Choose the ***most appropriate*** answer from the options given below:
A. (*a*) and (*d*) Only B. (*a*) and (*c*) Only
C. (*b*) and (*c*) Only D. (*a*) and (*b*) Only

47. Consider the following statements:
(*a*) Earth is farthest from the sun at the time of perihelion
(*b*) When perihelion occurs, it is winter season in the northern hemisphere
(*c*) Seasons on earth occur due to inclination in earth's axis of rotation

Choose the ***most appropriate*** answer from the options given below:
A. (*a*) and (*b*) Only B. (*b*) and (*c*) Only
C. (*a*) and (*c*) Only D. (*a*), (*b*) and (*c*)

48. Ferromagnesian minerals are:
(*a*) a group of silicates
(*b*) black, brown or green colour minerals
(*c*) a group of bicarbonates
(*d*) highly resistant to weathering and erosional process

Choose the ***most appropriate*** answer from the options given below:
A. (*a*), (*b*) and (*d*) Only
B. (*b*), (*c*) and (*d*) Only
C. (*a*) and (*b*) Only
D. (*c*) and (*d*) Only

49. Consider the following statements regarding clay minerals in soil:
(*a*) Some clay particles are technically not colloids yet they have colloid like properties
(*b*) There are four major types of colloids present in soil
(*c*) All types of clays are crystalline in nature
(*d*) Soil humus are not considered as colloids

Choose the ***most appropriate*** answer from the options given below:
A (*a*) and (*c*) Only B. (*b*) and (*c*) Only
C. (*a*) and (*b*) Only D. (*b*) and (*d*) Only

50. Consider the following statements:
(*a*) Richter magnitude is based upon the amplitude of the largest seismic wave produced during an earthquake
(*b*) An earthquake with Richter magnitude 7 produces 10 times larger displacement on the seismogram than does a magnitude 6
(*c*) S-waves travel faster than P waves through solid materials

Choose the ***most appropriate*** answer from the options given below:
A. (*a*) and (*b*) Only B. (*b*) and (*c*) Only
C. (*a*) and (*c*) Only D. (*a*), (*b*) and (*c*)

51. Consider the following statements regarding lines of regression between two variables X and Y.
(*a*) The correlation between X and Y is the geometric mean of the regression coefficients of Y on X and X on Y
(*b*) If the variables are uncorrelated, the two lines of regression (*i.e.*, Y on X and X on Y) are perpendicular to each other
(*c*) If the regression coefficient Y on X is greater than one, the coefficient of X on Y must also be greater than one

Choose the ***most appropriate*** answer from the options given below:
A. (*a*) and (*b*) only B. (*b*) and (*c*) only
C. (*a*) and (*c*) only D. (*a*), (*b*) and (*c*)

52. Energy crops:
(*a*) are fast growing plants
(*b*) can be grown on degraded, waste, saline or water logged lands
(*c*) can not be used to produce liquid fuels
(*d*) usually have high calorific values

Choose the ***most appropriate*** answer from the options given below:
A. (*a*) and (*b*) Only
B. (*b*) and (*c*) Only
C. (*a*), (*b*) and (*c*) Only
D. (*a*), (*b*) and (*d*) Only

53. Among the following effects of noise on people, identify the Auditory effects:
(*a*) Annoyance
(*b*) Speech interference
(*c*) Acoustical privacy
(*d*) Sleep interference
(*e*) Hearing loss

Choose the ***most appropriate*** answer from the options given below:
A. (*a*), (*b*) (*c*) and (*e*) Only
B. (*b*) and (*e*) Only
C. (*b*), (*c*) and (*e*) Only
D. (*a*), (*c*), (*d*) and (*e*) Only

54. In Isokinetic air sampling:
(*a*) the inlet is faced against the prevailing wind
(*b*) sampling flow rate is chosen so that inlet speed is same as the wind speed
(*c*) there should be least possibility of distortion of particles sampled

Choose the ***most appropriate*** answer from the options given below:
A. (*a*), (*b*) and (*c*) B. (*b*) and (*c*) Only
C. (*a*) and (*c*) Only D. (*a*) and (*b*) Only

55. Consider the following statements regarding organic carbon estimation following Walkley and Black method:
(*a*) Organic carbon estimated by this method excludes most of the less active organic matter
(*b*) 100% of the total oxidizable organic carbon is oxidized in this method
(*c*) Soil organic matter percentage can be calculated by multiplying estimated organic carbon percentage by 1.724
(*d*) K_2SO_4 and H_2SO_4 are used as reagents

Choose the ***most appropriate*** answer from the options given below:
A. (*b*) and (*d*) Only B. (*a*) and (*b*) Only
C. (*a*) and (*c*) Only D. (*b*) and (*c*) Only

56. Which of the following deposition mechanisms dominate(s) for particles in the size range 3-10 μm?
(*a*) Diffusion (*b*) Impaction
(*c*) Sedimentation

Choose the ***most appropriate*** answer from the options given below:
A. (*b*) only B. (*b*) and (*c*) only
C. (*a*) only D. (*a*) and (*c*) only

57. Consider the following statements regarding the 2012 application of vermicompost:
(*a*) Vermicompost is an excellent base for the establishment of beneficial microorganisms
(*b*) Presence of earthworms helps in aerating the soil
(*c*) Plants respond slowly compared to compost or farm yard manure
(*d*) Application of vermicompost augments the growth of N-fixing microbes
(*e*) Earthworm casts do not harbor Vesicular Arbuscular Micorrhizal (VAM) propagules

Choose the ***most appropriate*** answer from the options given below:
A. (*a*), (*b*) and (*e*) Only
B. (*a*), (*d*) and (*e*) Only
C. (*a*), (*b*) and (*d*) Only
D. (*b*), (*c*) and (*e*) Only

58. Consider the following statements regarding incineration of urban waste :
(*a*) Incineration of urban waste is a clean process
(*b*) Under ideal condition, incineration may reduce the volume of waste by 75–95%
(*c*) Ash is generated as by-product of incineration
(*d*) This process of pollutant abatement is inexpensive

Choose the ***most appropriate*** answer from the options given below:
A. (*a*) and (*b*) Only
B. (*b*) and (*c*) Only
C. (*b*), (*c*) and (*d*) Only
D. (*a*), (*b*) and (*d*) Only

59. Match List-I with List-II.

List-I	***List-II***
(*a*) Stenothermal	(*i*) Daphnia
(*b*) Eurythermal	(*ii*) Heteroneries
(*c*) Cyclomorphosis	(*iii*) Toads
(*d*) Circalunar rhythms	(*iv*) Fishes

Choose the ***correct*** answer from the options given below:

	(*a*)	(*b*)	(*c*)	(*d*)
A.	(*iv*)	(*iii*)	(*i*)	(*ii*)
B.	(*ii*)	(*iv*)	(*iii*)	(*i*)
C.	(*iv*)	(*iii*)	(*ii*)	(*i*)
D.	(*iii*)	(*ii*)	(*i*)	(*iv*)

60. Match List-I with List-II.

List-I (Mineral type)	***List-II (Geometric shape)***
(*a*) Helicitic	(*i*) Arranged like a star
(*b*) Micaceous	(*ii*) Consists of small ellipsoid or spheroids
(*c*) Oolitic	(*iii*) Consists of thin plate like lamelae
(*d*) Stellate	(*iv*) Twisted and curved, like coral branching

Choose the ***correct*** answer from the options given below:

	(*a*)	(*b*)	(*c*)	(*d*)
A.	(*iv*)	(*iii*)	(*i*)	(*ii*)
B.	(*iv*)	(*iii*)	(*ii*)	(*i*)
C.	(*i*)	(*ii*)	(*iii*)	(*iv*)
D.	(*i*)	(*ii*)	(*iv*)	(*iii*)

61. Match List-I with List-II.

List-I (Air Quality Index)	***List-II (Categorization)***
(*a*) 0–50	(*i*) Poor
(*b*) 51–100	(*ii*) Severe
(*c*) 201–300	(*iii*) Good
(*d*) 401–500	(*iv*) Satisfactory

Choose the ***correct*** answer from the options given below:

	(*a*)	(*b*)	(*c*)	(*d*)
A.	(*iii*)	(*iv*)	(*ii*)	(*i*)
B.	(*iii*)	(*iv*)	(*i*)	(*ii*)
C.	(*i*)	(*ii*)	(*iv*)	(*iii*)
D.	(*i*)	(*ii*)	(*iii*)	(*iv*)

62. Match List-I with List-II.

List-I (Water Quality Parameter)	***List-II (Chemical/Reagent used in Analysis)***
(*a*) Iron	(*i*) Barium Chloride
(*b*) Dissolved Oxygen	(*ii*) Phenanthroline
(*c*) Calcium	(*iii*) Murexide
(*d*) Sulphate	(*iv*) Manganous Sulphate

Choose the ***correct*** answer from the options given below:

	(*a*)	(*b*)	(*c*)	(*d*)
A.	(*i*)	(*iii*)	(*ii*)	(*iv*)
B.	(*ii*)	(*iv*)	(*iii*)	(*i*)
C.	(*ii*)	(*iii*)	(*i*)	(*iv*)
D.	(*iv*)	(*ii*)	(*iii*)	(*i*)

63. Match List-I with List-II.

List-I	***List-II***
(*a*) Animal Anatomical Waste	(*i*) White
(*b*) Waste sharp	(*ii*) Blue
(*c*) Discarded catheters	(*iii*) Yellow
(*d*) Disposable glasswares	(*iv*) Red

Choose the ***correct*** answer from the options given below:

	(*a*)	(*b*)	(*c*)	(*d*)
A.	(*ii*)	(*iii*)	(*iv*)	(*i*)
B.	(*iii*)	(*ii*)	(*iv*)	(*i*)
C.	(*iv*)	(*i*)	(*ii*)	(*iii*)
D.	(*iii*)	(*i*)	(*iv*)	(*ii*)

64. Match List-I with List-II.

List-I (Waste type)	***List-II (Toxic elements)***
(*a*) Wood preservatives	(*i*) Cadmium
(*b*) Food cans	(*ii*) Mercury
(*c*) Colored printing inks	(*iii*) Arsenic
(*d*) Fluorescent lamps	(*iv*) Lead

Choose the ***correct*** answer from the options given below:

	(*a*)	(*b*)	(*c*)	(*d*)
A.	(*iii*)	(*i*)	(*ii*)	(*iv*)
B.	(*iii*)	(*iv*)	(*i*)	(*ii*)
C.	(*iii*)	(*ii*)	(*iv*)	(*i*)
D.	(*iv*)	(*ii*)	(*iii*)	(*i*)

65. Match List-I with List-II.

List-I (Wild Animal/Plant)	***List-II (Schedule of Wildlife Protection Act)***
(*a*) Musk Deer	(*i*) III
(*b*) Himalayan Black Bear	(*ii*) VI
(*c*) Pitcher Plant	(*iii*) I
(*d*) Bison (Gaur)	(*iv*) II

Choose the ***correct*** answer from the options given below:

	(*a*)	(*b*)	(*c*)	(*d*)
A.	(*iii*)	(*i*)	(*ii*)	(*iv*)
B.	(*i*)	(*ii*)	(*iii*)	(*iv*)
C.	(*iv*)	(*iii*)	(*ii*)	(*i*)
D.	(*ii*)	(*iii*)	(*iv*)	(*i*)

66. Match List-I with List-II.

List-I (Pollutant)	List-II (Health Effects)
(a) Cadmium	(i) Severe skin condition 'Chloracne'
(b) Dioxin	(ii) Cancer
(c) Carbofuran	(iii) Weakening of bones
(d) Benzo (a) Pyrene	(iv) Impeded neuro-transmission

Choose the ***correct*** answer from the options given below:

	(a)	(b)	(c)	(d)
A.	(iv)	(iii)	(i)	(ii)
B.	(iv)	(i)	(ii)	(iii)
C.	(iii)	(iv)	(i)	(ii)
D.	(iii)	(i)	(iv)	(ii)

67. Match List-I with List-II.

List-I (Method)	List-II (Estimation of)
(a) X-Ray Fluorescence meter	(i) Functional groups
(b) Quartz Crystal Microbalance	(ii) Inorganic compounds
(c) Fourier Transform Infrared Spectro-meter	(iii) Multi-element analysis
(d) Laser Microprobe Mass Spectrometry	(iv) Particulate matter

Choose the ***correct*** answer from the options given below:

	(a)	(b)	(c)	(d)
A.	(i)	(iii)	(iv)	(ii)
B.	(iii)	(iv)	(ii)	(i)
C.	(iii)	(iv)	(i)	(ii)
D.	(i)	(iii)	(ii)	(iv)

68. Match List-I with List-II.

List-I (Hydropower projects)	List-II (River)
(a) Sardar Sarovar project	(i) Bhagirathi River
(b) Tehri Dam project	(ii) Narmada River
(c) Pong Dam	(iii) Mahanadi River
(d) Hirakund Dam	(iv) Beas River

Choose the ***correct*** answer from the options given below:

	(a)	(b)	(c)	(d)
A.	(i)	(ii)	(iv)	(iii)
B.	(iv)	(iii)	(ii)	(i)
C.	(iii)	(iv)	(i)	(ii)
D.	(ii)	(i)	(iv)	(iii)

69. Identify the correct sequence of the following data products of Indian satellites according to their spatial resolutions:

(a) Cartosat – 2 PAN
(b) Oceansat – 2 OCM
(c) Resourcesat – 2 AWIFS
(d) IRS – ID LISS – 3

Choose the ***correct*** answer from the options given below:

A. (c) > (a) > (b) > (d)
B. (b) > (d) > (c) > (a)
C. (c) > (b) > (d) > (a)
D. (b) > (c) > (d) > (a)

70. Identify the correct sequence of natural surfaces according to their albedo:

(a) Ocean (b) Fresh snow
(c) Grass (d) Desert Sand

Choose the ***correct*** answer from the options given below:

A. (a) < (b) < (c) < (d)
B. (c) < (a) < (d) < (b)
C. (c) < (a) < (b) < (d)
D. (a) < (c) < (d) < (b)

71. What is the correct order of abundance of following heavy metals in the earth's crust?

(a) Fe (b) Mg
(c) Al (d) Cu

Choose the ***correct*** answer from the options given below:

A. (a) > (c) > (b) > (d)
B. (a) > (c) > (d) > (b)
C. (c) > (a) > (b) > (d)
D. (c) > (a) > (d) > (b)

72. Identify the correct sequence in ascending order of the grade of metamorphism

(a) Gneiss (b) Slate
(c) Schist (d) Shale

Choose the ***correct*** answer from the options given below:

A. (a), (b), (c), (d) B. (d), (c), (b), (a)
C. (b), (d), (c), (a) D. (d), (b), (c), (a)

73. In the context of urban environment, arrange the following in order of increasing residence time.

(a) Formaldehyde
(b) Carbon monoxide
(c) Peroxyacetyl nitrate
(d) Hydroxyl radical

Choose the ***correct*** answer from the options given below :

A. (*a*) < (*d*) < (*b*) < (*c*)
B. (*a*) < (*b*) < (*d*) < (*c*)
C. (*d*) < (*a*) < (*c*) < (*b*)
D. (*b*) < (*c*) < (*a*) < (*d*)

74. Identify the correct sequence of Life Time (years) of the green house gases in increasing order:

(*a*) CH_4 (Methane)
(*b*) N_2O (Nitrous Oxide)
(*c*) CFC-12
(*d*) O_3 (Tropospheric)

Choose the ***correct*** answer from the options given below:

A. (*a*), (*d*), (*b*), (*c*) B. (*d*), (*a*), (*c*), (*b*)
C. (*b*), (*a*), (*d*), (*c*) D. (*b*), (*d*), (*a*), (*c*)

75. Identify the correct sequence of Net Heating Value (MJ/Kg) in increasing order for the following fuels.

(*a*) Charcoal (*b*) Bituminous coal
(*c*) Regular gasoline (*d*) Natural gas
(*e*) Oak wood

Choose the correct answer from the options given below:

A. (*a*), (*e*), (*b*), (*c*), (*d*)
B. (*e*), (*b*), (*a*), (*c*), (*d*)
C. (*b*), (*a*), (*e*), (*d*), (*c*)
D. (*e*), (*a*), (*b*), (*c*), (*d*)

76. Identify the correct sequence of conversion of a fertile nuclear material to a fissile material involving the following nuclei:

(*a*) Np^{239}_{146} (*b*) U^{239}_{147}
(*c*) Pu^{239}_{145} (*d*) U^{238}_{146}

Choose the ***correct*** answer from the options given below:

A. (*a*), (*b*), (*c*), (*d*) B. (*a*), (*b*), (*d*), (*c*)
C. (*b*), (*d*), (*a*), (*c*) D. (*d*), (*b*), (*a*), (*c*)

77. Identify the correct sequence of moisture content (%) in ascending order in the following categories of wastes:

(*a*) Animal solids and organic waste
(*b*) Trash
(*c*) Rubbish
(*d*) Garbage
(*e*) Refuse

Choose the ***correct*** answer from the options given below:

A. (*e*), (*d*), (*b*), (*c*), (*a*) B. (*c*), (*b*), (*d*), (*e*), (*a*)
C. (*a*), (*b*), (*c*), (*e*), (*d*) D. (*b*), (*c*), (*e*), (*d*), (*a*)

78. According to the Solid Waste Management Rules 2016, arrange the following metals in decreasing order of their permissible concentration (mg/kg) in the prepared compost:

(*a*) Chromium (*b*) Lead
(*c*) Cadmium (*d*) Copper

Choose the ***correct*** answer from the options given below:

A. (*a*), (*b*), (*c*), (*d*) B. (*b*), (*d*), (*a*), (*c*)
C. (*d*), (*b*), (*a*), (*c*) D. (*d*), (*a*), (*b*), (*c*)

79. Given below are two statements:

Statement I : Mean deviation is a better measure of dispersion than the quartile deviation.

Statement II : Mean deviation is obtained by dividing the algebraic sum of deviations about mean by total number of observations.

In the light of the above statements, choose the ***correct*** answer from the options given below:

A. Both Statement I and Statement II are true
B. Both Statement I and Statement II are false
C. Statement I is true, but Statement II is false
D. Statement I is false, but Statement II is true

80. Given below are two statements:

Statement I : The log-normal distribution is positively skewed.

Statement II : A negatively skewed distribution has its long tail to the left.

In the light of the above statements, choose the ***correct*** answer from the options given below:

A. Both Statement I and Statement II are true
B. Both Statement I and Statement II are false
C. Statement I is true, but Statement II is false
D. Statement I is false, but Statement II is true

81. Given below are two statements : One is labelled as Assertion (A) and the other is labelled as Reason (R).

Assertion (A) : In the hybrid car technology, cars run on both petrol and battery based electrical engines.

Reason (R) : Battery of the hybrid car is externally charged.

In the light of the above statements, choose the ***correct*** answer from the options given below:

A. Both (A) and (R) are true and (R) is the correct explanation of (A)

B. Both (A) and (R) are true, but (R) is NOT the correct explanation of (A)

C. (A) is true, but (R) is false

D. (A) is false, but (R) is true

82. Given below are two statements:

Statement I : Gasoline mixed with bio-fuels (ethanol) has generally more energy content than pure gasoline.

Statement II : Energy content per unit volume of ethanol is more than that of gasoline.

In the light of the above statements, choose the ***correct*** answer from the options given below:

A. Both Statement I and Statement II are true

B. Both Statement I and Statement II are false

C. Statement I is true, but Statement II is false

D. Statement I is false, but Statement II is true

83. Which article in Indian constitution recognizes the "Directive Principle of State Policy" for the protection of environment and wildlife?

A. Article 42 B. Article 21

C. Article 51A(g) D. Article 48A

84. Which of the following are included in the list of hazardous wastes as per Hazardous Waste Rules, 2016?

(*a*) Flyash

(*b*) Empty barrels contaminated with hazardous waste

(*c*) Red mud

(*d*) Chemical-containing residue arising from decontamination

Choose the ***most appropriate*** answer from the options given below:

A. (*a*), (*b*) and (*c*) only

B. (*b*) and (*d*) only

C. (*b*) and (*c*) only

D. (*a*), (*b*) and (*d*) only

85. The Biological Diversity Act 2002 provides the following provisions:

(*a*) Regulation of access to biodiversity

(*b*) Does not allow local communities for using their biological resources

(*c*) Establishment of state biodiversity boards

(*d*) Equitable sharing of benefits of biological resources with local communities

Choose the ***correct*** answer from the options given below:

A. (*a*), (*b*) and (*c*) only

B. (*b*), (*c*) and (*d*) only

C. (*a*), (*b*) and (*d*) only

D. (*a*), (*c*) and (*d*) only

86. The Government of India has introduced a scheme of eco-labelling of consumer products as "Ecomark".

(*a*) This scheme was introduced in 1986

(*b*) This scheme was introduced in 1991

(*c*) 'ISI' was given the mark for this scheme

(*d*) An 'earthen pitcher' was made the symbol for this scheme

Choose the ***most appropriate*** answer from the options given below:

A. (*a*) and (*d*) only B. (*a*) and (*c*) only

C. (*b*) and (*d*) only D. (*c*) and (*d*) only

87. Consider the following statement:

(*a*) Arithmetic Mean is greater than the geometric mean for two non-equal positive real numbers

(*b*) Correlation coefficient is a confirmatory tool to establish causal relationship between two variables

(*c*) Regression coefficient is independent of change of origin

Choose the correct answer from the option given below:

A. (*a*) and (*b*) only B. (*b*) and (*c*) only

C. (*a*) and (*c*) only D. (*a*), (*b*) and (*c*)

88. Which of the following are correct in the context of the Elephant Project?

(*a*) It was launched in February, 1992

(*b*) It was launched in April, 1973

(*c*) It is being implemented in 16 states

(*d*) Project is being executed in 50 reserves

(*e*) Project is being executed in 32 reserves

Choose the correct answer from the options given below:

A. (*b*), (*c*) and (*d*) only

B. (*a*), (*c*) and (*d*) only

C. (*a*), (*c*) and (*e*) only

D. (*b*), (*c*), (*d*) and (*e*) only

89. Identify the correct sequence of the given soil texture classes in decreasing order of stability of wet clods:

(*a*) Loam (*b*) Clay
(*c*) Sandy Loam (*d*) Silt Loam
(*e*) Clay Loam

Choose the ***correct*** answer from the options given below:

A. (*a*), (*b*), (*d*), (*e*), (*c*)
B. (*b*), (*e*), (*d*), (*a*), (*c*)
C. (*b*), (*d*), (*a*), (*c*), (*e*)
D. (*b*), (*e*), (*a*), (*c*), (*d*)

90. Given below are two statements:

Consider the following two statements with reference to Gaussian Plume Model.

Statement I : Turbulent diffusion causes mixing of pollutants at a rate faster than molecular diffusion in atmosphere.

Statement II : The distance from the stack, where maximum ground level concentration is observed, is relatively large when the atmosphere is more turbulent.

In the light of the above statements, choose the ***most appropriate*** answer from the options given below:

A. Both Statement I and Statement II are correct
B. Both Statement I and Statement II are incorrect
C. Statement I is correct, but Statement II is incorrect
D. Statement I is incorrect, but Statement II is correct

Directions (Q.No. 91 to 95): *Read the passage given below. Based on it answer the question.*

According to a study published recently in the journal Nature Climate Change, while black carbon has a large effect on snow darkening and resultant melting of snow, dust particles transported from as far as Saudi Arabia that get deposited in the Western Himalayan Region (WHR) have a large role to play in melting of snow, particularly at higher elevations. Dust transported as elevated, aerosol layers get deposited at 1 – 5 km elevations, black carbon emission is mostly a surface phenomenon and influences melting of snow from surface to about 3 km elevation.

Based on remote sensing data of spatial distribution of dust aerosol concentration over the Indian subcontinent and dust-induced snow albedo reduction over Himalayas during the period 2011-2016 and simulations, it has been inferred that the relative impacts of dust and black carbon vary with surface elevation of snow pack. This is in addition to snow-melt caused by warming due to climate change. Earlier studies have shown that the magnitude of snow mass decrease is about 1 mm per year at 1 km elevation, about 5 mm per year at 4.5 km elevation and about 3 mm per year at 6 km elevation.

Though black carbon has a larger snow albedo darkening effect than dust due to a larger mass absorption efficiency, the study found that radiative effects of dust deposited on snow are comparable to black carbon in the WHR at higher elevations. This is mainly because the deposition of the dust by mass is 100-1000 times more than black carbon. As the elevation increases, the influence of dust comes greater than black carbon and this coincides with maximum intensity of snow melt reduction seen at 3-5 km elevation. Between these two black carbon mainly contributes to snow melt at lower elevation while dust is the major contributor for snow melt at higher elevation.

Westerlies transport dust particles as elevated aerosol layers at maximum intensities mostly during the pre-monsoon period and this gets deposited at higher elevations in the WHR.

Due to global warming, snow cover at lower elevations in the Himalayas will occur less frequently or totally disappear compared with snow cover at higher elevations. The annual contribution of dust to snow melt will therefore likely increase in future as the black carbon effect at lower elevation weakness with dwindling snow pack.

91. Snow melt in Himalayas is on account of:

(*a*) Dust deposition
(*b*) Black carbon deposition
(*c*) Increase in albedo
(*d*) Climate change

A. (*a*) and (*b*) only
B. (*a*), (*b*), (*c*) and (*d*)
C. (*a*), (*b*) and (*c*) only
D. (*a*), (*b*) and (*d*) only

92. Maximum rate of snow mass reduction per annum is at elevation of:

A. 1 km B. 3-5 km
C. 6 km D. 2 km

93. Given below are two statements : One is labelled as Assertion (A) and the other is labelled as Reason (R):

Assertion (A) : Reduction in snow albedo is more in case of black carbon than dust

Reason (R) : Black carbon has higher mass absorption efficiency compared to dust.

In the light of the above statements, choose the ***correct*** answer from the options given below:

A. Both (A) and (R) are true and (R) is the correct explanation of (A)
B. Both (A) and (R) are true, but (R) is NOT the correct explanation of (A)
C. (A) is true, but (R) is false
D. (A) is false, but (R) is true

94. Given below are two statements : one is labelled as Assertion (A) and the other is labelled as Reason (R):

Assertion (A) : Radiative effects of dust deposited on snow are comparable to black carbon in the WHR at higher elevations.

Reason (R) : Both black carbon and dust darken the snow cover.

In the light of the above statements, choose the ***correct*** answer from the options given below:

A. Both (A) and (R) are true and (R) is the correct explanation of (A)
B. Both (A) and (R) are true, but (R) is NOT the correct explanation of (A)
C. (A) is true, but (R) is false
D. (A) is false, but (R) is true

95. The passage clearly brings out the finding that:

A. Black carbon causes global warming
B. Dust causes global warming
C. Dust modifies the radiative properties of snow cover to the same extent as black carbon
D. Black carbon and dust are competing agents in melting of snow packs

Directions (Q.No. 96 to 100): *Read the following passage carefully and answer the question:*

Ecologists and Economists have joined forces to estimate the value of the services that the World's ecosystems provide. There are many direct goods such as foods and indirect services, such as the assimilation of waste that ecological system's provide on a renewable basis. Many ecosystems provide more than one service. For example, swamps are important in flood control, water supply and waste treatment and as habitat. In turn, most services are provided by more than one ecosystem; for instance, many systems are involved in nutrient cycling. Robert Cōnstanza and his colleagues estimated that the World's ecosystems provide atleast US $ 33 trillion worth of services annually. This staggering figure is more than the total gross national product, which is around US $ 19 trillion per year. The majority of the services are currently outside the market system and include atmospheric gas regulation, waste treatment and nutrient cycling, which at US $ 17 trillion, was by far the most expensive services performed, but even if we eliminate this, the total annual value would still be a whopping US $ 16 trillion. About 63 percent of the estimated value of natural ecosystems is contributed by marine system; with most of the value coming from coastal systems (US $ 10.6 trillion per year). About 37 percent of the estimated value comes from terrestrial systems, mainly forests (US $ 4.7 trillion) and wetlands (US $ 4.9 trillion). If ecosystem services were actually paid for, the global price system would be very different from what it is today. The price of commodities would skyrocket. However, because ecosystem services are largely outside the market, they are usually ignored or grossly undervalued.

96. Ecosystem services which have no market value are:

(*a*) Providing food
(*b*) Nutrient cycling
(*c*) Atmospheric gas regulation
(*d*) Water supply

Choose the ***most appropriate*** answer from the options given below:

A. (*a*) and (*b*) only B. (*b*) and (*c*) only
C. (*a*) and (*d*) only D. (*c*) and (*d*) only

97. Which one of the following ecosystems provide maximum estimated value of ecosystem services?
A. Forest ecosystem
B. Coastal ecosystem
C. Grassland ecosystem
D. Desert ecosystem

98. Swamp ecosystems provide the following ecosystem services.
(*a*) Assimilation of waste
(*b*) Provide habitat for organisms
(*c*) Terrestrial fruits
(*d*) Flood control
Choose the ***most appropriate*** answer from the options given below:
A. (*a*) and (*c*) only
B. (*b*), (*c*) and (*d*) only
C. (*a*), (*b*) and (*d*) only
D. (*a*), (*b*) and (*c*) only

99. If the ecosystem services are paid for, the price of commodities will:
A. Increase marginally
B. Become very high
C. Remain unaffected
D. Decrease marginally

100. What was the estimated value per year for the global ecosystem services outside the market system?
A. US $ 19 trillion B. US $ 33 trillion
C. US $ 16 trillion D. US $ 17 trillion

ANSWERS

1. **(C):** A Hunting and Gathering Society is a human living in a society in which most or all food is obtained by foraging (collecting wild plants and pursuing wild animals). Hunting and Gathering Societies stand in contrast to agricultural societies, which rely mainly on domesticated species. Hunting and Gathering Society was humanity's first and most successful adaptation, occupying at least 90 per cent of human history. Following the invention of agriculture, hunter - gatherers who did not change have been displaced or conquered by farming or pastoralist groups in most parts of the world.

2. **(A):** Wangari Maathai (1940-2011) was the founder of the Green Belt Movement and the 2004 Nobel Peace Prize Laureate. She authored four books:
- The Green Belt Movement;
- Unbowed: A Memoir;
- The Challenge for Africa; and
- Replenishing the Earth.

As well as having been featured in a number of books, she and the Green Belt Movement were the subject of a documentary film, Taking Root: The Vision of Wangari Maathai (Marlboro Productions, 2008).

Wangari Muta Maathai was born in Nyeri, a rural area of Kenya (Africa), in 1940. The first woman in East and Central Africa to earn a doctorate degree, Professor Maathai became chair of the Department of Veterinary Anatomy and an associate professor in 1976 and 1977 respectively. In both cases, she was the first woman to attain those positions in the region.

3. **(B):** Entropy can also refer to the amount of energy available to humans. As a piece of wood is burned, for example, its available energy – also called 'exergy' – decreases as the wood is transformed into high entropy matter – carbon dioxide and other substances useless from an energy point of view, its original exergy dissipated as useless heat. Available energy corresponds to the useful part of energy, which can be transformed into work. The so-called Entropy Law (the Second Law of Thermodynamics) uses this definition of entropy to express the everyday experience that transformations of energy and matter are unidirectional. It states that the entropy of an isolated thermodynamic system never decreases, but strictly increases in irreversible transformations and remains constant in

reversible transformations. This places significant constraints on natural as well as technical processes. For example, the temperature of a cup of hot coffee left in a cold room will always decrease, never increase, to eventually reach equilibrium with room temperature. In this process, the entropy of the room has increased.

4. **(D):** Mercury occurs in the environment in different chemical forms. The most important chemical forms of mercury are elemental mercury (Hg^0), inorganic mercury (Hg^{2+}), monomethyl mercury (MMHg, CH_3Hg^+), and dimethyl mercury (DMHg, CH_3HgCH_3).

5. **(A):** A particular feature of calcium bicarbonate is that it only exists in the dissolved form; when it precipitates, it does so in the calcium carbonate form, one that is only slightly soluble and it can only remain in water when it is balanced out by available CO_2:

$$Ca(HCO_3)_2 \rightleftharpoons CaCO_3 + CO_2 + H_2O$$

As the CO_2 content has an influence on **pH**, we can conclude that, for a given mineralisation (fixed **CaH** and M-alk.), there will be a **pH** value for the equilibrium between this water and the calcium carbonate: this value is termed the **Langelier pH** or **saturation pH** hence the designation "**pH_S**" (the corresponding CO_2 content then being known as the balancing CO_2, a concept that will be quantified further on). Therefore, we can "classify" water on the basis of its **pH** compared with this **pH_S**:

- if **pH > pH_S**, water will tend to deposit $CaCO_3$ and is then designated as *scale-forming*;
- if **pH < pH_S**, water will tend to dissolve $CaCO_3$ and is then termed *aggressive.*

Carbonate calcium potential precipitation (CCPP) is an interesting parameter for quantifying what may be scale-forming or may have dissolving properties (pipes made from concrete) knowing that the CCPP is a level of concentration expressed in $CaCO_3$ (positive if water can cause scaling or negative if water is aggressive).

6. **(*):** *No option is correct or the question is wrong.*

7. **(B):** Gibbs free energy (G) is a state function defined with regard to system quantities only and may be used to predict the spontaneity of a process. A negative value for ΔG indicates a spontaneous process; a positive ΔG indicates a nonspontaneous process; and a ΔG of zero indicates that the system is at equilibrium. A number of approaches to the computation of free energy changes are possible.

8. **(D):** 1 MWh = 3.8 GJ

5000 MWh = 18000 GJ

$$\text{Efficiency of plant} = \frac{\text{Output}}{\text{Input}} \times 100$$

$$= \frac{(18000 + 3000)}{60000} \times 100$$

$$= \frac{48000}{60000} \times 100$$

$$= 80\%.$$

9. **(C):** Man-made compounds such as chlorofluorocarbons (CFCs), hydro fluorocarbons (HCFCs) and halons destroy ozone in the upper atmosphere (stratosphere), though they all vary in their Ozone Depletion Potential;

Compound	Ozone Depletion Potential
CFC–11	1.0
Halons	Ranges up to 10
HCFCs	0.01 to 1.0
Methyl Bromide	0.7

10. **(B):** ***Detrital*** sedimentary rocks form from detritus, the rock and mineral fragments that are transported by gravity, water, ice, or wind. Detrital sediments are classified by grain size.

Detritus is classified by its grain size. Grains larger than 2 millimeters are called ***gravel***. Grains between 1/16 mm and 2 mm are called ***sand***. Grains smaller than 1/16 mm are in the ***silt*** and ***clay*** size ranges, often referred to as mud.

Chalk is a non-clastic carbonate sedimentary rock that is form of limestone composed of the mineral calcite. It is soft, fine-grained and easily pulverized. Colour is white-to-grayish variety of limestone rock. It is composed of the shells of such minute marine organisms as foraminifera, coccoliths, and rhabdoliths. The purest varieties contain up to 99 per cent calcium carbonate in the form of the mineral calcite.

11. **(C):** U.S. Department of Agriculture (USDA) Classification of Soil Particle Size:

Type	Diameter (mm)
Gravel	> 2.0
Sand	0.05–2
Very Coarse Sand	1–2
Coarse Sand	0.5–1
Medium Sand	0.25–0.5
Fine Sand	0.10–0.25
Very Fine Sand	0.05–0.10
Silt	0.002–0.05
Clay	< 0:002

12. **(D):**

Rock Type	Hydraulic Conductivity (m/day)
Gravel	100–1000
Coarse Sand	20–100
Sand Gravel	5–100
Fine Sand	1–5
Clay	0.001–0.01
Fractured or weathered rock	0–300
Sandstone	0.001–1
Shale	Negligible
Limestone	Negligible

13. **(A):** Given Values are,

Latitude = 30° (sin 30° = 0.5)

Pressure = 1 mb (1 mb × 100 = 100 Pa)

Density of Air = 1.25 kg/m^3

Distance = 100 km

(100 km × 1000 = 100000 m)

$$V_g = \frac{P}{2\Omega \times \delta \times \sin\phi \times d}$$

Where,

V_g = Geostrophic wind Velocity

P = Pressure (in Pascal)

Ω = Angular Velocity of Earth (7.3×10^{-5})

δ = Density of Air

$\sin\phi$ = Latitude

D = Distance (in meters)

Now putting the given values in the equation,

$$V_g = \frac{100}{2 \times 7.3 \times 10^{-5} \times 1.25 \times 0.5 \times 100000}$$

V_g = ~11 m/s

14. **(A, B):** Alpha diversity describes the species diversity *within* a community at a small scale or local scale, generally the size of one ecosystem. Beta diversity describes the species diversity between two communities or ecosystems. Gamma diversity is studied at a very large scale—a biome—where species diversity is compared between many ecosystems. It could range over areas like the entire slope of a mountain, or the entire littoral zone of a sea shore. The internal relationship between α, β and γ diversity can be presented as $\alpha \times \beta = \gamma$.

15. **(C):** Factors affecting the formation of top soil.

When a soil deposits somewhere, it happens as a result of five major factors:

- Climate
- Time
- Topography
- Material
- Activities or organism

All of these factors collectively decide how long will it take for the soil to deposit at a certain location. For example, an area that involves too much human activity will keep eroding. Hence, it will take longer to get deposited.

Time taken for the formation of top 1 inch of soil

- As a result of all of the factors discussed above, the duration for the deposition of top layer of soil cannot be stated clearly.
- However, scientists found out that it takes **at least 100 years** to deposit top 1 inch of soil.

16. **(C):** The profundal zone is located below the thermocline where the sunlight does not penetrate. Again, the size of this zone depends on the age and water clarity of the pond or lake. The profundal zone typically has lower fish populations because of the lack of oxygen during many parts of the year.

17. **(D):** Slash and burn farming is a form of shifting agriculture where the natural vegetation is cut down and burned as a method of clearing the land for cultivation, and then, when the plot becomes infertile, the farmer moves to a new fresh plat and does the same again. This process is repeated over and over.

18. **(B):** A keystone species helps define an entire ecosystem. Without its keystone species, the ecosystem would be dramatically different or cease to exist altogether. In any arrangement or community, the "keystone" is considered one of the most vital parts. In a marine ecosystem, or any type of ecosystem, a keystone species is an organism that helps hold the system together. Without its keystone species, ecosystems would look very different.

19. **(B):** This region is the Kedarnath Wildlife Sanctuary which is spread across Chamoli and Rudraprayag districts of Uttarakhand. It is also known as Kedarnath Musk Deer Sanctuary because of the Himalayan Musk deer who form the flagship species of this reserve.

20. **(B):** According to standards of Central Pollution Control Board, permissible value of BOD is 30 mg/l and COD is 250 mg/l.

21. **(B)**

22. **(D):** Gel filtration (GF) chromatography separates proteins solely on the basis of molecular size. Separation is achieved using a porous matrix to which the molecules, for steric reasons, have different degrees of access—*i.e.*, smaller molecules have greater access and larger molecules are excluded from the matrix. Hence, proteins are eluted from the GF column in decreasing order of size. This unit describes the experimental theory behind gel filtration and contains many useful tables listing the properties and characteristics of currently available matrices.

23. **(A):** The Most Probable Number (MPN) technique is used to detect the number of microorganisms from foods, especially when the number of microorganisms is less than 10 g or mL of sample. Foods of different quantities (*e.g.*, 100, 10 or 1 g or mL) can be used in the MPN technique.

24. **(C):** The geothermal gradient is defined as the increase in temperature with depth in the Earth. In normal continental crust a typical geothermal gradient within the first 3 to 5 kilometers (2 or 3 miles) of Earth's surface is about 25°C/km. This gradient, however, is not sustained but decreases to no more than about 16°C/km at a depth of 40 km. Mountain-building processes have the effect of increasing the geothermal gradient, which results in the metamorphism of crustal rocks.

25. **(B):** The Betz limit is the theoretical maximum efficiency for a wind turbine, conjectured by German physicist Albert Betz in 1919. Betz concluded that this value is 59.3%, meaning that at most only 59.3% of the kinetic energy from wind can be used to spin the turbine and generate electricity.

26. (A): Carbon dioxide (CO_2) forms during coal combustion when one atom of carbon (C) unites with two atoms of oxygen (O) from the air. Because the atomic weight of carbon is 12 and that of oxygen is 16, the atomic weight of carbon dioxide is 44. Based on that ratio, and assuming complete combustion, 1 pound of carbon combines with 2.667 pounds of oxygen to produce 3.667 pounds of carbon dioxide.

Thus, production of Carbon dioxide (CO_2) on combustion of 1 kg of coal = 0.81 × 3.667 = ~3 kg

27. (D)

28. (C): Chironomus is a genus of nonbiting midges in the subfamily Chironominae of the bloodworm family, Chironomidae, containing several cryptic species that can only be distinguished by experts based on the characteristics of their giant chromosomes. The larvae of several species inhabit the profundal zone where they can reach relatively high densities. They use a combination of hemoglobin-like proteins and undulatory movements in their burrows to obtain oxygen in poorly oxygenated habitats.

29. (D): When water moves through the **soil**, it moves small colloidal-sized particles with it. These particles of clay, iron, **humus**, and calcium carbonate will be deposited in zones below the surface or in the **subsoil**. The zones are called illuvial zones and the process is referred to as illuviation. Illuvial zones are most often referred to as B horizons, and the subscript with the B designates the kind of material translocated (*i.e.*, B_t = clay accumulation).

30. (D): The haemoglobin is the respiratory pigment present in the red blood cells. It binds with the oxygen and transports it to the tissues from the lungs. The carbon monoxide is a harmful gas that shows higher affinity with the iron-containing heme group of the haemoglobin to form the carboxy-haemoglobin. Due to this, there is no haemoglobin left to combine with the oxygen. This causes oxygen deficiency in the tissues, called carbon monoxide poisoning.

31. (C): The environment ministry has decided that it will no longer regulate the ash content of coal used by thermal power plants. In May, 2020, the ministry issued a notification that overturned its January 2014 regulation that made it mandatory for all coal-based power plants located 500 kilometers or more from the pit-head or coal mine to use raw or blended or beneficiated coal with no more than 34 per cent ash content.

32. (B): Pyrolysis is the thermochemical decomposition of organic material at high temperature and in the absence of oxygen or in an atmosphere of inert gases. Pyrolysis process consists of both simultaneous and successive reactions when carbon-rich organic material is heated in a non-reactive atmosphere. Simply speaking, pyrolysis is the thermal degradation of organic materials in the absence of oxygen. Thermal decomposition of organic components in the waste stream starts at 350°C – 550°C and goes up to 700°C – 800°C in the absence of air/oxygen.

33. (B): Biogas is usually made up of around 50-70% methane (CH_4) and 25-45% carbon dioxide (CO_2), with other gases such as hydrogen (H_2), hydrogen sulphide (H_2S), water vapour (H_2O), nitrogen (N_2), oxygen (O_2), ammonia (NH_3) making up the rest. The exact percentages depend on a range of factors, such as retention time and operating temperature, however a rough estimate is:

- Methane (50-85%)
- Carbon dioxide (5-50%)
- Water vapour (0-10%)
- Hydrogen (0-1%)
- Hydrogen sulphide (0-3%)
- Nitrogen (0-5%)
- Oxygen (0-2%)

34. (B): The Convention on International Trade in Endangered Species of Wild Fauna and

Flora (CITES) is an international agreement to which States and regional economic integration organizations adhere voluntarily. CITES entered into force in July 1975. Currently there are 183 Parties (include countries or regional economic integration organizations).

India is one of the recognized mega-diverse countries of the world, harbouring nearly 7-8% of the recorded species of the world, and representing 4 of the 34 globally identified biodiversity hotspots (Himalaya, Indo-Burma, Western Ghats and Sri Lanka, Sundaland). India is also a vast repository of traditional knowledge associated with biological resources. So far, over 91,200 species of animals and 45,500 species of plants have been documented in the ten biogeographic regions of the country. Inventories of floral and faunal diversities are being progressively updated with several new discoveries through the conduct of continuous surveys and exploration.

India, being a CITES Party, actively prohibits the international trade of endangered wild species and several measures are in place to control threats from invasive alien species (*e.g.* certificates for exports, permits for imports, etc.).

35. (B): Discrete data is a numerical type of data that includes whole, concrete numbers with specific and fixed data values determined by counting.

Continuous data includes complex numbers and varying data values that are measured over a specific time interval.

Nominal data is classified without a natural order or rank, whereas ordinal data has a predetermined or natural order.

36. (C): Arrange the data in descending/ascending order:

4, 5, 5, 6, 6, 6, 7, 7, 8, 9

Median = is the simple average of the $n/2^{th}$ and the $(n/2 + 1)^{th}$ terms.

Here $n = 10$, $n/2^{th} = 5^{th}$ term, $(n/2 + 1)^{th} = 6^{th}$ term

Average of 5th term and 6th term = Average (6, 6) = 12/2 = 6.

37. (A): The standard Normal curve is the normal curve with mean $\mu = 0$ and standard deviation $\sigma = 1$. For the standard normal, probabilities are computed either by means of a computer/calculator of via a table. The table consists of two columns. One (on the left) gives a value for the variable z, and one (on the right) gives a value A(z), which can be interpreted in either of two ways:

The table consists of two columns. One (on the left) gives a value for the variable z, and one (on the right) gives a value A(z), which can be interpreted in either of two ways:

z	A(z)
1	0.8413

A(z) = the area under the standard normal curve ($\mu = 0$ and $\sigma = 1$) to the left of this value of z, shown as the shaded region in the diagram below.

A(z) = the probability that the value of the random variable Z observed for an individual chosen at random from the population is less than or equal to z.

A(z) = P(Z ≤ z). The shaded area is A(1) = 0.8413, correct to 4 decimal places.

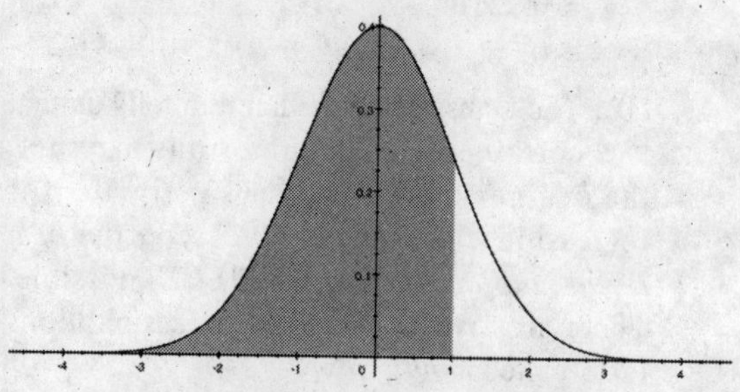

The section of the table shown above tells us that the area under the standard normal curve to the left of the value $z = 1$ is 0.8413. It also tells us that if Z is normally distributed with mean $\mu = 0$ and standard deviation $\sigma = 1$, then P (Z ≤ 1) = .8413.

38. (A): By solving the doubling time model for the growth rate, we can solve this problem by using below formula, where D = Doubling Time

$$D \approx \frac{70}{R}$$

$$R \cdot D \approx \frac{70}{R} \cdot R$$

$$RD \approx 70$$

$$\frac{RD}{R} \approx \frac{70}{D}$$

$$\text{Annual growth rate } R \approx \frac{70}{D}$$

$$R \approx \frac{70}{20}$$

Thus, the annual growth rate of the city is approximately 3.5%.

39. (D): The degrees of freedom is equal to the sum of the individual degrees of freedom for each sample. Since each sample has degrees of freedom equal to one less than their sample sizes, and there are *k* samples, the total degrees of freedom are *k* less than the total sample size: $df = N - k$.

40. (D): Coefficient of Determination (R^2)

(R^2) = Explained Variation/Total Variation
= 0.75/(0.75 + 0.25)
= 0.75/1
= 0.75.

41. (D): The Gauss Markov theorem tells us that if a certain set of assumptions are met, the ordinary least squares estimate for regression coefficients gives you the *best linear unbiased estimate (BLUE)* possible. There are five Gauss Markov assumptions (also called *conditions*):

1. **Linearity:** The parameters we are estimating using the OLS method must be themselves linear.
2. **Random:** Our data must have been randomly sampled from the population.
3. **Non-Collinearity:** The regressors being calculated aren't perfectly correlated with each other.
4. **Exogencity:** The regressors aren't correlated with the error term.
5. **Homoscedasticity:** No matter what the values of our regressors might be, the error of the variance is constant.

We can summarize the Gauss-Markov Assumptions succinctly in algebra, by saying that a linear regression model represented by

$$y_i = x_i' \beta + \varepsilon_i$$

and generated by the ordinary least squares estimate is the best linear unbiased estimate (BLUE) possible if

- $E\{\varepsilon_i\} = 0, i = 1, \ldots, N$
- $\{\varepsilon_1 \ldots \varepsilon_n\}$ and $\{x_1, \ldots, x_N\}$ are independent
- $\text{cov}\{\varepsilon_i, \varepsilon_j\} = 0, i, j = 1, \ldots, N\ I \neq j.$
- $V\{\varepsilon_1 = \sigma^2, i = 1, \ldots N$

Where:

- "ε" is the Greek letter epsilon, which measures error.
- Σ = Summation notation ("add up").

42. (C): The Ganges River originates in the Himalaya Mountains at Gomukh, the terminus of the Gongotri Glacier. When the ice of this glacier melts, it forms the clear waters of the Bhagirathi River. As the Bhagirathi River flows down the Himalayas, it joins the Alaknanda River, officially forming the Ganges River.

43. (C): Water has strong hydrogen bonds between molecules. These bonds require a lot of energy before they will break. This leads to water having a higher boiling point than if there were only weaker dipole-dipole forces. Water also has a high specific heat.

44. (B)

45. (D)

46. (A): Ginkgo biloba is the world's oldest living plant, and is known as a 'living fossil' because it has no close living relatives. It is found in fossils dating back 270 million years.

47. (B): Perihelion currently occurs around 3 January each year. This is in the northern hemisphere Winter. The seasons are mainly due to the obliquity of the Earth's axis of rotation, or axial tilt. At perihelion the Earth is about 147,000,000 km from the Sun.

Earth's tilted axis causes the seasons. Throughout the year, different parts of Earth receive the Sun's most direct rays. So, when the North Pole tilts toward the Sun, it's summer in the Northern Hemisphere. And when the South Pole tilts toward the Sun, it's winter in the Northern Hemisphere.

48. (C): Ferromagnesian Minerals: Silicate minerals in which cations of iron and magnesium form essential chemical components. The term is used to cover such minerals as the olivines, pyroxenes, amphiboles, and the micas biotite and phlogopite.

Single chain Pyroxene is another family of dark ferromagnesian minerals, typically black or dark green in colour. Members of the pyroxene family have a complex chemical composition that includes iron, magnesium, aluminum, and other elements bonded to polymerized silica tetrahedra.

49. (C): Soil colloids can be defined as the particle of soil with a diameter less than 1 μm. Soil is composed of a mixture of solids, liquids, and gases phases. The solid fragment of soils comprises an inorganic and organic material. There are four major types of colloids present in soil

- Layer silicate clays
- Iron and aluminum oxide clays (sesquioxide clays)
- Allophane and associated amorphous clays
- Humus.

50. (A): The first widely-used method, the **Richter scale,** was developed by Charles F. Richter in 1934. It used a formula based on the amplitude of the largest wave recorded on a specific type of seismometer and the distance between the earthquake and the seismometer.

The Richter scale is a **base-10 logarithmic** scale, meaning that each order of magnitude is 10 times more intensive than the last one. In other words, a two is 10 times more intense than a one and a three is 100 times greater. In the case of the Richter scale, the increase is in wave amplitude. That is, the wave amplitude in a level 6 earthquake is 10 times greater than in a level 5 earthquake, and the amplitude increases 100 times between a level 7 earthquake and a level 9 earthquake. The amount of energy released increases 31.7 times between whole number values.

51. (A): The **regression coefficient** is a statistical measure of the average functional relationship between two or more variables. In regression analysis, one variable is considered as dependent and the other(s) as an independent. Thus, it measures the degree of dependence of one variable on the other(s). The **geometric mean** between the two regression coefficients is equal to the **coefficient of correlation.**

Properties of regression line and correlation coefficient:

- If the correlation coefficient $r_{xy} = 0$, then the two lines of regression are perpendicular to each other.
- If the correlation coefficient $r_{xy} = +1$, then the two lines of regression are parallel to each other.

52. (D)

53. (B): Noise exposure can cause two kinds of health effects. These effects are non-auditory effects and auditory effects. Non-auditory effects include stress, related physiological and behavioural effects, and safety concerns. Auditory effects include hearing impairment resulting from excessive noise exposure. Hearing loss leading to the inability to understand speech in everyday situations can have a severe social effect. It can also affect cognitive performance and decrease attention to tasks.

54. (A): Isokinetic sampling techniques were developed to prevent skewed particulate concentration measurements due to inertial effects of particles as they enter a sampling nozzle. Basically, the idea is to sample at the same velocity as the gas stream so that the streamlines in the vicinity of the nozzle are straight. Attempts to avoid distorting the size distribution are made through isokinetic sampling, in which

- the sampler inlet velocity is matched with the free-stream air velocity, and
- the sampling probe is aligned parallel to air streamlines.

55. **(C):** Walkley-Black Method quantifies the amount of oxidizable organic matter in which OM is oxidized with a known amount of chromate in the presence of sulphuric acid. The remaining chromate is determined spectrophotometrically at 600 nm wavelength. The calculation of organic carbon is based on organic matter containing 58% carbon.

Equipment required:

- 500-mL Erlenmeyer flasks.
- 10-mL pipette.
- 10- and 20-mL dispensers.
- 50-mL burette.
- Analytical balance.
- Magnetic stirrer.
- Incandescent lamp.

Reagents:

- H_3PO_4, 85%.
- H_2SO_4, concentrated (96%).
- NaF, solid.
- Standard 0.167 M $K_2Cr_2O_7$: Dissolve 49.04 g of dried (105°C) $K_2Cr_2O_7$ in water and dilute to 1 L.
- 0.5 M Fe^{2+} solution: Dissolve 196.1 g of $Fe(NH_4)_2(SO_4)\cdot 6H_2O$ in 800 mL of water containing 20 mL of concentrated H_2SO_4 and dilute to 1 L. The Fe^{2+} in this solution oxidizes slowly on exposure to air so it must be standardized against the dichromate daily.
- Ferroin indicator: Slowly dissolve 3.71 g of o-phenanthroline and 1.74 g of $FeSO_4\cdot 7H_2O$ in 250 mL of water.

56. **(B):** In the respiratory tract, ***Inertial Impaction*** is the primary mechanism of deposition for particles >5 μm in diameter and is an important deposition mechanism for particles as small as 2 μm, depending on flow rate.

In the respiratory tract, deposition by ***Gravitational Sedimentation*** is most effective for particles in the size range of ~1–8 μm, with larger particles depositing mainly by inertial impaction and smaller particles depositing by Brownian diffusion.

The third main mechanism of deposition in the lung is that of ***Brownian Diffusion*** that results from the random motions of the particles caused by their collisions with gas molecules.

57. **(C):** Vermicomposting technology using earthworms as versatile natural bioreactors for effective recycling of organic wastes to the soil is an environmentally acceptable means of converting wastes into nutritious composts for crop production. The chief objective is to compost organic wastes not for the disposal of solid organic wastes but also to produce superior quality manure to feed our "nutrient/organic matter hungry" soils. Large volume of organic matter generated from agricultural activities, dairy farms and animal shelters usually dumped in corners emanating foul smell, can be utilized by properly composting it into a value-added end product. Briefly, when the earthworm consumes organic wastes, the substrate passes through earthworm's gut and gets digested in the intestine of earthworm with the aid of beneficial microbes.

58. **(B):** Waste Incineration is an alternative method of waste disposal to landfill. Waste incinerators use the process of combustion to convert the waste materials into carbon dioxide and water. Incineration residues usually consist of small quantities of HCl, S, and other volatile compounds and ash.

However, it is obvious that not all household waste materials are combustible. Reduction of waste volume by 75–95% is achieved with incineration. Therefore, it should be considered as a means of reducing the amount of waste to be disposed of by landfill rather than a method of ultimate disposal on its own. Waste Incinerators dispose of the ash by sending it to landfills, which is both costly and takes up physical space.

59. (A): Eurythermal Organisms are those which can tolerate a wide range of temperatures. Eg: Cow, Human, Monkey, Goats, Sheep.

Stenothermal Organisms are those which can tolerate a narrow range of temperatures. These organisms can be classified into two main groups.

Thermophilic: Species which are only able to survive at high temperatures. Eg: Few reptiles, Coral reefs, Fishes.

Cryophilic: Stenotherms which can only survive in regions with low temperatures. Eg: Arctic crustaceans, Salmons, Seals.

Cyclomorphosis: The occurrence of seasonal changes in the phenotype of an organism through successive generations. It occurs in small aquatic invertebrates that reproduce by parthenogenesis and give rise to several generations annually, such as rotifers and cladoceran crustaceans. Cyclomorphic species of Daphnia, for example, undergo changes in the shape of the head during the year; it is rounded from about midsummer to spring, and thereafter becomes helmet-shaped, reverting to the rounded shape at midsummer. Also, summer generations tend to be smaller and more transparent than at other times.

Circalunar Rhythm: A biorhythm that corresponds with the lunar cycle (approximately 29.5 days). The reproductive cycles of many organisms, especially marine organisms, are linked to changing levels of moonlight and the tidal cycle, both of which are governed by the phases of the moon.

60. (B) **61. (B)** **62. (B)**

63. (D) **64. (B)**

65. (*): *No option is correct or the question is wrong.*

66. (D): The toxic effect of cadmium on bone became evident at the outbreak of Itai-itai disease in Japan, where severe renal and skeletal damage in women was associated with consumption of heavily cadmium-polluted rice.

Chloracne is a rare skin eruption of blackheads, cysts and nodules, which has been linked directly to dioxin exposure. Mild forms may resemble teenage acne. Physicians sometimes have difficulty distinguishing chloracne from more common skin disorders.

Carbofuran, a carbamate pesticide, posed potential risks for the neurotransmitter systems.

Benzo[a]pyrene is a probable cancer-causing agent in humans. There is some evidence that it causes skin, lung, and bladder cancer in humans and in animals. If benzo(a)pyrene is on your skin when you are being exposed to sunlight or ultraviolet light, the risk of skin cancer is greater.

67. (C)

68. (D):

Hydropower projects	***Started in***	***River***
Sardar Sarovar Project	1961	Narmada River
Tehri Dam Project	1949	Bhagirathi River
Pong Dam	Construction on the dam began in 1961 and was completed in 1974	Beas River
Hirakund Dam	1946	Mahanadi River

69. (D):

Indian satellites	*Launch Year*	*Spatial Resolution*
Cartosat – 2 PAN	2007	1 meter
Oceansat – 2 OCM	2009	360 meters
Resourcesat – 2 AWIFS	2016	56 meters
IRS – ID LISS – 3	2010	24 meters

70. (D):

Natural Surfaces	*Albedo Effect*
Ocean	approximately 0.06
Fresh snow	0.96 to 0.98
Grass	0.25
Desert Sand	0.40

71. (C):

Heavy Metals Name	*Heavy Metals Symbol*	*Abundance in the Earth's Crust (ppm)*
Iron	Fe	56,300
Magnesium	Mg	23,300
Aluminium	Al	82,300
Copper	Cu	60

72. (D):

	Grade of Metamorphism
Gneiss	High Grade
Slate	Low Grade
Schist	Medium Grade
Shale	Very Low Grade

73. (C):

	Residence Time
Formaldehyde	0.1 and 1.2 days
Carbon monoxide	0.3 and 5.0 years
Peroxyacetyl nitrate	Upto 7 days
Hydroxyl radical	10^{-9} seconds

74. (B):

Green House Gases	*Life Time (years)*
CH_4 (Methane)	12 to 15 years
N_2O (Nitrous Oxide)	114 years
CFC-12	113 years
O_3 (Tropospheric)	23 days

75. (D):

Fuels	*Net Heating Value (MJ/kg)*
Charcoal	28 MJ/kg
Bituminous coal	22000 MJ/kg
Regular gasoline	49000000 MJ/kg
Natural gas	50000000 MJ/kg
Oak wood	18.5 to 19 MJ/kg

76. (D) **77. (D)**

78. (C):

Metals	*Permissible Concentration (mg/kg)*
Chromium	0.24 to 6.3 mg/kg
Lead	10 mg/kg
Cadmium	0.1 mg/kg
Copper	50 mg/kg

79. (C): The mean deviation is defined as a statistical measure that is used to calculate the average deviation from the mean value of the given data set. The mean deviation of the data values can be easily calculated using the below procedure.

- **Step 1:** Find the mean value for the given data values
- **Step 2:** Now, subtract the mean value from each of the data values given (Note: Ignore the minus symbol)
- **Step 3:** Now, find the mean of those values obtained in step 2.

Mean Deviation is the mean of all the absolute deviations of a set of data, whereas Quartile deviation is the difference between "first and third quartiles" in any distribution. Thus, Mean deviation is a better measure of dispersion than the quartile deviation.

80. (A): If one tail is longer than another, the distribution is skewed. These distributions are sometimes called asymmetric or asymmetrical distributions as they don't show any kind of symmetry. Symmetry means that one half of the distribution is a mirror image of the other half. For example, the normal distribution is a symmetric distribution with no skew. The tails are exactly the same.

A left-skewed distribution has a long-left tail. Left-skewed distributions are also called *negatively-skewed* distributions. That's because there is a long tail in the negative direction on the number line. The mean is also to the left of the peak. Log-normal distributions are positively skewed with long right tails due to low mean values and high variances in the random variables.

81. (C): Hybrid cars are powered by two engines: one petrol, one electric. Both work with each other to spin the wheels. This leads to lesser petrol being burned and therefore better fuel efficiency. When compared to conventional vehicles, hybrids offer better power and fuel efficiency as they combine the benefits of high fuel efficiency and low emissions. When hybrid vehicles are cruising or while braking, the result is excess power which is used to charge the batteries. This, in turn, aids higher fuel efficiency or range.

82. (B): The energy content of ethanol is about 33% less than pure gasoline. Ethanol contains less energy per gallon than gasoline, to varying degrees, depending on the volume percentage of ethanol in the blend.

83. (D): Article 48A lays down the directive principle for protection and improvement of environment and safeguarding of forests and wildlife. It reads as:

"The State shall endeavour to protect and improve the environment and to safeguard the forests and wildlife of the country."

This Article was added by the 42nd Amendment, 1976 and places an obligation on the State to protect the environment and wildlife. While not judicially enforceable, Article 48A may become enforceable under the ambit of the right to life under Article 21.

84. (B)

85. (D)

86. (C): To increase consumer awareness, the Government of India launched the eco-labelling scheme known as 'Ecomark' in 1991 for easy identification of environment-friendly products.The criteria follow a cradle-to-grave approach, i.e., from raw material extraction, to manufacturing, and to disposal. The Ecomark label is awarded to consumer goods that meet the specified environmental criteria and the quality requirements of Indian Standards. An earthern pot has been chosen as the logo for the Ecomark scheme in India.

87. (C): The arithmetic mean-geometric mean (AM-GM) inequality states that the arithmetic mean of non-negative real numbers is greater than or equal to the geometric mean of the same list. Further, equality holds if and only if every number in the list is the same.

The regression coefficients are independent of the change of the origin. But they are not independent of the change of the scale. It means there will be no effect on the regression coefficients if any constant is subtracted from the value of x and y.

88. (C): Project Elephant was launched in 1992 by the Government of India Ministry of Environment and Forests to provide financial and technical support to wildlife management efforts by states for their free-ranging populations of wild Asian Elephants. The project aims to ensure the long-term survival to the populations of elephants in their natural habitats by protecting the elephants, their habitats and migration corridors. Other goals of Project Elephant are supporting the research of the ecology and management of elephants, creating awareness of conservation among local people, providing improved veterinary care for captive elephants.

89. (B):

Soil Classes	*Stability of Wet Clods*
Loam	Dry—Clods moderately difficult to break
Clay	Dry—Clods cannot be broken with fingers without extreme pressure
Sandy Loam	Dry—Clods easily broken
Silt Loam	Dry—Clods difficult to break
Clay Loam	Dry—Clods very difficult to break with fingers

90. (C): The Gaussian plume model is the most common air pollution model. It is based on a simple formula that describes the three-dimensional concentration field generated by a point source under stationary meteorological and emission conditions. Gaussian plume model is based on the assumption:

- plume spread results primarily by molecular diffusion
- horizontal and vertical pollutant concentrations in the plume are normally distributed (double Gaussian distribution).

91. (D) **92. (B)** **93. (A)**
94. (B) **95. (D)** **96. (B)**
97. (B) **98. (C)** **99. (B)**
100. (D)

Previous Years' Paper (Solved)

National Testing Agency (NTA)

UGC-NET Junior Research Fellowship & Assistant Professor Eligibility Exam

ENVIRONMENTAL SCIENCE, June–2020

(Online Exam held on 29-09-2020)

PAPER-II

Note: *This paper contains* **hundred** (**100**) *objective type questions of* **two** (**2**) *marks each.* ***All*** *questions are* ***compulsory***.

1. Good absorbers are good emitters. This statement refers to which of the following laws?
A. Stefan's Law
B. Wien's Displacement Law
C. Planck's Law
D. Kirchhoff's Law

2. A sample of air has a relative humidity of 60%. Given that the Saturated Vapour Pressure of water is 2260 Pa, calculate the vapour pressure of the air at 20°C.
A. ~ 1460 Pa B. ~ 452 Pa
C. ~ 3767 Pa D. ~ 1356 Pa

3. Which among the following is short-lived species in the atmosphere?
A. CH_4 B. CO
C. N_2O D. OH radical

4. The chemical composition of CFC-113 is:
A. $CF_2ClCFCl_2$ B. $CFHClCFCl_2$
C. $CF_3CF_2Cl_2$ D. $CF_2HCF_2Cl_2$

5. Soil humic acids are:
A. Insoluble in alkali
B. Insoluble in acid
C. Soluble in acid
D. Insoluble in both acid and alkali

6. Volatile Organic Compounds (VOCs) are of great concern because:
A. Once such compounds are in the vapour state, they are difficult to control in the environment.
B. Most of them are ozone depleting substances
C. They contribute to a general increase in reactive hydrocarbons in the atmosphere
D. They are less soluble in water

7. Hyperthermophilic microorganisms prefer temperatures in excess of:
A. 45°C B. 80°C
C. 65°C D. 70°C

8. The most toxic form of mercury in water is:
A. Hg^{2+} B. $H_3C - Hg^+$
C. Hg^0 D. Hg^+

9. One Dobson unit, represents the ozone layer of thickness:
A. One-hundredth of a centimeter
B. One-tenth of a centimetre
C. One-hundredth of a millimeter
D. One-thousandth of a millimeter

10. The transitional zone (ecotone) between freshwater and terrestrial ecosystems is known as:
A. Riparian Zone B. Hyporheic zone
C. Benthic zone D. Epilimnetic zone

11. Which one of the following silicate clay minerals exhibits highest interlayer expansion?
A. Montmorillonite B. Vermiculite
C. Chlorite D. Kaolinite

12. Beside steam, next gas in order of abundance emitted from a volcanic eruption is:
A. Sulphur dioxide B. Nitrogen dioxide
C. Carbon dioxide D. Carbon monoxide

13. Heteromorphic rocks have:
A. Same mineral composition arising from similar magmas under different conditions of crystallization.
B. Different mineral composition arising from similar magmas under different conditions of crystallization.
C. Different mineral composition arising from different magmas under difierent conditions of crystallization.
D. Same mineral composition arising from different magmas under different conditions of crystallization.

14. A rock composed entirely of crystals is said to be:
A. Hypocrystalline B. Microcrystalline
C. Holocrystalline D. Holohyaline

15. A Si-solar cell has the minority carrier saturation current = 60 nAm^{-2} and solar radiation-induced current = 600 Am^{-2}. If the ambient temperature is 27°C, what is the open-circuit voltage of the solar cell?
A. ~ 0.6 V B. ~ 0.45 V
C. ~ 0.5 V D. ~ 1.5 V

16. Which one among the following Solar Collectors has the highest Concentration Ratio or CR value (a measure of the efficiency of the Solar Collectors)?
A. Compound Parabolic Collector with a plane receiver
B. Cylindrical Parabolic Collector
C. Fresnel Lens Collector
D. Paraboloid dish collector

17. The fast neutrons produced in the process of nuclear fission of ^{235}U, have an average energy of about:
A. 100 keV B. 1.0 Mev
C. 2.0 Mev D. 2.6 Mev

18. A small hydropower station based on the conversion of the kinetic energy of a river water generates power. If the flow of water is 10 m^3s^{-1} and the speed of water is 3 ms^{-1}, what is the maximum power the station can generate? (Assume efficiency of the power station to be 0.6)
A. 18 kW B. 27 kW
C. 36 kW D. 45 kW

19. The maximum cross-section for the fusion reaction $^2_1H + ^3_1H$ is reached at energies of nuclei at:
A. ~ 10 keV B. ~ 100 keV
C. ~ 1.0 keV D. ~ 17.6 keV

20. According to National Ambient Air Quality Standards (NAAQS), the annual lim its for PM_{10} and $PM_{2.5}$ in ecologically sensiiive areas (in $\mu g/m^3$) are:
A. 100 and 60, respectively
B. 60 and 40, respectively
C. 40 and 20, respectively
D. 40 and 15, respectively

21. At 1 atm pressure and 25°C temperature, NO_2 concentration of 80 ppb is equivalent to:
A. 40 $\mu g/m^3$ B. 160 $\mu g/m^3$
C. 240 $\mu g/m^3$ D. 150.4 $\mu g/m^3$

22. What is the sound pressure level (in dB) associated with a root mean square pressure of 100 Pa?
A. 148 dB B. 134 dB
C. 120 dB D. 110 dB

23. In the 'A' weighting network used in noise measurements, sounds of which of the following frequencies would require the least correction?
A. 31.5 Hz B. 125 Hz
C. 1000 Hz D. 12500 Hz

24. A N-fixing actinomycete associated with higher plants is:
A. Azospirillum B. Clostridium
C. Frankia D. Anabaena

25. Basel convention (1989) was designed to:
A. Reduce global waste generation
B. Control hazardous waste generation
C. Determine safe handling measures for hazardous waste
D. Prevent trans-boundary movement of hazardous waste between nations

26. Which of the following is NOT an epigeic earthworm species?
A. *Eisenia fetida*

B. *Eisenia andrei*
C. *Metaphire posthuma*
D. *Eudrilus eugeniae*

27. Which among the following is the major product of slow pyrolysis of biomass?
A. Biochar B. Biogas
C. Carbon monoxide D. Carbon dioxide

28. Which of the following are the dominant products of anaerobic digestion of municipal solid waste?
A. CO_2 and H_2 B. CH_4 and CO_2
C. CH_4, CO_2, and H_2 D. O_2 and H_2S

29. Ecological engineering is based on which one of the four classes of ecotechnology?
A. Use of ecosystems to reduce a pollution problem
B. Imitation of ecosystems to reduce pollution leading to constructed ecosystems
C. Recovery of ecosystems after significant disturbances
D. Use of ecosystems for benefit of humanity without destroying ecological balance

30. What is the maximum period valid for granting Environmental Clearance (EC) for mining projecs?
A. 30 Years B. 10 Years
C. 5 Years D. 20 Years

31. The Environmental Relief fund was created under:
A. Environmental Protection Act
B. Forest Conservation Act
C. Public Liability Insurance Act
D. Wildlife Protection Act

32. Which one of the categories of development projects does NOT require an Environmental Impact Assessment (EIA) report?
A. Category 'A' projects
B. Category 'B_2' projects
C. Category 'B_1' projects
D. Category 'B_1' and 'B_2' projects

33. According to Solid Waste Management Rules 2016, a landfill site should be at a distance of how many meters away from a pond?
A. 200 meters B. 150 meters
C. 100 meters D. 50 meters

34. In an objective type examination, hundred questions are given. One mark is given for each correct answer while 0.2 marks are deducted for each incorrect answer. The number of marks scored by students appearing in the examination is an example of:
A. Nominal variable
B. Ordinal variable
C. Discrete variable
D. Continuous variable

35. If the mean of two groups of 'm' and 'n' observations are 40 and 60 respectively, and the combined mean of two groups is 48, the ratio m : n is:
A. 2 : 3 B. 3 : 2
C. 1 : 2 D. 2 : 1

36. Which of the following is a correct statement regarding range as a measure of dispersion?
A. The range is independent of the change of origin and scale
B. The range is independent of the change of origin but not of the scale
C. The range is independent of the change of scale but not of the origin
D. The range is not affected by fluctuations of sampling

37. If $\Sigma x = 230$, $\Sigma x^2 = 6500$ and the numbers of observations N = 10, the value of standard deviation is:
A. 9 B. 10
C. 11 D. 12

38. Which of the following does NOT fall under the major goals of the National Mission for Green India?
A. To increase forest/tree cover to the extent of five million llectares.
B. To improve/enhance eco-system services like carbon sequestration and storage, hydrological services and biodiversity.
C. To increase forest-based livelihood income of about three million households.
D. To study the traditional knowledge systems for community participation in adaptation and mitigation strategies.

39. Under the GRIHA Rating Norms, a building securing 57 points on a 100 point scale, will be assigned which of the following star ratings?

A. Two star
B. Three star
C. Four star
D. Five star

40. The Brundtland Commission Report was entitled:

A. Limits to Growth
B. Our Common Future
C. Sustainable Development
D. Tragedy of Commons

41. Given below are two statements:

Statement I : In clear water, the reflectance is very high in the visible region of the electromagnetic spectrum.

Statement II : Pure water strongly absorbs radiation from the mid-infrared spectral region.

In light of the above statements, choose the ***correct*** answer from the options given below:

A. Both Statement I and Statement II are true
B. Both Statement I and Statement II are false
C. Statement I is correct, but Statement II is false
D. Statement I is incorrect but Statement II is true

42. Following are the examples of Persistent Organic Pollutants (POPs):

(*a*) Dioxin
(*b*) Volatile Organic Compounds (VOCs)
(*c*) Poly Chlorinated Biphenyl (PCBs)
(*c*) Furans
(*e*) Organochlorine pesticides

Choose the correct answer from the options given below:

A. (*a*), (*b*) and (*c*) only
B. (*a*), (*b*), (*c*) and (*d*) only
C. (*a*), (*d*), and (*e*) only
D. (*a*), (*c*), (*d*) and (*e*) only

43. Consider the following statements regarding the solubility of gases in water:

(*a*) The concentration of a dissolved gas in water is proportional to its partial pressure in the air.
(*b*) The solubility of a gas in water remains unaffected as other dissolved material in it increases.
(*c*) The solubility of a gas increases as temperature increases.
(*d*) The solubility of gases in water is governed by Henry's law.

Choose the correct answer from the options given below:

A. (*a*) and (*b*) only
B. (*b*) and (*c*) only
C. (*c*) and (*d*) only
D. (*a*) and (*d*) only

44. Consider the following statement regarding *ex-situ* bioremediation of contaminated soil:

(*a*) Bioremediation techniques can be applied at or very near the site of contamination.
(*b*) Biopiles and windrow composting are the most dominant *ex-situ* bioremediation techniques for treating contaminated soils.
(*c*) Biopiles can be formed with larger volumes of soil than windrows.
(*d*) Both biopiles and windrow composting are anaerobic processes.

Choose the correct answer from the options given below:

A. (*a*) and (*b*) only
B. (*b*) and (*d*) only
C. (*a*), (*b*) and (*c*) only
D. (*a*), (*b*) and (*d*) only

45. Diesel Exhaust Particles (DEP), known to manifest asthma-like features, are responsible for:

(*a*) Chronic airway inflammation
(*b*) Mucus hypersecretion
(*c*) Airway expansion
(*d*) Marked infiltration of eosinophils
(*e*) Airway hyperresponsiveness

Choose the correct answer from the options given below:

A. (*a*), (*c*), (*d*) and (*e*) only
B. (*a*), (*b*), (*c*) and (*d*) only
C. (*a*), (*b*), (*d*) and (*e*) only
D. (*b*), (*c*), (*d*) and (*e*) only

46. Consider the following statements regarding the phytoremediation of metal contaminated sites:

(*a*) Natural abilities of certain plant species are utilized to remove or stabilize toxic metals.
(*b*) Certain species termed hyperaccumulators can adsorb 50-100 times larger amounts of metals compared to most ordinary plants.
(*c*) The best candidates for removal by phytoremediation are arsenic and cadmium.
(*d*) The harvested hyperaccumulating plants can be recycled in agriculture.

Choose the correct answer from the options given below:
A. (*a*) only
B. (*a*) and (*b*) only
C. (*a*), (*b*) and (*c*) only
D. (*a*), (*c*) and (*d*) only

47. Given below are two statements:
Statement I : Many bacteria carry plasmids, which are much smaller pieces of DNA, also circular, and self-replicating.
Statement II : Plasmids are vitally important in the context of the environmental biotechnology in that they frequently carry the genes for degradative path-ways.

In light of the above statements, choose the ***most appropriate*** answer from the options given below:
A. Both Statement I and Statement II are correct
B. Both Statement I and Statement II are incorrect
C. Statement I is correct, but Statement II is incorrect
D. Statement I is incorrect, but Statement II is correct

48. Consider the following statements regarding reactions in moderately acidic soils:
(*a*) Base saturation is higher than that in the strongly acidic soils.
(*b*) Free aluminium ions are abundant in soil solutions.
(*c*) Aluminium hydroxy ions act as exchangeable cations.
(*d*) 'Small amounts of readily exchangeable hydrogen contributes to soil acidity.

Choose the correct answer from the options given below
A. (*a*) and (*b*) only
B. (*a*), (*b*) and (*c*) only
C. (*a*), (*c*) and (*d*) only
D. (*b*), (*c*) and (*d*) only

49. Given below are two statements.
Statement I : Cyclonic wind flow in the northern hemisphere is counter-clockwise.
Statement II : If you stand with your back to the wind in the northern hemisphere, low pressure will be to your left and high pressure will be to your right.

In light of the above statements, choose the ***most appropriate*** answer from the options given below:
A. Both Statement I and Statement II are correct
B. Both Statement I and Statement II are incorrect
C. Statement I is correct, but Statement II is incorrect
D. Statement I is incorrect, but Statement II is correct

50. What is the correct increasing order of following rocks by per cent volume in the earth's crust?
(*a*) Igneous rocks
(*b*) Sedimentary rocks.
(*c*) Metamorphic rocks

Choose the correct answer from the options given below:
A. (*a*), (*b*), (*c*) B. (*c*), (*b*), (*a*)
C. (*a*), (*c*), (*b*) D. (*b*), (*c*), (*a*)

51. What is the correct sequence in decreasing order of hardness among the following?
(*a*) Gypsum (*b*) Fluorite
(*c*) Feldspar (*d*) Topaz

Choose the correct answer from the options given below:
A. (*c*) > (*d*) > (*b*) > (*a*)
B. (*d*) > (*b*) > (*c*) > (*a*)
C. (*d*) > (*c*) > (*b*) > (*a*)
D. (*c*) > (*d*) > (*a*) > (*b*)

52. A random variable X follows Poisson distribution such that probabilties P(X = l) = P(X = 2). Now consider the following statements:

(*a*) The mean of this Poisson distribution is 2.

(*b*) The variance of this Poisson distribution is 2.

(*c*) Probability P(X = 0) is equal to e^{-2}

(*d*) Probability P(X = 0) = P(X = l)

Choose the correct answer from the options given below:

A. (*a*), (*b*) and (*c*) only
B. (*b*), (*c*) and (*d*) only
C. (*a*), (*b*) and (*d*) only
D. (*a*), (*c*) and (*d*) only

53. Identify the correct sequence of the following countries/group of countries credited with the highest to the lowest shares of cumulative CO_2 emissions to date.

(*a*) USA (*b*) China
(*c*) EU (*d*) India
(*e*) Japan

Choose the correct answer from the options given below:

A. (*a*), (*b*), (*c*), (*e*), (*d*)
B. (*a*), (*c*), (*e*), (*d*), (*b*)
C. (*a*), (*c*), (*b*), (*d*), (*e*)
D. (*a*), (*c*), (*b*), (*e*), (*d*)

54. Relative contribution (%) of the Green House Gases to global warming in decreasing order:

(*a*) Carbon dioxide (*b*) Methane
(*c*) CFC-12 (*d*) Nitrous oxide

Choose the correct answer from the options given below:

A. (*a*) > (*b*) > (*c*) > (*d*)
B. (*a*) > (*b*) > (*d*) > (*c*)
C. (*c*) > (*a*) > (*d*) > (*b*)
D. (*c*) > (*a*) > (*b*) > (*d*)

55. Consider the following statements regarding reactions of pesticides in soils:

(*a*) They may vaporize into the atmosphere without any chemical change.

(*b*) They do not move downward through the soil in solution form.

(*c*) They are resistant to microbial decay.

(*d*) They may be absorbed by plants.

Choose the ***most appropriate*** answer from the options given below:

A. (*a*) and (*d*) only
B. (*a*), (*b*) and (*d*) only
C. (*a*), (*c*) and (*d*) only
D. (*a*) and (*c*) only

56. Consider the following regarding the incineration process of solid waste.

(*a*) It is an oxidation process.

(*b*) The two major combustible chemical elements are carbon and hydrogen.

(*c*) Cellulose in the biowaste is transformed into organic acids.

(*d*) Excess source of air is not necessary.

Choose the correct answer from the options given below:

A. (*a*) and (*c*) only
B. (*b*) and (*c*) only
C. (*a*) and (*b*) only
D. (*b*) and (*d*) only

57. Given below are two statements: one is labelled as Assertion (A) and the other is labelled as Reason (R).

Assertion (A) : The risks from radioactive liquid wastes are caused under decontamination, solidification and disposal procedures.

Reason (R) : The chemicals in radioactive liquid wastes are hazardous in nature.

In light of the above statements, choose the most appropriate answer from the options given below:

A. Both (A) and (R) are correct and (R) is the correct explanation of (A)
B. Both (A) and (R) are correct, but (R) is NOT the correct explanation of (A)
C. (A) is correct, but (R) is not correct
D. (A) is not correct, but (R) is correct

58. Given below are two statements:

Statement I : Hazardous materials such as lead, mercury, and hexavalent chromium in one form or other are present in electronic wastes.

Statement II : Landfilling of electronic waste is the best operation from the environmental viewpoint.

In light of the above statements, choose the ***correct*** answer from the options given below:

A. Both Statement I and Statement II are true

B. Both Statement I and Statement II are false

C. Statement I is correct, but Statement II is false

D. Statement I is incorrect, but Statement II is true

59. Provision of Extended Producer's Responsibility (EPR) of producer, importer and brand owner for collecting back the waste generated by their product has been in the:

(*a*) Solid Waste Management Rules, 2016

(*b*) Construction & Demolition Waste Management Rules, 2016

(*c*) Plastic Waste Management Rules, 2016

(*d*) E-waste (Management) Rules, 2016

(*e*) Biomedical Waste Management Rules, 2016

Choose the ***correct*** answer from the options given below

A. (*a*), (*b*), (*d*) only

B. (*b*), (*c*), (*d*) only

C. (*c*), (*d*), (*e*) only

D. (*a*), (*b*), (*c*), (*d*) only

60. Given below are two statements:

Statement I : Increasing the productivity of forests to meet essential needs is one of the major objectives of the National Forest Policy, 1988.

Statement II : According to the National Forest Policy,1988, no forest-based enterprise should provide employment to local people on a priority basis.

In light of the above statements, choose the ***correct*** answer from the options given below:

A. Both Statement I and Statement II are true

B. Both Statement I and Statement II are false

C. Statement I is correct, but Statement II is false

D. Statement I is incorrect, but Statement II is true

61. Given below are two statements:

Statement I : Covariance between two variables X and Y determines whether the correlation between them is negative or positive.

Statement II : The product of the standard deviation of two variables X and Y can be both positive or negative.

In light of the above statements, choose the ***most appropriate*** answer from the options given below:

A. Both Statement I and Statement II are correct

B. Both Statement I and Statement II are incorrect

C. Statement I is correct, but Statement II is incorrect

D. Statement I is incorrect, but Statement II is correct

62. Consider the following statements regarding skewness:

(*a*) For a positively skewed distribution, the value of the mean is the greatest among the mean, median and mode.

(*b*) For a negatively skewed distribution, the median is greater than the mean.

(*c*) Karl Pearson's coefficient of skewness always lies between the limits ±1.

(*d*) Bowley's coefficient of skewness always lies between the limits ±1.

Choose the correct answer from the options given below

A. (*a*), (*b*) and (*c*) only

B. (*b*), (*c*) and (*d*) only

C. (*a*), (*c*), and (*d*) only

D. (*a*), (*b*) and (*d*) only

63. Consider the following statements about normal distribution:

(*a*) This distribution is applicable to continuous random variables.

(*b*) It is a symmetrical distribution.
(*c*) The mean of a standard normal distribution is 1.
(*d*) The standard deviation of the standard normal distribution is 1.

Choose the correct answer from the options given below:

A. (*a*), (*b*) and (*c*) only
B. (*b*), (*c*) and (*d*) only
C. (*a*), (*b*) and (*d*) only
D. (*a*), (*c*) and (*d*) only

64. Consider the following statements pertaining to sampling theory:

(*a*) The standard deviation of the sampling distribution of a statistic is known as its standard error.
(*b*) The precision of the sample estimate of some population parameter is the reciprocal of the standard error of the sampling distribution of the estimate.
(*c*) A Type-I error in hypothesis testing occurs when we accept a wrong null hypothesis.
(*d*) A Type-II error in hypothesis testing occurs when we reject a true null hypothesis.

Choose the correct answer from the options given below

A. (*a*) and (*b*) only
B. (*b*) and (*c*) only
C. (*a*) and (*c*) only
D. (*c*) and (*d*) only

65. Match List-I (Instrument) with List-II (Function).

List-I *(Instrument)*	**List-II** *(Function)*
(*a*) Campbell-Stokes Recorder	(*i*) To measure the visible light flux
(*b*) Pyraheliometer	(*ii*) To measure total solar irradiance on a plain surface
(*c*) Pyranometer	(*iii*) To measure direct beam solar irradiance
(*d*) Lux meter	(*iv*) To measure the sunshine duration

Choose the correct answer from the options given below:

Codes:

	(*a*)	(*b*)	(*c*)	(*d*)
A.	(*i*)	(*iii*)	(*ii*)	(*iv*)
B.	(*i*)	(*ii*)	(*iii*)	(*iv*)
C.	(*iv*)	(*iii*)	(*ii*)	(*i*)
D.	(*iv*)	(*i*)	(*ii*)	(*iii*)

66. Match List-I (Analysis) with List-II (Analytical techniques).

List-I ***(Analysis)***	***List-II*** ***(Analytical techniques)***
(*a*) To analyze organic compounds of pollutants	(*i*) SEM
(*b*) To analyze the elemental composition of pollutants	(*ii*) XRD
(*c*) Morphological analysis of pollutants	(*iii*) FTIR
(*d*) To analyze crystalline materials of pollutants	(*iv*) XRF

Choose the correct answer from the options given below:

Codes:

	(*a*)	(*b*)	(*c*)	(*d*)
A.	(*iii*)	(*ii*)	(*iv*)	(*i*)
B.	(*iv*)	(*iii*)	(*i*)	(*ii*)
C.	(*iii*)	(*iv*)	(*i*)	(*ii*)
D.	(*iv*)	(*iii*)	(*ii*)	(*i*)

67. Match List-I (Organism) with List-II (Ecosystem structure components).

List-I (Organism)	**List-II (Ecosystem structure components)**
(*a*) Earthworms	(*i*) Producer
(*b*) Grass	(*ii*) Secondary carnivore
(*c*) Frogs	(*iii*) Primary carnivore
(*d*) Hawks	(*iv*) Detrivore

Choose the correct answer from the options given below.

Codes:

	(*a*)	(*b*)	(*c*)	(*d*)
A.	(*iv*)	(*i*)	(*ii*)	(*iii*)
B.	(*ii*)	(*iii*)	(*iv*)	(*i*)
C.	(*iii*)	(*iv*)	(*i*)	(*ii*)
D.	(*iv*)	(*i*)	(*iii*)	(*ii*)

68. Match List I (Elements) with List II (Characteristics).

List-I (Elements)	List-II (Characteristics)
(*a*) Lithophile	(*i*) Occur mainly as sulfides
(*b*) Chalcophile	(*ii*) Gaseous elements do not generally form compounds
(*c*) Siderophile	(*iii*) Occur mainly in oxygen compounds
(*d*) Atmophile	(*iv*) Occur mainly as native elements

Choose the correct answer from the options given below:

Codes:

	(*a*)	(*b*)	(*c*)	(*d*)
A.	(*i*)	(*ii*)	(*iii*)	(*iv*)
B.	(*i*)	(*iv*)	(*iii*)	(*ii*)
C.	(*iii*)	(*iv*)	(*i*)	(*ii*)
D.	(*iii*)	(*i*)	(*iv*)	(*ii*)

69. Match List-I (Rock types) with List-II (Characteristics)

List-I (Rock types)	List-II (Characteristics)
(*a*) Rudaceous	(*i*) Rocks consisting mainly of silt and siltstones
(*b*) Arenaceous	(*ii*) Rocks consisting mainly of gravels, pebbles, cobbles, and boulders
(*c*) Silt rocks	(*iii*) Rocks consisting mainly of dust, mud, and clay
(*d*) Argillaceous	(*iv*) Rocks consisting mainly of sands

Choose the correct answer from the options given below:

Codes:

	(*a*)	(*b*)	(*c*)	(*d*)
A.	(*ii*)	(*i*)	(*iv*)	(*iii*)
B.	(*iv*)	(*ii*)	(*i*)	(*iii*)
C.	(*iv*)	(*i*)	(*iii*)	(*ii*)
D.	(*ii*)	(*iv*)	(*i*)	(*iii*)

70. Match List-I (Air pollutants) with List-II (Control Technique/ Equipment)

List-I (Air pollutants)	List-II (Control Technique/ Equipment)
(*a*) $PM_{2.5}$	(*i*) Selective catalytic reduction
(*b*) SO_2	(*ii*) Electrostatic precipitator
(*c*) NO_X	(*iii*) Cyclone collectors
(*d*) Coarse particulate matter	(*iv*) Scrubber

Choose the correct answer from the options given below:

Codes:

	(*a*)	(*b*)	(*c*)	(*d*)
A.	(*i*)	(*ii*)	(*iii*)	(*iv*)
B.	(*ii*)	(*iv*)	(*i*)	(*iii*)
C.	(*i*)	(*iv*)	(*ii*)	(*iii*)
D.	(*iv*)	(*i*)	(*iii*)	(*ii*)

71. Match List-I (Atmospheric stability) with List-II (Lapse Rate).

List-I (Atmospheric stability)	List-II (Lapse Rate)
(*a*) Absolutely Stable	(*i*) ELR = DALR
(*b*) Absolutely Unstable	(*ii*) ELR < DALR
(*c*) Conditionally Unstable	(*iii*) ELR > DALR
(*d*) Dry Neutral	(*iv*) SALR < ELR < DALR

Choose the correct answer from the options given below.

Codes:

	(*a*)	(*b*)	(*c*)	(*d*)
A.	(*ii*)	(*iii*)	(*i*)	(*iv*)
B.	(*ii*)	(*iii*)	(*iv*)	(*i*)
C.	(*iii*)	(*ii*)	(*iv*)	(*i*)
D.	(*iii*)	(*ii*)	(*i*)	(*iv*)

72. Match List-I (Statistical Test) with List-II (Applications).

List-I (Statistical test)	List-II (Applications)
(*a*) χ^2 -test	(*i*) Testing the significance of difference of means
(*b*) One-Way ANOVA	(*ii*) Testing the significance of a single mean
(*c*) Paired *t*-test	(*iii*) Testing the goodness of fit between theory and experiment
(*d*) Z-test	(*iv*) Comparing more than two sample means

Choose the correct answer from the options given below:

Codes:

	(*a*)	(*b*)	(*c*)	(*d*)
A.	(*i*)	(*ii*)	(*iii*)	(*iv*)
B.	(*ii*)	(*iii*)	(*iv*)	(*i*)
C.	(*iii*)	(*iv*)	(*i*)	(*ii*)
D.	(*iv*)	(*i*)	(*ii*)	(*iii*)

73. Match List-I (Environmentally significant Days) with List-II (Dates).

List-I (Environmentally significant Days)	List-II (Dates)
(*a*) World Ozone Day	(*i*) 16 September
(*b*) World Habitat Day	(*ii*) 21 March
(*c*) World Forest Day	(*iii*) 5 October
(*d*) World Water Day	(*iv*) 22 March

Choose the correct answer from the options given below:

Codes:

	(*a*)	(*b*)	(*c*)	(*d*)
A.	(*iv*)	(*iii*)	(*i*)	(*ii*)
B.	(*ii*)	(*i*)	(*iv*)	(*iii*)
C.	(*i*)	(*iii*)	(*ii*)	(*iv*)
D.	(*iii*)	(*i*)	(*iv*)	(*ii*)

74. Match List-I (Processes) with List-II (Energy Transfer).

List-I (Processes)	List-II (Energy Transfer)
(*a*) Conduction	(*i*) Energy is transferred by motion of a fluid
(*b*) Convection	(*ii*) Energy is transferred in the form of electromagnetic waves through a vacuum.
(*c*) Radiation	(*iii*) Energy is transferred between two points in a material at different temperatures
(*d*) Evaporation	(*iv*) Energy is lost through a phase change

Choose the correct answer from the options given below:

Codes:

	(*a*)	(*b*)	(*c*)	(*d*)
A.	(*ii*)	(*i*)	(*iii*)	(*iv*)
B.	(*ii*)	(*iv*)	(*iii*)	(*i*)
C.	(*iii*)	(*iv*)	(*ii*)	(*i*)
D.	(*iii*)	(*i*)	(*ii*)	(*iv*)

75. A strategy favoured by *r*-selection is:

A. Higher proportional allocation to non-reproductive activities.

B. Living in environments imposing high-density independent mortality.

C. Living in environments imposing high-density dependent regulation.

D. Higher proportional allocation to reproductive activities.

76. Traditionally membranes have been classified based on the minimum size of the contaminant that is excluded from passing through the particular membrane. Arrange the following in the correct sequence of decreasing pore size.

(*a*) Reverse Osmosis (*b*) Nanofiltration
(*c*) Microfiltration (*d*) Ultrafiltration

Choose the correct answer from the options given below:

A. (*a*), (*b*), (*c*), (*d*) B. (*d*), (*c*), (*b*), (*a*)
C. (*c*), (*d*), (*b*), (*a*) D. (*d*), (*c*), (*a*), (*b*)

77. For a given noise signal, what would be the correct order of noise indices in terms of increasing values?

(*a*) L_{10} (*b*) L_{50}
(*c*) L_1 (*d*) L_{90}

Choose the correct answer from the options given below:

A. (*c*) < (*a*) < (*b*) < (*d*)

B. (*a*) < (*b*) < (*c*) < (*d*)

C. $(d) < (c) < (b) < (a)$
D. $(d) < (b) < (a) < (c)$

78. Identify the correct sequence of steps involved in the development of a model.
(*a*) Validation (*b*) Formulation
(*c*) Identification (*d*) Solution
Choose the correct answer from the options given below:
A. (*a*), (*b*), (*c*), (*d*) B. (*b*), (*c*), (*d*), (*a*)
C. (*c*), (*b*), (*d*), (*a*) D. (*c*), (*d*), (*b*), (*a*)

79. Given below are two statements: One is labelled as Assertion (A) and other is labelled as Reason (R).
Assertion (A) : Plants generally reflect radiation highly in the near-infrared region of the electromagnetic spectrum.
Reason (R) : Plant leaves generally contain high chlorophyll content.
In light of the above statements, choose the correct answer from the options given below:
A. Both (A) and (R) are true and (R) is the correct explanation of (A)
B. Both (A) and (R) are true, but (R) is NOT the correct explanation of (A)
C. (A) is true, but (R) is false
D. (A) is false, but (R) is true

80. Given below are two statements: One is labelled as Assertion (A) and other is labelled as Reason (R).
Assertion (A) : Tropopause acts as a 'lid' limiting both convection and transport from the troposphere into the higher layers of the atmosphere.
Reason (R) : At tropopause height and at higher levels, the atmosphere is stable.
In light of the above statements, choose the correct answer from the options given below:
A. Both (A) and (R) are true and (R) is the correct explanation of (A)
B. Both (A) and (R) are true, but (R) is NOT the correct explanation of (A)
C. (A) is true, but (R) is false
D. (A) is false, but (R) is true

81. Given below are two statements: One is labelled as Assertion (A) and other is labelled as Reason (R).
Assertion (A) : Isomorphous substitution is the source of constant charges on soil silicate clays.
Reason (R) : Cations of comparable size substitute each other in respective tetrahedral and octahedral sheets in silicate clays.
In light of the above statements, choose the correct answer from the options given below:
A. Both (A) and (R) are true and (R) is the correct explanation of (A)
B. Both (A) and (R) are true, but (R) is NOT the correct explanation of (A)
C. (A) is true, but (R) is false
D. (A) is false, but (R) is true

82. Yaw control used in wind turbine generator is a:
A. Microprocessor-based control unit
B. The mechanism to keep the rotor axis along wind direction.
C. The mechanism to keep the rotor axis perpendicular to wind direction.
D. Gear mechanism to control the speed of the rotor when wind speed is extremely high

83. Given below are two statements: One is labelled as Assertion (A) and other is labelled as Reason (R).
Assertion (A) : Some countries are immune to the impacts of climate change.
Reason (R) : The net contribution of some countries is less than 1% towards the global CO_2 emissions as a whole.
In light of the above statements, choose the correct answer from the options given below:
A. Both (A) and (R) are true and (R) is the correct explanation of (A)
B. Both (A) and (R) are true, but (R) is NOT the correct explanation of (A)
C. (A) is true, but (R) is false
D. (A) is false, but (R) is true

84. Given below are two statements: One is labelled as Assertion (A) and other is labelled as Reason (R).

Assertion (A) : Solar and wind energy systems require quite large structures relative to power produced.

Reason (R) : Energy flux densities associated with solar energy and wind energy are on average small.

In light of the above statements, choose the ***most appropriate*** answer from the options given below:

A. Both (A) and (R) are correct and (R) is the correct explanation of (A)
B. Both (A) and (R) are correct, but (R) is NOT the correct explanation of (A)
C. (A) is correct, but (R) is not correct
D. (A) is not correct, but (R) is correct

85. Given below are two statements: One is labelled as Assertion (A) and other is labelled as Reason (R).

Assertion (A) : Hydrofluorocarbons (HFCs) and hydrochlorofluorocarbon (HCFCs) are used as substitute compounds for chlorofluorocarbons (CFCs).

Reason (R) : HCFCs and HFCs are quite susceptible to reaction with OH radicals in the troposphere.

In light of the above statements, choose the ***correct*** answer from the options given below:

A. Both (A) and (R) are true and (R) is the correct explanation of (A)
B. Both (A) and (R) are true, but (R) is NOT the correct explanation of (A)
C. (A) is true, but (R) is false
D. (A) is false, but (R) is true

86. Given below are two statements: One is labelled as Assertion (A) and other is labelled as Reason (R).

Assertion (A) : Regression analysis is suitable for two variables having a linear causal relationship between them.

Reason (R) : The causal relationship between two variables is never curvilinear.

In light of the above statements, choose the ***most appropriate*** answer from the options given below:

A. Both (A) and (R) are correct and (R) is the correct explanation of (A)
B. Both (A) and (R) are correct, but (R) is NOT the correct explanation of (A)
C. (A) is correct, but (R) is not correct
D. (A) is not correct, but (R) is correct

87. Given below are two statements.

Statement I : Leslie's matrix population model is a discrete and age-independent model.

Statement II : The first row in Leslie's projection matrix represents fertility.

In light of the above statements, choose the ***most appropriate*** answer from the options given below:

A. Both Statement I and Statement II are correct
B. Both Statement I and Statement II are incorrect
C. Statement I is correct, but Statement II is incorrect
D. Statement I is incorrect, but Statement II is correct

88. Arrange the environmental movements in chronological order.

(*a*) Silent Valley struggle
(*b*) Chipko movement
(*c*) Appiko movement
(*d*) Narmada Bachao movement

Choose the correct answer from the options given below:

A. (*a*), (*b*), (*c*), (*d*) B. (*b*), (*a*), (*c*), (*d*)
C. (*a*), (*d*), (*b*), (*c*) D. (*a*), (*b*), (*d*), (*c*)

89. Regarding Bharat Stage (BS-VI) vehicular emissions norms, choose the correct statements:

(*a*) BS (VI) emission norms are equivalent to Euro (VI) norms.
(*b*) BS (VI) norms require the up-gradation of engine and emission control technology

(*c*) BS(VI) norms are applicable to all categories of the vehicles including two, three and four-wheelers.
(*d*) BS (VI) norms do not require any change in fuel quality.
Choose the correct answer from the options given below:
A. (*a*), (*b*), (*c*) only
B. (*b*), (*c*), (*d*) only
C. (*a*), (*c*), (*d*) only
D. (*a*), (*b*), (*c*), (*d*) All

90. Which among the following atmospheric constituents have a negative radiative forcing?
(*a*) Tropospheric ozone
(*b*) Stratospheric ozone
(*c*) Sulphate Aerosol
(*d*) Nitrous oxide
Choose the correct answer from the options given below.
A. (*a*) and (*b*) only B. (*b*) and (*c*) only
C. (*c*) and (*d*) only D. (*a*) and (*d*) only

Directions (Qs. No. 91-95): *Read the given passage carefully and answer the questions that follow.*

The colour photograph of Earthrise, taken by Apollo 8 astronaut William A. Anders on December 24, 1968, is a powerful and eloquent image. One leading environmentalist has rightfully described it as "the most influential environmental photograph ever taken". Inspired by the photograph, economist Kenneth E. Boulding summed up the finite nature of our planet as viewed in the context of the vast expanse of space in his metaphor "Spaceship Earth". What had been perceived throughout human history as a limitless frontier had suddenly become a tiny sphere: limited in its resources, crowded by an ever-expanding human population, and threatened by our use of the atmosphere and the oceans as repositories for our consumptive wastes.

91. Perception of the planet Earth before 1968 was that it had:
A. Infinite resources
B. Limited resources
C. Finite carrying capacity
D. Scarce resources

92. Carrying capacity of the Earth is threatened by:
(*a*) Human population explosion
(*b*) Irrational use of atmosphere
(*c*) Dumping of consumptive wastes in the ocean
(*d*) Development of space technology
A. (*a*), (*c*) and (*d*) only
B. (*b*), (*c*) and (*d*) only
C. (*a*), (*b*) and (*c*) only
D. (*a*), (*b*) and (*d*) only

93. Perception about the planet Earth is that, it is a:
A. Tiny life support system
B. Vast life support system
C. Vast expanse of space
D. Limitless frontier in its extent

94. The metaphor "Spaceship Earth" was used to described the Earth as:
A. Tiny sphere in the vast universe
B. Repository of natural resources
C. Consisting of modern space infrastructure
D. Unmanned spacecraft

95. Inference of the passage is that the Earth is an ecosystem of:
A. Infinite carrying capacity
B. Infinite resources for exploitation
C. Finite carrying capacity
D. Unlimited power of self-sustenance

Directions (Qs. No. 96-100): *Read the given passage carefully and answer the questions that follow.*

The fermentation products prior to 1900 AD were confined to potable alcohol and vinegar. However, the first true large-scale breweries date from the 1700s AD when wooden vats of 1500 barrels capacity were introduced. By the mid-1800s AD, the role of yeasts in alcohol fermentation had been demonstrated independently by Cagniard-Latour, Schwann and Kutzing but it was Louis Pasteur who convinced the scientific world of the obligatory role of micro-organisms in the process. During the 1800s AD, Hansen started his pioneering work for isolating and propagating single yeast cells to produce pure culture. However, many traditional ale-producing breweries still use mixed yeast cultures. Vinegar was originally produced by leaving wine in shallow bowls or partially filled barrels where it was slowly oxidized to vinegar by the development of natural flora. The appreciation of the importance of air in the process led to the development of the 'generator'. Between the years, 1900 AD and 1940 AD, the most important advances were the development in the baker's yeast, solvent fermentation, citric acid production and lactic acid production.

96. Vinegar is a product of:
A. Solvent fermentation
B. Alcoholic fermentation
C. Aerobic fermentation
D. Anaerobic fermentation

97. Many traditional ale-producing breweries use:
A. Yeast pure culture
B. Mixed culture of bacteria
C. Mixed culture of yeasts
D. Bakers' yeast

98. Who among the following first developed the method of producing a pure culture of yeasts?
A. Cagniard-Latour
B. Hansen
C. Louis Pasteur
D. Schwann and Kutzing

99. In pre-1900s AD, which types of vessels were used in large-scale breweries?
A. Wooden
B. Copper
C. Steel
D. Mechanical fermenters

100. Which among the following is one of the oldest products of fermentation technology?
A. Bakers' yeast B. Yeast biomass
C. Lactic acid D. Alcohol

ANSWERS

1	**2**	**3**	**4**	**5**	**6**	**7**	**8**	**9**	**10**
D	D	D	A	B	C	B	B	C	A
11	**12**	**13**	**14**	**15**	**16**	**17**	**18**	**19**	**20**
A	C	B	C	A	D	C	B	B	B
21	**22**	**23**	**24**	**25**	**26**	**27**	**28**	**29**	**30**
D	B	C	C	D	C	A	B	*	A
31	**32**	**33**	**34**	**35**	**36**	**37**	**38**	**39**	**40**
C	B	A	C	B	B	C	D	B	B
41	**42**	**43**	**44**	**45**	**46**	**47**	**48**	**49**	**50**
D	D	D	C	C	B	A	C	A	D
51	**52**	**53**	**54**	**55**	**56**	**57**	**58**	**59**	**60**
C	A	D	B	A	C	A	C	D	C
61	**62**	**63**	**64**	**65**	**66**	**67**	**68**	**69**	**70**
C	D	C	A	C	C	D	D	D	B
71	**72**	**73**	**74**	**75**	**76**	**77**	**78**	**79**	**80**
B	C	C	D	D	C	D	C	B	A
81	**82**	**83**	**84**	**85**	**86**	**87**	**88**	**89**	**90**
A	B	D	A	A	C	D	B	A	B
91	**92**	**93**	**94**	**95**	**96**	**97**	**98**	**99**	**100**
A	C	A	A	C	C	C	B	A	D

* *No option is correct or the question is wrong.*

EXPLANATORY ANSWERS

1. According to Kirchhoff's law, $a = e$, or the absorptivity of a body equals its emissivity. A good absorber is a good emitter. As a good absorber is poor reflector, emitting (or radiating) ability of body is oppositely related to its ability to reflect. Therefore, good emitter (or radiator) is a poor reflector.

2. Relative Humidity = 60%

Saturation Vapour Density = 2260 Pa

Actual Vapour Pressure = ?

From, Relative Humidity

$$= \frac{\text{Actual Vapour Pressure}}{\text{Saturation Vapour Density}} \times 100\%$$

$$60 = \frac{\text{Actual Vapour Pressure}}{2260} \times 100$$

$\therefore$ Actual Vapour Pressure

$$= \frac{60 \times 2260}{100} = 1356 \text{ Pa.}$$

3. Upon interaction with water and oxygen moieties, CAPs generate hydroxyl radicals •OH and superoxide radical anions $O_2{\bullet}^-$. These short-lived species possess highly oxidising and cytotoxic properties, and are suggested to be one of the main causes of biomedical activity of cold plasma.

4. 1,1,2-Trichloro-1,2,2-trifluoroethane, also called trichlorotrifluoroethane or CFC-113, is a chlorofluorocarbon. It has the formula $Cl_2FC\text{-}CClF_2$. This colorless, volatile liquid is a versatile solvent.

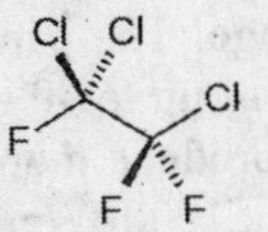

CFC-113 is a very unreactive chlorofluorocarbon. It remains in the atmosphere about 90 years, sufficiently long that it will cycle out of the troposphere and into the stratosphere. In the stratosphere, CFC-113 can be broken up by ultraviolet radiation (where sunlight in the 190-225 nm (UV) range), generating chlorine radicals (Cl•), which initiate degradation of ozone requiring only a few minutes.

5. Humic acids are insoluble in water at acid pH, whereas fulvic acids are also derived from humic substances but are soluble in water across the full range of pH. Humic and fulvic acids are commonly used as a soil supplement in agriculture, and less commonly as a human nutritional supplement.

6. Volatile organic compounds (VOCs) also referred to as solvents, are chemicals that evaporate easily at room temperature. VOCs are a class of liquid organic chemicals of variable lipophilicity and volatility.

VOCs are classified according to molecular structure or functional group. These include aliphatic hydrocarbons (many of which are chlorinated - halocarbons), aromatic hydrocarbons, alcohols, ethers, esters, aldehydes, etc. Solvents may be utilized individually or as mixtures containing several ingredients. Most VOCs contribute in varying degrees to the formation of ground levels of ozone.

7. Hyperthermophiles prefer high temperatures, e.g. above 80°C for optimal growth. They are able to thrive in such extreme temperatures because they contain enzymes that can function at high temperatures. They are an example of extremophiles. While they are able to live at high temperatures, most organisms would not be able to survive upon exposure to the same temperature.

8. The toxic effects of mercury depend on its chemical form and the route of exposure. Methylmercury [CH_3Hg] is the most toxic form. It affects the immune system, alters genetic and enzyme systems, and damages the nervous system, including coordination and the senses of touch, taste, and sight. Methylmercury is particularly damaging to developing embryos, which are five to ten times more sensitive than adults.

9. Ozone is measured as Dobson units. And a Dobson unit of gas is equal to a layer of gas, with a thickness of one-hundredth of a millimeter at the surface of the Earth. The ozone in the atmosphere is measured by about 300 Dobsons. Ozone is also known as a trace gas, meaning there are very few amounts in the atmosphere.

10. Riparian ecosystems are associated with water and occur as transition zones or ecotones between aquatic and terrestrial (upland) ecosystems. These transition zones have distinct vegetation and soil characteristics. Riparian ecosystems are uniquely characterized by the combination of high species diversity, high species densities, and high productivity. Continuous interactions occur between riparian, aquatic and adjacent terrestrial ecosystems through exchanges of energy, nutrients, and species.

11. Montmorillonite is a very soft phyllosilicate group of minerals that form when they precipitate from water solution as microscopic crystals, known as clay. Similar to many other clays, montmorillonite swells with the addition of water. Montmorillonites expand considerably more than other clays due to water penetrating the interlayer molecular spaces and concomitant adsorption. The amount of expansion is due largely to the type of exchangeable cation contained in the sample.

12. Volcanic gases are gases given off by active (or, at times, by dormant) volcanoes. These include gases trapped in cavities (vesicles) in volcanic rocks, dissolved or dissociated gases in magma and lava, or gases emanating from lava, from volcanic craters or vents. The principle components of volcanic gases are water vapour (H_2O), carbon dioxide (CO_2), sulfur either as sulfur dioxide (SO_2) (high-temperature volcanic gases) or hydrogen sulfide (H_2S).

The abundance of gases varies considerably from volcano to volcano, with volcanic activity and with tectonic setting. Water vapour is consistently the most abundant volcanic gas, normally comprising more than 60% of total emissions. Carbon dioxide typically accounts for 10 to 40% of emissions.

13. The phenomenon of rocks of different mineral composition arising from similar magmas under different conditions of crystallisation is termed heteromorphism by Lacroix, and the products are said to be heteromorphs of each other. Thus leucite-basalt is a heteromorph of mica-syenite, and allivalite of augitite.

14. Crystallinity is measured by the ratio subsisting between crystallized and non crystallized matter.

Types of Crystallinity

1. Holocrystalline
2. Holohyaline
3. Hemicrystalline/Hypocrystalline/ Merocrystalline

Holocrystalline: A rock composed entirely of crystals is said to be Holocrystalline. Holocrystalline texture is characterized by deep-seated or intrusive igneous rocks. Example: Granite, Gabbro, Syenite.

16. The light concentration process is typically characterized by the concentration ratio (C). By physical meaning, the concentration ratio is the factor by which the incident energy flux (I_o) is optically enhanced on the receiving surface.

The paraboloid dish solar concentrating system uses a parabolic concentrating dish to focus sunlight on a thermal cavity receiver. The receiver attains high temperature which in turn heats the water or thermal fluid inside the cavity. The heated fluid then transfer its heat to end industrial applications. The thermal energy attained is in 100 - 400 °C temperature range. The paraboloid can have a reflector area of up to 90 m^2. And a system like these can produce more than 50 kW of thermal output at 1000 W/m^2 solar insolation.

21. Concentrations of gaseous pollutants is sometimes given in units of mass per volume, and at other times in ppb or ppm.

ppb (*v*) is parts per billion by volume (i.e., volume of gaseous pollutant per 10^9 volumes of ambient air).

$\mu g/m^3$ is micrograms of gaseous pollutant per cubic meter of ambient air.

The conversion assumes an ambient pressure of 1 atmosphere and a temperature of 25 degrees Celsius.

SO_2	1 ppb = 2.62 μg/m^3
NO_2	1 ppb = 1.88 μg/m^3
NO	1 ppb = 1.25 μg/m^3
O_3	1 ppb = 2.00 μg/m^3
CO	1 ppb = 1.145 μg/m^3
Benzene	1 ppb = 3.19 μg/m^3

Hence 80 ppb = 80 × 1.88 = 150.4 μg/m^3.

22. From equation,

Lp = 20 log10 p + 94 [dB(re 2.0 × 10–5 pa)]

Lp = 20 log10 (100) + 94 = 40 + 94 = 134. [dB(re 2.0 × 10–5 pa)]

23. A-weighting is the most commonly used of a family of curves defined in the International standard IEC 61672:2003 and various national standards relating to the measurement of sound pressure level.The curves were originally defined for use at different average sound levels, but A-weighting, though originally intended only for the measurement of low-level sounds (around 40 phon), is now commonly used for the measurement of environmental noise and industrial noise.

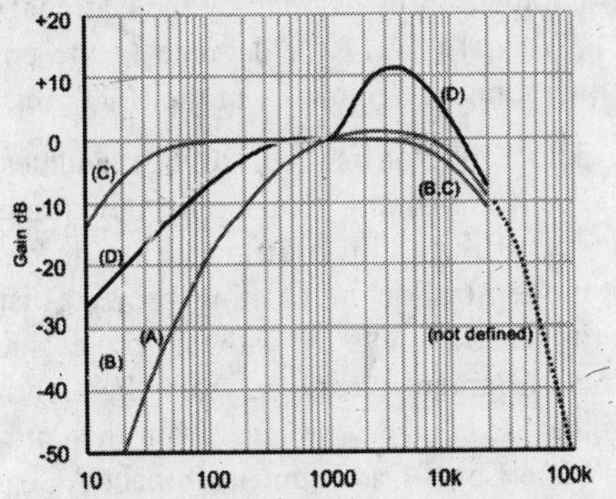

A-weighting (blue), B (yellow), C (red), and D-weighting (blk)

From graph we see that , In the 'A' weighting network used in noise measurements, sounds of 1000 Hz frequencies would require the least correction

24. ***Frankia*** is a genus of nitrogen-fixing, bacteria that live in symbiosis with actinorhizal plants, similar to the Rhizobium bacteria found in the root nodules of legumes in the family Fabaceae. Frankia also initiate the forming of root nodules. Most Frankia strains are specific to different plant species. The bacteria are filamentous and convert atmospheric nitrogen into ammonia via the enzyme nitrogenase, a process known as nitrogen fixation. Frankia can resist low concentration of heavy metals such as, Cu, Co, and Zn. Frankia may be an advantage for degraded soil. Frankia is a gram-positive Bacteria that is found on the roots of plants. The fact that Frankia is gram-positive means that the bacteria is made up of thick cell walls made out of protein called peptidologlycan. This helps with the resistance of the heavy metals that may be in the degraded soil.

25. The Basel Convention is an international treaty drafted in 1989 in response to public outcries against the indiscriminate dumping of hazardous waste. The convention went into force in 1992. It intends to reduce the movement of hazardous waste between nations and to prevent the "trade" in waste that resulted in developed countries' dumping hazardous waste in developing countries.

Under the convention, the movement of hazardous waste can take place only with written notification by the exporting state to the importing state and the approval of the importing state.

26. Vermicomposting, the conversion of organic waste into vermicompost, is mediated by the combined action of earthworms and microorganisms. Soil is not required in vermicomposting as the organic matter acts as both the substrate and food, and therefore only epigeic earthworms can be used in the process. Several earthworm species have been evaluated for their potential use in vermicomposting, including Eisenia fetida (Savigny), Eisenia andrei (Bouché), Dendrobaena veneta (Rosa), Dendrobaena hortensis (Michaelsen) Eudrilus eugeniae (Kinberg), and Perionyx excavatus (Perrier).

The species most commonly used in vermi-composting and vermiculture facilities world-wide are Eisenia andrei and Eisenia fetida.

27. Pyrolysis processes can be categorized as slow pyrolysis or fast pyrolysis. Fast pyrolysis is currently the most widely used pyrolysis system. Slow pyrolysis takes several hours to complete and results in biochar as the main product. On the other hand, fast pyrolysis yields 60% bio-oil and takes seconds for complete pyrolysis. In addition, it gives 20% biochar and 20% syngas.

28. Anaerobic digestion (AD) is a unique process where different microbial species decompose organic materials in the absence of oxygen. Anaerobic digestion is widely used for treating various waste streams such as municipal sludge or animal waste. For treating microalgae using anaerobic digestion, the digesting materials can be either raw algal biomass or the residue after oil extracted from the biomass.CH_4 and CO_2 are the dominant products of anaerobic digestion of municipal solid waste. Methane produced from anaerobic digestion can be used as a heat source or for electricity generation.

29. Ecological engineering may be based on one or more of the following four classes of ecotechnology:

1. Ecosystems are used to reduce or solve a pollution problem that otherwise would be (more) harmful to other ecosystems. A typical example is the use of wetlands for wastewater treatment.
2. Ecosystems arc imitated or copied to reduce or solve a pollution problem, leading to constructed ecosystems. Examples are fishponds and constructed wetlands for treating wastewater or diffuse pollution sources.
3. The recovery of ecosystems after significant disturbances. Examples are coal mine reclamation and restoration of lakes and rivers.
4. The use of ecosystems for the benefit of humanity without destroying the ecological balance (i.e., the utilization of ecosystems on an ecologically sound basis). Typical examples are the use of integrated agriculture and development of organic agriculture; this type of ecotechnology finds wide application in the ecological management of renewable resources.

30. Ahead of proposed auction of mines, including those bearing iron ore and limestone, the government has made it clear that firms having valid environment clearances (EC) for their projects are not required to obtain fresh green nod at the time of renewal of the leases.The maximum period of validity of the EC being given for mining lease for 30 years.

31. The Environment Relief Fund (ERF) was established under the Public Liability Act, 1991 (PLIA), to provide immediate relief to victims of accidents involving hazardous substances. Apart from contributions from hazardous industries that opt for insurance under the PLIA, the ERF consists of compensation awarded by the National Green Tribunal (NGT) for damage to the environment under Section 24 of the NGT Act, 2010.

32. The EIA Notification, 2006, mandates prior Environmental Clearance for new projects or activities including expansion or modernization of existing projects listed in its schedule. The 'A' category projects require environment clearance from the Centre and the 'B' category projects from the concerned State Level Environment Impact Assessment Authority.

Based on recommendations of the committee that was constituted in January 2013 under the chairmanship of Director - National Environmental Engineering Research Institute, Nagpur, with the objective of re-categorizing 'B' category projects and activities into categories 'B1' and 'B2' under the Environmental Impact Assessment Notification, 2006.

The projects categorized as B1 require EIA report for appraisal and also have to undergo public consultation process. The projects categorized as 'B2' are to be appraised based on the application accompanied with pre-feasibility report and other relevant documents.

33. The landfill site shall be 100 meter away from river, 200 meter from a pond, 200 meter from Highways, Habitations, Public Parks and water supply wells and 20 km away from Airports or Airbase. However in a special case, landfill site may be set up within a distance of 10 and 20 km away from the Airport/Airbase after obtaining no objection certificate from the civil aviation authority/Air force as the case may be. The Landfill site shall not be permitted within the flood plains as recorded for the last 100 years, zone of coastal regulation, wetland, critical habitat areas, sensitive eco-fragile areas.

34. Discrete random variables can take on either a finite or at most a countably infinite set of discrete values (for example, the integers). Their probability distribution is given by a probability mass function which directly maps each value of the random variable to a probability. For example, the value of X_1 takes on the probability P_1, the value of X_2 takes on the probability P_2, and so on. The probabilities P_1 must satisfy two requirements: every probability P_1 is a number between 0 and 1, and the sum of all the probabilities is 1. ($P_1 + P_2 + ... + P_k = 1$)

A discrete random variable has a countable number of possible values. Discrete random variable: obtained by counting values for which there are no in-between values, such as the integers 0, 1, 2, ...

Thus, The number of marks scored by students appearing in the examination is an example of discrete random variable.

35. Mean of m observation = 40

Mean of n observation = 60

Combined mean = 48

$$\therefore \quad 48 = \frac{m \times 40 + n \times 60}{m+n}$$

$$48(m + n) = 40m + 60n$$

$$48\left(\frac{m}{n}+1\right) = 40\frac{m}{n}+60$$

$$(48-40)\frac{m}{n} = 60 - 48$$

$$8\left(\frac{m}{n}\right) = 12$$

$$\therefore \quad \frac{m}{n} = \frac{12}{8} = \frac{3}{2}.$$

36. Dispersion is defined as deviation or scattering of values from their central values i.e, average (Mean, Median or Mode but preferably Mean or Median) . All measures of dispersions are independent of the change of origin but dependent on the change of scale.

37. Here we have

$\Sigma x = 230$, $\Sigma x^2 = 6500$ and $N = 10$

Standard deviation

$$\sigma = \sqrt{\frac{\Sigma x^2}{n} - \left(\frac{\Sigma x}{n}\right)^2} = \sqrt{\frac{6500}{10} - \left(\frac{230}{10}\right)^2}$$

$$= \sqrt{650-529}$$

$$= \sqrt{121} = 11.$$

38. The National Mission for Green India (GIM) is one of the eight Missions outlined under the National Action Plan on Climate Change (NAPCC). It aims at protecting; restoring and enhancing India's diminishing forest cover and responding to climate change by a combination of adaptation and mitigation measures.

Mission Goals

1. To increase forest/tree cover to the extent of 5 million hectares (mha) and improve quality of forest/tree cover on another 5 mha of forest/non-forest lands;
2. To improve/enhance eco-system services like carbon sequestration and storage (in forests and other ecosystems), hydrological

services and biodiversity; along with provisioning services like fuel, fodder, and timber and non-timber forest produces (NTFPs); and

3. To increase forest based livelihood income of about 3 million households.

40. Our Common Future, also known as the Brundtland Report, was published on October 1987 by the United Nations through the Oxford University Press. This publication was in recognition of Gro Harlem Brundtland's, former Norwegian Prime Minister, role as Chair of the World Commission on Environment and Development (WCED). Its targets were multilateralism and interdependence of nations in the search for a sustainable development path.

41. The spectral reflectance curve of healthy green vegetation has a significant minimum of reflectance in the visible portion of the electromagnetic spectrum resulting from the pigments in plant leaves. Reflectance increases dramatically in the near infrared. Stressed vegetation can also be detected because stressed vegetation has a significantly lower reflectance in the infrared.

The absorption of electromagnetic radiation by water depends on the state of the water.In liquid water the rotational transitions are effectively quenched, but absorption bands are affected by hydrogen bonding. In crystalline ice the vibrational spectrum is also affected by hydrogen bonding and there are lattice vibrations causing absorption in the far-infrared. Pure water strongly absorbs radiation from the midinfrared spectral region.

Hence Statement I is wrong but statement II is true.

42. Persistent organic pollutants (POPs) present in foods have been a major concern for food safety due to their persistence and toxic effects. They are all synthetic chemicals, either intentionally or nonintentionally produced/released. Some are pesticides, others are industrial products or unintended by-products resulting from industrial processes or combustions.

Persistent Organic Pollutants (POPs)

PESTICIDES	INDUSTRIAL CHEMICALS	UNINTENDED BYPRODUCTS
Aldrin Dieldrin Chlordane DDT Endrin Heptachlor Mirex Toxaphene	PCBs HCB	Dibenzodioxins Dibenzofurans

43. The pressure (p) of a gas in a solution is determined not only by its concentration, but also by its solubility coefficient. According to the Henry's law, when temperature is kept constant, the content of gas (n) dissolved in any solution is directly proportional to the partial pressure of a gas, i.e.,

$$n = pc,$$

where,

n = concentration (amount) of a gas in a solution,

p = partial pressure of gas and

c = solubility coefficient of the gas.

44. Ex-situ techniques involves the treatment of contaminated soil, away from the polluted site. Ex-situ bioremediation can be operated in two ways which include solid phase bioremediation and slurry phase bioremediation. Besides its high cost, these techniques are highly efficient, easy to control, faster and have great potential to treat large number of contaminants from the soil. Ex-situ techniques involve land farming, biopile, windrow, soil washing, composting, bioreactor, ion exchange, adsorption/absorption, pyrolysis and ultrasound technology. These techniques can be successfully applied for the treatment of fuel hydrocarbons, halogenated and non-halogenated organic compounds as well as for various pesticides.

45. Diesel exhaust particulates (DEPs) aggravate asthma-like pulmonary inflammation in a mouse model of asthma induced by a house dust extract (HDE) containing cockroach allergens and endotoxin.

46. One of phytoremediation categories, phytoextraction, can be used to remove heavy metals from soil using its ability to uptake metals which are essential for plant growth (Fe, Mn, Zn, Cu, Mg, Mo, and Ni). Some metals with unknown biological function (Cd, Cr, Pb, Co, Ag, Se, Hg) can also be accumulated. Some plants that are used in phytoextraction strategies are termed "hyperaccumulators." They are plants that achieve a shoot-to-root metal-concentration ratio greater than one. Nonaccumulating plants typically have a shoot-to-root ratio considerably less than one. Ideally, hyperaccumulators should thrive in toxic environments, require little maintenance and produce high biomass, although few plants perfectly fulfill these requirements.

47. Many bacteria carry plasmids, which are much smaller pieces of DNA, also circular and self-replicating. These are vitally important in the context of environmental biotechnology in that they frequently carry the genes for degradative pathways. Many of these plasmids may move between different bacteria where they replicate, thus making the metabolic capability they carry transferable. Bacteria show great promiscuity with respect to sharing their DNA.

Hence, Both Statement I and Statement II are correct.

49. In the Northern Hemisphere the motion of the winds about a cyclone, or low, will be an inblowing spiral and will have a counterclockwise direction; and the winds about an anticyclone will be an outblowing spiral and will have a clockwise direction. This is illustrated graphically in the figure. The relation of low and high pressure areas to the wind direction is happily expressed by the law known as Buys-Ballot's law, viz: "If you stand with your back to the wind, the region of low pressure will be on the left hand in the Northern Hemisphere, and on the right hand in the Southern Hemisphere; and high pressure will be on the right hand in the Northern Hemisphere, and on the left hand in the Southern Hemisphere."

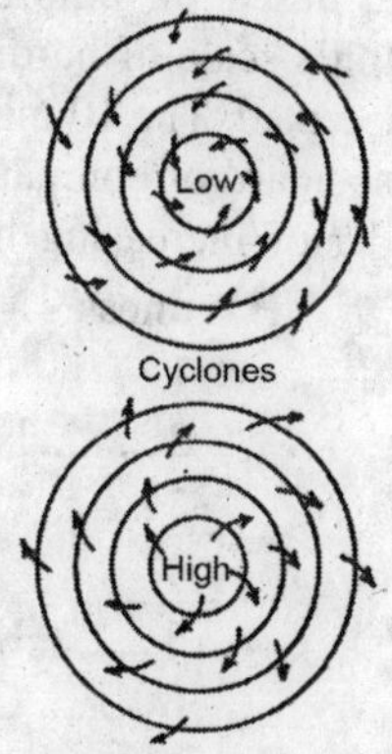

Hence, Both Statement I and Statement II are correct.

50. The rocks that make up the crust can be classified into three types.

- **Sedimentary Rocks**–rocks that are formed from the lithification of sediments, chemical precipitation or by direct biogenic deposition. Some common types are sandstone, shale, coal, limestone and coral.
- **Igneous Rocks**–rocks that cool from a magma. The two most common types are granite and basalt.
- **Metamorphic Rocks**–rocks that have been altered by high pressures, temperatures and/or chemical reaction while still in the solid state. Two common types are marble, which comes from limestone, and slate that comes from shale.

Increasing order of following rocks by per cent volume in the earth's crust : Sedimentary rocks < Metamorphic rocks < Igneous rocks.

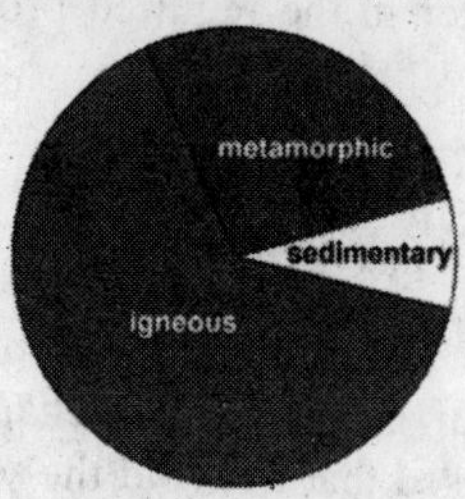

51. Hardness is a measure of the ability of a mineral to resist abrasion or scratching. A simple scale, based on empirical tests and known as Moh's scale of hardness, has been universally accepted. The 10 minerals selected to form the standard of comparison are listed below in order of increasing hardness:

Mineral	Hardness	Material
Talc	1	
Gypsum	2	Finger Nail
Calcite	3	Copper Penny
Fluorite	4	
Apatite	5	Knife Blade
Feldspar	6	Glass
Quartz	7	Porcelain
Topaz or Beryl	8	
Corundum	9	
Diamond	10	

52. We know that the density function of Poisson distribution is $\frac{e^{-\lambda}(\lambda)^x}{x!}$

Here, "X" is random variable and λ is the parameter of distribution.

Remember: Parameter of a distribution defines the character of the population.

So, if we got the value of parameter, we can find the probability for any value of random variable "X" that it assumes "(x)".

P(X = 1) = P(X = 2)

$\Rightarrow \quad \frac{e^{-\lambda}(\lambda)^1}{1!} = \frac{e^{-\lambda}(\lambda)^2}{2!}$

$\Rightarrow \quad 2e^{-\lambda}\,\lambda = e^{-\lambda}\,\lambda^2$

$\Rightarrow \quad 2\lambda = \lambda^2 \Rightarrow \lambda = 2$

Thus, we just need to put the value of parameter in the required probability.

$$P(X = 0) = \frac{e^{-\lambda}(\lambda)^0}{0!}$$

$\Rightarrow \quad P(X = 0) = e^{-2} = 0.1353.$

53. Carbon dioxide emissions are the primary driver of global climate change. It's widely recognised that to avoid the worst impacts of climate change, the world needs to urgently reduce emissions. The top 10 largest emitter countries account for 67.6% of the world total. Countries/group of countries credited with the highest to the lowest shares of cumulative CO_2 emissions: USA, EU, China, Japan, India.

54. Greenhouse gases are those that absorb and emit infrared radiation in the wavelength range emitted by Earth. Carbon dioxide (0.04%), nitrous oxide, methane and ozone are trace gases that account for almost 0.1% of Earth's atmosphere and have an appreciable greenhouse effect.

In order, the most abundant greenhouse gases in Earth's atmosphere are:

- Water vapour (H_2O)
- Carbon dioxide (CO_2)
- Methane (CH_4)
- Nitrous oxide (N_2O)
- Ozone (O_3)
- Chlorofluorocarbons (CFCs)
- Hydrofluorocarbons (includes HCFCs and HFCs).

55. Pesticides with high vapour pressures are easily lost to the atmosphere during application, and shortly thereafter they are lost from the soil through gaseous diffusion. Some highly vola-tile pesticides, however, may also move down-ward into aquifers. Roots are the principal absorbing organs for soil-applied pesticides.

56. Incineration is a chemical reaction in which carbon, hydrogen and other elements in the waste mix with oxygen in the combustion zone and generates heat. The air requirements for combustion of solid wastes are considerable.

57. Liquid RAW can be divided into process drains, floor drains and laundry drains based on the sources of waste generation. It is mainly generated from the clean-up and maintenance processes of reactor coolant and related systems containing radioactivity.The main sources of primary liquid radioactive waste (LRAW) from NPPs are pipelines leakages, water from spent nuclear fuel storage pools, solutions remaining after sorbent regeneration and spent decontamination solutions.The risks from radioactive liquid wastes are caused under decontamination, solidification and disposal procedures.

58. E-waste is a popular, informal name for electronic products nearing the end of their "useful life." Computers, televisions, VCRs, stereos, copiers, and fax machines are common electronic products. Many of these products can be reused, refurbished, or recycled. There are hazardous materials, such as lead, mercury, and hexavalent chromium, in circuit boards, batteries, and colour cathode ray tubes (CRTs) are present in electronic waste.

Land filling of electronic waste is not the best operation for the environmental viewpoint.

59. In the field of waste management, extended producer responsibility (EPR) is a strategy to add all of the environmental costs associated with a product throughout the product life cycle to the market price of that product. Extended producer responsibility legislation is a driving force behind the adoption of remanufacturing initiatives because it "focuses on the end-of-use treatment of consumer products and has the primary aim to increase the amount and degree of product recovery and to minimize the environmental impact of waste materials".

Provision of Extended Producer Responsibility (EPR) of producer, importer and brand owner for collecting back the waste generated by their product has been in the:

(*a*) Solid Waste Management Rules, 2016

(*b*) Construction & Demolition Waste Management Rules, 2016

(*c*) Plastic Waste Management Rules, 2016

(*d*) E-waste (Management) Rules, 2016

(*e*) Biomedical Waste Management Rules, 2016.

60. The basic objectives of the National Forest Policy, 1988 are:

- Maintenance of environmental stability through preservation and, where necessary, restoration of the ecological balance that has been adversely disturbed by serious depletion of forests.
- Conservation of the natural heritage by preserving the remaining natural forests with the vast variety of flora and fauna, which represents remarkable biological diversity and genetic resources.
- Substantial increase of forcst/tree cover through massive afforestation and social forestry programmes, especially on denuded, degraded and unproductive lands
- Meeting of the requirements of fuelwood, fodder, minor forest produce and small timber of the rural and tribal population
- Increasing the productivity of forests to meet essential national needs.
- Encouragement of efficient utilization of forest produce and maximization of wood substitution.
- Recognition of the rights of forest dependent communities.

61. Covariance measures the directional relationship between the returns on two assets. The covariance values of the variable can lie anywhere between $-\infty$ to $+\infty$. A negative value indicates a negative relationship whereas a positive value indicates a positive relationship between the variables. When the covariance value is zero, it indicates that there is no relationship between the variables.

62. Positive Skewness: A distribution in which more than half of the area under the curve is to be the right side of the mode, is a positively skewed distribution.The curve of this type of distribution have their right side more spread than the left one. This skewness is sometimes called skewed to the right. Thus, in a positively skewed distribution, its right tail is longer than left tail. Under such a distribution 'mean' is greater than the 'mode'. It is clear from figure 1.

$(\bar{X} > M > Z)$

$(Q_3 - M > M - Q_1)$

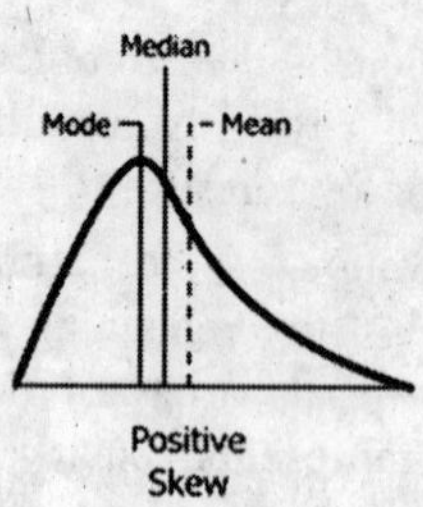

Figure 1

Negative Skewness: A distribution in which more than half of the area under the curve is to the left side of the mode is a negatively skewed distribution.Therefore, it is also called as skewed to the left. Thus, in a negatively skewed distribution, its left tail is longer than the right tail. Under such a distribution, mean is Less than mode. This fact can be made clear by following figure 2:

$\left(\bar{X} < M < Z\right)$

$(Q_3 - M < M - Q_1)$

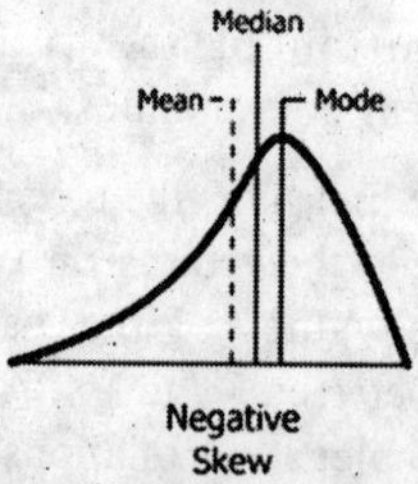

Figure 2

Karl Pearson's coefficient of skewness lies between –3 and +3.

Bowley's coefficient of skewness is bitterly used when the given distribution has open end class. Bowley's coefficient of skewness lies between –1 and +1.

63. A normal distribution serves as a good approximation to the distributions of a large number of continuous random variables. It is both continuous and symmetrical. The normal distribution is dependent upon its mean (μ) and its standard deviation (σ).

The standard normal distribution is a normal distribution with a mean of zero and standard deviation of 1. The standard normal distribution is centered at zero and the degree to which a given measurement deviates from the mean is given by the standard deviation.

64. The standard error (SE) of a statistic is the approximate standard deviation of a statistical sample population. The standard error is a statistical term that measures the accuracy with which a sample distribution represents a population by using standard deviation.

The precision of the sample estimate of some population parameter is the reciprocal of the standard error of the sampling distribution of the estimate.

65. (*i*) A Campbell-Stokes sunshine recorder concentrates sunlight through a glass sphere onto a recording card placed at its focal point. The length of the burn trace left on the card represents the sunshine duration.

(*ii*) A pyrheliometer is used to measure direct solar radiation from the sun and its marginal periphery. To measure direct solar radiation correctly, its receiving surface must be arranged to be normal to the solar direction.

(*iii*) A pyranometer is used to measure global solar radiation falling on a horizontal surface. Its sensor has a horizontal radiation-sensing surface that absorbs solar radiation energy from the whole sky (i.e. a solid angle of 2π *sr*) and transforms this energy into heat.

(*iv*) Lighting professionals use a light meter (also called an illuminance meter or lux meter) to measure the amount of light in a space/on a particular work surface. The light meter has a sensor that measures the light falling on it and provides the user with a measurable illuminance reading.

66. (*i*) Fourier Transform Infrared (FTIR) Spectroscopy is used to perform qualitative and quantitative analysis of organic compounds and to determines the chemical structure of many inorganic compounds.

(ii) Filters are measured by means of X-ray Fluorescence (XRF) based technique such as micro-XRF and grazing incidence XRF using synchrotron radiation, Mo or W excitation sources, after applying an automatized sample preparation method.

(iii) The use of Scanning Electron Microscope (SEM) has found application in the field of particulate air pollution for several years; its use has helped the study of particle morphology and single particles chemical composition.

(iv) XRD analysis can investigate crystalline material structure, including atomic arrangement, crystallite size, and imperfections.

67. 1. Primary producers are photosynthesizing organisms (the plants); which support the rest of the food chain.

2. Primary consumers are also called herbivores (eat plants); they eat the primary producers. Consumers cannot carry out photosynthesis and get their nutrients and energy by eating other things.

3. Secondary consumers eat the primary consumers, tertiary consumers eat the secondary consumers, and so on. They are all called carnivores because they eat meat. Omnivores eat both plants and meat. Scavengers, like vultures, consume animals that are already dead,

4. Detritivores, such as worms and ants, consume detritus (litter, debris and dung).

5. Decomposers, such as fungi and bacteria, complete the final breakdown of organic matter and return nutrient to the soil to fertilize the producers.

68. Lithophile, siderophile and chalcophile refer to the tendency of the element to partition into a silicate, metal, or sulfide liquid respectively.

Lithophile elements are those showing an affinity for silicate phases and are concentrated in the silicate portion (crust and mantle) of the earth.

Siderophile elements have an affinity for a metallic liquid phase. They are depleted in the silicate portion of the earth and presumably concentrated in the core.

Chalcophile elements have an affinity for a sulfide liquid phase. They are also depleted in the silicate earth and may be concentrated in the core.

Atmophile elements are generally extremely volatile (i.e., they form gases or liquids at the surface of the Earth) and are concentrated in the atmosphere and hydrosphere.

69. The factor of grade size is the one most used for the classification of sedimentary rocks. Four groups may be distinguished:

1. **Rudaceous:** Rocks consisting chiefly of gravel, pebbles, cobbles, or boulders. Loose materials of this class are gravels, pebble-beds, shingle, boulder-beds, scree, talus, etc. When cemented they form conglomerates and breccias.
2. **Arenaceous:** Rocks consisting chiefly of material of sand grade. Loose materials are sands; when consolidated they form sandstones, grits, arkoses, graywackes, etc.
3. **Silt Rocks:** Rocks consisting chiefly of material of silt grade. Silt and siltstones. This class is usually included either with the arenaceous or the argillaceous classes, but several distinct rock types occur in it, and the group is worthy of a separate designation.
4. **Argillaceous:** The clay rocks, consisting of the finest materials of rock decay. Dust, mud, clay, when more or less unconsolidated; mudstone and shale when compacted.

71. The ELR (Environmental Lapse Rate) is the actual rate at which the ambient temperature changes with height.

If no heat is exchanged with the surrounding air during this process, which is called "adiabatic cooling", the rate at which the air cools, the Adiabatic Lapse Rate (ALR) is a constant.

Stable – ELR less than DALR

- ELR < 10°C/km

Unstable - ELR greater than DALR

- ELR > 10°C/km

Neutral - no effect on vertical movement

- ELR = 10°C/km

73. 1. September 16 was designated by the United Nations General Assembly as the International Day for the Preservation of the Ozone Layer. This designation had been made on December 19, 2000, in commemoration of the date, in 1987, on which nations signed the Montreal Protocol on Substances that Deplete the Ozone Layer.

2. In 1985 the United Nations designated the 5th October every year as World Habitat Day. The idea is to reflect on the state of our towns and cities and the basic right of all to adequate shelter. It is also intended to remind the world of its collective responsibility for the future of the human habitat.

3. The International Day of Forests was established on the 21st day of March, by resolution of the United Nations General Assembly on November 28, 2012. Each year, various events celebrate and raise awareness of the importance of all types of forests, and trees outside forests, for the benefit of current and future generations.

4. World Water Day, held on 22 March every year since 1993, focuses on the importance of freshwater. World Water Day celebrates water and raises awareness of the 2.2 billion people living without access to safe water. It is about taking action to tackle the global water crisis. A core focus of World Water Day is to support the achievement of Sustainable Development Goal 6: water and sanitation for all by 2030.

74.

Mechanism	**Description/example**
Radiation	Transfer of heal energy via electromagnetic waves according to Boltzmann's equation: $Q = K\left(T_1^4 - T_2^4\right)$
Conduction	Transfer of energy between two solid objects in contact according to Fourier's equation: Q = KA*dt*/*dx*
Evaporation	Energy transferred during change of phase (water to gas): 58 kcal/g water evaporated
Convection	Transfer of heat energy occurring during the mass movement of gas or liquid.

75. The crucial evidence needed for *r*- and K-selection is whether an organism is allocating a greater proportion of its resources to reproductive activities (*r*-strategists) than another related one (K-strategist) under any and all D.D. and D.I. mortality conditions.

76. There are four levels of membrane filtration. These levels are (from largest to smallest pore size): microfiltration, ultrafiltration, nanofiltration, and reverse osmosis. Each level has a pore size range associated with it and is used to remove certain sized contaminants.

Comparison of Membrane Filtration Levels

Filtration Level	**Microfiltration**	**Ultrafiltration**	**Nanofiltration**	**Reverse Osmosis**
Pone Size Range	0.05-1.0 μm	0.005-0.5 μm	0.0005-0.01 μm	0.0001-0.001 μm
Target Contaminants	Particulate material like algae, Giardia, Crypto, bacteria, and clays	All substances removed by microfilters plus humic acids and some viruses	All substances removed by microfilters and ultrafilters plus dissolved metals and salts	All substances removed by micro-filters, ultrafilters, nanofilters plus smaller dissolved metals and salts

77. The commonly used values of n for the n-per cent exceeded level, Ln are 10, 50, and 90. L10 is the level exceeded for 10% of the time. For 10% of the time, the sound or noise has a sound pressure level above L10. For the rest of the time, the sound or noise has a sound pressure level at or below L10.These higher sound pressure levels are probably due to sporadic or intermittent events.

L50 is the level exceeded for 50% of the time. It is statistically the mid-point of the noise readings. It represents the median of the fluctuating noise levels.

L90 is the level exceeded for 90% of the time. For 90% of the time, the noise level is above this level. It is generally considered to be representing the background or ambient level of a noise environment. L90 is often used to quantify the background noise levels in assessments of noise pollution and nuisance noise from industrial sources.

79. Healthy plants have a high reflectance in the near-infrared between 0.7 and 1.3 μm. This is primarily due to healthy internal structure of plant leaves. As this internal structure varies amongst different plant species, the near infrared wavelengths can be used to discriminate between different plant species.

The contents of chlorophyll a are usually three times higher than chlorophyll b in the leaf tissue. The molecular formula for chlorophyll a is C5J H72 N4 O5 Mg and chlorophyll b is C55 H70 N4 O6 Mg. The chlorophyll molecule contains a porphyrin 'head' and a phytol 'tail'.

Hence , Both (A) and (R) are true, but (R) is NOT the correct explanation of (A)

80. The tropopause is a temperature inversion level (i.e., where a layer of relatively warm air lies above a colder one); the inversion thus acts as a 'lid' limiting both convection and transport from the troposphere into the higher layers of the Earth's atmosphere. Industrial pollutants from the Earth's surface are, therefore, only slowly diffused into the upper atmosphere from the troposphere.

The tropopause is the boundary in the Earth's atmosphere between the troposphere and the stratosphere. At tropopause height and at higher levels, the atmosphere is stable.

81. The wide variability in the electrochemical properties of silicate clays is due to the common process of isomorphous substitution. In this process, cations of comparable size substitute for Si, Ah and Mg ions in the respective tetrahedral and octahedral sheets. For example, the atomic radius of Al is only slightly larger than that of Si, and Al can therefore fit in the center of the tetrahedron to substitute for Si, Ions such as Fe and Zn can substitute for Al or Mg in the octahedral sheet due to their similar size. Isomorphous substitution can occur in either or both of the tetrahedral or octahedral sheets. Because of numerous ionic substitutions, silicate clays in soil are described by structural or unit layer formulae rather than simple chemical formulae.

82. All horizontal axis wind turbines use forced yawing, i.e. they use a mechanism which uses electric motors and gearboxes to keep the turbine yawed against the wind.

83. The net contribution of some countries is less than 1% towards the global CO_2 emissions as a whole.

84. Low energy flux density and large sunshine fluctuation are the fundamental characteristics of solar radiation, and they are also an insuperable barrier for humans in the large-scale exploitation and utilization of solar energy. In solar thermal plants, concrete, metals and glass are the most important materials for which, as with components of conventional thermal power stations, no significant environmental problems are foreseen.

85. Two of the chemical classes under consideration for replacing CFCs are hydrochlorofluorocarbons (HCFCs) and hydrofluorocarbons (HFCs). HCFCs contribute to the destruction of stratospheric ozone, but to a much lesser extent than CFCs.

HFCs and HCFCs are susceptible to attack by OH radicals in the troposphere (lower atmosphere). HFCs do not contain CI atoms and so do not have any ozone depletion potential associated with the well established chlorine catalytic cycle.

Hence, Both (A) and (R) are true and (R) is the correct explanation of (A).

86. Regression analysis is suitable for two variables having a linear causal relationship between them.

A curvilinear relationship is a type of relationship between two variables that has a pattern of correspondence or association between the two variables that change as the values of the variables change.

Hence, (A) is correct, but (R) is not correct.

87. Age-classified models place estimates of fertility and survival rates in a square "projection matrix". In the simplest case (Leslie matrix) the top row of the projection matrix represents age-specific fertility, while the subdiagonal represents age-specific survival. A common extension is to add an element at the lower right that represents survival of 'adults'. The remaining elements of the projection matrix are zero.

88. The Chipko movement or Chipko Andolan, was a forest conservation movement in India. It began in 1973 in Uttarakhand, then a part of Uttar Pradesh (at the foothills of Himalayas) and went on to become a rallying point for many future environmental movements all over the world.

Silent Valley struggle was started in 1973 by an NGO led by school teachers and the Kerala Sastra Sahithya Parishad(KSSP) to save the Silent Valley from being flooded by a hydroelectric project. The valley was declared as Silent Valley National Park in 1980.

The Appiko Movement, a movement similar to the Chipko Movement, was launched in September 1983 by the representatives of a Yuvak Mandali to save the Western Ghats in Southwest India. It was observed by the representatives of the Yuvak Mandali that in areas, which were easily accessible, there was an excessive concentration of trees reserved for felling, and there was also excessive damage to other trees during such course of felling.

Narmada Bachao Andolan is the most powerful mass movement, started in 1985, against the construction of huge dam on the Narmada river. Narmada is the India's largest west flowing river, which supports a large variety of people with distinguished culture and tradition ranging from the indigenous (tribal) people inhabited in the jungles here to the large number of rural population.

89. On February 19, 2016, the Indian Ministry of Road Transport and Highways (MoRTH) issued a draft notification of Bharat Stage (BS) VI emission standards for all major on-road vehicle categories in India.

BS VI proposal include enhanced OBD requirements for all vehicle classes, with first-ever OBD specifications for two- and three-wheeled vehicles, and the introduction of emission limits on nitrogen oxides (NOX), carbon monoxide (CO), and hydrocarbon (HC) for two-wheelers that are equivalent to proposed BS VI norms for light-duty gasoline passenger vehicles. Indian regulations for four-wheeled vehicles follow European Union regulatory pathways.

90. The radiative forcing due to tropospheric ozone and sulfate aerosol changes is evaluated using a radiative wideband model. Stratospheric ozone and Sulphate Aerosol have a negative radiative forcing.

Previous Years' Paper (Solved)

National Testing Agency (NTA)

UGC-NET Junior Research Fellowship & Assistant Professor Eligibility Exam

Environmental Sciences, December-2019*

PAPER-II

Note: *This paper contains* ***hundred (100)*** *objective type questions of* ***two (2)*** *marks each.* ***All*** *questions are* ***compulsory***.

1. What is the theoretical maximum fraction of power in the wind that can be extracted by a horizontal axis wind turbine?

A. ~27% B. ~59%
C. ~16% D. ~75%

2. Given below are two statements, one is labelled as Assertion (A) and the other is labelled as Reason (R).

Assertion (A) : There is a general pattern of increase in biodiversity from equator to poles.

Reason (R) : Due to high level of energy received in tropics, higher is the net primary production, which in turn supports large number of individuals, leading to high biodiversity.

In the light of above two statements, choose the correct options.

A. Both (A) and (R) are true and (R) is the correct explanation of (A).
B. Both (A) and (R) are true, but (R) is not the correct explanation of (A).
C. (A) is true, but (R) is false.
D. (A) is false, but (R) is true.

3. In comparison to its adjoining ecosystems, the biodiversity in the ecotone is:

A. lower B. higher
C. same D. extremely low

4. The ethical view, which argues that any resource of nature is meant for human use/ consumption is termed as:

A. Stewardship B. Utilitarian
C. Ecocentric D. Biocentric

5. Which among the following is the correct sequence of the elements in earth's crust in decreasing order?

A. Oxygen > Aluminium > Silicon > Iron
B. Oxygen > Silicon > Iron > Aluminium
C. Oxygen > Aluminium > Iron > Silicon
D. Oxygen > Silicon > Aluminium > Iron

6. The ability of an ecosystem to recover when the system has been disturbed by any perturbation is known as:

A. Resistance B. Homeostasis
C. Climax D. Resilience

7. Match List-I and List-II containing micro-organisms and processes associated with them:

List-I (Microorganisms)	*List-II (Processes)*
(*a*) Bacillus	(*i*) Denitrification
(*b*) Agrobacterium	(*ii*) Ammonification
(*c*) Rhizobium	(*iii*) Sulphur into Sulphate
(*d*) Thiobacillus	(*iv*) N-fixation

Choose the correct answer from the options given below:

	(*a*)	(*b*)	(*c*)	(*d*)
A.	(*i*)	(*iii*)	(*iv*)	(*ii*)
B.	(*ii*)	(*iv*)	(*i*)	(*iii*)

* *Online exam held on 5-12-2019.*

C.	*(iii)*	*(iv)*	*(ii)*	*(i)*
D.	*(ii)*	*(i)*	*(iv)*	*(iii)*

8. Which of the following statements in **incorrect**?

A. Thermosphere and stratosphere are characterized by an increase in temperature with altitude.

B. Troposphere and mesosphere are characterized by a decrease in temperature with altitude in general.

C. Lowest temperature is found at tropopause.

D. Lapse rates determine the vertical stability of the atmosphere.

9. Which one among the following is NOT a type of tidal power plant?

A. Single basin double-effect plant

B. Single basin with linked operation

C. Double basin with linked operation

D. Double basin with paired operation

10. The bioremediation technology which involves the addition of microbial culture is known as:

A. Enhanced Bioremediation

B. Bioaugmentation

C. Bioventing

D. Intrinsic Bioremediation

11. Match the celebration of days related to environment with their corresponding dates:

List-I ***(Days)***	***List-II*** ***(Dates)***
(a) Earth Day	*(i)* 2nd February
(b) International Ozone Day	*(ii)* 16th September
(c) International Biodiversity Day	*(iii)* 22nd April
(d) Wetland Day	*(iv)* 22nd May

Choose the correct answer from the options given below:

	(a)	*(b)*	*(c)*	*(d)*
A.	*(ii)*	*(iii)*	*(i)*	*(iv)*
B.	*(iv)*	*(ii)*	*(iii)*	*(i)*
C.	*(iii)*	*(ii)*	*(i)*	*(iv)*
D.	*(iii)*	*(ii)*	*(iv)*	*(i)*

12. Match the following iron oxides with their chemical formulae:

List-I ***(Iron Oxides)***	***List-II*** ***(Chemical Formulae)***
(a) Haematite	*(i)* $FeO.\ TiO_2$
(b) Magnetite	*(ii)* Fe_3O_4
(c) Ilmenite	*(iii)* $FeO.\ H_2O$
(d) Limonite	*(iv)* Fe_2O_3

Choose the correct answer from the options given below:

	(a)	*(b)*	*(c)*	*(d)*
A.	*(iv)*	*(ii)*	*(iii)*	*(i)*
B.	*(ii)*	*(iv)*	*(i)*	*(iii)*
C.	*(ii)*	*(iv)*	*(iii)*	*(i)*
D.	*(iv)*	*(ii)*	*(i)*	*(iii)*

13. Mean marks of 200 students in statistics are 47. The mean marks of top 25% students are 72 and that of bottom 25% students are 25. Which of the following are the mean marks of the remaining students?

A. 48.5 B. 47.5

C. 45.5 D. 44.5

14. Assuming the incoming solar radiation to be 100 units. Consider the following statements about the radiation budget of earth:

(a) About 51 units of solar radiation are absorbed by earth's surface.

(b) About 20 units of long-wave radiation emitted from earth's surface are lost to space directly without being absorbed by the atmosphere.

(c) About 19 units of solar radiation are absorbed by the atmosphere.

Which of the above statements are correct?

A. *(a)* and *(b)* only

B. *(b)* and *(c)* only

C. *(a)* and *(c)* only

D. *(a)*, *(b)* and *(c)* only

15. Consider the following statements regarding sampling:

(a) The sample mean is an unbiased estimate of the population mean.

(b) For small samples, the sample variance is an unbiased estimate of the population variance.

(c) If we reject the null hypothesis when it is actually true, we commit the type-I error in testing the hypothesis.

Which of the above statements are correct?

A. (a) and (b) only
B. (a) and (c) only
C. (b) and (c) only
D. (a), (b) and (c) only

16. Consider the following statements regarding Poisson Distribution:

(a) It is a continuous probability distribution.
(b) It is applicable when 'n' the number of trials is indefinitely large and 'p' the probability of success is indefinitely small.
(c) Its mean is equal to its variance.

Which of the above statements are correct?

A. (a) and (b) only B. (b) and (c) only
C. (a) and (c) only D. (a), (b) and (c) only

17. Match the following discontinuities with the boundaries they are found at:

List-I (Discontinuities)	List-II (Boundaries Between)
(a) Mohorovicic discontinuity	(i) Lower mantle and outer core
(b) Conrad discontinuity	(ii) Hydrosphere and crust
(c) Lehman discontinuity	(iii) Lower crust and upper mantle
(d) Gutenberg discontinuity	(iv) Outer core and inner core

Choose the correct answer from the options given below:

	(a)	(b)	(c)	(d)
A.	(iii)	(ii)	(iv)	(i)
B.	(i)	(iii)	(ii)	(iv)
C.	(iii)	(ii)	(i)	(iv)
D.	(iv)	(iii)	(ii)	(i)

18. In an objective type examination, there are 100 questions. One mark is awarded for each correct answer and 0.125 marks are deducted for each incorrect answer. The number of marks scored by the students in this examination is an example of which of the following types of variables?

A. Discrete B. Continuous
C. Nominal D. Ordinal

19. Given below are two statements, one is labelled as Assertion (A) and the other is labelled as Reason (R).

Assertion (A) : Isostacy is the corresponding state of balance between extensive blocks of earth's crust which rise to different levels and appear at the surface as mountains, plateaus, plains or ocean floor.

Reason (R) : There is a certain minimum depth below sea level where the pressure due to the weight of overlying material in each unit column is everywhere the same.

In the light of above two statements, choose the correct options.

A. Both (A) and (R) are true and (R) is the correct explanation of (A).
B. Both (A) and (R) are true, but (R) is not the correct explanation of (A).
C. (A) is true, but (R) is false.
D. (A) is false, but (R) is true.

20. Match the following commonly used separation equipments with their separates:

List-I (Equipment)	List-II (Separate)
(a) Electromagnetic Separator	(i) Heavy and light fraction
(b) Trommel Screen	(ii) Non-ferrous metals
(c) Air Classifier	(iii) Ferrous Metals
(d) Eddy Current Separator	(iv) Particulates

Choose the correct answer from the options given below:

	(a)	(b)	(c)	(d)
A.	(i)	(ii)	(iv)	(iii)
B.	(iii)	(iv)	(i)	(ii)
C.	(ii)	(iv)	(iii)	(i)
D.	(iii)	(i)	(iv)	(ii)

21. The probability density function of a continuous random variable x is given by

$$f(x) = \begin{cases} 3e^{-x} & \text{for } x > 0 \\ 0 & \text{for } x \le 0 \end{cases}$$

Which of the following would be the probability that x lies between 1 and 2?

A. $e^{-3} - e^{-6}$ B. $e^{-6} - e^{-3}$
C. $9(e^{-6} - e^{-3})$ D. $9(e^{-3} - e^{-6})$

22. Given below are two statements, one is labelled as Assertion (A) and the other is labelled as Reason (R).

Assertion (A): Himalayan states of India have greater hydropower potential.

Reason (R) : Hills provide an altitudinal gradient for the construction of dams.

In the light of above two statements, choose the correct options.

A. Both (A) and (R) are true and (R) is the correct explanation of (A).
B. Both (A) and (R) are true, but (R) is not the correct explanation of (A).
C. (A) is true, but (R) is false.
D. (A) is false, but (R) is true.

23. Solar insolation on a rectangular module (1.5 m × 2.0 m) of photovoltaic cells is 550 W/m^2. If the efficiency of the cells is 12%, what is the power output of the module?

A. 396 W B. 240 W
C. 99 W D. 198 W

24. Polar Stratospheric Clouds facilitate which of the following reactions in the development of ozone hole?

A. $Cl_2 + h\nu \rightarrow 2Cl$
B. $ClNO_3 + HCl \rightarrow Cl_2 + HNO_3$
C. $ClO + NO_2 + M \rightarrow ClNO_3 + M$
D. $Cl + O_3 \rightarrow ClO + O_2$

25. Sound emitted from a line source attenuates at which of the following rates as a result of geometrical spreading?

A. ~3 dB per doubling of distance from source
B. ~4 dB per doubling of distance from source
C. ~5 dB per doubling of distance from source
D. ~6 dB per doubling of distance from source

26. Which of the following chemical organic species is/are insoluble in acid or alkali?

A. Fulvic acid
B. Humic acid
C. Humin
D. Both humic acid and humin

27. Which among the following are considered as ecosystem services provided by forest ecosystem?

(*a*) Resins and gums
(*b*) Pollination by insects
(*c*) Climate regulation
(*d*) Timber

Choose the correct option:

A. (*a*) and (*b*) only B. (*b*) and (*c*) only
C. (*b*) and (*d*) only D. (*c*) and (*d*) only

28. Which one of the following is the important hotspot of biodiversity in India?

A. Ganga Basin B. Vindhyachal
C. Western Ghats D. Aravali Hills

29. Identify the correct sequence of the components of Producer Gas from biogasification of coal in decreasing order of their concentrations:

A. $CH_4 > H_2 > CO > N_2$
B. $H_2 > CO > CH_4 > N_2$
C. $N_2 > CO > H_2 > CH_4$
D. $N_2 > CH_4 > CO > H_2$

30. Given below are two statements, one is labelled as Assertion (A) and the other is labelled as Reason (R).

Assertion (A): Most of the world's geo-thermal sites are located in the circum-pacific belt known as 'Rim of Fire'.

Reason (R) : Geothermal fields require combination of three geological conditions—a natural underground source of water; an impermeable rock that traps water and allows formation of steam; and a large mass of hot rock in the vicinity of water system.

In the light of above two statements, choose the correct options.

A. Both (A) and (R) are true and (R) is the correct explanation of (A).
B. Both (A) and (R) are true, but (R) is not the correct explanation of (A).
C. (A) is true, but (R) is false.
D. (A) is false, but (R) is true.

31. Which one among the following is true in the context of enthalpy (H), internal energy (U), pressure (P) and volume (V) of a thermodynamic system?

A. H = U – PV B. H = U + PV
C. H = P + UV D. H = P – UV

32. In fast breeder nuclear reactor power plants, the ratio of fissile material produced to fissile material consumed is:

A. Zero B. 1
C. less than 1 D. greater than 1

33. Consider the following wavelengths:

(*a*) 0.94 μm (*b*) 1.14 μm
(*c*) 1.40 μm (*d*) 1.88 μm

Water vapours absorb strongly at which of the above wavelengths?

A. (*a*), (*b*) and (*c*) only
B. (*b*), (*c*) and (*d*) only
C. (*a*), (*c*) and (*d*) only
D. (*a*), (*b*), (*c*) and (*d*)

34. What is the total power per unit area available in a wind stream blowing at a speed of 5 m/s? (Given density of air = 1.226 J/kg.K/m^3)

A. 76.6 W/m^2 B. 15.3 W/m^2
C. 153.3 W/m^2 D. 30.6 W/m^2

35. In case of which of the following fossil fuels, the difference between the Gross Calorific Value and Net Calorific Value is maximum?

A. Natural Gas B. Petrol
C. Diesel D. Coal

36. Which of the following is/are the characteristic(s) of direct band gap semi-conductor Ga-As?

(*a*) less sharp absorption band
(*b*) large values of extinction coefficient

Choose the correct answer from options given below:

A. (*a*) only B. (*b*) only
C. (*a*) and (*b*) D. Neither (*a*) nor (*b*)

37. Given below are two statements, one is labelled as Assertion (A) and the other is labelled as Reason (R).

Assertion (A) : In soil, Chromium (III) predominates Chromium (VI).

Reason (R) : Chromium (VI) is easily reduced to Chromium (III) by organic matter in soil.

In the light of above two statements, choose the correct options.

A. Both (A) and (R) are true and (R) is the correct explanation of (A).
B. Both (A) and (R) are true, but (R) is not the correct explanation of (A).
C. (A) is true, but (R) is false.
D. (A) is false, but (R) is true.

38. Consider the following statements regarding water treatment:

(*a*) Alum is added to water as a coagulating agent.
(*b*) Residual chlorine is considered as a major disadvantage of using chlorination for disinfection of water.
(*c*) Addition of ammonia to water treated with chlorine leads to the formation of chloramines.

Which of the above statements are correct?

A. (*a*) and (*b*) only
B. (*b*) and (*c*) only
C. (*a*) and (*c*) only
D. (*a*), (*b*) and (*c*) only

39. The night-time tropospheric chemistry is dominated by which of the following chemical species?

A. Hydroxyl radicals B. Nitrate radicals
C. Nitrate ions D. Ozone molecules

40. Which is the most significant fingerprint of climate change with respect to biotic invasion?

A. Protozoa B. Mosquitoes
C. Bryophytes D. Gymnosperms

41. Which is the first company in India whose project was approved under the Clean Development Mechanism (CDM) of Kyoto Protocol?

A. Gujarat Fluorochemicals Ltd.
B. Jindal Steel and Power Ltd.
C. RSPL Ltd.
D. Inter-Ocean Shipping Private Ltd.

42. Which among the following is the correct order of stratification in lentic ecosystem from top to bottom?

A. Littoral zone, Limnetic zone, Profundal zone, Benthic zone
B. Limnetic zone, Littoral zone, Benthic zone, Profundal zone
C. Limnetic zone, Benthic zone, Profundal zone, Littoral zone
D. Littoral zone, Limnetic zone, Benthic zone, Profundal zone,

43. In ecological sampling, Importance Value Index refers to sum of which of the following?

(*a*) Relative density
(*b*) Relative frequency
(*c*) Relative abundance
(*d*) Relative dominance

Choose the correct answer from the options given below:

A. (*a*), (*b*) and (*c*) B. (*a*), (*c*) and (*d*)
C. (*b*), (*c*) and (*d*) D. (*a*), (*b*) and (*d*)

44. Which one among the following is NOT a form of precipitation?

A. Snow B. Sleet
C. Hail D. Fog

45. Given below are two statements, one is labelled as Assertion (A) and the other is labelled as Reason (R).

Assertion (A) : The increase in sea water acidity makes building and maintaining shells and other calcium carbonate structures difficult for calcifying organisms such as oyster and water corals.

Reason (R) : Increase in sea water acidity causes a decrease in bi-carbonate ion concentration.

In the light of above two statements, choose the correct options.

A. Both (A) and (R) are true and (R) is the correct explanation of (A).
B. Both (A) and (R) are true, but (R) is not the correct explanation of (A).
C. (A) is true, but (R) is false.
D. (A) is false, but (R) is true.

46. Which of the following surfaces exhibits maximum variation in albedo with respect to the angle of incidence of solar radiations?

A. Water B. Bare Soil
C. Sand D. Vegetation

47. Which of the following greenhouse gases has contributed the most to the global warming?

A. Methane B. Carbondioxide
C. Nitrous Oxide D. Ozone

48. If x and y are two variables that are not independent, then which of the following represents the variance $\text{Var}(ax + by)$ of their linear combination, where 'a' and 'b' are constants?

A. $a^2 \text{Var}(x) + b^2 \text{Var}(y)$
B. $a^2 \text{Var}(x) - b^2 \text{Var}(y)$
C. $a^2 \text{Var}(x) + b^2 \text{Var}(y) + 2ab \text{Cov}(x, y)$
D. $a^2 \text{Var}(x) + b^2 \text{Var}(y) - 2ab \text{Cov}(x, y)$

49. Given below are two statements, one is labelled as Assertion (A) and the other is labelled as Reason (R).

Assertion (A) : Between organophosphorus pesticides malathion and parathion, the former is more toxic than latter.

Reason (R) : Malathion is hydrolyzed by enzymes possessed by mammals to produce relatively non-toxic products.

In the light of above two statements, choose the correct options:

A. Both (A) and (R) are true and (R) is the correct explanation of (A).

B. Both (A) and (R) are true, but (R) is not the correct explanation of (A).

C. (A) is true, but (R) is false.

D. (A) is false, but (R) is true.

50. Consider the following statements:

Statement I : Objects at higher temperature emit higher amount of electromagnetic radiations.

Statement II : Objects with higher temperatures reach their maximum emissive intensity at longer wavelengths.

Which of the above statements is/are correct?

A. I and II both B. I only

C. II only D. Neither I nor II

51. According to Biomedical Waste Management Rules 2016 of the Government of India, which coloured non-chlorinated plastic bags should be used for the collection of human anatomical waste?

A. Yellow B. Red

C. White D. Blue

52. Consider the following statements:

(*a*) Chromium (III) chemical species is more toxic than Chromium (VI)

(*b*) Dimethylmercury chemical species is more toxic than methylmercury ion

(*c*) Arsenic (III) is more toxic than Arsenic (V)

Which of the above statements is/are correct?

A. (*b*) only B. (*a*), (*b*) and (*c*)

C. (*c*) only D. (*a*) and (*c*) only

53. In the context of gaseous pollutants control using packed towers, consider the following statements:

(*a*) The flow of the effluent gas through a packed tower is countercurrent

(*b*) The packing material should have a small surface to volume ratio

(*c*) The packing material is used to increase the contact time between the gaseous pollutant and liquid

Which of the above statements are correct?

A. (*a*) and (*b*) only

B. (*b*) and (*c*) only

C. (*a*) and (*c*) only

D. (*a*), (*b*) and (*c*) only

54. Consider the following characteristics of plant species:

(*a*) small size

(*b*) long life span

(*c*) low rate of growth

(*d*) production of large number of easily dispersed seeds

Which of the above characterize the early successional (pioneer) plant communities?

A. (*a*) and (*b*) only B. (*a*) and (*c*) only

C. (*b*) and (*c*) only D. (*a*) and (*d*) only

55. Above the earth's surface, 90% of the total atmospheric mass is confined within first:

A. 5 km B. 10 km

C. 20 km D. 30 km

56. Artesian Well is:

A. Artificial well

B. Natural well in fault planes

C. Water underneath the surface having sufficient hydraulic pressure

D. Water underneath the surface having very low hydraulic pressure

57. Which group of microorganisms dominate in glacial ecosystems?

A. Psychrophiles B. Thermophiles

C. Mesophiles D. Acidophiles

58. Identify the correct sequence of processes involved in chemical weathering of rocks:

A. Hydrolysis, Solution, Hydration, Oxidation, Carbonation

B. Solution, Hydrolysis, Hydration, Carbonation, Oxidation

C. Hydrolysis, Oxidation, Carbonation, Hydration, Solution

D. Hydrolysis, Hydration, Carbonation, Oxidation, Solution

59. Section 3B of the Forest (Conservation) Act, 1980 deals with the:

A. penalty for contravention of the provisions

B. cases in which offences are made by authorities

C. restriction on the state government for conversion of forests for non-forestry purposes

D. provision for using the natural resources from the forest by the community

60. Match List-I and List-II containing Acts and their year of enactment:

List-I (Act)	***List-II (Year of Enactment)***
(*a*) The Environment Protection Act	(*i*) 1980
(*b*) The Forest Conservation Act	(*ii*) 1981
(*c*) Water (Prevention & Control) Act	(*iii*) 1986
(*d*) Air (Prevention & Control) Act	(*iv*) 1974

Choose the correct answer from the options given below:

	(*a*)	(*b*)	(*c*)	(*d*)
A.	(*i*)	(*iii*)	(*iv*)	(*ii*)
B.	(*iii*)	(*i*)	(*iv*)	(*ii*)
C.	(*ii*)	(*iv*)	(*iii*)	(*i*)
D.	(*iv*)	(*ii*)	(*iii*)	(*i*)

61. Identify the INCORRECT statement about organophosphate pesticides from the following statements:

A. They are generally non-persistent.

B. They do not accumulate in the food chain.

C. They are toxic to humans.

D. They decompose and metabolize slowly.

62. Strike–slip faults are examples of plate movement which is:

A. perpendicular to the strike of the fault plane

B. parallel to the strike of the fault plane

C. at 45° to the strike of the fault plane

D. not in the faultzone

63. Consider the following statements about the Lotka-Volterra Model:

(*a*) Both the populations of prey and predator oscillate sinusoidically

(*b*) There is a phase difference of $\pi/2$ between the prey and predator populations

(*c*) Populations of prey and predator are directly proportional to each other

(*d*) Population of prey and predator are inversely proportional to each other

Which of the above statements are correct?

A. (*a*) and (*b*) only B. (*a*) and (*c*) only

C. (*a*) and (*d*) only D. (*b*) and (*d*) only

64. The landscape used by wild animals for their movement between forest patches, is called:

A. Wildlife Corridor B. Forest Edge

C. Public Corridor D. Resource Corridor

65. Given below are two statements, one is labelled as Assertion (A) and the other is labelled as Reason (R).

Assertion (A) : Aluminium Chloride is a good coagulant for treatment of raw water.

Reason (R) : Both the colloidal particles and Aluminium ions are positively charged.

In the light of above two statements, choose the correct options.

A. Both (A) and (R) are true and (R) is the correct explanation of (A).

B. Both (A) and (R) are true, but (R) is not the correct explanation of (A).

C. (A) is true, but (R) is false.

D. (A) is false, but (R) is true.

66. Which one among the following is the correct order of steps taken during the process of Environmental Impact Assessment (EIA)?

A. Scoping, Screening, Public Hearing, EIA, Issue of Environmental Clearance

B. Screening, Public Hearing, Scoping, EIA, Issue of Environmental Clearance

C. Screening, Scoping, EIA, Public Hearing, Issue of Environmental Clearance

D. Screening, EIA, Scoping, Public Hearing, Issue of Environmental Clearance

67. Consider the following changes with regard to dissolution of ammonia in water:

(*a*) increase in temperature
(*b*) decrease in pH of the solution
(*c*) increase in partial pressure of ammonia

The solubility of ammonia would increase by which of the above changes?

A. (*a*) and (*b*) only B. (*a*), (*b*) and (*c*)
C. (*b*) and (*c*) only D. (*a*) only

68. Consider the following gases:

(*a*) CO (*b*) CH_4
(*c*) HCFCs (*d*) CO_2
(*e*) SO_3

Those gases removed from the atmosphere by the process of oxidation are:

A. (*a*), (*b*), (*c*) and (*d*) only
B. (*a*), (*b*) and (*c*) only
C. (*a*), (*d*) and (*e*) only
D. (*a*), (*b*), (*c*), (*d*) and (*e*)

69. When a stable layer exists below the stack height and an unstable layer above, which of the following types of plume behaviour is expected to be observed?

A. Looping B. Coning
C. Fumigating D. Lofting

70. Which of the following statements is NOT correct with regard to chemical analysis by flame photometer?

A. The intensity of the colour tells us the amount of the element present.
B. The wavelength of the colour identifies the element present.
C. The ions absorb the energy from the flame and get excited.
D. When ion returns from excited state to ground state, it absorbs the radiation of a characteristic frequency.

71. Beaufort Scale is used to classify which of the following meteorological parameters?

A. Pressure B. Precipitation
C. Wind Direction D. Wind Velocity

72. How many years will it take for the population of a country to double, if it grows at the rate of 4 percent per year?

A. ~ 17.3 years B. ~ 13.8 years
C. ~ 15 years D. ~ 25 years

73. Which of the following particulate control devices has the poorest removal efficiency for particles in the sub-micron size range?

A. Electrostatic Precipitator
B. Fabric Filter
C. Cyclone
D. Venturi Scrubber

74. Which of the following measures of skewness is based on the distance of upper and lower quartiles from the median value in a dataset?

A. Karl Pearson's Coefficient of Skewness
B. Kelly's Measure of Skewness
C. Bowley's Coefficient of Skewness
D. Coefficient of Skewness based on moments

75. Which one of the following is NOT a constituent of photochemical smog?

A. Peroxy Benzoyl Nitrate
B. Ozone
C. Polycyclic Armoatic Hydrocarbons
D. Peroxy Acetyl Nitrate

76. Phytoremediation is an important tool for:

A. improving the health of diseased plants
B. removing dissolved oxygen from the aquatic ecosystem
C. eradicating the invasive species
D. removing toxic chemicals from the polluted ecosystem

77. Restoration of Doon Valley is an example of best practices of restoration of degraded ecosystem caused by:

A. over exploitation by the high influx of tourists
B. construction and widening of roads
C. limestone quarrying
D. massive civil works of building constructions

78. Consider the following statements regarding Chi-Square test:

(*a*) If X is a random variable following normal distribution with mean μ and standard deviation σ, then $\left(\frac{X-\mu}{\sigma}\right)^2$ is a Chi-square variate with 1 degree of freedom (*b*) It is an appropriate test for testing the goodness of fit of a model/theory to experimental data

(*c*) It involves computing the squares of the deviations of observed frequencies from the expected frequencies

Which of the above statements are correct?

A. (*a*) and (*b*) only B. (*b*) and (*c*) only

C. (*a*) and (*c*) only D. (*a*), (*b*) and (*c*)

79. 50 mm of rainfall was recorded during 30 min of rain in an area of 2.5 ha. The total volume of water that fell on that area during the rain would be:

A. 625 m^3 B. 1250 m^3

C. 18,750 m^3 D. 37,500 m^3

80. Which among the following radioactive species have a half life of more than 10 years?

(*a*) $_{36}Kr^{91}$ (*b*) $_{38}Sr^{90}$

(*c*) $_{55}Cs^{137}$ (*d*) $_{40}Zr^{91}$

Choose the correct option from those given below:

A. (*a*) and (*c*) only B. (*b*) and (*c*) only

C. (*a*) and (*d*) only D. (*c*) and (*d*) only

81. Gender is an example of which of the following types of variables?

A. Nominal B. Ordinal

C. Interval D. Ratio

82. Which of the following R_f values is not possible?

A. 0.0 B. 0.5

C. 1.0 D. 2.0

83. La Nina is a Spanish word meaning:

A. The little boy

B. The little girl

C. The son of the ocean

D. The daughter of the ocean

84. Two streams A and B are flowing with flow rates of 20 m^3/s and 5 m^3/s respectively. The concentration of a pollutant X in the two streams are 15 mg/l (stream A) and 50 mg/l (stream B). The two streams join each other. Assume that complete mixing of the streams occurs after joining and the pollutant is a conservative substance. The downstream concentration of the pollutant after the joining of two streams would be:

A. 30 mg/l B. 27 mg/l

C. 25 mg/l D. 22 mg/l

85. Influx of high nutrient load of nitrates and phosphates into an aquatic ecosystem contributes towards:

A. oligotrophication

B. poor primary production

C. extreme oligotrophication

D. eutrophication

86. Who was the woman activist, who initiated the Chipko movement in Reni village of Chamoli district in 1973?

A. Smt. Vimala Bahuguna

B. Smt. Gaura Devi

C. Smt. Ila Bhatt

D. Smt. Amrita Devi

87. As per the Coastal Regulation Zone (CRZ) Notification (1991), CRZ-I includes which of the following?

(*a*) Ecosensitive Zones

(*b*) Fishing Zones

(*c*) Intertidal Zones

(*d*) Development Zones

Choose the correct answer from the options given below:

A. (*a*) and (*b*) only B. (*b*) and (*c*) only

C. (*c*) and (*d*) only D. (*a*) and (*c*) only

88. Suppose a remote sensor records brightness levels in terms of digital numbers (DN) ranging from 0 to 255. The histogram of a scene recorded by the remote sensor shows the brightness values ranging from 60 to 158. A researcher wants to apply Linear Contrast Stretch to all the pixels in the scene. If DN′ represents the transformed brightness level of a pixel and DN represents its recorded brightness level, which of the following expressions would be the most appropriate?

A. $DN' = \left(\frac{DN - 60}{DN - 163}\right) \times 255$

B. $DN' = \left(\frac{DN-163}{DN-60}\right) \times 255$

C. $DN' = \left(\frac{DN-163}{158-60}\right) \times 255$

D. $DN' = \left(\frac{DN-60}{158-60}\right) \times 255$

89. The Article 48A of the Indian Constitution (Directive Principles of State Policy for Environmental Protection) was inducted in 1976 after the:

A. 42nd amendment B. 40th amendment
C. 28th amendment D. 14th amendment

90. Match the following parameters characterizing humidity of the atmosphere with their definitions:

List-I (Humidity Parameters)	***List-II (Definitions)***
(*a*) Relative Humidity	(*i*) Weight of water vapour per unit volume of air at a given temperature
(*b*) Absolute Humidity	(*ii*) Weight of water vapour per unit weight of total air at a given temperature
(*c*) Specific Humidity	(*iii*) Ratio of vapour pressure to the saturation vapour pressure in percentage at a given temperature
(*d*) Mixing Ratio	(*iv*) Weight of water vapour per unit weight of dry air at a given temperature

Choose the correct option from those given below:

	(*a*)	(*b*)	(*c*)	(*d*)
A.	(*i*)	(*iii*)	(*ii*)	(*iv*)
B.	(*iii*)	(*ii*)	(*i*)	(*iv*)
C.	(*iii*)	(*i*)	(*iv*)	(*ii*)
D.	(*iii*)	(*i*)	(*ii*)	(*iv*)

Directions (Qs. No. 91-95): *Based on the passage given below, answer the questions.*

Among the most interesting techniques for analyzing the earth's climatic history on a scale of hundred's to thousands of years are the study of ocean floor sediments and oxygen isotope analysis. Both methods are used to reconstruct past temperatures and each in part is related to the other. The seafloor sediments contain the remains of organisms that once lived near the surface. When such near surface organisms die, their shell slowly settle to the floor of the ocean, where they become part of the sedimentary record. One reason why seafloor sediments are useful recorders of worldwide climatic change is that the numbers and types of organisms living near the sea surface change as the climate changes.

We would expect that in any area of the ocean/atmosphere interface the average annual temperature of the surface water of the ocean would approximate that of the contiguous atmosphere. The temperature equilibrium established between surface sea water and the air above it should mean that changes in climate should be reflected in changes in organisms living near the surface of the deep sea.

The second technique, oxygen isotope analysis, is based on precise measurement of the ratio between two isotopes of oxygen: ^{16}O, which is the most common, and the heavier ^{18}O. Because the lighter isotope. ^{16}O, evaporates more readily from the oceans, precipitation (and hence the glacial ice that it may form) is enriched in ^{16}O. Of course, this leaves a greater concentration of the heavier isotope, ^{18}O, in the ocean water.

Thus during periods when glaciers are extensive the concentration of ^{18}O in seawater increases; conversely, during warmer interglacial periods when the amount of glacial ice drops dramatically, the amount of ^{18}O relative to ^{16}O in ocean water also drops. Ascertain microorganisms secrete their shells of calcium carbonate ($CaCO_3$), the prevailing $^{18}O/^{16}O$ ratio is reflected in the composition of these hard parts. Consequently, periods of glacial activity can be determined from variations in the oxygen isotope ratio found in shells of certain microorganisms buried in deep-sea sediments.

A second use of the $^{18}O/^{16}O$ ratio technique is its application to the study of cores taken from ice sheets, such as the one covers Greenland.

Here another cause for variation in the oxygen isotope ratio is used-namely, the ratio influenced by temperature. More ^{18}O is evaporated from the oceans when temperatures are high and less is evaporated when temperatures are low. Thus the heavy, isotope is more abundant in the precipitation of warm eras and less abundant during colder periods.

91. Which of the following is expected during the warmer periods?

A. Higher $\frac{^{18}O}{^{16}O}$ in ocean waters as compared to that in cold periods

B. Higher $\frac{^{18}O}{^{16}O}$ in the calcium carbonate shells of organisms as compared to that in cold periods

C. Higher $\frac{^{18}O}{^{16}O}$ in the glacial ice as compared to that in cold periods

D. Lower $\frac{^{18}O}{^{16}O}$ in the glacial ice as compared to that in cold periods

92. Consider the following statements regarding the ratio $\frac{^{18}O}{^{16}O}$:

(*a*) It is greater than one in ocean waters.
(*b*) It is less than one in glacial ice.

Which of the above statements are correct?

A. (*a*) only B. (*b*) only
C. Both (*a*) and (*b*) D. Neither (*a*) nor (*b*)

93. Given below are two statements, one is labelled as Assertion (A) and the other is labelled as Reason (R).

Assertion (A) : Seafloor sediments are useful recorders of worldwide climate change.

Reason (R) : Organisms living near the surface of deep sea are sensitive to variations in water temperature.

In the light of above two statements, choose the correct options.

A. Both (A) and (R) are true and (R) is the correct explanation of (A).
B. Both (A) and (R) are true, but (R) is not the correct explanation of (A).
C. (A) is true, but (R) is false.
D. (A) is false, but (R) is true.

94. Consider the following statements:

(*a*) Water molecules with ^{16}O evaporate more readily from the oceans.
(*b*) Water molecules with ^{18}O are found in greater concentration in glacial ice than in oceans.

Which of the above statements are correct?

A. (*a*) only B. (*b*) only
C. Both (*a*) and (*b*) D. Neither (*a*) nor (*b*)

95. Consider the following statements:

(*a*) The average annual temperature of the ocean surface water is close to the temperatures of contiguous atmosphere
(*b*) Changes in climate can be estimated from $\frac{^{18}O}{^{16}O}$ ratio in the calcium carbonate shells of organisms
(*c*) $\frac{^{18}O}{^{16}O}$ ratio in warmer periods is less in oceans as compared to that in cold periods.

Choose the correct option from those given below:

A. (*a*) and (*b*) only B. (*b*) and (*c*) only
C. (*a*) and (*c*) only D. (*a*), (*b*) and (*c*)

Directions (Qs. No. 96-100): *Based on the passage given below, answer the questions.*

Ozone and ultraviolet radiation are inseparable. It takes UV photons to form ozone from oxygen and UV photons to release the chlorine from CFCs to destroy ozone. Ozone depletion causes ground level UV radiation-an environmental hazard. The wavelength of the electromagnetic radiation that is visible to the human eye and photosynthetically active for plants lies between 400-700 nm. Wavelengths below 400 nm in the ultraviolet are invisible to the unaided human eye. The UV region is conventionally subdivided into UV-A (320-400 nm), UV-B (280-320 nm) and UV-C (200-280 nm). Natural UV is supplied exclusively by the sun, which radiates energy as a black body with an effective surface temperature of 6000 K. Outside the earth's atmosphere, the total solar radiation flux density of 1367 Wm^{-2} is the sum total of visible and IR (1254 Wm^{-2}), UV-A (85.7 Wm^{-2}),

UV-B (21.1 Wm^{-2}) and UV-C (6.4 Wm^{-2}). Close to the top of the earth's atmosphere, the spectrum is essentially extra-terrestrial. By an altitude of 40 km. Os absorption has already made a significant difference, reducing the flux most around 250 nm because that corresponds to the centre of the absorption band. At 20 km. above the surface, photon flux is almost same as the surface value, except for the residual peak at 200 nm. At this level, UV-C is effectively eliminated. Although UV-B is attenuated, the UV-C source flux increases towards the blue and Ozone absorption band weakens towards 300 nm. Both these influences combine to give a significant UV-B flux which is very sensitive to small shift in ozone aborption.

96. Which one of the following statement is NOT correct?
A. UV radiation forms as well as destroys ozone
B. UV radiation only destroys ozone
C. Ozone depletion causes ground level UV radiation
D. UV dissociates oxygen molecule to form oxygen radical

97. Which of the following UV radiation combinations occurs most on earth's surface in comparison to others?
A. UVA and UVB
B. UVB and UVC
C. UVC and UVA
D. UVA, UVB and UVC

98. The lowest contribution to solar constant at top of the atmosphere from electromagnetic radiation is in:
A. IR region
B. UVA region
C. UVB region
D. UVC region

99. The solar radiation flux, irrespective of wavelength bands, is same from earth's surface upto:
A. 40 km B. 30 km
C. 20 km D. 10 km

100. Ozone's absorption of UV radiation in stratosphere is maximum at:
A. 200 nm B. 250 nm
C. 300 nm D. 280 nm

ANSWERS

1	**2**	**3**	**4**	**5**	**6**	**7**	**8**	**9**	**10**
B	D	B	B	D	D	D	C	B	B
11	**12**	**13**	**14**	**15**	**16**	**17**	**18**	**19**	**20**
D	D	C	C	B	B	A	A	B	B
21	**22**	**23**	**24**	**25**	**26**	**27**	**28**	**29**	**30**
*	A	D	B, D	A	C	B	C	C	B
31	**32**	**33**	**34**	**35**	**36**	**37**	**38**	**39**	**40**
B	D	D	A	A	B	A	C	B	B
41	**42**	**43**	**44**	**45**	**46**	**47**	**48**	**49**	**50**
A	A	D	D	C	A	B	C	D	B
51	**52**	**53**	**54**	**55**	**56**	**57**	**58**	**59**	**60**
A	C	C	D	C	C	A	*	B	B
61	**62**	**63**	**64**	**65**	**66**	**67**	**68**	**69**	**70**
D	B	A	A	C	C	C	B	D	D
71	**72**	**73**	**74**	**75**	**76**	**77**	**78**	**79**	**80**
D	A	C	C	C	D	C	D	B	B
81	**82**	**83**	**84**	**85**	**86**	**87**	**88**	**89**	**90**
A	D	B	D	D	B	D	D	A	D
91	**92**	**93**	**94**	**95**	**96**	**97**	**98**	**99**	**100**
C	B	A	A	D	B	A	D	C	B

EXPLANATORY ANSWERS

1. Unfortunately, not all of the power in the wind can be extracted by a wind turbine. This is because some of the kinetic energy is carried downstream of the turbine in order to maintain air flow. This effect imposes a theoretical maximum efficiency of 59% for extracting power from the wind, known as the Betz limit.

The maximum power is generated when downstream of the turbine the wind speed is one-third of the upstream speed u_0 and at the turbine the wind speed is two-third of u_0; *i.e.*,

$$u_2 = \frac{1}{3}u_0 \text{ and } u_1 = (2/3)u_0.$$

2. The increase in biological diversity of some groups from the poles toward the equator is one of the most fundamental patterns of life on earth. Currently more than 30 different mechanisms and factors have been proposed and debated to explain the latitudinal gradient in species diversity. Due to high level of energy received in tropics, higher is the net primary production, which in turn supports large number of individuals, leading to high biodiversity. Hence, assertion is false but reason is true.

3. When a project site includes multiple ecosystems, additional consideration must be given to the unique characteristics that occur at the border ("ecotone") of two ecosystems. Ecotones have greater biodiversity than exists in either adjoining ecosystem. Because these edge areas maintain a source of replacements for each adjoining ecosystem, both ecosystems are more resilient to unexpected disturbance. Consequently, the development of designs that create or enhance ecotones is the most commonly available and cost-effective avenue to restoration for landscape architects. A typical location for ecotone development is at the cusp between a lawn/field and woodland border.

4. Economists typically employ Veblen's name in making two kinds of modification to their essentially individualistic and utilitarian model of consumer behaviour. The first, which is more specifically called the Veblen effect, involves recognizing that the price of a commodity is a culturally significant symbol in its own right, and not merely an index of economic worth or utility. The second, which embraces what are called the 'bandwagon' and 'snob' effects, involve recognition of the fact that an individual's consumption of goods is affected by the behaviour of other consumers. Either an individual's demand for goods or services is increased by the fact that others are seen to be consuming them (bandwagon), or decreased by the fact that others are consuming them (snob).

5. Given the abundance of oxygen and silicon in the crust, it should not be surprising that the most abundant minerals in the earth's crust are the silicates. Although the Earth's material must have had the same composition as the Sun originally, the present composition of the Sun is quite different. The elemental composition of the human body and life in general is quite different.

These general element abundances are reflected in the composition of igneous rocks.

Element	Approximate % by weight
Oxygen	46.6
Silicon	27.7
Aluminum	8.1
Iron	5.0
Calcium	3.6
Sodium	2.8
Potassium	2.6
Magnesium	2.1
All others	1.5

6. Discussion of resilience in the literature often involves the related concepts of resistance and robustness. These stability related properties are all concerned with the relationship between an imposed perturbation and a system's response. Resilience has been broadly articulated as a system's *ability to recover* from disturbance.

   As a simple distinction, resilience is concerned with the system's ability to recover its function post-disturbance, while resistance is concerned with the system's ability to maintain its function against a perturbation. In these contexts, resilience (or resistance) denotes the degree to which the *quantitative* value of any function of interest is recovered to (or maintained at) an initial or reference condition.

7. (*a*) *Bacillus macerans* performs ammonification with the production of ammonia from nitrate

   (*b*) *Agrobacterium tumefaciens* can grow anaerobically via denitrification.

   (*c*) Rhizobium is the bacteria that live in symbiotic association with the root nodules of the leguminous plants. Fixation of nitrogen cannot be done independently. That is why rhizobium requires a plant host. Rhizobium is a vital source of nitrogen to agricultural soils including those in arid regions. They convert dinitrogen into ammonia. Ammonia, being toxic in nature, is rapidly absorbed into organic compounds.

   (*d*) From all of the SOB, the only group that directly oxidize sulfide to sulfate in abundance of oxygen without accumulating elemental sulfur are the Thiobacilli. The other groups accumulate elemental sulfur, which they may oxidize to sulfate when sulfide is limited or depleted.

8. Air is all around us and it extends upwards for many kilometres as the Earth's atmosphere. The atmosphere is commonly described in terms of distinct layers, or regions. The main layers upwards from the Earth's surface are:

   - **Troposphere:** Most of the atmosphere is concentrated in this layer, which extends from the surface to an altitude of about 15 km. The temperature decreases rapidly in this region.
   - **Stratosphere:** This is a dry layer that lies above the troposphere and extends from 15 km to an altitude of about 50 km. Stratosphere is characterized by an increase in temperature because of the horizontal flow of jet streams. The stratosphere also contains the ozone layer.
   - **Mesosphere:** This layer is above the stratosphere in which the temperatures decline with altitude up to 85 km. It is the coldest region of the atmosphere, roughly reaching –85°C.
   - **Thermosphere:** This layer lies above the mesosphere. The temperature again rises with the increase in altitude in the thermosphere.
   - **Exposphere:** This is the topmost layer of the atmosphere. The density of air is so low here that temperature has no significance. The air in this region is filled with ultraviolet rays and zodiacal lights that are a reflection of the Sun on meteoric dust particles.

   Lapse rate: The fall in atmospheric temperature per increase in height. The average lapse rate within the troposphere is about 0.6°C per 100 metres, but the actual lapse rate varies considerably from day to day and from place to place. Lapse rate is some times negative, *i.e.*, temperature increases with height. This is called an inversion Lapse rates determine the vertical stability of the atmosphere

9. Tidal power plants can be broadly classified into the following four categories:

   (*i*) Single-basin single-effect plant

   (*ii*) Single-basin double-effect plant

   (*iii*) Double-basin with linked-basin operation

   (*iv*) Double-basin with paired-basin operation

10. Bioaugmentation is the addition of biocatalysts (generally bacteria, but it also could involve the addition of fungi, genes or enzymes) to degrade target pollutants, either *in situ* or *ex situ*. In most commercial applications, bioaugmentation involves the addition of mixed cultures of bacteria that have been derived from natural environments and demonstrated to be capable or rapid biodegradation of problematic contaminants.

11. (*a*) Earth Day is an annual event celebrated around the world on April 22 to demonstrate support for environmental protection. First celebrated in 1970, it now includes events coordinated globally by the Earth Day Network in more than 193 countries.

(*b*) September 16 was designated by the United Nations General Assembly as the International Day for the Preservation of the Ozone Layer. This designation had been made on December 19, 2000, in commemoration of the date, in 1987, on which nations signed the Montreal Protocol on Substances that Deplete the Ozone Layer.

(*c*) The International Day for Biological Diversity is a United Nations-sanctioned international day for the promotion of biodiversity issues. It is currently held on May 22. The International Day for Biological Diversity falls within the scope of the UN Post-2015 Development Agenda's Sustainable Development Goals.

(*d*) World Wetlands Day occurs annually on February 2, marking the date of the adoption of the Convention on Wetlands on February 2, 1971 when a small group of environmentalists signed an international agreement at the Ramsar Convention in Iran.

12. (*a*) Hematite, also spelled as haematite, is a common iron oxide with a formula of Fe_2O_3 and is widespread in rocks and soils. Hematite forms in the shape of crystals through the rhombohedral lattice system, and it has the same crystal structure as ilmenite and corundum..

(*b*) Magnetite is a rock mineral and one of the main iron ores, with the chemical formula Fe_3O_4. It is one of the oxides of iron, and is ferrimagnetic; it is attracted to a magnet and can be magnetized to become a permanent magnet itself. It is the most magnetic of all the naturally-occurring minerals on Earth.

(*c*) Ilmenite, also known as manaccanite, is a titanium-iron oxide mineral with the idealized formula $FeTiO_3$. It is a weakly magnetic black or steel-gray solid. From a commercial perspective, ilmenite is the most important ore of titanium. Ilmenite is the main source of titanium dioxide, which is used in paints, printing ink, fabrics, plastics, paper, sunscreen, food and cosmetics.

(*d*) Limonite is an iron ore consisting of a mixture of hydrated iron(III) oxide-hydroxides in varying composition. The generic formula is frequently written as $FeO(OH)\cdot nH_2O$. Limonite is one of the three principal iron ores, the others being hematite and magnetite, and has been mined for the production of iron since at least 2500 BCE.

13. Mean marks of 200 students = 47

Total marks of 200 students

$$= 200 \times 47 = 9400$$

Mean marks of top 25% students = 72

Total marks of top 25% students

$$= 200 \times \frac{25}{100} \times 72 = 3600$$

Mean marks of bottom 25% students = 25

Total marks of bottom 25% students

$$= 200 \times \frac{25}{100} \times 25 = 1250$$

Remaining marks

$$= 9400 - 3600 - 1250$$

$$= 4550$$

Remaining students

$$= 200 - 200 \times \frac{25}{100} - 200 \times \frac{25}{100} = 100$$

Hence, mean marks of remaining students

$$= \frac{4550}{100} = 45.5.$$

14. About 30% (30 units) of the incident solar radiation is reflected back to space. Two thirds of the reflected radiation, i.e., 20 units is reflected by clouds, 4 units are reflected by earth surface and the remaining 6 units are reflected by the atmosphere. Out of the remaining 70 units of the incident solar radiation, 19 units are absorbed by the atmosphere and clouds, while the remaining 51 units are absorbed at the earth surface. Out of 19 units of incident solar radiation absorbed during the passage through the atmosphere, 16 units are absorbed in cloud-free air by water vapour, ozone and dust particles, while 3 units are absorbed by clouds. The earth loses the 51 units of solar radiation, which it has absorbed through 21 units of net emission of long-wave infrared radiation from the earth surface (*i.e.,* upward emission of long-wave infrared radiation from the earth surface minus the downward emission of long-wave infrared radiation from the atmosphere to the surface), 23 units of latent heat flux through melting and evaporation of water and 7 units of sensible heat flux through conduction and convection processes.

15. The sample mean is a random variable that is an estimator of the population mean. The expected value of the sample mean is equal to the population mean μ. Therefore, the sample mean is an unbiased estimator of the population mean.

The investigator establishes the maximum chance of making type I and type II errors in advance of the study. The probability of committing a type I error (rejecting the null hypothesis when it is actually true) is called α (alpha) the other name for this is the level of statistical significance.

If a study of Tamiflu and psychosis is designed with α = 0.05, for example, then the investigator has set 5% as the maximum chance of incorrectly rejecting the null hypothesis.

The probability of making a type II error (failing to reject the null hypothesis when it is actually false) is called β (beta). The quantity (1 − β) is called power, the probability of observing an effect in the sample (if one), of a specified effect size or greater exists in the population.

16. The Poisson distribution can also be used for the number of events in other specified intervals such as distance, area or volume.

The Poisson distribution is popular for modeling the number of times an event occurs in an interval of time or space. The Poisson distribution can be applied to systems with a large number of possible events, each of which is rare. The number of such events that occur during a fixed time interval is, under the right circumstances, a random number with a Poisson distribution.

In Poisson Distribution mean is equal to its variance.

17. Earth's interior is made of different kinds of materials. Each of those materials are different from each other by their physical and chemical properties, such as temperature, density etc. Unique layers are there according to their characteristics inside the earth. All those layers are separated from each other through a transition zone. These transition zones are called discontinuities.

There are five discontinuities inside the earth.

Conrad Discontinuity: Transition zone between SIAL and SIMA.

Mohorovicic Discontinuity; Transition zone between the Crust and Mantle.

Repiti Discontinuity: Transition zone between Outer mantle and Inner mantle.

Gutenberg Discontinuity: Transition zone between Mantle and Core.

Lehman Discontinuity: Transition zone between Outer core and Inner core.

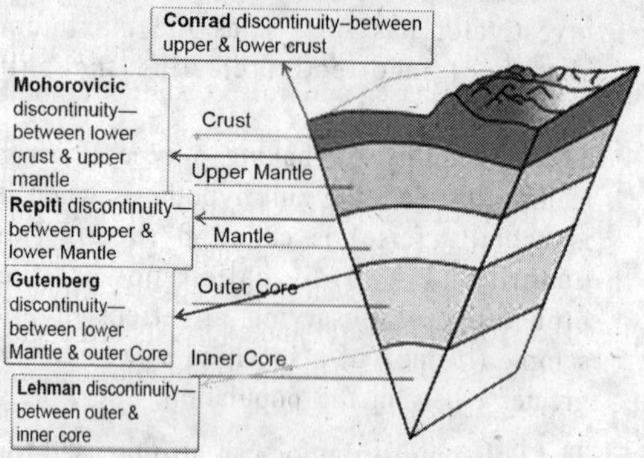

18. Variables that can only take on a finite number of values are called "discrete variables." All qualitative variables are discrete. Some quantitative variables are discrete, such as performance rated as 1, 2, 3, 4, or 5, or temperature rounded to the nearest degree.

In an objective type examination, there are 100 questions. One mark is awarded for each correct answer and 0.125 marks are deducted for each incorrect answer. The number of marks scored by the students in this examination is an example of discrete types of variables.

19. For the ideal condition of gravitational equilibrium that controls the heights of continents and ocean floors, in accordance with the densities of their underlying rocks, the term isostasy. Isostasy is the corresponding state of balance between extensive blocks of the Earth's crust which rise to different levels and appear at the surface as mountain ranges, plateaus, plains or ocean floors. The idea implies that there is a certain minimum depth below sea-level where the pressure due to the weight of the overlying material in each unit column is everywhere the same. In figure this level of uniform pressure is that of the base of the highest block.

Fig. *Wooden blocks of different heights floating in water (shown in front as a section through the tank), to illustrate the concept of isostatic balance between adjacent columns of the Earth's crust.*

20. (*a*) Electromagnetic separators are simple in design and operation. They extract ferrous metals from the wastestream by means of magnetic attraction. Configurations can vary from overhead to under the conveyor belt. Overhead electromagnets pulls waste up out of the wastestream as it travels underneath on the conveyor belt.

(*b*) The trommel screen system consisted of a cylindrical separation device that rotated to perform size separation.

(*c*) Air classifiers are sometimes used in MSW processing systems for separating components of low density and high air resistance, called the light fraction, from components of high density and low air resistance, called the heavy fraction. The light fraction consists largely of paper, cloth, and cardboard, but it also contains light plastics. The heavy fraction consists of metal, glass, stones and heavy plastics.

(*d*) An eddy current separator uses a powerful magnetic field to separate non-ferrous metals from waste after all ferrous metals have been removed previously by some arrangement of magnets. The device makes use of eddy currents to effect the separation. Eddy current separators are not designed to sort ferrous metals which become hot inside the eddy current field. This can lead to damage of the eddy current separator unit belt.

22. India is endowed with rich hydro-power potential; it ranks fifth in the world in terms of usable potential. The Himalaya is the home of many perennial rivers. Typical topography of the Himalaya is suitable for the construction of HEPs. Of the total identified hydro-power potential, 76 per cent is identified as the total hydro-power potential in the Himalayan States. Of this potential, 38.4 per cent is so far harnessed, 85.9 per cent is under construction, 53.46 per cent is going to be developed, which is under construction, and 86.6 per cent capacity is yet to be developed.

Hills provide an altitudinal gradient for the construction of dams.

23. Total Power Output = Total Area × Solar Irradiance × Conversion Efficiency

From question, we have

Total area = 1.5 m × 2 m = 3 m^2

Solar Irradiance = 550 W/m^2

Efficiency = 12% = 0.12

Hence, Total Power output

= 3 × 550 × 0.12 = 198 Watts.

24. Polar stratospheric clouds (PSCs) are clouds that form in the extremely cold and dry conditions that exist in the polar night regions of the stratosphere. PSCs are fundamental to an understanding of the Antarctic ozone hole. PSCs are important because they convert chlorine species that do not destroy ozone (like hydrochloric acid, HCl, and chlorine nitrate, $ClONO_2$) into forms that can destroy ozone.

There are two types of PSCs, referred to as Type I and Type II PSC.

PSC I provides a catalytic surface for a heterogeneous reaction between $ClNO_3$ and HCl that leads to regeneration of active chlorine.

$ClNO_3 + HCl \rightarrow Cl_2 + HNO_3$

and $2Cl + 2O_3 \rightarrow 2ClO + 2O_2$.

25. **Geometric Spreading** refers to the spreading of sound energy as a result of the expansion of the wavefronts. Geometric spreading is independent of FREQUENCY and has a major effect in almost all sound propagation situations. There are two common kinds of geometric spreading: *spherical* and *cylindrical spreading*. A line source will produce cylindrical spreading, resulting in a sound level reduction of 3 dB per doubling of distance.

26. Humin is insoluble, humic acid is soluble only in base, and fulvic acid is soluble in both acid and base. Because of their acid-base, sorptive, and complexing properties, both the soluble and insoluble humic substances have a strong effect upon the properties of water. In general, fulvic acid dissolves in water and exerts its effects as the soluble species. Humin and humic acid remain insoluble and affect water quality through exchange of species, such as cations or organic materials, with water.

27. **Pollination:** Insects and wind pollinate plants and trees, which is essential for the development of fruits, vegetables and seeds. Animal pollination is an ecosystem service mainly provided by insects but also by some birds and bats. Some 87 out of the 115 leading global food crops depend upon animal pollination including important cash crops such as cocoa and coffee.

28. The Western Ghats are one of the world's biodiversity hotspots with over 5,000 flowering plants, 139 mammals, 508 birds and 179 amphibian species. At least 325 globally threatened species occur here. The range covers 60,000 km^2 and forms the catchment area for a complex of river systems that drain almost 40% of India.

29. **Producer gas** is fuel gas that is manufactured from material such as coal, as opposed to natural gas. It can be produced from various fuels by partial combustion with air, usually modified by simultaneous injection of water or steam to maintain a constant temperature and obtain a higher heat content gas by enrichment of air gas with hydrogen.

The average composition of ordinary producer gas according to Latta was: CO_2 : 5.8%; O_2 : 1.3%; CO : 19.8%; H_2 : 15.1%;

CH_4 : 1.3%; N_2 : 56.7%; B.T.U. gross per cu.ft 136. Hence correct sequence is:

$N_2 > CO > H_2 > CH_4$.

31. **Enthalpy,** the sum of the internal energy and the product of the pressure and volume of a thermodynamic system. Enthalpy is an energy-like property or state function-it has the dimensions of energy (and is thus measured in units of joules or ergs), and its value is determined entirely by the temperature, pressure, and composition of the system and not by its history. In symbols, the enthalpy, H, equals the sum of the internal energy, E, and the product of the pressure, P, and volume, V, of the system: H = E + PV.

32. **Breeder reactors** are a type of nuclear reactor which produce more fissile materials than they consume. They are designed to extend the nuclear fuel supply for the generation of electricity, and have even been mistakenly called a potential renewable energy source.

An important concept for a breeder reactor is how much fissionable fuel is being produced compared to how much fuel is being used. This is known as the breeding ratio. For example for the breeding of plutonium, the ratio would be. the amount of plutonium produced to the amount of uranium-235 used. In the liquid metal fast breeder reactor (LMFBR), the breeding ratio is 1.4, however the actual achieved ratio is around 1.2.

34. Power available in wind

$= \frac{1}{8} \times$ air density $\times$ swept area $\times$ wind velocity

$= \frac{1}{8} \times 1.226 \times 1 \times 5 = 76.6$ W.m^2.

35. The terms net calorific value and gross calorific value of a fuel to generate motion or fuel to generate heat describe the amount of heat released in an energy source when it undergoes complete combustion with oxygen.

Net calorific value (H_i) = gross calorific value (H_s) – condensation heat

Gross calorific value (H_s) = net calorific value (H_i) + condensation heat

Therefore, the gross calorific value is always higher than the net calorific value.

The difference between the Gross Calorific Value and Net Calorific Value is maximum for natural gas.

36. Direct bandgap semiconductors (GaAs, InAs, InP, GaSb, InGaAs, GaAsSb), the photon absorption does not require assistant from lattice vibrations. The photon is absorbed and the electron is excited directly from the VB to CB without a change in its k-vector (crystal momentum $\hbar k$), since photon momentum is very small.

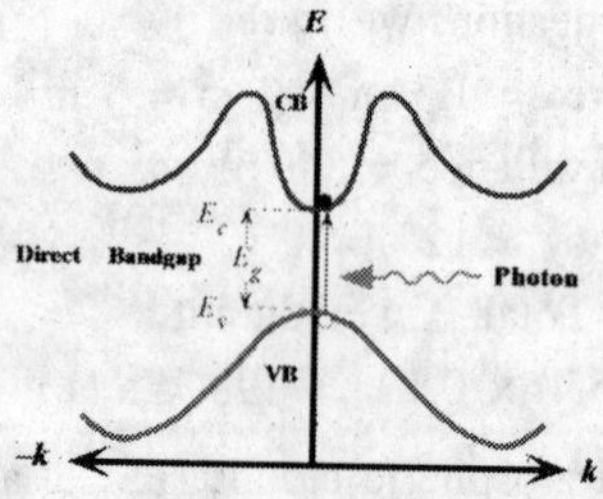

(a) GaAs (Direct bandgap)

$\eta k_{CB} - \eta k_{VB}$ = Photon momentum ≈ 0

Absorption coefficient α for direct bandgap semiconductors rise sharply with decreasing wavelength from λg (GaAs and InP).

37. The fate of chromium in soil is greatly dependent upon the speciation of chromium, which is a function of redox potential and the pH of the soil. In most soils, chromium will be present predominantly in the chromium (III) state. Under oxidizing conditions, chromium (VI) may be present in soil as CrO_4^{2-} and $HCrO_4^-$. In deeper soil, where anaerobic conditions exist, chromium (VI) will be reduced to chromium (III) by S^{2-} and Fe^{2+} present in soil. The reduction of chromium (VI) to chromium (III) is possible in aerobic soils that contain appropriate organic energy sources to carry out the redox reaction. The reduction of chromium (VI) to chromium (III) is facilitated by low pH.

38. The goal of disinfection of public water supplies is the elimination of the pathogens that are responsible for waterborne diseases.

The transmission of diseases such as typhoid and paratyphoid fevers, cholera, salmonell-osis, and shigellosis can be controlled with treatments that substantially reduce the total number of viable microorganisms in the water. Presedimentation to remove suspended matter, coagulation with alum or other agents, and filtration reduce the organic material in the raw water and, thus, the disinfectant demand. Water, particularly surface waters, may also contain synthetic organic molecules whose demand for disinfectant will be determined by their structure. Ammonia and amines in raw water will react with chlorine to yield chloramines that do have some biocidal activity, unlike most products of these side reactions.

39. The chemistry of the nighttime troposphere is usually dominated by reactions of NO_3. This radical can oxidize a number of nonmethane hydrocarbons (NMHCs) and sulphur containing compounds such as dimethyl sulphide (DMS), and it also provides a route for the conversion of the oxides of nitrogen ($NO\bullet = NO + NO_2$) to nitric acid (HNO_3).

40. Climate change, particularly global warming is said to be caused mainly by the greenhouse effect, and the resulting increase in global temperatures is causing diseases and vectors to spread to higher altitudes in mountainous regions and to higher latitudes that were previously free of the infections.

Vector-borne diseases are transmitted by arthropods including ticks and various types of mosquitoes and their spread is enhanced by rainfall, high humidity and high temperature. Malaria is a serious vector-borne disease caused by Plasmodium species is sadly fast spreading widely due to climate change. People in developing countries are most likely to be affected by the impact of climate change on malaria's expansion. Mosquitoes is the most significant fingerprint of climate change with respect to biotic invasion.

41. Gujarat Fluorochemicals Ltd (GFL) is a part of the \$2 billion group of companies. It is a family-owned professionally managed business group, with interest in diverse businesses, including industrial gases, refrigerants, chemicals, carbon credits, cryogenic engineering, renewable energy, and entertainment.

Gujarat Fluorochemicals Ltd has been at the forefront in bringing the concept of carbon credits to India. GFL's Clean Development Mechanism (CDM) projects were the first in the world to seek registration by the CDM Executive Board, a body of the United Nations Framework Convention on Climate Change (UNFCCC). GFL is the largest CDM player in India.

42. Based on the availability of light, lentic ecosystem have well defined and characteristic stratification:

(*a*) **Littoral zone:** It is the shallow water zone near the shore of a lake or pond in which light penetrates up to the bottom. It is typically occupied by rooted and floating aquatic plants. Aquatic life is richest and most abundant in this littoral zone. In ponds and lakes, littoral zone is relatively large.

(*b*) **Limnetic zone:** It is the near-surface zone in the open water that extends up to the depth of effective light penetration and is usually surrounded by littoral zone. Planktons (both phytoplankton and zooplankton) and nektons (fishes) are the abundant biotic forms of the limnetic zone.

Both littoral and limnetic zones constitute the euphotic zone where light penetrates and production is greater than respiration ($P/R > 1$).

(*c*) **Profundal zone:** The deep water zone present beyond the depth of effective light penetration is the profundal zone. This is also termed as aphotic zone were light does not reach and respiration is greater than production ($P/R < 1$). Producers are absent and heterotrophs usually inhabit this zone. The consumers are mainly detritus feeders and carnivores. Such profundal zones are usually present in marine and deep freshwater ecosystems, but are usually small or even absent in shallow waterbodies (like ponds).

(*d*) **Compensation level:** Between the limnetic and profundal zone lies another strata where production equals respiration (i.e., P/R = 1) is known as compensation level.

(*e*) **Benthic zone:** Benthic zone is the bottom region of both littoral and profundal zones. In this zone the dead bodies of plants and animals, organic debris and the materials washed in by inflowing water settle and mainly decomposition takes place. The major community constituents are bacteria, fungi, chironomid larvae, bottom dwelling annelids, clams, etc.

43. Importance Value Index (IVI): IVI is the sum of the relative frequency, relative density and relative dominance. The relative values are calculated as follows:

Relative Frequency

$$= \frac{\text{Frequency of a species}}{\text{Frequency of all species}} \times 100$$

Relative Density

$$= \frac{\text{Density of a species}}{\text{Density of all species}} \times 100$$

Relative Dominance

$$= \frac{\text{Basal area of a species}}{\text{Basal area of all species}} \times 100$$

44. Some of the common forms of precipitation are: rain, snow, drizzle, glaze, slet and hail.

Snow: Snow is another important form of precipitation. Snow consists of ice crystals which usually combine to form flakes. When fresh, snow has an initial density varying from 0.06 to 0.15 g/cm^3 and it is usual to assume an average density of 0.1 g/cm^3. In India, snow occurs only in the Himalayan regions.

Sleet: It is frozen raindrops of transparent grains which form when rain falls through air at subfreezing temperature. In Britain, sleet denotes precipitation of snow and rain simultaneously.

Hail: It is a showery precipitation in the form of irregular pellets or lumps of ice of size more than 8 mm. Hails occur in violent thunderstorms in which vertical currents are very strong.

45. Ocean acidification is affecting the entire world's oceans, including coastal estuaries and waterways. Many economies are dependent on fish and shellfish and people worldwide rely on food from the ocean as their primary source of protein.

Carbonate ions are an important building block of structures such as sea shells and coral skeletons. Decreases in carbonate ions can make building and maintaining shells and other calcium carbonate structures difficult for calcifying organisms such as oysters, clams, sea urchins, shallow water corals, deep sea corals, and calcareous plankton.

46. Albedo is the measure of the diffuse reflection of solar radiation out of the total solar radiation and measured on a scale from 0, corresponding to a black body that absorbs all incident radiation, to 1, corresponding to a body that reflects all incident radiation.

Surface albedo is defined as the ratio of radiosity to the irradiance (flux per unit area) received by a surface . Water surfaces exhibits maximum variation in albedo with respect to the angle of incidence of solar radiations.

47. Carbon dioxide (CO_2) has contributed the most to climate change. CO_2 remains in the atmosphere longer than the other major heat-trapping gases emitted as a result of human activities. It takes about a decade for methane (CH_4) emissions to leave the atmosphere (it converts into CO_2) and about a century for nitrous oxide (N_2O).

After a pulse of CO_2 is emitted into the atmosphere, 40% will remain in the atmosphere for 100 years and 20% will reside for 1000 years, while the final 10% will take 10,000 years to turn over. This literally means that the heat-trapping emissions we release today from our cars and power plants are setting the climate our children and grandchildren will inherit.

48. The variance of a random variable X is a measure of its dispersion around its mean, E(X) defined as:

$Var[X] = \sigma_x^2 = E[(X - E[X]^2]$

$= E[(X - \mu_x)^2] = E[X^2] - \mu_x$

Important Properties of Variance

1. $Var[a] = 0$
2. $Var[aX + b] = a^2 Var[X]$
3. $Var[X + Y] = Var[X] + Var[Y] + 2Cov[X, Y]$
4. $Var[X - Y] = Var[X] + Var[Y] - 2Cov[X, Y]$
5. $Var[aX + bY] = a^2\ Var[X] + b^2\ Var[Y] + 2abCov[X, Y]$.

49. Malathion has two carboxyester linkages, which are hydrolyzable by carboxylase enzymes to relatively nontoxic products as shown by the following reaction:

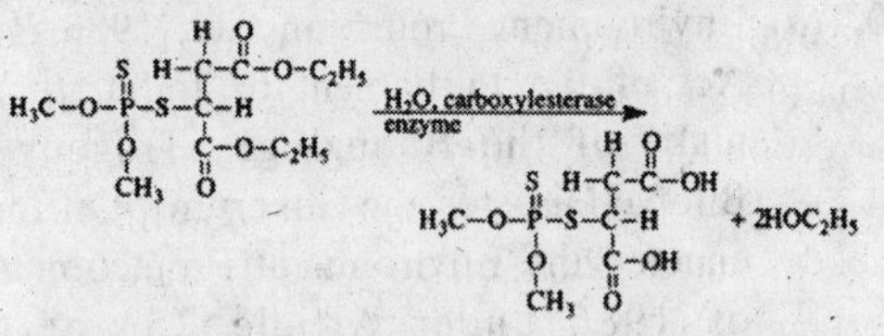

The enzymes that accomplish malathion hydrolysis are possessed by mammals, but not by insects, so that mammals can detoxify malathion, whereas insects cannot; therefore, malathion is selectively toxic to insects.

Other OP compounds include malathion, which is much less toxic than parathion and is used more in horticulture; dithion, diazinon, hexaethyltetraphosphate (HETP), tetraethylpyrophosphate (TEPP), octamethylpyrophosphamide (OMPA) and demeton are other pesticides of this group.

50. Objects that have a very high temperature emit energy at a greater rate or intensity than objects at a lower temperature.

Thus, as the temperature of an object increases, more total radiation is emitted each second. This can be expressed mathematically as

$E = \sigma T^4$ (Stefan-Boltzmann law)

where E is the maximum rate of radiation emitted by each square meter of surface area of the object, σ (the Greek letter sigma) is the Stefan-Boltzmann constant, * and T is the object's surface temperature in degrees Kelvin. This relationship, called the Stefan-Boltzmann law.

51. According to Biomedical Waste Management Rules 2016 of the Government of India, yellow colored non-chlorinated plastic bags should be used for the collection of human anatomical waste.

52. Arsenic is a ubiquitous element with several different forms. The toxicity of arsenic is determined by its form. The prevalent valences are the +3 and the +5 form. Arsenic is found in both an organic form and an inorganic form with valence numbers ranging from +3 to +5. As^{+3}, or arsenite, is more toxic than arsenate, or As^{+5}.

53. Packed towers are typically designated by the flow arrangement used for gas-liquid contact or by the material used as packing for the bed. The most common flow configuration for packed towers is countercurrent flow. A wet-film scrubber uses packing to provide a large contact area between the gas and liquid phases, turbulent mixing of the phases, and sufficient residence time for the exhaust gas to contact the liquid. These conditions are ideal for gas absorption. Large contact area and good mixing are also good for particle collection; however, once collected, the particles tend to accumulate and plug the packing bed.

55. Atmospheric layers are characterized by variations in temperature resulting primarily from the absorption of solar radiation; visible light at the surface, near ultraviolet radiation in the middle atmosphere, and far ultraviolet radiation in the upper atmosphere. Earth's atmosphere is mainly composed of nitrogen and oxygen. Although our atmosphere extends upward for many hundreds of kilometers, 90% of the atmosphere's mass is confined within a 20 km of the earth's surface.

56. **Artesian well,** well from which water flows under natural pressure without pumping. It is dug or drilled wherever a gently dipping, permeable rock layer (such as sandstone) receives water along its outcrop at a level higher than the level of the surface of the ground at the well site. At the outcrop the water moves down into the aquifer (water-bearing layer) but is prevented from leaving it, by impermeable rock layers (such as shale) above and below it. Pressure from the water's weight (hydrostatic pressure) forces water to the surface of a well drilled down into the aquifer; the pressure for the steady upflow is maintained by the continuing penetration of water into the aquifer at the intake area.

57. A **thermophile** is an organism—a type of extremophile—that thrives at relatively high temperatures, between 41 and 122 °C (106 and 252 °F). Many thermophiles are archaea. Thermophilic eubacteria are suggested to have been among the earliest bacteria.

The glacial ecosystems have very unique characteristics, which cannot be seen in other ecosystems. Thermophiles group of micro-organisms dominate in glacial ecosystem.

58. Biotic weathering is often treated separately, although the processes can be related to either physical or chemical processes. Biotic activity can cause or aid chemical processes, and physical effects can be significant. The most important chemical processes are solution, carbonation, hydration, hydrolysis, oxidation and reduction, and organic complexing.

59. The **Forest (Conservation) Act, 1980** an Act of the Parliament of India to provide for the conservation of forests and for matters connected therewith or ancillary or incidental thereto. It was further amended in 1988. The act came into force on 25 October 1980. It has five sections.

Section 3 of the Act deals with constitution of Advisory Committee. It gives Central Government the power to constitute a committee of such number of person as it may deem fit to advise the Government with regard to- (i) the grant of approval for the purpose which is prohibited in section of this act; or (ii) any other matter connected with the conservation of forests which may be referred to it by the Central Government.

Section 3A deals with Penalty for contravention of the provisions of the Act. It states that Whoever contravenes or abets the contravention of any of the provisions of Section 2, shall be punishable with simple imprisonment for a period which may extend to fifteen days.

Section 3B deals with cases in which the offence is made by Authorities or Government Departments. In such cases it says that the Head of the Department shall be considered Guilty, although if he proves that it was done without his knowledge or that he exercised all due diligence to prevent the commission of such offence.

60. (*a*) Environment Protection Act, 1986 is an Act of the Parliament of India. In the wake of the Bhopal gas Tragedy or Bhopal Disaster, the Government of India enacted the Environment Protection Act of 1986 under Article 253 of the Constitution. Passed in March, 1986, it came into force on 19 November, 1986.

(*b*) The Forest Act, 1980 an Act of the Parliament of India to provide for the conservation of forests and for matters connected therewith or ancillary or incidental thereto. It was further amended in 1988.

(*c*) Water Act 1974 aims to prevent and control water pollution. Under Water Act, 1974, pollution control boards were created, who are responsible for implementation of its provisions. One of the important provision of the Water Act,

1974 is to maintain and restore the 'wholesomeness' of our aquatic resources.

(*d*) The Air (Prevention and Control of Pollution) Act, 1981 provide for the prevention, control and abatement of air pollution, for the establishment, with a view to carrying out the aforesaid purposes, of Boards, for conferring on and assigning to such Boards powers and functions relating thereto and for matters connected therewith.

61. **Organo Phosphates:** They are not persistent, but are more acutely toxic to humans than the organo chlorines that they have replaced. They are rapidly absorbed through the skin, lungs, and gastrointestinal tract. The exposed humans have shown a range of symptoms such as tremor, confusion, slurred speech, muscle twitching (jerking) and convulsions. Organo phosphates such as parathion, malathion, diazinon, tetraethyl prophosphate (TEPP), and diamethoate are effective against wide range of insects.

62. A strike-slip fault is present where the movement of blocks bounding the fault is parallel to the strike of the fault. A right-slip, right strike-slip, or right-lateral fault is a strike-slip fault along which strike-slip or strike-separation movement on the side or block of the fault opposite the observer has moved right (strike slip) or seemingly to the right (strike separation).

63. We can use them to draw several conclusions about the cyclic variation of the predator and prey on such trajectories.

1. The sizes of the predator and prey populations vary sinusoidally with period $2\pi/\sqrt{ac}$. This period of oscillation is independent of the initial conditions.
2. The predator and prey populations are out of phase by one-quarter of a cycle. The prey leads and the predator lags.
3. The amplitudes of the oscillations are Kc/γ for the prey and $\sqrt{ac}K/\alpha$ for the predator and hence depend on the initial conditions as well as on the parameters of the problem.
4. The average populations of predator and prey over one complete cycle are c/γ and a/α, respectively.

64. Wildlife movement corridors, also called dispersal corridors or landscape linkages as opposed to linear habitats, 1 are linear features whose primary wildlife function is to connect at least two significant habitat areas (Beier and Loe 1992). These corridors may help to reduce or moderate some of the adverse effects of habitat fragmentation by facilitating dispersal of individuals between substantive patches of remaining habitat, allowing for both long-term genetic interchange and individuals to re-colonize habitat patches from which populations have been locally extirpated.

65. Alum is widely used as a **coagulant** in most of the water treatment plants in spite of its limitations on the temperature, turbidity, pH. Inorganic polyvalent Aluminium salt has been used as a coagulant for treatment of water worldwide. When dose to raw water, inorganic coagulants decrease its alkalinity.

66. The environmental impact assessment in India was started in 1976-77 when the Planning Commission asked the then Department of Science and Technology to examine the river-valley projects from environmental angle.

The EIA Cycle and Procedures: The EIA process in India is made up of the following phases:

1. Screening
2. Scoping and consideration of alternatives
3. Baseline data collection
4. Impact prediction
5. Assessment of alternatives
6. Delineation of mitigation measures
7. Environmental impact statement
8. Public hearing
9. Environmental management plan
10. Decision making
11. Monitoring and clearance conditions.

68. The atmosphere is an oxidizing medium. Many environmentally important trace gases are removed from the atmosphere mainly by oxidation: greenhouse gases such as CH_4, toxic combustion gases such as CO, agents for stratospheric O_3 depletion such as HCFCs, and others.

It is thought that oxidation of species emitted from the Earth's surface, such as CO and CH_4, required transport to the stratosphere followed by reaction with OH in the stratosphere:

$CO + OH \rightarrow CO_2 + H$ (R4)

$CH_4 + OH \rightarrow CH_3 + H_2O$ (R5).

69. Lofting Plume: Under conditions of strong super adiabatic lapse rate just above the stack and negative lapse rate (inversion) just below the opening of stack, lofting plume is obtained.

The upward mixing of plume is very rapid and turbulent, but downward mixing is less because the downward movement is prevented by inversion.

The dispersion of pollutants therefore becomes rapid and pollutants cannot come down to the ground. Such kind of a plume is ideal for dispersion of air pollutants and protection of living beings to a great extent.

70. Flame photometry is a method used for the determination of elements which can be easily excited, for example, alkali and alkaline earth metals. This method is based upon the measurement of intensity of radiation emitted, in the visible region, when a metal atom is introduced into a flame. The wavelength of the radiation (or the colour), emitted tells us what the element is, and the intensity of the radiation tells us how much of the element is present.

71. Beaufort Wind Scale. One of the first scales to estimate wind speeds and the effects was created by Britain's Admiral Sir Francis Beaufort (1774-1857). He developed the scale in 1805 to help sailors estimate the winds via visual observations. The scale starts with 0 and goes to a force of 12.

73. Cyclone separators provide a method of removing particulate matter from air or other gas streams at low cost and low maintenance. The efficiency of cyclones greatly depends on the size of the particulate, the larger particle being removed at higher efficiency than smaller particles.

Among Electrostatic Precipitator, Fabric Filter, cyclone and Venturi Scrubber, cyclone has the poorest removal efficiency for particles in the sub-micron size range.

74. Bowley's Coefficient of Skewness: This method is based on quartiles, i.e., second absolute measure of skewness. The formula for calculating skewness is:

$$Sk_B = \frac{(Q_3 - M_d) - (M_d - Q_1)}{(Q_3 - M_d) + (M_d - Q_1)} = \frac{Q_3 + Q_1 - 2M_d}{Q_3 - Q_1}$$

This method is particularly useful in case of open end distributions and where extreme values are present or when class-intervals are unequal. Skewness should be measured by this Bowley's method also when positional measures are called for.

If the value of this coefficient is zero, it is a symmetrical distribution. For positive value, it is a positively skewed distribution and for a negative value it is a negatively skewed distribution. The range of variation under this formula is ± 1. But the main drawback of this measure is that it is based on central 50% of the data and it ignores the remaining 50% of the data i.e., 25% of the data below Q_1 and 25% of the data above Q_3.

75. Peroxy acetyl nitrate (PAN) is the most abundant peroxy acyl nitrate and is an important component of photochemical smog in urban areas. PAN is largely responsible for the eye irritation experienced in smog episodes and, because of its phytotoxic nature, can damage agricultural crops. Other members of the peroxy acyl nitrate family include peroxy propyl nitrate, $C_2H_5C(O)O_2NO_2$, and peroxy benzoyl nitrate, $C_6H_5C(O)O_2NO_2$, which are found at levels ranging from a few per cent to 30% of that of PAN. Photolysis of NO_2 is an important source of tropospheric ozone and is responsible for the formation of photochemical smog in polluted air masses.

76. **Phytoremediation** is an eco-friendly and advantageous technique for the cleaning of contaminated media. The mechanism involves is absorption of pollutants through roots, accumulation in body tissues, decompose and transforming pollutants to a less harmful forms.

77. Doon valley and Mussoorie hills (Garhwal Himalayas of Uttarakhand, India) till early eighties faced a serious threat due to heavy limestone quarrying with 105 working mines in this region. After the cessation of mining activity restoration of these sites was undertaken by different agencies. The ecological restoration interventions were initiated in these areas during 1988-1989. Ecology of this region was adversely affected by large scale limestone quarrying.

78. Pearson's chi-squared test is used to assess three types of comparison: goodness of fit, homogeneity, and independence.

- A test of goodness of fit establishes whether an observed frequency distribution differs from a theoretical distribution.
- A test of homogeneity compares the distribution of counts for two or more groups using the same categorical variable (e.g. choice of activity—college, military, employment, travel—of graduates of a high school reported a year after graduation, sorted by graduation year, to see if number of graduates choosing a given activity has changed from class to class, or from decade to decade).
- A test of independence assesses whether observations consisting of measures on two variables, expressed in a contingency table, are independent of each other.

79.

$$50 \text{ mm} = 50 \times 10^{-3}$$

$$1 \text{ hectare} = 10000 \text{ m}^2$$

$$\text{Volume of water} = 5 \times 10^{-3} \times 2.5 \times 10^4$$

$$= 1250 \text{ m}^3.$$

80. Several radioactive isotopes were released in huge quantities, contaminating many thousands of square kilometers and directly affecting hundreds of thousands of people. The most significant releases were of ^{131}I, ^{90}Sr, ^{137}Cs, ^{239}Pu, ^{238}U, and ^{235}U. Estimates are that the total amount of radiation released was about 100 million curies.

These radioactive species have a half life of more than 10 years.

81. A categorical or discrete variable is one that has two or more categories (values). There are two types of categorical variable, nominal and ordinal. A nominal variable has no intrinsic ordering to its categories. For example, gender is a categorical variable having two categories (male and female) with no intrinsic ordering to the categories. An ordinal variable has a clear ordering. For example, temperature as a variable with three orderly categories (low, medium and high).

83. In Spanish, "la niña" means "the little girl." It got its name as a direct response to the phrase "El Niño," which means "the little boy," the Spanish diminutive often used to denote the Christ Child.

84.

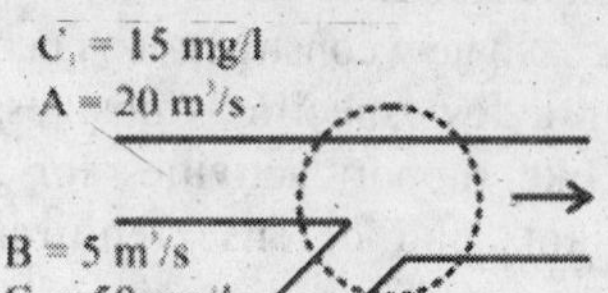

$$C_d = \frac{20 \times 15 + 5 \times 50\,(\text{mg/L.m}^3/\text{s})}{(20+5)\ \text{m}^3/\text{s}}$$

$$= 22 \text{ mg/L}.$$

85. Nitrogen in water is measured as the common form nitrate (NO_3^-) that is dissolved in water and readily absorbed by photosynthesizers such as algae. The common form of phosphorus measured is phosphate (PO_4^{3-}), which is strongly attracted to sediment particles as well as dissolved in water. In excess amounts, both nutrients can cause an increase in aquatic plant growth that can disrupt the light, temperature, and oxygen levels in the water below and lead to eutrophication and hypoxia (low dissolved oxygen in water) forming a "dead zone" of no biological activity. Sources of nitrates and phosphorus include wastewater treatment plants, runoff from fertilized lawns and agricultural lands, faulty septic systems, animal manure runoff, and industrial waste discharge.

86. Gaura Devi was born in 1925 in a village named Lata in the state of Uttarakhand. She moved to a nearby village named Reni by the Alaknanda River. By the age of 22 she was a widow with a child. Her new village was near to the border with Tibet. Gaura Devi was elected to lead the Mahila Mangal Dal (Women's Welfare Association) in the wake of the Chipko movement. The organization worked on the protection of community forests.

87. The Coastal Regulation Zone has been classified as CRZ-I, CRZ-II and CRZ-III in the state for the purpose of regulation of the permitted activities.

CRZ-I: Ecological sensitive area and the area between High Tide Line (HTL) and Low Tide Line (LTL). No new construction is permitted except for a few specified most essential activities like support activities for atomic energy plants and defense requirements, facilities required for disposal of treated effluents and other port related water front activities.

88. The linear contrast stretch would be applied to each pixel in the image uses the algorithm

$$DN' = \left(\frac{DN - MIN}{MAX - MIN}\right) \times 225$$

Where,

DN′ = digital number assigned to pixel in output image

DN = original digital number of pixel in input image

MIN = minimum value of input image, to be assigned a value of 0 in the output image (60)

Max = maximum value of input image, to be assigned a value of 255 in the output image (158)

Thus, required expression is:

$$DN' = \left(\frac{DN - 60}{158 - 60}\right) \times 225.$$

89. The 42nd amendment introduced Article 48A, part of the Directive Principles of State which read, "The State shall endeavour to protect and improve the environment and to safeguard the forests and wildlife of the country." Article 51A (g), part of the Fundamental Duties read, "It shall be the duty of every citizen of India... to protect and improve the natural environment...".

90. Humidity is the amount of moisture (Water vapour) in the air.

Absolute humidity: Absolute humidity is the total amount of water vapour present in a given volume of air. It does not take temperature into consideration. Absolute humidity in the atmosphere ranges from near zero to roughly 30 grams per cubic meter when the air is saturated at 30°C.

Relative humidity: The relative humidity of an air-water mixture is defined as the ratio of the partial pressure of water vapour (H_2O) in the mixture to the saturated vapour pressure of water at a given temperature. Thus the relative humidtiy of air is a function of both water content and temperature.

Specific humidity: Specific humidity (or moisture content) is the ratio of water vapour mass to the air parcel's total (*i.e.,* including dry) mass and is sometimes referred to as the humidity ratio. Specific humidity is approximately equal to the "mixing ratio", which is defined as the ratio of the mass of water vapour in an air parcel to the mass of dry air for the same parcel.

Previous Paper (Solved)

National Testing Agency (NTA)

UGC-NET-Junior Research Fellowship & Assistant Professor Eligibility Online Exam

Environmental Science, June-2019*

PAPER-II

Note: *This paper contains **hundred** (**100**) objective type questions of **two (2)** marks each. **All** questions are **compulsory**.*

1. Wind rose reveals

(*a*) Percentage of time winds persist in a specific direction

(*b*) Most probable direction of winds

(*c*) Percentage duration for which wind speeds are in a given range

(*d*) Wind energy potential

Select the correct answer from the options given below:

A. (*a*) and (*b*) only

B. (*b*), (*c*) and (*d*) only

C. (*a*), (*b*) and (*d*) only

D. (*a*), (*b*) and (*c*) only

2. An aeroplane causes a sound of level 110 dB on taking off. What is the sound level of 5 such identical aeroplanes taking off simultaneously?

A. ~117 dB B. ~115 dB

C. ~113 dB D. ~110 dB

3. Given below are two statements, one labelled as Assertion (A) and the other labelled as Reason (R).

Assertion (A): The occurrence of acid rain over the Indian landmass is extremely rare.

Reason (R): The alkaline dust and ammonia (NH_3) produced from agricultural areas neutralise the acid formation in the atmosphere.

Choose the correct answer from the options given below.

A. Both (A) and (R) are true and (R) is the correct explanation of (A)

B. Both (A) and (R) are true, but (R) is not the correct explanation of (A)

C. (A) is true, but (R) is false

D. (A) is false, but (R) is true

4. The largest unit, in which gene flow is possible, is:

A. Population B. Genus

C. Species D. Family

5. Moderate disturbance in an ecosystem:

A. Increases biodiversity

B. Decreases biodiversity

C. Has no effect on biodiversity

D. Increases carrying capacity

6. Which is the first mineral to form in cooling magma?

A. Olivine

B. Quartz

C. Mica

D. Potassium feldspar

7. In order of intensity of different components of electromagnetic radiation emitted from sun reaching earth's surface, identify the correct sequence:

A. ultraviolet > visible > infrared

B. ultraviolet < visible < infrared

C. ultraviolet > infrared > visible

D. ultraviolet < infrared < visible

* Exam held on 25 June, 2019

8. Given below are two statements, one labelled as Assertion (A) and the other labelled as Reason (R).

Assertion (A): Biogas production is reduced in winters.

Reason (R): Methanogenesis occurs at mesophilic temperatures.

Choose the correct answer from the options given below.

A. Both (A) and (R) are true and (R) is the correct explanation of (A)
B. Both (A) and (R) are true, but (R) is not the correct explanation of (A)
C. (A) is true, but (R) is false
D. (A) is false, but (R) is true

9. Electrostatic precipitator (ESP) is good for controlling:

A. VOCs
B. Greenhouse gases
C. Fine particulate matter
D. Sulphur compounds

10. Which of the following modes of energy generation has maximum conversion efficiency?

A. Hydroelectric
B. Thermoelectric
C. Hydrogen fuel cell
D. Geothermal

11. Which method is most appropriate for separating tin cans from aluminium cans in municipal solid waste?

A. Shear shredding
B. Manual sorting
C. Pelletizing
D. Magnetic field separation

12. Which of the following is a primary air pollutant?

A. Surface Ozone B. Sulphate
C. Nitrate D. Black Carbon

13. Which among the following CAN NOT be categorized as VOCs?

A. Polycyclic Aromatic Hydrocarbons
B. Halocarbons
C. Non-methane Hydrocarbons
D. Oxygenates

14. Given below are two statements, one labelled as Assertion (A) and the other labelled as Reason (R).

Assertion (A): The organic matter helps in formation and stabilization of soil texture.

Reason (R): Humified organic matter has an affinity for water and can absorb and hold water upto several times of its dry weight.

Choose the correct answer from the options given below.

A. Both (A) and (R) are true and (R) is the correct explanation of (A)
B. Both (A) and (R) are true, but (R) is not the correct explanation of (A)
C. (A) is true, but (R) is false
D. (A) is false, but (R) is true

15. Which toxic metal is present in the colour printing inks of magazine pages?

A. Lead B. Cadmium
C. Arsenic D. Mercury

16. What per cent of visible radiation accounts for total solar radiation incident on top of atmosphere?

A. 7 B. 41
C. 56 D. 75

17. Ground truth data in remote sensing is collected for:

(*a*) Analysis of remote sensing data
(*b*) Accuracy assessment
(*c*) Calibration of remote sensing sensors

Choose the correct option:

A. (*a*), (*b*) and (*c*) B. (*a*) and (*c*) only
C. (*b*) and (*c*) only D. (*a*) and (*b*) only

18. Fulvic acid molecules in soil humus are:

(*a*) Randomly coiled
(*b*) More polar
(*c*) Highly charged
(*d*) Smaller molecules than humic acid molecules

Choose the correct options:

A. (*a*), (*b*) and (*c*) only

B. (*b*), (*c*) and (*d*) only
C. (*a*), (*c*) and (*d*) only
D. (*b*) and (*d*) only

19. Fire occurrence in the forests depends on:
(*a*) Fuel load
(*b*) Vegetation type
(*c*) Distance from the habitations
Choose the correct options:
A. (*a*) and (*b*) only B. (*a*), (*b*) and (*c*)
C. (*b*) and (*c*) only D. (*a*) and (*c*) only

20. Predators and parasites are similar in that, both can be characterised by
A. +/+ interaction B. +/–interaction
C. –/–interaction D. +/0 interaction

21. Two important characteristics of any population are:
A. Diversity and density
B. Frequency and density
C. Abundance and dispersion
D. Density and dispersion

22. A country has population of 350 million and an annual growth rate of population 2.0% at $t = 0$. There after the population stabilizes at 1.4 billion. How long it will take for the population to reach 0.7 billion?
A. ~41.2 years B. ~17.9 years
C. ~5 years D. ~35.0 years

23. Consider the following simple regression equation of dependent variable (Y) and explanatory variable (X):

$$Y = a + bX + \in$$

Given the following data: $S^2 = 250$, residual variance = 5, $b = 0.2$ and $a = 0.5$. What will be the overall variance Sy^2?
A. 15 B. 55
C. 45 D. 10

24. Which microbial metabolism involves immobilisation of soluble metal species by forming complexing agents like metal sulphides, metal carbonates and metal phosphates?
A. Biosorption B. Bioaccumulation
C. Solubilization D. Bioprecipitation

25. Hardness of minerals depends on:
A. Chemical composition and physical makeup
B. Physical makeup and atomic constitution
C. Parent material
D. Chemical composition and atomic constitution

26. Major attributes of a restored ecosystem are:
(*a*) Representation of all functional groups
(*b*) Amelioration of physical environment
(*c*) Resilience and integrity
(*d*) Absence of potential threats
Choose the correct options:
A. (*a*) and (*b*) only
B. (*a*), (*b*), (*c*) and (*d*)
C. (*b*), (*c*) and (*d*) only
D. (*a*), (*c*) and (*d*) only

27. Match List-I (ISO Standards) with List-II (Environmental Management Aspects):

List-I (ISO Standards)	**List-II (Environmental Management Aspects)**
(*a*) ISO 14010	(*i*) Environmental auditing
(*b*) ISO 14020	(*ii*) Environmental aspect in product standard
(*c*) ISO 14050	(*iii*) Environmental labelling standard
(*d*) ISO 14060	(*iv*) Environmental terms and definitions

Choose the correct answer from the options given below:

	(*a*)	(*b*)	(*c*)	(*d*)
A.	(*i*)	(*ii*)	(*iv*)	(*iii*)
B.	(*iv*)	(*iii*)	(*i*)	(*ii*)
C.	(*i*)	(*iii*)	(*iv*)	(*ii*)
D.	(*iv*)	(*ii*)	(*iii*)	(*i*)

28. Match List-I (NGO Movements) with List-II (Years of Struggle):

List-I (NGO Movements)	**List-II (Years of Struggle)**
(*a*) Silent Valley Struggle	(*i*) 1973
(*b*) Chipko Movement	(*ii*) 1978
(*c*) Appiko Movement	(*iii*) 1980
(*d*) Gandhamardan Movement	(*iv*) 1983

Choose the correct answer from the options given below:

	(a)	(b)	(c)	(d)
A.	(ii)	(iii)	(iv)	(i)
B.	(iii)	(ii)	(iv)	(i)
C.	(iv)	(i)	(iii)	(ii)
D.	(ii)	(i)	(iv)	(iii)

29. Saturation vapour pressure at a given temperature is 900 mbar while it is 600 mbar at dew point temperature. What will be the relative humidity?

A. 90% B. 66.7%
C. 60% D. 76.6%

30. Simultaneous measurement of humidity Y(%) and temperature X(°C) at a given site are given as under:

Y :	30	40	45	60	65
X :	40	35	30	25	20

The correlation coefficient between Y and X is:

A. –0.987 B. 0.826
C. 0.621 D. –0.360

31. What is the required solar panel area for photovoltaic cells with efficiency of 20% and incident solar radiation of 400 W/m^2 to run an electric geyser of 2 kW?

A. 2.5 m^2 B. 25 m^2
C. 37.5 m^2 D. 0.25 m^2

32. Which type of earthworms are most suitable for vermicomposting?

A. Anecic
B. Epigeic
C. Endogeic
D. Both endogeic and epigeic

33. The first state to be declared as an organic state of the country is:

A. Sikkim B. Uttarakhand
C. Himachal Pradesh D. Kerala

34. In an urban atmosphere the concentration of CH_4 and OH radical is 5×10^{19} molecules m^3 and 1.8×10^{12} molecules m^{-3} respectively. The rate constant for 2nd order reaction between OH and methane is 8.36×10^{-21} m^3 $mol^{-1}s^{-1}$. What is the instantaneous rate of oxidation of CH_4?

A. 3.26×10^{11} molecules $m^{-3}s^{-1}$
B. 2.52×10^{12} molecules $m^{-3}s^{-1}$
C. 7.52×10^{11} molecules $m^{-3}s^{-1}$
D. 7.52×10^{12} molecules $m^{-3}s^{-1}$

35. Which instrument is used to measure total irradiance?

A. Pyrheliometer B. Anemometer
C. Pyranometer D. Hygrometer

36. Mycorrhizae enhance plant nutrition mainly by:

A. Providing sugar to root cells
B. Absorbing water and minerals
C. Converting atmospheric nitrogen to ammonia
D. Enhancing root growth

37. Which Article of the Indian Constitution was used by Government of India to enact the Environmental Protection Act (EPA), 1986?

A. 48 A B. 253
C. 251 D. 51 A(g)

38. Maximum concentration of hydroxyl radical in earth's atmosphere is observed at:

A. The equator, in middle of troposphere
B. The poles, in middle of troposphere
C. The equatorial surface
D. The Tropic of Cancer

39. Match List-I (Ozone Depleting Substances) with List-II (Chemical Formulas):

List-I (Ozone Depleting Substances)	**List-II (Chemical Formulas)**
(a) CFC-12	(i) $CF_2ClCFCl_2$
(b) CFC-113	(ii) $CClF_2CF_3$
(c) CFC-114	(iii) CF_2Cl_2
(d) CFC-115	(iv) CF_2ClCF_2Cl

Choose the correct answer from the options given below:

	(a)	(b)	(c)	(d)
A.	(iii)	(ii)	(i)	(iv)
B.	(iii)	(i)	(ii)	(iv)
C.	(iii)	(i)	(iv)	(ii)
D.	(iv)	(iii)	(ii)	(i)

40. Which of the following biomes has the largest area?

A. Grassland B. Desert

C. Taiga D. Rain forest

41. A thermal power plant emits SO_2 at the rate of 500×10^8 μg/s. Its stack has an effective height of 200 m where wind speed is 5.0 m/s. If the horizontal and vertical dispersion coefficients are 400 m and 200 m, respectively, the downwind ground level concentration of SO_2 at a distance of 2 km will be:

A. ~241.4 μg/m^3 B. ~206.5 μg/m^3

C. ~75.8 μg/m^3 D. ~180.6 μg/m^3

42. Which is the correct hierarchical level of organisation in ecology?

A. Organism, population, community, ecosystem, biome, landscape, ecosphere

B. Organism, population, community, ecosystem, landscape, biome, ecosphere

C. Organism, community, population, ecosystem, landscape, biome, ecosphere

D. Organism, population, community, landscape, ecosystem, biome, ecosphere

43. Given below are two statements, one labelled as Assertion (A) and the other labelled as Reason (R):

Assertion (A): The power output from a windmill is maximum for an optimal wind speed.

Reason (R): The turbulence in the atmosphere influences wind energy production.

Choose the correct answer from the options given below.

A. Both (A) and (R) are true and (R) is the correct explanation of (A)

B. Both (A) and (R) are true, but (R) is not the correct explanation of (A)

C. (A) is true, but (R) is false

D. (A) is false, but (R) is true

44. In a typical solar pond which region has the salt concentration gradient?

A. Surface convective zone

B. Non-convective zone

C. Lower convective zone

D. Entire solar pond

45. Which energy conversion process is involved in syngas production from biomass?

A. Combustion B. Gasification

C. Pyrolysis D. Fermentation

46. Given below are two statements, one labelled as Assertion (A) and the other labelled as Reason (R):

Assertion (A): In the Himalayas north-facing slopes have luxuriant growth of forests, whereas shruby drought-resistant vegetation inhabits the south-facing slopes.

Reason (R): South-facing slopes in the northern hemisphere receive more sunlight than nearby north-facing slopes and, therefore, are warmer and drier.

Choose the correct answer from the options given below.

A. Both (A) and (R) are true and (R) is the correct explanation of (A)

B. Both (A) and (R) are true, but (R) is not the correct explanation of (A)

C. (A) is true, but (R) is false

D. (A) is false, but (R) is true

47. Removal of decomposers from an ecosystem will lead to:

A. Increase in number of herbivores

B. Reduction in nutrient cycling

C. Increased number of carnivores

D. Decreased number of carnivores

48. A stream of waste water having BOD of 20.0 mg/L discharges water at the rate 1.0 m^3/s into river with flow rate 8.0 m^3/s and BOD of 5.0 mg/L. Assuming complete and instantaneous mixing, what is the resultant BOD just downstream from the point of discharge?

A. ~12.5 mg/L B. ~6.7 mg/L

C. ~15.0 mg/L D. ~1.5 mg/L

49. If s^2 is the variance of a sample of size N drawn from a normal population with variance

σ^2, then $\frac{Ns^2}{\sigma^2}$ has which one of the following distributions with (N – 1) degrees of freedom?

A. Chi-square B. Normal
C. Student's *t* D. Poisson

50. Match List-I (Clay Minerals) with List-II (Cation Exchange Capacity in cmol(+) kg^{-1}):

List-I (Clay Minerals)	List-II (Cation Exchange Capacity in cmol (+) kg^{-1})
(*a*) Vermiculite	(*i*) 5–25
(*b*) Smectite	(*ii*) 20–40
(*c*) Illite	(*iii*) 100–120
(*d*) Kaolinite	(*iv*) 150–160

Choose the correct answer from the options given below:

	(*a*)	(*b*)	(*c*)	(*d*)
A.	(*iv*)	(*i*)	(*iii*)	(*ii*)
B.	(*iii*)	(*ii*)	(*iv*)	(*i*)
C.	(*i*)	(*ii*)	(*iii*)	(*iv*)
D.	(*iv*)	(*iii*)	(*ii*)	(*i*)

51. In an ideal magnetohydrodynamic (MHD) generator, the velocity of fuel gas is increased by a factor of 1.5 and the magnetic field is increased by a factor of 2. By what factor, the maximum power produced from the MHD generator would increase?

A. 3 B. 6
C. 9 D. 4.5

52. An ozone analyser shows 100 ppb concentration at 1 atmosphere or atm and 25°C. Convert the observed concentration of ozone in μg/m^3.

A. 96.0 B. 196.2
C. 200.0 D. 48.92

53. Computation of radiative forcing due to Greenhouse Gas does NOT involve:

A. Concentration of the Greenhouse Gases present in the atmosphere
B. Lapse rate of the atmosphere
C. Wavelength at which the gas molecules absorb
D. Intensity of the absorption per molecule

54. Ozone depleting potential is measured with reference to:

A. CFC-11 B. CFC-12
C. HCFC-22 D. CFC-113

55. Match List-I (Gases) with List-II (Measurement Techniques):

List-I (Gases)	List-II (Measurement Techniques)
(*a*) Ozone	(*i*) IR Absorption
(*b*) NO_X	(*ii*) Pulsed Fluorescence
(*c*) SO_2	(*iii*) Chemiluminescence
(*d*) CO	(*iv*) Ultraviolet Absorption

Choose the correct answer from the options given below:

	(*a*)	(*b*)	(*c*)	(*d*)
A.	(*i*)	(*ii*)	(*iii*)	(*iv*)
B.	(*iv*)	(*iii*)	(*ii*)	(*i*)
C.	(*ii*)	(*iv*)	(*i*)	(*iii*)
D.	(*iv*)	(*ii*)	(*iii*)	(*i*)

56. Which forest type has the highest percentage cover in the country?

A. Tropical deciduous
B. Tropical evergreen
C. Temperature deciduous
D. Mangrove

57. Arrange the following biomes in the increasing order of primary productivity:

(*a*) Savannah
(*b*) Boreal forests
(*c*) Temperate forests
(*d*) Temperate grasslands

Choose the correct option:

A. (*a*), (*c*), (*b*) and (*d*)
B. (*c*), (*b*), (*a*) and (*d*)
C. (*c*), (*a*), (*d*) and (*b*)
D. (*b*), (*c*), (*d*) and (*a*)

58. Which of the following types of coal has maximum ash content (%)?

A. Anthracite
B. Sub-Bituminous
C. Lignite
D. High volatile Bituminous

59. Which among the following substances is responsible for global cooling instead of global warming?

A. Black carbon B. Nitrous oxide
C. Sulphate aerosols D. HCFC

60. In a population, where the allele frequency shifts by a random chance, the mechanism of evolution at work is:
A. Co-evolution B. Mutation
C. Natural selection D. Genetic drift

61. Major environmental impacts of the Tehri dam in the Central Himalaya are:
(*a*) Submergence of fertile agricultural lands
(*b*) Reservoir-induced seismicity
(*c*) Increased incidences of landslides in the reservoir rim
(*d*) Loss of biodiversity

Choose the correct option:
A. (*a*) and (*b*) only
B. (*a*) and (*c*) only
C. (*a*) and (*d*) only
D. (*a*), (*b*), (*c*) and (*d*)

62. Greenhouse gas CO_2 has very strong absorption band in the wavelength region:
A. 4 – 10 μm B. >13.0 μm
C. 2 – 3.5 μm D. 0.7 – 2 μm

63. Given below are two statements, one labelled as Assertion (A) and the other labelled as Reason (R):

Assertion (A): Sounds with a frequency <100 Hz (base notes) need to be of a higher energy before damage to ear occurs.

Reason (R): Human ear has variable frequency response.

Choose the correct answer from the options given below:
A. Both (A) and (R) are true and (R) is the correct explanation of (A)
B. Both (A) and (R) are true, but (R) is not the correct explanation of (A)
C. (A) is true, but (R) is false
D. (A) is false, but (R) is true

64. For a $H^2 + H^3$ fusion reaction if the desired confinement for the ionized fuel is 2 seconds, what must be the minimum concentration of ions per cubic meter for net gain of energy?
A. 0.25×10^{19} B. 2.5×10^{19}
C. 5×10^{19} D. 2×10^{19}

65. Sustainable development presupposes:
(*a*) Maintenance of ecosystem integrity
(*b*) Improvement in economic and social conditions of people
(*c*) Perpetual availability of ecosystem services

Choose the correct option:
A. (*a*), (*b*) and (*c*) B. (*a*) and (*b*) only
C. (*a*) and (*c*) only D. (*b*) and (*c*) only

66. In a breeder reactors:
A. Neutrons first convert a fertile material into fissile material and then sustain the fission reaction
B. Neutrons first start the fission reaction and fissile material is a by-product
C. Fissile material produces fertile material
D. Ratio of amount of fissile material produced to fissile material consumed should be less than one

67. Spring tides occur:
A. When sun and moon are at right angle with respect to earth
B. In spring season
C. During half-moons
D. When sun, moon and earth are aligned linearly

68. Given below are two statements, one is labelled as Assertion (A) and the other labelled as Reason (R).

Assertion (A): Refuse derived fuel from municipal solid waste has higher energy content than raw municipal solid waste.

Reason (R): Combustible organic material gets concentrated in fuel pellets produced from municipal solid waste.

Choose the correct answer from the options given below:
A. Both (A) and (R) are true and (R) is the correct explanation of (A)
B. Both (A) and (R) are true, but (R) is not the correct explanation of (A)

C. (A) is true, but (R) is false

D. (A) is false, but (R) is true

69. Given below are two statements, one labelled as Assertion (A) and the other labelled as Reason (R):

Assertion (A): Strategic Environmental Assessment (SEA) is a more advanced tool in environmental management.

Reason (R): SEA is applicable at the level of policy, planning and programmes.

Choose the correct answer from the options given below:

A. Both (A) and (R) are true and (R) is the correct explanation of (A)

B. Both (A) and (R) are true, but (R) is not the correct explanation of (A)

C. (A) is true, but (R) is false

D. (A) is false, but (R) is true

70. Spectral response pattern of leaves in healthy vegetation in SWIR region of EMR is primarily a function of:

A. Chlorophyll content

B. Leaf parenchyma

C. Water content of the leaf

D. Presence of waxy layer on epidermis

71. Match List-I (Soil Type) with List-II (Degree of Compressibility):

List-I (Soil Type)	**List-II (Degree of Compressibility)**
(*a*) Softy Clay	(*i*) Low
(*b*) Clay	(*ii*) High
(*c*) Silt	(*iii*) Medium
(*d*) Sandy Clay	(*iv*) Very High

Choose the correct answer from the options given below:

	(*a*)	(*b*)	(*c*)	(*d*)
A.	(*ii*)	(*i*)	(*iii*)	(*iv*)
B.	(*iv*)	(*iii*)	(*i*)	(*ii*)
C.	(*iii*)	(*ii*)	(*iv*)	(*i*)
D.	(*iv*)	(*ii*)	(*iii*)	(*i*)

72. Given below are two statements, one labelled as Assertion (A) and the other labelled as Reason (R).

Assertion (A): Carbon dioxide content in soil air is more than atmospheric air.

Reason (R): Carbon dioxide released from automobile exhaust and industries gets sequestered in the soil.

Choose the correct answer from the options given below:

A. Both (A) and (R) are true and (R) is the correct explanation of (A)

B. Both (A) and (R) are true, but (R) is not the correct explanation of (A)

C. (A) is true, but (R) is false

D. (A) is false, but (R) is true

73. Landslide incidences in the Himalayas have increased due to:

(*a*) Increased rainfall

(*b*) Deforestation

(*c*) Construction of new roads

Choose the correct option:

A. (*a*) and (*b*) only B. (*b*) and (*c*) only

C. (*c*) only D. (*b*) only

74. For a negatively skewed distribution, which is the correct relation?

A. Arithmetic mean < Median < Mode

B. Arithmetic mean < Mode < Median

C. Arithmetic mean > Mode > Median

D. Median = Mode > Arithmetic mean

75. Given below are two statements, one labelled as Assertion (A) and the other labelled as Reason (R):

Assertion (A): Hydroxides of Aluminium (III) or Iron (III) are quite effective in removing colloidal clay particles from turbid water.

Reason (R): Hydroxides from positively charged flocs attract and carry down negatively charged colloidal clay particles.

Choose the correct answer from the options given below:

A. Both (A) and (R) are true and (R) is the correct explanation of (A)

B. Both (A) and (R) are true, but (R) is not the correct explanation of (A)

C. (A) is true, but (R) is false
D. (A) is false, but (R) is true

76. Cartagena Protocol deals with:
A. Waste management
B. Protection of plant variety
C. Natural resource management
D. Biosafety

77. Which of the following parameters provides information on ignition quality of diesel?
A. Octane number B. Cetane number
C. Iodine value D. Acid value

78. A lake has 2.5 mgL^{-1} of dissolved organic carbon. The dissolved organic matter concentration in the lake is approximately:
A. 6.25 mgL^{-1} B. 4.25 mgL^{-1}
C. 3.25 mgL^{-1} D. 2.75 mgL^{-1}

79. Remote sensing data from which of the following remote sensing satellites is most suitable for urban ecological studies?
A. RISAT-2
B. CARTOSAT-2
C. LANDSAT-8
D. RESOURCESAT-2 WiFS

80. If x and y are two variables with independent frequency distributions with means μ_x and μ_y and variances σ_x^2 and σ_y^2, then the population variance of their difference σ_{x-y}^2 is:
A. $\sigma_x^2 + \sigma_y^2$ B. $\sigma_x^2 - \sigma_y^2$
C. $\mu_x\sigma_x^2 + \mu_y\sigma_y^2$ D. $\mu_x\sigma_x^2 - \mu_x\sigma_y^2$

81. Which is an exotic epigeic earthworm used widely for vermicomposting in India?
A. *Perionyx excavatus*
B. *Eudrilus eugeniae*
C. *Drawida willsi*
D. *Lampito mauritii*

82. What type of rock will be formed when the lava cools and crystallizes?
A. Intrusive igneous B. Extrusive igneous
C. Metamorphic D. Sedimentary

83. A container has 3 white balls and 2 black balls identical in size. Two balls are drawn randomly without replacement. The probability that the two balls are of different colours is:
A. $\frac{2}{5}$ B. $\frac{3}{5}$
C. $\frac{3}{10}$ D. $\frac{2}{10}$

84. Municipal Solid Waste (Management and Handling) Rules, 2000 were replaced by:
A. Solid Waste (Management and Handling) Rules, 2016
B. Solid Waste Management Rules, 2016
C. Municipal Solid Waste (Management and Handling) Rules, 2016
D. Solid Waste Management (Handling) Rules, 2018

85. UNEP awarded 'Champion of Earth' for the year 2018 for environmental contribution towards:
(*a*) Air pollution abatement
(*b*) Beating plastic pollution
(*c*) Establishing International Solar Alliance
(*d*) Swachh Bharat Abhiyan

Choose the correct answer from the options given below:
A. (*a*) and (*d*) only B. (*b*) and (*d*) only
C. (*a*) and (*b*) only D. (*b*) and (*c*) only

86. Match List-I (Property) with List-II (Ecological Level):

List-I (Property)	**List-II (Ecological Level)**
(*a*) Fragmentation	(*i*) Community
(*b*) Assembly	(*ii*) Ecosystem
(*c*) Integrity	(*iii*) Population
(*d*) Dispersion	(*iv*) Landscape

Choose the correct answer from the options given below:

	(*a*)	(*b*)	(*c*)	(*d*)
A.	(*ii*)	(*iii*)	(*iv*)	(*i*)
B.	(*iii*)	(*i*)	(*ii*)	(*iv*)
C.	(*iv*)	(*i*)	(*ii*)	(*iii*)
D.	(*i*)	(*iii*)	(*ii*)	(*iv*)

87. Atmospheric Scale Height (H) is the height over which pressure decreases by a factor of:

A. *e* B. 10
C. π D. 2

88. Consider a normal distribution *f*(*x*) of variable *x*. What percentage of variable values deviate from the mean by more than $2\sigma_x$?

A. ~0.26% B. ~2.64%
C. ~31.74% D. ~4.56%

89. In the model of $\overline{r}$ and $\overline{k}$ selection, rate of increase of two species are portrayed as function of:

(*a*) Population density
(*b*) Resource density
(*c*) Habitat
(*d*) Size

Choose the correct answer from the options given below:

A. (*a*) and (*c*) B. (*a*) and (*b*)
C. (*b*) and (*d*) D. (*c*) and (*a*)

90. A windmill has 10 m diameter and efficiency of 40%. Wind velocity at normal temperature and pressure is 10 m/s and the density of air is 1.29 kg/m^3. The expected power output from the windmill is:

A. 20.0 kW B. 20.27 kW
C. 10.27 kW D. 10.0 kW

91. According to National Ambient Air Quality Standards (NAAQS) annual average concentration (μg/m^3) for SO_2 and NO_2 in ecologically sensitive areas are:

A. 20 and 60 respectively
B. 80 and 47 respectively
C. 50 and 20 respectively
D. 20 and 30 respectively

92. A 100 mL sample of paper industry effluent is digested in acidified dichromate solution and by back titration it is found that 5×10^{-4} mol of dichromate has been consumed in chemical oxidation. What is COD (mgO_2L^{-1}) of the sample?

A. 120 B. 620
C. 240 D. 310

93. Acid mine drainage from underground mines occurs as:

A. Non-point discharge
B. Point discharge
C. Spoil tip drainage
D. Slurry lagoon drainage

94. Given below are two statements, one labelled as Assertion (A) and the other labelled as Reason (R):

Assertion (A): If BOD level of water in a reservoir is less than 5 mgL^{-1}, it is highly polluted.

Reason (R): High BOD means high microbial activity.

Choose the correct answer from the options given below.

A. Both (A) and (R) are true and (R) is the correct explanation of (A)
B. Both (A) and (R) are true, but (R) is not the correct explanation of (A)
C. (A) is true, but (R) is false
D. (A) is false, but (R) is true

95. Match List-I (Environmental Pollutant) with List-II (Instruments Used for Analysis):

List-I (Environmental Pollutant)	**List-II (Instruments Used for Analysis)**
(*a*) PAHs	(*i*) AAS
(*b*) Heavy metals	(*ii*) UV-Vis spectrophotometer
(*c*) Sulphate ions	(*iii*) Electrophoresis
(*d*) Nucleotides	(*iv*) HPLC

Choose the correct answer from the options given below:

	(*a*)	(*b*)	(*c*)	(*d*)
A.	(*i*)	(*ii*)	(*iii*)	(*iv*)
B.	(*ii*)	(*iii*)	(*iv*)	(*i*)
C.	(*i*)	(*ii*)	(*iv*)	(*iii*)
D.	(*iv*)	(*i*)	(*ii*)	(*iii*)

96. Which one among the following do all the terrestrial biomes have in common?

A. Annual average rainfall in excess of 25 cm
B. Clear boundaries between adjacent biomes

C. Vegetation demonstrating adjacent stratification
D. Biodiversity pattern that is directly proportional to latitude

97. The marks of students in a certain course averaged 75 over a period of years. A class of 50 students has a mean marks 70 with a standard deviation of 10. To test whether this lower mean can be attributed to ordinary sampling variation, *t*-statistic is required. The value of *t* is:
A. –3.5 B. –0.5
C. –2.5 D. +1.5

98. As per the amended rules for the implementation of Forest Rights Act of 2006, the transit passes for the transport of minor forest produce are issued by:
A. Gram Sabha
B. Forest Department
C. Biodiversity Monitoring Committee
D. District Level Committee

99. As per Occupational Safety and Health Administration, hazard communication pictogram of flame over circle represents the hazardous waste, to be an:
A. oxidizer B. acutely toxic
C. explosive D. irritant

100. First State to make rainwater harvesting compulsory in India is:
A. Haryana
B. Tamil Nadu
C. Gujarat
D. Madhya Pradesh

ANSWERS

1	2	3	4	5	6	7	8	9	10
D	A	A	C	A	A	D	A	C	C
11	**12**	**13**	**14**	**15**	**16**	**17**	**18**	**19**	**20**
D	D	A	D	A,B	B	A	B	B	B
21	**22**	**23**	**24**	**25**	**26**	**27**	**28**	**29**	**30**
D	A	A	D	D	B	C	D	B	A
31	**32**	**33**	**34**	**35**	**36**	**37**	**38**	**39**	**40**
B	B	A	C	C	B	B	A	C	C
41	**42**	**43**	**44**	**45**	**46**	**47**	**48**	**49**	**50**
*	B	B	B	B	A	B	B	A	D
51	**52**	**53**	**54**	**55**	**56**	**57**	**58**	**59**	**60**
C	B	B	A	B	A	*	C	C	D
61	**62**	**63**	**64**	**65**	**66**	**67**	**68**	**69**	**70**
D	B	B	C	A	A	D	A	A	C
71	**72**	**73**	**74**	**75**	**76**	**77**	**78**	**79**	**80**
D	C	B	A	A	D	B	B	B	A
81	**82**	**83**	**84**	**85**	**86**	**87**	**88**	**89**	**90**
B	A	B	B	D	C	A	D	B	B
91	**92**	**93**	**94**	**95**	**96**	**97**	**98**	**99**	**100**
D	C	B	D	D	D	A	A	A	B

EXPLANATORY ANSWERS

1. The wind rose is the time honoured method of graphically presenting the wind conditions, direction and speed, over a period of time at a specific location. To create a wind rose, average wind direction and wind speed values are logged at a site, at short intervals, over a period of time, *e.g.* 1 week, 1 month, or longer. The collected wind data is then sorted by wind direction so that the percentage of time that the wind was blowing from each direction can be determined.

2. Sound emitted by 5 such aeroplanes

$$L_{\Sigma} = 10 \log_{10}\left(10^{\frac{L_1}{10}} + 10^{\frac{L_2}{10}} + 10^{\frac{L_3}{10}} + 10^{\frac{L_4}{10}} + 10^{\frac{L_5}{10}}\right)$$

According to the question,

$$L_1 = L_2 = L_3 = L_4 = L_5 = 110 \text{ dB}$$

$$\therefore L_{\Sigma} = 10\log_{10}\left(10^{\frac{110}{10}} + 10^{\frac{110}{10}} + 10^{\frac{110}{10}} + 10^{\frac{110}{10}} + 10^{\frac{110}{10}}\right)$$

$$= 10\log_{10}\left(10^{11} + 10^{11} + 10^{11} + 10^{11} + 10^{11}\right)$$

$$= 10\log_{10}\left(5 \times 10^{11}\right)$$

$$= 10\log_{10}(5) + 10\log_{10}(10^{11})$$

$$= 10 \times 0.69 + 10 \times 11$$

$$= 6.9 + 110 \approx 117 \text{ dB.}$$

3. Acid rain has many baneful effects. It upsets chemical balance in water bodies, releasing toxic metals. This causes serious health problems to people. Acid rain also triggers leaching of important nutrients from the soil, affecting plants. When snow with acid deposit melts, higher concentration of acid gets released, affecting fish. Acid rains also cause corrosion in buildings—the Taj Mahal being a case in point.

The occurrence of acid rain over the Indian landmass is extremely rare because the alkaline dust and ammonia produced from agricultural areas neutralizes the acid formation in the atmosphere.

4. The species level is highly embedded in current ecological theory and practice. It is widely accepted that within— and between-species interactions are different in kind. Niche theory is usually conjoined with a view that the species level provides a fundamental break. Gause's theory of competitive exclusion talks about the ability of species needing to differentiate in order to live in the same environment. The species level is likewise highly embedded in studies of population genetics. The species is thought to be the largest unit in which gene flow is possible, thus the largest group that can actually evolve as a unit.

5. Disturbance, defined here as any process that removes biomass from the community, has long been recognized as influencing species coexistence and the maintenance of biodiversity. As a result, there is a considerable body of research examining the effects of disturbance on species diversity, much of which focuses on testing the intermediate disturbance hypothesis. In ecology, a **disturbance** is a temporary change in environmental conditions that causes a pronounced change in an ecosystem. Disturbances often act quickly and with great effect, to alter the physical structure or arrangement of biotic and abiotic elements. Disturbance can also occur over a long period of time and can impact the biodiversity within an ecosystem. Major ecological disturbances may include fires, flooding, storms, insect outbreaks and trampling. Earthquakes, various types of volcanic eruptions, tsunami, firestorms, impact events, climate change, and the devastating effects of human impact on the environment (anthropogenic disturbances) such as clearcutting, forest clearing and the introduction of invasive species can be considered major disturbances.

6. Olivine has a very high crystallization temperature compared to other minerals. That makes it one of the first minerals to crystallize from a magma. During the slow cooling of a magma, crystals of olivine may form and then settle to the bottom of the magma chamber because of their relatively high density.

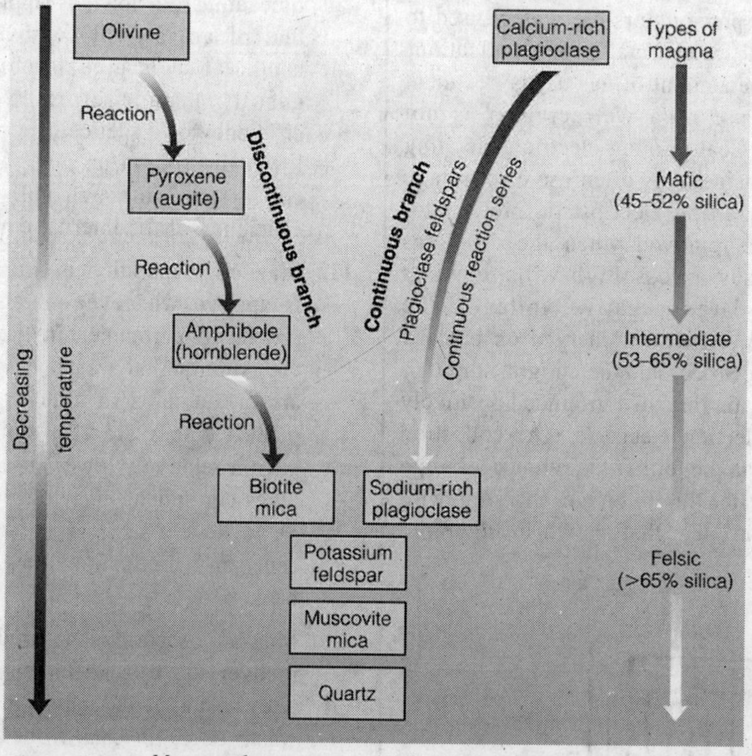

Magma changes as crystallization takes place along the two branches

7. The electromagnetic spectrum covers electromagnetic waves with frequencies ranging from below one hertz to above 10^{25} hertz, corresponding to wavelengths from thousands of kilometers down to a fraction of the size of an atomic nucleus. This frequency range is divided into separate bands, and the electromagnetic waves within each frequency band are called by different names; beginning at the low frequency (long wavelength) end of the spectrum these are: radio waves, microwaves, infrared, visible light, ultraviolet, X-rays, and gamma rays at the high-frequency (short wavelength) end.

Class			Frequency	Wavelength	Energy
Visible	NUV	Near ultraviolet	3 PHz	100 nm	12.4 eV
	NIR	Near infrared	300 THz	1 µm	1.24 eV
	MIR	Mid infrared	30 THz	10 µm	124 meV
	FIR	Far infrared	3 THz	100 µm	12.4 meV

8. The biogas production decreased with temperature decrease in winter, while acetate and propionate were accumulated. The lower biogas production in winter might be explained by poor degradation of organic matter and higher solubility of biogas at a lower temperature.

The optimum mesophilic temperature of biogas production from blends of agro-based wastes was determined under constant supply of heat. Methanogenesis occurs at mesophilic temperature.

9. Electrostatic precipitators are widely used to trap fine particulate matter in applications where a large amount of gas needs treatment and where use of a wet scrubber is not appropriate. Coal-burning electric generating plants and incinerators often use electrostatic precipitators. In an electrostatic precipitator particles are removed when the dirty gas stream passes across high-voltage wires carrying a large negative voltage. The particles are electrically charged on passage past these electrodes and then migrate through the electrostatic field to a grounded positively charged collection electrode. The collection electrode can be either a cylindrical pipe surrounding the high-voltage charging wire or a flat plate, like that shown in Figure.

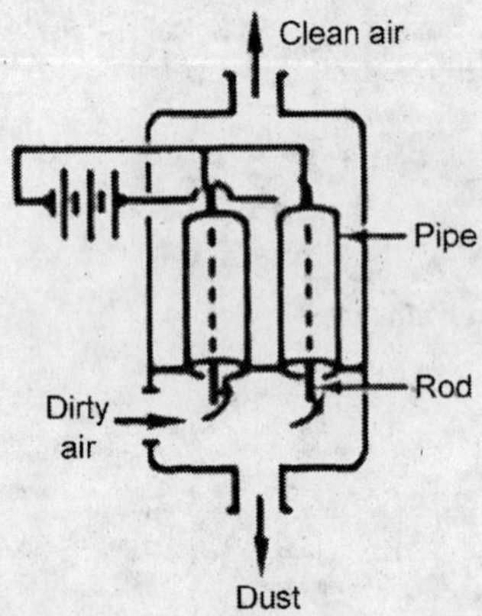

Fig.: *Electrostatic precipitator*

10. The major drivers for the development of fuel cell technology are efficiency and low emissions. The efficiency of fuel cells versus the internal combustion engine is often misrepresented. These two technologies are intrinsically different and have different efficiency-power characteristics. While an internal combustion engine has the maximum efficiency at or near its maximum power, the fuel cell system has its maximum efficiency at partial load. Because of that, the efficiency of a hydrogen-fuelled fuel cell propulsion system in a typical driving schedule, where an automobile engine operates most of the time at partial load, is approximately twice that of an internal combustion engine. If another fuel is used (such as methanol or gasoline) and reformed onboard, the efficiency of a fuel cell propulsion system is lower than the efficiency of a hydrogen fuel cell system, although still higher than the efficiency of the internal combustion engine.

11. Magnetic separation is a unit operation that is applied whenever metals with magnetic properties participate in the composition of the commingled waste. Magnetic separators are encountered in almost all the recycling plants, as they are very simple in operation, have a relatively lower cost compared to the other equipment of a solid-waste processing plant, have a high efficiency (80 to 95 per cent) and production rates, and short pay-back period.

Magnetic separation is used to separate and recover (1) ferrous metals from scrap and alloys, slag, mixed metals in source-separated waste (*e.g.*, tin cans from aluminium cans), (2) ferrous items from automobile shredding, municipal solid wastes (tin cans, wires, household equipment, etc.) and combustion residues.

12. The major primary air pollutants that are linked to direct emissions from on-road vehicles include soot (black carbon), carbon monoxide (CO), and nitric oxide (NO).

Black carbon is the sooty black material emitted from gas and diesel engines, coal-fired power plants, and other sources that burn fossil fuel. It comprises a significant portion of particulate matter or PM, which is an air pollutant.

Aerosol black carbon (BC) is a widespread environmental pollutant, which is generated from combustion processes of carbonaceous materials at high temperature. Being the principal light absorbing aerosol species with specific absorption coefficients ranging from 11 to 12 m^2g^{-1} at 650 nm, BC absorbs radiation that lowers the single scattering albedo.

13. Volatile organic compounds:

The general category of VOCs consists of many chemicals, including non-methane hydrocarbons (for example, alkanes, alkenes, and aromatics), halocarbons (for example, trichloroethylene), and oxygenates (alcohols, aldehydes, and ketones). There is a preponderance of carcinogens among VOCs - for example, benzene, polyaromatic hydrocarbons, 1,3-butadiene, many of the halocarbons. Owing to the carcinogenicity of benzene and polyaromatic hydrocarbons, no safe levels are recommended by WHO.

Petroleum and gasoline consist of blends of over 250 diverse hydrocarbons. Many of these are toxic. Some, such as benzene, are carcinogenic. Hydrocarbons escape into the air during refilling, from the gasoline tank and carburetor during normal operation, and from engine exhaust. Transportation sources account for 30-50% of all hydrocarbon emissions into the atmosphere.

14. The presence of organic matter is of great importance in the formation and stabilization of soil structure. Polymers of the FA and HA fractions are adsorbed on mineral surfaces by a variety of mechanisms, primarily involving the functional groups - carboxyls, carbonyl (C = O), alcoholic-OH, phenolic-OH, amino (= NH) and amine ($-NH_2$).

So, Assertion (A) is false.

Humified organic matter has an affinity for water and can absorb and hold water up to several times its dry weight.

So, Reason (R) is true.

15. It is well known that certain heavy metals like lead, cadmium and chromium are serious health hazards even if ingested in small quantities. It is especially for lead and cadmium. Children face a greater risk in view of the susceptibility of their immature central nervous system.

One source of lead, cadmium and chromium that children are likely to come into contact with is coloured magazines and comics. Hankin and co-workers (1973) found that the coloured inks used in American magazines contained a very high level of lead. Values of 1140–3170 ppm of lead were reported.

16. Solar radiation is radiant (electromagnetic) energy from the sun. It provides light and heat for the Earth and energy for photosynthesis. This radiant energy is necessary for the metabolism of the environment and its inhabitants. The three relevant bands, or ranges, along the solar radiation spectrum are ultraviolet, visible (PAR), and infrared. Of the light that reaches Earth's surface, infrared radiation makes up 49.4% of while visible light provides 42.3%. Ultraviolet radiation makes up just over 8% of the total solar radiation. Each of these bands has a different impact on the environment.

The amount and intensity of solar radiation that a location or body of water receives depends on a variety of factors. These factors include latitude, season, time of day, cloud cover and altitude. Not all radiation emitted from the sun reaches Earth's surface. Much of it is absorbed, reflected or scattered in the atmosphere. At the surface, solar energy can be absorbed directly from the sun, called direct radiation, or from light that has been scattered as it enters the atmosphere, called indirect radiation.

17. Ground truth is a term used in various fields to refer to information provided by direct observation (*i.e.* empirical evidence) as opposed to information provided by inference. In remote sensing, "ground truth" refers to information collected on location. Ground truth allows image data to be related to real features and materials on the ground. The collection of ground truth data enables calibration of remote-sensing data, and aids in the interpretation and analysis of what is being sensed. Examples include cartography, meteorology, analysis of aerial photographs, satellite imagery and other techniques in which data are gathered at a distance.

Generally, ground truth is used to assist with (1) image analysis and interpretation (e.g., image classification) of remotely sensed imagery, (2) remote sensor calibration, and (3) accuracy assessment of image analysis results.

18. Humus has traditionally been extracted with a strong alkali, such as sodium hydroxide, which acts by separating the negatively charged organic matter from clays, and by hydrolysing and depolymerizing the large organic molecules. Approximately 25% of the FA is aromatic. FA molecules are smaller, more highly charged and more polar than HA. Charge repulsion causes the FA molecules to be more linear than the randomly coiled HA molecules. They do not precipitate in acid solutions and are susceptible to leaching.

19. A **wildfire**, **wildland fire** or **rural fire** is an uncontrolled fire in an area of combustible vegetation occurring in rural areas. Depending on the type of vegetation present, a wildfire can also be classified more specifically as a **brush fire**, **bush fire**, **desert fire**, **forest fire**, **grass fire**, **hill fire**, **peat fire**, **vegetation fire**, or **veld fire.**

High-severity wildfire creates complex early seral forest habitat (also called "snag forest habitat"), which often has higher species richness and diversity than unburned old forest. Many plant species depend on the effects of fire for growth and reproduction. Wildfires in ecosystems where wildfire is uncommon or where non-native vegetation has encroached may have strongly negative ecological effects.

Wildfire behaviour and severity result from a combination of factors such as available fuels, physical setting, and weather. Strategies for wildfire prevention, detection, control and suppression have varied over the years. One common and inexpensive technique is controlled burning: intentionally igniting smaller fires to minimize the amount of flammable material available for a potential wildfire.

20. In evolutionary biology, **parasitism** is a relationship between species, where one organism, the **parasite**, lives on or in another organism, the host, causing it some harm, and is adapted structurally to this way of life. The entomologist E. O. Wilson has characterised parasites as "predators that eat prey in units of less than one".

Name	Description	Effect
Competition	Organisms of two species use the same limited resource and have a negative impact on each other.	-/-
Predation	A member of one species, predator, eats all or part of the body of a member of another species, prey.	+/-
Herbivory	A special case of predation in which the prey species is a plant	+/-
Mutualism	A long-term, close association between two species in which both partners benefit	+/+
Comm-ensalism	A long-term, close association between two species in which one benefits and the other is unaffected	+/0
Parasitism	A long-term, close association between two species in which one benefits and the other is harmed	+/-

21. Characteristics of Population Ecology

Ecologists use various terms when understanding and discussing populations of organisms. A population is all of one kind of species residing in a particular location. *Population size* represents the total number of individuals in a habitat. *Population density* refers to how many individuals reside in a particular area.

Population Size is represented by the letter N, and it equals the total number of individuals in a population. The larger a population is, the greater its generic variation and therefore its potential for long-term survival. Increased population size can, however, lead to other issues, such as overuse of resources leading to a population crash.

Population Density refers to the number of individuals in a particular area. A low-density area would have more organisms spread out. High-density areas would have more individuals living closer together, leading to greater resource competition.

Population Dispersion: Yields helpful information about how species interact with each other. Researchers can learn more about populations by studying the way they are distributed or dispersed.

Population distribution describes how individuals of a species are spread out, whether they live in close proximity to each other or far apart, or clustered into groups.

- *Uniform dispersion* refers to organisms that live in a specific territory. One example would be penguins. Penguins live in territories, and within those territories the birds space themselves out relatively uniformly.
- *Random dispersion* refers to the spread of individuals such as wind-dispersed seeds, which fall randomly after travelling.
- *Clustered or clumped dispersion* refers to a straight drop of seeds to the ground, rather than being carried, or to groups of animals living together, such as herds or schools. Schools of fish exhibit this manner of dispersion.

24. Metal Immobilization: The contact of soluble metal species with microbial cells results in *in-situ* transformations of the targeted species. As a consequence, the metals are immobilized by the microbial biomass. Soluble metal and metalloid species may be sequestered from water streams via their interaction with microbial cells by active (i.e. metabolic/ energy dependent) and passive (i.e. non metabolic/energy independent) processes. Metabolically mediated immobilization of metal species by active microbial cells includes different mechanisms such as bio-precipitation and biological reduction/ oxidation. Passive metal uptake by microbial cells is described by the general term biosorption and includes different mechanisms of physico-chemical interaction between the microbial cell biopolymers and the metal species such as complexation, chelation, ion exchange and precipitation.

Both living/metabolizing and non-metabolizing microbial cells may be used in technology development for:

1. The removal of metals from aqueous industrial effluents.
2. Metal recovery from industrial process streams.
3. Bioremediation of contaminated surface waters and groundwater.

Microorganisms influence the chemical state - speciation and hence the mobility of the metals by numerous and complex mechanisms ranging from direct processes like metal transformation and intracellular uptake, to more indirect processes via production of substances that render the metals more or less mobile.

Microbially-mediated metal transformations

- May involve phase changes of metals;
- Are responsible for metal cycling in ecosystems.
- Are of use in biohydrometallurgy and bioremediation.
- Are much more often caused by prokaryotes than by eukaryotes.

25. It is a fairly constant and diagnostic property of minerals. Hardness may be defined as the resistance, which a mineral offers to an external deformation action such as scratching, abrasion, rubbing or indentation. Hardness of a mineral depends on its chemical composition and atomic constitution.

Broadly speaking hardness of minerals as determined conventionally is a qualitative property determined in relative terms. It was in 1822 that Austrian mineralogist F. Mohs proposed a relative, broadly quantitative "scale of hardness" of minerals assigning values between 1 and 10. Since then, the Mohs' Scale of Hardness for Minerals has been universally adopted.

The Mohs' scale of hardness comprises ten minerals arranged in order of ascending hardness; the softest is assigned a value of 1 and the hardest a value of 10.

Table: Mohs' Scale of Hardness for Minerals

Hardness	*Standard Minerals*	*Composition*
1.	TALC	$Mg_3[Si_4O_{10}][OH]_2$
2.	GYPSUM	$CaSO_4.2H_2O$
3.	CALCITE	$CaCO_3$
4.	FLUORITE	CaF_2
5.	APATITE	$Ca_5[PO_4]_3F$
6.	ORTHOCLASE	$KAlSi_3O_8$
7.	QUARTZ	SiO_2
8.	TOPAZ	$Al_2[SiO_4][F,OH]_2$
9.	CORUNDUM	Al_2O_3
10.	DIAMOND	C

Three facts need careful consideration in determining hardness of a mineral on Mohs scale:

First: Hardness is only a relative property. If Talc has H = 1 and Quartz H = 7, it does not indicate quartz is seven times harder than talc.

Second: Hardness is an anisotropic property; a mineral may show different values in different directions. Most commonly, however, this difference is negligible except in the case of a mineral kyanite where H = 4.5 along the length and H = 6.5 across the length of a crystal.

Third: Hardness decreases on decomposition of a mineral due to atmospheric attack on its surface. Hence, it must be checked on unweathered and unaltered surfaces only.

26. An ecosystem is *'recovered and restored'- when* it contains sufficient biotic and abiotic resources to continue its development without further assistance. It will be self-sustaining both structurally and functionally. It will demonstrate resilience to normal ranges of environmental stress and disturbance. The nine attributes listed below provide a basis for determining when restoration has been accomplished. Some attributes are readily measured. Others must be assessed indirectly (i.e. functional aspects of ecosystem).

1. Comparison of characteristic of species of restored ecosystem, namely, the reference ecosystem.
2. The species composition in the restored ecosystem should be consisting of indigenous species to the greatest extent as practicable.
3. All functional groups necessary for the continued development and/or stability of the restored ecosystem are represented.
4. The physical environment of the restored ecosystem is capable of self-sustaining and reproducing species necessary for its continued stability or development along the desired trajectory.
5. The restored ecosystem apparently functions normally for its ecological stage of development, and signs of dysfunction are absent.
6. The restored ecosystem is suitably integrated into a larger ecological matrix or landscape, with which it interacts through abiotic and biotic flows and exchanges.

7. Potential threats to the health and integrity of the restored ecosystem from the surrounding landscape have been eliminated or reduced as much as possible.
8. The restored ecosystem is sufficiently resilient to endure the normal periodic stress events in the local environment that serve to maintain the integrity of the ecosystem.
9. The restored ecosystem is self-sustaining to the same degree as its reference ecosystem and has the potential to persist indefinitely under existing environmental conditions. Nevertheless, aspects of its biodiversity, structure and functioning may change as part of normal ecosystem development and may fluctuate in response to normal periodic stress and occasional disturbance events of greater consequence. As in any intact ecosystem, the species composition and other attributes of a restored ecosystem may evolve as environmental conditions change.

27. ISO (the International Organization for Standardization) is a worldwide federation of national standards bodies (ISO member bodies). The work of preparing International Standards is normally carried out through ISO technical committees. Each member body interested in a subject for which a technical committee has been established has the right to be represented on that committee. International organizations, governmental and non-governmental, in liaison with ISO, also take part in the work. ISO collaborates closely with the International Electrotechnical Commission (IEC) on all matters of electrotechnical standardization.

By 1996, the evolution of quality management focus on environmental quality issues prompted the adoption of new sets of standards. These new standards, like the ISO 9000 series, deal with the guidelines and principles of environmental management systems to make businesses aware and concerned about the growing need of environmental protection. These new standards are known as ISO 14000 series.

This committee was to focus in the following areas:

- environmental management systems (EMS);
- environmental auditing;
- environmental labelling;
- environmental performance evaluation (EPE);
- life cycle assessment (LCA);
- terms and definitions;
- environmental aspects in product standards (EAPS).

ISO 14010: Guidelines for environmental auditing - general principles of environmental auditing

ISO 14020: General principles for all environmental labels and declarations

ISO 14050: Terms and definitions

ISO 14060: Guide for the inclusion of environmental aspects in product standards.

28. **(*a*) Save Silent Valley Movement**

- **Year:** 1978
- **Place:** Silent Valley, an evergreen tropical forest in the Palakkad district of Kerala, India.
- **Leaders:** The Kerala Sastra Sahitya Parishad (KSSP) an NGO, and the poet-activist Sughathakumari played an important role in the Silent Valley protests.
- **Aim:** In order to protect the Silent Valley, the moist evergreen forest from being destroyed by a hydroelectric project.

What was it all about: The Kerala State Electricity Board (KSEB) proposed a hydroelectric dam across the Kunthipuzha River that runs through Silent Valley. In February 1973, the Planning Commission approved the project at a cost of about ₹ 25 crores. Many feared that the project would submerge 8.3 sq km of untouched moist evergreen forest. Several NGOs strongly opposed the project and urged the government to abandon it. In January 1981, bowing to unrelenting public pressure, Indira Gandhi declared that Silent Valley will be protected. In June 1983 the Center re-examined the issue through a commission chaired by Prof. M.G.K. Menon. In November 1983 the Silent Valley Hydroelectric Project was called off. In 1985, Prime Minister Rajiv Gandhi formally inaugurated the Silent Valley National Park.

(*b*) Chipko Movement

- **Year:** 1973
- **Place:** In Chamoli district and later at Tehri-Garhwal district of Uttarakhand.
- **Leaders:** Sundarlal Bahuguna, Gaura Devi, Sudesha Devi, Bachni Devi, Chandi Prasad Bhatt, Govind Singh Rawat, Dhoom Singh Negi, Shamsher Singh Bisht and Ghanasyam Raturi.
- **Aim:** The main objective was to protect the trees on the Himalayan slopes from the axes of contractors of the forest.

What was it all about: Mr. Bahuguna enlightened the villagers by conveying the importance of trees in the environment which checks the erosion of soil, cause rains and provides pure air. The women of Advani village of Tehri-Garhwal tied the sacred thread around trunks of trees and they hugged the trees, hence it was called 'Chipko Movement' or 'hug the tree movement'. The main demand of the people in these protests was that the benefits of the forests (especially the right to fodder) should go to local people.

(*c*) Appiko Movement

- **Year:** 1983
- **Place:** Uttara Kannada and Shimoga districts of Karnataka State.
- **Leaders:** Appiko's greatest strengths lie in it being neither driven by a personality nor having been formally institutionalised. However, it does have a facilitator in Pandurang Hegde. He helped launch the movement in 1983.
- **Aim:** Against the felling and commercialization of natural forest and the ruin of ancient livelihood.

What was it all about: It can be said that Appiko movement is the southern version of the Chipko movement. The Appiko Movement was locally known as "Appiko Chaluvali". The locals embraced the trees which were to be cut by contractors of the forest department. The Appiko movement used various techniques to raise awareness such as foot marches in the interior forest, slide shows, folk dances, street plays etc. The second area of the movement's work was to promote afforestation on denuded lands. The movement later focused on the rational use of ecosphere through introducing alternative energy resource to reduce pressure on the forest. The movement became a success. The current status of the project is – stopped.

(*d*) Save Gandhamardan Movement

- **Year:** 1980
- **Place:** Odisha: mass movements against industries and mines.

The first major popular struggle against mining in Odisha took place in the early 1980s, when a project run by the Bharat Aluminium Company (BALCO), a large public-sector organisation, was set up at Gandhamardan, in west Odisha. The area is 'rich in bio-diversity and is the home to countless threatened or endangered plant and animal species. It is also a place of great spiritual significance. In addition, Gandhamardan provides a life-support system for about 100,000 people. The forests are especially important for marginal farmers and the landless, who account for roughly 30 per cent of the population, providing them with resources for their very survival.

29. **Dewpoint:** If the air is gradually cooled while maintaining the moisture content constant, the relative humidity will rise until it reaches 100%. This temperature, at which the moisture content in the air will saturate the air, is called the dewpoint.

Relative Humidity:

The amount of water vapour in the air at any given time is usually less than that required to saturate the air. The relative humidity is the per cent of saturation humidity, generally calculated in relation to saturated vapour density.

$$\text{Relative Humidity} = \frac{\text{Actual vapour density}}{\text{Saturation vapour density}} \times 100\%$$

$$\text{Here, R.H.} = \left(\frac{600}{900}\right) \times 100 = 66.7\ \%.$$

32. Earthworms are members of phylum Annelida and class Oligochaeta, living in different strata of soil. More than 4400 species of earthworms are found worldwide. They occur in diverse habitats, vary greatly in size, and feed upon a variety of organic materials. Mainly they are burrowing animals and feed on dead organic matter, living bacteria, rotifers, nematodes, fungi, and other microorganisms. Earthworms based on ecological and trophic niche are divided into three main categories: epigeic, anecic, and endogeic. Most suitable species for vermicomposting are epigeic because these live in organic horizons and feed primarily on decaying organic matter. Among the epigeic earthworms, *E. fetida* and *Eisenia andrei* are most commonly used in vermicomposting because both earthworms are peregrine and ubiquitous with a worldwide distribution, resilient, and have wide temperature tolerance.

33. Sikkim was on 18 January 2016 declared as the first organic farming state of India. The declaration was made by the Prime Minister Narendra Modi while inaugurating the Sikkim Organic Festival 2016 in Gangtok, Sikkim.

Besides making the declaration, the Prime Minister also handed over the Organic Certificate to Sikkim Chief Minister Pawan Chamling.

On this occasion, he also launched three new orchid species developed in Sikkim. The new species are

- Cymbidium Sardar (after Sardar Patel)
- Cymbidium Deen Dayal (after Deen Dayal Upaddhyay)
- Cymbidium Namo (after Narendra Modi)

The Sikkim Organic Festival 2016 was held on the sidelines of the 2-day long National Conference on Sustainable Agriculture and Farmers Welfare that began on 17 January 2016.

35. A **pyranometer** is a type of actinometer used for measuring solar irradiance on a planar surface and it is designed to measure the solar radiation flux density (W/m^2) from the hemisphere above within a wavelength range 0.3 μm to 3 μm.

To make a measurement of irradiance, it is required by definition that the response to "beam" radiation varies with the cosine of the angle of incidence. This ensures a full response when the solar radiation hits the sensor perpendicularly (normal to the surface, sun at zenith, 0° angle of incidence), zero response when the sun is at the horizon (90° angle of incidence, 90° zenith angle), and 0.5 at a 60° angle of incidence. It follows that a pyranometer should have a so-called "directional response" or "cosine response" that is as close as possible to the ideal cosine characteristic.

Thermopile pyranometers are frequently used in meteorology, climatology, climate change research, building engineering physics and in photovoltaic systems.

They are usually installed horizontally in meteorological stations and typically mounted in the 'plane of array' (with the sensor surface parallel to the solar panel) when used for monitoring of photovoltaic systems.

36. Mycorrhizae are symbiotic association between a fungus and roots of vascular plants. The fungal hyphae of the Mycorrhizae help the plant by absorbing water and minerals more efficiently from the soil. Thus they indirectly help in enhancing plant nutrition.

Mycorrhizae not only help plants to take up nutrients and water but also increase the resistance of plant against disease and pathogenic organisms. Graham indicated that mycorrhizae - inoculated citrus plant has more resistance against pathogens. Mycorrhizae also can help control pests such as pathogenic fungi and nematodes by releasing antibiotics into the soil which reduce the risk of infection.

37. The Environment (Protection) Act, 1986, has provisions for a fairly comprehensive coverage to deal with various aspects, including pollution, environmental degradation and protection of ecologically important areas. The Act provides for setting up of new institutional mechanisms where called for. It has empowered the concerned authorities to issue necessary directions, including closure of installations/activities causing pollution or environmental degradation. Stringent penalties with imprisonment and fine have also been prescribed in the Act.

The Environment (Protection) Act, 1986, was promulgated under Article 253 of the constitution following the leakage of methyl isocyanate gas from the Union Carbide factory in Bhopal. Brought into force from November 19, 1986, the Act sought to deal with aspects relating to hazardous chemicals and sitting of industries. It also highlighted the need for providing teeth for taking deterrent action, where warranted.

The Environment (Protection) Act, 1986, enables the central government to:

1. Take all necessary measures for protecting the quality of environment.
2. Co-ordinate the action of state governments, officers and other authorities under this Act or under any other law that is related to the objects of this Act.
3. Plan and execute a nationwide programme for prevention, control and abatement of environmental pollution.
4. Lay down standards for discharge of environmental pollutants.
5. Empower any person to enter, inspect, take samples and test.
6. Establish or recognise environmental laboratories.
7. Appoint or recognise government analysts.
8. Lay down standards for the quality of environment.
9. Lay down procedures and safeguards for handling hazardous substances.
10. Restrict areas in which any industries, operations or processes may not be carried out or shall be carried out subject to certain safeguards.
11. Lay down safeguards for prevention of accidents and take remedial measures in case of such accidents.
12. Constitute an authority or authorities for exercising its powers.
13. Issue directions to any person, officer or authority, including the power to direct closure, prohibition or regulation of any industry, operation or process, or stoppage or regulation of supply of electricity, water or any other service.
14. Require any person, officer, state government or authority to furnish any prescribed information.

15. Delegate powers to any officer or state government or authority.

38. The troposphere and the stratosphere are separated by a boundary called the tropopause, whose altitude varies from about 16 km in the tropics to about 8 km near the poles. The troposphere is characterized by rapid vertical transport and mixing caused by weather disturbances.

The troposphere is an oxidizing medium. The dominant oxidizing species in the troposphere is the hydroxyl radical, OH. Virtually, all organic compounds, carbon monoxide, CO, methane, CH_4, and most nitrogen- and sulphur-containing species react with the hydroxyl radical in the atmosphere. Because of this, OH is often referred to as the 'atmosphere's detergent.' Reaction of OH with an organic molecule initiates an oxidation process, similar in many respects to combustion of an HC fuel.

The basic ingredients for the formation of hydroxyl are NO and NO_2, water vapour, ozone and radiation at wavelengths shorter than 315 nm: in simple terms, NO_2 is very reactive and may form O_3, which in turn may yield hydroxyl. NO_2 is mainly created through oxidization of NO, itself an indirect product of biomass burning, high temperature combustion and microbial actions in the soil.

39. Chlorofluorocarbons (CFCs) are artificially made chemical compounds used as refrigerants, cleaning solvents, aerosol propellants, and blowing agents for foam packaging in many commercial applications. They typically consist of chlorine, fluorine, carbon, and hydrogen. Freon®, a trade name, is often used to refer to them. CFCs do not spontaneously occur in nature.

These are also the properties which make them useful for many applications. Table lists some of the most important CFCs and gives their atmospheric lifetimes.

Table: Estimated CFC Lifetimes (WMO, 1994)

Name	*Chem Formula*	*Conc (1992)*	*Lifetime*
CFC-11	$CFCl_3$	0.27 ppbv	50 years
CFC-12	CF_2Cl_2	0.50 ppbv	100 years
CFC-113	$C_2F_3Cl_3$	0.082 ppbv	85 years
CFC-114	$C_2F_4Cl_2$	0.020 ppbv	300 years
	CCl_4	0.13 ppbv	42 years

40. The taiga is the largest uninterrupted forest area on earth; its average width measures 1,500 km and covers 8% of the lands above sea level. Rainfall is poor, generally about 400-600 mm, and decreases in the far north: sometimes just about 150 mm, like in many deserts. In southern Europe, conifer forests can be found between 1500 and 2000 metres a.s.l., and in many respects they resemble the taiga of northern plains.

Taiga, also called **boreal forest**, biome (major life zone) of vegetation composed primarily of cone-bearing needle-leaved or scale-leaved evergreen trees, found in northern circumpolar forested regions characterized by long winters and moderate to high annual precipitation. The taiga, "land of the little sticks" in Russian, takes its name from the collective term for the northern forests of Russia, especially Siberia.

42. Ecological systems are hierarchical in nature – at each level, components interact with the physical environment (matter and energy)

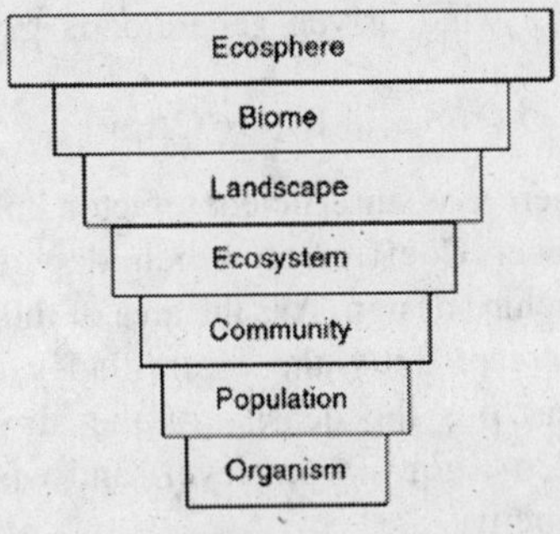

Fig.: *Most commonly recognized ecological hierarchy. The organism is the simplest level within this hierarchy while the ecosphere is the most complex*

and produce functioning systems. The most recognized ecological hierarchy, from the simplest to the most complex, is illustrated in Figure. This hierarchy organizes the living systems on the planet into seven levels. Each level is composed of the levels below (i.e., populations are composed of organisms, communities are composed of populations, ecosystems are composed of communities, etc.). Energy and material can flow among levels. It is important to note that ecological systems need not be confined to the traditional ecosystem level of the hierarchy. An ecological system can be any system with biotic and abiotic components. Further, most ecological system are hierarchical and Figure may not explain all ecological phenomena well - for example, nutrient cycling does not fit well within this hierarchy; however, this is a fundamental ecological process that transcends the levels of organization diagrammed in Figure. The complexity of ecological systems is a result, in part, from the interactions across these levels. At any given level in the hierarchy, interactions among components of lower levels produce emergent, irreducible properties that cannot be predicted from studying individual components of these lower levels.

43. The wind is a source of free energy which has been used since ancient times in windmills for pumping water or grinding flour.

The power **P** available in the wind impinging on a wind driven generator is given by:

$$\mathbf{P} = \frac{1}{2}\mathbf{C}\mathbf{A}\boldsymbol{\rho}\boldsymbol{v}^3$$

where **C** is an efficiency factor known as the Power Coefficient which depends on the machine design, **A** is the area of the wind front intercepted by the rotor blades (the swept area), **ρ** is the density of the air (averaging 1.225 Kg/m³ at sea level) and **v** is the wind velocity.

Note that the power is proportional to area swept by the blades, the density of the air and to the cube of the wind speed. Thus doubling the blade length will produce four times the power and doubling the wind speed will produce eight times the power.

Atmospheric turbulence is the set of seemingly random and continuously changing air motions that are superimposed on the wind's average motion. Atmospheric turbulence impacts wind energy in several ways, specifically through power performance effects, impacts on turbine loads, fatigue and wake effects, and noise propagation.

44. Salinity gradient solar ponds are large bodies of water that act as solar collectors and heat storages. A solar pond is a simple and low-cost solar energy system that collects solar radiation and stores it as thermal energy for a relative longer period.

Because of movement and mixing of the fluid both at the top and the bottom, the solar pond is characterized by three zones: a surface convective zone, a non-convective concentration gradient zone, and a lower convective zone (Fig.). The *surface convective zone* (SCZ) usually has a small thickness, around 10 to 20 cm. It has a low, uniform concentration, which is close to zero, as well as a fairly uniform temperature, which is close to the ambient air temperature. The *non-convective zone* (NCZ) is much thicker and occupies more than half the depth of the pond. Both concentration and temperature increase with depth in this zone. It serves principally as an insulating layer and reduces heat losses in the upward direction. Some of the heat collection also takes place in this zone and it serves also as part of the thermal storage. The *lower convective zone* (LCZ) is comparable in thickness to the non-convective zone. Both the concentration and the temperature are nearly constant in this zone. It serves as the main heat-collection as well as thermal-storage medium. The lower convective zone is often referred to as the storage zone or as the bottom layer.

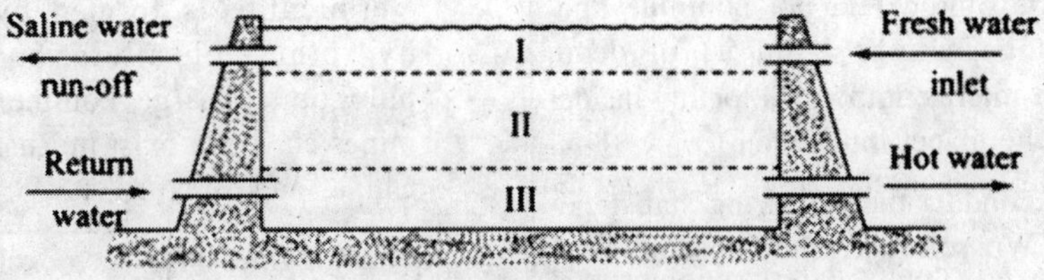

I — Surface convective zone SCZ
II — Concentration gradient zone NCZ
III — Lower convective zone LCZ

Fig.: *Schematic diagram of a solar pond*

45. **Gasification** is a **process** that converts organic- or fossil fuel-based carbonaceous materials into carbon monoxide, hydrogen and carbon dioxide. This is achieved by reacting the material at high temperatures (>700°C), without combustion, with a controlled amount of oxygen and/or steam. Biomass gasification is a renewable alternative that has the potential to decrease CO_2 emissions. However, efficient energy and resource utilization is essential. Previous works had shown that biomass is most cost-effectively used for heating purposes or electricity generation. But to increase the overall efficiency, biomass gasification could be integrated in industrial processes. The gasification is an old thermo-chemical conversion technology with a change of the chemical structure of the biomass at 800 – 1000°C in the presence of a gasifying agent (for instance air, oxygen, steam, CO_2, or mixtures of these components) enables the promotion of steam reforming reactions and thus it consists another method of producing a H_2 rich gas from biomass. Gasification is a thermochemical process for destruction of feedstocks (i.e. biomass, lignocellulosic residues, agriculture waste, refuse derived fuel and organic wastes) to produce energy carrier.

46. Mountains have a significant effect on the amount of sunlight reaching an area, as well as on local temperature and rainfall. South-facing slopes in the Northern Hemisphere receive more sunlight than nearby north-facing slopes and are therefore warmer and drier. These abiotic differences influence species distribution; for example, in many mountains of western North America, spruce and other conifers occupy the north-facing slopes, whereas shrubby, drought-resistant plants inhabit the south-facing slopes.

In the himalaya north facing slopes have luxuriant growth of forest whereas shrubs drought resistant vegetation inhibits the south facing slopes.

47. Decomposers, such as fungi, bacteria and invertebrates, play a critical role in nutrient cycling and without them the earth's ecosystem may not support life as we know it. Carbon in the atmosphere is taken up by plants and phytoplankton and converted into proteins, carbohydrates and fats. Decomposers are able to break down this material and release carbon back into the atmosphere and the cycle can begin again. Without decomposers, the carbon would remain locked in dead organisms and could only be released through combustion. If all decomposers were to die off, these nutrient cycles would be severely disrupted and the essential elements, perhaps with the exception of carbon, would not be available for life to continue. Nitrogen and phosphorus would be locked in dead material. In all probability, life as we know it would not continue and there would be a huge build up of dead material with many compounds locked inside these bodies.

49. Suppose we conduct the following statistical experiment. We select a random sample of size n from a normal population, having a standard deviation equal to σ. We find that the standard deviation in our sample is equal to s. Given these data, we can define a statistic, called **chi-square,** using the following equation:

$$\chi^2 = [(n - 1) \times s^2]/\sigma^2$$

The distribution of the chi-square statistic is called the chi-square distribution.

50. Clay minerals likely are the most utilized minerals ... not just as the soils that grow plants for foods and garment, but a great range of applications, including oil absorbants, iron casting, animal feeds, pottery, china, pharmaceuticals, drilling fluids, waste water treatment, food preparation and paint.

There are four type of clays:

Kaolinite- also includes dickite and nacrite; formed by the decomposition of orthoclase feldspar (e.g. in granite); kaolin is the principal constituent in china clay.

Illite- also includes glauconite (a green clay sand) and are the commonest clay minerals; formed by the decomposition of some micas and feldspars; predominant in marine clays and shales.

Smectites or montmorillonites - also includes bentonite and vermiculite; formed by the alteration of mafic igneous rocks rich in Ca and Mg; weak linkage by cations (e.g. Na^+) Ca^{++}) results in high swelling/shrinking potential

Vermiculite is a hydrous phyllosilicate mineral. It undergoes significant expansion when heated. Exfoliation occurs when the mineral is heated sufficiently, and the effect is routinely produced in commercial furnaces. Vermiculite is formed by weathering or hydrothermal alteration of biotite or phlogopite. Large commercial vermiculite mines currently exist in Russia, South Africa, China, and Brazil.

Clay Minerals	Clay exchange capacity (in mol/kg)
Vermiculite	150-160
Smectite	100-120
Illite	20-40
Kaolinite	5-25

52. Concentration of Ozone (O_3) = 100 ppb

Temp. = 25°C = 25 + 273.15 = 298.15

Pressure = 1 atm.

Concentration in (μg/m^3)

$$= \frac{100 \times 12.187 \times 48}{298.15}$$

$$= 100 \times 1.962 = 196.2 \ \mu g/m^3.$$

53. The GCMs are 3-dimensional meteorological models that attempt to capture the ensemble of radiative, dynamical, and hydrological factors controlling the Earth's climate through the solution of fundamental equations describing the physics of the system. In these models, a radiative perturbation associated with increase in a greenhouse gas (radiative forcing) triggers an initial warming; complex responses follow involving for example enhanced evaporation of water vapour from the ocean (a positive feedback, since water is a greenhouse gas), changes in cloud cover, and changes in the atmospheric or oceanic circulation. There is still considerable doubt regarding the ability of GCMs to simulate perturbations to climate, and indeed different GCMs show large disagreements in the predicted surface warmings resulting from a given increase in greenhouse gases.

Computation of radiative forcing due to greenhouse gases involved:

1. Concentration of greenhouse gases present in the atmosphere.

2. Wavelength at which gas molecules absorb.
3. Intensity of the absorption per molecules.

54. Some chemicals can damage the earth's protective ozone layer. This layer is composed of ozone molecules in the stratosphere, which extends from about 15 to 50 kilometers above the Earth's surface. Stratospheric ozone is a naturally-occurring gas that filters the sun's ultraviolet (UV) radiation.

Ozone depleting substances (ODS), including chlorofluorocarbons (CFCs), halons, and several other chemicals, are responsible for thinning the stratospheric ozone layer. Ozone depleting substances vary in their capacity to destroy ozone molecules, so scientists have developed a method for characterizing the relative depletion caused by different ODS. Ozone Depleting Potential (ODP) is the ratio of calculated ozone column change for each mass unit of a gas emitted into the atmosphere relative to the calculated depletion for the reference gas CFC 11 (ODP = 1.0). This allows different chemicals to be compared using a common unit (CFC 11-equivalents). For example, a chemical such as Halon 2402 (ODP = 6) is six times more detrimental to the stratospheric ozone layer than CFC 11.

55. Although the National Survey had measured high urban concentrations successfully, some major defects became apparent in the 1980s:

- Urban smoke and SO_2 concentrations had declined to such low levels that the relatively crude methods of the National Survey no longer offered adequate sensitivity.
- The network had naturally been concentrated in urban areas so that there were relatively few rural measurements.
- There was no capability at all to measure ozone or its precursors, which had by that time been identified as major factors in poor air quality.
- There was no capability to measure the most toxic organic compounds, which were by then known to be carcinogenic at very low concentrations.
- Although the existing National Survey results were appropriate to show compliance with the Commission of the European Communities (CEC) directive on SO_2 and TSP, there was no corresponding capability for the directive on NO_2.

The following pollutants (at least) are measured at each site:

O_3 – by ultraviolet absorption

NO_x – by chemiluminescence

SO_2 – by pulsed fluorescence

CO – by infrared (IR) absorption

PM_{10} – by tapered element oscillating microbalance (TEOM)

56. Tropical Deciduous Forests in India are the most widespread. Commonly also known as Monsoon forests, in the world, they are found in the belt along the equator, between the tropics of Cancer and Capricorn as well as the humid subtropics.

Africa, India, South America, Central America and small islands in the Pacific are some of the places where they grow.

In India, they grow in the states of Madhya Pradesh, Uttar Pradesh, Bihar, Chhattisgarh, Odisha, and parts of Maharashtra.

This type of forest is a biome and as previously stated, known for the falling and shedding of leaves during the autumn season.

In such forests, the vast majority of tree species as well as other vegetation that make up the forest shed their leaves during the cold winter and re-grow new leaves in the next spring season which is also known as the Monsoon Season.

This forest has a distinct ecosystem, understory growth as well as complex soil dynamics.

58. Characteristics of the Different Ranks of Coals

Rank (from lowest to highest)	*Properties*
Lignite	1. The lowest rank of coal that has been transformed into a brown-black coal from peat.
	2. Contains recognizable plant structures.
	3. Excessive moisture (25%–50%).
	4. Heating value less than 8300 BTU/lb on a mineral matter free basis.
	5. Carbon content between 60% and 70% on a dry ash-free basis.
Sub-bituminous	1. Denser and harder than lignite.
	2. Lower moisture content (12%-25%).
	3. With higher carbon content (71%-77%) on dry ash-free basis.
	4. Heating value much higher than lignite or sub-bituminous coal.
	5. On the basis of hating value, it is subdivided into sub-bituminous A. Sub-bituminous B. and sub-bituminous C ranks.
Bituminous	1. Alternate bright and dull bandings.
	2. Harder and denser than sub-bituminous coal.
	3. Carbon content between 77% and 87% on dry ash-free basis.
	4. Heating value much higher than lignite or sub-bituminous coal.
	5. On the basis of volatile content, bituminous, coals are subdivided into low volatile bituminous, medium volatile bituminous, and high volatile bituminous.
Anthracite	1. Anthracite is the highest rank of coal.
	2. Carbon content over 87% on dry ash-free basis.
	3. Anthracite coal generally has the highest heating value per ton on a mineral matter free basis.
	4. It is often subdivided into semi-anthracite, anthracite, and meta-anthracite on the basis of carbon content.

59. **Global cooling** was a conjecture, especially during the 1970s, of imminent cooling of the Earth culminating in a period of extensive glaciation. Human activity — mostly as a by-product of fossil fuel combustion, partly by land use changes — increases the number of tiny particles (aerosols) in the atmosphere. These have a direct effect: they effectively increase the planetary albedo, thus cooling the planet by reducing the solar radiation reaching the surface; and an indirect effect: they affect the properties of clouds by acting as cloud condensation nuclei.

60. Genetic drift is a random change in allele frequencies over time, brought about by chance.

Random change in allele frequencies can lead to a loss of genetic diversity and to the homozygous condition. This is a possible outcome of genetic drift in all populations; it simply happens faster in small ones. When all of the individuals of a population have become homozygous for one allele, we say that fixation has occurred. Once an allele is fixed, its frequency will not change again unless mutation or gene flow introduces new alleles.

Bottlenecks and the Founder Effect

Genetic drift is pronounced when a few individuals rebuild a population or start a new one, such as occurs after a bottleneck—a drastic reduction in population size brought about by severe pressure.

61. The study reveal the impact of dam-building activities on human lives and livelihoods. Due to high population density, dams have displaced Indian citizens for decades. Major environmental impact of the Tehri dam in the central Himalaya are loss of biodiversity.

62. Atmospheric absorption in the thermal wavelength regions is dominated by the presence of H_2O and CO_2 absorption bands. Water vapour absorbs both solar near-infrared and thermal longwave radiation. The important absorption bands are in the near-infrared bands, the 6.3 μm vibration-rotation band, and the pure rotation band at wavelengths longer than 15 μm. CO_2 is active mainly in the 15 μm vibration-rotation band. The ozone (O_3) 9.6 μm vibration-rotation band appears in a region without other strong absorptions.

63. The human idea of 'loudness' is complicated by the fact that the human ear is more sensitive to some frequencies than others. Sounds with a frequency <100 Hz (bass notes) need to be of a higher energy before damage occurs than sounds in the most sensitive 1–5 kHz range.

65. Ecosystem integrity, albeit a useful concept, in sustainable natural resources management, poses a number of problems that science has yet to resolve. The concept is vague and often does not incorporate the dynamic view of ecosystems. Ecosystem integrity is a complex issue. A single indicator may not provide an operational definition. Integrity presupposes "unimpaired state", the quality or condition of being "whole" or "complete".

The new and wider goal in promoting sustainable development allows seeing its priority not only for environmental movement traditionally related to those issues but also for all civil society. In its turn, such an approach allowed identifying a sustainable development support movement as a priority for civil society action taken by economic and social councils, sustainable development institutions, national councils and social fora for sustainable development.

66. The neutrons generated by the fission reaction serve two activities. First they convert a fertile material into fissile material and then sustain the fission reaction for the fissile material so formed. These two reactions are called breeder reactions as they produce more fissile material than they consume in the process. The nuclear reactor in which such a reaction occurs is called a breeder reactor.

In case of U^{238} to Pu^{239} breeders, neutrons are not slowed down by a moderator, so they are known as Fast Breeder Reactors (FBRs). According to estimates the natural supply of fissile element will last for decades and that of fertile elements for hundred years provided that fast breeder reactors (FBRs) are used.

67. The ocean responds simultaneously to inertia and to the gravitational force of both the sun and moon. If earth, the moon, and the sun are all in a line (as shown in Figure a), the lunar and solar tides will be additive, resulting in higher high tides and lower low tides. But if the moon, earth, and sun form a right angle (as shown in Figure b), the solar tide will tend to diminish the lunar tide. Because the moon's contribution is more than twice that of the sun, the solar tide will not completely cancel the lunar tide.

The large tides caused by the linear alignment of the sun, earth, and moon are called spring tides. During spring tides and high tides are very high and low tides very low. These tides occur at two-week intervals corresponding to the new and full moons. Neap tides occur when the moon, earth, and sun form a right angle. During neap tides, high tides are not very high and low tides not very low.

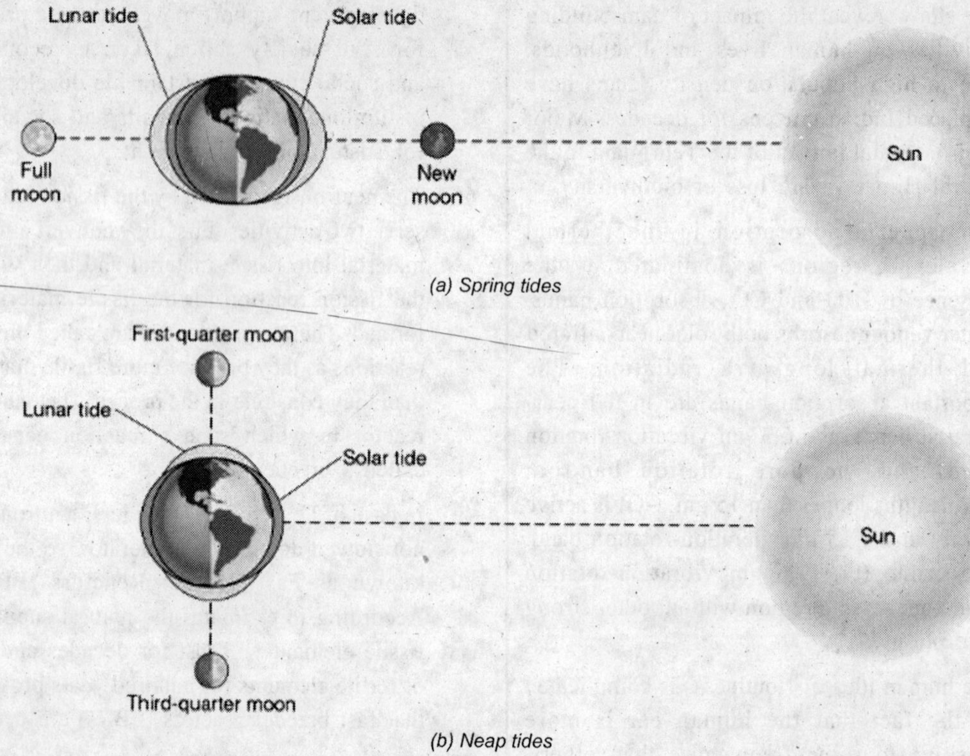

Fig.: *Relative positions of the sun, moon, and earth during spring and neap tides. (a) At the new and full moons, the solar and lunar tides reinforce each other, making spring tides, the highest high and lowest low tides. (b) At the first and third-quarter moons, the sun, earth, and moon form a right angle, creating neap tides, the lowest high and the highest low tides.*

68. Refuse derived fuel from municipal solid waste has higher energy content than raw municipal solid waste.

Refuse-derived fuel is produced from municipal solid waste, waste wood, commercial waste, industrial waste, sewage sludge, etc. In the United Kingdom, refuse-derived fuel is produced from raw municipal solid waste or source-separated municipal solid waste.

70. The spectral variation of canopy reflectance is mostly governed by the absorption properties of the elements, hence the leaves, since their intrinsic scattering properties show very little spectral variation. The relationship between canopy reflectance and leaf reflectance measured at the red edge over sugar beet canopies was used to simulate canopy reflectance from leaf reflectance spectra measured over the whole spectral domain.

Spectral reflectance data were collected from detached snapbean leaves in the laboratory with a multiband radiometer. Four experiments were designed to study the spectral response resulting from changes in leaf cover, relative water content of leaves, and leaf water potential. Spectral regions included in the analysis were red NIR and mid-IR. The red and mid-IR bands showed sensitivity to changes in both leaf cover and relative water content of leaves. The NIR was only highly sensitive to changes in leaf cover. Results provided evidence that mid-IR reflectance was governed primarily by leaf moisture content, although soil reflectance was an important factor when leaf cover was less than 100 per cent. High correlations between leaf water potentials and reflectance were attributed to covariances with relative water content of leaves and leaf cover.

71. Identification of Fine-Grained Soil Fractions from Manual Test

Material	Dry Strength	Dilatency Reaction	Toughness of Plastic Thread	Plasticity Description
Sandy silt	None-very low	Rapid	Weak, soft	None-low
Silt	Very low-low	Rapid	Weak, soft	None-low
Clayey silt	Low-medium	Rapid-slow	Medium stiff	Slight-medium
Sandy clay	Low-high	Slow-none	Medium stiff	Slight-medium
Silty clay	Medium-high	Slow-none	Medium stiff	Slight-medium
Clay	High-very high	None	Very stiff	High
Organic silt	Low-medium	Slow	Weak, soft	Slight
Organic day	Medium-very high	None	Medium stiff	Medium-high

72. The gaseous phase, or *soil air,* is a mixture of gases, and its content and composition are determined by soil-water-plant relationships. Whereas atmospheric air contains 20% oxygen, 0.03% carbon dioxide, and 78% nitrogen by volume, soil air tends to be lower in oxygen (<20%) and higher in carbon dioxide, (CO_2) content (>0.03%). In soil air, the CO_2 content may be 10 times or considerably higher than that in atmospheric air. It can reach levels of 5% but can be as low as 0.3%. Soil air in direct contact with plant roots, generally in the form of *films,* often contains ≥90% CO_2.

Here Assertion (A) is true and Reason (R) is false.

73. Human impacts such as building construction, deforestation, and the collapse of agricultural terraces were associated with smaller landslides, while geological factors showed no significant correlations with landslide volume. Road engineering factors such as the location of another road upslope and the collapse of roadcut retaining wall also proved unimportant. However, the height of the roadcut, channel incision undermining the roadcut and, especially, the steepness of the hillside upslope proved significant.

74. A skewed distribution is one in which many more values fall on one side of the mean than on the other side of the mean. This imbalance creates a difference between the mean and the median.

In a negatively skewed distribution, more values are above the mean, but the mean is lowered by some extremely low values below it. Figure illustrates a negatively skewed distribution. Notice that most of the x-axis values in the distribution are at the high end, to the right, and the smaller number of extremely low values at the low end are pulling the mean to the left of the median. Thus, in a negatively skewed distribution, the tail is on the left, at the lower end of x-axis values.

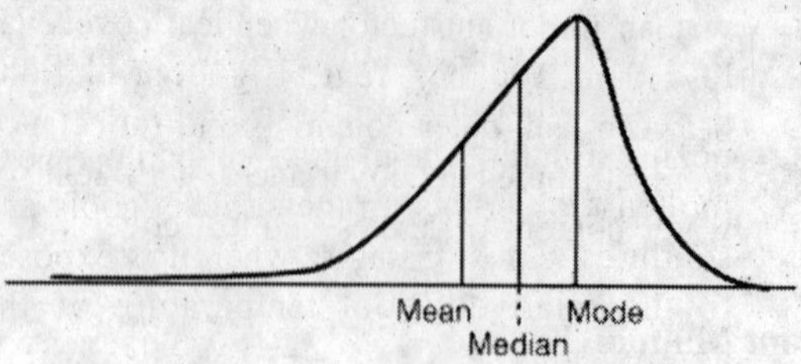

Fig.: *Negatively skewed distribution*
(tail is on the left, at the low end of the x-axis values)

75. Preliminary purification by flocculation is necessary, if the untreated water has a high turbidity, particularly as a result of colloidal or soluble organic impurities. Iron or aluminium salts are added to the water, so that iron(III) or aluminium hydroxide is precipitated:

$$Al_2(SO_4)_3 + 6\,H_2O \rightarrow 2\,Al(OH)_3\downarrow + 3\,H_2SO_4$$

$$FeSO_4Cl + 3\,H_2O \rightarrow Fe(OH)_3\downarrow + H_2SO_4 + HCl$$

$$Fe_2(SO_4)_3 + 6\,H_2O \rightarrow 2\,Fe(OH)_3\downarrow + 3\,H_2SO_4$$

Hydroxyl from positively charged flocs attract and carry down negatively charged colloidal clay particles.

76. The *Cartagena Protocol on Biosafety to the Convention on Biological Diversity* is an international agreement which aims to ensure the safe handling, transport and use of living modified organisms (LMOs) resulting from modern biotechnology that may have adverse effects on biological diversity, taking also into account risks to human health. It was adopted on 29 January 2000 and entered into force on 11 September 2003.

The Protocol seeks to protect biological diversity from the potential risks posed by living modified organisms resulting from modern biotechnology. It establishes an advance informed agreement (AIA) procedure for ensuring that countries are provided with the information necessary to make informed decisions before agreeing to the import of such organisms into their territory.

77. Cetane number: An engine rating method is the only reliable method of determining the ignition quality of a diesel fuel.

Cetane has a low auto-ignition temperature of 202°C and a short ignition delay which ensures smooth combustion in a diesel engine. 1-MN has a high auto-ignition temperature of 529°C and a long ignition delay. Heptamethylnonane has an auto-ignition temperature of 472°C and an ignition delay that is between cetane and 1-MN.

Cetane Index (CI): Cetane index is a calculated value, derived from fuel density and volatility. Cetane index usually gives a reasonably close approximation to real cetane number, which is derived from measurement in a real engine. Cetane index is widely used for routine monitoring of diesel fuel ignition quality. The calculated cetane index has mainly served as an alternative method of determining the ignition quality of diesel fuel to minimize the need for engine tests.

79. CARTOSAT-2 is a remote sensing satellite. Cartosat-2B weighed 694 kilograms at launch and is capable of steering its panchromatic camera up to plus or minus 26 degrees along its north-south and east-west axes to facilitate frequent imaging of any area in its field of view.

81. Epigeic (litter dweller): Epigeic worms live 10-30 cm deep beneath the soil and feed on humic substances and mineral matter. They are oesophageal, detritivorous, live in litter, and also consume litter. They have small size and are uniformly pigmented.

Litter dwellers or epigeic earthworms, such as *Eudrilus eugeniae, Eisenia fetida,* and *Perionyx excavates,* are the most suitable species for vermicomposting. The properties required for worms used in vermicomposting are as follows:

- Earthworms used for vermicomposting should consume high biomass and also be able to convert organic biomass at a high rate.

- They should be tolerant to changing environmental conditions.
- They should be able to feed on different types of organic feed materials.
- Population growth rate should be high in species chosen for vermicomposting.
- Process of vermicomposting is more feasible when a mixture of different species of earthworms is used rather than a single species.
- Species of earthworm selected for vermicomposting should be disease resistant.

82. Lava rock, also known as igneous rock, is formed when volcanic lava or magma cools and solidifies. It is one of the three main rock types found on Earth, along with metamorphic and sedimentary. Typically, eruption occurs when there is an increase in temperature, a decrease in pressure or a change in composition.

Igneous rocks are divided into two groups, intrusive or extrusive, depending upon where the molten rock solidifies.

Intrusive Igneous Rocks:

Intrusive, or plutonic, igneous rock forms when magma is trapped deep inside the Earth. Great globs of molten rock rise toward the surface. Some of the magma may feed volcanoes on the Earth's surface, but most remains trapped below, where it cools very slowly over many thousands or millions of years until it solidifies. Slow cooling means the individual mineral grains have a very long time to grow, so they grow to a relatively large size. Intrusive rocks have a coarse grained texture.

Extrusive Igneous Rocks:

Extrusive, or volcanic, igneous rock is produced when magma exits and cools above (or very near) the Earth's surface. These are the rocks that form at erupting volcanoes and oozing fissures. The magma, called lava when molten rock erupts on the surface, cools and solidifies almost instantly when it is exposed to the relatively cool temperature of the atmosphere.

83. Number of white ball = 3

Number of black ball = 2

Total number of ball = 3 + 2 = 5

Number of ways of selecting 2 balls out of 5 balls = ${}^5C_2$

Now, two balls are of different colours

Then, number of ways of selecting 1 white ball = ${}^3C_1$

and number of ways of selecting 1 black ball = ${}^2C_1$

$$\text{Required probability} = \frac{{}^3C_1 \times {}^2C_1}{{}^5C_1}$$

$$= \frac{3\times 2}{\left(\frac{5\times 4}{2}\right)} = \frac{6}{10} = \frac{3}{5}.$$

84. Waste management in India falls under the purview of the Union Ministry of Environment, Forests and Climate Change (MoEF&CC). In 2016 this ministry released the Solid Waste Management (SWM) Rules, 2016, these rules replaced the Municipal Solid Wastes (Management and Handling) Rules, 2000 which had been in place for 16 years.

Some of the highlights of the Solid Waste Management (SWM) Rules, 2016 are:

- Waste segregation at source is mandatory. Waste generators have to segregate waste into three streams - Organic or Biodegradable waste, Dry waste (plastic, paper, metal, wood, etc.) and Domestic Hazardous waste (diapers, napkins, mosquito repellants, cleaning agents etc.). Further, bulk waste generators such as hotels, hospitals etc. are expected to treat organic waste either onsite or by collaborating with the urban local body.

- Municipalities and urban local bodies have been directed to include informal waste pickers and rag pickers into their waste management process. This is the first time that national policy has acknowledged and included the informal sector into the waste management process. India has over 1.5 million subsistence informal waste pickers and including them into the formal waste management system represents an opportunity for urban local bodies to streamline their operations, while provide the waste pickers with better income opportunities.
- FMCG product manufacturers that use non-biodegradable packaging for their products must put in place a system to collect the packaging waste generated due to their production.
- Urban local bodies have been given a provision to charge bulk generators a user fee to collect and process their waste, additionally spot fines may be levied on user's burning garbage or throwing it in a public place.
- No non-recyclable waste having a calorific value of 1,500 Kcal/kg or more should be disposed in the landfills. It should either be utilized for generating energy or can be used for preparing refuse derived fuel. Or it can be used for co-processing in cement or thermal power plants.

85. United Nations Environment has bestowed Prime Minister Narendra Modi and French president Emmanuel Macron with the 2018 'Champion of the Earth' award for their leadership in promotion of solar energy.

86. (*i*) Fragmentation is a natural process; however, human activities increase the extent of fragmentation. Landscape ecology is one way to study how invasive species are influenced by fragmentation and other changes. Over time there have been different ideas of how temporal and spatial patterns of invasion are influenced by landscape processes.

(*ii*) Assembly is a community for women who want to be brave with their lives; a space to connect with others and enjoy the simple pleasures of food, creativity and exploring what it means to put our most courageous selves into the world.

(*iii*) The concept of Ecosystem Integrity is heavily discussed. A huge amount of definitions are used. Two of them:

- Supporting and maintaining a balanced, integrated adaptive community of organisms having a species composition, diversity, and functional organisation comparable to that of a natural habitat of the region. (Jorgensen/Müller, 2000)
- Ecosystem Integrity is a framework:
  - Precaution of ecological risks
  - Preserving the power of nature
  - Long-term development
  - Basis for human life
  - Protection of processes and structures being precautional for self-regulation.

(*iv*) **Dispersion** or distribution patterns show the spatial relationship between members of a **population** within a habitat. Individuals of a **population** can be distributed in one of three basic patterns: uniform, random, or clumped.

87. The atmospheric scale height

$$H \equiv \frac{k_B \overline{T}}{\overline{m}g}.$$

In terms of scale height, the pressure relative to its reference value thus varies with z as

$$\frac{p(z)}{p_0} = \exp\left(-\frac{z}{H}\right).$$

At altitude $z = H$, the pressure is just $1/e$ of its reference value (p_0); at $z = 2H$, the pressure has fallen another factor of e, that is to $1/e^2$

of p_0, and so on. Scale height provides a concise measure of the rate with which pressure decreases with altitude; pressure decreases by a factor of e for each increment of H in altitude.

89. In ecology, *r*/K **selection theory** relates to the selection of combinations of traits in an organism that trade off between quantity and quality of offspring. The focus on either an increased quantity of offspring at the expense of individual parental investment of *r*-strategists, or on a reduced quantity of offspring with a corresponding increased parental investment of K-strategists, varies widely, seemingly to promote success in particular environments.

In *r*/K selection theory, selective pressures are hypothesised to drive evolution in one of two generalized directions: *r*- or K-selection. These terms, *r* and K, are drawn from standard ecological algebra as illustrated in the simplified Verhulst model of population dynamics.

$$\frac{dN}{dt} = rN\left(1 - \frac{N}{K}\right)$$

where *N* is the population, *r* is the maximum growth rate, K is the carrying capacity of the local environment, and dN/dt, the derivative of *N* with respect to time *t*, is the rate of change in population with time. Thus, the equation relates the growth rate of the population *N* to the current population size, incorporating the effect of the two constant parameters *r* and K. (Note that decrease is negative growth.) The choice of the letter K came from the German *Kapazitätsgrenze* (capacity limit), while *r* came from *rate*.

93. Generally, acid mine drainage from underground mines occurs as point discharges. A major source of acid mine drainage may result from the closure of a mine. When a mine is abandoned and dewatering by pumping ceases, the water level rebounds. However, the workings often act as drainage systems so that the water does not rise to its former level.

94. **BOD indicates** the amount of putrescible organic matter present in water. Therefore, a low **BOD** is an indicator of good quality water, while a **high BOD indicates** polluted water. Dissolved oxygen (DO) is consumed by bacteria when **large** amounts of organic matter from sewage or other discharges are present in the water.

If BOD level of water in a reservoir is less than 5 mg/L, it is low polluted.

95. (*i*) High-performance liquid chromatographic (HPLC) method with fluorescence detection was developed for the quantification of polycyclic aromatic hydrocarbons (PAHs) in human hair.

(*ii*) **Ultraviolet–visible spectroscopy** or **ultraviolet–visible spectrophotometry** (**UV–Vis** or **UV/Vis**) refers to absorption spectroscopy or reflectance spectroscopy in part of the ultraviolet and the full, adjacent visible spectral regions. This means it uses light in the visible and adjacent ranges.

(*iii*) **Electrophoresis** is a technique commonly used in the lab to separate charged molecules, like DNA, according to size. Gel **electrophoresis** is a technique commonly used in laboratories to separate charged molecules like DNA.

96. Terrestrial ecosystems are known for their diversity; they are grouped into large categories called biomes. Grouping these ecosystems into just a few biome categories obscures the great diversity of the individual ecosystems within them.

Terrestrial biomes on Earth are each distinguished by characteristic temperatures and amount of precipitation. Comparing the annual totals of precipitation and fluctuations in precipitation from one biome to another provides clues as to the importance of abiotic factors in the distribution of biomes.

Temperature variation on a daily and seasonal basis is also important for predicting the geographic distribution of the biome and the vegetation type in the biome. The distribution of these biomes shows that the same biome can occur in geographically distinct areas with similar climates.

98. The Union ministry of tribal affairs has notified the amended rules for the implementation of the Forest Rights Act (FRA) of 2006. The new rules say that forest dwellers can transport minor forest produce (MFP) by "any appropriate means of transport" and mandate that transit passes for the same will be issued by a committee constituted by the Gram Sabha.

The draft rules issued in July were silent on transit passes. "This would have led to a threat of opening up of forest for unsustainable use. But allowing the forest department to issue transit passes, as has been done so far, would have defeated the purpose. The ministry has done the right thing by empowering gram sabha to issue transit passes,"

According to the new rule, the committee constituted under the gram sabha will prepare conservation and management plan for community forest resources after forest dwellers' rights on such resources are recognised.

99. As of June 1, 2015, the Hazard Communication Standard (HCS) will require pictograms on labels to alert users of the chemical hazards to which they may be exposed. Each pictogram consists of a symbol on a white background framed within a red border and represents a distinct hazard(s). The pictogram on the label is determined by the chemical hazard classification.

Flame Over Circle

100. The feasibility of rainwater harvesting in a particular locality is highly dependent upon the amount and intensity of rainfall. Other variables, such as catchment area and type of catchment surface, usually can be adjusted according to household needs. As rainfall is usually unevenly distributed throughout the year, rainwater collection methods can serve as only supplementary sources of household water. The viability of rainwater harvesting systems is also a function of the quantity and quality of water available from other sources, household size, per capita water requirements, and budget available.

Tamil Nadu was the first state to make rainwater harvesting compulsory for every building to avoid groundwater depletion. The scheme was launched in 2001 and has been implemented in all rural areas of Tamil Nadu. It gave excellent results within five years, and slowly every state took it as role model. Since its implementation, Chennai saw a 50% rise in the water table in five years and the water quality significantly improved.

Previous Paper (Solved)

UGC-NET-Junior Research Fellowship & Assistant Professor Exam

Environmental Science, July-2018*

PAPER-II

Note: *This paper contains* ***hundred (100)*** *objective type questions of* ***two (2)*** *marks each.* ***All*** *questions are* ***compulsory***.

1. For a thermally comfortable, seated bare bodied person at 25°C, the maximum energy loss is due to:
A. Radiation B. Convection
C. Conduction D. Evaporation

2. High concentrations of pollutants at ground level during winter season are due to:
A. Radiation inversion
B. Subsidence inversion
C. Frontal inversion
D. Landscape induced inversion

3. The theme 'Transforming our world : 2030 Agenda' pertains to:
A. Protection of ozone layer
B. Climate change - Action plans
C. Sustainable development goals
D. Millennium development goals

4. At a latitude of 30°, there is pressure gradient of 5.0 mb per 100 km. Given the density of air ~ 1.25 kg/m^3, the geostrophic winds will have velocity (m/s):
A. 5.48 m/s B. 54.86 m/s
C. 109.72 m/s D. 27.43 m/s

5. The basic nature of lithosphere does not arise from element(s):
A. Na and K B. Ca
C. Mg D. Si

6. If the tropospheric lapse rate be 6.5°C/km and if T denotes temperature and Z denotes the altitude then:

A. $\frac{dT}{dZ} = 6.5°C/km$

B. $\frac{dT}{dZ} = -6.5°C/km$

C. $\frac{dZ}{dT} = 6.5°C/km$

D. $\frac{dZ}{dT} = -6.5°C/km$

7. Identify the statement, which best describes the second law of thermodynamics:
A. The internal energy of the universe is constant.
B. Energy can be neither created nor destroyed.
C. At absolute zero, entropy of a substance is considered to be zero.
D. When an isolated system undergoes a spontaneous change, the entropy of the universe increases.

8. Tropical cyclones occur on:
A. Meso - scale B. Micro - scale
C. Planetary scale D. Synoptic scale

9. If e and p are vapour pressure of water and total pressure of moist air, the equation of state for moist atmosphere can be written as:

A. $PV \simeq RT\left[1+\frac{e}{p}\right]$

B. $PV \simeq RT\left[1-\frac{e}{p}\right]$

* Exam held on 08 July, 2018

C. $PV = RT\left[1 + 0.38\frac{e}{p}\right]$

D. $PV = RT\left[1 + 0.62\frac{e}{p}\right]$

10. Select the **incorrect** statement about the redox potential of aqueous solutions:

A. As the concentration of molecular oxygen increases, the redox potential increases.

B. As the concentration of hydrogen ions increases, the redox potential increases.

C. As the concentration of molecular oxygen decreases, the redox potential decreases.

D. As the concentration of hydrogen ions decreases, the redox potential increases.

11. Match the List-I and List-II. Identify the **correct** answer from the codes given below:

List-I (Analyte)	**List-II (Method)**
(*a*) Lead	(*i*) Winkler Method
(*b*) Dissolved oxygen	(*ii*) Gravimetric Method
(*c*) SO_2	(*iii*) GC-MS
(*d*) PAH	(*iv*) West Gaeke Method

Code :

	(*a*)	(*b*)	(*c*)	(*d*)
A.	(*iii*)	(*iv*)	(*ii*)	(*i*)
B.	(*i*)	(*ii*)	(*iii*)	(*iv*)
C.	(*ii*)	(*iii*)	(*iv*)	(*i*)
D.	(*ii*)	(*i*)	(*iv*)	(*iii*)

12. The main acidic component of the present atmosphere is:

A. HCl B. NO_x

C. SO_2 D. CO_2

13. Identify the **incorrect** statement regarding PCBs:

A. These are water soluble and hence bioaccumulate.

B. These are fire resistant.

C. These are stable at high temperatures.

D. These have high electrical resistance.

14. Toxicity of which of the following metals is **not** due to reaction with sulfhydryl group?

A. Arsenic B. Cadmium

C. Lead D. Chromium

15. By chemical reaction, the hydroxyl radicals fail to remove which of the following trace gases from the atmosphere?

A. CO B. NO

C. SO_2 D. CFCs

16. How many gram of acetic acid (molar mass = 60 g/mole) are present in 100 ml of 0.1 M acetic acid?

A. 0.6 g B. 0.06 g

C. 6.0 g D. 60.0 g

17. Three coloured sheets of equal thickness are placed in a light beam. Each sheet absorbs 20% of light incident upon it. What is the intensity of light transmitted after the third plate?

A. 9.0% B. 10.5%

C. 51.2% D. 40.0%

18. In a volumetric titration, a 20 ml aqueous HCl solution, needs 10 ml of 0.1 N NaOH for complete neutralization.

The concentration of HCl solution is:

A. 0.2 N B. 0.002 N

C. 0.01 N D. 0.05 N

19. The best way for assessing the organic component of a water sample is the determination of:

A. TOC B. COD

C. BOD D. DO

20. Biogas produced by the anerobic digestion is a mixture of:

A. CO_2, SO_2, N_2O, CH_4 and H_2O

B. CO, CO_2, H_2S, CH_4 and natural gas

C. CH_4, CO_2, NH_3, H_2S and H_2O

D. CO_2, NH_3, C_2H_5OH and H_2O

21. The percentage concentration of which of the following ions is highest in sea water?

A. Bicarbonate B. Chloride

C. Sulphate D. Sodium

22. In which of the following ecosystems, the food web involves more species and more trophic levels?

A. Rain forest B. Ocean
C. Desert D. Glacier

23. Given below are two statements. One labelled as Assertion (A) and the other labelled as Reason (R):

Assertion (A) : The available energy of an ecosystem decreases with the length of food chain.

Reason (R) : At each transfer of energy in food chain, a large proportion of potential energy is lost as heat.

Choose the **correct** answer:

A. Both (A) and (R) are correct and (R) is the correct explanation of (A).
B. Both (A) and (R) are correct and (R) is not the correct explanation of (A).
C. (A) is true, but (R) is false.
D. (A) is false, but (R) is true.

24. The origin of eukaryotic cell on earth took place:

A. 1500 Million years ago
B. 1850 Million years ago
C. 850 Million years ago
D. 1000 Million years ago

25. Ratio of energy transfer at different trophic levels in the food chain is called:

A. Metabolic efficiency
B. Ecological efficiency
C. Energy flow rate
D. Food chain complexity

26. At which stage of ecological succession, an ecosystem exhibits, photosynthesis (P) = Respiration (R):

A. Pioneer stage B. Mid seral stage
C. Climax stage D. Early seral stage

27. The species determining the ability of large number of other species to persist in a community, are called:

A. Indicator species B. Keystone species
C. Dominant species D. Endemic species

28. Biodiversity:

(*a*) Increases towards the Arctic region
(*b*) Decreases towards the Arctic region
(*c*) Increases towards the equator
(*d*) Decreases towards the equator

Choose the **correct** code :

A. (*a*) and (*d*) B. (*a*) and (*b*)
C. (*a*) and (*c*) D. (*b*) and (*c*)

29. Arctic Tundra is situated around:

A. 66.5° N B. 55.5° N
C. 45° N D. 66.5° S

30. Main limiting factor governing primary productivity in pelagic zone of the ocean is:

(*a*) Light
(*b*) Available nutrients
(*c*) Number of primary producers
(*d*) Tidal current

Choose the **correct** code:

A. (*a*) only
B. (*a*) and (*b*) only
C. (*a*), (*b*) and (*c*) only
D. (*a*), (*b*), (*c*) and (*d*)

31. The nature of food web at the developmental stage of a succession is:

A. linear, predominantly grazing
B. linear, predominantly detritus
C. weblike, predominantly detritus
D. weblike, predominantly grazing

32. Based on the casualties reported worldwide, which one of the following is most deadly airborne bacterial disease?

A. Diphtheria B. Whooping cough
C. Pneumonia D. Meningitis

33. Match the List-I and List-II. Identify the **correct** answer from the code given below:

List-I (Endangered animals)	**List-II (Distribution)**
(*a*) Lion tailed Macaque	(*i*) Himalayan foothills
(*b*) Golden Langur	(*ii*) Jammu and Kashmir
(*c*) Spotted Linsang	(*iii*) Western Ghats
(*d*) Pallas's cat	(*iv*) Central and Eastern Himalayas

Code :

	(*a*)	(*b*)	(*c*)	(*d*)
A.	(*ii*)	(*i*)	(*iii*)	(*iv*)
B.	(*iii*)	(*i*)	(*iv*)	(*ii*)
C.	(*iv*)	(*iii*)	(*ii*)	(*i*)
D.	(*i*)	(*ii*)	(*iv*)	(*iii*)

34. Reproductive isolation of populations leads to:
A. infertility
B. population explosion
C. speciation
D. population decline

35. In the context of local environment, heleoplankton refers to:
A. Saltwater plankton B. Pond plankton
C. Stream plankton D. Lake plankton

36. According to India State Forest Report (ISFR), 2017 of MOEFCC, GOI, the increase in forest cover of the country with reference to the year 2015 is:
A. 1.8% B. 2.0%
C. 2.2% D. 1.0%

37. Which one of the following is a cultivable species of tropical earthworm?
A. Elsenia fetida
B. Lumbricus rubellus
C. Drawida nepalensis
D. Polypheretima elongata

38. Slow downslope movement of water saturated rock mass which is not confined to a definite channel, is called:
A. Soil creep B. Debris flow
C. Mudslide D. Solifluction

39. Isogons are the points which join beds of:
A. Equal dip amount
B. Same strike direction
C. Equal thickness
D. Opposite strike direction

40. Match the List-I and List-II. Identify the **correct** answer from the code given below:

List-I (Ecosystem service)	**List-II (Function)**
(*a*) Provisioning	(*i*) Nutrient cycling
(*b*) Regulating	(*ii*) Recreational
(*c*) Cultural	(*iii*) Carbon sequestration
(*d*) Supporting	(*iv*) Pharmaceuticals

Code :

	(*a*)	(*b*)	(*c*)	(*d*)
A.	(*i*)	(*ii*)	(*iii*)	(*iv*)
B.	(*iv*)	(*iii*)	(*ii*)	(*i*)
C.	(*i*)	(*iv*)	(*iii*)	(*ii*)
D.	(*iv*)	(*iii*)	(*i*)	(*ii*)

41. Cartostat-2 satellite has a spatial resolution of:
A. better than 1 m B. 2 m
C. 5.8 m D. 23 m

42. L-band in microwave remote sensing provides information about scattering from:
(*a*) Volume (*b*) Soil
(*c*) Canopy (*d*) Trunks and boles
Choose the **correct** code:
A. (*a*) only B. (*a*), (*b*), only
C. (*a*), (*b*), (*c*) only D. (*a*), (*b*), (*d*) only

43. In temperate lakes upwelling replenishes nutrients turnover during:
(*a*) Autumn and spring
(*b*) Autumn and winter
(*c*) Summer and winter
(*d*) Summer and spring
Choose the **correct** code:
A. (*a*) only B. (*b*) only
C. (*c*) only D. (*d*) only

44. Soil pollution is caused by:
(*a*) Industrial waste (*b*) Agrochemicals
(*c*) Petrochemicals (*d*) Detergents
Choose the **correct** code:
A. (*a*) and (*b*) only
B. (*b*), (*c*) and (*d*) only
C. (*a*), (*b*), (*c*) and (*d*)
D. (*c*) and (*d*) only

45. In an aquifer having a coefficient of permeability $k = 0.1$ mm/s and water table sloping at a rate of 1 m over a distance of 200 m, the value of groundwater flow is:
A. 0.005 mm/s B. 0.0010 mm/s
C. 0.0015 mm/s D. 0.0025 mm/s

46. Seismic waves travel faster through:

A. Gas B. Liquid
C. Solid D. Lava

47. Urban Heat Island effect is best studied using remote sensing in the following spectral region:

(*a*) 0.5-0.9 μm (*b*) 3-5 μm
(*c*) 10-12 μm (*d*) 3-6 cm

Choose the **correct** code:

A. (*a*) only B. (*a*) and (*b*) only
C. (*a*) and (*c*) only D. (*a*) and (*d*) only

48. In landscape ecological studies, the term landscape process includes:

(*a*) The exchange of materials and energy
(*b*) Exchange or movement of organisms
(*c*) Patch, matrix and corridor
(*d*) Porosity

Choose the **correct** code:

A. (*a*) only
B. (*a*) and (*b*) only
C. (*a*), (*b*) and (*c*) only
D. (*a*), (*b*), (*c*) and (*d*)

49. A drowned river valley estuary is formed when?

A. a barrier island or sand bar separates a section of the coast where fresh water enters.
B. sea level rose at the end of the last glacial age invading low lands and rivers.
C. a deep valley is created by retreating glaciers.
D. land sinks due to movements of the crust.

50. Fringing reef generally develops:

A. as a narrow band close to a shore.
B. at some distance from the coast.
C. as a ring around central lagoon.
D. as a patch in the pelagic zone of the sea.

51. According to River Continuum Concept of Vannote et. al (1980), the major sources of energy in medium-sized streams are:

(*a*) Fine particulate organic matter
(*b*) Coarse particulate organic matter
(*c*) Algae
(*d*) Aquatic plants

Choose the **correct** code:

A. (*a*) only
B. (*b*) and (*c*) only
C. (*a*), (*c*) and (*d*) only
D. (*a*), (*b*), (*c*), and (*d*)

52. Self-purification of running streams may be due to:

A. oxidation, sedimentation and coagulation
B. sedimentation, dilution and oxidation
C. dilution, sedimentation and coagulation
D. dilution, oxidation and coagulation

53. Given below are two statements. One labelled as Assertion (A) and the other labelled as Reason (R):

Assertion (A) : The efficiency of a PV cell is limited by the quantum processes involving incident photons and the electrons in the cell.

Reason (R) : The band gap energy of the semiconducting material used to fabricate PV cell is less in comparison to the energies of photons of insolation.

Choose the correct answer:

A. Both (A) and (R) are correct and (R) is the correct explanation of (A).
B. Both (A) and (R) are correct and (R) is not the correct explanation of (A).
C. (A) is true, but (R) is false.
D. (A) is false, but (R) is true.

54. Given below are two statements. one labelled as Assertion (A) and the other labelled as Reason (R):

Assertion (A) : The recoverable renewable energy is a fraction of the resource base of the renewable sources available in the world.

Reason (R) : Much of the renewable energy is either of high entropy or too inaccessible to use.

Choose the **correct** answer :

A. Both (A) and (R) are correct and (R) is the correct explanation of (A).
B. Both (A) and (R) are correct and (R) is not the correct explanation of (A).
C. (A) is true, but (R) is false.
D. (A) is false, but (R) is true.

55. Given below are two statements. One labelled as Assertion (A) and the other labelled as Reason (R):

Assertion (A) : Tidal range is a critical factor in determining whether an estuary would be useful for tidal power generation.

Reason (R) : Tidal power is proportional to tidal range.

Choose the **correct** answer:

A. Both (A) and (R) are correct and (R) is the correct explanation of (A).
B. Both (A) and (R) are correct and (R) is not the correct explanation of (A).
C. (A) is true, but (R) is false.
D. (A) is false, but (R) is true.

56. A single solar cell on illumination by insolation of about 800 Wm^{-2} produces a voltage of 0.5 V and a current upto 2.0 A. The efficiency of the solar cell is 12.5%. The area of the cell is:

A. 2×10^{-2} m^2 B. 5×10^{-3} m^2
C. 4×10^{-4} m^2 D. 10^{-2} m^2

57. If the ion density in a high temperature fusion plasma consisting of deuterium and tritium fuel is 2.5×10^{20} m^{-3}, the minimum confinement time required for nuclear fusion to produce net energy will be:

A. 0.5 s B. 0.4 s
C. 0.25 s D. 4.0 s

58. At present, which geothermal resource is exploited on commercial scale in the world?

A. Magma B. Hot dry rock
C. Geopressured D. Hydrothermal

59. Which of the following substances has the maximum energy content (MJ/m^3)?

A. Methane gas B. Liquid butane
C. Natural gas D. Hydrogen gas

60. Given below are two statements. One labelled as Assertion (A) and the other labelled as Reason (R):

Assertion (A) : The nuclei of elements such as plutonium and uranium have extremely large energy potentials.

Reason (R) : They are in states of thermodynamic non-equilibrium.

Choose the correct answer:

A. Both (A) and (R) are **correct** and (R) is the correct explanation of (A).
B. Both (A) and (R) are correct and (R) is not the correct explanation of (A).
C. (A) is true, but (R) is false.
D. (A) is false, but (R) is true.

61. In a nuclear fission reaction involving U_{92}^{235} and a slow neutron, the mass defect is found to be 0.223 u. How much energy will be released from 5.0 gram of U_{92}^{235}? ($1u = 1.66 \times 10^{-27}$ kg)

A. 426.7 GJ B. 85.3 GJ
C. 170.6 GJ D. 42.6 GJ

62. Which of the following biofuels is produced from acidification and distillation of woody crops?

A. Methanol B. Ethanol
C. Producer gas D. Esters

63. How thick a sound barrier be made if it is to attenuate efficiently sound transmitted at 5.0 kHz?

A. ~ 2.0 cm B. ~ 3.3 cm
C. ~ 6.6 cm D. ~ 2.0 m

64. Identify the most reducing water sample as inferred from pE values given below:

A. pE = 15 B. pE = 12
C. pE = 7 D. pE = 5

65. Given below are two statements. One labelled as Assertion (A) and the other labelled as Reason (R):

Assertion (A) : In an unpolluted and dust free atmosphere, rainwater pH is ~ 5.6.

Reason (R) : Dissolution of carbon dioxide in rainwater produces hydrogen ions.

Choose the correct answer :

A. Both (A) and (R) are **correct** and (R) is the correct explanation of (A).
B. Both (A) and (R) are correct and (R) is not the correct explanation of (A).

C. (A) is true, but (R) is false.
D. (A) is false, but (R) is true.

66. As per BIS, the recommended pH for drinking water is:
A. 5.0 - 6.5 B. 6.5 - 8.5
C. 7.5 - 9.0 D. 8 - 10

67. In the disinfection of water by chlorine, the most reactive chlorine species is:
A. Cl_2 B. ClO^-
C. HOCl D. Cl^-

68. Given below are two statements. One labelled as Assertion (A) and the other labelled as Reason (R) :

Assertion (A) : Black carbon contributes to global warming.

Reason (R) : Black carbon behaves like a black body.

Choose the **correct** answer :
A. Both (A) and (R) are correct and (R) is the correct explanation of (A).
B. Both (A) and (R) are correct and (R) is not the correct explanation of (A).
C. (A) is true, but (R) is false.
D. (A) is false, but (R) is true.

69. Which of the following air pollutants are responsible for photochemical smog?
(*a*) Oxides of nitrogen
(*b*) Ozone
(*c*) Unburnt hydrocarbons
(*d*) Sulphur dioxide

Choose the **correct** code:
A. (*a*), (*b*) and (*d*) only
B. (*a*), (*b*) and (*c*) only
C. (*c*) and (*d*) only
D. (*a*) and (*c*) only

70. Temporary hardness is caused by:
A. Calcium sulphate
B. Magnesium sulphate
C. Magnesium carbonate
D. Magnesium chloride

71. Bioremediation of soil is **not** achieved readily if :
A. Contaminant is a lighter molecule.
B. Contaminant has high aromaticity.
C. Contaminant is a polar molecule.
D. Contaminant is non-halogenated.

72. Given below are two statements. One labelled as Assertion (A) and the other labelled as Reason (R):

Assertion (A) : Traffic policemen in urban centres generally suffer from oxygen deficiency.

Reason (R) : Carbon dioxide forms a very strong complex with haemoglobin.

Choose the **correct** answer:
A. Both (A) and (R) are correct and (R) is the correct explanation of (A).
B. Both (A) and (R) are correct and (R) is not the correct explanation of (A).
C. (A) is true, but (R) is false.
D. (A) is false, but (R) is true.

73. A bar graph whose bars are drawn in decreasing order of frequency is:
A. histogram
B. frequency polygon
C. pareto chart
D. cumulative bar chart

74. If four groups of vehicles consisting of 5, 10, 12 and 8 cars reported the gaseous pollutant emissions of 1.2 kg, 2.1 kg, 3.0 kg and 1.5 kg per day respectively, then the mean emission of gaseous pollutant from all cars is:
A. 4.43 kg/day B. 2.14 kg/day
C. 4.80 kg/day D. 3.12 kg/day

75. A sample of 10 measurements of diameter of trees in a survey gives a mean of 43.8 cm and a standard deviation of 0.6 cm. Given t = 2.26, the 95% confidence limit for the actual diameter is in between:
A. 41.54 and 46.06 cm
B. 43.348 and 44.252 cm
C. 43.20 and 44.812 cm
D. 43.252 and 44.348 cm

76. In a fish population of a pond it is believed that males and females are in equal proportion. If out of 200 fish in a catch, 120 are male and 80 are female, then the Chi square (χ^2) value is:

A. 8 B. 4
C. 16 D. 12

77. In multiple regression analysis, the value that refers to the extent of possible variance in the dependent variable that can be accounted for, by the independent variable is:

A. R Value
B. Adjusted R^2 Value
C. '*r*' Value
D. 1/R Value

78. A population size at $t = 0$ is 80 and has a growth rate of 0.12. If the population follows logistic growth, what is the growth rate constant if the carrying capacity is 240?

A. 5.32 B. 9.60
C. 0.18 D. 3.80

79. In a city of area (8 km × 8 km), the vehicular traffic is releasing 10^{-5} g/m^2 – s of CO during the winter season between 4 pm and 8 pm. During this period mixing height is 100 m. The wind is blowing in the city at a speed of 4.0 m/s along the side of the city. If the initial concentration of CO at 4 pm was negligible, the estimated concentration of CO after 4 hours should be:

A. 0.2 mg/m^3 B. 3.2 mg/m^3
C. 2.0 mg/m^3 D. 20.0 mg/m^3

80. In the Gaussian plume model, the effective stack height is the sum of actual stack height and the plume rise which depends on:

(*a*) buoyancy of exhaust gases
(*b*) momentum of exhaust gases
(*c*) stability of the atmosphere
(*d*) emission rate of the pollutants

Choose the **correct** code :

A. (*a*), (*b*) and (*d*) B. (*a*), (*b*), (*c*) and (*d*)
C. (*a*), (*c*) and (*d*) D. (*a*), (*b*) and (*c*)

81. Given below are two statements. One labelled as Assertion (A) and the other labelled as Reason (R):

Assertion (A) : Global shipping is a source of net cooling of atmosphere.

Reason (R) : Ships are responsible for significant amounts of sulphur emissions.

Choose the **correct** answer:

A. Both (A) and (R) are correct and (R) is the correct explanation of (A).
B. Both (A) and (R) are correct and (R) is not the correct explanation of (A).
C. (A) is true, but (R) is false.
D. (A) is false, but (R) is true.

82. Given below are two statements. One labelled as Assertion (A) and the other labelled as Reason (R):

Assertion (A) : Ozone depletion in stratosphere causes melanoma.

Reason (R) : Ozone is a gas which largely absorbs UV - A radiation.

Choose the **correct** answer:

A. Both (A) and (R) are correct and (R) is the correct explanation of (A).
B. Both (A) and (R) are correct and (R) is not the correct explanation of (A).
C. (A) is true, but (R) is false.
D. (A) is false, but (R) is true.

83. Identify the **incorrect** statement with regard to saline and alkaline soil:

A. These show white incrustation of salts of calcium, magnesium and sodium on the soil surface.
B. These soils are infertile.
C. These soils are poor in drainage.
D. These soils are pervious.

84. Given below are two statements. One labelled as Assertion (A) and the other labelled as Reason (R):

Assertion (A) : Phosphorus limits eutrophication if nitrogen is eight times more abundant (weight wise) than phosphorus in fresh water.

Reason (R) : About eight times more nitrogen (weight wise) is required than phosphorus for plant growth.

Choose the **correct** answer :

A. Both (A) and (R) are correct and (R) is the correct explanation of (A).
B. Both (A) and (R) are correct and (R) is not the correct explanation of (A).

C. (A) is true, but (R) is false.
D. (A) is false, but (R) is true.

85. World Biodiversity day is celebrated every year on:

A. March 22 B. May 22
C. July 22 D. November 22

86. To achieve its objectives, the International Solar Alliance aims to mobilize financial investment over:

A. Z 1 trillion B. Z 100 billion
C. Z 500 billion D. Z 200 billion

87. A Ramsar site not able to perform its ecological functions comes under:

A. Montreal protocol
B. Montreux record
C. Montreal record
D. Montreaux protocol

88. Which of the following bacterium is called as the superbug that could clean up oil spills?

A. Bacillus denitrificans
B. Pseudomonas denitrificans
C. Pseudomonas putida
D. Bacillus subtillis

89. For the scientific research or investigations, the chief wildlife warden may grant the permission to public to enter a sanctuary under the section:

A. 35 of The wildlife (Protection) Act 1972
B. 28 of The Wildlife (Protection) Act 1972
C. 72 of The Indian Forest Act 1922
D. 73 of The Indian Forest Act 1927

90. Power to issue notification reserving the trees or class of trees in a protected forest lies with:

A. Ministry of Environment, Forest and Climate Change, GOI
B. Biodiversity Board
C. State Government
D. Central Government

91. In which stage of decomposition of landfilled waste, the bacteria acetogen helps to reduce the pH of leachate and allows heavy metals to be solubilized?

A. Aerobic Phase
B. Acid Phase
C. Unsteady Methanogenisis Stage
D. Steady Methanogenisis Stage

92. Choose the **correct** sequence in resource recovery for mixed solid waste:

A. Screening → Air classifier → Shredder → Magnetic separation
B. Magnetic separation → Shredder → Screening → Air classifier
C. Shredder → Screening → Air classifier → Magnetic separation
D. Screening → Shredder → Magnetic separation → Air classifier

93. Onsight mulching and composting of waste is a component of integrated solid waste management under the process of:

A. recycling
B. disposal
C. source reduction
D. disinfection

94. Match the List-I and List-II. Identify the **correct** answer from the code given below:

List-I (Waste types)	**List-II (Disposal methods)**
(*a*) Human tissues	(*i*) Disinfection and shredding
(*b*) Laboratory wastes	(*ii*) Disinfection and discharge into drains
(*c*) Waste sharps	(*iii*) Autoclaving
(*d*) Liquid waste	(*iv*) Incineration and deep burial

Code :

	(*a*)	(*b*)	(*c*)	(*d*)
A.	(*iv*)	(*iii*)	(*i*)	(*ii*)
B.	(*ii*)	(*iii*)	(*iv*)	(*i*)
C.	(*iii*)	(*iv*)	(*ii*)	(*i*)
D.	(*iv*)	(*iii*)	(*ii*)	(*i*)

95. Which of the following materials are used as landfill sealants for the control of gas and leachate?

(*a*) Fly ash

(*b*) Lime
(*c*) Bentonite
(*d*) Butyl rubber

Choose the **correct** code:
A. (*a*) and (*b*) only
B. (*b*) and (*c*) only
C. (*c*) and (*d*) only
D. (*d*) and (*a*) only

96. Select the **correct** sequence with reference to Environmental Management System ISO1401:
A. Environmental policy → Implementation and operation → Checking and corrective action → Management review
B. Implementation and operation → Checking and corrective action → Management review → Environmental policy
C. Implementation and operation → Environmental policy → Checking and corrective action → Management review
D. Checking and corrective action → Management review → Implementation and operation → Environmental policy

97. Match the List-I and List-II. Identify the **correct** answer from the code given below:

List-I (EIA process)	List-II (Features)
(*a*) Environmental Baseline	(*i*) Systematic Appraisal of EIS
(*b*) Development Action	(*ii*) Avoid, reduce and remedy for impacts
(*c*) Mitigation measures	(*iii*) Rationale of the project
(*d*) Review	(*iv*) Establishment of present and future state of environment

Code:

	(*a*)	(*b*)	(*c*)	(*d*)
A.	(*iv*)	(*iii*)	(*ii*)	(*i*)
B.	(*i*)	(*ii*)	(*iii*)	(*iv*)
C.	(*ii*)	(*iii*)	(*iv*)	(*i*)
D.	(*iii*)	(*iv*)	(*i*)	(*ii*)

98. The type of project in 'B' category in the schedule attached with EIA notification of 14th September 2006, needs environmental clearance from:
(*a*) Central Govt. without the recommendation of the Expert Appraisal Committee.
(*b*) State Govt. on the recommendation of the State Expert Appraisal Committee.
(*c*) State Environmental Impact Assessment Authority on the recommendation of State Expert Appraisal Committee.

Choose the **correct** code:
A. (*a*) and (*b*) only
B. (*b*) and (*c*) only
C. (*c*) only
D. (*c*) and (*a*) only

99. Match the List-I and List-II. Identify the **correct** answer from the code given below:

List-I (Process)	List-II (Description)
(*a*) Development action	(*i*) Compensation for adverse impacts
(*b*) Environmental baseline	(*ii*) Development stages and processes
(*c*) Impacts prediction	(*iii*) Establishment of future and present state of environment
(*d*) Mitigation measures	(*iv*) Magnitude of identified change in environment

Code :

	(*a*)	(*b*)	(*c*)	(*d*)
A.	(*ii*)	(*iii*)	(*iv*)	(*i*)
B.	(*iii*)	(*iv*)	(*i*)	(*ii*)
C.	(*iv*)	(*i*)	(*ii*)	(*iii*)
D.	(*i*)	(*ii*)	(*iii*)	(*iv*)

100. Battelle - Columbus environmental evaluation system is used to assess the impact of:
A. Mining development projects.
B. Pulp and paper mill projects.
C. Water resources projects.
D. Highway projects.

ANSWERS

1	2	3	4	5	6	7	8	9	10
D	A	C	B	D	B	D	D	C	D
11	**12**	**13**	**14**	**15**	**16**	**17**	**18**	**19**	**20**
D	D	A	D	D	A	C	D	A	C
21	**22**	**23**	**24**	**25**	**26**	**27**	**28**	**29**	**30**
B	B	A	B	B	C	B	D	A	C
31	**32**	**33**	**34**	**35**	**36**	**37**	**38**	**39**	**40**
A	B	B	C	B	D	D	D	A	B
41	**42**	**43**	**44**	**45**	**46**	**47**	**48**	**49**	**50**
A	D	A	C	*	C	C	B	B	A
51	**52**	**53**	**54**	**55**	**56**	**57**	**58**	**59**	**60**
C	B	C	A	C	D	B	D	B	A
61	**62**	**63**	**64**	**65**	**66**	**67**	**68**	**69**	**70**
A	A	C	D	A	B	C	A	B	C
71	**72**	**73**	**74**	**75**	**76**	**77**	**78**	**79**	**80**
B	C	C	B	B	A	B	C	A	D
81	**82**	**83**	**84**	**85**	**86**	**87**	**88**	**89**	**90**
A	C	D	A	B	*	B	C	B	C
91	**92**	**93**	**94**	**95**	**96**	**97**	**98**	**99**	**100**
B	D	C	A	C	A	A	C	A	C

Error in Questions/Option

EXPLANATORY ANSWERS

1. The evaporative heat transfer rate can be increased by increasing the surrounding air velocity and/or by reducing the moisture content of surrounding air. Since the body temperature depends on the heat balance, which in turn depends on the conditions in the surroundings, it is important that the surrounding conditions should be such that the body is able to maintain the thermal equilibrium with minimum regulatory effort.

A sedentary person at neutral condition loses about 40 % of heat by evaporation, about 30% by convection and 30 % by radiation. However, this proportion may change with other factors. For example, the heat loss by evaporation process is maximum at 25°C for a thermally comfortable, seated bare bodied person.

2. This measured increase in air temperature just above the ground is known as a radiation inversion because it forms mainly through radiational cooling of the surface. Since radiation inversions occur on most clear, calm nights, they are also called nocturnal inversions.

Cold Air at the Surface : A strong radiation inversion occurs when the air near the ground is much colder than the air higher up. Ideal conditions for a strong inversion and, hence, very low nighttime temperatures exist when the air is calm, the night is long, and ther air is fairly dry and cloud-free.

A windless night is essential for a strong radiation inversion because a stiff breeze tends to mix the colder air at the surface with the warmer air above.

3. The Sustainable Development Goals (SDGs) (or Global Goals for Sustainable Development) are a collection of 17 global goals set by the United Nations Development Programme. The formal name for the SDGs is: "Transforming our World: the 2030 Agenda for Sustainable Development." That has been shortened to "2030 Agenda." The goals are broad and interdependent, yet each has a separate list of targets to achieve. Achieving all 169 targets would signal accomplishing all 17 goals. The SDGs cover social and economic development issues including poverty, hunger, health, education, global warming, gender equality, water, sanitation, energy, urbanization, environment and social justice.

5. **Lithosphere :** The external rock crust of the earth, the lithosphere, extends from the earth's surface, which is partly covered with water, to a depth of 70 kilometres (45 miles). Its geochemical structure is intense of scientific and economic interest. The minerals and rocks that form the earth's crust consist of elements of widely varying abundance. Gold and platinum, for instance, occur very rarely. Iron, on the other hand, occurs frequently. Precise information regarding the geophysical composition of the lithosphere is available at present for only the outer surface down to a depth of 16 kilometres (10 miles).

   At about 46% abundance, oxygen (in the form of its various compounds) is the most common element in the lithosphere. It is followed in second place by silicon, with about 28%. Silicon does not occur in the lithosphere in its pure form any more than oxygen does. Silicon is often present in compounds with oxygen, particularly in the chemically inactive and consequently very durable compound quartz. Third place is taken with 8% by aluminium, which plays an important part in the composition of silicates and in particular is a basic component in the formation of alumina. In fourth place is iron (5%), which is found everywhere—if only in small quantities—and is often present in rock in the form of red iron ore, magnetite or brown ore. Following them in declining order of importance come calcium, sodium, potassium and magnesium.

6. The decrease of an atmospheric variable with height, the variable being temperature unless otherwise specified. In general, a lapse rate is the negative of the rate of temperature change with altitude change, thus $\Gamma = -\frac{dT}{dz}$ where Γ (sometimes L) is the lapse rate given in units of temperature divided by units of altitude. T is temperature, and z is altitude.

   The lapse rate of nonrising air-commonly referred to as the normal, or environmental, lapse rate-is highly variable, being affected by radiation, convection, and condensation; it averages about 6.5 °C per kilometre (18.8 °F per mile) in the lower atmosphere (troposphere). It differs from the adiabatic lapse rate, which involves temperature changes due to the rising or sinking of an air parcel. Adiabatic lapse rates are usually differentiated as dry or moist.

7. The change in entropy of the system ΔS is given as

$$\Delta S = q_{rev}/T \qquad ...(i)$$

   The second law of thermodynamics may also be stated in terms of entropy as the change in entropy of an isolated system is always positive when it undergoes a spontaneous process. All natural processes are spontaneous and irreversible and hence are accompanied by a net increase in entropy. Thus, the entropy of the universe (an isolated system) increases with every change that occurs in nature. When the entropy of the universe reaches a maximum and an equilibrium is attained it will result in an entropic doom. Using these ideas Clausius put forth the first law of thermodynamics as 'the energy of the universe is constant' and that of second law as 'the entropy of the universe tends always to a maximum'.

8. Tropical cyclones (TCs) always develop from synoptic-scale disturbances. Tropical Cyclones are low pressure systems that form over warm tropical waters and have gale force winds (sustained winds of 63 km/h or greater and gusts in excess of 90 km/h) near the centre. Technically, they are defined as a non-frontal low pressure system of synoptic scale developing over warm waters having organised convection and a maximum mean wind speed of 34 knots or greater extending more than half-way around near the centre and persisting for at least six hours.

9. In the range of atmospheric conditions that we would be interested in, it is perfectly possible to assume that water vapour satisfies the ideal gas law. The specific gas constant for water vapour (R_v) would be simply the ratio of the universal gas constant to the molecular mass of water and has a value 461 J deg^{-1} kg^{-1}. For our purposes, it is sufficiently accurate to assume that both dry air and water vapour separately satisfy the equation of state for an ideal gas. Hence it would be important to obtain the equation of state for moist air (*i.e.*, a mixture of dry air and water vapour). While deriving the equation of state for dry air, we defined a mean molecular mass for the dry air by taking the weighted harmonic mean of the molecular masses of the constituents of the dry air. In a similar manner the mean molecular mass of moist air can be defined as

$$\frac{1}{M_{\text{moist}}} = \frac{1}{(m_d + m_v)}\left[\frac{m_d}{M_d} + \frac{m_v}{M_v}\right] \quad ...(i)$$

where the subscripts *d* and *v* refer to dry air and water vapour, respectively. The above expression can be written in term of M_d, mixing ratio $w\left(w = \frac{m_v}{m_d}\right)$ and the ratio of the molecular masses $\frac{M_v}{M_d} = \varepsilon$ as

$$\frac{1}{M_{\text{moist}}} = \frac{1}{M_d}\frac{m_d}{(m_d + m_v)}\left[1 + \frac{m_v/m_d}{M_v/M_d}\right] \quad ...(ii)$$

$$\frac{1}{M_{\text{moist}}} = \frac{1}{M_d}\frac{(1 + w/\varepsilon)}{(1 + w)} \quad ...(iii)$$

Using the above expression for the mean molecular mass of moist air, the equation of state for moist air can be written as

$$p\alpha = \frac{R}{M_d}\frac{(1 + w/\varepsilon)}{(1 + w)}T = R_{sp}\frac{(1 + w/\varepsilon)}{(1 + w)}T \quad ...(iv)$$

10. The oxidation-reduction protential, also called the redox potential, expresses the equilibrium that exists in a solution, at any given time, between oxidized and reduced substances. The redox potential, expressed in millivolts (mV), is determined by measuring the electromotive force of a solution.

The normal hydrogen electrode which is the reference point of most measurements is a platinum electrode plated with platinum black, immersed in a solution which is 1 N with respect to hydrogen ions, and in equilibrium with hydrogen gas of atmospheric pressure. To this electrode the potential zero has been ascribed by convention. Upon increasing the ph (decreasing the hydrogen ion concentration) the potential of the hydrogen electrode decreases in linear fashion.

11. Gravimetric analysis is a technique through which the amount of an analyte (the ion being analyzed) can be determined through the measurement of mass. Gravimetric analyses depend on comparing the masses of two compounds containing the analyte. An example of a gravimetric analysis is the determination of chloride in a compound. In order to do a gravimetric analysis, a cation must be found that forms an insoluble compound with chloride. This compound must also be pure and easily filtered. The solubility rules indicate that Ag^+, Pb^{2+}, and Hg_2^{2+} form insoluble chlorides.

The Winkler Method is a technique used to measure dissolved oxygen in freshwater systems. Dissolved oxygen is used as an indicator of the health of a water body, where higher dissolved oxygen concentrations are correlated with high productivity and little pollution. This test is performed on-site, as delays between sample collection and testing may result in an alteration in oxygen content.

Sulphur dioxide is a major air pollutant, commonly formed by the combustion of sulphur-bearing fuels.

Since its inception in 1956, the West-Gaeke method seems to be the one most widely used for the determination of atmospheric sulphur dioxide (SO_2). It is most important for workers in the field to have an exact idea of its accuracy, reproducibility, and limitations; particularly when they are trying to detect small differences in its concentration.

Polycyclic aromatic hydrocarbons (PAHs) consist of two or more aromatic rings. More rings usually equals higher lipophilicity and lower vapour pressure. Gas chromatography coupled to mass spectrometry (GC/MS) is a well-established technique for analysing PAHs. It is cheap, time efficient and provides good sensitivity, selectivity and resolution. The difficulty with analysing PAHs in GC/MS lies in that many PAHs have the same mass. The isomeric PAHs have the same ion fragmentation and chemical structure. This will make them impossible to separate in the mass spectrometer, and importance of a good chromatographic separation is imperative. In order to get the best possible separation, selection of column and oven program optimisation is necessary.

12. Carbon dioxide, (CO_2), a colourless gas having a faint, sharp odour and a sour taste; it is a minor component of Earth's atmosphere (about 3 volumes in 10,000), formed in combustion of carbon-containing materials, in fermentation, and in respiration of animals and employed by plants in the photosynthesis of carbohydrates. The main acidic component of the present atmosphere is CO_2.

13. PCBs are fire resistant and stable at high temperature and have a high electrical resistance. They were widely used as insulating materials in transformers, electrical capacitors, and condensers, and are still present in older equipment. PCBs also were used extensively as platicizers in the plastics industry. Plastics tend to be brittle; the addition of PCBs makes them more flexible and resistant to cracking.

PCBs were spread widely in the environment and entered surface waters in industrial discharges and in particulates from incinerators. When plastic wastes and other PCB-containing materials are burned, PCB vapours condense on airborne particles that then fall directly onto water or reach water in runoff from the land. PCBs are now found in the body fat of animals living in the furthest corners of the Earth, including polar bears in the Arctic and albatrosses on remote Pacific Islands.

14. A sulfhydryl is a functional group consisting of a sulphur bonded to a hydrogen atom. The sulfhydryl group, also called a thiol, is indicated in chemistry nomenclature by "-thiol" as a suffix and "mercapto-" or "sulfanyl" as a prefix. Thiols have great affinity for soft metals.

Toxicity of chromium is not due to reaction with sulfhydryl group.

15. The CFCs are not generally broken down in the troposphere. They are only removed from the atmosphere by photolysis, by the highly energetic short wave UV radiation, or possibly by reaction with singlet oxygen ($O(^1D)$), both mechanisms in the stratosphere (Fisher et al., 1990). The average lifetime of CFCs in the atmosphere is of the order of 50 to several hundred years.

16.

$$\text{Concentration} = 0.1 \text{ mol.L}^{-1}$$

$$\text{Volume} = 100 \text{ mL.}$$

$$\text{Concentration} = nV.$$

So, $n = C \times V$

Thus, $0.1L \times 0.1.\ mol\ L^{-1} = 0.01.mol$

Now, 1 mol = 60 g of CH_3COOH

So, 0.01 mol = 0.6 g CH_3COOH

17. Let, light incident on first plate is 100 candela.

Then, light transmitted from first plate

$$= 100 \times \frac{(100-20)}{100} = 80 \text{ candela.}$$

Again, light transmitted from second plate

$$= 80 \times \frac{(100-20)}{100} = 64 \text{ Candela.}$$

In last, light transmitted from third plate

$$= 64 \times \frac{(100-20)}{100} = 51.2 \text{ Candela.}$$

Thus, light transmitted from third plate (in per cent) = 51.2%

18. The reaction is:

$$HCl + NaOH \rightarrow H_2O + NaCl$$

For complete neutralization,

$$N_1.V_1 = N_2.V_2$$

$$N_1 \times 20 = 0.1 \times 10$$

$$\therefore \quad N_1 = \frac{1}{20} = 0.05 \text{ N.}$$

19. Total organic carbon (TOC) is a measure of the total amount of carbon in organic compounds in an aqueous system. It has become an important parameter used to monitor overall levels of organic compounds present.

Generally, the determination of TOC is done by thermal or wet chemical oxidation, so that CO_2 is formed, which is subsequently measured by a NDIR detector. TOC measurements are well suited for online measurements since its provides fast and meaningful results depending on the function of the process analyser. The TOC takes a special position in well-known regulatories.

BOD, biochemical oxygen demand: The BOD indicates the content of oxygen needed to decompose organic compounds in waste water by bacteria. In most cases the special factor BOD_5 is perceived as the BOD, which requires a detailed definition (5 represents the 5 days analysis time). For the determination of BOD_5 there are nitrification inhibitors added to the samples, which suppress the degradation of nitrogen compounds. Consequently, it results in the determination of the decomposition of carbon compounds only.

COD, chemical oxygen demand: The COD value has been developed analogically to the BOD measurement. Since there are many organics which are rather hard or not possible to decompose biologically, a parameter has been defined indicating the amount of oxygen which would be needed when all organic ingredients would be oxidised completely. As, according to the name, the oxidation takes place chemically, the chemical oxygen demand can only be defined indirectly.

TOD, total oxygen demand: According to its name, this parameter defines the total oxygen demand of the water sample. It is based on the same principle as the COD. To define the TOD the sample is thermally oxidised in an oven and the emerging oxygen is measured directly in the carrier gas by a NDIR detector. The TOD value can be affected by inorganic compounds. However, these influences are generally very small and thus enables a mathematically compensation.

20. Biogas is a fuel gas formed by a mixture of CH_4 (=2/3) and CO_2 (=1/3), plus some traces of gases like H_2S and NH_3. Biogas is mainly produced from anaerobic digestion of high moisture content biomasses such as manure, waste streams from food processing plants, agriculture residues, or sludges and biosolids from municipal effluent treatment plants. Microalgal biomasses have been also investigated for the production of biogas.

Briefly, anaerobic digestion involves the breakdown of biodegradable materials by microorganisms in the absence of oxygen. There are four phases in biogas production: (1) hydrolysis by anaerobic microorganisms that use enzymes to break down high molecular organic substances such as proteins, carbohydrates, and fats into low molecular compounds like amino acids, sugars, and fatty acids, respectively, with production of hydrogen and carbon dioxide; (2) acidogenesis where acid-forming bacteria promote the decomposition of the previous products into organic acids, carbon dioxide, hydrogen sulphide (H_2S), and ammonia (NH_3); (3) acetogenesis where acid bacteria form acetate, CO_2, and H_2; and (4) methanogenesis where methane-forming bacteria convert acetates to methane, carbon dioxide, and alkaline water. Additionally, H_2 and CO_2 formed in the previous steps are converted to CH_4. About 30% of the total methane is produced by this route.

21. In the past, salinity of seawater was measured by evaporating the water and weighing the amount of salt remaining. Since that approach is difficult and inaccurate, electrical conductivity of seawater is now used to measure salinity.

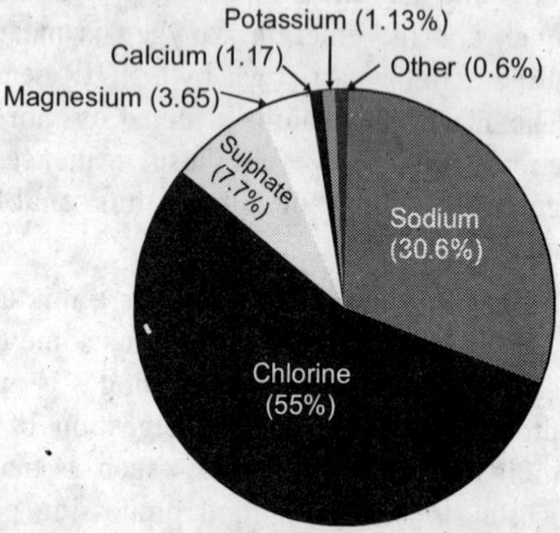

Salts in Seawater

22. **An Aquatic Food Chain and Food Web:**

- Generally, in the aquatic (*e.g.*, marine) food chain, microscopic single cell plankton algae are in the first trophic level and are called producers.
- Small invertebrates called zooplankton and some fish feed on the algae. These herbivores form the second trophic level.
- Other fish and invertebrates feed on these herbivores, and forming the third trophic level. These are the carnivores.
- In the oceans, food webs involve more species. In the ocean, seal feeds at several trophic levels. It may start from second trophic level to fourth trophic levels.

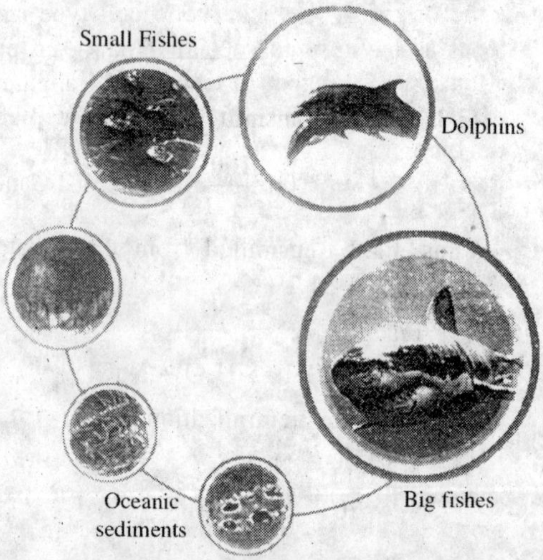

Fig. : Marine Food Chain

Food Chain Involves both Aquatic and Land Organisms: In this type of food chain, the planktons in aquatic body serve as first trophic level and the small fishes that feed on planktons form second trophic level. Big fishes that feed on small fishes are included in third trophic level and humans or hawks which feed on big fishes are on the fourth trophic level.

Plankton →	Small fishes →	Big fishes →	Humans or Hawks
1st	2nd	3rd	4th
Trophic level	Trophic level	Trophic level	Trophic level

23. The transfer of food energy from the source in plants through a series of organisms, with repeated eating and being eaten, is referred to as a food chain. At each transfer a large proportion, 80 to 90 per cent, of the potential energy is lost as heat. Therefore, the number

of 'links' in a sequence is limited, usually four or five. The number of consumers that can be supported by a given primary production output very much depends on the length of the food chain; each link in the chain decreases the available energy by about one order of magnitude.

24. The origin of eukaryotic cell on earth took place 1850 Million years ago.

Among major events in biologic evolution, the origin of the eukaryotic cell type stands out as having had special impact—an event that both changed the course and apparently altered the rate of early evolutionary advance. Although paleobiologic data can be expected to provide only limited insight into the mode of origin of eukaryotes, evidence indicative of the timing of this event should be preserved in the fossil record. Assessment of such evidence, however, is likely to be difficult. The earliest eukaryotes seem certain to have been simple, microscopic unicells. Such eukaryotes, similar in gross morphology to their prokaryotic precursors, would be expected to be difficult to distinguish from prokaryotes in the early fossil record.

25. Energy transfers along the food chain were studied for the first time by Lindeman. Lindeman demonstrated that all the functions of an ecosystem could be discribed in terms of energy by the knowledge of two attributes of each trophic level (*i*) the level of energy storage (*ii*) efficiency of energy transfer.

Lindeman calculated in energy which entered in each of the trophic levels and also the energy which passed along to the next level and determined the efficiency of each trophic level and utilization of energy. According to him the rate of change of energy present in any trophic level is determined by the rate of absorption of energy less the rate at which energy is lost. Thus, the ratios of energy flowing between various trophic levels are expressed as ecological efficiency.

Ecological efficiency: The efficiency of transfer of energy from one trophic level to the next is called ecological efficiency. Coefficient of ecological efficiency is the ratio of energy assimilated at a given trophic level to that assimilated at the previous trophic level.

Coefficient of ecological efficiency = $\frac{P_t}{I_t}$.

26. Ecological succession is the process of change in the species structure of an ecological community over time.

Climax concept: According to classical ecological theory, succession stops when the sere has arrived at an equilibrium or steady state with the physical and biotic environment. Barring major disturbances, it will persist indefinitely. This end point of succession is called climax.

Climax community: The final or stable community in a sere is the climax community or climatic vegetation. It is self-perpetuating and in equilibrium with the physical habitat. There is no net annual accumulation of organic matter in a climax community. The annual production and use of energy is balanced in such a community.

Characteristics

- The vegetation is tolerant of environmental conditions.
- It has a wide diversity of species, a well-drained spatial structure, and complex food chains.
- The climax ecosystem is balanced. There is equilibrium between gross primary production and total respiration, between energy used from sunlight and energy released by decomposition, between uptake of nutrients from the soil and the return of nutrient by litter fall to the soil.
- Individuals in the climax stage are replaced by others of the same kind. Thus, the species composition maintains equilibrium.
- It is an index of the climate of the area. The life or growth forms indicate the climatic type.

27. Some biologists have used the term 'keystone species' to identify those species which may influence the ability of large numbers of others to persist in the community. The basic assumption is that within biological communities, certain species are important in determining the ability of large numbers of other species to persist in the community. Examples of keystone species include the starfish, the Ochre sea star in rocky tidal communities, lobsters in subtidal communities, sea otters in marine kelp forests or Old World fruit bats in tropical forests. Protecting keystone species is seen by some as a priority because if such a species is lost, numerous others may disappear – causing an 'extinction cascade'. The term has also been applied to resources, to denote elements of a habitat that are critical to many species in the community.

28. The reason for this differential distribution of biodiversity is that at the equator, there is favourable environmental conditions for speciation as well as for sustaining both variety and number of organisms. This region is represented by tropical rain forests. As we move away from tropic $23\frac{1}{2}N° - 66\frac{1}{2}N°$, the biodiversity decreases because harsh conditions exist in temperature areas during the cold winter season. Beyond $66\frac{1}{2}N° -$ very harsh conditions prevail for most of the year in Arctic polar region and the biodiversity reaches to the maximum decline.

29. The artic tundra's are mostly found in the Northern Hemisphere but some have been found in the Southern Hemisphere in islands near Antarctica and in the Antarctica Peninsula. There are five main arctic tundra's in the world and they lie in North America, Northern Europe and Northern Asia. They are called Northern Alaska, Scandinavian, Siberian, Canada and Greenland tundra. The Tundra is about 3 million square miles long and covers about 20% of the earth's surface. The latitude of which the tundra is located in 55 degrees-75 degrees N. They are in one way all connected. They share the same location, climate, flora and fauna.

The Alaskan tundra lies in Northern Alaska covering all of the state of Alaska.

The Scandinavian tundra lies in the largest peninsula in Europe, Scandinavia and it extends from the Arctic Circle to the North and Baltic Sea.

The Siberian tundra lays in Siberia a vast region of Russia. It extends from the Ural Mountains to the Pacific Ocean.

The Canadian tundra lies in the beautiful country of Canada and the tundra extends from the Mackenzie delta to the Hudson Bay and NE Labrador.

The Greenland tundra lies in Northern Greenland and it's about 11,563,300 km^2 (4,464,600 sq. mi) in space.

30. The standing stock of pelagic primary producers is conveniently expressed as the difference between growth and reduction of the standing stock by grazing or by sinking out of the euphotic zone. The rate of growth is determined largely by environmental variables such as the light regime, temperature, and nutrient supply. In polar regions these variables are generally quite different than those in lower latitudes. The atmospheric light regime, for instance fluctuates extremely through the season at high latitudes. Sea ice affects the submarine light regime profoundly, and the formation and melting of ice affect the stability of the water column.

31. The tabular model of ecological succession presented by Odum. The table presents trends that might be expected in the development of ecosystems during the developmental stages to the mature, or climax, community.

Ecosystem Attributes	Developmental Stages	Mature Stages
Community Energetics		
Gross production/ community respiration (P/R ratio)	Greater or less than 1	Approaches I
Gross production/ standing crop biomass (P/B ratio)	High	Low
Biomass supported/ unit energy flow (B/E ratio)	Low	High
Net community production	High	Low
Food chains	Linear, predominantly grazing	Weblike, predominantly detritus

32. An airborne disease is any disease that is caused by pathogens that can be transmitted through the air. Such diseases include many of considerable importance both in human and veterinary medicine. The relevant pathogens may be viruses, bacteria, or fungi, and they may be spread through breathing, talking, coughing, sneezing, raising of dust, spraying of liquids, toilet flushing or any activities which generates aerosol particles or droplets.

Whooping cough (pertussis): This is a contagious, bacterial illness that causes the airways to swell. The hacking cough that results is persistent and generally treated with antibiotics early on to prevent damage. Based on the casualties reported worldwide, whooping cough is most deadly airborne bacterial disease. Worldwide, there are about 16 million cases of whooping cough every year resulting in 195,000 deaths. In 2014, there were 32,971 reported cases in the United States.

33. India is located at the confluence of Oriental, Palaearctic and Ethiopian biogeographical realms and Indian mammals are the admixture of the three realms. Mammals are considered as the dominant animals in terrestrial and non-terrestrial ecosystems.

The lion-tailed macaque (Macaca silenus), or the wanderoo, is an Old World monkey endemic to the Western Ghats of South India. The hair of the lion-tailed macaque is black. Its outstanding characteristic is the silver-white mane which surrounds the head from the cheeks down to its chin, which gives this monkey its German name Bartaffe - "beard ape". The lion-tailed macaque is a diurnal rainforest dweller. It is a good climber and spends a majority of its life in the upper canopy of tropical moist evergreen forests. Unlike other macaques, it avoids humans.

Gee's golden langur, or simply the golden langur, is an Old World monkey found in a small region of western Assam, India and in the neighbouring foothills of the Black Mountains of Bhutan. It is one of the most endangered primate species of India.

The Spotted Linsang is a linsang found in the forests of the central and eastern Himalaya. It is short, light coloured, and has a slender body with a pointed head and small limbs. It stalks its prey by crawling on its belly, when it is often mistaken for a python or other heavy-built poisonous snakes due to its slender appearance. Its diet consists of insects, rodents, lizards, birds and small mammals.

The surface of the Jammu and Kashmir State is generally mountainous intercepted with lovely valleys and drained by perennial rivers. The Pallas cat is found in Ladakh, Turkestan and Mangolia. A live full grown male measures 1'-1" and tail 8.5". The hair on its body give a curious silvery appearance of shades of brown marked with blackish brown. On the back, the sides have cross stripes of deep brown. The lower portions are pure white. The limbs in parts are tawny marked with black. The head is marked with irregular spots. The fur is very dense silky and long.

34. The mechanisms of reproductive isolation are a collection of evolutionary mechanisms, behaviours and physiological processes critical for speciation. They prevent members of different species from producing offspring, or ensure that any offspring are sterile. These barriers maintain the integrity of a species by reducing gene flowbetween related species. Reproductive isolation of populations leads to population explosion.

The mechanisms of reproductive isolation have been classified in a number of ways. Zoologist Ernst Mayr classified the mechanisms of reproductive isolation in two broad categories: pre-zygotic for those that act before fertilization (or before mating in the case of animals) and post-zygotic for those that act after it. The mechanisms are genetically controlled and can appear in species whose geographic distributions overlap (sympatric speciation) or are separate.

35. The plankton are minute, microscopic organisms of plants & animal origin. They spend their whole life in the water. For their movement, they depend on the mercy of physical conditions of the water body and environment *e.g.*, depth, water current, wind, light, air etc.

Plankton are distinguished as holoplankton and meroplankton: the former remain planktonic throughout their lives and the latter only for a short period, *e.g.*, glochidium larvae of freshwater mussels. Plankton are sometimes referred to by their habitat. The plankton species from ponds are called heleoplankton, of lakes limnoplankton, of running water potamoplankton (rheoplankton) and of salt water haliplankton. The pseudoplankton are those which occupy the upper layer of water accidentally. Examples of these include creeping organisms which rise up through the aquatic vegetation and are accidentally caught in the plankton collection.

36. The Ministry of Environment, Forest and Climate Change (MoEFCC) has released India State of Forest Report (ISFR) 2017. It has revealed that total forest and tree cover in India has increased of over 8,021 sq km (about 80.20 million hectare) which is one per cent increase from 2015.

The increase in the forest cover has been observed as 6,778 sq km and that of tree cover as 1,243 sq km. The total forest and tree cover is 24.39% of geographical area of the country. The increase in forest cover has been observed in Very Dense Forest (VDF) which absorbs maximum carbon dioxide from the atmosphere. It is followed by increase in forest cover in open forest.

India's tree and forest cover has registered an increase of 1% or 8,021 sq. km in two years since 2015, according to the latest assessment by the government.

37. Earthworms' release "cast" at the opening of their burrows. Epigeic earthworms release the castings exclusively on soil surface. Their castings may be granular or spindle like masses that may be 2 to 3 cm high heaps as in Eudrilus eugeniae or Perionyx excavates. Polypheretima elongata is a cultivable species of tropical earthworm. Polypheretima elongata and Pontoscolex corethrurus excrete the ingested soil as sticky, thick lumps on soil surface.

38. **Solifluction :** The word solifluction, which literally means "soil flow", refers to the relatively slow downslope movement of water-saturated soil and/or regolith. Solifluction is most common in high-latitude or high-elevation tundra regions that have *permafrost,* a subsurface layer of permanently frozen ground. Above the permafrost layer lies the active layer, which freezes during winter and thaws during summer. During the summer thaw of the centimeters to meters-thick active layer, the permanently frozen ground beneath it prevents downward percolation of melted soil water. As a result, the active layer becomes a heavy, water-saturated soil mass that, even on a gentle incline, sags slowly downslope by the force of gravity until the next surface freeze arrives. Movement rates are typically only several centimeters per year.

39. Ramsay's classification of folds is based on the dip isogon. A dip isogon is the line joining points of equal dip as shown in Fig. Two common types of folds are the similar and parallel folds. In similar folds the bedding shape remains the same from bed to bed whereas in parallel folds the bedding thickness remains unaltered from bed to bed.

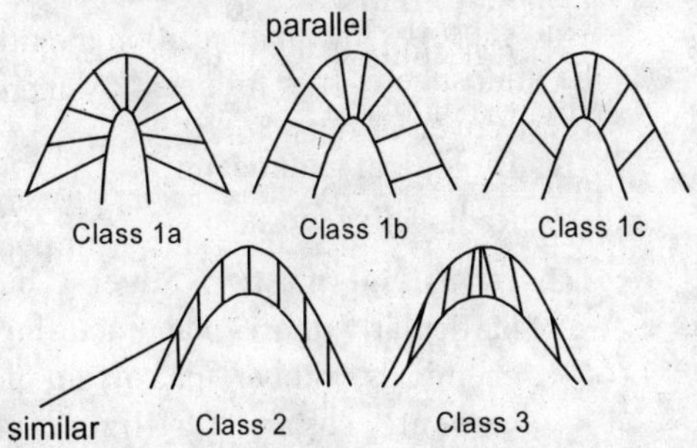

Fig.

40. The role of biotic and abiotic components of the landscape in creating a healthy environment. Any ecosystem provides a service as a process that provides something of value. These services provide positive benefits to human beings and may be large or small and direct or indirect. There are four major categories of ecosystem services; provisioning, regulating, supporting and cultural services. A provisioning service provides a benefit extracted from nature such as food and food security, drinking water, and medicines or pharmaceuticals. Regulating services include carbon sequestration, climate regulation, pollination and erosion control. Supporting services are nutrient cycling, the water cycle, soil formation, photosynthesis and primary production. Cultural services are non-material benefits of the environment to people such as art, spirituality, well-being, discovery, recreation and tourism. Ecosystem services are negatively impacted by runoff, pollution, invasive species, overharvest, habitat destruction, erosion, deforestation and human development. Economists and others have attrempted to value ecosystem services at various dollar amounts but the complexity of the services makes economic valuation difficult.

41. Cartosat-2, the twelfth in the Indian Remote Sensing (IRS) satelite series, is an advanced remote sensing satellite capable of providing scene-specific spot imagery.

Cartosat-2, launched on January 10, 2007 by PSLV-C7, carries a single panchromatic camera onboard capable of providing better than 1-meter spatial resolution imagery, with a swath of 9.6 km. The satellite has high agility with capability of steering along and across the track up to + 450 to facilitate imaging of any area more frequantly. It was placed in a sun synchronous polar orbit of a nominal altitude of 630 km with a re-visit of 4-5 days and can be brought to a special orbit of 560 km with revisit periods of 4 days and 1 days respectively.

Cartosat-2 satellite has been providing operational services to the user community. The data from the satellite is being used for cartographic applications at the cadastral level, urban and rural infrastructure development and management, as well as applications in Land Information System (LIS).

42. Microwave remote sensing observations for atmospheric chemistry have been obtained from ground, aircraft, balloon, and satellite platforms. 'Microwave' is used here to denote heterodyne measurements at centimeter, millimeter, and submillimeter wavelengths. The spectral range of interest extends, roughly, from the 1.35 cm wavelength (22 GHz frequency, 1 GHz = 10^9 Hz) H_2O spectral line through the 0.12 mm wavelength (2.5 THz frequency, 1 THz = 10^{12} Hz) OH lines.

At L-band (1.4 GHz), soil contribution is dominant for most low vegetation covers. As frequency increases, the screening effect of vegetation increases. Thus, at 5 GHz, for low vegetation cover, the soil and vegetation contributions are similar in magnitude, while at 10 GHz the vegetation effects become dominant. L-band in microwave remote sensing provides information about scattering from Volume, Soil and Trunks and boles.

Although sensors in the L-band (1-2 GHz) provide the most reliable surface soil moisture estimates, these radiometers are operating at higher frequencies due to the technical challenges of constructing L-band antennae long enough (4-6 m) to provide adequate resolution and complex processing to obtain well-calibrated L-band brightness temperature data.

43. In freshwater systems, the recycling of nutrients occurs in response to air temperature changes. The nutrients at the bottom of lakes are recycled twice each year: in the spring and fall turnover. The spring and fall turnover is a seasonal process that recycles nutrients and oxygen from the bottom of a freshwater ecosystem to the top of a body of water. These turnovers are caused by the formation of a thermocline: a layer of water with a temperature that is significantly different from that of the surrounding layers. In wintertime, the surface of lakes found in many northern regions is frozen. However, the water under the ice is slightly warmer, and the water at the bottom of the lake is warmer yet at 4°C to 5 °C (39.2°F to 41°F). Water is densest at 4°C; therefore, the deepest water is also the densest. The deepest water is oxygen poor because the decomposition of organic material at the bottom of the lake uses up available oxygen that cannot be replaced by means of oxygen diffusion into the water due to the surface ice layer.

In springtime, air temperatures increase and surface ice melts. When the temperature of the surface water begins to reach 4°C, the water becomes heavier and sinks to the bottom. The water at the bottom of the lake is then displaced by the heavier surface water and, thus, rises to the top. As that water rises to the top, the sediments and nutrients from the lake bottom are brought along with it. During the summer months, the lake water stratifies, or forms layers, with the warmest water at the lake surface.

44. The soil pollution is caused on account of the following wastes:

I. Industrial waste

II. Agricultural waste

III. Urban waste

IV. Biological pathogens

V. Radioactive waste

I. Industrial waste : Several industries particularly those manufacturing paper, chemicals, rubber, petroleum products, cement, sugar, fertilizers, textile, pesticides as well as tanneries and oil refineries throw harmful waste causing soil pollution. The furnaces also throw fly ash which not only pollutes the soil but also the air and waster. The pollution of soil is mainly due to excessive addition of carbonates, bicarbonates, sulphates, sulphites, chlorides and fluorides of Na, Ca, K, Fe, Mn and Mg. Besides, the suspended solids, the paper factory waste is rich in chlorides whereas the steel factory waste contains cyanides and phenols. The distillaries add potassium salts and nitrogenous waste whereas the textile mill's waste is rich in chloride ions. The solid waste (sludge) from a paper mill has been accumulated as a kilometer long hillock at Saharanpur. The waste from different industries also deposits Ni, Cu, Ba, Mo, As and Hg in traces.

II. Agricultural waste : The agricultural waste includes fertilizers, pesticides, farm waste and fumigants. The fertilizers contain plant nutrients particularly N, P and K, but the soil also gets polluted mainly due to organic pollutants presents as impurities. Besides, different types of biocides such as DDT, aldrin, dieldrin, chordane etc. also cause soil pollution. The waste added due to domestic pets also pollutes the soil. The fecal matter of pigs is rich in phosphates and those of other animals contains numerous pathogenic micro-organisms.

III. Urban waste : The urban waste includes, sewage and solid waste discarded as refuse. This refuse includes several billion tonnes of rubbish material such as domestic waste, paper, plastic, metallic containers and cartons, waste clothes, shoes and reading material. While some of the wastes are biodegradable, some are non-degradable.

IV. Biological pathogens : The soil contains numerous organisms such as algae, fungi, bacteria, viruses, protozoans, nematodes, annelids, insects and rodents. These forms may be pathogenic or non-pathogenic. There are many pathogenic forms present in the human and animal excreta which may cause soil-borne diseases in plants and animals including human beings.

V. Radioactive waste : It is discussed separately under radioactive pollution.

46. Seismic waves are the same—only *bigger*. Seismic waves vibrate the ground just as a sound wave will vibrate the air and your eardrum. Seismic waves travel through rock and dirt instead of air. A seismic wave that transfers its energy into the water can create a tsunami.

Seismic waves radiate out in all directions from the point of rock and plate movement. Because seismic waves so closely match ocean waves, scientists use the same terms to describe seismic waves.

- Period (T) : The time between beginning and end of one complete wave.
- Amplitude (A) : The size of the movement in the ground as the wave passes.
- Frequency (f) : The number of waves that pass one spot in a given period of time.
- Speed (V) : How fast the seismic waves travel. Seismic waves can race through the Earth at up to 4 miles per second (14,400 mph).

47. Urban heat island (UHI) is a climatic phenomenon where urban areas have higher air temperature than their rural surroundings due to the anthropogenic modifications of land surfaces. There are two types of urban heat islands, surface and atmospheric UHI. A combination of factors leads to the development of the UHI. UHI is measured by surface temperature, which can vary between the city and rural area by up to 5°C.

Many Factors contribute to UHI, such as: building material thermal properties, urban design geometry (urban canyon), anthropogenic factors and altered land cover. Building material reflectance is generally low so they reflect less and absorb more energy which leads to increasing temperatures at surface level. Building materials have high remittance values so they release heat quickly and stay cooler. Top of atmosphere and land surface brightness temperature differences generally range from 1 Kelvin to 5 Kelvin in the 10-12 μm spectral regions, and such differences depend on the atmospheric conditions.

48. Ecology is the scientific study of interaction between organisms and their environment. It includes both biotic and abiotic factors.

The ecological studies are all about connections of all life forms in earth and their various types of ecology.

Organism Ecology : This is the study of organism respond to stimuli caused by physical environment. The organisms adapt the environment either happily or ignoring away from its effect. A physical change in environment will show the change in behaviour or physical attributes.

Population Ecology : The natural process is that, all organisms will grow and die. The factors by which they will populate are the size of colony, birth and death rate, population growth rate.

Community Ecology : The association of populations of two or more different species occupying the same geographical area. Competition, mutualisms are key interactions to maintaining a community.

Ecosystem Ecology : This is the community of living organisms along with non-living environment like air, water, soil.

Landscape Ecology : The exchange of energy, materials, organisms and other products between the ecosystems is known as landscape ecology.

Global Ecology : The effect of change in energy and matter exchange on the function and distribution of organism in environment.

49. An estuary is a partially enclosed coastal body of brackish water with one or more rivers or streams flowing into it, and with a free connection to the open sea. The banks of many estuaries are amongst the most heavily populated areas of the world, with about 60% of the world's population living along estuaries and the coast. As a result, many estuaries suffer degradation from a variety of factors including: sedimentation from soil erosion from deforestation, overgrazing, and other poor farming practices; overfishing; drainage and filling of wetlands.

Drowned river valleys are also known as coastal plain estuaries. In places where the sea level is rising relative to the land, sea water progressively penetrates into river valleys and the topography of the estuary remains similar to that of a river valley. This is the most common type of estuary in temperate climates. The width-to-depth ratio of these estuaries is typically large, appearing wedge-shaped (in cross-section) in the inner part and broadening and deepening seaward.

50. Fringing reefs are the most common types of reefs, developing near shore where hard surfaces occur. Their name describes their growth in a narrow band or "fringe". A distinctive element of fringing reefs is the inner reef flat, which is the widest part of the reef, separating the land from the outer reef slope. The reef flat is a shallow, low-gradient structure that is often exposed at low tide, unlike the reef slope, which is quite steep. The reef flat has far less diversity and quantity of corals than does the reef slope, consisting mainly of sediment, rubble, and a greater proportion of seaweeds and seagrasses.

51. Since two concepts, river continuum and flood pulse have been proposed to provide conceptual bases for ecological prediction of flora and fauna within riverine studies as well as for riverine ecological planning. The river continuum concept, first presented by Vannote and his colleagues, provides a framework for predicting variability in a biological community from headwater streams to river mouth.

According to Vannote's hypothesis, which is based on the physical geomorphological theory, structural and functional characteristics of stream communities are selected to conform to the most probable position or mean state of the physical system. As a river changes from headwaters to the lower reaches, there will be a change in the relationship between the production and consumption (respiration) of the material (P/R ratio). Riverine communities can be separated into three main groups, headwaters (orders 1-3), medium-sized streams (orders 4-6) and large rivers (orders > 6).

According to River Continuum Concept of Vannote, the major sources of energy in medium-sized streams are Fine particulate organic matter, Coarse particulate organic matter and Aquatic plants . In a middle order stream, energy inputs change as stream broadens. Due to a forest canopy reduction and upstream processing, shading and

CPOM's contribution decreases because fine particulate matter (FPOM) occurs. Without forest canopy shading, sunlight supports significant periphyton production.

52. Self Purification of Running Streams: The phenomenon is constantly taking place in flowing streams. The various actions involved are physical, chemical and biological and may be explained as due to

(*a*) Dilution
(*b*) Sedimentation
(*c*) Reduction
(*d*) Oxidation, and
(*e*) Sunlight.

(*a*) **Dilution :** As the putrescible organic matter is discharged into the flowing water, it is rapidly dispersed or diluted in it, the action resulting in diminishing the potential nuisance of sewage. This process is further accelerated by the joining in with the main stream of surface tributaries and underground streams.

(*b*) **Sedimentation :** This also helps in self-purification by the separation of the settleable solids in sewage in the form of sludge deposits. It may be pointed out that out of the four forms in which solids occur in sewage *viz*., suspended, dissolved, colloidal and settleable, it is the last form which is most stable and easily separates out.

(*c*) **Reduction :** It occurs due to the hydrolysis of organic matter either chemically or biologically. Anacrobic organisms liquefy, splitting complex organic constituents of sewage with the evolution of odours and gases and in this way paving the way of stabilization by oxidation.

(*d*) **Oxidation :** As soon as the organic matter meets the water, it starts getting oxidized owing to the development of the oxidizing organisms in water. The process goes on till the organic matter has been completely oxidized, the oxygen demand is then fully satisfied and the stream is said to have purified itself. It is, therefore, essential for the stream to have initially dissolved oxygen in it. Oxygen is also contributed through the dilution received from tributaries, through aeration by the action of wind or by the action of microscopic organisms.

(*e*) **Sunlight :** It is effective in the self-purification through its stabilizing and bleaching effects on bacteria and through the biological action of certain micro-organisms deriving energy from the sun, converting themselves into food for other forms of life, absorbing carbon dioxide and giving off oxygen–a process commonly known as photosynthesis.

53. A PV device's ability to effectively convert solar radiation to electric current is described by external quantum efficiency (EQE, η_{ext}) and spectral response (SR). EQE is a measure of how well the PV cell converts incident light to current, including all losses, defined as:

$$\eta_{ext} = I_{sc} I_{ph}$$

I_{ph} is the maximum possible photocurrent, assuming all photons incident upon the cell create electron-hole pairs with an energy greater than the band-gap energy of the PV material. The efficiency of a PV cell is limited by the quantum processes involving incident photons and the electrons in the cell.

The solar irradiance (average incoming solar radiation) consists of many colours, ranging from low-energy infrared photons to high-energy ultraviolet photons with all the visible-light photons between, distributed as shown in Figure. Each solar cell material responds to a narrow range of these energies, corresponding to its characteristic band gap. Photons with energy lower than the band gap

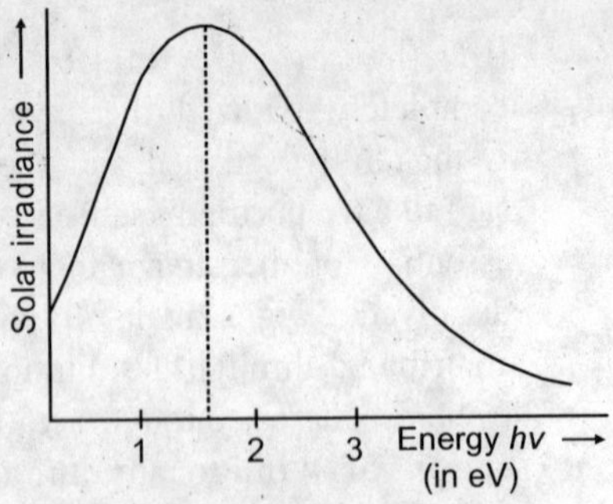

Fig. : Solar Radiation Spectrum

escape unabsorbed; photons with higher energy are absorbed, but their excess energy is wasted as heat that decreases the efficiency of the cell. Thus, to achieve the maximum efficiency in converting light to electrical power, semiconductor with band gap ~1.5 eV or slightly lower is preferred.

54. The recoverable renewable energy is a fraction of the resource base of the renewable sources available in the world. Because Much of the renewable energy is either of high entropy or too inaccessible to use.

55. To smooth power production, the estuary would normally be emptied gradually over a period of 3-4 hours on each tidal cycle, which means that a lot of power generation occurs when the difference in height is less than the full tidal range, reducing overall output.

Tidal range is a critical factor in determining whether an estuary would be useful for tidal power generation, because its dependence on R^2 means a small increase in tidal range gives a larger increase in potential energy available. The gravitational forces that cause tides result in a relatively small tidal range in the open oceans, of around 0.5 m. At coasts and in estuaries the range can be much greater. As the tidal swell approaches land, the water gets shallower and the moving water banks up, increasing its height.

56. From question, we have voltage (V) = 0.5 V

Current (I) = 2.0 A

and, Solar irradiance = 800 W/m^2

efficiency of the cell = 12.5%

Hence, area of the cell (A)

$$= \frac{\text{V.I.}}{(\eta.\text{Solar irradiance})}$$

$$= \frac{0.5 \times 2}{\frac{12.5}{100} \times 800} = 10^{-2}\ \text{m}^2$$

57. Conditions for Fusion : In addition to providing a sufficiently high temperature to enable the particles to overcome the coulomb barrier, that temperature must be maintained for a sufficient confinement time and with a sufficient ion density in order to obtain a net yield of energy from a fusion reaction. The overall conditions which must be met for a yield of more energy than is required for the heating of the plasma are usually stated in terms of the product of ion density and confinement time, a condition called Lawson's criterion.

Lowson's criterion for fustion

$$= \frac{n\tau \geq 10^{14}\ \text{s/cm}^3}{n\tau \geq 10^{16}\ \text{s/cm}^3}$$

$$= \frac{\text{deuterium-tritium fusion}}{\text{deuterium-deuterium fusion}}$$

Thus, for minimum time

$$t = \frac{(10^{14} \times 10^6)}{(2.5 \times 10^{20})}$$

$$= 0.4\ \text{s}$$

58. Geothermal energy is recognised to be a safe, reliable, environmentally benign energy, which produces renewable energy resources to generate electricity and/or heating and cooling while producing very low levels of greenhouse-gas (GHG) emissions. At present, hydrothermal geothermal resource is exploited on commercial scale in the world. At present, geothermal production of heat and power is on-going in a number of geological environments where the temperatures and depths of the reservoirs vary accordingly. Many high-temperature (>180°C) hydrothermal systems are associated with recent volcanic activity and are found near plate tectonic boundaries, or at crustal and mantle hot spot anomalies. Intermediate – (100 to 180°C) and low-temperature (<100°C) systems are also found in continental settings with or without (in case of Enhanced Geothermal Systems : EGS) hydrothermal resources.

59. Energy content or calorific value is the same as the heat of combustion, and can be calculated from thermodynamical values, or measured in a suitable apparatus.

A known amount of the fuel is burned at constant pressure and under standard conditions (0°C and 1 bar) and the heat released is captured in a known mass of water in a calorimeter. If the initial and final temperatures of the water is measured, the energy released can be calculated using the equation

$$H = \Delta T\ mC_p$$

where H = heat energy absorbed (in J), ΔT = change in temperature (in °C), m = mass of water (in g), and C_p = specific heat capacity (4.18 J/g°C for water). The resulting energy value divided by grams of fuel burned gives the energy content (in J/g). Liquid butane has the maximum energy content (MJ/m^3).

60. Fission is the break-up of heavy nuclei that are already likely to release energy as shown by their natural radioactivity; these are the 'fuels' of conventional nuclear power stations and basic nuclear weapons. The nuclei of elements with highest nuclear mass (e.g., plutonium and uranium) have extremely large energy potentials and are in states of thermodynamic non-equilibrium. This means that if the nuclei are disrupted, they decay into more stable forms and release energy as radiation and thermal energy. The energy released is so great that the combined masses of the residue nuclei are measurably less than the masses of the initial nuclei, *i.e.*, mass is significantly transformed into energy. This is explained by Einstein's mass defect formula, probably the most famous equation in science.

$$\Delta E = \Delta m.c^2$$

where ΔE is the energy released, Δm is the mass deficit and c is the speed of light.

62. A biofuel is a fuel that is produced through contemporary biological processes, such as agriculture and anaerobic digestion, rather than a fuel produced by geological processes such as those involved in the formation of fossil fuels, such as coal and petroleum, from prehistoric biological matter.

Biofuels can be derived directly from plants (*i.e.*, energy crops), or indirectly from agricultural, commercial, domestic, and/or industrial wastes. Renewable biofuels generally involve contemporary carbon fixation, such as those that occur in plantsor microalgae through the process of photosynthesis. Other renewable biofuels are made through the use or conversion of biomass (referring to recently living organisms, most often referring to plants or plant-derived materials).

Example of biofules:

Gaseous biofuels: Used for heating and cooking, and in engines for electricity and heat generation, and occasionally for transport, *e.g.*,

- Biogas (methane, CH_4 and CO_2) from anaerobic digestion of plant and animal wastes.

Liquid biofuels: Used mainly for transport fuels, *e.g.*,

- Oils from crop seeds (*e.g.*, rape, sunflower)
- Esters produced from such oil
- Ethanol from fermentation and distillation
- Methanol from acidification and distillation of woody crops.

Solid biofuels, e.g.

- Wood from plantations, forest cuttings, timber yards and other wastes

- Charcoal from pyrolysis
- Refuse-derived fuels *e.g.*, compressed pellets.

64. Reduction potential (pE,) is a measure of the tendency of a chemical species to acquire electrons and thereby be reduced. Reduction potential is measured in volts (V), or millivolts (mV). Each species has its own intrinsic reduction potential; the more positive the potential, the greater the species' affinity for electrons and tendency to be reduced. ORP is a common measurement for water quality.

The most reducing water sample has pE = 5

- Redox is expressed in units of "pe". analogous to pH.

$$pe = \log [e] \text{ (or Eh = 2.3 RT pE/F)}$$

where $[e]$ is the electron concentration or activity.

- "pe" is derived from the equilibrium constant (K) for an oxidation-reduction reaction at equilibrium.

$$K = \frac{[\text{reduced species}]}{[\text{oxidized species}]\,[e^-][H^+]}$$

Oxidized species + e^- + H^+ $\leftrightarrow$ reduced species

$$K = \frac{[\text{reduced} \times \text{species}]}{[\text{oxidized} \times \text{species}]\,[e^-][H^+]}$$

$$\log K = \log[\text{red}] - \log[\text{ox}] - \log[e^-] - \log[H^+]$$

$$\log K = -p_{\text{red}} + p_{\text{ox}} + pe + pH$$

If we assume [oxidized] = [reduced] = 1 (*i.e.*, at standard state), then,

$$\log K = pe + pH$$

The Nernst Equation can be used to relate this equation to measured Pt-electrode voltage (Eh, E_h, E_H);

$$pe = pE = \frac{F}{2.3RT}Eh$$

or $Eh = 2.3 \text{ RT } pE/F$

where, Eh = measured redox potential as voltage

R = the Universal Gas Constant (= 8.31 JK^{-1} mot^{-1})

T = temperature in degrees Kelvin

F = Faraday constant (= 23.1 kal V^{-1} equ v^{-1})

2.3 = conversion from natural to base-10 logarithms

- pE is a given environment is controlled by this reaction.

$$Fe^{3+} + e \rightarrow Fe^{2+} \qquad (\therefore n = 1)$$

- $\{Fe^{3+}\} = 10^{-5}$
- $\{Fe^{2+}\} = 10^{3}$

$$pE = pE^\circ + \frac{1}{n}\left\{\frac{oxid}{reduc}\right\}$$

$$pE^\circ = \frac{\log(K)}{n} = 13.0$$

$$\therefore \quad pE = 13.0 + \log\left(\frac{10^{-5}}{10^{-3}}\right) = 11.0$$

$$\{e^-\} = 10^{-11}$$

65. Normal rainwater has a pH of 5.6 (slightly acidic). This is because it is exposed to the carbon dioxide in the atmosphere. The carbon dioxide gets dissolved in the rainwater and forms carbonic acid (H{–2}CO{–3}).

Rainwater with pH value below 5.6 is considered as acid rain. There are both natural and non-natural sources of materials that cause pH of rain water to change.

Increasing pollution results in acid rains. Generally rainwater is pure and potable. The pH of drinking water falls in the range of 6.5- 8.

66. The usability for drinking water was determined on the basis of its pH, TH and TDS as per BIS and WHO norms (Table 1). The composite map generated by crossing classified spatial distribution maps for these parameters depicts the study area into different zones of unique combination of all the classes present in the input maps, and thus demonstrates the overall suitability for domestic use. Groundwater quality was found to be good for domestic use in about 88% of the district area while in rest 12% of the area falling in Kalayat and Rajaund blocks, the quality was moderate to doubtful due to TDS and pH exceeding maximum permissible limits.

Table: Standards for drinking Water

Parameter	WHO (2004)		BIS : 10500 (1998)	
	HDL	MPL	HDL	MPL
pH	7-8.5	6.5-9.2	6.5-8.5	No Relaxation
TDS mg/1	500	1500	500	2000
TH mg/1	100	500	300	600

HDL: Highest desired limit,
MPL: Maximum permissible limit

Hypochlorous Acid: HOCI is overall the most effective disinfectant of the chlorine species present in dilute solution at the pH values associated with water and wastewater treatment. Because HOCI is uncharged and has a relatively low molecular weight, it is better able than other chlorine species to penetrate cells walls; and it reacts more rapidly than other chlorine species, in both oxidative and substitution reactions, with organic matter, including critical components of cells.

The hypochlorous acid produced is a weak acid with pKa = 7.53; it partially dissociates in water to form the hypochlorite ion as follows:

$$HOCl \rightleftarrows H^+ + OCl^- \qquad (i)$$

As result, pH is critical in determining the dominant species in solution. The quantity of HOCl and OCl^- present in water is called the free available chlorine. The time to reach equilibrium is very short (less than one second).

Ammonia is commonly present in wastewater Hypochlorous acid reacts with ammonia and with many of its complex derivatives to produce chloramines in accordance with the following reactions

$$NH_3 + HOCl \rightarrow H_2O + NH_2Cl \text{ (monochloramine)} \quad ...(ii)$$

$$NH_2Cl + HOCl \rightarrow H_2O + NHCl_2 \text{ (dichloramine)} \quad ...(iii)$$

$$NHCl_2 + HOCl \rightarrow H_2O + NCl_3 \text{ (nitrogen trichloride)} \quad ...(iv)$$

68. It is generally agreed that as much as 40% of current net warming

(1) (10-20% of gross warming

(2) is attributable to black carbon

(3) Because of its large effect on radiative forcing and relatively short residence time in the atmosphere.

(4) black carbon presents some unique opportunities for postponing the effects of climate change. Whereas CO_2 has a life of up to about 40 years.

(5) black carbon remains in the atmosphere for as little as several weeks.

(6) As such, reducing emissions of black carbon can have an immediate near term impact on atmospheric warming. Furthermore, since black carbon is considered responsible for about 30% of the arctic melting, black carbon emission reductions can rapidly reduce the rate at which arctic ice is melting and avert associated consequences. Black carbon reduction policies can also result in large health benefits especially to citizens of developing countries.

69. Photochemical smog is formed as a result of the reaction of sunlight with hydrocarbons and nitrogen oxides. Ozone, nitric oxide, acrolein, formaldehyde, and peroxyacetyl nitrate (PAN) are common components of photochemical smog. The formation of photochemical smog can be summarized as follows: Burning of fossil fuels leads to the emission of hydrocarbons and nitrogen dioxide in the atmosphere. High concentrations of these pollutants in air results in their interaction with sunlight as follows:

$NO_2(g) \rightarrow NO(g) + O(g)$
Nitrogen dioxide Nitric oxide

$O(g) + O_2(g) \rightarrow O_3(g)$

$O_3(g) + NO(g) \rightarrow NO_2(g) + O_2(g)$

While ozone is toxic in nature, both NO_2 and O3 are oxidizing agents. They react with the unburnt hydrocarbons in air to produce formaldehyde, PAN, and acrolein.

$$3CH_4 + 2O_3 \rightarrow 3CH_2 = O + 3H_2O$$
Formaldehyde

70. According to the nature of hardness hard water is classified as:

(*i*) Temporary hard water

(*ii*) Permanent hard water

Temporary Hard Water : The sample of hard water whose hardness can be removed by easy means such as boiling is called temporary Hard water. Such hardness of water is known as temporary hardness. It is caused by the presence of soluble bicarbonates of calcium and magnesium in water.

(A) Removal of Temporary hardness: Temporary hardness of water is due to the presence of bicarbonate of calcium and magnesium in it. Such hardness can be removed by (*i*) boiling, (*ii*) by Clark's process.

(*i*) **By boiling :** When temporary hard water is boiled, the soluble bicarbonates of calcium and magnesium ore decomposed with the formation of corresponding carbonates which are insoluble in water.

$Ca(HCO_3)_2 \rightarrow CaCO_3 \downarrow + CO_2 + H_2O$

$Mg (HCO_3)_2 \rightarrow MgCO \downarrow CO_2 + H_2O$

(*ii*) **Clasics method :** In this process, temporary hardness of water is removed by treating it with calculated amount of slaked lime $Ca(OH)_2$. Slaked lime reacts with calcium and magnesium bicarbonates as follows:

$$Ca(HCO_3)_2 + Ca(OH)_2 \rightarrow 2CaCO_3 + 2H_2O$$

$$Mg (HCO_3)_2 + 2Ca (OH)_2 \rightarrow 2CaCO_3 \downarrow + Mg (OH)_2 + 2H_2O$$

71. Bioremediation is a process used to treat contaminated media, including water, soil and subsurface material, by altering environmental conditions to stimulate growth of micro-organisms and degrade the target pollutants.

Bioremediation of soils is currently a relevant issue, because it implies a process in which organic contaminants in the subsoil are biodegraded and can become mineralized so that eventually they become non-toxic compounds. The contaminant does not enter another physical state because it is degraded. Bioremediation of soil is not achieved readily if Contaminant has high aromaticity.

Bioremediation is aimed at maintaining the maximal possible growth of microorganisms until the carbon source (organic contaminant) decreases and, consequently, the microbial population decreases.

Physical and chemical factors are needed for an efficient bioremediation process; including water, temperature, pH, oxygen, major and minor nutrients.

72. It has been presumed that a concentration of CO below 1 part per 10,000 in air is not dangerous to most healthy persons, but individuals with heart or respiratory diseases may be harmed by this level. An important phenomenon in regard to CO, because of its tenacity in binding with hemoglobin, is that relatively low concentrations in air can rapidly result in accumulation of carboxy-hemoglobin (HbCO) in the blood. At 1:10,000 CO concentration in air, within relatively few minutes a human being will equilibrate to a stead y-state blood concentration of about 10% HbCO, which , in most people, will not produce symptoms. In fact, an individual accustomed to smoking (and inhaling) a pack or more of cigarettes per day will probably carry a HbCO concentration of 5 to 10% at all times. Similar concentrations are also regularly observed in persons who are surrounded by automobile traffic in their work environment, such as traffic policemen.

73. **Pareto Diagrams :** A Pareto diagram is a special bar graph in which the bars are arranged in descending order of magnitude. The purpose of Pareto analysis, using Pareto diagrams, is to identify the major problems in a product or process or, more generally, to identify the most significant causes for a given effect. This allows a developer to prioritize problems and decide which problem area to work on first. Pareto diagrams (charts) can be helpful in determining whether efforts toward process improvement are producing results. These diagrams are useful when the process is stable; they are not: effective if used on a chaotic process because the process is not ready for improvement. The process must first be stabilized through the use of control charts. Root cause analysis is performed using Pareto diagrams.

74. Total gaseous pollutant emissions by all car

$= 5 \times 1.2 + 10 \times 2.1 + 12 \times 3 + 8 \times 1.5$

$= 6 + 21 + 36 + 12 = 75$ kg

Total number of cars

$= 5 + 10 + 12 + 8 = 35$ cars.

Mean emissions of gaseous pollutant from all

$$= \frac{75}{35} = 2.14 \text{ kg/day}$$

75. The 95% confidence limits are given by

$$\bar{X} \pm t\left(\frac{s}{\sqrt{N-1}}\right)$$

From question, $\bar{X} = 43.8$ cm

$s = 0.6$ cm

$N = 10$

The required 95% confidence limits are

$$43.8 \pm 2.26\left(\frac{0.6}{\sqrt{10-1}}\right)$$

$= (43.8 = 0.452)$ cm

Thus, we can 95% confident that the true lies between $(43.8 - 0.452) = 43.348$

and $(43.8 + 0.452) = 44.252$ cm.

77. The adjusted R-squared compares the explanatory power of regression models that contain different numbers of predictors. The adjusted R-squared is a modified version of R-squared that has been adjusted for the number of predictors in the model. The adjusted R-squared increases only if the new term improves the model more than would be expected by chance. It decreases when a predictor improves the model by less than expected by chance. The adjusted R-squared can be negative, but it's usually not. It is always lower than the R-squared.

80. **Gaussian Dispersion Equation :** If the emission source is at ground level with no effective plume rise then

$$C(x, y, z) = \frac{Q}{\pi\sigma_y\sigma_z\bar{u}}\exp\left[-\frac{1}{2}\left(\frac{y^2}{\sigma_y^2}+\frac{z^2}{\sigma_z^2}\right)\right]$$

Plume Rise : H is the sum of the physical stack height and plume rise.

$$H = \Delta h_{plume\ rise} + h_{actual\ stack}$$

And it depends on buoyancy of exhaust gases, momentum of exhaust gases and stability of the atmosphere.

81. International shipping has been a fast growing sector of the global economy and its share of total anthropogenic emissions is significant, having effects on climate, air quality, and human health. The nature of the contribution to climate change is complex: In addition to warming by CO_2 emissions, ship emissions of sulphur dioxide (SO_2) cause cooling through effects on atmospheric particles and clouds, while nitrogen oxides (NO_x) increase the levels of the greenhouse gas (GHG) ozone (O_3) and reduce the GHG methane (CH_4), causing warming and cooling, respectively. The result is a net global mean radiative forcing (RF) from the shipping sector that is strongly negative, leading to a global cooling effect today.

82. The stratospheric ozone layer absorbs most of the harmful ultraviolet B (UVB) radiation (shortwave UV rays measuring 280-315 nanometers, or nm) emitted by the sun. In small amounts, UVB radiation is helpful to life (*e.g.*, for the production of vitamin D).

Research has shown that even small amounts of UV-B radiation can cause considerable harm. UV-B damages the genetic material of DNA and is related to some types of skin cancer. It is important to note, however, that UV-B radiation has always had this effect on humans. In recent years non-melanoma skin cancer has become more prevalent in many parts of the world because people are spending more time in the Sun and are exposing more of their skin in the process.

83. Saline-alkali soils: These soils are both saline and alkali. There can be all stages in transition with varying degree of dominance of salt content and pH. According to movement of soluble salts, formation of saline-alkali and non-saline alkali soils depends. Soil contains Na-clay as well as excess soluble salts.

If the soluble sodium salts are not leached out due to the insufficiency of rain water, they remain in the soil. The soil thus contains Na-clay and excess soluble, salts in solution. Such soils are known as saline-alkali soils. They are thus, developed as a result of the combined process of salinization and alkalization. In spite of the presence of sodium clay (Na-clay) the soil remains friable and possesses aggregate (flocculated). This is because the presence of sodium salts does not allow the sodium clay to get dispersed and keeps it flocculated.

Thus, this soil behaves more or less like saline soils. If due to much water soluble salts are leached down, and soil contains Na-clay only. Thus, this soil behaves more or less as non-saline-alkali soil. Therefore, the soil structure becomes un-favourable for the entry and movement of air and water.

84. Extensive use of fertilizers results in significant concentrations of nutrients particularly nitrogen, in agricultural runoff. If eroded soil reaches the lake, both phosphorus and the nitrogen in the soil contribute to eutrophication. Erosion is often caused by deforestation which also results from unwise planning and management of the resource.

Soils that have been fertilized for several years using only or primarily, poultry litter, dairy wastes and other animal manures, can begin to test "high" or "excessive" in phosphorus, since application rates of these substances are generally based on their nitrogen content. Animal manures commonly have similar nitrogen and phosphorus contents, and most crops will utilize 5 to 10 times more nitrogen than phosphorus, therefore, phosphorus will begin to accumulate in the soil under such management practices.

85. The International Day for Biological Diversity (or World Biodiversity Day) is a United Nations sanctioned international day for the promotion of biodiversity issues. It is currently held on May 22. From its creation by the Second Committee of the UN General Assembly in 1993 until 2000, it was held on December 29 to celebrate the day the Convention on Biological Diversity went into effect. On December 20, 2000, the date was shifted to commemorate the adoption of the Convention on May 22, 1992 at the Rio Earth Summit, and partly to avoid the many other holidays that occur in late December.

86. Make solar energy affordable for the poorest, the Alliance underscores the importance of channelling capital, reducing costs through financial mechanisms, promoting universal access to energy and supporting the creation of common standards to guarantee appropriate product quality in the use of products by member countries.

To achieve these objectives, the Alliance aims to implement financial instruments to mobilize over \$1 trillion in solar energy investment by 2030.

87. Sites on the List at which changes in ecological character have occurred, are occurring, or are likely to occur can be placed by the Contracting Party concerned on a special register known as the Montreux Record, a list of Ramsar Sites requiring priority conservation attention. These sites may benefit from the application of the Ramsar Advisory Mission mechanism, by which the Ramsar Secretariat organizes technical missions to seek solutions and provide advice to the relevant authorities. Article 3.2 of the Convention commits the Parties to make themselves awar.

88. Pseudomonas putida is a Gram-negative, rod-shaped, saprotrophic soil bacterium. Based on 16S rRNA analysis, P. putida was taxonomically confirmed to be a Pseudomonas species and placed, along with several other species, in the P. putida group, to which it lends its name.

Dr. Ananda Mohan Chakraborthi introduced plasmid from different strains in to single cell of *Pseudomonas putida.* The result was new genetically engineered bacterium which would be used in cleaning oil spills called "Super bug".

89. **Regulation with Respect to Energy:** There are restrictions on entry to a sanctuary or a national park for persons other than a public servant. Only after obtaining a permit from the Chief Wildlife Warden, any person may enter or reside in a sanctuary or a national park for all or any of the following purposes:

(*a*) investigation or study of wild life,

(*b*) photography,

(*c*) scientific research,

(*d*) tourism,

(*e*) transaction of lawful business with any person residing in the sanctuary.

90. The Indian Forest Act, 1927 was largely based on previous Indian Forest Acts implemented under the British. The most famous one was the Indian Forest Act of 1878. Both the 1878 act and the 1927 one sought to consolidate and reserve the areas having forest cover, or significant wildlife, to regulate movement and transit of forest produce, and duty leviable on timber and other forest produce. It also defines the procedure to be followed for declaring an area to be a Reserved Forest, a Protected Forest or a Village Forest. It defines what is a forest offence, what are the acts prohibited inside a Reserved Forest, and penalties leviable on violation of the provisions of the Act.

91. Biodegradation increase BOD levels in leachate and reduces the pH level, and then gasification generates gas from organic acids, thereby reducing BOD levels and increasing pH. Decomposition in landfills is divided into five phases; initial adjustment (Phase I), transition (Phase II), acidification (Phase III), methane fermentation (Phase IV), and maturation (Phase V) (Tchobanoglous).

Phase I : Initial Adjustment Phase : During this phase, aerobic conditions occur where organic biodegradable materials undergo microbial decomposition facilitated by air trapped within the landfill. Leachate generated from this phase is characterized by entrained particulate matter and small amounts of organic substances from aerobic degradation.

Phase II : Transition Phase : In this phase, biological decomposition of waste occurs. Transformation from aerobic to anaerobic environment occurs as the oxygen in waste cell decreases with more carbon dioxide being produced.

During the initial aerobic phase, oxygen present in landfill is rapidly consumed; resulting in the production of CO_2 and the leachate temperatures can be increased. The aerobic phase in a landfill lasts only a few days because oxygen is not replenished once the waste is covered and the pH in this early stage becomes neutral. When the condition turns anaerobic, the hydrolytic, fermentative, and acetogenic bacteria becomes dominant, resulting in an accumulation of carboxylic acids. Consequently, chemical oxygen demand (COD) and pH in the leachate are reduced by the end of this phase as more volatile organic acids and CO_2 are produced.

Phase III : Acid Phase : This phase is also known as the acetogenic phase and is governed by acidogenic bacteria (acid formers). In this phase, oxygen in the landfill is consumed by aerobic bacteria. Development of organic acids and dissolved CO_2 reduces leachate pH to 5 or lower (Salem et at., 2008). Therefore, the heavy metals become soluble, and essential nutrients are removed from the leachate because of the decreasing pH. Ammonium and metal concentrations also rise, and complex molecules are degraded.

Phase IV : Methane Fermentation Phase : In this phase, methanogen conditions are established after several months or years, and leachate becomes neutral or slightly alkaline. Methanogenic bacteria consume acids and produce methane and carbon dioxide. Under stablized methanogenic conditions, landfill gas is composed of approximately 55% to 60% methane and 40% to 45% carbon dioxide, with trace amounts of other gases. The pH in this phase increases to neutral values of 7 or 8.

Phase V : Maturation Phase : In this phase, nutrients and substrates become limited, and biological decomposition is less active. Aerobic conditions may return after conversion of biodegradable waste to carbon dioxide and methane gas. Landfill gas is depleted, and then the leachate stabilizes. Leachate often contains humic and fulvic acids, which are difficult to biodegrade. The slow degradation of these resistant organic materials may continue with the production of humic-like substances.

92. Resource recovery is using wastes as an input material to create valuable products as new outputs. The aim is to reduce the amount of waste generated, therefore reducing the need for landfill space and also extracting maximum value from waste. Resource recovery delays the need to use raw materials in the manufacturing process. Materials found in municipal solid waste can be used to make new products. Plastic, paper, aluminium, glass and metal are examples of where value can be found in waste.

Mechanical separation usually involves the use of several type of unit processes, five of which are size reduction, screening, air classification, magnetic separation, and non-ferrous (*e.g.*, aluminium) separation [1-5]. Table 1lists unit processes relevant to separation, as well as most of the types of mechanical unit processes that have been incorporated into waste processing facilities implemented to date.

Table: Mechanical unit processes used in waste processing facilities

- Size reduction
- Air classification
- Screening
- Magnetic separation
- Glass separation
- Non-ferrous separation
- Densification
- Conveyors.

The sequence of the processes for mixed waste processing varies, although either size reduction or a preliminary screening (trommel) usually is the first step.

The correct sequence in resource recovery for mixed solid waste is → Screening → Shredder Magnetic separation → Air classifier.

93. Integrated Solid Waste Management (ISWM) can be defined in many ways but it is probably best to think of it as a way of using a combination of waste management techniques to treat the different types of waste in ways that are environmentally, financially and socially sustainable. ISWM should be based on the waste hierarchy and focus on using the 3 Rs while finding a suitable way of dealing with the remaining waste. It also depends on collaboration among all the organisations and individuals involved in waste management.

Introducing ISWM means adopting all of the beneficial practices that have been described in previous study sessions and ensuring that they all work together effectively. It has a number of advantages for the different sectors of society. Here are some examples:

1. **Reduction and reuse at source :** reducing waste at the source and reusing wastes means that less waste has to be collected. This lowers costs for residents, businesses and the local authority. Also, the pollution generated in transporting the waste and at the disposal site is reduced. Waste reduction and reuse means that there is less pollution from manufacturing and a reduced need to import goods. Finally, society benefits because people have the use of items that they may not otherwise be able to afford.
2. **Waste separation at source :** Many ISWM schemes require householders and businesses to separate reusable and recyclable materials from the rest of the waste and sort them by type. This helps to make people more aware of what they throw away and means that the material separated for recycling is of a higher quality and has a higher selling price. In alternative schemes, where recyclable materials are extracted from mixed wastes at the transfer station, there is a greater health risk to those who do this work and also to those who work in the recycling industry.

94. ***14th International Conference on Humanizing Work and Work Environment HWWE-2016***

Table: Categories of Biomedical Wastes

Waste Category	Waste Class and Description	Treatment and Disposal (Option)
No. 1	Human Anatomical Wastes *i.e.*, Human tissues, organs, waste body parts	Incineration/deep burial
No. 2	Animal Wastes *i.e.*, animal tissue, organs, body parts, carcases, body fluid, blood and blood products, items contaminated with blood and fluids, wastes from surgery treatment and autopsy and wastes of experimental animals used in research, and the waste generated by veterinary hospitals, colleges, animal houses and livestock farms.	Incineration/deep burial
No. 3	Microbiology & Biotechnology Waste *i.e.* wastes from laboratory, culture stocks or specimens of micro-organisms, live or attenuated vaccines, human and animal cell culture used in research and infections agents from research and industrial laboratories, wastes from production of biological dishes and devices used for transfer of cultures etc.	Local autoclaving/ microwaving/incineration

No. 4	Waste Sharps *i.e.*, Needles, syringes, scalpels, blades, glass, that is capable of causing puncture and cuts. This includes both used and unused sharps.	Disinfection using chemical treatment/autoclaving microwave, shredding and disposal in landfill/recycling (for PVC and plastics).
No. 5	Discarded Medicines *i.e.*, wastes comprising of outdated, contaminated and discarded medicines.	Incineration or destruction and disposal in landfills.
No. 6	Solied Wastes *i.e.*, wastes generated from soiled cotton, dressings, plaster casts, linens, beddings, material contaminated with blood including the packaging materials.	Incineration autoclaving/ microwaving.
No. 7	Solid Waste *i.e.*, wastes generated from disposable items other than the waste sharps such as tubing S. catheters, intravenous sets etc.	Disinfection by chemical treatment an autoclaving/ microwaving and multilation/shredding.
No. 8	Liquid Waste *i.e.*, waste generated from laboratory and washing, cleaning, house-keeping and disinfecting activities.	Disinfection by chemical treatment and discharge into drain.
No. 9	Incineration ash *i.e.*, ash from incineration of any biomedical waste.	Disposal in municipal landfill.
No. 10	Chemical Waste *i.e.*, chemicals used in production of biological, chemicals used in disinfection, as insecticides, etc.	Chemical treatment and discharge into drains for liquids and secured landfill for solids.

95. ***Table : Landfill sealants for the control of gas and leachate movement***

Sealant		Remarks
Classification	**Representative types**	
Compacted soil		Sould contain some clay or fine silt.
Compacted clay	Bentonites, illites, kaolinites	The most commonly used sealant for landfills: these type of sealant would have a layer of thickness varies from 6 to 48 in and the layer must be continuous to prevent any disfiguration of the protective layer and are not allowed to dry out or it would eventually cracked.
Inorganic chemicals	Sodium carbonate, silicate or pyrophosphate	Use depends on local soil characteristics.
Synthetic chemicals	Polymers, rubber latex	Experimental; use in field not well established.

Synthetic membrane liners	Polyvinyl chloride, butyl rubber, hypalon, poluethylene, nylon-reinforced liners.	Commonly used for leachate control; increased usage for control of landfill gas.
Asphalt	Modified asphalt, rubber-impregnated asphalt, asphalt-covered polyethylene fabric, asphalt concrete.	The layer must be sufficiently thick enough to maintain continuity under differential settling conditions as could be impose by the landfilling process and leachate accumulation.
Others	Gunite concrete, soil cement, plastic soil cement	Not commonly used for control of leachate and gas movement because of shrinkage cracks after construction.

96. The introduction to ISO 14001 clearly states that it:

Does not establish absolute requirements for environmental performance beyond commitment, in the policy, to compliance with applicable legislation and regulation and to continual improvement. Thus, two organizations carrying out similar activities but having different environmental performance may both comply with its requirements.

ISO 14001 is a Five Step Process : The elements of ISO 14001 are organized around five steps:

1. Environmental policy;
2. Planning;
3. Implementation and operation;
4. Checking and corrective action;
5. Management review.

Each step is briefly described below:

Environmental Policy : An organization drafts a policy setting out its intentions in relation to the environment. A policy must contain commitments to:

- Continual improvement;
- Prevention of pollution;
- Complying with relevant environmental legislation and other relevant requirements.

ISO 14001 defines 'continual improvement' as: The process of enhancing the environmental management system in order to achieve improvements in environmental performance in line with the organization's environmental policy.

'Prevention of pollution' is defined as: Use of processes, practices, materials or products that avoid, reduce or control pollution, which may include recycling, treatment, process changes, control mechanisms, efficient use of resources and material substitution.

Planning : The organization must then set itself objectives and targets relating to its three policy commitments and devise a plan to meet these objectives and targets.

Implementation and operation : Having devised its plan, the organization must then put in place of the various elements necessary for its successful implementation and operation.

Checking and corrective action : Having implemented its plan, the organization must then check to see whether it has been successful in meeting its objectives and targets. If any have not been met, then corrective action must be taken. The entire management system must be periodically audited to see that it meets the requirements of the standard.

Management review : Management must periodically review the system to ensure its continuing effectiveness and suitablity. Changes are made to the system as and when necessary.

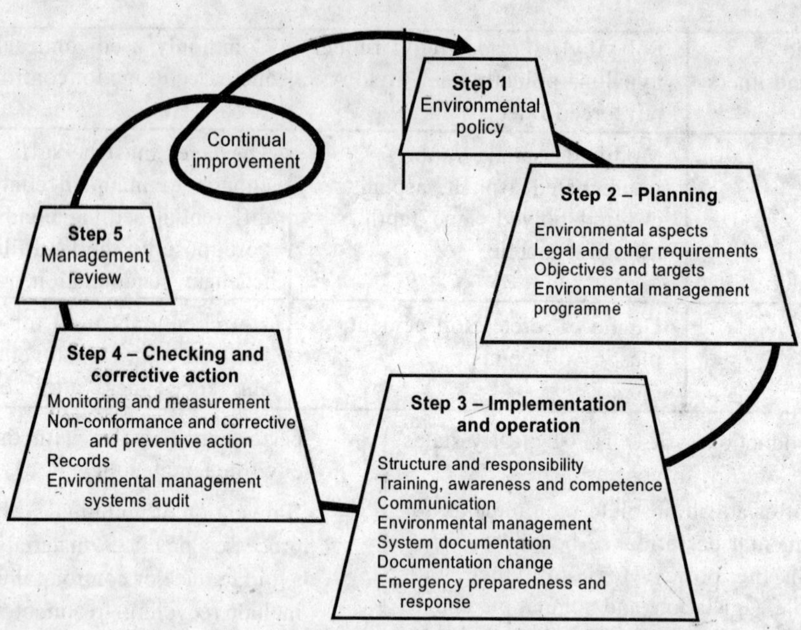

Fig. : The Five Steps and the Elements of ISO 14001

97. • The description of the project/development action includes a clarification of the purpose and rationale of the project, and an understanding of its various characteristics – including stages of development, location and processes.

• The description of the environmental baseline includes the establishment of both the present and future state of the environment, in the absence of the project, taking into account changes resulting from natural events and from other human activities.

• Mitigation involves the introduction of measures to avoid, reduce, remedy or compensate for any significant adverse impacts. In addition enhancement involves the development of beneficial impacts where possible.

• Review involves a systematic appraisal of the quality of the EIS, as a contribution to the decision-making process.

98. All projects or activities included as Category 'B' in the Schedule, including expansion and modernization of existing projects or activities as specified in sub paragraph (*ii*) of paragraph 2, or change in product mix as specified in sub paragraph (*iii*) of paragraph 2, but excluding those which fulfill the General Conditions (GC) stipulated in the Schedule, will require prior environmental clearance from the State/Union territory Environment Impact Assessment Authority (SEIAA). The SEIAA shall base its decision on the recommendations of a State or Union territory level Expert Appraisal Committee (SEAC) as to be constituted for in this notification. In the absence of a duly constituted SEIAA or SEAC, a Category 'B' project shall be treated as a Category 'A' project;

B.(*ii*) Expansion and modernization of existing projects or activities listed in the Schedule to this notification with addition of capacity beyond the limits specified for the concerned sector, that is, projects or activities which cross the threshold limits given in the Schedule, after expansion or modernization;

B.(*iii*) Any change in product - mix in an existing manufacturing unit included in Schedule beyond the specified range.

99. ***Table : Components of the EIA process***

Component	Propose
Project screening	To narrow the application of assessment to those projects that may have significant environmental impacts
Scoping	To identify at an early stage, from all of a project's possible impacts and from all the alternatives that could be addressed, those that are the key significant issues.
Consideration of alternatives	To ensure that the proponent has considered various feasible approaches (*e.g.*, alternative location/scale/ processes) and the 'no action' option.
Project description	To elarify the purpose and rationale of the project and to identify its various characteristics (including stages of development, location and processes).
Environmental baseline description	To establishment both the present and future state of the environment (in the absence of the project), taking into account changes resulting from natural events and from other human activities.
Key impacts	To bring together the previous steps so that all potentially significant environmental impacts (adverse and beneficial) are indentified and into account.
Impact prediction	To identify the magnitude and other dimensions of any identified change in the environment due to the project.
Assessment	To assess the relative importance of the predicted impacts and thus focus on key adverse impacts.
Mitigation	The introduction of measures to avoid/reduce/remedy or compensate for any significant adverse impacts
Public consultation	To ensure the quality, comprehensiveness and effectiveness of the EIA, as well as to ensure that the public's views are taken into consideration.
Environmental statement	To present the outcomes of the assessment process and the proposed mitigation measures. If done badly, much good work in the EIA may be negated.
Review	To provide a systematic appraisal of the quality of the ES, as a contribution to the decision-making process.
Decision-making	Consideration by the relevant authority of the ES (including the consultation process), together with other material considerations.
Monitoring	Recording the outcomes associated with development impacts, after a decision to proceed.

100. The environmental evalution system was designed by the Battelle Columbus Laboratories in the United States to assess impacts of water-resource development, water-quality management plans, highways, nuclear power plants, and other projects.

The Battelle environmental evaluation system for water resources is described in Table. The human concerns are separated into four main categories: (*a*) ecology; (*b*) physical/chemical; (*c*) aesthetics; and (*d*) human interest/social. Each category contains a number of components that have been selected specifically for use in all U.S. Bureau of Reclamation water-resource development projects.

Table : The Battelle environmental classification for water-resource development projects (the numbers in parentheses are relative weights)

Ecology	**Physical/Chemical**
Terrestrial species and populations	***Water quality***
Browsers and grazers (14)	Basin hydrologic loss (2)
Crops (14)	Biochemical oxygen demand (25)
Natural vegetation (14)	Dissolved oxygen (31)
Pest species (14)	Fecal coliforms (18)
Upland game birds (14)	Inorganic carbon (22)
	Inorganic nitrogen (25)
Aquatic species and populations	Inorganic phosphate (28)
Commercial fisheries (14)	Pesticides (16)
Natural vegetation (14)	pH (18)
Pest species (14)	Stream flow variation (28)
Sport fish (14)	Temperature (28)
Water fowl (14)	Total dissolved solids (25)
	Toxic substances (14)
Terrestrial habitats and communities	Turbidity (20)
Food web index (12)	
Land use (12)	***Air quality***
Rare and endangered species (12)	Carbon monoxide (5)
Species diversity (14)	Hydrocarbons (5)
	Nitrogen oxides (10)
Aquatic habitats and communities	Particulate matter (12)
Food web index (12)	Photochemical oxidants (5)
Rare and endangered species (12)	Sulphur oxides (10)
River characteristics (12)	Other (5)
Species deversity (14)	
	Land pollution
	Land use (14)
	Soil erosion (14)
	Noise pollution
	Noise (4)
Aesthetics	**Human interest/social**
Land	***Education/Scientific***
Geologic surface material (6)	Archeological (13)
Relief and topographic character (16)	Ecological (13)
Width and alignment (10)	Geological (11)
	Hydrological (11)
Air	
Order and visual (3)	***Historical***
Sounds (2)	Architecture and styles (11)
	Events (11)
Water	Persons (11)
Appearance of water (10)	Religions and cultures (11)
Land and water interface (16)	Western Frontier (11)

Previous Paper (Solved)

UGC-NET-Junior Research Fellowship & Assistant Professor Exam

Environmental Science, November-2017*

PAPER-II

Note: *This paper contains **fifty (50)** objective type questions of **two (2)** marks each. **All** questions are **compulsory**.*

1. The innermost layer of the earth is made up of:

A. Silicon and alumina
B. Silicon and magnesium
C. Silicon and nickel
D. Nickel and iron

2. The heat is distributed through a vertical mixing process called:

A. Advection B. Diffusion
C. Convection D. Turbulance

3. Which of the following statement(s) is/are true for an isothermal process?

(*a*) There is no change in enthalpy
(*b*) There is no change in internal energy
(*c*) There is change in temperature

Choose the correct code:

A. (*a*) only B. (*b*) and (*c*) only
C. (*a*) and (*b*) only D. (*a*), (*b*) and (*c*)

4. Match the List-I and List-II. Identify the correct answer from the code given below:

List-I (Aerosol)	**List-II (Source)**
(*a*) Primary natural aerosol	(*i*) Organic matter from biogenic gases
(*b*) Secondary natural aerosol	(*ii*) Soot from biomass burning
(*c*) Primary anthro-pogenic aerosol	(*iii*) Sulphate aerosol from powerplant SO_2 emissions
(*d*) Secondary anthro-pogenic aerosol	(*iv*) Soil dust

Code:

	(*a*)	(*b*)	(*c*)	(*d*)
A.	(*i*)	(*ii*)	(*iii*)	(*iv*)
B.	(*ii*)	(*iii*)	(*iv*)	(*i*)
C.	(*iii*)	(*iv*)	(*i*)	(*ii*)
D.	(*iv*)	(*i*)	(*ii*)	(*iii*)

5. Which of the following is not a heavy metal?

A. Lead B. Mercury
C. Bismuth D. Aluminum

6. The dominant dissolved carbon dioxide species in sea water is:

A. Bicarbonate ion
B. Carbonate ion
C. Carbonic acid
D. Aquated carbon dioxide

7. A solution of chemical 'A' having its 0.14 mol L^{-1} concentration has an absorbance of 0.42. Another solution of 'A' under the same conditions has an absorbance of 0.36. What is the concentration of this solution of 'A'?

A. 0.108 mol L^{-1} B. 0.35 mol L^{-1}
C. 0.12 mol L^{-1} D. 0.10 mol L^{-1}

8. Which one of the following is not a soil micronutrient?

A. Sulphur B. Boron
C. Iron D. Zinc

9. If life of NO_2 be 0.693 day, its residence time is:

A. 1.44 days B. 1.0 day
C. 0.693 day D. 0.48 day

10. The general molecular formula of PAN type compound is:

* Exam held on 05 November, 2017

A. $C_X H_Y OONO_2$ B. $C_X H_Y OO_2NO_2$
C. $C_x H_x OO_2NO_2$ D. $C_x H_Y ONO_2$

11. In an ecosystem, which one of the following is a micro-consumer?
A. Herbivores B. Omnivores
C. Carnivores D. Saprotrophs

12. A structure with hundreds of species non-linearly interlinked for their livelyhood is called:
A. Guild B. Food chain
C. Food web D. Pyramid

13. The process of examination of change in species diversity between ecosystems is a measure of:
A. Alpha diversity B. Beta diversity
C. Gamma diversity D. Genetic diversity

14. Red tide is caused by:
A. Diatoms B. Dianoflagillates
C. Navicula D. Desmids

15. The unidirectional series of changes from an uninhabited water body to a water body inhabited by a stable aquatic community are called:
A. Eutrophication B. Succession
C. Regeneration D. Reclamation

16. Under the clear Sunny day, the maximum depth of the ocean at which photosynthesis can occur is:
A. 10 m B. 250 m
C. 80 m D. 600 m

17. The organism likely to be most similar to the first life form that evolved on the earth is:
A. Blue - green algae
B. Methane producing bacteria
C. Protozoan
D. Red algae

18. A landform that results from free fall of rocks is called:
A. Alluvial fan B. Debris flow
C. Talus slope D. Valley fills

19. In India lignite is mined in:
A. Neyveli B. Jharia
C. Singrauli D. Singareni

20. Tree height can be measured using remote sensing data from:
A. Resourcesat B. Landsat
C. Cartosat D. RISAT

21. Ecosystem restoration deals with restoring:
A. Ecosystem integrity
B. Biodiversity
C. Physical environment
D. Ecosystem resistance

22. A single solar cell (10 cm × 10 cm) produces a voltage of 0.5 V and a current upto 2.5 A. If the solar insolation is 800 W/m^2, the efficiency of the solar cell is:
A. ~ 15.6 % B. ~ 24.6 %
C. ~ 12.3 % D. ~ 10.2 %

23. Which of the following atoms is not fissile?
A. $^{238}_{92}U$ B. $^{235}_{92}U$
C. $^{233}_{92}U$ D. $^{239}_{94}U$

24. Which of the following fuels has minimum nitrogen content?
A. Crude oil B. CNG
C. Producer gas D. LPG

25. Maximum sulfur content is found in which grade of coal?
A. Bituminous B. Sub - bituminous
C. Lignite D. Anthracite

26. Which of the following solar cell materials has maximum efficiency?
A. Cd Te, thin film
B. Si, polycrystalline
C. Amorphous Si : Ge : H film
D. Ga As, single crystal

27. Noise level of 70 dB corresponds to sound intensity of:
A. 10^{-5} Wm^{-2} B. 10^{-7}Wm^{-2}
C. 10^{-4}Wm^{-2} D. $10^{-3.5}$Wm^{-2}

28. At 25°C and 1 atm. pressure, 1 ppm concentration of SO_2 is equivalent to:
A. 1310 μg/m^3 B. 1826 μg/m^3
C. 2620 μg/m^3 D. 5240 μg/m^3

29. Given below are two statements. One labelled as **Assertion (A)** and the other labelled as **Reason (R)**:

Assertion (A) : Arsenic (III) is more toxic than arsenic (V).

Reason (R) : Arsenic (V) binds the sulfhydryl group more strongly than arsenic (III).

Choose the **correct** answer:

A. Both (A) and (R) are correct and (R) is the correct explanation of (A).
B. Both (A) and (R) are correct and (R) is not the correct explanation of (A).
C. (A) is true, but (R) is false.
D. (A) is false and (R) is true.

30. The half life period of a radioactive substance is 32 h. How much time it would take for its 75% disintegration?

A. 16 h B. 96 h
C. 128 h D. 64 h

31. Match the List-I and List-II. Identify the correct answer from the code given below:

List-I (Pesticides)	**List-II (Target)**
(*a*) Avicide	(*i*) Fish
(*b*) Disinfectant	(*ii*) Plants
(*c*) Herbicide	(*iii*) Birds
(*d*) Piscicide	(*iv*) Micro-organisms

Code:

	(*a*)	(*b*)	(*c*)	(*d*)
A.	(*i*)	(*ii*)	(*iii*)	(*iv*)
B.	(*ii*)	(*i*)	(*iii*)	(*iv*)
C.	(*iii*)	(*iv*)	(*ii*)	(*i*)
D.	(*iv*)	(*ii*)	(*i*)	(*iii*)

32. Nitrogen fixation in nature is not accomplished by:

A. Lightning
B. Cyanobacteria
C. Rotifers
D. Bacteria in root nodules of Leguminous plants

33. Which country has opted out of Paris Agreement on climate change?

A. USA B. Canada
C. Australia D. Russia

34. Under the EIA notification of 14th September, 2006, preparation of EIA is not required for the projects falling in the:

A. Category 'A' projects
B. Category 'B' projects
C. Category B_1 projects
D. Category B_2 projects

35. Which type of projects usually require an EIA?

A. Community garden development
B. Mining and mineral development projects
C. Outdoor recreation
D. Development of community wells

36. Match the List-I and List-II. Identify the correct answer from the code given below:

List-I (Series)	**List-II (Environmental labelling)**
(*a*) ISO 14021	(*i*) Principles and procedures
(*b*) ISO 14022	(*ii*) Self declaration of environmental claims
(*c*) ISO 14023	(*iii*) Symbols
(*d*) ISO 14024	(*iv*) Testing and verification methods

Code:

	(*a*)	(*b*)	(*c*)	(*d*)
A.	(*i*)	(*ii*)	(*iii*)	(*iv*)
B.	(*ii*)	(*iii*)	(*iv*)	(*i*)
C.	(*iii*)	(*iv*)	(*i*)	(*ii*)
D.	(*iv*)	(*i*)	(*iii*)	(*ii*)

37. Match the List-I and List-II. Identify the correct answer from the code given below:

List-I (Acts)	**List-II (Year)**
(*a*) Environmental Protection Act	(*i*) 1991
(*b*) Air (Prevention and Control of Pollution) Act	(*ii*) 1977
(*c*) Water (Prevention and Control of Pollution) Act	(*iii*) 1981
(*d*) Public Liability Insurance Act	(*iv*) 1986

Code:

	(*a*)	(*b*)	(*c*)	(*d*)
A.	(*i*)	(*ii*)	(*iii*)	(*iv*)
B.	(*ii*)	(*iii*)	(*iv*)	(*i*)
C.	(*iii*)	(*iv*)	(*i*)	(*ii*)
D.	(*iv*)	(*iii*)	(*ii*)	(*i*)

38. Articles 21, 48-A and 51-A(g), which aim to protect and improve the environment and safe guard forests and wildlife, incorporate which of the following principles of environmental law?

A. Polluter pays principle
B. Precautionary principle
C. Principle of strict liability
D. Moral duty of the state

39. Which is the correct classification of forests under the Indian Forest Act, 1927?

A. Grasslands, tropical forests, wetlands
B. Protected forest, reserved forest, village forest
C. Wildlife sanctuary, national parks, biosphere reserve
D. Private forest, social forest, town forest

40. Hardening of the steel releases the hazardous waste containing:

A. Brine sludge containing mercury
B. Cyanide - nitrate containing sludge
C. Lead bearing residues
D. Tar containing waste

41. Red coloured containers in the hospitals are used to dump:

A. Waste from laboratory cultures
B. House keeping waste
C. Human anatomical waste
D. Waste sharps

42. Mercury pollution is considered hazardous to human health because,

A. Mercury is a pure metal and hard to digest
B. Mercury accumulates and its concentration increases high up in the food chain
C. Mercury is highly soluble in water and easily absorbed by human body
D. Mercury is heavy and is not dispersed by the wind

43. In the context of Gaussian Plume Dispersion model assumptions, consider the following statements:

(*a*) The pollutants have the same density as the air surrounding them.
(*b*) The atmosphere is stable.

Choose the correct code:

A. Both (*a*) and (*b*) are true
B. (*a*) is true, (*b*) is false
C. (*a*) is false, (*b*) is true
D. Both (*a*) and (*b*) are false

44. Graphically depicting a group of numerical data through their Quartile is:

A. Histogram B. Frequency polygon
C. Box plot D. Pie chart

45. If, out of 50 fish of a pond, 12 had no ectoparasite and remaining had varying numbers of parasites on them, then how many of fish had at least one parasite?

A. 4 B. 24
C. 38 D. 16

46. In a One-way ANOVA, explained variance was found to be 8.0 and unexplained variance was 3.67. The F-ratio is:

A. 0.46 B. 4.26
C. 2.0 D. 2.18

47. In total global emissions of CO_2, India's contribution is about :

A. ~ 3% B. ~ 6%
C. ~ 9% D. ~ 12%

48. According to IPCC, in order to restrict global mean temperature rise to 2°C by the year 2050, global energy related CO_2 emissions (reference year 2005) need to be cut down by the year 2050 by:

A. ~ 50% B. ~ 90%
C. ~ 40% D. ~ 30%

49. Global average water consumption (L/person/day) is:

A. ~ 53 B. ~ 20
C. ~ 42 D. ~ 80

50. In a city, half a million cars travel approximately 20 km on a given day. The average HC emission rate is 2.0 g per car km. Assuming that the average molecular weight of all the emitted HCs is equal to that of CH_4, how much volume of HC is released in the city each day?

A. 1.4×10^4 m^3/day B. 2.8×10^4 m^3/day
C. 6.1×10^4 m^3/day D. 11.3×10^4 m^3/day

ANSWERS

1	2	3	4	5	6	7	8	9	10
D	C	C	D	D	A	C	A	B	B
11	**12**	**13**	**14**	**15**	**16**	**17**	**18**	**19**	**20**
D	C	B	B	B	B	B	C	A	C
21	**22**	**23**	**24**	**25**	**26**	**27**	**28**	**29**	**30**
A	A	A	D	A	D	A	C	C	D
31	**32**	**33**	**34**	**35**	**36**	**37**	**38**	**39**	**40**
C	C	A	D	B	B	D	B	B	B
41	**42**	**43**	**44**	**45**	**46**	**47**	**48**	**49**	**50**
A	B	B	C	C	D	B	A	A	B

EXPLANATORY ANSWERS

1. The Earth comprises of four separate layers. Most of the geologist believes that as the Earth cooled the heavier, the materials denser sank into the center, and the lighter ones rose towards the top. Due to this, the outermost layer is made of lightest materials such as rocks and granites and the innermost layer consists of nickel and iron.

Our Earth consists of four different layers namely:

- Inner core
- Outer core
- Mantle
- Crust

Inner Core: It is the center and the hottest layer of the Earth. The inner core is solid and made up of iron and nickel with temperature up to 5,500°C. Due to its immense heat energy, the inner core is more like the engine room of the Earth.

2. Vertical mixing, in the atmosphere or oceans, an upward and downward movement of air or water that occurs as a result of the temperature gradients. In the atmosphere vertical mixing is sometimes discernible as a form of atmospheric turbulence.

When the surface of Earth is substantially warmer than the overlying air, mixing will spontaneously occur in order to redistribute the heat. This process, referred to as free convection or natural convection, occurs when the environmental lapse rate — the rate of change of an atmospheric variable, such as temperature or density, with increasing altitude of temperature — decreases at a rate greater than 1°C per 100 metres.

3. An isothermal process is a thermodynamic process in which the temperature stays constant. In isothermal processes, there is no change in internal energy because internal energy is directly related to temperature.

For an ideal gas the internal energy (U) depends on temperature. Hence, if temperature is constant (isothermal process), the internal energy remains constant and hence, $\Delta U = 0$.

Enthalpy change (ΔH) can be directly measured using coffee-cup calorimeter and when we measure heat change (q_P) at constant pressure we actually measure change in enthalpy (ΔH).

We know that $\Delta H = \Delta U + \Delta n\ RT$ and since for isothermal process ΔT as well ΔU are equal to zero and hence, $\Delta H = 0$.

4. Global sources of major aerosol types

Natural	**Primary**	Soil dust (mineral aerosol), sea salt, volcanic dust, primary organic aerosols
	Secondary	Sulphates from biogenic gases, sulphates from volcanic SO_2, organic matter from biogenic VOCs, nitrate from NO_x
Anthropogenic	**Primary**	Industrial dust (except soot), black carbon (includes biomass burning)
	Secondary	Sulphate from SO_2, nitrates from NO_x, organic matter from biogenic VOCs

5. Heavy metals are generally defined as metals with relatively high densities, atomic weights, or atomic numbers. The criteria used, and whether metalloids are included, vary depending on the author and context. In metallurgy, for example, a heavy metal may be defined on the basis of density, whereas in physics the distinguishing criterion might be atomic number, while a chemist would likely be more concerned with chemical behaviour. The definitions encompass up to 96 out of the 118 known chemical elements; only mercury, lead and bismuth meet all of them.

6. When CO_2 from the atmosphere comes into contact with seawater, it can become dissolved into the water where is undergoes chemical reactions to form a series of products, as described in the following:

1. CO_2 (dissolved gas) + $H_2O \Leftrightarrow$ H_2CO_3 (carbonic acid)
2. H_2CO_3 (carbonic acid) $\Leftrightarrow$ H+ + HCO_3^- (hydrogen ion + bicarbonate)
3. $HCO_3^- \Leftrightarrow H^+ + CO_3^{-2}$ (hydrogen ion + carbonate)

The amount of CO_2 as dissolved gas is what controls the concentration of CO_2. This concentration depends strongly on the temperature — it is low in cold water and it is high in warm water, which means that the colder parts of the ocean absorb CO_2 from the atmosphere and the warm parts of the ocean release CO_2 into the atmosphere.

All of these reactions mean that in seawater, you can find all of these different forms or species of inorganic carbon co-existing, dissolved in seawater. In reality though, bicarbonate (HCO_3^-) is the dominant form of inorganic carbon; carbonate (CO_3^{2-}) and dissolved CO_2 are important, but secondary.

7. Beer's law governs the amount of radiation absorbed and indicates that absorbance is directly proportional to concentration. Thus, as the concentration of a compound dissolved in a given solvent increases, the absorbance of the solution should also increase proportionally.

Concentration of Solution A

$$= \frac{0.14 \times 0.36}{0.42} = 0.12 \text{ mol/L}.$$

8. Micronutrients are essential for plant growth and play an important role in balanced crop nutrition. They include boron (B), copper (Cu), iron (Fe), manganese (Mn), molybdenum (Mo), zinc (Zn), nickel (Ni) and chloride (Cl). They are as important to plant nutrition as primary and secondary macronutrients, though plants don't require as much of them. A lack of any one of the micronutrients in the soil can limit growth, even when all other nutrients are present in adequate amounts. They constitute in total less than 1% of the dry weight of most plants.

9. Residence times can be determined for a reservoir itself (such as the water in a lake) or for a substance within it (such as a contaminant). The residence time for any reservoir can be determined by taking the ratio of the total amount (mass or volume) of the reservoir to the flux.

The residence time can be calculated as the reciprocal of the sum of all first order rate constants.

Residence time of substance

$$= \frac{\text{amount of substance}}{\text{total of all removal rates}}$$

$$= \frac{1}{\Sigma \text{ removal rate constants}}$$

Half-life: $t_{1/2} = \frac{\ln 2}{k} = \frac{0.693}{k}$

Residence time: $\tau = \frac{1}{k}$, where *k*' represents the sum of all first order (or *pseudo*-first order) rate constants

Therefore;

Half-life = 0.693 × (Residence time)

$$\Rightarrow \quad \text{Residence time} = \frac{\text{Half life}}{0.693}$$

$$= \frac{0.693}{0.693} = 1 \text{ day.}$$

10. **Peroxyacyl nitrates** (also known as **Acyl peroxy nitrates**, **APN** or **PAN**s) are powerful respiratory and eye irritants present in photochemical smog. They are nitrates produced in the thermal equilibrium between organic peroxy radicals by the gas-phaseoxidation of a variety of volatile organic compounds (VOCs), or by aldehydes and other oxygenated VOCs oxidizing in the presence of NO_2.

For example, peroxyacetyl nitrate, $CH_3COOONO_2$:

Hydrocarbons + O_2 + NO_2 + light → $CH_3COOONO_2$

The general equation is:

$C_xH_yO_3 + NO_2 \rightarrow C_xH_yO_3NO_2$

They are good markers for the source of VOCs as either biogenic or anthropogenic, which is useful in the study of global and local effects of pollutants.

11. **Microconsumers or Saprotrophs:** The organisms which decompose complex compounds and dead cells and release in organic substances and belong chiefly in the group of bacteria, fungi. Item 1 to 2 - abiotic component u-6 biotic community.

12. A food web is a series of interacting food chains. Food chains show the order in which animals consume food. Food chains and food webs are made up of Producers, Consumers, and Decomposers. It is a structure with hundreds of species non-linearly interlinked for their livelihood.

13. (*a*) **Alpha diversity** [within-community diversity]: the diversity within a site, or quadrant. Also called as the local diversity.

(*b*) **Beta diversity** [between-community diversity] : the change in species composition from site to site. Also called as species turnover. Higher the heterogenecity in the habitats in a region, greater is the beta diversity.

(*c*) **Gamma diversity:** the diversity of a landscape, or of all sites combined. Also called as regional diversity.

(*d*) **Genetic diversity**

1. Genetic variation is the cornerstone of all biodiversity.
2. It enables a population to adapt to its environment and to respond to natural selection. The more individuals there are, the greater the chance of genetic variation. Species with a small population of individuals have limited variability and, therefore, have limited ability to respond to change.
3. The amount of genetic variation is the basis of speciation.
4. Genetic diversity within a species often increases with environmental variability.

14. Red tides are caused by an explosive growth and accumulation of certain microscopic algae, predominantly dinoflagellates, in coastal waters. Some species of dinoflagellates produce toxins that are among the most potent known to man. These harmful algae blooms, or HABs for short, pose a serious and recurring threat to human health, wildlife, marine ecosystems, fisheries, coastal aesthetics and our economy. The most troublesome species in the Gulf of Mexico is *Karenia brevis*. Like other dinoflagellates these tiny, single-celled organisms photosynthesize using chlorophyll like a plant yet they are mobile with the use of two flagella that propel them through the water column.

15. Two important subclasses of lakes are ponds, which typically are small lakes that intergrade with wetlands, and water reservoirs. Over long periods of time, lakes, or bays within them, may gradually become enriched by nutrients and slowly fill in with organic sediments, a process called succession.

Succession is recognizable only if the colonization of plant communities takes place in artificial small and shallow ponds, lakes, etc. where wave action speeds up the process by allowing the erosion of soil towards edge regions. In this way, the filling process also speeds up quickly and consequently the body of water disappears within few years time.

16. Photosynthesis is the process by which plants and other organisms, also known as photoautotrophs, use energy from sunlight to produce glucose. This process can occur both on land and underwater.

Photosynthesis can occur underwater as long as enough light is available. In the ocean, significant amounts of photosynthetically active radiation can be detected as deep as 250 m below the surface. Within this euphotic zone (sunlight zone), photosynthesis can occur. This process only requires light, carbon dioxide, and water. As long as a photosynthesizing organism, on land or underwater, has enough of these molecules, it can produce glucose and oxygen.

17. Genetically, the earliest bacteria are thought to have been archaebacteria, a classification that includes methane-producing bacteria, halophiles that survive conditions too hypersaline (salt-rich) for most other organisms, and sulfur bacteria able to tolerate the extreme heat radiating from earth's interior.

18. Rockfall talus slopes result from the accumulation of rockfall debris from discrete rockfall events over long periods of time. The plan morphology of talus slopes depends on the form of the cliffs supplying the debris and the morphology of the surface on which the debris accumulates. Relatively simple cliffs, straight in plan view and of uniform or similar geology, tend to produce sheet (straight) rockfall talus slopes lacking.

19. In 1935, the presence of black particles was discovered and the analysis led to the discovery of lignite reserves beneath the areas in and around Neyveli village. Lignite or brown coal occurs in (*i*) Neyveli in Tamil Nadu, (*ii*) Pallu fields in Rajasthan (*iii*) Masi in Kashmir and (*iv*) Parts of Assam, Meghalaya and other hilly tracts on the foothills of the Himalayas. By far the largest deposits occur in Neyveli in South Arcot district of Tamil Nadu. The Neyveli Lignite Corporation was formed as a corporate Body in 1956 by the Government of India and the mining of lignite started in 1962. The first thermal power station was commissioned in 1962 with assistance from U.S.S.R.

India is the fifth largest coal producing country in the world. The coal production was 295.09 million tons and lignite production was 20.01 million tons in 1996-97.

20. The **Cartosat** series of satellites are a type of earth observation satellites indigenously built by India. Up till now 6 Cartosat satellites have been launched by ISRO. The Cartosat series is a part of the Indian Remote Sensing Programme. They were specifically launched for Earth's resource management and monitoring.

Indian Earth Observation Satellite Cartosat-1 data were evaluated for the estimation of biophysical variables, including as tree height, crown diameter, canopy density and canopy gap, that are crucial for the estimation of stand volume, biomass and generation of site index. Investigations were carried out at a site covering the major dominant forest species grown in India. Cartosat-1 stereo data were analysed in conjunction with differential global positioning system (DGPS) measurements to generate a digital elevation model (DEM) and an orthoimage, which were used to estimate the biophysical variables. Analysis using grey level co occurrence texture measures was performed for separation of forest species, homogeneity of the classes of forest stands, stratification and measurement of crown area, canopy gap and stand density. Field measurements of tree height, diameter at breast height (DBH), stand density, age and crown diameter were conducted for each stand. Empirical models for the estimation of DBH were developed and validated with Cartosat 1 derived height and crown diameter.

21. Ecosystem Restoration is the "process of assisting the recovery of an ecosystem that has been degraded, damaged or destroyed". Ecosystem Restoration should be an important component of conservation and sustainable development programmes so that the livelihoods of people depending on these degraded ecosystems can be sustained.

The time has come to bridge the gap between the discipline of restoration ecology and communities around the world attempting to restore the ecological integrity of their surrounding landscapes.

22. The efficiency of a solar cell is determined as the fraction of incident power which is converted to electricity and is defined as:

$$P_{max} = V_{OC} I_{SC} FF$$

$$\eta = \frac{V_{OC} I_{SC} FF}{P_{in}}$$

Where:

V_{OC} is the open-circuit voltage;

I_{SC} is the short-circuit current;

FF is the fill factor and

η is the efficiency.

$$\eta = \frac{0.5 \times 2.5}{800 \times 0.1 \times 0.1} \times 100$$

$$= 15.6\%.$$

23. In nuclear engineering, **fissile material** (nuclide) is material that is capable of undergoing fission reaction after absorbing thermal (slow or low energy) neutron. These materials are used to fuel thermal nuclear reactors, because they are capable of sustaining a nuclear fission chain reaction.

For heavy nuclides with atomic number of higher than 90, most of fissile isotopes meet the **fissile rule**:

Fissile isotopes have $2 \times Z - N = 43 \pm 2$ (example for ^{235}U: $2 \times 92 - 143 = 41$)

where Z is number of protons and N is number of neutrons.

- **Fissile material** consist of fissionable isotopes that are capable of undergoing nuclear fission **only after capturing a thermal neutron**. ^{238}U is not fissile isotope, because ^{238}U cannot be fissioned by thermal neutron. ^{238}U does not meet also alternative requirement to fissile materials. ^{238}U is not capable of sustaining a nuclear fission chain reaction, because neutrons produced by fission of ^{238}U have lower energies than original neutron (usually below the threshold energy of 1 MeV). Typical fissile materials: ^{235}U, ^{233}U, ^{239}Pu, ^{241}Pu.
- **Fertile material** consist of isotopes that are not fissionable by thermal neutrons, but **can be converted into fissile isotopes**

(after neutron absorption and subsequent nuclear decay). Typical fertile materials: **^{238}U, ^{232}Th**.

25. Coal is a readily combustible rock containing more than *50 per cent* by weight of carbonaceous material formed from compaction and indurations of variously altered plant remains similar to those in peat.

- **Lignite** increases in maturity by becoming darker and harder and is then classified as sub-bituminous coal. After a continuous process of burial and alteration, chemical and physical changes occur until the coal is classified as bituminous - dark and hard coal.
- **Bituminous coal** ignites easily and burns long with a relatively long flame. If improperly fired bituminous coal is characterized with excess smoke and soot.
- **Anthracite coal** is the last classification, the ultimate maturation. Anthracite coal is very hard and shiny.

Typical Sulfur Content in Coal

- Anthracite Coal : *0.6 - 0.77 weight %*
- Bituminous Coal : *0.7 - 4.0 weight %*
- Lignite Coal : *0.4 weight %*

26. The primary objective of the worldwide photovoltaic (PV) solar cell research and development is to reduce the cost of PV cells and modules to a level that will be competitive with conventional ways of generating power.

Photovoltaic conversion efficiencies greater than 20% can be achieved by using single-crystal silicon or single junction GaAs semiconductor materials. Extraordinary progress has been made in recent years in achieving record-level efficiencies of 22% and 24% in single-crystal Si materials grown by the Czochralski (CZ) and 3 Float Zone (FZ) methods, respectively.

28. Concentration (μg/m³)

$$= \frac{\text{ppm} \times \text{molecular weight (g/mol)} \times 1000\ (\mu\text{g*L/m}^3\text{*g})}{24.5\ (\text{L/mol})}$$

$$= \frac{1 \times 64.2 \times 1000}{24.5} = 2620\ \mu\text{g/m}^3.$$

29. Arsenic is one of the most toxic metals derived from the natural environment. The major cause of human arsenic toxicity is from contamination of drinking water from natural geological sources rather than from mining, smelting, or agricultural sources.

Unbound arsenic also exerts its toxicity by generating reactive oxygen intermediates during their redox cycling and metabolic activation processes that cause lipid peroxidation and DNA damage. As III, especially, binds thiol or sulfhydryl groups in tissue proteins of the liver, lungs, kidney, spleen, gastrointestinal mucosa, and keratin-rich tissues (skin, hair, and nails).

31. Pesticides and Their Targets

Pesticide Type	**Target Organism**
Acaricide	Mites
Algicide	Algae
Avicide	Birds
Bactericide	Bacteria
Disinfectant	Microorganisms
Fungicide	Fungi
Herbicide	Plants
Insecticide	Insects
Larvicide	Insect larvae
Molluscicide	Snails, slugs
Nematicide	Nematodes
Piscicide	Fish
Rodenticide	Rodents
Termiticides	Termites

32. The process of converting free nitrogen gas of atmosphere into compounds of nitrogen (which can be used by plants) is called fixation of nitrogen. Nitrogen gas of the atmosphere can be fixed in three ways:

1. Fixation by bacteria
2. Fixation by algae
3. Fixation by lightning

1. **Fixation of nitrogen by bacteria:** The root nodules of certain leguminous plants (like peas, beans, etc.) contain nitrogen fixing bacteria called rhizobium. These nitrogen fixing bacteria convert nitrogen gas to nitrogen compounds, which can then be used by plants. Some non-leguminous plants like alnus and ginkgo also convert atmospheric nitrogen to usable nitrogen compounds for plants.

2. **Fixation of nitrogen by blue green algae:** Algae is the simplest green plant. Blue-green algae is also able to do nitrogen fixation. The nitrogen-fixing blue-green algae is found in paddy fields.

   Thus the two living organisms which can do fixation of nitrogen are rhizobium bacteria and blue-green algae. The fixation of nitrogen by bacteria and algae is called biological fixation of nitrogen. Most of the nitrogen in nature is fixed by this method.

3. **Fixation of nitrogen by lightning:** During lightning in the sky, a high temperature is produced, and the nitrogen gas present in the atmosphere reacts with oxygen, also present in the atmosphere to form nitrogen oxides. These nitrogen oxides dissolve in rain-water to form a very dilute solution of nitric acid which comes down to the Earth. This nitric acid reacts with the alkalies of soil (like limestone) to form nitrates. These nitrates get stored in the soil. In this way, the atmospheric nitrogen gets fixed. The nitrates present in the soil are then absorbed by the plants.

33. The United States withdraw from the Paris climate agreement, "In order to fulfill my solemn duty to protect America and its citizens, the United States will withdraw from the Paris climate accord," Trump said. Withdrawing, he said, "represents a reassertion of America's sovereignty."

He added that he hoped to "begin negotiations to reenter either the Paris accord or really entirely new transition on terms that are fair to the United States."

34. The objective of EIA Notification 2006 is to address the limitations in the old EIA Notification (1994). Therefore, various modifications have been incorporated in the old Notification, which the ministry claims have been done after taking into account the feedback from the different stakeholders.

EIA Notification 2006: Projects in Schedule-1 have been divided into two categories, Category A and B.

Category A project will require clearance from Central Government (MEF). Category B will require clearance from State Government. However, the state government will first classify if the B project falls under B1 or B2 category. B1 projects will require preparation of EIA reports while remaining projects will be termed as B2 projects and will not require EIA report.

This has the potential of being a good move as decentralization of power may speed up the project clearance process. However, it may be misused and there is an urgent need to build the capacity of the state regulators to deal with their new responsibilities.

36. ISO 14021: Environmental labels and declarations. Self-declaration of environmental claims: guidelines, definitions and usage of terms. This document is currently at the ISO DIS voting stage. It is expected to be completed and published by the end of the second quarter of 1998. This standard was combined with ISO 14022 and ISO 14023.

ISO 14022: Environmental labels and declarations. Self-declaration of environmental claims: symbols. Currently this document is at the ISO committee draft (CD) voting stage. It is expected to be completed and published by the first quarter of 1999. This standard was combined with ISO 14021 and ISO 14023.

ISO 14023: Environmental labels and declarations. Self-declaration of environmental claims: testing and verification methodologies. This document is currently at the ISO CD voting stage. It is expected to be completed and published by the first quarter of 1999. This standard was combined with ISO 14021 and ISO 14023.

ISO 14024: Environmental labels and declarations. Environmental labeling Type I: guiding principles and procedures. This document is currently at the ISO DIS voting stage. It is expected to be completed and published by the end of 1998.

37. 1. **Rules framed under the Air (Prevention and Control of Pollution) Act, 1981:** Under section 54 of the Air (Prevention and Control of Pollution) Act, 1981 confers that every state government shall make their rules of the respective state. Similarly, under section 53 of Air Act, 1981, the central government framed the Air (Prevention and Control of Pollution) Rules 1982.

2. **Rules frame under the Environment (Protection) Act, 1986:** The Environment (Protection) Act, 1986 under sections 6 and 25 empowers that the Government of India formulated the Environment (Protection) Rules, 1986. In exercise of powers conferred by sections 6, 8 and 25 of the Environment (Protection) Act, 1986, the Government of India formulated the following Rules.

(*a*) The hazardous wastes (Management and Handling) Rules, 1989

(*b*) The manufacture, storage, and import of hazardous chemicals Rules, 1989

(*c*) The chemical accidents (Emergency Planning, Preparedness and Response) Rules, 1996

(*d*) The biomedical wastes (Management and Handling) Rules, 1998.

3. **The Water (Prevention and Control of Pollution) Cess Act, 1977:** This Act was passed in 1977. This Act deals with the various provisions relating to levy and collection of a cess on water consumed by person carrying on certain industries and by local authorities, with a view to augment the resources of the Central and the State Boards constituted under the Water (Prevention and Control of Pollution) Act, 1974 for the Prevention and Control of Water Pollution.

4. **Rules framed under National Environment Appellate Authority Act, 1997 and Public Liability Insurance Act, 1991:** Under section 22 of the National Environment Appellate Authority Act, 1997 the central government made the National Environment Appellate Authority (Appeal) Rules 1997. Similarly, Under section 22 read with section 13 of the National Environment Appellate Authority Act, 1997 (22 of 1997) the central government of India made the National Environment Appellate Authority (Financial and Administrative powers) Rules, 1998. In exercise of the powers conferred by section 23 of the Public Liability Insurance Act 1997, the central government made the Public Liability Insurance Rules, 1991.

38. Article 21 of the constitution of India provides for the right to life and personal liberty. It states that "no person shall be deprived of his life or personal liberty except according to procedure established by law." In Rural Litigation and Entitlement.

In addition, the Constitution (Forty Second Amendment) Act 1976 explicitly incorporated environmental protection and improvement as a part of state policy. Article 48A, a Directive Principle of State Policy, provides that: The State shall endeavour to protect and improve the environment and safeguard the forests and wildlife of the country'. Moreover, article 51A (g) imposes a similar resonsibility on every citizen to protect and improve the natural environment including forest, lakes, rivers and wildlife, and to have compassion for living creatures ..... 'Therefore, protection of natural environment and compassion for living creatures were made the positive fundamental duty of every citizen. Both the provisions substantially send the same message. Together, they highlight the national consensus on the importance of the protection and improvement of the environment.

39. The Indian Forest Act was enacted to preserve and safeguard the forests generally in India. The Act makes various provisions for such conservation of forests and in the scheme it provides for a State Government to constitute any forest land or waste land, which are property of Government or which the Government has proprietary rights, as a reserved forest.

Although the Indian Forest Act deals specifically with (*i*) reserved forests; (*ii*) village forest, viz., reserved forest which have been assigned to any village community; and (*iii*) protected forests. The preamble and other provisions of the Forest Act are wide enough to cover all categories of forests. This Act is one curtailing proprietary rights of individuals and so the Act and the notifications issued under it must be construed strictly where the rights of individuals are trenched upon.

40. Hardening involves heating of steel, keeping it at an appropriate temperature until all pearlite is transformed into austenite, and then quenching it rapidly in water or oil. The temperature at which austentizing rapidly takes place depends upon the carbon content in the steel used. The heating time should be increased ensuring that the core will also be fully transformed into austenite. The microstructure of a hardened steel part is ferrite, martensite, or cementite.

Hardening of steel releases hazardous waste containing cyanide-, nitrate-, or nitrite-containing sludge and spent hardening salt.

41. Red coloured disinfected containers or bags be used for the disposal of microbial and biological wastes and the soiled wastes. Waste of category 3, 6 and 7 are to be kept together in red container.

The hazardous hospital waste has been divided into various categories, such that each category should contain different type of waste, also requiring different treatment procedures, according to nature of component. The categories 3, 6 and 7 are discussed below.

Category 3: Microbiological and biotechnological wastes, such as waste from laboratory culture, specimens from microorganisms, vaccines, cell cultures, toxins, dishes, devices used to transfer cultures are included under the category 3. Their treatment and disposal options are- local autoclaving or micro waving or incineration.

Category 6: This includes soiled wastes, contaminated with blood and body fluids including cotton, dressing, soiled plasters, linen etc. Their treatment and disposal options are- autoclaving, micro waving or incineration.

Category 7: This category of hospital waste consists of solid wastes such as tubes, catheters, IV sets etc. Their recommended disposal is by means of chemical disinfection, autoclaving, micro waving, mutilation and shredding.

42. Methylmercury is special among organic mercury compounds because large numbers of people are exposed to it and its toxicity is better understood. Methylmercury in food, such as fish, is a particular health hazard because it is easily taken up into the body through the stomach and intestines.

It is a poison for the nervous system. Exposure during pregnancy is of most concern, because it may harm the development of the unborn baby's brain. Some studies suggest that small increases in exposure may affect the heart and circulatory system.

Moreover, there is some evidence at present that methylmercury can cause cancer in humans, but it is far from conclusive: the International Agency for Research on Cancer (IARC) has classified methylmercury as "possibly carcinogenic to humans".

43. Gaussian model: The Gaussian model is perhaps the oldest (circa 1936) and perhaps the most commonly used model type. It assumes that the air pollutant dispersion has a Gaussian distribution, meaning that the pollutant distribution has a normal probability distribution. Gaussian models are most often used for predicting the dispersion of continuous, buoyant air pollution plumes originating from ground-level or elevated sources. Gaussian models may also be used for predicting the dispersion of non-continuous air pollution plumes (called *puff models*). The primary algorithm used in Gaussian modeling is the *Generalized Dispersion Equation For A Continuous Point-Source Plume.*

44. In descriptive statistics, a box plot or boxplot is a convenient way of graphically depicting groups of numerical data through their quartiles. Box plots may also have lines extending vertically from the boxes (whiskers) indicating variablility outside the upper and lower quartiles, hence the terms box-and-whisker plot and box-and-whisker diagram. Outliers may be plotted as individual points.

Advantages of Box and Whisker Plot

1. It helps us to learn how the data is spread in the series.
2. The graph is not sophisticated. It is clear and easy to understand.
3. It uses the range and the median values.
4. It is easy to compare the stratified data using the Box Whisker Plot.

Disadvantages of Box and Whisker Plot

1. Original data is not clearly shown in the Box Plot.
2. Mean and mode cannot be identified using the Box Plot.
3. It can be easy misinterpreted.
4. If large outliers are present, the Box Plot is more likely to give an incorrect representation.

45. Total number of fish in the pond $n(F) = 50$

Number of fishes without ectoparasite $n(A) = 12$

Number of fishes with atleast one parasites

$$= n(F) - n(A)$$
$$= 50 - 12 = 38.$$

46. To use the F-test to determine whether group means are equal, it's just a matter of including the correct variances in the ratio. In one-way ANOVA, the F-statistic is this ratio:

$$F = \text{variation between sample means} / \text{variation within the samples}$$
$$= \frac{8}{3.67} = 2.18.$$

47. India and China are among the world's biggest contributors to fossil fuel emissions with India's carbon dioxide discharge increasing by a whopping 7.7 per cent last year.

Indian CO_2 emissions increased by a whopping 7.7 per cent, with those from coal growing 10.2 per cent, said the report coinciding with the UN climate talks in Warsaw, the Polish capital.

48. Global CO_2 emissions would have to start coming down by about 2015 and by 2050 should be around 50-85% below the year 2000 levels. For a 550 ppm CO_2 equivalent stabilization level (leading to about 3°C warming), global CO_2 emissions should start declining no later than about 2030 and should be 5-30% below 2000 levels by 2050.

49. We use water not just to drink or shower or wash our clothes, we use it through the products we consume too. The average person will need 5 liters of water to drink daily, to survive in a moderate climate with little activity. An average American uses 100 to 175 gallons of water per day. Globally, we consume around 4 trillion cubic meters of fresh water a year!

Agriculture alone can consume 75 to 90% of a region's available freshwater. Global average water consumption (L/person/day) is 53.

PAPER-III

Note: *This paper contains* ***seventy five (75)*** *objective type questions of* ***two (2)*** *marks each.* ***All*** *questions are compulsory.*

1. The sum of the internal energy and product of pressure and volume is known as:

A. Enthalpy

B. Gibbs free energy

C. Entropy

D. Helmholtz free energy

2. If at latitude $\phi = 30°$, pressure gradient is 15 mb per 1000 km, the geostrophic wind velocity will be:

A. ~ 20.54 m/s B. ~ 15.92 m/s

C. ~ 7.96 m/s D. ~ 10.27 m/s

3. In a cloud free weather, there is an atmospheric window, which is transparent to terrestrial radiation in the wavelength band:

A. 1618 nm - 23400 nm

B. 2168 nm - 4610 nm

C. 12500 nm - 17000 nm

D. 7000 nm - 13500 nm

4. If $\Gamma_{env} < \Gamma_d$, where Γ_{env} and Γ_d are environmental and dry adiabatic lapse rates respectively, which of the following types of plume emitted from a stack of a thermal power plant is observed?

A. Fanning B. Fumigating

C. Looping D. Coning

5. Out of the following two statements, identify the correct one(s):

(*a*) An aqueous solution of sodium carbonate is alkaline.

(*b*) An aqueous solution of carbon dioxide is acidic.

A. (*a*) is correct, (*b*) is incorrect

B. (*a*) is incorrect, (*b*) is correct

C. Both (*a*) and (*b*) are incorrect

D. Both (*a*) and (*b*) are correct

6. The photodissociation of NO_2 yields which oxygen species?

A. $O(^3P)$ B. $O(^1D)$

C. O^+ D. O^-

7. The vapour pressure of bromobenzene above its ideal dilute aqueous solution of molality 0.1 mol kg^{-1} is 24.0 kPa. Calculate the Henry's law constant of bromobenzene:

A. 240 kPa kg mol^{-1}

B. 220 kPa kg mol^{-1}

C. 460 kPa kg mol^{-1}

D. 400 kPa kg mol^{-1}

8. In the Spectrophotometric Study, if a sample has transmittance of 50%, then its absorbance is:

A. 0.5 B. 0.3

C. 1.0 D. 0.7

9. Given below are two statements. One labelled as **Assertion (A)** and the other labelled as **Reason (R):**

Assertion (A): Sandy soil helps promote good drainage and aeration.

Reason (R): Sandy soil particles have size in the range 0.05 – 2.0 mm.

Choose the **correct** answer:

A. Both (A) and (R) are correct and (R) is the correct explanation of (A).

B. Both (A) and (R) are correct and (R) is not the correct explanation of (A).

C. (A) is true, but (R) is false.

D. (A) is false and (R) is true.

10. Night–time tropospheric chemistry is dominated by which of the following radicals?

A. NO_3 B. OH
C. HO_2 D. O

11. Given below are two statements. One labelled as **Assertion (A)** and the other labelled as **Reason (R):**

Assertion (A): Chlorine, which is widely used as an effective and relatively inexpensive disinfectant in water, generates toxic organochlorine compounds in water.

Reason (R): Hypochlorous acid reacts rapidly with humic acids and hydroxobenzenes.

Choose the **correct** answer:

A. Both (A) and (R) are correct and (R) is the correct explanation of (A).
B. Both (A) and (R) are correct and (R) is not the correct explanation of (A).
C. (A) is true, but (R) is false.
D. (A) is false and (R) is true.

12. In the context of argentometric titration of chloride ions in a water sample, identify the **incorrect** statement:

A. Titrant is silver nitrate solution
B. Indicator is potassium chromate
C. Colour of the end - point is lemon - yellow
D. pH of water sample should be less than 5

13. The reaction of OH radicals with which of the following species generates hydrogen atom?

A. CH_4 B. NH_3
C. CO D. NO_2

14. Which of the following statements is true for an ideal dilute solution?

A. Solute and solvent both obey Raoult's law
B. Solute obeys Raoult's law and solvent obeys Henry's law
C. Solute obeys Henry's law and solvent obeys Raoult's law
D. Solute and solvent both obey Henry's law

15. Given below are two statements. One labelled as **Assertion (A)** and the other labelled as **Reason (R):**

Assertion (A): The living components of ecosystems are not immortal.

Reason (R): Depending on the biological longevity, all living systems become abiotic constituents.

Choose the **correct** answer:

A. Both (A) and (R) are correct and (R) is the correct explanation of (A).
B. Both (A) and (R) are correct and (R) is not the correct explanation of (A).
C. (A) is true, but (R) is false.
D. (A) is false and (R) is true.

16. The movement of energy from primary producers to consumers is effected by:

A. The process of eating
B. The rate of rainfall
C. The rate of evaporation
D. The rate of transpiration

17. The result of removal of primary producers and subsequent reduction in population size leading to change in community attributes is referred to as:

A. Top - down cascade
B. Bottom - up cascade
C. Population decline
D. Community collapse

18. The amount of accumulated dead organic matter in different forest types:

A. Decreases from pole to equator.
B. Increases from tropic of cancer to tropic of Capricorn.
C. Increases from pole to equator.
D. Stabilizes at any point between two poles.

19. Which one of the following termite gut microbe contributes to degradation of cellulose?

A. *Trichonympha* sp. B. *Enterococcus* sp.
C. *Enterobacter* sp. D. *Citrobacter* sp.

20. Match the List-I and List-II. Identify the correct answer from the code given below:

List-I (Group of Plankton)	**List-II (Example)**
(*a*) Macroplankton	(*i*) Rotifera
(*b*) Nanoplankton	(*ii*) Copepoda
(*c*) Mesoplankton	(*iii*) Pyrrophyta
(*d*) Microplankton	(*iv*) Amphipoda

Code:

	(*a*)	(*b*)	(*c*)	(*d*)
A.	(*iii*)	(*iv*)	(*i*)	(*ii*)
B.	(*ii*)	(*i*)	(*iv*)	(*iii*)
C.	(*i*)	(*ii*)	(*iii*)	(*iv*)
D.	(*iv*)	(*iii*)	(*ii*)	(*i*)

21. The size of the Femtoplankton is in the range:

A. 0.2 - 2.0 μm B. < 0.2 μm

C. > 5.0 μm D. 0.5 - 1.0 μm

22. As of July 2017, the total number of National Parks existing in India is:

A. 127 B. 103

C. 97 D. 100

23. Given below are two statements. One labelled as **Assertion (A)** and the other labelled as **Reason (R):**

Assertion (A) : Some infectious particles loose their infectious - ability in territories closer to equator, with high average of daily sunshine hours.

Reason (R): UV incidence can determine the survival of infectious particles.

Choose the **correct** answer:

A. Both (A) and (R) are correct and (R) is the correct explanation of (A).

B. Both (A) and (R) are correct and (R) is not the correct explanation of (A).

C. (A) is true, but (R) is false.

D. (A) is false and (R) is true.

24. An organism that represents both primary producer and primary consumer of an aquatic ecosystem is:

A. Phytoplankton B. Bacterioplankton

C. Benthic algae D. Zooplankton

25. Given below are two statements. One labelled as **Assertion (A)** and the other labelled as **Reason (R):**

Assertion (A): The $^{18}O/^{16}O$ ratio in a natural system can be used as a thermometer.

Reason (R): The fractions of $^{18}O/^{16}O$ depend on temperature.

Choose the **correct** answer:

A. Both (A) and (R) are correct and (R) is the correct explanation of (A).

B. Both (A) and (R) are correct and (R) is not the correct explanation of (A).

C. (A) is true, but (R) is false.

D. (A) is false and (R) is true.

26. Most suitable spectral region for studying Urban Heat Island (UHI) effect is:

A. 3 - 5 μm B. 8 - 10 μm

C. 10 - 12 μm D. 1 - 3 μm

27. Which factor(s) may affect species richness on island?

(*a*) Area of the island

(*b*) Distance from the mainland

(*c*) Shape of the island

Choose the **correct** code:

A. (*a*) and (*b*) only B. (*b*) and (*c*) only

C. (*a*) and (*c*) only D. (*a*), (*b*) and (*c*)

28. Delineation of water - nonwater boundary in remote sensing is best done using:

A. 0.5 - 0.6 μm B. 0.6 - 0.7 μm

C. 0.7 - 0.9 μm D. 1 - 3 μm

29. Environmentalists oppose the mining of antarctic mineral resources because:

A. The demand for minerals is expected to decline as the world's nations become more industrialized.

B. Environment of Antarctica is extremely vulnerable and fragile to the disturbance that would occur with the development.

C. Territorial claims to Antarctica are unresolved.

D. Currenty known reserves of minerals and metals are considered inexhaustible.

30. Which of the following statements is not true for the solubility of CO_2 in seawater?

A. It increases with increase in partial pressure of CO_2.

B. It increases with increase in pH.

C. It increases with increase in temperature.

D. It decrease with increase in salinity.

31. What was the theme for the International Ozone Day (year 2017)?

A. 'Caring for all life under the Sun'
B. 'Ozone : All there is between you and UV'
C. 'Ozone and Climate : Restored by a World United'
D. '30 years of healing Ozone Together'

32. Given below are two statements. One labelled as **Assertion (A)** and the other labelled as **Reason (R):**

Assertion (A): OTEC power plants have low efficiences.

Reason (R): Efficiency is governed by 2nd law of thermodynamics.

Choose the **correct** answer:
A. Both (A) and (R) are correct and (R) is the correct explanation of (A).
B. Both (A) and (R) are correct and (R) is not the correct explanation of (A).
C. (A) is true, but (R) is false.
D. (A) is false and (R) is true.

33. Given below are two statements. One labelled as **Assertion (A)** and the other labelled as **Reason (R):**

Assertion (A): The efficiency of a silicon solar cell decreases with increase in temperature.

Reason (R): The intrinsic resistance of the solar cell increases with rise in temperature.

Choose the **correct** answer:
A. Both (A) and (R) are correct and (R) is the correct explanation of (A).
B. Both (A) and (R) are correct and (R) is not the correct explanation of (A).
C. (A) is true, but (R) is false.
D. (A) is false and (R) is true.

34. Given below are two statements. One labelled as **Assertion (A)** and the other labelled as **Reason (R):**

Assertion (A): The rotor blades of wind - turbine execute rotational motion when moving air impinges on them.

Reason (R): The momentum of the moving air is transferred to the moving blades.

Choose the **correct** answer:
A. Both (A) and (R) are correct and (R) is the correct explanation of (A).
B. Both (A) and (R) are correct and (R) is not the correct explanation of (A).
C. (A) is true, but (R) is false.
D. (A) is false and (R) is true.

35. A tidal power station has basin area = 10,000 m^2 and water trapped at height = 2.0 m above low tide. If the density of sea water is 1025 kgm^{-3}, the potential energy available for every tidal period is:

A. ~ 201 MJ B. ~ 402 MJ
C. ~ 240 MJ D. ~ 480 MJ

36. A typical fission reaction involving an atom of $^{235}_{92}U$ leads to a mass defect = 0.37×10^{-27} kg. How much energy is going to be released by 1.0 g of $^{235}_{92}U$?

A. 3.33×10^{-11} MJ B. 2.23×10^{12} MJ
C. 2.56×10^{4} MJ D. 8.53×10^{4} MJ

37. Given below are two statements. One labelled as **Assertion (A)** and the other labelled as **Reason (R):**

Assertion (A) : To exploit renewable energy, quite large structures are required relative to the power produced.

Reason (R): Power flux densities of renewable energy sources are appreciably lower compared to fossil fuels.

Choose the **correct** answer:
A. Both (A) and (R) are correct and (R) is the correct explanation of (A).
B. Both (A) and (R) are correct and (R) is not the correct explanation of (A).
C. (A) is true, but (R) is false.
D. (A) is false and (R) is true.

38. Biodiesel is produced from oils and fats using:
A. Transesterification
B. Anaerobic digestion
C. Pyrolysis
D. Fermentation

39. On take - off, an aeroplane generates noise level of 120 dB. If 5 such aeroplanes take - off simultaneously what will be the noise level?

A. ~ 126.98 dB B. ~ 124.98 dB

C. ~ 123.86 dB D. ~ 122.98 dB

40. CRIEGEE intermediate is formed in which of the following atmospheric reactions?

A. Olefin and Ozone

B. Ethane and Ozone

C. Acedaldehyde and Ozone

D. NO_2 and Ozone

41. In the purification of drinking water, the purpose of aeration is not to:

A. Remove dissolved gases such as H_2S

B. Remove volatile organic compounds

C. Oxidize soluble Fe^{2+} to Fe^{3+}

D. Precipitate colloidal particles

42. Which of the following is an organocarbamate insecticide?

A. Parathion B. Chloropyritos

C. Aldicarb D. Malathion

43. A bag containing a mixed feitilizer is labelled 5 - 10 - 5. It indicates:

A. 5% P ; 10% N ; 5% K

B. 5% N ; 10% P_2O_5 ; 5% K_2O

C. 5% N_2O ; 10% PH_3 ; 5% K_2O

D. 5% N ; 10% PH_3 ; 5% K_2O

44. The bioremediation technique of a contaminated soil does not require the fulfilment of which of the following conditions?

A. Waste must be present in a physical form that is susceptible to microbes.

B. Waste must be susceptible to biodegradation.

C. Environmental conditions such as pH, temperature and oxygen level must be appropriate.

D. Microbes of any type must be available.

45. Given below are two statements. One labelled as **Assertion (A)** and the other labelled as **Reason (R):**

Assertion (A): Organophosphate insecticides have lower values of partition coefficient, Kow, than organochlorine pesticides.

Reason (R): Organophosphate insecticide molecules have lower ability to form hydrogen bonds with water than organochlorine pesticides.

Choose the **correct** answer:

A. Both (A) and (R) are correct and (R) is the correct explanation of (A).

B. Both (A) and (R) are correct and (R) is not the correct explanation of (A).

C. (A) is true, but (R) is false.

D. (A) is false and (R) is true.

46. Given below are two statements. One labelled as **Assertion (A)** and the other labelled as **Reason (R):**

Assertion (A): NOX and volatile organic compounds (VOCs) are primary precursors in photochemical smog formation.

Reason (R): NOX and VOCs form oxidants by thermal reactions.

Choose the **correct** answer:

A. Both (A) and (R) are correct and (R) is the correct explanation of (A).

B. Both (A) and (R) are correct and (R) is not the correct explanation of (A).

C. (A) is true, but (R) is false.

D. (A) is false and (R) is true.

47. The dominant species, which removes hydroxyl radical in troposphere, is:

A. CH_4 B. CO

C. NO D. NO_2

48. Match the List-I and List-II. Identify the correct answer from the code given below:

List-I (EIA methods)	List-II (Features)
(*a*) Overlays	(*i*) Environmental Evaluation System
(*b*) Networks	(*ii*) Adaptive environmental assessment
(*c*) Battelle Columbus	(*iii*) Environmental Systems as a complex web
(*d*) Simulation modelling	(*iv*) Composite impact by superimposing maps

Code:

	(*a*)	(*b*)	(*c*)	(*d*)
A.	(*i*)	(*ii*)	(*iii*)	(*iv*)
B.	(*ii*)	(*iii*)	(*iv*)	(*i*)
C.	(*iii*)	(*iv*)	(*i*)	(*ii*)
D.	(*iv*)	(*iii*)	(*i*)	(*ii*)

49. The baseline studies in EIA pertain to:
A. Collection of demographic data only
B. Prediction of significant residual environmental impact
C. Existing environmental setting of the proposed development area
D. Selection of the best project option available

50. Which one of the following steps is not included in the scoping process?
A. Baseline descriptions and potential additional data collection needs
B. Description of environmental impacts and creation of contingency plan
C. Defining a set of criteria to assess the project
D. Setting of experts team that will conduct EIA

51. A company conducted an environmental risk assessment to evaluate the possible impacts of releasing various levels of pollutants from a chemical plant. An environmental risk assessment should focus on:
A. Beneficial aspects of the products produced by the plant
B. The legislative requirements related to the human health effects as a result of exposure to the pollutant
C. The quantification of hazards to the local environment from pollutants released
D. Detailed outline of the management process to reduce the health effects related to exposure to the pollutants

52. In EIA the multi - attribute utility theory is used to describe:
A. The identification of the alternatives to be evaluated and structuring of environmental parameters
B. Existing environmental quality of study area
C. The socio - economic status of the area
D. The risk involved in a development project

53. Under the Air Act, 1981, which body is empowered to set standard for ambient air quality?
A. MOEFCC
B. Ministry of Home Affairs
C. Central Pollution Control Board (CPCB)
D. State Ministry of Home Affairs

54. What is meant by the doctrine of riparian rights?
A. Prevention is better than cure.
B. One who pollutes the water, must pay for it.
C. Every owner has a right to get unpolluted water without alteration.
D. All of the above.

55. Which environmental legislation in India makes it compulsory to obtain prior approval of the Central Government for diversion of forest lands for non - forest purposes?
A. Environment (Protection) Act, 1986
B. Indian Forest Act, 1927
C. Forest Conservation Act, 1980
D. Traditional forest - Dwellers (Forest rights) Act, 2006

56. The Lime stabilization and drying of biosolids ensure:
(*a*) Creating unfavourable condition to vector
(*b*) High pH of contents in biosolids
(*c*) Reduction of all toxic elements
Choose the **correct** answer:
A. (*a*), (*b*) and (*c*) B. (*a*) and (*c*) only
C. (*a*) and (*b*) only D. (*b*) and (*c*) only

57. Which one of the following waste may undergo exothermic self - accelerating decomposition?
A. Organic peroxides
B. Arsenic bearing sludges
C. Organo - Chlorines
D. Vinylchlorides

58. According to Plastic Waste (Management and Handling) Rules 2011, recycling of the plastic should be done according to:

A. IS/ISO 14852 : 1991
B. IS/ISO 17088 : 2008
C. IS 9833 : 1981
D. IS 14534 : 1998

59. Which of the following is not a Millennium Development Goal?
A. Ensuring environmental sustainability
B. Eradicating extreme hunger and poverty
C. Developing global partnership for development
D. Achieving universal energy security

60. The definition of 'air pollutant' as per section 2(a) of Air Act, 1981 includes:
A. Liquid and gaseous substances
B. Solid, liquid and gaseous substances including noise
C. Gaseous substances
D. Solid, liquid and gaseous substances

61. In a population of 210 individuals, 72 are smokers and 138 are non - smokers. If a person is selected with an equal chance to each category, what is the probability of that person being a smoker?
A. 0.25 B. 0.50
C. 0.34 D. 0.75

62. If the mean value ($\overline{X}$) of a normally distributed data is 10 and number of observation (n) = 36 with an standard deviation (sd) of 0.3, then 90% confidence interval is:
A. 10 ± 0.08 B. 10 ± 8.23
C. 10 ± 0.16 D. 10 ± 4.15

63. Consider a tall stack emitting a pollutant at the rate 5.0 gms^{-1} in the atmosphere where wind is blowing in X-direction with an average velocity of 2.0 ms^{-1} at the stack height. What will be the maximum ground level concentration if the effective stack height is 30.0 m and the Gaussian plume is assumed with dispersion parameters σ_y = 50.0 m and σ_z = 30.0 m?
A. ~ 180 μgm^{-3} B. ~ 320 μgm^{-3}
C. ~ 240 μgm^{-3} D. ~ 415 μgm^{-3}

64. Which of the following material(s) are used as land fill liner for the control of gas and leachate movement?
(*a*) Sand (*b*) Bentonite
(*c*) Fly ash (*d*) Butyle rubber
Choose the **correct** code:
A. (*a*) and (*b*) only B. (*a*) and (*c*) only
C. (*c*) and (*d*) only D. (*b*) and (*d*) only

65. Assume that the population (N) of a species follows the logistic growth represented by following equation:

$$\frac{dN}{dt} = 0.8N - 0.01N^2$$

At what value of N, the population exhibits maximum growth?
A. 40 B. 80
C. 160 D. 800

66. Given below are two statements. One labelled as **Assertion (A)** and the other labelled as **Reason (R):**

Assertion (A) : In regression analysis, smaller the p - values, the more significant is the result of the experiment.

Reason (R) : The magnitude of p - value is an indicator of the association between the changes in the predictor's value and the changes in the response variable.

Choose the **correct** answer:
A. Both (A) and (R) are correct and (R) is the correct explanation of (A).
B. Both (A) and (R) are correct and (R) is not the correct explanation of (A).
C. (A) is true, but (R) is false.
D. (A) is false and (R) is true.

67. The mean and median of a moderately skewed distribution are 21 and 20 respectively. The mode of the distribution is:
A. 24 B. 12
C. 18 D. 26

68. The 90th percentile value for the data : 6, 6, 6.5, 7.0, 7.5, 6.5, 6, 7.5 and 8 is:
A. 7.50 B. 6.50
C. 7.75 D. 7.00

69. Given below are two statements. One labelled as **Assertion (A)** and the other labelled as **Reason (R):**

Assertion (A): Sustainable mountain development should be the global priority.

Reason (R): Mountain people are particularly vulnerable to impacts of climate change and natural disasters.

Choose the **correct** answer:

A. Both (A) and (R) are correct and (R) is the correct explanation of (A).

B. Both (A) and (R) are correct and (R) is not the correct explanation of (A).

C. (A) is true, but (R) is false.

D. (A) is false and (R) is true.

70. In the total global ecological footprint, which country has the maximum share:

A. USA B. China

C. India D. Brazil

71. Given below are two statements. One labelled as **Assertion (A)** and the other labelled as **Reason (R):**

Assertion (A): Climate change induced monsoon variability may have serious consequences for Indian agriculture.

Reason (R): Two third (2/3rd) of area under cultivation in India is rain dependent.

Choose the **correct** answer:

A. Both (A) and (R) are correct and (R) is the correct explanation of (A).

B. Both (A) and (R) are correct and (R) is not the correct explanation of (A).

C. (A) is true, but (R) is false.

D. (A) is false and (R) is true.

72. Namami Gange (Integrated Ganga Conservation Mission / Programme under National Ganga River Basin Authority) programme was launched in which year?

A. 2014 B. 2015

C. 1989 D. 2012

73. Which state in India is pioneer in making rain water harvesting as a compulsory measure in towns to avoid ground water depletion?

A. Kerala

B. Arunachal Pradesh

C. Tamil Nadu

D. Maharashtra

74. Environmental education:

(*a*) Increases public awareness

(*b*) Provides knowledge of environmental issues

(*c*) Does not provide disciplinary focus

(*d*) Sensitizes individuals about the necessity of sustainable development

Choose the **correct** answer:

A. (*a*), (*c*) and (*d*) only

B. (*a*), (*b*) and (*d*) only

C. (*b*), (*c*) and (*d*) only

D. (*a*), (*b*), (*c*) and (*d*)

75. The greenhouse gas, ozone, absorbs and emits long wave radiation near the wavelength :

A. 9.6 μm B. 11.2 μm

C. 6.9 μm D. 17.3 μm

ANSWERS

1	**2**	**3**	**4**	**5**	**6**	**7**	**8**	**9**	**10**
A	B	D	A	D	A	A	B	A	A
11	**12**	**13**	**14**	**15**	**16**	**17**	**18**	**19**	**20**
A	D	C	C	A	A	B	A	A	D
21	**22**	**23**	**24**	**25**	**26**	**27**	**28**	**29**	**30**
B	B	B	B	A	C	D	C	B	C
31	**32**	**33**	**34**	**35**	**36**	**37**	**38**	**39**	**40**
A	A	A	B	A	D	A	A	A	A

41	42	43	44	45	46	47	48	49	50
D	C	B	D	C	C	B	D	C	B
51	52	53	54	55	56	57	58	59	60
D	A	C	C	C	C	A	D	D	B
61	62	63	64	65	66	67	68	69	70
C	A	B	D	A	C	C	C	B	B
71	72	73	74	75					
A	A	C	B	A					

EXPLANATORY ANSWERS

1. *The* enthalpy *of a system may be defined as the sum of the internal energy and the product of pressure and volume of the system.*

The *physical significance of enthapy* may be put as under:

The **enthlpy** *of a substance is the amount of energy stored within the substance, i.e., available for conversion into heat.*

Like internal energy, *the heat content or enthalpy of a substance is also a state function, i.e.,* depends only on the state of the system and is independent of the manner by which the state has been attained.

Enthalpy change: Like internal energy, the absolute value of enthalpy of a substance cannot be determined. However, the change in the enthalpy when a system undergoes a change can be determined experimentally accurately and that serves our purpose.

A relation between enthalpy change and internal energy change exists as follows:

$$\Delta H = \Delta E + P\,\Delta V$$

where $\Delta E = E_2 - E_1$ represents the change in internal energy

and $\Delta V = V_2 - V_1$ represents the change in volume of the system

Thus, enthalpy change *of a system may be defined as the sum of internal energy change and the pressure-volume work done.*

If q_p is the heat absorbed at constant pressure, then $q_p = \Delta H$

Thus, enthalpy change *is the heat absorbed or evolved at constant pressure.*

2. **Hint:** The speed of the geostrophic wind can be approximated by

$$V_g \cong \frac{1}{pf}\left|\frac{\Delta p}{\Delta n}\right|$$

where Δp is the difference in pressure between adjacent isobars (in Pascals, not millibars), and Δn is the horizontal distance between the two adjacent isobars.

4. **Plume Types:** Plume types are important because they help us understand under what conditions there will be higher concentrations of contaminants at ground level.

Looping Plume

- High degree of convective turbulence
- Super adiabatic lapse rate — strong instabilities
- Associated with clear daytime conditions accompanied by strong solar heating & light winds
- High probability of high concentrations sporadically at ground level close to stack.
- Occurs in unstable atmospheric conditions.

Coning Plume

- Stable with small-scale turbulence
- Associated with overcast moderate to strong winds

- Roughly 10° cone
- Pollutants travel fairly long distances before reaching ground level in significant amounts
- Occurs in neutral atmospheric conditions

Fanning Plume

- Occurs under large negative lapse rate
- Strong inversion at a considerable distance above the stack
- Extremely stable atmosphere
- Little turbulence
- If plume density is similar to air, travels downwind at approximately same elevation

Fumigation

- Most dangerous plume: contaminants are all coming down to ground level.
- They are created when atmospheric conditions are stable above the plume and unstable below.
- This happens most often after the daylight sun has warmed the atmosphere, which turns a night time fanning plume into fumigation for about a half an hour.

5. (*a*) **Sodium carbonate** acts as an alkali because when dissolved in **water**, it dissociates into the weak acid: carbonic acid and the strong alkali: **sodium** hydroxide.

$H_2O \rightarrow 2H^+ + OH^-$

$NaCO_3 \rightarrow Na^+ + CO_3(2^-)$

Net reaction:

$H_2O + NaCO_3 \rightarrow H_2CO_3 + NaOH$

(*b*) Carbon dioxide (CO_2) gas dissolved in water can cause water to become acidic.

The acidity of water from dissolved CO_2 can be reduced by a base such as baking soda (sodium bicarbonate).

6. The photochemical dissociation of NO_2 illustrates the importance of photochemistry, because one of the products is atomic oxygen.

Many photochemical reactions in the atmosphere yield atoms or free radicals and these are much more reactive than molecular species. The oxygen atoms generated in the photodissociation of nitrogen dioxide can subsequently lead to the formation of ozone:

$$O + O_2 + M \rightarrow O_3 + M$$

where M is a third body, *i.e.*, a molecule such as N_2 that carries off excess energy that might disrupt the ozone molecule. Ozone produced by this reaction may photodissociate:

$$O_3 + h\nu \rightarrow O(^3P)$$

where ^3P describe the spectral state of the atom.

7. The Henry's law constant is defined here as the ratio of the aqueous-phase concentration of a chemical to its equilibrium partial pressure in the gas phase.

Thus, Hengy's law constant

$$= \frac{24}{0.1} = 240 \text{ kPa kg/mol.}$$

8. The amount of monochromatic light absorbed by a sample is determined by comparing the intensities of the incident light (Io) and transmitted light (I). The ratio of the intensity of the transmitted light (I) to the intensity of the incident light (Io) is called ***transmittance (T)***.

$$T = I/Io$$

From the transmittance or % transmittance, one can calculate the quantity known as ***absorbance (A)***. Absorbance is the amount of light absorbed by a sample. It is calculated from T or %T using the following equations:

$$A = -\log_{10} T \quad \text{or} \quad A = \log_{10}(1/T)$$

$$A = \log_{10}\left(\frac{1}{0.5}\right)$$

$$= \log_{10}(2) = 0.3.$$

9. Sandy soils have a higher percentage of macro pores. Typically, sandy soils never become water logged and allow water to percolate downward more rapidly than clay soils. Typically, moisture content in sandy soils is relatively low when compared to clay soils.

The terms sand, silt, and clay refer to particle size; sand is the largest and clay is the smallest. Gravel particles are larger than 2 millimeters (mm), sand particles are 0.05-2 mm, silt particles are 0.002-0.05 mm, and clay is smaller than 0.002 mm.

10. The night-time oxidant, NO_3 is predominantly formed in the troposphere by the reaction of NO_2 and ozone, and therefore, the regional distribution follows the same pattern as ozone and NO_x.

11. Chlorine (Cl_2) is the most common disinfectant in water treatment because it is easy to use and has effective germicide properties and a low cost. However, chlorine also reacts with dissolved organic material and produces disinfection byproducts, such as trihalomethanes (chloroform) and haloacetic acids. Chlorine, which is widely used as an effective and relatively inexpensive disinfectant in water, generates toxic organochlorine compounds in water because Hypochlorous acid reacts rapidly with humic acids and hydroxobenzenes.

12. Argentometric is a process of determining the content of a substance based on precipitation reaction from component of the test substance, using precipitation of Ag^+.

Titrations with Ag^+ are called argentometric titrations. For argentometric titrations, three classical methods based on colour indicators can be used for end point detection.

Preparation of standard $AgNO_3$ solution:

- Titrate the sample with 0.1 mole $Liter^{-1}$ silver nitrate solution. Although the silver chloride that forms is a white precipitate, the chromate indicator initially gift the cloudy solution faint lemon-yellow colour.
- The endpoint of the titration is identified as the first appearance of a red-brown colour of silver chromate.

13. Carbon monoxide is used to generate hydrogen atom. The reaction is like this:

$$OH + CO \Rightarrow CO_2 + H(atom)$$

Hydroxyl radicals are capable of oxidizing carbon monoxide by hydrogen abstraction.

14. *In an ideally dilute solution, the solvent obeys Raoult's law and the solutes obey Henry's law.*

Henry's law states that the vapour partial pressure of solute i above an ideally dilute solution is proportional to the mole fraction of i in the solution.

Raoult's law states that the vapour pressure of a solution is equal to the sum of the vapour pressures of each volatile component if it were pure multiplied by the mole fraction of that component in the solution. As a result, adding more components to a solution decreases each partial vapour pressure because the mole fraction decreases. Raoult's law can be used to calculate the molecular mass of an unknown solute.

At sufficiently high dilutions, all nonelectrolyte solution become ideally dilute. For less dilute solutions, the solution is no longer ideally dilute and shows deviations from Raoult's and Henry's laws.

15. An ecosystem can be described simply as the collection of all living and non-living components in a particular area. The living components of the environment are known as biotic factors. Biotic factors include plants, animals, and micro-organisms. The non-living components of the environment are known as abiotic factors. Abiotic factors include things such as rocks, water, soil, light, etc.

The living components of ecosystems are not immortal. Because depending on the biological longevity, all living systems become abiotic constituents.

16. In ecology, **energy flow**, also called the **calorific flow**, refers to the flow of energy through a food chain, and is the focus of study in **ecological energetics**. In an ecosystem, ecologists seek to quantify the relative importance of different component species and feeding relationships. The movement of energy from primary producers to consumers is affected by the process of eating.

17. **Trophic cascades** occur when predators in a food web suppress the abundance or alter the behaviour of their prey, thereby releasing the next lower trophic level from predation (or herbivory if the intermediate trophic level is a herbivore).

    The trophic cascade is an ecological concept which has stimulated new research in many areas of ecology. For example, it can be important for understanding the knock-on effects of removing top predators from food webs, as humans have done in many places through hunting and fishing.

    A **top-down cascade** is a trophic cascade where the food chain or food web is disrupted by the removal of a top predator, or a third or fourth level consumer. On the other hand, a **bottom-up cascade** occurs when a primary producer, or primary consumer is removed, and there is a reduction of population size through the community.

18. In some communities dead organic matter accumulates, but in most forest environments the rate at which litter is added to the soil equals the rate at which it is removed by decomposition. The amount of dead organic matter measured in forests at different latitudes is greatest towards the poles and least at the equator (Table). As the total biomass per unit area in a forest is *greatest* at the equator, this means that almost all of the organic matter in a tropical rainforest is tied up in the living organisms.

Table: The amount of accumulated dead organic matter in different forest types is greatest in forests near the poles and decreases towards the equator.

Forest type	Mass of organic matter in the forest layer
Tropical rainforest	2 tons/ha
Subtropical forest	10 tons/ha
Broad-leaved forest	15-30 tons/ha
Taiga	30-45 tons/ha
Shrub tundra	85 tons/ha

19. Termites depend upon the microbes in their gut or digestive tract to digest the complex sugars in wood into simpler molecules that they can use for food. Cellulose is a major sugar in wood and it is broken down in the hindgut of the termite by microbes into molecules called short-chain fatty acids.

    Cellulose degradation: Protists reside in the termite gut ingest wood particles in the form of cellulose and degrade it within their cells. Cellulolytic protists known as Trichonympha and mixotricha produce cellulases and various glycolytic enzymes that can break down cellulose and convert it into an intermediate product, malate. In addition, they carry specific anaerobic energy- generating organelle, hydrogenosome, where transferred malate from the cytoplasm is further fermented to produce CO_2, H_2, and acetate with the help of hydrogenase enzyme. During this fermentation process, ATP is also produced in the way and stored as energy available for both microbes and termite.

20. **Plankton** (singular **plankter**) are the diverse collection of organisms that live in large bodies of water and are unable to swim against a current. They provide a crucial source of food to many large aquatic organisms, such as fish and whales.

    Plankton are also often described in terms of size. Usually the following divisions are used:

Group	Size range (ESD)	Examples
Megaplankton	> 20 cm	metazoans; *e.g.* jellyfish; ctenophores; salps and pyrosomes (pelagic Tunicata): Cephalopoda; Amphipoda
Macroplankton	2-20cm	metazoans; *e.g.* Pteropods; Chaetognaths; Euphausiacea (krill); Medusae; ctenophores; salps, doliolids and pyrosomes (pelagic Tunicata); Cephalopoda; Janthinidae (one family of gastropods); Amphipoda
Mesoplankton	0.2-20 mm	metazoans; *e.g.* copepods; Medusae; Cladocera; Ostracoda; Chaetognaths; Pteropods; Tunicata; Heteropoda
Microplankton	20-200 μm	large eukaryote protists; most phytoplankton; Protozoa Foraminifera; tintinnids; other ciliates; Rotifera; juvenile metazoans - Crustacea (copepod nauplii)
Nanoplankton	2-20 μm	small eukaryote protists; Small Diatoms; Small Flagellates; Pyrrophyta; Chrysophyta; Chlorophyta; Xantnopnyta
Picoplankton	0.2-2 μm	small eukaryotic protists; bacteria; Chrysophyta
Femtoplankton	< 0.2 μm	marine viruses

21. Femtoplankton is the plankton composed of cells smaller than 0.2 micrometers.

22. An area, whether within a sanctuary or not, can be notified by the state government to be constituted as a National Park, by reason of its ecological, faunal, floral, geomorphological, or zoological association or importance, needed to for the purpose of protecting & propagating or developing wildlife therein or its environment. No human activity is permitted inside the national park except for the ones permitted by the Chief Wildlife Warden of the state under the conditions given in CHAPTER IV, WPA 1972.

There are 103 existing national parks in India covering an area of 40,500.13 km^2, which is 1.23% of the geographical area of the country.

Name of State & Union Territory	State Area km^2	No. of NPs	Area km^2	% of State Area
1. Andhra Pradesh	1,60,205	2	356.02	0.22
2. Arunachal Pradesh	33,743	2	2,290.82	2.74
3. Assam	78,438	5	1,977.79	2.52
4. Bihar	94,163	1	335.65	0.38
5. Chhattisgarh	1,35,191	3	2,899.08	2.14
6. Goa	3,702	1	107.00	2.89
7. Gujarat	1,96,022	4	480.12	0.24
8. Haryana	44,212	2	48.25	—

24. Bacterioplankton are the bacterial component of the plankton. They are comprised of prokaryotes. Some of them serve as primary producers and others as primary consumers in aquatic ecosystems (*e.g.*, marine and freshwater ecosystems). Primary producer bacterioplankton are those that are capable of photosynthesis, *e.g.*, blue-green algae (cyanophyta). It should be noted though that cyanophyta are also referred to as phytoplankton since they are also regarded as one of the photosynthetic algal groups. However, they are the only algal group that is prokaryotic and therefore are also considered as bacteria. Bacterioplankton are ecologically essential since they are involved in the remineralization processes of organic material. They drive global biogeochemical cycling of elements (*e.g.*, carbon fixation, nitrogen fixation, denitrification, nitrification, etc.). Many of them are saprotrophic as they obtain energy from organic material they consume.

25. Oxygen isotope ratio cycles are cyclical variations in the ratio of the abundance of oxygen with an atomic mass of 18 to the abundance of oxygen with an atomic mass of 16 present in some substances, such as polar ice or calcite in ocean core samples, measured with the isotope fractionation. The ratio is linked to water temperature of ancient oceans, which in turn reflects ancient climates. The calculated ratio of the masses of each present in the sample is then compared to a standard, which can yield information about the temperature at which the sample was formed.

^{18}O is two neutrons heavier than ^{16}O and causes the water molecule in which it occurs to be heavier by that amount. The addition of more energy is required to vaporize $H_2{}^{18}O$ than $H_2{}^{16}O$, and $H_2{}^{18}O$ liberates more energy when it condenses. In addition, $H_2{}^{16}O$ tends to diffuse more rapidly.

Because $H_2{}^{16}O$ requires less energy to vaporize, and is more likely to diffuse to the liquid surface, the first water vapour formed during evaporation of liquid water is enriched in $H_2{}^{16}O$, and the residual liquid is enriched in $H_2{}^{18}O$. When water vapour condenses into liquid, $H_2{}^{18}O$ preferentially enters the liquid, while $H_2{}^{16}O$ is concentrated in the remaining vapour.

As an air mass moves from a warm region to a cold region, water vapour condenses and is removed as precipitation. The precipitation removes $H_2{}^{18}O$, leaving progressively more $H_2{}^{16}O$-rich water vapour. This distillation process causes precipitation to have lower $^{18}O/^{16}O$ as the temperature decreases. Additional factors can affect the efficiency of the distillation, such as the direct precipitation of ice crystals, rather than liquid water, at low temperatures.

Due to the intense precipitation that occurs in hurricanes, the $H_2{}^{18}O$ is exhausted relative to the $H_2{}^{16}O$, resulting in relatively low $^{18}O/^{16}O$ ratios. The subsequent uptake of hurricane rainfall in trees, creates a record of the passing of hurricanes that can be used to create a historical record in the absence of human records.

26. Urban development has some negative impacts on the global environmental quality, including air quality, temperature increases and landscape alteration. It also leads to conversion of agricultural land and loss of biodiversity (Santamouris et al., 2001) . Urban heat island (UHI) is a climatic phenomenon where urban areas have higher air temperature than their rural surroundings due to the anthropogenic modifications of land surfaces.

There are two types of urban heat islands, surface and atmospheric UHI. A combination of factors leads to the development of the UHI. UHI is measured by surface temperature, which can vary between the city and rural area by up to 5°C.

The split-window algorithms have been widely used for estimating LST from two thermal bands in the 10.5 - 12.5 μm region with given surface emissivity.

27. Islands have relatively low species richness, but there are some islands such as Galapagos, Hawaii, Madagascar and Mauritius which possess a very high biodiversity. Islands are recognized as hotspots of endemicity and evolutionary marvels. Islands play a vital role as refuges of biodiversity.

The Theory of Island Biogeography is determined by two factors. The first is the effect of distance from the **mainland**. The mainland is where new immigrant species originally inhabited. The second is the effect of island size.

These two factors establish how many species an island can hold at equilibrium. **The equilibrium species number** is the species richness of an island at which immigration balances extinction and which remains roughly constant.

29. Antarctica and its surrounding waters are under pressure from a variety of forces that are already transforming the area, scientists warn.

The most immediate threats are regional warming, ocean acidification and loss of sea ice, all linked to global levels of carbon dioxide. Environmentalists oppose the mining of antarctic mineral resources because Environment of Antarctica is extremely vulnerable and fragile to the disturbance that would occur with the development.

Last year nearly 20,000 tourists visited the Antarctic Peninsula, according to the International Association of Antarctica Tour Operators. There are also more researchers, and there is more exploration for minerals and other resources. An increase in visitors means more disturbances to the fragile ecosystem, more pollution and more opportunities to bring organisms onto the continent from elsewhere in the world.

30. The CO_2 system in the ocean is dependent upon five major parameters: salinity, temperature, pressure, biologic activity and carbonate precipitation (or dissolution). Increased temperature will increase reaction rates of the CO_2 species, but also will decrease the solubility of gaseous CO_2 in sea water. Thus, in an open system (where CO_2 can enter or escape) pH will increase with increasing temperature; in a closed system (such as the deep sea), in which CO_2 cannot readily escape, pH will fall with increasing temperature. The decrease in pH is in response to increases in K_1' and K_2' which cause further dissociations and the release of hydrogen.

The solubilities of CO_2 and H_2CO_3 are inversely related to salinity, while the solubilities of HCO_3^- and $CO_3^=$ are directly related. Pressure increases the solubility of CO_2 and the dissociation constants increase at the following rates:

$\Delta pK_1' = -0.48 \times 10^{-4}\ \Delta z$

$\Delta pK_2' = -0.18 \times 10^{-4}\ \Delta z$

where z = depth in meters (SVERDRUP and others, (1942).

Biologic activity (photosynthesis and respiration) has perhaps the greatest effect upon the CO_2 system in the oceans:

$$H_2O + CO_2 \underset{\text{respiration}}{\overset{\text{photosynthesis}}{\rightleftharpoons}} \underset{\text{(organic matter)}}{HCOH} + O_2$$

During photosynthesis, the partial pressure of CO_2 decreases and pH increases. During respiration, CO_2 increases and pH decreases.

31. The theme for the 2017 International Day for the Preservation of the Ozone Layer to be marked on September 16 is: 'Caring for all life under the sun'. This year, to mark the 30th anniversary of the Montreal Protocol celebration, the Ozone Secretariat in cooperation with the Government of Canada hosted the Ozone Awards to be held in Montreal, Canada. That would recognize the achievements of individuals, groups and organizations that have demonstrated extraordinary commitment and contribution in the past 10 years.

32. OTEC power systems operate as cyclic heat engines. They receive thermal energy through heat transfer from surface sea water warmed by the sun, and transform a portion of this energy to electrical power. The Second Law of Thermodynamics precludes the complete conversion of thermal energy in to electricity. A portion of the heat extracted from the warm sea water must be rejected to a colder thermal sink. The thermal sink employed by OTEC systems is sea water drawn from the ocean depths by means of a submerged pipeline. A steady-state control volume energy analysis yields the result that net electrical power produced by the engine must equal the difference between the rates of heat transfer from the warm surface water and to the cold deep water. The limiting (*i.e.*, maximum) theoretical Carnot energy conversion efficiency of a cyclic heat engine scales with the difference between the temperatures at which these heat transfers occur. For OTEC, this difference is determined by T and is very small; hence, OTEC efficiency is low. Although viable OTEC systems are characterized by Carnot efficiencies in the range of 68%, state-of-the-art combustion steam power cycles, which tap much higher temperature energy sources, are theoretically capable of converting more than 60% of the extracted thermal energy into electricity. The low energy conversion efficiency of OTEC means that more than 90% of the thermal energy extracted from the ocean's surface is 'wasted' and must be rejected to the cold, deep sea water. This necessitates large heat exchangers and seawater Sow rates to produce relatively small amounts of electricity.

33. Solar cell performance decreases with increasing temperature, fundamentally owing to increased internal carrier recombination rates, caused by increased carrier concentrations. The operating temperature plays a key role in the photovoltaic conversion process. Both the electrical efficiency and the power output of a photovoltaic (PV) module depend linearly on the operating temperature. The various correlations proposed in the literature represent simplified working equations which can be apply to PV modules or PV arrays mounted on free-standing frames, PV-Thermal collectors, and building integrated photovoltaic arrays, respectively. The electrical performance is primarily influenced by the material of PV used. Numerous correlations for cell temperature which have appeared in the literature involve basic environmental variables and numerical parameters which are material or system dependent.

34. Wind is essentially a moving gas and like all matter, it is formed of particles. Motion means kinetic energy, so what wind turbines do is capture the kinetic energy in the wind. This energy can then be transferred from one medium into another, namely into electric energy.

There are three essential parts to a wind turbine. The *rotor blades* act as "barriers" to the wind. When the wind forces the blades to move, kinetic energy is transferred from the wind to the blades. Then, the wind-turbine *shaft* is connected to the center of the rotor and acts as a bridge between the rotor and the third component, the *generator*. When the rotor spins, the shaft spins as well, transferring the wind's kinetic energy into the shaft's rotational energy. The shaft then transfers this mechanical, rotational energy from the rotor to the generator.

37. The power densities realized by harnessing these energy flows are appreciably lower than the power densities of fossil fuel-based systems, something that even often uncritical proponents of wind and solar energy—the new renewables, in addition to the two traditional renewable energies, hydro energy and fuelwood—cannot ignore. Thus, to exploit renewable energy, quite large structures are required relative to the power produced.

38. Biodiesel is an alternative fuel similar to conventional or 'fossil' diesel. Biodiesel can be produced from straight vegetable oil, animal oil/fats, tallow and waste cooking oil. The process used to convert these oils to Biodiesel is called transesterification.

Biodiesel can be produced from straight vegetable oil, animal oil/fats, tallow and waste oils. There are three basic routes to biodiesel production from oils and fats:

- Base catalyzed transesterification of the oil.
- Direct acid catalyzed transesterification of the oil.
- Conversion of the oil to its fatty acids and then to biodiesel.

The Transesterification process is the reaction of a triglyceride (fat/oil) with an alcohol to form esters and glycerol. A triglyceride has a glycerine molecule as its base with three long chain fatty acids attached. The characteristics of the fat are determined by the nature of the fatty acids attached to the glycerine. The nature of the fatty acids can in turn affect the characteristics of the biodiesel. During the esterification process, the triglyceride is reacted with alcohol in the presence of a catalyst, usually a strong alkaline like sodium hydroxide. The alcohol reacts with the fatty acids to form the mono-alkyl ester, or biodiesel and crude glycerol. In most production methanol or ethanol is the alcohol used (methanol produces methyl esters, ethanol produces ethyl esters) and is base catalysed by either potassium or sodium hydroxide. Potassium hydroxide has been found to be more suitable for the ethyl ester biodiesel production, either base can be used for the methyl ester. A common product of the transesterification process is Rape Methyl Ester (RME) produced from raw rapeseed oil reacted with methanol.

39. The logarithmic properties of the decibel are best illustrated by a few examples: Two equal noises when sounded simultaneously will produce a noise 3 decibels higher in sound level than either alone; 10 equal noise sources, when sounded simultaneously, will produce a noise 10 decibels higher than one alone; a hundred will produce a noise 20 decibels higher than one alone; a thousand will produce a noise 30 decibels higher than one alone; and 10,000 will produce a noise 40 decibels higher than one alone.

The sound insulation of a wall R, can be defined as

$$R = 10 \log(I_i/I_t)$$

where I_i and I_t are the incident and transmitted sound intensities.

Here, $\dfrac{I_i}{I_t} = 5$

$10 \log(5) = 6.98$

So, $R' = R + 6.98$

$= 120 + 6.98 = 126.98$ dB

Hence, five such aeroplane will produces 126.98 dB noise while take-off.

40. The presence of the double bond renders alkenes susceptible to reaction with ozone. Reactions with ozone are, in fact, competitive with the daytime OH radical reactions and the nighttime NO_3 radical reaction as a tropospheric loss process for the alkenes. The ozone-alkene reaction proceeds via initial O_3 addition across the olefinic C=C bond, forming a cyclic 1,2,3-trioxolane intermediate species, referred to as the primary ozonide (denoted POZ). The POZ is formed with a large amount of excess energy, which results in rapid decomposition of the POZ to a stable ketone or aldehyde and a carbonyl oxide reactive intermediate, referred to as a *Criegee intermediate.* In the case of asymmetrically substituted alkenes, two pairs of products are formed:

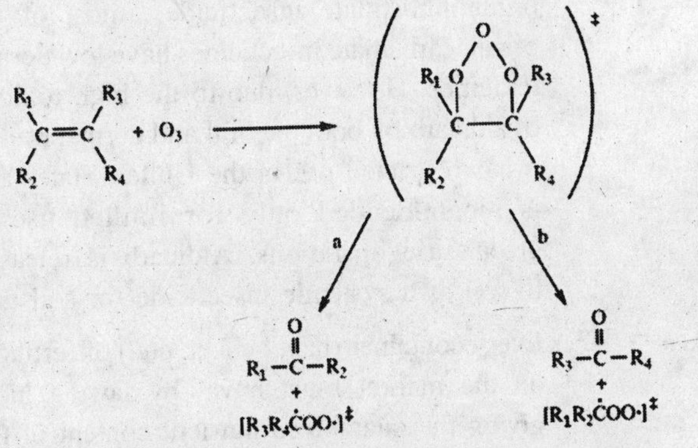

The relative importance of the reaction pathways *a* and *b* are generally assumed to be equal. The Criegee intermediates are represented as biradicals. The simplest Criegee intermediate is CH_2OO, which is formed in the ozonolysis of ethene and 1-alkenes.

41. Aeration water treatment is effective for management of dissolved gases such as radon, carbon dioxide, some taste and odor problems such as methane, and hydrogen sulfide, as well as volatile organic compounds, like MTBE or industrial solvents. It is also effective in precipitating dissolved iron and manganese. Aeration raises the pH of water.

Aeration of water Removal of dissolved gases (*e.g.*, H_2S) and organosulfur compounds

Removal of volatile organic compounds

Oxidation of Fe^{2+} to Fe^{3+} and precipitation as insoluble $Fe(OH)_3$.

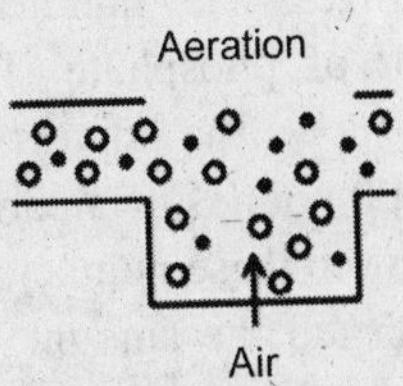

42. Organocarbamate pesticides are one of several classes of insecticides: including compounds such as carbaryl, aldicarb, and zectran. The organocarbamates are not broad-spectrum insecticides, and some common household insect pests are relatively immune to the effects of these chemicals. Unlike the organophosphate insecticides, most of the organocarbamate insecticides have low dermal toxicities. However, due to the high toxicity of aldicarb by both the oral and dermal routes, it has restricted use in the United States and is recommended only for limited use in greenhouse operations. Aldicarb is released to soil as a systemic insecticide for soil use.

43. Every container (bag, bucket, etc.) of fertilizer on the market must have, by law, a label giving the guaranteed nutrient content of the fertilizer. The information required on the label and the way in which the information is given are specified by the fertilizer law. The information on the label is the guaranteed amount of the primary nutrients given in a series of three numbers, such as 5-10-5, and is referred to as the "fertilizer grade." A fertilizer grade gives the minimum guaranteed primary nutrient content as percentage of total nitrogen (N), percentage of available phosphate (P_2O_5), and percentage of water-soluble potash (K_2O). The fertilizer grade always specifies the nutrient content in this order:

Nitrogen (N) → 5-10-5 ← Soluble Potash (K_2O)
↑
Available Phosphate (P_2O_5)

The first number indicates the pounds of nitrogen (N) contained in each 100 pounds of fertilizer. The middle figure refers to the amount of phosphate (P_2O_5), and the last figure shows the pounds of potash (K_2O) in each 100 pounds of a particular fertilizer. By referring to these numbers printed on the bag, you can tell the amount, of each nutrient in the fertilizer. This labeling is the same nationwide.

44. Bioremediation is defined as the acceleration of the natural metabolic process whereby microorganisms alter and break down organic molecules into other substances. In situ bioremediation involves the placement of amendments directly into contaminated media, whereas ex situ bioremediation transfers the contaminated media to a selected site for treatment.

The bioremediation technique of a contaminated soil require the fulfilment of:

Waste must be present in a physical form that is susceptible to microbes.

Waste must be susceptible to biodegradation.

Environmental conditions such as pH, temperature and oxygen level must be appropriate.

Organic contaminants aré often classified as biodegradable, persistent or recalcitrant, depending on their behaviour in the environment:

Biodegradable: they undergo a biological transformation.

Persistent: they do not undergo biodegradation in certain environments.

Recalcitrant: they resist biodegradation in a wide variety of environments.

45. Organophosphorus group of pesticides are known to be the best insecticides and acaricides, and also they are equally effective as fungicides, nematicides, herbicides, plant growth regulators, insect chemosterilants and rodenticides. All organophosphorus pesticides are derived from phosphoric acid. Pesticides containing phosphorus include phosphates, phosphoronates, phosphoroamides, pyrophosphates and their sulphur analogues. Organophosphorus pesticides offer a broad range of toxicity to insect-pests, and are generally among the most toxic of all pesticides to vertebrate animals. Organochlorine pesticides are, in general, of lower toxicity than organophosphorus pesticides, but are causing environmental problems due to their higher persistence and higher toxicity. The organophosphorus pesticides are easily degradable and consequently less persistent and are often preferred to organochlorines in conventional agricultural applications. Organophosphorus compounds are highly effective and rapid in its action on aphides, spider mites, small caterpillars and many other insects. It is highly toxic to man and other animals. In water solution, it gets easily decomposed by hydrolysis into non-toxic water-soluble products.

46. Nitrogen oxides (the mixture of NO and NO_2 together referred to as NOx) and volatile organic compounds (VOCs) are primary air pollutants, released in the atmosphere by automobiles and industrial processes. Nitrogen dioxide absorbs ultraviolet light and formation of nitric oxide and atomic oxygen takes place. Ozone is generated by the reaction of oxygen gas with this atomic oxygen. Ozone, aldehydes and peroxyacetyl nitrate so formed are thus secondary air pollutants. Photochemical smog is a mixture of primary and secondary air pollutants.

NOX and VOCs form antioxidants by thermal reactions.

47. Carbon monoxide (CO) is the dominant sink of OH in most of the troposphere, and that CH_4 is next in importance. The resulting OH lifetime is of the order of one second. Because of this short lifetime, atmospheric concentrations of OH are highly variable; they respond rapidly to changes in the sources or sinks.

48. Overlay maps are a series of transparencies used to identify, predict, assign relative significance to and communicate impacts, normally at a scale larger than local.

(*i*) The composite impact of the project is found by superimposing the overlay maps and noting the relative intensity of total shading. Unshaded areas would be those where development project would have no impacts. Overlay maps are easy to represent and understand.

(*ii*) Network methods explicitly recognize that environmental systems consist of a complex web of relationships, and try to reproduce that web. Impact identification using networks involves following in effects of development through changes in the environmental parameters in the model.

(*iii*) The use of simulation modelling, adaptive environmental assessment, has been advocated as a means of assessing a wide range of development proposals and environmental management schemes as a means of accommodating the behaviour of ecosystems. It has been used to assess forest pest management, fish stock management, tourist development, regional development, hydroelectric development and a water-resource study.

(*iv*) The Battelle Environmental Evaluation System (EES) is a methodology for conducting environmental impact analysis developed at Battelle Columbus Laboratories by an interdisciplinary research team under contract with the U.S. Bureau of Reclamation. It is based on a hierarchical assessment of environmental quality indicators.

The system is based on a classification consisting of four levels:

- Level I: Categories,
- Level II: Components,
- Level III: Parameters, and
- Level IV: Measurements.

49. Baseline studies are perhaps the most commonly recognized, and yet least understood, element of EIA. The term usually refers to the collection of background information on the environmental and socioeconomic setting for a proposed development project and it is normally one of the first activities undertaken in an EIA. A baseline studies programme may be designed around the results of a scoping exercise. Whether it involves the collation of existing information or requires the acquisition of new data through field sampling, baseline studies frequently account for a large part of the overall cost of an EIA.

Environmental impact assessments are often conducted under severe time restrictions and, since it is relatively easy to collect information and data, there is a tendency to give too much emphasis to baseline studies early in the assessment process. The result is that there is often a great deal of information made available on the environmental setting of a particular project, but it may be irrelevant to the resolution of certain critical questions raised at later stages in the EIA.

50. **Scoping** is the process of determining which are the most critical issues to study and will involve community participation to some degree. It is at this early stage that EIA can most strongly influence the outline proposal.

Steps included in the scoping process:

(*a*) Set up the team of experts that will conduct the EIA.

(*b*) Describe the project area and the area of the project influence.

(*c*) Outline project alternative for preparation, implementation and closure.

(*d*) Conduct public meetings and stakeholder consultations; integrate comments and collected feedback into project planning and alternatives.

(*e*) Create a set of environmental, biological and socioeconomic areas that will be used in the assessment.

(*f*) Define a set of criteria to assess the project.

(*g*) Identify a set of data for baseline descriptions and potential additional data collection needs.

(*h*) Start inserting this information in the appropriate section of the TOR.

51. Risk assessment provides a basis for risk management. However, while risk assessment is a scientific procedure, risk management is more pragmatic, involving decisions and actions that aim at preventing, or reducing to acceptable levels, the occurrence of agents which may pose hazards to the health of workers, surrounding communities and the environment, also accounting for the socio-economic and public health context.

The classical steps in occupational hygiene practice are:

- the recognition of the possible health hazards in the work environment
- the evaluation of hazards, which is the process of assessing exposure and reaching conclusions as to the level of risk to human health
- prevention and control of hazards, which is the process of developing and implementing strategies to eliminate, or reduce to acceptable levels, the occurrence of harmful agents and factors in the workplace, while also accounting for environmental protection.

52. In decision theory, a **multi-attribute utility** function is used to represent the preferences of an agent over bundles of goods either under conditions of certainty about the results of any potential choice, or under conditions of uncertainty. In EIA the multi - attribute utility theory is The identification of the alternatives to be evaluated and structuring of environmental parameters.

53. Ambient air quality refers to the condition or quality of air surrounding us in the outdoors. National Ambient Air Quality Standards are the standards for ambient air quality set by the Central Pollution Control Board (CPCB) that is applicable nationwide. The CPCB has been conferred this power by the Air (Prevention and Control of Pollution) Act, 1981.

Ambient Air Quality Standards in India

The Air (Prevention and Control of Pollution) Act 1981 was enacted by the Central Government with the objective of arresting the deterioration of air quality. The Air (Prevention and Control of Pollution) Act 1981 describes the main functions of the Central Pollution Control Board (CPCB) as follows:

- To advise the Central Government on any matter concerning the improvement of the quality the air and the prevention, control and abatement of air pollution.
- To plan and cause to be executed a nation-wide programme for the prevention, control and abatement of air pollution.
- To provide technical assistance and guidance to the State Pollution Control Board.
- To carry out and sponsor investigations and research related to prevention, control and abatement of air pollution.
- To collect, compile and publish technical and statistical data related to air pollution; and
- To lay down and annul standards for the quality of air.

54. The *Indian Easements Act,* 1882 is one of the earlier statutes dealing with the rights of individuals *inter se* in regard to pollution of waters. The Act has, in fact, codified the common law doctrine of riparian rights to unpolluted waters. The illustrations (f) and (h) of section 7 of the Act in particular, refer to water pollution. Illustration (f) says: "The right of every owner of land, within his own limits, the water which naturally passes or percolates by, over or through his land shall not, before so passing or percolating, be unreasonably polluted by other persons."

Illustration (h) among others, protects the right of every riparian owner to get water of a natural stream, a natural lake or pond into or out of which a natural stream flows from any material alteration in temperature of water. There seems to have been an overlapping in illustrations (f) and (h) in regard to alteration in temperature as this aspect is covered under unreasonable pollution.

55. The Indian Forest Act of 1927 led to the Forest Conservation Act of 1980. This law applied to all the lands, which are notified as forests in the government records and is not restricted to reserved and protected forests. It restricts the power of the state governments by making it mandatory for them, to seek permission from the central government for any non-forest use of forest lands, including de-reservation of forest and diversion of forest land.

The states, where de-reservation was practiced, had regularized encroachments and resettled 'project affected people' from development projects such as dams. The need for a new legislation became urgent. The Act made it possible to retain a greater control over the frightening level of deforestation in the country and specified penalties for offenders.

56. Alkaline or lime stabilization is a very simple process. Its principal advantages over other stabilization processes include low cost and simplicity of operation. However, lime stabilization accomplished at a pH of 10.0–11.0, may allow odors to return during storage owing to pH decay. To eliminate this problem and reduce pathogen levels, addition of sufficient quantities of lime to raise and maintain the biosolids pH to 12.0 for 2 h is required. The lime-stabilized biosolids readily dewaters with mechanical equipment and is generally suitable for application on an agricultural land or disposal in a sanitary landfill.

57. Organic substances which contain the bivalent -0-0- structure and may be considered derivatives of hydrogen peroxide, where one or both of the hydrogen atoms have been replaced by organic radicals. Organic peroxides are thermally unstable substances, which may undergo exothermic self-accelerating decomposition. In addition, they may have one or more of the following properties:

(*i*) be liable to explosive decomposition;

(*ii*) burn rapidly;

(*iii*) be sensitive to impact or friction;

(*iv*) react dangerously with other substances;

(*v*) cause damage to the eyes.

58. The Recycled Plastics Manufacture and Usage Rules, 1999 came to be called the Plastic Waste (Management and Handling) Rules, 2011 from 4 February 2011. Under these rules, the use of carry bags and sachets or containers made of recycled plastic or compostable plastic for storing, carrying dispensing, or packaging food is prohibited. Recycling of plastic is to be undertaken strictly in accordance with the Bureau of Indian Standards specifications IS: 14534:1998 entitled 'The Guidelines for Recycling of Plastics' amended from time to time.

59. The **Millennium Development Goals (MDGs)** were the eight international development goals for the year 2015 that had been established following the Millennium Summit of the United Nations in 2000, following the adoption of the United Nations Millennium Declaration. All 191 United Nations member states at that time, and at least 22 international organizations, committed to help achieve the following Millennium Development Goals by 2015:

1. To eradicate extreme poverty and hunger
2. To achieve universal primary education
3. To promote gender equality and empower women
4. To reduce child mortality
5. To improve maternal health
6. To combat HIV/AIDS, malaria, and other diseases
7. To ensure environmental sustainability
8. To develop a global partnership for development.

60. Act of 1981 'air pollution means the presence in the atmosphere of any air pollutant' (section 2 b). The term 'air pollutant means any solid, liquid or gascous substance including noise present in the atmosphere in such concentration as may be or tend to be injurious to human beings or other living creatures or plants or property or environment' (section 2a).

61. Total population $n(S) = 210$

Number of somker $n(A) = 72$

Number of non-smoker = 138

$$\text{Probability of selecting a smoker} = \frac{n(A)}{n(S)}$$

$$= \frac{72}{210} = 0.34.$$

62. $$\text{Confidence Interval} = \bar{X} \pm 1.74 \frac{\sigma}{\sqrt{n}}$$

Here, $\bar{X} = 10$, $\sigma = 0.3$, $n = 36$.

$$\text{So, Confidence Interval} = 10 \pm 1.74 \times \frac{(0.3)}{\sqrt{36}}$$

$$= 10 \pm 1.74 \frac{(0.3)}{6}$$

$$= 10 \pm 0.08.$$

64.

Classification	Representative types
(*i*) Compound clay	Bentonides, illites, kaolinites.
(*ii*) Inorganic chemicals	Sodium carbonates, silicate or pyrophosphate.
(*iii*) Synthetic chemicals	Polymers, rubber latex.
(*iv*) Synthetic membrane	PVC, buyl rubber, hypation, poly-thene, nylon reinforced liners.
(*v*) Asphalt	Modified asphalt, asphalt-covered polypropylene fabric, asphalt concrete.
(*vi*) Others	Gunite concrete, soil cement, plastic soil cement.

The seal material should be more impermeable than the soil. So sand will not be a suitable material. Flyash and lime themselves produce pollutants which dissolve in water. Therefore these materials cannot be used ads sealants.

65. $$\frac{dN}{dt} = 0.8\ N - 0.01\ N^2$$

For maximum growth, $\frac{d^2N}{dt^2} = 0$

$$\frac{d^2N}{dt^2} = 0.8 - 0.01\ (2N)$$

$$\Rightarrow \quad \frac{d^2N}{dt^2} = 0.8 - 0.02\ N$$

For maximum growth, $0.8 - 0.02\ N = 0$

$$N = \frac{0.8}{0.02} = 40.$$

66. A p-value is used in hypothesis testing to help you support or reject the null hypothesis. The p-value is the evidence **against** a null hypothesis. The smaller the p-value, the strong the evidence that you should reject the null hypothesis. P-values are expressed as decimals although it may be easier to understand what they are if you convert them to a percentage. For example, a p value of 0.0254 is 2.54%. This means there is a 2.54% chance your results could be random.

On the other hand, a large p-value of 0.9 (90%) means your results have a 90% probability of being completely random and *not* due to anything in your experiment. Therefore, the smaller the p-value, the more important ("significant") your results.

67. In a moderately symmetric distribution, the mean, median and mode are connected by the formula:

$$\text{Mode} = 3\ \text{Median} - 2\ \text{Mean}$$
$$= 3 \times 20 - 2 \times 21$$
$$= 60 - 42 = 18.$$

68. Arranging data in ascending order:
6, 6, 6, 6.5, 6.5, 7, 7.5, 7.5, 8
to get 90th percentile of these,
we have $0.9 \times n$
Here, $n = 9$
So, $0.9 \times 9 = 8.1$
Thus, average of 8th and 9th value will give 90th percentile *i.e.*,

$$\frac{7.5+8}{2} = 7.75.$$

70. China's total Ecological Footprint has dramatically increased in the past 15 years and surpassed that of the United States in the early 2000s. China is now the nation with the world's largest total Ecological Footprint. Two factors that drive increasing total Ecological Footprint are increasing per capita Ecological Footprint (a measure of increasing consumption) and population growth.

It is widely known that China has the world's largest population. Over the last 30 years, however, China's population growth rate has stabilized and started to decrease.

71. Climate change refers to a long-term change in the state of climate, that can be identified by changes in the means and/or changes in the variability.

Climate change also include gradual and/or abrupt changes of the frequencies and intensities of extreme events.

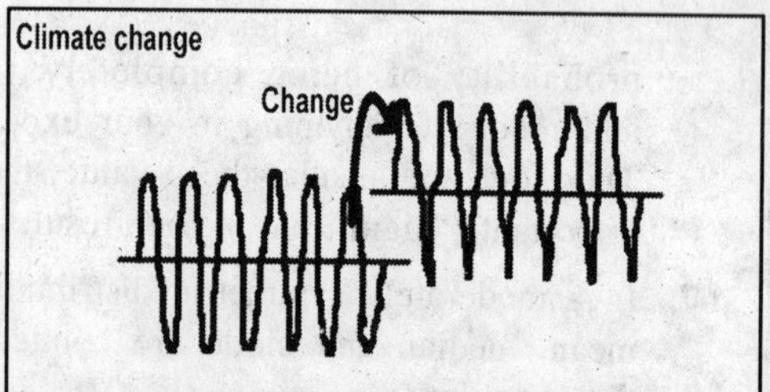

Change of the chatecteristics of climate. Here, a change in the mean state is shown.

Climate Change and Indian Agriculture

- Large country with diverse climate
- Two thirds area rain dependent
- High monsoon dependency
- Diverse seasons, crops and farming systems
- Close link between climate and water resources
- Small holdings, poor coping mechanisms and low penetration of risk management products

72. **'Namami Gange Programme'**, is an Integrated Conservation Mission, approved as 'Flagship Programme' by the Union Government in June 2014 with budget outlay of ₹ 20,000 Crore to accomplish the twin objectives of effective abatement of pollution, conservation and rejuvenation of National River Ganga.

The key achievements under Namami Gange programme are:

1. **Creating Sewerage Treatment Capacity:** 63 sewerage management projects under implementation in the States of Uttarakhand, Uttar Pradesh, Bihar, Jharkhand and West Bengal. 12 new sewerage management Projects launched in these states.Work is under construction for creating Sewerage capacity of 1187.33 (MLD). Hybrid Annuity PPP Model based two projects has been initiated for Jagjeetpur, Haridwar and Ramanna, Varanasi.
2. **Creating River-Front Development:** 28 River-Front Development projects and 33 Entry level Projects for construction, modernization and renovation of 182 Ghats and 118 crematoria has been initiated.
3. **River Surface Cleaning:** River Surface cleaning for collection of floating solid waste from the surface of the Ghats and River and its disposal are afoot and pushed into service at 11 locations.
4. **Bio-Diversity Conservation:** Several Bio-Diversity conservation projects are namely: Biodiversity Conservation and Ganga Rejuvenation, Fish and Fishery Conservation in Ganga River, Ganges River Dolphin Conservation Education Programme has been initiated. 5 Bio-Diversity center's at Dehradun, Narora, Allahabad, Varanasi and Barrackpore has been developed for restoration of identified priority species.
5. **Afforestation:** Forestry interventions for Ganga through Wildlife Institute of India; Central Inland Fisheries Research Institute and Centre for Environment Education has been initiated. Forestry interventions for Ganga has been executed as per the Detailed Project Report prepared by Forest Research Institute, Dehradun for a period of 5 years (2016-2021) at project cost of ₹ 2300 Crores. Work has been

commenced in 7 districts of Uttarakahnd for medicinal plants.

6. **Public Awareness:** A series of activities such as events, workshops, seminars and conferences and numerous IEC activities were organized to make a strong pitch for public outreach and community participation in the programme. Various awareness activities through rallies, campaigns, exhibitions, shram daan, cleanliness drives, competitions, plantation drives and development and distribution of resource materials were organized and for wider publicity the mass mediums such as TV/Radio, print media advertisements, advertorials, featured articles and advertorials were published. Gange Theme song was released widely and played on digital media to enhance the visibility of the programme. NMCG ensured presence at Social Media platforms like Facebook, Twitter, You Tube etc.

7. **Industrial Effluent Monitoring:** Real Time Effluent Monitoring Stations (EMS) has been installed in 572 out of 760 Grossly Polluting Industries (GPIs). Closure notice have been issued to 135 GPIs so far and others have been given deadlines for compliance to stipulated norms and for installations of online EMS.

8. **Ganga Gram:** Ministry of Drinking Water and Sanitation (MoDWS) identified 1674 Gram Panchayats situated on the bank of River Ganga in 5 State (Uttarakhand, Uttar Pradesh, Bihar, Jharkhand, West Bengal). ₹ 578 Crores has been released to Ministry of Drinking Water and Sanitation (MoDWS) for construction of toilets in 1674 Gram Panchayats of 5 Ganga Basin States. Out of the targeted 15, 27,105 units, MoDWS has completed construction of 8,53,397 toilets. Consortium of 7 IITs has been engaged in the preparation of Ganga River basin Plan and 65 villages has been adopted by 13 IITs to develop as model villages. **UNDP** has been engaged as the executing agency for rural sanitation programme and to develop Jharkhand as a model State at an estimated cost of ₹ 127 Crore.

YOUR SPACE

Previous Paper (Solved)

UGC-NET-Junior Research Fellowship & Assistant Professor Exam

Environmental Science, January-2017*

PAPER-II

Note: *This paper contains **fifty** (**50**) objective type questions of **two** (**2**) marks each. **All** questions are compulsory.*

1. Which of the following methods is generally not adopted for the safe disposal of biomedical waste?
A. Incineration
B. Hydroclaving
C. Landfilling
D. Shredding after disinfection

2. Which of the following prompted the Govt. of India to enact Environment (Protection) Act, 1986?
A. River Ganga Water Pollution
B. Endosulfan tragedy in Kerala
C. London Smog
D. Bhopal Gas Tragedy

3. Protection and improvement of environment and safeguarding of forest and wildlife is emphasized in constitution of India under the Article
A. 48 A B. 21
C. 47 D. 46

4. Environmental Relief Fund was established under the provisions of
A. The Environment (Protection) Act, 1986
B. The Indian Wild Life (Protection) Act, 1972
C. The Public Liability Insurance Act, 1991
D. The Forest (Conservation) Act, 1980

5. A type of lake that forms in the depression of the earth's crust between two parallel faults is known as
A. Grade lake B. Surface lake
C. Graben lake D. Glacial lake

6. In case of plumes from a tall stack located on flat terrain 'Lofting' type of plume behaviour is observed when in the atmosphere
A. inversion conditions prevail below the stack height.
B. strong lapse rate conditions exist.
C. inversion conditions exist above the stack height.
D. weak lapse rate conditions exist.

7. Turbulent updrafts and downdrafts flows are an example of
A. Synoptic scale phenomena
B. Planetary scale phenomena
C. Meso-scale phenomena
D. Micro-scale phenomena

8. A niche of the species where there is no competition from other species is called
A. hyper volume niche
B. habitat
C. fundamental niche
D. realized niche

9. Dissipative process of energy during photosynthesis in a plant is
A. Decomposition
B. Senescence
C. Respiration
D. Mineralization of humus

10. Which of the following substances is generally not considered toxic?
A. Carbonic acid B. Carbon monoxide
C. Acetaldehyde D. Benzene

* Exam held on 22 January, 2017

11. Percentage of tropospheric ozone in relation to total atmospheric ozone is about
A. 90% B. 10%
C. 50% D. 80%

12. Among the following, which one is the most hazardous chemical in the atmosphere?
A. Dioxin B. Carbon monoxide
C. Halons D. CFCs

13. The technique, which is fastest for measuring organic carbon is,
A. COD B. BOD_5
C. BOD_7 D. TOC

14. With increase in temperature, the specific conductivity of water
A. remains unchanged
B. increases
C. decreases
D. makes the water turbid

15. According to ZSI (GOI), which one of the following birds declined by 99%?
A. Sparrow
B. Pink-headed Duck
C. Pond heron
D. White backed Vulture

16. According to Convention on International Trade in Endangered species (CITES) COP 17, which one of the following is transferred from CITES Appendix II to Appendix I by January 2017.
A. Gorilla B. Pangolin
C. Tapir D. Mongoose

17. Taxonomic diversity of a region with several ecosystems is:
A. Alpha diversity B. Beta diversity
C. Gamma diversity D. Sigma diversity

18. Soil water available to roots is
A. Surface water
B. Hygroscopic water
C. Gravitational water
D. Capillary water

19. C_4 plants are commonly found in
A. Arid and hot environment
B. Humid and low temperature environment
C. Temperature environment
D. Semi-humid and rainy environment

20. The point at which the light intensity is just enough to produce energy by photosynthesis which equal to the energy used in respiration is called
A. Equal point
B. Regulatory point
C. Compensation point
D. Complementary point

21. The global pattern of prevailing winds drives the cell-like circulation pattern of ocean currents called
A. Trade winds B. Gyres
C. Jet Streams D. Shallow drifts

22. As the number of species in a food web increases
A. Food chain length tends to increase
B. System tends to be unstable
C. Energy flow decreases
D. System tends to collapse completely

23. Each degree of latitude on the earth's surface represents approximately
A. 91 km B. 101 km
C. 111 km D. 121 km

24. Remote sensing satellites for earth observation are normally located in
A. Elliptical orbit
B. Sun-synchronous orbit
C. Geo-synchronous orbit
D. Equatorial orbit

25. Asian Ministerial Conference on Disaster Risk Reduction–2016 (AMCDRR–2016) was held in
A. Bangkok B. Beijing
C. New Delhi D. Colombo

26. Groundwater movement depends on the following characteristics of rock materials.
(*a*) Porosity
(*b*) Permeability
(*c*) Specific yield
(*d*) Specific retention capacity
Choose the correct code:
A. (*a*) only
B. (*a*) and (*b*) only
C. (*a*), (*b*) and (*c*) only
D. (*a*), (*b*), (*c*) and (*d*)

27. Magma starts to crystallise when it loses heat during its upward rise to shallower level from a deep source. Which among the following is Bowen's Reaction Series?

A. Pyroxene, Hornblende, Olivine, Mica, Quartz

B. Olivine, Pyroxene, Hornblende, Mica, Quartz

C. Hornblende, Olivine, Mica, Pyroxene, Quartz

D. Olivine, Pyroxene, Hornblende, Mica, Quartz

28. A 2000 MW dam has maximum head of 200 m. What is the rate of falling water on the turbines? (Neglect losses)

A. ~ 102.00 m^3/s

B. ~ 1560.24 m^3/s

C. ~ 1020.41 m^3/s

D. ~ 800.00 m^3/s

29. A hydro power plant has a reservoir storage capacity of 2×10^3 m^3 and its maximum head is 500 m. What is its potential energy?

A. ~ 10 PJ B. ~ 18.6 PJ

C. ~ 27.5 PJ D. ~ 49 PJ

30. The maximum efficiency of hydrogen fuel cell is

A. 0.96 B. 0.92

C. 0.83 D. 0.72

31. In a biogas digestor having biomass and animal wastes as feed, for optimum methane production, the value of pH should be such that initially

A. pH is in the range 6.6 to 7

B. pH < 6.2

C. pH is in the range 7 to 7.2

D. pH is in the range 7.6 to 8

32. Which of the following statements is true in relation to solar flat plate collectors? Glazing (glass or plastic) above the absorber plate?

A. Reduces convection losses

B. Reduces conduction losses

C. Reduces conduction and radiation losses

D. Enhances the absorption of solar radiation onto the absorber plate.

33. Marine pollution is caused by

(*a*) Sewage

(*b*) Land runoff

(*c*) Oil spills

(*d*) Ocean mining

Choose the correct code:

A. (*a*), (*c*), and (*d*) only

B. (*c*) and (*d*) only

C. (*a*), (*b*), (*c*) and (*d*)

D. (*d*), (*c*), (*b*) only

34. Which of the following wave properties is *not* taken advantage of in controlling noise?

A. Absorption

B. Damping

C. Interference

D. Diffraction

35. The reaction $O_2 \rightarrow 2O$, which occurs in the stratosphere, does not occur in the troposphere to produce ozone due to

A. lower tropospheric temperature

B. absence of $\lambda < 242$ nm radiation

C. high air pressure

D. high gas molecule concentrations

36. The most important global sink process for aerosols is

A. Interception

B. Sedimentation

C. Impaction

D. Wet deposition

37. Identify the correct sequence with reference to environmental clearance process for new projects :

A. Appraisal → Screening → Scoping → Public Consultation

B. Screening → Scoping → Public Consultation → Appraisal

C. Scoping → Public Consultation → Appraisal → Screening

D. Public Consultation → Appraisal → Screening → Scoping

38. Which of the following elements has the longest oceanic residence time?

A. Iron B. Lead

C. Calcium D. Sodium

39. The purpose of offshore islands is focussed for site or landscape restoration to
A. provide linkage between movement and genetic interchange of species.
B. foster populations of endangered species without native or introduced predators.
C. increase the availability of habitats.
D. increase the stabilization of surface cover and protect the animal corridor on land.

40. Match the List-I and List-II. Identify the correct answer from the codes given below:

List–I (Series)	***List–II (Life Cycle Analysis)***
(*a*) ISO 14040	1. Interpretation
(*b*) ISO 14041	2. Impact assessment
(*c*) ISO 14042	3. Principles and framework
(*d*) ISO 14043	4. Inventory Analysis

Codes:

	(*a*)	(*b*)	(*c*)	(*d*)
A.	1	2	3	4
B.	4	3	2	1
C.	1	4	2	3
D.	4	1	3	2

41. Which of the following can be used for valuing environmental amenities?
(*a*) Hedonic pricing
(*b*) Travel cost
(*c*) Contingent valuation
Choose the correct code:
A. (*a*) only B. (*b*) only
C. (*a*), (*b*) and (*c*) D. (*b*) and (*c*) only

42. A graphical representation where frequencies are plotted against class intervals is called
A. Stem and leaf plot B. Pie chart
C. Histogram D. Box plot

43. Which one of the following is a density–independent factor that limits the size of the natural population?
A. Predation B. Territoriality
C. Severe drought D. Sex ratio

44. In a multiple regression analysis, if the variance of the observed variable Y is 1.57 and variance of the residue is 0.52, then R-square value is
A. 0.85 B. 0.67
C. 0.72 D. 0.52

45. The median value of the following data:
1, 2, 3, 5, 8 and 100 ; is
A. 3 B. 5
C. 4 D. 20

46. Exchangeable Sodium Percentage (ESP) > 40, and pH > 9.8 are characteristic of
A. Acidic soil
B. Weak saline soil
C. Strongly saline soil
D. Eroded soil

47. The climate meet COP-22 was held in which country?
A. Morocco
B. South Africa
C. Malaysia
D. Indonesia

48. In an aquatic system, the presence of noxious gases such as H_2S and CH_4 is associated with
A. abundant algal growth
B. oxygen depletion
C. absence of macrophytic vegetation
D. excess of dissolved oxygen

49. Severe drought is declared if
A. Deficit of rainfall is more than 50 per cent of the normal.
B. Deficit of rainfall varies between 25-45 per cent of the normal.
C. Rainfall deficit exceeds 25 per cent of the normal.
D. Rainfall deficit is between 15-25 per cent of the normal.

50. The Global Warming Potential (GWP) of a substance depends on
(*a*) the spectral band of its absorbing wavelengths.
(*b*) its residence time in atmosphere.
(*c*) its number of carbon molecules.
(*d*) concentration of the substance.

Choose the correct answer:
A. (*a*), (*b*) and (*c*) only
B. (*b*), (*c*) and (*d*) only
C. (*a*), (*c*) and (*d*) only
D. (*b*), (*d*) and (*a*) only

ANSWERS

1	2	3	4	5	6	7	8	9	10
C	D	A	C	C	A	D	C	C	A
11	**12**	**13**	**14**	**15**	**16**	**17**	**18**	**19**	**20**
B	A	D	B	D	B	C	D	A	C
21	**22**	**23**	**24**	**25**	**26**	**27**	**28**	**29**	**30**
B	A	C	B	C	D	*	C	*	C
31	**32**	**33**	**34**	**35**	**36**	**37**	**38**	**39**	**40**
A	A	C	D	B	D	B	D	B	*
41	**42**	**43**	**44**	**45**	**46**	**47**	**48**	**49**	**50**
C	C	C	B	C	C	A	B	A	D

* *Error in Questions.*

EXPLANATORY ANSWERS

1. **Biomedical waste** is any kind of waste containing infectious materials.
   There are mainly five technology options available for the treatment of biomedical waste. They can be grouped as follows:
   - Chemical processes
   - Thermal processes
   - Mechanical processes
   - Irradiation processes
   - Biological processes

   Chemical processes : These processes use chemicals that act as disinfectants. Sodium hypochlorite, dissolved chlorine dioxide, peracetic acid, hydrogen peroxide, dry inorganic chemical and ozone are examples of such chemicals. Most chemical processes are water-intensive and require neutralising agents.

   Thermal processes : These processes utilise heat to disinfect. Depending on the temperature they operate, it is been grouped into two categories, which are Low-heat systems and High-heat systems

   Low-heat systems (operates between 93 -177 °C) use steam, hot water, or electromagnetic radiation to heat and decontaminate the waste. Autoclave & Microwave are low heat systems.

   High-heat systems employ combustion and high temperature plasma to decontaminate and destroy the waste. Incinerator & Hydroclaving are high heat systems.

   Mechanical processes : These processes are used to change the physical form or characteristics of the waste either to facilitate waste handling or to process the waste in conjunction with other treatment steps. The two primary mechanical processes are

   Compaction : Used to reduce the volume of the waste

   Shredding : Used to destroy plastic and paper waste to prevent their reuse. Only the disinfected waste can be used in a shredder.

   Irradiation processes : In these processes, wastes are exposed to ultraviolet or ionizing radiation in an enclosed chamber. These systems require post shredding to render the waste unrecognizable.

   Biological processes : Biological enzymes are used for treating medical waste. It is claimed that biological reactions will not only decontaminate the waste but also cause the destruction of all the organic constituents so that only plastics, glass, and other inert will remain in the residues.

2. In the wake of the Bhopal Tragedy, the Government of India enacted the Environment Protection Act of 1986 under Article 253 of

the Constitution. Passed in March 1986, it came into force on 19 November 1986. It has 26 sections. The purpose of the Act is to implement the decisions of the United Nations Conference on the Human Environments they relate to the protection and improvement of the human environment and the prevention of hazards to human beings, other living creatures, plants and property. The Act is an "umbrella" legislation designed to provide a framework for central government coordination of the activities of various central and state authorities established under previous laws, such as the Water Act and the Air Act.

3. **Environmental values** are also emphasized in the Constitution of India in the following articles:

   Article 51A(g) : The constitution expects citizen of the country to 'protect and improve the natural environment including forests, lakes, rivers and wildlife and to have compassion for all living creatures'.

   Article 48A : The state shall endeavour to protect and improve the environment and to safeguard the forests and wildlife in the country.

   Value education in the context of the environment must teach us the following:

   (*i*) Environmental values.
   (*ii*) Values for nature.
   (*iii*) Values for culture.
   (*iv*) Values for social justice.
   (*v*) Values for human heritage.
   (*vi*) Values for equitable use of resources.
   (*vii*) Values for sharing common property resources.
   (*viii*) Values to stop/minimize environmental degradation.

4. Deposit of amount payable for damage to environment

   1. Where any amount of compensation is ordered to be paid under any award by the Tribunal on the ground of any damage to environment, that amount shall be remitted to the authority specified under sub-section (3) of section 7A of the Public Liability Insurance Act, 1991 for being credited to the Environmental Relief Fund established under that section.
   2. The amount of compensation credited to the Environmental Relief Fund under sub-section (1) may be utilised by such person or authority, in such manner and for such purposes of environment as may be prescribed.

5. In geology, a graben is a depressed block of the Earth's crust bordered by parallel faults.

   A graben is a valley with a distinct escarpment on each side caused by the displacement of a block of land downward. Graben often occur side-by-side with horsts. Horst and graben structures indicate tensional forces and crustal stretching.

   Graben are produced from parallel normal faults, where the displacement of the hanging wall is downward, while that of the footwall is upward. The faults typically dip toward the center of the graben from both sides. Horsts are parallel blocks that remain between graben; the bounding faults of a horst typically dip away from the center line of the horst. Single or multiple graben can produce a rift valley.

6. When the reverse condition of the fumigation occurs the plume is said to be lofting (Fig.).

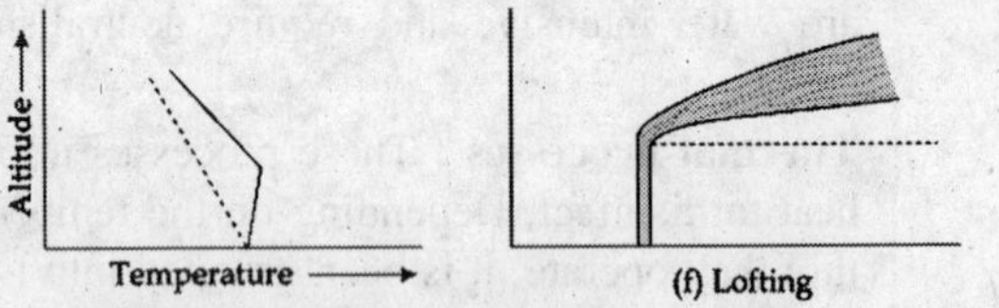

Fig. : *Plume behaviour (Lofting)*

Under this condition the lapse rate above the plume is unstable while below the plume is stable. When the pollutants are emitted from elevated source, they move above the inversion layer and are dispersed well vertically. This is also very suitable condition for dispersion of pollutants. Under these conditions the pollution ground level gets minimum.

7. **Microscale :** The size of microscale is less than 2 km. The time scale is a few seconds to a few minutes. Some examples of microscale are turbulent flow (updrafts and downdrafts).

8. A fundamental niche is the term for what an organism's niche would be in the absence of competition from other species.
Generally, however, there are competitors for the same lifestyle. Rabbits compete with groundhogs for food. Grasses compete with shrubs for soil, and bacteria compete with mold for nutrients among the leaf litter. The niche that a species actually inhabits, taking into account interspecific competition, is its realized niche.

Examples of Fundamental Niches

The male red-winged blackbird's mating call can be heard in the marshes in early spring. At that time, they hold the prime real estate in the marsh. However, as the season progresses, the more aggressive tri-colour blackbirds move in. The tri-colours take over the best territory and force the red-wings to choose the leftovers. The entire marsh represents the red-winged blackbirds' fundamental niche.

9. Dissipative processes are also at work within the biosphere, even under conditions of a steady state of minimum entropy production. These dissipative processes are exemplified by such processes as respiration and senescence that degrade photosynthesized molecules and structures back into smaller molecules such as CO_2, H_2O and less complex mineral compounds and structures. Ordering and dissipative processes in the soil-plant ecosystem can be categorized. Soil and land degradation occur when dissipative processes become excessive; *e.g.,* soil profile destruction by erosion resulting from tillage and poor residue management or overgrazing.

10. **Table :** *Toxic Gases Found in House Fire Smoke*

Substance	Source	Effect
Ammonia	Melamine resins	Inflammation
Aldehydes (acrolein, acetaldehyde, formaldehyde)	Wood, cotton, paper	Inflammation
Benzene	Petroleum products	Irritation and coma
Carbon dioxide	Organic materials	Asphyxiation and coma
Carbon monoxide	Organic materials	Asphyxiation and coma
Hydrogen chloride	Polyvinyl chloride	Inflammation
Hydrogen cyanide	Polyurethanes	Cellular asphyxia
Isocyanate	Polyurethanes	Inflammation and bronchospasm
Organic acids (acetic and formic acid)	Wood, cotton, paper	Inflammation
Oxides of nitrogen and sulphur	Nitrocellulose film	Pulmonary edema
Phosgene	Polyvinyl chloride	Inflammation

11. There are only 10 per cent of atmospheric ozone resides in the troposphere, it plays a critical role in the chemistry of the region. Photolysis of ozone in the presence of water (H_2O) is the primary source of the hydroxyl radical (OH), which for example, partly determines the removal rates of such climatically important trace gases as methane and the chlorofluorocarbons.

12. Doxin is one of the most toxic chemical known.

Combustion : Dioxins form during poorly controlled combustion in municipal-waste incinerators and other combustion sources– they are products of incomplete combustion. Dioxin particles released into air settle onto vegetation, and are eaten by cattle and other animals. Animals concentrate dioxins in their fat. Humans receive about 90% of their total exposure to dioxins when they eat contaminated fatty meat such as hamburgers and fatty dairy products.

Chlorine-using processes : A pulp mill using elemental chlorine to bleach pulp releases trace amounts of dioxins into their effluent. Released into a river, most dioxin is not soluble; most attaches to sediment particles. Bottom-feeding creatures ingest dioxins as they eat the tiny organisms living there. From there, dioxins biomagnify in the food web.

13. Total Organic Carbon (TOC) is one of the simplest and fastest to measure. Total organic carbon (TOC) is the amount of carbon found in an organic compound and is often used as a non-specific indicator of water quality or cleanliness of pharmaceutical manufacturing equipment. TOC may also refer to the amount of organic carbon in soil, or in a geological formation, particularly the source rock for a petroleum play; 2% is a rough minimum. For marine surface sediments, average TOC content is 0.5% in the deep ocean, and 2% along the eastern margins .

14. Pure water is not a good conductor of electricity, because electrical current in liquids is conducted by dissolved ions. But, as the concentration of ions in water increases, the conductivity increases. The measurement of conductivity or specific conductance is an excellent indicator of the degree of mineralization of a water.

The conductance of a water sample will decrease with decreasing temperature, and it can be adjusted to 25 °C (k_{25}) with the equation

$$k_{25} = \frac{k_m}{1+0.0191(T-25)}$$

where k_m = measured k at any temperature (T in °C). This equation assumes that the specific conductance measurement has been corrected for the cell constant—the value necessary to adjust for variation in the dimensions of the electrode. Specific conductance increases with increasing temperature.

15. Out of nine species of vultures, the population of three species—White-backed Vulture *(Gyps bengalensis),* Slender-billed Vulture *(Gyps tenuirostris)* and Long-billed Vulture *(Gyps indicus)* has declined by 99%. The Red-headed Vulture *(Sarcogyps calvus)* has also suffered a rapid decline in the recent past. Vultures keep the environment clean, by scavenging on animal carcasses. The decline in vulture populations has associated disease risks, including increased risk of spread of rabies and anthrax, besides adversely impacting the observance of last rites by the Parsis in the Towers of Silence.

Habitat: Forests, villages etc.

Distribution: Across India.

Threats: A major threat to vultures is the painkiller diclofenac used by veterinarians to treat cattle. When vultures consume these carcasses, diclofenac enters their system, but they are unable to metabolize it. Accumulation of diclofenac results in gout-like symptoms such as neck-drooping, ultimately leading to death.

16. The 17th meeting of the Conference of the Parties to CITES (CoP17) took place between 24th September and 4th October 2016 in Johannesburg, South Africa.

The CITES CoP is a meeting of CITES Parties to review the implementation of the Convention. The CoP provides a forum for Parties to:

- Review progress in the conservation of species listed under CITES
- Consider, and where appropriate adopt, proposals to amend the lists of species under CITES
- Recommend measures to improve the effectiveness of the Convention
- Make provisions (including budget matters) necessary to allow the CITES Secretariat to function effectively.

The 17th meeting of the Conference of the Parties to CITES (CoP17) African pangolin species from Appendix II to Appendix I.

17. Biodiversity can be measured by the numbers and types of different species, or the genetic variations within and between species. The Ecologists use different indices to measure biodiversity. Whittaker emphasized on species richness or species evenness as common matrices to measure the species and land diversity. Three indices are commonly used by ecologists to measure biodiversity. These are known as alpha, beta and gamma.

The **Alpha diversity** refers to the diversity within a particular area, and is measured by counting the number of taxa within the ecosystem. It refers to the concept of species richness in a particular habitat or ecosystem.

The **Beta Diversity** is species diversity between ecosystems. For this the numbers of taxa are compared that are unique to each of the ecosystem. If the species composition of a particular community changes from place to place in a particular area, we may say that the beta diversity in that area is high. However, if the whole area is occupied by the species, the beta diversity is said to be low.

The **Gamma Diversity** is a measure of the overall diversity for different ecosystems within a region. In other words, the gamma diversity is defined as the rate of coming up of additional species due to geographical replacements for a given type of habitat in different types of localities.

18. **Capillary water** is that fraction of soil water that is held in the small spaces of the soil against the force of gravity by adhesive forces between water molecules and soil particles; about 75% of this soil water is available to plants. This water is held in the interspaces or thin capillaries between the soil particles after the gravitational water has drained down. It is held against the force of gravity by capillary forces and is called capillary water. The capillary water is readily available to plants for absorptions. Capillary water is important because cohesive forces permit both upward and lateral movement. Often it is the rate, not the distance traversed, that is the critical factor influencing the relative importance of capillary flow.

19. C_4 plants tend to be most abundant in warm, fairly dry environments. The C_4 system is especially often found in grasses in semi-arid environments such as the western and especially the southwestern parts of the North American prairies (no trees have the C_4 metabolism). There is a gradient in C_4 abundance going from cool to warm, and from wet to dry. However, the pattern is not always quite as expected.

A C_4 plant, avoids photorespiration because it shuttles the fixed carbon to have the final sugar-making reaction occur in special cells deep within its leaf that aren't producing any oxygen. And concentrating CO_2 at high levels relative to oxygen also helps suppress photorespiration. Having special "CO_2-gathering" cells that take up CO_2 without producing any CO_2 through photorespiration helps to ensure maximum efficiency in CO_2 uptake (it is like a vacuum cleaner for CO_2), in terms of "stomatal opening time" and water loss. Hence, in a C_4 plant stomata need not be open for as long to take up a unit of carbon, and—for this reason too—water use is more efficient. Thus, the C_4 plant loses less water per unit time per unit of carbon fixed. This should help it to do better in dry environments.

20. Daily and seasonal variations in light intensity affect plant growth; at least 1% intensity of full sunlight is necessary to trigger photosynthesis. Plants are said to have reached a compensation point when the light intensity is enough to produce an equivalent amount of energy by photosynthesis that is being used in respiration. From there, photosynthesis increases linearly, up to between 10 and 20% of full sunlight, when light saturation may be reached. Beyond the saturation point, light intensity may actually impair photosynthesis by causing photooxidation of recently produced photosynthetic products or by increasing the breakdown rate of chlorophyll beyond its renewal rate. Inadequate light intensity limits the radiant energy available for photosynthesis. Only 1–2% of total radiant energy is absorbed and converted into chemical energy through photosynthesis.

21. This global pattern of prevailing winds drives the cell-like circulation pattern of ocean currents called gyres. Most currents are called "drifts" because they lag far behind the average speeds of the surface winds, averaging only about 8 km hr^{-1}. Variations in water temperature, density, and salinity are another major source of oceanic circulation. For example, increases in salinity or decreases in temperature make water denser and cause it to sink. Cold currents of the polar areas sink and flow toward the equator, while warm currents from the equator flow toward the higher Latitudes transporting heat.

22. It appears that the average number of feeding links per species (linkage density) increases as the size of the web (*i.e.,* number of species) increases. This implies that the number of prey that a predator will eat increases in proportion to the total number of species in that community. However, the number of links relative to all possible links (connectance) decreases as the number of groups in a food web increases. Martens suggested that this might reflect an increase in ecosystem stability. However, Christensen and Pauly conclude that any interpretation of connectance is ambiguous due to the binary nature of its scoring.

23. Lines of latitude are always parallel with each other and, therefore, are also known as parallels. Any number of parallels can be designated using degrees, minutes, and seconds. Neglecting Earth's oblate shape, one degree of latitude is anywhere equivalent to approximately 111 km. Important lines of latitude usually shown on maps or globes are the Tropic of Cancer, Tropic of Capricorn, Arctic Circle, Antarctic Circle, and the equator.

Important Parallels of Latitudes

Equator : The equator is the line of 0° latitude and is so named because it divides the Earth into two equal halves.

Tropic of Cancer : It lies at an angle of 23½ °N of the equator.

Tropic of Capricorn : It lies at an angle of 23½ °S of the equator.

Arctic Circle : It lies at an angle of 66½ °N of the equator.

Antarctic Circle : It lies at an angle of 66½ °S of the equator.

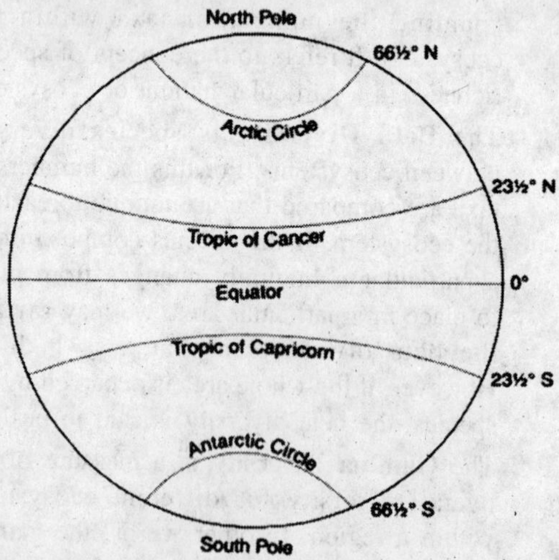

Fig. : *Important Parallels of Latitudes*

- The lines of latitude are horizontal and parallel, running from east to west.
- The equator is the largest line of latitude as it encircles the earth in the middle.
- The lines of latitudes become progressively shorter as they near the poles.
- All the lines of latitudes are circles, except the North and South Poles, which are points.
- If the lines of latitude are 1° apart from each other, there will be 90 parallels in the Northern.

  Hemisphere and 90 parallels in the Southern Hemisphere (total 181 parallels including the equator).
- Each degree of latitude is divided into 60 minutes, and each minute is divided into 60 seconds.

24. Sun-synchronous Orbit

An orbit is said to be sun-synchronous, if the orbit precession of the satellite compensates for the Earth's rotation around the sun. For near-Earth satellite orbits (altitude < 1000 km) sun-synchronous orbits are polar orbits at an orbital inclination and altitude such that a satellite passes over a given site always at the same local time. The orbital nodes maintain a near constant solar time. The satellite always crosses the equatorial plane at the same local time. This means that the sun position (lighting conditions) is always the same (within certain limits) for a repeat observations of any given site. There are advantages and disadvantages to the measurement at constant sun–angle depending on the application. Varying sun angles may be of importance to geologists to reveal subtle structural details not visible at higher sun angles.

25. India had host the Asian Ministerial Conference for Disaster Risk Reduction (AMCDRR) from 3 November to 5 November 2016.

Prime Minister Narendra Modi inaugurated the conference that was held in New Delhi in collaboration with the United Nations Office for Disaster Risk Reduction (UNISDR). The Conference was focus on partnership with governments and stakeholders to imbibe the practices in the region's development narrative.

Key Highlights of the Conference

- The conference aims at transforming the commitments of governments and stakeholders during the Sendai Conference into national and local action.
- The meet was focus on collaboration, consultation and partnership with governments and stakeholders to mainstream DRR in the region's development narrative.
- The conference adopted the Asian Regional Plan for implementation of the Sendai Framework endorsed by the Asian countries.
- It was also consolidate the political commitment of governments towards preventing and reducing risk as well as strengthening resilience in the form of a political declaration.

26. Movement of groundwater depends on rock and sediment properties and the groundwater's flow potential. Porosity, permeability, specific yield and specific retention are important properties of groundwater flow. Porosity is the volume of pore space relative to the total volume (rock and/or sediment + pore space). Primary porosity (% pore space) is the initial void space present (intergranular) when the rock formed. Secondary porosity (% added openings) develops later. It is the result of fracturing, faulting, or dissolution. Grain shape and cementation also affect porosity.

Permeability is the capability of a rock to allow the passage of fluids. Permeability is dependent on the size of pore spaces and to what degree the pore spaces are connected. Grain shape, grain packing, and cementation affect permeability.

Specific yield (S_y) is the ratio of the volume of water that drained from a rock (due to gravity) to the total rock volume. Grain size has a definite effect on specific yield. Smaller grains have larger surface areas. Larger surface areas mean more surface tension. Fine-grained sediment will have a lower specific yield than more coarsely-grained sediment. Sorting of material affects groundwater movement. Poorly sorted material is less porous than well-sorted material.

Specific retention (S_r) is the ratio of the volume of water a rock can retain (in spite of gravity) to the total volume of rock.

Specific yield plus specific retention equals porosity.

$$S_r + S_y = \Phi$$

Porosity, permeability, specific yield, and specific retention are all components of hydraulic conductivity.

27. By using Bowen's Reaction Series (Fig.) illustrating the order of crystallization of minerals from a magma, depending on temperature, it becomes apparent how such a varied collection of rocks may be formed from a single source. At the highest temperatures, the rocks formed tend to be free or virtually free of fieldspars, containing olivine and pyroxene, and are called ultrabasic. Basic rocks contain a calcium rich plagioclase feldspar, and a pyroxene; intermediate rocks, a plagioclase in between calcium and sodium rich and an amphibole, with less than 10% quartz; acid rocks, a sodic plagioclase and/or an alkali feldspar, and more than 10% quartz. So, the minerals which crystallize out at any particular temperature combine to form a representative rock type, leaving the chemical composition of the still molten portion of the magma changed. Hence, as the high temperature minerals become crystallized out, elements such as Mg, Fe and Ca, are taken from the melt, along with relatively small amounts of silica combined with these as a silicate radical. Thus, the melt is enriched in Al, Na and silica, and the lower temperature minerals and hence, rocks are rich in these.

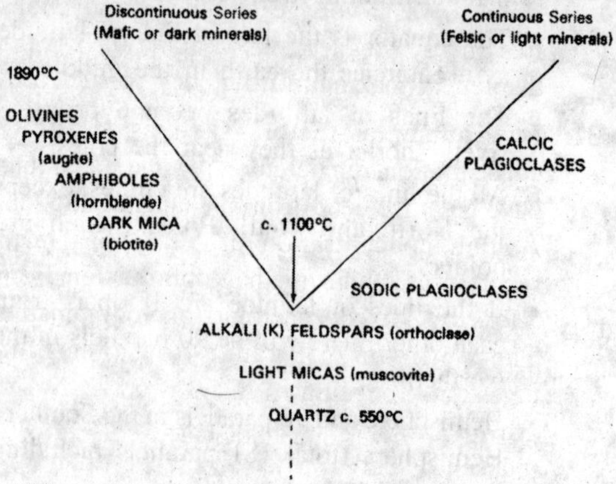

Fig. : *Bowen's Reaction Series showing the order of crystallization of common rock forming minerals from a silicate magma*

28. We know that 1 m³/sec = 1000 *l*/sec

Again from formula,

$$\text{Power (w)} = \text{Net head } (m) \times \text{Flow } (l/\text{sec}) \times 9.8 \text{ (m/sec}^2)$$

$$2 \times 10^9 = 200 \times \text{Flow } (l/\text{sec}) \times 9.8$$

$$\text{Flow } (l/\text{sec}) = \frac{10^7}{9.8}$$

$$= 10.2041 \times 10^5$$

$$\text{Flow (m}^3/\text{sec}) = 10.2041 \times 10^2$$

$$\text{Flow} = 1020.41 \text{ m}^3/\text{sec.}$$

30. The thermal efficiency of fuel cell is given by the ratio of useful electrical energy produced to the enthalpy formation of fuel and is given by Eq. and rewritten as follows.

$$\eta_{FC} = \frac{\Delta G}{\Delta H}$$

where ΔG is change in Gibbs free energy and ΔH is the enthalpy of formation of the reaction. In practice, the actual efficiency of fuel cell is given as follows.

$$\eta = 0.83 \times \left(\frac{V_{CELL}}{V_{IDEAL}}\right)$$

where V_{CELL} = The actual voltage of fuel cell; V_{IDEAL} = The voltage obtained from Gibbs free energy for the ideal case and 0.83 is the theoretical maximum efficiency of fuel cell.

31. Environmental factors such as substrate concentration, temperature, pH and metal ions have great influences on methane production. A high concentration of VFAs has been reported to inhibit methane production from VFAs by mixed anaerobic microorganisms. The optimum pH range for anaerobic digestion producing methane is 6.8–7.2. The growth rate of methanogens can be greatly reduced when the pH value is less than 6.6. An excessively alkaline pH can lead to the disintegration of microbial granules and subsequent failure of the digestion process. Therefore, a buffer is needed in the methane production process in order to provide the resistance to significant and rapid pH changes in the system. Buffer capacity is proportional to the concentration of bicarbonate. $NaHCO_3$ has been widely used to create a buffer system during the anaerobic digestion process. Speece found that an alkalinity to COD concentration ratio (w/w) of 1.2–1.6 was required to sufficiently maintain the pH at approximately 6.6 during the anaerobic digestion of carbohydrate waste to produce methane. It is obviously seen that in order to achieve a maximum methane production, the key environmental factors should be optimized.

32. Flat-plate collector is one of the most important components of a solar water heater. Flat-plate collectors are the simplest and most commonly used collectors for converting the sun's radiation into useful heat. They are designed for applications requiring energy delivery at moderate temperature (less than 100°C) as in water and space heating. They have the advantages of using both beam and diffuse solar radiation, not requiring orientation towards the sun and requiring little maintenance. A conventional flat-plate collector is made up of a flat absorbing plate, normally metallic upon which solar radiation falls and is absorbed, changing to heat energy. The absorb plate is usually black in colour for optimum collection and its area is the same as the area intercepting the radiation. To reduce convective and radiative heat losses from the absorber, one or two transparent covers (glazing) are generally placed above the absorber plate.

They usually be made from glass or plastic.

Flat Plate Collector

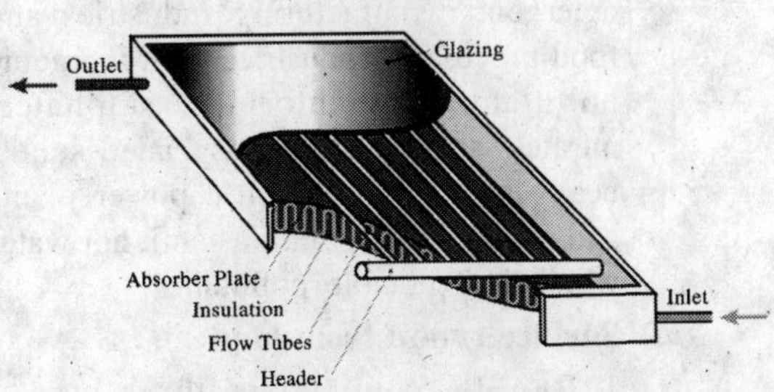

33. **Marine Pollution :** Oceans are the ultimate sink of all natural and man-made pollutants. Rivers discharge their pollutants into the sea. The sewerage and garbage of coastal cities are also dumped into the sea. The other sources of oceanic pollution are navigational discharge of oil, grease, detergents, sewage, garbage, and radioactive wastes. Capsized oil tankers, offshore oil mining and soil exploration operations and oil-refineries mainly contribute to oil pollution of marine ecosystem. An accidental discharge of petroleum in oceans and estuaries is called oil spills.

The water pollutants are generated by different sources and activities, some of these are briefly described below:

(*i*) **Household detergents and domestic sewage :** Domestic sewage is mainly the liquid wastes from kitchen, toilets and other household domestic activities. In most cases they are discharged into a river or a water body nearby. A mere 0.1% impurities make domestic sewage unfit for human use.

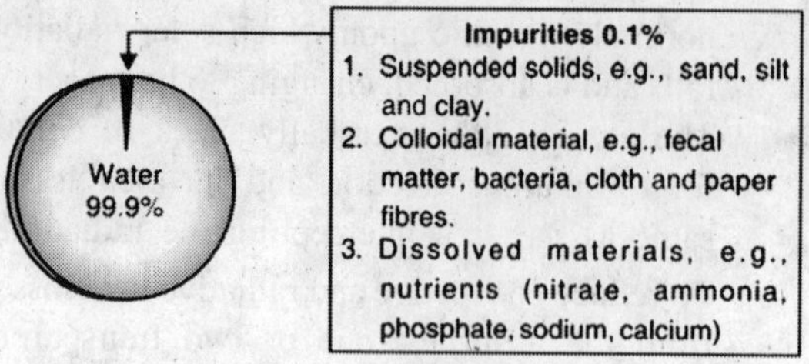

Fig. : *Composition of domestic sewage*

(*ii*) **Industrial waste and effluents :** Small and large scale industries like iron and steel industries, chemical plants, soap and detergent manufacturing industries and food processing industries emit inorganic pollutants like chlorides, sulphates, nitrates, acids, alkalis, suspended solids, heavy metals, etc. Electric power plants and nuclear power stations emit hot water which is a notable pollutant.

(*iii*) **Surface runoff from land**

1. Runoff from agricultural land—Pesticide residues and inorganic residues of fertilisers.
2. Runoff from urban areas—Contain biodegradables organic pollutants.
3. Runoff from industries—Contain heavy metals, acids and various inorganic compounds.

(*iv*) **Oil spills :** An oil spill is the accidential discharge of oil from various sources/activities like by:

(*a*) Capsized oil tankers : Oil, grease, petroleum products

(*b*) Offshore oil mining and oil exploration operations and oil refineries : Oil, grease, petroleum products

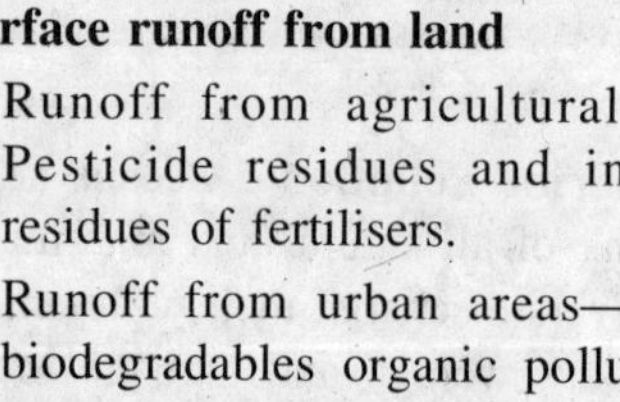

Fig. : *Oil spill damages the biodiversity, birds smeared with oil lose capability to fly.*

Oil spills cause the death of plankton fish and marine birds as shown in the accompanying figure. They are extremely harmful to coral reefs and drastically damage the marine biodiversity.

34. Controlling noise : Methods of controlling noise take advantage of some of its wave properties, including absorption, damping, reflection and interference.

Sound-proofing materials absorb noise over a wide range of frequencies. They are materials like expanded polystyrene, fibreglass or even old egg cartons, that are soft and/or contain air pockets, so absorbing the vibrations. These are used in recording studios to reduce incoming noise, and in noisy developments such as clubs or theatres to prevent excess noise escaping to nearby residential areas. The choice of material will depend upon the frequency range of the noise to be controlled, as certain materials absorb more effectively at certain frequencies. Sound insulation is important in walls and ceilings, particularly between neighbouring properties and in apartment blocks. The sound insulation of a wall, R, can be defined as

$$R = 10 \log\left(\frac{I_i}{I_t}\right)$$

where I_i and I_t are the incident and transmitted sound intensities. This gives the difference in decibel levels at each side of the barrier. It will be reduced in the case of sounds transmitted directly to the wall rather than through the air, for instance where residents in the flat upstars have their hi-fi speakers on the floor. Sound insulation is frequency dependent. To be effective, sound-proofed areas must be solid and without cracks, as sound will be transmitted effectively through quite small holes or cracks reducing any noise insulation significantly.

35. The ozone is produced by the photolysis of oxygen molecules into oxygen atoms, shown in Reaction (1), followed by the reaction of one oxygen atom with an oxygen molecule:

O_2 + UV light → O + O $\lambda < 242$ nm ...(1)

$O + O_2 + M \rightarrow O_3 + M$ ...(2)

Net: $2\ O_2$ + UV light → $O + O_3$

In Reaction (1), the ultraviolet light required to dissociate the O_2 molecules must have a wavelength less than 242 nm. The oxygen atoms formed in Reaction (1) react with an oxygen molecule to form ozone in Reaction (2). The third molecule, M, is needed to remove the excess energy and can be any other molecule in the atmosphere.

This reaction does not occur in the troposphere to produce ozone due to absence of $\lambda < 242$ nm radiation.

36. For the aerosol in the accumulation mode, the wet deposition is thought to be more of importance. Thus, for sea salt aerosol, dry and wet depositions are the most important sink-processes. The wet deposition process refers to the removal of any species from the atmosphere by precipitation, either by in-cloud or below-cloud scavenging. The in-cloud process is thought to be most important for small sea salt aerosol, which effectively form cloud condensation nuclei, whereas larger aerosol are removed by falling raindrops (below-cloud scavenging). Dry deposition refers to removal mechanisms that do not involve precipitation. For dry deposition of aerosol processes such as gravitational sedimentation, turbulent transfer, Brownian diffusion and impaction are considered.

37. The environmental clearance process comprises of four stages, namely, Stage (1) Screening; Stage (2) Scoping; Stage (3) Public Consultation and Stage (4) Appraisal.

Screening : Screening refers scrutiny of category 'B' projects seeking prior environmental clearance made in Form-1 by the concerned State Level Expert Appraisal Committee for determining whether or not the project requires further environmental studies for preparation of EIA for its appraisal depending upon the nature and location specificity of the project.

Scoping : Scoping refers to the process by which the EAC in the case of Category 'A' projects or activities, and SEAC in the case of Category 'B1' projects or activities determine detailed and comprehensive TORs addressing all the relevant environmental concerns for the preparation of EIA report.

Public Consultation : Public Consultation refers to the process by which the concerns of local affected persons and others who have plausible stake in the environmental impacts of the project or activity are ascertained.

Appraisal : Appraisal means the detailed scrutiny by the Expert Appraisal Committee or State Level Expert Appraisal Committee of the application and other documents submitted by the applicant for grant of environmental clearance.

38. Oceanographers call the time it takes for a substance to be removed from the ocean its *residence time.* Sodium and chloride have the longest residence times of the six major constituents. This explains why table salt is found in the sea in such abundance. Rivers actually add this common salt to oceans very slowly. The other elements have relatively short residence times. For example, potassium lasts seven million years, calcium one million years.

39. The ecological restoration of islands, or island restoration, is the application of the principles of ecological restoration to islands and island groups. Islands, due to their isolation, are home to many of the world's endemic species, as well as important breeding grounds for seabirds and some marine mammals. The purpose of offshore islands is focussed for site or landscape restoration to foster populations of endangered species without native or introduced predators.

41. Estimating Benefits for Nonmarket Goods

Clearly one of the problems with using benefit-cost analysis to help make regulatory decisions is the difficulty involved in estimating the monetary value of nonmarket goods and services, such as improved water quality or the reduced number of sick days. The three techniques that are most commonly used include hedonic pricing (inferring effects of regulations based on changes in the values of market goods such as houses), travel cost and contingent valuation. Each method has its strengths and weaknesses.

42. Histogram : It is the most commonly used graphical representation of grouped frequency distribution. Variable characters of the different groups are indicated on the horizontal line (x-axis) and frequencies (number of observation) are indicated on the vertical line (y-axis). Frequency of each group forms a column or rectangle. Such diagram is called *histogram.* The area of rectangle is proportional to the frequency of the correspondence class interval and the total area of the histogram is proportional to the total frequency of all the class intervals. A histogram may be drawn by using following steps:

- Set of vertical bars the areas of which are proportional to frequencies represented.
- The difference of histogram from bar diagram is that bar diagram is one dimensional and only the length of the bar has its significance while in histogram both length and width matters.
- When class intervals are equal, frequency is taken on y-axis, the variables on x-axis and adjacent rectangles are constructed.
- When the class intervals are unequal, a correction for unequal class intervals must be made.

The following frequency distribution is represented graphically in the form of histogram.

Age group (years)	*No. of males*
15-20	15
20-25	20
25-30	40
30-35	60
35-40	50

Here, we will take class boundaries along the horizontal axis and frequencies along with vertical axis. From the data shown above a histogram is drawn, which is presented in fig.

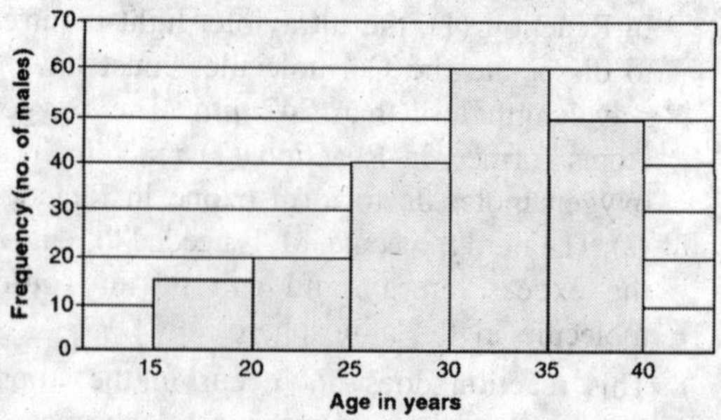

Fig. : *Histogram depiciting number of males in different age groups.*

43. Density independent factors influence population size without regard for the population's density. They include events like severe drought or a prolonged cold period, either of which can cause widespread mortality independent of population density. A graph of density-independent effects on populations would show instantaneous, rather than gradual, drops in population size, and these changes would occur at different starting densities.

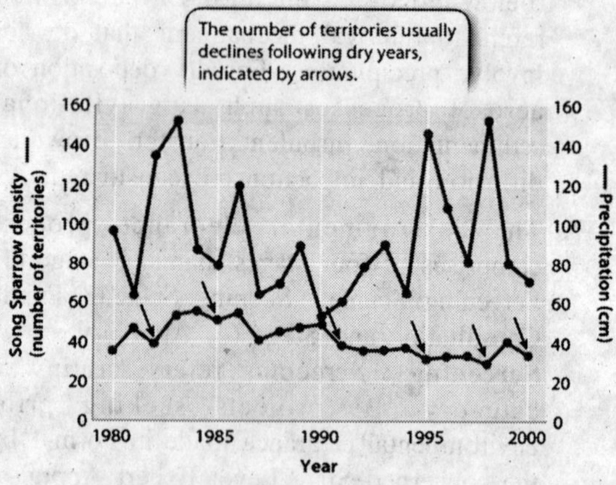

Fig. : *Density-independent effects on population size. Independent of population density, extreme weather (such as drought) lowers the quality of habitat for Song Sparrows, reducing the number of territories occupied.*

44. R-squared $(R^2) = 1 - \left[\dfrac{SS_{Error}}{SS_{Total}}\right]$

$$= 1 - \frac{0.52}{1.57}$$

$$= 1 - 0.33 = 0.67.$$

45. Data in ascending order: 1, 2, 3, 5, 8, 100

Number of term N = 6

So, medium (M)

$$= \text{Mean of } \frac{N}{2}\text{th term and } \left(\frac{N}{2}+1\right)\text{th term}$$

$$= \frac{3+5}{2} = \frac{8}{2} = 4.$$

47. COP-22 was held in Marrakech, in the North-African country of Morocco, on 7-18 November 2016. A focal issue of COP-22 is that of water scarcity, water cleanliness, and water-related sustainability, a major problem in the developing world, including many African states. Prior to the event a special initiative on water was presided by Charafat Afailal, Morocco's Minister in Charge of Water and Aziz Mekouar, COP-22 Ambassador for Multilateral Negotiations. Another focal issue was the need to reduce greenhouse emissions and utilize low-carbon energy sources. Mr. Peter Thompson, President of the UN General Assembly, called for the transformation of the global economy in all sectors to achieve a low emissions global economy.

48. Organic matter in water is broken down by microorganisms, especially bacteria, either aerobically (using oxygen) or, once the oxygen dissolved in water is depleted, anaerobically (without oxygen). The organic matter content of water is described by its biochemical oxygen demand (BOD), a measure of the amount of oxygen needed to break down the organic matter aerobically. Anaerobic decay produces a variety of noxious gases, such as hydrogen sulphide (H_2S) and methane (CH_4), the presence of which in a body of water signals oxygen depletion.

49. Meteorological drought is defined as the deficiency of precipitation from expected or normal levels over an extended period of time (*i.e.*, normal levels accommodate upto 10% deviation from long term average). Meteorological drought usually precedes other kinds of drought and is said to occur when the seasonal rainfall received over an area is less than 25% of its long-term average value. It is classified as moderate drought if the rainfall deficit is 26-50% and severe drought when the deficit exceeds 50% of the normal.

50. **Global warming potential (GWP)** is a relative measure of how much heat a greenhouse gas traps in the atmosphere. It compares the amount of heat trapped by a certain mass of the gas in question to the amount of heat trapped by a similar mass of carbon dioxide. A GWP is calculated over a specific time interval, commonly 20, 100, or 500 years. GWP is expressed as a factor of carbon dioxide.

The substances subject to restrictions under the Kyoto protocol either are rapidly increasing their concentrations in Earth's atmosphere or have a large GWP.

The GWP depends on the following factors:

- The absorption of infrared radiation by a given species
- The spectral location of its absorbing wavelengths
- The atmospheric lifetime of the species

Thus, a high GWP correlates with a large infrared absorption and a long atmospheric lifetime. The dependence of GWP on the wavelength of absorption is more complicated. Even if a gas absorbs radiation efficiently at a certain wavelength, this may not affect its GWP much if the atmosphere already absorbs most radiation at that wavelength. A gas has the most effect if it absorbs in a "window" of wavelengths where the atmosphere is fairly transparent. The dependence of GWP as a function of wavelength has been found empirically and published as a graph.

PAPER-III

Note: *This paper contains* ***seventy five*** *(75) objective type questions of* ***two*** *(2) marks each.* ***All*** *questions are compulsory.*

1. Given below are two statements. One labelled as Assertion (A) and the other labelled as Reason (R):
   Assertion (A) : Vertical velocity often equals or exceeds horizontal velocity in mesoscale meteorological systems.
   Reason (R) : Rising thermals are susceptible to undergo non-hydrostatic processes such as buoyant acceleration or acceleration through a narrow mountain pass.
   Choose the correct answer:
   A. Both (A) and (R) are correct and (R) is the correct explanation of (A).
   B. Both (A) and (R) are correct and (R) is not the correct explanation of (A).
   C. (A) is true, but (R) is false.
   D. (A) is false and (R) is true.

2. Given below are two statements. One labelled as Assertion (A) and the other labelled as Reason (R):
   Assertion (A) : Geostrophic wind velocity is independent of latitude.
   Reason (R) : Geostrophic wind velocity is determined by pressure gradient force only.
   Choose the correct answer:
   A. Both (A) and (R) are correct and (R) is the correct explanation of (A).
   B. Both (A) and (R) are correct and (R) is not the correct explanation of (A).
   C. (A) is true, but (R) is false.
   D. (A) is false and (R) is true.

3. Mixing height during night is typically in the range
   A. < few hundred metres
   B. 1 km – 2 km
   C. 2 km – 3 km
   D. 3 km – 4 km

4. At a given urban location, the temperature at an elevation of 25 m above ground is 15 °C. If the inversion conditions prevail and the environmental lapse rate is 1.25 °C per 100 m, the temperature at an elevation of 200 m will be
   A. 12.5 °C B. 17.5 °C
   C. 12.75 °C D. 17.25 °C

5. When the temperature of the atmosphere falls at a rate greater than the dry adiabatic lapse rate, the atmosphere is
   A. stable
   B. highly stable
   C. unstable
   D. conditionally unstable

6. Gross Primary Productivity (GPP) of an ecosystem is
   A. net rate of carbon gain by the plant after respiration losses.
   B. total energy used to convert the sugar during growth.
   C. photosynthetic fixation rate of atmospheric carbon dioxide.
   D. rate of release of oxygen through respiration of a plant.

7. The oxygen atom species, which reacts with water to form hydroxyl radical, is produced by the photodissociation of
   A. O_2 B. O_3
   C. NO_2 D. H_2O

8. Match the List–I and List–II given below:

List–I (Element)	*List–II (Classification)*
(*a*) Sodium	1. Chalcogen
(*b*) Calcium	2. Alkali Metal
(*c*) Chromium	3. Alkaline Earth Element
(*d*) Sulphur	4. Transition Element

Choose the correct answer:

Codes:

	(*a*)	(*b*)	(*c*)	(*d*)
A.	2	3	4	1
B.	1	2	3	4
C.	3	1	2	4
D.	4	2	1	3

9. Identify the incorrect statement about carbon isotopes:
A. C-13 is less abundant in vegetation than in oceans.
B. C-12 is most abundant in nature.
C. C-14 is absent in fossil fuels.
D. C-13 is used for carbon-dating.

10. Among the following insecticides, which one is relatively more soluble in water?
A. Aldicarb B. Carbaryl
C. Malathion D. Aldrin

11. At 25 °C, hydrogen ion concentration in an environmental aqueous solution is found to be 5×10^{-4} mol L^{-1}. This implies that the concentration of hydroxyl ions is
A. 2×10^{-3} mol L^{-1} B. 1×10^{-7} mol L^{-1}
C. 2×10^{-11} mol L^{-1} D. 2×10^{-19} mol L^{-1}

12. Identify the incorrect statement about humus.
A. Humus acts as a reservoir of nitrogen for plants.
B. By decaying, humus supplies nitrogen to plants.
C. Its rate of decay and rate of nitrogen release follow plant growth.
D. Rate of nitrogen release to plants is slow during warm growing season and fast during winter months.

13. Match the List–I and List–II. Identify the correct answer from the codes given below:

List–I (Terms)	***List–II (Chromatographic action)***
(*a*) Effluent	1. The eluted solute
(*b*) Eluate	2. The mobile phase
(*c*) Eluent	3. The solute-mobile phase mixture which exits the column
(*d*) Eluite	4. The stream flowing out of the column

Codes:

	(*a*)	(*b*)	(*c*)	(*d*)
A.	1	3	2	4
B.	2	4	3	1
C.	3	1	2	4
D.	4	3	2	1

14. A textile industry effluent containing 1×10^{-6} mol L^{-1} of an organic dye has 0.6 absorbance in a cell of 1.0 cm path length. The molar extinction coefficient of the dye is
A. 6×10^{4} L mol^{-1} cm^{-1}
B. 6×10^{-7} L mol^{-1} cm^{-1}
C. 1.66×10^{-5} L mol^{-1} cm^{-1}
D. 6.0×10^{6} L mol^{-1} cm^{-1}

15. Characteristics of successful invasive plant species are:
(*a*) Rapid growth and early flowering.
(*b*) High phenotypic plasticity
(*c*) Production of large number of seeds
Choose the correct answer:
A. (*a*) only B. (*a*) and (*b*) only
C. (*b*) and (*c*) only D. (*a*), (*b*) and (*c*)

16. Drugs that prevent the formation of bacterial cell wall are
A. Quinolones B. Beta-lactams
C. Tetracyclines D. Aminoglycocides

17. As a result of El Niño, it has been observed that phytoplankton productivity increases in Eastern Indian Ocean around Indonesia and Gulf of Mexico. This increase is probably due to
(*a*) Increased rainfall
(*b*) More nutrient inflow
(*c*) Turbulence in surface waters
Codes:
A. (*a*) and (*b*) only B. (*b*) and (*c*) only
C. (*a*) and (*c*) only D. (*a*), (*b*) and (*c*)

18. Vermi composting process depends on
(*a*) Quality of organic resources
(*b*) Types of earthworms
(*c*) Moisture content of the organic wastes
Choose the correct answer:
A. (*a*) only B. (*a*) and (*b*) only
C. (*b*) and (*c*) only D. (*a*), (*b*) and (*c*)

19. Photosynthesis in plants is associated with
(*a*) decrease in entropy
(*b*) increase in entropy
(*c*) increase in Gibbs free energy
Choose the correct answer:
A. (*a*) only B. (*b*) only
C. (*b*) and (*c*) only D. (*a*), (*b*) and (*c*)

20. The predominant bioparticulate allergens in the air are
A. Insect debris and house dust mites
B. Pollen grains and fungal spores
C. Animal dander and house dust
D. Wool particles and cockroach calyx

21. The enhancement of the fitness of a recipient individual by acts that reduce the evolutionary fitness of the donor individual is
A. Amensalism B. Altruism
C. Commonsalism D. Parasitism

22. The greater proportion of the edges in a national park indicates a
(*a*) less functional habitat
(*b*) highly functional habitat
(*c*) degraded habitat
Choose the correct answer:
A. (*a*) only B. (*a*) and (*c*) only
C. (*b*) and (*c*) only D. (*a*), (*b*) and (*c*)

23. The change in species composition that is imposed by factors external to the biotic community is known as
A. Autogenic succession
B. Allogenic succession
C. Xerarch
D. Hydrarch

24. Which ecosystem type produces maximum litter mass?
A. Tropical rain forest
B. Tropical seasonal forest
C. Temperate deciduous forest
D. Boreal forest

25. Cyclomorphism is a phenomenon observed in certain planktonic crustaceans and is generally attributed as a response to
(*a*) changes in environmental variables of water.
(*b*) ensure adaptive significance.
(*c*) growth, reproduction and sudden genetic change
Codes:
A. (*a*) and (*c*) only B. (*b*) and (*c*) only
C. (*a*) and (*b*) only D. (*a*), (*b*) and (*c*)

26. Microbes in the environment are likely to be
I. living in biofilms on surfaces
II. non-culturable
III. living solitary and planktonic lines
Choose the correct code:
A. I only B. II and III only
C. I and III only D. I and II only

27. Which magma type contains the greatest amount of silica?
A. Basaltic B. Andesitic
C. Rhyolitic D. Peridotic

28. Match the List–I and List–II and choose the correct answer from the codes given below:

List–I (Stratigraphic Unit)	***List–II (Deposits)***
(*a*) Bailadila Group	1. Mn
(*b*) Nallamalai Group	2. Phosphorite
(*c*) Udaipur Group	3. Banded Iron Formation
(*d*) Sansar Group	4. Pb-Zn

Codes:

	(*a*)	(*b*)	(*c*)	(*d*)
A.	3	4	2	1
B.	4	1	3	2
C.	1	2	4	3
D.	2	3	1	4

29. Which group of following factors determine the discharge of a stream?
A. Width, length and depth
B. Width, length and velocity
C. Width, depth and velocity
D. Length, depth and run-off

30. Which among the following zones has the highest erosion rate in the journey of a river?
A. Head water
B. Potamon
C. Mouth
D. Sediment transforming zone

31. In the decreasing order of hardness on Moh's scale, choose the correct sequence from the following:
A. Quartz, Feldspar, Calcite, Talc
B. Feldspar, Calcite, Talc, Quartz
C. Talc, Quartz, Feldspar, Calcite
D. Quartz, Calcite, Feldspar, Talc

32. Wind transport of materials entails the following processes:
I. Saltation
II. Reptation
III. Suspension
IV. Creep
Choose the correct answer:
A. I, II, III, IV
B. II, III and IV only
C. III and IV only
D. I and II only

33. According to Darcy's law for ground water movement, velocity is proportional to
A. Hydraulic gradient.
B. Square of hydraulic gradient.
C. Square root of hydraulic gradient.
D. Reciprocal of hydraulic gradient.

34. Which of the following types of coal has maximum ash content (%)?
A. Anthracite
B. Sub-Bituminous
C. Lignite
D. High volatile Bituminous

35. Given below are two statements. One labelled as Assertion (A) and the other labelled as Reason (R):
Assertion (A): The amount of energy available in a single fusion event is small compared to a fission event.
Reason (R) : Isotopes of hydrogen are much lighter than uranium.
Choose the correct answer:
A. Both (A) and (R) are correct and (R) is the correct explanation of (A).
B. Both (A) and (R) are correct and (R) is not the correct explanation of (A).
C. (A) is true, but (R) is false.
D. (A) is false and (R) is true.

36. Given below are two statements. One labelled as Assertion (A) and the other labelled as Reason (R):
Assertion (A): The thermal efficiency of nuclear reactors is lower than that of fossil fuelled steam plants.
Reason (R) : Temperature of water generating stream in a nuclear reactor has relatively lower values compared to fossil fuelled steam plants.
Choose the correct answer:
A. Both (A) and (R) are correct and (R) is the correct explanation of (A).
B. Both (A) and (R) are correct and (R) is not the correct explanation of (A).
C. (A) is true, but (R) is false.
D. (A) is false and (R) is true.

37. Given below are two statements. One labelled as Assertion (A) and the other labelled as Reason (R):
Assertion (A): Natural gas contributes less to smog formation than gasoline.
Reason (R) : Unburnt CH_4 molecules are considerably less reactive with respect to the free radical chemistry for smog than the hydrocarbon molecules with more than one C atom.
Choose the correct answer:
A. Both (A) and (R) are correct and (R) is the correct explanation of (A).
B. Both (A) and (R) are correct and (R) is not the correct explanation of (A).
C. (A) is true, but (R) is false.
D. (A) is false and (R) is true.

38. Consider ocean waves of amplitude 2.0 m and wavelength 200 m. Assuming the gravity to be the only active force, the power available per metre perpendicular to the propagation of the wave is
A. 86.24 kW m^{-1}
B. 172.48 kW m^{-1}
C. 344.90 kW m^{-1}
D. 800.00 kW m^{-1}

39. A wind mill has cross-sectional area 25.0 m^2. The wind speed is 6.0 m/s. What will be the power generated by the wind mill in the Betz limit?
A. ~ 2.064 kW
B. ~ 3.483 kW
C. ~ 11.162 kW
D. ~ 18.321 kW

40. Given below are two statements. One labelled as Assertion (A) and the other labelled as Reason (R):

Assertion (A): The power output from an OTEC system installed at a tropical site is steady.

Reason (R) : At tropical sites, the temperatures of warm surface water and cold water in the depth of ocean hardly vary from season to season.

Choose the correct answer:

A. Both (A) and (R) are correct and (R) is the correct explanation of (A).
B. Both (A) and (R) are correct and (R) is not the correct explanation of (A).
C. (A) is true, but (R) is false.
D. (A) is false and (R) is true.

41. An electric power plant based on solar energy uses collectors with concentrators which can achieve temperature of about 700 °C to operate a heat engine to generate electricity. If the solar insolation is 1 kW/m^2, how much total collector area will be required to supply on average 10 MW of electricity? (Take ambient air temperature to be 25 °C)

A. $5.15 \times 10^3\ m^2$ B. $1.44 \times 10^3\ m^2$
C. $3.18 \times 10^3\ m^2$ D. $10.61 \times 10^3\ m^2$

42. The potency factor of $CHCl_3$ is 6.1×10^{-3} kg-day/mg. The concentration in drinking water that would result in 2×10^{-6} risk for a 70-kg man, who drinks 2L/day throughout of his life, is

A. 11.4 μg/L B. 20.6 μg/L
C. 6 μg/L D. 25 μg/L

43. Which of the following compounds used for disinfection of water is not stable but is prepared *in situ?*

A. Cl_2 B. $Ca(OCl)_2$
C. NaOC*l* D. HOC*l*

44. Identify the incorrect statement from the following regarding soil pollution by heavy metals:

A. Soils act as a sink for heavy metals.
B. Humic materials have great affinity for heavy metal cations.
C. Humic materials extract heavy metals from soil water by forming complexes.
D. Complexes formed by humic acids are normally water soluble.

45. A point source of noise produces a sound of 60 dB at a distance of 10 m from it. If the sound is measured at a distance of 40 m, what will be its value?

A. 48 dB B. 54 dB
C. 57 dB D. 44 dB

46. Identify the incorrect statement with regard to water purification by coagulation.

A. Particles suspended in water are in colloidal form.
B. Suspended particles carry a positive charge.
C. Suspended particles due to similar charge repel each other.
D. When alum is added it works as a coagulant.

47. In relation to drinking water source without conventional treatment but after disinfection, water parameters and their permissible values are given in the lists given below:

Match the List–I and List–II. Identify the correct answer from the codes given below:

List–I (Water parameters)	*List–II (Permissible values)*
(*a*) Total coliform organism MPN per 100 ml	1. 6.5 – 8.5
(*b*) pH	2. < 50 per 100 mL
(*c*) DO	3. 2 mg/L or less
(*d*) BOD (5 days, 20 °C)	4. 6 mg/L or more

Codes:

	(*a*)	(*b*)	(*c*)	(*d*)
A.	2	1	4	3
B.	2	1	3	4
C.	3	4	2	1
D.	4	2	3	1

48. Given below are two statements. One labelled as Assertion (A) and the other labelled as Reason (R):

Assertion (A) : Ozone depletion is much less over arctic stratosphere than over Antarctic stratosphere.

Reason (R) : Antarctic atmosphere is on an average about 10 °C cooler than the arctic stratosphere.

Choose the correct answer:

A. Both (A) and (R) are correct and (R) is the correct explanation of (A).

B. Both (A) and (R) are correct and (R) is not the correct explanation of (A).

C. (A) is true, but (R) is false.

D. (A) is false and (R) is true.

49. Match the List–I and List–II. Identify the correct answer from the codes given below:

List–I ***(Water type)***	***List–II*** ***(Conductivity*** ***($\mu S\ cm^{-1}$))***
(*a*) Fresh water	1. > 500
(*b*) Clean tap water	2. < 300
(*c*) Clean upland river	3. 60 – 100
(*d*) Organically enriched river	4. 2 – 4

Codes:

	(*a*)	(*b*)	(*c*)	(*d*)
A.	4	3	2	1
B.	1	4	3	2
C.	2	1	4	3
D.	3	2	1	4

50. Match the List–I and List–II. Identify the correct answer from the codes given below :

List–I ***(Auditing types)***	***List–II*** ***(Set of terms)***
(*a*) Implementation audit	1. External review of the procedures used
(*b*) Performance audit	2. Compare actual with predicted impacts
(*c*) Project impact audit	3. To cover full operation
(*d*) Procedures audit	4. To cover a start-up

Codes:

	(*a*)	(*b*)	(*c*)	(*d*)
A.	3	4	1	2
B.	4	3	2	1
C.	1	2	3	4
D.	2	3	4	1

51. Given below are two statements. One labelled as Assertion (A) and the other labelled as Reason (R):

Assertion (A) : The ecological restoration is a difficult proposition both in principle and in practice.

Reason (R) : Identity and population sizes of plants and animals once present at a particular site are largely unknown.

Choose the correct answer:

A. Both (A) and (R) are correct and (R) is the correct explanation of (A).

B. Both (A) and (R) are correct and (R) is not the correct explanation of (A).

C. (A) is true, but (R) is false.

D. (A) is false and (R) is true.

52. During the EIA process under the EIA notification of September 14, 2006, no public hearing is required for

(*a*) all A′ category projects

(*b*) all 'B_1' category projects

(*c*) all 'B_2' category projects

Choose the correct code:

A. (*a*) only B. (*a*) and (*b*) only

C. (*b*) and (*c*) only D. (*c*) only

53. Given below are two statements. One labelled as Assertion (A) and the other labelled as Reason (R):

Assertion (A) : Evaporation of surface water is reduced due to black carbon in atmosphere.

Reason (R) : Presence of aerosols having black carbon is responsible for dimming effect.

Choose the correct answer:

A. Both (A) and (R) are correct and (R) is the correct explanation of (A).

B. Both (A) and (R) are correct and (R) is not the correct explanation of (A).
C. (A) is true, but (R) is false.
D. (A) is false and (R) is true.

54. Match the List–I and List–II. Identify the correct answer from the codes given below:

List–I (Methods)	*List–II (Description)*
(*a*) Network Method	1. Possible impacts by composite environmental parameters.
(*b*) Overlays Method	2. Structured approaches by involving scaling-weighing techniques.
(*c*) Checklists Method	3. Environmental systems as a complex web of relationships.
(*d*) Adhoc Method	4. Spatial distribution of environmental impacts using GIS.

Codes:

	(*a*)	(*b*)	(*c*)	(*d*)
A.	4	3	2	1
B.	1	2	3	4
C.	4	1	3	2
D.	3	4	2	1

55. In environmental Impact Assessment, the baseline studies describe the
A. socio-economic mapping of the area.
B. consequences of the development activity.
C. assessment of the risk involved during project implementation.
D. environmental setting existing in the project area.

56. An ecosystem restoration project should have the outcomes which are
I. Specific
II. Measurable
III. General
IV. Realistic
V. Time bound
Choose the correct code:
A. I, II, III, V B. I, II, IV, V
C. II, III, IV, V D. I, II, III, IV

57. When applied to field populations, Lotka-Volterra equations suffer from the following:
I. Competition coefficients are assumed to be constant.
II. Carrying capacity is assumed to be constant.
III. There are no time lags.
IV. Maximal rate of increase is assumed to be constant.
Choose the correct answer:
A. I and II only B. II and III only
C. II, III and IV only D. I, II, III and IV

58. In a city, the daily per capita inhalation (m^3) values of contaminated air over a period of 5 days are 6.3, 6.3, 6.2, 6.4 and 5.8, respectively. The sample mean with standard deviation of the data is
A. 6.2 ± 0.02 B. 6.2 ± 0.23
C. 6.0 ± 0.15 D. 6.2 ± 0.18

59. The population (N) of fish in a pond follows the logistic equation $\frac{dN}{dt} = 0.1\,N - 0.001\,N^2$.
What is the maximum sustainable yield?
A. 100 B. 50
C. 25 D. 200

60. Given below are two statements. One labelled as Assertion (A) and the other labelled as Reason (R):
Assertion (A): For power stations and polluting industries, tall stacks are installed.
Reason (R) : The maximum ground level concentration of a pollutant released from a stack is inversely proportion to the height of the stack.
Choose the correct answer:
A. Both (A) and (R) are correct and (R) is the correct explanation of (A).
B. Both (A) and (R) are correct and (R) is not the correct explanation of (A).
C. (A) is true, but (R) is false.
D. (A) is false and (R) is true.

61. Consider a box model for an airshed over a city and assume that the initial concentration of a pollutant is zero and that the air entering the box is clean. If the length of the box is 10 km and the wind speed along the length of the box is 5 m/s, what is the time taken for the pollutant concentration to reach ~ 95% of its final value?
A. 1 h 40 minutes
B. 1 h 7 minutes
C. 33 minutes 20 seconds
D. 2 h 13 minutes 20 seconds

62. For a sample size $n = 16$, the mean $(\overline{X})$ value and standard deviation (S) are found to be 5.667 and 0.934, respectively. If the population mean is $\mu = 5.2$, then t – statistic is
A. 0.5 B. 0.47
C. 1.76 D. 2.0

63. Which of the following are sources of the greenhouse gas methane (CH_4)?
(*a*) Coal mining areas
(*b*) Ruminants
(*c*) Wetlands
(*d*) Low land paddy
Choose the correct answer:
A. (*a*), (*b*) and (*c*) only
B. (*b*) and (*c*) only
C. (*b*), (*c*) and (*d*) only
D. (*a*), (*b*), (*c*) and (*d*)

64. Which of the following convention/protocols/ treaties is legally binding on the signatory countries?
A. Basel Convention B. Montreal Protocol
C. Kyoto Protocol D. Paris Agreement

65. For untreated municipal wastewater, BOD/ COD ratio is in the range
A. 1.3 – 3 B. 0.3 – 0.8
C. 3.0 – 6.5 D. > 10

66. Organic wetland soils have
I. High porosity
II. Low density
III. High Ion exchange capacity
IV. Low nutrient availability
Choose the right answer:
A. I, II, III, IV B. II, III, IV only
C. III, IV only D. I, II only

67. Consider following statements about the ozone hole?
I. Ozone formation and destruction keeps on happening.
II. Ozone destruction rate is higher than its formation rate.
III. Ozone destruction rate is equal to its formation rate.
Choose the correct answer:
A. I only B. I and II only
C. I and III only D. III only

68. Consider following statements about an estuary:
I. Estuary is the ecotonal region between fresh water and oceanic water.
II. This area is highly productive.
III. This area is highly unproductive.
Choose the correct answer:
A. I only B. I and II only
C. III only D. I and III only

69. The ionic species, O^+, O_2^+ and N_2^+ are found generally in
A. Troposphere B. Stratosphere
C. Mesosphere D. Heterosphere

70. As part of recently signed international agreement on phasing out synthetic hydrofluorocarbons (HFCs), India will start phasing them out from the year
A. 2019 B. 2024
C. 2028 D. 2032

71. In the tropospheric ozone formation reaction sequence, which of the following chemical species does not act as a catalyst?
A. OH B. HO_2
C. NO_2 D. O_2

72. Which of the following are useful indicators of pollution potential of organic effluents?
(*a*) Total Organic Carbon (TOC)
(*b*) Biological Oxygen Demand (BOD)
(*c*) Turbidity
(*d*) Conductivity

Choose the correct code:
A. (*a*) and (*b*) only B. (*a*) and (*c*) only
C. (*b*) and (*d*) only D. (*a*), (*b*), (*c*) and (*d*)

73. Which of the following power plants releases radioactive materials as well as hazardous metals such as lead and arsenic under normal operating conditions?
A. Nuclear power plant
B. Solar power installations
C. Hydro power
D. Coal based thermal power plants

74. Match the List-I and List-II. Identify the correct answer from the codes given below :

List–I (Convention)	***List–II (Purpose)***
(*a*) Paris Convention 1992	1. Transboundary Movement of Waste
(*b*) Vienna Convention 1985	2. Protection of Marine Environment
(*c*) Bamako Convention 1998	3. Protection of ozone layer
(*d*) Basel Convention 1992	4. Ban on import of hazardous waste to Africa

Codes:

	(*a*)	(*b*)	(*c*)	(*d*)
A.	2	3	4	1
B.	3	4	1	2
C.	4	1	2	3
D.	1	2	3	4

75. Match the List-I and List-II. Identify the correct answer from the codes given below:

List–I (Colour Codes)	***List–II (Hospital Wastes)***
(*a*) Yellow Bags	1. Infected metal sharps
(*b*) Red Bags	2. Outdated Medicine bottles
(*c*) Blue Bags	3. Used Catheters
(*d*) Black Carboy	4. Infectious waste placenta

Codes:

	(*a*)	(*b*)	(*c*)	(*d*)
A.	4	3	2	1
B.	3	2	1	4
C.	2	1	4	3
D.	1	4	3	2

ANSWERS

1	**2**	**3**	**4**	**5**	**6**	**7**	**8**	**9**	**10**
A	*	A	D	C	C	B	A	D	A
11	**12**	**13**	**14**	**15**	**16**	**17**	**18**	**19**	**20**
C	D	D	*	D	B	A	D	A	B
21	**22**	**23**	**24**	**25**	**26**	**27**	**28**	**29**	**30**
B	B	B	D	C	C	C	A	C	A
31	**32**	**33**	**34**	**35**	**36**	**37**	**38**	**39**	**40**
A	A	A	C	B	A	A	B	A	A
41	**42**	**43**	**44**	**45**	**46**	**47**	**48**	**49**	**50**
*	A	D	D	A	B	A	C	A	B
51	**52**	**53**	**54**	**55**	**56**	**57**	**58**	**59**	**60**
B	D	A	D	D	B	D	B	B	C
61	**62**	**63**	**64**	**65**	**66**	**67**	**68**	**69**	**70**
A	D	D	B	B	A	B	B	D	C
71	**72**	**73**	**74**	**75**					
D	A	D	A	A					

* *Error in Questions.*

EXPLANATORY ANSWERS

1. Mesoscale meteorology is the study of weather systems smaller than synoptic scale systems but larger than microscale and storm-scale cumulus systems. Horizontal dimensions generally range from around 5 km to several hundred kilometers. Examples of mesoscale weather systems are sea breezes, squall lines, and mesoscale convective complexes.

Vertical velocity often equals or exceeds horizontal velocities in mesoscale meteorological systems due to nonhydrostatic processes such as buoyant acceleration of a rising thermal or acceleration through a narrow mountain pass.

2. The geostrophic wind speed is a function of latitude, pressure gradient and air density. Hence, assertion is false.

The geostrophic wind is a theoretical wind calculated from surface pressure data. A balance is assumed between the flow of air from high to low pressure regions and the effects of the rotation of the Earth as manifested in the "Coriolis Effect". The geostrophic wind flows parallel to the isobars, and a good approximation to the actual wind in the free atmosphere.

The geostrophic wind is the horizontal equilibrium wind (V_G), blowing parallel to the isobars, which represents the exact balance between the horizontal pressure gradient force:

$$-\left(\frac{1}{\rho}\right)\Delta_H p$$

and the horizontal component of the Coriolis Force:

$$fV_G$$

where $\Delta_H p$ is the horizontal pressure gradient, ρ is the air density, and f is the Coriolis parameter.

3. Mixing height (also called mixing depth) is the height above ground level through which relatively vigorous vertical mixing occurs. Low mixing heights mean that the air is generally stagnant with very little vertical motion; pollutants usually are trapped near the ground surface. High mixing heights allow vertical mixing within a deep layer of the atmosphere and good dispersion of pollutants. Mixing heights usually are lowest late at night or early morning and highest during mid to late afternoon. This daily pattern often causes smoke to be concentrated in basins and valleys during the morning and dispersed aloft in the afternoon. Average night mixing heights range from 300 m (~980 ft) to over 900 m (~2,900 ft) above ground level. The highest morning mixing heights occur in coastal areas that are influenced by moist marine air and cloudiness that inhibit radiation cooling at night.

4. Lapse rate, $\dfrac{\Delta T}{\Delta Z} = \dfrac{T_2 - T_1}{Z_2 - Z_1}$

$$\frac{1.25}{100} = \frac{T_2 - 15°C}{200 - 25}$$

$$\frac{1.25}{100} = \frac{T_2 - 15}{175}$$

$$T_2 - 15 = \frac{1.25 \times 175}{100}$$

$$T_2 - 15 = 2.1875$$

$$T_2 = 15 + 2.1875$$

$$\Rightarrow \quad T_2 = 17.1875°.$$

5. Unstable Atmosphere : If the temperature of the atmosphere falls at a rate greater than Γ, the lapse rate is said to be *superadiabatic,* and the atmosphere is unstable. Using Figure, we can see that this is so. The actual lapse rate is shown by the solid line. If we capture a balloon full of polluted air at elevation A and adiabatically displace it 100 m vertically to elevation B, the temperature of the air inside the balloon will decrease from 21.15° to 20.15°C. At a lapse rate of –1.25°C/100 m, the temperature of the air outside the balloon will decrease from 21.15° to 19.90°C. The air inside the balloon will be warmer than the air outside; this temperature difference gives the balloon buoyancy. It will behave as a hot gas and continue to rise without any further mechanical effort. Thus, mechanical turbulence is enhanced and the atmosphere is unstable. If we adiabatically displace the balloon downward to elevation C, the temperature inside the balloon would rise at the rate of the dry adiabat. Thus, in moving 100 m, the temperature will increase from 21.15° to 22.15°C. The temperature outside the balloon will increase at the superadiabatic lapse rate to 22.40°C. The air in the balloon will be cooler than the ambient air and the balloon will have a tendency to sink. Again, mechanical turbulence (displacement) is enhanced.

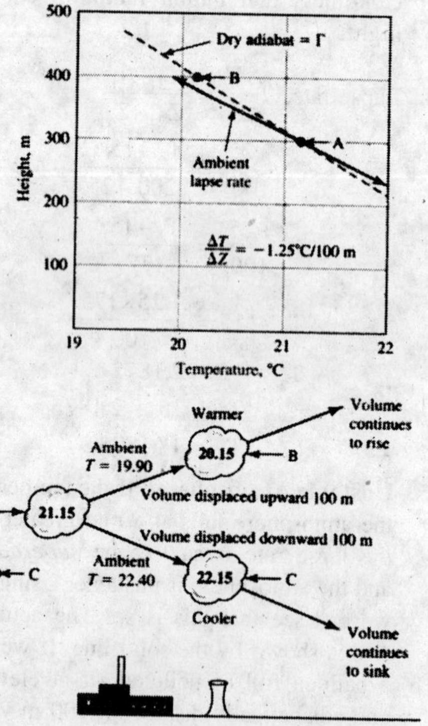

Fig. : *Unstable atmosphere*

6. The photosynthetic fixation rate of atmospheric carbon dioxide is called gross primary productivity (GPP). Net primary productivity (NPP) is the net rate of carbon gain after respiration losses (R). This can be expressed as: NPP = GPP – R. Net production, which accumulates as biological mass in plant organs over time, is referred to as biomass and can be expressed in terms of dry weight (g) or energy content (kcal). The overall photosynthetic efficiency of plants, measured as the amount of solar energy available to them that they actually covert to biomass is typically about 1% or less.

7. The hydroxyl radical (OH) is one of the most important of the trace species in the troposphere, even though its globally averaged concentration is only a few tenths of a pptv (~10^{12} OH m^{-3}; or 3OH per 10^{13} air molecules). The hydroxyl radical is produced by the high-energy photodissociation of ozone:

$O_3 + h\nu \rightarrow O_2 + O(^1D)$ ($\lambda < 320$ nm)

Here, $O(^1D)$ is an excited state of the oxygen atom. We should know that the stratospheric ozone layer absorbs almost all photons with wavelengths less than ~300 nm, steadily decreasing amounts of radiation up to ~330 nm.

8. By convention, the groups in the periodic tables are assigned certain names:

- group 1 – "alkali metals"
- group 2 – "alkaline earth metals"
- group 3 to 12 – "transition metals"
- group 13 – "boron group elements"
- group 14 – "carbon group elements"
- group 15 – "pnictogens"
- group 16 – "chalcogens"
- group 17 – "halogens"
- group 18 – "noble gases".

9. (*i*) Carbon-13 isotope, is less common in vegetation or fossil fuels formed from long-dead vegetation and is more abundant in carbon found in the oceans and in volcanic or geothermal emissions.

(*ii*) C-12 for the most common carbon isotope and C-14 for the rare isotope.

(*iii*) C-14 is absent in fossil fuels.

(*iv*) C-13 is not used for carbon-dating.

10. Aldicarb : Technically pure aldicarb is a white crystal, and sparingly miscible in water and most organic solvents. For instance, the solubility of aldicarb in acetone is 34%, in ethanol 25%, and in toluene 10%. Aldicarb is extremely toxic to animals. The acute oral and dermal LD_{50} value for rat is 0.6 to 0.8 mg/kg and 2.5 to 3.0 mg/kg respectively. The female rat is more sensitive than the male rat.

11. Given that, $[H^+] = 5 \times 10^{-4}$ mol/L

and from $K_w = [H^+][OH^-]$

where K_w is the dissociation constant for water

At 25°C, $K_w = 1 \times 10^{-14}$

$$1 \times 10^{-14} = 5 \times 10^{-4} \times [OH^-]$$

$$[OH^-] = \frac{1\times10^{-14}}{5\times10^{-4}}$$

$$= 2 \times 10^{-11} \text{ mol/L}$$

13. Effluent : The mobile phase that exits the column.

Eluate : The solute-mobile phase mixture which exits the column.

Eluent : Another word for the mobile phase.

Eluite : The eluted solute.

Elute : The use of elution chromatography.

Elution : The passing of mobile phase through the chromatographic bed to transport solutes.

15. Characteristics of Successful Invasive Plant Species : Rapid growth and early flowering. • Able to cope with a range of nutritional conditions. • High phenotypic plasticity. • Different growth forms depending on the ecosystem type. • Large numbers of seeds produced that are easily dispersed. • Seed set in a wide range of temperatures and photo-periods. • Germination "polymorphisms" (*i.e.*, some germinate early, some late).

16.

Antimicrobial action	Examples of antibiotics
Antimetabolites interrupt metabolic pathways causing death, such as blocking nucleic acid synthesis	Sulphonamides
Cell wall agents prevent formation of cross-linking in cell walls so bacteria are killed by lysis (bursting)	Beta-lactams, *e.g.*, penicillins, glycopeptides
Cell membrane agents damage the cell membrane, so metabolites leak out or water moves in, killing the bacteria	Some penicillins, cephalosporins
Protein synthesis inhibitors interrupt or prevent transcription and/or translation of microbial genes, so protein production is affected	Tetracyclines, chloramphenicol
DNA gyrase inhibitors stop bacterial DNA coiling up so it no longer fits within the bacterium	Quinolone

17. El Nino is a climate cycle in the Pacific Ocean with a global impact on weather patterns. The cycle begins when warm water in the western tropical Pacific Ocean shifts eastward along the equator toward the coast of South America. Normally, this warm water pools near Indonesia and the Philippines. As a result of El Nino, it has been observed that phyto-plankton productivity increases in Eastern Indian Ocean around Indonesia and Gulf of Mexico. This increase is probably because of increase in rainfall and more nutrient inflow.

18. Vermicompost is the product of the composting process using various species of worms, usually red wigglers, white worms, and other earthworms, to create a heterogeneous mixture of decomposing vegetable or food waste, bedding materials, and vermicast. This process of producing vermicompost is called vermicomposting. Vermicast (also called worm castings, worm humus or worm manure) is the end-product of the breakdown of organic matter by an earthworm. These castings have been shown to contain reduced levels of contaminants and a higher saturation of nutrients than do organic materials before vermicomposting. Vermicompost contains water-soluble nutrients and is an excellent, nutrient-rich organic fertilizer and soil conditioner. It is used in farming and small scale sustainable, organic farming.

19. Photosynthesis in green plants results in the conversion of simple substances like CO_2 and H_2O into an enormously complex organism. There is a very large decrease in entropy associated with the growth of a plant, but it comes at the expense of an enormous increase in entropy in the Sun to produce the light that is essential for photosynthesis to occur. It is a pessimistic but accurate view that anything we do will always add to the disorder of the universe.

20. Aerobiology is a branch of science which studies these airborne bio-particles with respect to their source, take off, dispersal, deposition and their effect on other organisms. Pollen grains and fungal spores form an important constituent of airspora (airborne spores) all over the world. The atmosphere also contains an incredible diversity of pollen grains and fungal spores and they are very light weight. Pollen grains are amongst the earliest known aeroallergens and are found to be the major cause of bronchial asthma and allergic rhinitis. Seasonal pollen grains and fungal spores are the most predominant allergens in the air.

21. In biology, altruism refers to behaviour by an individual that increases the fitness of another individual while decreasing the fitness of the actor. Altruism in this sense is different from the philosophical concept of altruism, in which an action would only be called "altruistic" if it was done with the conscious intention of helping another. In the behavioural sense, there is no such requirement. As such, it is not evaluated in moral terms—it is the consequences of an action for reproductive fitness that determine whether the action is considered altruistic, not the intentions, if any, with which the action is performed.

22. Edge effects were seen in the majority of species; however, the magnitude of these effects was influenced by the ecotone type. At the assemblage level, more species avoided edges in the ecotone with tree plantations compared with open habitats. The effect of edges on the calculated habitat suitability was either positive or negative, depending on the function that best described the response of the species to edges and whether they avoided edges or penetrated into the less-preferred habitat. In general, forest species penetrated deeper into tree plantations but moved only short distances into open habitats.

23. **Allogenic succession** is definded as the changes in species composition that are imposed by factors external to the biotic community. Physical factors, which produce allogenic succession, such as fire, wind, snow-storm, flood, landslide, or changes induced by climate change. These processes are controlled by forces external to the ecosystem in question and they cause ecosystem disturbance—they alter the rates and patterns of ecosystem change expected from autogenic succession.

24. In the boreal forests, tree stands, mosses and dwarf shrubs produce the majority of the litterfall, which becomes a component of humus as it decomposes.

25. The term cyclomorphosis has been applied to the cyclic morphological changes that supposedly occur with fairly strict seasonality in certain freshwater plankton. Seasonal changes in the morphology within populations involve the alternation of different morphs in time. Forms with external protuberances *e.g.,* helmets, crests, peaks of the head, humps or spikes of the carapace, spines, elongation of the antennules, usually alternate with forms lacking these exuberances. Cyclomorphosis has been reported for some planktonic algae, rotifers and crustaceans. It ensure adaptive significance and changes in environmental variables of water.

26. A **biofilm** is any group of microorganisms in which cells stick to each other and often these cells adhere to a surface. These adherent cells are frequently embedded within a self-produced matrix of extracellular polymeric substance (EPS). Microbes form a biofilm in response to many factors, which may include cellular recognition of specific or non-specific attachment sites on a surface, nutritional cues, or in some cases, by exposure of planktonic cells to sub-inhibitory concentrations of antibiotics. When a cell switches to the biofilm mode of growth, it undergoes a phenotypic shift in behaviour in which large suites of genes are differentially regulated.

27. Rhyolitic magma has the greatest silica content, with silica making up about 70 per cent of the magma. Basaltic and andesitic magma have lower silica contents at 50 per cent and 60 per cent, respectively.

Magma with a higher silica content is more viscous, meaning it is thicker and doesn't flow as easily. The more explosive volcanic eruptions are caused by this more viscous magma, which means that rhyolitic magma causes the most explosive eruptions.

Rhyolitic magma contributes to the explosive character of siliceous lava flows and lava domes. The Vulcanian and Plinian types of volcanic eruptions feature rhyolitic magma. Eruptions involving rhyolitic magma produce obsidian and pumice rocks, and rhyolitic volcanoes are typically cinder cone volcanoes.

29. Stream flow or discharge is the volume of water that moves through a specific point in a stream during a given period of time. Discharge is usually measured in units of cubic feet per second (cfs). To determine discharge, a cross-sectional area of the stream or river is measured. Then, the velocity of the stream is measured using a Flow Rate Sensor.

Flow velocity is influenced by the slope of the surrounding terrain, the depth of the stream, the width of the stream, and the roughness of the substrate or stream bottom.

Factors Influencing Flow Velocity:

- Depth of stream channel
- Width of stream channel
- Roughness of stream bottom
- Slope or incline of surrounding terrain

30. Rivers are part of the hydrological cycle. Water generally collects in a river from precipitation through a drainage basin from surface runoff and other sources such as groundwater recharge, springs, and the release of stored water in natural ice and snowpacks (*e.g.*, from glaciers). Potamology is the scientific study of rivers while limnology is the study of inland waters in general. A river begins at a source (or more often several sources), follows a path called a course, and ends at a mouth or mouths. The water in a river is usually confined to a channel, made up of a stream bed between banks. Head water has the highest erosion rate in the journey of a river.

31. Abrasives are hard substances capable of wearing down soft surfaces by cutting, grinding or polishing action. Some of the commonly used abrasives include diamond, quartz, emery, corundum, carborundum, alundum and boron carbide in the form of powder, paste, sheet, or wheel. The most important property of abrasives is their hardness usually measured in Moh's scale or Vicker's scale. Diamond is rated as the hardest substance with a maximum value of 10 on the Moh's scale. Others in the decreasing order of hardness include corundum. (9) topaz or emery, (8) quartz, (7) feldspar, (6) apatite, (5) fluorite, (4) calcite, (3) gypsum (2) and talc, (1).

32. Wind transport encompasses four processes—saltation, reptation, suspension, and creep (Figure):

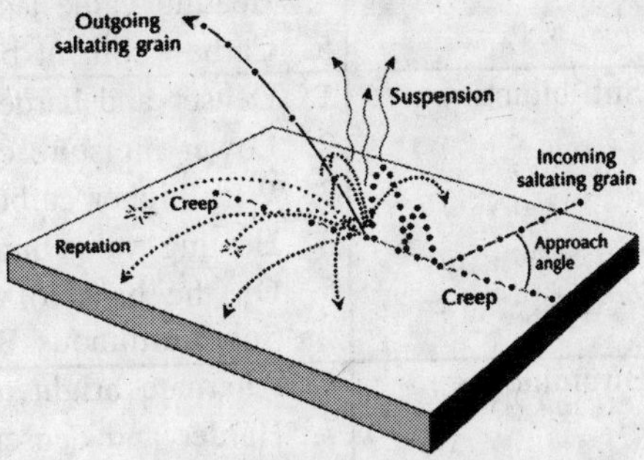

Fig. : *Modes of grain transport by wind.*

1. **Saltation :** Sand grains bound, land, and rebound, imparting, renewed impetus to other sand grains. Such motion is confined to short distances and heights of about 2 m.
2. **Reptation :** On hitting the surface, saltating grains release a small splash-like shower of particles that make small hops from the point of impact. This process is reptation.

3. **Suspension :** Particles of silt and clay lifted into the atmosphere become suspended and may be carried great distances. Sand particles may be lifted into the lower layers of the atmosphere, as in sandstorms, but will fall out near the point of takeoff. Dust particles may be carried around the globe. Dust storms may carry 100 million tonnes of material for thousands of kilometres. A dramatic dust storm, which carried in estimated 2 million tonnes of dust, engulfed Melbourne, Australia, on 8 February 1983.
4. **Creep** and related near-surface activity. Coarse sand and small pebbles inch forward by rolling and sliding with the momentum gained from the impact of jumping sand particles and down the tiny craterslopes produced by an impacting particle.

33. The rates and direction of flow between two points are described by Darcy's law, or

$$Q = -KA\ (dh/dL)$$

where Q is the rate of flow through the media, K is the hydraulic conductivity of the material, A is the total cross-sectional area of the porous medial including both pores and particles, h is the head, and L is the length of the porous media. According to Darcy's law, the rate of ground water movement is proportional to the hydraulic gradient, dh/dL. The proportionality factor, K, is known as the hydraulic conductivity. High values of hydraulic conductivity mean that the material readily transmits water. Among other things, hydraulic conductivity depends on the size, shape, and connectivity of pores and fractures in the aquifer.

34. Characteristics of the Different Ranks of Coals

Rank (from lowest to highest)	*Properties*
Lignite	1. The lowest rank of coal that has been transformed into a brown-black coal from peat. 2. Contains recognizable plant structures. 3. Excessive moisture (25%–50%). 4. Heating value less than 8300 BTU/lb on a mineral matter free basis. 5. Carbon content between 60% and 70% on a dry ash-free basis.
Sub-bituminous	1. Denser and harder than lignite. 2. Lower moisture content (12%-25%). 3. With higher carbon content (71%-77%) on dry ash-free basis. 4. Heating value much higher than lignite or sub-bituminous coal. 5. On the basis of hating value, it is subdivided into sub-bituminous A. Sub-bituminous B. and sub-bituminous C ranks.
Bituminous	1. Alternate bright and dull bandings. 2. Harder and denser than sub-bituminous coal. 3. Carbon content between 77% and 87% on dry ash-free basis. 4. Heating value much higher than lignite or sub-bituminous coal. 5. On the basis of volatile content, bituminous, coals are subdivided into low volatile bituminous, medium volatile bituminous, and high volatile bituminous.
Anthracite	1. Anthracite is the highest rank of coal. 2. Carbon content over 87% on dry ash-free basis. 3. Anthracite coal generally has the highest heating value per ton on a mineral matter free basis. 4. It is often subdivided into semi-anthracite, anthracite, and meta-anthracite on the basis of carbon content.

37. Natural gas is formed in the earth's crust as a result of transformation of organic matter due to heat and pressure of overlying rock. Natural gas mainly consists of saturated aliphatic hydrocarbons like methane. Components such as carbon dioxide, hydrogen sulphide, nitrogen and helium constitute an insignificant proportion of natural gas composition. Natural gas is the cleanest of all fossil fuels and the main products of combustion of natural gas are carbon dioxide and water vapour. The combustion of natural gas releases very small amounts of nitrogen oxides (NOx), sulphur dioxide (SO_2), carbon dioxide (CO_2), carbon monoxide (CO), other reactive hydrocarbons and virtually no particulate matter.

Natural gas contributes less to smog formation than gasoline. Unburnt CH_4 molecules are considerably less reactive with respect to the free radical chemistry for smog than the hydrocarbon molecules with more than one C atom.

Natural gas can be used in many ways to help reduce the emissions of pollutants into the atmosphere as it emits fewer harmful pollutants and an increased reliance on natural gas can potentially reduce the emission of many of these harmful pollutants.

39. Power generated by the wind in the Betz limit

$$= A \times (V)^3 \times 38\%$$

$$= 25 \times (6)^3 \times \frac{38}{100} \approx 2.064 \text{ kW}.$$

40. Ocean thermal energy conversion (OTEC) uses the temperature difference between cooler deep and warmer shallow or surface seawaters to run a heat engine and produce useful work, usually in the form of electricity. OTEC is a base load electricity generation system.

Among ocean energy sources, OTEC is one of the continuously available renewable energy resources that could contribute to base-load power supply. At tropical sites, the temperatures of warm surface water and cold water in the depth of ocean hardly vary from season to season, and the power output from an OTEC system installed at a tropical site is steady.

43. Disinfection of water:

$$Cl_2 + H_2O \rightleftarrows HCl + HOCl$$

$$HOCl \rightleftarrows H^+ + OCl^-$$

The hypochlorous acid (HOCl) and hypochlorite ions (OCl^-) are responsible for the disinfection of water. The action of chlorine is directly proportional to the pH value of water. At high pH value, say above 8.50, chlorine is not a suitable bacterial removal. Disinfection is rapid when pH of water is below 7.0. Chlorine is applied for disinfection as free chlorine, chloramines and bleaching powder.

The term free chlorine is used to indicate the sum of hypochlorous acid, hypochlorite ions and molecular chlorine existing in a sample of water. Free chlorine is available in gaseous or liquid forms. Chlorine is not stable in water, but when it is mixed in water with ammonia, stable compounds known as chloramines are formed. These compounds have adequate and good disinfecting properties and especially used for disinfecting swimming pools. They also remove odour from water to some extent.

46. The process of chemically neutralizing the negative charge on colloidal matter in waste waters to form small floc particles is called "coagulation." Most colloidal suspended matter in water carries a negative charge by nature. It can consist of emulsified oil particles, solid particles, dirt, metal fines, or biological particles. These particles will not settle until this charge is neutralized. Water treatment polymers that carry a positive charge and low molecular weight (coagulants) can be added to the water to neutralize the colloidal charges.

47. Surface water quality classes used in India

Class	*Criteria*
A	1. Total coliform organisms MPN/100 ml shall be 50 or less. 2. pH between 6.5 and 8.5 3. Dissolved oxygen 6 mg/L or more. 4. BOD 5 days 20°C 2 mg/L or less.

B
1. Total coliform organisms MPN/100 ml 500 or less.
2. pH between 6.5 and 8.5.
3. Dissolved oxygen 5 mg/L or more.
4. BOD 5 days 20°C 3 mg/L or less.

C
1. Total coliform organisms MPN/100 mL 5000 or less.
2. pH between 6 and 9.
3. Dissolved oxygen 4 mg/L or more.
4. BOD 5 days 20°c 3 mg/L or less

D
1. pH between 6.5 and 8.5.
2. Dissolved oxygen 4 mg/L or more.
3. Free ammonia (as N) 1.2 mg/L or less.

E
1. pH between 6.0 and 8.5.
2. Electrical conductivity at 25°C μmhos/cm Max. 2250.
3. Sodium absorption ratio max. 26
4. Boron max. 2 mg/L.

Below-E : Not meeting A, B, C, D & E criteria.

Note : Class A is suitable for drinking water without conventional treatment but after disinfection.

Class B suitable for outdoor bathing (organized).

Class C suitable for drinking water after conventional treatment and disinfection.

Class D suitable for propagation of wild life and fisheries.

Class E suitable for irrigation, industrial cooling controlled waste disposal.

48. Ozone depletion occurs in the Arctic stratosphere, but much less than over Antarctica. The Arctic winter stratosphere has fewer and shorter-lived stratospheric clouds than the Antarctic stratosphere. Thus, assertion is true. The winter Antarctic stratosphere is on the average more than 10 K colder than the Arctic stratosphere, the Antarctic polar vortex lasts longer, and the winter build-up of ozone is weaker. Hence, reason is false.

50. Auditing is a term frequently used to describe a systematic process of examining, documenting, and verifying that EIA procedures and outcomes correspond to its objectives and recommendations. This process can be undertaken during and/or after project construction and draws upon surveillance reports and monitoring data. The main types of audits related to post-decision activities are as follows:

- **Implementation audit :** It essentially "polices" projects to ensure that recommended mitigation measures are in place and operated correctly.
- **Performance audit :** It is regarded as a management activity that examines the response of personnel concerned with the project operation to potential environmental problems and determines whether the actions required to deal with a major environmental incident are satisfactory.
- **Project impact audits :** It is designed to identify environmental changes that have occurred as a consequence of a development.
- **Predictive techniques audit :** It is to assess the accuracy and utility of predictive techniques by a comparison of actual consequences with the predicted environmental impacts of a project.
- **EIA procedure audit :** It includes any or all of the previously mentioned audits with the intention of improving procedures in general rather than individual EIAs.
- **Compliance audit :** It is undertaken to verify that the project complies with environmental standards and regulatory requirements.

52. Environmental Impact Assessment (EIA) is an important tool for integrating the objectives of environmental management into the decision making process to ensure environmentally sound and sustainable development. Earlier, any developmental project/activity were reviewed keeping in view the technical feasibility and financial viability of the project only. However, with the introduction of concept of EIA the environmental considerations have also been included as one of the factors to be considered while deciding about the feasibility and sustainability of any developmental/industrial project/activity. In fact, the main purpose of EIA is to mitigate adverse environmental impacts of any project/activity and bringing them to an acceptable level and to project the community likely to be affected by the proposed project.

The EIA notification has undergone several amendments incorporating provisions for "Public Hearing" and bringing in several important projects/activities into the purview of EIA, requiring "Environmental Clearance" by Ministry of Environment and Forest (MoEF), Govt of India. To further improve the EIA procedure in India, EIA notification was revised on September 14th, 2006. According to the notification, different projects/developmental activities have been divided into 8 major heads requiring "Environmental Clearance" (EC) either from Central Government, *i.e.,* MoEF (Category 'A') or at State Level from State Environmental Impact Assessment Authority (SEIAA) (Category 'B'). The category 'B' has been further divided into category 'B1' (project requires to submit EIA report) and 'B2' project activities which don't require EIA report). All categories 'A' and 'B1' projects necessarily have to carry out EIA studies along with the "public hearing" as per the procedure stipulated in the notification.

53. Evaporation of surface water is reduced due to black carbon in atmosphere.

Black carbon aerosols absorb incoming solar radiation, which both reduces radiation reaching the surface and cools the surface, but they also warm the troposphere by absorbing solar radiation with peak heating at 2–6 km in the atmosphere. The effect of cooling the surface and warming above is to make the atmosphere more stable, which tends to reduce precipitation as well. These aerosol effects taken together can lead to a weaker hydrological cycle, a weaker monsoon circulation, less freshwater availability, and drought. In addition, black carbon aerosols nucleate more cloud droplets, making the clouds more reflective and less efficient in producing precipitation. These effects have been noted in southern Asia, where there is a persistent brown haze due to aerosols from biomass burning and fossil fuel consumption. Hence, reason is correctly explain the assertion.

54. **Ad Hoc methods :** This is the most common approach to impact assessment. Basically ad hoc methods indicate broad areas of likely impact by listing composite environmental parameters (for example, flora and fauna) likely to be affected by development activities.

Checklist Methods : Checklists annotate the environmental features or factors that need to be addressed when identifying the impacts of projects and activities. They can vary in complexity and purpose, from a simple checklist to a structured methodology or system that also assigns significance by scaling and weighting the impacts.

Checklists provide a systematized means of identifying impacts. They also have been developed for application to particular types of projects and categories of impacts (such as dams or road building)

Networks Methods : Networks illustrate the cause-effect relationship of project activities and environmental characteristics. They are, therefore, particularly useful in identifying and depicting secondary impacts (indirect, cumulative, etc). Simplified networks, used in conjunction with other methods, help to ensure that important second-order impacts are not omitted from the investigation.

Overlays Methods : Overlays and geographic information systems Overlays can be used to map impacts spatially and display them pictorially.

A modern version of the overlay method is the computer-based geographical information system (GIS). In simple terms, a GIS stores, retrieves, manipulates and displays environmental data in a spatial format. A set of maps or overlays of a given area provide different types of information and scales of resolution. The use of GIS for EIA purposes is not as widespread as commonly imagined. The main drawbacks are the lack of appropriate data and the expense of creating a usable system.

55. Baseline studies will characterize and document the existing environmental conditions prior to development. Those environmental elements that have a likelihood of being affected by the proposed project will be the focus of data collection. Knowledge of baseline environmental conditions is important for two reasons: first, to form a basis for the assessment and second, to provide a record of initial conditions, which will be essential both during operations, and when project decommissioning takes place.

In the baseline Studies, the environmental assessment will include a description of the project location on a national, regional and local basis with increasingly more detailed maps. The regional and local geology and geography lead into a description of the local terrestrial habitat. Descriptions of climate, surface water hydrology, hydrogeology, soil, water and air quality, and natural radiological conditions are required in the baseline document. Any rare or endangered animal or plant species in the area of the project must be identified. A description of resource use including land use, agriculture, livestock, wildlife harvesting, fishing, tourism, etc. is also an integral part of the document. Finally, a description of the socio-economic environment indicating the inhabitants of the areas potentially impacted areas and the nature of their livelihood and culture will round out the description of baseline conditions.

56. The goals and objectives of a river restoration are to identify, usually in a short but clear sentence, the desired outcome or results of any action to restore the river. This is a critical step in the overall planning process in order to avoid failed or poorly performing restoration as well as to evaluate the restoration project after the completion of the project. General and broad scopes and expressions of the objectives can make the project team lose focus and how well to perform for the restoration. Narrowing the objectives reduces any ambiguity for the project team. The objectives of river restoration should be:

• Specific • Realistic • Achievable • Measurable

57. The Lotka–Volterra equations can also be written in a more general form for a community composed of *n* different species:

$$\frac{dN_i}{dt} = r_i N_i \left(\frac{\{K_i - N_i - \Sigma\alpha_{ij} N_j\}}{K_i} \right)$$

where the *i* and *j* subscripts denote species and range from 1 to *n* and the summation is from 1 to *n* over all other species.

Implicit in the Lokta-Volterra competition equations are a number of assumptions; some can be relaxed, although the Mathematics rapidly become unmanageable. Maximal rates of increase, competition coefficients, and carrying capacities are all assumed to be constant and immutable; they do not vary with population densities, community composition, or anything else. As a result, all inhibitory relationships within and between populations are strictly linear, and every N_1 individual is identical as is every N_2 individual.

Also there is no time lag in this equation.

59. For maximum sustainable yield

$$\frac{dy}{dN} = 0$$

Here, $y = \frac{dN}{dt} = 0.1\ N - 0.001\ N^2$

$$\frac{dy}{dN} = 0.1 - 0.001\ (2N)$$

So, $0.1 - 0.002N = 0 \Rightarrow N = \frac{0.1}{0.002} = 50.$

60. Some countries set minimum heights for industrial stacks (chimneys) on the assumption that the taller the stack the greater the dispersion of pollutants away from the point of origin. Wind speeds normally increase with height, so tall stacks emit pollutants into stronger winds, which encourage dispersion and dilution. Tall stacks are needed for industrial plants located in valleys and basins because these locations are prone to low-level temperature inversions. The tall stacks enable emitted plumes to penetrate an inversion. Thus assertion is true.

For continuous source the following type of Gaussian Distribution is assumed normally.

$$C(x, y, z) = \frac{Q}{\pi\sigma_y\sigma_z\bar{u}} \exp-\left\{\left(\frac{h^2}{2\sigma_z^2}\right)+\left(\frac{y^2}{2\sigma_y^2}\right)\right\}$$

Where,

C = Concentration (g/m^3)

Q = Pollutant release rate (g/s)

σ_y, σ_z = Crosswind and vertical plume standard deviations (m)

$\bar{u}$ = Mean wind speed (m/s) at h_s, the height of the stack

h = Effective stack height (m)

x, y = Downwind and crosswind distances.

From the above equation it is seen that C, the ground level (Z = 0) concentration of a pollutant at a point (x, y) downwind from a source is proportional to the rate of emission (Q). Further, it is inversely proportional to the wind speed ($\bar{u}$), and to the parameters σ_y and σ_z. Also, it can be shown that the maximum ground level concentration of a gaseous pollutant is inversely proportional to the square of the effective stack height.

Hence, reason is false.

62. Given datas: Mean ($\bar{X}$) = 5.667

Standard deviation (S) = 0.934

Population mean (μ) = 5.2

Sample size (n) = 16

Test statistic = ?

From formula

Test statistic (z)

$$= \frac{\bar{X}-\mu}{\frac{S}{\sqrt{n}}} = \frac{5.667-5.2}{\frac{0.934}{\sqrt{16}}} = \frac{0.467}{\frac{0.934}{4}}$$

$$= \frac{0.467}{0.2335} = 2.$$

63. Methane (CH_4) is one of the most widespread greenhouse gases (GHGs) emitted from paddy fields and other sources such as wetlands, ruminants, coal mines as well as anthropogenic activities such as leakage from natural gas systems and the raising of livestocks. The concentration of CH_4 in the atmosphere is increasing due to discrepancy in CH_4 emanation and its removal. The lifetime of CH_4 in the atmosphere in 8–12 years, but it is more efficient in trapping radiation and 23–30 times more potential than CO_2 Global surface temperature has increased by 0.8 °C in the last 100 years and CH_4 also contributed to this phenomenon as a potent GHG.

64. All over the world, efforts are on to save the ozone layer. The United Nations formed a committee which drafted an agreement that calls for a stepwise reduction of CFCs. This agreement, called the Montreal Protocol, came into effect in 1987. Under this legally binding agreement, the consumption and production of CFCs and halons is to be stopped within a stipulated time. The committee keeps a regular check on the amount of ozone depleting substances in the world. It also provides technical and financial assistance to developing countries to reduce CFC consumption. Under the Montreal Protocol, all the signatory countries have to assess their consumption and production of ODS every year.

65. Typical values for the ratio of BOD/COD for untreated municipal wastewater are in the range from 0.3 to 0.8. If the BOD/COD ratio for untreated wastewater is 0.5 or greater, the waste is considered to be easily treatable by biological means. If the ratio is below about 0.3, either the waste may have some toxic components or acclimated microorganisms may be required in its stabilization. The corresponding BOD/TOC ratio for untreated wastewater varies from 1.2 to 2.0. In using these ratios it important to remember that they will change significantly with the degree of treatment the waste has undergone, as reported in Table.

Type of wastewater	*BOD/COD*	*BOD/TOC*
Untreated	0.3–0.8	1.2–2.0
After primary settling	0.4–0.6	0.8–1.2
Final effluent	0.1–0.3A[a]	0.2–0.5[b]

a : CBOD/COD

b : CBOD/TOC

66. Organic soils, or histosols, develop under conditions of almost continuous saturation where drainage is poor, anaerobic conditions prevail, and litter production exceeds decomposition. If soils become deficient in oxygen because they are waterlogged, oxidation of organic matter is limited and rate of decomposition slows because anaerobic decomposition processes are much less efficient than aerobic ones.

Organic soils typically have lower bulk density (dry weight per volume less than 1 g/cm^3) and a higher porosity (volume of water held per volume of soil) and higher water holding capacity than mineral soils. Consequently, flooded organic soils can often hold more water than flooded mineral soils. In spite of higher porosity, organic soils may have low to high hydraulic conductivities, indicating that they may impede horizontal or vertical groundwater flows. Thus, organic soils can act as an aquitard to seal a wetland and increase hydroperiod. Organic soils typically have a lower stock of available plant nutrients than mineral soils and are less capable of storing some cations and anions in wastewater effluents.

67. Ozone is constantly being produced and destroyed in a natural cycle in the environment.

Large increases in stratospheric chlorine and bromine, however, have upset that balance. In effect, they have added a siphon downstream, removing ozone faster than natural ozone creation reactions can keep up. Therefore, ozone levels fall.

Research has shown that ozone depletion occurs over the latitudes that include North America, Europe, Asia and much of Africa, Australia and South America. Over the U.S., ozone levels have fallen 5–10%, depending on the season. Thus, ozone depletion is a global issue and not just a problem at the South Pole. Reductions in ozone levels will lead to higher levels of UVB reaching the Earth's surface. The sun's output of UVB does not change; rather, less ozone means less protection, and hence more UVB reaches the Earth. Studies have shown that in the Antarctic, the amount of UVB measured at the surface can double during the annual ozone hole.

68. **Estuarine ecology :** River mouths, coastal bays, tidal marshes and any other semi-enclosed coastal body of water which is influenced by tidal action and in which sea water is constantly in interaction with fresh-water are called estuaries. Hence they are 'transitional ecotones' between freshwater and marine habitats. Drowned river valleys, ford-type estuaries, bar-built estuaries, estuaries created by tectonic processes and river delta estuaries are some of the types of estuaries. Various estuaries have various amounts of salinity value, some being homogenous, whole others not. Estuaries are highly productive because of their 'being trapped' in between the sea and the freshwater ecosystem.

69. **Composition of the heterosphere**

Above the turbopause (about 100 km), the Earth's atmosphere begins to have a composition that varies with altitude. This is essentially because, in the absence of mixing, the density of a gas falls off exponentially with increasing altitude, at a rate that depends on the molecular mass of the gas. Higher mass constituents, such as oxygen and nitrogen, fall off more quickly than lighter constituents such as helium, molecular hydrogen, and atomic hydrogen. Thus, as the altitude increases in the heterosphere, the atmosphere is dominated successively by helium, molecular hydrogen, and atomic hydrogen. The precise altitude of the heterosphere and the layers it contains varies significantly with temperature.

70. The Kigali deal on HFCs is in fact fiendishly complicated and has taken years to negotiate in various technical and political forums. The final agreement, announced on Saturday morning caps and reduces the use of HFCs in a gradual process beginning in 2019.

Worldwide use of HFCs has soared in the past decade as rapidly growing countries such as

China and India adopted air-conditioning in homes, offices and cars. But HFC gases are thousands of times more destructive to the climate than carbon dioxide, and scientists say their growing use threatens to undermine the Paris accord, agreed last year by 195 countries.

Rich countries, including the US, Japan and Europe, will start phasing out synthetic HFCs in 2019, China in 2024, and India and less ambitious countries in 2028.

71. Hydroxyl radicals are present in the atmosphere at very low concentrations. Since the hydroxyl radical is reformed in the atmospheric photooxidation of hydrocarbons, it effectively acts as a catalyst for the oxidation of hydrocarbons. Figure illustrates the role of the hydroxyl radical in initiating a chain of reactions that oxidize hydrocarbons, forming peroxy radicals that can oxidize NO to NO_2 and re-form hydroxyl radicals. The NO_2 can photolyze, leading to the formation of ozone.

$$NO_2 + OH + M \rightarrow HNO_3 + M$$

NO_2 may also photolyze and produce a ground state O atom, which will go on to produce ozone:

$$NO_2 + h\nu \rightarrow NO + O \ (\lambda < 410 \text{ nm})$$

$$O_2 + O + M \rightarrow O_3 + M$$

72. The key measurands relate to the composite loading of organic compounds in the water (the sources of which are familiar to us all and need not be detailed) and provide general indicators of pollution level, rather than specific chemical contaminant levels. These are biological oxygen demand (BOD), chemical oxygen demand (COD), total organic carbon (TOC) and dissolved oxygen (DO). Water returned to natural courses with low oxygen levels or with contaminants which consume oxygen significantly will have a damaging effect on the plant and animal life in the water.

BOD is a measure of the biodegradable substances in a sample, COD the oxygen required to oxidise the organic and inorganic substances present. TOC indicates the total carbon compounds present but does not differentiate between degradable and nondegradable compounds. DO in a sample is lowered if BOD or COD are high. Typically, BOD is used to indicate final pollutant load in effluent. Either COD, TOC or DO act as control parameters for the blending and treatment processes. The parameters are related and not usually all measured on the same site.

73. Coal Based Thermal power plants which generated electricity by burning coal releases radioactive materials during it's normal operation. Radioactive leakage may occur from a Nuclear plant, but only due to a fault or damages. Hydroelectric or solar power plants can't produce radioactive materials or toxic bi-products.

74. Paris Convention 1992:

Regional Sea Agreements Relevant to Pollution

Two regional agreements focusing on regional sea management may serve as avenues for controlling land-based pollution: Paris Convention for the Protection of the Marine Environment of the North-East Atlantic, 1992 and the Convention on the Protection of the Marine Environment of the Baltic Sea Area, 1992 and this often referred to as the Helsinki Convention, 1992.

The Vienna Convention for the Protection of the Ozone Layer, 1985

The conference of the plenipotentiaries for a Convention for the Protection of the Ozone Layer took place in Vienna on 18-22 March 1985. Thirty-four countries attended the meeting, including ten developing countries. Attending, as observers, were China, industrial organizations – including two from Europe – and the International Chamber of Commerce. The United Nations Industrial Development Organization (UNIDO), WMO, the European Economic Community and OECD were also present. No environmental NGO was present.

Basel Convention 1992

The Basel Convention on the Control of Transboundary Movements of Hazardous Wastes and their Disposal (the Basel Convention) entered into force on 5 May 1992. The Convention regulates the transboundary import and export of hazardous wastes and obliges Parties to ensure that such wastes are managed and disposed of in an environmentally sound manner.

Bamako Convention 1998

Many African states considered the Basel Convention insufficient, and in 1998, the Organization for African Unity adopted the Bamako Convention on the Ban of Import into Africa and the Control of Transboundary Movement and Management of Hazardous Wastes within Africa to address specific regional concerns regarding hazardous waste.

The provisions of the Bamako Convention generally correspond to those of the Basel Convention, with a few important distinctions. First, the Bamako Convention defines waste in a much broader context, including radioactive wastes that are subject to any international control system. Parties must also strive to apply the precautionary approach in their activities. Most importantly, Parties to the Bamako Convention commit to prohibit and criminalize the importation of all hazardous wastes, for any reason, into Africa from non-contracting parties. Additionally, it bans the dumping of hazardous wastes at sea by contracting parties or in internal waters by non-contracting parties, and it requires Parties to impose strict, unlimited liability, along with joint and several liability, on those parties that generate hazardous waste.

75. Table : *Colour-coding system for waste, recommended by the DH*

Colour receptacle	*Waste type and management*
Yellow	Infectious waste that has an additional characteristic that means that it must be incinerated in a suitably licensed or permitted facility. Examples: anatomical waste, chemically contaminated samples and diagnostic kits, medicinally contaminated infectious waste; and Category A (as specified in the Carriage Regulations) pathogens (often when in culture form) as these are capable of causing permanent disability, life-threatening or fatal disease.
Orange	Infectious waste, for example, incontinence pads, stoma bags and soiled wound dressings where the patient has an infection and the causative agent is likely to be in the waste. For example, the stoma bag of a patient with a gastrointestinal infection. A used wound drain would always go into this waste steam. This waste steam must not contain non-infectious waste or infectious waste with additional characteristics (chemicals, medicines, anatomical waste), which mean it must be incinerated.
Purple	Waste consisting of, or contaminated with cytotoxic and/or cytostatic products.
Yellow with black stripe	Offensive/hygiene waste, such as stoma bags, incontinence pads, catheter bags and soiled wound dressings, when they are not considered infectious. In the community, a patient who is self-managing can put small amounts of these items into their domestic waste stream.
Red	Anatomical waste, which includes recognisable body parts and placenta.
Black (or clear)	Domestic waste which is similar to waste generated at home. Domestic waste should not contain any infectious materials, sharps or medicinal products. Examples: Non-recyclable packaging, such as crisp packets, polystyrene cups, flowers.
Blue	Medicinal waste.

Previous Paper (Solved)

UGC-NET-Junior Research Fellowship & Assistant Professor Exam

Environmental Science, July-2016*

PAPER-II

Note: *This paper contains **fifty (50)** objective type questions of **two (2)** marks each. **All** questions are compulsory.*

1. Photoionization of gas molecules maintain the temperature profile of which atmospheric layer?

A. Troposphere B. Stratosphere
C. Mesosphere D. Thermosphere

2. Around the mid latitude, the surface winds are generally

A. Gradient B. Geostrophic
C. Subgeostrophic D. Cyclonic

3. How many biogeographic regions are reported to exist in India?

A. Five B. Seven
C. Ten D. Three

4. Energy transfer and nutrient flow through various trophic levels can be described as

A. Linear
B. Cyclic
C. Linear and cyclic respectively
D. Cyclic and linear respectively

5. The highest rate at which individuals can be harvested without reducing the population size is called maximum sustainable yield of a

A. Population B. Community
C. Ecosystem D. Landscape

6. Leslie matrix population model is generally used to determine

(*a*) the growth of population.
(*b*) the age distribution within population over time.
(*c*) the prey-predator interactions.

Choose the correct answer:

A. (*a*) only B. (*a*) and (*c*) only
C. (*b*) and (*c*) only D. (*a*) and (*b*) only

7. If ΔN_n is equal to production of new individual in the population, Δt and N represent time and initial number of individuals of a population, then natality rate per unit of population is

A. $\frac{\Delta N_n}{\Delta t}$ B. $\frac{\Delta N_n}{N\Delta t}$

C. $\Delta N_n - N\Delta t$ D. $\frac{N\Delta t}{\Delta N_n}$

8. In a health survey, 38 of 120 men and 24 of 80 women are found to be affected by nicotine by smoking. What is the probability of a randomly selected male being a smoker?

A. 0.32 B. 0.19
C. 0.38 D. 0.12

9. If for a sample size (N) of 64, the mean $(\overline{X})$ and standard deviation (SD) are found to be 82 and 6. Then standard error (SE) for the mean is

A. 0.75 B. 0.14
C. 10.4 D. 2.2

10. 'Public hearing' is not mandatory for project like

A. building construction project
B. mining project
C. oil refinery project
D. river valley project

* Exam held on 10 July, 2016

11. The preparedness for prevention of chemical accidents and emergency in industry should be made according to the statutory framework of

(*a*) The National Environmental Tribunal Act, 1975

(*b*) The Public Liability Insurance Act, 1991

(*c*) The Factories Act, 1948

(*d*) The Water (Prevention and Control of Pollution) Act, 1974

Choose the correct answer:

A. (*a*), (*b*) and (*c*) only
B. (*b*), (*c*) and (*d*) only
C. (*b*) and (*c*) only
D. (*a*), (*b*), (*c*) and (*d*)

12. The term (life) of a patent from the date of filing is

A. 5 years B. 100 years
C. 20 years D. 50 years

13. According to the Hazardous Waste (Management and Handling) Rules, 1989, the limit for Polyaromatic Hydrocarbons (PAH) in waste oil suitable for recycling should be less than

A. 8% B. 10%
C. 6% D. 15%

14. The main objectives of the Wildlife (Protection) Act, 1972 are

(*a*) Restricting hunting, killing or overexploitation of species.

(*b*) Protection of wildlife, preservation of natural habitats and environment.

(*c*) Recognizing the right of people to a healthy environment.

Choose the correct answer:

A. (*a*) and (*b*) only B. (*b*) and (*c*) only
C. (*a*) and (*c*) only D. (*a*), (*b*) and (*c*)

15. The signing ceremony of Paris agreement on climate change was held on April 22, 2016 at UN headquarters. The agreement will be open for signatures by the countries till

A. December 22, 2016
B. April 21, 2017
C. December 21, 2017
D. March 21, 2018

16. The committee, which reviews the EIA and EMP reports of developmental projects in Ministry of Environment, Forest and Climate Change, is called

A. Project Assessment Committee
B. Environment Appraisal Committee
C. Project Evaluation Committee
D. Environmental Clearance Committee

17. In EIA, after official notification, time given to hold public hearing is

A. 10 days B. 15 days
C. 30 days D. 50 days

18. The corporate social responsibility has been made mandatory since

A. 2010 B. 2014
C. 2015 D. 2013

19. The guiding principles for the National Land Utilization Policy are as follows:

(*a*) Inclusive growth, poverty eradication and gender equality – equal opportunities.

(*b*) Balanced development and intergenerational justice.

(*c*) Efficient utilization of resources and mitigation of impacts.

(*d*) Integrated and comprehensive development planning.

Choose the correct answer:

A. (*a*) and (*b*) only
B. (*a*), (*b*) and (*c*) only
C. (*b*), (*c*) and (*d*) only
D. (*a*), (*b*), (*c*) and (*d*)

20. Degradation of different categories of pesticides by soil microorganism is called

A. Biotransformation
B. Biomineralization
C. Bioaugmentation
D. Biomagnification

21. Given below are two statements. One labelled as Assertion (A) and the other labelled as Reason (R):

Assertion (A) : CO can contribute to the photochemical smog problem in cities.

Reason (R) : It aids in formation of surface ozone.

Choose the correct answer:

A. Both (A) and (R) are correct and (R) is the correct explanation of (A).

B. Both (A) and (R) are correct and (R) is not the correct explanation of (A).

C. (A) is true but (R) is false.

D. (A) is false but (R) is true.

22. For spherical aerosol particles smaller than about 30 μm and with density much greater than air, their settling velocity varies with their size (d) as

A. $\propto d$ B. $\propto d^{-1}$

C. $\propto d^{-2}$ D. $\propto d^2$

23. Given below are two statements. One labelled as Assertion (A) and the other labelled as Reason (R):

Assertion (A) : Sound barriers alongside motorways in urban areas are very effective in controlling noise.

Reason (R) : They act as reflectors of sound back into motorways and upwards.

Choose the correct answer:

A. Both (A) and (R) are correct and (R) is the correct explanation of (A).

B. Both (A) and (R) are correct and (R) is not the correct explanation of (A).

C. (A) is true but (R) is false.

D. (A) is false but (R) is true.

24. The effect of sulphate aerosol in the Earth's atmosphere is to

A. decrease precipitation

B. destroy ozone

C. cool global climate

D. warm global climate

25. Solar radiation of average energy ~ 1.25 eV and intensity 500 W/m^2 are incident on the surface of a solar flat plate collector. What is the approximate photon flux density impinging on the surface of the collector?

A. ~ 5×10^{22} photons m^{-2} s^{-1}

B. ~ 2×10^{22} photons m^{-2} s^{-1}

C. ~ 2.5×10^{20} photons m^{-2} s^{-1}

D. ~ 2.5×10^{21} photons m^{-2} s^{-1}

26. A solar pond based electricity generation plant has an efficiency of 5% and power output of 500 mW. If the solar insolation is 1000 W/m^2, what is the area of solar pond?

A. 5 km^2 B. 10 km^2

C. 1.0 km^2 D. 20 km^2

27. Intended nationally determined contribution of India envisages reduction in carbon intensity by 2030 below 2005 level by what percentage?

A. 22–25 % B. 33–35 %

C. 35–40 % D. 40–50 %

28. By the year 2022, India's target of producing power from wind energy is

A. 50 GW B. 60 GW

C. 75 GW D. 120 GW

29. Which among the following surfaces has maximum albedo?

A. Leafy crops B. Dry sand

C. Calm sea water D. Dark asphalt

30. A wetland ecosystem has a very high Biological Oxygen Demand (BOD). Which of the following statement about such a wetland is correct?

A. It has high level of microbial pollution.

B. It has very low level of microbial pollution.

C. There is no microbial pollution.

D. It is highly turbid.

31. Desertification is the process of

A. increase in desert area

B. sand dune movement

C. land degradation

D. arid zone management

32. Ecological restoration is the process of rebuilding a degraded ecosystem till

A. it becomes pollution free and provides solace to the people.

B. it becomes free of disturbance.

C. its structure and functions are restored.

D. it starts providing some ecosystem services.

33. Consider the following four statements about wetland ecosystems:

(*a*) They are the transitional zones between terrestrial and aquatic ecosystems.

(*b*) They are highly productive.
(*c*) They are the source of greenhouse gases.
(*d*) They normally occur in the floodplain of rivers.

Choose the correct answer:
A. (*a*) and (*b*) only
B. (*a*), (*b*) and (*c*) only
C. (*b*), (*c*) and (*d*) only
D. (*a*), (*b*), (*c*) and (*d*)

34. In soil conservation programme, the tillage where residues of previous crops are left in the soil is called
A. Reduced tillage
B. No tillage
C. Conservation tillage
D. Contour plowing

35. Which of the following will provide the most valuable information for determining risk of mass wasting of an area?
A. Seismometer
B. Analysis of stereo satellite data
C. Measurement of acceleration due to gravity
D. Geological map of the region

36. The rapid downslope movement of ice or snow is called as
A. Mudflow B. Solifluction
C. Lahars D. Avalanches

37. The landform created by subglacial meltwater is known as
A. Moraine B. Eskers
C. Cirques D. Kames

38. Among the following gases, which is not emitted by volcano?
A. NO_x B. SO_x
C. CO_2 D. H_2S

39. In remote sensing, ground truth data is generally required for
(*a*) calibration of sensor
(*b*) analysis of remotely sensed data
(*c*) accuracy assessment

Choose the correct answer:
A. (*a*) only B. (*b*) and (*c*) only
C. (*a*), (*b*) and (*c*) D. (*a*) and (*b*) only

40. A species the population of which is low enough for it to be at risk of becoming extinct, but not low enough that it is in imminent danger of extinction is called
A. Endangered species B. Threatened species
C. Vulnerable species D. Rare species

41. Landscape mosaic comprises
A. matrices and patches
B. patches and corridors
C. matrices, patches and corridors
D. matrices and corridors

42. Which of the following country is not a megadiversity centre of biodiversity?
A. Columbia B. India
C. Brazil D. Argentina

43. Sclerophyllous leaves are the characteristic features of
A. Chaparral Vegetation
B. Grassland Vegetation
C. Tropical Vegetation
D. Alpine Vegetation

44. Among the plants listed below, which is not producing allergenic pollen grain?
A. Mango B. Neem
C. Fan Palm D. Pine

45. A species having a dominating influence on the structure and function of a community or ecosystem is known as
A. Fundamental species
B. Functional species
C. Keystone species
D. Indicator species

46. Which of the following trace atmospheric gases is not an acid rain precursor?
A. Dimethyl sulphide B. Hydrogen sulphide
C. Nitrous oxide D. Nitric oxide

47. According to WHO report 2015, out of 20 most polluted cities of the world, India has
A. 12 B. 18
C. 10 D. 13

48. With respect to sea, increase in CO_2 abundance is not responsible for which of the following?
A. Increase in pH of sea water.

B. Increase in concentration of bicarbonate ions.
C. Coral bleaching.
D. Enhanced dissolution of calcareous materials.

49. Elements that cycle in the environment and that also have a gaseous phase at some point in their cycle include which of the following?
(*a*) Phosphorus
(*b*) Sulphur
(*c*) Carbon
Choose the correct answer:
A. (*a*) only B. (*b*) only
C. (*b*) and (*c*) only D. (*a*) and (*c*) only

50. Poor aeration and high water holding capacity are characteristic features of
A. Sandy soil B. Loam soil
C. Clay soil D. Sandy Loam soil

ANSWERS

1	**2**	**3**	**4**	**5**	**6**	**7**	**8**	**9**	**10**
D	B	C	C	C	D	B	B	A	A
11	**12**	**13**	**14**	**15**	**16**	**17**	**18**	**19**	**20**
A	C	C	D	B	B	C	B	D	A
21	**22**	**23**	**24**	**25**	**26**	**27**	**28**	**29**	**30**
A	D	C	C	D	B	B	B	B	A
31	**32**	**33**	**34**	**35**	**36**	**37**	**38**	**39**	**40**
C	C	D	C	C	D	B	A	C	B
41	**42**	**43**	**44**	**45**	**46**	**47**	**48**	**49**	**50**
C	D	A	A	C	C	D	A	C	C

EXPLANATORY ANSWERS

1. The **thermosphere** is the layer of the Earth's atmosphere directly above the mesosphere and directly below the exosphere. Within this layer of the atmosphere, ultraviolet radiation causes photoionization/photo-dissociation of molecules, creating ions in the ionosphere.

2. The **geostrophic wind** is the theoretical wind that would result from an exact balance between the Coriolis effect and the pressure gradient force. This condition is called geostrophic balance.

The geostrophic wind neglects frictional effects, which is usually a good approximation for the synoptic scale instantaneous flow in the midlatitude mid-troposphere. Although ageostrophic terms are relatively small, they are essential for the time evolution of the flow and in particular are necessary for the growth and decay of storms.

3. Biogeographic classification of India is the division of India according to biogeographic characteristics. Biogeography is the study of the distribution of species (biology), organisms, and ecosystems in geographic space and through geological time. There are ten biogeographic zones in India.

1. Trans Himalayan zone,
2. Himalayan zone,
3. Desert zone,
4. Semiarid zone,
5. Western ghat zone,
6. Deccan plateau zone,
7. Gangetic plain zone,
8. North east zone,
9. Coastal zone, and
10. Islands present near the shore line.

5. In population ecology and economics, maximum sustainable yield or MSY is theoretically, the largest yield (or catch) that can be taken from a species' stock over an indefinite period. Fundamental to the notion of sustainable harvest, the concept of MSY aims to maintain the population size at the point of maximum growth rate by harvesting the individuals that would normally be added to the population, allowing the population to continue to be productive indefinitely. Under the assumption of logistic growth, resource limitation does not constrain individuals' reproductive rates when populations are small, but because there are few individuals, the overall yield is small. MSY is extensively used for fisheries management.

6. In applied mathematics, the Leslie matrix is a discrete, age-structured model of population growth that is very popular in population ecology. The Leslie matrix (also called the Leslie model) is one of the most well known ways to describe the growth of populations (and their projected age distribution), in which a population is closed to migration, growing in an unlimited environment, and where only one sex, usually the female, is considered.

The Leslie matrix is used in ecology to model the changes in a population of organisms over a period of time. In a Leslie model, the population is divided into groups based on age classes.

9. Standard Error Formula:

$$SE_{\bar{x}} = \frac{s}{\sqrt{n}}$$

where,

$SE_{\bar{x}}$ = Standard Error of the Mean

s = Standard Deviation of the Mean

n = Number of Observations of the Sample

From question,

$s = 6, n = 64$

$$SE_{\bar{x}} = \frac{6}{\sqrt{64}} = \frac{6}{8} = 0.75$$

10. The concept of Public Hearing was introduced for the first time in the Environment Impact Assessment *vide* Notification S.O. 60 (E) dated 27.01.1994 and subsequently formalized *vide* Notification S.O. 318 (E) dated 10.04.1997 making amendment in the Environment Impact Assessment Notification, 1994. Whereas, the Industrial Estates were added in the Schedule to the EIA Notification mandating the requirement of environmental clearance *vide* notification S.O. 801 (E) dated 7.07.2004. In between, the above two notifications, another notification No. S.O. 737 (E) dated 1st August, 2001 introducing the concept of exemption from public hearing for certain category of projects and activities in the process of environmental clearance was published. The said notification reads as "However, Public Hearing is not required in respect of (*i*) small scale industrial undertakings located in (*a*) notified/ designated industrial areas/industrial estates or (*b*) areas earmarked for industries under the jurisdiction of industrial development authorities; (*ii*) widening and strengthening of Highways; (*iii*) mining projects (major minerals) with lease area up to twenty-five hectares (*iv*) units located in Export Processing Zones, Special Economic Zones and (*v*) Modernization of existing irrigation projects."

12. The term of a patent is the maximum period during which it can be maintained in force. It is usually expressed in a number of years either starting from the filing date of the patent application or from the date of grant of the patent.

"The term of protection available (for patents) shall not end before the expiration of a period of twenty years counted from the filing date."

Consequently, in most patent laws nowadays, the term of patent is 20 years from the filing date of the application. This however does not forbid the states party to the WTO from providing, in their national law, other type of patent-like rights with shorter terms. Utility models are an example of such rights. Their term is usually 6 or 10 years.

14. Wildlife Protection Act of 1972 is a comprehensive legislation that was enacted by the Government of India in 1972. The first comprehensive legislation relating to protection of wild life was passed by the Parliament and it was assented by the President on 9th September, 1972 and came to be known as The Wild Life (Protection) Act, 1972.

Objective of Wildlife Protection Act of 1972

The main objective behind the enactment of Wildlife Protection Act of 1972 was to control poaching and illegal trading of wildlife in the country. The act also aims at providing a powerful legal framework for conserving the wildlife by introduction of regulations such as prohibition of hunting, protection and management of wildlife habitats, establishment of protected areas, regulation and control of trade in parts and products derived from wildlife and management of zoos. The protected areas under the Act are categorized as National Parks, Wildlife Sanctuaries, Tiger Reserves, Conservation Reserves and Community Reserves.

15. The Paris Agreement calls for the Agreement to be open for signature from 22 April, 2016 to 21 April, 2017. To mark the first day that the Agreement will be open for signing (which coincides with Earth Day), United Nations Secretary-General Ban Ki-moon invited leaders from all countries to attend a high-level signing ceremony to accelerate climate action and to drive the political momentum towards ratification and early entry into force of the Paris Agreement.

17. **Public Consultation** - All Category A and Category B1 projects or activities have to undertake public consultation except for 6 activities for which public consultation has been exempted. Some of the projects exempted include expansion of roads and highways, modernization of irrigation projects, etc. Some of these may have potential, social and environmental impact. The responsibility for conducting the public hearing still lies with the state PCBs. Member-Secretary of the concerned State Pollution Control Board or Union Territory Pollution Control Committee has to finalise the date, time and exact venue for the conduct of public hearing within 30 days of the date of receipt of the draft Environmental Impact Assessment report, and advertise the same in one major National Daily and one Regional vernacular Daily. A minimum notice period of 30 days will be given to the public for furnishing their responses.

The public consultation will essentially consist of two components - a public hearing to ascertain the views of local people and obtaining written responses of interested parties.

18. India became the first country in the world to write CSR into legislation in April 2014, forcing companies to invest in sustainability programs. This should spell great news for development in India but business leaders are split over the effectiveness of such a law.

19. **Guiding Principles for the National Land Utilization Policy**

1st Principle: ***Human beings are at the centre***—Human beings are at the centre of concerns for sustainable development. They are entitled to a healthy and productive life in harmony with nature.

2nd Principle: ***Inclusive growth, poverty eradication and gender equality-equal opportunities***—Inclusive growth, poverty eradication and gender equality are indispensable requirements for sustainable development of India, and must be addressed in all policies, plans and programmes.

3rd Principle: ***Balanced development and intergenerational justice***—Developmental sectors and activities must be planned in a balanced manner to meet economic, social and environmental needs of present and future generations, and should aim to minimize any large-scale displacement of population.

4th Principle: ***Efficient utilisation of resources and mitigation of impacts***—Long-term planning for optimum utilisation of land

and saving scarce land resource is essential and as far as possible, projects should be set up on recycled lands, wastelands, degraded lands or un-irrigated lands provided these are not performing any other important function like biodiversity, water resources etc.

5th Principle: ***Integrated and comprehensive development planning***—Development planning must be comprehensive, sustainable, and integrated vertically (national, state, regional and local levels) taking into consideration the interest of all other sectors and stakeholders.

6th Principle: ***The States are custodian of land***—States are custodian of land and state governments must eliminate unsustainable patterns of land utilisation/land management and provide necessary legal and institutional support to facilitate capacity building and participatory, transparent and comprehensive land use planning.

7th Principle: ***Harmonization with existing policy, legislative and regulatory framework***—The existing constitutional provisions and rights, the existing laws, rules, standards, procedures, guidelines and stipulations brought out by various ministries, departments and institutions of the Government of India, as applicable to land utilisation policy shall continue to be in force for taking decisions on land matters and land use changes.

23. A noise barrier (also called a soundwall, sound berm, sound barrier, or acoustical barrier) is an exterior structure designed to protect inhabitants of sensitive land use areas from noise pollution. Noise barriers are the most effective method of mitigating roadway, railway, and industrial noise sources - other than cessation of the source activity or use of source controls.

24. Aerosols are minute particles suspended in the atmosphere. When these particles are sufficiently large, we notice their presence as they scatter and absorb sunlight. Their scattering of sunlight can reduce visibility (haze) and redden sunrises and sunsets. As a direct effect, the aerosols scatter sunlight directly back into space. As an indirect effect, aerosols in the lower atmosphere can modify the size of cloud particles, changing how the clouds reflect and absorb sunlight, thereby affecting the Earth's energy budget.

27. On the domestic front, India continued to take ambitious targets in its actions against climate change. As a part of its contributions to the global climate change mitigation efforts, India announced its intended nationally determined contribution (INDC) which set ambitious targets for domestic efforts against limate change. Including other efforts, the country has set itself an ambitious target of reducing its emissions intensity of its gross domestic product (GDP) by 33-35 per cent by 2030, compared to 2005 levels, and of achieving 40 per cent cumulative electric power installed capacity from non-fossil fuel-based energy resources by 2030.

28. India has committed to generating 60 GW (60,000 MW) of wind power by 2030, while the Prime Minister has given a much tighter deadline of 2022. Where are we in relation to this goal in terms of actual generation, installed capacity and capacity being installed.

"We have a target for renewable energy generation of 175 gigawatts by 2022. We have got off to a good start with nearly 12 GW likely to be installed by 2016, more than three times the current capacity," Prime Minister Narendra Modi said during the inauguration of India's pavilion at the ongoing Paris climate change conference.

Of the target capacity, 100 GW would be from solar power, 60 GW from wind, 10 GW from biomass and 5 GW from small hydro power, according to the Union ministry of new and renewable energy.

29. Sand surface had a higher albedo (0.266) than BSCs (0.226) when the surfaces were very dry. However, sand surface albedo became increasingly lower than that of BSCs when the surfaces were in wet conditions and when the soil moisture exceeded a critical value. The changes in soil surface albedo from sand dune to BSCs after revegetation in shallow soil profiles associated with the variation of the surface soil moisture can be seen as an indicator of the degree of sand dune stabilization when compared with the original shifting sand dune soil.

31. Desertification can be considered to be a subset of land degradation, occurring in more arid areas; though land degradation is usually defined as being caused by human actions. The main direct actions are over-clearing, over-grazing and over-cultivation. There is a host of more complex direct and underlying causes including the introduction and spread of exotic plants, animals, pests and diseases, fire, economic pressures, people's attitudes, perceptions and knowledge, actions or inactions by government agencies, and inappropriate government policies.

32. Interestingly, ecosystem restoration can give to the science of ecology as well as take from it because it represents and experimental application of our knowledge of ecosystem function and structure. As Bradshaw put it, "Ecologists working in the field of ecosystem restoration are in the construction business and, like their engineering colleagues, can soon discover if their theory is correct by whether the airplane falls out of the sky, the bridge collapses, or the ecosystem fails to flourish."

36. Avalanche is a rapid, downslope movement of snow, ice, water, rock, soil, vegetation, etc., mixed in various proportions. The term avalanche is used most often when snow or ice is the major component.

Avalanches require a combination of steep slopes and a heavy snowfall. A common trigger is the deposition of wet snow over ice or a hard crust, with failure occurring at the base of the snow. Alternatively, high winds can produce a cornice, which may break off, causing an avalanche on the slope below.

37. **Eskers** are the chief landform created by subglacial meltwater. Minor forms include sediment-filled Nye channels and moulin kames, which are somewhat fleeting piles of debris at the bottom of a moulin (a pothole in a glacier that may extend from the surface to the glacier bed). Esker is an Irish word and is now applied to long and winding ridges formed mostly of sand and gravel and laid down in a meltwater tunnel underneath a glacier.

38. The major volcanic gases emitted from basaltic magma are H_2O, CO_2, SO_2, H_2, CO, H_2S, HCl and HF. The most abundant gas is water vapour (H_2O), followed by carbon dioxide (CO_2) and sulphur dioxide (SO_2).

41. To understand landscape ecology, we have to focus on some of its important principles: landscape composition, structure, function and change.

– Structure involves the variety of habitat patches or ecosystems and thier patterns- the size and arrangement of patches, stands, or ecosystems—including the sequence of pools in a stream, vertical layering of vegetation.

43. Mediterranean Shrublands or Chaparral biome is found along the coasts of the Mediterranean Sea, California, Central Chile, south-western part of South Africa and south-western parts of Australia.

The dominant shrubs that occupy these regions are stunted and tough in their ability to with-stand hot-summer drought and due to this, the chaparral vegetation is also known as sclerophyllous. It averages as metre or two in height and has deep, well developed roots, leathery and uneven low branches.

45. A keystone species is a species that has a disproportionately large effect on its environment relative to its abundance. Such species are described as playing a critical role in maintaining the structure of an ecological community, affecting many other organisms in an ecosystem and helping to determine the types and numbers of various other species in the community.

47. World Health Organization (WHO) has revealed a report with the most polluted cities across the world according to WHO's guidelines. The most shameful thing about this list is that, out of 20 most polluted cities of the world, 13th are Indian cities.

50. In suspension, particles of largest dimensions will settle first and those of smaller dimensions will settle afterwards. Individual soil separates are identified on the basis of their respective diameter ranges. Soil separates (sand, silt and clay) differ not only in their sizes but also in their bearing on some of the important factors affecting plant growth, such as, soil aeration, workability, movement and availability of water and nutrients.

PAPER-III

Note: *This paper contains* ***seventy five (75)*** *objective type questions of* ***two (2)*** *marks each.* ***All*** *questions are compulsory.*

1. In India audit on conservation and protection of tigers in all 28 Tiger reserves was conducted in

A. 2001 B. 2004

C. 2006 D. 2007

2. In the screening stage of EIA, the impact level of a development project is not discernible, then what step should be adopted?

A. Scoping stage ought to be initiated

B. Detailed EIA study ought to be conducted

C. A rapid EIA study ought to be conducted

D. The project may not be given environmental clearance

3. Biodiversity hotspots are regions of high

A. stationary population of common species

B. richness of endemic species

C. migratory population

D. richness of dominant species

4. Given below are two statements. One labelled as Assertion (A) and the other labelled as Reason (R):

Assertion (A) : Ocean Thermal Energy Conversion (OTEC) plants have very low efficiencies.

Reason (R) : The temperature difference between warm surface water and cold deeper ocean water is not all that great.

Choose the correct answer:

A. Both (A) and (R) are correct and (R) is the correct explanation of (A).

B. Both (A) and (R) are correct and (R) is not the correct explanation of (A).

C. (A) is true, but (R) is false.

D. (A) is false, but (R) is true.

5. In respect of geothermal power production, identify the correct sequence of the countries:

A. Iceland > Russia > Japan > USA

B. Japan > Iceland > USA > Russia

C. USA > Iceland > Japan > Russia

D. USA > Japan > Iceland > Russia

6. Among the forest types of India, which category of forest covers maximum geographical area:

A. Tropical grassland

B. Mangrove forest

C. Tropical deciduous forest

D. Temperate evergreen forest

7. The overall diversity of a landscape comprising several ecosystems is known as

A. Alpha diversity B. Beta diversity

C. Gamma diversity D. Delta diversity

8. The ratio between the amount of radiation emitted by earth upto the wavelength at which maximum radiation is emitted and total amount of radiation emitted by earth is approximately

A. ~ 25% B. ~ 50%

C. ~ 40% D. ~ 66%

9. Milankovitch cycles refer to
A. Shifts in the temperature of surface water in the middle latitudes of the Pacific Ocean.
B. The timing of the northern lights in the thermosphere.
C. The changes in the Earth's rotation and orbit around the sun that may trigger climate variation.
D. Upwelling and down-welling in the ocean.

10. El Niño and La Niña phenomena
A. decrease water temperatures in the eastern Pacific Ocean
B. increase water temperatures in the Gulf of Mexico
C. occur in a definite pattern every ten years
D. cause changes in global temperature and precipitation pattern

11. Given below are two statements. One labelled as Assertion (A) and the other labelled as Reason (R):
Assertion (A) : At a constant temperature, the solubility of ammonia in water increases with decrease in pH.
Reason (R) : The solubility of all gases increase with decrease in pH.
Choose the correct answer:
A. Both (A) and (R) are correct and (R) is the correct explanation of (A).
B. Both (A) and (R) are correct and (R) is not the correct explanation of (A).
C. (A) is true, but (R) is false.
D. (A) is false, but (R) is true.

12. Given below are two statements. One labelled as Assertion (A) and the other labelled as Reason (R):
Assertion (A) : Temperature of sea water generally decreases with increasing latitude.
Reason (R) : Surface layers of sea water tend to contract and sink in cold waters.
Choose the correct answer:
A. Both (A) and (R) are correct and (R) is the correct explanation of (A).
B. Both (A) and (R) are correct and (R) is not the correct explanation of (A).
C. (A) is true, but (R) is false.
D. (A) is false, but (R) is true.

13. A normal sand dune is characterized by
A. Gentle windward and steeper leeward sides.
B. Both gentle sides.
C. Steeper windward and gentle leeward sides.
D. Both steeper sides.

14. Given below are two statements. One labelled as Assertion (A) and the other labelled as Reason (R):
Assertion (A) : The distribution of animals over the world is much more complex and irregular compared to plants.
Reason (R) : The animals are mobile and therefore capable of more rapid dispersal.
Choose the correct answer:
A. Both (A) and (R) are correct and (R) is the correct explanation of (A).
B. Both (A) and (R) are correct and (R) is not the correct explanation of (A).
C. (A) is true, but (R) is false.
D. (A) is false, but (R) is true.

15. Consider the following statements in case of Gaussian Plume Model.
(*a*) The wind speed is constant both in time and with elevation.
(*b*) The emission rate from the source is constant.
(*c*) The pollutant is conservative.
Choose the answer:
A. (*a*) only B. (*b*) only
C. (*a*) and (*b*) only D. (*a*), (*b*) and (*c*)

16. A stream flowing at 5.0 m^3/s converges with another stream with the same flow rate. The concentration of the phosphate upstream to the junction is 10.0 mg/L and that in the other stream is 5.0 mg/L. The downstream concentration of phosphate is
A. 2.5 mg/L B. 5.0 mg/L
C. 7.5 mg/L D. 10 mg/L

17. Lotka-Volterra model for an ecosystem can be used to study
(*a*) oscillations in prey-predator population.
(*b*) effect of predator on prey population.
(*c*) effect of prey on predator population.
Choose the correct answer:
A. (*a*) and (*b*) only
B. (*b*) and (*c*) only
C. (*a*) and (*c*) only
D. (*a*), (*b*) and (*c*)

18. In an ecosystem following logistic growth model initial population was 900 with growth rate constant of 0.1. If the carrying capacity of the ecosystem is 1000, what is the instantaneous rate of change of population?
A. 10 B. 25
C. 1.1 D. 9

19. Choose an appropriate hypothesis testing method for the condition where the variance is an unknown parameter of a population of independent observations:
A. Z-test B. χ^2-test
C. t-test D. F-test

20. For sampling error of 1.96σ; where σ is the standard deviation, and at critical value of 1.96, the significance level is
A. 5.0 % B. 1.0 %
C. 2.7 % D. 4.5 %

21. Qualitatively a sampling error in a survey based environmental experiment is the sum of
A. Frame error + Response error + Chance error
B. Frame error + Non-sampling error
C. Chance error + Frame error + Systematic error
D. Non-sampling error + Chance error + Systematic error

22. Ecosensitive zones are declared by the Ministry of Environment, Forest and climate change, Govt. of India under the provisions of
A. Forest Act, 1927
B. Forest (Conservation) Act, 1980
C. Environment (Protection) Act, 1986
D. Biological Diversity Act, 2002

23. Basel convention on trans-boundary movement of hazardous waste and disposal was adopted in the year
A. 1969 B. 1979
C. 1999 D. 1989

24. Which method reduces the volume of waste but could release toxic air emissions into the atmosphere?
A. Biological treatment
B. Sanitary landfill
C. Incineration
D. Chemical treatment

25. As per CRZ (Coastal Regulation Zone) 2011 Notification, which of the following activities is permitted?
A. Dumping of untreated sewage, effluents or solid waste.
B. Traditional fishing and allied activities.
C. Construction of Housing Complexes.
D. Infrastructural projects.

26. Match the List-I and List-II. Identify the correct answer from the codes given below:

List-I (Biomedical Waste)	**List-II (Treatment/Disposal)**
(*a*) Human tissues	(*i*) Incineration
(*b*) Scalpels	(*ii*) Autoclaving
(*c*) Solid plaster casts	(*iii*) Microwave mutilation
(*d*) Catheters	(*iv*) Deep burial

Codes:

	(*a*)	(*b*)	(*c*)	(*d*)
A.	(*iv*)	(*ii*)	(*i*)	(*iii*)
B.	(*iii*)	(*i*)	(*iv*)	(*ii*)
C.	(*ii*)	(*iv*)	(*iii*)	(*i*)
D.	(*i*)	(*iii*)	(*ii*)	(*iv*)

27. An organisation implementing an EMS under ISO 14001 should set environmental targets in order to achieve environmental objectives within a specified time-frame. The target should be
A. implemented on a trial basis
B. generic in nature
C. related to financial aspects
D. measurable and specific

28. ISO 14001 requires an organisation to
A. set improvement targets for every department.
B. define a quality policy within the defined scope of its EMS.
C. define the scope of its EMS.
D. define the scope of its audit.

29. Cost-benefit analysis is performed during
A. Design phase
B. Feasibility study phase
C. Implementation
D. Maintenance phase

30. Given below are two statements. One labelled as Assertion (A) and the other labelled as Reason (R):

Assertion (A) : The ecosystem surrounding a river gets damaged due to the construction of a dam on it.

Reason (R) : The area in upper catchment of the river gets inundated.

Choose the correct answer:
A. Both (A) and (R) are correct and (R) is the correct explanation of (A).
B. Both (A) and (R) are correct and (R) is not the correct explanation of (A).
C. (A) is true but (R) is false.
D. (A) is false but (R) is true.

31. Match the List-I and List-II. Identify the correct answer from the codes given below:

List-I (Auditing)	**List-II (Actions)**
(a) Implementation audit	*(i)* External review
(b) Predictive techniques audit	*(ii)* Initial activities
(c) Performance audit	*(iii)* Validation of impacts
(d) Procedures audit	*(iv)* Comprehensive operational activities

Codes:

	(a)	*(b)*	*(c)*	*(d)*
A.	*(ii)*	*(iii)*	*(iv)*	*(i)*
B.	*(iii)*	*(iv)*	*(i)*	*(ii)*
C.	*(iv)*	*(i)*	*(ii)*	*(iii)*
D.	*(i)*	*(ii)*	*(iii)*	*(iv)*

32. The interaction matrix developed by Leopold consists of how many parameters?
A. 30 B. 60
C. 70 D. 90

33. Given below are two statements. One labelled as Assertion (A) and the other labelled as Reason (R):

Assertion (A) : The goal of the National Land Utilisation Policy is to achieve improvement of livelihood, food and water security under the umbrella of sustainable development in India.

Reason (R) : The National Land Utilisation Policy envisages a guiding framework for state specific needs, potentials, priorities and legal provisions.

Choose the correct answer:
A. Both (A) and (R) are correct and (R) is the correct explanation of (A).
B. Both (A) and (R) are correct and (R) is not the correct explanation of (A).
C. (A) is true but (R) is false.
D. (A) is false but (R) is true.

34. Which of the following is a major photochemical oxidant?
A. PAN
B. Ozone
C. Aldehydes
D. Peroxybenzoyl nitrates (PBzN)

35. In terms of toxicity, identify the correct sequence:
A. Arsenic > Cadmium > Methylene chloride
B. Cadmium > Arsenic > Methylene chloride
C. Methylene chloride > Cadmium > Arsenic
D. Methylene chloride > Arsenic > Cadmium

36. Upwelling of oceanic waters is important for
A. enrichment of nutrients in pelagic waters.
B. balancing water circulation pattern in oceans and seas.
C. making the pelagic waters nutrient deficient.
D. helping survival of benthic organisms.

37. Arrange the following in terms of increasing productivity:

(*a*) Antarctica sea (*b*) Arctic sea
(*c*) Dead sea (*d*) Arabian sea

Choose the correct answer:

A. (*c*) < (*a*) < (*d*) < (*b*)
B. (*c*) < (*a*) < (*b*) < (*d*)
C. (*d*) < (*b*) < (*c*) < (*a*)
D. (*a*) < (*c*) < (*d*) < (*b*)

38. Match the List-I and List-II. Identify the correct answer from the codes given below:

List-I (Process/Event)	**List-II (Consequences/Links)**
(*a*) Assimilative capacity	(*i*) DO, BOD, Coliform
(*b*) Critical water parameter	(*ii*) Cadmium
(*c*) Itai-Itai disease	(*iii*) Blue baby syndrome
(*d*) Excess nitrate in water	(*iv*) Waste discharge

Codes:

	(*a*)	(*b*)	(*c*)	(*d*)
A.	(*i*)	(*ii*)	(*iii*)	(*iv*)
B.	(*iv*)	(*i*)	(*ii*)	(*iii*)
C.	(*ii*)	(*i*)	(*iii*)	(*iv*)
D.	(*ii*)	(*iii*)	(*i*)	(*iv*)

39. Which type of plume behaviour one would expect from a tall stack located on a flat terrain if adiabatic lapse rate (Γ) and environmental lapse rate (Γ_{env}) are as shown in the diagram below:

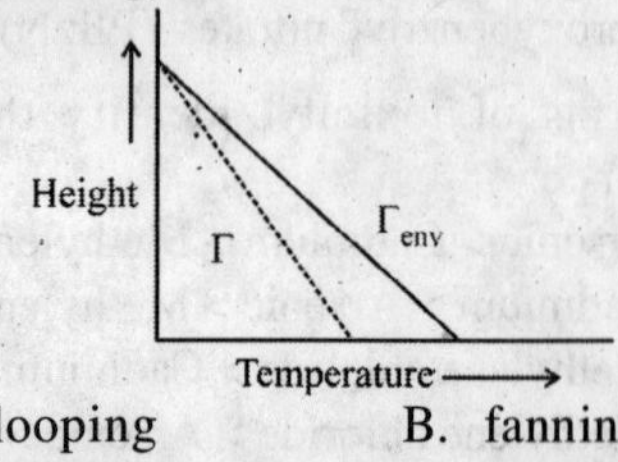

A. looping B. fanning
C. coning D. trapping

40. A road carrying heavy traffic has an average noise level of 90 dB when measured at a distance of 10 metres. What would be the noise level at 20 metres distance?

A. 87 dB B. 84 dB
C. 60 dB D. 45 dB

41. When biomass is converted to CO and H_2O, the energy made available is ~450 kJ per mol of carbon per unit of reduction level. What would be the heat of combustion per gram of methane?

A. 28.125 kJ/g B. 56.25 kJ/g
C. 67.5 kJ/g D. 135 kJ/g

42. Given below are two statements. One labelled as Assertion (A) and the other labelled as Reason (R):

Assertion (A) : Hydrogen, as a fuel, when burned, does produce some amount of pollution.

Reason (R) : Heat produced during combustion of hydrogen chemically combines N_2 and O_2 in atmosphere to produce NO_x.

Choose the correct answer:

A. Both (A) and (R) are correct and (R) is the correct explanation of (A).
B. Both (A) and (R) are correct and (R) is not the correct explanation of (A).
C. (A) is true but (R) is false.
D. (A) is false but (R) is true.

43. Given standard enthalpies for methane, carbon dioxide and water vapour as ~75 kJ/mol, 394 kJ/mol and 240 kJ/mol, respectively. What is the net heat of combustion of methane?

A. – 799 kJ/mol B. – 802 kJ/mol
C. + 1598 kJ/mol D. + 799 kJ/mol

44. In an ideal magnetohydrodynamic power plant, the speed of flow of the hot ionized gas is *u* m/s. The maximum power output from the plant varies as

A. $\propto u$ B. $\propto u^{3/2}$
C. $\propto u^2$ D. $\propto u^3$

45. An ideal wind turbine located on a hill top produces electrical power. If wind speed changes by 5%, by what percentage the electrical power will change?

A. 12.5 % B. 25 %
C. 30 % D. 15 %

46. A person working in a nuclear reactor is exposed to a beam of thermal neutrons and receives a dose of 20 millirads per hour for an exposure of 12 minutes. What is the equivalent dose in millirems, the person is exposed to?

A. 4 B. 8
C. 12 D. 16

47. What is the approximate increase in radiative forcing if the CO_2 concentration increases from 400 ppm to 800 ppm?

A. ~ 4.37 W/m^2 B. ~ 3.81 W/m^2
C. ~ 2.72 W/m^2 D. ~ 1.62 W/m^2

48. Given below are two statements. One labelled as Assertion (A) and the other labelled as Reason (R):

Assertion (A) : Large parts of India have already become water stressed.

Reason (R) : Climate change may be the main reason.

Choose the correct answer:

A. Both (A) and (R) are correct and (R) is the correct explanation of (A).
B. Both (A) and (R) are correct and (R) is not the correct explanation of (A).
C. (A) is true, but (R) is false.
D. (A) is false, but (R) is true.

49. Ecosystem degradation refers to

(*a*) loss or decrease in biodiversity.
(*b*) modification in structure of abiotic components.
(*c*) impairment of ecosystem processes such as nutrient cycling.

Choose the correct answer:

A. (*a*) only B. (*a*) and (*b*) only
C. (*b*) and (*c*) only D. (*a*), (*b*) and (*c*)

50. In addition to their role in ozone depletion, CFCs play a role in global warming by

A. reducing the albedo of the earth's surface
B. absorbing solar radiation
C. blocking UV-B radiation on earth
D. absorbing terrestrial radiation

51. Given below are two statements. One labelled as Assertion (A) and the other labelled as Reason (R):

Assertion (A) : As per equilibrium theory of island biogeography, distance of the islands from the mainland determines the dispersal rate of new species.

Reason (R) : Size of an island is important in determining number of species.

Choose the correct answer:

A. Both (A) and (R) are correct and (R) is the correct explanation of (A).
B. Both (A) and (R) are correct and (R) is not the correct explanation of (A).
C. (A) is true, but (R) is false.
D. (A) is false, but (R) is true.

52. Given below are two statements. One labelled as Assertion (A) and the other labelled as Reason (R):

Assertion (A) : All cloud processes have implications for climate change.

Reason (R) : Clouds strongly affect the flux of both shortwave and infra-red light through atmosphere.

Choose the correct answer:

A. Both (A) and (R) are correct and (R) is the correct explanation of (A).
B. Both (A) and (R) are correct and (R) is not the correct explanation of (A).
C. (A) is true, but (R) is false.
D. (A) is false, but (R) is true.

53. Using remote sensing for height measurement of trees, which microwave band is most suitable?

A. X B. C
C. S D. L

54. For public use, Survey of India publishes topographical maps on 1 : 50,000 scale. These maps use

A. UTM projection and WGS 84 datum
B. Polyconic projection and WGS84 datum
C. UTM projection and Modified Mount Everest datum
D. Polyconic projection and Modified Mount Everest datum

55. Sub-geostrophic winds in the earth-atmospheric system are caused by the balance involving

A. pressure gradient force, Coriolis force and frictional force
B. pressure gradient force and Coriolis force
C. pressure gradient force and frictional force
D. Coriolis force and frictional force

56. Which one of the following is not a set of polymorphous minerals?

A. Calcite, aragonite, vaterite
B. Quartz, coesite, tridymite
C. Graphite, anthracite, diamond
D. Kyanite, alusite and sillimanite

57. Match the List-I and List-II. Identify the correct answer from the codes given below:

List-I (**Geological events**)	**List-II** (**Processes**)
(*a*) Exfoliation dome	(*i*) Landform change
(*b*) Rift valleys	(*ii*) Ultisols
(*c*) Palaeomagnetism	(*iii*) Mechanical weathering
(*d*) Pedogenesis	(*iv*) Seafloor spreading

Codes:

	(*a*)	(*b*)	(*c*)	(*d*)
A.	(*i*)	(*ii*)	(*iii*)	(*iv*)
B.	(*ii*)	(*i*)	(*iv*)	(*iii*)
C.	(*iii*)	(*i*)	(*iv*)	(*ii*)
D.	(*iv*)	(*ii*)	(*i*)	(*iii*)

58. Given below are two statements. One labelled as Assertion (A) and the other labelled as Reason (R):

Assertion (A) : Soil development begins with physical, chemical and biological weathering of rocks.

Reason (R) : Anthropogenic factors play a major role in soil formation.

Choose the correct answer:

A. Both (A) and (R) are correct and (R) is the correct explanation of (A).
B. Both (A) and (R) are correct and (R) is not the correct explanation of (A).
C. (A) is true but (R) is false.
D. (A) is false but (R) is true.

59. The most common ferromagnesian rock forming minerals are as follows:

A. Amphibole and Biotite Mica
B. Muscovita mica and Quartz
C. Galena and Pyrite
D. Calcite and Dolomite

60. Underground coal mine fires can best be monitored by remote sensing technique in the spectral region

A. 3–5 μm B. 10–12 μm
C. 1–3 μm D. 1–10 mm

61. Our inability to address the conflict between short term individual well-being and long term societal welfare is responsible for the

A. Tragedy of the population
B. Tragedy of the community
C. Tragedy of the environment
D. Tragedy of the commons

62. Proportion of representation of each species allows ecologists to compare different communities through graphical representation. Such a graph is called

A. Rank abundance curve
B. Species accumulation curve
C. Survivorship curve
D. Sigmoid curve

63. Lincoln index is a mark-recapture method used in animals to estimate the

A. total population density
B. total number
C. total frequency
D. total dominance

64. K-selected population during ecological succession tends to dominate in

A. mature stages B. early stages
C. pioneer stages D. seral stages

65. Evolution can be viewed as

(*a*) genetic change over time
(*b*) a process of descent with modification
(*c*) a sudden change in organism
(*d*) a man-made change in oraganism

Choose the correct code:

A. (*a*) and (*b*) only B. (*b*) and (*c*) only
C. (*c*) and (*d*) only D. (*a*) and (*d*) only

66. Given below are two statements. One labelled as Assertion (A) and the other labelled as Reason (R):

Assertion (A) : C_4 photosynthesis lowers photorespiratory energy loss.

Reason (R) : The greater supply of CO_2 lowers the rate of O_2 uptake by rubisco substantially reducing photorespiration.

Choose the correct answer:

A. Both (A) and (R) are correct and (R) is the correct explanation of (A).
B. Both (A) and (R) are correct and (R) is not the correct explanation of (A).
C. (A) is true, but (R) is false.
D. (A) is false, but (R) is true.

67. Symbiotic blue-green algal biofertilizer is obtained from

A. *Nostoc* species
B. *Rhizobium* species
C. *Azolla* mass culture
D. *Azospirillum* mass culture

68. With reference to smog consider the following statements:

(*a*) Los Angeles smog is oxidizing.
(*b*) London smog is reducing.

Choose the correct answer:

A. Both (*a*) and (*b*) are false.
B. Both (*a*) and (*b*) are true.
C. (*a*) is false, but (*b*) is true.
D. (*a*) is true, but (*b*) is false.

69. Match the List-I and List-II. Identify the correct answer from the codes given below:

List-I (Chemical Species)	**List-II (Measurement Techniques)**
(*a*) DO	(*i*) West-Gaeke Method
(*b*) SO_2	(*ii*) Non-dispersive infrared analyser
(*c*) CO	(*iii*) Chemiluminescence
(*d*) NO	(*iv*) Winkler's Method

Codes:

	(*a*)	(*b*)	(*c*)	(*d*)
A.	(*iv*)	(*i*)	(*ii*)	(*iii*)
B.	(*iii*)	(*ii*)	(*i*)	(*iv*)
C.	(*ii*)	(*iii*)	(*iv*)	(*i*)
D.	(*i*)	(*iv*)	(*iii*)	(*ii*)

70. Disintegration of $^{88}_{226}Ra$ yields $^{86}_{222}Rn$ owing to the emission of

A. two β-particles
B. one α-particle
C. γ-radiation
D. one β-particle followed by an α-particle

71. Given below are two statements. One labelled as Assertion (A) and the other labelled as Reason (R):

Assertion (A) : Temperature in stratosphere increases with increase in altitude.

Reason (R) : Photodissociation of O_2 in stratosphere makes the lapse rate positive.

Choose the correct answer:

A. Both (A) and (R) are correct and (R) is the correct explanation of (A).
B. Both (A) and (R) are correct and (R) is not the correct explanation of (A).
C. (A) is true, but (R) is false.
D. (A) is false, but (R) is true.

72. At 15 °C, a manufacturer dissolves CO_2 at 2.4 atm in water in a bottle. If Henry's law constant of CO_2 in water be 0.045 mol L^{-1} atm^{-1} at 15 °C, calculate the concentration of CO_2 dissolved in water.

A. 5.6 mol L^{-1}
B. 0.019 mol L^{-1}
C. 0.098 mol L^{-1}
D. 0.108 mol L^{-1}

73. Match the List-I and List-II. Identify the correct answer from the codes given below:

List-I (Pesticides)	**List-II (Purpose)**
(*a*) Malathion	(*i*) Molluscicide
(*b*) Metaldehyde	(*ii*) Fungicide
(*c*) Diethyl Tolumide (DEET)	(*iii*) Insecticide
(*d*) Chloroneb	(*iv*) Insect repellant

Codes:

	(*a*)	(*b*)	(*c*)	(*d*)
A.	(*iv*)	(*ii*)	(*i*)	(*iii*)
B.	(*i*)	(*iii*)	(*ii*)	(*iv*)
C.	(*ii*)	(*iv*)	(*iii*)	(*i*)
D.	(*iii*)	(*i*)	(*iv*)	(*ii*)

74. Which of the following is not an Advanced Oxidation Process for the treatment of waste water?

A. PhotoFenton Process
B. Photocatalytic TiO_2 Process
C. UV/H_2O_2 Process
D. Acidified Potassium Dichromate Oxidation Process

75. If a material containing humic substances is extracted with a strong base, and the resulting solution is acidified, products are

(*a*) humin (*b*) humic acid
(*c*) fulvic acid

Choose the correct answer:

A. (*a*) only B. (*a*) and (*b*) only
C. (*a*), (*b*) and (*c*) D. (*b*) and (*c*) only

ANSWERS

1	2	3	4	5	6	7	8	9	10
C	C	B	A	C	C	C	A	C	D
11	**12**	**13**	**14**	**15**	**16**	**17**	**18**	**19**	**20**
C	B	A	A	D	C	D	D	B	A
21	**22**	**23**	**24**	**25**	**26**	**27**	**28**	**29**	**30**
A	C	D	C	B	A	D	C	B	B
31	**32**	**33**	**34**	**35**	**36**	**37**	**38**	**39**	**40**
A	D	A	B	A	A	B	B	A	A
41	**42**	**43**	**44**	**45**	**46**	**47**	**48**	**49**	**50**
B	A	A	C	D	B	A	C	D	D
51	**52**	**53**	**54**	**55**	**56**	**57**	**58**	**59**	**60**
B	A	D	A	A	C	C	C	A	B
61	**62**	**63**	**64**	**65**	**66**	**67**	**68**	**69**	**70**
D	A	A	A	A	A	C	B	A	B
71	**72**	**73**	**74**	**75**					
C	D	D	D	C					

EXPLANATORY ANSWERS

1. The IX Plan proposal for the continuation of the Centrally Sponsored Scheme (CSS) "Project Tiger" was approved by the Government in June 1999 with the direction that for monitoring purposes, a master plan for development of each of the reserves should be prepared.

Achievement of physical targets was to be compared with the master plan. PTD stated in March 2006 that the Management Plans (MPs) of the Tiger Reserves were the master plans.

3. Nowadays there is serious concern about the effectiveness of existing strategies for biodiversity protection. A central issue in conservation is to identify biodiversity-rich areas to which conservation resources should be directed. Based on the observation that some parts of the world have far more species than others, the area-based approaches are widely advocated for species conservation planning. Areas with high concentrations of endemic species (species that are found nowhere else on Earth) and with high habitat loss are often referred to as "hotspots". The hotspot approach can be applied at any geographical scale and both in terrestrial and marine environments.

4. Ocean Thermal Energy Conversion (OTEC) plants have very low efficiencies. OTEC works best when the temperature difference between the warmer, top layer of the ocean and the colder, deep ocean water is about 36°F (20°C). These conditions exist in tropical coastal areas, roughly between the Tropic of Capricorn and the Tropic of Cancer. To bring the cold water to the surface, ocean thermal energy conversion plants require an expensive, large-diameter intake pipe, which is submerged a mile or more into the ocean's depths.

5. **Geothermal power** is power generated by geothermal energy. Technologies in use include dry steam power stations, flash steam power stations and binary cycle power stations.

Installed geothermal electric capacity

Country	Capacity (MW) 2007	Capacity (MW) 2010	Capacity (MW) 2013	Capacity (MW) 2015	Share of national generation (%)
USA	2687	3086	3389	3450	0.3
Iceland	421.2	575	664	665	30.0
Japan	535.2	536	537	519	0.1
Russia	79	82	97	82	

6. Temperate Deciduous Forests are those, which consist of predominantly broad-leafed trees. Deciduous forests are of two types: Temperate and Tropical. Temperate deciduous forests occur in areas of moderate temperature and rainfall with chilly winters. It covers maximum geographical area. Species belonging to these forests drop leaves in autumn. The deciduous forests in tropical areas shed leaves only by December (in the Northern Hemisphere) when water becomes scarce. The tropical monsoon deciduous forests are found in areas receiving an annual rainfall of 100 to 200 cms in India, with a distinct dry and rainy season and minimum temperature. The deciduous forest can further be divided into Moist and Dry.

7. Diversity is a combination of two factors; the number of species present, species richness, and the distribution of individuals among the species are referred to as evenness or equitability. Whittaker distinguishes three types of diversity:
   1. *Alpha*-diversity – diversity within a particular area or ecosystem.
   2. *Beta*-diversity – the change in diversity between ecosystems, and
   3. *Gamma*-diversity – the overall diversity of a landscape comprising of several ecosystem.

   The two most widely used species diversity indices are Shannon and Simpson indices. They are adopted by ecologists to describe the average degree of uncertainty in predicting the species of an individual picked at random from a given community.

9. **Milankovitch cycles** describes the collective effects of changes in the Earth's movements upon its climate, named after Serbian geophysicist and astronomer Milutin Milankovic, who in the 1920s had theorized that variations in eccentricity, axial tilt, and precession of the Earth's orbit determined climatic patterns on Earth through orbital forcing.

10. The ENSO cycle, both El Niño and La Niña, causes global changes of both temperatures and rainfall.

13. Sand dunes form when the wind carries small particles of sand that are deposited against an obstacle, such as a shrub, rock, tree or any other kind of obstruction. As small particles of sand are deposited around the obstacle,

the dune grows in size, forming rows that grow perpendicular to the wind's direction. The wind will continue to erode the sand particles that were deposited on the windward side of the dune and deposit them on the leeward side of the dune. Sand dunes migrate when erosion by the wind forces the sand particles to move by saltation on the upwind slope. These particles are then deposited on the slip face, creating repose angles of 30-34°.

14. Zoogeographic Regions

1. Distribution of animals over the world is more complex and irregular than plants because they are mobile.
2. Broad distribution of animals is reflective of the distribution of energy and food diversity: (*a*) richest faunal assemblages are in the permissive environment of the humid tropics (*b*) sparsest representations of both species and individuals are in the dry lands and cold lands.

15. Point Source Gaussian Plume Model

Model Structure and Assumptions

- pollutants released from a "virtual point source".
- advective transport by wind.
- dispersive transport (spreading) follows normal (Gaussian) distribution away from trajectory.
- constant emission rate.
- wind speed constant with time and elevation.
- pollutant is conservative (no reaction).
- terrain is flat and unobstructed.
- uniform atmospheric stability.

17. The **Lotka-Volterra equations,** also known as the **predator-prey equations,** are a pair of first-order, non-linear, differential equations frequently used to describe the dynamics of biological systems in which two species interact, one as a predator and the other as prey.

The Lotka-Volterra model makes a number of assumptions about the environment and evolution of the predator and prey populations:

1. The prey population finds ample food at all times.
2. The food supply of the predator population depends entirely on the size of the prey population.
3. The rate of change of population is proportional to its size.
4. During the process, the environment does not change in favour of one species and genetic adaptation is inconsequential.
5. Predators have limitless appetite.

22. The Environment (Protection) Act (EPA), 1986, under the jurisdiction of the Indian Ministry of Environment and Forests (MoEF) is officially considered to be the umbrella legislation to regulate environment degradation and pollution. It also attempts to provide a critical framework to enable the coordination of bodies such as Pollution Control Boards set up through air and water related legislations that precede the EPA.

23. The Basel Convention on the Control of Transboundary Movements of Hazardous Wastes and their Disposal was adopted on 22 March 1989 by the Conference of Plenipotentiaries in Basel, Switzerland, in response to a public outcry following the discovery, in the 1980s, in Africa and other parts of the developing world of deposits of toxic wastes imported from abroad.

24. Incineration is a waste treatment process that involves the combustion of organic substances contained in waste materials. Incineration of waste materials converts the waste into ash, flue gas, and heat. The ash is mostly formed by the inorganic constituents of the waste, and may take the form of solid lumps or particulates carried by the flue gas. The flue gases must be cleaned of gaseous and particulate pollutants before they are dispersed into the atmosphere. In some cases, the heat generated by incineration can be used to generate electric power.

Incineration reduces the volume of waste but could release toxic air emissions into the Atmosphere.

25. The dwelling units of the traditional coastal communities including fisherfolk, tribals as were permissible under the provisions of the CRZ notification, 1991, but which have not obtained formal approval from concerned authorities under the aforesaid notification shall be considered by the respective Union territory CZMAs and the dwelling units shall be regularized subject to the following condition, namely–

(*i*) These are not used for any commercial activity.

(*ii*) These are not sold or transferred to non-traditional coastal community.

28. The ISO 14000 family includes most notably the ISO 14001 standard, which represents the core set of standards used by organizations for designing and implementing an effective Environmental Management System (EMS). ISO 14001 sets out the criteria for an Environmental Management System (EMS). It does not state requirements for environmental performance, but maps out a framework that a company or organization can follow to set up an effective EMS. It can be used by any organization that wants to improve resource efficiency, reduce waste, and drive down costs. Using ISO 14001 can provide assurance to company management and employees as well as external stakeholders that environmental impact is being measured and improved. ISO 14001 can also be integrated with other management functions and assists companies in meeting their environmental and economic goals..

29. A unique problem-set of the smaller-size software project is that technically qualified personnel for performing feasibility studies and cost-benefit analysis are often not available. Therefore, linking the feasibility study to risk analysis and cost-benefit analysis techniques may result in no feasibility study being performed. Since in most system development projects it is important that some form of feasibility study be executed, to the highest degree of rigor that circumstances permit, then it is preferable to consider risk analysis and cost-benefit analysis as alternative phases.

32. Simple 'interaction matrices' as developed by Leopold *et al.* display project actions or activities along one axis with appropriate environmental factors listed along the other (Canter 1996). Leopold *et al.* (1971) constructed a generic interaction matrix based on about 100 categories of action and 90 categories of 'environmental item'. To use the 'Leopold' matrix, each action and its potential for creating an impact must be considered for each environmental item or receptor. Where an impact is anticipated, the matrix is marked with a diagonal line in the appropriate cell. It is also possible to indicate the possibility of beneficial or detrimental impacts using + or – signs, respectively.

34. Photochemical oxidants are the products of reactions between NO_x and a wide variety of volatile organic compounds (VOCs). The most well known 'oxidants' are ozone (O_3), peroxyacetyle nitrate (PAN) and hydrogen peroxide (H_2O_2). The main impact on the natural environment is mostly due to elevated O_3. Excessive concentrations of tropospheric (ground level) O_3 have toxic effects on both plants and human health.

49. Environmental degradation is the deterioration of the environment through depletion of resources such as air, water and soil; the destruction of ecosystems and the extinction of wildlife. It refers to loss or decrease in biodiversity, modification in structure of abiotic components and impairment of ecosystem processes such as nutrient cycling.

50. CFCs were phased out via the Montreal Protocol due to their part in ozone depletion. This anthropogenic compound is also a greenhouse gas, with a much higher potential to enhance the greenhouse effect than CO_2.

52. All cloud processes have the potential to change as the climate state changes. Cloud feedbacks are of intense interest in the context of climate change. Any change in a cloud process that is caused by climate change - and in turn influences climate - represents a cloud-climate feedback. Because clouds interact so strongly with both sunlight and infrared light, small changes in cloudiness can have a potent effect on the climate system. Many possible types of cloud-climate feedbacks have been suggested, involving changes in cloud amount, cloudtop height and/or cloud reflectivity. The literature shows consistently that high clouds amplify global warming as they interact with infrared light emitted by the atmosphere and surface. There is more uncertainty, however, about the feedbacks associated with low-altitude clouds, and about cloud feedbacks associated with amount and reflectivity in general.

53. Interaction of SAR microwaves with canopies, trees and soil is of interest. The longer wavelengths (*e.g.,* L-band 15-20 cm) penetrate the canopy, and its backscatter data contains information that relates to leaves, branches, stems and soil conditions; the longer the wavelength the greater the penetration. It has been proven that radar is sensitive to the structure of the canopy. The received backscatter intensity represented in the image is a composition of interactions with the crown, the trunk and the ground surface. Using fully polarimetric SAR it is possible to derive a relationship between backscatter, texture and crop status.

54. **Open Series Maps (OSM)** – These are prepared on 1:250,000; 1:50,000 and 1:25,000 scales for the use of general public/civilians for supporting development activities in the country. Technically maps of this series are based on WGS-84 Datum and UTM Projection. They do not contain grid and classified information; therefore, they are kept under unrestricted category. They can be obtained from all map sale centre and other authorized agents deputed all over the country. Few sheets are also printed in Hindi and other regional languages.

55. An air parcel initially at rest will move from high pressure to low pressure because of the pressure gradient force (PGF). However, as that air parcel begins to move, it is deflected by the Coriolis force to the right in the northern hemisphere (to the left on the southern hemisphere). As the wind gains speed, the deflection increases until the Coriolis force equals the pressure gradient force. At this point, the wind will be blowing parallel to the isobars. When this happens, the wind is referred to as geostrophic.

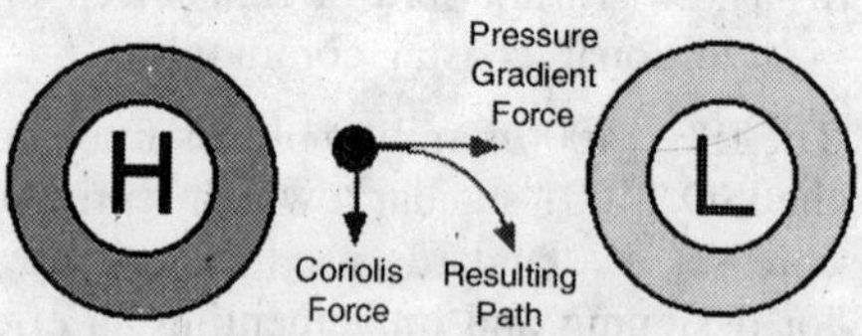

57. Exfoliation refers to the *spalling,* or breaking off, of curved rock shells roughly parallel or concentric to the surface. Exfoliation is especially common in granite and was once thought to be caused by temperature changes. However, this process may actually be related to both chemical and physical weathering processes. Exfoliation that produces thin sheets or spalls a few millimeters or so thick is associated with hydration, a chemical weathering process.

A rift valley is a lowland region that forms where Earth's tectonic plates move apart, or rift. Rift valleys are found both on land and at the bottom of the ocean, where they are created by the process of seafloor spreading. Rift valleys differ from river valleys and glacial valleys in that they are created by tectonic activity and not the process of erosion.

Paleomagnetists led the revival of the continental drift hypothesis and its transformation into plate tectonics. Apparent polar wander paths provided the first clear geophysical evidence for continental drift, while marine magnetic anomalies did the same for seafloor spreading. Paleomagnetism continues to extend the history of plate tectonics back in time and are applied to the movement of continental fragments, or terranes.

Pedogenesis is the process of soil formation as regulated by the effects of place, environment, and history. Pedogenesis is studied as a branch of pedology, the study of soil in its natural environment. Other branches of pedology are the study of soil morphology, and soil classification. The study of pedogenesis is important to understanding soil distribution patterns in current (soil geography) and past (paleopedology) geologic periods.

59. Ferromagnesian silicates contain iron and magnesium. Since these two metal ions are nearly identical in size, they easily substitute for one another in the crystal structure. Ferromagnesian silicates are usually dark in colour. Olivine, pyroxene, amphibole and biotite mica are ferromagnesian silicates.

61. Our inability to address the conflict between short term individual well-being and long term societal welfare is responsible for the tragedy of the commons.

62. A rank abundance curve or Whittaker plot is a chart used by ecologists to display relative species abundance, a component of biodiversity. It can also be used to visualize species richness and species evenness. It overcomes the shortcomings of biodiversity indices that cannot display the relative role different variables played in their calculation.

The rank abundance curve visually depicts both species richness and species evenness. Species richness can be viewed as the number of different species on the chart *i.e.,* how many species were ranked. Species evenness is reflected in the slope of the line that fits the graph (assuming a linear, *i.e.,* logarithmic series, relationship). A steep gradient indicates low evenness as the high-ranking species have much higher abundances than the low-ranking species. A shallow gradient indicates high evenness as the abundances of different species are similar.

63. **Mark and recapture** is a method commonly used in ecology to estimate an animal population's size. A portion of the population is captured, marked, and released. Later, another portion is captured and the number of marked individuals within the sample is counted. Other names for this method is the Lincoln method.

The Lincoln-Petersen method (also known as the Petersen-Lincoln index or Lincoln index) can be used to estimate population size if only two visits are made to the study area. This method assumes that the study population is "closed".

64. K-selected species possess relatively stable populations and tend to produce relatively low numbers of offspring; however, individual offspring tend to be quite large in comparison with *r*-selected species. *K*-selected species are characterized by long gestation periods lasting several months, slow maturation (and thus extended parental care), and long life spans. In addition, they tend to inhabit relatively stable biological communities, such as late-successional or climax forests.

65. "Evolution" commonly is used more narrowly to refer to the specific theory that all organisms have descended from common ancestors, also known as the "theory of descent with modification," or to refer to one explanation for the process by which change occurs, the "theory of modification through natural selection". The term also is used with reference to a comprehensive theory that includes both the non-causal pattern of descent with modification and the causal mechanism of natural selection.

Evolution can be viewed as genetic change over time or as a process of descent with modification. Biological evolution is change in organisms over time.

68. The London smog has been called reducing or sulphurous smog. This type is identified by high concentrations of sulphur dioxide (SO_2) and particulate matter. London smog is therefore composed of air pollutants that are emitted directly by combustion processes and are called "Primary pollutants".

The Los Angeles smog is an oxidizing smog formed from the photochemical reactions of nitrogen oxides and volatile organic hydrocarbons, which are primary pollutants released from the combustion of fossil fuels in automobiles, power plants, etc.

70. When one α-particle emitted from a radioactive substance, its atomic number is decreases by two and its mass number is decreases by 4.

$$^{226}_{88}Ra \xrightarrow[\alpha-\text{particle}]{} {}^{222}_{86}Rn \; .$$

71. The air at the surface up to around 10 kilometers is called the troposphere. The reason it is warmer at the surface is simple. The air is warmed by heat given off by the Earth! The farther away from the surface the air moves, the less heat there is to absorb.

The stratosphere lies roughly 12 to 50 km above the surface and is marked by a temperature profile that increases with height. This is due to the absorbtion by ozone of the sun's UV radiation and is in sharp contrast to the lower atmosphere. There it generally gets colder as you go higher due to the expansion of gases as the pressure decreases. Technically, the stratosphere has a negative 'lapse rate' (temperature increases with height), while the lower atmosphere's lapse rate is positive.

72. When a gas is dissolved in a liquid, the concentrations will eventually reach equilibrium between the source of the gas and the solution. Henry's Law shows the concentration of a solute gas in a solution is directly proportional to the partial pressure of the gas over the solution.

$$P = K_H C; \text{ where}$$

P is the partial pressure of the gas above the solution

K_H is the Henry's Law constant for the solution

C is the concentration of the dissolved gas in solution.

$$P = 2.4 \times 0.045$$
$$= 0.108 \text{ mol/L}^{-1}$$

75. The most important class of complexing agents that occur naturally is the humic substances. These are degradation-resistant materials formed during the decomposition of vegetation that occur as deposits in soil, marsh sediments, peat, coal, lignite, or in almost any location where large quantities of vegetation have decayed. They are commonly classified on the basis of solubility. If a material containing humic substances is extracted with a strong base, and the resulting solution is acidified, the products are (1) a nonextractable plant residue called humin; (2) a material that precipitates from the acidified extract, called humic acid; and (3) an organic material that remains in the acidified solution, called fulvic acid. Because of their acid-base, sorptive, and complexing properties, both the soluble and insoluble humic substances have a strong effect upon the properties of water. In general, fulvic acid dissolves in water and exerts its effects as the soluble species. Humin and humic acid remain insoluble and affect water quality through exchange of species, such as cations or organic materials, with water.

Previous Paper (Solved)

UGC–NET Environmental Science

Junior Research Fellowship and Assistant Professor Exam

December–2015

PAPER-II

Note : *This paper contains **fifty (50)** objective type questions of **two (2)** marks each. **All** questions are **compulsory**.*

1. Which one of the following elements contributes maximum to the earth crust by weight?
A. Iron B. Silicon
C. Oxygen D. Carbon

2. The lowest temperature is observed in which layer of the atmosphere?
A. Troposphere B. Stratosphere
C. Mesosphere D. Thermosphere

3. Which of the following gases has the lowest residence time?
A. CO_2 B. N_2O
C. CFCs D. CH_4

4. Which of the following statement is **incorrect**?
A. Chromium (VI) is highly toxic
B. Methyl mercury is most toxic mercury species
C. Arsenic (III) is more toxic than arsenic (V)
D. Cadmium is a criteria pollutant

5. The most abundant functional group present in fulvic acid, commonly found in soils, is:
A. Peptide group
B. Carboxylate group
C. Phenolic group
D. Amino group

6. The source of Stratospheric NO_x is:
A. Atmospheric N_2
B. Tropospheric N_2O
C. Tropospheric NO
D. Tropospheric NO_2

7. In troposphere, which of the following processes does **not** generate hydroxyl radical?
A. $O(^1D) + H_2O$ B. $O(^3P) + H_2O$
C. HCHO + hν D. HNO_2 + hν

8. The most common form of lead present in pesticide is:
A. Lead acetate B. Lead arsenate
C. Lead azide D. Lead telluride

9. Consider the following four statements about benzo[a]pyrene:
(*a*) It is a group I carcinogen
(*b*) It is a polycyclic aromatic hydrocarbon
(*c*) Its molecular formula is $C_{20}H_{12}$
(*d*) It has four benzene rings

Choose the **correct** code:
A. (*a*) and (*b*) only
B. (*a*), (*b*) and (*c*) only
C. (*b*), (*c*) and (*d*) only
D. (*a*), (*b*), (*c*) and (*d*)

10. Given below are two statements. One labelled as **Assertion (A)** and the other labelled as **Reason (R)**.

Assertion (A): Radon is an inert gas and it is radioactive.

Reason (R): All inert gases are radioactive.

Choose the **correct** answer:
A. Both (A) and (R) are correct and (R) is the correct explanation of (A).
B. Both (A) and (R) are correct and (R) is not the correct explanation of (A).
C. (A) is true, but (R) is false.
D. (A) is false, but (R) is true.

11. Most of Epiphytes are examples of type of biotic interactions called:

A. Mutualism B. Coevolution
C. Commensalism D. Parasitism

12. Inhalation of airborne mold spore leads to disease in man such as:
A. Bronchitis
B. Allergy
C. Cardiac congestion
D. Eye irritation

13. Biological diversity is mainly a function of:
(*a*) Latitude
(*b*) Longitude
(*c*) Distance from sea

Choose the **correct** answer:
A. (*a*) only B. (*a*) and (*b*) only
C. (*b*) and (*c*) only D. (*a*), (*b*) and (*c*)

14. The ability of a living system to be restored through secondary succession after a more severe disturbance is known as:
A. Rehabilitation B. Resistance
C. Resilience D. Restoration

15. The characteristic feature of the background extinction is disappearance of a species at a:
A. low rate B. fast rate
C. lapse rate D. intrinsic rate

16. Speciation means:
A. Natural process of extinction of different species
B. Artificial process of extinction of different species
C. One species splits into two or more different species naturally
D. Characterisation of different species

17. Topological modelling is a well organized cluster of functions in GIS to process:
(*a*) Spatial data
(*b*) Attribute data
(*c*) Physico-chemical data
(*d*) Species richness data

Choose the **correct** code:
A. (*a*) and (*b*) only
B. (*b*) and (*c*) only
C. (*a*), (*b*) and (*c*) only
D. (*a*), (*b*), (*c*) and (*a*)

18. A rock body or formation which may be porous enough to hold enough quantity of water but which by virtue of its other properties does not allow an easy and quick flow through it, is called:
A. Aquitard B. Aquifuge
C. Aquiclude D. Aquifer

19. For many decades, geologists noted the high number of earthquakes and active volcanoes occurring around the rim of the Pacific Ocean basin. This is called:
A. Volcanic ring B. Ring of fire
C. Earthquake zone D. Volcanic hot spot

20. Inversion that occurs near Earth's Surface is called:
A. Radiation inversion
B. Advectional inversion
C. Subsidence inversion
D. Cold-air-drainage inversion

21. The radiation flux emitted per unit solid angle in a specified direction by a unit area of source is called:
A. irradiance B. radiance
C. exitance D. radiant flux

22. Mean residence time of soil organic matter in an ecosystem is maximum in:
A. Tropical rain forest
B. Boreal forest
C. Temperate coniferous forest
D. Dry deciduous forest

23. Worst affected area by Indian Ocean Tsunami of December 2004 in India was:
A. Andaman and Nicobar Islands
B. Tamil Nadu
C. Andhra Pradesh
D. Odisha

24. Consider solar insolation of 400 W/m^2 incident on a single solar cell of area 100 cm^2. If only 15% of the photons cause electron - hole pairs and the average energy of incident photons is ~1 eV, the short circuit current of the cell is:
A. 1.2 A B. 1.5 A
C. 1.6 A D. 1.8 A

25. For which of the following renewable resources of energy, sun is not directly responsible?

A. Wind B. Biomass
C. OTEC D. Tidal

26. In terms of the calorific value, identify the **correct** sequence:

A. Methane > hydrogen > ethanol > methanol
B. Hydrogen > methane > ethanol > methanol
C. Methane > hydrogen > methanol > ethanol
D. Hydrogen > ethanol > methane > methanol

27. At a given location the wind speeds are predominantly in the range 6 to 6.4 m/s. This location's wind power class will be termed as:

A. Fair B. Good
C. Excellent D. Outstanding

28. Which of the following nuclides does **not** undergo fission with low energy (slow) neutrons?

A. 235 U B. 238 U
C. 239 Pu D. 233 U

29. According to CPCB standards, the annual average concentration of $PM_{2.5}$ should not exceed:

A. 60 $\mu g\ m^{-3}$ B. 40 $\mu g\ m^{-3}$
C. 80 $\mu g\ m^{-3}$ D. 100 $\mu g\ m^{-3}$

30. Which of the following is a secondary aerosol?

A. Pollens
B. Virus
C. Sodium Chloride
D. Ammonium Sulphate

31. In the colorimetric determination of ambient SO_2 by WEST-GAEKE method, the absorbance of the coloured complex should be measured at which of the following wavelengths?

A. 550 nm B. 650 nm
C. 450 nm D. 350 nm

32. A healthy human ear, before experiencing pain, can detect sound pressure levels as high as:

A. 50 Pa B. 100 Pa
C. 200 Pa D. 1000 Pa

33. The resultant of two noise levels of 80 dB and 50 dB will be about:

A. ~80 dB B. ~82 dB
C. ~60 dB D. ~130 dB

34. The half life of radioactive iodine –131 is:

A. 30 years B. 15 years
C. 5 years D. 8 days

35. Which of the following best describes the function of the environmental management plan as a part of the environmental statement?

A. It describes the environmental impacts of the proposal.
B. It describes the baseline environmental data.
C. It describes the project proposal in detail.
D. It describes the actions and auditing procedures needed.

36. India submitted its INDCs related to climate change to the UN recently. What does INDCs stand for?

A. Intended Nationally Devoted Contributions
B. Intended Nationally Determined Contributions
C. Intended Notified Decisive Contributions
D. India's Nationally Determined Contributions

37. Formal EIA became an integral part of Environmental Management in India by a Notification for the first time in:

A. 1988 B. 1990
C. 1992 D. 1994

38. EIA is necessary because:

(*a*) Development is not good for environment
(*b*) Environmental impacts of development are in public interest
(*c*) There is growing interest in sustainability

Choose the **correct** answer:

A. (*a*) only B. (*b*) only
C. (*b*) and (*c*) only D. (*a*), (*b*) and (*c*)

39. A moist air parcel at 24°C has a mixing ratio of 10 g per kg. Its virtual temperature is:

A. ~25.81°C B. ~20.68°C
C. ~ 31.25°C D. ~28.12°C

40. The Vienna Convention is basically related to:
A. International trade in endangered species
B. Protection of O_3 layer
C. Biodiversity conservation
D. Preservation of cultural environment

41. According to Wildlife Protection Act in India, who is the authority to issue permission to hunt rogue animals?
A. Chief Minister of the State
B. Chief Wildlife Warden
C. Conservator of Forest
D. Deputy Commissioner

42. According to MOEF (now MOEFCC) notification of 1992, for labelling cosmetics as environment friendly product, the presence of fluoride (F) in tooth paste/powder should not exceed:
A. 20 ppm B. 50 ppm
C. 100 ppm D. 10 ppm

43. Which one of the following methods converts decomposed liquid or solid hazardous organic waste effectively?
A. Open incineration
B. Plasma incineration
C. Sanitory landfill
D. Bioremidiation

44. For a bi-variate sample, the correlation coefficient is 0.25 and it is found to be significantly different from zero at 5% level of significance. Given $t_{0.05}$ = 1.645, what is the minimum size of the sample?
A. 43 B. 50
C. 55 D. 63

45. Which one of the following is non-probability sampling?
A. Convenience probability
B. Stratified
C. Cluster
D. Systemic

46. A parametric test generally used to compare sample variance to a theoretical population variance, is:
A. F - test B. Z - test
C. t - test D. χ^2 - text

47. From a random sample of 36 fish caught in a sample, the mean length $(\overline{X})$ and sample standard deviation (sd) were found to be 30 cm and 6 cm respectively. If at 95% confidence level z is 1.96, then the mean length of fish in this population is in the range:
A. $27 < X < 33$ B. $27.5 < X < 32.5$
C. $24 < X < 36$ D. $28.04 < X < 32$

48. One of the natural causes of occurrence of inland soil alkalinity is the presence of:
A. Sodium hypochlorite
B. Potassium nitrate
C. Sodium chloride
D. Sodium carbonate

49. The Supreme Court of India directed the government to implement environmental education in all educational institutions as compulsory subject in:
A. 1976 B. 2003
C. 1988 D. 2014

50. Organic wetland soils have:
A. high cation capacity
B. high bulk density
C. low porosity
D. high nutrient availability

ANSWERS

1	2	3	4	5	6	7	8	9	10
C	C	D	D	B	B	B	B	B	C
11	**12**	**13**	**14**	**15**	**16**	**17**	**18**	**19**	**20**
C	B	A	C	A	C	A	C	B	A

21	22	23	24	25	26	27	28	29	30
B	B	A	A	D	B	C	B	B	D
31	**32**	**33**	**34**	**35**	**36**	**37**	**38**	**39**	**40**
A	C	A	D	D	B	D	C	A	B
41	**42**	**43**	**44**	**45**	**46**	**47**	**48**	**49**	**50**
B	D	B	A	A	D	D	D	B	A

EXPLANATORY ANSWERS

1. This table includes the average weight percentage each element contributes to the composition of the earth's crust.

Table: ***Weight percentages of the earth's crust***

Element	Weight %
Oxygen	46.7
Silicon	27.7
Aluminum	8.15
Iron	5.00
Calcium	3.65
Sodium	2.85
Potassium	2.60
Magnesium	2.10
Hydrogen	.15
Phosphorus	.15
Total	**99.05**

2. The mesopause is the temperature minimum at the boundary between the mesosphere and the thermosphere atmospheric regions. Due to the lack of solar heating and very strong radiative cooling from carbon dioxide, the mesosphere is the coldest region on Earth with temperatures as low as –100°C (–148°F or 173 K). The altitude of the mesopause for many years was assumed to be at around 85 km (52 mi.), but observations to higher altitudes and modelling studies in the last 10 years have shown that in fact the mesopause consists of two minima - one at about 85 km and a stronger minimum at about 100 km.

5. Fulvic acids: The fraction of humic substances that is soluble in water under all pH conditions. They remain in solution after removal of humic acid by acidification. Fulvic acids are light yellow to yellow-brown in colour.

Fulvic acids contain more functional groups of an acidic nature, particulary COOH. The total acidities of fulvic acids (900 - 1400 meq/100 g) are considerably higher than for humic acids (400 - 870 meq/100 g).

6. Nitrogen substances: Nitrous oxide (N_2O). The dominant sources of N_2O are natural, but anthropogenic contributions are becoming increasingly important. Nitrous oxide is the primary source of stratospheric NO_x, which play a vital role in controlling the abundance of stratospheric ozone.

Nitrogen oxides (NO_x). Ground-level sources of NO_x play a major direct role only in tropospheric photochemical processes and an indirect role in stratosphere photochemistry, whereas injection of NO_x close to the tropopause may lead directly to a change in upper tropospheric and stratospheric ozone.

8. Most common form of lead present in pesticide is Lead arsenate. Lead arsenate is a pentavalent form of inorganic arsenic. It normally exists as white crystals with no discernible odour. Lead arsenate contains 22% arsenic and is very slightly soluble in cold water. The melting point of lead arsenate is 1042°C, the density is 7.80 and the molecular weight is 347.12.

9. Benzo[a]pyrene is a polycyclic aromatic hydrocarbon found in coaltar with the formula $C_{20}H_{12}$. Its metabolites are mutagenic and highly carcinogenic, and it is listed as a Group

I carcinogen by the IARC. The compound is one of the benzopyrenes, formed by abenzene ring fused to pyrene, and is the result of incomplete combustion at temperatures between 300°C (572°F) and 600°C.

11. Commensalism is an interaction that benefits one species but has little, if any, effect on the other species. One example is some kinds of silverfish insects that move along with columns of army ants to share the food left over during their raids. The army ants receive no apparent harm or benefit from the silverfish.

Birds can benefit from trees by making their nests in them. But generally this does not affect the trees in any way. Another example is plants called *epiphytes* such as some types of orchids and bromeliads, which attach themselves to the trunks or branches of large trees in tropical and subtropical forests.

12. The molds that produce airborne toxins that can cause serious symptoms, such as breathing difficulties, memory and hearing loss, dizziness, flu-like symptoms, and acid reflux. Common ailments from toxigenic mold—including allergies (hypersensitivity after initial toxicity), and excessive bruising—usually can be treated and reduced after people leave their contaminated environment.

13. The word "biodiversity" is a contracted version of "biological diversity". The Convention on Biological Diversity defines biodiversity as: "the variability among living organisms from all sources including, *inter alia*, terrestrial, marine and other aquatic ecosystems and the ecological complexes of which they are a part; this includes diversity within species, between species, and of ecosystems."

14. **Resilience:** The ability of a living system to be restored through secondary succession after a more severe disturbance.

16. Under certain circumstances, natural selection can lead to an entirely new species. In this process, called speciation, one species splits into two or more different species. For sexually reproducing organisms, a new species forms when one population of a species has evolved to the point where its members can no longer breed and produce fertile offspring with members of another population that did not change or that evolved differently.

17. A geographic information system or geographical information system (GIS) or geospatial information system is a system designed to capture, store, manipulate, analyze, manage, and present all types of spatial or geographical data. The acronym GIS is sometimes used for geographic information science (GIScience) to refer to the academic discipline that studies geographic information systems and is a large domain within the broader academic discipline of geoinformatics.

18. **Aquiclude:** A rocky body or formation which may be porous enough to hold enough quantity of water but which by virtue of its other properties does not allow an easy and quick flow through it. It is to be treated as a practically impermeable rock mass. Compacted clay formations are the best examples of aquicludes.

19. The greater depths of the oceans are found in trenches at the margins of the oceans. Excepting the Indonesia, Antilles, and Scotia deeps, the major trenches are found in the Pacific Ocean floor. However, as pointed out by Uyeda, in a broad sense, even these three exceptions may be regarded as part of the Pacific margin because they comprise the belts of active volcanoes, sometimes called the Ring of Fire around the Pacific. These are also belts of high seismic activity and margins with trenches are Pacific-type or active margins.

20. *Ground surface inversion* also called as *radiation inversion* occurs near the earth's

surface due to radiation mechanism. This is also called as non-advectional inversion because it occurs in static atmospheric condition characterized by no movement of air whether horizontal or vertical (it may be noted that air is never static). Such inversion normally occurs during the long cold winter nights in the snow-covered regions of the middle and high latitudes. In fact, surface inversion is caused due to excessive nocturnal cooling of the ground surface due to rapid rate of loss of heat from the ground through outgoing longwave terrestrial radiation. Thus, the air coming in contact with the cool ground surface also becomes cold while the air layer lying above is relatively warm. Consequently, temperature inversion develops because of cold air layer below and warm air layer above.

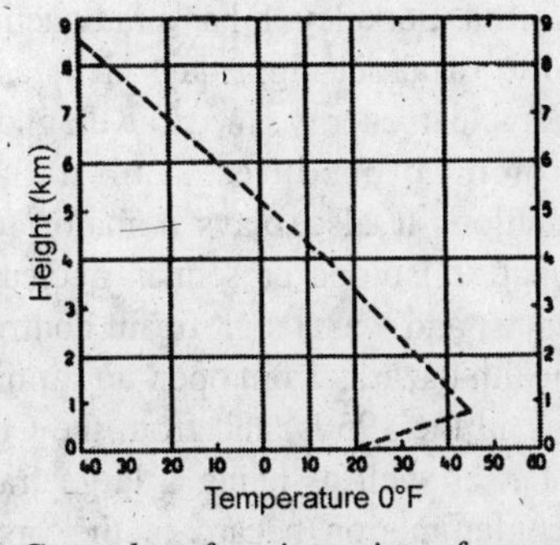

Fig.: *Ground surface inversion of temperature*

21. **Radiance:** An element of surface with an area dS emits a flux $d\mathbf{F}$ in a direction specified by an angle ψ with respect to the normal. When the element is projected at right angles to the direction of the flux, its projected area is $dS \cos \psi$ which is the apparent or effective area of the surface viewed from an angle ψ. The radiance of the element in this direction is the flux emitted in the direction per unit solid angle, or $d\mathbf{F}/\omega$, divided by the projected area $dS \cos \psi$. In other words, radiance is equivalent to the intensity of radiant flux observed in a particular direction divided by the apparent area of the source in the same direction. This quantity may be expressed in W m^{-2} sr^{-1}.

22. The boreal forest is the world's largest land-based biome. Spreading over continents and covering many countries, the boreal plays a significant role in the planet's biodiversity and even its climate. In Boreal forest mean residence time of soil organic matter in an ecosystem is maximum.

23. **The Asian Tsunami, 26 December 2004:** The Asian Tsunami, which occurred on 26 December 2004, was generated by a great underwater earthquake—the Indian Ocean earthquake, also known as the Sumatra-Andaman earthquake.

    Affected areas: The Asian Tsunami has been one of the deadliest disasters in modern times. It killed large numbers of people and inundated coastal areas across south and south-east Asia, including parts of Indonesia, Sri Lanka, Thailand and India. Coastal areas of other south Asian countries like Malaysia, Myanmar, Bangladesh and Maldives, and east African countries like Somalia, Kenya, Tanzania and Madagascar also suffered serious damage. In India, the coastal areas of Andhra Pradesh, Tamil Nadu, Kerala, Pondicherry and Andaman and Nicobar Islands were the worst affected. The Indira Point in the Nicobar Islands, which was the southernmost point of India, was completely submerged, as were a few other islands.

25. Renewable energy is not always connected to the Sun. We can use energy that is created from the earth's heat to heat and cool our homes and other buildings. This source is geothermal energy. Geothermal energy is also a reliable source for the production of electricity.

    Our earth is made up of seven continents, which are surrounded by oceans, which provide two important sources of energy. Tides and wind create waves. Tidal energy is renewable, and wave energy is consistently renewable with wind, water, and tides. That is not all there is! The difference in temperature of ocean water from the icy cold depths to the shallower, warmer water that has been heated by the Sun is also a source of energy.

26. The Calorific Value:

Fuel	Higher Calorific Value (Gross Calorific Value-GCV)		Lower Calorific Value (Net Calorific Value - NCV)
	kJ/kg	Btu/lb	kJ/kg
Ethanol	29700	12800	
Hydrogen	141790	61000	121000
Kerosene	46200		43000
Lignite	16300	7000	
Methane	55530		50000
Methanol	23000		

28. Uranium-238 (238U) is fissionable, but because it cannot sustain a neutron chain reaction, it is not fissile. Neutrons produced by fission of 238U have lower energies than the original neutron (they behave as in an inelastic scattering), usually below 1 MeV (*i.e.*, a speed of about 14,000 km/s), the fission threshold to cause subsequent fission of 238U, so fission of 238U does not sustain a nuclear chain reaction.

Fast fission of 238U in the secondary stage of a nuclear weapon contributes greatly to yield and to fallout. The fast fission of 238U also makes a significant contribution to the power output of some fast-neutron reactors.

30. Atmospheric particulate matter - also known as particulate matter (PM) or particulates - are microscopic solid or liquid matter suspended in the Earth's atmosphere. The term aerosol commonly refers to the particulate/air mixture, as opposed to the particulate matter alone.

In the presence of ammonia, secondary aerosols often take the form of ammonium salts; *i.e.* ammonium sulphate and ammonium nitrate (both can be dry or in aqueous solution); in the absence of ammonia, secondary compounds take an acidic form as sulphuric acid (liquid aerosol droplets) and nitric acid (atmospheric gas), all of which may contribute to the health effects of particulates.

31. SO_2 forms a complex salt with sodium tetra chloromercurate. Formaldehyde and pararosalinine dye are added to obtain a red purple colour (under controlled pH) the intensity of which can be measured at 550 nm wave length colorimetrically. (West-Gaeke method).

32. **Human Acoustics:** The human ear is a remarkable organ, which is capable of hearing sound pressures as low as 2×10^{-5}Pa (Pascals) to as high as 200 Pa before experiencing pain. The audible frequency response for a good ear ranges between 16 to 20,000 Hz. Sounds below 16 Hz are called infrasound, while those above 20,000 Hz are called ultrasound. The audio sense of human ear is most sharp in the frequency range of 2,000 to 5,500 Hz.

34. Iodine-131 (^{131}I), is an important radioisotope of iodine discovered by Glenn Seaborg and John Livingood in 1938 at the University of California, Berkeley. It has a radioactive decay half-life of about eight days. It is associated with nuclear energy, medical diagnostic and treatment procedures, and natural gas production. It also plays a major role as a radioactive isotope present in nuclear fission products, and was a significant contributor to the health hazards from open-air atomic bomb testing in the 1950s, and from the Chernobyl disaster, as well as being a large fraction of the contamination hazard in the first weeks in the Fukushima nuclear crisis. This is because I-131 is a major uranium, plutonium fission product, comprising nearly 3% of the total products of fission (by weight).

36. India has submitted its Intended Nationally Determined Contributions (INDCs) at midnight on 1st October to The United Nations Framework Convention on Climate Change (UNFCCC), making it one of the last countries to submit its climate action plan in run up to the climate change conference—Conference of Parties (COP21)—that will be held in Paris this December. A total of 146 countries, representing 87 per cent of global greenhouse gas emissions have submitted their INDCs to UNFCCC before the deadline.

37. Environmental Impact Assessment (EIA) is the formal process used to predict the environmental consequences (positive or negative) of a plan, policy, program, or project prior to the decision to move forward with the proposed action.

In India, EIAs of development projects were first started in 1977-78 when the Department of Science and Technology took up environmental appraisal of river valley projects. Subsequently, various other projects were brought under the purview of EIA. It was, however, in 1994 when EIA was made mandatory in India under the Environmental Protection Act of 1986.

40. The Vienna Convention for the Protection of the Ozone Layer is a Multilateral Environmental Agreement. It was agreed upon at the Vienna Conference of 1985 and entered into force in 1988. In terms of universality, it is one of the most successful treaties of all time, having been ratified by 197 states as well as the European Union.

41. The Chief Wildlife Warden may, on an application, grant to any person a permit to enter or reside in a sanctuary for the following purposes;

(*a*) Investigation or study of wildlife and any purpose ancillary or incidental thereto;

(*b*) Photography

(*c*) Scientific research

(*d*) Tourism

(*e*) Transaction of lawful business with any person in the sanctuary

42. Tooth Paste/Tooth Powder: For the purpose of formulation of these products, the ingredients listed in IS : 6356 (1979) and ISL: 5383 (1978) shall only be used. Moreover, tooth paste shall not be fluoridated and presence of fluoride (F) as impurity shall not exceed the limit of 10 ppm.

43. Incineration is a disposal method in which solid organic wastes are subjected to combustion so as to convert them into residue and gaseous products. This method is useful for disposal of residue of both solid waste management and solid residue from waste water management. This process reduces the volumes of solid waste to 20 to 30 per cent of the original volume. Incineration and other high temperature waste treatment systems are sometimes described as "thermal treatment". Incinerators convert waste materials into heat, gas, steam, and ash.

Incineration is carried out both on a small scale by individuals and on a large scale by industry. It is used to dispose of solid, liquid and gaseous waste. It is recognized as a practical method of disposing of certain hazardous waste materials (such as biological medical waste). Incineration is a controversial method of waste disposal, due to issues such as emission of gaseous pollutants.

45. In non-probability sampling designs, the elements in the population do not have any probabilities attached to their being chosen as sample subjects. This means that the findings from the study of the sample cannot be confidently generalized to the population. However, the researchers may at times be less concerned about generalisability than obtaining some preliminary information in a quick and inexpensive way. Sometimes non-probability could be thee only way to collect the data.

Examples of non-probability sampling include:

- **Convenience, haphazard or accidental sampling:** Members of the population are chosen based on their relative ease of access. To sample friends, co-workers, or shoppers at a single mall, are all examples of convenience sampling. Such samples are biased because researchers may unconsciously approach some kinds of respondents and avoid others and respondents who volunteer for a study may differ in unknown but important ways from others.

- **Snowball sampling:** The first respondent refers an acquaintance. The friend also refers a friend, and so on. Such samples are biased because they give people with more social connections an unknown but higher chance of selection but lead to higher response rates.
- **Judgmental sampling or purposive sampling:** The researcher chooses the sample based on who they think would be appropriate for the study. This is used primarily when there is a limited number of people that have expertise in the area being researched, or when the interest of the research is on a specific field or a small group. Different types of purposive sampling include:
- **Deviant case:** The researcher obtains cases that substantially differ from the dominant pattern (a special type of purposive sample). The case is selected in order to obtain information on unusual cases that can be specially problematic or specially good.
- **Case study:** The research is limited to one group, often with a similar characteristic or of small size.
- **Ad hoc quotas:** A quota is established (*e.g.* 65% women) and researchers are free to choose any respondent they wish as long as the quota is met.

46. The chi-square value is often used to judge the significance of population variance *i.e.,* we can use the test to judge if a random sample has been drawn from a normal population with mean (μ) and with a specified variance (σ_P^2). The test is based on χ^2-distribution. Such a distribution we encounter when we deal with collections of values that involve adding up squares. Variances of samples require us to add a collection of squared quantities and, thus, have distributions that are related to χ^2-distribution. If we take each one of a collection of sample variances, divide them by the known population variance and multiply these quotients by $(n - 1)$, where n means the number of items in the sample, we shall obtain a χ^2-distribution. Thus,

$$\frac{\sigma_S^2}{\sigma_P^2}(n-1) = (d.f.)$$ would have the same distribution as χ^2-distribution with $(n - 1)$ degree of freedom.

48. Alkali, or alkaline, soils are clay soils with high pH (> 8.5), a poor soil structure and a low infiltration capacity. Often they have a hard calcareous layer at 0.5 to 1 metre depth. Alkali soils owe their unfavourable physico-chemical properties mainly to the dominating presence of sodium carbonate, which causes the soil to swell and difficult to clarify/settle.

49. In 2003, the Supreme Court (SC) of India mandated compulsory Environmental Education (EE) at all stages of education throughout the country. It directed the National Council of Education Research and Training (NCERT) to prepare a model syllabus for this purpose. In 2004, NCERT published the first edition of the syllabus, which the Supreme Court approved and directed all the boards and councils for school education in the country to adopt, to suitably modify their existing syllabi and textbooks, or to develop them a new.

50. Table: Comparison of Mineral and Organic Soils in Wetlands

	Mineral Soil	Organic Soil
Organic content, per cent	Less than 20-35	Greater than 20-35
Organic carbon, per cent	Less than 12-20	Greater than 12-20
pH	Usually circumneutral	Acid
Bulk density	High	Low
Porosity	Low (45-55%)	High (80%)
Hydraulic conductivity	High (except for clays)	Low to high
Water holding capacity	Low	High
Nutrient availability	Generally high	Often low
Cation exchange capacity	Low, dominated by major cations	High, dominated by hydrogen ion
Typical wetland	Riparian forest, some marshes	Northern peatland, southern swamps, and marshes

PAPER-III

Note : *This paper contains* ***seventy five (75)*** *objective type questions of* ***two (2)*** *marks each.* ***All*** *questions are* ***compulsory****.*

1. Which one of the following statements is not true in the case of point source Gaussian Plume Model?
A. Wind speeds are constant in time
B. Pollutants are conservative
C. Rate of emission of pollutants from the stack is constant
D. The ground level concentration is inversely proportional to effective stack height

2. Consider the simple regression equation $Y = a + bX$ between the variables Y and X. If the standard deviation S_X and S_Y are 3 and 2 respectively and correlation coefficient $r = 0.75$, the estimate of b is:
A. 0.25 B. 0.5
C. 1.125 D. 1.5

3. Consider two normal populations with variances of 10 and 20, respectively. If two independent random samples drawn from the two populations are of the sizes 30 and 24 and their variances 10 and 15 respectively, the value of static $F_{(29,23)}$ is:
A. 1.33 B. 2.50
C. 1.56 D. 3.0

4. A normal population has $\sigma^2 = 6$. The sum of squares of deviations of 15 sample values from their mean being 120, what is the χ^2 (chi-square) value?
A. 9 B. 48
C. 20 D. 1.33

5. Choose the correct sequence of phases associated with a population growth that exhibits logistic model represented by $\frac{dN}{dt} = rN\left(1 - \frac{N}{k}\right)$.
A. Stationary phase → Exponential phase → Lag phase
B. Lag phase → Stationary phase → Exponential phase
C. Lag phase → Exponential phase → Stationary phase
D. Exponential phase → Stationary phase → Lag phase

6. The toxic substances of special concern emitted during incineration process from waste to energy plants are:
(*a*) Carbon monoxide (*b*) Carbon dioxide
(*c*) Dioxins (*d*) Furans
Choose the **correct** answer:
A. (*a*) and (*b*) only B. (*b*) and (*c*) only
C. (*a*) and (*d*) only D. (*c*) and (*d*) only

7. Sanitary land fills have following properties. They:
(*a*) reduce trash volume in a short time
(*b*) release CH_4 and CO_2
(*c*) eventually produce leachate which contaminate ground water
Choose the **correct** answer:
A. (*a*) and (*b*) only B. (*b*) only
C. (*a*) and (*c*) only D. (*a*), (*b*) and (*c*)

8. For providing information related to environment to decision makers, policy makers, scientists and environmental engineers all over the country, ENVIS was established in the year belonging to:
A. Sixties B. Seventies
C. Eighties D. Nineties

9. The total radiative forcing of all major and minor green-house gases in the year 2014 is estimated to be:
A. ~ 2.51 W/m^2 B. ~ 2.93 W/m^2
C. ~ 1.87 W/m^2 D. ~ 2.7 W/m^2

10. For the range of temperatures observed in the earth's atmosphere, the saturation mixing ratio (W_s) and the total pressure are related as:

A. $W_s \propto \frac{1}{p}$ B. $W_s \propto p$

C. $W_s \propto p^{3/2}$ D. $W_s \propto p^{-3/2}$

11. A thermal power plant based on coal produces 100 MW of electrical power with conversion efficiency of 30%. If the ash content of coal is 5% and net heating value is 30 MJ per kg, how much ash is produced daily?

A. 48 metric tons B. 24 metric tons

C. 90 metric tons D. 60 metric tons

12. Under which section of Wildlife (Protection) Act 1972, the state government can declare an area closed to hunting for a specified period?

A. Section 35 B. Section 27

C. Section 38-A D. Section 37

13. Which one of the following criteria should **not** contribute to the process of establishing significance of the impact of a developmental project on environment?

A. Sensitivity of surrounding environment

B. Probability of the impact occurring

C. Views and values of the developer

D. Views and suggestions of the public

14. The following benefits may accrue as a result of environmental audit:

(*a*) Material audit leads to improvement in the production efficiency and cost

(*b*) Pollution monitoring leads to environmental quality improvement

(*c*) Approach towards zero discharge and zero emission leads to clean development

(*d*) Incentive for pollution abatement in the form of reduction in import tax leads to cleaner environment

Choose the **correct** answer:

A. (*a*) only

B. (*b*) and (*c*) only

C. (*b*) and (*d*) only

D. (*a*), (*b*), (*c*) and (*d*)

15. Environmental Impact Assessment (EIA) was incorporated under which one of the following legislations?

A. Air (Prevention and Control of Pollution) Act 1981

B. Wildlife (Protection) Act, 1981

C. Indian Forest Act, 1927

D. Environmental (Protection) Act 1986

16. A company operating a vehicle Manufacturing plant has developed Environmental Management System (EMS) to enhance its performance and to improve quality of its products. The key aspects of this EMS would include:

A. Audit of manufacturing plant safety procedure

B. Maximizing returns to stakeholders of the company

C. The development of an overall framework for environmental affairs of the company

D. The aspects of costs involved in developing an environmental policy.

17. Best practice in scoping requires:

(*a*) A site visit

(*b*) Relevant experience of other similar developmental projects

(*c*) Employing formal scoping techniques

Choose the **correct** answer:

A. (*a*) only B. (*a*) and (*b*) only

C. (*b*) and (*c*) only D. (*a*), (*b*) and (*c*)

18. Match the **List-I** and **List-II**. Identify the **correct** answer from the codes given below:

List-I (Stages in EIA)	**List-II (Actions in EIA)**
(*a*) Screening	(*i*) Reduce or avoid the impacts
(*b*) Scoping	(*ii*) Establish present and future stages of environment
(*c*) Baseline description	(*iii*) Early indication of crucial impacts
(*d*) Mitigation measures	(*iv*) Narrowing the application of EIA

Codes:

	(*a*)	(*b*)	(*c*)	(*d*)
A.	(*iv*)	(*iii*)	(*ii*)	(*i*)
B.	(*i*)	(*iv*)	(*iii*)	(*ii*)
C.	(*ii*)	(*i*)	(*iv*)	(*iii*)
D.	(*iii*)	(*ii*)	(*i*)	(*iv*)

19. The decision making process in EIA generally **does not** include:
A. Cost-benefit analysis
B. Procedural information
C. Socio-economic aspects
D. Operational management

20. Which of the following actions may be recommended for acidified lakes?
A. Ammoniation B. Liming
C. Ozonation D. Chlorination

21. Given below are two statements. One labelled as **Assertion (A)** and the other labelled as **Reason (R).**

Assertion (A): All types of aerosols contribute to radiative forcing.

Reason (R): Aerosol effectively absorb electromagnetic radiations.

Choose the **correct** answer:
A. Both (A) and (R) are correct and (R) is the correct explanation of (A).
B. Both (A) and (R) are correct and (R) is not the correct explanation of (A).
C. (A) is true, but (R) is false.
D. (A) is false, but (R) is true.

22. Given below are two statements. One labelled as **Assertion (A)** and the other labelled as **Reason (R).**

Assertion (A): The efficiency of fuel cells is not limited by the second law of thermodynamics.

Reason (R): There is no intermediate heat to work conversion in a fuel cell.

Choose the **correct** answer:
A. Both (A) and (R) are correct and (R) is the correct explanation of (A).
B. Both (A) and (R) are correct and (R) is not the correct explanation of (A).
C. (A) is true, but (R) is false.
D. (A) is false, but (R) is true.

23. Given below are two statements. One labelled as **Assertion (A)** and the other labelled as **Reason (R).**

Assertion (A): A wind rose with approximately equal length spokes (or petals) represents great variation of wind direction over a given duration.

Reason (R): The length of the spokes is a measure of wind speeds in a given duration.

Choose the **correct** answer:
A. Both (A) and (R) are correct and (R) is the correct explanation of (A).
B. Both (A) and (R) are correct and (R) is not the correct explanation of (A).
C. (A) is true, but (R) is false.
D. (A) is false, but (R) is true.

24. Given below are two statements. One labelled as **Assertion (A)** and the other labelled as **Reason (R).**

Assertion (A): Large scale OTEC development may exacerbate the green-house effect.

Reason (R): Methane is a green-house gas.

Choose the **correct** answer:
A. Both (A) and (R) are correct and (R) is the correct explanation of (A).
B. Both (A) and (R) are correct and (R) is not the correct explanation of (A).
C. (A) is true, but (R) is false.
D. (A) is false, but (R) is true.

25. In a spectrophotometric cell of 2.0 cm path length, the solution of a substance shows the absorbance value of 1.0. If the molar absorptivity of the compound is 2×10^4 L mol^{-1} cm^{-1}, calculate the concentration of the substance in solution. What is the concentration of the substance in that solution?
A. 2.5×10^{-5} mol L^{-1}
B. 4.0×10^{-4} mol L^{-1}
C. 1.0×10^{4} mol L^{-1}
D. 5.0×10^{-4} mol L^{-1}

26. In order to obtain useful fusion energy from a thermonuclear fusion reactor, if the confinement time of the D + T Plasma ions is 1 μ sec, the ion density (per m^3) must be:

A. $\geq 10^{26}$ m^{-3} B. $\geq 10^{23}$ m^{-3}
C. $\geq 10^{20}$ m^{-3} D. $\geq 10^{14}$ m^{-3}

27. Which of the following is **not** a detrivore?
A. Vultures B. Earthworms
C. Insects D. *Hydrilla*

28. Secondary succession begins at:
A. base rock
B. newly cooled lava
C. burnt forest
D. newly created shallow pond

29. Given below are two statements. One labelled as **Assertion (A)** and the other labelled as **Reason (R).**

Assertion (A): It is generally agreed that life on earth began between 3.5 and 4.5 billion years ago.

Reason (R): The first form of life was the anaerobic bacteria as environment was devoid of oxygen.

Choose the **correct** answer:
A. Both (A) and (R) are correct and (R) is the correct explanation of (A).
B. Both (A) and (R) are correct and (R) is not the correct explanation of (A).
C. (A) is true, but (R) is false.
D. (A) is false, but (R) is true.

30. The total number of Sustainable Development Goals (SDGs) announced by UN in 2015 are:
A. 15 B. 17
C. 19 D. 21

31. The total area of productive ecosystem required to support the population sustainably is known as:
A. Ecological footprint
B. Ecological handprint
C. Carrying capacity
D. Ecological services

32. Carrying capacity of a population determines that a particular habitat for a given species can sustain:
A. Minimum Population
B. Maximum Population
C. Average Population
D. A Fraction of Migrating Population

33. Which one of the following is the most productive ecosystem?
A. Lakes and Streams
B. Estuaries
C. Continental shelf
D. Open ocean

34. A measure that combines the number of species and their relative abundances compared with one another is termed:
A. Species richness
B. Species evenness
C. Species diversity
D. Species relationships

35. The figures of humanity's global footprint (million hectares) for different countries estimated by WWF and Global Footprint Network in 2008 fall in the sequence:
A. US > China > European Union > Japan > India
B. China > US > Japan > India > European Union
C. European Union > US > China > Japan > India
D. US > European Union > China > India > Japan

36. A common features of the synoptic and mesoscale motions in the atmosphere is that their:
A. Vertical motion component is more in magnitude than the horizontal wind component.
B. Vertical motion component is roughly comparable to horizontal wind component.
C. Vertical motion component is an order of magnitude smaller than the horizontal wind component.
D. Properties can be studied by conventional synoptic networks.

37. The shape of a plume from a tall stack located on a flat terrain is found to be of "fanning" type. It implies that the atmosphere is under the condition of:

A. Strong lapse rate
B. Weak lapse rate
C. Inversion
D. Weak lapse rate below inversion

38. Given below are two statements. One labelled as **Assertion (A)** and the other labelled as **Reason (R).**

Assertion (A): Thunderstorm is a violent convective event accompanied by thunder and lightening.

Reason (R): Thunderstorm is not associated with vertical air movement, humidity and instability.

Choose the **correct** answer:

A. Both (A) and (R) are correct and (R) is the correct explanation of (A).
B. Both (A) and (R) are correct and (R) is not the correct explanation of (A).
C. (A) is true, but (R) is false.
D. (A) is false, but (R) is true.

39. According to National Ambient Air Quality Standards in India, the permissible 24 hour average concentration of lead in ambient air of an industrial area is:

A. 1.0 μg/m^3 B. 2.0 μg/m^3
C. 3.03 μg/m^3 D. 4.0 μg/m^3

40. Peat soils, which have undergone prolonged drought in the forests are prone for:

(*a*) ground forest fire
(*b*) underground forest fire
(*c*) tree crown fire

Choose the **correct** code:

A. (*a*) only B. (*b*) only
C. (*a*) and (*b*) only D. (*a*), (*b*) and (*c*)

41. Insect pests can be controlled by the use of:

(*a*) Insecticide
(*b*) Pheromones
(*c*) Juvenile Hormones
(*d*) Nitrophosphate

Choose the **correct** answer:

A. (*a*) only
B. (*a*) and (*b*) only
C. (*a*), (*b*) and (*c*) only
D. (*a*), (*b*), (*c*) and (*d*)

42. Dioxins and Furans are two toxic gaseous pollutants which can be measured by:

A. GC - MS B. TLC
C. ICP - AES D. AAS

43. Based on the pE value for four water samples given below, the concentration of dissolved oxygen shall be highest in:

A. pE = –4.1 B. pE = 13.9
C. pE = 1.0 D. pE = 7.0

44. A total of 10 instantaneous sound pressure level measurements at 10 sec intervals for a traffic site are given in the table below:

S. No.	1	2	3	4	5	6	7	8	9	10
SPL (dB)	71	75	70	78	80	84	76	74	75	74

The estimated L_{90} from these measurement is:

A. ~71 dB B. ~70 dB
C. ~74 dB D. ~75 dB

45. The composition of rhizospheric micro organisms are dependent on the soil:

(*a*) Texture (*b*) Organic matter
(*c*) pH (*d*) Elasticity

Choose the **correct** answer:

A. (*a*) only
B. (*a*) and (*b*) only
C. (*a*), (*b*) and (*c*) only
D. (*a*), (*b*), (*c*) and (*d*)

46. Given below are two statements. One labelled as **Assertion (A)** and the other labelled as **Reason (R).**

Assertion (A): The fundamental goal of a dose - response assessment is to obtain a mathematical relationship between the amount of a toxicant that a human is exposed to and the risk that there will be.

Reason (R): To apply dose - response data obtained from animal bioassay to humans, a scalling factor must be introduced.

Choose the **correct** answer:

A. Both (A) and (R) are correct and (R) is the correct explanation of (A).
B. Both (A) and (R) are correct and (R) is not the correct explanation of (A).
C. (A) is true, but (R) is false.
D. (A) is false, but (R) is true.

47. Tropical grasslands with scattered trees are also known as:

A. Taigas B. Steppe
C. Savannas D. Meadows

48. On 18th April 2015, Global Alliance to Eliminate Lead Paint (GAELP) announced the goal of eliminating lead paint around the world by:

A. 2020 B. 2025
C. 2028 D. 2022

49. The form of coal/fuel in the ascending order of heating value can be best represented as:

A. Lignite < Peat < Bituminous < Anthracite
B. Bituminous < Lignite < Peat < Anthracite
C. Peat < Lignite < Bituminous < Anthracite
D. Peat < Lignite < Anthracite < Bituminous

50. In India wetland conservation is presently done by the Ministry of Environment, Forest and Climate Change under:

A. National Wetland Conservation Programme
B. National Plan for Conservation of Aquatic Ecosystems
C. National Lake Conservation Programme
D. Coastal Regulation Zone

51. Soil salination is **not** caused by:

A. Agricultural area with high ground water irrigation
B. Coastal swampy area
C. Flood prone area
D. Upland lateritic area with waste water irrigation

52. Ground water occurs under:

(*a*) Unconfined condition in shallow aquifers
(*b*) Semi-confined aquifers
(*c*) Confined aquifers

Choose the **correct** answer:

A. (*a*) only B. (*a*) and (*b*) only
C. (*b*) and (*c*) only D. (*a*), (*b*) and (*c*)

53. DEM (Digital Elevation Model) is best represented using:

A. Vector Data Models
B. Raster Data Models
C. Coverage Data Structure
D. Non-topological Data Structure

54. Delta are classified into six basic types taking cognissance and importance of:

(*a*) Rivers (*b*) Waves
(*c*) Tides

Choose the **correct** answer:

A. (*a*) only B. (*a*) and (*b*) only
C. (*a*) and (*c*) only D. (*a*), (*b*) and (*c*)

55. Large elongated depression with steep walls formed by the downward displacement of a block of the earth surface between nearly parallel faults or fault system:

A. Thrust faults B. Horst
C. Grabben D. Rift Valley

56. Which form of scattering in visible region in the atmosphere is not dependent on wavelength?

(*a*) Rayleigh (*b*) Mie
(*c*) Non-selective

Choose the **correct** answer:

A. (*a*) only B. (*a*) and (*b*) only
C. (*c*) only D. (*b*) and (*c*) only

57. Best spatial configuration for designing a core natural area is:

A. Circular B. Rectangular
C. Square D. Triangle

58. Ecosystem resilience is the capacity of an ecosystem to sustain its:

(*a*) Fundamental function
(*b*) Structure
(*c*) Feedbacks in the face of a spectrum of shock and perturbations

Choose the **correct** answer:

A. (*a*) and (*b*) only B. (*b*) and (*c*) only
C. (*a*) and (*c*) only D. (*a*), (*b*) and (*c*)

59. With regard to ozone depletion over Antarctica, select the false statement:

A. Circumpolar vortex acts as a reaction chamber
B. Polar Stratospheric Clouds (PSCs) are formed within the vortex

C. There is very low temperature inside the vortex

D. The heterogenous reaction $ClONO_2(s) + HCl(g) \rightarrow Cl_2(g) + HNO_3(s)$ takes over PSCs

60. Match the **List-I** and **List-II.** Choose the **correct** answer from the codes given below:

List-I (Horizon)	List-II (Type/Characteristics)
(*a*) A - horizon	(*i*) Subsoil
(*b*) O - horizon	(*ii*) Leaf litter
(*c*) C - horizon	(*iii*) Parent material
(*d*) B - horizon	(*iv*) Top soil

Codes:

	(*a*)	(*b*)	(*c*)	(*d*)
A.	(*iv*)	(*ii*)	(*iii*)	(*i*)
B.	(*i*)	(*iii*)	(*iv*)	(*ii*)
C.	(*ii*)	(*iv*)	(*i*)	(*iii*)
D.	(*iii*)	(*i*)	(*ii*)	(*iv*)

61. A laboratory analysis of a waste water sample indicated BOD of 750 mg L^{-1} with rate constant (K) 0.20 day^{-1} at 20°C. The 5-day BOD at 20°C is:

A. 675 mg L^{-1} B. 650 mg L^{-1}

C. 400 mg L^{-1} D. 600 mg L^{-1}

62. A stream with a flow of 0.2 m^3/sec and a chloride concentration of 50 mg/L receives a discharge of mine drainage water with a flow of 0.05 m^3/sec and chloride concentration of 1500 mg/L. The downstream concentration of chloride is:

A. 150 mg/L B. 200 mg/L

C. 340 mg/L D. 380 mg/L

63. Four students **(List-A)** working independently in a chromatographic analysis **(List-B)** reported the Retention Factor (R_f) values:

List-A (Students)		List-B (R_f Values)
(*a*) R	→	(*i*) 0
(*b*) S	→	(*ii*) 0.5
(*c*) T	→	(*iii*) 1.3
(*d*) U	→	(*iv*) 1.0

The result of which student(s) is (are) definitely **incorrect**:

A. R and U B. S and T

C. S, T and U D. T

64. The mechanism of the formation of gaseous N_2O_5 from NO_2 and O_2 gases in the gas phase within clouds is:

$$NO_2(g) + O_3(g) \rightarrow NO_3(g) + O_2(g) \quad (i)$$

$$NO_3(g) + NO_2(g) \rightarrow N_2O_5(g) \quad (ii)$$

The experimentally determined rate law is

$$-d\,[NO_2(g)]\,/dt = K\,[NO_2(g)]\,[O_3(g)]$$

Based on the information provided which of the following statement is **incorrect**?

A. Overall reaction is : $2NO(g) + O_3(g) \rightarrow N_2O_5(g) + O_2(g)$

B. The reaction intermediate is NO_3

C. The rate determining step is reaction (*i*)

D. The rate reaction (*ii*) is slower than the rate of reaction (*i*)

65. In a rain water sample of pH = 8.45, the dominant species of dissolved sulphur dioxide shall be:

A. $SO_2 \cdot H_2O$ B. HSO_3^-

C. SO_3^{2-} D. $S_2O_5^{2-}$

66. An aquifer of sand has a saturated column of cross-sectional area 0.2 m × 5 m and a depth of 3 m. If the specific yield of sand is 25%, how much water can be extracted from the aquifer?

A. 0.5 m^3 B. 0.75 m^3

C. 1.2 m^3 D. 1.5 m^3

67. Atmospheric life times of CFCs is typically in the range:

A. 50 - 102 years B. 140 - 200 years

C. 200 - 400 years D. 152 - 210 years

68. With respect to CO_2, Global Warming Potential (GWP) for N_2O over a time horizon of 100 years is estimated to be:

A. 156 B. 210

C. 296 D. 240

69. The green-house gas N_2O strongly absorbs infra-red radiations of wavelength(s):
A. ~4.5 μm
B. ~7.8 μm and 8.6 μm
C. ~9.6 μm
D. ~10.6 μm

70. By the year 2022, Indian government has set a new target of Solar Power generation of:
A. 4 GW B. 60 GW
C. 75 GW D. 100 GW

71. Match the **List-I** and **List-II.** Identify the **correct** answer from the codes given below the lists.

List-I (Causes)	List-II (Effects)
(*a*) Soil organisms	(*i*) Algal bloom
(*b*) Phosphorous assimilation	(*ii*) Chronic obstructive pulmonary diseases
(*c*) Water pollution	(*iii*) Decomposition
(*d*) Air pollution	(*iv*) Complexing agent

Codes:

	(*a*)	(*b*)	(*c*)	(*d*)
A.	(*i*)	(*ii*)	(*iii*)	(*iv*)
B.	(*iii*)	(*iv*)	(*i*)	(*ii*)
C.	(*ii*)	(*iii*)	(*iv*)	(*i*)
D.	(*iv*)	(*ii*)	(*i*)	(*iii*)

72. The Wavelengths that are most important in the context of stratospheric ozone depletion are:
A. 280 - 320 nm B. 400 - 700 nm
C. 700 - 900 nm D. > 900 nm

73. Remote sensing satellites such as RESOURCESAT are usually placed in polar:
(*a*) Low Earth Polar orbit
(*b*) Sunsynchronous orbit
(*c*) Geosynchronous orbit

Codes:
A. (*b*) and (*c*) only B. (*a*) and (*b*) only
C. (*a*) and (*c*) only D. (*a*), (*b*) and (*c*)

74. Gills of marine fishes perform the functions of the following:
A. Water loss and salt excretion
B. Water gain and salt excretion
C. Water uptake and solute uptake
D. Water loss and solute uptake

75. The instrument used for determination of soil water loss by percolation, evapotranspiration and run off is called:
A. Lysimeter
B. Rain Gauze
C. Soil moisture meter
D. Soil porosity meter

ANSWERS

1	**2**	**3**	**4**	**5**	**6**	**7**	**8**	**9**	**10**
D	B	A	C	C	D	B	C	B	A
11	**12**	**13**	**14**	**15**	**16**	**17**	**18**	**19**	**20**
A	D	C	D	D	C	D	A	D	B
21	**22**	**23**	**24**	**25**	**26**	**27**	**28**	**29**	**30**
C	A	C	B	A	A	D	C	B	B
31	**32**	**33**	**34**	**35**	**36**	**37**	**38**	**39**	**40**
A	B	B	C	D	C	C	C	A	C
41	**42**	**43**	**44**	**45**	**46**	**47**	**48**	**49**	**50**
C	A	B	A	C	B	C	A	C	B
51	**52**	**53**	**54**	**55**	**56**	**57**	**58**	**59**	**60**
C	D	B	D	D	C	A	D	D	A
61	**62**	**63**	**64**	**65**	**66**	**67**	**68**	**69**	**70**
A	C	D	D	C	B	A	C	B	D
71	**72**	**73**	**74**	**75**					
B	A	B	A	A					

EXPLANATORY ANSWERS

1. Assumptions in Gaussian plume model:

(*i*) Steady-state conditions, which imply that the rate of emission from the point source is constant.

(*ii*) Homogeneous flow, which implies that the wind speed is constant both in time and with height (wind direction shear is not considered).

(*iii*) Pollutant is conservative and no gravity fallout.

(*iv*) Perfect reflection of the plume at the underlying surface, *i.e.* no ground absorption.

(*v*) The turbulent diffusion in the *x*-direction is neglected relative to advection in the transport direction (*x*), which implies that the model should be applied for average wind speeds of more than 1 m/s ($\bar{u}$ > 1 m/s).

(*vi*) The coordinate system is directed with its *x*-axis into the direction of the flow, and the *v* (lateral) and *w* (vertical) components of the time averaged wind vector are set to zero.

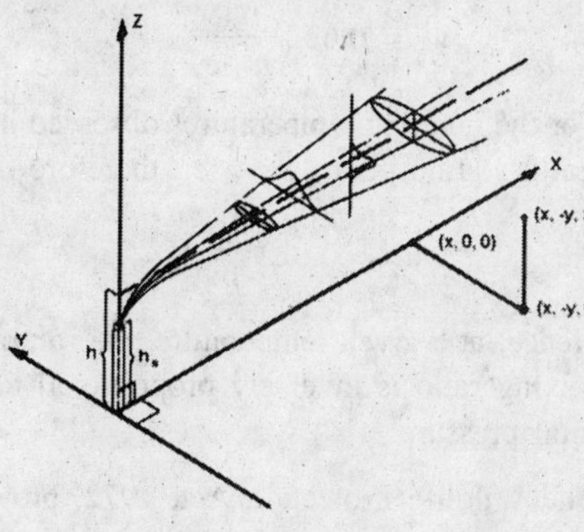

Fig.: *Cross section of a Gaussian plume profile in the horizontal and vertical directions.*

(*vii*) The terrain underlying the plume is flat.

(*viii*) All variables are ensemble averaged, which implies long-term averaging with stationary conditions.

2. For simple linear regression,

$$b = r\frac{s_y}{s_x}, \qquad b_0 = \bar{y} - b_1\bar{x}$$

Given that $r = 0.75$,

$s_x = 3, \quad s_y = 2$

$$b = 0.75 \times \frac{2}{3} = 0.5.$$

5. Four characteristic phases of the growth cycle are recognized.

1. **Lag Phase:** Immediately after inoculation of the cells into fresh medium, the population remains temporarily unchanged. Although there is no apparent cell division occurring, the cells may be growing in volume or mass, synthesizing enzymes, proteins, RNA, etc., and increasing in metabolic activity.
2. **Exponential (log) Phase:** The exponential phase of growth is a pattern of balanced growth wherein all the cells are dividing regularly by binary fission, and are growing by geometric progression. The cells divide at a constant rate depending upon the composition of the growth medium and the conditions of incubation.
3. **Stationary Phase:** Exponential growth cannot be continued forever in a **batch culture** (*e.g.* a closed system such as a test tube or flask). Population growth is limited by one of three factors: 1. exhaustion of available nutrients; 2. accumulation of inhibitory metabolites or end products; 3. exhaustion of space, in this case called a lack of "biological space".
4. **Death Phase:** If incubation continues after the population reaches stationary phase, a death phase follows, in which the viable cell population declines. During the death phase, the number of viable cells decreases geometrically (exponentially), essentially

the reverse of growth during the log phase.

6. Dioxins and furans are chemicals that are created by burning chlorine in the presence of hydrocarbons and oxygen. Hydrocarbons (the bulk of the TDF itself, as well as coal, wood or gas it's co-fired with) and oxygen (from the air) are readily available when TDF is incinerated. Dioxins and furans are produced by tire incineration because tires contain chlorine. The manufacture of synthetic rubber for tires uses up to 25% aromatic extender oils, a toxic waste product of oil refining which can contain chlorine.

7. Landfills produce both gaseous and aqueous emissions. Biomass in landfills quickly depletes oxygen by aerobic biodegradation of microorganisms in the landfill,

   $\{CH_2O\}$ (biomass) + $O_2 \rightarrow CO_2 + H_2O$

   emitting carbon dioxide. Over a period of many decades the buried biodegradable materials undergo anaerobic biodegradation

   $$2\{CH_2O\} \rightarrow CO_2 + CH_4$$

   releasing methane as well as carbon dioxide. Although often impractical and too expensive, it is desirable to reclaim the methane as fuel, and some large sanitary landfills are major sources of methane. Released methane is a greenhouse gas and can pose significant explosion hazards to structures built on landfills.

8. Realising the importance of Environmental Information, the Government of India, in December, 1982, established an Environmental Information System (ENVIS) as a plan programme. The focus of ENVIS since inception has been on providing environmental information to decision makers, policy planners, scientists and engineers, research workers, etc. all over the country. Since environment is a broad-ranging, multi-disciplinary subject, a comprehensive information system on environment would necessarily involve effective participation of concerned institutions/organisations in the country that are actively engaged in work relating to different subject areas of environment. ENVIS has, therefore, developed itself with a network of such participating institutions/organisations for the programme to be meaningful.

10. **Saturation mixing ratios**

    The *saturation mixing ratio* w_s, with respect to water is defined as the ratio of the mass m_{vs} of water vapour in a given volume of air that is saturated with respect to a plane surface of pure water to the mass m_d of the dry air. That is

    $$w_s = \frac{m_{vs}}{m_d}$$

    Because water vapour and dry air both obey the ideal gas equation

    $$w_s = \frac{p'_{vs}}{p'_d} = \frac{e_s}{(R_y T)} \bigg/ \frac{(p-e_s)}{(R_d T)}$$

    where p'_{vs} is the partial density of water vapour required to saturate air with respect to water at temperature T, p'_d is the partial density of the dry air and p is the total pressure. Combining the equations, we obtain

    $$w_s = 0.622\frac{e_s}{p-e_s}$$

    For the range of temperatures observed in the Earth's atmosphere, $p >> e_y$; therefore

    $$w_s = 0.622\frac{e_s}{p}$$

    Hence, at a given temperature, the saturation mixing ratio is inversely proportional to the total pressure.

12. The Wildlife Protection Act, 1972, provides for protection to listed species of flora and fauna and establishes a network of ecologically-important protected areas. The Act consists of 60 Sections and VI Schedules-divided into Eight Chapters. The Wildlife Protection Act, 1972 empowers the central

and state governments to declare any area a wildlife sanctuary, national park or closed area. There is a blanket ban on carrying out any industrial activity inside these protected areas. It provides for authorities to administer and implement the Act; regulate the hunting of wild animals; protect specified plants, sanctuaries, national parks and closed areas; restrict trade or commerce in wild animals or animal articles; and miscellaneous matters. The Act prohibits hunting of animals except with permission of authorized officer when an animal has become dangerous to human life or property or as disabled or diseased as to be beyond recovery.

Section-37: Declaration of closed area: (1) The State Government may, by notification, declare any area closed to hunting for such period as may be specified in the notification. (2) No hunting of any wild animal shall be permitted in a closed area during the period specified in the notification referred to in sub-section (1).

15. Under the Environment (Protection) Act, 1986 EIA for projects was made mandatory in India in 1994 with the objective to predict environment impact of projects, find ways and means to reduce adverse impacts, and if these impacts were too high, to disallow such projects.

16. The key to effective environmental management is the use of a systematic approach to planning, controlling, measuring and improving an organization's environmental efforts. Potentially significant environmental improvements (and cost savings) can be achieved by reviewing and improving your organization's management processes. Not all environmental problems need to be solved by installing expensive pollution control equipment.

18. **Screening:** Screening helps to focus resources on those projects most likely to have significant impacts, those where the impacts are uncertain and those where environmental management input is likely to be required.

Scoping: Scoping is a crucial part of the impact assessment process and involves the identification and 'narrowing-down' of potential environmental impacts to ensure that the assessment focuses on the key issues for decision-making. It also offers a crucial opportunity to involve local people in determining the scope and focus of the impact assessment.

The description of the environmental baseline includes the establishment of both the present and future state of the environment, in the absence of the project, taking into account changes resulting from natural events and from other human activities.

Mitigation involves the introduction of measures to avoid, reduce, remedy or compensate for any significant adverse impacts.

20. **Liming:** The only sure way to prevent acidification of freshwater bodies is to reduce the emissions of acid pollutants in the first place . At present, the main way of reversing acidification in freshwaters is liming the water body or its surrounding catchment. The main liming method is to add the lime directly to the water body.

Acidified lakes in Sweden have been restored in the short-term by liming. Liming provides only a temporary solution, hence it is far better to attack the source of the problem by reducing emissions of acidifying pollutants.

22. **Fuel cells:** A fuel cell converts chemical energy of a fuel into electricity directly, with no intermediate combustion cycle. Since there is no intermediate 'heat to work' conversion, the efficiency of fuel cells is not limited by the second law of thermodynamics, unlike conventional 'fuel → heat → work → electricity' systems. The efficiency of conversion from chemical energy to electricity by a fuel cell may theoretically be 100%.

27. **Detritivore:** Organisms that eat dead things, also known as decomposers.

Decomposer: Organisms that break down dead organisms by consuming them.

Decomposers are like nature's garbage collectors. Common detritivores include vultures, many types of insects, fungi, and bacteria but hydrilla is not a detrivore.

28. Secondary succession is one of the two types of ecological succession of plant life. As opposed to the first, primary succession, secondary succession is a process started by an event (*e.g.,* forest fire, harvesting, hurricane) that reduces an already established ecosystem (*e.g.,* a forest or a wheat field) to a smaller population of species, and as such secondary succession occurs on pre-existing soil whereas primary succession usually occurs in a place lacking soil.

30. On September 25th 2015, countries adopted a set of goals to end poverty, protect the planet and ensure prosperity for all as part of a new sustainable development agenda. Each goal has specific targets to be achieved over the next 15 years.

The total number of sustainable development Goals (SDGs) announced by UN in 2015 are 17.

1. No Poverty, 2. Zero Hunger, 3. Good Health and Well-Being, 4. Quality Education, 5. Gender Equality, 6. Clean Water and Sanitation, 7. Affordable and Clean Energy, 8. Decent Work and Economic Growth, 9. Industry, Innovation and Infrastructure, 10. Reduced Inequalities, 11. Sustainable Cities and Communities, 12. Responsible Consumption and Production, 13. Climate Action, 14. Life Below Water, 15. Life on Land, 16. Peace, Justice and Strong Institutions, 17. Partnerships for the Goals.

31. **Total Ecological Impact and Ecological Footprint:** The concept of an ecological footprint is concerned with determining how much productive land and water area in various ecosystems is required to support a region's human population indefinitely at current consumption levels. This approach essentially inverts traditional carrying-capacity measures that are concerned with the maximum size of population that a given ecological region can sustain indefinitely.

Related to the ecological footprint concept is the notion of total ecological impact—the total human impact on ecosystems of the resource degradation and pollution caused by human production and consumption activities.

32. **Carrying capacity (K):** The maximum population of a given species that a particular habitat can sustain indefinitely without degrading the habitat. The growth rate of a population decreases as its size nears the carrying capacity of its environment because resources such as food and water begin to dwindle.

33. An estuary is a partially enclosed body of water along the coast where freshwater from rivers and streams meets and mixes with salt water from the ocean. Estuaries and the lands surrounding them are places of transition from land to sea and freshwater to salt water. Although influenced by the tides, they are protected from the full force of ocean waves, winds, and storms by barrier islands or peninsulas. Estuaries are among the most productive ecosystems in the world. Many species of animals rely on the sheltered waters of estuaries for food, secure places to breed and migration stopovers.

34. Biodiversity is one of the primary interests of ecologists, but quantifying the species diversity of ecological communities is complicated. In addition to issues of statistical sampling, the rather arbitrary nature of delineating an ecological community, and the difficulty of positively identifying all of the species present, species diversity itself has two separate components: (1) The number of species present (species richness). (2) Their relative abundances (termed dominance or evenness).

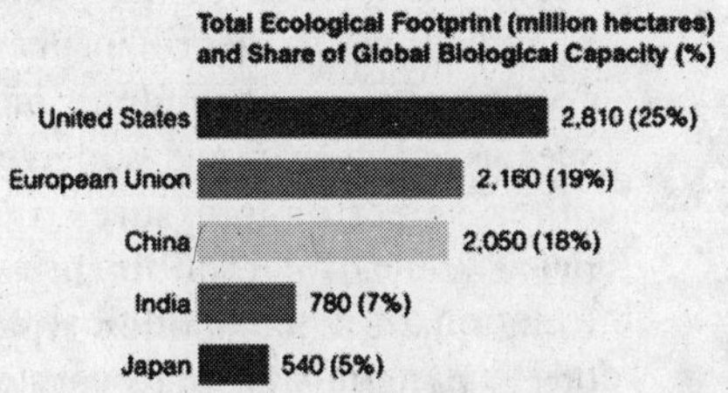

35. The per capita ecological footprint is an estimate of how much of the earth's renewable resources an individual consumes.

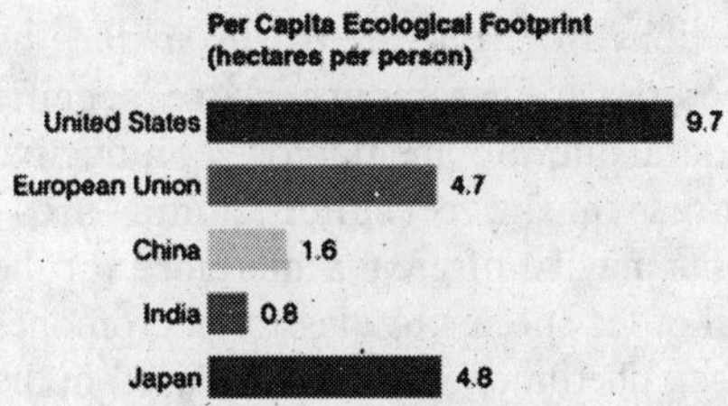

36. A common features of the synoptic and mesoscale motions in the atmosphere is that their Vertical motion component is an order of magnitude smaller than the horizontal wind component.

The vertical component of atmospheric motions, typically on the order of 1 – 10 cm/sec., is generally much weaker than its horizontal counterpart, often by 2 orders of magnitude when examined at the synoptic scale. In spite of their relatively small magnitude, vertical motions are necessary in maintaining the global energy cycle and shaping the temperature structure of the atmosphere.

37. Plume Behaviour: One way to quickly determine the stability of the lower atmosphere is to view the shape of a smoke trail, or *plume,* from a tall stack located on flat terrain. Visible plumes usually consist of pollutants emitted from a smoke stack into the atmosphere. The formation and fate of the plume itself depend on a number of related factors: (1) the nature of the pollutants, (2) meteorological factors (combination of vertical air movement and horizontal air flow), (3) source obstructions, and (4) local topography, especially downwind. Overall, maximum ground-level concentrations will occur in a range from the vicinity of the smokestack to some distance downwind.

When the atmosphere is slightly stable or neutral, a typical plume *cones.* This is likely to occur on cloudy days or sunny days between the breakup of a radiation inversion and the development of unstable daytime conditions. When the atmosphere is highly unstable, a *looping plume* forms. In the looping plume, the stream of emitted pollutants undergoes rapid mixing, and the wind causes large eddies, which may carry the entire plume down to the ground, causing high concentrations close to the stack before dispersion is complete. In an extremely stable atmosphere, usually in the early morning during a radiation inversion, a *fanning plume* spreads horizontally, with little mixing. When an inversion layer occurs a short distance above the plume source, the plume is said to be *fumigating.* Ground-level pollutant concentrations can be very high when fumigation occurs. Sufficiently tall stacks can prevent fumigation in most cases. When inversion conditions exist below the plume source, the plume is said to be *lofting.* When conditions are neutral, the plume issuing from a smoke stack tends to rise directly into the atmosphere. When an inversion layer prevails both above and below the plume source, the plume issuing from a smokestack tends to be *trapped.*

39. The environmental quality is based on three physical parameters *viz.* Air quality, Water quality and Noise level.

Lead (Pb): No systematic date is available to compare the status of lead (Pb) in the district. But the present data show that average concentration of Pb (0.45) lies within the limit of National Ambient Air Quality Standard (NAAQS) for residential area (1.0 μg/m^3).

41. Insect pheromones: Pheromones serve as a means of communication between animals like light and sound. They transfer informations from one animal to another by smell or taste. Pheromones evoke specific behavioural, developmental or reproductive responses in the recipients, and these responses may be of great importance for the survival of the species. A class of pheromones called sex pheromones are mainly used in the behavioural control of insect pests. A trap containing female sex pheromones is placed in the pest infested region. The males aggregate at the trap and are destroyed. Natural pheromone of gypsy moth, *Prothetria dispar,* a pest of forest can be used for its control. A synthetic compound gypture, similar to the hormone of gypsy moth, has become important in insect control. If the air is filled with synthetic pheromones, the males would fail to locate the females for insemination. This method is called 'male inhibition technique'.

In another method, early death of the insect pests can be brought about by the introduction of juvenile hormone at the late stage of larval development. The larva develops into giant larva (immature adult) which die quickly without attaining maturity. Insecticide can also be used to insect pests.

42. Gas chromatography (GC) is a dynamic method of separation and detection of volatile organic compounds. GC separates the gaseous components of a mixture by partitioning them between the inert gas mobile phase and a stationary phase.

Mass Spectrometry: Mass spectrometry (MS) is a technique that is used to measure the mass of atoms or molecules. To obtain a mass spectrum, gaseous sample atoms are introduced into the source of the MS where they are ionized. Dioxins and Furans are two toxic gaseous pollutants that are created by burning chlorine in the presence of hydrocarbon and oxygen and measured by GC-MS method.

45. The plant root zone hosts not only an increase in the numbers of micro-organisms, but also a rich variety of microbial species. The actual composition of the rhizosphere microbial community is dependent on host plant species, plant age, and soil type as well as other selection pressures including the presence of xenobiotic compounds Rhizosphere communities typically consist of (1) bacteria which are very abundant and reproduce rapidly under favourable conditions, and (2) fungi which form mycelia on plant roots and extend into the surrounding soil to seek nutrients. Aerobic bacteria, particularly Pseudomonads, are generally abundant in the root zone and play an important role in organic contaminant degradation. The composition of rhizospheric micro organisms are also depends on the soil pH and its texture.

47. Grasslands are large areas of grass with scattered trees. They can be divided into two types—tropical grasslands or savannas and temperate grasslands. They are often given local names like veldts in South Africa, pampas in Argentina, outback or scrub in Australia, steppe on Central Asia and prairies in North America.

Tropical Grasslands

Location: Tropical grasslands, also known as savannas, are found between 20° north and south of the Equator. They cover large parts of Africa, Australia, South America and India.

48. At the April 18 Global Citizen 2015 Earth Day, the Global Alliance to Eliminate Lead Paint (Lead Paint Alliance), co-led by the United Nations Environment Programme (UNEP) and the World Health Organization (WHO), announced the goal of eliminating lead paint around the world by 2020. The event in Washington, DC, was organized by the Global Poverty Project and Earth Day Network to commemorate the 45th anniversary of the first Earth day.

49. Coal is the principal energy source, particularly in India because of its large deposits and availability. According to geological order of formation, coal may be of the following types: (1) Peat, (2) Lignite, (3) Subbituminous, (4) Bituminous, (5) Subanthracite, and (6) Anthracite, with increasing percentages of carbon. After anthracite, graphite is formed. Anthracite contains more than 86% fixed carbon (in amorphous form) and less volatile matter. Volatile matter helps in the ignition of coal. So, it is often difficult to burn anthracite. Bituminous coal is the largest group containing 46-86% of fixed carbon and 20-40% of volatile matter. It can be low-volatile, medium-volatile and high-volatile. The lower the volatility, the higher the heating value. Lignite is the lowest grade of coal containing moisture as high as 30% and high volatile matter. According to ASTM (American Society of Testing and Materials), peat is not regarded as a rank of coal. Peat contains up to 90% moisture and is not attractive as a utility fuel. Rank carries the meaning of degree of maturation (carbonisation) and is a measure of carbon content in coal. Lignite is considered to be low rank and anthracite to be high rank.

50. National Plan for Conservation of Aquatic Eco-systems (NPCA) will help promote better synergy and avoid overlap of administrative functions. It will be governed by a uniform policy and clear guidelines, and will operate through the implementation of sustainable conservation plans. The principal objectives of NPCA will be holistic conservation and restoration of lakes and wetlands through an integrated and multidisciplinary approach with a common regulatory framework.

This will enable enhancement of water quality, as well as enrichment of biodiversity and the ecosystem. The scheme will also contribute to reduction of pollution loads and improvement in goods and services provided by these water bodies to stakeholders, say ministry officials.

The new scheme includes within its scope the conservation and management of lakes and wetlands, the maintenance of an inventory and information system on these water bodies, a national-level directive on criteria for lakes and wetlands, a regulatory framework, the inclusion of capacity building at state government and local body levels, and evaluation.

51. Soil salinity is the salt content in the soil; the process of increasing the salt content is known as salinization. Salts occur naturally within soils and water. Salination can be caused by natural processes such as mineral weathering or by the gradual withdrawal of an ocean. It can also come about through artificial processes such as water irrigation in agriculture area and Upland lateritic area. Salinity from irrigation can occur over time wherever irrigation occurs, since almost all water (even natural rainfall) contains some dissolved salts. Water in excess of plant needs is called the leaching fraction. Salination from irrigation water is also greatly increased by poor drainage and use of saline water for irrigating agricultural crops.

53. A digital elevation model (DEM) is a digital model or 3D representation of a terrain's surface — commonly for a planet, moon, or asteroid — created from terrain elevation data.

A DEM can be represented as a raster (a grid of squares, also known as a heightmap when representing elevation) or as a vector-based triangular irregular network (TIN). The TIN DEM dataset is also referred to as a primary (measured) DEM, whereas the Raster DEM is referred to as a secondary (computed) DEM.

54. Deltas are discrete shoreline protuberances formed where a river enters a standing body of water and supplies sediments more rapidly than they can be redistributed by basinal processes, such as tides and waves. In that sense, all deltas are river-dominated and deltas are fundamentally regressive in nature. The morphology and facies architecture of a delta is controlled by the proportion of wave, tide, and river processes; the salinity contrast between inflowing water and the standing body of water, the sediment discharge and sediment caliber, and the water depth into which the river flows. The geometry of the receiving basin (and proximity to a shelf edge) may also have an influence. The simple classification into river-, wave-, and tide-dominated end members must be used with caution because the number of parameters that control deltas is more numerous.

55. **Rift valley:** It is a Elongated depression, trough, or graben in the earth's crust, bounded on both sides by normal faults and occurring on the continents or under the oceans. The central flat block forming the trough slips downward relative to the crustal blocks on either side. The appearance is that of a fallen keystone in a broken arch. Rift valleys form by tensional forces, typically those associated with the initiation of plate separation. The development of a rift valley in a continent is believed to be a precursor to the breakup of the continent and the development of a new ocean basin by seafloor spreading. Rift valleys, such as the Red Sea and the African rift valleys, are commonly the sites of volcanism and the locus of much earthquake activity.

56. Scattering is a condition whereby suspended particles and molecules in the atmosphere redirect solar radiation in every direction. The Solar radiation reaches the Earth's surface by a direct transmission as well as an indirect transmission from scattering by particulates. A portion of the scattered energy is redirected back toward space, and a portion is re-scattered by other particulates. If we did not have scattering, we would not be able to see light when standing in shadows, because there would be no redirected light that our eyes could detect. There are 3 defined types of scattering: Rayleigh, MIE, and Non-selective scattering, Rayleigh scattering happens at the upper atmosphere and occurs when atmospheric particles have a diameter smaller than the incident wavelength. Since Blue and UV light is more readily scattered than red light, we generally see the sky as blue. MIE scattering is caused by particulates that exist in the Earth's lower atmosphere, and when particulates are roughly equal to the incident wavelength. Dust, smoke, and water droplets in the lower atmosphere cause Mie scattering to create a dark or grey appearance in the sky. Non-selective scattering is caused by particles much larger than the incident wavelength and occurs in the very lowest portion of the atmosphere to the Earth's surface. Non-selective scattering by aerosols is the primary cause of haze. Non-selective scattering in visible region in the atmosphere is not dependent on wavelength.

57. The best spatial configuration for a core natural area is circular.

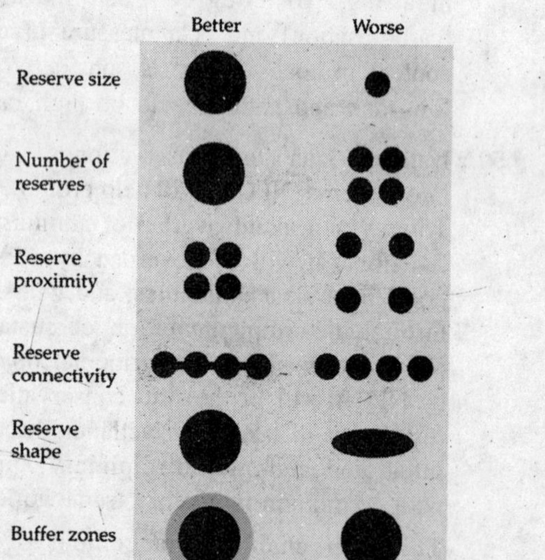

Fig.: *The Best Spatial Configurations for a Core Natural Area*

58. Ecosystem resilience is the capacity of an ecosystem to sustain its fundamental function, structure, and feedbacks in the face of a spectrum of shocks and perturbations Ecosystems are particularly resilient to those fluctuations to which organisms are well-adapted, including day-night or seasonal cycles of light and temperature.

60. A Horizon or Surface Soil:

- It is the part of top soil.
- In this layer, organic matter is mixed with mineral matter.
- It is the layer of mineral soil with the most organic matter accumulation and soil life.
- This layer is depleted of (eluviated of) iron, clay, aluminum, organic compounds, and other soluble constituents.
- When depletion is pronounced, a lighter coloured "E" subsurface soil horizon is apparent at the base of the "A" horizon.

O Horizon:

- Layers dominated by organic material.
- Some O layers consist of undecomposed or partially decomposed litter (such as leaves, needles, twigs, moss, and lichens).
- They may be on top of either mineral or organic soils.

C Horizon or Parent Rock:

- Weathered parent material accumulates in this layer, *i.e.* the parent material in sedimentary deposits.
- It is a layer of large unbroken rocks.
- This layer may accumulate the more soluble compounds (inorganic material).

B Horizon or Subsoil

- It is subsurface layer reflecting chemical or physical alteration of parent material.
- This layer accumulates all the leached minerals from A and E horizon.
- Thus iron, clay, aluminum and organic compounds accumulate in this horizon [illuviation (opposite of eluviation)].

62. Using mass balance equation

$0.2 \times 50 + 0.05 \times 1500$

$= (0.2 + 0.05) \times$ downstream concentration

i.e., downstream concentration = 340 mg/L.

63. In chromatography, a retardation factor (R_f) describes the ratio of time spent in the stationary phase relative to time spent in the mobile phase basically is the distance travelled by the compound divided by the distance travelled by the solvent can be determined using Equation.

$$R_f = \frac{\text{Migration Distance of Substance}}{\text{Migration Distance of Solvent Front}}$$

An R_f value will always be in the range 0 to 1: if the substance moves at all, it moves along the direction the solvent ("mobile phase") does less, but cannot move further than the solvent does. R_f values are only useful if they are between these two extremes. So, student T with R_f values 1.3 is definitely incorrect.

67. Molina and Rowland estimated in 1974 the average lifetime of a molecule of CFC-11 in the atmosphere at 40 to 80 years, and at 75 to 150 years for CFC-12. These predictions have been confirmed by measurements over the last 23 years which have shown their actual atmospheric lifetimes to be about 50 years for CFC-11 and 100 years for CFC-12.

68. The global warming potential (GWP) of a GHG is a relative measure of its ability to act as a GHG with respect to carbon dioxide. For example, nitrous oxide has a 100-year GWP of 296. This means that 1 tonne of nitrous oxide gas emitted into the atmosphere is the same as the emission of 296 tonnes of carbon dioxide.

69. The green-house gas N_2O strongly absorbs infra-red radiations of wavelength(s) ~7.8 μm and 8.6 μm.

70. The Government has up-scaled the target of renewable energy capacity to 175 GW by the year 2022 which includes 100 GW from solar, 60 GW from wind, 10 GW from bio-power and 5 GW from small hydro-power. Stepping up capacity target under the Jawaharlal Nehru National Solar Mission (JNNSM) by five times now India is aiming to generate reaching 1,00,000 MW solar power by 2022. The target will principally comprise of 40 GW Rooftop and 60 GW through Large and Medium Scale Grid Connected Solar Power Projects. With this ambitious target, India will become one of the largest Green Energy producers in the world, surpassing several developed countries. The total investment in setting up 100 GW will be around ₹ 6,00,000 crore.

72. High levels of UV-B radiation (280 to 320 nm wavelength) are responsible for many biologically harmful effects in both plants and animals. Some effects include DNA damage, eye cataracts, skin cancer, and immune system suppression in animals, as well as lower growth rates and depressed rates of leaf photosynthesis in plants. Results of calculations of the transmission of UV-B through the atmosphere indicate that a 1% decrease in ozone results in a 1.3% to 2% increase in the UV-B levels at the surface of the earth.

73. Indian earth observation system began with the launch of *remote sensing satellites* from 1988 onwards: with the largest constellation of IRS satellites in operation today. They fall into two broad categories: satellites in *medium-earth* orbits at 10,000 km above the earth (in a sun-synchronous polar orbit) carrying payload up to 1500 kg; and satellites in *low-earth* polar orbit with payloads 1000-1200 kg or less. The Polar Satellite Launch Vehicle (PSLV) is now India's workhorse launcher, which has launched its ninth IRS satellite CARTOSAT-1 (2005) for cartographic applications and a small satellite HAMSAT, as piggyback, for amateur radio (HAM) operators.

IRS-P6, called RESOURCESAT-1 (2003), was a multi-institutional endeavour at 620 km high, with academic and private participation from IIT Chennai, M/S Godrej, Bharat Aluminium Company (BALCO), Hindustan Aeronautics (HAL) and Bharat Electronics (BEL) for making data products available to end-users. It is placed in low earth polar sunsynchronous orbit.

74. Freshwater fishes adapted very successfully to their aquatic habitats. Thus, when some freshwater fishes returned to the sea about 200 mya, their blood and body fluids were less salty than (hypotonic to) their surroundings. They tended to lose water osmotically and to take in salt. To compensate for fluid loss, many marine bony fishes drink seawater. They retain the water and excrete salt by the action of specialized cells in their gills. Very little urine is excreted by the kidneys; the kidneys have only small (or no) glomeruli.

75. A lysimeter is a measuring device which can be used to measure the amount of actual evapotranspiration which is released by plants, usually crops or trees. By recording the amount of precipitation that an area receives and the amount lost through the soil, the amount of water lost to evapotranspiration can be calculated.

A lysimeter is most accurate when vegetation is grown in a large soil tank which allows the rainfall input and water lost through the soil to be easily calculated. The amount of water lost by evapotranspiration can be worked out by calculating the difference between the weight before and after the precipitation input.

Previous Paper (Solved)

UGC–NET Environmental Science, June–2015*

PAPER-II

Note : *This paper contains* ***fifty (50)*** *objective type questions of* ***two (2)*** *marks each. All questions are compulsory.*

1. An endotherm's basal metabolic rate stays constant throughout a range of environmental temperatures known as the:

I. Lower critical temperature zone
II. Thermoneutral zone
III. Higher critical temperature zone

Choose the correct answer:

A. I only B. II only
C. I and II only D. II and III only

2. Which state has the largest coastline in India?

A. West Bengal B. Karnataka
C. Gujarat D. Odisha

3. Indicators for sustainable development are:

I. environmental pressures
II. environmental quality
III. society's response

Choose the correct answer:

A. I and II only B. II and III only
C. I and III only D. I, II and III

4. Stoichiometric calculations are based on:

A. Moles B. Atomic weight
C. Atomic number D. Loss of mass

5. BOD of the effluents discharged on land for irrigation should not exceed:

A. 30 mg/L B. 100 mg/L
C. 300 mg/L D. 60 mg/L

6. Which of the following adds to the carbon dioxide concentration in atmosphere?

I. Volcanic action
II. Respiration
III. Photosynthesis
IV. Decay of organic matter

Choose the correct answer:

A. I and III only
B. II only
C. I, II and IV only
D. I, II, III and IV

7. Corrosion normally occurs when an electrochemical cell is set up on a metal surface. The corroded area is:

A. cathode
B. anode
C. electrolyte
D. entire metal surface

8. Acid sulphate soils are characteristic of marine coastal plains in areas rich in:

I. Organic matter
II. Brackish water
III. Mangrove swamps

Choose the correct answer:

A. I only B. I and II only
C. II only D. I, II and III

9. The amount of energy at one trophic level divided by the amount of energy at the trophic level immediately below it is termed as:

A. Trophic efficiency
B. Consumption efficiency
C. Assimilation efficiency
D. Production efficiency

10. Blue whale is placed under the category of:

A. Endangered species
B. Critically endangered species
C. Vulnerable species
D. Extinct species

* Exam held on 28-06-2015

11. Maximum density of detritivorus micro organisms in pond ecosystem are present in:
A. Limnetic zone B. Photic zone
C. Littoral zone D. Benthic zone

12. Species diversity show a marked pattern as one moves from equator to the poles. Species diversity:
A. increases as one moves towards the poles from the equator
B. decreases as one moves from equator to poles
C. remains constant as one moves from equator to poles
D. is highest in the arctic and antartic regions

13. Coral reefs are mainly distributed globally in:
A. Temperate waters
B. Tropical waters
C. Antartic waters
D. Arctic waters

14. Most common soil borne bacterial pathogen that manipulates plant by injecting its DNA segment into plant cell is:
A. *Acidaminococcus fermentans*
B. *Clostridium thermoacetium*
C. *Rhizobium leguminosarum*
D. *Agrobacterium tumefaciens*

15. Which among the following are the best tools/techniques to study landscape fragmentation?
I. Remote sensing
II. Geodesy
III. Cartography
IV. Geographical Information System
Choose the correct answer:
A. I and II only
B. I, III and IV only
C. II, III and IV only
D. I, II, III and IV

16. An earthquake's epicentre is:
A. usually in the lower part of the mantle
B. determined by analysing S-wave arrival time at seismic stations
C. determined by analysing P-wave arrival time at seismic stations
D. a point on the surface directly above the focus

17. Water entrapped at the time of formation of the sedimentary rocks is called:
A. Meteoric water B. Connate water
C. Juvenile water D. Ground water

18. Which of the following pairs of igneous rocks have the same mineral composition?
A. Granite – basalt
B. Andesite -- rhyolite
C. Basalt – gabbro
D. Pumic – basalt

19. Traps for petroleum and natural gas formed by deformation such as folding and fracturing of rocks are known as:
A. Lithification traps
B. Reservoir traps
C. Structural traps
D. Stratigraphic traps

20. In which one of the following areas does radiant drainage fully develop?
A. On a point bar
B. Around an ox-bow lake
C. Near a delta
D. Around a volcano

21. Which of the following countries produce highest amount of hydropower?
A. Australia B. Canada
C. Italy D. India

22. A solar cell of area 10 cm × 10 cm produces a voltage of 0.6 V and a current upto 2A. If solar insolation is 1000 Wm^{-2}, the efficiency of the solar cell is:
A. 15% B. 12%
C. 25% D. 24%

23. An ocean wave has a height of 3 m and has time period of 10 sec. The power available for extraction from this wave in the units of kW per meter of the wavefront is approximately:
A. 30 B. 45
C. 90 D. 300

24. In the case of Silicon solar cell (Eg = 1.12 eV), the maximum wavelength of solar radiations for production of electron-hole pairs is:

A. ~ 560 nm B. ~ 480 nm
C. ~ 720 nm D. ~ 1100 nm

25. The share of India in the total annual GHG emissions of the world is approximately:

A. 5 - 7% B. 10 - 12%
C. 17 - 20% D. 20 - 25%

26. In biogas, the percentage (%) of methane is in the range of:

A. 50 - 70% B. 30 - 40%
C. 70 - 90% D. 40 - 50%

27. Indira Gandhi canal passes through the following state:

I. Punjab II. Haryana
III. Uttar Pradesh IV. Rajasthan

Choose the correct answer:

A. I, II only B. I, II, III only
C. I, II, IV only D. I, II, III, IV

28. Trichloromonofluoromethane is:

I. Freon-II
II. A spray can propellent
III. A chlorofluorocarbon

Choose the correct answer:

A. I only B. II and III only
C. I and III only D. I, II and III

29. Which of the following air pollutants are released by thermal power plants?

I. Oxides of nitrogen
II. Oxides of sulphur
III. Ammonia
IV. Carbon monoxide

Choose the correct answer:

A. I, III and IV only B. II and III only
C. I, II and IV only D. I, II, III and IV

30. The Noise Index L_{eq} for a specific duration is a measure of:

A. acoustic energy content
B. average noise amplitude
C. sum of instantaneous sound pressure levels
D. fluctuations in noise levels

31. When DDT enters the human body, it is:

A. water soluble and easily excreted in urine
B. stored in the bones
C. fat soluble and stored in fat tissues
D. processed by enzymes and becomes a different compound which is toxic

32. In which EIA guidelines notification, developmental projects were categorized as 'A' and 'B' in India?

A. EIA guidelines notification, 1994
B. EIA guidelines notification, 1986
C. EIA guidelines notification, 2006
D. EIA guidelines notification, 2000

33. Three important rivers of Indian sub-continent have their source near the Mansarovar lake in Tibet. These rivers are:

A. Indus, Jhelum, Ganga
B. Indus, Sutlej, Yamuna
C. Indus, Sutlej, Brahmaputra
D. Yamuna, Brahmaputra, Gandak

34. Which state in India has the highest area of wastelands under barren/stony/rock category?

A. Jammu and Kashmir
B. Himachal Pradesh
C. Arunachal Pradesh
D. Uttarakhand

35. During clearance of any developmental project, the minimum distance required for site selection from eco-sensitive zone is:

A. 5 km B. 10 km
C. 15 km D. 20 km

36. Which of the following are true regarding 'Jhum' cultivation in India?

I. It is largely practiced in N-E India
II. Fertility is exhausted in a few years
III. It is referred as 'Slash and Burn' technique

Choose the correct answer:

A. I, II, and III B. I and II only
C. II and III only D. I and III only

37. Compensatory afforestation provisions are covered under the Environment Act names as:

A. Indian Forest Act (Revised), 1982
B. Environment Protection Act, 1986

C. Forest Conservation Act, 1980
D. Public Liability Insurance Act, 1981

38. When a disaster has occurred, the early action in a Disaster Management Plan could be:
A. Response and Rescue
B. Warning and preparedness
C. Relief and Rehabilitation
D. Shelter and Food supply

39. An environmental problem associated with landfill waste disposal site is:
I. Methane production
II. Ground water pollution
III. Incomplete decomposition
Choose the correct answer:
A. I and II only B. I, II and III
C. I and III only D. II and III only

40. Eco-labelling of commercial products is regulated by:
A. ISO 14020 B. ISO 14010
C. ISO 14030 D. ISO 14040

41. Which one of the following is not a part of 'Waste Reduction' strategy?
A. Reduced use of raw material
B. Material Reuse
C. Recycling of waste
D. Decreased toxicity

42. The expanded form of ISWM is:
A. International Standards of Waste Management
B. Indian Standards for Waste Material
C. Integrated Solid Waste Management
D. International Solid Waste Management

43. Municipal Solid Waste (Handling and Management) rule and Biomedical Waste (Handling and Management) rule were implemented in the years respectively:
A. 2000 and 1998 B. 1998 and 2002
C. 1996 and 1998 D. 1990 and 1985

44. If a phosphorous limited lake having surface area equal to 80×10^6 m^2 is fed by stream with flow rate 20 m^3/s that has phosphorous concentration of 0.01 mg/L, then the phosphorous loading from the incoming stream is:
A. 4.0 g/s B. 0.2 g/s
C. 0.4 g/s D. 0.6 g/s

45. If K is the carrying capacity of a population N in an ecosystem following the logistic growth, its growth rate becomes zero when:
A. N/K = 0
B. Mortality > Natality
C. N/K = 1
D. N = Half of the carrying capacity of the habitat

46. A good sample design should result in:
A. A truely representative sample
B. Highly varied sampling error
C. Low level of confidence
D. Unsystemic bias

47. The mean of a Poisson's distribution is 8. Its standard deviation is:
A. 2 B. $2\sqrt{2}$
C. 4 D. $\frac{8}{5}$

48. Destructive powers of Tsunami result mainly from its:
A. Incredible Height
B. Unpredictability
C. Momentum and long wavelength
D. Cold water

49. Which one of the following is **not** correct for drip irrigation?
A. Drip consists of a network of perforated plastic tubing below the ground surface
B. Drip irrigation increases fertilizer use and water pollution from fertilizer run-off
C. Small holes in the tubing drops off water at a slow rate close to plant roots
D. This technique was developed in Israel in the 1960's

50. The non-formal Environmental Education in India provides support to:
I. Eco-clubs
II. GLOBE
III. Environmental appreciation courses
Choose the correct answer:
A. I and II only B. II and III only
C. I and III only D. I, II and III

ANSWERS

1	2	3	4	5	6	7	8	9	10
B	C	D	A	B	C	B	D	A	A
11	12	13	14	15	16	17	18	19	20
D	B	B	D	B	D	B	C	C	D
21	22	23	24	25	26	27	28	29	30
B	B	C	D	A	A	C	B	C	A
31	32	33	34	35	36	37	38	39	40
C	C	C	A	B	A	C	A	B	A
41	42	43	44	45	46	47	48	49	50
D	C	A	B	C	A	B	C	B	A

SOME SELECTED EXPLANATORY ANSWERS

2. Gujarat—longest coast line 1600 km, dotted with 41 ports; 1 major, 11 intermediate and 29 minor ports. Andhra Pradesh is the second longest coast line 972 km (604 mi).

3. Environmental and sustainable development indicators proliferated in the wake of the Rio Earth Summit's call for indicators of sustainable development.

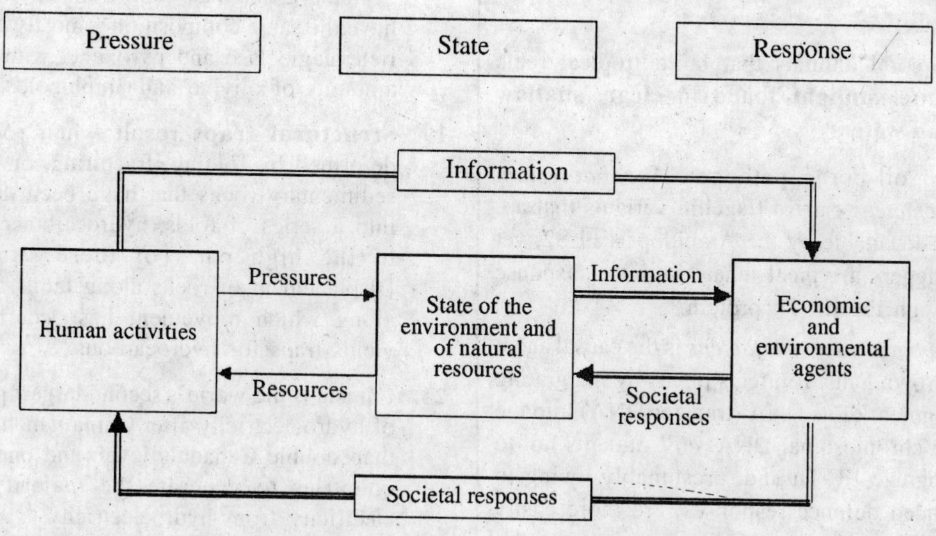

7. Corrosion normally occurs when an electrochemical cell is set up on a metal surface. The area corroded is the anode, where the following oxidation reaction occurs, illustrated for the formation of a divalent metal ion from a metal, M:

$$M \rightarrow M^{2+} + 2e^-$$

9. Trophic levels are the feeding position in a food chain such as primary producers, herbivore, primary carnivore, etc. Green plants form the first trophic level, the producers. Herbivores form the second trophic level, while carnivores form the third and even the fourth trophic levels.

Trophic efficiency is the transfer of energy through tropic levels, the trophic level is the same as the food chain.

Trophic efficiency

$$= \frac{\text{Amount of energy at } n^{\text{th}} \text{ trophic level}}{\text{Amount of energy at } (n+1)^{\text{th}} \text{ trophic level}}$$

10. Blue whales are the largest mammals that ever lived, but they are also an endangered species. Due to aggressive hunting and environmental changes, these ocean-dwellers could become extinct.

13. Coral reefs are found in all three of the Earth's oceans that have portions in the tropics—the Atlantic, Pacific and Indian.

However, coral reefs are **not randomly scattered** throughout each of these great ocean basins.

Because the global distribution of coral reefs is largely determined by the ecological requirements of the reef-building corals themselves.

The coral animals that build tropical reefs require **sunlight** found in **clear, shallow ocean waters**.

14. The soil-borne pathogen *Agrobacterium tumefaciens* carries flagellin variants that are non-detectable by the Arabidopsis FLS2, yet it triggers a typical innate immune response through the EF-Tu protein.

Agrobacterium tumefaciens is the causal agent of crown galls. It infects plants by integrating a segment of its DNA (transfer DNA) into the host chromosomal DNA. *efr1* mutants fail to recognize EF-Tu and, presumably owing to reduced defence responses, are more easily transformed by Agrobacterium.

16. The epicentre, epicentre or epicentrum is the point on the Earth's surface that is directly above the hypocentre or focus, the point where an earthquake or underground explosion originates.

17. **Sources of Ground water:** There are three sources of ground water:

- **Connate Water:** Water entrapped in the interstices of a sedimentary rock at the time the rock was deposited.
- **Meteoric Water:** Meteoric water originates in the atmosphere, falls as precipitation and becomes groundwater by infiltration. Meteoric water constitutes the bulk of groundwater and this is evident in the fluctuation of water level in wells during the rainy season when the level goes up, and in summer season when the level goes down.
- **Juvenile Water:** Juvenile water is that water which is considered to have been generated in the interior of the Earth and have reached the upper levels of the Earth's surface for the first time. It is also called magmatic water.

18. **Basalt-Gabbro:** *Basalt* and *Gabbro* are the aphanitic and phaneritic rocks that crystallize from mafic magma (45-52% silica). Thus, both have the same composition—mostly calcium-rich plagioclase and pyroxene, with smaller amounts of olivine and amphibole.

19. **Structural traps** result when rocks are deformed by folding, fracturing, or both. In sedimentary rocks that have been deformed into a series of folds, hydrocarbons migrate to the high parts of these structures. Displacement of rocks along faults fractures along which movement has occurred also yields traps for hydrocarbons.

21. Canada is the world's second largest producer of hydroelectricity after China which is more than double Canada's level, and one of few countries to generate the majority of its electricity from hydroelectricity.

- Hydropower produced 63 per cent of Canada's electricity production in 2010.
- Canada is the world's second largest hydropower producer, generating 363 TWh/year.
- Every province with the exception of Prince Edward Island produces hydropower to varying degrees.
- There is 163, 173 megawatts of undeveloped hydro potential in Canada.

22. Efficiency of the Solar Cell

$$= \frac{\frac{\text{Voltage} \times \text{Current}}{\text{Area(in m}^2)} \times 100}{\text{Solar insolation}}$$

$$= \frac{\frac{0.6 \times 2}{10 \times 10} \times 100}{100 \times 100} \times 1000 = 12\%.$$

26. Biogas is a mixture of different gases produced by the breakdown of organic matter and is used as a renewable energy source that exerts a very small carbon footprint. The composition of biogas is typically 40-60 per cent methane, 40-50 per cent carbon dioxide, and the remainder being water, hydrogen sulfide, and other impurities. The composition of a specific biogas depends on the type of waste it is being obtained from, what it's being purified for, as well as the purpose for which the biogas is being used.

27. Indira Gandhi Canal is the largest canal in India. The canal is 650 km long and starts from the Harike Barrage, a few kilometers below the confluence of the Sutlej and Beas rivers in Punjab. It flows through Punjab, Haryana, and Rajasthan, with the major length of the canal flowing through Rajasthan. The canal terminates near Jaisalmer in Rajasthan.

30. The most common general noise indice is: The equivalent sound pressure level $L_{eq,T}$, defined in ISO 1996–1, expresses the level of a continuous noise that would have the same total acoustic energy as a fluctuating noise measured for the same specific period

$$T : L_{eq,T} = 10\log_{10}\left(\frac{1}{T}\int_0^T \frac{p^2(t)}{p_0^2}\,dt\right)[dB].$$

31. DDT is fat soluble and is disseminated by air and water to terrestrial and aquatic ecosystems. When DDT enters a water environment, it is taken up by aquatic animals and becomes part of the food chain, accumulating and concentrating in the fat of predatory species. DDT also remains residual in upper soil layers and accumulates in many terrestrial animal species.

33. The Indus River originates in the northern slopes of the Kailash range near Lake Manasarovar in Tibet. While the Sutlej river originates from the Rakas Lake (Rakshas Tal), which is connected to the Manasarovar lake by a stream, in Tibet and the Brahmaputra river also originated from Manasarovar lake in tibet.

35. Restrictions have been imposed for any project operations in wildlife, sanctuaries, national parks, near the national monuments, areas of cultural heritage, ecological fragile areas rich in biological diversity, gene pool etc. Prior environmental clearance is required in respect of any project to be located within 10 km of the boundary of reserve forests or a designated ecologically sensitive area or within 25 km of the boundary of national park or sanctuary.

40. **Eco-labels** and **Green stickers** are labelling systems for food and consumer products. Eco-labels are voluntary, but green stickers are mandated by law. This International Standard establishes guiding principles for the development and use of environmental labels and declarations. It is intended that other applicable standards in the ISO 14020 series be used in conjunction with this International Standard.

41. Waste minimisation can be defined as "systematically reducing waste at source". It means:

- Prevention and/or reduction of waste generated
- Efficient use of raw materials and packaging
- Efficient use of fuel, electricity and water
- Improving the quality of waste generated to facilitate recycling and/or reduce hazard
- Encouraging re-use, recycling and recovery.

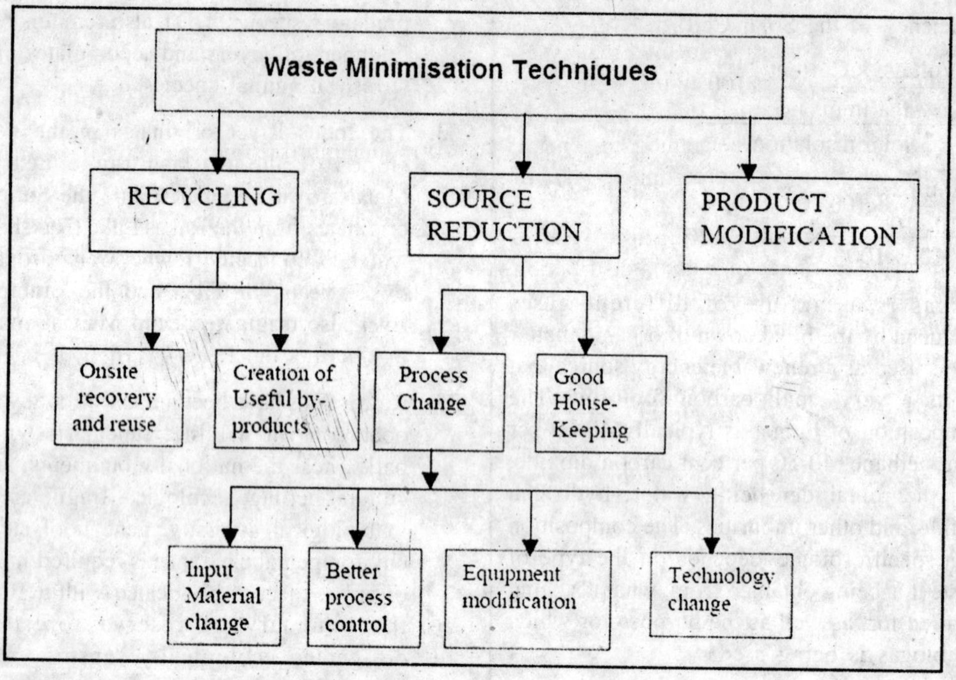

42. ISWM stand for Integrated Solid Waste Management. There is a clear need for strategies to redesign conventional waste generation systems in such a way that they can effectively and efficiently handle growing amounts of waste with diversified waste streams. To respond to this need, the work plan for the focal area on integrated solid waste management (ISWM) proposes to promote an integrated approach to solid waste management, which will enable local/ national authorities to reduce the overall amount of waste generated and to recover valuable materials for recycling and for the generation of energy.

44. Phosphorous loading from the incoming stream is

$$OC_{in} = 20 \text{ m}^3/\text{sec} \times 0.01 \text{ mg/l} \times 1\frac{g/l}{mg/l}$$

$$= 0.2 \text{ g/sec.}$$

45. **Logistic population growth model** follows an S-shaped or sigmoid growth form. In this the population increases slowly at first, then more rapidly, before slowing to an equilibrium level where the population may fluctuate around a maximum. This equilibrium density is termed the carrying capacity and is represented by K in the following model (logistic growth equation):

$$\frac{dN}{dt} = \frac{rN(K-N)}{K}$$

where r is the intrinsic rate of growth and N is the population size. Note that, as N increases, N/K approaches one and the population growth rate keeps falling. When $N = K$, the pupulation growth rate (dN/dt) becomes zero.

46. Characteristics of a good sample design as under:

- Sample design must result in a truly representative sample.
- Sample design must be such which results in a small sampling error.
- Sample design must be viable in the context of funds available for the research study.

- Sample design must be such so that systematic bias can be controlled in a better way.
- Sample should be such that the results of the sample study can be applied, in general, for the universe with a reasonable level of confidence.

47. Properties of Poisson Distribution

1. Mean and Variance of Poisson distribution are same, each equal to λ.
2. Poisson distribution is always a skewed distribution.

∴ Standard deviation

$$S.D. = \sqrt{8} = 2\sqrt{2}.$$

48. Tsunamis (seismic sea waves) are triggered by earthquakes or volcanic eruptions beneath the ocean floor. These waves have wavelengths of approximately 160 kilometers and a speed of 600 to 700 kilometers per hour. Their high speed gives them great momentum and large destructive power.

PAPER-III

Note : *This paper contains* ***seventy five (75)*** *objective type questions of two (2) marks each.* ***All*** *questions are compulsory.*

1. Biological zonation in the ocean is determined by:

I. Ocean depth
II. Light availability
III. Bottom substrate

Choose the correct answer :

A. I only
B. I and II only
C. I, II and III
D. II and III only

2. Given below are two statements. One labelled as Assertion (A) and the other labelled as Reason (R):

Assertion (A): Methanogenic archae (methanogens) grow in swamps and sewage.

Reason (R): Methanogens are obligate anaerobes.

Choose the correct answer :

A. Both (A) and (R) are correct and (R) is the correct explanation of (A).
B. Both (A) and (R) are correct and (R) is not the correct explanation of (A).
C. (A) is true, but (R) is false.
D. (A) is false, but (R) is true.

3. Filamentous Cyanobacteria differentiate 5 to 10% of their vegetative cells into heterocysts. Heterocysts are characterized by :

I. Thick cell wall
II. Only PSI activity
III. Nitrogenase activity

Choose the correct answer :

A. I only
B. I and II only
C. II and III only
D. I, II and III

4. A critically endangered species :

A. Do not exist in wild habitat
B. Face extremely high risk of extinction in immediate future
C. Face high risk of extinction in the medium term future
D. Will not face any risk of extinction in future 1000 years

5. Which of the following characteristics of desert animals are physiological adaptation to conserve water ?

I. Thick outer covering
II. Release dry faeces
III. Avoid exposure to direct sunlight

Choose the correct answer :

A. I and III only
B. II and III only
C. I and II only
D. I, II and III

6. The balance between photosynthesis and photorespiration is related to :

I. The ratio of O_2 and CO_2 in the atmosphere

II. Temperature
III. Kranz anatomy
IV. The ratio of CO_2 and H_2O

Choose the correct answer :
A. I and II only
B. II, III and IV only
C. I, II and III only
D. I, II, III and IV

7. Individual organism respond to environmental change through short-term adjustment(s) by :
A. Physiological changes
B. Cytological changes
C. Genetic changes
D. Phytochemical and genetic alterations

8. The hurricanes have spatial scale of :
A. 100 Km - 1000 Km
B. 10 Km - 100 Km
C. 100 m - 100 Km
D. 100 m - 10 Km

9. In SDS - PAGE :
A. Polymeric proteins are not only converted into monomers, but monomers are also denatured by SDS.
B. Polymeric proteins converted into monomeric units, but monomers are not denatured.
C. Polymeric proteins are retained as single unit.
D. SDS donot have any negative impact on native structure of monomers.

10. Which of the following is the major source of mercury pollution in India ?
A. Coal based thermal power plants
B. Pesticides manufacturing
C. Dental amalgam fillings
D. Electrical and electronic gadgets

11. A non-metal 'X' occurs in nature in free state. It combines with hydrogen to form a gas, which is colourless and highly toxic. Apart from this, 'X' is oxidized to 'XO_2' which is a colourless, pungent and irritating gas. 'X' represents :
A. Sulphur B. Carbon
C. Phosphorus D. Nitrogen

12. Elemental carbon influences the regional climate because :
A. It influences the radiative flux in the atmosphere due to its absorbing properties.
B. It reacts with other pollutants.
C. It coagulates with other atmospheric pollutants.
D. Its concentration is usually more in the atmosphere.

13. Bioremediation of xenobiotics (like melathion) through hydrolysis involves their detoxification by :
A. Removal of water
B. Addition of water
C. Both removal and addition of water
D. Removal of phosphate

14. To determine the cation-exchange capacity, it is necessary to calculate the total positive charge associated with ions like :
A. Ca^{2+}, Mg^{2+}, K^+, Na^+
B. Ca^{2+}, Mn^{2+}, Fe^{3+}, Cr^{3+}
C. Mg^{2+}, Fe^{3+}, Ni^{2+}, Cd^{2+}
D. K^+, BO^{2+}, Pb^{2+}, Hg^{2+}

15. Given below are two statements. One labelled as Assertion (A) and the other labelled as Reason (R) :

Assertion (A): Organometals/organometalloids such as trimethylarsine and dimethylmercury are more toxic to living systems (including humans) compared to their inorganic forms.

Reason (R): Organometals/organometalloids are more hydrophilic than their inorganic forms and hence can move easily across lipid bilayer.

Choose the correct answer :
A. Both (A) and (R) are correct and (R) is the correct explanation of (A).
B. Both (A) and (R) are correct and (R) is not the correct explanation of (A).
C. (A) is true, but (R) is false.
D. (A) is false, but (R) is true.

16. Project elephant was launched in the year :

A. 1973 B. 1985

C. 1992 D. 1998

17. Biological communities in a stream vary based on :

I. Water velocity

II. Allochthonous material

III. Size of the particle on the stream bed

IV. Depth of the stream

Choose the correct answer :

A. I and II only

B. I, II and III only

C. II, III and IV only

D. I, II, III and IV

18. Champion and Seth (1968) classify Indian forests based on :

I. Floristic Composition

II. Precipitation

III. Distance from Sea

Choose the correct answer :

A. I Only B. I and II only

C. II only D. I, II and III

19. Which one of the following statements is **not** correct ?

A. The solubility of gases varies considerably with pressure.

B. Hydrocarbons chiefly occur in coal, natural gas and petroleum.

C. Polynuclear aromatic hydrocarbons are present in coal tar and fossil fuels.

D. All hydrocarbons are hydrophilic in nature.

20. Gauss exclusion principle states that :

A. Complete competitors co-exist

B. Complete competitors cannot co-exist

C. Complete competitors tend to co-operate

D. Symbionts evolve into complete competitors

21. Parasites in a population/community can :

I. Influence host population cycles

II. Change ecological communities

III. Change community structure

Choose the correct answer :

A. I, II and III

B. II and III only

C. III only

D. I only

22. Long-term patterns of evolution are shaped by large scale process(s) such as :

I. Speciation

II. Mass extinction

III. Adaptive radiation

Choose the correct answer:

A. I only B. II and III only

C. I and III only D. I, II and III

23. Match the List-I with List-II. Identify the correct answer from the codes given below the lists :

List–I (Organism)	***List–II (Interaction)***
(*a*) *Albugo* and Indian mustard	(*i*) Symbiosis
(*b*) *Penicillium* and *Staphyllococcus*	(*ii*) Ammensalism
(*c*) Lichens	(*iii*) Commensalism
(*d*) Barnacles and whales	(*iv*) Parasitism

Codes:

	(*a*)	(*b*)	(*c*)	(*d*)
A.	(*i*)	(*ii*)	(*iii*)	(*iv*)
B.	(*ii*)	(*i*)	(*iv*)	(*iii*)
C.	(*iv*)	(*ii*)	(*i*)	(*iii*)
D.	(*iv*)	(*iii*)	(*ii*)	(*i*)

24. Extreme of seasonal variation (as much as 80°C swing) from summer to winter is represented by :

A. Boreal forest

B. Tropical forest

C. Deciduous forest

D. Evergreen forest

25. Aeromycoflora can be trapped and quantified by :

A. Rotorod air sampler

B. Anderson air sampler

C. Gregory air sampler

D. Respirable dust sampler

26. Which among the following frequencies in microwave region of electromagnetic spectrum is better suited for determination of tree height ?

A. C - band (4 - 8 GHz)
B. X - band (8 - 12.5 GHz)
C. P - band (0.3 - 1.0 GHz)
D. K - band (18 - 26.5 GHz)

27. Which of the common mineral is not a silicate?

A. Quartz B. Calcite
C. Pyroxene D. Feldspar

28. Which among the following is the best model in GIS spatial relationships?

A. Spaghetti model
B. Topological model
C. Relational database model
D. Parent-child model

29. One of the warning signs of an impending volcanic eruption is volcanic tremor, which is :

A. A change in ground levels
B. Inflation of a volcano as magma rises
C. Ground shaking lasting for minutes or hours
D. Emission of large quantities of gases

30. Time slot for measuring thermal inertia (TI) differences between land and water is :

A. 1000 hrs. B. 1100 hrs.
C. 1200 hrs. D. 1400 hrs.

31. Slump is a complex slide which consists of :

A. Curved shear surface
B. Curved and planar shear surfaces
C. Planar shear surface
D. No definite shear surface

32. In rainwater harvesting, the purpose of percolation tank is :

A. Recharge ground water only
B. Surface water supply for irrigation
C. Both surface water supply and ground water recharge
D. Drinking water supply

33. Which of the following minerals causes fluoride pollution in the groundwater ?

A. Fluorite and Apatite
B. Olivine and Haematite
C. Calcite and Magnetite
D. Quartz and Orthoclase

34. Indian monsoon is greatly influenced by :

I. Sea surface temperature in pre-monsoon season
II. El Nino
III. La Nina
IV. Depression over Tibet

Choose the correct answer :

A. I and II only
B. II and III only
C. III and IV only
D. IV only

35. The important continental silicate mineral weathering process of lowering carbon dioxide levels is :

A. Hydrolysis B. Oxidation
C. Carbonation D. Reduction

36. The set of processes by which soil and rock are loosened and move downhill are called :

A. Erosion B. Saltation
C. Weathering D. Abrasion

37. Wind mills are most suited for :

I. Deserts
II. Offshore
III. High altitude
IV. Roof tops

Choose the correct answer :

A. I and II only
B. II and III only
C. I and III only
D. II, III and IV only

38. Main source of energy for a tropical cyclone formation comes from :

I. Heat of condensation of water vapours in the atmosphere
II. Torrential rains
III. Large ocean waves

Choose the correct answer :

A. I only
B. II only
C. III and II only
D. I and III only

39. In the following nuclear fusion reaction $^{2}_{1}D$ + $^{2}_{1}D$ = $^{3}_{2}He$ + $^{1}_{0}n$ + E the value of the energy E is :

A. 17.6 MeV B. 18.3 MeV
C. 4.03 MeV D. 3.27 MeV

40. Fast neutrons produced in nuclear fission reactions involving ^{235}U have average energy of the order of :

A. 2 MeV B. 5 MeV
C. 100 MeV D. 200 MeV

41. As the population growth rate increases the doubling time :

A. Increase B. Double
C. Remain constant D. Decrease

42. A tidal estuary of tidal range 2 m has trapped water area 5000 m^2. If g = 9.8 m/s^2, the maximum energy available per tidal cycle is:

A. 2.45 kW B. 9.8 kW
C. 98 kW D. 19.6 kW

43. The power (P) from an ocean wave varies with time period (T) of the wave as :

A. $P \propto T$ B. $P \propto T^2$
C. $P \propto \frac{1}{T}$ D. $P \propto \frac{1}{T^2}$

44. With reference to pre-industrial times, the present day average global surface temperature is higher approximately by :

A. ~ 0.56 °C B. ~ 0.85 °C
C. ~1.3 °C D. ~1.5 °C

45. Burning of 1 mol of CH_4 liberates 890 kJ of energy and 1 mol of CO_2. Since 1 mol of CO_2 has 12 g of carbon, the higher heating value (HHV) of methane is :

A. 13.5 gC/MJ B. 18.5 gC/MJ
C. 12.0 gC/MJ D. 10.0 gC/MJ

46. pH of 1 mM HCl is :

A. 1 B. 2
C. 3 D. 11

47. Priority air pollutants included in the air quality index for urban areas in India are :

A. CO, NO_x, PM_{10} and $PM_{2.5}$, SO_x, O_3, ammonia and Pb
B. CO, NO_x, SO_x and Pb
C. NO_x, SO_x, O_3, and Pb
D. PM_{10} and $PM_{2.5}$, NO_x, SO_x, O_3, and Pb

48. Present day advanced anaerobic digestors can generate power in the range :

A. 2 - 10 MW
B. 20 - 100 MW
C. 100 - 200 MW
D. 200 - 500 MW

49. Cement dust is characterized by very fine particulates. Which of the following air pollution control devices is appropriate for removing them from hot exhaust gases emanating from cement kiln?

A. Baghouse
B. Cyclones
C. Venturi scrubber
D. Electrostatic precipitator

50. The sources of aliphatic hydrocarbons in indoor environment are :

A. Paints, adhesives and gasoline
B. Aerosol sprays and solvents
C. Spirits and cleansers
D. Solvents and vinyl flooring

51. Given the following data of sound pressure levels measured at equal intervals: 60 dB, 62 dB, 63 dB, 59 dB, 60 dB, 80 dB, 58 dB, 59 dB, 65 dB, 57 dB, 62 dB. The value of the background noise level (L_{90}) is :

A. 62.5 dB B. 57 dB
C. 61 dB D. 58 dB

52. The air-to-fuel ratio (A/F) for complete combustion in an internal combustion engine is about :

A. 14.6 B. 11.2
C. 12.1 D. 15.5

53. Phytovolatilization of mercuric pollutants involves volatalization of mercury in :

A. Elemental state

B. Ionic state

C. Organic state

D. Both ionic and organic state

54. Match the List - I with List - II. Identify the correct answer from the codes given below the lists :

List–I	***List–II***
(*a*) Texture	(*i*) Vertical zonation
(*b*) Profile	(*ii*) Land degradation
(*c*) Erosion	(*iii*) Planting tree
(*d*) Conservation	(*iv*) Mineral particle size

Codes :

	(*a*)	(*b*)	(*c*)	(*d*)
A.	(*iv*)	(*i*)	(*ii*)	(*iii*)
B.	(*i*)	(*ii*)	(*iii*)	(*iv*)
C.	(*ii*)	(*iii*)	(*iv*)	(*i*)
D.	(*iii*)	(*iv*)	(*i*)	(*ii*)

55. Environmental Management Plan is associated with :

A. EIS

B. Environmental audit

C. ISO 14000

D. LCA

56. ISO 14000 is connected with :

A. Adoption of environmental safety guideline

B. Energy audit in industries

C. Adoption of clean development

D. Adoption of environmental management system in industry/organisation

57. CAPART in India stands for :

A. Committee for Advancement and Promotion of Rural Technology

B. Council for Advancement of Rural Technology

C. Council for Advancement of People's Action and Rural Technology

D. Committee for Advancement and Privatization of Rural Technology

58. EIA of Port and Harbour projects involve impact assessment on :

I. Biological environment

II. Air environment

III. Soil environment

IV. Social environment

Choose the correct answer :

A. I only

B. II only

C. III only

D. I, II and IV only

59. Which act provided provisions for enforcing levy and collection of a tax on water consumed by industries ?

A. Water (prevention and control of pollution) Act 1974

B. Water (prevention and control of pollution) Cess Act 1977

C. Environment (protection) Act 1986

D. Public Liability Insurance Act 1991

60. Disaster risk reduction in degraded wilderness areas is better achieved using :

A. People's participation

B. Ecosystem based management

C. Strengthening of people's economic conditions

D. Afforestation

61. The major conventions of Rio Earth Summit are :

A. CBD and climate change

B. Kyoto protocol and Montreal protocol

C. CDM and Nagoya protocol

D. Basel convention and Bameco convention

62. If $\Gamma_s < \Gamma_e < \Gamma_d$ where Γ_s, Γ_e and Γ_d are saturated adiabatic lapse rate, environmental lapse rate and dry adiabatic lapse rate, the atmosphere is :

A. Stable

B. Conditionally unstable

C. Unstable

D. Neutral

63. Match the List–I with List–II. Identify the correct answer from the codes given below the lists:

List–I (Tests)	*List–II (Application)*
(*a*) Z-test	(*i*) Judging the significance of differences between means of two small samples
(*b*) t-test	(*ii*) Judging the significance of mean, median, mode
(*c*) Chi-square (χ^2) test	(*iii*) Compare the variance of two - independent samples
(*d*) F-test	(*iv*) Compare sample variance to a theoretical population variance

Codes:

	(*a*)	(*b*)	(*c*)	(*d*)
A.	(*ii*)	(*i*)	(*iv*)	(*iii*)
B.	(*iii*)	(*ii*)	(*i*)	(*iv*)
C.	(*iv*)	(*iii*)	(*ii*)	(*i*)
D.	(*i*)	(*iv*)	(*iii*)	(*ii*)

64. Chocolates of 250 g produced in a factory were observed to have standard deviation of 2 g. A random sample of 20 chocolates showed a standard deviation of 1.5 g. What is the χ^2 value for the sample ?

A. 7.2 B. 6.0
C. 12.0 D. 33.3

65. Which one of the following would indicate that a dataset is NOT distributed in a bell - shape?

A. The range is equal to 5 standard deviation
B. The range is larger than the inter quartile range
C. The mean is much smaller than the median
D. There are no outliers

66. In a random sample of $x = 16$, the mean $(\overline{X})$ is 40, and the standard deviation (sd) is 4.0. The 95% confidence interval (Z = 1.96) for the mean is :

A. ±4.0 B. ±1.96
C. ±0.25 D. ±0.30

67. The title of the Brundtland report is :

A. Caring for Earth
B. Caring of Biosphere
C. Our Common Future
D. The Silent Spring

68. According to Gaussian Plume Model, the maximum ground level concentration (C) varies with height (H) of chimney:

A. $C \propto \frac{1}{H}$ B. $C \propto H^{-2}$
C. $C \propto H^{-1/2}$ D. $C \propto H^{-3/2}$

69. Given below are two statements. One labelled as Assertion (A) and the other labelled as Reason (R) :

Assertion (A): A wetland of international importance is brought under the 'Montreux Record'.

Reason (R): The country in which the wetland is located should enact a law to prohibit any human activity within five kilometers from the edge of the wetland.

Choose the correct answer :

A. Both (A) and (R) are correct and (R) is the correct explanation of (A).
B. Both (A) and (R) are correct and (R) is not the correct explanation of (A).
C. (A) is true, but (R) is false.
D. (A) is false, but (R) is true.

70. Which of the following methods related to fly ash utilization has future ecofriendly and economic benefits?

I. Direct application to cropland
II. Converting to Bricks
III. Using as a road-sub-base material

Codes:

A. I and II only B. II and III only
C. I and III only D. I, II and III

71. Which of the following is NOT one of the twelve principles of green chemistry?

A. Minimize or eliminate the need for waste cleanup by emphasizing waste prevention
B. Minimize energy consumption

C. Maximize use of products from green plants
D. Avoid the use and generation of hazardous substances that may harm humans or the environment

72. Match the List-I with List-II. Identify the correct answer from the codes given below the lists :

List–I *(Halocarbons)*	*List–II* *(Atmospheric residence time)*
(*a*) CF_4	(*i*) ~ 50 years
(*b*) CF_2Cl_2	(*ii*) ~ 50,000 years
(*c*) $CFCl_3$	(*iii*) ~ 65 years
(*d*) CF_3Br	(*iv*) ~ 102 years

Codes :

	(*a*)	(*b*)	(*c*)	(*d*)
A.	(*ii*)	(*iv*)	(*i*)	(*iii*)
B.	(*iii*)	(*i*)	(*ii*)	(*iv*)
C.	(*iv*)	(*ii*)	(*iii*)	(*i*)
D.	(*i*)	(*iii*)	(*iv*)	(*ii*)

73. Climate change has become a buzz word throughout the world. In case of the Himalayas the best way to infer whether there is a climate change or not is to :
I. Monitor tree line
II. Monitor migration of glaciers
III. Study alteration in species composition

Choose the correct answer :
A. I only B. I and II only
C. II only D. I, II and III

74. Landslide hazards in the Himalayan region are the consequence of :
I. Road cutting
II. Seismic activity
III. Deforestation
IV. Urbanization

Choose the correct answer :
A. I only
B. I and II only
C. I, II and III only
D. I, II, III and IV

75. Consider the following International agreements.
I. The International Treaty on Plant Genetic Resources for Food and Agriculture
II. The United Nations Convention to Combat Desertification
III. The World Heritage Convention

Which of the above has/have a bearing on the biodiversity ? Choose the correct answer:
A. I and II only B. III only
C. I and III only D. I, II and III

ANSWERS

1	2	3	4	5	6	7	8	9	10
C	A	D	B	C	C	A	A	A	A
11	**12**	**13**	**14**	**15**	**16**	**17**	**18**	**19**	**20**
A	A	B	A	C	C	D	B	D	B
21	**22**	**23**	**24**	**25**	**26**	**27**	**28**	**29**	**30**
A	D	C	A	B	C	B	B	C	D
31	**32**	**33**	**34**	**35**	**36**	**37**	**38**	**39**	**40**
B	A	A	A	A	A	A	A	D	D
41	**42**	**43**	**44**	**45**	**46**	**47**	**48**	**49**	**50**
D	C	A	B	A	C	A	A	D	A
51	**52**	**53**	**54**	**55**	**56**	**57**	**58**	**59**	**60**
D	A	A	A	B	D	C	D	B	B
61	**62**	**63**	**64**	**65**	**66**	**67**	**68**	**69**	**70**
A	B	A	A	C	B	C	B	C	B
71	**72**	**73**	**74**	**75**					
C	A	D	D	D					

SOME SELECTED EXPLANATORY ANSWERS

1. Marine biological zones are determined by ocean depth, light availability, and the stability of the bottom substrate.

Marine Biological Zones

- Nearshore zones reflect the influence of tides and substrate stability
- Shallow ocean zones are diverse and productive
- Open ocean and deep benthic zones are determined by light availability and proximity to the bottom
- Marine biological zones have been impacted by human activities

2. Methanogens (methane generators) live in reducing environments, and represent about one-half of all known species of archaeans. All known methanogens, for example *Methanococcus* and *Methanobacterium* species, belong to the Euryarchaeota. Methanogens are obligate anaerobes, meaning they are killed by oxygen. They are found in the anoxic (oxygen-lacking) sediments of, for instance, swamps and marshes, as well as in more moderate environments, such as the rumen of cattle and sheep; the large intestine of dogs and humans; and the hindguts of insects such as termites and cockroaches. Methanogens generate energy by converting at least ten different substrates such as carbon dioxide and hydrogen gas, methanol, or acetate into methane gas (CH_4), which is released into the atmosphere.

4. Critically Endangered species face an extremely high risk of extinction in the wild in the immediate future, whilst Endangered species face a high risk of extinction in the wild in the near future. Those categorised as Vulnerable face a high risk of extinction in the medium term.

7. Aquatic crustaceans respond to environmental change in a number of ways. In order to avoid the most immediate effects, individuals move away from the problem and show a range of unusual behaviours, such as the aggregation of both predators and prey to avoid bouts of hypoxia. Physiological responses further enhance the ability of individuals to survive relatively short-term changes in either O_2, temperature, or pH levels in the surrounding water. Compensatory responses are observed in a range of crustacean species and are focused on adjustments in respiratory physiology, including acid-base homeostasis and ion regulation. Survival depends on the ability to maintain the most appropriate conditions for protein function. The physiological responses and consequent survival of aquatic crustaceans to simultaneous changes in environmental pH and either temperature or O_2 over the longer term remain to be studied.

8. A hurricane is a type of tropical cyclone or severe tropical storm that forms in the southern Atlantic Ocean, Caribbean Sea, Gulf of Mexico, and in the eastern Pacific Ocean.

9. SDS (sodium dodecyl sulphate) is a detergent (soap) that can dissolve hydrophobic molecules but also has a negative charge (sulphate) attached to it. Therefore, if a cell is incubated with SDS, the membranes will be dissolved, all the proteins will be solubilized by the detergent, plus all the proteins will be covered with many negative charges. The end result has two important features: (1) all proteins retain only their primary structure and (2) all proteins have a large negative charge which means they will all migrate towards the positive pole when placed in an electric field. All proteins converted into monomers and monomers are also denatured by SDS.

10. The major sources of mercury pollution in India are chloralkali industries, industrial processes in thermal power plants, steel and cement industries, coal fired power and heat production, mercury-containing products such as thermometers, blood pressure equipment, pesticides, dental amalgam, and waste incineration processes.

16. Elephant (*Elephas maximus*) is the largest terrestrial mammal of India. Project Elephant (PE) was launched by the Government of India in the year 1992 as a Centrally Sponsored Scheme with following objectives:

1. To protect elephants, their habitat & corridors
2. To address issues of man-animal conflict
3. Welfare of captive elephants

18. Champion and Seth classified forest into five major groups based on climatic factors, precipitation and floristic composition. These major groups have been further divided into 16 type groups based on temperature and moisture content. A few of these type groups have been further divided into several subgroups. Ultimately the type groups have been classified into 221 forest types and subtypes based on location specific climate factors and vegetation formation. Structure, physiognomy, floristics, temperature, edaphic factors, and moisture are all used as characters to define the types. Previous classification systems and profile diagrams were also used as input data for classification. The system is valid even now, to prepare working plans and for silvicultural practises.

20. In ecology, the **competitive exclusion principle**, sometimes referred to as **Gauss's law of competitive exclusion** or just **Gauss's law**, is a proposition that states that two species competing for the same resource cannot coexist at constant population values, if other ecological factors remain constant. When one species has even the slightest advantage or edge over another then the one with the advantage will dominate in the long term. One of the two competitors will always overcome the other, leading to either the extinction of this competitor or an evolutionary or behavioural shift toward a different ecological niche. The principle has been paraphrased into the maxim **"complete competitors cannot coexist"**.

21. Parasite-modified changes in predator-prey dynamics can have ramifications throughout the community, affecting community structure and productivity.

24. The **Boreal forest** is the world's largest land-based biome. Spreading over continents and covering many countries, the Boreal plays a significant role in the planet's biodiversity and even its climate. The seasonal variation from summer to winter is represented by boreal forest.

27. Calcite is a carbonate mineral and the most stable polymorph of calcium carbonate. The other polymorphs are the minerals aragonite and vaterite. Aragonite will change to calcite at 380-470 °C, and vaterite is even less stable.

28. A GIS topology is a set of rules and behaviours that model how points, lines, and polygons share coincident geometry. For example:

- Adjacent features, such as two counties, will have a common boundary between them. They share this edge.
- The set of county polygons within each state must completely cover the state polygon and share edges with the state boundary.

Topology has long been a key GIS requirement for data management and integrity. In general, a topological data model manages spatial relationships by representing spatial objects (point, line, and area features) as an underlying graph of topological primitives—nodes, faces, and edges. These primitives, together with their relationships to one another and to the features whose boundaries they represent, are defined by representing the feature geometries in a planar graph of topological elements.

30. **Thermal Inertia** is the degree of slowness with which the temperature of a body approaches that of its surroundings and which is dependent upon its absorptivity, its specific heat, its thermalconductivity, its dimensions, and other factors.

Thermal inertia is an important parameter in geological and agricultural applications. Time slot for measuring thermal inertia (TI) differences between land and water is 1400 hrs.

31. A **slump** is a form of mass wasting that occurs when a coherent mass of loosely consolidated materials or rock layers moves a short distance down a slope. Movement is characterized by sliding along a concave-upward or planar surface. Causes of slumping include earthquake shocks, thorough wetting, freezing and thawing, undercutting, and loading of a slope.

32. In scientific terms, water harvesting broadly refers to collection and storage of rain water and also other activities such as harvesting surface water, extracting ground water, prevention of losses through evaporation and seepage. In general, water harvesting is the activity of direct collection of rain water, collected rain water can be stored for direct use or can be recharged into ground water.

RWH helps conserve and augment the storage of ground water aquifers, thereby improving the ground water table. In coastal areas over extraction of ground water leads to saline water intrusion. Therefore recharging the ground water aquifer helps arrest the saline water intrusion. Continuous recharge of ground water using rain water helps improve the ground water quality considerably.

36. **Erosion:** The set of all processes by which soil and rock are loosened and moved downhill or downwind.

41. A useful way to demonstrate growth rate is to present it as *doubling time,* or the number of years for a human population to double its size. The doubling time can be calculated according to the following relationship:

doubling time = 0.70/growth rate

This relationship is derived from the formula for calculating compound interest at the bank and is an approximation. It is useful to remember that a growth rate in any population compounds itself since the individuals entering the population will ultimately reproduce and add more people to that population. As the growth rate increases, the doubling time decreases.

45. Balanced chemical oxidation reaction of methane:

$$CH_4 + 2O_2 = CO_2 + 2H_2O$$

Burning 1 mol of CH_4 liberates 890 kJ of energy while producing 1 mol of CO_2. Since 1 mol of CO_2 has 12g of carbon, the HHV carbon intensity of methane is

$$\text{HHV carbon intensity} = \frac{12\text{g}}{890\text{kJ}}$$

$$= 0.0135 \text{ gC/kJ} = 13.5 \text{ gC/MJ}.$$

46. mM HCl = 10^{-3} M HCl

HCl dissociates completely, so

$$[H^+] = \text{M HCl}$$

$$[H^+] = 10^{-3}$$

$$pH = -\log[H^+]$$

$$= -\log 10^{-3}$$

$$pH = 3.$$

50. The sources of aliphatic hydrocarbons (octane, decane, undecane) in indoor environment are paints, adhesives, gasoline, combustion sources, etc.

52. Internal combustion engines burn a mixture of fuel and air; the air is the source of oxygen needed to engage in the chemical reaction with the fuel known as combustion,, or burning. In standard engines, the ratio of air to fuel is set at or very near that which ensures that there is sufficient oxygen in the mixture to burn all of the fuel, yet not an excess amount of air.

A stoichiometric air/fuel ratio (A/F) of approximately 14.6, when gasoline is the fuel, which yields lower fuel economy for complete combustion in an internal combustion engine.

53. Phytovolatilization is a process, in which plants take up contaminants from soil and release them as volatile form into the atmosphere through transpiration. The process occurs as growing plants absorb water and organic contaminants. As water travels from the roots to the leaves along the vascular system of the plant, it is changed and modified along the way. Then, some of the contaminants move through the plants to the leaves and evaporate or volatilize into the atmosphere. Phytovolatilization has been primarily used to remove mercury; the mercuric ion is converted into less toxic elemental mercury.

56. The ISO 14000 family of standards provides practical tools for companies and organizations of all kinds looking to manage their environmental responsibilities.

57. **Council for Advancement of People's Action and Rural Technology** (CAPART) is a nodal organization for rural development. The main purpose of this organization is to promote and organize the joint venture emerging between the Government of India and the voluntary organizations pertaining to the development of the rural sector. The voluntary organizations are responsible for motivating and promoting the rural sector towards change.

59. An Act to provide for the levy and collection of a cess on water consumed by persons carrying on certain industries and by local authorities, with a view to augment the resources of the Central Board and the State Boards for the prevention and control of water pollution constituted under the Water (Prevention and Control of Pollution) Act, 1974.

Levy and Collection of Cess

1. There shall be levied and collected a cess for the purpose of the Water (Prevention and Control of Pollution) Act, 1974 (6 of 1974) and utilisation thereunder.
2. The cess under sub-section (1) shall be payable by—

   (*a*) every person carrying on any specified industry; and

   (*b*) every local authority

60. Disasters can have adverse consequences on the environment and on ecosystems in particular, which could have immediate to long-term effects on the populations whose life, health, livelihoods and well-being depend on a given environment or ecosystem.

Environmental degradation also contributes to risk by increasing socio-economic vulnerability to hazard impacts, as the capacity of damaged ecosystems to meet people's needs for food and other products is reduced. Appropriate management of ecosystems can therefore play a critical role in reducing vulnerability and enhancing resilience of local communities, as healthy socioecological systems are better able to prevent, absorb and recover from disasters.

61. The three major Rio Conventions—on Biodiversity, Climate Change and Desertifi-

cation—derive directly from the 1992 Earth Summit. The three conventions are intrinsically linked, operating in the same ecosystems and addressing interdependent issues.

Convention on Biological Diversity

The objectives of the CBD are the conservation of biological diversity, the sustainable use of its components, and the fair and equitable sharing of the benefits arising from commercial and other utilization of genetic resources. The agreement covers all ecosystems, species, and genetic resources.

63. The important parametric tests are: the z-test, the t-test, the Chi-square (χ^2) test and the F-test.

(*a*) **The z-test:** This test is widely used for testing the significance of statistics such as mean, median, mode, coefficient of correlation and others. This test is used even when binomial distribution or 't' distribution is applicable on the presumption that such a distribution tends to approximate normal distribution as the sample size (n) becomes larger. The elevant test statistic, 'z', is calculated and compared with its probable value at a specified level of significance for judging the significance of the measure concerned.

(*b*) **The t-test:** This test is suitable for testing the significance of a sample mean or for judging the significance of difference between the means of two samples, when the samples are less than 30 in number and when the population variance is not known. When two samples are related, the paired t-test is used. The t-test can also be used for testing the significance of the coefficients of simple and partial correlations. The relevant test statistic, 't', is calculated from the sample data, and it is compared with its corresponding critical value in the t-distribution table for rejecting or accepting a null hypothesis.

(*c*) **The Chi-square (χ^2) test:** The chi-squared calculation is between observed and expected values. This approach applies whether we are looking at comparing a theoretical with an empirical distribution, testing a sample variance against the population variance (expected), or using a contingency table.

Use the basic chi-squared formula to calculate a value

$$\chi^2 = \sum_i \frac{(\text{observed}_i - \text{expected}_i)^2}{\text{expected}_i}$$

(*d*) **The F-test:** This test is based on F-distribution which is a distribution skewed to the right, and tends to be more symmetrical, as the number of degrees of freedom in the numerator and denominator increase. The F-test is used to compare the variances of two independent samples. It is also used in the analysis of variance (ANOVA) for testing the significance of more than two sample means at a time. It is also used for judging the significance of multiple correlation coefficients.

66. The module on confidence intervals provided methods for estimating confidence intervals for various parameters. Confidence intervals for every parameter take the following general form:

Point Estimate ± Margin of Error

In the module on confidence intervals we derived the formula for the confidence interval for μ as

$$\bar{X} \pm Z\frac{\sigma}{\sqrt{n}}$$

For this question, Z is the value from the table of probabilities of the standard normal distribution for the desired confidence level (*e.g.*, Z = 1.96 for 95% confidence), mean = ± 1.96.

67. **Our Common Future**, also known as the **Brundtland Report**, from the United Nations World Commission on Environment and Development (WCED) was published in 1987.

Its targets were multilateralism and interdependence of nations in the search for a sustainable development path. The report sought to recapture the spirit of the United Nations Conference on the Human Environment—the Stockholm Conference—which had introduced environmental concerns to the formal political development sphere. *Our Common Future* placed environmental issues firmly on the political agenda; it aimed to discuss the environment and development as one single issue.

68. In the Gaussian equation, it is assumed that the plume spread has a Gaussian distribution in both the horizontal and vertical planes. The standard deviation of the plume concentration distribution in the horizontal (crosswind) is denoted by sigma $y(\sigma_y)$ and the corresponding concentration distribution in the vertical is denoted by sigma $z(\sigma_z)$. These are frequently referred to as dispersion or diffusion coefficients. The values for these diffusion coefficients vary depending on the height above the surface, the surface roughness, sampling time, wind speed and distance downwind from the source.

$$\text{Concentration (c)} \propto \frac{1}{\{\text{height(H)}\}^2}$$

72. A halocarbon is an organic chemical molecule composed of at least one carbon atom bound covalently with one or more halogen atoms. The residence time (or atmospheric lifetime) of a halocarbon is defined by its rate of removal or sink. The average atmospheric lifetime not only controls the build-up of the halocarbon in the atmosphere, but also impacts on the global distribution of halocarbons and the role in evaluating the impact of individual species on the stratospheric and tropospheric ozone depletion, climate change, regional pollution and on future scenarios, and finally determines the timescale for the atmosphere to recover after emissions cease.

	Lifetime (years)	Radiative forcing (Wm^{-2}/ppb)
CF_4	50000	0.08
CCl_3F	50	0.25
CCl_2F_2	10	0.32
$CBrF_3$	65	0.32

74. The sudden movement of rock, debris or earth along the slope is called landslide.

The various causes of landslides are-

(*a*) **Natural causes:**

1. Landslides are generally associated with natural calamities like earthquake, volcanic eruptions, floods, cloudburst, etc
2. Long spell of rainfall
3. Loose soil cover and sloping terrain

(*b*) **Anthropogenic causes:**

1. Rapid urbanization and changes in land use patterns
2. Rampant deforestation and mining activities like blasting and quarrying, etc
3. Increased industrialisation leading to climate change and weather disturbances
4. Change in river flow due to construction of dams, barriers, etc.

Previous Paper (Solved)

UGC–NET Environmental Sciences, December–2014

PAPER-II

Note : *This paper contains* ***fifty (50)*** *objective type questions of* ***two (2)*** *marks each. All questions are compulsory.*

1. Thermal stratification of aquatic ecosystems takes place in
A. tropical lakes B. temperate lakes
C. glacier lakes D. meandering rivers

2. The scale length of pressure variations in atmosphere in vertical direction is about
A. 3 km B. 4.8 km
C. 7 km D. 12 km

3. Which radioactive element is considered as an indoor pollutant?
A. Oxygen – 18 B. Nitrogen – 15
C. Carbon – 13 D. Radon

4. In a closed thermodynamic system, across its boundaries
A. no transfer of heat is possible.
B. no transfer of work is possible.
C. transfer of heat is possible but not of work.
D. transfer of heat and work is possible.

5. In an urban area, moist air at 27 °C has a mixing ratio of 50 gm per kg. Its virtual temperature is
A. 33.69 °C B. 38.15 °C
C. 36.15 °C D. 32.30 °C

6. Under aerobic biodegradation of DDT, which of the following compound is formed?
A. DDD B. DDE
C. DDN D. DDS

7. Among the following heavy metals, which has highest concentration in earth's crust?
A. Chromium B. Copper
C. Nickel D. Zinc

8. Composition-wise halons are related to
A. CFCs B. Halides
C. Hydrocarbons D. Peptides

9. Which of the following gases has highest absorption co-efficient for solubility in water?
A. Hydrogen B. Nitrogen
C. Oxygen D. Carbon dioxide

10. Quantity of glucose (MW 180) required to prepare 1000 ml of 5% solution is
A. 5 g B. 50 g
C. 900 g D. 9000 g

11. Endemic species are
A. Uniformly distributed across the landscape
B. Widely distributed
C. Restricted to a particular area
D. Continuously distributed globally

12. Which of the following is the *in-situ* biodiversity conservation site?
A. Arboretum B. Botanical garden
C. Biosphere reserve D. Orchidarium

13. The largest unit of climax communities representing well defined climatic zone is referred to as
A. Biosphere B. Biome
C. Biota D. Landscape

14. An active, adaptive control process which is able to maintain the overall balance is known as
A. Bohr's Hypothesis B. Miller Hypothesis
C. Gaia Hypothesis D. Kepler's Law

15. Niche of an organism is
A. Address B. Profession
C. Location D. Range

16. Out of the total fresh water volume of the frozen form constitutes

A. 60% B. 70%
C. 80% D. 50%

17. If Q = stream flow, P = precipitation, E = evapotranspiration, ΔS = net change in storage and ΔT = net underground transfers, then the basic water balance equation is

A. $Q = (P + E) - (\Delta S + \Delta T)$
B. $Q = (P - E) - (\Delta S + \Delta T)$
C. $Q = (P - E) + (\Delta S + \Delta T)$
D. $Q = (P - E) - (\Delta S - \Delta T)$

18. Particles with a diameter smaller than 0.002 mm are classed as

A. Cobble B. Pebble
C. Silt D. Colloids

19. Water storage capacity of which soil is maximum?

A. Sandy loam B. Loam
C. Clay loam D. Heavy clay

20. Which among the following is not a hot desert?

A. Sahara B. Kalahari
C. Thar D. Gobi

21. In an ideal MHD power generator, the maximum power P output varies with the velocity (u) of conducting fuel as

A. $P_{max} \propto u$ B. $P_{max} \propto u^2$
C. $P_{max} \propto u^3$ D. $P_{max} \propto u^{3/2}$

22. Which is the most efficient energy source for producing electricity?

A. Nuclear power B. Hydro power
C. Wind power D. Solar power

23. Which of the following types of coal has highest water content?

A. Anthracite
B. Bituminous coal
C. Lignite
D. Subbituminous coal

24. Energy intensity is the amount of energy

A. produced per unit gross domestic product
B. consumed per unit gross domestic product
C. produced per year per unit area of the country
D. consumed per year per unit area of the country

25. Which is the cleanest fuel for power generation?

A. Coal B. Uranium
C. Hydrogen D. Water

26. The mountain that rises a kilometre or more above the surrounding sea floor is called

A. Oceanic island B. Atoll
C. Seamount D. Island arc

27. Which form of As is most toxic?

A. As^{+3} B. As^{+2}
C. As^{+6} D. As^{+4}

28. Noise climate is represented by

A. $L_{10} - L_{90}$ B. L_{eq}
C. L_{50} D. $(L_{10} - L_{90})^2 / 60$

29. The classical smog is mainly composed of

A. NO_x and smoke particulates
B. O_3 and SO_2
C. SO_2 and NO_x
D. SO_2 and smoke particulates

30. According to National Ambient Air Quality Standards the annual average concentration of SPM in a residential area should not exceed

A. 80 $\mu g/m^3$ B. 100 $\mu g/m^3$
C. 140 $\mu g/m^3$ D. 200 $\mu g/m^3$

31. "Blue baby syndrome" is caused due to intake of water high in

A. Ammonia B. Nitrates
C. Sulphates D. Sulphides

32. EIA of mining activities involve impact assessment on

I. Geological Environment
II. Biological Environment
III. Aerial Environment

Codes :

A. I only B. II and III only
C. I and III only D. I, II and III

33. Accreditation of Environmental Consultant Organizations in India is done by
A. Ministry of Environment, Forest and Climate Change
B. Central Pollution Control Board
C. Ministry of Earth Sciences
D. Quality Council of India

34. Life Cycle Assessment (LCA) does not include
A. Life Cycle Inventory of the product
B. Quantitative improvement in the process of the product
C. Life Cycle Impact Analysis
D. Emergency Preparedness Plan

35. A developmental project requires both environmental clearance as well as approval under
A. Water Act, 1974
B. Forest (Conservation) Act, 1980
C. National Environmental Tribunal Act, 1995
D. Air Act, 1981

36. The best practice of disposal of construction and demolition (C & D) debris is
A. Incineration B. Recycling
C. Land fills D. Solidification

37. Pyrolysis of Solid Waste refers to
A. High temperature aerobic incineration
B. High temperature anaerobic distillation of waste for energy generation
C. Ambient aerobic distillation
D. Ambient anaerobic distillation

38. Kyoto Protocol of 1997 introduced the concept of carbon trading in the year of
A. 2000 B. 2004
C. 2001 D. 2002

39. Citizen's Charter on Environment in the Constitution of India is embodied in
A. Article 48 B. Article 48A
C. Article 49A D. Article 51A

40. United Nation's Conference on Environment and Development was held in
A. December, 1993 B. June, 1992
C. December, 1995 D. November, 1996

41. The geometric mean of the numbers 4, 6 and 9 is
A. 6 B. 8
C. 5 D. 7

42. A complete enumerate of all items in the population is
A. Unrestricted sampling
B. Non-probability sampling
C. Census
D. Sample survey

43. The term 'parameter' is an attribute associated with the data pertaining to
A. sample
B. population
C. descriptive statistics
D. sampling technique

44. A solar cell of surface area = 5 cm^2 delivers a current of 0.1 A at 0.6 V. If the intensity of solar radiation impinging on the solar cell is 1.0 kW/m^2, the efficiency of the solar cell is
A. 6% B. 3%
C. 30% D. 12%

45. **Assertion (A) :** Living systems exposed to drought salinity and freezing show enhanced levels of osmolytes.
Reason (R) : Drought, salinity and freezing stress induce water deficit.
In the context of the two statements, which one of the following is correct?
A. Both (A) and (R) are true and (R) is the correct explanation of (A).
B. Both (A) and (R) are true, but (R) is not the correct explanation of (A).
C. (A) is true, but (R) is false.
D. (A) is false, but (R) is true.

46. UN Decade of Education for Sustainable Development is
A. 2000 – 2009 B. 2005 – 2014
C. 2010 – 2019 D. 2020 – 2031

47. Two kinds of the values distinguished in environmental ethics are
A. Instrumental value and intrinsic value
B. Direct use values and social values

C. Social values and existence value
D. Indirect use value and aesthetic value

48. The natural sources of methyl bromide in the atmosphere is
A. Ocean
B. Volcanoes
C. Landslide
D. Vegetation

49. The part of an actual resource which can be developed profitably in the future is
A. Non-renewable resources
B. Potential resources
C. Reserved resources
D. Stock resources

50. Trophic state index of aquatic ecosystem is determined by the concentration of
A. Chlorophyll-a
B. NO_3^-
C. PO_4^{-3}
D. NO_2^-

ANSWERS

1	2	3	4	5	6	7	8	9	10
B	C	D	D	C	B	B	A	D	B
11	**12**	**13**	**14**	**15**	**16**	**17**	**18**	**19**	**20**
C	C	B	C	B	B	C	D	D	D
21	**22**	**23**	**24**	**25**	**26**	**27**	**28**	**29**	**30**
B	A	C	B	C	C	A	A	D	C
31	**32**	**33**	**34**	**35**	**36**	**37**	**38**	**39**	**40**
B	D	D	D	B	C	B	D	D	B
41	**42**	**43**	**44**	**45**	**46**	**47**	**48**	**49**	**50**
A	C	B	D	A	B	A	A	C	A

SOME SELECTED EXPLANATORY ANSWERS

1. An important feature of most lakes is that the water is divided into layers (strata) which tend not to mix. Many temperate lakes exhibit thermal stratification. In the summer the top few metres of the lake may reach a temperature of 20°C, a pleasant temperature for swimming. However, at a depth of 20 m, the summer temperature may be only 5°C. Most humans would die from hypothermia within an hour of being in water this cold. In winter the reverse happens; the surface of the lake is *colder* than lower down. Stratification can be understood if one remembers that water is densest at 4°C. Consequently, water that is either cooler or warmer than this will rise.

2. The atmosphere is considerably thinner in its vertical extent (scale height 7 km) than in its horizontal extent. The largest scales of motion are in the horizontal direction and form the basis for the general circulation of the atmosphere.

3. Radon is a dangerous indoor air pollutant that comes from the ground through rocky soil. Radon is a radioactive gas, whose decay particles cling to dust and can mutate lung tissue. The concentration of radon varies widely, both regionally and within regions. Energy conservation work probably has little effect on radon concentrations. However, all housing specialists should be aware of radon's danger, radon testing procedures, and radon mitigation strategies.

4. A **thermodynamic system** is the content of a macroscopic volume in space, along with its walls and surroundings; it undergoes thermodynamic processes according to the principles of thermodynamics. The walls of a closed system allow transfer of energy as heat and as work, but not of matter, between it and its surroundings. The walls of an *open system* allow transfer both of matter and of energy.

5. $T_v = T\ (1 + 0.61\ W)$

$$= (273+27)\left(1+0.61\times\frac{50}{1000}\right)$$

$$= 300\ (1 + 0.61 \times 0.05)$$

$$= 300\ (1 + 0.0305)$$

$$= 300\ (1.0305)$$

$$= 309.15\ K = 36.15°C.$$

6. During biodegradation of DDT, both DDE and DDD are formed in soils. Both metabolites may undergo further transformation but the extent and rate are dependent on soil conditions and, possibly, microbial populations present in soil. DDT under both aerobic and anaerobic conditions, forming 4-chlorobenzoic acid and DDE, respectively. Biodegradation of DDT and its metabolites involves cometabolism, a process in which the microbes derive nutrients for growth and energy from sources other than the compound of concern. DDE, the dominant DDT metabolic found, is often resistant to biodegradation under aerobic and anaerobic conditions. In laboratory experiments with marine sediments, DDT has been shown to degrade to DDE and DDD under anaerobic and anaerobic conditions, respectively.

7. Copper is a reddish metal that occurs naturally in rock, soil, water, sediment, and at low levels air. Its average concentration in the earth's crust is about 50 parts copper per million parts soil (ppm) or, stated another way, 50 grams of copper per 1,000,000 grams of soil (1.8 ounces or 0.11 pounds of copper per 2,200 pounds of soil). Copper also occurs naturally in all plants and animals. It is an essential element for all known living organisms including humans and other animals at low levels of intake.

8. Chlorofluorocarbons (CFCs) and halons are man-made chemicals that exist as gases or liquids. Chlorofluorocarbons contain chlorine, fluorine and carbon. Halons are similar but contain bromine or iodine. They are neither toxic nor flammable.

9. Solubility of gases in a liquid is generally expressed in terms of volume rather than weight. It is generally expressed in terms of *absorption coefficient* (α) *which is defined as the volume of gas, reduced to 0°C and 1 atm pressure (STP), dissolved in unit volume of the solvent at the experimental temperature under a partial pressure of 1 atm of the gas.* Higher the absorption coefficient higher is the solubility of the gas. Absorption coefficient of some common gases in water at 20°C are given in the table.

Table : *Absorption Coefficient of some gases at 20°C*

He	N_2	H_2	O_2	CO_2	H_2S	HQ	NH_3
0.009	0.015	0.017	0.028	0.88	2.62	442	710

11. **Endemism** is the ecological state of a species being unique to a defined geographic location, such as an island, nation, country or other defined zone, or habitat type; organisms that are indigenous to a place are not endemic to it if they are also found elsewhere. The extreme opposite of endemism is cosmopolitan distribution. Another term for a species that is endemic is precinctive, which applies to species (and subspecific categories) that are restricted to a defined geographical area. A native species, such as a native plant, is one that is considered to have been endemic for a relatively long period of time.

12. In-situ conservation is on site conservation or the conservation of genetic resources in natural populations of plant or animal species, such as forest genetic resources in natural populations of tree species. It is the process of protecting an endangered plant or animal species in its natural habitat, either by protecting or cleaning up the habitat itself, or by defending the species from predators.

In India following types of natural habitats are being maintained:

1. National parks
2. Wildlife sanctuaries
3. Biosphere reserves

Biosphere Reserves: It is a special category of protected areas where human population also forms a part of the system. They are large protected area of usually more than 5000 sq.km.

14. An active, adaptive control process, able to maintain the Earth in over-all balance, is known as the Gaia hypothesis.

The updated Gaia hypothesis proposes that Earth's atmosphere, oceans, and land masses are held in equilibrium by the living inhabitants of the planet, which includes millions of species besides humans. The Gaia concept suggests that this living world keeps itself in worldwide environmental balance. One example of this balancing act takes place in the oceans. Salts are constantly added to the oceans by physical and chemical processes, raising salinity. Eventually, affected seas (like the Dead Sea) reach an uninhabitable salinity level. According to the Gaia hypothesis, the sea's salinity is controlled biologically through the mutual action of ocean organisms. In fact, living sea creatures, primarily algae and protozoa, have processed and removed salt throughout geological time, balancing salinity levels that allow life to thrive.

15. The concept of the ecological niche is an important one; it helps us to understand how organisms in an ecosystem interact with each other. The ecological niche of an organism depends not only on where it lives but also on what it does. By analogy, it may be said that the habitat is the organism's "address", and the niche is its "profession", biologically speaking.

16. Over 70% of our Earth's surface is covered by water. Although water is seemingly abundant, the real issue is the amount of fresh water available.

- 97.5% of all water on Earth is salt water, leaving only 2.5% as fresh water
- Nearly 70% of that fresh water is frozen in the icecaps of Antarctica and Greenland; most of the remainder is present as soil moisture, or lies in deep underground aquifers as groundwater not accessible to human use.
- Only ~1% of the world's fresh water is accessible for direct human uses. This is the water found in lakes, rivers, reservoirs and those underground sources that are shallow enough to be tapped at an affordable cost. Only this amount is regularly renewed by rain and snowfall, and is therefore available on a sustainable basis.

18. Clay particles range downward in diameter from 0.002 mm or 2 microns to smaller than 0.001 micron. Clay particles finer than about 0.01 micron are classed as *colloids.* A property of mineral colloids is their ability to remain in suspension indefinitely in water, once the particles have become dispersed (separated one from another). A colloidal suspension appears clouded or murky.

19. The plant-available water-holding capacity of soil varies from around 50 to 400 mm per metre of soil depth. The maximum volume of water available to a plantation therefore depends on the depth of its root zone and on the water storage properties of the soil. In general, Water storage capacity of heavy clay soil is maximum.

20. Gobi is a cold desert, and it is not uncommon to see frost and occasionally snow on its dunes. Besides being quite far north, also is situated on a plateau about 910-1,520 meters above sea level, further contributing to its low temperature. Generally temperate desert climate is typical continental, with extremely low winter temperatures (–40° C) and very hot summers (temperatures can rise up to 40 Celsius). The extreme temperature difference between winter and summer, and that between day and night can be explained by lack of water. Thus, the difference in temperature within 24 hours can reach 32° C.

22. Nearly a third of the world's energy demands are met through nuclear power plants. The waste and potential environmental hazards posed are minimal, however, when compared with other major energy sources, such as fossil fuels. The electricity produced by nuclear energy, if produced using coal, would release nearly 147 million metric tons of carbon dioxide into the atmosphere. With nuclear energy, waste production is smaller and contained. The total volume of nuclear waste produced since the nuclear power industry began is only enough to fill a football field to a depth of about 15 yards. This is easily managed and held on site or in underground repositories, safely out of environmental or public contact.

23. **Lignite coal**—The softest of the four types of coal. It is a brownish black in color, very crumbly and primarily used for the generation of electricity. Because of its color, it is often referred to as "brown coal." Lignite is the result of millions of tons of plants and trees that decayed in a swampy atmosphere about 50-70 million years ago. The material on top of the lignite deposits in North Dakota and Montana - called *overburden* - was deposited by runoff from the west as the Rocky Mountains formed. The heating content of lignite is approximately 4,000-8,000 Btu's per pound. The carbon content of lignite is 25%-35% and it has a very high water content - about 35 percent.

24. **Energy intensity** is a *measure* of the *energy efficiency* of a nation's *economy*. It is calculated as units of *energy* per unit of *GDP*.

- High energy intensities indicate a high price or cost of converting energy into GDP.
- Low energy intensity indicates a lower price or cost of converting energy into GDP. Energy Intensity as defined here is not to be confused with Energy Use Intensity (EUI), a measure of building energy use per unit area.

25. In many ways, hydrogen is the perfect fuel. It is the cleanest burning and the most efficient. Hydrogen can produce electricity and electricity can produce hydrogen, creating an energy loop that is renewable and harmless to the environment. Hydrogen combines chemically with most elements, so it has been utilized as an industrial chemical in a wide range of applications for many years. In vehicles, hydrogen can be used as a fuel in two ways: to produce electricity in a fuel cell for the cleanest option; or in an internal combustion engine where emissions are still significantly reduced compared with other fuels.

26. A **seamount** is a mountain rising from the ocean seafloor that does not reach to the water's surface (sea level), and thus is not an island. Seamounts are typically formed from extinct volcanoes that rise abruptly and are usually found rising from the seafloor to 1,000-4,000 metres in height. They are defined by oceanographers as independent features that rise to at least 1,000 metres above the seafloor. The peaks are often found hundreds to thousands of meters below the surface, and are therefore considered to be within the deep sea.

28. **Noise Climate (NC)**

Noise Climate = $L_{10} - L_{90}$

where L_{90} = the level exceeded for 90% of the time of record

L_{10} = level exceeded for 10% of the time of record.

29. Smoke-fog like condition is known as smog. Classical smogs occur in cold humid climate and are result of buildup of sulphur dioxide and particulate matter from fuel combustion. Classical smog is chemically reducing smog with high concentration of SO_2.

31. There are two health concerns when drinking water with high levels of nitrates or nitrites. The first health concern is with infants being at risk for **"blue baby syndrome",** also called **methemoglobinemia:**

- Poisoning can occur when infants drink formula made with nitrate or nitrite contaminated tap water.
- The infant's blood is less able to carry oxygen due to the poisoning.
- Affected infants develop a blue-grey color and need emergency medical help immediately.
- Infants under six months of age are more susceptible.

The second health concern with nitrates and nitrites is the formation of chemicals called **nitrosamines** in the digestive tract. Nitrosamines are being studied for long term links to cancer. No standards have been set for this yet.

33. Quality Council of India (QCI) was set up jointly by the Government of India and the Indian Industry represented by the three premier industry associations i.e. Associated Chambers of Commerce and Industry of India (ASSOCHAM), Confederation of Indian Industry (CII) and Federation of Indian Chambers of Commerce and Industry (FICCI), to establish and operate national accreditation structure and promote quality through National Quality Campaign. It is among the world's leading national apex quality facilitation, accreditation and surveillance organisations, to continuously improve the climate, systems, processes and skills for total quality.

35. The environmental clearance process is required for 39 types of projects and covers aspects like screening, scoping and evaluation of the upcoming project. The main purpose is to assess impact of the planned project on the environment and people and to try to abate/minimise the same.

Issues of clearance or rejection letter: When a project requires both environmental clearance as well as approval under the Forest (Conservation) Act, 1980. Proposals for both are required to be given simultaneously to the concerned divisions of the ministry. The processing is done simultaneously for clearance/rejection, although separate letters may be issued. If the project does not involve diversion of forest land, the case is processed only for environmental clearance.

37. **Pyrolysis** is a thermochemical decomposition of organic material at elevated temperatures in the absence of oxygen (or any halogen). It involves the simultaneous change of chemical composition and physical phase, and is irreversible. The word is coined from the Greek-derived elements *pyro* "fire" and *lysis* "separating".

Pyrolysis of Solid Waste refers to High temperature anaerobic distillation of waste for energy generation.

38. In response to the threat of climate change, UN passed the Kyoto Protocol in 1997, which was gradually ratified by 156 countries, and later infamously rejected by the world's biggest polluters - the US and Australia. The protocol sets the target of reducing emissions by an average of 5.2 percent below 1990 greenhouse gas levels by the year 2012. Russia and Canada ratify the Kyoto Protocol to the UNFCCC bringing the carbon treaty into effect on 16 February 2005.

39. The chapter on fundamental duties of the Indian Constitution clearly imposes duty on every citizen to protect environment. Article 51-A (g), says that "It shall be duty of every citizen of India to protect and improve the natural environment including forests, lakes, rivers and wild life and to have compassion for living creatures."

40. The **United Nations Conference on Environment and Development (UNCED),** also known as the Rio Summit, Rio Conference, and Earth Summit was a major United Nations' conference held in Rio de Janeiro from 3 to 14 June 1992.

41. Geometric mean (G.M.) = $\{4.6.9\}^{\frac{1}{3}}$

$$= \sqrt[3]{216} = 6.$$

42. Surveys are used as a tool to collect information from some or all units of a population and compile the information into a useful form. There are two different types of surveys that can be used to collect information in different circumstances to satisfy differing needs. These are *sample surveys* and *censuses.*

Sample Surveys: In a sample survey, only part of the total population is approached for information for the topic under study. These data are then 'expanded' or 'weighted' to make inferences about the whole population. We define the sample as the set of observations taken from the population for the purpose of obtaining information about the population.

Censuses: A census is a collection of information from all units in the population or a 'complete enumeration' of the population. We use a census when we want accurate information for many subdivisions of the population. Such a survey usually requires a very large sample size and often a census offers the best solution.

46. The United Nations Decade of Education for Sustainable Development (2005-2014), for which UNESCO is the lead agency, seeks to integrate the principles, values, and practices of sustainable development into all aspects of education and learning, in order to address the social, economic, cultural and environmental problems we face in the 21st century.

47. Values are an assessment of measure of the worth of something. Two broad types of values can be distinguished in environmental ethics:

1. *Instrumental* is the value that something has as a means to an end. So money might be good only because it leads to other good things (purchase of goods). Putting monetary value on environmental goods, or considering nature in terms of natural resources and ecosystem services, are typical expressions of instrumental value in relation to nature.
2. *Instrinsic* is the value that a thing has in itself, or for its own sake, or in its own right. Money for example is not intrinsically good (unless you are a collector of historic or different currencies) whereas most other goods might arguably be considered as having some intrinsic value. Environmentalism as a soical movement in the mid-twentieth century grew from an appreciation of the intrinstic value for nature.

A third type of value can be associated with the valuer as against the valued. Here, value is linked with obligations and the boundaries of the *moral community*–who or what is worthy of respect (past, present, future generations? other animals? all living organisms? ecosystems? biosphere? universe? multiverse?).

3. Personal (or individual) is the internally held value of the valuer usually attached to character traits such as having integrity. Behind any value is a valuer with particular perspectives on the world guided by personal values. Two perspectives on the environment based on personal values can be distinguished–anthropocentric and ecocentric.

49. **Natural resources** occur naturally within environments that exist relatively undisturbed by humanity, in a natural form. A natural resource is often characterized by amounts of biodiversity and geodiversity existent in various ecosystems.

Considering their stage of development, natural resources may be referred to in the following ways:

- *Potential resources*–Potential resources are those that exist in a region and may be used in future. For example *petroleum* occurs with sedimentary rocks in various regions, but until the time it is actually drilled out and put into use, it remains a potential resource.
- *Actual resources*–Actual resources are those that have been surveyed, their quantity and quality determined and are being used in present times. The development of an actual resource, such as *wood processing* depends upon the technology available and the cost involved.
- *Reserve resources*–The part of an actual resource which can be developed profitably in the future is called a reserve resource.
- *Stock resources*–Stock resources are those that have been surveyed but cannot be used by organisms due to lack of technology. For example: *hydrogen.*

50. Quantitive evaluation of trophic state conditions has been aided by use of simple trophic state indices. The most widely used TSIs are those developed by Carlson (1977), based on Secchi disk transparency and on concentrations of total phosphate and chlorophyll *a*. These strongly intercorrelated parameters are, respectively, the best quantified physical, chemical and biological measures of trophic conditions, and Carlson developed a simple index based on each parameter.

PAPER-III

Note : *This paper contains **seventy five (75)** objective type questions of **two (2)** marks each. **All** questions are compulsory.*

1. Which of the following ranges of scale lengths represents meso-scale motions in atmosphere?

A. 30 km – 400 km

B. 500 m – 10 km

C. 1 km – 2 km

D. 100 m – 1 km

2. Rayleigh scattering in the atmosphere is caused by

A. molecules larger than the wavelength

B. molecules equal to the size of wavelength

C. molecules whose size is much smaller than the wavelength

D. molecules and particles of all sizes

3. Wind rose is a

A. graphical representation of wind velocity vector over a period of time in a polar diagram.

B. graphical representation of wind velocity vector in a spherical coordinate system over a period of time.

C. graphical representation of horizontal and vertical wind speeds over a period of time in polar diagram.

D. graphical representation of instantaneous wind velocity at a particular time.

4. The key groups of organic molecules that help in chelation of metal ions are

I. –COOH

II. –SH

III. $-CH_3$

IV. –CHO

Choose the correct answer from the codes given below:

A. I only

B. I and II only

C. II, III and IV only

D. I, II and IV only

5. Geostrophic winds are the result of the balance between
A. coriolis force and pressure gradient force
B. coriolis force and centrifugal force
C. pressure gradient force and frictional force
D. pressure gradient force and centrifugal force

6. A possible mechanism for photochemical smog inhibition is to add compounds like diethylhydroxylamine (DEHA) as it reacts with
A. hydrocarbon
B. nitrogen dioxide
C. PAN
D. hydroxyl radicals

7. In the determination of sulphur dioxide by p-rosaniline method, the end product is
A. p-rosaniline sulfonic acid
B. methyl p-rosaniline
C. p-rosaniline methyl sulfonic acid
D. sulfo methyl p-rosaniline

8. Number of molecules present in 10 ml of proline is
A. 6.023×10^{23} B. 6.023×10^{20}
C. 6.023×10^{18} D. 6.023×10^{17}

9. Nitrogenous biochemical oxygen demand refers to the quantity of O_2 needed to convert
A. N_2 to NO_3^-
B. N_2 to NH_4^+
C. NH_4^+ to NO_3^-
D. Protein to $CO_2 + H_2O + NO_2$

10. Beer-Lambert's law defines
A. The degree of absorption of monochromatic light by a homogeneous medium
B. Atomic absorption spectrophotometry
C. Atomic emission spectrophotometry
D. Gas chromatography

11. Chemically phytochelatins are
A. Proteins B. Polysaccharides
C. Lipids D. Polypeptides

12. Mixture of organic pollutants X and Y were separated using paper chromatography and the R_f values obtained for X and Y were 0.75 and 0.25, respectively. Which relationship holds good for the solubility of these pollutants in mobile phase?
A. $X > Y$ B. $X < Y$
C. $X = Y$ D. $X + Y = 1$

13. Overall reaction of Winkler's method is

$$4S_2O_3^{2-} + 4H^+ + O_2 \rightarrow 2S_4O_6^{2-} + 2H_2O$$

This equation indicates:
A. One mole of O_2 is equivalent to one mole of thiosulphate.
B. One mole of O_2 is equivalent to two moles of thiosulphate.
C. One mole of O_2 is equivalent to three moles of thiosulphate.
D. One mole of O_2 is equivalent to four moles of thiosulphate.

14. Return of an ecosystem to a condition prior to disturbance refers to as
A. Rehabilitation B. Restoration
C. Rejuvenation D. Reclaimation

15. **Assertion (A) :** Shade loving species show better natural regeneration under highly disturbed condition.
Reason (R) : Heliophilic species needs more exposure to light for better natural regeneration.
In the context of the two statements, which one of the following is correct?
A. Both (A) and (R) are true and (R) is the correct explanation of (A).
B. Both (A) and (R) are true, but (R) is not the correct explanation of (A).
C. (A) is true, but (R) is false.
D. (A) is false, but (R) is true.

16. Which one of the following enzymes work under strict anaerobic conditions to fix atmospheric nitrogen?
A. Nitrate reductase
B. Nitrite reductase
C. Transaminase
D. Nitrogenase

17. Predatory strategy followed by an alligator for hunting is

A. Chase B. Stalk
C. Ambush D. Camouflage

18. In a tropical peat forest, the carbon storage (tonnes/ha) is typically in the range

A. 3000 – 6000 B. 13000 – 16000
C. 300 – 600 D. 300 – 1600

19. Which one of the following bacterial species convert NO_2^- to NO_3^- ?

A. *Nitrosomonas* B. *Nitrobacter*
C. *Rhizobium* D. *Azospirillum*

20. **Assertion (A) :** Living system adapted to low temperatures invariably show higher unsaturated to saturated fatty acid in membrane lipids.

Reason (R) : Fluidity of membranes is directly proportional to unsaturated to saturated fatty acids in membrane lipids.

In the context of the two statements, which one of the following is correct?

A. Both (A) and (R) are true and (R) is the correct explanation of (A).
B. Both (A) and (R) are true, but (R) is not the correct explanation of (A).
C. (A) is true, but (R) is false.
D. (A) is false, but (R) is true.

21. Which of the following is/are produced during fermentation?

I. Ethanol
II. Citrate
III. Lactate
IV. Succinate

Choose the correct answer from the codes given below:

A. I only B. I and II only
C. I and III only D. II and IV only

22. Salinity of the ocean varies from 2.0% to 4.2% in

A. Red Sea and Gulf of Kachchh
B. Black Sea and Omura Bay
C. Baltic Sea and Persian Gulf
D. Mediterranean Sea and Bay of Fundy

23. Uranium in Indian agricultural soils is mainly contributed by

A. Weathering of Uranium rich minerals
B. Excess addition of NPK fertilizers
C. Excess addition of pesticides
D. Excess addition of fungicides

24. Loamy sand contains

A. > 80% silt and > 80% clay
B. 10% silt and 5% clay
C. 15 to 30% silt and 10 to 15% clay
D. > 80% silt and < 20% clay

25. Spectral reflectance of leaf is highest for which band?

A. Blue B. Green
C. Near infrared D. Middle infrared

26. Match the List–I with List–II and choose the correct answer from the given codes:

List–I (Elements)	***List–II (Concentration in Earth's Crust by weight %)***
(*a*) Oxygen	(*i*) 8.13
(*b*) Aluminium	(*ii*) 46.60
(*c*) Iron	(*iii*) 27.72
(*d*) Silicon	(*iv*) 5.00

Identify the correct code:

Codes :

	(*a*)	(*b*)	(*c*)	(*d*)
A.	(*i*)	(*iv*)	(*iii*)	(*ii*)
B.	(*iii*)	(*ii*)	(*i*)	(*iv*)
C.	(*ii*)	(*i*)	(*iv*)	(*iii*)
D.	(*iv*)	(*iii*)	(*ii*)	(*i*)

27. Indian Microwave Remote Sensing Satellite is

A. RISAT B. Resourcesat
C. IRS D. Bhaskara

28. Mount Etna in Sicily and Mauna Loa in Hawaiian Islands are the most noteworthy examples of

A. shield volcanoes
B. plug dome
C. strato volcanoes
D. pyroclastic cones

29. Match the List–I with List–II and choose the correct answer from the given codes:

List–I (Mineral Deposit)	***List–II (Top producer)***
(*a*) Bauxite	(*i*) Peru
(*b*) Copper	(*ii*) India
(*c*) Mica	(*iii*) USA
(*d*) Guano	(*iv*) Australia

Identify the correct code :

Codes :

	(*a*)	(*b*)	(*c*)	(*d*)
A.	(*i*)	(*ii*)	(*iii*)	(*iv*)
B.	(*iv*)	(*iii*)	(*ii*)	(*i*)
C.	(*iii*)	(*i*)	(*iv*)	(*ii*)
D.	(*ii*)	(*iv*)	(*i*)	(*iii*)

30. Which of the following fuels has the highest HHV carbon intensity?
A. Natural gas B. Oil
C. Bituminous coal D. Nuclear fuel

31. If fission of 1 atom of U^{235} produces 200 MeV energy, how much energy will be produced by 1 metric ton of U^{235}?
A. 4.1×10^7 MJ B. 8.2×10^7 MJ
C. 1.23×10^8 MJ D. 2×10^5 MJ

32. The Green Climate Fund recently set up to help poor countries adapt to climate impacts envisages financial support to the extent of (in $ per year)
A. 100 bn B. 30 bn
C. 10 bn D. 3 bn

33. Which of the following biomass conversion processes produces biogas from crop residues?
A. Anaerobic digestion
B. Fermentation
C. Pyrolysis
D. Aerobic digestion

34. Which among the following is superior carbon fixer per unit area for bioenergy generation?
A. Trees B. Shrubs
C. Blue-green algae D. Crops

35. Energy flow in ecosystem is governed by
A. First law of thermodynamics
B. Second law of thermodynamics
C. Planck's law
D. Kirchoff's law

36. Average number of carbon in diesel ranges between
A. $C_{18} - C_{24}$ B. $C_{10} - C_{16}$
C. $C_4 - C_6$ D. $C_{25} - C_{30}$

37. Knocking effect in the gasoline cannot be reached by one of the following additives:
A. $(C_2H_5)_4Pb$ B. BTX
C. Kerosene D. n-Butane

38. Radioactive mineral available in the Indian coastal region is
A. Rutile B. Monazite
C. Apatite D. Magnetite

39. Thermal pollution in the coastal region is caused by
(*i*) Atomic power plants
(*ii*) Thermal power plants
(*iii*) Industrial plants
(*iv*) Tourism industry
Choose the correct answer from the codes given below:
Codes :
A. (*i*), (*ii*) and (*iii*) only B. (*i*) and (*ii*) only
C. (*iii*) and (*iv*) only D. (*ii*) and (*iii*) only

40. **Assertion (A) :** Metallic contaminants are toxic to the microorganism.
Reason (R) : Heavy metal tends to precipitate in the form of phosphatic compounds and decrease soil fertility.
In the context of the two statements, which one of the following is correct?
A. Both (A) and (R) are true and (R) is the correct explanation of (A).
B. Both (A) and (R) are true, but (R) is not the correct explanation of (A).
C. (A) is true, but (R) is false.
D. (A) is false, but (R) is true.

41. A point source of sound produces a noise of 70 dB at a distance of 20 m from it. What will be the noise level at 80 m from it?
A. 35 dB B. 64 dB
C. 58 dB D. 52 dB

42. Stratospheric ozone absorbs UV radiations principally in the wavelength of range

A. 320 – 400 nm
B. 230 – 320 nm
C. < 290 nm
D. 180 – 240 nm

43. If Γ_d, Γ_s and Γ represent dry adiabatic, saturated adiabatic lapse rate and environ-mental lapse rate, respectively, the condition for unstable atmosphere is

A. $\Gamma > \Gamma_d$ B. $\Gamma < \Gamma_d$
C. $\Gamma < \Gamma_s$ D. $\Gamma < \Gamma_s < \Gamma_d$

44. At initial time (t_0) number of *E. coli* per ml was 10. If generation time is 30 minutes, what would be number of cells per ml after a duration of 4 hours?

A. 256 B. 2560
C. 240 D. 300

45. Emission inventories involved in urban air quality assessment include parameters on

(*i*) SO_2, NO_x, particulate matter pollutants
(*ii*) Industry, traffic, domestic sources
(*iii*) Fuel type, gasoline, wood as energy carrier

Choose the correct answer from codes given below:

Codes:

A. (*i*) and (*ii*) only
B. (*ii*) and (*iii*) only
C. (*i*) and (*iii*) only
D. (*i*), (*ii*) and (*iii*)

46. Assertion (A) : Leopold matrix can be expanded or contracted.

Reason (R) : Leopold matrix is a checklist designed to show possible interactions between developmental activities and set of environmental characteristics.

In the context of the two statements, which one of the following is correct?

A. Both (A) and (R) are true and (R) is the correct explanation of (A).
B. Both (A) and (R) are true, but (R) is not the correct explanation of (A).
C. (A) is true, but (R) is false.
D. (A) is false, but (R) is true.

47. In Battele environment evaluation system the total parameter importance units is lowest for

A. Ecology
B. Environmental Pollution
C. Aesthetics
D. Human interest

48. ISO 14040 is

A. Environmental Management : Life cycle assessment principle and framework.
B. Environmental Management – environmental assessment of sites and organization.
C. Guidelines for environmental audit – general principle.
D. Environmental Management – vocabulary.

49. Given below are stages within each tier of risk assessment:

(*i*) identification of consequences
(*ii*) hazard identification
(*iii*) probability assessment
(*iv*) assessment of consequences as well as significance of risk
(*v*) magnitude assessment for consequences

Which one of the following code represent correct sequences?

A. (*ii*), (*i*), (*v*), (*iii*), (*iv*)
B. (*i*), (*ii*), (*iii*), (*iv*), (*v*)
C. (*iii*), (*ii*), (*iv*), (*v*), (*i*)
D. (*iv*), (*ii*), (*i*), (*iii*), (*v*)

50. Ecolabels are indicators of

(*i*) Acceptable level of environmental impact of a product.
(*ii*) Environmental performance of a product.
(*iii*) Claims of environmental friendliness of a product.

Choose the correct answer from the codes given below:

A. (*i*), (*ii*), (*iii*) B. (*i*) and (*ii*) only
C. (*i*) only D. (*ii*) only

51. Ecosystem diversity can be best studied using the

A. Topographical maps
B. Geoinformatics
C. Geodesy
D. Geology

52. Biennial assessment of forest cover in India is done by

A. Indian Institute of Remote Sensing, Dehradun
B. Forest Research Institute, Dehradun
C. Indian Institute of Forest Management, Bhopal
D. Forest Survey of India, Dehradun

53. Soil moisture using remote sensing techniques is determined best in

A. Optical region
B. Thermal region
C. Microwave region
D. Infrared region

54. Which one of the following statements is not connected to ISO 14000 series of Environmental Management?

A. Promotes eco-labelling of the product
B. It is based on the recommendation of TC-207 committee
C. Make the environmental audit mandatory
D. Promotes human rights and women empowerment

55. As per colour coding of plastic bags for biomedical wastes, match the List–I with List–II and choose the correct answer from the codes given below:

List–I *(Colour Code)*	*List–II* *(Option for disposal)*
(*a*) Yellow plastic bags	(*i*) Disposal in secured land fills
(*b*) Black plastic bags	(*ii*) Incineration and deep burials
(*c*) Blue/White plastic bags	(*iii*) Autoclaving and chemical treatment
(*d*) Red plastic bags	(*iv*) Microwave treatments and destruction

Codes :

	(*a*)	(*b*)	(*c*)	(*d*)
A.	(*iv*)	(*iii*)	(*ii*)	(*i*)
B.	(*i*)	(*iv*)	(*iii*)	(*ii*)
C.	(*ii*)	(*i*)	(*iv*)	(*iii*)
D.	(*iii*)	(*ii*)	(*i*)	(*iv*)

56. Given below is a list of natural disasters:

(*i*) Hudhud cyclone
(*ii*) Chernobyl nuclear plant disaster
(*iii*) Tsunami in Indian Ocean
(*iv*) Bhopal gas tragedy

Which is the correct chronological sequence for the above events in the codes given below?

Codes:

A. (*iii*), (*i*), (*ii*), (*iv*) B. (*ii*), (*iii*), (*i*), (*iv*)
C. (*iv*), (*ii*), (*iii*), (*i*) D. (*i*), (*ii*), (*iii*), (*iv*)

57. Benchmarking in environmental management refers to

A. Potential risk assessment.
B. Reporting of environmental performance.
C. Assessment of organization's business processes against the best-in-class operations to improve the performance.
D. Setting of environmental standards to be followed by environmental managers.

58. Basel convention is related to

A. Control of ozone depletion.
B. Control of water pollution.
C. Transboundary movement of hazardous wastes and their disposal.
D. Environmental auditing.

59. Concept of intergenerational equity on natural resources refers to

A. Legal obligations of present generation to future generations.
B. Moral obligation of the present generation to future generation.
C. Equitable responsibility of pollution generating industries.
D. Prudent use of resources inherited from previous generation.

60. Which among the following is not correct in regard to the sources of nitrate in the soils?

(*i*) Microbial breakdown of soil organic matter, organic manure and plant residues.
(*ii*) Fertilizers which add nitrate and that formed by microbial oxidation of NH_4^+ from ammonium fertilizers or urea.
(*iii*) Addition from the atmosphere.

(*iv*) Pesticides containing nitrogen atoms.
Choose the correct answer from the following codes:

Codes:

A. (*i*) B. (*ii*)
C. (*iii*) D. (*iv*)

61. Which one of the following protozoan is related to water borne disease?

A. *Spumella* sp.
B. *Entamoeba histolytica*
C. *Paramoecium*
D. *Plasmodium vivax*

62. Match the List–I with List–II, choose the correct answer from the given codes:

List–I (Group of Analysis)	***List–II (Test)***
(*a*) Unidimensional analysis	(*i*) Testing of hypothesis
(*b*) Multivariate analysis	(*ii*) Measure of central tendency
(*c*) Interferential analysis	(*iii*) Two-way ANOVA
(*d*) Bivariate analysis	(*iv*) Canonical analysis

Codes :

	(*a*)	(*b*)	(*c*)	(*d*)
A.	(*i*)	(*iii*)	(*iv*)	(*ii*)
B.	(*ii*)	(*iv*)	(*i*)	(*iii*)
C.	(*iii*)	(*i*)	(*ii*)	(*iv*)
D.	(*iv*)	(*ii*)	(*iii*)	(*i*)

63. The differences between crude birth rate and crude death rate in a population is called

A. Population momentum
B. Demographic transition rate
C. Net migration rate
D. Rate of natural increase

64. Which set of stoichiometric coefficient correctly balance the equation?
(*a*) H_2O_2 + (*b*) $KMnO_4$ + (*c*) H_2SO_4 → (*d*) K_2SO_4 + (*e*) $MnSO_4$ + (*f*) H_2O + (*g*) O_2
Select the correct answer from the codes given below :

Codes :

	(*a*)	(*b*)	(*c*)	(*d*)	(*e*)	(*f*)	(*g*)
A.	1	1	1	1	1	1	1
B.	1	2	3	1	2	4	3
C.	2	5	3	2	1	8	5
D.	5	2	3	1	2	8	5

65. Assertion (A) : The hypothesis testing can proceed on the basis of null hypothesis.
Reason (R) : If null hypothesis is true probabilities to different possible sample result can be assigned to it.
In the context of the two statements, which one of the following is correct?

A. Both (A) and (R) are true and (R) is the correct explanation of (A).
B. Both (A) and (R) are true, but (R) is not the correct explanation of (A).
C. (A) is true, but (R) is false.
D. (A) is false, but (R) is true.

66. The advantage of Leslie matrices are

I. Stable age distribution is not required for valid population projections.
II. Can derive finite rate of population change.
III. Requires large amount of data on population structure.

Choose the correct answer from the codes given below:

Codes :

A. I and III only B. I only
C. I and II only D. II and III only

67. Important characteristics of χ^2 test are

I. As a non-parametric test, it is based on frequencies.
II. It is not useful for estimation and to test hypothesis.
III. Can be applied to a complex contingency table.

Choose the correct answer from the codes given below:

Codes :

A. I and II only B. I and III only
C. II and III only D. I, II and III

68. The quantity of 0.2% solution needed to prepare 1000 mL of 10 ppm solution is

A. 5 mL B. 10 mL
C. 20 mL D. 200 mL

69. Which one of the following international events was not related to climate change?
A. UN framework convention on climate change, 1992.
B. Montreal Protocol, 1987
C. Stockholm conference on "Human and Environment", 1972
D. Kyoto Protocol, 1997

70. Which of the following has the lowest Ozone depletion potential?
A. HCFC – 22 B. HCFC – 123
C. Halon – 1211 D. CFC – 12

71. Assertion (A) : Rain water harvesting, primarily aims at artificial recharge of ground water to uplift the ground water table.
Reason (R) : Under rain water harvesting, the primary aim is to let the rain water infiltrate into the underground aquifer.
In the context of the two statements, which one of the following is correct?
A. Both (A) and (R) are true and (R) is the correct explanation of (A).
B. Both (A) and (R) are true, but (R) is not the correct explanation of (A).
C. (A) is true, but (R) is false.
D. (A) is false, but (R) is true.

72. For environmental mass awareness, ***Paryavaran Vahini*** Scheme was launched in the year
A. 1988 B. 2003
C. 1992 D. 1998

73. Disaster Management Act in India came into existence in the year
A. 2003 B. 2005
C. 1998 D. 2006

74. Which one of the following is most reactive oxygen species?
A. ${}^{1}O_2$ B. $\dot{O}_2^-$
C. H_2O_2 D. $O\dot{H}$

75. If we move through the group I elements from top to bottom we first encounter Lithium, Sodium and Potassium. If we move further which elements we will encounter in sequence?
A. Caesium, Calcium, Rubidium
B. Rubidium, Caesium, Francium
C. Rubidium, Caesium, Rhodium
D. Magnesium, Rubidium, Francium

ANSWERS

1	2	3	4	5	6	7	8	9	10
A	C	A	D	A	D	C	C	C	A
11	**12**	**13**	**14**	**15**	**16**	**17**	**18**	**19**	**20**
D	A	D	B	D	D	C	A	A	A
21	**22**	**23**	**24**	**25**	**26**	**27**	**28**	**29**	**30**
C	C	B	C	C	C	A	A	B	C
31	**32**	**33**	**34**	**35**	**36**	**37**	**38**	**39**	**40**
B	A	A	C	A	B	C	B	B	A
41	**42**	**43**	**44**	**45**	**46**	**47**	**48**	**49**	**50**
C	B	A	B	D	A	C	A	A	B
51	**52**	**53**	**54**	**55**	**56**	**57**	**58**	**59**	**60**
B	D	C	D	C	C	C	C	B	D
61	**62**	**63**	**64**	**65**	**66**	**67**	**68**	**69**	**70**
B	B	D	B	A	C	D	A	C	B
71	**72**	**73**	**74**	**75**					
B	C	B	D	B					

SOME SELECTED EXPLANATORY ANSWERS

1. Mesoscale meteorology is the study of weather systems smaller than synoptic scale systems but larger than microscale and storm-scale cumulus systems. Horizontal dimensions generally range from around 5 kilometers to several hundred kilometers. Examples of mesoscale weather systems are sea breezes, squall lines, and mesoscale convective complexes.
Mesocyclone: A horizontal atmospheric rotation on a scale between 4 and 400 km. It is a rotation within a thunderstorm typically surrounding a small area of low pressure. Typically within thunderstorms the rotation is 4-12 km across and 4-10 km in height.
Mesoscale: On a scale of 4 km to 400 km.

2. **Rayleigh Scattering:** It is largely due to gas molecules and other very small particles, many times smaller than the wavelength of radiation under consideration, such as visible light (0.4–0.7 μm) by pure gas molecules of size 10^{-4} μm, in a clean atmosphere. Rayleigh scattering is inversely proportional to the fourth power of the wavelength. The scattering is accomplished through absorption and re-emission of radiation by atoms and molecules. For a wavelength ratio of 1:2 between 0.4 μm (blue) and 0.8 μm (beyond red), the ratio of scattered light is 16:1. This is the reason for bluish appearance of clear sky.

3. A **wind rose** is a graphic tool used by meteorologists to give a succinct view of how wind speed and direction are typically distributed at a particular location. Using a polar coordinate system of gridding, the frequency of winds over a long time period is plotted by wind direction, with color bands showing wind ranges. The directions of the rose with the longest spoke show the wind direction with the greatest frequency.

5. The **geostrophic wind** is the theoretical wind that would result from an exact balance between the Coriolis effect and the pressure gradient force. This condition is called geostrophic balance. The geostrophic wind is directed parallel to isobars (lines of constant pressure at a given height). This balance seldom holds exactly in nature. The true wind almost always differs from the geostrophic wind due to other forces such as friction from the ground. Thus, the actual wind would equal the geostrophic wind only if there were no friction and the isobars were perfectly straight.

6. A possible mechanism for photochemical smog inhibition is to add compounds like diethylhydroxylamine (DEHA) as it reacts with hydroxyl radicals. Diethylhydroxylamine (DEHA) reacts with gas-phase hydroxyl radicals on every third collision, whereas the corresponding reaction in aqueous solution is considerably slower. The high gas-phase reactivity explains the predicted inhibitory effect of DEHA in atmospheric smog processes.

9. **Biochemical oxygen demand (BOD)** is the amount of dissolved oxygen needed by aerobic biological organisms in a body of water to break down organic material present in a given water sample at certain temperature over a specific time period. It is the amount of oxygen required for microbial metabolism of organic compounds in water. This demand occurs over some variable period of time depending on temperature, nutrient concentrations, and the enzymes available to indigenous microbial populations.
The first step in the process, conversion of ammonia to nitrite and then to nitrate, is called nitrification. The process is summarized in the following equations:

$$NH_4 + 3/2\ O_2 \rightarrow NO_2^- + 2H^+ + H_2O$$

$$NO_2^- + 1/2O \rightarrow NO_3^-$$

Nitrification Process

It is important to note that this process requires and consumes oxygen. This contributes to the BOD or biochemical oxygen demand of the sewage. The process is mediated by the bacteria *Nitrosomnas* and *Nitrobacter* which require an aerobic (presence of oxygen) environment for growth and metabolism of nitrogen. Thus, **the nitrification process must proceed under aerobic conditions.**

10. **Beer's law:** The physical law stating that the quantity of light absorbed by a substance dissolved in a nonabsorbing solvent is directly proportional to the concentration of the substance and the path length of the light through the solution; the law is sometimes also referred to as the Beer-Lambert law or the Bouguer-Beer law. Beer's law is commonly written in the form $A = \varepsilon cl$, where A is the absorbance, c is the concentration in moles per liter, l is the path length incentimeters, and ε is a constant of proportionality known as the molar extinction coefficient. The law is accurate only for dilute solutions; deviations from the law occur in concentrated solutions because of interactions between molecules of the solute, the substance dissolved in the solvent.

11. Phytochelatins are small, cysteine-rich peptides capable of binding heavy metal ions via thiolate coordination. They primarily form a M_r 3600 complex with cadmium. Phytochelatins are assumed to be involved in the accumulation, detoxification, and metabolism of metal ions such as cadmium, zinc, copper, lead and mercury in plant cells.

13. **Winkler Method for Determining Dissolved Oxygen (DO):** An accurate method of measuring the amount of DO in water is the Winkler method. Oxygen dissolved in water is able to oxidize manganese (II) ions in alkaline solution to manganese (IV) ions. The alkali is necessary to convert the manganese (II) sulphate to manganese hydroxide, which is readily oxidized.

    The titration end point can be easily detected visually from blue to colorless, the overall reaction of the Winkler method is:

    $$2S_2O_3^{2-} + 2H^+ + ½O_2 \rightarrow S_4O_6^{2-} + H_2O$$

    The above reaction indicates that 1 mol of O_2 is equivalent to 4 mol of thiosulphate $\left(S_2O_3^{2-}\right)$ in the final titration. The DO can be calculated by the following equation:

    $$DO\ (mg/L) = \frac{N \times V \times 8000}{V_S}$$

    where N and V are the normality and volume (mL) of $Na_2S_2O_3$, respectively, Vs is the sample volume (typically 200 mL is withdrawn from 300 mL sample).

14. Restoration is ... the return of an ecosystem to a close approximation of its condition prior to disturbance. In restoration, ecological damage to the resource is repaired. Both the structure and the functions of the ecosystem are recreated ... The goal is to emulate a natural, functioning, self-regulating system that is integrated with the ecological landscape in which it occurs.

17. **Ambush predators** or **sit-and-wait predators** are carnivorous animals or other organisms, such as some nematophagous fungi and carnivorous plants, that capture or trap prey by stealth or by strategy (typically not conscious strategy), rather than by speed or by strength.

    Alligator gars *(Atractosteus spatula)* are relatively passive, seemingly sluggish solitary fish, but voracious ambush predators. They are opportunistic night predators and are primarily piscivores, but they will also ambush and eat water fowl and small mammals that may be floating on the surface. Their method of ambush is to float a few feet below the surface, and wait for unsuspecting prey to swim within reach. They lunge forward, and with a sweeping motion grab their prey, impaling it on their double rows of sharp teeth.

19. Ammonia is very soluble. It moves in the soil rapidly and is acted upon by microorganisms of the category of chemosynthetic autotrophs. The nitrifying bacteria which convert ammonia into nitrite is *Nitrosomonas* and which converts nitrite into nitrate is *Nitrobacter.*

$$NH_4 + 2O_2 \xrightarrow{\text{Nitrosomonas}} 2H_2O + NO_2$$

$$NO_2^- + 1/2O_2 \xrightarrow{\text{Nitrobacter}} NO_3^- .$$

22. Although the average salinity of the oceans is 3.5 per cent, it varies geographically. High rainfall near the equator dilutes salinity to 3.45 per cent. Conversely, in dry subtropical regions, where evaporation is high and low precipitation, salinity can be as high as 3.6 per cent. Salinity varies more dramatically along coastlines. The Baltic Sea is a shallow ocean basin fed by many large, fresh water rivers and diluted further by rain and snow. As a result, its salinity is as low 2.0 per cent. In contrast, the Persian Gulf has low rainfall; high evaporation; and few large, inflowing rivers; its salinity exceeds 4.2 per cent.

24. **Loamy Sand:** This category contains 70 to 85 percent sand, 0 to 30 percent silt, and 10 to 15 percent clay. Because loamy sand contains more clay than does sand, it is slightly cohesive and can be molded into a ball that will maintain its form under gentle pressure. Soil squeezed between the thumb and forefinger, will not form a ribbon.

25. When solar radiation hits a target surface, it may be **transmitted, absorbed** or **reflected**. Different materials reflect and absorb differently at different wavelengths. The reflectance spectrum of a material is a plot of the fraction of radiation reflected as a function of the incident wavelength and serves as a unique signature for the material. In principle, a material can be identified from its spectral reflectance signature if the sensing system has sufficient **spectral resolution** to distinguish its spectrum from those of other materials. This premise provides the basis for multispectral remote sensing.

27. **Radar Imaging Satellite 1,** or **RISAT-1,** is an Indian remote sensing satellite which was built and is operated by the Indian Space Research Organisation (ISRO). The second RISAT satellite to be launched, it uses C-band 5.35 GHz Synthetic Aperture Radar for earth observation irrespective of the light and weather conditions of the area being imaged.

28. **Shield volcanoes** are huge, gently sloping volcanoes built of very thin lava spreading out in all directions from a central vent. They have wide bases several miles in diameter with steeper middle slopes and a flatter summit. The gentle convex slopes give them an outline like a medieval knight's shield. Eruptions are not generally explosive, more like liquid overflowing around the edges of a container. Mount Etna in Sicily and Mauna Loa in Hawaiin Islands are the most noteworthy examples of shield volcanoes. The world's largest volcano, Mauna Loa in Hawaii, is a shield volcano. Mauna Loa is about 55,770 feet (17,000 meters) from its base beneath the ocean to the summit, which is 13,681 feet (4,170 meters) above sea level. It is also one of the Earth's most active volcanoes and is carefully monitored. The most recent eruption was in 1984.

30. The calorific value of a fuel is the **quantity of heat produced by its combustion—**at constant pressure and under "normal" ("standard") conditions.

Higher Calorific Value (or Gross Calorific Value–GCV, or Higher Heating Value–HHV)– the water of combustion is entirely condensed and that the heat contained in the water vapor is recovered.

Table : *Carbon Intensity of Fossil Fuels Based on High-Heating Values (HHV)**

	Energy Density (kJ/kg)	Carbon Content (%)	Carbon Intensity (kgC/GJ)
Anthracite coal	34,900	92	26.4
Bituminous coal	27,330	75	27.4
Crude oil	42,100	80	19.0
Natural gas	55,240	77	13.9

* *HHV includes latent heat in exhaust water vapour.*

32. The Green Climate Fund (GCF) is a cornerstone of the emerging architecture of the global climate regime. The volume of funds must be sufficient to inspire developing countries confidence in the commitment of developed countries to support climate action and inspire developing countries to put sufficient effort into creating projects and programs to make good use of this funding. ECO wonders how serious developed countries are about the GCF, really. As soon as the GCF is fully operational, and the institutional arrangements are in place for direct access by developing countries, ECO suggests that regular contributions to the GCF increase rapidly, surpassing USD$10 billion annually. This must also scale up further to account for a substantial part of the $100 billion committed by developed countries by 2020.

33. Anaerobic digestion is the natural biological process which stabilizes organic waste in the absence of air and transforms it into biofertilizer and biogas. Anaerobic digestion is a reliable technology for the treatment of wet, organic waste. Organic waste from various sources is biochemically degraded in highly controlled, oxygen-free conditions circumstances resulting in the production of biogas which can be used to produce both electricity and heat.

An anaerobic digestion plant produces two outputs, biogas and digestate, both can be further processed or utilized to produce secondary outputs. Biogas can be used for producing electricity and heat, as a natural gas substitute and also a transportation fuel. A combined heat and power plant system (CHP) not only generates power but also produces heat for in-house requirements to maintain desired temperature level in the digester during cold season.

35. The first laws of thermodynamics deals with the conservation of matter and energy and states that energy cannot be created or destroyed but can only change from one form to another. For example, the energy of visible light is absorbed by green plants through photosynthesis; it is changed into chemical energy stored in the glucose molecules. Almost all living organisms including plants consume glucose in respiration and use the stored chemical energy for their metabolic activity. Some of the energy is dissipated as heat, another form of energy.

37. **Knocking** in spark-ignition internal combustion engines occurs when combustion of the air/fuel mixture in the cylinder does not start off correctly in response to ignition by the spark plug, but one or more pockets of air/fuel mixture explode outside the envelope of the normal combustion front. ***Knocking effect in the gasoline cannot be reached by additive like kerosene.***

38. **Monazite** is a reddish-brown phosphate mineral containing rare earth metals. It occurs usually in small isolated crystals. Monazite is an important ore for thorium, lanthanum, and cerium. It is often found in placer deposits. India, Madagascar, and South Africa have large deposits of monazite sands. The deposits in India are particularly rich in monazite. It has a hardness of 5.0 to 5.5 and is relatively dense, about 4.6 to 5.7 g/cm^3.

42. The UV (ultraviolet) region of solar radiation covers the wavelength range 100-400 nm and is divided into three bands:

- UV-A (315-400 nm)
- UV-B (280-315 nm)
- UV-C (100-280 nm)

Stratospheric ozone levels are near their lowest point since measurements began, so current UV-B radiation levels are thought to be close to their maximum. Total stratospheric content of ozone-depleting substances is expected to reach a maximum before the year 2000. All other things being equal, the current ozone losses and related UV-B increases should be close to their maximum.

47. The Battelle Environmental Evaluation System (EES) is a methodology for conducting environmental impact analysis developed at Battelle Columbus Laboratories by an interdisciplinary research team under contract with the U.S. Bureau of Reclamation. It is based on a hierarchical assessment of environmental quality indicators. In Battele environment evaluation system the total parameter importance units is lowest for aesthetics.

48. ISO 14040:2006 describes the principles and framework for life cycle assessment (LCA) including: definition of the goal and scope of the LCA, the life cycle inventory analysis (LCI) phase, the life cycle impact assessment (LCIA) phase, the life cycle interpretation phase, reporting and critical review of the LCA, limitations of the LCA, the relationship between the LCA phases, and conditions for use of value choices and optional elements.

49. With regards to the risk assessment undertaken at each tier of the framework, it is important that the following are taken into account:

- Have the hazards been identified?
- Have the consequences been identified?
- Have the magnitudes of consequences been determined?
- Have the probabilities of the consequences been determined?
- Has the significance of the risk been determined?

51. **Geoinformatics** is the science and the technology which develops and uses information science infrastructure to address the problems of geography,geosciences and related branches of engineering.

Geoinformatics has been described as "the science and technology dealing with the structure and character of spatial information, its capture, its classification and qualification, its storage, processing, portrayal and dissemination, including the infrastructure necessary to secure optimal use of this information" or "the art, science or technology dealing with the acquisition, storage, processing production, presentation and dissemination of Geoinformation".

52. **Forest Survey of India** (FSI) is a government organization in India under the union Ministry of Environment and Forests for conducting forest surveys and studies. The organization came into being in June, 1981. It is head-quartered at Dehradun of Uttarakhand in India.

53. Satellite sensors can observe large areas but the spatial resolution of these is dependent on microwave frequency, antenna dimensions, and height above the earth's surface. The higher the sensor, the lower the spatial resolution and at low elevations the spacecraft would use more fuel. Higher spatial resolution requires larger diameter antennas that in turn require more fuel to maintain in space.

56. (*a*) The **Bhopal disaster,** also referred to as the **Bhopal gas tragedy,** was a *gas leak* incident in India, considered *the world's worst industrial disaster.*

It occurred on the night of 2-3 December 1984 at the *Union Carbide India Limited* (UCIL) pesticide plant in Bhopal, Madhya Pradesh. Over 500,000 people were exposed to *methyl isocyanate (MIC)* gas and other chemicals. The toxic substance made its way into and around the *shanty towns* located near the plant.

(*b*) The **Chernobyl disaster** was a catastrophic nuclear accident that occurred on 26 April 1986 at the Chernobyl Nuclear Power Plant in Ukraine (then officially the Ukrainian SSR), which was under the direct jurisdiction of the central authorities of the Soviet Union. An explosion and fire released large quantities of radioactive particles into the atmosphere, which spread over much of the western USSR and Europe.

(*c*) **The 2004 Indian Ocean earthquake** occurred at 00:58:53 UTC on 26 December with an epicentre off the west coast of Sumatra, Indonesia. The event is known by the scientific community as the **Sumatra-Andaman earthquake.** The resulting tsunami was given various names, including the **2004 Indian Ocean tsunami, South Asian tsunami, Indonesian tsunami,** the **Christmas tsunami** and the **Boxing Day tsunami.**

(*d*) Very Severe Cyclonic Storm Hudhud was a strong tropical cyclone that caused extensive damage and loss of life in eastern India and Nepal during October 2014.

Hudhud originated from a low pressure system that formed under the influence of an upper-air cyclonic circulation in the Andaman Sea on October 6. Hudhud intensified into a cyclonic storm on October 8 and as a Severe Cyclonic Storm on October 9.

57. Benchmarking, a management approach for implementing best practices at best cost, is a recent concept in the healthcare system. Benchmarking is often thought to consist simply of comparing indicators and is not perceived in its entirety, that is, as a tool based on voluntary and active collaboration among several organizations to create a spirit of competition and to apply best practices. The key feature of benchmarking is its integration within a comprehensive and participatory policy of continuous quality improvement (CQI). Conditions for successful benchmarking focus essentially on careful preparation of the process, monitoring of the relevant indicators, staff involvement and inter-organizational visits.

58. The Basel Convention is to protect human health and the environment against the adverse effects of hazardous wastes. Its scope of application covers a wide range of wastes defined as "hazardous wastes" based on their origin and/or composition and their characteristics, as well as two types of wastes defined as "other wastes" - household waste and incinerator ash.

The provisions of the Convention center around the following principal aims:

- the reduction of hazardous waste generation and the promotion of environmentally sound management of hazardous wastes, wherever the place of disposal;
- the restriction of transboundary movements of hazardous wastes except where it is perceived to be in accordance with the principles of environmentally sound management; and
- a regulatory system applying to cases where transboundary movements are permissible.

59. Intergenerational equity is a concept that says that humans 'hold the natural and cultural environment of the Earth in common both with other members of the present generation and with other generations, past and future'. It means that we inherit the Earth from previous generations and have an obligation to pass it on in reasonable condition to future generations.

63. In demographics, the **rate of natural increase (NIR)** is the crude birth rate minus the crude death rate of a population. When looking at countries, it gives an idea of what position in the Demographic Transition Model, but to find out how much a country is growing, the population growth rate should be observed. The formula for the rate of natural increase is: (Crude birth rate – Crude death rate) / 10, where birth and death rates are in per mile. The result is the rate of natural increase in percentage form.

72. Paryavaran Vahini, was launched in 1992-93 to create environmental awareness and to ensure active public participation by involving the local people in activities related to environmental protection. Paryavaran Vahinis are proposed to be constituted in 194 selected districts all over the country which have a high incidence of pollution and density of tribal and forest population. The Vahinis also play a watch-dog role by reporting instance of environmental pollution, deforestation, poaching, etc.

73. The Disaster Management Act, 2005 came into the statute book on 26 December 2005 by a Gazette notification, exactly on the first anniversary of the devastating tsunami of 2004, which killed nearly 13,000 people in India alone and affected 18 million people. The Act provides a legal and institutional framework for "the effective management of disasters and for matters connected there with or incidental thereto." It provides for establishment of *National Disaster Management Authority (NDMA),* State Disaster Management Authority (SDMA) and *District Disaster Management Authorities (DDMA)* at the National, State and District levels with adequate financial and administrative powers and creation of the National Institute of Disaster Management (NIDM) with the mandate of undertaking training and capacity building, Develop Training Modules on various aspects of Disaster management, Undertake Research and Documentation, Formulate and implement comprehensive *HRD Plan* covering all aspects of DM, Provide assistance in national level policy formulation and Provide assistance to state governments and State Training Institutions.

Previous Paper (Solved)

UGC-NET Environmental Science, June 2014

PAPER-II

Note : *This paper contains* ***fifty (50)*** *objective type questions of* ***two (2)*** *marks each. All questions are compulsory.*

1. For a clear night and with windspeeds < 3 m/s, the atmosphere is

A. stable B. slightly unstable
C. neutral D. slightly stable

2. Assertion (A) : Chemosynthesis plays an important role in 'S' cycle.

Reason (R) : In chemosynthesis, some sulphur compounds act as source of energy.

Codes:

A. Both (A) and (R) are true and (R) is the correct explanation.
B. Both (A) and (R) are true and (R) is not the correct explanation.
C. (A) is true, but (R) is false.
D. (A) is false, but (R) is true.

3. Which of the following is ***NOT*** a correct statement?

A. Tropics are the warmest and wettest regions.
B. Subtropical high pressure zones create dry zones at about 30° N and S.
C. Temperature and precipitation are lowest at the poles.
D. Temperature is lowest and precipitation is highest at the poles.

4. Protecting nature and the wilderness for its own sake is referred as

A. Deep ecology B. Shallow ecology
C. Self ecology D. Selfless ecology

5. For the analysis of oxides of Nitrogen, which of the following set of reagents are used?

A. Sulphanilic acid, NEDA, H_2O_2, HNO_3
B. Sulphamic acid, NEDA, H_2O_2, HNO_3
C. Sulphamic acid, Nicotine, H_2O, HNO_3
D. Sulphomolybdic acid, NEDA, H_2O_2, H_2SO_4

6. Number of ions of cadmium present in $3n$ moles of cadmium nitrate is

A. 18.069×10^{23} B. 18.069×10^{20}
C. 18.069×10^{17} D. 18.069×10^{14}

7. Which one of the following organisms is a free living nitrogen fixer?

A. *Rhizobium* B. *Azotobacter*
C. *Frankia* D. *Dorylimes*

8. Which one of the following has highest bioconcentration factor (BCF)?

A. DDT B. DDE
C. Chlordane D. Heptachlor

9. Consider an Ocean Thermal Energy Conversion (OTEC) process operating between 30°C and 5°C. What would be the maximum possible efficiency for an electricity generator station operating with these temperatures?

A. 8% B. 15%
C. 25% D. 40%

10. The process of 'Nebulisation' in Atomic Absorption Spectrophotometry is to

A. convert the liquid sample to gaseous form.
B. convert the liquid sample into small droplets.
C. sublimate the sample.
D. solubilization of the solute.

11. Individuals of a plant species occurring in a particular area constitute

A. fauna B. flora
C. flora and fauna D. population

12. A local population genetically, structurally and functionally adapted to its local environment is called

A. ecotype B. ecophene
C. ecad D. ecocline

13. Mycorrhizae is an example of

A. Ammensalism B. Commensalism
C. Parasitism D. Symbiosis

14. The entire series of communities of biotic succession from pioneer to climax community is known as

A. Troph B. Sere
C. Population D. Biome

15. In which of the following ecosystems the pyramid of biomass is inverted?

A. Forest B. Grassland
C. Pond D. Desert

16. The first National Park established in India is

A. Kaziranga National Park
B. The Jim Corbett National Park
C. Hazaribagh National Park
D. Gir National Park

17. The animals that rest or swim on the surface of the lakes are called

A. Nektons B. Neustons
C. Benthos D. Peritons

18. Which of the following is an example of *in situ* conservation of biodiversity?

A. Captive breeding
B. Seed bank
C. National park
D. Pollen bank

19. A biome contains

A. many ecosystems
B. many communities
C. many populations
D. a single ecosystem

20. In Bhopal gas tragedy, the quantity of Methyl Isocyanate leaked into the atmosphere was around

A. ~ 180 tonnes B. ~ 60 tonnes
C. ~ 112 tonnes D. ~ 40 tonnes

21. What is the sequence of arrival of seismic waves at a recording station?

A. P-wave, S-wave, L-wave, R-wave.
B. S-wave, P-wave, R-wave, L-wave.
C. R-wave, L-wave, P-wave, S-wave.
D. S-wave, L-wave, R-wave, P-wave.

22. The presence of ammonia in groundwater may indicate a nearby

A. coal mine
B. municipal solid waste dumping site
C. thermal power plant
D. granite quarry

23. Given below are statements in the context of a truly vertical aerial photograph:

(*i*) The principal point, nadir point and isocentre coincide.
(*ii*) Isocentre is the centre from where the radial displacements of images take place.
(*iii*) Tilt is a character of vertical aerial photograph

Identify the correct answer from the codes given below:

A. (*i*) only
B. (*i*) and (*ii*) only
C. (*i*) and (*iii*) only
D. (*ii*) and (*iii*) only

24. Kaolinite is a type of clay Mineral with layers of silicon and aluminium in the ratio of

A. 1 : 1 B. 1 : 2
C. 2 : 1 D. 3 : 1

25. In an ideal Magneto Hydro Dynamic Power Generator, the separation between the plates = 0.5 m, magnetic flux density = 2 Wb/m^2 and average fuel velocity = 500 m/sec. The voltage developed across the plates will be

A. 500 V B. 1000 V
C. 2000 V D. 5000 V

26. If the wind speed in a certain area increases by a factor of 2 from 4 m/s to 8 m/s, the power output from an ideal wind mill will increase by a factor of

A. 4 B. 8
C. 16 D. 2

27. Under Jawaharlal Nehru Solar Mission of Government of India, a total of 20,000 MW of utility Grid Power (including roof to solar power) is sought to be installed by the year.
A. 2020 B. 2022
C. 2025 D. 2030

28. In which country dry steam deposits have been used as such for electricity generation?
A. Italy B. Iceland
C. Austria D. New Zealand

29. The resources which are unlimited and where quality is not degraded are termed as
A. renewable B. reusable
C. immutable D. exhaustible

30. The most toxic form of mercury in water is
A. $2\ Hg^+$ B. $Hg2^+$
C. $CH_3^-Hg^+$ D. Hg°

31. Hardness of water is due to the presence of
A. Calcium and Magnesium ions
B. Strontium and Nitrate ions
C. Sodium and Chloride ions
D. Potassium and Nitrite ions

32. Principal constitutents of atmospheric brown clouds are
I. Soot
II. Soil dust
III. Fly ash
IV. Sulphates and nitrates
Identify the correct code:
A. I and II only B. I and IV only
C. II, III and IV only D. I, II, III and IV

33. The famous 'London Smog' was observed in the year
A. 1750 B. 1952
C. 1972 D. 2000

34. The permissible limit of day time industrial noise as recommended by WHO is
A. 80 dB B. 75 dB
C. 90 dB D. 76 dB

35. Surface litter layer on ground soil is also known as
A. 'O' horizon B. 'A' horizon
C. 'B' horizon D. 'C' horizon

36. Which one of the following represents the correct Uranium decay series?
A. Uranium → Radium → Radon → Polonium
B. Uranium → Radon → Radium → Polonium
C. Uranium → Radium → Polonium → Radon
D. Uranium → Radon → Polonium → Radium

37. Hydropower projects with large reservoirs affect the environment by release of
A. CO B. CO_2
C. CH_4 D. NO_2

38. Terms of reference is fixed at which stage of EIA process?
A. Screening stage
B. Scoping stage
C. Detailed EIA stage
D. Project Appraisal stage

39. Arrange the functions associated with EIA in a sequential manner
(*i*) Identification
(*ii*) Prediction
(*iii*) Defining the scope
(*iv*) Impact evaluation and analysis

Codes :

A.	(*i*)	(*iii*)	(*iv*)	(*ii*)
B.	(*ii*)	(*iv*)	(*i*)	(*iii*)
C.	(*iii*)	(*i*)	(*ii*)	(*iv*)
D.	(*iv*)	(*ii*)	(*iii*)	(*i*)

40. The role of State Pollution Control Board in EIA is
(*i*) Public hearing/consultation
(*ii*) Issue of NOC
(*iii*) Collecting environmental data
(*iv*) Survey of fauna and flora

Codes :
A. (*i*) and (*iii*) only B. (*i*) and (*ii*) only
C. (*iii*) and (*iv*) only D. (*ii*) and (*iii*) only

41. Percentage of carbon in a typical municipal solid waste ranges from
A. 50 – 60% B. 40 – 50%
C. 30 – 40% D. 20 – 30%

42. Which one of the following has maximum destruction and removable efficiency?
A. Incineration
B. Biological Treatment
C. Chemical Treatment
D. Landfill

43. Wastes are known to be corrosive if the pH is
A. ≤ 2 B. ≤ 3
C. ≤ 4 D. ≤ 5

44. Hazardous Waste Management and Handling Rule was enacted in the year
A. 1989 B. 1979
C. 1969 D. 1999

45. For a given set of data 5, 8, 12, 15 and 20, the comparison of geometric ($\overline{G}$), harmonic ($\overline{H}$) and arithmetic mean ($\overline{X}$) will be
A. $\overline{H} > \overline{G} > \overline{X}$ B. $\overline{H} > \overline{G} < \overline{X}$
C. $\overline{H} < \overline{G} < \overline{X}$ D. $\overline{H} < \overline{G} > \overline{X}$

46. Algal bloom follows a population growth pattern, which is
A. J-shaped
B. S-shaped
C. Exponential
D. Linear

47. *t*-distribution is approximately normal for sample size η
A. ≥ 30 B. ≥ 10
C. ≥ 15 D. ≥ 20

48. Two sets of data consisting of 10 and 20 observations have same mean 8 with standard deviations of 1 and 2, respectively. If the two data sets are combined, then the variance is
A. 3
B. 2
C. 5
D. 1.5

49. Match the List-I with List-II and choose the correct answer from the given codes:

List–I (Event)	***List–II (Date)***
(*a*) Earth Day	(*i*) 5th June
(*b*) World Environment Day	(*ii*) 3rd October
(*c*) Ozone Day	(*iii*) 22nd April
(*d*) World Nature Day	(*iv*) 16th September

Codes :

	(*a*)	(*b*)	(*c*)	(*d*)
A.	(*i*)	(*ii*)	(*iv*)	(*iii*)
B.	(*iii*)	(*i*)	(*iv*)	(*ii*)
C.	(*ii*)	(*i*)	(*iii*)	(*iv*)
D.	(*iv*)	(*iii*)	(*ii*)	(*i*)

50. CBD stands for
A. Convention on Biological Diversity
B. Conservation Biodiversity Development
C. Conservation Association for Biodiversity and Management
D. Cumulative Plan for Biological Diversity

ANSWERS

1	2	3	4	5	6	7	8	9	10
A	A	D	A	A	D	B	A	A	B
11	**12**	**13**	**14**	**15**	**16**	**17**	**18**	**19**	**20**
D	A	D	B	C	B	B	C	A	D
21	**22**	**23**	**24**	**25**	**26**	**27**	**28**	**29**	**30**
A	B	A	A	A	B	B	A	C	C
31	**32**	**33**	**34**	**35**	**36**	**37**	**38**	**39**	**40**
A	D	B	B	A	A	C	B	C	B
41	**42**	**43**	**44**	**45**	**46**	**47**	**48**	**49**	**50**
A	A	A	A	C	A	A	A	B	A

Some Selected Explanatory Answers

1. Relation between the Monin-Obukhov Length, L and Other Meteorological Stability Conditions

Description	Time and weather	Wind speed u	Monin-Obukhov Length, L	Pasquill-Gifford stability class
Very stable	Clear night	< 3 m/s	10 m	F
Stable	↓	2–4 m/s	50 m	E
Neutral	Cloudy or windy	Any	> |100 m|	D
Unstable	↓	2-6 m/s	–50 m	B or C
Very unstable	Sunny	< 3 m/s	– 10 m	A

3. On a global scale the effects of **latitude** are of greatest importance. The highest temperatures are recorded in low latitudes in the tropics between 0° and 23½° north and south of the Equator. Lowest temperatures are recorded in polar latitudes north and south of 66½°. There is a gradual decrease in temperature between the Equator and the Poles because of reduced **insolation**. The lowest precipitation **amounts** at **high latitudes** are on the plateau of Antarctica and in the central area of Greenland.

4. In the 1970s, a new thinking on environmental concerns began to emerge, protecting nature and the wilderness for its own sake, which is now referred to as 'Deep Ecology'. It recognizes the intrinsic value of all living beings and looks upon mankind as a small segment of a great living community of life-forms. It teaches that the well-being and flourishing of human and non-human life on Earth have value in themselves and that these values are independent of the usefulness of the non-human world for human purposes. Deep Ecologists on the other hand stress that wilderness preservation is a means to achieve the conservation and protection of biological diversity. Thus, it is not enough to protect the fragments that are that left of the wilderness, but we must also attempt to restore degraded areas to their former natural ecological state.

7. **Azotobacter** are free living bacteria which grow well on a nitrogen free medium. These bacteria utilize atmospheric nitrogen gas for their cell protein synthesis. This cell protein is then mineralised in soil after the death of Azoto-bacter cells thereby contributing towards the nitrogen availability of the crop plants. Azotobacter naturally fixes atmospheric nitrogen in the rhizosphere. Azotobacter uses carbon for its metabolism from simple or compound substances of carbonaceous in nature. Besides carbon, Azotobacter also requires calcium for nitrogen fixation.

8. Some compounds with very high bioconcentration factors, 10^3 to 10^4, show lower than expected EM values, (See Table). Since the accumulation values for DDT, PCB, hexachlorobenzene (HCB), and di-2-ethylhexyl phthalate (DEHP) in the real aquatic environment are high, the laboratory data should also rank these compounds among the highest in accumulative potential.

Table : *Predicting the more accumulative compounds*

Compounds	Bioconcentration Factors	Ecological Magnification	
	Trout Muscle	Terrestrial and Aquatic	Aquatic
PCB	12,400 ± 2290	11,900	17,840

Compounds	Bioconcentration Factors: Trout Muscle	Ecological Magnification: Terrestrial and Aquatic	Ecological Magnification: Aquatic
HCB	7,880 ± 350	287	343
DDT	1,390 (191)	84,545	16,950
DEHP	800 (143)	130	3

10. Nebulization is where the sample is converted to a fine mist of finely divided droplets but using a jet of compressed gas.

Pneumatic nebulization is the technique used in most atomic spectroscopy determinations. The sample solution is introduced through an orifice into a high-velocity gas jet, usually the oxidant. The sample stream may intersect the gas stream in either a parallel or perpendicular manner. Liquid is drawn through the sample capillary by the pressure differential generated by the high velocity gas stream passing over the sample orifice. The liquid stream begins to oscillate, producing filaments. Finally, these filaments collapse to form a cloud of droplets in the aerosol modifier or spray chamber. In the spray chamber the larger droplets are removed from the sample stream by mixer paddles or broken up into smaller droplets by impact beads or wall surfaces.

11. A population is the set of individuals of a species that live in a particular area at the same time and that can interbreed with each other. **Population genetics** deals with the abundance of different alleles within a population and the manner in which the abundance of a particular allele increases, decreases, or remains the same with time.

12. **Ecotypes (Ecological or Physiological races).** These are genetically adapted local populations that evolve from a species having a wide range of distribution.

14. The first commodity, which inhabit a bare area is called pioneer community. It has very little diversity and takes longest time to change the environment for invasion of the next community. The last and stable community in the area is called climax community. It is in perfect harmony with the physical environment. It is also termed as **climatic climax community**. It has maximum diversity and niche specialization. The intermediate communities between pioneer and climax communities are called **seral** or **transitional communities.** The entire series of communities of biotic succession from pioneer to climax community is known as **sere.**

15. **Pyramid of biomass:** It is based upon the total biomass (dry matter) at each trophic level in a food chain. The pyramid of biomass can also be *upright* or *inverted*. Fig. (*a, b*) show pyramids of biomass in a forest and an aquatic ecosystem. The pyramid of biomass in a forest is upright in contrast to its pyramid of numbers. This is because the producers (trees) accumulate a huge biomass while the consumers' total biomass feeding on them declines at higher trophic levels, resulting in broad base and narrowing top.

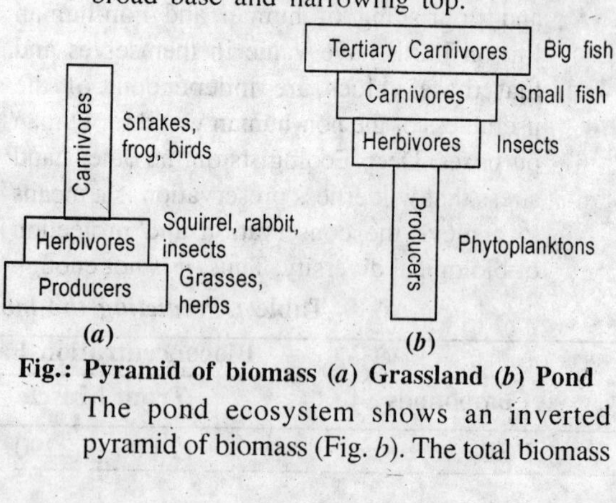

Fig.: Pyramid of biomass (*a*) Grassland (*b*) Pond

The pond ecosystem shows an inverted pyramid of biomass (Fig. *b*). The total biomass of producers (phytoplanktons) is much less as compared to herbivores (zooplanktons, insects), Carnivores (Small fish) and tertiary carnivores (big fish). Thus the pyramid takes an inverted shape with narrow base and broad apex.

16. Jim Corbett National Park: Jim Corbett National Park was India's first national park, located near Nainital in the state of Uttaranchal. It was established as a national park in 1936 under the United Provinces National Parks Act of India. It is known for its varied wildlife, and as the site for the launching of Project Tiger. The park is named after Jim Corbett, a legendary hunter-turned-conservator, best known for despatching a number of man-eating tigers and leopards in this region in the first half of the 20th century.

18. Conserving wild plants and animals in their original habitats or natural surroundings is referred to as *in situ* conservation. Conserving wild plants and animals in forests, national parks or sanctuaries are examples of *in situ* conservation.

24. Kaolinite and Halloysite, 1:1 Minerals: 1:1 clay minerals are composed, for their silicate part, by a two layer structure where one layer is occupied exclusively by silicon cations and the other in large majority by aluminium ions. The aluminium is in octahedral coordination with oxygen atoms, shared with Si cations, and hydroxyl cations. This mineral is highly hydrated (hydrogen content) and therefore less thermally stable than the 2:1 minerals. The ratio of Si to Al is very near one. The kaolinite structure is not subject to cation substitutions for the most part and its composition is thus near Al, Si, O and H.

28. *Dry steam,* that is, steam accompanied by very little water, is the simplest system and is produced by some reservoirs. The steam can be used directly to power turbines for the generation of electric power. It has been used in Italy for electricity generation.

29. Classification of Natural Resources: Resources may be classified on the basis of the following:

1. Availability

(*i*) **Inexhaustible:** These resources are unlimited in quantity and quality. With the passage of time quality may be degraded but not the quantity.

(*ii*) **Exhaustible:** Quantity and quality of these resources may be exhausted soon.

2. Renewed Capability

(*i*) **Renewable:** Resources which can be renewed along with their exploitation. For example, forest, solar energy.

(*ii*) **Non-renewable:** These cannot be regene-rated if exploited on a large scale. For example, mineral, water and so on.

3. Quality

(*i*) **Immutable:** Quality of these resources are not degraded by human activity. For example, tidal power, wind, atomic power.

(*ii*) **Mutable:** Quality may be degraded by man's activity. For example, water, hydropower.

4. Method used

(*i*) **Maintainable:** The method used for consumption by human being.

(*ii*) **Non-maintainable:** Total quantity static when consumption occurs.

5. Origin

(*i*) **Biotic:** (Organic) Biotic resources are obtained from biosphere. For example, crops, birds, animals and so on.

(*ii*) **Abiotic:** (Inorganic) Resources composed of non-living matter. For example, land, water, minerals.

31. Hardness of water is of two types: *Temporary hardness and Permanent hardness.*

Temporary hardness: When hardness of water is due to the presence of soluble bicarbonates of calcium and magnesium, it is called temporary hardness. Temporary hardness of water can be removed by boiling. Temporary hardness is also called **carbonate hardness.**

Permanent hardness: It is due to the presence of sulphates and chlorides of magnesium and calcium, *i.e.,* $CaCl_2$, $CaSO_4$, $MgCl_2$ and $MgSO_4$. This type of hardness is called permanent hardness because it can not be removed simply by boiling. Permanent hardness is also called **non-carbonate hardness.**

33. When a thick fog engulfed London from December 5 to December 9, 1952, it mixed with black smoke emitted from homes and factories to create a deadly smog. This smog killed approximately 12,000 people and shocked the world into starting the environmental movement.

34. **Table : Allowable noise limits (India)**

Area zone	*Day-time limits dB(A)*	*Night-time limits dB(A)*
Industrial Area	75	70
Commercial Area	65	55
Residential Area	55	45
Silence zone	50	40

36. The *uranium decay series* consist of a group of nuclides that, when their mass number is divided by 4, have a remainder of 2 (the $4n + 2$ series). The parent of this series is ^{238}U with a natural abundance of 99.3%; it undergoes α-decay with a half-life of 4.46×10^9 y. The stable end product of the uranium series is ^{206}Pb, which is reached after 8 α- and 6 β-decay steps.

The specific activity of ^{238}U is 12.44 MBq/kg ^{238}U. However, because *natural uranium* consists of 3 isotopes, ^{238}U, ^{235}U and ^{234}U, whose isotopic abundances are 99.2745%, 0.7200% and 0.0055%, respectively, the specific activity of natural uranium is 25.4 MBq/kg.

The uranium decay series provides the most important isotopes of elements radium, radon and polonium, which can be isolated in the processing of uranium minerals.

38. Scoping was also introduced as a term which included the generation of Terms of Reference, on the basis of which the EIA report had to be made by Project Proponents. These terms of reference had to be devised by the Expert Appraisal Committee at center and State expert Appraisal Committee at the state level. This enhanced the role and burden on the expert committees.

42. Incineration has maximum destruction and removal efficiency.

43. **Corrosivity:** An aqueous waste is corrosive if it is strongly acidic with a pH of 2 or less, or strongly alkaline with pH of 12.5 or more. Also considered corrosive is a liquid waste capable of corroding steel at a rate of 6.35 mm per year as determined by the National Association of Corrosive Engineers. Examples of corrosive substances are highly alkaline compounds such as caustic soda or strong acids such as sulphuric and nitric acids.

44. **Hazardous Waste Management in India:** In India the need to manage hazardous wastes on scientific lines was felt only after the occurrence of Bhopal accident in the mid eighties (2, December, 1984). The Government then started thinking about the hazardous waste substances and their effect on human health and on the environment. In order to cover the environment as a whole entity, the Ministry of Environment and Forests (MOEF) enacted the law, Environment (Protection) Act 1986. Subsequent to this Act, in order to prevent indiscriminate disposal of hazardous waste, the MOEF initiated the Hazardous Wastes (Handling and Manage-ment) Rules in 1989. Though the Hazardous Waste Handling Rules were enacted in 1989 only, the response towards their implementation was very poor. It may be because of liberalized policy and the pace of industrialization has been accelerated, which was resulted in the increasing amounts of hazardous waste generated and released into the environment every year.

45. Arithmetic mean ($\bar{X}$)

$$= \frac{5+8+12+15+20}{5} = 12$$

Harmonic mean ($\bar{H}$)

$$= \frac{1}{\frac{\left(\frac{1}{5}+\frac{1}{8}+\frac{1}{12}+\frac{1}{15}+\frac{1}{20}\right)}{5}} = 2.625$$

Geometric mean ($\bar{G}$)

$$= \sqrt{A.M. \times H.M.}$$

$$= \sqrt{12 \times 2.625}$$

$$= 5.6125$$

Hence, $\bar{H} < \bar{G} < \bar{X}$

47. The *t*, or Student's *t*, distribution is an unbounded distribution having a mean of zero and a variance that depends on the scale parameter *v*, which is sometimes termed the "degrees of freedom". As *v* increases toward infinity, the *t* distribution approaches the standard normal density function. In general, the standard normal distribution can be used instead of the *t* distribution for sample sizes greater than 30.

PAPER-III

***Note :** This paper contains **seventy five (75)** objective type questions of **two (2)** marks each. **All** questions are compulsory.*

1. Chemosynthesis involves CO_2 fixation using energy derived from
A. Sunlight
B. Infrared radiation
C. UV-radiation
D. Inorganic and Organic compounds

2. Wind in the mountain-valley regions are of
A. Microscale B. Mesoscale
C. Macroscale D. Synoptic scale

3. In tropical region an aircraft is flying at an altitude of 10 km. At that altitude the tempera-ture is – 40 °C. What is the ambient temperature on the ground?
A. 24°C B. 40°C
C. 30°C D. 20°C

4. Assertion (A) : Upper atmosphere shields life on earth.
Reason (R) : Ultraviolet radiations are absorbed in the upper atmosphere.
Choose the correct answer:
Codes:
A. Both (A) and (R) are true and (R) is the correct explanation of (A).
B. Both (A) and (R) are true, but (R) is not the correct explanation of (A).
C. (A) is true and (R) is false.
D. (A) is false and (R) is true.

5. The molar extinction coefficient of proline ninhydrin complex at 520 nm is 0.34 μM^{-1} cm^{-1}. A solution of the proline ninhydrin complex has an absorbance of 0.68 in a one centimeter cuvette. The concentration (μM) of proline is
A. 0.5 B. 0.2312
C. 2.312 D. 2

6. The principal components of photochemical smog in urban areas are
A. SO_2 and NO_2
B. SPM and CO
C. SPM and NO_2
D. Oxides of Nitrogen, Hydrocarbons and Ozone.

7. The amount of a particular gas dissolved in water depends on
(*i*) its solubility in water.
(*ii*) its partial pressure at the air/water interface or sediment/water interface.
(*iii*) the water temperature.
(*iv*) the levels of salts in the water.
Identify the correct answer:
A. (*i*) and (*ii*) only
B. (*ii*), (*iii*) and (*iv*) only
C. (*i*), (*ii*) and (*iii*) only
D. (*i*), (*ii*), (*iii*) and (*iv*)

8. A 50 ml solution of pH = 1 is mixed with a 50 ml solution of pH = 2. The pH of the mixture will be nearly

A. 0.76 B. 1.26
C. 1.76 D. 2.26

9. The solubility product of the following type of reaction:

$Al(OH)_3 \longrightarrow Al^{3+} + 3\overset{\ominus}{O}H$ is

A. Ksp = (Al) (OH)
B. Ksp = $(Al^{3+})(3\overset{\ominus}{O}H)$
C. Ksp = $(Al^{3+})(\overset{\ominus}{O}H)^3$
D. Ksp = $(Al^{3+})(\overset{\ominus}{O}H)$

10. Cells grown in medium containing isotope sulphur 35 will show radio labelling in

A. membrane lipids
B. membrane proteins
C. glycogen
D. nucleic acid

11. A stream flowing at 10.0 m^3/s has a tributary feeding it with a flow of 5.0 m^3/s. The stream concentration of chloride upstream at the junction is 20.0 mg/L and the tributary chloride concentration is 40 mg/L. Treating chloride as a conservative substance and assuming complete mixing of the two streams, find the down stream concentration.

A. 26.7 mg/L B. 30.2 mg/L
C. 22.6 mg/L D. 35.2 mg/L

12. Assume that dilution factor *p* for an unseeded mixture of waste and water is 0.03. The DO of the mixture is initially 9.0 mg/L and after 5 days, it has dropped to 3.0 mg/L. The reaction rate constant 'K' has been found to be 0.22 / day. Five day BOD of the water will be

A. 200 mg/L B. 150 mg/L
C. 100 mg/L D. 75 mg/L

13. Nudation is generally caused by

A. migration of species
B. climate change
C. invasion of foreign species
D. modification of habitat

14. Which one of the following is the best tool to study the interacting residues in protein-ligand interaction?

A. X-ray crystallography
B. Circular dichroism spectroscopy
C. UV–V is spectroscopy
D. Fluorescence spectroscopy

15. During centrifugation, if the centrifugal force is F_c, buoyant force is F_b, and frictional force is F_f, which of the following equations expresses the sedimentation of the molecule?

A. $F_C = F_b - F_f$ B. $F_C = F_b + F_f$
C. $F_C = \frac{F_b - F_f}{2}$ D. $F_C = \frac{F_b + F_f}{2}$

16. Match the List-I with List-II and choose the correct answer from the given codes:

List-I (*Lakes*)	*List-II* (*Characteristics*)
(*a*) Oligotrophic lakes	(*i*) More nutrient concentration
(*b*) Dystrophic lakes	(*ii*) Magmatic water
(*c*) Eutrophic lakes	(*iii*) Low nutrient concentration
(*d*) Volcanic lakes	(*iv*) Low pH and high humic acid conditions

Codes :

	(*a*)	(*b*)	(*c*)	(*d*)
A.	(*i*)	(*ii*)	(*iii*)	(*iv*)
B.	(*ii*)	(*i*)	(*iv*)	(*iii*)
C.	(*iii*)	(*iv*)	(*i*)	(*ii*)
D.	(*iv*)	(*iii*)	(*ii*)	(*i*)

17. The earthworm used for composting is

(*a*) *Crassiclitellata excavata*
(*b*) *Octochaetona serrata*
(*c*) *Lumbricus terrestris*
(*d*) *Eisenia foetida*

Choose the correct answer:

A. (*a*) and (*b*) only B. (*b*) and (*d*) only
C. (*b*) and (*c*) only D. (*a*) and (*d*) only

18. The amount of the living material present in different trophic levels at a given time is called

(*a*) standing crop (*c*) standing state

(*b*) biomass (*d*) biosphe

Choose the correct answer:

A. (*a*) and (*c*) are correct

B. (*d*) is correct

C. (*b*) is correct

D. (*c*) and (*b*) are correct

19. Many orchids use trees as a surface to grow. This is an example of

A. Commensalism B. Mutualism

C. Parasitism D. Predation

20. The *r*-strategist is a

A. small organism that has a short life, produces many offsprings and does not reach carrying capacity.

B. small organism that has a longer life, produces offsprings and does not reach carrying capacity.

C. small organism that has a short life, produces numerous offsprings and reach carrying capacity.

D. medium organism that has a short life, produces numerous offsprings and reach carrying capacity.

21. Under the Rhino relocation project, during 1987, Rhinoes were introduced in

A. Assam B. Meghalaya

C. West Bengal D. Madhya Pradesh

22. Which of the following is an endangered bird species?

A. Kashmir stag

B. Great Indian Bustard

C. Hangul

D. Black buck

23. In India, Crocodile breeding project started for the first time in

A. Tamil Nadu B. West Bengal

C. Odisha D. Goa

24. Identify the correct sequence of materials in terms of their porosity.

A. Sand > clay > gravel

B. Clay > sand > gravel

C. Gravel > sand > clay

D. Gravel > clay > sand

25. For an aquifer of gravel having cross sectional area of 4 m^2 and a depth of 2.5 m, how much water could potentially be extracted? (The porosity and specific yield of gravel are 25% and 20% respectively.)

A. 0.5 m^3 B. 0.25 m^3

C. 0.125 m^3 D. 1 m^3

26. The layers formed by thermal stratification in lakes are

A. Epilimnion, Midlimnion, Hypolimnion

B. Epilimnion, Oligolimnion, Hypolimnion

C. Epilimnion, Dystrolimnion, Hypolimnion

D. Epilimnion, Thermocline, Hypolimnion

27. On an aerial photograph, the focal length (f) of the camera lens is 6 inches and flying height (H) over the datum line is 15,000 ft. What is scale of the aerial photograph?

A. 1 : 30,000 B. 1 : 10,000

C. 1 : 5,000 D. 1 : 25,000

28. Which of the following substrate will have highest reflectance value?

A. Silt loam with 20% moisture.

B. Clay with 36% moisture.

C. Silt loam with 0.8% moisture.

D. Clay with 2% moisture.

29. Assertion (A) : For sustainable development of a region, proper land use planning is required.

Reason (R) : Land use planning involves inputs of soil types, rock types, seismicity, weather pattern and socio-economic conditions of a region.

Codes:

A. Both (A) and (R) are true and (R) is the correct explanation of (A).

B. Both (A) and (R) are true, but (R) is not the correct explanation of (A).

C. (A) is true and (R) is false.

D. (A) is false and (R) is true.

30. Tundra is biome characterized by

A. stunted trees and permanently frozen sub-surface soil.

B. coniferous trees and permanently frozen sub-surface soil.

C. lack of trees and permanently frozen sub-surface soil.
D. evergreen trees and permanently frozen sub-surface soil.

31. Acid mine drainage occurs when
A. the combined action of O_2, H_2O and certain bacteria cause sulphur in coal to form H_2SO_4.
B. the combined action of H_2O and certain bacteria cause sulphur in coal to form H_2SO_4.
C. the combined action of O_2 and certain bacteria cause sulphur in coal to form H_2SO_4.
D. the combined action of SO_2 and certain bacteria with coal to form H_2SO_4.

32. In accordance with Saffir-Simpson hurricane scale, a cyclonic storm of category 5 should have wind speeds
A. > 69 ms^{-1} B. 50 – 58 ms^{-1}
C. 59 – 69 ms^{-1} D. 33 – 42 ms^{-1}

33. **Assertion (A) :** Large scale OTEC development may not be good for environment.
Reason (R) : Release of CO_2 from ocean depths into the atmosphere could exacerbate GHG effect.
Codes:
A. Both (A) and (R) are true and (R) is the correct explanation of (A).
B. Both (A) and (R) are true, but (R) is not the correct explanation of (A).
C. (A) is true, but (R) is false.
D. Both (A) and (R) are false.

34. In a methane fuel cell, what will be the voltage of the cell and its efficiency? (Given: $\Delta G° = 8 \times 10^5$ Joules/gm-mole $\Delta H° = 8.8 \times 10^5$ Joules/gm-mole and Faraday's constant = 96500 coulomb/gm-mole)
A. ~ 1.23 Volts, ~ 90.9%
B. ~ 1.04 Volts, ~ 90.9%
C. ~ 1.15 Volts, ~ 11%
D. ~ 2.13 Volts, ~ 92%

35. The coefficient of performance for an ideal wind mill is
A. 3/8 B. 5/16
C. 2/5 D. 16/27

36. Assume that the energy released during the combustion of methane is 900 kJ/mol. Its carbon intensity is
A. 13.3 gc/MJ B. 15.3 gc/MJ
C. 19.7 gc/MJ D. 24.2 gc/MJ

37. In a nuclear fusion reactor it is envisaged to use a liquid blanket of Li to absorb fast neutrons from D + T reaction. How many neutrons are produced as a result of ${}^7_3Li + {}^1_0n$?
A. 1 B. 2
C. 3 D. 4

38. In an ideal MHD power plant, the electrical efficiency corresponding to maximum power production is
A. 50% B. 75%
C. 25% D. 100%

39. Energy intensity is a measure of
A. effectiveness of energy utilisation
B. energy produced per unit area
C. energy produced per unit volume
D. energy produced per unit area per unit time

40. One of the criteria for characterizing a region as ABC hotspot is that the annual mean anthropogenic Aerosol Optical Depth (AOD) is greater than
A. 0.3 B. 0.5
C. 0.8 D. 0.1

41. The resultant of two noise levels of 50 dB and 55 dB is
A. 58 dB B. 55.41 dB
C. 52.5 dB D. 56.19 dB

42. Which of the following is used as a coagulant for removal of phosphates in water?
A. Aluminium sulphate
B. Iron sulphate
C. Copper sulphate
D. Potassium chromate

43. Which of the following radionuclides has the longest half-life?

A. C^{14} B. Sr^{90}
C. I^{131} D. Cs^{137}

44. Under anaerobic conditions nitrogenase catalises

A. breakdown of atmospheric nitrogen
B. oxidation of atmospheric nitrogen
C. reduction of atmospheric nitrogen
D. hydrolysis of nitrogenous compounds

45. Size range of atmospheric aerosols is

A. 5 nm – 100 µm
B. 100 µm – 150 µm
C. 150 µm – 200 µm
D. 0.01 nm – 5 nm

46. Which one of the following is used as microbial indicator of water contamination?

A. Coliform bacteria
B. Giardia
C. Cryptosporidium
D. Tobacco mosaic virus

47. Elevated salt and Na^+ concentrations in soils are highly toxic to many plants, but relatively high tolerance level (to this toxicity) is seen in

A. Sugarbeet B. Sugarcane
C. Onion D. Lettuce

48. Which of the following hydrocarbons is emitted by vegetation?

A. Ocimene B. Xylene
C. Acrolein D. 1, 3-Pentadions

49. For particles of size > 5 µm, the efficiency of cyclones can be as high as

A. 50% B. 60%
C. 80% D. 90%

50. Given the following parameters of a primary settling chamber:
Diameter = 50 m, Depth = 2.5 m, average detention time = 2 hours.
How much quantity of waste water is being treated?

A. ~ 58928 m^3/day B. ~ 48321 m^3/day
C. ~ 45321 m^3/day D. ~ 25321 m^3/day

51. A flat surface type electrostatic precipitator (ESP) has the following parameters: collector plate area A = 4600 m^2, volumetric flow rate Q = 200 m^3/s and effective drift velocity of flue gas = 0.15 m/s.
What is the efficiency of the ESP?

A. ~ 0.968 B. ~ 0.981
C. ~ 0.975 D. ~ 0.922

52. **Assertion (A) :** Cost-benefit analysis for assess-ment of natural systems is not merely concerned with the effects on environmental quality but seeks the conditions for sustainable use of the natural resources of a region.
Reason (R) : Cost-benefit analysis is not useful for small scale development projects, but is better suited for the analysis and evaluation of a regional development plan.
Identify the correct answer:
Codes:

A. Both (A) and (R) are true and (R) is the correct explanation.
B. Both (A) and (R) are true, but (R) is not the correct explanation.
C. (A) is true and (R) is wrong.
D. Both (A) and (R) are wrong.

53. Battelle-Columbus weighting – scaling checklist methodology for water-resources projects obtains base line data on how many environmental parameters?

A. 40 B. 78
C. 68 D. 50

54. Match List-I with List-II and choose the correct answer from the codes given below:

List-I	*List-II*
(*a*) Checklists methods	(*i*) Involve preparation of a set of trans-parent maps, which represent the spatial distribution of an environmental characteristics
(*b*) Overlays methods	(*ii*) Highly structured approaches involving importance weightings for factors and

		application of scaling techniques
(*c*) Adhoc methods	(*iii*)	Identification and evaluation of interactions between various activities and environmental parameters
(*d*) Matrices methods	(*iv*)	Indicate broad areas of possible impacts by listing composite environmental parameters.

Codes :

	(*a*)	(*b*)	(*c*)	(*d*)
A.	(*i*)	(*ii*)	(*iii*)	(*iv*)
B.	(*iv*)	(*ii*)	(*i*)	(*iii*)
C.	(*ii*)	(*i*)	(*iv*)	(*iii*)
D.	(*iii*)	(*iv*)	(*ii*)	(*i*)

55. Match List-I with List-II and choose the correct answer from the codes given below:

List-I (Criteria of EIA Methodology)	***List-II (Component)***
(*a*) Impact identification	(*i*) Magnitude
(*b*) Impact measurement	(*ii*) Specificity
(*c*) Impact communication	(*iii*) Depth of analysis
(*d*) Impact interpretation	(*iv*) Comprehensive overall perspective

Codes :

	(*a*)	(*b*)	(*c*)	(*d*)
A.	(*i*)	(*iv*)	(*iii*)	(*ii*)
B.	(*ii*)	(*i*)	(*iv*)	(*iii*)
C.	(*iii*)	(*iv*)	(*i*)	(*ii*)
D.	(*iv*)	(*iii*)	(*ii*)	(*i*)

56. Significant hazard/accident factor to be considered under risk assessment of distillaries are

A. toxic gas release and human accident
B. pressure wave and heat radiation
C. toxic gas release and radiation
D. pressure wave and toxic gas release

57. If 'I' is the impact of the population on the environment, 'P' is the size of the population, 'A' is the per capita affluence or consumption and 'T' is the damage caused by technologies, then which of the following equation is correct?

A. I = (P × A)/T B. I = P × A × T
C. I = T/(P × A) D. I = P/(A × T)

58. According to Environment (Protection) Act, 1986 permissible limits of oil and grease in the effluents to be discharged into public sewers is

A. 10 mg/*l* B. 20 mg/*l*
C. 25 mg/*l* D. 30 mg/*l*

59. 'Reed swamp stage' is also referred to as

A. submerged stage
B. woodland stage
C. rooted floated stage
D. amphibious stage

60. Match List-I with List-II and choose the correct answer from the given codes:

List-I (Ecosystem types)	***List-II (Characteristics)***
(*a*) Coral reefs	(*i*) Still water
(*b*) Deltas	(*ii*) Saline water
(*c*) Wetlands	(*iii*) Brackish water
(*d*) Rivers	(*iv*) Fresh water

Codes :

	(*a*)	(*b*)	(*c*)	(*d*)
A.	(*i*)	(*ii*)	(*iii*)	(*iv*)
B.	(*ii*)	(*iii*)	(*i*)	(*iv*)
C.	(*ii*)	(*i*)	(*iv*)	(*iii*)
D.	(*iii*)	(*iv*)	(*i*)	(*ii*)

61. Maximum energy content (KJ/kg) in a typical municipal solid waste is found in

A. Plastic B. Leather
C. Wood D. Textile

62. Public Liability Insurance Act was enacted in the year

A. 1991 B. 1993
C. 1995 D. 1997

63. A sample size of 17 observations is selected from a normal population with mean = 50. The sample mean and variance are 48 and 8 respectively. The value of *t*–statistic is

A. 0.25 B. –2.82
C. –2.2 D. 0.71

64. A class has equal number of boys and girls. The mean and standard deviation of their weights are $\bar{X}_g = 40$ kg, $S_g = 2$ kg for girls and $\bar{X}_b = 50$ kg, $S_b = 2$ kg for boys. What is the combined variance of the weights of the whole class?

A. 29 B. 16
C. 8 D. 19

65. For a simple regression analysis involving the dependent variable Y and explanatory variable X, the following data is given : No. of observations N = 40, $\Sigma X^2 = 2000$, $\Sigma Y^2 = 2000$, $\bar{X} = 20$, $\bar{Y} = 5$, standard error of estimate of Y on X, $S_{YX} = 4$. The explained variance is

A. 360 B. 860
C. 500 D. 580

66. A ψ^2 distribution with 10 degrees of freedom has variance

A. 10 B. 20
C. 5 D. 40

67. The rank of the matrix

$$\begin{bmatrix} 1 & 1 & 1 \\ 1 & -1 & -1 \\ 3 & 1 & 1 \end{bmatrix}$$ is

A. 2
B. 3
C. 1
D. Not possible to determine

68. Which of the following is not an eigenvector of the matrix $\begin{bmatrix} 2 & 0 \\ 0 & 5 \end{bmatrix}$?

A. $\begin{bmatrix} 1 \\ 0 \end{bmatrix}$ B. $\begin{bmatrix} 0 \\ 1 \end{bmatrix}$

C. $\begin{bmatrix} 0 \\ 2 \end{bmatrix}$ D. $\begin{bmatrix} 1 \\ 1 \end{bmatrix}$

69. Assertion (A) : Ground level concentration of pollutants decreases when taller stacks are used.

Reason (R) : The ground level concentration varies inversely proportional to the height of the stacks.

Codes:

A. Both (A) and (R) are true and (R) is the correct explanation of (A).
B. Both (A) and (R) are correct, but (R) is not the correct explanation of (A).
C. (A) is true and (R) is false.
D. Both (A) and (R) are false.

70. Assume that 5.3 billion people live in less developed countries, where average birth rate is 23 and infant mortality rate is 53. Then the total death due to infant mortality are

A. 6.5×10^6/year B. 5.3×10^6/year
C. 7.3×10^6/year D. 8.5×10^6/year

71. Which of the following act as 'natural sink for carbon'?

I. Trees II. Oceans
III. Soils

Choose the correct code:

A. I only B. I and II only
C. I, II and III D. II and III only

72. Match List-I with List-II and choose the correct answer from the codes given below:

List-I (GHGs)	***List-II (Atmospheric Lifetime) (Years)***
(*a*) CFC-12	(*i*) 12
(*b*) Methane	(*ii*) 50-200
(*c*) CO_2	(*iii*) 114
(*d*) N_2O	(*iv*) 100

Codes :

	(*a*)	(*b*)	(*c*)	(*d*)
A.	(*iii*)	(*iv*)	(*i*)	(*ii*)
B.	(*ii*)	(*iii*)	(*iv*)	(*i*)
C.	(*iv*)	(*i*)	(*ii*)	(*iii*)
D.	(*i*)	(*ii*)	(*iii*)	(*iv*)

73. REDD[+] initiatives include

I. Forest carbon partnership facility
II. Forest investment programme
III. Sanitation for all
IV. Food security for all

Choose the correct code:

A. I and IV only B. I and II only
C. I, II and III only D. III and IV only

74. Match List-I with List-II and choose the correct answer from the codes given below:

List-I (Environment Related Treaties)	***List-II (Year)***
(*a*) CITES	(*i*) 1989
(*b*) Basel	(*ii*) 1973
(*c*) UNFCCC	(*iii*) 1997
(*d*) Kyoto Protocol	(*iv*) 1992

Codes :

	(*a*)	(*b*)	(*c*)	(*d*)
A.	(*iii*)	(*ii*)	(*i*)	(*iv*)
B.	(*iv*)	(*iii*)	(*ii*)	(*i*)
C.	(*i*)	(*iv*)	(*iii*)	(*ii*)
D.	(*ii*)	(*i*)	(*iv*)	(*iii*)

75. Identify the correct sequence with reference to sensitization about environmental problems.

A. Knowledge → Awareness → Attitude → Skill → Evaluation ability → Participation

B. Knowledge → Awareness → Skill → Attitude → Participation → Evaluation ability

C. Awareness → Knowledge → Attitude → Skill → Evaluation ability → Participation

D. Awareness → Knowledge → Participation → Attitude → Skill → Evaluation ability

ANSWERS

1	2	3	4	5	6	7	8	9	10
D	B	A	B	D	D	D	B	C	B
11	**12**	**13**	**14**	**15**	**16**	**17**	**18**	**19**	**20**
A	A	B	A	B	C	B	A	A	A
21	**22**	**23**	**24**	**25**	**26**	**27**	**28**	**29**	**30**
A	B	C	B	A	D	A	C	A	C
31	**32**	**33**	**34**	**35**	**36**	**37**	**38**	**39**	**40**
A	A	A	B	D	A	B	A	A	A
41	**42**	**43**	**44**	**45**	**46**	**47**	**48**	**49**	**50**
D	A	D	C	A	A	A	A	D	A
51	**52**	**53**	**54**	**55**	**56**	**57**	**58**	**59**	**60**
A	A	B	C	B	B	B	A	D	B
61	**62**	**63**	**64**	**65**	**66**	**67**	**68**	**69**	**70**
A	A	B	A	A	B	A	D	C	A
71	**72**	**73**	**74**	**75**					
C	C	B	D	C					

Some Selected Explanatory Answers

1. The principal exception to the creation of organic matter through photosynthesis is *chemosynthesis*. In chemosynthesis, chemical reactions rather than light provide the energy to "fix" CO_2. Regardless of the energy source, however, fixation of CO_2 involves the Benson-Calvin Cycle and RUBISCO. Chemosynthesis typically results in carbon isotope fractionations similar to those of photosynthesis. Thus large carbon isotope fractionations are the signature of both photosynthesis and chemosynthesis.

6. Smog is a type of *air pollution.* Smog is a mixture of smoke and fog, hence the name (SMoke + fOG = SMOG). Victorian-era London was famous for its thick smogs, which resulted from the city's frequent, naturally occurring, heavy fogs that combined with smoke from coal fires which were used to heat homes. The main components of photochemical smog are *nitrogen oxides, Volatile Organic Compounds, (VOCs), tropospheric ozone,* and PAN *(peroxyacytyl nitrate).* All of these substances are very chemically reactive and are irritating to humans and other living things.

8. $[H_3O^+]$ in solution with pH = 1 = 10^{-1} M

$[H_3O^+]$ in solution with pH = 2 = 10^{-2} M

$$M_1V_1 + M_2V_2 = M_3V_3$$

$$10^{-1} \times 50 + 10^{-2} \times 50 = M_3 \times 100$$

$$M_3 = \frac{1}{2}[10^{-1} + 10^{-2}] = 5.5 \times 10^{-2}$$

$[H_3O^+]$ after mixting = 5.5×10^{-2}

pH = $-\log 5.5 \times 10^{-2}$ = 1.26

Hence, the choice B is correct.

10. *Sulphur-35* is used to label proteins and nucleic acids. *Cysteine* is an *amino acid* containing a *thiol* group which can be labelled by S-35. For *nucleotides* that do not contain a *sulphur* group, the oxygen on one of the phosphate groups can be substituted with a sulphur. This *thiophosphate* acts the same as a normal phosphate group, although there is a slight bias against it by most *polymerases.* The maximum theoretical specific activity is 1,494 Ci/mmol (55.28 PBq/mol).

11.

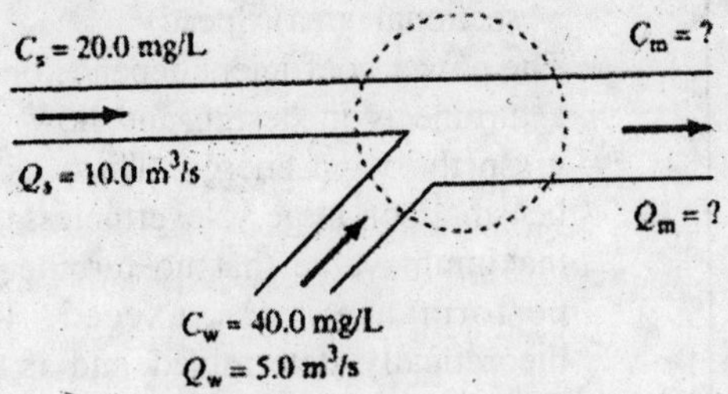

Fig.: *Flow rate and chloride concentrations for example stream and tributary.*

In problems of this sort, it is much easier simply to leave the mixed units in the expression, even though they may look awkward at first, and let them work themselves out in the calculation. The downstream concentration of chlorides is thus

$$C_m = \frac{(20.0 \times 10.0 + 40.0 \times 5.0)\text{mg/L} \cdot \text{m}^3/\text{s}}{(10.0 + 5.0)\ \text{m}^3/\text{s}}$$

$$= 26.67 \text{ mg/L}$$

14. X-ray crystallography is essentially a form of very high resolution microscopy. It enables us to visualize protein structures at the atomic level and enhances our understanding of protein function. Specifically we can study how proteins interact with other molecules, how they undergo conformational changes, and how they perform catalysis in the case of enzymes. Armed with this information we can design novel drugs that target a particular protein, or rationally engineer an enzyme for a specific industrial process.

16. Types of Lakes: Some important types of lakes are:

(*a*) **Oligotrophic** lakes which have low nutrient concentrations.

(*b*) **Eutrophic** lakes which are overnourished by nutrients like nitrogen and phosphorus, usually as a result of agricultural run-off or municipal sewage discharge. They are covered with "algal blooms", *e.g.* Dal lakes.

(*c*) **Dystrophic** lakes that have low pH, high humic acid content and brown waters, *e.g.* Bog lakes.

(*d*) **Endemic** lakes that are very ancient, deep and have endemic fauna which are restricted only to that lake, *e.g.* the Lake Baikal in Russia: the deepest lake, which is now suffering a threat due to industrial pollution.

(*e*) **Desert salt** lakes that occur in arid regions and have developed high salt concentrations as a result of high evaporation, *e.g.* great salt lake, Utah; Sambhar lake in Rajasthan.

(*f*) **Volcanic** lakes that receive water from magma after volcanic eruptions, *e.g.* many lakes in Japan. They have highly restricted biota.

(*g*) **Meromictic** lakes that are rich in salts and are permanently stratified, *e.g.* lake Nevada.

(*h*) **Artificial lakes or impoundments** that are created due to construction of dams, *e.g.* Govindsagar lake at Bhakra-Nangal.

19. Commensalism occurs when one population is benefited but the other is unaffected (+, 0). Small epiphytes such as bromeliads and orchids, which grow on the surfaces of large trees without obvious detriment to the tree, might be an example.

20. R-strategies principally operates to maximize reproductive rates in harsh, unstable environment or during habitat disturbance, while there are only a little competition exist. This R-strategies favour a "gambling" strategies.

22. Endangered Species – Endangered species are those species whose number has been reduced to a critical level. This reduction is specifically attributed to loss of natural habitat of animals. Endangered species are near extinction and may become extinct if causal factors continue operating. Among the important endangered animals are charismatic species such as the tiger, the elephant, the rhino etc. Some others include Indian wild ass, the hangul or Kashmiri stag, the Golden langoor, the Pygmy hog and a host of others. There are also endangered bird species, like the Siberian crane, the Great Indian bustard, the Florican and several birds of prey.

26. Thermal stratification can occur in lakes as well as the ocean. Lakes can be classified according to their mixing regimes. The warm, oxygenated and less dense layer above the thermocline (or metalimnion) is called the epilimnion (Fig-*b*.).

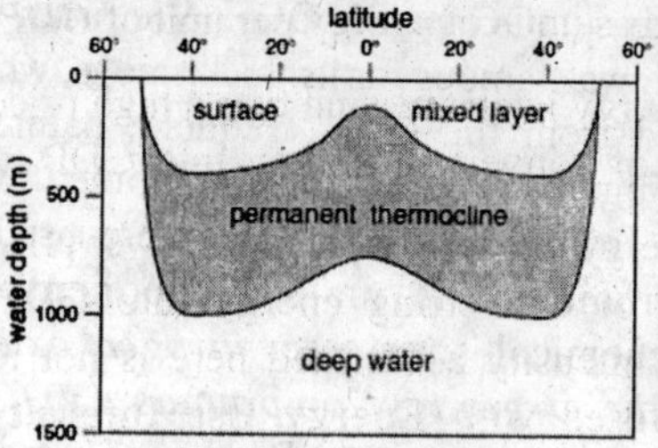

Fig. (*a*) : *Generalised thermal Stratification of the oceans.*

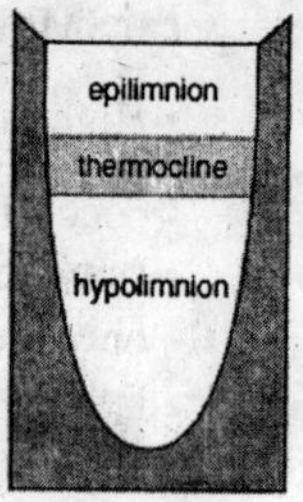

Fig. (*b*) : *Corresponding nomenclature for lakes*

The lower layer is termed the hypolimnion and contains colder denser water, which may become depleted in oxygen. Circulation within each layer is independent; it is likely to be more sluggish in the hypo-limnion because it is not affected by wind action.

30. Tundra is the coldest of all the biomes. Tundra comes from the Finnish word **tunturia**, meaning treeless plain. It is noted for its frost-molded landscapes, extremely low temperatures, little precipitation, poor nutrients, and short growing seasons. Dead organic material functions as a nutrient pool. The two major nutrients are nitrogen and phosphorus. Nitrogen is created by biological fixation, and phosphorus is created by precipitation.

35. Power of a wind turbine

= (A coefficient) (Power in the wind)

This coefficient must, obviously, be smaller than 1. It is called **power coefficient.**

Wind turbine power

= ½(Power coefficient) (Density) (Cross-sectional area)(Speed)^3

The power coefficient depends on how good a turbine is in design and how well it can grasp the wind energy. Thus, its value can be small or large. Nevertheless, there is a maximum value that no turbine in its best performance can exceed. It can be theoretically determined and is called the **Betz limit**.

The value for ***Betz limit*** is 16/27 = 0.59.

39. Energy intensity is a *measure* of the *energy efficiency* of a nation's *economy*. It is calculated as units of *energy* per unit of *GDP*.

- High energy intensities indicate a high price or cost of converting energy into GDP.
- Low energy intensity indicates a lower price or cost of converting energy into GDP. Energy intensity as defined here is not to be confused with **Energy Use Intensity** (EUI), a measure of building energy use per unit area.

42. Aluminium sulphate is used in water purification for removal of phosphate and of colloidal matter, for the coagulation of which the high charge on the cation is very effective. Aluminium in food, however, is suspected of causing Alzheimer's disease.

44. $N_2 + 6H^+ + 6e^- \rightarrow 2HN_3$

$12ATP \rightleftharpoons 12(ADP + Pi)$

Nitrogenase catalyzes proton reduction in the absence of nitrogen gas.

46. Coliform bacteria are the natural part of the microbial flora of the intestinal tract of warm-blooded mammals, including man. Coliform bacteria can also be found in soil, vegetation and other animals. The coliform group is relatively easy to culture in the lab and therefore, has been selected as primary indicator bacteria for the presence of disease causing organism. Coliform bacteria are normally non-pathogenic organisms and are only mildly infectious. For this reason these bacteria are relatively safe to work with in the laboratory. If large number of coliform is found in water, there is a high probability of presence of other pathogenic viruses, bacteria, protozoa and helminthes.

48. Ocimene hydrocarbons is emitted by vegetation.

57. I = PAT is the lettering of a formula put forward to describe the impact of human activity on the environment.

$I = P \times A \times T$

In words:

Human Impact (I) on the environment equals the product of P = Population, A = Affluence, T = Technology. This describes how our growing population, affluence, and technology contribute toward our environmental impact.

59. Reed-swamp stage. This stage is also known as **amphibious** stage as the plants of community are rooted but most parts of their shoots (assimilatory organs) remain exposed to air. Species of *Scirpus, Typha, Sagittaria* and *Phragmites* etc. are the chief plants of this stage. They have well-developed rhizomes and form a very dense vegetation. The water level is by now very much reduced and finally becomes unsuitable for the growth of these amphibious species.

62. The Public Liability Insurance Act, 1991– This law has been enacted to provide for public liability insurance for the purpose of providing immediate relief to the persons affected by accident occurring while handling any hazardous substance and the matters connected therewith or incidental there to. The act came into force with effect from the 1 April 1991. The main rules under this act were notified on the 1 May 1991, and other notifications under various provisions of the Act have also been issued.

63. $t\text{-statistic} = \dfrac{\bar{X} - \mu}{\sigma / \sqrt{n}}$

$$= \frac{48 - 50}{\sqrt{8}/\sqrt{17}} = \frac{-2\sqrt{17}}{2\sqrt{2}} \cong -2.82$$

64.

	Boys	**Girls**
Number :	n	n
Mean Wts :	50 kg	40 kg
Standard deviation :	2 kg	2 kg
Variance :	4 kg	4 kg

Combined variance

$$\sigma_{12}^2 = \frac{N_1\sigma_1^2 + N_1 d_1^2 + N_2\sigma_2^2 + N_2 d_2^2}{N_1 + N_2}$$

Here, $N_1 = N_2 = n$, $\sigma_1 = \sigma_b = 4$, $\sigma_2 = \sigma_g = 4$

To find the value of d_1 and d_2 we will calculate combined mean of the boys and girls

$$a_{12} = \frac{N_1 d_1 + N_2 d_2}{N_1 + N_2} = \frac{(50+40)n}{2n} = 45 \text{ kg}$$

$$d_1 = 50 - 45 = 5 \text{ kg}$$
$$d_2 = 40 - 45 = -5 \text{ kg}$$

Substituting the values in the above formula we get:

$$\sigma_{12}^2 = \frac{4n + 25n + 4n + 25n}{2n}$$

$$= \frac{58}{2} = 29.$$

67. $$\begin{bmatrix} 1 & 1 & 1 \\ 1 & -1 & -1 \\ 3 & 1 & 1 \end{bmatrix} = \frac{1}{2}\begin{bmatrix} 2 & 2 & 2 \\ 1 & -1 & -1 \\ 3 & 1 & 1 \end{bmatrix} \{R_1 \to 2R_1\}$$

$$= \begin{bmatrix} 3 & 1 & 1 \\ 1 & -1 & -1 \\ 3 & 1 & 1 \end{bmatrix} \{R_1 \to R_1 + R_2\}$$

68. Given matrix $= \begin{bmatrix} 2 & 0 \\ 0 & 5 \end{bmatrix}$

Eigen values $= \begin{bmatrix} 2-\lambda & 0 \\ 0 & 5-\lambda \end{bmatrix} = 0$

$$= (2-\lambda)(5-\lambda) = 0$$

$\therefore \quad \lambda = 2, 5$

Eigen vector for $\lambda = 2$

$$= \begin{bmatrix} 2-2 & 0 \\ 0 & 5-2 \end{bmatrix} \begin{bmatrix} x_1 \\ x_2 \end{bmatrix} = \begin{bmatrix} 0 \\ 0 \end{bmatrix}$$

$$= \begin{bmatrix} 0 & 0 \\ 0 & 3 \end{bmatrix} \begin{bmatrix} x_1 \\ x_2 \end{bmatrix} = \begin{bmatrix} 0 \\ 0 \end{bmatrix}$$

so, eigen vector would be $\begin{bmatrix} 0 \\ 1 \end{bmatrix}$ or $\begin{bmatrix} 0 \\ 2 \end{bmatrix}$

again, eigen vector for $\lambda = 5$

$$= \begin{bmatrix} 2-5 & 0 \\ 0 & 5-5 \end{bmatrix} \begin{bmatrix} x_1 \\ x_2 \end{bmatrix} = \begin{bmatrix} 0 \\ 0 \end{bmatrix}$$

$$= \begin{bmatrix} -3 & 0 \\ 0 & 0 \end{bmatrix} \begin{bmatrix} x_1 \\ x_2 \end{bmatrix} = \begin{bmatrix} 0 \\ 0 \end{bmatrix}$$

$\therefore$ eigen vector would be $\begin{bmatrix} 1 \\ 0 \end{bmatrix}$

$$= \frac{1}{2}\begin{bmatrix} 0 & 0 & 0 \\ 1 & -1 & -1 \\ 3 & 1 & 1 \end{bmatrix} \{R_1 \to R_1 - R_3\}$$

Hence, Rank of the given matrix is 2.

70. Population of the developed countries = 5.3 billion

Average birth rate = 23%

and Infant mortality rate = 53%

So, total death due to infant mortality

$$= 5.3 \times 10^7 \times \frac{23}{100} \times \frac{53}{100}$$

$$= 6.46 \times 10^6 \cong 6.5 \times 10^6/\text{year}.$$

74.

Agreement type and name	*Date adopted*	*Secretariat*
Atmosphere Conventions:		
United Nations Framework Convention on Climate Change (UNFCCC)	1992	UN
Kyoto Protocol to the United Nations Framework Convention on Climate Change	1997	UN
Convention on International Trade in Endangered Species (CITES)	1973	UNEP
Basel Convention on the Control of Transboundary Movements of Hazardous Wastes and their Disposal	1989	UNEP

Previous Paper (Solved)

UGC-NET ENVIRONMENTAL SCIENCE DECEMBER 2013

PAPER-II

Note : *This paper contains* ***fifty (50)*** *objective type questions, each question carrying* ***two (2)*** *marks. All questions are compulsory.*

1. Mesoscale Meteorological Phenomena occur over areas of horizontal distance in the range (km)

A. 100 – 200 km B. 1 – 100 km
C. 10 – 50 km D. 1 – 10 km

2. The Indian monsoon period is from

A. October to November
B. December to February
C. June to September
D. March to May

3. Which of the following is not a reactive oxygen species?

A. Hydrogen peroxide
B. Hydroxyl ion
C. Singlet oxygen
D. Superoxide anion

4. If air quality standard for carbon monoxide is 9.0 ppmV, the percentage as in mg/m^3 at 1 atm. at 25°C is

A. 10.3 mg/m^3 B. 15.2 mg/m^3
C. 20.0 mg/m^3 D. 5.6 mg/m^3

5. Azaridine, Ethylene dibromide, Bis (chloromethyl) ether are

A. Alkylating agents
B. Hydrocarbons
C. Hydrazines
D. Aromatic amines

6. Normality of 0.25 M phosphoric acid is

A. 0.25 B. 0.50
C. 0.75 D. 2.50

7. Match List–I with List–II and choose the correct answer from the codes given below :

List–I **(Air Pollutants)**	*List–II* **(Sources / Activities)**
(*a*) Carbon monoxide	1. Coal burning
(*b*) Nitrogen oxide	2. Cigarette Smoking
(*c*) Sulphur dioxide	3. Chemical reaction with VOCs
(*d*) Ozone	4. Power and Industrial Plant

Codes :

	(*a*)	(*b*)	(*c*)	(*d*)
A.	2	4	1	3
B.	1	2	3	4
C.	3	1	4	2
D.	4	3	2	1

8. The gaseous material which is used for the synthesis of Methyl isocyanate is

A. Chloranil B. Sevin
C. Phosgene D. Chlorine

9. During the determination of COD, sulphanilic acid is added, because

A. it maintains the acidic nature
B. it precipitates the mercury ions
C. it oxidises nitrites to nitrates
D. it reacts with ferrous ammonium sulphate

10. Which year was declared as International Year of Biodiversity?

A. 2002 B. 2010
C. 2020 D. 1972

11. The forest biome characterised by 3-4 tree species/km^2 is

A. Tropical B. Temperate
C. Boreal D. Taiga

12. Which of the following is a type of biodiversity extinction caused primarily due to anthropogenic activities?

A. Carboniferous rain forest collapse
B. Permian — Triassic extinction
C. Cretaceous paleogene extinction
D. Holocene extinction

13. The chemical used in a fermenter with molasses as a substrate is

A. Diammonium sulphate
B. Diammonium phosphate
C. Diammonium nitrate
D. Diammonium chloride

14. Which of the following is an example of lotic ecosystem?

A. Stream ecosystem
B. Pond ecosystem
C. Bog ecosystem
D. Wetland ecosystem

15. Which pyramid is always straight?

A. Pyramid of biomass
B. Pyramid of number
C. Pyramid of energy
D. Pyramid of number and biomass

16. Which of the following type of materials present in a landslide suggest that the movement was rotational?

A. Rockflow, Debris flow, Earthflow
B. Rock slump, Debris slump, Earth slump
C. Rockfall, Debris fall, Earth fall
D. Rock topple, Debris topple, Earth topple

17. Which of the following parameters is not a good indicator of contamination in ground water?

A. BOD
B. Nitrates
C. Silica
D. Chlorides

18. On an aerial photograph, the distance between the principal point and the conjugate principal point is called

A. Relief
B. Tilt
C. Photo-base
D. Focal length

19. An equatorial west to east remote sensing satellite orbiting the earth at an altitude of 36,000 km is called

A. Sun-synchronous satellite
B. Geostationary satellite
C. Space shuttle
D. Stereo imager

20. Which state of Cr (Chromium) is most toxic?

A. Cr^{4+} B. Cr^{3+}
C. Cr^{5+} D. Cr^{6+}

21. **Assertion (A) :** Groundwater may get seriously contaminated in coastal areas.

Reason (R) : Groundwater overdrafts near coastal areas can contaminate groundwater supplies by allowing salt water to intrude into freshwater aquifers.

Codes :

A. Both (A) and (R) are true and (R) is the correct explanation of (A).
B. Both (A) and (R) are true, but (R) is not the correct explanation of (A).
C. (A) is true and (R) is false.
D. (A) is false and (R) is true.

22. **Assertion (A) :** Tropical and subtropical seas are most suitable for OTEC.

Reason (R) : There is a certain minimum vertical gradient (> 25°C/km) required for OTEC to become feasible.

Codes :

A. Both (A) and (R) are true and (R) is the correct explanation of (A).
B. Both (A) and (R) are true, but (R) is not the correct explanation of (A).
C. (A) is true, but (R) is false.
D. (A) is false, but (R) is true.

23. On burning a certain amount of fuel a total of 500 million tonnes of CO_2 is released to the atmosphere. If the entire amount of CO_2 remains in the atmosphere, what will be the rise in the concentration of CO_2 in ppm?

A. ~ 0.236 ppm B. ~ 0.128 ppm
C. ~ 2.312 ppm D. ~ 1.216 ppm

24. A thermal power station has a heat rate of 12 mJ/kWh. Its thermal efficiency is

A. 30% B. 36%
C. 40% D. 25%

25. Assume that world coal production is 6.1 billion tons per year and estimated total recoverable resources of coal is 1.1 trillion tons. How long it would take to use up those reserves at current rate of production?

A. ~ 180 years B. ~ 150 years
C. ~ 120 years D. ~ 90 years

26. In a salt gradient solar pond, the salinity generally varies from top to bottom of the pond as

A. < 5% to ~ 20%
B. ~ 10% to ~ 30%
C. ~ 20% to ~ 35%
D. ~ 20% to ~ 40%

27. Which region among the following is not Atmospheric Brown Cloud (ABC) hotspot?

A. East-Asia
B. South Africa
C. Amazon Basin in South America
D. Australia

28. Prolonged exposure to high levels of noise causes

(*i*) Hearing loss
(*ii*) Constriction of blood vessels
(*iii*) Gastric ulcers
(*iv*) Toxicity

Identify the correct answer :

A. (*i*), (*ii*) and (*iv*) only
B. (*i*), (*iii*) and (*iv*) only
C. (*i*), (*ii*) and (*iii*) only
D. (*i*), (*ii*), (*iii*) and (*iv*)

29. *Azolla pinnata* is a

A. Blue green algae B. Green algae
C. Red algae D. Fern

30. Assertion (A) : Eruption of the volcano Mt. Pinatobu in 1991 spewed sulphur clouds into the upper reaches of the atmosphere. The following three years were cooler.

Reason (R) : Sulphate aerosols reflect sunlight away from the Earth.

Codes :

A. Both (A) and (R) are correct and (R) is the correct explanation of (A).
B. Both (A) and (R) are correct and (R) is not the correct explanation of (A).
C. (A) is correct (R) is incorrect.
D. Both (A) and (R) are incorrect.

31. Photolysis of NO_2 occurs due to radiations of wavelength

A. < 600 nm
B. < 550 nm
C. < 480 nm
D. < 390 nm

32. The efficiency of removing SO_2 from the flue gas by limestone in wet scrubbers can be as high as

A. 30%
B. 50%
C. 70%
D. 90%

33. The depth of the oxidation ponds is typically

A. 1–2 m B. 2–5 m
C. 5–10 m D. 10–20 m

34. In EIA the baseline data describes

A. The environmental consequences by mapping
B. Existing environmental status of the identified study area
C. Assessment of risk on the basis of proposal
D. Demographic and socioeconomic data

35. Which one of the following does not belong to EIA methods used for assessing the impacts of developmental activities on the environment?

A. Checklist B. Adhoc
C. Network D. Flexible

36. The EIA report of a hydropower project would be valid upto how many years after the environmental clearance of the project?

A. 5 years B. 6 years
C. 30 years D. 10 years

37. If in the screening stage of EIA, the impact level of a developmental project is not discernible, then what step should be adopted?

A. Scoping stage is to be followed.
B. A rapid EIA study is to be co[illegible]
C. Detail EIA study is to be [illegible]
D. The project shoul[illegible] Environmental Clear[illegible]

38. The Committee which reviews the Environmental Impact Assessment and Environmental Management plan reports of a developmental project in Ministry of Environment and Forest is called

A. Project Assessment Committee
B. Project Appraisal Committee
C. Project Evaluation Committee
D. Project Estimate Committee

39. In a typical municipal solid waste, least percentage of Ash is found in

A. Textiles B. Plastic
C. Leather D. Rubber

40. Highly inflammable liquid/chemicals have flash point

A. lower than 23°C
B. between 23 and 26°C
C. between 27 and 31°C
D. between 32 and 40°C

41. Which one of the following does not contribute to climate change?

A. NO B. O_3
C. SF_6 D. HFCs

42. A population (X) in an ecosystem follows logistic growth curve. If the carrying capacity of the system is K, the growth realisation factor is

A. $\frac{K-X}{X}$ B. $\frac{K-X}{K}$

C. $\frac{K-X}{K^2}$ D. (K – X)

43. Which one of the following conditions would indicate that the dataset is **not** bell shaped?

A. The mean is much smaller than median
B. The range is equal to five times the standard deviation.
C. The range is larger than interquartile range.
D. The range is twice the standard deviation.

44. For degrees of freedom (*df*) > 1, the mean (μ) of the *t*-distribution is

A. Zero B. 1
C. depends on *df* D. 2

45. Which of the following is an eigen value of the matrix $\begin{bmatrix} 3 & -1 \\ 4 & -2 \end{bmatrix}$?

A. 2 B. 0
C. 1 D. 3

46. Suppose a 70 kg person drinks 2L of water everyday for 70 years with a chloroform concentration of 0.10 mg/L (the drinking water standard), upper bound cancer risk for these individual will be

A. 17 in 1 million B. 25 in 1 million
C. 37 in 1 million D. 5 in 1 million

47. What is Ecomark?

A. Label given to recycled products
B. Label given to an environment friendly products
C. Land mark indicating the boundaries of bioparks
D. Label given to non-recyclable products

48. An important source of Arsenic in Municipal Solid Water (MSW) is

A. Pigments in plastics
B. Rubber products
C. Batteries
D. Household pesticides

49. Which of the following is **not** a nonformal Environment Education and Awareness Programme?

A. Global Learning and Observations to Benefit the Environment (GLOBE)
B. National Environment Awareness Campaign (NEAC)
C. Eco-clubs
D. Environmental Education in School System

50. REDD stands for

A. Recurring Emission from Deforestation and Forest Degradation
B. Reducing Environmental Degradation and Forest Degradation
C. Reducing Emissions from Deforestation and Forest Degradation
D. Reducing Emissions from Degradable Deposits of Wastes

ANSWERS

1	2	3	4	5	6	7	8	9	10
B	C	B	A	A	C	A	C	C	B
11	**12**	**13**	**14**	**15**	**16**	**17**	**18**	**19**	**20**
B	D	B	A	C	B	C	C	B	D
21	**22**	**23**	**24**	**25**	**26**	**27**	**28**	**29**	**30**
A	A	A	A	A	A	D	C	D	A
31	**32**	**33**	**34**	**35**	**36**	**37**	**38**	**39**	**40**
D	D	A	B	D	D	B	B	A	A
41	**42**	**43**	**44**	**45**	**46**	**47**	**48**	**49**	**50**
A	B	A	A	A	A	B	D	D	C

SOME SELECTED EXPLANATORY ANSWERS

1. Mesoscale metrology is the study of weather system smaller than synoptic scale systems but larger than microscale and strom scale cumulus systems. Horizontal dimension generally range from around 1–100 km. Example of mesoscale weather systems are seabreezes, squallines and mesoscale convective complexes.

2. The Indian monsoon period is from June to September. Monsoon is traditionally defined as a seasonal reversing wind accompanied by corresponding changes in precipitation, but is now used to describe seasonal changes in atmosphere circulation and precipitation associated with the asymmetric heating of land and sea.

3. Reactive oxygen species (ROS) are chemically reactive moleculus containing oxygen, Examples include oxygen ions and peroxides. ROS are formed as a natural by product of the normal metabolism of oxygen and have important roles in cell signaling and homeostasis. However, during times of environment stress (*e.g.*, UV or heat exposure), ROS levels can increase dramatically. This may result in significant demage to cell structures. Cumulatively, this is known as oxidative stress. ROS are also generated by exogenous sources such as ionizing, radiation.

Damaging Effects : Normally, cells defend themselves against ROS damage with enzymes such as alpha-1 microglobulin, superoxide dismutases, catalases, lactoperoxidases, glutathioxins. Small molecule antioxidants such as ascorbic acid (Vitamin C), tocopherol (Vitamin E), uric acid glutathione also play important roles as cellular antioxidants. In a similar manner, polyphenol antioxidants assist in preventing ROS damage by scavenging free radicals. In contrast, the antioxidant ability of the extra cellular space is less, *e.g.*, the most important plasma antioxidant in humans is uric acid.

Effects of ROS on cell metabolism are well documented in a variety of species. These include not only roles in apoptosis (programmed cell death) but also positive effects such as the induction of host defence genes and mobilisation of ion transport systems. This implicates them in control of cellular function. In particular, platelets involved in wound repair and blood homeostasis release ROS to recruit additional platelets to sites of injury. These also provide a link to the adaptive immune system via the recruitment of leukocytes.

Reactive oxygen species are implicated in cellular activity to a variety of inflammatory responses including cardiovascular disease. They may also be involved in hearing impairment via cochlear damage induced by elevated sound levels in ototoxicity of drugs such as cisplatin and in congenital deafness in both animals and humans. ROS are also implicated in meditation of apoptosis or programmed cell death and ischaemic injury. Specific examples include stroke and heart attack.

In general, harmful effects of reactive oxygen species on the cell are most often.

1. Damage of DNA
2. Oxidations of polyunstaurated fatty acids in lipids.
3. Oxidations of amino acids in proteins.
4. Oxidatively inactivate specific enzymes by oxidation of co-factors.

10. The UN-declared 2010 as international year of Biodiversity.

Biodiversity plays a vital role in human sciences, culture and its diversity, education and communication, contributes in a multidisciplinary way to taking the root causes of biodiversity erosion and loss due to unsustainable development. During the year, UNESCO has lead several activities which aimed to educate and to raise public awareness on the reasons for conserning biodiversity and to catalyte further international action for its sustainable use.

11. Temperate Forest : Temperate forest occurs in eastern North America, north-eastern Asia, and Western and Central Europe well defined seasons with a distinct winter characterize this forest biome. Moderate climate and a growing season of 140-200 days during 4-6 forst-trees months distinguish temperate forests.

- Temperature varies from –30°C to 30°C.
- Precipitation (75-150 cm) is distributed evenly throughout the year.
- Soil is fertile, enriched with decaying litter.
- Canopy is moderately dense and allows light to penetrate, resulting in well-developed and richly diversified understory vegetation and stratification of animals.
- Flora is characterized by 3-4 tree species per square kilometre (3-4 tree species/km^2) Trees are distinguished by broad leaves that are lost annually and include such species as oak, hickory, beech, hemlock, maple, basswood, cottonwood, elm, willow, and spring-flowering herbs.
- Fauna is represented by squirrels, rabbits, skunks, birds, deer, mountain black lion, bobeat, timber wolf, fox and bear.

  Further sub-divisions of this groups are determined by seasonal distribution of rainfall.
- Moist conifer and evergreen broad-leave forests : Wet winters and dry summers (rainfall is concentrated in the winter months and winters are relatively mild).
- Dry conifer forests : Dominate higher elevation zones; low precipitation.
- Mediterraneam forests : Precipitation is concentrated in winter, less than 100 cm per year.
- Temperate coniferous : Mild winters high annual precipitation (greater than 200 cm).
- Temperate broad-leaved rainforests : Mild, frost-free winters, high precipitation (more than 150 cm) evenly distributed throughout the year.

Only scattered remnants of original temperate forests remain.

12. Holocene extiction : The Holocene extinction, sometimes called the sixth Extinction, is name proposed to describe the extinction event of species that has occurred during the present Holocene epoch (since around 10,000 BC). The large number of extinctions span numerous families of plants and animals including mammals, birds, amphibians, reptiles and arthropods. Although 875 extinctions occurring between 1500 and 2009 have been documented by International union for conservation of Nature and Natural Resources, the vast majority are undocumented. According to the species-area theory and based on upper-bound estimating, the present rate of extinction may be up to 140,000 species per year.

The Holocene extinction includes the disappearance of large mammals known as megafauna, starting between 9,000 and 13,000 years ago, the end of the last Ice Age. This may have been due to the extinction of the mammoth that had maintained grasslands that became brich forests without the mammoths. The new forest and the resulting forest fires may have induced climate change. Such disappearances might be the result of the proliferation of modern humans which led to climate change. These extinctions, occurring near the Pleistocene-Holocene boundry are sometimes referred to as the quaternary extinction event. The Holocene extinction continuous into the 21st century.

There is no general agreement on whether to consider this as merely part of the quaternary extinction event, or just a result of human caused changes. Only during these most recent parts of the extinction can be characterized by humanity's presence.

13. Diammonium Phosphate (DAP) (chemical formula $(NH_4)_2HPO_4$, IUPAC name diammonium hydrogen phosphate) is a series of water-soluble ammonium phosphate salts that can be produced when ammonia reacts with phosphoric acid. Solid diammonium phosphate shows a dissociation pressure of ammonia as given by the following expression and equation,

$(NH_4)_2\ HPO_4(s)\ NH_3(g) + NH_4H_2\ PO_4(s)$

log P mmHg = 3063/T + 175 log

T + 3.3

Where, P = the resultant dissociation pressure of ammonia

T = absolute temperature (K)

At 100°C, the dissociation pressure of diammonium phosphate is approximately 5 mmHg.

Uses : DAP is used as a fertilizer. When applied as plant food, it temporally increases the soil pH, but over a long term the treated ground becomes more acidic than before upon nitrification of the ammonium. It is incomplete with alkaline chemical because its ammonium ion is more likely to convert to ammonia in a high pH environment. The average pH in solution in 7.5–8. The typical formulation is 18–46–0 (18% N, 46% P_2O_5, 0% K_2O).

DAP can be used as a fire retardant. It lowers the combustion temperature of the national, decreases maximum weight loss rates and causes an increase in the production of residue or char. These are important effects in fighting wildfiers as lowering the pyrolysis temperature and increasing the amount of char formed reduces that amount of available fuel and can lead to the formation of a firebreak. It is the largest component of some popular commercial firefighting products.

DAP is also used as a yeast nutrient in wine making and brecuing mead; as an addtive in some brands of cigarettes purportedly as a nicotine enhancer; to prevent afterglow in matches, in purifying sugar; as a flux for soldering tin, copper, zinc and brass; and to control precipitation of alkali-soluble and acid-insoluble colloidal dyes on wool.

15. "Pyramid of Energy is a graphic representation of the amount of energy trapped per unit time and area in different trophic level of a food chain with producers forming the base and the top carnivors at the tip."

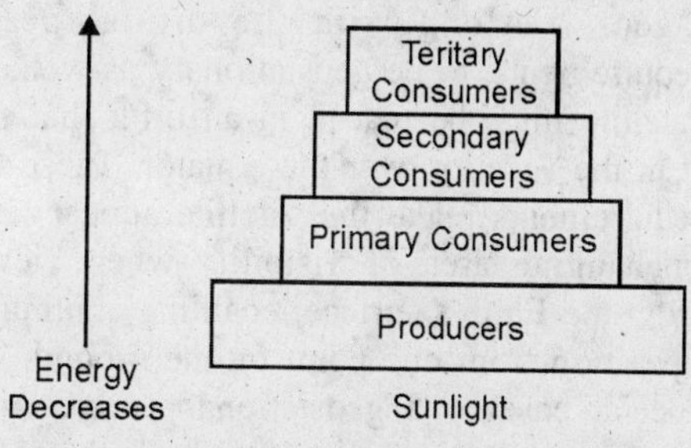

Representation of Pyramid of Energy

Pyramid of energy is always upright. It is so because at each transfer about 80-90% of the energy available at lower trophic level is used upto overcome its entrophy and to perform metabolic activities. Only 10% of the energy is available to next tropic level (as per lindermann's ten per cent rule).

19. A Geostationary satellite is a satellite in geosynchronous orbit, with an orbital period the same as the Earth's rotation period. Such a Satellite returns to the same position in the sky after each sidereal day and over the course of a day traces out a path in the sky that is typically some form of analemma. A special case of geosynchronous satellite is the geo stationary satellite, which has a geostationary orbit a circular geosynchronous orbit directly above the Earth's equator. Another type of geosynchronous orbit used by satellites is the Tundra elliptical orbit.

Geosynchronous satellites have the advantage of remaining permanently in the same area of the sky, as viewed from a particular location on Earth, and so permanently within view of a given ground station. Geostationary satellites have the special property of remaining permanently fixed in exactly the same position in the sky, meaning that ground based anternnas do not need to track them but can remain fixed in one direction. Such satellite are often used for communication purposes; a geosynchronous network is a communication network based on communication with or through geosynchronous satellites.

Definition : The term "geosynchronous" refers to the satellite's orbital period being exactly one sidereal day which enables it to be synchronized with the rotation of the Earth ('geo-'). Along with the orbital period requirements, to be geostationary as well, the satellite must be placed in an orbit that puts it in the vicinity over the equator. These two requirements make the satellite appear in an unchanging area of visibility when viewed from the Earth's surface, enabling continuous operation from one point on the ground. The special case of a geostationary orbit is the most common type of orbit for communications satellites. If a geosynchronous satellite's orbit is not exactly aligned with the Earth's equator, the orbit is known as an inclined orbit. It will appear (when viewed by someone on the ground). As the angle between the orbit and the equator decreases, the magnitude of this oscillation becomes smaller; when the orbit lies entirely over the equator in circular orbit, the satellite remains stationary relative to the Earth's surface. it is said be geostationary.

20. Chromium is a hard steel-gray metal that is highly resistant to oxidation, even at high temperatures. It is the sixth most abundant element in the earth's crust, where it is combined with iron and oxygen in the form of chromite ore.

Chromium is used in three basic industries:

- Metallurgical,
- Chemical, and
- Refractory (heat-resistant applications)

Chromium exists in series of oxidation states from –2 to +6 valence. The most important stable states are O (elemental metal), +3 (trivalent), and +6 (hexavalent). Chromium in chromite ore is in the trivalent state; industrial processes also produce the elemental metal and hexavalent chromium.

Cr^{6+} is generally considered 1,000 times more toxic than Cr^{3+}.

Cr^{3+} is an essential dietary mineral in low doses. Cr^{6+} compounds are carcinogenic.

Therefore Cr^{6+} state of Cr (chromium) is most toxic.

21. Ground water is get seriously contaminated in coastal areas. It overdrafts near the coastal areas can contaminated ground water supplies by allowing salt water to introduce into freshwater aquifers. Hence, both (A) and (R) are true and R is correct explanations of A.

22. Ocean thermal energy conversion (OTEC) uses the temperature difference between cooler and warmer shallow or surface ocean waterstorum a heat engine and produced a useful work. In ocean, the temperature difference between surface and deep water is greatest in the tropics, although still a modest 20 to 25°C. In OTEC, the tropical and subtropical seas are most suitable and there is minimum vertical gradient >25°C/km required for OTEC to become feasible.

27. Atmospheric Brown Cloud (ABC) hotspot observe as widespread layers of browish haze, regional scale plumes of air pollutants, consisting of many aerosol particles, such as black carbon (BC), and precursor gases which produce aerosols and ozone. ABCs and their interaction with buildup of greenhouse gases significantly effect, the regional climate, hydrological cycle, glacial melting, agriculture and human health.

Atmospheric Brown Cloud (ABC) hotspot regions are :

• East Asia (Eastern China, Thiland, Vietname, Combodia), • Indonesian region, • South Africa extending southerwords from Sub-Saharan Africa into Angola, Zambia and Zimbabwe, the American basin in South America.

29. Azolla pinnata is a species of fern known by several common names including feathered mosquitofern and water velvet. It is native to much of Africa, Asia from China to Japan, India and the Phillippines, and parts of Australia. It is an aquatic plant, its frond floating upon the surface of the water. It grows in quiet and slow-moving water bodies, because swift currents and waves break up the plant. This is a with a triangular frond measuring up to 2.5 centimeters in length which floats on the water. The frond is made up of many rounded or angular ovelapping leaves each 1 or 2 millimeters long. They are green, blue-green or dark red in colour and coated in tiny hairs, giving them a velvety appearance. The hairs make the top surface of the leaf water-repellent, keeping the plant afloat even after being pushed under. A water body may be coated in a dense layer of the plants, which form a velvety mat that crowds out other plants. The hairlike roots extend out into the water. The leaves contain the cyanobacterium Anabaena azolle, which is a symbiont that fixes nitrogen from the atmosphere that the fern can use.

This gives the fern the ability to grow in habitats that are low in nitrogon. The plant reproduces vegetatively when branches break off the main axis, or sexually when sporocarps on the leaves release spores.

It is present in New Zealand as an introduced species and an invasive weed that has crowded out a native relative, Azolla rubra. Therefore Azolla pinnata is a fern.

30. In 1991, the erruption of the Vocano Mt. Pinatobu spewed sulphur(s) clouds into the upper atmospheres. The sulphate aerosols reflect light of the sun away from the surface of the earth. Therefore, both the statements are true and farmer is correct explanation of later.

45. $\begin{vmatrix} 3 & -1 \\ 4 & -2 \end{vmatrix}$

We know that the eigenvalue are the roots of equation, then characterstic equations

$$\begin{vmatrix} 3-\lambda & -1 \\ 4 & -2-\lambda \end{vmatrix}$$

Solving this, we get the result $\lambda = 2$.

47. Ecomark or Eco mark is a certification mark issued by the Bureau of Indian Standards (The National Standards Organisation of India) to products conforming to a set of Standards aimed at the least impact on ecosystem. The marking scheme was started in 1991. One of the purposes of the mark inereasing awareness among the consumers towards reducing environment impact. The mark is issued to various product categories and the development of standards for more products is in progress.

Eco-mark Pre-Inked Stamps : Produced using the most environmently friendly manufacturing methods, eco-mark offers the quality you expect at a price that fits your budget. Eco-mark is a pre-inked stamp with a self-inker 'look' without the messy ink pads or noise of a conventional self-inker. The new wrap around lens cover gives you ideal space to advertise your company information. Several private label options are available. Therefore, Label given to an invironmental friendly products.

50. **REDD** involves some kind of incentive for changing are used. As such, it offers a new way of curbing CO_2 emission through paying for actions that prevent forest loss or degradation. These transfer mechanisms can include carbon trading, or paying for forest management. It stands for reducing emissions from Deforestation and forest Degration.

PAPER-III

Note : This paper contains ***seventy five (75)*** *objective type questions of* ***two (2)*** *marks each.* ***All*** *questions are compulsory.*

1. For an overcast day or night, the atmosphere is

A. stable B. neutral

C. slightly stable D. unstable

2. Assertion (A) : The energy flow in an ecosystem follows the law of thermodynamics.

Reason (R) : The energy flow in an ecosystem is unidirectional and during the transformation of energy from one trophic level to the other, 80–90% of energy is lost.

Codes :

A. Both (A) and (R) are true and (R) is the correct explanation of (A).

B. Both (A) and (R) are true, but (R) is not the correct explanation of (A).

C. (A) is true, but (R) is false.

D. (A) is false, but (R) is true.

3. Match the List–I with List–II and identify the correct answer from the given codes :

List–I **(Thermodynamic Variables) (Symbols have their usual meanings.)**	***List–II*** **(Expression)**
(*a*) ΔG	1. $\Delta E + P\Delta V$
(*b*) ΔG°	2. $-n\,FE^\circ$
(*c*) ΔS	3. $RT\ln\frac{V_1}{V_2}$
(*d*) ΔH	4. $nR\ln\frac{V_2}{V_1}$

Codes :

	(*a*)	(*b*)	(*c*)	(*d*)
A.	2	4	1	3
B.	3	2	4	1
C.	3	1	4	2
D.	2	3	4	1

4. The environmental lapse rate during day time is governed by

(*i*) Wind speed

(*ii*) Sunlight

(*iii*) Topographical features

(*iv*) Cloud cover

The correct answer is

A. (*i*) and (*ii*) only

B. (*ii*) and (*iii*) only

C. (*i*), (*ii*) and (*iii*) only

D. (*i*) and (*iv*) only

5. The wavelength range of UV–C radiations is

A. 200–280 nm B. 180–240 nm

C. 320–400 nm D. 240–300 nm

6. In a gas chromatography experiment, the retention factor (R_f) values for pollutant 'A' and pollutant 'B' in a mixture of pollutants were 0.5 and 0.125, respectively. If the distance travelled by solvent front is 12 cms, the distance (in cms) travelled by pollutant 'A' and pollutant 'B' will be

A. 6 and 1.5 B. 3 and 1.5

C. 0.5 and 0.125 D. 1.5 and 3

7. Using the following equations, which can be determined correctly?

$$Ca(HCO_3)_2 \xrightarrow{\Delta} CaCO_3 + H_2O + CO_2$$

(by heating)

or

$$Ca(HCO_3)_2 + Ca(OH)_2 \longrightarrow 2CaCO_3 + 2H_2O$$

(by addition of lime)

A. Carbon dioxide

B. Carbonates

C. Bicarbonates

D. Carbonates and Bicarbonates

8. Assume that a river having dissolved oxygen 0.5 g/m^3, BOD 0.3 g/m^3 flowing at 80 m^3/sec. converge with another river having Dissolved Oxygen 0.7 g/m^3. BOD 0.6 g/m^3 flowing at a rate of 60 m^3/sec. If after the confluence the Dissolved Oxygen is 0.59 g/m^3, then the BOD is

A. 0.83 g/m^3 B. 0.43 g/m^3

C. 0.73 g/m^3 D. 0.92 g/m^3

9. Cells grown in a medium containing phosphorous –32 will show radio labelling in
A. Starch B. Glycogen
C. Proteins D. Nucleic acids

10. C^{14} has a half-life of 5700 years. The fraction of the C^{14} atoms that decays per year is
A. 1.216×10^{-4} B. 0.52×10^{-3}
C. 0.78×10^{-4} D. 2.81×10^{-4}

11. **Assertion (A) :** Marine biodiversity tends to be highest in mid-latitudes in all oceans and along coasts in the Western Pacific.
Reason (R) : Sea surface temperature along coasts in the Western Pacific is highest.
Codes :
A. Both (A) and (R) are true and (R) is the correct explanation of (A).
B. Both (A) and (R) are true, but (R) is not the correct explanation of (A).
C. (A) is true, but (R) is false.
D. (A) is false, but (R) is true.

12. "Double digging" is a method of
A. Bio-intensive agriculture
B. Deforestation
C. Aforestation
D. Water conservation

13. The rate of replacement of species along a gradient of habitats pertains to
A. Alpha diversity B. Beta diversity
C. Gamma diversity D. Species diversity

14. Match the List–I and List–II. Choose the correct answer from the given codes :

List–I **(Vegetation development)**	***List–II*** **(Nomenclature of succession)**
(*a*) On a rock	1. Psammosere
(*b*) On sand	2. Lithosere
(*c*) In aquatic habitat	3. Xerosere
(*d*) In dry habitat	4. Hydrosere

Codes :

	(*a*)	(*b*)	(*c*)	(*d*)
A.	2	1	4	3
B.	1	2	3	4
C.	3	4	2	1
D.	4	3	1	2

15. If individuals of a species remain alive only in captivity or other human controlled conditions, the species is said to be
A. Ecologically extinct
B. Mass extinct
C. Wild extinct
D. Anthropogenic extinct

16. Which of the following symbolises correct sequence in hydrosere?
A. Diatoms → Wolffia → Hydrilla → Cyperus → Populus
B. Hydrilla → Wolffia → Cyperus → Populus → Diatoms
C. Cyperus → Diatoms → Hydrilla → Wolffia → Populus
D. Diatoms → Hydrilla → Wolffia → Cyperus → Populus

17. Which of the following is not a class of aquatic ecosystems based on salinity levels?
A. Stagnant water ecosystem
B. Freshwater ecosystem
C. Brackish ecosystem
D. Marine ecosystem

18. The K-strategists are
(*a*) large organisms which have relatively longer life
(*b*) provide care for their offsprings
(*c*) organisms that stabilise their population at carrying capacity for the area
Choose the correct answer ;
A. (*a*) and (*b*) only B. (*a*) and (*c*) only
C. (*b*) and (*c*) only D. (*a*), (*b*) and (*c*)

19. Limnetic zone in freshwater ecosystem is characterised by
A. Presence of rooted vegetation
B. Absence of rooted vegetation
C. Presence of large proportion of lime
D. Absence of phytoplankton

20. Match the List–I with List–II, choose the correct answer from the given codes :

List–I **(Plants)**	***List–II*** **(Family)**
(*a*) *Camellia caduca*	1. Orchidaceae
(*b*) *Picea brachytyla*	2. Theaceae
(*c*) *Colchicum luteum*	3. Pinaceae
(*d*) *Arachnantha clarkei*	4. Liliaceae

Codes :

	(*a*)	(*b*)	(*c*)	(*d*)
A.	4	2	3	1
B.	1	2	3	4
C.	2	1	4	3
D.	2	3	4	1

21. Vegetation cover shows maximum reflectance in which of the following regions of the electromagnetic radiation spectrum?
A. Ultraviolet B. Near infrared
C. Middle infrared D. Visible

22. During remote sensing of the vegetation cover, the spectral reflection of vegetation over electromagnetic radiation spectrum depends upon
A. Pigmentation in the leaf
B. Structure of the leaf
C. Moisture content of the leaf
D. All the above characters

23. Given below are statements in the context of biogeochemical cycles :
(*i*) Ecosystems are black boxes for many of the processes that take place within them.
(*ii*) Ecosystem boundaries are permeable to some degree or other.
(*iii*) The energy and nutrients can be transferred to and from one ecosystem to another via imports and exports.

Identify the correct answer from the codes given below:
A. (*i*) and (*ii*) only B. (*ii*) and (*iii*) only
C. (*i*) and (*iii*) only D. (*i*), (*ii*) and (*iii*)

24. The volume of ejecta and the column height for a volcano are $10^{8.5}$ m^3 and 24 km, respectively. What is its volcanic explosivity index value?
A. 2 B. 8
C. 7 D. 4

25. In the context of material balance in hydrological cycle, which of the following equations is correct for oceans?
A. Input + change in storage = output
B. Precipitation + inflow = evaporation
C. Input – change in storage = output
D. Precipitation – inflow = evaporation

26. In disaster management which steps are followed in post-disaster recovery phase?
A. Relief, rehabilitation, reconstruction, learning–review
B. Risk Assessment, mitigation, preparedness, emergency plans.
C. Relief, mitigation, emergency plans.
D. Learning–review, emergency plans, preparedness.

27. Permafrost represents
A. permanently frozen subsurface soil
B. frozen leaves of Oak trees
C. frozen needles of pine trees
D. temporarily frozen subsurface soil

28. Assertion (A) : Estuaries are productive ecosystems.
Reason (R) : Large amounts of nutrients are introduced into the basin from the rivers that run into them.
Choose the correct answer :
A. Both (A) and (R) are true, and (R) is the correct explanation of (A).
B. Both (A) and (R) are true, but (R) is not the correct explanation of (A).
C. (A) is true and (R) is false.
D. (A) is false and (R) is true.

29. A confined aquifer of thickness 25 m has two wells 200 m apart along the direction of flow of water. The difference in their hydraulic heads is 1 m. If hydraulic conductivity is 50 m/day, the rate of flow of water per day per metre of distance perpendicular to the flow of water is
A. 25 m^3/day per metre
B. 50 m^3/day per metre
C. 5 m^3/day per metre
D. 1 m^3/day per metre

30. Which of the following material has the highest hydraulic conductivity?
A. Clay B. Sandstone
C. Limestone D. Quartzite

31. Which of the following energy sources is not renewable on human time scale?
A. Solar B. Hydrothermal
C. Geothermal D. Biomass

32. For a solar flat plate collector the following data is given : Useful heat gain = 28 watts/m^2 per hour, solar radiation intensity = 350 watts/m^2 per hour and the factor to convert beam radiation to that on the plane of the collector = 1.2. The collector efficiency is

A. ~ 6.6% B. ~ 4.8%
C. ~ 12.2% D. ~ 15.2%

33. For the reaction in a hydrogenoxygen fuel cell,

$$H_2 + \frac{1}{2}O_2 = H_2O(l)$$

Given $\Delta G° = 240$ kJ/gm – mole of H_2 and Faraday's constant = 96,500 Coulomb/gm mole.
The developed voltage in the fuel cell will be

A. ~ 1.13 Volts
B. ~ 2.13 Volts
C. ~ 1.51 Volts
D. ~ 1.24 Volts

34. Identify the correct sequence of the fuels in order of their increasing carbon intensity :

A. Natural gas < Oil < Bituminous coal < Nuclear
B. Oil < Coal < Natural gas < Nuclear
C. Nuclear < Coal < Natural gas < Oil
D. Nuclear < Natural gas < Oil < Bituminous coal

35. In nuclear thermal reactors, which of the following is not used as moderator?

A. Normal water B. Heavy water
C. Graphite D. Liquid Helium

36. The minimum temperature gradient (°C/km) required for OTEC is about

A. 20 B. 10
C. 40 D. 60

37. A solar pond has electricity generating capacity of 600 MWe. If the efficiency of solar energy to electric generation process was 2% and solar energy supply rate was 300 W/m^2, what is the area of solar pond?

A. 100 km^2 B. 90 km^2
C. 60 km^2 D. 180 km^2

38. Which of the following causes warming of atmosphere but cooling of the earth's surface?

A. Ozone
B. Black carbon aerosols
C. All Greenhouse gases
D. Sulphates and nitrates

39. Assertion (A) : For noise level surveys in urban areas, weighting A is used for measurements.
Reason (R) : Weighting A filters out unwanted signals.
Codes :

A. Both (A) and (R) are true and (R) is the correct explanation of (A).
B. Both (A) and (R) are true, but (R) is not the correct explanation of (A).
C. (A) is true, but (R) is false.
D. Both (A) and (R) are false.

40. Noise levels of 80 dB refers to a sound pressure level of

A. 0.2 Pa B. 0.02 Pa
C. 20 Pa D. 200 Pa

41. Asphyxiation is caused by

A. HCN, $COCl_2$ B. NO_x
C. $CHCl_3$ D. AsH_3

42. Sequence of a typical sewage treatment plant operation process will be

A. Aeration → Flocculation → Sedimentation → Recarbonation → Filtration → Disinfection
B. Aeration → Sedimentation → Flocculation → Filtration → Recarbonation → Disinfection
C. Flocculation → Aeration → Recarbonation → Sedimentation → Filtration → Disinfection
D. Sedimentation → Flocculation → Aeration → Filtration → Recarbonation → Disinfection

43. Which one of the following isotopes has maximum half-life period?

A. Rn^{222}
B. Pb^{210}
C. Ti^{210}
D. Bi^{210}

44. Match the List–I with List–II and identify the correct answer from given codes :

List–I **(Aerosols)**	*List–II* **(Constituents)**
(*a*) Dust	1. Small gas borne particles resulting from combustion
(*b*) Mist	2. Black carbon
(*c*) Smoke	3. Suspended small liquid droplets
(*d*) Atmospheric Brown Cloud	4. Solid suspended particles

Codes :

	(*a*)	(*b*)	(*c*)	(*d*)
A.	4	3	2	1
B.	3	4	1	2
C.	2	1	3	4
D.	1	2	3	4

45. Assertion (A) : Chloroflurocarbons deplete ozone.

Reason (R) : These compounds contain chlorine, bromine and fluorine.

Codes :

A. Both (A) and (R) are true and (R) is the correct explanation of (A).
B. Both (A) and (R) are true, but (R) is not the correct explanation of (A).
C. (A) is true, but (R) is false.
D. (A) is false, but (R) is true.

46. Which of the following organic compounds is not of biogenic origin?

A. Isoprene B. α-pinene
C. Myrcene D. Acrolein

47. Which of the following is used as plant indicator for detection of presence of SO_2 and HF in air?

A. Lichen B. Orchid
C. Apricot D. Tobacco

48. Integrated Gasification Combined Cycle (IGCC) technology is best at removing

A. NO_2 and CO
B. CO and SO_2
C. Particulates and sulphur
D. NO_2 and SO_2

49. A wastewater treatment plant in a city treats 50,000 m^3 wastewater generated per day. For an average flow rate of 25 m^3 per day per sq. metre, what should be the diameter of the circular primary settling tank?

A. 50.4 m B. 30.6 m
C. 20 m D. 25.8 m

50. An Electrostatic Precipitator (ESP) with collector plate area = 5000 m^2 treats a flue gas with drift velocity = 0.12 m/s with 98% efficiency. The volumetric flow rate (m^3/s) of the flue gas is

A. ~ 175.2 B. ~ 213.5
C. ~ 153.4 D. ~ 198.9

51. Assertion (A) : Urban heat islands contribute to build up of pollutants in cities.

Reason (R) : Urban heat islands produce a somewhat stable air mass in the city's atmosphere.

Codes :

A. Both (A) and (R) are correct and (R) is the correct explanation of (A).
B. Both (A) and (R) are correct, but (R) is not the correct explanation of (A).
C. (A) is true, but (R) is false.
D. Both (A) and (R) are false.

52. Match List–I with List–II and choose the correct answer from the codes given below :

List–I **(Analytical functions)**	*List–II* **(Activity under the function)**
(*a*) Defining scope of EIA	1. Critical Assessment of impacts
(*b*) Identification of impacts	2. Estimation of the probability that a particular impact will occur
(*c*) Prediction of Impacts	3. Description of the existing environment system
(*d*) Impact Evaluation and Analysis	4. Deciding important issues and concerns

Codes :

	(*a*)	(*b*)	(*c*)	(*d*)
A.	3	4	1	2
B.	4	3	2	1
C.	2	1	3	4
D.	1	2	4	3

53. A drawback of checklists is

A. Preliminary analysis is available in scaling checklist
B. Checklists are too general or incomplete
C. Checklists summarises information to make it available to experts
D. Ecosystem functions can be clearly understood from weighting methods

54. If EIU_j = environmental impact units for jth alternative, EQ_{ij} = environmental – quality – scale value for i^{th} factor and j^{th} alternative, PIU_i = parameter importance units for i^{th} factor, then what is the correct formulation for the index expressed in environmental impact units (EIU_i)?

A. $EIU_i = \sum_{i=1}^{n} \left(\frac{E}{Q_{ij}} \right) PIU_i$

B. $EIU_i = \sum_{i=1}^{n} \left(\frac{Q_{ij}}{E} \right) PIU_i$

C. $EIU_i = \sum_{i=1}^{n} EQ_{ij}\, PIU_i$

D. $EIU_i = \sum_{i=1}^{n} \frac{PIU_i}{EQ_{ij}}$

55. Match List–I with List–II and choose the correct answer from the codes given below :

List–I **(Scales used in EIA methods)**	*List–II* **(Example)**
(*a*) Nominal	1. Temperature (degrees)
(*b*) Ordinal	2. Species classification
(*c*) Interval	3. Map scale
(*d*) Ratio	4. Worst to best

Codes :

	(*a*)	(*b*)	(*c*)	(*d*)
A.	1	2	3	4
B.	4	3	2	1
C.	3	1	4	2
D.	2	4	1	3

56. Risk assessment in EIA does not involve

A. Maximum credible analysis
B. Hazard and operability studies
C. Preparation of disaster management plan
D. Assessment of economic benefit arising out of a project

57. In a gravity flow autoclave, medical waste is subjected to a temperature

A. > 120°C B. < 100°C
C. > 300°C D. > 800°C

58. Hierarchy of priorities in hazardous waste management is

A. Eliminate generation → Reduce generation → Recycle/Reuse → Treatment → Disposal
B. Reduce generation → Eliminate generation → Recycle/Reuse → Treatment → Disposal
C. Eliminate generation → Reduce generation → Treatment → Recycle/Reuse → Disposal
D. Reduce generation → Eliminate generation → Treatment → Recycle/Reuse → Disposal

59. Public Liability Insurance Act was enacted in the year

A. 1991 B. 1993
C. 1995 D. 1997

60. Match List–I with List–II and choose the correct answer from the codes given below :

List–I **(Convention)**	*List–II* **(Year)**
(*a*) Convention for the protection of the ozone layer	1. 1979
(*b*) Conservation of migratory species of wild animals	2. 1985
(*c*) Kyoto protocol	3. 1982
(*d*) UN Convention on the law of the sea	4. 1997

Codes :

	(*a*)	(*b*)	(*c*)	(*d*)
A.	2	1	4	3
B.	2	4	3	1
C.	3	1	2	4
D.	1	2	3	4

61. Match List–I with List–II and choose the correct answer from the codes given below :

List–I **(Acts)**	*List–II* **(Year when enacted)**
(*a*) Wildlife Protection Act	1. 1980
(*b*) Forest Conservation Act	2. 1972
(*c*) Air (Prevention and Control of Pollution) Act	3. 1974
(*d*) Water (Prevention and Control of Pollution) Act	4. 1981

Codes :

	(*a*)	(*b*)	(*c*)	(*d*)
A.	2	1	4	3
B.	1	2	3	4
C.	3	2	1	4
D.	4	3	2	1

62. Assertion (A) : χ^2 distribution is a non-parametric distribution.

Reason (R) : χ^2 is a sample statistic having no corresponding population parameter.

Codes :

A. Both (A) and (R) are correct and (R) is the correct explanation of (A).

B. Both (A) and (R) are correct, but (R) is not the correct explanation of (A).

C. (A) is true, but (R) is false.

D. Both (A) and (R) are false.

63. In a simple regression analysis of y on x, the standard error of estimate of y on x, $S_{yx} = 5$, number of observations N is 30, and $\Sigma y^2 = 2000$. The unexplained variance is

A. 1500 B. 750

C. 500 D. 250

64. Two normal populations have variances $\sigma_1^2 = 10$ and $\sigma_1^2 = 20$. Two random samples of sizes 25 and 20, independently selected from these populations have variances of $S_1^2 = 8$ and $S_2^2 = 15$, respectively. What is the $F_{(24, 19)}$ statistic?

A. 1

B. 2

C. 2.81

D. 3.6

65. Assertion (A) : A matrix is non-singular if and only if none of its eigen values is zero.

Reason (R) : The product of the eigen values equals the determinant of a matrix.

Codes :

A. Both (A) and (R) are correct and (R) is the correct explanation of (A).

B. Both (A) and (R) are correct, but (R) is not the correct explanation of (A).

C. (A) is correct, but (R) is false.

D. Both (A) and (R) are false.

66. In Gaussian Plume Model assume $\sigma_z = cx$, where c is a constant and ratio of σ_y to σ_z to be a constant. If H is the effective height of the stack, the maximum concentration at a distance (x) from the stack is proportional to

A. H^{-1} B. H^{-2}

C. $\exp(-H^2)$ D. $H^{-3/2}$

67. The Pearson Linear correlation coefficient (r) for the following paired data (x, y) : (2, 1.4) (4, 1.8), (8, 2.1), (8, 2.3), (9, 2.6) is

A. 0.623 B. −0.572

C. 0.957 D. 0.823

68. In a rough terrain the wind speed at a height of 10 m is 2.5 m/s. The wind speed at an elevation of 300 m will be

A. 4.9 m/s B. 1.2 m/s

C. 3.6 m/s D. 7.9 m/s

69. In the context of REDD$^+$ initiatives the land clearing in forest areas is primarily concerned with

A. Physical resources of the area

B. Ecology of the area

C. Carbon budget of the area

D. Water resources of the area

70. What was the objective of Basel Convention (1989) under UNEP?

I. Minimize generation of hazardous wastes in terms of quantity and hazardousness

II. Disposal of hazardous wastes as close to the source of generation as possible.

III. Reduce the movement of hazardous wastes.

Choose the correct code :

A. I and II only B. II and III only

C. I, II and III D. I only

71. Global Warming Potential (GWP) of a greenhouse gas (GHG) is a comparison of global warming impact between

A. 1 kg of GHG and 1 kg of methane
B. 1 kg of GHG and 1 kg of CO_2
C. 1 kg of GHG and 1 kg of N_2O
D. 1 kg of GHG and 1 kg of CFC-11

72. Which of the following mixture of gases is called biogas?

A. CO_2, CH_4, NH_3, H_2S, H_2O (vapour)
B. CO, CH_4, NH_3, H_2S, H_2O (vapour)
C. CO_2, CH_4, N_2O, NH_3, H_2O (vapour)
D. CO_2, NO_x, H_2O, CH_4

73. Environmental ethics deal with moral relationship of human beings to

A. the value and moral status of the environment and its non-human contents
B. the values that are important to development and economic growth
C. the conservation values of selected species
D. the development of genetically modified organisms

74. The major source of BaP (Benzo-a-pyrene) in atmospheric environment is

A. residential wood burning
B. gasoline
C. coal tar
D. cooked meat

75. Match the List–I with List–II and choose the correct answer from the codes given below :

***List–I* (Materials)**	***List–I* (Applications)**
(*a*) Trichloroethylene	1. Gasoline
(*b*) Toluene	2. Wood treatment
(*c*) Zinc	3. Dry cleaning
(*d*) Phenol	4. Mining

Codes :

	(*a*)	(*b*)	(*c*)	(*d*)
A.	3	1	4	2
B.	2	3	1	4
C.	1	4	2	3
D.	4	2	3	1

ANSWERS

1	2	3	4	5	6	7	8	9	10
B	A	B	C	A	A	D	B	D	A
11	**12**	**13**	**14**	**15**	**16**	**17**	**18**	**19**	**20**
A	A	B	A	C	D	A	D	B	D
21	**22**	**23**	**24**	**25**	**26**	**27**	**28**	**29**	**30**
B	D	D	D	B	A	A	A	C	B
31	**32**	**33**	**34**	**35**	**36**	**37**	**38**	**39**	**40**
C	A	D	D	D	A	A	B	C	A
41	**42**	**43**	**44**	**45**	**46**	**47**	**48**	**49**	**50**
A	A	B	A	C	D	A	C	A	C
51	**52**	**53**	**54**	**55**	**56**	**57**	**58**	**59**	**60**
A	B	B	C	D	D	A	A	A	A
61	**62**	**63**	**64**	**65**	**66**	**67**	**68**	**69**	**70**
A	A	B	A	A	B	C	A	C	C
71	**72**	**73**	**74**	**75**					
B	A	A	A	A					

SOME SELECTED EXPLANATORY ANSWERS

1. Atmospheric Stability and Instability

Atmospheric stability : The resistance of the atmosphere to vertical motion.

Temperature distribution and lapse rates, where that temperatures normally increases as we get closer to the earth's surface. This is due in part to the greater molecular activity of denser, more compressed air at lower attitudes. These conditions change throughout a 24-hour period, as the daytime solar heating and nighttime heat loss to and through the atmosphere distributions.

Temperature Distribution of vertically moving air

The term 'adiabatic process' which simply means warning by compression, or cooling by expansion, without a transfer of heat or mass into a system. As air moves up or down within the atmosphere, it is affected by this process. This temperature difference will be 5-1/2 degree decreases per 1000 feet increase in attitude. This is also terned the dry adiabatic lapse rate. The atmosphere may or may not have a temperature distribution that fits the dry adiabatic lapse rate.

The actual lapse rate may be greater of less the dry adiabatic lapse rate and may change by levels in the atmosphere. This variation from the dry adiabatic lapse rate is what determines whether the air is stable or unstable. If the air is unstable. The vertical movement of air is encouraged and this tend to increase fire activity. If the air is stable, vertical movement of air is discouraged, and this usually. The importance of the atmosphere property will became evident by the time we have completed this unit.

Dry Lapse Rates : The actual temperature lapse rate in a given portion of the atmosphere could range from a plus 15 per 1000 feet to a minus 15 per 1000 feet. These would represent the extremes of very stable air to very unstable air. Rather than be concerned with all of these degrees of stability or instability, we usually describe the atmosphere as falling into one of five conditions.

The vertical air temperature distribution in the atmosphere is highly variable. For dry air it ranges as follows:

1. **Very stable :** Temperature increases with increase in altitude. This is a 'plus' temperature lapse rate, or an inversion.
2. **Stable :** Temperature lapse rate is less than the dry adiabatic rate, but temperature decreases with altitude increase.
3. **Neutral :** Temperature lapse rate is the same as the dry adiabatic rate of 5.5 degrees Fahrenheit per 1000 feet increase.
4. **Unstable :** Temperature lapse rate is greater than the dry adiabatic rate. It may be 6 degrees Fahrenheit or more.
5. **Very Stable :** Temperature lapse rate is much greater than the dry adiabatic rate and it called super-adiabatic.

Therefore (B) Neutral : the temperature lapse rate is the same as the dry adiabatic rate of 5.5 degree Fahrenheit per 1000 feet increase.

2. In the ecosystem, the flow energy follows the law of thermodynamics, it is because the flow of energy in the ecosystemic is unidirectional. The energy is lost from one trophic level to other is 80-90% during the transfarmation of energy. Hence, both the statements are true and reason (R) is the correct explanation of assertion (A).

3. (*a*) $\Delta G = RT \ln \frac{V_1}{V_2}$

(*b*) $\Delta G^\circ = -n FE^\circ$

(*c*) $\Delta S = nR \ln \frac{V_2}{V_1}$

(*d*) $\Delta H = \Delta E + P\Delta V$

5. **Electro-magnetic Spectrum :** The electro-megnetic spectrum is a way of visualizing the frequency and wavelength proportions of different forms of energy. Electromagnetic radiation has properties of both waves and particles. We divide the electromagnetic spectrum in the UV range for medical purposes.

- UVA is found in the region between 320 and 400 nm (nm = Nanometer = 1 billionth of a meter) and is the least powerful wavelength band of UV radiation.
- UVB is found in the region between 280 and 320 nm. It comprises the wavelengths primarily associated with erythema (sunburn), is also necessary for the production of vitamin D in the skin and is primarily responsible for stimulating increased milamine production.

UV–B wavelength (at 305 nm) have 1,000 times more erythemal power than UVA wavelengths.

UV–C is found in the region between approximately 200-280 nm and is called germicidal UV because of its proven effectiveness in killing single cell organisms. Solar radiations in the UVC range is absorbed almost entirely by the atmosphere and that is fortunate considering that even a short overexposure to UVC is very harmful to eyes and causes severe erythema (sunburn). UVC is emitted by High Intensity Discharge (HID) lamps, therefore these lamps require special filter glass, its contain the output of the UVC spectrum.

Therefore the wavelength range of UV-C radiations is 200-280 nm.

9. The cells grown in a medium containing phospherous (P-32) will show radio labelling in nucleic acids.

11. In the Western Pecific Ocean, the marine biodiveristy tends to be highest in mid-latitudes in all oceans along coasts. It is because the temperature of surface of sea/ocean along the coasts in the western pacific is the highest.

Hence, both (A) and (R) are true and (R) is the correct explanation of (A).

14. (*a*) Lithosene – rock
(*b*) Psammosere – sand
(*c*) Hydroser – aquatic (life) aquatic
(*d*) Xerosere – dry habitate.

16. The symbolises correct sequence in hydrosere is

Diatoms → hydrilla → wolffia cyperus → populus.

17. The eco-systems in the hydrosphere are callled aquatic eco-system. For example, include ponds, lakes, rivers, open ocean, coral reefs, estuaries months of rivers or oceans inlets (where salt water and fresh mix and coastal and island wettends) such as swamps marshes and pairie pothdes that are covered with water all or part of the lime. The major differences between these eco-systems are the result of differences in the amount of various nutrients in the depth of sunlight presentation and differences in average water temperature. Therefore, all the class of aquatic eco-systems based on the salinity levels are freshwater eco-systems, brackish eco-system and the marine eco-system. Hence (A) is not a clause of aquatic ecosystem based on the salinity level.

18. **K- Strategists :** These are large organisms that have relatively longer life and provide care for their offsprings.

The organism which stablise their population at the carrying capacity for the area. Hence, all the statements (A), (B) and (C) are correct.

20. Theaceae → *Camellia caduca*
Pinaceae → *Picea brachytyla*
Liliaceae → *Colchicum luteum*
Orchidaceae → *Arachnantha clarkei*

Hence option (D) is correct.

23. **Biogeochemical Cycles :** The eco-systems are black boxes for many of the processes that

takes place within them. The boundries of the eco-systems are the permeable to some degree, from one eco-systems to another eco-system via imparts and exports, the energy and the nutrients are transformed. Hence, all the statements are correct. Therefore, (D) is the correct option.

31. Geothermal energy is thermal energy generated and stored in the earth. Thermal energy is the energy that determines the temperature of matter. The geothermal energy of the Earth's crust originates from the original formation of the planet (20%) and form radioactive decay of minerals (80%). The geothermal gradient, which is the difference in temperature between the core of the planet and its surface, drives a continuous conduction of thermal energy in the form of heat from the core to the surface. Geothermal energy is cost effective reliable, sustainable and environmentally friendly, but has historically been limited to areas near tectonic plate boundaries. Recent technological advances have dramatically expanded the range and size of viable resources, especially for applications such as home heating, opening a potential for widespread exploitation. Geothermal wells release greenhouse gases trapped deep within the earth, but these emissions are much lower per energy unit than those of fossil fuels. As a result, geothermal power has the potential to help mitigate global warming if widely deployed in place of fossil fuels.

The Earth geothermal resources are theoretically more than adequate to supply humanity's energy needs, but only a very small fraction may be profitably exploited. Drilling and exploration for deep resources is very expensive. Forecasts for the future of geothermal power depend on assumptions about technology, energy prices, subsidies, and interest rates. Pilot programs like EWEB's customer opt in Green Power Program show that customers would to pay a little more for a renewable energy source like geothermal. But as a result of government assisted research and industry experience, cost of generating geothermal power has decreased by 25% over the past two decades. In 2001, geothermal energy cost between two and ten US conts per kWh.

35. **Liquid Helium :** The chemical element helium exists in a liquid form only at the extremely low temperature of –269 degrees celsius (about 4 kelvin or –452.2 degrees Fahrenheit). Its boiling point and critical point depend on which isotope of helium is present : the common isotope helium 4 or the rare isotope helium-3. These are the only two stable isotopes of helium. The density of liquid helium-4 at its boiling point and a pressure of one atmosphere (101.3 kilo pascals) is about 125 grams per liter.

38. **Black Carbon Aerosols :** The sun provides the energy that drives Earth's climate, but not all of the energy that reaches the top of the atmosphere finds its way to the surface. That is because aerosols and clouds seeded by them reflect about a quarter of the sun's energy back to space. Aerosols play an important role in Earth's climate. Most aerosols are brighter than land or ocean, and cool the earth by reflecting sunlight back to space. Different aerosols scatter or absorb sunlight to varying degrees, depending on their physical properties. Climatologists describe these scattering and absorbing properties as the 'direct effect' of aerosole on Earth's radiation field. However, since aerosols comprise such a broad collection of particles with different properties, the overall effect is anything but simple.

Although most aerosols reflect sunlight, some also absorb it. An aerosols effect on light depends primarily on the composition and colour of the particles. Broadly speaking, bright coloured or translucent particles tend to reflect radiation in all directions and back towards space. Darker aerosols can absorb significant amounts of light.

Pure sulfates and nitrates reflect nearby all radiation they encounter cooking the atmosphere. Black carbon in contrast, absorbs radiation readily, warming the atmosphere but also shading the surface organic carbon, sometimes called brown carbon or organic matter, has a warming influence on the atmosphere depending on the brightness of the underlying ground. Dust impacts radiation to varying degrees, depending on the composition of the minerals that comprise the dust grains, and whether they are coated with black or brown carbon. Salt particles tend to reflect all the sunlight they encounter. Black carbon aerosols, similar to the 500 in a chimney, absorb sunlight rather than reflecting it. This warms the layer of the atmosphere carrying the black carbon, but also shades and cools the surface below.

Aerosols can have a major impact on climate when they scatter light. In 1991 the eruption of Mount Pinatubo in the Phillippines ejected more than 20 million tons of sulfer dioxide–a gas that reacts with other substances to produce sulfate aerosol as high as 60 kilometers (37 miles) above the surface, creating particles in the stratosphere. Those bright particles remained above the clouds and didn't get washed from the sky by rain; they settled only after several years climatologists predicted global temperatures would drop as a result of that global sulfate infusion. They were right: Following the eruption, global temperatures abruptly dipped by about a half-dgree (0.6°C) for about two years. And Pinatubo isn't a unique event large, temperature–altering eruptions occur about once per decade. Large volcanic eruptions may lift sulfate aerosols into the stratosphere, which usually cools the global, climate for the following year or two.

In addition to scattering or absorbing radiation, aerosols can albebo, of the planet. Bright surfaces reflect radiation and cool the climate, whereas darker surfaces absorb radiation and produce a warming effect. White sheets of sea ice, for example, reflect a great deal of radiation, whereas darker surfaces, such as the ocean, tend to absorb solar radiation and have a net warming effect.

Aerosols particularly black carbon, can alter reflectively by depositing a layer of dark residue on ice and other bright surfaces. In the Arctic especially, aerosols from wildfires and industrial pollution are likely hastening the meling of ice.

Dark aerosols dramatically change the reflectivity of the Earth's surface when they land on snow. Black ash covered the summit of New Zealand's Mount Ruapehu after an eruption in 2007, but was soon covered by fresh snow, long-term accumulation of black carbon aerosols in the Arctic and Himalaya is leading to increased melting of snow.

Scientists believe the cooling from sulfates and other reflective aerosols. Overwhelms the warming effect of black carbon and other absorbing aerosols over the planet.

Despite considerable advances in recent decades, estimating the direct climate impacts of aerosols remains an immature science of the 25 climate models considered by the Fourth. Intergovernmental Panel on climate (IPCC), only a handful considered the direct effects of aerosols types other than sufates.

Therefore Black carbon aerosols causes warming of atmosphere but cooling of the earth's surface.

41. Asphyxia or asphyxiation is a condition of severaly deficient supply of oxygen to the body that arises from abnormal breathing. An example of asphyxia is choking. Asphyxia causes generalized hypoxia, which primarily affects the tissues and organs. There are many circumstances that can induce asphyxia, all of which are characterized by an inability of an individual to acquire sufficient oxygen through breathing for an extended period of time. These circumstances can include but are not limited to the constriction or obstruction of airways, such as from asthma, laryngospasm, or simple blockage from the pressure of foreign materials; from being in environments where oxygen is not readily accessible, such as underwater, in a low oxygen atmosphere, or in a vaccum; environments where sufficiently oxygenated air is present, but cannot be adequately breathed because of air contamination such as excessive smoke. Asphyxia can cause come or death.

48. An Integrated Gastrification combined cycle (IGCC) is a technology that uses a gas fier to turn coal and other carbon based fuels into gas, i.e., synthesis gas. It then removes the impurities from the synthesis gas before it is combusted some of these pollutants, such as particulates and sulphur can be turn into reusable by-products. This results in the lower emission of sulphur dioxides parculates and mercurry (Hg) with additional process equipments. The carbon in the synthesis gas can be shifted to hydrogen (H_2) via the water gas shift reaction, resulting is nearly carbon free fuel. This resulting CO_2 from the shift reaction can be compressed and stored. Excess heat from the primary combstion and synthesis gas fixed generation is then passed to a steam cycle similar to the combined cycle. This results in improved efficiency composed to conventional pulverized coal.

61. (*a*) **Wildlife Protection Act :** In India, the Wildlife Protection Act of 1972 was amended thrice (in 1983, 1986 and 1991). The wildlife crime control Bureau has been constituted through amendment of the Wildlife (Protection) Act, 1972 in 2008. The powers and function of the bureau have been defined u/s 38Z of the act. Wildlife Protection Act, 1972 aimed at rational and modern wildlife management.

(*b*) **Forest Conservation Act, 1980 :** The Forest Conservation Act, 1980, amended in 1988.

(*c*) **Air (Prevention and Control of Pollution) Act, 1981 :** The Central Enactment came into force from 16-05-1981. This act was intended to achive effective contral over air pollution caused by various regions. The Act contemplates establishment of the central and state Boards rested with wide powers to enable them to devise means to improve the quality of air and to prevent, control or abate pollution in the country.

The Act is visualized as a measure to implemented some of the decisions taken at the UN conference on Human Environment held at Stockholm in June 1972 to take appropriates steps for the prevention of the natural resources of the earth and central the pollution.

(*d*) **The Water (Prevention and Control of Pollution) Act, 1974 :** This comprehensive piece of legistation was passed under Article 252 of the constitution mainly with the object of prevention and control of water pollution. The act contemplates establishment of the Central Board of Prevention and Control of Water Pollution and similar Boards at the state level. The penalties against the pollution vary from regrous imprisonment for 6 months to 6 years.

62. χ^2 distribution is a non-parametric distribution, because it is a sample statistic having no corresponding population parameter. Then, both (A) and (R) are true and former is correct explanation of latter.

72. CO_2, CH_4, NH_3, H_2S, H_2O (vapour)

Biogas typically refers to a mixture of gases produced by the breakdown of organic matter in the absence of oxygen. Biogas can be produced from regionally available raw materials such as recycled waste. It is a renewable energy source and it many cases exerts a very small carbon footprint.

Biogas is produced by anaerobic digestion with anaerobic bacteria or fermentation of biodegrable materials such as manure, sewage, municipal waste, green waste, plant material and crops. It is primarily methane (CH_4) and carbon dioxide (CO_2) and may have small amounts of hydrogen sulphide (H_2S), moisture and siloxanes.

The gases methance, hydrogen and carbon monoxide (CO) can be combusted or oxidized with oxygen. This energy release allows biogas to be used as a fuel; it can be used for any heating purpose, such as cooking. It can also be used in gas engine to convert the energy in the gas into electricity and heat.

Biogas can be compressed, the same way natural gas is compressed to CNG and used to power motor vehicles. In the UK, for example, biogas is estimated to have the potential to replace around 17% of vehicle fuel. It qualifies for renewable energy subsidies in some parts of the world. Biogas can be cleaned and upgraded to natural gas thousands when it becomes bio methane.

Previous Paper (Solved)

UGC-NET ENVIRONMENTAL SCIENCE, JUNE 2013

PAPER-II

Note : *This paper contains **fifty (50)** objective type questions, each question carrying **two (2)** marks. Attempt **all** the questions.*

1. **Assertion (A) :** Every country should integrate the principles of sustainable development into its policies and programmes.
   Reason (R) : Environmental resources are a Nation's wealth.
   Choose the correct code from the following:
   A. Both (A) and (R) are true and (R) is the correct explanation of (A).
   B. Both (A) and (R) are true, but (R) is not the correct explanation of (A).
   C. (A) is true, but (R) is false.
   D. (A) is false, but (R) is true.
2. Wind rose represents statistical distribution of
   A. Wind velocity in vector form
   B. Wind speeds in scalar form
   C. Wind speeds in π diagram
   D. Wind speeds in the form of histograms
3. In the redox reaction given below, which one of the substrates in forward reaction is oxidized?
   $$2Fe^{3+} + H_2 \rightarrow 2Fe^{2+} + 2H^+$$
   A. Fe^{3+} B. H_2
   C. H^+ D. Fe^{2+}
4. If soil in a given area is wetted and allowed to drain till percolation is stopped, the amount of water thus retained is called
   A. Storage capacity
   B. Capillary capacity
   C. Hygroscopic capacity
   D. Field capacity
5. Quantity of 5M HCl required for preparing 1000 ml of 0.1 M HCl is,
   A. 20 ml B. 2 ml
   C. 200 ml D. 100 ml
6. The method which can be used for the softening of water having high calcium, high magnesium-carbonate hardness and some non-carbonate hardness
   A. single-stage lime process.
   B. excess lime process.
   C. single stage lime-soda ash process.
   D. excess lime-soda ash process.
7. Spotted deer, Asiatic wild ass, Black buck are,
   A. Endangered species B. Vulnerable species
   C. Threatened species D. Key species
8. Specific mortality of members of a population is expressed by
   A. Life table
   B. Survivorship curve
   C. Rate of mortality
   D. Rate of fecundity
9. Which group of vertebrate comprises maximum number of endangered species?
   A. Fish B. Amphibia
   C. Reptiles D. Birds
10. Under anaerobic condition denitrifying *Pseudomonas* changes,
    A. Nitrate to molecular nitrogen
    B. Nitrate to ammonia
    C. Nitrate to Nitrite
    D. Nitrite to Nitrate
11. The Phenomenon of having higher number of species in ecotone is called
    A. Dominance effect B. Edge effect
    C. Abundance D. Frequency
12. Which specific common feature is not found in zooplankton and rabbit ?
    A. Both are animals
    B. Both are primary consumers
    C. Both are carnivores
    D. Both are herbivores

13. The following exogenous and endogenous factors are the cause of extinction of animal species :

I. Ecological niche
II. Decrease in reproductive potency.
III. Lesser adaptability to fluctuating environment.

Choose the correct answer from the codes given below:

Codes :

A. I only B. II only
C. I and II D. I, II and III

14. Positive mass balance of glaciers has been recently reported from

A. Eastern Himalayas B. Nepal Himalayas
C. Western Himalayas D. Karakoram

15. Which of the following will lead to reduction in greenhouse gases in atmosphere?

A. Increased chemical weathering of rocks.
B. Volcanic eruption
C. Lowering of mean sea level
D. An increase in melting of glacial ice

16. The unconsolidated material with highest permeability is

A. Landslide with clayey component
B. Altered volcanic ash
C. Well sorted alluvial sand
D. Buried mud flows

17. Which of the following component of cryosphere has the longest life ?

A. Sea ice B. Icebergs
C. Valley glaciers D. Ice sheets

18. Aerobic bacteria is most active in

A. Moist and saturated soil
B. Moist and non-saturated soil
C. Alluvial soil
D. Permafrost

19. Andisols are formed by

A. Biological activity B. Erosion by wind
C. Erosion by waves D. Volcanoes

20. In case of photovoltaic cell, the maximum theoretical efficiency of conversion is

A. ~ 45% B. ~ 30%
C. ~ 25% D. ~ 50%

21. Consider an ideal wind power generator, if the wind speed increases 3 times, the power output would increase by how many times?

A. 3 B. 9
C. 27 D. 81

22. Identify the correct sequence in increasing order of total CO_2 emissions from various countries at present.

A. Britain < India < China < USA
B. India < Britain < China < USA
C. Britain < USA < India < China
D. Britain < India < USA < China

23. Arsenic compounds cause

A. Dwarfism B. Dermatitis
C. Thyrotoxicosis D. Wilson's disease

24. What is the pE value in an acid mine water sample having

$[Fe^{2+}] = 7.03 \times 10^{-3}$ M and
$[Fe^{3+}] = 3.71 \times 10^{-4}$ M

A. 10.5 B. 12.5
C. 14.5 D. 18.5

25. **Assertion (A) :** Chronic exposure to ozone is a possible contributor to forest decline.

Reason (R) : Surface ozone is a greenhouse gas.

Identify the correct code:

A. Both (A) and (R) are true and (R) is the correct explanation of (A).
B. Both (A) and (R) are true, but (R) is not the correct explanation of (A).
C. (A) is true, but (R) is false.
D. (A) is false, but (R) is true.

26. Identify the most dominant pollutant in terms of its concentration levels in urban atmosphere.

A. Oxides of nitrogen B. Oxides of sulphur
C. Particulate matter D. Carbon monoxide

27. The main constituents of photochemical smog are

A. Oxides of sulphur and CO
B. Oxides of sulphur and hydrocarbons
C. Oxides of nitrogen and CO
D. Oxides of nitrogen, hydrocarbons and ozone

28. The air borne fraction of carbon is

A. ~ 0.72 B. ~ 0.62
C. ~ 0.46 D. ~ 0.38

29. The noise index L_{eq} is used for noise standards in ambient environment of urban areas. The prescribed duration of the integration associated with L_{eq} is

A. 12 hours
B. 8 hours
C. 1 hour
D. 30 minutes

30. In alkaline soils, which of the following is not present in soluble state?

A. Phosphorous
B. Calcium
C. Nitrates
D. Potassium

31. Which one of the following is not a post audit activity under environmental audit process?

A. Review of draft report by Law department.
B. Issue of final report to functional specialist.
C. Develop action plan to establish responsibility.
D. Report audit findings.

32. Which one of the following pairs is correctly matched?

A. Specification for environmental management system	ISO 14001
B. Environmental performance evaluation	ISO 14040
C. Guidelines for environmental auditing	ISO 14000
D. Environmental labels and declaration	ISO 14004

33. In accordance with the Indian EIA notification 2006, within how many days if Environmental Appraisal Committee do not specify the Terms of Reference, the proponent can go ahead with its own Terms of Reference.

A. 15 days B. 45 days
C. 60 days D. 90 days

34. Which is the correct sequence for impact assessment process in EIA ?

A. Description of Environment → Identification of impacts → Prediction of impacts → Evaluation of impacts → Identification of mitigation needs.
B. Identification of impacts → Prediction of impacts → Evaluation of impacts → Identification of mitigation needs.
C. Identification of impacts → Description of Environment → Prediction of impacts → Evaluation of impacts → Identification of mitigation needs.
D. Prediction of impacts → Identification of impacts → Description of environment → Evaluation of impacts → Identification of mitigation needs.

35. Quantifying the energy and raw material requirement as a part of life cycle assessment, is termed as

A. Life Cycle improvement analysis.
B. Life Cycle impact analysis.
C. Life Cycle inventory.
D. Life Cycle pre-requisites.

36. Which of the following pertains to "high-waste approach" in dealing with the solid and hazardous wastes?

A. Burying and burning
B. Recycling
C. Composting
D. Reusing

37. **Assertion (A) :** Dumping of sewage to river water may decrease oxygen even below 4 mg/l.
Reason (R) : Dumping of sewage pollutes river water heavily.
Identify the correct answer:

A. Both (A) and (R) are true with (R) being the correct explanation.
B. Both (A) and (R) are true, but (R) is not the correct explanation.
C. (A) is true, but (R) is wrong.
D. Both (A) and (R) are wrong.

38. In most of the studies, a large sample size is anticipated to

A. get a low level of precision.
B. maximize the sampling error.
C. get a high level of precision.
D. maximize the standard deviation.

39. The geometric mean of 4, 8 and 16 is

A. 9.3 B. 8.0
C. 4.8 D. 10.2

40. The covariance between two data of N observations each represented by variables X and Y is given by (A)

A. $\frac{\Sigma(X-\overline{X})(Y-\overline{Y})}{N^2}$

B. $\frac{\Sigma(X-\overline{X})^2(Y-\overline{Y})^2}{N}$

C. $\frac{\Sigma(X-\overline{X})^2(Y-\overline{Y})^2}{N^2}$

D. $\frac{\Sigma(X-\overline{X})(Y-\overline{Y})}{N}$

41. The mean and standard deviation of a Binomial distribution are 9 and 1, respectively. The first moment of the distribution is

A. 9
B. 3
C. 1
D. 0

42. Which one of the following is used in manufacturing flexible plastic bags and sheets?

A. Polystyrene (PS)
B. Polyethylene terephthalate (PET)
C. Low density polyethylene (LDPE)
D. TEFLON

43. Which one of the following is a non-formal environment education and awareness programme?

A. Environmental appreciation courses.
B. National Environment Awareness Campaign.
C. Environmental Education in school system.
D. Environmental Management Business Studies.

44. Bioparks are conceived, developed and managed with a goal of conservation of biodiversity through

(*i*) development of educational and scientific activities.
(*ii*) promoting silviculture and monoculture.
(*iii*) promoting local community welfare without harming the natural habitat.

Choose the correct answer from the codes:

Codes :

A. (*i*) and (*ii*)
B. (*ii*) and (*iii*)
C. (*i*) and (*iii*)
D. (*i*), (*ii*) and (*iii*)

45. In about a 7 metre deep pond the series of vegetation development will be

A. Submerged → Floating → Reed → Herb
B. Floating → Submerged → Reed → Herb
C. Floating → Reed → Submerged → Herb
D. Submerged → Reed → Floating → Herb

46. In terrestrial ecosystems, roughly how much NPP ends up being broken down by decomposers?

A. 90%
B. 70%
C. 50%
D. 10%

47. Which of the following BOD level waste water is permitted to be released inlands by industries under water (Prevention and Control of Pollution) Act, 1974 ?

A. 30 mg/l
B. 80 mg/l
C. 100 mg/l
D. 150 mg/l

48. Hydraulic conductivity is a function of

A. medium alone
B. fluid alone
C. either fluid or medium
D. both fluid and medium

49. Dachigan sanctuary is associated with

A. Hangul
B. Rhinoceros
C. Barking deer
D. Leopard

50. Rio + 20 summit was held in

A. Durban
B. Johannesburg
C. Rio de Janeiro
D. Cancun

ANSWERS

1	2	3	4	5	6	7	8	9	10
B	A	B	D	A	D	B	B	D	A
11	**12**	**13**	**14**	**15**	**16**	**17**	**18**	**19**	**20**
B	C	D	D	A	C	D	B	D	A
21	**22**	**23**	**24**	**25**	**26**	**27**	**28**	**29**	**30**
C	D	B	C	B	D	D	C	B	A
31	**32**	**33**	**34**	**35**	**36**	**37**	**38**	**39**	**40**
D	A	C	A	C	A	A	C	B	A
41	**42**	**43**	**44**	**45**	**46**	**47**	**48**	**49**	**50**
D	C	B	C	A	A	A	D	A	C

SOME SELECTED EXPLANATORY ANSWERS

2. The movement of air from higher pressure to lower pressure is an attempt to balance out the pressure differences. As the wind travels it is diverted to its right in the northern hemisphere and to its left in the southern hemisphere *i.e.*, The velocity of wind is represented in the vector form.

Wind rose is a diagram indicating the frequency and strengths of winds in a definite locality for a given period of years.

3. Redox reaction : A chemical reaction in which change in valency of elements takes place is called redox reaction. In these reactions, both oxidation and reduction processes take place simultaneously. One substance is oxidised and other is reduced in these reactions.

In the reaction,

$2Fe^{3+} + H_2 \rightarrow 2Fe^{2+} + 2H^+$

H_2 is one of the substrates in forward reaction that is oxidised.

4. When a soil holds all the water it can, but no gravitational water, it is said to be its field capacity. This is generally defined as the water content of an undistributed soil after it is saturated by rainfall and drainage of gravitational water has completely stopped. In practice for determining field capacity, soil is thus sampled about 48 hrs after rain. This value for a soil may be taken as constant. Thus, field capacity of soil may be taken as the total amount of capillary, hygroscopic and combined water plus water vapours.

5. 0.1 M HCl is required 1000 ml

$\therefore$ 1 M HCl is required $= 1000 \times 0.1$

$\therefore$ 5 M HCl is required $= \dfrac{1000 \times 0.1}{5} = 20$ Ml.

6. The hardness of water is due to presence of the bicarbonates of calcium and magnesium. Excess of lime-soda ash method can be used for the softening of water having high calcium, high magnesium carbonate hardness and some non-carbonate hardness.

7. Vulnerable species are likely to move into this endangered category in the near future if the causal factors continue to operate. These are species, whose populations have been seriously depleted and also those whose populations are still abundant throughout their range. Spotted deer, asiatic wild ass, black buck etc. are the examples of vulnerable species.

8. Mortality may be expressed as the number of individuals dying in a given period (death per time) or as the specific rate terms of units of the total population.

A birth-death ratio $\left(100 \times \frac{\text{births}}{\text{deaths}}\right)$ is called vital index. For a population, the important thing is not which members die but which members survive. Thus, survival rates are of much interest than the death rates.

Survival rates are generally expressed by survivorship curves.

Survivorship curves : The pattern of mortality with age is best illustrated by survivorship curves which plot the number surviving to a particular age. There are three general types of survivorship curves which represent different nature of survivors in different types of population

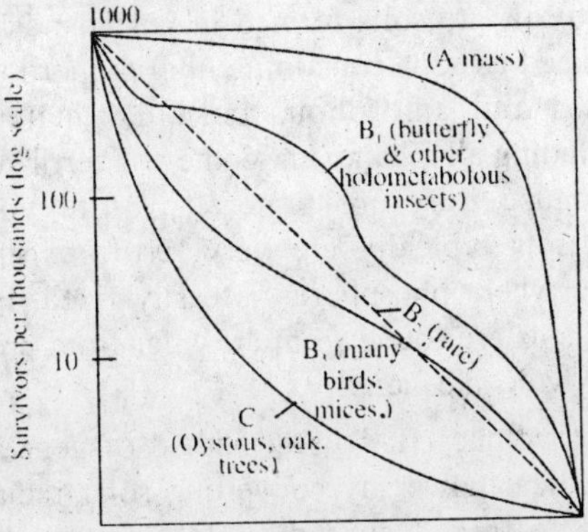

9. Birds group of vertebrate comprises maximum number of endangered species.

10. Ammonia is changed to nitrite by nitrite bacteria (e.g., nitrosomonas, nitrococcus) which is then oxidised to nitrate by nitrate bacteria. There are some bacteria which reduce nitrates and change them into free nitrogen. They are called denitrifying bacteria (e.g., Thiobacillus, denitrificans, pseudomonas denitrificans).

11. Ecotone is a translational area of vegetation between two different plant communities, such as forest and grassland. It has some of the characteristics of each bordering biological community and often contains species not found in the overlapping communities. An ecotone may exist along a broad belt or in a small pocket, such as forest clearing, where two local communities blend together. The influence of the two bordering communities on each other is known as the edge effect. An ecotonal area often has a higher density of organisms of one species and a greater number of species then are found in either flanking community.

12. Zooplankton and rabbit are the small animals, they depend on plants only. They are called herbivores. Carnivores are the animals they depend upon the flesh of animals. That's why their specific common feature is not found in zooplankton and rabbit.

13. An ecological niche is a description of all the physical, chemical and biological factors that a species needs to live, grow and reproduce in an ecosystem, decrease in reproductivity, potency and lesser adaptability to fluctuating environmental factors are the cause of extinction of animal species.

14. **Mass balance glaciers :** Crucial to the survival of a glacier is its mass balance, the difference between accumulation and ablation (sublimation and melting). Climate change may cause variations in both temperature and snowfall, causing changes in mass balance. Changes in mass balance control a glacier's long-term behaviour and are the most sensitive climate indicators on a glacier. From 1980-2008 the mean cumulative mass loss of glaciers reporting mass balance to the World Glacier Monitoring Service is –12m. This includes 19 consecutive years of negative mass balances.

A glacier with a sustained negative balance is out of equilibrium and will retreat, while one with a sustained positive balance is out of equilibrium and will advance. Glacier retreat results in the loss of the low elevation region of the glacier. Since higher elevations are cooler than lower ones, the disappearance of the lowest portion of the glacier reduces overall ablation, thereby increasing mass balance and potentially reestablishing equilibrium. However, if the mass balance of a significant portion of the accumulation zone of the glacier is negative, it is in disequilibrium with the local climate. Such a glacier will melt away with a continuation of this local climate. The key symptom of a glacier in disequilibrium is thinning along the entire length of the glacier. For example, Easton Glacier will likely shrink to half its size, but at a slowing rate of reduction, and stabilize at that size, despite the warmer temperature, over a few decades. However, the Grinnell Glacier will shrink at an increasing rate until it disappears. The difference is that the upper section of Easton Glacier remains healthy and snow-covered, while even the upper section of the Grinnell Glacier is bare, melting and has thinned. Small glaciers with shallow slopes such as Grinnell Glacier are most likely to fall into disequilibrium, if there is a change in the local climate.

In the case of positive mass balance, the glacier will continue to advance expanding its low elevation area, resulting in more melting. If this still does not create an equilibrium balance the glacier will continue to advance. If a glacier is near a large body of water, especially an ocean, the glacier may advance until iceberg calving losses bring about equilibrium. Positive mass balance of glaciers has been recently reported from Karakoram.

15. Greenhouse gases : The best known greenhouse gas is carbon dioxide CO_2. It is breathed out or otherwise given off by living organisms as they undergo aerobic respiration, and is taken in by green plants during photo-synthesis. A small amount of CO_2 in atmosphere is an absolute necessity for life on the earth, without it the planet would be too cold to support living organisms and plants would lack an essential raw ingradient. But excess of CO_2 will cause the earth's surface to heating abnormally.

17. The cryosphere is those portions of earth's surface where water is in solid form, including sea ice, lake ice, river ice, snow cover glaciers, ice caps and ice sheets and frozen ground. Thus, there is a wide overlap with the hydrosphere. The cryosphere is an integral part of the global climate-system with important linkages and feedbacks generated through its influence on the surface energy and moisture fluxes, clouds, hydrology atmospheric and oceanic circulation.

18. Moist and non-saturated soil : When soil temperatures are below 50°F, these bacterias are fairly inactive. Also, the bacteria require aerobic conditions (unsaturated soil water conditions) to nitrify ammonium.

Thus, the amount of nitrification that occurs in the soil is largely dependent on the soil temperature and the time elapsed from application until the soil becomes saturated with water.

19. Andisols are soils formed in volcanic ash and defined as soils containing high proportions of glass and amorphous colloidal materials, including allophane, imogolite and ferrihydrite. Because they are generally quite young, andisols typically are very fertile except in case where phosphorus is easily fixed. Fossil andisols are found from areas far from present day volcanic activity.

20. Photovoltaics (PV) is a method of generating electrical power by converting solar radiation into direct current electricity using semiconductors that exhibit the photovoltaic effect. Photovoltaic power generation employs solar panels composed of a number of solar cells containing a photovoltaic material. Materials presently used for photovoltaics include monocrystalline silicon, polycrystalline silicon, amorphous silicon, cadmium telluride, and copper indium gallium selenide/sulphide. Due to the increased demand for renewable energy sources, the manufacturing of solar cells and photovoltaic arrays has advanced considerably in recent years.

The maximum theoretical efficiency of conversion is about 45%. In August, the university of New South Wales set a record with a solar cell that could convert 43% of light that struck it into electricity.

22. The emission of carbon due to burning of fossil fuels are produced disproportionately by the people of the industriallized countries. Indeed, the wealthiest nations of the world's population burn nearly 70% of the fossil fuels. China is the biggest single contributor, after USA of the world's CO_2 emission. The correct sequence in increasing order of total CO_2 emissions from various countries at present is :

Britain < India < USA < China.

25. Both A and R are true, but R is not the correct explanation of A.

26. Carbon monoxide is a colourless, odourless inflammable, toxic gas present in large quantities in the waste water from burned gases, especially in exhaust fumes from motor vehicles. This is the pollutant which is mostly produced by mankind, who generates more than 70% of its total volume. The toxic effect of carbon monoxide arises from the fact that it combines with the RBCs pigment haemoglogbin so as impedes the combination that normally occurs in the lungs of oxygen with haemoglobin. It thus arrests the transport of oxygen through the blood and leads to symptoms similar to those occur in suffocation. Carbon monoxide (CO) has a 500 times greater affinity to bind with haemoglobin than oxygen. No person should be exposed to CO at a concentration greater than 35 ppm.

27. Photochemical Smog : Smog formed from atmospheric pollutants that are generated under the influence of solar radiations. It manifests itself in the form of a more or less dense haze covering the town which restricts visibility by the blurring, it contrasts due to dissipation of light. The dissipation of light caused by aerosols generated by chemical reactions occasioned by smog. Initial products of reactions are sulphur dioxide, nitrogen oxide various hydrocarbons. Many important reactions include formation of Ozone.

28. The air borne fraction is a scalling factor defined as the ratio of the annual increase in atmospheric CO_2 to the CO. It represents the proportion of human emitted CO_2 that remains in the atmosphere. The fraction average about 46% meaning that approx. half the human emitted CO_2 is absorbed by ocean and land surface.

29. Alkali or Alkaline soils are clay soils with high pH > 8.5, a poor soil structure and a low infiltration capacity. Also they have a hard calcareous layer at 0.5 to 1 m depth. Alkali soils owe their unfavourable physico-chemical properties mainly to the dominating presence of sodium carbonate, phosphorous is not present in soluble state.

31. Report audit findings is not a post audit activity under environmental audit process.

32. Specification for environmental management system – ISO 14001.

33. The draft notification further to amend the Environment Impact Assessment Notification, 2006 published in the Gazette of India, Extraordinary, Part II, Section 3, Subsection (ii) vide number S. 1533 (E) dated the 14th September, 2006, which the Central Government proposes to make, in exercise of the powers conferred by sub-section (1) and clause (v) of sub-section (2) of section 3 of the Environment (Protection) Act, 1986 (29 of 1986), is hereby published for the information of the public likely to be affected thereby and notice is hereby given that the said notification will be taken into consideration after the expiry of sixty days (60 days) from the date on which copies of the Official Gazette containing this notification is made available to the public.

34. Description of environment → Identification of impacts → Prediction of impacts → Evalution of impacts → Identification of mitigation needs.

35. Life Cycle Inventory (LCI) database helps in Life Cycle Assesment (LCA). Practioners answer questions about the environmental impact.

36. Fossil fuels, non renewable natural resources that originate in the earth's crust are being extracted from the earth at breakneck speed simply for human consumption. The chronology ratio of mineral formation to mineral extraction is remarkably high.

There are two ways to manage municipal solid waste (MSW). The high waste approach involves leaving it somewhere burning it or burying it.

Landfills the symbol of the high waste approach, have the proven reputation of preventing MSW from degrading, not to mention attracting a lot of traffic noise, and dust to the surrounding areas.

37. Both (A) and (R) are correct and Reason (R) is not the correct explanation of A.

39. Here terms, $n = 3$

$\because$ GM = $\sqrt[3]{4 \times 8 \times 16}$

$= \sqrt[3]{512} = 8.$

40. The covariance between two data of N observations is given by $\dfrac{\Sigma(X-\overline{X})(Y-\overline{Y})}{N^2}$.

42. Low density polyethylene (LDPE) is a thermoplastic made from the monomer ethylene. It was the first grade of polyethylene, produced by using high pressure process via free radical polymerisation. The EPA estimates 5.7% of LDPE is recycled. LDPE is defined by a density range of 0.910–0.940 g cm^{-3}. It is not reactive at room temperatures except by strong oxydising agents and some solvents come swelling. It can withstand temperatures at 80°C continuously and 95°C for a short time. Made in tranlucent or opaque variations, it is quite flexible and tough but breakable.

43. National Environment Awareness compaign is a non-formal environment education and awareness programme. It is designed for any group, participitating in social, economic and cultural development of the community. They form groups or clubs and arrange exhibition, public lectures, meetings, environment compaigns, etc.

46. NPP (Net Primary Productivity) is the primary measure of biomass accumulation within an ecosystem. Net primary productivity can be calculated by simple formula where the total amount of productivity is adjusted for total productivity losses through maintenance of biological processes.

$NPP = GPP - R_{producer}$

In the terrestrial ecosystem roughly 90% NPP ends up being broken down by decomposers.

47. Regulating marine pollution is the Water (Prevention and Control of Pollution) Act, 1974 (amended up to 1988), which is operative up to 5 km from the shoreline in all coastal States and Union Territories. The enforcement of this Act rests with Central and State Pollution Control Boards. In the case of marine areas, sea water is categorized into five zones, with minimum standards evolved by the Indian Standards Institution (ISI) for the permissible quantities and concentrations of pollutants in each zone.

The prevention and control of marine pollution is one of the responsibilities of the Coast Guard, under the Coast Guard Act, 1978. The prevention and control of marine pollution by oil from ships and liabilities for oil pollution damage are addressed in amendments to the Merchant Shipping Act, 1958, which address provisions of the International Convention for the Prevention of Pollution from Ships (MARPOL) in accordance with the amendments to the 1954 Oil Pollution Convention.

Implementation and enforcement of pollution-related legislation rests with the Central and State Pollution Control Boards and the State Departments of Environment. BOD level waste water is permitted to be released in lands by industries under (PCPA) act 1974 is 30 mg/l.

48. Hydraulic conductivity, symbolically represented as K, is a property of vascular plants, soil or rock, that describes the ease with which a fluid (usually water) can move through pore spaces or fractures. It depends on the *intrinsic permeability* of the material and on the degree of saturation, and on the density and viscosity of the fluid. Saturated hydraulic conductivity,

K_{sat}, describes water movement through saturated media. It is a function of both fluid and medium.

49. Dachigan Sanctuary is associated with Hangul.

50. The UN General Assembly in December 1989 responding to the report of the Brundtland commission decided to hold an international conference on issues concerning environment and development in Rio de Janeiro in June 1992, with the object of a new evolving a new global partnership for saving the earth planet and for sustainable development for the future.

It was decided that the UNCED would beat the level of Heads of State and Government. This made it the first ever earth summit. The Reo Earth marked the 20th anniversary of the Stockholm conference and the founding of the UNTEP, the head for the scintific understanding phenomenon like climatic change acid, rain, global warming, ozone depletion.

The Heads of State and Government assembled at Rio to have the last chance to draw up an action plan, based on global partnership to 'save' the earth planet for future generation.

PAPER-III

Note : This paper contains ***seventy five (75)*** *objective type questions, of* ***two (2)*** *marks each.* ***All*** *questions are compulsory.*

1. Most of the day to day weather changes are associated with which scale in meteorology?

A. Micro scale B. Meso scale

C. Synoptic scale D. Planetary scale

2. Match the List-I with List-II and choose the correct answer from the codes given below:

List-I (Date)	**List-II (Event)**
(*a*) 5th June	1. National Pollution Prevention Day
(*b*) 2nd December	2. World Environment Day
(*c*) 22nd May	3. World Forest Day
(*d*) 21st March	4. Bio-diversity Day

Codes :

	(*a*)	(*b*)	(*c*)	(*d*)
A.	2	1	4	3
B.	3	2	4	1
C.	4	3	2	1
D.	1	4	3	2

3. 'Fanning' smoke stack plumes are observed when

A. there is an inversion above the ground surface.

B. there is unstable atmosphere.

C. there is neutrally stable atmosphere.

D. the stack height is below an inversion layer.

4. The cyclonic winds are generated by the approximate balance between

A. Pressure gradient force and coriolis force

B. Centrifugal force and coriolis force

C. Centrifugal force, coriolis force and frictional drag force.

D. Centrifugal force and pressure gradient force.

5. Mixing height is determined by

A. adiabatic lapse rate and environmental lapse rate.

B. vertical profile of wind speeds and adiabatic lapse rate.

C. vertical profiles of wind speeds and ambient temperature.

D. wind speeds and solar insolation.

6. United Nations has declared "UN Decade of Education for sustainable Development' and the decade identified for this education is

A. 2006–2015

B. 2005–2014

C. 2011–2020

D. 2012–2021

7. Halon–1301 is a

A. Fire extinguisher B. Solvent

C. Refrigerant D. Aerosol propellant

8. Which of the following is a primary pollutant in atmospheric air?

A. Cl_2 B. SO_3

C. Nitrates D. Sulphates

9. Hardness is expressed on the Mohs scale, which ranges from

A. 1 to 10 B. 1 to 14
C. –14 to 14 D. 1 to 100

10. The halon H-1211 has the following chemical composition :

A. CF_2 Cl Br B. CCl_2 FBr
C. CCl_2 F_2 D. CBr_2 Cl F

11. The most toxic among the chlorinated hydrocarbons is

A. Aldrin B. DDT
C. Endrin D. Heptachlor

12. Agent orange is a

A. Weedicide B. Fungicide
C. Nematicide D. Rodenticide

13. Major source of SO_2 is

A. Cement Industry
B. Forest fires
C. Thermal Power Stations
D. Volcanic activity

14. Match each water contaminant in Column-I with its preferred method of removal in Column-II.

Column–I	Column–II
(*a*) Mn^{2+}	1. Activated Carbon
(*b*) Ca^{2+} and HCO_3^-	2. Raise pH by addition of Na_2CO_3
(*c*) Trihalomethane	3. Addition of lime
(*d*) Mg^{2+}	4. Oxidation

Codes :

	(*a*)	(*b*)	(*c*)	(*d*)
A.	4	3	1	2
B.	3	2	4	1
C.	2	4	3	1
D.	1	2	4	3

15. Reverse Osmosis (RO) operated at 200–1200 psig removes particles ranging from

A. 0.0001 to 0.001 μm B. 0.01 to 10 μm
C. 0.1 to 1.0 μm D. 0.1 to 2.0 μm

16. Coagulation is a chemical process, in which charged particles or colloids undergo

A. Stabilization B. Destabilization
C. Attraction D. Precipitation

17. Water has the following chemical composition:

$[Ca^{2+}]$ = 15 mg/L;
$[Mg^{2+}]$ = 10 mg/L;
$[SO_4^{2-}]$ = 30 mg/L;

The total hardness of water will be

A. 80 mg/L as $CaCO_3$ B. 55 mg/L as $CaCO_3$
C. 160 mg/L as $CaCO_3$ D. 40 mg/L as $CaCO_3$

18. Two water samples were collected.

Sample # 1 : pH = 9, but no carbonate or other dissolved proton donors or acceptors.

Sample # 2 : pH = 8.3, but it contains dissolved $NaHCO_3$ at a concentration of 0.01/mg/L

Which of the following is true based on the above observations.

A. Sample # 1 will have more alkalinity.
B. Sample # 2 will have more alkalinity.
C. Sample # 1 and sample # 2 will have exactly same alkalinity.
D. Alkalinity cannot be estimated.

19. Two soil samples, A and B, at different soil moisture levels are placed in contact with each other. Water will more likely move from soil A to soil B if their water potential, expressed in kPa, are :

A. A = –5; B = +5 B. A = –5; B = –5
C. A = –20; B = –10 D. A = –30; B = –40

20. Blue baby syndrome is caused by

A. Carbon monoxide B. Nitrate
C. Fluoride D. Mercury

21. Assertion (A) : For solar cell fabrication, those semiconducting materials which have band-gap energies in the range 1-1.8 eV are most suitable.

Reason (R) : The maximum solar irradiance is around a wavelength corresponding to 1.5 eV.

Identify the correct Code:

A. Both (A) and (R) are correct and (R) is the correct explanation of (A).
B. Both (A) and (R) are correct and (R) is not the correct explanation of (A).
C. (A) is true, but (R) is false.
D. (A) is false, but (R) is true.

22. Assertion (A) : State factors (external factors) control the overall structure of an ecosystem and the way things work within it.

Reason (R) : The state factors are not themselves influenced by the ecosystem.
Identify the correct code:
A. (A) is correct (R) is incorrect.
B. Both (A) and (R) are correct, but (R) is not correct explanation of (A).
C. Both (A) and (R) are correct and (R) is correct explanation of (A).
D. Both (A) and (R) are incorrect.

23. Assertion (A) : When energy is transferred between trophic levels, the successive level in the pathway have lesser available energy compared to the preceding level.
Reason (R) : Whenever energy is transformed, there is loss of energy through the release of heat.
A. Both (A) and (R) are true and (R) is the correct explanation.
B. Both (A) and (R) are true and (R) is not the correct explanation.
C. (A) is true and (R) is false.
D. (A) is false and (R) is true.

24. Assertion (A) : The ecosystem surrounding a river gets damaged due to construction of a dam.
Reason (R) : The area gets inundated with large volume of water.
Identify the correct answer:
A. Both (A) and (R) are true, with (R) being the correct explanation.
B. Both (A) and (R) are true, but (R) is not the correct explanation.
C. (A) is true, but (R) is wrong.
D. Both (A) and (R) are wrong.

25. Assertion (A) : Soils rich in clay minerals have high levels of organic matter.
Reason (R) : Clay soils tend to have low decomposition rates.
Identify the correct answer:
A. Both statements are correct and (R) is correct explanation of (A).
B. Both statements are correct, but (R) is not correct explanation of (A).
C. Statement (A) is correct, but (R) is incorrect.
D. Statement (A) is incorrect, but (R) is correct.

26. Assertion (A) : Nitrogen cycle is an endogenic biogeochemical cycle.
Reason (R) : Atmospheric N_2 can be fixed by certain prokaryotes in the soil.
Choose correct answer:
A. Both (A) and (R) are true and (R) is the correct explanation of (A).
B. Both (A) and (R) are true, but (R) is not the correct explanation of (A).
C. (A) is true, but (R) is false.
D. (A) is false, but (R) is true.

27. Match the following :

Column–I	**Column–II**
(*a*) Nekton	1. Associated with surface film water
(*b*) Neuston	2. Found at the bottom of an aquatic ecosystem.
(*c*) Benthos	3. Active swimmer, against water current.
(*d*) Plankton	4. Incapable of independent movement.

Choose the correct answer from the Codes:
Codes :

	(*a*)	(*b*)	(*c*)	(*d*)
A.	1	3	4	2
B.	2	4	1	3
C.	3	1	2	4
D.	4	2	3	1

28. Which of the following is not a major biome of India?
A. Tropical rain forest biomes
B. Tropical deciduous forest biomes
C. Temperate needle leaf forest biomes
D. Mountains and glaciers

29. To survive and avoid competition for the same resources, a species usually occupies only part of its fundamental niche in a particular community or ecosystem. This is called
A. Geographic isolation
B. Mutualism
C. Realized Niche
D. Broad Niche

30. Which of the following is *not* a characteristic feature of community?
A. Populations of different species occupying a particular place.

B. Complex interacting network of plants, animals and microbes.
C. Different species interacting with one another and with their environment of matter and energy.
D. Groups of interacting individuals of different species.

31. Which of the following food chain is correct?
A. Krill → Adelie Penguins → Emperor Penguins → Leopard Seal
B. Krill → Crabeater Seal → Leopard Seal → Killer Whale
C. Krill → Leopard Seal → Emperor Penguins → Killer Whale
D. Krill → Crabeater Seal → Killer Whale → Leopard Seal

32. The observation that individuals of a population are uniformly distributed suggests that
A. Density of population is low.
B. Resources are distributed unevenly.
C. The members of the population are neither attracted to nor repelled by one another.
D. The members of the population are competing for access to a resource.

33. Which of the following biomes is correctly paired with the description of its climate?

A. Tropical forests	—	nearly constant day length and temperature
B. Tundra	—	long summers, mild winters
C. Savanna	—	cool temperature year-round, uniform precipitation during the year
D. Temperate grasslands	—	relatively short growing season, mild winters.

34. Cellulose and hemicellulose are not resistant to decay but are broken down more slowly. They are considered
A. Labile B. Moderately labile
C. Recalcitrant D. Nonlabile

35. The parasitic gall formation is related to
A. Host-specific antibodies
B. Parasite specific cysts
C. Parasite specific enzymes
D. Host specific hormones

36. What is the estimate of volume of water yield for saturated pond aquifer of 1 metre width and 2 metre depth and length of 4 metre. Consider the porosity of sand to be 35% and specific yield to be 25%?
A. 2.8 m^3 B. 28 m^3
C. 0.28 m^3 D. 280 m^3

37. Arrange the following climate proxies in ascending order of time scales:
(*i*) Lithological records
(*ii*) Pollens
(*iii*) Tree rings
(*iv*) Historical records
A. (*iv*), (*iii*), (*i*), (*ii*)
B. (*iv*), (*iii*), (*ii*), (*i*)
C. (*iv*), (*ii*), (*i*), (*iii*)
D. (*iv*), (*i*), (*iii*), (*ii*)

38. Acid drainage is more in mining of
A. Granite
B. Bauxite
C. Lime stone
D. Base metal sulphide

39. Geothermal gradient in Earth is
A. Uniform throughout.
B. Higher in continental lithosphere.
C. Higher in subduction zones.
D. Lower at mid oceanic ridges.

40. Coal mining areas are affected by
(*i*) Land subsidence
(*ii*) Fire hazard
(*iii*) Radioactive waste
(*iv*) Air pollution
A. (*i*) and (*ii*)
B. (*i*), (*ii*) and (*iii*)
C. (*i*), (*ii*) and (*iv*)
D. (*i*), (*ii*), (*iii*) and (*iv*)

41. Radioactive elements are concentrated in
A. Earth's core B. Earth's mantle
C. Mid-Oceanic ridges D. Earth's crust

42. What led to maximum number of fatalities during Indonesian 2004 Earthquake?
A. Death on account of openings on surface
B. Fires generated due to earthquake
C. Epidemic diseases
D. Tsunami

43. Maximum carbon in the world is found in
A. Oceans B. Coal mines
C. Antarctica D. Forests

44. The highest seismic domain in India is
A. The Himalayas
B. The Western ghats
C. The Indogangetic plains
D. The Dharwar craton

45. Earth's core is mainly composed of
A. Iron
B. Nitrogen
C. Carbon
D. Magnesium

46. Gasification is
A. the high temperature (~ 750 – 850 °C) conversion of solid, carbonaceous fuel into flammable gas mixtures.
B. the high temperature (~ 750 – 850 °C) conversion of solid, carbonaceous fuel into liquid.
C. the low temperature (~ 250 – 350 °C) conversion of solid, carbonaceous fuel into flammable gas mixture.
D. the low temperature (~ 250 – 350 °C) conversion of solid, carbonaceous fuel into liquid.

47. In case of magneto hydrodynamic power generation, for maximum power output, the efficiency is
A. 0.25 B. 0.5
C. 0.75 D. 0.4

48. Which combination of radiative fluxes plays the all important role in climate change?
A. Visible and infrared
B. Visible and UV
C. Visible, UV and infrared
D. UV, microwaves and infrared

49. The climate sensitivity parameter is defined as the rate of change of
A. surface temperature with albedo of earth
B. surface temperature with CO_2 concentration in atmosphere
C. precipitation with earth's temperature
D. surface temperature with radiative forcing.

50. Which of the following fuels has highest carbon intensity?
A. Natural gas B. Oil
C. Bituminous coal D. Biomass

51. Solid waste treatment by pyrolysis involves
A. Autoclaving
B. Heating in presence of air
C. Heating in presence of acetic acid
D. Heating in absence of air

52. In which year Wildlife Protection Act was enacted ?
A. 1962 B. 1972
C. 1982 D. 1992

53. According to National Ambient Air Quality Standards, the annual average concentration of Sulphur dioxide in residential areas in India is
A. 20 $\mu g/m^3$ B. 40 $\mu g/m^3$
C. 60 $\mu g/m^3$ D. 80 $\mu g/m^3$

54. Which of the following statements is correct in the context of Environmental Impact Assessment?
A. The process considers broad range of potential alternatives.
B. It provides early warning of cumulative effects.
C. Focusses on sustainability agenda.
D. Focusses on standard agenda.

55. Match the List-I with List-II and choose the correct answer from the codes given below:

List–I (Components)	List–II (Dimensions)
(*a*) Equitable utilization of natural resources	1. Social dimensions
(*b*) Benefit to disadvantaged group	2. Economic dimensions
(*c*) Creation of additional value	3. Environmental dimensions
(*d*) Elimination of toxic substances	4. Political dimensions

Codes :

	(*a*)	(*b*)	(*c*)	(*d*)
A.	4	1	2	3
B.	4	1	3	2
C.	3	2	1	4
D.	2	4	1	3

56. Among the following, which one does not belong to EIA process?
A. Establishment of base line environmental condition.
B. Identification, Prediction and assessment of impact.
C. Suggesting the mitigation measures.
D. Developing EMS auditing procedures.

57. According to Gaussian Plume Model, the ground level concentration (C) of a pollutant varies with effective height (H) as (σ is the vertical dispersion coefficient):

A. $C \propto \frac{1}{H}$

B. $C \propto e^{-\frac{H^2}{\sigma^2}}$

C. $C \propto e^{-\frac{H}{\sigma}}$

D. $C \propto H^{-2}$

58. In a multiple regression analysis, an examination of variances revealed that explained sum of squares per degree of freedom and residual sum of squares per degree of freedom were 250 and 100, respectively. What is the F-ratio?
A. 6.25 B. 5.25
C. 0.4 D. 2.5

59. A source of air pollution is emitting a pollutant at the rate S(mg/hours) inside a room of volume V(m^3). The air of the room is being changed n times per hour. If k is pollutant decay rate constant, the concentration C(t) of the pollutant at any given instant of time under well mixed conditions is given by

A. $C(t) = \left(\frac{S}{nV}\right)(1 - e^{-nt})$

B. $C(t) = \left(\frac{S/V}{n+k}\right)(1 - e^{-nt})$

C. $C(t) = (S/nV)\,(n + k)$

D. $C(t) = \left(\frac{nV}{S}\right)(1 - e^{-nk})$

60. Which one of the following is *not* an eigenvalue of the matrix?

$$\begin{bmatrix} -1 & 2 & 2 \\ 2 & 2 & 2 \\ -3 & -6 & -6 \end{bmatrix}$$

A. 0 B. −2
C. −3 D. 3

61. A sample of 17 measurements of the diameter of a spherical particle gave a mean = 5 μm and a standard deviation = 0.5 μm. Assuming t-statistic for 16 degrees of freedom $t_{0.05} \approx 2$, the 95% confidence limits of actual diameter are
A. 4.75 and 5.25 μm. B. 4.00 and 6.00 μm.
C. 4.9 and 5.1 μm. D. 4.5 and 5.5 μm.

62. "Hot spots" are areas,
(*i*) extremely rich in species
(*ii*) with high endemism
(*iii*) extremely scarce in species
(*iv*) under constant threat
Choose the correct answer from the codes:
Codes :
A. (*i*) and (*ii*)
B. (*ii*) and (*iii*)
C. (*ii*), (*iii*) and (*iv*)
D. (*i*), (*ii*) and (*iv*)

63. A paddy field is an example of
A. Fresh water ecosystem
B. Terrestrial ecosystem
C. Auto ecosystem
D. Engineered ecosystem

64. Which pyramid cannot be inverted in a stable ecosystem?
A. Pyramid of energy
B. Pyramid of biomass
C. Pyramid of number
D. Pyramid of dry weight

65. Which one of the following environmental factors is responsible for cyclomorphism in animals?
A. Moisture
B. Temperature
C. Photoperiod
D. Wind

66. Sr^{90} can enter and accumulate in the body through
A. Drinking water
B. Inhaling contaminated air
C. Food chain
D. Skin

67. Which one of the following is a neurotoxic?
A. Organophosphate B. Nitric oxide
C. 2, 4-D D. Cuprous oxide

68. If 0.05 M proline-ninhydine complex has an absorbance of 0.15 at 520 nm in a 1 cm curvette, its molar extinction coefficient will be
A. 50 m M^{-1} cm^{-1} B. 0.1 M^{-1} cm^{-1}
C. 1 M^{-1} cm^{-1} D. 3 M^{-1} cm^{-1}

69. Which bacterium found in soil is anaerobic?
A. *Clostridium* Sp B. *Azatobacter* Sp
C. *Bacillus* Sp D. *Thiobacillus* Sp

70. Particles of sizes < 1 μm are most efficiently removed by
A. Cyclones
B. Scrubbers
C. Bag filter
D. Electrostatic Precipitator

71. The attenuation of sound by reactive type silencers is based on
A. absorption of sound waves
B. scattering of sound waves
C. impedance discontinuity
D. interference of sound waves

72. "Farmer's lung" is a classic example for
A. Psittacosis
B. Extrinsic allergic alveolitis
C. Legionnaire's disease
D. Aspergillosis

73. The lichen and moss stages occur in
A. Lithosere B. Psamosere
C. Hydrosere D. Hydrarch

74. The mean of a data following Poisson distribution is 4. The second moment of the distribution is:
A. 4 B. 2
C. 1 D. 0

75. Which of the following rivers has maximum melt water component in its discharge?
A. Indus B. Ganges
C. Brahmaputra D. Narmada

ANSWERS

1	2	3	4	5	6	7	8	9	10
C	A	A	D	A	B	A	A	A	A
11	**12**	**13**	**14**	**15**	**16**	**17**	**18**	**19**	**20**
C	A	D	A	A	B	A	B	D	B
21	**22**	**23**	**24**	**25**	**26**	**27**	**28**	**29**	**30**
A	B	B	B	A	D	C	D	C	C
31	**32**	**33**	**34**	**35**	**36**	**37**	**38**	**39**	**40**
B	D	A	B	C	A	B	C	B	C
41	**42**	**43**	**44**	**45**	**46**	**47**	**48**	**49**	**50**
D	D	A	A	A	A	B	A	D	C
51	**52**	**53**	**54**	**55**	**56**	**57**	**58**	**59**	**60**
D	B	C	D	A	D	B	D	A	D
61	**62**	**63**	**64**	**65**	**66**	**67**	**68**	**69**	**70**
A	D	D	A	B	C	A	D	A	D
71	**72**	**73**	**74**	**75**					
C	B	A	A	A					

SOME SELECTED EXPLANATORY ANSWERS

1. Scale in meteorology is the interdisciplinary scientific study of the atmosphere that focuses on weather processes and short term forecasting (in contrast with climatology). Studies in the filled stretch back millennia, though significant progress in meteorology did not occur until the 18th century, saw breakthrough occur after observing networks developed across several countries. Breakthrough in weather forecasting were achieved in the latter half of the twentieth century, after development of computer. Most of the day weather changes are associated with planetary scale.

2. 5th June : World Environment Day
   2nd December : National Pollution Prevention Day
   22nd May : Biodiversity Day
   21st March : World Forest Day.

3. Tall smoke stacks emit the pollution from the inversion aloft. This fume does not pollute the nearby area. Otherwise, the smoke stack forms a fumigating plume that can cause health problems to those in the nearby area. There are also their plumes sometimes created by the smoke stack. It depends on how the power plant releases the exhaust into the air and how outside forces impact the exhaust, the smoke stack can develop a coning plume, a looping plume, a lofting plume or a fumigation.

4. **Cyclonic winds :** The cyclones are irregular wind movements involving closed air circulation around a low pressure centre. This closed air circulation is caused by atmospheric disturbances over and above the surface of the earth, coupled with the earth's rotation which imparts to these disturbances a whirling motion. Cyclones are associated with destructive and violent disturbances, such a heavy squalls and torrential rainfall. The cyclonic winds are generated by the balance between centrifugal force and pressure gradient force.

6. **UN Decade of Education for Sustainable Development:** Education for Sustainable Development allows every human being to acquire the knowledge, skills, attitudes and values necessary to shape a sustainable future. Education for Sustainable Development means including key sustainable development issues into teaching and learning for example, climate change, disaster risk reduction, biodiversity, poverty reduction, and sustainable consumption. It also requires participatory teaching and learning methods that motivate and empower learners to change their behaviour and take action for sustainable development. Education for Sustainable Development consequently promotes competencies like critical thinking, imagining future scenarios and making decisions in a collaborative way. Education for Sustainable Development requires far-reaching changes in the way education is often practised today. UNESCO is the lead agency for the UN Decade of Education for Sustainable Development (2005-2014).

7. **Halon–1301 :** Halon-1301 was introduced as an effective gaseous fire suppression agent in the 1960s, and was used around valuable materials, such as aircraft, mainframe computers, and telecommunication switching centers, usually in total flooding systems. It was also widely used in the maritime industry to add a third level of protection, should the main and emergency fire pumps become inoperable or ineffective. It is a fire extinguisher.

   It is considered good practice to avoid all unnecessary exposure to Halon 1301, and to limit exposures to concentrations of 7 per cent and below to 15 minutes. Exposure to Halon 1301 in the 5 to 7 per cent range produces little, if any, noticeable effect. At levels between 7 and 10 per cent, mild central nervous system effects such as dizziness and tingling in the extremities have been reported. In practice, the operators of many Halon 1301 total flooding systems evacuate the space on impending agent discharge.

8. **Primary Pollutant in atmospheric Air :** Global satellite data showed that stratospheric ozone levels were decreasing over most of the southern polar latitudes. This pattern, widely referred to as the 'ozone hole' (more accurately, ozone thinning), proved to be caused by high chlorine radical concentrations, as well as by bromine radicals (Br), which also trigger catalytic cycles with chlorine to consume ozone.

The source of the high chlorine radicals was found to be a fast reaction of the chlorine reservoirs HCl and $ClNO_3$ at the surface of icy particles formed at the very cold temperatures of the Antarctic wintertime stratosphere and called polar stratospheric clouds (PSCs). HCl and $ClNO_3$ react on PSC surfaces to produce molecular chlorine (Cl_2) and nitric acid. Cl_2 then rapidly photolyzes in spring to release chlorine atoms and trigger ozone loss.

Ozone depletion has worsened since 1985. Today springtime ozone levels over Antarctica are less than half of levels recorded in the 1960s, and the 2006 Antarctic Ozone hole covered 29 million square kilometers, tying the largest value previously recorded in 2000. In the 1990s, ozone loss by the same mechanism was discovered in the Arctic springtime stratosphere, although Arctic ozone depletion is not as extensive as in Antarctica because temperatures are not as consistently cold. Cl_2 is a primary pollutant in atmospheric air.

9. **Mohs Scale:** The Mohs scale of mineral hardness characterizes the scratch resistance of various minerals through the ability of a harder material to scratch a softer material. It was created in 1812 by the German geologist and mineralogist Friedrich Mohs and is one of the several definitions of hardness in materials science.

The Mohs scale of mineral hardness is based on the ability of one natural sample of matter to scratch another mineral. The sample of matter used by Mohs are all different minerals.

Minerals are pure substances found in nature. Rocks are made up of one or more minerals. As the hardest known naturally occurring substance, when the scale was designed, diamonds are at the top of the scale. The hardness of material is measured against the scale by finding the hardest material that the given material can scratch and the softest material that can scratch the given material. For example, if some material is scratched by apatite but not by fluorite, its hardness on the Mohs scale, which ranges from 1 to 10.

10. **Halon H-1211 :** Halon-1211 and Halon-1301 are low toxicity, chemically stable compounds that as long as contained in cylinders, are easily recyclable. Halon-1211 is a CFC, production of new Halon has ceased. There is no cost effective means of safety effectively of the halon-1211. Hence, recycling and reusing the existing supply intelligently and responsibly to protect lives and property is the wisest solution. The halon H-1211 has the chemical composition of CF_2ClBr.

11. Chlorinated Hydrocarbons are a group of chemicals composed of carbon, chlorine and hydrogen. As pesticides, they are also referred to by several other names, including chlorinated organics, chlorinated insecticides and chlorinated synthetics. Although the first chlorinated hydrocarbon was synthesized in 1874, its insecticidal properties were not discovered until 1939 by the Swiss chemist, Paul Müller. It was introduced as DDT in 1942 during World War II and its subsequent use is responsible for saving millions of lives from vectored diseases such as typhus and malaria. The advantages of these synthetic chemicals over previously used botanical or natural insecticides were improved efficacy, lower use rates, lower costs and greater persistence. As with most of the chlorinated hydrocarbons, DDT has been banned for use in the United States, but is still used in some developing countries for combating insect vectors of disease. Other members of this chemical group no longer in use in the United States include aldrin, dieldrin, heptachlor, mirex, chlordecone, and chlordane. Others remaining registered are

active ingredients of various home and garden products and some agricultural, structural, and environmental pest control products. One particular subgroup of these chemicals, known as cyclodienes, were especially persistent, which made them useful for controlling structural pests such as termites. Their persistence is attributed to their long soil-life and stability in the presence of the untraviolet radiation from sunlight. Many structures treated with one of these compounds are still protected today. One cyclodiene still registered for use, endosulfan, is less persistent. The Environmental Protection Agency determined that the potential for environmental contamination from the persistent members of this group of chemicals was sufficient to issue a ban on their use. The most toxic among the chlorinated hydrocarbons is Endrin.

12. Agent Orange or Herbicide Orange (HO) is one of the herbicides and defoliants used by the U.S. military as part of its herbicidal warfare program, Operation Ranch Hand, during the Vietnam War from 1961 to 1971. A 50:50 mixture of 2,4,5-T and 2,4-D, it was manufactured for the U.S. Department of Defense primarily by Monsanto Corporation and Dow Chemical. The 2,4,5-T used to produce Agent Orange was contaminated with 2,3,7,8-tetrachlorodibenzodioxin (TCDD), an extremely toxic dioxin compound. It was given its name from the colour of the orange-striped 55 US gallon (208) barrels in which it was shipped and was by far the most widely used of the so-called "Rainbow Herbicides".

During the Vietnam War, between 1962 and 1971, the United States military sprayed nearly 2,00,00,000 US gallons (7,60,00,000) of material containing chemical herbicides and defoliants mixed with jet fuel in Vietnam, eastern Laos and parts of Cambodia, as part of Operation Ranch Hand. The program's goal was to defoliate forested and rural land, depriving guerrillas of cover, another goal was to induce forced draft urbanization, destroying the ability of peasants to support themselves in the countryside, and forcing them to flee to the U.S. dominated cities, thus depriving the guerrillas of their rural support and food supply.

The US began to target food crops in October 1962, primarily using Agent Blue. In 1965, 42 per cent of all herbicide spraying was dedicated to food crops. Rural-to-urban migration rates dramatically increased in South Vietnam, as peasants escaped the war and famine in the countryside by fleeing to the U.S.-dominated cities. The urban population in South Vietnam nearly tripled: from 2.8 million people in 1958, to 8 million by 1971. The rapid flow of people led to a fast-paced and uncontrolled urbanization; an estimated 1.5 million people were living in Saigon slums.

United States Air Force records show that at least 6,542 spraying missions took place over the course of Operation Ranch Hand. By 1971, 12 per cent of the total area of South Vietnam had been sprayed with defoliating chemicals, at an average concentration of 13 times the recommended USDA application rate for domestic use. In South Vietnam alone, an estimated 10 million hectares (25 million acres, 39,000 square miles) of agricultural land was ultimately destroyed. In some areas, TCDD concentrations in soil and water were hundreds of times greater than the levels considered safe by the U.S. Environmental Protection Agency. Overall, more than 20% of South Vietnam's forests were sprayed at least once over a nine-year period. Hence, Agent Orange is weedicide.

13. SO_2 : Sulphur dioxide belongs to the family of gases called sulphur oxides. SO_2 forms when substances containting sulphur are burned usually coal, diesel, or oil and during some industrial processes. SO_2 affects respiratory systems and aggravates cardiovascular disease. It can harm vegetation, including agricultural crops. Mixed with moisture in the atmosphere, SO_2 can create acid rain, which can harm humans, animals and vegetation as well as erode buildings. The major source of SO_2 is volcanic activity.

14. Mn^{2+} → oxidation
$Ca^{2+}HCO_3$ → addition of lime
Trihalomethane → activated carbon
Mg^{2+} → raise pH by addition of Na_2CO_3.

15. **Reverse Osmosis (RO) :** The process of movement of solvent through a semipermeable membrane from the solution to the pure solvent by applying excess pressure on solution side is known as reverse osmosis. This process is used for distillation of sea water obtaining drinking water. It operates at 200–1200 psig, removes particles, ranging from 0.001 to 0.001 μm.

16. The use of nitrate-contaminated drinking water to prepare infant formula is a well-known risk factor for infant methemoglobinemia. Affected infants develop a peculiar blue-gray skin colour and may become irritable or lethargic, depending on the severity of their condition. The condition can progress rapidly to cause coma and death if it is not recognized and treated appropriately. Two cases of blue baby syndrome were recently investigated. Both cases involved infants who became ill after being fed formula that was reconstituted with water from private wells. Water samples collected from these wells during the infants, illnesses contained nitrate-nitrogen concentrations of 22.9 and 27.4 mg/L.

21. Both (A) and (R) are correct and (R) is correct explanation of (A).

22. Both (A) and (R) are correct and (R) is not the correct explanation of (A).

23. Both (A) and (R) are correct and (R) is not the correct explanation of (A).

24. Both (A) and (R) are true, but (R) is not the correct explanation of (A).

34. Using the organic phosphorus fractionation system suggested by Bowman and Cole, this paper studied the dynamics of labile, moderately labile, moderately resistant, and highly resistant organic phosphorus in rhizosphere and non-rhizosphere soil at different development stages of larch, and their relationships with soil available phosphorus and tree growth yield. The results showed that the main components of soil organic phosphorus in larch plantation were moderately labile and moderately resistant organic phosphorus, amounted to 77.07%-86.68% of the total organic phosphorus. The labile and moderately labile organic phosphorus in rhizosphere soil were the main sources of soil available phosphorus at different development stages of larch. The contents of total organic phosphorus, labile organic phosphorus, moderately resistant organic phosphorus and highly resistant organic phosphorus in rhizosphere soil decreased with stand ages from young stand to near mature stand, but increased from near mature stand to mature stand. No apparent change the moderately labile organic phosphorus content was found over stand ages in rhizosphere soil. The contents of various organic phosphorus forms presented a fluctuating increasing tendency in non-rhizosphere soil as stand ages increased. There was a close relationship between the increments of periodic average diameter at breast height and periodic average height and the contents of soil labile organic phosphorus and available phosphorus. Cellulose and hemicelluse are not resistance to decay but are broken down more slowly. They are considered as moderatory labile.

35. In fact, most galls contain both the parasitic larvae of a gall wasp, and the parasitic larvae of a wasp which feeds on the parasitic larvae of the gall wasp. (It's like an Escher drawing! But with parasitic wasps.)

Another interesting fact is that many gall wasps practice parthenogenesis, which is where the female reproduces without any interaction with a male. Some species practice blended methods (sometimes reproducing sexually, and other times using parthenogenesis) and other species alternate generations (with one generation reproducing sexually, and the next generation reproducing through parthenogenesis). Hence, the parasitic gall information is related to parasite specific enzymes.

37. Historical records → Tree rings → Pollens → Lithological records.

38. **Acid drainage :** When rock surfaces are exposed to air and rain, a reaction can occur with the elements in the rock which results in a change in the characteristics of the water that drains off. If the rock contains sulphides, a natural oxidation process can acidify the water. This is known as acid drainage (also acid rock drainage (ARD) or acid mine drainage (AMD)). As the water becomes more acidic, its capacity to leach out other elements from the rock, such as metals, increases. The resulting drainage can become very acidic and contain a number of harmful constituents. In some cases, elements from the rock can leach out into contact water without acidification and result in water contamination—this is known as metal leaching (ML). In either case, polluted water drains away from the exposed rock and can have significant impacts on surrounding water bodies (rivers, lakes, coastal areas, groundwater) and the wildlife or people who come in contact with these sources. Acid drainage is more in mining of lime stone.

Although this is natural process, mining activities can trigger this phenomenon by exposing large surface areas of rock to water and oxygen. Rock is exposed on the walls of open pits and underground structures–but the most significant newly exposed rock surfaces are in the fragmented pieces of waste rock that are removed from the ground and placed in dumps.

39. The geothermal gradient of 25°C/km is thought to be restricted to the upper part of the earth's crust. If it continued at this rate uniformly from the surface, the internal temperature of the earth would be greater than 2,000°C within the lithosphere—a temperature that far exceeds the melting temperatures for all rocks at the depth. Since the crust and upper mantle are solid and brittle, this gradient cannot extend to these depths, where it is more likely about 1°C/km. Recent laboratory studies have suggested the temperature is about 4,800°C at the base of the lower mantle and about 7,000°C in the inner core. The heat flow is the amount of heat from the earth's interior that is lost at the surface. The heat is probably generated by a still–cooling core or by the radioactive decay of elements such as uranium and thorium. Areas of higher heat flow are generally related to magnatic activity or tectonic forces that bring wedges of hot mantle rock (mangle plumes) into thin or faulted crustal areas.

40. Coal mining areas are affected by Land subsidence, fire hazard and air pollution.

41. Uranium, thorium and potassium are the main elements contributing to natural terrestrial radioactivity. The isotopes ^{228}U, ^{235}U, ^{232}Th and ^{40}K decay with half-lives so long that significant amounts remain in the earth, providing a continuing source of heat. The slow decay of these isotopes also provides the basis for radiometric age dating and isotopic modelling of the evolution of the earth and its crust. There is a complex interplay between their heat production and the processes involved in crust formation. The phenomena such as volcanism, earthquakes, and large-scale hydrothermal activity associated with ore deposition reflect the dissipation of heat energy from the earth much of which derived from natural radioactivity.

42. On the morning of December 26, 2004 a magnitude 9.3 earthquake struck off the Northwest coast of the Indonesian island of Sumatra. The earthquake resulted from complex slip on the fault where the oceanic portion of the Indian Plate slides under Sumatra, part of the Eurasian Plate. The earthquake deformed the ocean floor, pushing the overlying water up into a tsunami wave. The tsunami wave devastated nearby areas where the wave may have been as high as 25 metres (80 feet) tall and killed nearly 3,00,000 people from nations in the region and tourists from around the world. The tsunami wave itself also travelled the globe, and was measured in the Pacific and many other places by tide gauges. Measurements in California exceeded 40 cm in height, while New Jersey saw water level fluctuations as great as 34 cm. Eyewitness accounts, photos, and videos provided unprecedented documentation of the event.

44. Northeast India is seismically, one of the six most active regions of the world, the other five being Mexico, Taiwan, California, Japan and Turkey. It is placed in zone 5, the highest zone, of the seismic zonation map of India. It lies at the junction of Himalayan arc to the north and Burmese arc to the east. The region has experienced 18 large earthquakes ($M \geq 7$) during the last hundred years including the great earthquakes of Shillong (1897, M = 8.7) and Assam-Tibet border (1950, M = 8.7). Besides, several hundred small and micro earthquakes have also been recorded in the region. The high seismicity in the region is attributed to the collision tectonics between the Indian and the Eurasian plate in the north and subduction tectonics along the Indo-Myanmar range (IMR) in the east.

45. Earth's core is structured in a solid inner core, mainly composed of iron, and a liquid outer core. The temperature at the inner core boundary is expected to be close to the melting point of iron at 330 gigapascal (GPa). Despite intensive experimental and theoretical efforts, there is litle consensus on the melting behaviour of iron at these extreme pressures and temperatures. We present static laser-heated diamond anvil cell experiments up to 200 GPa using synchrotron-based fast X-ray diffraction as a primary melting diagnostic. When extrapolating to higher pressures, we conclude that the melting temperature of iron at the inner core boundary is 6230 ± 500 kelvin. This estimation favours a high heat flux at the core-mantle boundary with a possible partial melting of the mantle.

46. Gasification is a processs that converts organic or fossil based carbonaceous materials into carbon monoxide, hydrogen and carbon dioxide. This is achieved by reacting the material at high temperatures ~750°C-850°C, without combustion, with a controlled amount of oxygen and/or steam. The resulting gas mixture is called syngas (from synthesis gas or synthetic gas) or producer gas and is itself a fuel. The power derived from gasification and combustion of the resultant gas is considered to be a source of renewable energy, if the gasified compounds were obtained from biomass.

The advantage of gasification is that using the syngas is potentially more efficient than direct combustion of the original fuel because it can be combusted at higher temperatures or even in fuel cells, so that the themodynamic upper limit to the efficiency defined by Carnot's rule is higher or not applicable. Syngas may be burned directly in gas engines, used to produce methanol and hydrogen, or converted via the Fischer–Tropsch process into synthetic fuel. Gasification can also begin with material which would otherwise have been disposed of such as biodegradable waste. In addition, the high-temperature process refines out corrosive ash elements such as chloride and potassium, allowing clean gas production from otherwise problematic fuels. Gasification of fossil fuels is currently widely used on industrial scales to generate electricity.

51. Pyrolysis is a thermochemical decomposition of organic material at elevated temperatures in the absence of oxygen (or any halogen). It involves the simultaneous change of chemical composition and physical phase, and is irreversible.

Pyrolysis is a type of thermolysis, and is most commonly observed in organic materials exposed to high temperatures. It is one of the processes involved in charring wood, starting at 200-300°C (390-570°F). It also occurs in fires where solid fuels are burning or when vegetation comes into contact with lava in volcanic eruptions. In general, pyrolysis of organic substances produces gas and liquid products and leaves a solid residue richer in carbon content, char. Extreme pyrolysis, which leaves mostly, carbon as the residue, is called carbonization.

The process is used heavily in the chemical industry, for example, to produce charcoal, activated carbon, methanol and other chemicals from wood, to convert ethylene dichloride into vinyl chloride to make PVC, to produce coke from coal, to convert biomass into syngas and biochar, to turn waste into safely disposable substances, and for transforming medium-weight hydrocarbons from oil into lighter ones like gasoline. These specialized uses of pyrolysis may be called various names, such as dry distillation, destructive distillation, or cracking.

Pyrolysis also plays an important role in several cooking procedures, such as baking, frying, grilling and caramelizing. In addition, it is a tool of chemical analysis, for example, in mass spectrometry and in carbon-14 dating. Indeed, many important chemical substances, such as phosphorus and sulfuric acid, were first obtained by this process. Pyrolysis has been assumed to take place during catagenesis, the conversion of buried organic matter to fossil fuels. It is also the basis of pyrography. In their embalming process, the ancient Egyptians used a mixture of substances, including methanol, which they obtained from the pyrolysis of wood.

52. In 1972, new wildlife protection act was passed under this act, possession, trapping, shooting of wild animals alive or dead, serving their meat in eating houses, their transport and export are all controlled and watched by special staff. This acts prohibits hunting of females and young ones. Under this act, threatened species are absolutely protected and the rest afford graded protection according to their state of population size.

53. Literature comparing national ambient air quality standards (AAQSs) globally is scattered and sparse. Twenty-four hour AAQSs for particulate matter <10 μm in aerodynamic diameter (PM_{10}) and sulphur dioxide (SO_2) in 96 countries were identified through literature review, an international survey, and querying an international legal database. Eighty three per cent of the 96 countries with information on the presence or absence of AAQSs, have 24-h AAQSs for either PM_{10} or SO_2. The annual average concentration of SO_2 in residential areas in India by National Ambient Air Quality Standards is 60 $\mu g/m^3$.

56. Environmental management System (EMS): It EMS is that aspect of the total management structure of the organisation which addresses the immediate as well as long term impact of its products, services and processes on the enviornment. EMS is a tool, which is used by organisations world over to facilitate the implementation of environmental policy of the respective governments.

57. The Gaussian plume model is a (relatively) simple mathematical model that is typically applied to point source emitters, such as coal-burning electricity-producing plants. Occassionally, this model will be applied to non-point source emitters, such as exhaust from automobiles in an urban area.

One of the key assumptions of this model is that over short periods of time (such as a few hours) steady state conditions exists with regard to air pollutant emissions and meteorological changes. Air pollution is represented by an idealized plume coming from the top of a stack of some height and diameter. One of the primary calculations is the effective stack height. As the gases are heated in the plant (from the burning of coal or other materials), the hot plume will be thrust upward some distance above the top of the stack—the effective stack height. We need to be able to calculate this vertical displacement, which depends on the stack gas exit velocity and temperature, and the temperature of the surrounding air. According to Gaussian plume model, the grand level concentration (c), $C \propto e^{-H/\sigma}$.

58. In oceanic biogeochemistry, the f-ratio is the fraction of total primary production fuelled by nitrate (as opposed to that fuelled by other nitrogen compounds such as ammonium). This fraction is significant because it is assumed to be directly related to the sinking (export) flux of organic marine snow from the surface ocean by the biological pump. The ratio was originally defined by Richard Eppley and Bruce Peterson in one of the first papers estimating global oceanic production.

F-ratio =

$$\frac{\text{Sum of squares per degree of freedom}}{\text{Residual sum of squares per degree of freedom}}$$

$$= \frac{250}{100} = 2.5.$$

60. We have, $A - \lambda I = \begin{bmatrix} -1 & 2 & 2 \\ 2 & 2 & 2 \\ -3 & -6 & -6 \end{bmatrix} - \begin{bmatrix} \lambda & 0 & 0 \\ 0 & \lambda & 0 \\ 0 & 0 & \lambda \end{bmatrix}$

$$= \begin{bmatrix} -1-\lambda & 2 & 2 \\ 2 & 2-\lambda & 2 \\ -3 & -6 & -6-\lambda \end{bmatrix}$$

$\Rightarrow \quad -(1 + \lambda) \{(\lambda - 2)(6 + \lambda) + 12\} + 2 \{-6 + 12 + 2\lambda\} + 2 \{-12 + 3(2 - \lambda)\} = 0$

$\Rightarrow \quad -(1 + \lambda) \{\lambda^2 + 4\lambda - 12 + 12\} + 2 (2\lambda + 6) + 2 \{-6 - 3\lambda\} = 0$

$\Rightarrow \quad -(1 + \lambda)^2 \{\lambda^2 + 4\lambda\} + 12 + 4\lambda - 12 - 6\lambda = 0$

$\Rightarrow \quad -\lambda (1 + \lambda)^2 \{\lambda + 4\} - 2\lambda = 0$

$\Rightarrow \quad -\lambda \{\lambda^2 + 5\lambda + 4 + 2\} = 0$

$\Rightarrow \quad -\lambda (\lambda + 2)(\lambda + 3) = 0$

$\therefore \quad \lambda = 0, -2, -3$

Hence, 3 is not eigenvalue. Therefore option (C) is correct.

62. Hot spot are areas that are extremely rich in species, have high endemism and are under constant threat. Among the 25 hot spots of the world, two are found in India extending into neighbouring countries—the western Ghats/Sri Lanka and the Indo-Myanmar region (covering the eastern Himalayas.) These areas are particularly rich in floral wealth and endemism, not only in flowring plants but also in repetiles, amphibians, swallow-tailed butterflies and some mammals.

63. An ecosystem that is fully designed and controlled by man is called Engineered eco-systems. A paddy field or a fish pond can be quoted as an example for engineered type of eco-system.

64. Pyramid of energy : The energy pyramids give the best picture of overall nature of the ecosystem. Here, number and weight of organisms at any level depends not on the amount of fixed energy present at any one time in the level just below but rather on the rate at which food is being produced. In contrast with the pyramids of numbers and biomass which are pictures of the standing situations, the pyramid of energy is a picture of the rates of passage of food mass through the food chain. Pyramid energy cannot be invested in a stable ecosystem.

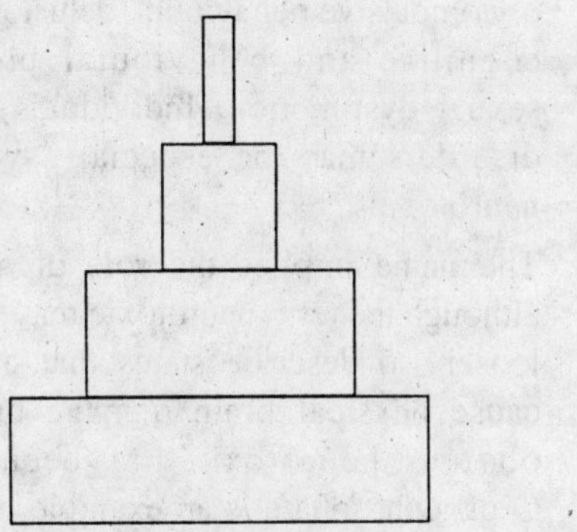

Pyramid of energy

65. The temperature is an environment factor and is responsible for cyclomorphism in animals.

66. Everyone is exposed to small amounts of strontium-90, since it is widely dispersed in the environment and the food chain. Dietary intake of Sr-90, however, has steadily fallen over the last 30 years with the suspension of nuclear weapons testing. People who live near or work in nuclear facilities may have increased exposure to Sr-90. The greatest concern would be the exposures from an accident at a nuclear reactor, or an accident involving high-level wastes. Sr^{90} can enter and accumulates in the body through drinking water.

67. Neurotoxicity occurs when the exposure to natural or artificial toxic substances, which are called neurotoxins, alters the normal activity of the nervous system in such a way as to cause damage to nervous tissue. This can eventually disrupt or even kill neurons, key cells that transmit and process signals in the brain and other parts of the nervous system. Neurotoxicity can result from exposure to substances used in chemotherapy, radiation treatment, drug therapies, certain drug abuse and organ transplants, as well as exposure to heavy metals, certain foods and food additives, pesticides, industrial and/or cleaning solvents, cosmetics, and some naturally occurring substances. Symptoms may appear immediately after exposure or be delayed. They may include limb weakness or numbness, loss of memory, vision, and/or intellect, uncontrollable obessive and/ or compulsive behaviours, delusions, headache, cognitive and behavioural problems and sexual dysfunction. Individuals with certain disorders may be especially vulnerable to neurotoxins.

The name implies the role of a neurotoxin, although the term neurotoxic may be used more loosely to describe states that are known to cause physical brain damage but where no obvious neurotoxin has been identified. Organophosphate is an example of neurotoxic.

69. Clostridium sporogenes is the name given to strains of Clostridium botulinum that do not produce botulinum neurotoxins. Like other strains of C. botulinum, it is an anaerobic Gram-positive, rod-shaped bacterium that produces oval, subterminal endospores and is commonly found in soil. It is being investigated as a way to deliver cancer-treating drugs to tumours in patients.

Clostridium sporogenes is often used as a surrogate for C. botulinum when testing the efficacy of commercial sterilisation.

70. An electrostatic precipitator (ESP), or electrostatic air cleaner is a particulate collection device that removes particles from a flowing gas (such as air) using the force of an induced electrostatic charge. Electrostatic precipitators are highly efficient filtration devices that minimally impede the flow of gases through the device, and can easily remove fine particulate matter such as dust and smoke from the air stream. The particles sizes < 1 μm are most efficiently removed by ESP.

In contrast to wet scrubbers which apply energy directly to the flowing fluid medium, an ESP applies energy only to the particulate matter being collected and therefore is very efficient in its consumption of energy (in the form of electricity).

71. The sound generated by the unsteady motion of a vortex filament moving over a flat boundary with a sharp flow impedance discontinuity is studied theoretically. Theoretical results show that the vortex filament undergoes significant accelerating or decelerating motions and radiates sound at the instant when it moves across the plane of impedance discontinuity. The accelerations and decelerations of the vortex filament are shown to be the major mechanisms of sound generation. The sound so produced has a large low-frequency content such that the change in the flow impedance affects only the sound generation process but not the subsequent sound propagation to the far field. The attenuation of sound by reactive type silencers is based on impedence discontinuity.

72. Farmer's lung is a hypersensitivity pneumonitis induced by the inhalation of biologic dusts coming from hay dust or mold spores or other agricultural products. It results in a type III hypersensitivity, inflammatory response and can progress to become a chronic condition which is considered potentially dangerous. While inhaled allergens often provoke the creation of IgE antibodies that circulate in the bloodstream, these types of immune response are most often initiated by exposure to thermophilic actinomycetes (most commonly Saccharopolyspora rectivirgula), which generates IgG-type antibodies. Following a subsequent exposure, IgG antibodies combine with the inhaled allergens to form immune complexes in the walls of the alveoli in the lungs. This causes fluid, protein and cells to accumulate in the alveolar wall which slows blood-gas interchange and compromises the function of the lung.

73. **Lithosere** is a type of Xerosere originating on bare rock surfaces. The original substratum is deficient in water and lacks any organic matter having only minerals in disintegrated unweathered state. The pioneers to colonise this primitive substratum are crustose type of lichens and moss stages.

74. **Poisson distribution** is the distribution of a discrete random variable whose probability of occurrence is very small but the mean and variance of the distribution are equal and finite. Thus, the Poisson distribution is the distribution of a rare event with a finite mean and variance. The equality of mean and variance is important property of Poisson distribution.

75. The large area of the Indus river flow in the Himalayas. The Tibetan Plateau contains the world's third-largest store of ice. Qin Dahe, the former head of the China Meteorological Administration, said the recent fast pace of melting and warmer temperatures will be good for agriculture and tourism in the short term, but issued a strong warning:

"Temperatures are rising four times faster than elsewhere in China, and the Tibetan glaciers are retreating at a higher speed than in any other part of the world. In the short term, this will cause lakes to expand and bring floods and mudflows. In the long run, the glaciers are vital lifelines of the Indus River. Once they vanish, water supplies in Pakistan will be in peril."

Hence, Indus river has maximum melt water component in its discharge.

Previous Paper (Solved)

UGC-NET ENVIRONMENTAL SCIENCE, DECEMBER 2012

PAPER-II

Note : *This paper contains **fifty** (50) objective type questions, each carrying two (2) marks. Attempt **all** the questions.*

1. Assertion (A): Biosphere constitutes an excellent life-support system which is sustainable and can fulfil all human needs.

Reason (R): The size and productivity of the Biosphere is limited by availability of water, nutrients and environmental conditions. Identify the correct code :

Codes :

A. Both (A) and (R) are true and (R) is the correct explanation of (A).
B. Both (A) and (R) are true, but (R) is not the correct explanation of (A).
C. (A) is true but (R) is false.
D. (A) is false but (R) is true.

2. Geostrophic wind occurs when pressure gradient force balances

A. Coriolis force
B. Frictional force
C. Centripetal force
D. Coriolis and frictional force together

3. Scales of Meteorology are in the following order starting from the least

A. Macro –, Micro –, Meso –
B. Macro–, Meso–, Micro–
C. Meso–, Macro–, Micro–
D. Micro–, Meso–, Macro–

4. When the full potential of physical, chemical and biological factors, a species can use if there is no competition, it is called

A. Fundamental niche
B. Ecological niche
C. Realized niche
D. Competitive exclusion

5. The uppermost zone of atmosphere of earth, where shortwave ultraviolet radiations are absorbed, is

A. Troposphere B. Stratosphere
C. Mesosphere D. Thermosphere

6. Which of the following oxides of nitrogen is the major air pollutant released from automobile exhausts?

A. NO B. N_2O
C. NO_2 D. N_2O_3

7. Match List-I with List-II which contains pollutant gases and their threshold (safe limit) values as per WHO standards :

List-I (Pollutant gas)	**List-II (Thresholds)**
(*a*) CO	(*i*) 2 ppm
(*b*) SO_2	(*ii*) 50 ppm
(*c*) NO	(*iii*) 0.08 ppm
(*d*) PAN	(*iv*) 25 ppm

Identity the correct code :

Codes :

	(*a*)	(*b*)	(*c*)	(*d*)
A.	(*ii*)	(*iii*)	(*i*)	(*iv*)
B.	(*iv*)	(*ii*)	(*i*)	(*iii*)
C.	(*ii*)	(*i*)	(*iv*)	(*iii*)
D.	(*iii*)	(*iv*)	(*ii*)	(*i*)

8. The band labelled as UV-C which is lethal to micro-organisms is

A. 0.29 – V 0.32 μm
B. 0.2 – V 0.29 μm
C. 0.17 – V 0.2 μm
D. 0.07 – V 0.21 μm

9. Which of the following species in the atmosphere is called atmospheric detergent?

A. Chlorine radical B. Hydroxyl radical
C. Methyl radical D. Ozone radical

10. The pOH of a 0.001 M solution of HCl is

A. 12 B. 10
C. 11 D. 13

11. Identify the pair (element-health effect) which is correctly matched :

A. Lead – Methaemoglobinemia
B. Arsenic – Kidney damage
C. Mercury – Nervous disorder
D. PAN – Hypoxemia

12. Which of the following organisms can act as primary consumer, secondary consumer, tertiary consumer or scavenger in different types of food chains?

A. Raven
B. Tiger
C. Snake
D. Phytoplanktones

13. The tendency of biological systems to resist change and to remain in a state of equilibrium is called

A. Homeostatis
B. Feedback mechanism
C. Ecological efficiency
D. Carrying capacity

14. If different categories of threatened species are written in a sequence, what is the correct order?

A. Extinct → Vulnerable → Rare → Endangered
B. Vulnerable → Rare → Endangered → Extinct
C. Vulnerable → Rare → Extinct → Endangered
D. Rare → Vulnerable → Endangered → Extinct

15. Which of the following is not a type of *ex situ* conservation method?

A. Botanical garden
B. Zoological park
C. Wildlife sanctuaries
D. Gene banks

16. As a consequence of succession the P/B ratio (Gross production/Standing crop biomass) is changed. It is

A. high during developmental stages and low at mature stage.
B. low during developmental stages and high at mature stage.
C. > 1 or < 1 at developmental stages and approximately 1 at mature stage.
D. remaining unchanged at all stages.

17. Preparation of hazard-zoning map in case of landslide prone regions involves comprehensive investigation of

A. details of structural and lithological settings.
B. geomorphic features relating to instability of slopes.
C. seismicity pattern of the region.
D. All of the above

18. If ap = specified value of peak acceleration, N = mean rate of occurrence of earthquake per year, t_{ep} = time interval of consideration (exposure period) and F_{ap} = probability that an observed acceleration is less than or equal to ap, then the cumulative probability distribution of peak acceleration for epoch — dependent seismic hazard map is given by which formula?

A. $F_{max}\ t_{ep} = \exp\{-Nt(1 - Fap)\}$
B. $F_{max} = \exp\{-Nt(1 - F_{ap})\}\ .\ t_{ep}$
C. $F_{max}\ tep = \exp\{-t(1 - F_{ap})N\}$
D. All of the above

19. Assertion (A): In oceans, Na has the longest residence time, within an order of magnitude of the age of the oceans.

Reason (R): The long residence time of Na reflects a lack of reactivity of sodium in the marine environment by not being readily incorporated in the common sedimentary minerals, nor being removed by biological reactions.

Identify the correct code :

Codes:

A. Both (A) and (R) are true and (R) is the correct explanation of (A).
B. Both (A) and (R) are true, but (R) is not the correct explanation of (A).
C. (A) is true, but (R) is false.
D. (A) is false, but (R) is true.

20. According to Goldieh the decreasing order of stability of following minerals of igneous rocks towards weathering is

A. Muscovite > Quartz > Potash feldspar > Biotite
B. Biotite > Potash feldspar > Muscovite > Quartz
C. Quartz > Muscovite > Potash feldspar > Biotite
D. Potash feldspar > Quartz > Muscovite > Biotite

21. In universal polar stereographic coordinate system the eastings and northings are computed using which projection method?
A. Polar aspect stereographic projection
B. Non-polar aspect stereographic projection
C. Polar aspect mercator projection
D. Non-polar aspect mercator projection

22. Pitchblende is an ore of
A. Nickel B. Chromium
C. Molybdenum D. Uranium

23. Copper (Cu) is classified according to its geochemical affinity as
A. Siderophile element
B. Chalcophile element
C. Lithophile element
D. Atmophile element

24. If 'a' is the fractional wind speed decrease at the wind turbine, the maximum extraction of power from the wind occurs when 'a' is equal to
A. 1/2 B. 1/3
C. 1 D. 3/5

25. In the following fusion energy reaction
$D + T = {}_0n^1 + X$
identify X
A. Li B. H_2
C. He^3 D. He_4

26. **Assertion (A):** Natural gas is a very attractive ecofriendly fuel.

Reason (R): It produces few pollutants and less carbon dioxide per unit energy than any other fossil fuel on combustion.

Identify the correct answer :

Codes:
A. Both (A) and (R) are true and (R) is the correct explanation of (A).
B. Both (A) and (R) are true and (R) is not the correct explanation of (A).
C. (A) is true but (R) is false.
D. (A) is false but (R) is true.

27. **Assertion (A):** Solar photovoltaic cells are expensive.

Reason (R): Solar photovoltaic cells are fabricated from crystalline silicon and operate only at 10-12% efficiency.

Identify the correct answer :

Codes:
A. Both (A) and (R) are true and (R) is the correct explanation of (A).
B. Both (A) and (R) are true and (R) is not the correct explanation of (A).
C. (A) is true but (R) is false.
D. (A) is false but (R) is true.

28. Human activities add 7-9 gigatons of CO_2 per annum into the atmosphere. Major contributor to this CO_2 is
A. Burning of fossil fuels
B. Clearing of forests for agriculture
C. Fermentation industries
D. Cement industries

29. According to WHO, maximum permissible level of chlorides in drinking water is
A. 100 mg/L B. 200 mg/L
C. 600 mg/L D. 800 mg/L

30. Wilting coefficient of a loam represents
A. the minimum water content of the soil at which plants can no longer obtain water
B. water holding capacity
C. capillary water
D. field capacity

31. Which one of the following techniques can be used for determining the level of cadmium in soil?
A. UV – Visible spectrophotometer
B. Atomic Absorption Spectrophotometer
C. XRD
D. IR spectrometer

32. For noise control in automobiles, the exhaust muffler attenuates sound by
A. Absorption
B. Destructive interference
C. Reducing velocity of hot gases
D. Absorption and destructive interference

33. Five particles (< 2-3 μm) can be effectively collected from industrial stacks by
A. Fabric filters
B. Cyclone separators
C. Venturi scrubbers
D. Settling chambers

34. Soil fulvic acids are strong chelators of

A. Iron (II)

B. Iron (III)

C. Both A and B

D. $Fe(OH)_3$

35. Natural source of polycyclic aromatic hydrocarbons (PAHs) is

A. Root exudates

B. Anaerobic bacteria

C. Aerobic bacteria

D. Grass fires

36. Match the 'phase' with the 'activity' in Environmental Audit. Identify the correct answer from the codes given below the lists :

List-I (Phase)	List-II (Activity)
(*a*) Pre-Audit	(*i*) Human input-output analysis in relation to economy
(*b*) On-site Audit	(*ii*) Reviewing audit-check lists
(*c*) Post-Audit	(*iii*) Records/Documents Review

Codes:

	(*a*)	(*b*)	(*c*)
A.	(*ii*)	(*iii*)	(*i*)
B.	(*i*)	(*iii*)	(*ii*)
C.	(*i*)	(*ii*)	(*iii*)
D.	(*iii*)	(*ii*)	(*i*)

37. Match the Impact Assessment Methodologies (List-II) with the corresponding environments (List-I). Identify the correct answer from the codes given below the lists.

List-I	List-II
(*a*) Air	(*i*) Ecosystem models
(*b*) Biological	(*ii*) Gaussian models
(*c*) Water	(*iii*) Mass balance approach
(*d*) Land	(*iv*) G.I.S.

Codes :

	(*a*)	(*b*)	(*c*)	(*d*)
A.	(*ii*)	(*i*)	(*iii*)	(*iv*)
B.	(*i*)	(*ii*)	(*iv*)	(*iii*)
C.	(*iii*)	(*iv*)	(*ii*)	(*i*)
D.	(*iv*)	(*iii*)	(*i*)	(*ii*)

38. Public hearing is conducted

A. Prior to site selection

B. Prior to approval of Terms of Reference

C. After preparation of EIA

D. After environmental clearance

39. IAIA stands for

A. International Association of Impact Assessment

B. Indian Association of Impact Assessment

C. International Assembly of Impact Assessment

D. Indian Assembly of Impact Assessment

40. Municipal Solid Wastes (MSWs) have the heating value typically in the range

A. 9,300 to 12,800 kJ/kg

B. 1000 to 2500 kJ/kg

C. 1780 to 2830 kJ/kg

D. 530 to 780 kJ/kg

41. The Motor Vehicles Act, 1938 was amended in which year?

A. 1972 B. 1980

C. 1988 D. 1986

42. The following statistical test is used to ascertain whether there is significant difference between the variances of two sets of observations:

A. t-test B. F-test

C. Chi square test D. Regression

43. The population (N) of an ecosystem obeys the growth equation

$$\frac{dN}{dt} = \alpha N - \beta N^2$$

where α and β are constants. The maximum sustainable yield of this ecosystem will be

A. $\alpha - \beta N$ B. α/β

C. $\alpha/2\beta$ D. α^2/β

44. The geometric mean of the following data: 4, 10, 25, 10

is

A. 10 B. 5

C. 12.25 D. $\frac{100}{49}$

45. If the mean and variance of a Poisson distribution are μ and σ, then the following relation is correct.

A. $\sigma = \mu^2$ B. $\sigma = \sqrt{\mu}$

C. $\sigma^2 = \mu$ D. $\sigma = 2\mu$

46. In the Gaussian Plume Model, the plume rise varies with Buoyancy Flux Parameter F as

A. F B. $F^{\frac{1}{2}}$

C. $F^{\frac{1}{3}}$ D. $F^{\frac{1}{4}}$

47. United Nations Conference on Environment, also termed as Earth Summit, was held in 1992 in which city?

A. Rio de Janeiro B. Kyoto

C. Stockholm D. Copenhagen

48. In which part of India, the tropical Western Ghats are situated?

A. Punjab B. Rajasthan

C. Gujarat D. Kerala

49. Variety of different species, genetic variability among individuals within each species and variety of ecosystems constitute the so called

A. Species diversity

B. Genetic diversity

C. Biological diversity

D. Ecological diversity

50. Baba Amte was the leader of

A. Appiko Movement

B. Chipko Movement

C. Narmada Bachao Andolan

D. Tehri Dam Movement

ANSWERS

1	2	3	4	5	6	7	8	9	10
D	A	D	A	D	A	C	B	B	C
11	12	13	14	15	16	17	18	19	20
D	A	A	B	C	A	D	A	A	C
21	22	23	24	25	26	27	28	29	30
A	D	B	B	D	A	A	A	C	A
31	32	33	34	35	36	37	38	39	40
B	C	C	C	D	A	A	C	A	A
41	42	43	44	45	46	47	48	49	50
C	B	C	A	A	C	A	D	C	C

SOME SELECTED EXPLANATORY ANSWERS

2. An air parcel initially at rest will move from high pressure to low pressure because of the pressure gradient force (PGF). However, as that air parcel begins to move, it is deflected by the Coriolis force to the right in the northern hemisphere (to the left on the southern hemisphere). As the wind gains speed, the deflection increases until the Coriolis force equals the pressure gradient force. At this point, the wind will be blowing parallel to the isobars. When this happens, the wind is referred to as geostrophic wind.

3. Microclimatology—Microclimatological studies often measure small-scale contrasts, such as between hilltop and valley or between city and surrounding country. They may be of an extremely small scale, such as one side of a hedge contrasted with the other, a plowed furrow versus level soil, or opposite leaf surfaces. Climate in the micro scale may be effectively modified by relatively simple human efforts.

Meso Climatology—Meso climatology embraces a rather indistinct middle ground between macro climatology and microclimatology. The areas are smaller than those of macro climatology are and larger than those of microclimatology, and they may or may not be climatically representative of a general region.

Macroclimatology—Macro climatology is the study of the large-scale climate of a large area or country. Climate of this type is not easily modified by human efforts. However, continued pollution of the Earth, its streams, rivers, and atmosphere, can eventually make these modifications

4. **Fundamental niche:** The full range of environmental conditions and resources an organism can possibly occupy and use, especially when limiting factors are absent in its habitat.

   The fundamental niche describes the potential area and resources an organism is capable of using. But the presence of limiting factors such as direct competition with other organisms, the organism tends to occupy a niche narrower than this.

5. The thermosphere is the layer of the Earth's atmosphere directly above the mesosphere and directly below the exosphere. Within this layer, ultraviolet radiation (UV) causes ionization.

   At these high altitudes, the residual atmospheric gases sort into strata according to molecular mass (see turbosphere). Thermospheric temperatures increase with altitude due to absorption of highly energetic solar radiation.

6. Petrol on combustion produces carbon monoxide, hydrocarbons, nitrogen oxides, aldehydes, sulphur compounds, organic acids and ammonia and carbon particles. Incomplete combustion of petrol produces a hydrocarbon, 3, 4 benzpyrene. There is more pollution during acceleration and deceleration than during constant speed. Nitrous oxides, produced as a result of combusting fuel at excessive temperatures, contribute significantly to car pollution. Nitrogen oxide is a major cause of acid rain. Over the years, better techniques have reduced the amount of nitrous oxide released from cars but these gases are still responsible for around 8% of global warming.

9. Hydroxyl radicals are often called the "detergent" of the atmosphere because they control the atmosphere's capacity to cleanse itself of pollutants. Here, we show that the reaction of electronically excited nitrogen dioxide with water can be an important source of tropospheric hydroxyl radicals. Using measured rate data, along with available solar flux and atmospheric mixing ratios, we demonstrate that the tropospheric hydroxyl contribution from this source can be a substantial fraction (50%) of that from the traditional $O(^1D) + H_2O$ reaction in the boundary-layer region for high solar zenith angles. Inclusion of this chemistry is expected to affect modeling of urban air quality, where the interactions of sunlight with emitted NO_x species, volatile organic compounds, and hydroxyl radicals are central in determining the rate of ozone formation.

10. pH = –log [H^+]

    pOH = –log [OH^–]

    Since the HCl is strong acid and dissociates completely hence

    [H^+] from HCl is 0.001M.

    The pH = –log [0.001]
    = –(–3)
    = 3

    pOH = 14 – pH = 14 – 3 = 11 **Answer**

13. **Homeostatis:** The ability or tendency of an organism or cell to maintain internal equilibrium by adjusting its physiological processes.

    Any self-regulating process by which a biological or mechanical system maintains stability while adjusting to changing conditions. Systems in dynamic equilibrium reach a balance in which internal change continuously compensates for external change in a feedback control process to keep conditions relatively uniform. An example is temperature regulation mechanically in a room by a thermostat or biologically in the body by a complex system controlled by the hypothalamus, which adjusts breathing and metabolic rates, blood-vessel dilation, and blood-sugar level in response to changes caused by factors including ambient temperature, hormones, and disease.

14. The World Conservation Union (IUCN) is the foremost authority on threatened species, and treats threatened species not as a single category, but as a group of four categories, depending on the degree to which they are threatened:

They are written in a sequence as:

Vulnerable → Rare → Endangered → Extinct.

15. Ex-situ conservation means literally, "off-site conservation". It is the process of protecting an endangered species of plant or animal outside its natural habitat; for example, by removing part of the population from a threatened habitat and placing it in a new location, which may be a wild area or within the care of humans. While ex-situ conservation comprises some of the oldest and best known conservation methods, it also involves newer, sometimes controversial laboratory methods.

They are meant to protect and conserve particular species of wildlife. They are not bound by state legislation. Killing, hunting or capturing of any animal species is prohibited. Forestry and other activities such as grazing of domestic animals are permitted as long as these activities do not adversely affect the wild life.

22. Lindgren defines an ore mineral as "a mineral which may be used for the extraction of one or more metals." A uranium ore mineral is therefore a mineral possessing such physical and chemical properties and occurring in a deposit in such concentrations that it may be used for the profitable extraction of uranium, either alone or together with one or more other metals. Pitchblende is Amorphous, dense, black, pitchy form of the crystalline uranium oxide mineral uraninite; it is one of the primary mineral ores of uranium. Pitchblende is found in granular masses and has a greasy lustre. Three chemical elements were first discovered in pitchblende: uranium, polonium, and radium.

23. Copper is a chalcophile element forming several minerals, including chalcopyrite $CuFeS_2$, covellite CuS, and malachite $Cu_2CO_3(OH)_2$, but is more widely dispersed at trace levels in mica (biotite), pyroxene and amphibole, thus showing a greater affinity for mafic than for felsic igneous rocks. Copper can occur in its metallic form in nature (i.e., native copper), and is one of the seven metals known in antiquity. Copper may be redistributed during low-grade metamorphism and metasomatism (Senior and Leake 1978), but its mobility is more restricted at higher metamorphic grades (Nicollet and Andriambololona 1980). In common with other chalcophile elements, Cu is strongly concentrated into sulphide minerals during hydrothermal mineralisation.

28. Burning wood or allowing trees to rot does not increase the amount of carbon dioxide in the atmosphere, as long as old trees are replaced by new ones which absorb as much carbon as the old ones had done. This is essentially part of the natural cycle, in which carbon is continually added to and removed from the atmosphere. But deforestation does increase the amount of carbon dioxide in the atmosphere, because new trees are not allowed to replace those removed.

The most important way in which we add to the amount of carbon dioxide in the atmosphere is by burning fossil fuels. The burning of fossil fuels is a primary source of increased atmospheric carbon dioxide. Motor vehicle exhaust and the burning of fuel oil in ships and factories or power plants puts lots of CO_2 into the air. We also burn a lot of coal worldwide, and this also ups CO_2 output by people. Additionally, the burning of wild lands (either by accident or on purpose) is increasing the amount of combustion byproducts (including CO_2) in the air.

29. Environmental impact of chlorides are not usually harmful to human health; however, the sodium part of the table salt has been linked to heart and kidney diseases. Sodium chloride may impact a salty taste at 250 mg/l; however, calcium or magnesium chloride is usually detected by taste until levels of 1000 mg/l are reached. Public drinking water standards require chloride level not to exceed 250 mg/l. Chlorides may get into surface water from several sources including: rocks contain chlorides, agricultural run-off, waste water from industries, oil well wastes, and effluent waste water from waste water treatment plants. Chlorides can corrode metals and affect the taste of food products. Chlorides can contaminate fresh water streams and lakes. Fish and aquatic communities cannot survive in high level of chlorides. Therefore, water that is used in industry or proceeds for any use has a recommended maximum chloride level.

30. If the roots of a plant are well established in a mass of soil, the plant gradually reduces the water content until permanent wilting occurs. The water remaining in the soil under this condition has been termed non-available by previous writers. We have found, however, that plants can reduce the soil moisture content somewhat below the point corresponding to the permanent wilting of the leaves, so that the water content at the wilting point is not strictly non-available. In fact, this loss of water from the soil to the air goes on through the plant tissues even after the death of the plant, and appears to be limited only by the establishment of a state of equilibrium between the soil and the air. The plant during the drying stage acts simply as a medium for the transference of water, and while the rate of loss is reduced, the final result is the same as if the air and soil were in direct contact. By means of the wax seal method, which effectually prevents all direct loss of water from the soil, we have been able to demonstrate conclusively that there is a continued loss of water from the soil through the plant long after wilting occurs.

31. Quantitative determination of cadmium can be performed using a variety of methods and techniques, including:

- Atomic absorption spectroscopy (AAS) with either a graphite furnace (GFAA, EPA Method 213.2) or flame (FAA, EPA Method 231.1)
- Inductively coupled plasma techniques (ICP) using optical emission spectroscopy (ICP-OES) or atomic emission spectroscopy (ICP-AES, EPA method 200.7)
- Mass spectrometry (ICP-MS, EPA method 200.8)
- Electrochemical techniques such as adsorptive cathodic stripping voltametry (ACSV) [8, 9], potentiometric stripping analysis (PSA) [10], and liquid chromatography [10] are also used to analyze and separate cadmium (Cd (II)).

32. The most common element used to silence generator exhausts are reactive mufflers. Reactive mufflers are available in a wide range of cost and performance. The noise is reduced by forcing the exhaust air to pass through a series of tubes and chambers.

Each element in the muffler has sound reduction properties that vary greatly with acoustic frequency, and it is the mixing and matching of these elements that constitutes muffler design.

35. Sources of PAHs can be both natural and anthropogenic.

Natural sources include:

- forest and grass fires
- oil seeps
- volcanoes
- chlorophyllous plants, fungi, and bacteria

39. IAIA is the leading global network on best practice in the use of impact assessment for informed decision making regarding policies, programs, plans and projects.

The name of the South African Affiliate of the International Association for Impact

Assessment (IAIA) will be the "International Association for Impact Assessment - South African Affiliate (IAIAsa)" herein after referred to as the "Affiliate".

41. After the coming into force of the Motor Vehicles Act, 1988, Government received a number of representations and suggestions from the state govt. transport operators and members of public regarding the inconvenience faced by them because of the operation of some of the provisions of the 1988 Act. A Review Committee was, therefore, constituted by the Government in March, 1990 to examine and review the 1988 Act.

43. Let population of ecosystem at time t is P then $P = \alpha N - \beta N^2$

For maximum sustainable yield

$$\frac{dP}{dN} = 0$$

$$\frac{dP}{dN}(\alpha N - \beta N^2) = 0$$

$$\alpha - 2\beta N = 0$$

$$N = \frac{\alpha}{2\beta}$$

44. Geometric mean of the series

a, b, c, d

$$\text{G.M.} = \sqrt[4]{abcd}$$

$$= \sqrt[4]{4 \times 10 \times 25 \times 10}$$

$$= \sqrt[4]{10 \times 10 \times 10 \times 10}$$

$$= 10.$$

45. The *mean* of a data set is simply the arithmetic average of the values in the set, obtained by summing the values and dividing by the number of values. Recall that when we summarize a data set in a frequency distribution, we are approximating the data set by "rounding" each value in a given class to the class mark. With this in mind, it is natural to define the mean of a frequency distribution by

$$\mu = \frac{1}{n}\sum_{i=1}^{n} f_i x_i = \sum_{i=1}^{n} p_i x_i$$

The *variance* of a data set is the arithmetic average of the squared differences between the values and the mean. Again, when we summarize a data set in a frequency distribution, we are approximating the data set by "rounding" each value in a given class to the class mark. Thus, the variance of a frequency distribution is given by

$$\sigma^2 = \frac{1}{n}\sum_{i=1}^{n} f_i (x_i - \mu)^2 = \sum_{i=1}^{n} p_i (x_i - \mu)^2$$

The *standard deviation* is the square root of the variance:

$$\sigma = \mu^2$$

47. The United Nations Conference on Environment and Development (UNCED), also known as the Rio Summit, Rio Conference, and Earth Summit was a major United Nations conference held in Rio de Janeiro from 3 June to 14 June 1992.

48. Western ghats are the continuous range of mountains, rising up from the India's Malabar Coast. The average elevation of the western ghats is approximately 1200 meters. Starting at south of Tapti river (near the border of Gujarat and Maharashtra), Western Ghats cover 1600 Km, and pass through states like Maharashtra, Goa, Kerala, Karnataka and Tamil Nadu. The mountain range of Western Ghats end at Kanyakumari, which is the southern end of India.

50. Baba Amte, (1914-2008), was one of India's most respected social and moral leaders. Most of his life he devoted to the care and rehabilitation of leprosy patients. His community of a few thousand patients at Anandwan has done much to dispel prejudice against the victims of leprosy. In 1990 he left Anandwan with the words: "I am leaving to live along the Narmada... Narmada will linger on the lips of the nation as a symbol of all struggles against social injustice."

PAPER-III

Note : This paper contains seventy five (75) objective type questions, each question carrying two (2) marks. All questions are compulsory.

1. In a multiple regression model, the f-ratio is used to test the
A. Variance of the data
B. Standard error of mean
C. R^2 value
D. Overall goodness of fit of the model.

2. If the mean of a sample is 20, the standard error of mean is 1 and the t-statistic for 95% level of confidence is 2.5, the population mean will be in the range
A. 17.5 to 22.5 B. 15 to 25
C. 20 to 25 D. 15 to 20

3. The third moment about the mean of a distribution of a set of observations is a measure of
A. Mode B. Skewness
C. Kurtosis D. Variance

4. Consider an air shed over a city in the form of a rectangular box. The wind velocity is 5 m/sec normal to left face of the box. The length of the box along the direction of wind is 10 km and mixing height is 1 km. Assuming rapid mixing of the pollutants which are conservative in nature, the concentration of the pollutants in the city would reach 63% of its final value in
A. 2,000 sec B. 5,000 sec
C. 10,000 sec D. 1,000 sec

5. Which one of the following states of mercury is volatile?
A. Organic B. Ionic
C. Atomic D. All of the above

6. Molar extinction coefficient of H_2O_2 at 240 nm is 0.04 M^{-1} cm^{-1}. The concentration of H_2O_2 in a solution which has absorbance of 0.6 in a 3 cm curette will be
A. 5 M B. 10 M
C. 15 M D. 20 M

7. A reference solution is to be prepared with 5 PPM parabenzopyrene (molecular weight = 252). The quantity of parabenzopyrene required for preparing one litre 5 PPM solution is
A. 252 mg B. 25.2 mg
C. 5 mg D. 252 μg

8. Which one of the following is a peroxyl radical?
A. OH° B. R°
C. RO° D. ROO°

9. Depending upon the amount of net primary productivity the various ecosystems can be arranged in a decreasing sequence of yield.
A. Tropical seasonal forest – Tropical rain forest – Temperate Grassland – Woodland and Shrubland.
B. Tropical seasonal forest – Tropical rain forest – Woodland and Shrubland – Temperate Grassland
C. Tropical rain forest – Temperate Grassland – Woodland and Shrubland – Tropical seasonal forest.
D. Tropical rain forest – Tropical seasonal forest – Woodland and Shrubland – Temperate Grassland.

10. Which of the following is a correct sequence of secondary seral vegetation development on any habitat?
A. Ecesis – Invasion – Aggregation – Stabilization
B. Ecesis – Aggregation – Invasion – Stabilization
C. Aggregation – Invasion – Ecesis – Stabilization
D. Invasion – Ecesis – Aggregation – Stabilization

11. What is common feature among the following?
Abies delavayi
Aconitum diennorrhzum
Adinandra griffthii
Aglaia perviridis
A. All have been extinct.
B. All are gymnosperms.

C. All are identified as endangered species.
D. All are angiosperms.

12. Raunkiaer's normal biological spectrum for phanerogamic flora of the world exhibits one of the following sequence of occurrence (%) of different life forms.
A. Phanerophytes, Hemicryptophytes, Therophytes, Cryptophytes, Chaemophytes.
B. Phanerophytes, Hemicryptophytes, Therophytes, Chaemophytes, Cryptophytes.
C. Phanerophytes, Hemicryptophytes, Cryptophytes, Chaemophytes, Therophytes.
D. Phanerophytes, Chaemophytes, Hemicryptophytes, Cryptophytes, Therophytes.

13. One of the following categories of earthworms is most suitable for wasteland reclamation.
A. Epigeic B. Anecic
C. Endogeic D. None of the above

14. How many mega-bio-diverse countries have been identified in the world?
A. 2 B. 12
C. 17 D. 35

15. Which one of the following is an *Ex-situ* method of biodiversity conservation?
A. Seed storage B. DNA Bank
C. Tissue culture D. All of the above

16. Which one of the following is a methyl isocyanate (MIC) based pesticide?
A. Sevin (Carbaryl)
B. Temix (Aldicarb)
C. Furadon (Carbofuran)
D. All of the above

17. The sequence of fossil fuels in the order of higher to lower heating value is as follows :
A. Coal, Petroleum, Natural Gas, Hydrogen.
B. Hydrogen, Natural Gas, Petroleum, Coal.
C. Hydrogen, Coal, Natural Gas, Petroleum.
D. Natural Gas, Petroleum, Coal, Hydrogen.

18. Natural ore of radioactive materials does not contain which one of the following isotope?
A. U^{235} B. Pu^{239}
C. U^{238} D. Th^{232}

19. The process of splitting bigger hydrocarbon into smaller hydrocarbon molecules is called
A. Pyrolysis
B. Thermal decomposition
C. Cracking
D. Combustion

20. Which one of the following is a complex in organic fertilizer?
A. Urea B. Super phosphate
C. Potash D. NPK

21. The sequence of ease of decomposition of organic compounds in soil is
A. Lignin – Hemicellulose – Starch – Crude protein – Fat
B. Crude protein – Starch – Fat – Lignin – Hemicellulose
C. Starch – Crude protein – Hemicellulose – Fat – Lignin
D. Fat – Starch – Lignin – Hemicellulose – Crude protein

22. Which one of the following radionuclides has the lowest half life period?
A. C^{14} B. Sr^{90}
C. I^{131} D. Cs^{137}

23. Match the rules mentioned in Column-I with year of enforcement mentioned in Column-II.

Column-I	Column-II
(*a*) Hazardous Wastes (Management and Handling) Rules	1. 2000
(*b*) Biomedical Solid Wastes (Management and Handling) Rules.	2. 1978
(*c*) Municipal Solid Wastes (Management and Handling) Rules	3. 1989
(*d*) The Water (Prevention and Control of Pollution) Cess Rules	4. 1998

Choose the correct code:

Codes:

	(*a*)	(*b*)	(*c*)	(*d*)
A.	3	4	1	2
B.	4	1	2	3
C.	2	4	3	1
D.	1	3	4	2

24. Average composition of biodegradable waste in Municipal Solid Waste (MSW) of India is

A. 30-35% B. 40-45%

C. 55-65% D. 60-70%

25. The treatment method recommended for the human anatomical waste generated from hospitals is

A. Chemical disinfection

B. Autoclaving

C. Incineration

D. All of the above

26. Match the waste class mentioned in Column-I with Colour Code of the Collection Container mentioned in Column-II.

Column-I	Column-II
(*a*) Human Anatomical Waste	1. Blue
(*b*) Waste Scrap	2. Green
(*c*) Discarded glass ware	3. Red
(*d*) Disposable plastics	4. White

Choose the correct code:

Codes:

	(*a*)	(*b*)	(*c*)	(*d*)
A.	2	3	1	4
B.	4	2	3	1
C.	1	2	3	4
D.	3	1	4	2

27. Which of the following is true when frequency of occurrence of risk is remote but possible?

A. Risk is acceptable.

B. Risk reduction measures should be implemented.

C. Risk is unacceptable.

D. Both A and B are true.

28. Given below are two statements, one labelled as Assertion (A) and the other labelled as Reason (R).

Assertion (A): Indirect impacts are more difficult to measure, but can ultimately be more important.

Reason (R): In areas where wildlife is plentiful, such as Africa, new roads often lead to the rapid depletion of animals.

Choose the correct answer.

Codes:

A. Both (A) and (R) are true and (R) is the correct explanation.

B. Both (A) and (R) are true, but (R) is not the correct explanation.

C. (A) is true, but (R) is false.

D. (A) is false, but (R) is true.

29. An earthquake measuring over 8 on Richter Scale is rated as

A. Destructive B. Major

C. Great D. Damaging

30. Given below are two statements, one labelled as Assertion (A) and the other labelled as Reason (R).

Assertion (A): It is difficult to judge how changes in localized gas samples represent more general conditions in the Volcano.

Reason (R): The composition of the juvenile gases emitted from volcanic vents offen show considerable variation over short periods and distances.

Choose the correct answer.

Codes:

A. Both (A) and (R) are true and (R) is the correct explanation of (A).

B. Both (A) and (R) are true, but (R) is not the correct explanation of (A).

C. (A) is true, but (R) is false.

D. (A) is false, but (R) is true.

31. In a false - colour set, human visual perception is limited to how many independent coordinates?

A. Three B. Four

C. One D. Five

32. If D = Detector Dimension, F = Focal Length, H = Flying Height, then Ground Resolution Element (GRE) is equal to

A. (D/F) × H B. D/F

C. H/F D. D/H

33. Darkest level of the associated colour (RGB) would have brightness value equal to

A. 0 B. 256

C. 255 D. 2047

34. The efficiency of a MHD power generator for applied electric field $\vec{E}$, magnetic field $\vec{B}$ and velocity of hot ionized gas $\vec{U}$ is

A. $\frac{|\vec{E}|}{|\vec{U}||\vec{B}|}$ B. $\frac{|\vec{U}||\vec{B}|}{|\vec{E}|}$

C. $\frac{|\vec{E}|^2}{|\vec{U}||\vec{B}|^2}$ D. $\frac{|\vec{E}|^2}{|\vec{U}||\vec{B}|^2}$

35. Match the List-I with List-II and choose the correct answer from the codes given below :

List-I (Constituents of Particulate matter)	**List-II (Sources)**
(*a*) Si	1. Natural Resources
(*b*) PAH	2. Incomplete combustion of fossil fuels
(*c*) SO_4^{2-}	3. Elements largely introduced by Human Activities
(*d*) Pb	4. Reactions of a gas in atmosphere

Choose the correct code :

Codes:

	(*a*)	(*b*)	(*c*)	(*d*)
A.	1	2	4	3
B.	2	3	4	1
C.	2	4	1	3
D.	3	4	2	1

36. For aerosol particles having sizes > 1 μm, the terminal settling velocity (V_T) of an aerosol particle varies with its diameter (D) as

A. $VT \propto D$ B. $V_T \propto D^2$

C. $V_T \propto D^3$ D. $V_T \propto D^{3/2}$

37. Scale lengths associated with synoptic scale phenomenon in atmosphere are typically in the range

A. 10 — 100 km

B. 200 — 40,000 km

C. 10,000 — 100,000 km

D. 1 — 10 km

38. Assume that the atmosphere is isothermal at 25°C and the estimated maximum daily surface temperature is 35°C, the mixing height is (take adiabatic lapse rate to be 1°C per 100 m)

A. 3.5 km B. 2.5 km

C. 1.5 km D. 1 km

39. The wavelengths of UV-A radiations are in the range

A. 200 - 240 nm B. 240 - 280 nm

C. 280 - 320 nm D. 320 - 400 nm

40. Two sounds of 80 dB and 85 dB superimpose at a location. What is the resultant sound at that location?

A. ~ 82 dB B. ~ 87 dB

C. ~ 91 dB D. ~ 165 dB

41. The coefficient of performance of a wind turbine for maximum power output is

A. 13/18 B. 5/8

C. 16/27 D. 11/17

42. Which of the following does not have a direct role in climate change?

A. Sulphate and nitrate aerosols

B. Black carbon aerosols

C. Surface ozone

D. Nitric oxide

43. Which method is used to separate molecules on the basis of their sizes?

A. Ion exchange chromatography

B. Molecular exclusion chromatography

C. Adsorption chromatography

D. Thin layer chromatography

44. Which type of support media is used in different types of electrophoresis?

A. Agarose gel

B. Polyacrylamide gel

C. Sodium dedecyl sulphate polyacrylamide gel

D. All of the above

45. Which of the following categories of plants get benefitted more due to elevation of CO_2 level?

A. C_3 plants B. C_4 plants

C. CAM plants D. All of the above

46. Aquifers that extend continuously from the land surface through material of high permeability are

A. Aquitards B. Auicludes

C. Confined aquifers D. Unconfined aquifers

47. Which one of the following is used to determine ambient concentration of suspended particulate matter?
A. Cascade impactor B. Kjeldahl's Flask
C. Sacchi Disk D. Folin-Wu method

48. Which of the following laws states that the solubility of a gas in a liquid is proportional to the partial pressure of that gas in contact with liquid?
A. Hick's law
B. Henry's law
C. Hardy-Weinburg law of equilibrium
D. 2nd Law of Newton

49. Maximum CaO is found in
A. Bauxite B. Limonite
C. Limestone D. Siderite

50. The sequence of chemical constituents in order of their abundance in a majority of sedimentary rocks is
A. $SiO_2 > TiO_2 > Al_2O_3 > Fe_2O_3$
B. $SiO_2 > Al_2O_3 > Fe_2O_3 > TiO_2$
C. $SiO_2 > Fe_2O_3 > Al_2O_3 > TiO_2$
D. $SiO_2 > Fe_2O_3 > TiO_2 > Al_2O_3$

51. The primary producers in the marine ecosystem are
A. Eubacteria and Algae
B. Cyanobacteria and Algae
C. Algae and Protozoans
D. All of the above

52. Mycorrhizae can be used as biofertilizers because they
A. fix nitrogen
B. fix CO_2
C. solubilise phosphate
D. kill pathogens

53. Given below are two statements, one labelled as Assertion (A) and the other labelled as Reason (R).

Assertion (A): Some plants with mycorrhizal fungi are able to occupy habitats that otherwise could not inhabit.

Reason (R): The importance of mycorrhizal plant interaction is attested by the fact that 95% of all plants have mycorrhizae.

Choose the correct answer :

Codes:
A. Both (A) and (R) are true and (R) is the correct explanation of (A).
B. Both (A) and (R) are true but (R) is not the correct explanation of (A).
C. (A) is true, but (R) is false.
D. (A) is false, but (R) is true.

54. An interactive association between two populations in which one population benefits from the association, while the other is not affected, is
A. Mutualism B. Neutralism
C. Commensalism D. Symbiosis

55. The method for downstreaming of ethanol from fermentation broth is
A. Filtration B. Flow cytometry
C. Distillation D. Flame Photometry

56. The country which uses maximum nuclear power is
A. U.S.A. B. Japan
C. France D. Germany

57. Which bacteria removes copper from low grade copper ore?
A. *Thiobacillus sp*
B. *Bacillus thuringiensis*
C. *Rhizobium sp*
D. All of the above

58. Which of the following is *not* a part of Geographic Information System (GIS)?
A. Projection
B. Overlay
C. Reclassification
D. Measuring distance and connectivity

59. Ultrafiltration can remove
A. Suspended solids B. Bacteria
C. Protozoa D. All of the above

60. A good automobile fuel, in addition to having high calorific value, should have
A. High ignition temperature
B. High viscosity
C. Low ignition temperature
D. Moderate ignition temperature

61. Reserve food material in algae is
A. Starch B. Cellulose
C. Protein D. None of the above

62. The biodegradability of xenobiotics can be characterized by
A. Rate of CO_2 formation
B. Rate of O_2 consumption
C. Ratio of BOD to COD
D. All of the above

63. The soil borne plant pathogens could be controlled by
A. Lowering pH B. Increasing pH
C. Adding lime D. All of the above

64. A selective Lignin degrading fungus belongs to
A. Soft – rot B. Brown – rot
C. White – rot D. Red – rot

65. The drastic reduction in the number of intestinal pathogens during activated sludge process is the overall result of
A. Competition
B. Competition and adsorption
C. Predation, competition and adsorption
D. Competition, adsorption, predation and settling

66. Which of the following disinfection method does not result in synthesis of organochlorine?
A. Chlorination B. Chloroamination
C. Ozonation D. None of the above

67. An organism's niche is
A. the way the organism uses the range of physical and biological conditions in which it lives.
B. all the biological and physical factors in the organism's environment.
C. the function role played by the organism where it lives.
D. the range of temperature that the organism needs to live.

68. The pyramid of biomass is invented in
A. Forest ecosystem
B. Greenland ecosystem
C. Aquatic ecosystem
D. All of the above

69. Which of the following chemicals of anthropogenic origin mimics the effect of estrogen in animals?
A. Alkyl phenol
B. Polychlorinated biphenyl
C. O, p' - DDT
D. All of the above

70. "Black Foot" disease in human beings caused due to use of water contaminated with
A. Mercury B. Cadmium
C. Silver D. Arsenic

71. Largest amount of fresh water is present in
A. Lakes B. Rivers
C. Glaciers D. Polar Ice

72. A threatened species is
A. only endangered species
B. only vulnerable species
C. only rare species
D. All of the above

73. Given below are two statements, one labelled as Assertion (A) and the other labelled as Reason (R).

Assertion (A): Animals adopt various strategies to survive in hostile environment.

Reason (R): Praying mantis is green in colour which emerges with plant foliage.

Choose the correct code:

Codes:
A. Both (A) and (R) are true, with (R) being the correct explanation of (A).
B. Both (A) and (R) are true but (R) is not the correct explanation of (A).
C. (A) is true, but (R) is false.
D. Both (A) and (R) are false.

74. Given below are two statements, one labelled as Assertion (A) and the other labelled as Reason (R).

Assertion (A): Increasing temperature in the environment influences gonadal growth in fish.

Reason (R): Increase in day length causes increase in environmental temperature in summer.

Choose the correct code:

Codes:
A. Both (A) and (R) are true, and (R) is the correct explanation of (A).

B. Both (A) and (R) are true, but (R) is not the correct explanation of (A).
C. (A) is true, and (R) is false.
D. (A) and (R) are false.

75. Match Column-I with Column-II:

Column-I	Column-II
(*a*) The Rio Summit	1. 1997
(*b*) Johannesburg Earth Summit	2. 1972
(*c*) Kyoto Protocol	3. 1992
(*d*) The Stockholm Conference	4. 2002

Codes:

	(*a*)	(*b*)	(*c*)	(*d*)
A.	3	4	1	2
B.	1	2	3	4
C.	4	3	2	1
D.	2	1	4	3

ANSWERS

1	**2**	**3**	**4**	**5**	**6**	**7**	**8**	**9**	**10**
D	A	B	A	C	A	C	D	D	B
11	**12**	**13**	**14**	**15**	**16**	**17**	**18**	**19**	**20**
C	B	C	C	D	D	B	B	C	D
21	**22**	**23**	**24**	**25**	**26**	**27**	**28**	**29**	**30**
C	C	A	B	C	D	A	B	C	A
31	**32**	**33**	**34**	**35**	**36**	**37**	**38**	**39**	**40**
A	A	A	A	A	B	B	D	D	A
41	**42**	**43**	**44**	**45**	**46**	**47**	**48**	**49**	**50**
C	D	B	D	A	D	A	B	C	B
51	**52**	**53**	**54**	**55**	**56**	**57**	**58**	**59**	**60**
B	C	A	C	C	C	A	A	D	D
61	**62**	**63**	**64**	**65**	**66**	**67**	**68**	**69**	**70**
A	D	A	C	D	C	C	C	D	D
71	**72**	**73**	**74**	**75**					
D	D	C	A	A					

SOME SELECTED EXPLANATORY ANSWERS

1. Significance Testing and Goodness of Fit

In linear regression, we tested for a significant relationship by looking at the *t* or F-ratios. In multiple regression, the two ratios test two different hypotheses. As before, the *t* test is used to determine if a slope equals zero. Thus, in this case, we have two tests to perform:

Expenditures	**SAT Scores**
$H_0 : \beta_2 = 0$	$H_0 : \beta_2 = 0$
$H_A : \beta_1 \neq 0$	$H_A : \beta_2 \neq 0$

The *t* ratio and significance level in each row of the table of coefficients tell us whether to reject each of the null hypotheses. In this instance, at the .05 level of significance, we reject in both cases, due to the very low P-values. That is to say, both independent variables have statistically significant relationships to tuition.

The F-ratio in a multiple regression is used to test the null hypothesis that all of the slopes are equal to zero:

$$H_0 : \beta_1 = \beta_2 = 0 \text{ vs. } H_A : H_0 \text{ is not true.}$$

Note that the alternative hypothesis is different from saying that all of the slopes are nonzero. If one slope were zero and the other were not, we would reject the null in the F test. In the two t tests, we would reject the null in one, but fail to reject it in the other.

Finally, let's return to r^2, the coefficient of multiple determination. In the prior sessions, we noted that the output reports both r^2 and "adjusted" r^2. It turns out that adding any x variable to a regression model will tend to inflate r^2. To compensate for that inflation, we adjust r^2 to account for both the number of x variables in the model, and for the sample size. When working with multiple regression analysis, we generally want to consult the adjusted figure.

3. Skewness is asymmetry in a statistical distribution, in which the curve appears distorted or skewed either to the left or to the right. Skewness can be quantified to define the extent to which a distribution differs from a normal distribution.

In a normal distribution, the graph appears as a classical, symmetrical "bell-shaped curve." The **mean**, or average, and the **mode**, or maximum point on the curve, are equal.

- In a perfect normal distribution (green solid curve in the illustration below), the tails on either side of the curve are exact mirror images of each other.
- When a distribution is skewed to the left (red dashed curve), the tail on the curve's left-hand side is longer than the tail on the right-hand side, and the mean is less than the mode. This situation is also called negative skewness.
- When a distribution is skewed to the right (blue dotted curve), the tail on the curve's right-hand side is longer than the tail on the left-hand side, and the mean is greater than the mode. This situation is also called positive skewness.

8. The analog of the perhydroxyl radical in which the H atom is replaced by an organic group is called a peroxyl radical (ROO •). Peroxyl radicals do not dissociate to O_2~ because of the stability of the carbon-oxygen bond. The principal pathway of peroxyl radical formation in biological systems is autoxidation.

13. By their activity in the soil, earthworms offer many benefits: increased nutrient availability, better drainage, and a more stable soil structure, all of which help improve farm productivity.

14. The **megadiverse countries** are a group of countries that harbor the majority of the Earth's species and are therefore considered extremely *biodiverse. Conservation International* identified 17 megadiverse countries in 1998. All are located in, or partially in, the *tropics.*

India is one of the 17 Megabiodiverse countries in the world and accounts for 7-8 % of the recorded species. The State of Assam is a constituent unit of the Eastern Himalayan Biodiversity Region; one of the two biodiversity "Hot Spots" in the country. The climatic condition and wide variety in physical features witnessed in Assam have resulted in a diversity of ecological habitats such as forests, grasslands, wetlands, which harbour and sustain wide ranging floral and faunal species placing.

15. Ex-situ conservation means literally, "off-site *conservation*". It is the process of protecting an *endangered species* of plant or animal outside its natural habitat; for example, by removing part of the *population* from a threatened *habitat* and placing it in a new location, which may be a wild area or within the care of humans. While ex-situ conservation comprises some of the oldest and best known conservation methods, it also involves newer, sometimes controversial laboratory methods.

Ex-situ conservation, while helpful in man's efforts to sustain and protect our environment, is rarely enough to save a species from extinction. It is to be used as a last resort, or as a supplement to *in-situ conservation* because it cannot recreate the habitat as a whole: the entire *genetic variation* of a species, its *symbiotic* counterparts, or those elements which, over time, might help a species adapt to its changing surroundings. Instead, ex-situ conservation removes the species from its natural ecological contexts, preserving it under semi-isolated conditions whereby natural evolution and adaptation processes are either temporarily halted or altered by introducing the specimen to an unnatural habitat. In the case of *cryogenic* storage methods, the preserved specimen's adaptation processes are frozen altogether.

17. The calorific value of a fuel is the **quantity of heat produced by its combustion** - at constant pressure and under "normal" ("standard") conditions (i.e. to *0°C* and under a pressure of *1,013 mbar*).

Hydrogen	141,790
Natural gas	43,000
Petroleum	43,000
Coal (Lignite - Anthrasite)	15,000 - 27,000

18. Plutonium-239 is an *isotope* of *plutonium.* Plutonium-239 is the primary *fissile* isotope used for the production of *nuclear weapons,* although *uranium-235* has also been used and is currently the secondary isotope. Plutonium-239 is also one of the three main isotopes demonstrated usable as fuel in *nuclear reactors,* along with *uranium-235* and *uranium-233.* Plutonium-239 has a *half-life* of 24,100 years.

19. Cracking is the process whereby complex *organic molecules* such as *kerogens* or heavy *hydrocarbons* are broken down into simpler molecules such as light hydrocarbons, by the breaking of *carbon*-carbon *bonds* in the precursors. The *rate* of cracking and the end products are strongly dependent on the *temperature* and presence of *catalysts.* Cracking is the breakdown of a large *alkane* into smaller, more useful *alkanes* and *alkenes.*

22. A **radionuclide** is an *atom* with an unstable *nucleus,* characterized by excess energy available to be imparted either to a newly created radiation particle within the nucleus or via *internal conversion.* During this process, the radionuclide is said to undergo *radioactive decay,* resulting in the emission of *gamma ray*(s) and/or *subatomic particles* such as *alpha* or *beta particles.* These emissions constitute *ionizing radiation.* Radionuclides occur naturally, or can be produced artificially.

The half-life of Carbon-14 is 5730 years. The half-life of Sr-90 is 29.1 years, I-131 has a half-life of 8 days. Cs-137 has a biological half-life of 70 days.

24. Municipal Solid Waste

Garbage is generally referred to "Waste" and is also termed as rubbish, trash, junk, unwanted or undesired material. As per the Municipal Solid Waste (Management & Handling) Rule, 2000 garbage is defined as Municipal Solid Waste which includes commercial and residential wastes generated in a municipal or notified areas in either solid or semi-solid form excluding industrial hazardous wastes but including treated bio-medical wastes. Municipal solid waste consists of household waste, construction and demolition debris, sanitation residue, and waste from streets. This garbage is generated mainly from residential and commercial complexes.

Average composition of biodegradable waste in Municipal Solid Waste (MSW) of India is 40 – 45%.

25. Incineration is a *waste treatment process* that involves the *combustion* of *organic* substances contained in waste materials. Incineration and other high temperature waste treatment systems are described as "*thermal treatment*". Incineration of waste materials converts the waste into *ash, flue gas,* and heat. The ash is mostly formed by the *inorganic* constituents of the waste, and may take the form of solid lumps or *particulates* carried by the flue gas. The flue gases must be cleaned of gaseous and particulate pollutants before they are dispersed into the *atmosphere.* In some cases, the heat generated by incineration can be used to generate *electric power.*

27. Acceptable risk: That risk for which the probability of a hazard-related incident or exposure occurring and the severity of harm or damage that may result are as low as reasonably practicable (ALARP) and tolerable in the setting being considered.

29. A logarithmic scale used to rate the strength or total energy of earthquakes. The scale has no upper limit but usually ranges from 1 to 9. Because it is logarithmic, an earthquake rated as 5 is ten times as powerful as one rated as 4. An earthquake with a magnitude of 1 is detectable only by seismographs; one with a magnitude of 7 is a major earthquake. The Richter scale is named after the American seismologist Charles Francis Richter.

Less than 2.0: Micro - *not felt.*

2.0-2.9: Minor - *not felt, but recorded.*

3.0-3.9: Minor - *felt, but rarely causes damage.*

4.0-4.9: Light - *noticeable shaking of items, damage unlikely.*

5.0-5.9: Moderate - *damage to poorly constructed buildings, unlikely damage to specially designed buildings.*

6.0-6.9: Strong - *destructive for up to 100 miles across populated areas.*

7.0-7.9: Major - *serious damage over large areas.*

8.0-8.9: Great - *serious damage over areas of several hundred miles.*

9.0-9.9: Great - *devastating damage in areas thousands of miles across.*

31. Human visual perception is limited to three independent coordinates.

39. Ultraviolet (UV) "light" is a type of *electromagnetic radiation.* UV light has a shorter *wavelength* than *visible light.* The solar UV spectrum is continuous, it is a scientific convenience to describe the light within three specific wavebands - UVA, UVB and UVC - classified according to their wavelength. UVA is long wavelength (320-400 nm) UV and accounts for up to 95 per cent of the solar UV radiation reaching the Earth's surface. It can penetrate into the deeper layers of the skin and has for years been thought to play a major part in skin aging and wrinkling. Importantly, recent studies strongly suggest that it may also initiate and exacerbate the development of skin cancers. UVA rays are present during all daylight hours and throughout the winter months.

43. A method of separating and identifying the components of a complex mixture by differential movement through a two-phase system, in which the movement is effected by a flow of a liquid or a gas (mobile phase) which percolates through an adsorbent (stationary phase) or a second liquid phase chromatograph.

48. Henry's law helps to predict the amount of each gas which will go into solution, but different gases have different solubilities and this also affects the rate. The constant of proportionality in Henry's law must take this into account. For example, in the gas exchange processes in respiration, the solubility of carbon dioxide is about 22 times that of oxygen when they are in contact with the plasma of the human body.

49. Limestone containing about 45% CaO and above is usually preferred for the manufacturing of cement. Limestone Lumps are calcareous sedimentary rock composed of mineral calcite ($CaCO_3$) which upon calcination yields lime (CaO) for commercial use. Besides, Limestone Lumps are used as fluxing material in Ferro-alloys, pelletization plants, foundries and in the production of sponge from iron, as refining materials in the production of sugar; as an additive in glass industry; as a coating material in fertilizers industry; and in the cooking of range and grass in the paper industry.

51. Algae are primary producers in freshwater and marine ecosystems. Exponentially-growing cultures of selected fresh water algae or Cyanobacteria are exposed over multiple generations under defined conditions. Usually five concentrations in a geometric row are tested, but in some cases a limit test is performed.

54. In *ecology*, **commensalism** is a class of relationship between two organisms where one organism benefits but the other is neutral. An example of commensalism: *cattle egrets* foraging in fields among *cattle* or other livestock. As cattle, *horses*, and other livestock graze on the field, they cause movements that stir up various insects. As the insects are stirred up, the cattle egrets following the livestock catch and feed upon them. The egrets benefit from this relationship because the livestock have helped them find their meals, while the livestock are typically unaffected by it.

56. France with about 80% of their electricity generated by nuclear power. France is the world's largest net exporter of electricity due to its very low cost of generation, and gains over Euro 3 billion per year from this. France has been very active in developing nuclear technology. Reactors and fuel products and services are a major export.

58. Ultrafiltration is a separation process using membranes with pore sizes in the range of 0.1 to 0.001 micron. Typically, ultrafiltration will remove high molecular-weight substances, colloidal materials, and organic and inorganic polymeric molecules. Low molecular-weight organics and ions such as sodium, calcium, magnesium chloride, and sulfate are not removed. Because only high-molecular weight species are removed, the osmotic pressure differential across the membrane surface is negligible. Low applied pressures are therefore sufficient to achieve high flux rates from an ultrafiltration membrane. Flux of a membrane is defined as the amount of permeate produced per unit area of membrane surface per unit time.

60. The criteria for an ideal fuel is as follows :

1. The fuel should have high calorific value. A fuel that gives more calories per unit of weight would be an ideal choice. We have seen earlier that fuels that have oxygen in them have less calorific value.
2. The fuel should have a suitable ignition temperature. We have seen that a fuel will catch fire only if its ignition temperature is reached. If the ignition temperature is too low, then the fuel is not suitable as it will cause fire easily. If the ignition temperature is too high, then again it is not suitable, as reaching the ignition temperature will not be practical. Thus the ignition temperature of an ideal fuel should not be too high nor too low.
3. The fuel should have low content of non combustible materials. Non combustible materials in a fuel are its impurities. When heated these impurities may cause pollution and give out undesirable harmful gases. Thus an ideal fuel should not pollute the air by emanating harmful gases.

61. Algae can either be **autotrophic or heterotrophic** in nature. Most of them are **photoautotrophic** i.e. they need only **light and Carbon Dioxide** as their chief source of energy and carbon. **Chemoheterotrophic** algae require **other external organic compounds** as carbon and energy sources **Reserved food materials** present in algae include Starch, Oils, Floridean starch, Laminarin, Paramylon, soluble carbohydrates and Chrysolaminarin..

67. A niche is the role an organism plays in its environment. The organism uses physical & biological conditions to perform their role. Say for example, the niche of vultures is to feed on dead bodies.

70. Black foot disease has caused significant economic damage in California grape vineyards since the 1990s. Young vines are most susceptible. Plant symptoms are black, sunken root lesions, necrotic root crowns and black vascular streaking. Leaves appear scorched or water stressed and may be chlorotic. Vines are often stunted and may be killed.

71. Most of the world's ice is in Antarctica which is covered to an average depth of more than two kilometers of ice (2133 meters or 7000 feet). Ice at the North Pole is not nearly as thick. There is also a significant amount of ice on Greenland. Total water on earth (estimated): 326,000,000 cubic miles (1360,000,000 cubic km); 3% of that is fresh. 90% of all fresh water is frozen in ice.

Previous Paper (Solved)

UGC-NET ENVIRONMENTAL SCIENCE, JUNE 2012

PAPER-II

Note : *This paper contains **fifty (50)** objective type questions, each carrying **two (2)** marks. Attempt **all** the questions.*

1. If the standard deviation of a population is 20 and the standard error of mean is 4, then the sample size is

A. 25 B. 80
C. 5 D. 100

2. In a multiple regression model, the explained variance per d.f. is 50 and unexplained variance per d.f. is 10. The F-ratio is

A. 2.5 B. 5
C. 25 D. 0.2

3. Which one of the following is not a random sampling method?

A. Stratified Sampling
B. Cluster Sampling
C. Systematic Sampling
D. Judgement Sampling

4. In the Gaussian Plume Model, the plume size is estimated considering buoyancy of exhaust gases, stack diameter, wind speed and stability of the atmosphere. The plume size Δh depends on inside radius of stack (r) as

A. $\Delta h \propto r$ B. $\Delta h \propto r^{1/3}$
C. $\Delta h \propto r^{2/3}$ D. $\Delta h \propto r^2$

5. The acidity of normal rain water is due to

A. CO_2 B. Cl_2
C. NO_2 D. SO_2

6. Per cent of water on the world's surface representing fresh water is

A. 97 B. 50
C. 10 D. 3

7. Concentration of CO_2 in present day atmosphere is

A. ~ 220 ppm B. ~ 280 ppm
C. ~ 360 ppm D. ~ 390 ppm

8. Hardness of diamond is due to

A. Coordinate bonding
B. Covalent bonding
C. Electrovalent bonding
D. van der Waals forces

9. In biological systems sulphur is largely bound in

A. Lipids
B. Proteins
C. Nucleic acids
D. Proteins and nucleic acids

10. pH of 0.01 M HNO_3 is

A. 0.1 B. 1
C. 2 D. 10

11. Which is a correct food chain in the Antarctic ecosystem?

A. Phytoplankton – Krill – Carnivorous Plankton – Emperor Penguin
B. Phytoplankton – Krill – Carnivorous Plankton – Squid – Elephant Seal – Leopard Seal
C. Phytoplankton – Herbivorous Zoo Plankton – Carnivorous Plankton – Adelic Penguin – Emperor Penguin
D. Herbivorous Zoo Plankton – Phytoplankton – Carnivorous Plankton – Elephant Seal – Leopard Seal

12. Given below are two statements, one labelled as Assertion (A) and the other labelled as Reason (R) :

Assertion (A) : The phosphorous cycle in an ecosystem is a sedimentary cycle.

Reason (R) : Phosphorous does not occur naturally as gas.

A. Both (A) and (R) are true and (R) is the correct explanation of (A).
B. Both (A) and (R) are true, but (R) is not the correct explanation of (A).

C. (A) is true, but (R) is false.
D. (A) is false, but (R) is true.

13. Pyramid of trophic levels is always upright in case of

A. Biomass B. Energy
C. Number D. All of the above

14. Which of the following is a correct match?

A. Periyar – Kerala
B. Ranthambore – M.P.
C. Panna – U.P.
D. Bandhvgarh – Bihar

15. Replacement of existing communities by any external condition is termed

A. Primary succession
B. Secondary succession
C. Autogenic succession
D. None of the above

16. The area where two major communities meet and blend together is termed as

A. Ecotype B. Biotype
C. Ecotone D. Meeting place

17. Indian wolf has become an important animal because

A. It's name appears in Red Data Book.
B. It is only an important member of food chain of almost all Indian forests.
C. Wild dogs disappeared due to their presence.
D. It has been chosen as a State animal.

18. Walkley and Black rapid titration method is used for the determination of

A. Organic carbon content of soil
B. Nitrate content of soil
C. Phosphate content of soil
D. Fluoride content of soil

19. Which one of the following is an endoenzyme in soil?

A. Cellulase B. Invertase
C. Protease D. Dehydrogenase

20. Of the following humic groups which is not soluble in both acid and alkali?

A. Fulvic acid B. Humic acid
C. Humin D. All of the above

21. The sources of thermal pollution are

A. Power plants
B. Cooling forests
C. Industrial effluents
D. All of the above

22. Which one of the following radionuclides has the longest half life?

A. C^{14} B. Sr^{90}
C. I^{131} D. Cs^{137}

23. What is the importance of the 42nd Amendment to the Constitution brought in the year 1976?

A. Insertion of Article 48-A
B. Insertion of Article 51-A (g)
C. Insertion of Article 48-A and 51-A (g)
D. None of the above

24. Who issues the Ecomark notification?

A. Ministry of Environment and Forest, Govt. of India
B. Ministry of Human Health and Family Welfare, Govt. of India
C. Department of Science and Technology, Govt. of India
D. Bureau of Indian Standards

25. Which one of the following is a waste recycling method of solid waste management?

A. Pelletisation B. Composting
C. Incineration D. Sanitary Landfill

26. A hazardous waste is characterised by

A. Ignitibility B. Reactivity
C. Toxicity D. All of the above

27. How many hot spots have been identified in the world and Indian Subcontinent respectively?

A. 17, 2 B. 12, 3
C. 35, 2 D. 17, 3

28. Which one of the following chemical species of mercury is highly toxic to living system?

A. Mercurous ion B. Mercuric ion
C. Organo mercurials D. Atomic mercury

29. Natural gas is composed primarily of

A. Methane
B. n-butane
C. n-octane
D. A mixture of n-octane and n-butane

30. Which of the following is true regarding the Leopold interaction matrix used in Environmental Impact Assessment Process?

A. It can be expanded.
B. It can be contracted.
C. It can be contracted and expanded.
D. It cannot be contracted and expanded.

31. Which of the following can be considered in Environmental Risk Assessment?
A. Exposure period
B. Potency of a toxic material
C. Quality of models
D. All of the above

32. In India, Environmental Impact Assessment report of a proposed river valley project after environmental clearance is applicable for a maximal period of how many years?
A. 5 B. 10
C. 30 D. 2

33. An earthquake is rated as 'major' if its magnitude in Richter Scale is in the range of
A. 4.0-4.9 B. 7.0-7.9
C. 6.0-6.9 D. 5.0-5.9

34. What is the proportion of the frequency of occurrence of La Nina compared to El Nino?
A. Half B. One-third
C. Twice D. Two-third

35. An element in soil will be considered as a trace element if its concentration is
A. 1-2 wt % B. $<$ 0.1 wt %
C. $>$ 2 wt % D. $<$ 1 wt %

36. Which of the following is correct about attribute data in Geographic Information System?
A. Attributes are pieces of data that are connected or related to the points, lines or polygons mapped in the GIS.
B. Attribute data can be analysed to determine patterns of importance.
C. Attribute data is entered directly into a database where it is associated with element data.
D. All of the above

37. At Nadir, the LISS-IV camera in IRS-P6 has a spatial resolution of
A. 5.8 m B. 5.9 m
C. 5.7 m D. 5.6 m

38. Which one of the following can be estimated by Flame Photometer?
A. Sodium and Potassium
B. Cadmium and Cobalt
C. Chlorine and Bromine
D. Mercury and Arsenic

39. The contribution of CO_2 towards global warming has been estimated to be about
A. 57-60% B. 60-75%
C. 80-85% D. 45-55%

40. The principal components of photochemical smog in urban areas are
A. SO_2 and NO_2
B. SPM and CO
C. SPM and NO_2
D. Hydrocarbons and Ozone

41. Match List-I and List-II and choose the correct answer from the codes given below:

List-I (Aerosol Constituents)	List-II (Sources)
(i) Si	1. Gases in the ambient atmosphere
(ii) V	2. Natural sources
(iii) Benzo(a)pyrene	3. Combustion of certain kinds of fuel oil
(iv) Sulphuric acid droplets	4. Incomplete combustion

Codes:

	(i)	(ii)	(iii)	(iv)
A.	2	4	3	1
B.	3	1	2	4
C.	4	1	2	3
D.	1	4	3	2

42. A river flowing at 20.0 m^3/sec has a tributary feeding into it with a flow rate of 5.0 m^3/sec. Upstream from the point of junction. The fluoride concentration is 5 mg/L in the river and 10 mg/L in the tributary. Assuming fluoride to be conservative substance and rapid mixing in the river, the downstream concentration in the river is
A. 6 mg/L B. 8 mg/L
C. 8.5 mg/L D. 7.5 mg/L

43. The power obtained from a horizontal wind turbine operating at maximum efficiency is proportional to its diameter (D) as

A. D B. D^2

C. $D^{3/2}$ D. $\sqrt{D}$

44. Noise of 90 dB for 8 hours represents 100% dose. If the noise of 93 dB is for 1 hour duration, it represents a dose of

A. 25% B. 50%

C. 75% D. 100%

45. Scale lengths associated with mesoscale phenomenon in atmosphere are typically in the range

A. 10-500 m B. 1-200 km

C. 100-1000 km D. 1000-10,000 km

46. When an atmosphere has an isothermal profile, it is

A. very stable

B. slightly stable

C. unstable

D. very unstable (turbulent)

47. The wavelength range of UV-C radiation is

A. 320-400 nm B. 280-320 nm

C. 100-1500 nm D. 240-280 nm

48. Lightening in the atmosphere produces

A. NO B. CO

C. CO_2 D. NH_3

49. The maximum tidal energy potential in India is

A. in Gulf of Khambhat

B. in Gangetic delta in Sundarbans

C. along the coast of Odisha

D. along the coast of Chennai

50. The maximum theoretical efficiency of a silicon solar cell can be

A. 45% B. 30%

C. 12% D. 50%

ANSWERS

1	2	3	4	5	6	7	8	9	10
A	B	D	C	A	D	D	B	B	C
11	**12**	**13**	**14**	**15**	**16**	**17**	**18**	**19**	**20**
B	B	B	A	B	C	A	A	D	C
21	**22**	**23**	**24**	**25**	**26**	**27**	**28**	**29**	**30**
D	D	C	A	B	D	C	C	A	C
31	**32**	**33**	**34**	**35**	**36**	**37**	**38**	**39**	**40**
D	B	B	A	B	D	A	A	A	D
41	**42**	**43**	**44**	**45**	**46**	**47**	**48**	**49**	**50**
A	A	B	A	B	B	D	A	A	A

PAPER-III

Note : This paper contains ***seventy five*** *(75) objective type questions, each question carrying two (2) marks.* ***All questions are compulsory.***

1. If the standard deviation of a population is 20, the population and sample means are 35 and 33, respectively and the t-statistic at 95% confidence level is 2.5, the sample size is

A. 100 B. 125

C. 250 D. 625

2. For 5 degrees of freedom, the variance of χ^2 distribution is

A. 10 B. 5

C. 16 D. 4

3. Identify the random sampling method among the following :

A. Judgement sampling

B. Quota sampling
C. Convenience sampling
D. Stratified sampling

4. Consider a Box model for an urban area. Assuming that the pollutants are conservative and that the mixing is rapid inside the Box, the concentration (C) of pollutants varies with the mixing height as

A. $C \propto \frac{1}{H}$ B. $C \propto \frac{1}{H^2}$

C. $C \propto \frac{1}{\sqrt{H}}$ D. $C \propto H^{-3/2}$

5. At higher pH, majority of iron is present as
A. Fe^{2+}
B. Fe^{3+}
C. Fe^{2+} and Fe^{3+}
D. $Fe(OH)_2$ and $Fe(OH)_3$

6. In living organisms phosphorous is largely associated with
A. Carbohydrate B. Lipids
C. Nucleic acids D. Proteins

7. Molar extinction coefficient of malondialdehyde at 532 nm is 0.155 $M^{-1}cm^{-1}$. The concentration of malondialdehyde in a solution which has absorbance of 0.31 in a 1 cm curette will be
A. 0.5 M B. 1.0 M
C. 1.5 M D. 2.0 M

8. pOH of 0.001 M solution of HCl is
A. 0.1 B. 1
C. 10 D. 11

9. The molecular weight of DDT is 354.5. The quantity of DDT required to prepare one litre of 10 ppm DDT solution is
A. 10 mg B. 35.45 mg
C. 354.5 mg D. 354.5 μg

10. Which one of the following is referred to as superoxide radical?
A. O B. O_2
C. $O_2^{\circ -}$ D. O_3

11. The net primary productivity of an ecosystem is
A. the gross primary productivity minus plant respiration
B. the primary productivity at herbivore level
C. the primary productivity at consumer level
D. the productivity at top consumer level minus respiration at all levels

12. Which of the following habitats has not been included as Indian biodiversity hot spots?
A. The Eastern Ghats
B. The Western Ghats
C. North-Eastern Hills
D. South-Eastern Hills

13. The area of the biosphere which is protected entirely, without any experimentation and research and no biotic interference, is known as
A. Undisturbed zone B. Buffer zone
C. Core zone D. Principal zone

14. When a mixture of Azospirillum, Azotobacter and Vibrio was applied to rhizosphere, fixation of atmospheric nitrogen was increased. It was due to activity of
A. All the three
B. Azospirillum and Vibrio
C. Azotobacter and Vibrio
D. Azotobacter and Azospirillum

15. Which type of forests are found at an altitude of 5300 ft chiefly on mountains of Himalayas and Nilgiri?
A. Dry deciduous forest
B. Moist tropical forest
C. Temperate forest
D. Tropical moist deciduous forest

16. The sequence of events that occur during primary succession is as follows :
A. Nudation – Colonisation – Ecesis – Aggregation
B. Aggregation – Colonization – Ecesis – Nudation
C. Ecesis – Nudation – Aggregation – Colonization
D. Nudation – Ecesis – Colonization – Aggregation

17. As per Raunkaiers law of frequency, five different frequency classes (A, B, C, D and E) in a natural undisturbed community exhibit one of the following relationship :

A. $A < B > C \gtreqless D < E$

B. $A > B > C \gtreqless D < E$

C. $A < B > C \gtreqless D > E$

D. $A < B < C \gtreqless D > E$

18. Which one of the following category of earthworms is most suitable for Vermicomposting?

A. Epigeic B. Anecic
C. Endogeic D. All of the above

19. Which one of the following is an in situ method of biodiversity conservation?

A. Reserve forest B. National parks
C. Sanctuaries D. All of the above

20. Match the contaminant in Column-I with the disease in Column-II :

Column-I	Column-II
(i) Mercury	1. Methamoglobinemia
(ii) Nitrate Nitrogen	2. Itai Itai
(iii) Cadmium	3. Silicosis
(iv) Coal	4. Minamata

Choose the correct code :

Codes :

	(i)	(ii)	(iii)	(iv)
A.	2	3	4	1
B.	3	4	2	1
C.	1	2	3	4
D.	4	1	2	3

21. Which of the following types of coal contains higher percentage of volatile matter?

A. Peat B. Lignite
C. Bituminous D. Anthracite

22. Carbon dioxide evolved from soil mainly comes from

A. Microbial respiration
B. Root respiration
C. Soil animals respiration
D. All of the above

23. Which one of the following pesticides persists for a long period in soil?

A. Lindane B. Monocrotophos
C. Carbaryl D. Parathion

24. Organic matter (OM) content of soil can be calculated from organic carbon (OC) by using the formula

A. OM (%) = OC (%) × 1.724
B. OM (%) = OC (%) × 1.247
C. OM (%) = OC (%) × 1.472
D. OM (%) = OC (%) × 1.427

25. The problem of thermal pollution can be alleviated by using

A. Cooling ponds
B. Cooling towers
C. More efficient electricity generating plants
D. All of the above

26. According to Recycled Plastics (Manufacture and Usage) Rules 1999, the minimum thickness of carry bags shall not be less than

A. 10 microns B. 20 microns
C. 30 microns D. 50 microns

27. Match the Act mentioned in Column-I with the year of enactment mentioned in Column-II :

Column-I	Column-II
(i) The Water (Prevention and Control of Pollution) Act	1. 2002
(ii) The Air (Prevention and Control of Pollution) Act	2. 1986
(iii) The Environmental (Protection) Act	3. 1974
(iv) The Biological Diversity Act	4. 1981

Choose the correct code :

Codes :

	(i)	(ii)	(iii)	(iv)
A.	1	4	3	2
B.	3	4	2	1
C.	3	2	1	4
D.	2	4	3	1

28. Which one of the following is not an energy recovery method of solid waste management?

A. Pelletisation B. Biomethanation
C. Pyrolysis D. Composting

29. The colour code of the container for collection of waste scrap generated from Hospitals is

A. Red B. Blue
C. White D. Green

30. Given below are two statements, one labelled as Assertion (A) and the other labelled as Reason (R) :

Assertion (A) : When quantitative probabilistic risk assessment is performed on hazardous waste sites they usually turn out to be of relatively low threats.

Reason (R) : In hazardous waste sites the chance of exposure is low because of isolation of drinking water supplies and prevention of access.

Choose the correct answer :

A. Both (A) and (R) are true and (R) is the correct explanation of (A).
B. Both (A) and (R) are true, but (R) is not the correct explanation of (A).
C. (A) is true, but (R) is false.
D. (A) is false, but (R) is true.

31. In India, an Environment Impact Assessment report of a proposed mining project after environmental clearance is applicable for a maximal period of how many years?

A. 5 years B. 10 years
C. 30 years D. 2 years

32. An increase of one unit of Richter Scale represents an increase in amplitude by a factor of

A. 10 B. 100
C. 1000 D. 2

33. Which rare earth element is not present in the earth's crust but for commercial purpose comes from the Nuclear reactors?

A. Promethium B. Lanthanum
C. Cerium D. Samarium

34. To display green colour in the monitor the amount of RGB should be

A. 255 : 0 : 0 B. 255 : 255 : 255
C. 0 : 0 : 0 D. 0 : 255 : 0

35. When the temperature range in geothermal resource is generally low, electrical power generation from such resources require the use of secondary low boiling point fluid. This is generally known as

A. Rankine cycle
B. Production well cycle
C. Flash stem cycle
D. Hard Dry Rock cycle

36. The Global Warming Potential (GWP) is the least for which of the following greenhouse gases?

A. CH_4 B. CO_2
C. N_2O D. SF_6

37. The maximum specific power output (p) from a MHD power generator varies with the velocity (u) of hot ionized gas as

A. $p \propto u$ B. $p \propto u^2$
C. $p \propto u^{3/2}$ D. $p \propto u^3$

38. Given below are two statements. One labelled as Assertion (A) and the other labelled as Reason (R).

Assertion (A) : Electrostatic precipitators (ESPs) can be harmful if not operated properly.

Reason (R) : Corona discharge in ESPs produces ozone.

Choose the correct answer :

A. Both (A) and (R) are correct and (R) is the correct explanation of (A).
B. Both (A) and (R) are correct and (R) is not the correct explanation of (A).
C. (A) is true, but (R) is false.
D. Both (A) and (R) are false.

39. Given below are two statements. One labelled as Assertion (A) and the other labelled as Reason (R) :

Assertion (A) : Vegetation hedges are the best way to control noise.

Reason (R) : Vegetation hedges scatter noise.

Choose the correct answer.

A. Both (A) and (R) are correct and (R) is the correct explanation of (A).
B. Both (A) and (R) are correct, but (R) is not the correct explanation of (A).
C. (A) is true, but (R) is false.
D. (A) is false, but (R) is true.

40. If w and ws are mixing ratio and saturation mixing ratio respectively; T and Td are the ambient temperature and dew point temperature respectively, then identify the correct expression of relative humidity (RH).

A. $RH = \frac{\text{w at Td}}{\text{w at T}}$ B. $RH = \frac{\text{w at T}}{\text{w at Td}}$

C. $RH = \frac{\text{ws at Td}}{\text{ws at T}}$ D. $RH = \frac{\text{ws at T}}{\text{ws at Td}}$

41. Identify mesoscale phenomenon.
A. Tornado B. Sea breeze
C. Cyclone D. Eddies

42. For elevations less than few hundred metres, if the wind speeds are u_1 and u_2 at elevations z_1 and z_2 respectively, the following equation holds $\left(\frac{u_1}{u_2}\right) = \left(\frac{z_1}{z_2}\right)^p$. The value of the exponent p is
A. ≤ 0.6 B. $= 1$
C. ≥ 0.6 D. negative

43. Given below are two statements. One labelled as Assertion (A) and the other labelled as Reason (R).

Assertion (A) : Noise gets attenuated more in dry atmosphere.

Reason (R) : Moist air is less denser than dry air.

Choose the correct answer :
A. Both (A) and (R) are true and (R) is the correct explanation of (A).
B. Both (A) and (R) are true and (R) is not the correct explanation of (A).
C. (A) is true, but (R) is false.
D. (A) is false, but (R) is true.

44. $OH^{\bullet}$ radicals in atmosphere play a role of
A. scavenger B. acidifier
C. reducing agent D. greenhouse gas

45. The slow neutrons initiating nuclear fission with U^{235} have energies of the order of
A. 0.25 MeV B. 0.15 MeV
C. 0.25 eV D. 0.025 eV

46. The most suitable range of wind speeds for wind power generation is
A. 1-5 m/s B. 4-12 m/s
C. 10-20 m/s D. 20-50 m/s

47. For energy to be produced from nuclear fusion of Deuterium (D) and Tritium (T), the mixture of D + T has to be heated up to energies of at least
A. 1 KeV B. 10 KeV
C. 500 eV D. 1 MeV

48. Element contaminating the water body is determined and quantified by using one of the following methods :
A. Colorimeter
B. Spectrophotometer
C. Atomic absorption spectrometer
D. All of the above

49. In which type of chromatography four modes viz, Absorption, partition, Ion exchange and exclusion, are present?
A. HPLC
B. Liquid-liquid chromatography
C. Ion-exchange chromatography
D. Adsorption chromatography

50. The metal which is generally absorbed by plants along with Zn and causes "Ouch Ouch" disease in human beings is
A. Pb B. Cd
C. Hg D. Cr

51. Radioactive isotopes of which of the elements in human body decay every second?
A. K^{40} and C^{14}
B. C^{14} and N^{6}
C. N^{16} and K^{40}
D. None of the above

52. Which of the following techniques is most appropriate for determining crystalline structure of environmental samples?
A. Infrared spectroscopy
B. X-ray diffraction
C. Microspectrophotometry
D. Raman spectroscopy

53. Which one of the following is the most predominant element in a majority of igneous rocks?
A. Al B. Fe
C. O D. Si

54. Match the entries in Group-I with the process parameters in Group-II :

Group-I	Group-II
(i) Clark electrode	1. Dissolved Oxygen
(ii) Redox Probe	2. pH
(iii) Load cell	3. Liquid level
(iv) Diaphragm gauge	4. Vessel pressure

Choose the correct code :

Codes :

	(i)	(ii)	(iii)	(iv)
A.	1	2	3	4
B.	2	1	4	3
C.	1	4	3	2
D.	4	3	2	1

55. Which one of the following is used to determine total organic matter by Walkley and Black method?
A. KOH and H_2SO_4
B. $Na_2S_2O_3$ and H_2SO_4
C. $K_2Cr_2O_7$ and H_2SO_4
D. HNO_3 and H_2SO_4

56. As per WHO standards the maximum permissible level of coliform organisms per 100 ml of drinking water is
A. 10 B. 100
C. 150 D. 1000

57. Progressive increase in concentration of a xenobiotic compound when it passes through the food chain is called
A. Biomagnification
B. Hyper accumulation
C. Bioaccumulation
D. None of the above

58. Highest level of biotic interaction is
A. Mutualism B. Predation
C. Parasitism D. Amensalism

59. Which one of the following is considered as indicator of aquatic pollution?
A. Rotifers B. Copepods
C. Mysids D. Calanoids

60. Poorly nourished lakes are known as
A. Oligotrophic B. Eutrophic
C. Mesotrophic D. Xerotrophic

61. Identify a sampling method which is not non-destructive.
A. Sub-surface coring
B. Using of neutron probes to measure soil water
C. Fourier transform infrared spectroscopy
D. Time domain refractometry to measure soil water

62. Ministry of Environment and Forests amended the EIA notification making public hearing mandatory for environmental clearance on
A. 27th January 1996
B. 10th April 1997
C. 27th January 1997
D. None of the above

63. The allochthonous microorganisms of an ecosystem are
A. Indigenous microorganisms
B. Migrant
C. Parasitic
D. Pathogenic

64. The rate of evaporation of oil spilled into the sea depends on
A. The elemental concentration of sea water
B. The composition of sea water microflora
C. Composition of the crude oil
D. The temperature of the sea

65. The most dangerous and heat resistant spoilage organism in canning industry is
A. Clostridium cellulolyticum
B. Bacillus subtilis
C. E.coli
D. Clostridium botulinum

66. Oxygen concentrations in compost developed in static piles usually
A. Ten times lower than in ambient air
B. Five times lower than in ambient air
C. Two times more than in ambient air
D. Five times more than in ambient air

67. If a bacterium with a 20 minute generation time is grown under optimal conditions (37°C), one cell would multiply to 10^3 (1000) cells in 3.3 hours, then how much time it will take to multiply to 10^6 cells?
A. 5.3 hrs. B. 6.6 hrs.
C. 9.9 hrs. D. 6.3 hrs.

68. The biodegradation of plant material is slow because of presence of
A. Cellulose B. Xylene
C. Extensin/protein D. Lignin

69. The widely used aerobic suspension type of liquid waste treatment system is
A. Rotating Biological Contactor (RBC)
B. Percolating filter
C. Activated sludge process
D. Septic tank

70. The treatment designed to remove non-biodegradable organic pollutants and mineral nutrients from waste water is
A. Lagoons
B. Imhoff tank
C. Secondary treatment
D. Tertiary treatment

71. An ecotype is
A. Genetically different forms of the same organisms
B. Genetically similar forms of the same organisms
C. Morphologically different forms of the same organisms
D. Both A and B

72. Ultraviolet radiations are lethal due to inactivation of
A. Proteins, nucleic acids and pigments
B. Minerals, water and air
C. Carbohydrates, fats and vitamins
D. O_2, CO_2 and water

73. The following are the characters of species diversity :
(i) More richness
(ii) More evenness
(iii) More dominance
(iv) Less dominance
(v) Less richness
(vi) Less evenness

Point out the combination of conditions in which species diversity of an ecosystem will be more.
A. (i), (ii) and (iii)
B. (v), (ii) and (iii)
C. (i), (ii) and (iv)
D. (i), (vi) and (iv)

74. Given below are two statements, one labelled as Assertion (A) and the other labelled as Reason (R).

Assertion (A) : If natality is greater than mortality, it leads to population explosion.

Reason (R) : The scientific study of various species of human population is called demography.

Choose the correct answer :
A. Both (A) and (R) are true and (R) is the correct explanation of (A).
B. Both (A) and (R) are true, but (R) is not the correct explanation of (A).
C. (A) is true, but (R) is false.
D. Both (A) and (R) are false.

75. Match Column-I with Column-II :

Column-I	Column-II
(i) Chipko Movement	1. Medha Patkar
(ii) Narmada Bacchao Andolan	2. Al Gore
(iii) Climate Change	3. Rachel Carson
(iv) Silent Spring	4. Sundarlal Bahuguna

Choose the correct code :

Codes :

	(i)	(ii)	(iii)	(iv)
A.	1	2	3	4
B.	2	3	4	1
C.	4	1	2	3
D.	3	4	1	2

ANSWERS

1	2	3	4	5	6	7	8	9	10
D	A	D	A	D	C	D	D	A	C

11	12	13	14	15	16	17	18	19	20
A	D	C	D	C	A	B	A	D	D
21	**22**	**23**	**24**	**25**	**26**	**27**	**28**	**29**	**30**
A	A	A	A	D	B	B	D	B	A
31	**32**	**33**	**34**	**35**	**36**	**37**	**38**	**39**	**40**
C	A	A	D	A	B	B	A	D	C
41	**42**	**43**	**44**	**45**	**46**	**47**	**48**	**49**	**50**
B	A	B	A	D	B	B	D	A	B
51	**52**	**53**	**54**	**55**	**56**	**57**	**58**	**59**	**60**
A	B	C	A	C	A	A	B	A	A
61	**62**	**63**	**64**	**65**	**66**	**67**	**68**	**69**	**70**
A	B	B	C	D	B	B	D	C	D
71	**72**	**73**	**74**	**75**					
A	A	C	B	C					

YOUR SPACE

YOUR SPACE